BRITISH SUBMARINES
in Two World Wars

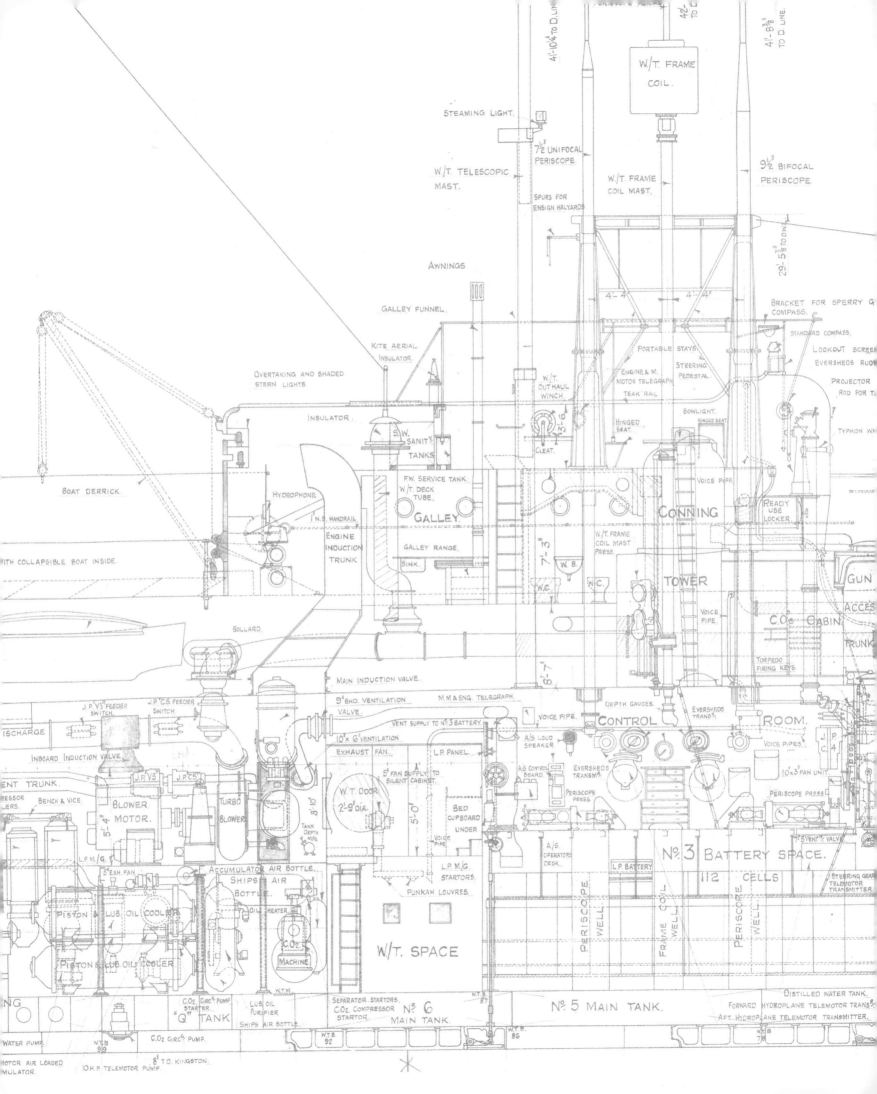

BRITISH SUBMARINES
in Two World Wars

NORMAN FRIEDMAN

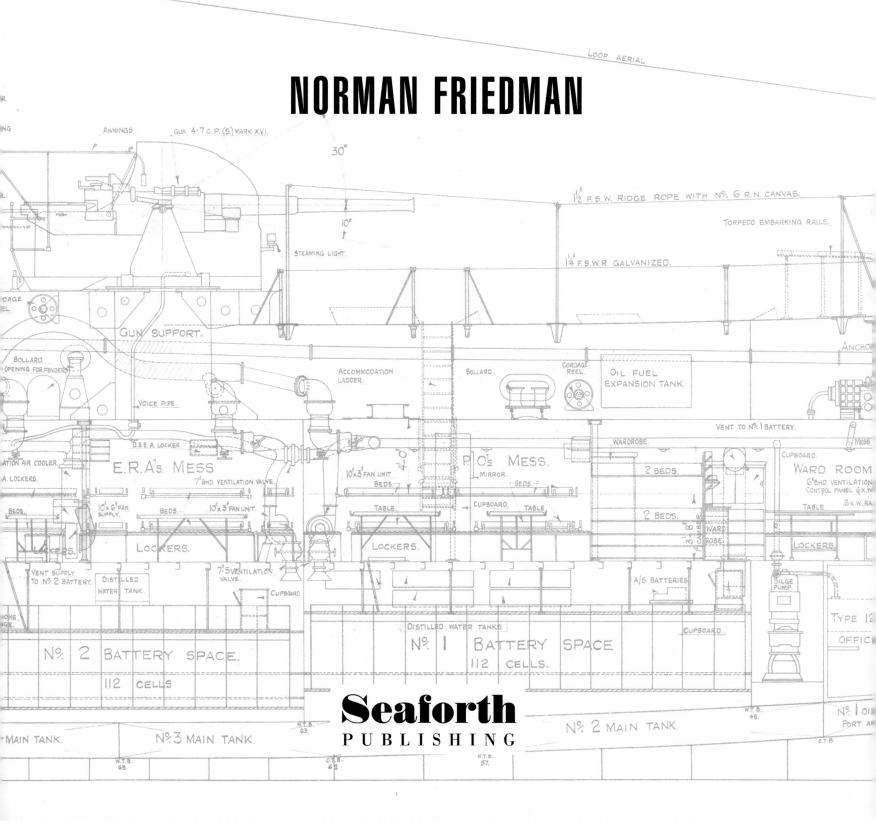

Seaforth

PUBLISHING

Copyright © Norman Friedman 2019

This edition first published in Great Britain in 2019 by
Seaforth Publishing,
An imprint of Pen & Sword Books Ltd,
47 Church Street,
Barnsley
South Yorkshire S70 2AS

www.seaforthpublishing.com
Email: info@seaforthpublishing.com

British Library Cataloguing in Publication Data
A catalogue record for this book is available from the British Library

978-15267-3816-5 (Hardback)
978-15267-3818-9 (Kindle)
978-15267-3817-2 (ePub)

Pen & Sword Books Limited incorporates the imprints of Atlas, Archaeology, Aviation, Discovery,
Family History, Fiction, History, Maritime, Military, Military Classics, Politics, Select, Transport,
True Crime, Air World, Frontline Publishing, Leo Cooper, Remember When, Seaforth Publishing,
The Praetorian Press, Wharncliffe Local History, Wharncliffe Transport, Wharncliffe True Crime
and White Owl.

Typeset and designed by Ian Hughes, Mousemat Design Limited
Printed and bound in China

CONTENTS

ABBREVIATIONS

ADT = Assistant Director of Torpedoes
AEL = Admiralty Engineering Laboratory
AIO = Action Information Organisation
ANCS = Assistant Chief of the Naval Staff
A(S) = Admiral (Submarines)
ASD = Anti-Submarine Division
ASW = anti-submarine warfare
BHP = brake horsepower
BIR = Board of Invention and Research
CIC = Combat Information Center
CID = Committee of Imperial Defence
CNS = Chief of the Naval Staff
COPP = Combined Operations Pilotage Party
EinC = Engineer-in-Chief
DA = director (or deflection) angle
DASD = Director, ASW Division
DCNS = Deputy Chief of the Naval Staff
DCT = director control tower
DDOD = Deputy Director of Operations Division
DEE = Director of Electrical Engineering
D/F = direction-finding
DGD = Director of Gunnery Division
DNA&T = Director of Naval Artillery and Torpedoes
DNC = Director of Naval Construction
DNE = Director, Naval Equipment
DNI = Director of Naval Intelligence
DNO = Director of Naval Ordnance
DOD = Director of Operations Division
D of D = Director of Dockyards
DTD = Director of Tactical Division
DSD = Director Signals Department

DSR = Director, Scientific Research
DTASW = Director of Torpedo, Anti-Submarine and Mine Warfare
DTM = Director of Torpedoes and Mining
DTSD = Division of Training and Staff Duties
FOSM = Flag Officer Submarines
HA = high angle (gun)
HE = hydrophone effect
H/F = high frequency
HP = high pressure/horsepower
HTP = high-test (hydrogen) peroxide
ICS = Inspecting Captain of Submarines
KBB = Kelvin, Bottomley and Baird
LA = low angle (gun)
LP = low pressure
M/F = medium frequency
NHHC = Naval History and Heritage Command (US)
NID = Naval Intelligence Department
PDH = Portable Directional Hydrophone
RA(S) = Rear Admiral (Submarines)
RCNC = Royal Corps of Naval Constructors
RDH = revolving directional hydrophone
RPM = revolutions per minute
SLC = *Siluro lenta corsa* (low-speed torpedo)
S/T = sound telegraphs
STD = Submarine Torpedo Director
TBS = Talk Between Ships (US)
TDC = Torpedo Data Computer (US)
VA(S) = Vice Admiral (Submarines)
WRT = water round torpedoes
W/T = wireless telegraphy

ACKNOWLEDGEMENTS

No book like this can be written without considerable help. I am extremely grateful to Andrew Choong and Jeremy Michell of the Brass Foundry outstation of the National Maritime Museum. The Brass Foundry is the repository of the Covers on which this book is largely based, of original British warship plans, of photographs and of other British warship design documents I have used. George Malcolmson, currently archivist of the Royal Navy Museums and formerly head of the Royal Navy Submarine Museum, provided both documents and valuable advice. Dr Ian Buxton provided Vickers weight data otherwise entirely unavailable. Stephen McLaughlin provided data on early Vickers submarine projects, including export proposals. For other assistance with submarine policy and details I am grateful to Rear Admiral James Goldrick RAN (Ret) and to John Perryman of the Royal Australian Navy Seapower Centre. I would like to thank Peter T Hulme of the Barrow Submariners Association for invaluable advice. I also found the Association's website extremely helpful. I would like to thank the staffs of the Public Record Office at Kew and of the US National Archives and Records Administration at College Park for access to (and assistance with) their vast collections of documents; Admiralty Librarian Jennie Wraight; and also the staffs of the US Navy Department Library and the Library of Congress. For photographs I thank Dr Josef Straczek; Mr Perryman; photo curator David Colomari (as well as his predecessor Chuck Haberlein) of the US Navy History and Heritage Command; A D Baker III; Dr David Stevens; Janis Jorgenson, photo curator of the US Naval Institute; John A Gourley; David C Isby; and the State Library of Victoria. I could not have written without the loving support, encouragement and advice of my wife Rhea.

CHAPTER 1
THE ROYAL NAVY AND THE SUBMARINE, 1901–1945

The Royal Navy did not invent the submarine, but by 1914 it was the world's leading submarine operator. It was extremely innovative. For example, it originated the specialised anti-submarine submarine which became so important after the Second World War. Its First World War fleet submarines can be seen as forebears of modern fast nuclear submarines intended for direct support of battle groups. By 1914 the Royal Navy considered submarines integral to its strategy. Like the rest of the Royal Navy's ships, submarines were much affected by the strategic shifts of the interwar years, from an emphasis on European waters to the Far East and then back to European waters. These shifts are visible in the design of British submarines. British submarine design was also much affected by the interwar attempts at arms control, particularly the 1930 London Naval Treaty. This book is limited to the period through 1945, because afterwards submarine roles and technology changed drastically. The period after 1945 will be covered in a separate volume.

The Royal Navy did not buy submarines until 1901 not because of some innate conservatism but because up to that point submarines did not affect its strategy. It kept close watch on foreign submarine developments, the question always being when (and if) submarines matured to the point that they might affect British naval operations.[1] For example, the Royal Navy acquired plans of the Confederate submarine *H.L. Huntley*, which had successfully attacked the Union sloop *Housatonic* off Charleston in 1864. In the 1880s British officers witnessed the trials of the Garrett-Nordenfelt submarine off Stockholm.

Through the latter part of the nineteenth century the British faced a French commerce-raiding threat, which would have been prosecuted by cruisers. The main British countermeasure was to bottle up the cruisers in the limited number of French naval ports. The French battle fleet would have tried to support a break-out. By 1900 the French development first of harbour and then of seagoing torpedo boats had forced the projected British blockade well out to sea. In the narrow waters of the Channel, the French were expected to deploy their large torpedo boats against shipping; the British built their early destroyers specifically to deal with any French torpedo boats which got to sea. By this time the French already had submarines capable of operating in their harbours, but the Royal Navy had already

HMS *Venturer*, the first (and so far the only) submarine to have sunk another submarine while both were submerged, in her case off Norway on 9 February 1945. She detected the snorkelling U-boat by its noise and then sighted a periscope on the bearing indicated (she never sighted the exhaust plume of the snorkel, but the noise made it clear that the U-boat was using it). She stalked the U-boat, plotting her course and speed by Asdic, confirmed by a few periscope sightings. Lieutenant J S Launders fired a full four-torpedo salvo at an estimated range of 2000 yds, the torpedoes set for depths of 30ft and 34ft in the knowledge that the U-boat had to stay close to the surface to snorkel. It helped that U-boats were instructed to set their periscopes to look out over the top of the snorkel. One torpedo hit, sinking *U 864*. *Venturer* also sank four transports and another U-boat. She was transferred to the Royal Norwegian Navy in August 1946. (John Lambert collection)

abandoned an earlier strategy of attack at source – of going into those harbours to destroy the French navy. The Royal Navy recognised that the French might try raiding British ports, but it did not adopt French-style harbour defence submarines. Instead British naval ports were defended by shore batteries manned by the Royal Garrison Artillery and controlled minefields operated by the Royal Engineers.

The situation changed when the French completed the seagoing submarine *Gustav Zéde*.[2] She was essentially a surface torpedo boat hull wrapped around a submarine pressure hull. The French claimed, and the British accepted, that she could cross the Channel. The British now needed their own submarine to gauge what the French could do and against which to develop defences. They could not buy a French submarine, so they turned to the only other currently successful type, the US Holland. Despite considerable publicity, Holland's Electric Boat Company had not yet exported any such craft; the Admiralty was its first customer. After some discussion of having one or more boats built in the United States, Electric Boat licensed Vickers to build submarines in the United Kingdom. The Admiralty granted Vickers a ten-year monopoly of Admiralty submarine orders. The Royal Navy bought five near-duplicates of Holland's first submarine (which the US Navy had bought). Vickers soon acquired control of Electric Boat itself, the two companies splitting world rights.

Many in Britain argued that it was urgent to buy submarines to match those in foreign navies, to maintain a balance. It was generally admitted that submarines would not fight other submarines. This was not a particularly good argument given the rather different strategic requirements of the Royal Navy and its foreign competitors. Within the Admiralty it was accepted that destroyers, which were already considered the antidote to surface torpedo craft, would be the main antidote to submarines. They could be supplemented by contact mines laid off enemy submarine bases. The first submarine purchase coincided roughly with the end of the Boer War and thus with a need to cut defence spending.

Prime Minister Balfour convened a defence review, which ultimately found a definite role for the new submarines. That happened indirectly. The Cabinet Defence Committee began taking testimony in January 1903.[3] The first item to be considered was defence of the United Kingdom against invasion, a role shared by army and navy. An invader had to secure control of a deep-water port to land artillery and cavalry as well as supplies. The main defences of British ports were shore batteries and controlled minefields. The Admiralty argued that the fleet was the most important line of defence, but many in the Cabinet were not convinced. Captain Jackson, who as attaché had reported the successful French submarine trials in 1899 (and thus had triggered the British submarine programme), argued that submarines would be an inexpensive way to protect the ports. He was now assistant to the Director of Naval Ordnance. Jackson was backed by the Captain of HMS *Vernon*. Captain Prince Louis of Battenberg, who as Director of Naval Intelligence was in effect director of the naval staff, disliked the idea because it might divert funds from the blue-water Royal Navy.

Perhaps surprisingly, Jackson's idea gained army support. In 1903 the new Secretary of State for War was H O Arnold-Foster, who in 1901 had been a strong submarine supporter as the new Parliamentary and Financial Secretary to the Admiralty. Now he wrote to First Lord Selborne that he supported the transfer of port defence to submarines. The idea gained support through the winter of 1903. In November 1903 senior submarine officer (Inspecting Captain of Submarines)

The first big shift in British submarine policy was towards 'overseas' submarines which could operate effectively off the German coast. They made the pre-war concept of an 'observational blockade' practical – but they lacked the wireless range to transmit back what they saw. Initially the only solution was linking ships operating in the North Sea; it was not until 1916 that submarines were fitted with long-range wireless. *D 1*, the first 'overseas' submarine, shows her radio antennae (the X-shaped objects along separate wires). The short mast aft is an auxiliary periscope, not a radio mast. (NHHC)

Bacon was ordered to survey army mining depots as potential future submarine bases. In December he asked for and was given Director of Naval Construction (DNC) assistance in the design of the next class of submarines. The War Office sought to kill the idea by linking it to proposed Admiralty responsibility for all coast defence batteries and maritime fortresses. This was hardly the way to increase funding for the blue-water navy, so Selborne backed away from submarine-based coast defence. However, in the course of the defence review Balfour had become fascinated by submarines. Meanwhile, in September 1903 Admiral Sir John Fisher was appointed CinC Portsmouth as a holding

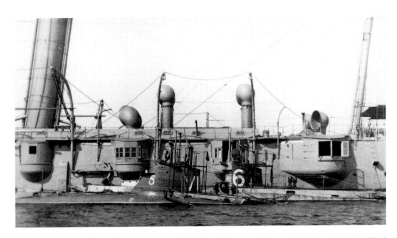

The first British submarines were conceived for harbour defence, but they gained a kind of strategic mobility using mobile tenders (depot ships). During the First World War the Royal Navy was able to relocate its anti-U-boat submarine force rapidly by moving their tenders. Here *A 5* and *B 6* (inboard) lie alongside the former cruiser HMS *Thames*. The conning tower of *A 5* has been considerably lengthened. Initially the 'A'-class submarines had Roman numbers (I through XIII) painted on their conning towers, as here; it is not clear why the outboard boat bears both the number 5 and the Roman number 6. Only the hatchway in the bridge structure was watertight; note the freeing holes in its outside, the ventilators, and the pair of magnetic compasses aft, outside the magnetic influences of the hull. (Dr Josef Straczek)

The big 'J'-class submarines were well-adapted to the observational blockade mission, although they had not been conceived for it. After the war they were given to the Royal Australian Navy – which could not afford to maintain and operate them, and soon had to discard them. Here *J 4* and *J 5* and another unidentified 'J'-boat lie alongside at Garden Island, with the cruiser *Sydney* in the background. (RAN Historical Section via Dr Josef Straczek)

appointment pending his accession as First Sea Lord the following year. He was now responsible, through Bacon, for the embryonic British submarine force. He also came into direct contact with Balfour, because he was one of three members of a committee set up to reorganise British army headquarters.

Fisher and Balfour discussed the implications of submarines for imperial defence at length and both became convinced of their importance. Fisher seems to have been responsible for including submarines in the 1904 fleet manoeuvres, ensuring that the rules offered them a fair chance.[4] After becoming First Sea Lord in October 1904, Fisher quickly pushed through the adoption of submarines as the chief means of defending naval bases, both at home and abroad. The development of submarines as an arm of the fleet, not just a means of understanding a new threat, had begun.

Buying Submarines

For the Royal Navy, submarines were a radically new technology. The navy followed much the same pattern as it had with an earlier new technology, that of fast surface torpedo craft. Initially it accepted that the new type of craft had to bought from one or more specialist builders, who were best equipped to understand what was and was not practicable. During this initial period British naval constructors learned the arcane art of specialist design. After a time they were deemed capable of designing the new type of craft and Admiralty designs largely superseded private ones. In the case of torpedo boats and then destroyers, the key private firms were Thornycroft and Yarrow. They continued to offer their own designs, some of which the Admiralty bought as late as the First World War. After the war all British destroyers were Admiralty designs developed by the Royal Corps of Naval Constructors (RCNC). Only recently has this pattern changed, the design agent for British surface warships now being BAE.

For submarines, there was a single private builder: Vickers. It bought a construction licence from Electric Boat and there was clearly considerable technology transfer. Within a few years Vickers was designing its own submarines. From 1905 on, the Admiralty (DNC Department) produced sketch designs which Vickers elaborated. Thus an account of the 'J'-class submarine (1914) states that Vickers engineers were unable to fit the desired power plant and had to settle for an alternative. The initial sketch surely came from DNC.

Vickers seems to have broken the technology connection with Electric Boat by about 1906. The Royal Navy would not have wanted its new submarine designs shared with the US company, which was building virtually all US submarines at the time. For that matter, the US Navy would not have accepted continued transfer of Electric Boat designs for its submarines. There is, moreover, evidence that Vickers was unfamiliar with some export submarines advertised by Electric Boat.

The Vickers monopoly expired in 1911. By that time Royal Navy submariners were visiting foreign yards, particularly in France and in Italy, and they were reporting that foreign submarines were superior. Whether or not that was true, the Admiralty felt justified in buying several foreign-designed submarines. Vickers continued to be the principal British submarine design agent through the First World War, but after the war the Royal Navy bought only Admiralty designs. The Vickers monopoly extended to diesels. As in the case of submarines, officers visiting foreign builders returned impressed with what they had seen. It may well be argued that they had seen the foreign engines at their best and Vickers engines at their best and worst, but there was certainly a feeling that the monopoly was harmful. In 1917 the Admiralty created a machinery research establishment, the Admiralty Engineering Laboratory (AEL). It was intended to perform basic research to support all potential diesel builders, but ultimately AEL designed its own engines. During the interwar period the Royal Navy tried a number of foreign-built diesels; it is not clear how well they performed.

The Submarine Organisation

From the outset, the Director of Naval Construction (DNC) was responsible for British submarine design, as he was for all other warship designs. He was responsible to the Board of Admiralty, whose Third Sea Lord (Controller) drew up building programmes and was, in theory, responsible for the outline characteristics of new warships. Engines were the responsibility of Engineer-in-Chief (EinC), but batteries and motors were controlled by Director of Electrical Engineering (DEE). Submarine weapons and, initially, wireless were controlled by Director of Naval Ordnance (DNO); pre-war wireless development was conducted by DNO's HMS *Vernon*, the torpedo and mining establishment. In 1920 a separate signals organisation was set up under Director Signals Department (DSD). It was responsible for underwater sound as well as for W/T. Under DNO was a Director of Torpedoes and Mining (DTM). Note that director and department were often used interchangeably, so that DNO was also the Department of Naval Ordnance. DNC was not only the chief warship designer but also the chief of the technical departments, acting as technical advisor to the Board of Admiralty. There was also a Director, Naval Equipment (DNE), who often applied staff considerations to machinery proposals.

Because they were so different from other warships, submarines were subject to a specially-chosen chief, who was involved in design as well as in operations. Initially that was the Inspecting Captain of

Submarines (ICS); in 1912 the submarine service was led by a commodore. Beginning in 1918 the service was led by a flag officer, initially Rear Admiral (Submarines) or RA(S). Since as yet there were no submariners senior enough to hold flag rank, until 1929 RA(S) was a non-submariner depending on his submariner chief of staff for key advice.[5] In 1940 Vice Admiral Max Horton was appointed chief submariner, VA(S) and from that time on the appointment (a Rear Admiral) was styled Admiral (Submarines) or A(S). Beginning in 1944 the chief submariner was styled Flag Officer Submarines (FOSM). Although FOSM generally did not lay down submarine characteristics,

Like all other British warships, British submarines reflected larger themes in British naval, and national, strategy. Between the two World Wars that centred on the Far East. Here *Medway* tends four large long-range submarines in Hong Kong in 1931. (US Naval Institute)

Before the First World War, Winston Churchill when First Lord hoped that groups of large fast submarines could replace increasingly unaffordable battleships; the submarine officers warned him that what he envisaged was a step too far. Once war broke out, Churchill's naval guru Admiral Lord Fisher was able to realise this idea in the form of the 'K'-class. *K 15* is shown late in the war, modified for better seakeeping with a high 'swan' bow. Note her two wireless mass and the torpedoes stowed on deck, presumably for torpedo-firing exercises. (RAN Historical Section via Dr Josef Straczek)

The mission envisaged in the 1920s was reconnaissance: it was considered essential that the Far East fleet commander know when the Japanese fleet sortied, and in which direction it was headed. The US Navy saw its own submarines in much the same way, and in its war games it assumed that Japanese submarines would be stationed around Pearl Harbor for the same warning purpose. Warning required long-range radio (wireless). Here *Oxley*, *Oberon* and *Otway* lie together alongside. The bow of HMS *Oberon*, the prototype long-range patrol submarine, shows a stub tripod which supported the bow end of a long flat-top radio antenna. The other two submarines show net-cutters, their bows shaped for that purpose. (US Navy)

Money was so tight in the early 1930s that the Royal Navy built small 'S'-class submarines which would have been almost useless in its Far East war plan – they would have been limited to operating near bases. During the Second World War, however, the class was revived because it was ideal for the North Sea and the Mediterranean, places not considered likely areas of naval warfare until the late 1930s. HMS *Snapper* is shown in the 1930s. (John Lambert collection)

he certainly had enormous influence. In this book I have used FOSM and A(S) interchangeably.

The first ICS was Reginald Bacon, who was appointed special assistant to Controller in March 1901 with responsibility for overseeing the construction of the new Vickers-built Holland boats. Bacon was appointed in about May 1901, with special responsibility for organising the submarines for the projected anti-submarine warfare (ASW) experimental programme. Bacon managed to postpone the ASW programme in order to train the new submarine crews; he emphasised the need to determine the more general capabilities of the craft. Bacon was closely associated with Admiral Fisher and he was the First Sea Lord's Private Secretary in 1904–5. Presumably he had a good deal to do with Fisher's enormously increased interest in submarines at about this time.

Bacon was succeeded by Captain Edgar Lees, who resigned in 1906 to become managing director of the Whitehead Torpedo Factory. He was succeeded by Captain Sydney S Hall (initially Commander Hall, promoted Captain 1908). After leaving his post as ICS, Hall commanded the cruiser *Diana* and, more importantly, served as Secretary to the Royal Commission on Fuel Oil. Admiral Fisher also served on the commission and used it to promote his ideas on the future of submarine warfare. In 1914 Hall was commanding the armoured cruiser *Roxburgh*, but when Fisher returned to the Admiralty he chose Hall to supervise the crash submarine production programme he considered essential. Now a Commodore, Hall returned to head the submarine service in 1915–18.

Hall's successor was Captain Roger Keyes, also a Fisher protégé. Unlike Hall, Keyes was not an experienced submarine officer. He therefore set up a committee of submarine officers to advise him on future submarine construction.[6] They were responsible for the May 1912 proposal to differentiate between coastal and overseas submarines and they laid out requirements for both types. From 1910 on there was also another Submarine Committee, which was actually the Admiralty's *anti*-submarine committee, the name being chosen for concealment. The use of submarine officers was deliberate, the idea being to keep the submariners' attack tactics in mind. This was not Keyes' committee. As a measure of its perceived importance, it was led by a Rear Admiral.

Keyes considered the Vickers monopoly harmful and he actively encouraged experimentation with the two major foreign submarine configurations, the Italian Laurenti (which he favoured) and the French Laubeuf. Hall considered Keyes' experiments wasteful and wrote to Fisher later that the multiplication of types was just the thing his committee (which Hall saw as a protective screen around Keyes) would promote. Keyes was promoted Commodore 2nd Class in 1912 and in this book is often styled Commodore (S) rather than ICS. Keyes left his post as Commodore (S) to become Chief of Staff for the Dardanelles operation and was not afterwards associated with submarines. Hall returned as Commodore (S) on 8 February 1915 and served through the First World War. Despite his disdain for committees, Hall found himself presiding over a Submarine Development Committee in 1915–16. It was responsible for the wartime 'L' and 'M' classes.

During the First World War, the growing submarine force was run by a remarkably small staff: Commodore (S) and two commanders (one for personnel, acting as chief of staff) and one for battery and periscope matters; there were also a W/T officer and an Engineer Commander and a Secretary. The Commanders visited boats building and attended trials. Operations were handled by the Admiralty, communicating directly with the Captains (S) commanding the flotillas. The Admiralty also arranged for the entry and training of personnel.[7]

During the period covered by this book, the Admiralty underwent

The 'T' class was the best that could be done before 1939; with limited numbers (and endurance) it was associated with a different Far Eastern war plan. Four 'T'-class submarines lie alongside HMS *Adamant* in Fremantle, 1945. Their size was limited to hold down their cost; to provide sufficient firepower, they were given external torpedo tubes (the muzzles of the bow tubes are visible). They show the Oerlikons adopted for protection against air attack, and the outboard boat has a 0.303in machine gun near her 4in gun. Note also the additional protection provided to the 4in guns of the outboard boats, which were using their guns more to attack small Japanese craft. (Alan C Green via State Library of Victoria)

two major reorganisations, both of which affected submarine design. The first, in 1912, was the creation of a formal War Staff. It was a direct consequence of a 1911 meeting of the Committee of Imperial Defence (CID) at which Prime Minister Asquith asked both First Sea Lord (Admiral Sir A K Wilson) and the Director of Military Operations what their services would do in the event of a war; the meeting was called because of the 1911 Agadir crisis. It emerged that Wilson had not shared his war plan with any of his senior commanders. Secretary of State for War Haldane pointed to Wilson's failing as a

Perhaps the greatest surprise of the Second World War was that the small 'U'-class, conceived for training, was ideal for the tough submarine war in the Mediterranean. HMS *Unique* is shown in 1942. (John Lambert collection)

symptom of a wider problem: the navy should have a staff like the army's. In retrospect, he seems to have been interested mainly in creating an issue which would have justified making him First Lord. Asquith, who badly wanted to move Winston Churchill out of the Home Office (where he had been far too aggressive), saw an opportunity and moved him to the Admiralty (Churchill had really wanted the War Office) with a mandate to remove Wilson and to create a War Staff. Initially it comprised an Operations Division, an Intelligence Division and a Mobilisation Division.

The Royal Navy already had a staff incorporated in its Naval Intelligence Department (NID), so the reorganisation was more about appearance than reality. In theory the new War Staff strove to develop design requirements in line with war plans; for example it pointed out that British destroyers lacked the endurance to carry out their wartime roles. The staff's important pre-war contribution to British submarines was that it recognised that overseas submarines were a preferable substitute for surface ships in the observational blockade essential to

current British strategy. In so doing it highlighted the need for many more overseas submarines ('E' class, at the time). It seems unlikely that the War Staff became involved in Churchill's attempt to build the much larger Ocean Submarine he favoured, which became the 'K' class.

The Admiralty was reorganised again in 1917, a much larger and more elaborate staff being created.[8] The reorganisation is significant for this book, as the various divisions of the Admiralty figure prominently in accounts of discussions leading up to submarine designs. First Sea Lord was now double-hatted as both the senior Sea Lord on the Board of Admiralty and as Chief of the Naval Staff (CNS). Two additional Naval Lords were appointed as Deputy Chief and Assistant Chief of the Naval Staff (DCNS and ACNS). In the autumn of 1917 the Board was grouped into two committees, an Operations

Committee headed by First Sea Lord and a Maintenance Committee headed by Second Sea Lord (including Third Sea Lord). A Plans Division and a Training Division were formed.[9] The Operations Committee seems to have conceived the 'R' class ASW submarine.

A Staff Duties Division was set up in December 1917; it was responsible for coordinating Staff Requirements, the basis for, among other things, new ship (including submarine) designs. It was also responsible for training, hence became DTSD (training and staff duties). In a further reorganisation in 1920 a Tactical Section was created to help with fighting instructions, manoeuvres and tactics. At the same time the staff was split into a strategic part under DCNS and a tactical part under ACNS.

Further staff divisions were created to deal with particular technical areas, beginning with Director of Naval Artillery and Torpedoes (DNA&T), which in theory was the staff organisation responsible for requirements for weapons. By 1921 there were separate gunnery and torpedo sections. Director of Torpedo Department (DTD) took considerable responsibility for submarine design.

Among many other things, the Naval Staff was given responsibility for the outline requirements (Staff Requirements) to which new ships, including submarines, were designed. Since the Staff was also responsible for war plans, in theory the reorganisation aligned the requirements for new ships with intentions for their use. The Staff was, for example, responsible for the evolving Far East war plan, which shaped British warship design up through at least the mid-1930s.

The final British submarine design of this era was the 'A' class, in effect an enlarged 'T'-class submarine with much more internal space and much better air-conditioning. These submarines are generally said to have been designed for the Far East – they had great range and could deal with much hotter temperatures – but they were conceived well before the war in Europe was winding down. HMS *Anchorite* is shown on 18 November 1947.

CHAPTER 2
MAKING SUBMARINES WORK[1]

Submarines took centuries to develop because their designers had to solve several difficult interlocked problems. The key problem is that once a submarine is heavier than water, it will simply continue to sink.[2] Something is needed to maintain depth, as well as fore-and-aft stability. The submarine also has to surface on demand and to fire weapons without suddenly surfacing (broaching) because of the weight suddenly expelled. It needs some means of underwater propulsion, generally without any access to air. Unless that confers very long range, a seagoing submarine also needs a separate means of propulsion on the surface. To further complicate matters, the underwater volume of the submarine must equate to its weight. A slightly overweight surface ship sinks slightly deeper into the water; the history of warships is full of ships so overweight that they submerged their side armour. An overweight submarine cannot simply sink deeper. To only a limited extent overweight may be balanced off by reducing the volume of ballast tanks (i.e., increasing underwater volume). Modern submarines generally incorporate additional weight in the form of lead, which can be removed to allow for a degree of growth in service.

Through the nineteenth century inventors tried and failed to build effective submarines. Typically, tanks were flooded sufficiently to put the submarine underwater. Because weights varied and volumes were difficult to calculate, these tanks typically were not full. They were said to have a free surface. When the submarine tipped up or down, the water in a partly-empty tank would rush to the low end, tipping the submarine further and making recovery difficult at best. Such submarines were therefore prone to plunge or to tip up by the bow.

Holland Solves the Problem

The problem seems to have been solved for the first time by John L Holland, an Irishman who moved to the United States. A schoolteacher, Holland was initially fascinated by the problem of flight. He then turned to submarines, offering one to the Fenians, an Irish society dedicated to forcing the British out of Ireland. Since British power was based on the Royal Navy, it seemed to Holland's Fenian sponsors that a submarine could cancel that out.

Holland's initial interest in flight was probably crucial, because it appears that he realised that in effect a submarine was flying underwater. It could maintain depth dynamically rather than by the weight of its ballast. That meant relying on the force generated by water flowing over the submarine's hydroplanes. This flying analogy is not obvious, because hydroplanes are so small, but the far greater density of water compensates for small size and low speed.[3]

Given hydroplanes, Holland did not have to adjust the weight of ballast to force his boat underwater. He could dive with full ballast tanks (no free surface). Even then his boat could maintain the positive buoyancy he preferred as a safety measure.[4] For that matter, a Holland submarine could run awash, because its tanks did not have to be adjusted to provide just enough positive buoyancy to keep a limited volume above water. Holland could compensate for drastic weight change (as in firing a torpedo) with small tanks whose minimal free surface would cause little trouble with trim.

All modern submarines employ Holland's concept. The main

A submarine is like an aircraft flying underwater, its direction determined by its control surfaces. This is the after end of the preserved *Holland No 1*, at the Royal Navy Submarine Museum at Gosport. The stern planes are slightly depressed, which would have pointed the submarine down. John Holland succeeded where many submarine inventors failed by emphasising dynamic control by planes with water flowing over them, rather than control simply by ballasting the submarine down. Earlier submarines dove with partly-filled tanks. When they tipped up or down, the water ran in that direction, ruining their stability. Holland's submarines dove with their main ballast tanks full; the only partly-empty tanks were so small that they could not destabilise the submarine. (John A Gourley)

From the 'Hollands' through the 'C' class, Royal Navy submarine had single hulls, their ballast tanks internal. Because there was little space for these tanks, the submarine had to be close to neutral buoyancy even when surfaced, with little freeboard and therefore little seakeeping ability. This is the launch of HMS *B 1*, 25 October 1904. (Author's collection)

The control room of a First World War 'J'-class submarine, looking aft, shows the wheels which operated forward and aft planes by actuating remote power (telemotors). Also visible is the eyepiece of a periscope. Ballast controls were on the opposite side. (Dr Josef Straczek)

For better seakeeping, a submarine had to have a greater reserve of buoyancy – a greater difference between her surfaced and submerged (ballasted) displacements. She needed more volume for her main ballast tanks. The Royal Navy provided that in the form of saddle tanks like that shown on board *E 19*, shown being launched on 13 May 1915. Against that advantage, saddle tanks added considerable drag, precluding high surface speed. However, the saddle tank provided sufficient beam for broadside torpedo tubes, which the pre-war British submariners considered extremely important. The equivalent double-hulled 'G' class needed a pronounced bulge extending outboard to accommodate their broadside tubes. (NHHC)

development since Holland has been the ability to hover by continuously venting or pumping small ballast tanks, but it is insignificant compared to Holland's basic discovery.

Holland built a small one-man submarine in 1878. It was successful enough to convince the Fenians to finance a larger one incorporating an internal combustion engine, the *Fenian Ram*. Holland later claimed that the French gained access to his ideas when they visited the construction site and that in effect he had been responsible for early French submarine design. As for the *Ram*, the British naval attaché in the United States monitored construction and sought to prevent delivery. Ultimately Holland fell out with the

Fenians. They seized his boat; Holland stole it back. It survives as a museum exhibit.

Unfortunately for Holland, the US Navy of the 1880s had little interest in submarines. Holland was unable to build a fully practical submarine until 1898. The US Navy was finally quite interested and it was evident to foreign (including British) observers that a fully practicable submarine finally existed. It appears that the French submarines which triggered the British submarine programme employed Holland's basic idea.

Propulsion

In his 1898 submarine Holland solved not only the buoyancy and stability problems but also the propulsion problem. It was already clear that a submarine could be driven underwater by an electric motor fed by storage batteries. The French built a series of small harbour submarines, which relied on shore power for charging. That drastically limited their mobility. The question was how to provide sufficient power for the submarine to recharge her batteries. If she could do so, she could enjoy useful range. The charging engine would also propel the submarine on the surface. It had to be compact (internal volume was limited) and it would have to be shut down quickly when the submarine dived. It would also have to start up quickly once the submarine surfaced. In the 1890s only steam engines were powerful enough, but they satisfied none of these conditions. Even after shutting down, a boiler would retain considerable heat, which would be a problem. Steam power required numerous openings in the submarine's hull, which might be difficult to shut quickly for diving. Also, boilers required considerable time to start up. When the US Navy finally bought a submarine from Holland, it specified steam power (in USS *Plunger*) and the result failed. Holland had to finance his own ultimately successful submarine, his sixth.

The key was the rapidly-developing internal combustion engine, which was beginning to power land vehicles. It had no external boiler

and it could start and stop quickly. Holland adopted a 50 HP gasoline (Otto) engine he saw at an industrial fair. Similar engines powered many early submarines. Their fuel turned out to be their main drawback. Gasoline forms an explosive vapour. That is useful inside a cylinder, but dangerous outside. Gasoline fumes also turned out to be intoxicating.

By the time Holland was building his gasoline-powered submarine, the alternative power plant which would become standard was being tested: the diesel. Like a gasoline engine, a diesel takes its power from hot gas expanding in a cylinder, driving a piston. Both engines follow a cycle in which air is sucked in, fuel is burned, the piston is driven down the cylinder, the burned gas is expelled and the cycle repeats to ingest fresh air. The difference is in how the air is heated to make it expand. In a gasoline engine, a fuel-air mixture is ignited by a spark-plug. The resulting controlled explosion heats the air.

A diesel has no spark-plug. Instead, it uses the heat of compression to ignite its fuel. Compression requires a stronger cylinder head, which is why diesels were heavier than their gasoline counterparts. Like a gasoline engine, a diesel sucks in air on a down stroke. The piston then rises to compress (and therefore heat) air in the cylinder. During this stroke fuel is fed into the cylinder, either by air blast (using an engine-driven compressor) or by a fuel injection pump (solid injection). Problems with compressors led Vickers to adopt solid injection before the First World War, when all other diesel makers were using air blast. The amount can be metered, in principle providing just enough to be thoroughly burned (errors produce a smoky exhaust). Dissatisfaction with smoky exhausts led the Royal Navy to drop solid injection about when other navies were adopting it and solid injection was revived only late in the 1930s. At that time, an important selling point was that the required (and often unreliable) air compressor could be elim-

As Commodore (S), Roger Keyes thought that British submarine design was being hobbled by the Vickers monopoly – which also meant by existing designs. He became interested in the Italian Laurenti designs, which were double-hulled – ballast tanks completely (or almost completely) surrounded the pressure hull to form a ship-shaped envelope better adapted to high speed. All of the fast British submarines of the First World War used Laurenti hull structures. The first such submarines, derived from Laurenti designs, were coastal submarines built by Scotts'. S 2, shown at her launch on 14 April 1915, was one of them. (R A Burt)

The 'J' class were much larger Laurenti-type submarines. J 1 is shown at Cockatoo Dockyard near Sydney, 18 November 1919. Note her centreline screw. (Australian National Maritime Museum via Dr Josef Straczek)

inated, making for a more compact engine or for an extra cylinder in the same space.

The heat generated by compression ignites the fuel-air mixture as the piston reaches the top of its up-stroke.[5] The heated air expands, pushing the piston down and generating power. The next stroke pushes the exhausted mixture of air and gas out of the cylinder in preparation for a repeated cycle. This engine operates in a four-stroke cycle, only one of which is a power stroke. The alternative is two strokes, giving more frequent power strokes. On the down (power) stroke exhaust valves are opened and then scavenging air ports are uncovered by the piston. The air blown into the cylinder through these ports pumps out remaining exhaust gas and fills the cylinder. As in a four-stroke engine, on the up stroke the air in the cylinder is compressed and mixed with fuel. A two-stroke engine is lighter than its four-stroke equivalent, but its working temperature is higher, affecting the piston and cylinder head. Nearly all Royal Navy diesels operated on a four-stroke cycle, but through the interwar period it seemed that the two-stroke cycle offered the kind of power output required for the desired high surface speed.

There was an important rub. A diesel fires its cylinders in alternating order. The crankshaft feels a series of separate thrusts, so it twists as it turns. The twisting motion translates into vibration, which is present no matter how well the engine is balanced. The long propeller shaft also twists, since the propeller feels resistance from the water and thus fights the turning motion of the shaft. All diesels have critical speeds at which torsional vibration damages them. The problem seems not to have been well understood before the end of the First World War, perhaps because engines rarely ran near their critical speeds. After that navies became concerned with the critical speed problem. It

helped doom the big *X 1*. The US Navy adopted diesel-electric drive largely because it allowed engines to run at safe speeds without affecting propeller speed.

Weight and space always count, so diesel designers sought more compact lighter-weight engines. The faster the engine runs, the more strokes per minute, the higher the power for a given combination of cylinder bore (diameter) and stroke. Power per cylinder could also be increased by raising the gas pressure in the cylinder. During the interwar period there was also supercharging, increasing the amount of air in the cylinder so that more fuel could be burned and useful pressure increased. British submarines typically had muffler tanks outside the pressure hull, in which diesel exhaust was cooled and silenced. Beyond that the exhaust was typically underwater.

Submarines were driven under water by electric motors fed by batteries. Since motors could function as generators, they were also used to charge batteries on the surface (and when the submarine snorkelled). Typically, diesels were clutched to the motor/generators, which were also clutched to the propeller shafts. A two-shaft submarine might use one engine to charge batteries (the shaft trailing), while running on the other. Alternatively, both engines might run generators while clutched to the propellers. Typically, propellers could not be equally efficient surfaced and submerged, but attempts to use controllable-pitch or variable-pitch propellers failed. During the interwar period the Royal Navy adopted tandem motors (two motors, connected in series, on each shaft) to limit motor

In dry-dock to be broken up, *J 5* shows her ship form. The larger of the two openings in her side is for her broadside torpedo tube, an important feature of contemporary British submarines. (Alan C Green via State Library of Victoria)

The big interwar submarines were double-hulled, giving them a good underwater form and considerable reserve buoyancy on the surface. Smaller submarines had saddle tanks. This is HMS *Proteus* at her launch, 23 July 1929. (US Naval Institute)

diameter for a given output. They were typically water-cooled with air ventilation, air being forced through the motors by a separate motor-driven fan.

During the First World War, the Germans fitted their long-range U-cruisers with auxiliary battery-charging diesels, so that they could run at maximum speed on their main diesels when on the surface. In a very few cases the Royal Navy followed suit. The small 'U' and 'V'-class submarines used diesel-electric propulsion, the diesels never driving propellers directly. Instead they drove generators, the propellers always being motor-driven.

Motors were typically used for manoeuvring inside harbours, even when the main diesels were reversible. Typically, diesels used compressed air to reverse and constant reversing would use up their air supply too quickly.

Metallurgy limited what a single cylinder of reasonable size could produce. For that reason, the First World War 'K' class was steam-powered, a steam turbine demanding much less space for a given output. On the other hand, steam caused many difficulties and it was

abandoned after 1918. The French navy tried steam and found that it had to revert to it when its diesel programme foundered. Steam came back only with nuclear power.

Typical British interwar practice was to group batteries in sections of 112 cells each, normally connected in parallel, with 220-volt output. Some submarines had one split battery section, which could be set up in parallel or in series, in the latter case producing 330 volts. Typically batteries accounted for 10 per cent of the total submerged displacement of a submarine. When they were being charged, batteries gassed (gave off hydrogen) and could therefore be an explosion risk, particularly at the low finishing charging rate. Battery spaces were therefore ventilated, to keep the percentage of hydrogen in the battery compartment to within 2 per cent.

Battery power was typically enough to drive a submerged

HMS *Sickle* shows the top of her starboard saddle tank in a late-war photo (note the antenna for her Type 291W air-warning radar abaft her second periscope).

submarine at full speed for an hour or at a much lower speed for much longer. Before the First World War, endurance at very low speed seems not to have been a significant consideration, but afterwards it certainly was and attention was paid to controllability at very low speed.

Planes

Quite early the Royal Navy provided planes (hydroplanes) fore and aft; it experimented with conning tower planes on an 'A'-class submarine, but did not adopt them. For diving the forward planes were pointed down to bring down the bow, the after planes being pointed up to bring the stern up. If the submarine had more or less neutral buoyancy (having been trimmed down before diving), this sufficed to bring her under. Once submerged, depth was controlled by the fore planes and angle by the after ones. Beginning during the First World War, planes were remotely controlled using telemotors.

In early submarines the planes were sometimes called side rudders or diving rudders and during the Second World War their movement was still described as changes in helm.

Hull Structure and Tankage

Holland's submarines had *single hulls*: all tankage was inside their pressure hulls. They consumed internal volume, but that was not much of a problem in a small submarine. Typically, the upper part of the main tanks was recessed to take the battery. A single hull made for a streamlined form, but limited tank volume and therefore reserve buoyancy. That affected seakeeping and endurance. When the Kingstons (valves) on the bottoms of the tanks were open, the flat upper parts of the tanks became, in effect, the pressure hull. Kingstons thus had to be closed soon after diving, not only to resist pressure but also to protect against depth-charging.

The larger the submarine, the more ballast tankage it needed and the more tankage would encroach on the space inside the pressure hull. The simplest solution was to add tanks to the outside of the pressure hull. Because they did not have to resist sea pressure (they were full when the submarine dived), they could be lightly built. With the Kingstons open, the water in them could be blown out to surface the submarine. Tank capacity could easily exceed that of a single-hull

submarine, so on the surface such a submarine could have much more reserve buoyancy. Such a submarine would also have more waterplane area, offering greater stability when surfaced. However, the hull form was less efficient either surfaced or submerged. That was no great problem at moderate speeds, but it mattered at high surface speed, as in the fleet submarines.

The alternative was to wrap a second hull around the pressure hull, using the spaces between the two for tankage, including ballast tanks. As in the saddle-tank submarine, the outer hull can be lightly built. However, a small double-hull submarine had too little space between the hulls and the structure involved added weight. Overall, a saddle-tank submarine is simpler to build and to maintain, because less of its pressure hull is covered by tankage. The British First World War 'E' class typified the saddle-tank solution; the corresponding double-hull submarine was the 'G' class.

Tanks were blown by air pressure; submarines had HP (high pressure) and LP (low pressure) systems. HP air was stored in grouped pressure tanks, which could be filled by on-board compressors. Air injection fuel pumps were fed by HP air, with an alternative feed from the diesel compressors used to blow air into the cylinders. The parallel LP system was fed by blowers.

In British parlance, the tanks which were always completely filled

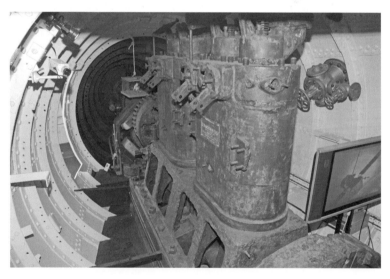

The quality of machinery, particularly engines and batteries, largely determined whether submarines could operate effectively. The earliest British submarines used gasoline engines, the only ones compact enough. This is the 160 BHP four-cylinder Wolseley engine of the preserved *Holland No 1*, showing the cylinder heads and the water jackets (for cooling) surrounding each pair of cylinders. The springs surrounded the stems of the valves atop the cylinders, which admitted air and vaporised fuel. The shafts and rods driving the valves are all gone. Visible abaft the engine is the flywheel geared to the crankshaft (below the cylinders). According to surviving accounts, the engine was actually mounted horizontally, with a weight on the other side for balance. Each cylinder was balanced to avoid vibration. The engine was the only part of the submarine *not* designed by Electric Boat; Wolseley was a British company which Vickers soon bought for its engine expertise (the Wolseley engines in the 'B' and 'C' classes were described as Vickers engines, but Wolseley continued to market cars under its own name). Wolseley gasoline engines powered the later Vickers gasoline submarines of the 'A' through 'C' classes, cylinder size and power gradually increasing. Abaft the flywheel was the motor-generator. The gasoline tank was right forward under the torpedo tubes. Note the canary cage – as in a mine, the canary would fall over before the air became too foul for humans to breathe. (John A Gourley)

The starboard twelve-cylinder main engine of a 'J'-class submarine gives some idea of the complexity and the sheer size of a First World War diesel, in this case an enlarged version of the Vickers engine first used in the 'D' class. The cylinders were largely enclosed by the plated enclosure, at the bottom of which was the crankshaft. Hoses atop each cylinder carried water to cool the exhaust valves. Barely visible at top right is a spring surrounding one of the valves leading down into the cylinder. The pipe at the top of the engine, with tubes leading from it, is probably the 'common rail' which fed fuel to the cylinders at high pressure. The main complaint against wartime Vickers solid (fuel) injection engines was that they burned their fuel incompletely, producing too much smoke. They also vibrated far more than their German counterparts. Cylinders were mounted in groups of four, tied together by the visible rods. Each had a cup to catch splashing lubricating oil, a measure of how much was used. (Dr Josef Straczek)

were the main tanks; other tanks were used for trimming, compensating and for consumables such as fuel oil. Trimming meant maintaining neutral buoyancy. Some adjustment had to be made for different water density, as the weight of the main tanks would vary. The less adjustment required, the smaller trimming tanks could be. Conversely, limiting the volume of trimming tanks limited the range of water density in which the submarine could operate.

In the earliest submarines, all the ballast tanks had Kingstons, valves opening beneath them through which they could be filled or emptied. However, during the First World War crash-diving was frequently necessary. Kingstons were typically left open (later they were often not even fitted). On the surface ballast tanks would be filled with low-pressure air, the vents atop the tanks being closed. This was 'riding the vents'. When the vents were opened, water flooded in from below. All internal main tanks had Kingstons, which protected them at depths at which the pressure exceeded the test pressure of the tanks. In addition to the main tanks, submarines generally had bow buoyancy tanks in their superstructures (above the pressure hull) to improve seakeeping. They were generally open to the sea at the bottom, their freeing holes above the normal waterline; in some cases they had spray-tight flaps. Their vents were remotely controlled (by telemotor). Larger submarines also had auxiliary tanks at the ends of the submarine to quickly adjust their trim when diving.

With the advent of crash-diving during the First World War, submarines were given Q (quick-dive) tanks slightly forward of amidships. Rapidly flooding a Q tank gave the submarine both a bow-down angle and extra weight to put her underwater. Q tanks were typically pressure-proof, so that they could be blown at depth (for crash-surfacing); they were closed off by Kingstons and vents, blown by HP air.

Before the Second World War many British submarines had drop keels, their droppable sections weighing about 10 tons each. They could be slipped quickly in an emergency to restore buoyancy. The sections were controlled by a wheel connected to rod gearing.

Submarines had to be able to fire torpedoes without broaching due to the lost weight. That required special tanks, which could replace the volume (weight) of a fired torpedo. Similar considerations applied to other consumables, including gun ammunition.

In all of these cases, in pre-1945 submarines the pressure hull was typically surmounted by a free-flooding superstructure, including a flat upper deck to be used when the submarine rode on the surface. The Royal Navy often described the free-flooding structure as a superstructure. A pressure-tight extension above the pressure hull, from which the submarine could be conned, was termed a conning tower in analogy to the conning towers of surface ships. Eventually it was surrounded by a free-flooding fairwater and surmounted by a bridge to be used when the submarine was surfaced. The conning tower supported periscope standards and it contained the hatchway leading down into the submarine. Before such arrangements became standard, many early submarines were conned from a low tower (with deadlights) when running awash, typical practice being to come up periodically to allow observation of either a target or of the submarine's surroundings. It was some time before submarine commanders shifted to rely on periscopes, running submerged when anywhere near a potential target or threat.

Diving Depth

Through this book there are numerous references to designed diving depth, which ultimately means the depth at which the pressure hull collapses. Calculation of collapse depth is extremely complicated and much more so for anything with a shape more complicated than a simple cylinder. No submarine was tested to collapse before trials after the Second World War and the first British model simulations, using cylinders with various kinds of framing, were conducted just before the war.[6] Initial design depths were based on the 'boiler formula' previously used to determine the breaking point of cylindrical boilers due to internal steam pressure. It related strength to thickness. Through the end of the First World War diving depth was not a very important figure, since a submarine was invisible once submerged. In the North Sea, a submarine which could dive to about 150ft could lie on the bottom.[7] Deeper diving became important after the war and that in turn required a more sophisticated way of calculating diving depth in terms of submarine structure.

Modern designers distinguish between operational depth, test depth and collapse depth. It appears that typical practice by the early 1930s was to take collapse depth as twice operational depth. In theory test and operational depths were the same, but officers often dove to 10 per cent more than operational depth to give crews confidence in their submarines. Submarines generally operated above their rated depths. Modes of collapse were identified fairly early, but computing what it took to overcome them had to await sophisticated post-1945 analysis using computers. The main modes were overall collapse, typically of a whole compartment between bulkheads; buckling between frames; and yielding of plating between frames (stretching leading to pleating). Of these, buckling between frames was typically due to depth-charging. Overall collapse was the most difficult to calculate. Typically, riveted hulls failed when the rivets sheared. Typical practice was to overdesign the frames by judgement, making failure between frames the main issue. It could be calculated using the boiler formula.[8]

In 1933, R L Payne described the current state of submarine structural knowledge.[9] By this time it was generally understood that the best pressure hull cross section was a circle, the ideal being a cylinder stiffened by framing. In the past, the emphasis had been on the frames and on stresses forcing them inwards, with relatively little attention paid to the plating between frames and stresses along that plating. During the war, however, the Germans were compelled to rethink submarine structures and they looked more at stresses along the length of the pressure hull. It turned out that the stress along the length of the pressure hull was greater than that forcing the frames in and that bulkheads actually increased local stress on plating. The hull had to be thicker near the bulkheads rather than, as before, thinner (in the expectation that the bulkhead helped prop up the plating). Yet another new consideration was that a hull might suddenly collapse by distortion. In that case the frames might tip over as the pressure hull was squeezed down. Payne concluded that systematic model tests were needed.

DNC had to contend with what he considered misinterpretation of experiments. In 1934 RA(S) attacked existing submarine designs as insufficiently protected against depth-charging.[10] Based on tests of underwater protection of surface ships, RA(S) argued that a double hull should be adopted. He thought that a depth charge would cause the inner hull to rupture, while the outer hull survived and could withstand full depth. DNC pointed out that RA(S) was describing a water-backed protection system, in this case consisting of a holding bulkhead behind a water layer, the outside of which was the outer hull. This system was widely adopted before the Second World War – for surface ships. In a submarine, devoting the available weight to a single pressure hull would buy the greatest protection. DNC also pointed to the value of moving all oil inside the pressure hull so that leaks could not give the submarine away.

The limits of interwar knowledge are evident in remarks DNC Sir Stanley Goodall made when he inspected the captured *U 570* (HMS *Graph*) in October 1941. He could not see why she had so thick a pressure hull and such flimsy frames. In fact the Germans had learned to size their frames more precisely.[11]

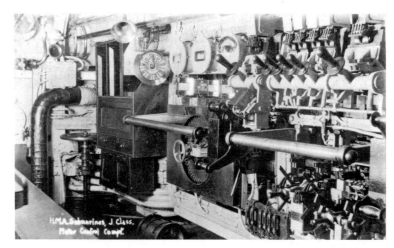

The motor control compartment of a 'J'-class submarine. British submarines (and most others) generally had their batteries in two or three sections, connected as two sets. Grouper Up or Down meant connecting them in series (maximum voltage) or parallel (minimum) for high or low speed. Battery cells were not individually controlled. Typically each shaft was driven either by a pair of motors or by two windings in one motor. The two motors could be connected in series (or one could be cut out) for various speeds and (as generators) for various rates of charge to the battery. For example, for medium speed one set of windings could be used at maximum battery output. Visible at right are the main motor switches. One was used for starting, others for setting various combinations of motor or generator functions. The motors could be used to start submarine diesels; air starting (from the submarine's tanks) was the alternative. (Dr Josef Straczek)

As an example of what was not understood in the 1920s, Folio 39 of the *Thames* Cover gives a series of results from a 15 February 1929 work book, with additional data for the 'G' class. Two methods of analysis had been tried and both were given:

	'L'	X 1	Odin	'G'
Diving Depth (ft)	150	500	500	300
Pressure Hull Diameter (ft-in)	15–9	19–9	16–9	17–10
Frame spacing (in)	21	18	21	21
Plating (in)	½	1	⅞	⅝
Crush I (ft)	640	2940	2300	920
Crush II (ft)	590	660	550	1920
Ratio Crush/Dive:				
I	4.3	5.88	4.60	3.07
II	3.9	1.30	1.10	6.1

Method I assumed that the frame bars were rigid, so its crush depth was set by plating thickness and frame spacing. It did not reflect the strength given by the plate framing adopted in the 'G' design. Method II assumes that the frame and frame spaces of plating formed a continuous circular ring. A calculation of the crush depth of the 'G' design which took into account external plating gave the enormous crush depth of 30,800ft, but this did not take into account the reduced section at the top. The 1920ft figure took into account the reduced cross section at the top of the hull, but not the external plating. Disregarding the strong framing, the 'G' design was not quite up to the standard of previous submarines. However, taking that framing into account, the 'G' design was much better than any predecessor. The 'boiler formula' gave substantially lower figures, perhaps about 500ft. During wartime, *Clyde* managed 300ft but her hull was distorted in the process.

CHAPTER 3
BEGINNINGS

In 1900 only two successful submarines existed: the French *Gustave Zedé* and the US *Holland No*. As there was no question of the French selling a submarine to their enemies the British, if the Admiralty wanted a submarine it had either to buy from Holland or finance a wholly British design. For years the Admiralty had quietly killed British submarine designs so as to hold back progress in submarine development, on the reasonable theory that submarines could not help the Royal Navy but could most certainly harm it. Now that both the French and the Americans had produced usable submarines, Controller

A 5 on the surface, showing her rudimentary bridge and her drowned exhausts, emerging from the sides of her hull below her conning tower. One pipe emerged from each row of eight cylinders. In *A 1–A 4* the two pipes merged into a main exhaust pipe below the waterline, which passed through a large vertical U-bend atop the hull and then passed into a muffle box whose closure could be operated from inside the boat. *A 5* and the other 'A'-class submarines had considerably enlarged conning towers with periscopes passing up through them. The number on her conning tower is her pennant number, which did not correspond to her designation. (R A Burt)

Rear Admiral Sir A K Wilson saw no point in inspiring foreign development by sponsoring any new British work. Better to limit submarine innovation while working hard on anti-submarine measures. Thus in 1900 Holland was the only viable candidate for a British submarine. In 1900 that meant the Electric Boat Company controlled by Isaac L Rice, which had financed the construction of the successful *Holland* of 1898, buying up Holland's patents. Rice now wanted to make good on his investment. He planned to tour Europe, offering to sell patent rights to European companies.[1]

Initially Controller wanted a single Holland boat for ASW experiments.[2] Rice envisaged building a single boat in the United States and then accepting further orders or charging the Admiralty a royalty. DNC pointed to the high price Rice expected. By the autumn of 1900 Controller wanted a total of five submarines: one for each of the two torpedo schools (*Vernon* and *Defiance*) and three for the ports at which

Holland No 5 approaches Portsmouth Harbour in her original form, with a very low conning tower. As designed, these submarines had no periscopes; the commander was expected to porpoise periodically, looking out through the deadlights in the conning tower in which he stood. The periscope, which was stowed horizontally, was added by ICS Reginald Bacon. It was mounted on a ball joint. Bacon later wrote that he invented it because he considered it pointless to be completely blind when underwater; he hit on the idea of a tube projecting above the surface. He began by installing a prism to bend the light down the tube, then added a wide-angle lens at the top. He first tested his periscope on the stern of HMS *Vernon*, lying on his back and looking up; then he added another prism at the bottom so that he could look out while sitting up. Bacon's tube was fitted to the first Holland boat in time for her trials. Bacon thought it was the first tried in England, and possibly the first in any country. Production instruments were made by Sir Howard Grubb. The earliest periscopes suffered badly from moisture in the air in the tube, which could condense on the lenses as the tube cooled due to water rushing past it. Presumably it would be stayed up before the submarine dived. Note the projecting support for the low conning tower, which was solid only in *Holland No 1*. (Dr David Stevens)

After the 'A' class had taller conning towers fitted, the 'Hollands' were refitted similarly (about 1908). *Holland No 2* is shown at Barrow, with a new periscope rising out of her conning tower. The new conning towers retained deadlights. When the 'Hollands' were used as targets in anti-submarine experiments before the war, they proved vulnerable because the deadlights could be smashed by explosions, flooding them. That may have given an exaggerated sense of how vulnerable submarines were to shellfire. Note the surface steering wheel and the magnetic compass aft, outside the hull. As yet there were no reliable gyrocompasses to make it possible to steer a steady course submerged. The compass heading could be seen by the helmsman via a 'compass periscope tube' leading from the compass. There was a duplicate compass inside the hull, at least in the 'A' and later classes, but the strong varying magnetic field of the motor-generator badly disrupted magnetic compasses. In 1912 the Submarine Committee strongly pressed for gyrocompasses, at least for overseas submarines. After trials, the Sperry gyrocompass was chosen in favour of the Anschutz, and most British submarines had such compasses from 1914 on. (Dock Museum VPA 3441)

the destroyers would practice ASW attacks.[3] He proposed to ask Rice for five submarines of the improved 'Holland' type (Electric Boat Design 7), to be delivered in England; Rice would also provide an instructional crew. Rice met Controller on 16 October. He pointed out that building the submarines in the United States would inevitably excite press interest and make it impossible to keep the project secret. He explained further that it would be a great advantage to him and to Electric Boat if the submarines, except perhaps the first, were built in the United Kingdom.

Meanwhile Rice negotiated an exclusive licensing agreement with Vickers for all European navies. Three days after his first meeting he returned to the Admiralty with a Vickers representative; he told Controller and DNC that Vickers was now Electric Boat licensee for Europe. The company would be fully informed of both the current Holland patents and of any further improvements the company made. The five boats were offered to the Royal Navy at the same price Electric Boat had charged the US Navy, $170,000 (about £34,000 each).[4] Soon Rice agreed to have Vickers build the boats and to waive a desired royalty on further submarine construction. They became *Holland Nos 1–5*. Subsequent submarines built through the early 1920s were given class letters and numbers, e.g. *A 3*. The submarine project was definitely agreed with Vickers in December 1900 and the submarines were bought under the 1901–2 Estimates.

The 'Hollands' were extremely simple, without internal subdivision and with stern but not bow planes. Their stern planes ('diving rudders') were abaft their propellers, like the usual rudders, for maximum effect. These diving rudders were generally distinguished from stand-alone hydroplanes which were not abaft the propeller. This distinction became important when the Royal Navy developed the twin-screw 'D' class described below. They were powered by four-stroke Wolseley (i.e., British) gasoline engines rated at 160 BHP,

A 1 runs on the surface as completed, showing her pennant number in Roman form (XI). She and her sisters were designed with rudimentary bridges; note the steering wheel being operated by the sailor on the platform built atop the conning tower. The rudimentary platform forward of the conning tower was installed in 1905. This photograph was therefore taken after *A 1* had been rebuilt after having been rammed and sunk by the liner *Berwick Castle* on 18 March 1904. She was sunk as a target in October 1911. Unlike the 'Hollands', these and later submarines did not run noticeably stern-down. (NHHC)

HM SUBMARINE BOATS *1–5*. External views. (Drawn by John Lambert)

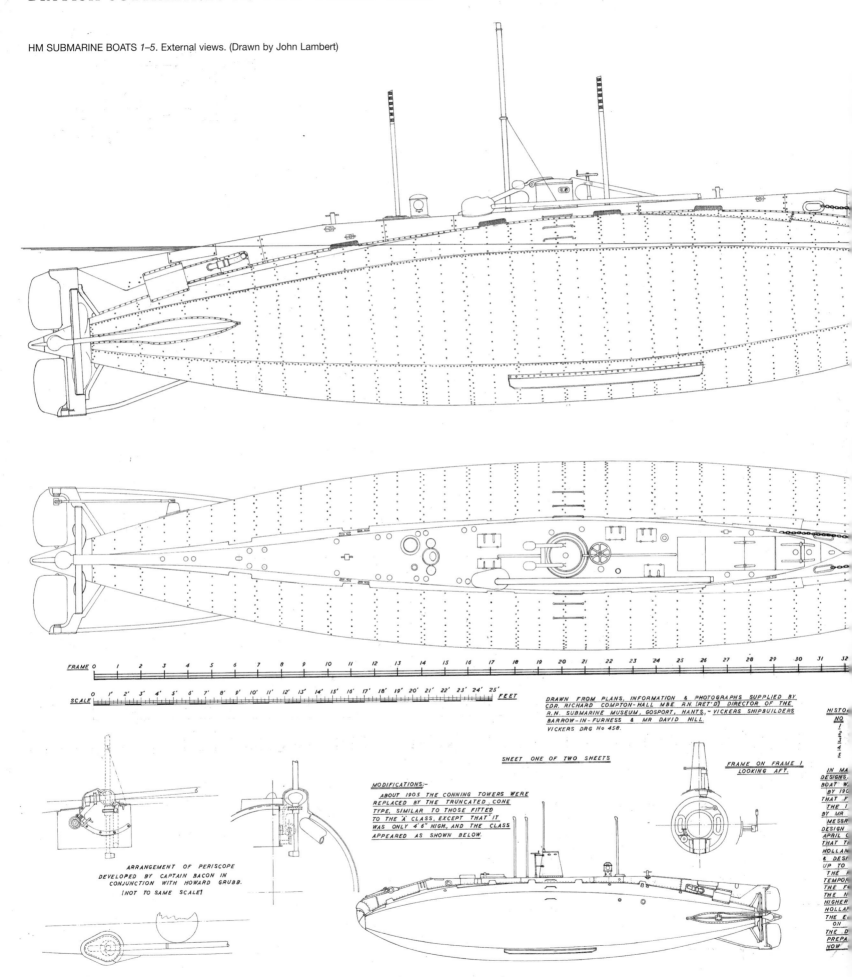

FRAME 0 1 2 3 4 5 6 7 8 9 10 11 12 13 14 15 16 17 18 19 20 21 22 23 24 25 26 27 28 29 30 31 32

SCALE 0 1' 2' 3' 4' 5' 6' 7' 8' 9' 10' 11' 12' 13' 14' 15' 16' 17' 18' 19' 20' 21' 22' 23' 24' 25' FEET

DRAWN FROM PLANS, INFORMATION & PHOTOGRAPHS SUPPLIED BY
CDR. RICHARD COMPTON-HALL M.B.E. R.N. [RET'D] DIRECTOR OF THE
R.N. SUBMARINE MUSEUM, GOSPORT, HANTS. - VICKERS SHIPBUILDERS
BARROW-IN-FURNESS & MR DAVID HILL.
VICKERS DRG No 458.

SHEET ONE OF TWO SHEETS

FRAME ON FRAME I
LOOKING AFT.

MODIFICATIONS:-
ABOUT 1905 THE CONNING TOWERS WERE
REPLACED BY THE TRUNCATED CONE
TYPE, SIMILAR TO THOSE FITTED
TO THE 'A' CLASS, EXCEPT THAT IT
WAS ONLY 4'6" HIGH, AND THE CLASS
APPEARED AS SHOWN BELOW.

ARRANGEMENT OF PERISCOPE
DEVELOPED BY CAPTAIN BACON IN
CONJUNCTION WITH HOWARD GRUBB.
[NOT TO SAME SCALE]

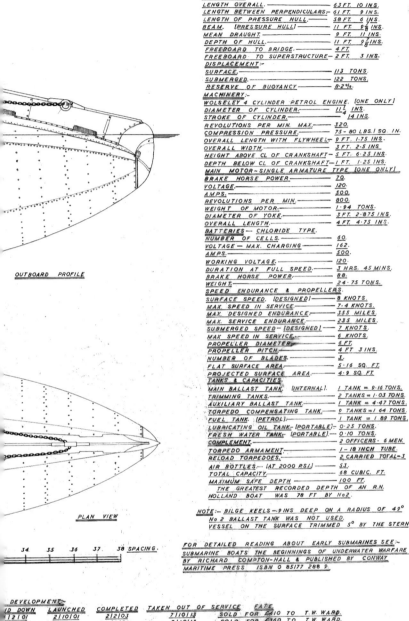

CLASS DATA

DIMENSIONS:-
LENGTH OVERALL. — 63 FT. 10 INS.
LENGTH BETWEEN PERPENDICULARS — 61 FT. 9 INS.
LENGTH OF PRESSURE HULL. — 58 FT. 6 INS.
BEAM. [PRESSURE HULL] — 11 FT. 9¾ INS.
MEAN DRAUGHT. — 9 FT. 11 INS.
DEPTH OF HULL. — 11 FT. 9¾ INS.
FREEBOARD TO BRIDGE. — 4 FT.
FREEBOARD TO SUPERSTRUCTURE — 2 FT. 3 INS.
DISPLACEMENT:-
SURFACE. — 113 TONS.
SUBMERGED. — 122 TONS.
RESERVE OF BUOYANCY. — 8·2%.
MACHINERY:-
WOLSELEY 4 CYLINDER PETROL ENGINE. [ONE ONLY]
DIAMETER OF CYLINDER. — 11½ INS.
STROKE OF CYLINDER. — 14 INS.
REVOLUTIONS PER MIN. MAX. — 320.
COMPRESSION PRESSURE. — 75 - 80 LBS./SQ. IN.
OVERALL LENGTH WITH FLYWHEEL — 9 FT. 1·75 INS.
OVERALL WIDTH. — 3 FT. 2·5 INS.
HEIGHT ABOVE CL OF CRANKSHAFT - 5 FT. 6·25 INS.
DEPTH BELOW CL OF CRANKSHAFT - 1 FT. 1·25 INS.
MAIN MOTOR - SINGLE ARMATURE TYPE [ONE ONLY]
BRAKE HORSE POWER. — 70.
VOLTAGE. — 120.
AMPS. — 500.
REVOLUTIONS PER MIN. — 800.
WEIGHT OF MOTOR. — 1·94 TONS.
DIAMETER OF YOKE. — 3 FT. 2·875 INS.
OVERALL LENGTH. — 4 FT. 4·75 INS.
BATTERIES — CHLORIDE TYPE.
NUMBER OF CELLS. — 60.
VOLTAGE - MAX. CHARGING — 162.
AMPS. — 500.
WORKING VOLTAGE. — 120.
DURATION AT FULL SPEED. — 3 HRS. 45 MINS.
BRAKE HORSE POWER. — 88.
WEIGHT. — 24·75 TONS.
SPEED ENDURANCE & PROPELLERS.
SURFACE SPEED. [DESIGNED] — 8 KNOTS.
MAX. SPEED IN SERVICE. — 7·4 KNOTS.
MAX. DESIGNED ENDURANCE. — 355 MILES.
MAX. SERVICE ENDURANCE. — 235 MILES.
SUBMERGED SPEED - [DESIGNED] — 7 KNOTS.
MAX SPEED IN SERVICE. — 6 KNOTS.
PROPELLER DIAMETER. — 6 FT.
PROPELLER PITCH. — 4 FT 3 INS.
NUMBER OF BLADES. — 1.
FLAT SURFACE AREA. — 5·16 SQ. FT.
PROJECTED SURFACE AREA. — 4·9 SQ. FT.
TANKS & CAPACITIES.
MAIN BALLAST TANK. [INTERNAL]. — 1 TANK = 9·16 TONS.
TRIMMING TANKS. — 2 TANKS = 1·03 TONS.
AUXILIARY BALLAST TANK. — 1 TANK = 4·47 TONS.
TORPEDO COMPENSATING TANK. — 0 TANKS = 1·64 TONS.
FUEL TANK. [PETROL]. — 1 TANK = 1·89 TONS.
LUBRICATING OIL TANK- [PORTABLE]. — 0·25 TONS.
FRESH WATER TANK- [PORTABLE]. — 0·10 TONS.
COMPLEMENT. — 2 OFFICERS - 6 MEN.
TORPEDO ARMAMENT. — 1 - 18 INCH TUBE.
RELOAD TORPEDOES. — 2 CARRIED TOTAL = 3.
AIR BOTTLES - [AT 2000 P.S.I.] — 53.
TOTAL CAPACITY. — 68 CUBIC. FT.
MAXIMUM SAFE DEPTH. — 100 FT.
THE GREATEST RECORDED DEPTH OF AN R.N.
HOLLAND BOAT WAS 78 FT BY No2.

NOTE:- BILGE KEELS - 9 INS. DEEP ON A RADIUS OF 49°
No 2 BALLAST TANK WAS NOT USED.
VESSEL ON THE SURFACE TRIMMED 5° BY THE STERN.

OUTBOARD PROFILE

PLAN VIEW

34   35   36   37   38 SPACING.

FOR DETAILED READING ABOUT EARLY SUBMARINES SEE:-
SUBMARINE BOATS THE BEGINNINGS OF UNDERWATER WARFARE
BY RICHARD COMPTON-HALL & PUBLISHED BY CONWAY
MARITIME PRESS ISBN 0 85177 288 9.

DEVELOPMENT.

LAID DOWN	LAUNCHED	COMPLETED	TAKEN OUT OF SERVICE	FATE
1·2·01	21·10·01	2·12·03	7·11·13	SOLD FOR £410 TO T.W. WARD.
1·2·01	21·1·02	1·18·02	7·11·13	SOLD FOR £360 TO T.W. WARD.
1·2·01	9·5·02	19·11·03	7·11·13	SOLD FOR £405 TO T.W. WARD.
	23·1·02	2·8·02	17·10·12	SUNK BY GUNFIRE DURING EXPERIMENTS 11·17
	10·6·02	19·11·03		LOST WHILST ON TOW FROM PORTSMOUTH TO SHEERNESS 8·17.

1893 THE U.S. GOVERNMENT MADE AN APPROPRIATION OF $200 000 FOR A SUBMARINE BOAT & ADVERTISED FOR
IRISH AMERICAN JOHN PHILIP HOLLAND [1841-1914] RECIEVED A CONTRACT IN 1895 & THE HOLLAND TORPEDO
ARMED, LATER TO BECOME THE ELECTRIC BOAT COMPANY.
BRITISH GOVERNMENT HAD TAKEN NO STEPS TO OBTAIN SUBMERSIBLES ALTHOUGH THE ADMIRALTY KNEW
& OTHER NATIONS WERE CONDUCTING EXPERIMENTS.
NAVY ESTIMATES PUBLISHED - 113·01 CONTAINED THE FOLLOWING STATEMENT - "FIVE SUBMARINE VESSELS, INVENTED
AND, HAVE BEEN ORDERED, THE FIRST OF WHICH SHOULD BE DELIVERED NEXT AUTUMN."
LAR TO THOSE BUILDING IN THE U.S.A. IN FACT THE FIRST R.N. HOLLAND CARRIED OUT SEA TRIALS IN
KERS SONS & MAXIM AT BARROW-IN-FURNESS WERE GIVEN THE CONTRACT, THE FIVE BOATS OF HOLLAND'S
SOME MONTHS BEFORE THE U.S.S. ADDER CARRIED OUT HERS, THUS VICKERS CAN CLAIM WITH JUSTIFICATION
THE SENIOR SUBMARINE CONSTRUCTORS. SUCH WAS THE COMPANYS ENTERPRISE THAT THEY SOON IMPROVED
DESIGN WITH THE R.Ns A, B, C & D CLASSES. ONLY FROM 1913 WERE OTHER U.K. SHIPBUILDERS ABLE TO BUILD
BRITISH SUBMARINES. U.S. PRACTICE WAS TO NUMBER FRAMES FROM AFT COMMENCING WITH 'O' & CONTINUED
'E' CLASS.
OF Nos 1-5 WAS £35000 EACH, INCLUDING DELIVERY TO A SELECTED BRITISH NAVAL PORT. No1 WAS
COMPLETED WITHOUT HER ARMAMENT. FIRST DIVING TRIALS TOOK PLACE ON 5·2·02 & DEEP SEA TRIALS
DURING APRIL. No1 NOT BEING COMPLETED UNTIL NEARLY A YEAR LATER. SHE SANK DURING MANOEVRES OFF
LIGHTSHIP ON 18·3·04. SHE WAS RAISED AFTER ONE MONTH & AFTER REPAIRS WENT BACK INTO SERVICE.
CONNING TOWERS WERE FITTED TO THE CLASS - 1905-06.
No1 WAS LOST WHILST ON TOW FROM PORTSMOUTH TO T.W. WARD LTD OF SHEFFIELD WHILST 1·5 MILES OFF
ONE LIGHTHOUSE, TOWED BY THE TUG ENFIELD. SHE WAS LOST DURING HEAVY WEATHER IN NOVEMBER 1913.
DAY 14 APRIL 1981 THE MINE HUNTER H.M.S. BOSSINGTON MADE SONAR CONTACT WITH HOLLAND No1. BY MIDNIGHT
VESSEL SEAFORTH CLANSMAN HAD IDENTIFIED HER, THEN DURING 9-23 AUGUST 1982 NAVAL DIVING PARTY 1007
HER FOR LIFTING & RECOVERY. SHE WAS SUCCESSFULLY SALVAGED IN SEPTEMBER. SHE IS
DISPLAY AT THE R.N. SUBMARINE MUSEUM AT GOSPORT, VERY NEAR TO H.M.S. DOLPHIN.

L/S/52/A

© JOHN LAMBERT 15·8·83

---

driving their single propellers directly via their motor-generators. The lack of subdivision was later considered a major virtue, because it allowed officers to supervise all operations in the submarine. As yet there were no telemotors (introduced about 1915), so all valves had to be operated individually, by hand.

The Royal Navy's 'Hollands' differed from Holland's American submarines mainly in having periscopes ('optical tubes'); the American submarines were conned by coming awash periodically, their commanding officers peering through deadlights let into a low conning tower.[5] While the boats were being built Captain Bacon, who was superintending construction, wrote to DNC and Controller that he feared difficulties in steering the boats underwater with only the stern planes and a positive buoyancy of 500lbs. He wanted additional hydroplanes fore and aft fitted to one of the boats for trials.[6] DNC's deputy H S Deadman pointed out that unless the planes were arranged symmetrically around the centre of gravity of the boat, they might exert a turning force, which would be even worse if one plane were damaged. More importantly, any interference with plans supplied by Electric Boat would become an excuse allowing the firm to disclaim all responsibility in the event of some mishap. Moreover, it was understood that no such problems had occurred in the United States; boats were able to maintain depth within a foot and it was easy to level the boat out after it dove at the usual 10° angle.

Holland No 1 ran her first diving trials on 5 February 1902, deep sea trials following in April. Reportedly the 'Hollands' were only moderately successful and their gasoline engines caused considerable trouble. They were erratic when submerged and they had poor surface qualities. However, they had excellent diving qualities and could submerge from full buoyancy in three minutes.[7] In 1903, having operated the 'Hollands', Captain Bacon wrote that their curse was their limited horizon when surfaced.[8] They were difficult to trim in a seaway except after considerable experience. Their periscopes had to be so long that they could not be retracted into the submarine; to take them down, the internal part had to be removed. Finally, their submerged speed was too low, so that too many were needed. Bacon added that the new 'A' class would overcome these defects.

This is one of *A 2* through *A 6*, all of which had the sharply raked bridge fairwater. Later units (and *A 5* and *A 6* as modified) had the fairwater extended so that it continued almost all the way under the bridge platform. These later units also had very visible engine exhausts extending down into the water from below the after part of the fairwater. Surviving 'A'-class submarines served during the First World War for training and as harbour defence craft. (R A Burt)

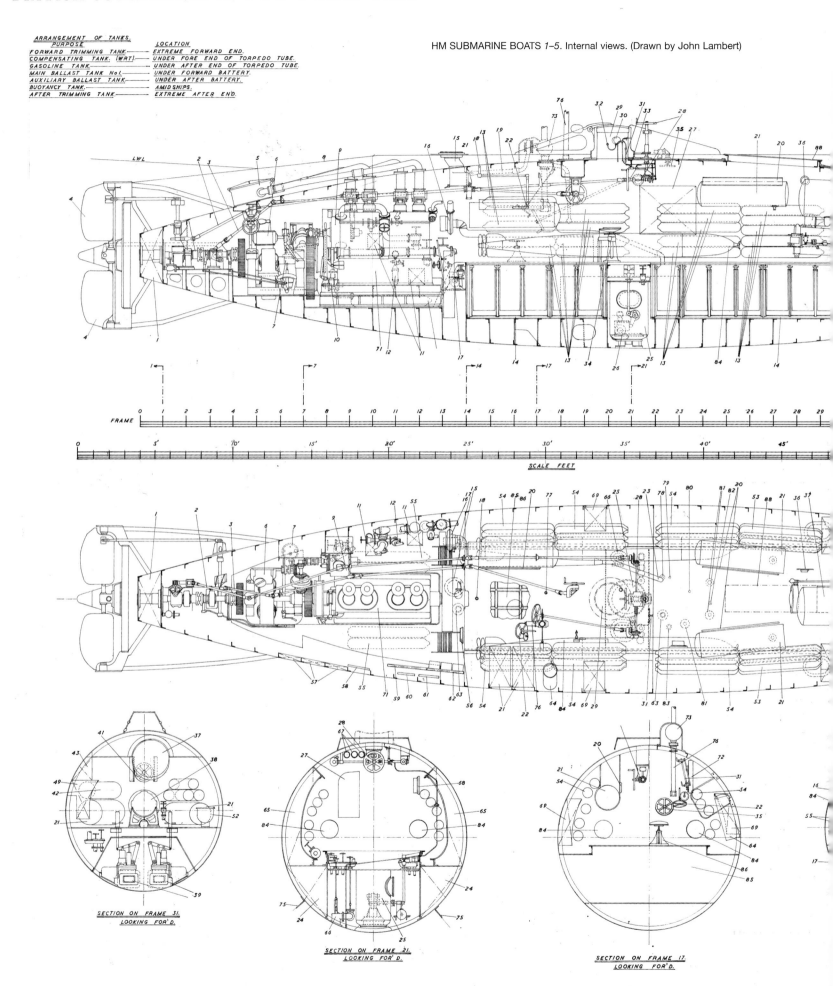

ARRANGEMENT OF TANKS.

PURPOSE	LOCATION
FORWARD TRIMMING TANK.	EXTREME FORWARD END.
COMPENSATING TANK. [WRT]	UNDER FORE END OF TORPEDO TUBE.
GASOLINE TANK.	UNDER AFTER END OF TORPEDO TUBE.
MAIN BALLAST TANK No.I.	UNDER FORWARD BATTERY.
AUXILIARY BALLAST TANK.	UNDER AFTER BATTERY.
BUOYANCY TANK.	AMIDSHIPS.
AFTER TRIMMING TANK.	EXTREME AFTER END.

HM SUBMARINE BOATS *1–5*. Internal views. (Drawn by John Lambert)

SECTION ON FRAME 31. LOOKING FOR'D.

SECTION ON FRAME 21. LOOKING FOR'D.

SECTION ON FRAME 17. LOOKING FOR'D.

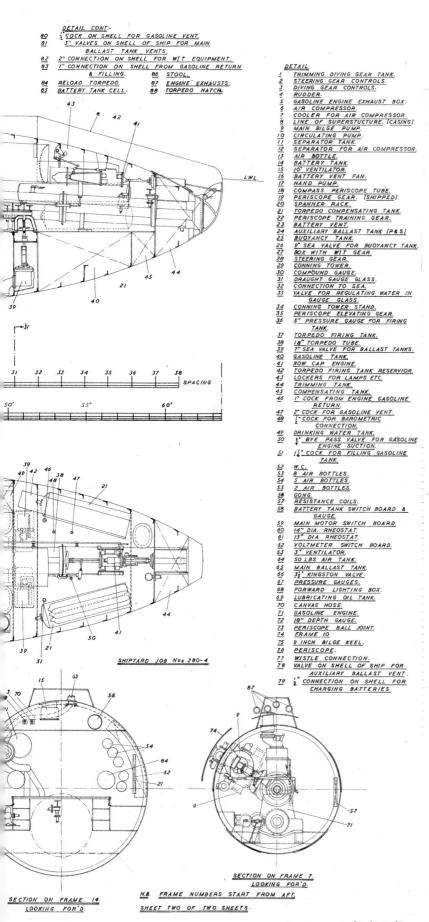

DETAIL CONT:-
80 ½" COCK ON SHELL FOR GASOLINE VENT.
81 3" VALVES ON SHELL OF SHIP FOR MAIN BALLAST TANK VENTS.
82 2" CONNECTION ON SHELL FOR W/T EQUIPMENT.
83 1" CONNECTION ON SHELL FROM GASOLINE RETURN & FILLING.
84 RELOAD TORPEDO.
85 BATTERY TANK CELL.
86 STOOL.
87 ENGINE EXHAUSTS.
88 TORPEDO HATCH.

DETAIL
1 TRIMMING DIVING GEAR TANK.
2 STEERING GEAR CONTROLS.
3 DIVING GEAR CONTROLS.
4 RUDDER.
5 GASOLINE ENGINE EXHAUST BOX.
6 AIR COMPRESSOR.
7 COOLER FOR AIR COMPRESSOR.
8 LINE OF SUPERSTUCTURE. (CASING).
9 MAIN BILGE PUMP.
10 CIRCULATING PUMP.
11 SEPARATOR TANK.
12 SEPARATOR FOR AIR COMPRESSOR.
13 AIR BOTTLE.
14 BATTERY TANK.
15 10" VENTILATOR.
16 BATTERY VENT FAN.
17 HAND PUMP.
18 COMPASS PERISCOPE TUBE.
19 PERISCOPE GEAR. (SHIPPED).
20 SPANNER RACK.
21 TORPEDO COMPENSATING TANK.
22 PERISCOPE TRAINING GEAR.
23 BATTERY VENT.
24 AUXILIARY BALLAST TANK (P&S)
25 BUOYANCY TANK.
26 9" SEA VALVE FOR BUOYANCY TANK.
27 BOX WITH W/T GEAR.
28 STEERING GEAR.
29 CONNING TOWER.
30 COMPOUND GAUGE.
31 DRAUGHT GAUGE GLASS.
32 CONNECTION TO SEA.
33 VALVE FOR REGULATING WATER IN GAUGE GLASS.
34 CONNING TOWER STAND.
35 PERISCOPE ELEVATING GEAR.
36 5" PRESSURE GAUGE FOR FIRING TANK.
37 TORPEDO FIRING TANK.
38 18" TORPEDO TUBE.
39 7" SEA VALVE FOR BALLAST TANKS.
40 GASOLINE TANK.
41 BOW CAP ENGINE.
42 TORPEDO FIRING TANK RESERVOIR.
43 LOCKERS FOR LAMPS ETC.
44 TRIMMING TANK.
45 COMPENSATING TANK.
46 1" COCK FROM ENGINE GASOLINE RETURN.
47 2" COCK FOR GASOLINE VENT.
48 ½" COCK FOR BAROMETRIC CONNECTION.
49 DRINKING WATER TANK.
50 ½" BYE PASS VALVE FOR GASOLINE ENGINE SUCTION.
51 1½" COCK FOR FILLING GASOLINE TANK.
52 W.C.
53 8 AIR BOTTLES.
54 5 AIR BOTTLES.
55 2 AIR BOTTLES.
56 GONG.
57 RESISTANCE COILS.
58 BATTERY TANK SWITCH BOARD & GAUGE.
59 MAIN MOTOR SWITCH BOARD.
60 14" DIA. RHEOSTAT.
61 15" DIA RHEOSTAT.
62 VOLTMETER SWITCH BOARD.
63 3" VENTILATOR.
64 50 LBS AIR TANK.
65 MAIN BALLAST TANK.
66 3½" KINGSTON VALVE.
67 PRESSURE GAUGES.
68 FORWARD LIGHTING BOX.
69 LUBRICATING OIL TANK.
70 CANVAS HOSE.
71 GASOLINE ENGINE.
72 18" DEPTH GAUGE.
73 PERISCOPE BALL JOINT.
74 FRAME 10.
75 9 INCH BILGE KEEL.
76 PERISCOPE.
77 WISTLE CONNECTION.
78 VALVE ON SHELL OF SHIP FOR AUXILIARY BALLAST VENT.
79 1½" CONNECTION ON SHELL FOR CHARGING BATTERIES.

SHIPYARD JOB Nos 280-4

SECTION ON FRAME 7 LOOKING FOR'D.

SECTION ON FRAME 14. LOOKING FOR'D.

N.B. FRAME NUMBERS START FROM AFT

SHEET TWO OF TWO SHEETS.

© JOHN LAMBERT 21/8/83

L/S/52/B

B 2 as completed, a considerably enlarged 'A'-boat. One noticeable difference was a substantial casing, rather than a deck built over the pressure hull. It stopped short of the bow in a vertical line, rather than the sloped fairing line of the earlier class. Another was a pair of forward planes on the fore side of the conning tower (first tested on board *A 7*). *B 1* differed from the others in having a sharply sloping stern and a more sharply sloping bridge fairwater (altered in 1908, but the stern remained). (US Naval Institute)

Having superintended the construction of the 'Hollands', Bacon became the first Inspecting Captain of Submarines (ICS), in effect chief of the infant British submarine service. He pressed for a more seaworthy follow-on.[9] The 1902–3 Estimates provided four submarines of a considerably enlarged 'A' class (*A 1–A 4*). *A 1* was designed for Bacon by Vickers. She was 100ft long, compared to 63ft for the 'Hollands'. Rated displacement was nearly twice that of the 'Hollands', 204 tons rather than 122 tons. The lines were sent to the testing tank, whose chief R E Froude suggested modifications to give them better speed at economical power. Of the four, *A 2–A 4* were modified as Froude suggested. They were 99ft long. These submarines seem to have been considered far more successful than the small 'Hollands'. They were much larger than the improved 'Hollands' ('B' class), which Electric Boat was soon designing for the US Navy and thus probably marked a departure from any dependence on US designs.

Apart from greater size, the most visible change was a 7ft high conning tower, installed at Bacon's suggestion. It housed periscopes. This innovation having proven successful, in June 1905 a high conning tower was ordered for at least one of the original 'Hollands' (*No. 2*).[10] Oddly, the refit was justified by Holland's fitting conning towers to submarines for Japan and Russia, rather than by experience with the 'A' class.

A 1 turned out to be handier below water than the 'Hollands'. She behaved well at sea and could keep her depth even at quite moderate speeds, in contrast to earlier boats, which had to run at full speed submerged and had to be trimmed very carefully.[11] Bacon considered her 350 BHP engine promising, but not powerful enough (he had hoped for 500 BHP). For *A 2–A 4* the Admiralty asked for an additional torpedo tube as well as some minor improvements. By May 1903 Vickers was developing a more powerful gasoline engine, which produced 750 BHP on trial. Development turned out to be protracted.[12] Bacon later wrote that it was the most powerful light oil (petrol)

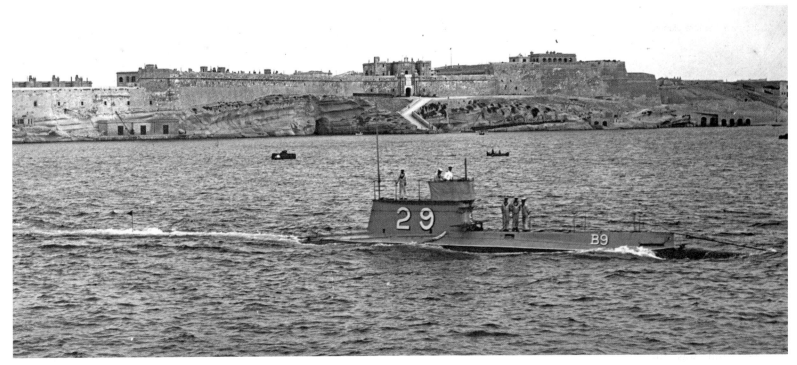

engine the Royal Navy was likely to need; its development also provided invaluable experience. *A 5* had it, plus further improvements.[13] Estimated surface speeds given in 1906 were 9 knots for *A 1* (350 BHP), *A 2* 10.5 knots at 450 BHP and *A 5* 11 knots at 600 BHP.[14]

By 1903 there were two major engine developments in prospect. One was to replace the horizontal engines then on board submarines with vertical ones. EinC wrote that from a mechanical point of view a vertical engine offered such advantages that 'every endeavour should be made to fit vertical engines in the new boats'. The only problem was that the centreline of the crankshaft would be below the centreline of the boat. The engine would either be geared to a centreline shaft or connected to it via a universal joint, to avoid producing offset thrust.

The second possibility was a heavy oil engine, though not necessarily a diesel. By this time some of EinC's advisors already had considerable experience with such engines; in May Bacon wrote to Vickers asking whether any non-gasoline engine was considered to have material advantages over the gasoline engine currently under test.[15] Was EinC in a position to submit such a design to Vickers with a view to having one made for trial?[16] Bacon wanted Vickers to experiment with vertical engines burning both heavy and light (gasoline) oil.

EinC wrote that although the internal combustion engine, particularly the heavy oil engine, was still in an early stage of development, the petrol engine must give way to it

on the scores of greater safety, reduced cost of running (the heavy oil can be purchased at about ½ to ⅓ the price of gasoline) and also the power which can be produced in a single cylinder . . . Explosion of a mixture of gasoline vapour and air is comparatively sharp and with an explosion of such a nature it is difficult to calculate the real stresses which come upon the piston, connecting rods and crank shaft, while with a heavier oil the combustion is slower, a more steady pressure is obtained and a more uniform turning moment produced on the crank shaft. The temperature of ignition of the gasoline explosion being lower it will always be more sensitive to change of conditions

At Malta, *B 9* shows her considerably enlarged fairwater, with a bridge on top protected by a canvas cheater. It covered the magnetic compass visible on board *B 2*. The casing was cut down sharply abaft it, much reducing the submarine's apparent length. This modification was carried out beginning in 1909–10 with *B 1*. Submarines of this type were sent abroad in the summer of 1912 to provide local defence for key overseas bases: *B 9*, *B 10* and *B 11* to Malta, and *B 6*, *B 7* and *B 8* to Gibraltar. *C 36–C 38* went to Hong Kong, arriving on 20 April 1911 after a 72-day journey. *B 11* was the first British submarine to penetrate the Dardanelles, sinking the Turkish battleship *Messudieh*. By October 1916, *B 8* and *B 10* had machine guns (with portable mountings), the only ships of their class apparently to have gun armament. (NHHC)

within the cylinder and therefore ignition more uncertain, a difficulty which will be accentuated with increased diameter . . . attempts to increase the power in a single cylinder of a gasoline motor will entail more or less risk of failure and recourse should be had to increase the number of cylinders when an increase of power is desired.

The Vickers gasoline engine in the later 'A', 'B' and 'C' classes already needed sixteen cylinders to generate 600 BHP and any addition would make it longer and hence more difficult to accommodate. That was apart from the complication of balancing more and more pistons to limit vibration and the increasing maintenance effort required to handle more cylinders.[17]

EinC proposed using the existing Hornsby-Ackroyd engine, already widely used ashore, which could burn low-volatility heavy oil (flashpoint not less than 200° F). Hornsby had already produced 125 BHP in a single cylinder and it seemed likely that he could scale up to 150. To accommodate such engines, EinC wanted at least the later 'A'-boats to have vertical engine installations. To Bacon the important point was that a design for a four-cylinder 600 HP heavy oil engine existed. The greater weight of a heavy oil engine could be balanced by its greater efficiency, hence by a reduction in fuel. Hornsby expected to build the first engine in about nine months, plus three months to erect and test it in the shop. The company was willing to license

B 5 shows her fore planes and her enlarged bridge. (R A Burt)

further production to Vickers. EinC proposed testing the new engine in one of the new 'A'-boats.[18]

It turned out that the Hornsby engine had to be rebuilt after preliminary running and in June 1905 its manufacturer had to accept lower RPM. When trials were eventually run in September 1907 it failed to develop even 400 BHP. It was paid for pro rata on the power obtained and was finally installed in the power station at Simonstown.[19] Other firms were approached during 1905. Vickers experimented with full diesels; in October 1905 it offered to guarantee 500 BHP and to complete and install an engine within six months. This offer was accepted in December 1905, subject to the engine being fully suitable for *A 13* and that it should use oil with a flashpoint of 150° F (and be able to use oil with a 200° flashpoint). It was soon clear

that the experimental Vickers engine could not develop the guaranteed power. Vickers therefore rebuilt it. Running in October 1906, it developed only 450 BHP. Vickers was given three months both to improve performance and to obtain data for the engines planned at that time for *D 1*. In March 1907 serious defects developed; the first official trial was at the end of August 1907. This time the guaranteed power was obtained, but further improvements were considered necessary. A satisfactory trial followed in September 1907, although when running on Texas oil the engine developed less power with a smoky exhaust. A year later *A 13* made her first run, to Portsmouth. The Admiralty officer who monitored it wrote that despite minor problems, particularly with the air compressor (which were common at the time) the engine was superior to existing petrol engines.[20]

The 'C' class began as slightly modified 'B'-boats; this is *C 3* as built, with a small fairwater similar to that of the 'B' class. (RAN Historical Section via Dr Josef Straczek)

C 9 shows her initial fairwater and her two periscopes. Note that she no longer had planes on her fairwater. (NHHC)

The *A 13* diesel provided crucial experience for *D 1*, which required two 600 BHP engines. The company's *D 1* engine was a fresh design, introducing the cylinder Vickers later used for the 'E', 'J', 'K' and 'L' classes. Its general design was approved in June 1907, but satisfactory shop trials were not completed until early 1909, the submarine being completed late that year. It ran satisfactory trials in January 1910. Other submarines of the class had improved engines.

To Bacon, the obvious direction of future development was better seakeeping. The *A 2* class was useful mainly off harbours and coasts. Their minimum surfaced speed was 11–12 knots (10 knots cruising at half power); submerged speed was 8–8.5 knots for 4 hours or 6 knots for 8–9 hours. Radius of action was 400nm. They were able to remain at sea for three days to ride out any ordinary bad weather.

Bacon proposed a further experimental submarine (which he called the 'B' type) in a 7 November 1903 memo to Controller.[21] Machinery would repeat that of the 'A' class. The two most important improvements would be increased radius of action and increased habitability. Both could be obtained by enlarging the boat (to carry more fuel) and providing a more suitable superstructure to add to the crew's comfort and freedom. All of this would cost speed, so Bacon asked what speed was essential. Surface speed was valuable strategically but not tactically, because on sighting a target a submarine would immediately dive, steering by compass. For that matter, a submarine could not remain on the surface in daylight for fear that her bow wave would be seen. Bacon therefore considered 10–12 knots sufficient surface speed. It was not worth sacrificing radius of action or any other quality to gain higher surface speed. This was very different from the case of a destroyer or surface torpedo boat, for which high speed was vital tactically, both in attacking and in escaping after an attack. Because she was invisible when submerged, the submarine could approach her target and also escape afterwards.

Submerged speed was vital tactically, but it was difficult to secure. Bacon stated that the submerged power needed to drive a boat at a given speed was about proportional to her displacement.[22] Since the submerged submarine was always slower than the target, the obvious tactic was for the submarine to steer at right angles to the course of the target until ahead of her. That defined what would later be called limiting lines of approach, within which a submarine could attack but outside which she could not. He could compare the value of various submerged speeds against a target making 15 knots, which in 1902 was reasonable for a major unit. For example, the advantage of 8 knots over 6 knots submerged was 4:3. That gain was hardly commensurate with the sacrifice involved in raising submarine speed, particularly since submarines would generally work in groups, at least some of which would probably be in favourable attacking positions.

Existing submarines were designed to discharge their batteries at a 4-hour rate at most; a few knots could be gained if the batteries discharged at a higher rate. Speed could be gained by adding motor rather than battery weight. For example, instead of designing for four hours at 8 knots Bacon could ask for two hours at 8 knots, retaining the normal underwater speed of 6 knots for four hours. His best captain preferred to manoeuvre submerged at 4 knots 'and his attacks are by far the most successful'; high submerged speed might not always be desirable. Bacon concluded that he wanted a normal submerged speed

Like the 'B' class, the 'C' class were given enlarged fairwaters. This is *C 13* as modified, her fore planes having been relocated to her bow. Often submarines ran with a canvas cheater around the fore end of the fairwater. Submarines were modified in 1909–11, probably beginning with *C 13* and *C 14*. (NHHC)

Later 'C'-class submarines (*C 19* onwards) had a different enlarged fairwater, lower at the after end. Their planes were relocated to their bows; the two bow planes are just visible right forward. There was a single periscope. This is *C 34*. (Alan C. Green via State Library of Victoria)

of 6 knots for four hours, with the ability to attain 8 knots for two hours. Submerged radius of action was of little importance, but the time the boat could stay down would determine whether she could escape pursuit after an attack. Bacon considered eight hours sufficient.

Bacon considered two loaded torpedo tubes, as in a destroyer, sufficient; no destroyer in a manoeuvre had ever found them inadequate. It was uninspiring to submariners that their only defence was 'to skulk below water . . . – and for destroyers to know that submarines will probably not shed their teeth in firing torpedoes at them'. He therefore pressed for a gun sufficient to disable a pursuing destroyer – a 12pdr – which could be loaded from the conning tower. To him the knowledge that a submarine could approach a destroyer unseen and then fire point-blank a shell sufficient to sink it, would make destroyers 'far more careful how they not only dog submarines, but how they loiter near our ports'.

Bacon therefore proposed a 135ft boat (300 tons) with the same (improved) engine as *A 2* (12 knots surfaced) and a sixth more battery power giving 200 HP for four hours or 300 HP for two hours, coupled to a heavier motor giving 6 knots for four hours or 8 knots for two hours. Surface radius of action should be 800 miles. The submarine should have an additional superstructure for the crews' use as well as sleeping accommodation.[23]

DNC had no objection to passing these requirements to Vickers.[24] Controller (Rear Admiral W H May) agreed and proposed to order the tenth submarine in the current programme to the new 'B' design. First Lord Kerr agreed, except for the gun; he was not enthusiastic about using submarines against destroyers and considered it risky to stow cordite with the very inflammable material inside a submarine (meaning gasoline). He asked for a meeting of the Naval Lords, which was arranged for 22 December. They approved the 'B' submarine except for its gun. On 15 January 1904 Vickers was sent a letter asking for a design, to be prepared in conjunction with Bacon, for a single

C 32 shows her enlarged fairwater. The big low structure abaft the bridge covered the magnetic compass. She is probably alongside HMS *Victory* at Portsmouth. (NHHC)

SUBMARINE BOATS *C 19* AND *C 20* AS FITTED. Profile and plan of superstructure. (© National Maritime Museum M1061)

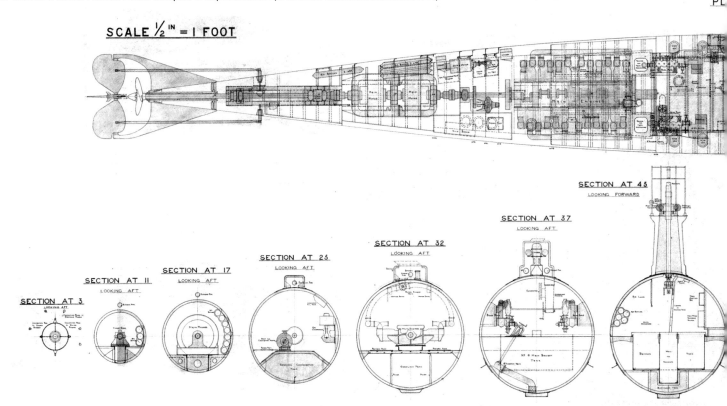

SUBMARINE BOATS *C 19* AND *C 20* AS FITTED. Plan of flat and sections. (© National Maritime Museum M1060)

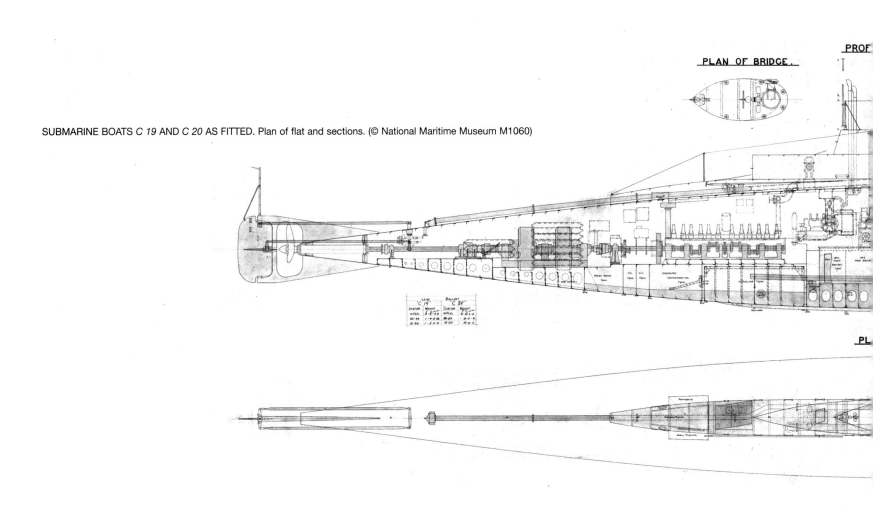

OF FLAT

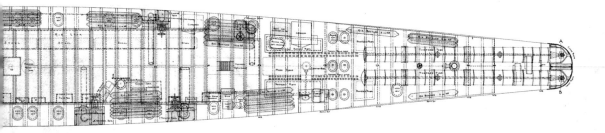

SECTION AT 56
LOOKING FORWARD

SECTION AT 62
LOOKING FORWARD

SECTION AT 67
LOOKING FORWARD

SECTION AT 72
LOOKING FORWARD

SECTION AT 79
LOOKING FORWARD

SECTION AT 82
LOOKING FORWARD

SECTION AT AB
LOOKING FORWARD

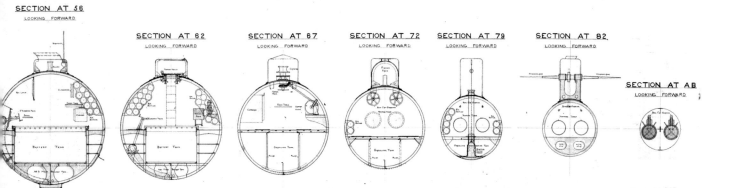

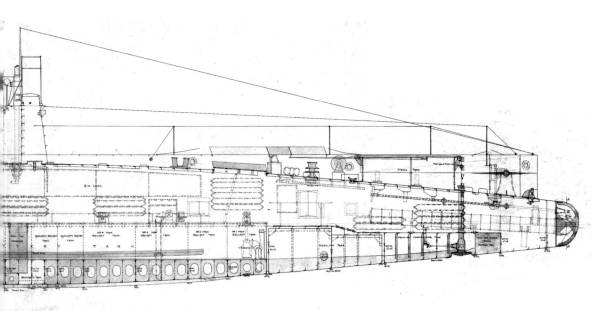

OF SUPERSTRUCTURE.

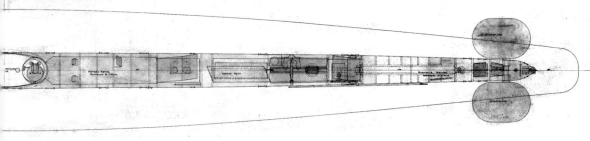

C 22, probably after mid-1915, when boats' own designations were used as their pennant numbers and painted on their fairwaters. The jumping wires were a wartime addition. Bow planes are barely visible right forward. (NHHC)

enlarged boat, 135ft long, displacing 300 tons, with battery power of 200 HP for two hours rather than 150 HP for four hours and a motor capable of producing 300 HP when desired. She had to be laid down during the 1903–4 financial year (ending 31 March), because she was part of the 1903–4 Programme. Vickers understood the need for speed, so on 22 January it sent in its tender. The company proposed a 125-footer, which would cost £48,883 compared to £40,215 for an 'A'-boat. The design actually built was a 135-footer.

Each of the 1903–4 and 1904–5 Programmes included ten new submarines of, respectively, the 'A' and 'B' classes (the first of the 'B' class was built under the 1903–4 Programme).[25] Another ten submarines were planned for 1905–6. There was apparently no question but that they would be repeat 'B'-boats. However, ICS proposed a series of improvements which would justify a new class designation: the 'C' class.[26] They would have four- rather than three-bladed propellers, for higher speed and greater efficiency. The motor would have two armatures rather than the previous three, each offering a greater range of speeds (underwater BHP increased by 50 per cent). The battery would be watertight, with 160 cells rather than 159; the main fuses and main switches would be combined. All terminals and switches would be as high as possible in the boat, to keep them dry. The hydroplanes would be pivoted near the balancing point of the submarine. All of these changes (and others) were proposed after the boats were ordered, so ICS had to limit the extra cost involved.

This finally seemed to be the basis for a large class of standard submarines: C 1–C 11 in the 1905–6 Programme, C 12–C 18 in 1906–7, C 19–C 30 in 1907–8, C 31–C 32 in 1908–9 and C 33–C 38 in 1909–10. Vickers built two more for Japan. There were actually several sub-classes. Overall, changes, particularly larger conning

towers and bridges, superstructures and different hydroplanes all increased resistance and cost underwater speed. On the other hand, the 'C'-boats had greater underwater power. Vickers' design figure was apparently 7.5 knots on 300 BHP submerged, although DNC later claimed only 7 knots.[27] Rated surface speed remained at 12 knots but endurance increased to 910nm at full speed and 1360nm at half power. Since the battery could not be enlarged, it could not run the larger motor for as long. The full-discharge time at full speed was reduced from 4 hours to 2 hours 20 minutes (500 amps), so at 7 knots endurance underwater was about 14nm. The design figure was 50nm at 4.5 knots.

C 19 and later boats had redesigned tail frames, a new propeller, a redesigned engine exhaust and a new low-resistance conning tower with a fixed bridge. The improvements bought as much as 1.5 to 2 knots (at 294 RPM) over the previous units. On 10 May 1912 C 22 made 8.65 knots at 294 RPM (650 amps). The previous best was C 13 with her conning tower modified to match the later design; she had gained half a knot compared to earlier units.

In 1908 ICS (Captain S S Hall) proposed giving up the four forward cylinders (out of sixteen) of the gasoline engines of the 'A' class (A 5–A 12) and to fit them with bow hydroplanes. DNC agreed; the propellers fitted could not absorb the full power of the engine and at high speed the boats tended to go down by the bow. This change applied to later 'C'-class submarines. The modified engines had the same 600 BHP rating as earlier ones, but presumably that was unrealistic.

A New Generation

In June 1905 the Submarine Boat Design Committee met to consider what should be built under the 1906–7 Programme.[28] The 'Hollands' and their successors ('A', 'B' and 'C' classes) all had cigar-shaped hulls with all ballast tanks inboard, hence of limited capacity, meaning that the boats had limited reserve buoyancy, typically about 12 per cent. Habitability was poor, there were no watertight bulkheads and speed was low both surfaced and submerged. Given very low reserve buoyancy, a boat with her conning tower hatch open might nose down into a wave and flood. British submariners knew that the French and the Italians were building boats with much greater reserve buoyancy, for better seakeeping. The French publicised a comparison between what they termed a true submarine (with very little sacrificed for surface seakeeping) and a submersible. The true submarine *Émeraude* had 7 per cent reserve of buoyancy; the submersible *Pluviose* had about 40 per cent. The trials strongly favoured the submersible, the French abandoning construction of submarines with poor seakeeping.

To get the desired ship qualities, the French designer Laubeuf wrapped a ship-like outer hull around a circular-section (hence strong) pressure hull, fairing the outer hull into the pressure hull below the waterline. The space between pressure hull and outer hull provided the desired reserve buoyancy. At least at first, Laubeuf's submarines were

not quite double-hulled, but they did show that reserve buoyancy was worthwhile. Laubeuf's early submarines were sometimes described as pressure hulls wrapped in outer hulls of torpedo-boat form.

In Italy Laurenti employed single-hull ends with ballast tanks amidships in the form of a watertight structure almost completely surrounding his pressure hull. He did not use a circular-section pressure hull. The outer structure was divided into upper watertight 'baling spaces' which could be flooded using valves and lower spaces which could be flooded from below via Kingstons, valves set into the ship's bottom. Normally the Kingstons were open. On the surface the lower tanks were filled with air, the submarine 'riding the vents'. Watertight flats separated the upper and lower spaces. With the flats watertight, reserve buoyancy would be 65 per cent; overall, the ballast tankage amounted to 28 per cent of displacement. Laurenti had rejected inherently strong circular-section pressure hulls in order to shape his outer hulls for high surface speed, using deep framing for strength. When the Royal Navy adopted double-hulled designs, almost all were based on Laurenti practice.

The chief requirements in 1905 seems to have been greater reserve buoyancy and also greater resistance to plunging in a swell. The latter translated as longitudinal stability. Neither Laubeuf nor Laurenti designs seem to have been considered, possibly because DNC had not

Although not considered an overseas submarine, *D 1* was in effect their prototype: she introduced saddle tanks and twin power trains. The magnetic compass was moved into the casing (it was accessible via a hatch). There was also a stern torpedo tube. The vertical object right aft was the base of a portable torpedo crane serving the after tube. *D 1* was conceived with a secondary conning tower aft. As she was built, it was reduced to a protected hatch abaft which a second periscope protruded. It is shown raised. She sometimes had a topside rudder, but it is absent from this photograph. The class typically had this rudder in 1909–12 but not later. (NHHC)

yet come into much contact with either. Only in 1909 did ICS (Captain S S Hall) report in detail on Laubeuf and Laurenti designs, probably due to the visit of Laurenti's Swedish submarine *Hvalen* to Portsmouth.[29]

DNC offered the Submarine Boat Design Committee two alternative designs, 'C2' and 'D', each with greater reserve buoyancy. 'C2' was a single-hull submarine, like the earlier designs, with added tankage atop the hull. 'D' was more radical, adding a pair of saddle tanks alongside the hull. They contained the bulk of her water ballast, 99 tons. Five internal tanks under the batteries carried another 29 tons (on completion, it turned out that *D 1* needed only 13 tons in these tanks). Since the hull did not have to contain most of the ballast, reserve buoyancy (as set by tank volume) could be much greater than before. Moreover, as the boat grew larger, pressure hull diameter did not have to keep increasing. That limited the submarine's draft and it also helped limit wasted space inside the pressure hull. Overall, water ballast in 'D' amounted to about a quarter of total displacement. The corresponding figure for a 'B'-boat was 29 tons (1/11th of submerged displacement).

'D' added hydroplanes ('side rudders') on the sides of the hull forward of the stern. They were considered very desirable in such large boats. Captain Bacon, former head of the submarine service, pointed out that the 'B' class already had hydroplanes on their conning towers, where they were less subject to injury than they would be on the boats' hulls (as in the 'D' design). Because these hydroplanes were out of the water until the submarine was nearly underwater, they could not contribute to controlling diving near the surface.

'D' offered considerably increased displacement, 414 tons when surfaced and more battery power (212 cells rather than 159) at a cost of about £10,000 beyond that of a 'B'-boat. Freeboard would be 3ft 7in, compared to 2ft 5in to the top of the hull (2ft 10in to the top of the superstructure) of a 'B'-boat. ICS Captain Lees pointed to the greater safety of Design 'D' due to its greater reserve buoyancy and also greater economy at low speed. The number of torpedo tubes doubled to two and 'D' had twin screws. Petrol stowage would be doubled. Greater size would buy increased accommodation, sufficient to provide reliefs. The endurance (in terms of fuel) of the 'C' class was already more than her crew could manage. The new submarine could operate longer away from her base, which was the beginning of attempts to build submarines suitable for overseas work. Lees pointed out that although 'D' was somewhat larger than previous British submarines, she would still be somewhat smaller than some of the French submarines.

The fairwater of *D 1* shows her forward periscope. Light coming through the footholds on the side shows that the conning tower occupied only a small fraction of the fairwater. The circular object is the raised conning tower hatch. In addition, there was a telescoping radio mast. Between it and the fore periscope was a wheel to be used for surface steering. (NHHC)

The fairwater of *D 2* shows both periscopes as well as the wheel and pelorus to be used on the surface. (NHHC)

The designers adopted a flat deck forward so that the two bow torpedo tubes could be installed one above the other. The form with a bow flattened vertically and a stern flattened transversely was considered well adapted to depth-keeping. By adopting twin screws, the designers could provide for two stern torpedo tubes, something no previous British submarine had. They also claimed that dividing power between two screws made for greater efficiency at the power and RPM ranges available from the gasoline engine for which the submarine was designed.

The designers pointed out that they had not gained very much space in the new design. It was 12ft longer than 'B', of which the main engines absorbed about 9ft and the battery probably more than 3ft. It had been difficult to find space for gasoline and for compensating tanks. Water jacketing around the gasoline added considerable weight, limited gasoline capacity and much complicated the design. The designers commented that the submarine could be greatly improved by lengthening and, by implication, by eliminating gasoline. At this stage the submarine was 153ft long overall; as built it was 163ft long.

Numbers mattered; was the more expensive submarine worthwhile? Extra battery power would be expensive when batteries had to be replaced. Captain Bacon, formerly head of the submarine service, doubted that adding reliefs would really extend submarines' endurance, as crews could not well remain on board for more than about three days even in good weather. As for armament, Bacon suggested that the 'B' class might be modified to accommodate three torpedoes.

None of this killed the proposed new design; Controller ruled that the matter was too important to decide at once. The first step would be to try the hull-mounted planes, which could be fitted to the last boat of the 'B' class. The questions of increased buoyancy and size would be deferred. Even so, the merits of the two designs were compared. DNC pointed out that 'C2' offered increased freeboard as well as greater surface speed and crew comfort in smooth water. Although the two submarine captains (Bacon and Lees) did not see increased freeboard as a great advantage, on the whole they preferred 'D' to 'C2'. They saw saddle tanks as protection. 'D' required less depth and was somewhat better shaped for diving and for steering steadily in the horizontal plane when dived. It was provisionally agreed that 'D' was preferable and that DNC should seek to improve it further.

This conference also agreed that heavy oil should replace gasoline as the submarine fuel as soon as possible.[30] Not long afterwards (4 July) EinC proposed adopting a diesel engine for the new submarines. It would be about twice the weight and 1½ times the volume of the gasoline engine, but it would need only about half the weight (and less than half the volume) of gasoline fuel; the fuel would also cost less than half as much per gallon.[31] Bacon did not want any boat designed for such an engine until the planned trials in *A 13* had succeeded. Manufacturers were 'apt to take a rosy view of the difficulties

D 2 shows the humped casing characteristic of the 'E' and 'L' classes derived from the 'D' class, in this case beginning at the bridge fairwater and extending well aft. Presumably it accommodated the muffler and other piping. The bow planes were underwater. Note the topside rudder aft. It was not in D 1. Later units of the class also lacked it. (NHHC)

attending producing an engine varying perhaps only slightly from their standard types'. Bacon disliked the high compression of a diesel; he thought that other heavy oil engines would give better results. Considerable weight would be saved by eliminating the water jacket around the fuel tank, allowing for more oil and a greater radius of action. If the diesel was not adopted, the 'D' design could accommodate the existing gasoline engine (twelve cylinders on each shaft), but not a longer engine.

The 'D'-class design offered a straight (flat) upper deck, giving much greater longitudinal stability or stiffness (resistance to plunging). On the surface a 'C'-boat had a longitudinal metacentric height of 27ft, compared to 163ft in a 'D'-boat (at the design stage the figures were 39ft and 145ft). 'D' also had a greater transverse metacentric height, 21in rather than 7in at the design stage. This was a mixed blessing: the 'D'-boat would have shorter rolling and pitching periods and would roll and pitch heavily in weather which would not much affect a 'B'-boat. On the other hand, filled saddle tanks would steady a 'D'-boat. In the 'D'-boat the reserve of buoyancy increased to 28 per cent. Surface and submerged speeds increased. The additional internal space improved habitability, although there was no particular effort to improve accommodation. There were still no internal bulkheads.

As 'D' was so much larger than earlier submarines, she would use a different diving technique.[32] Existing submarines dived by inclining stern planes, which in turn tipped the boat down. Their propellers drove them under. The force driving the boat down was water pressure on the surface of the inclined hull, which overcame the upward pressure from the stern planes and also the buoyancy of the boat.

Except with a very small reserve of buoyancy, it would be difficult to hold or alter depth. A much larger submarine with a large reserve of buoyancy had to rely on forces generated by diving planes. To do that, the designers added forward planes ('side rudders'). The stern planes would be larger and would supply most of the diving force. The forward planes would bring the boat level or to a desired trim.

Diving would be a protracted process. First the boat would trim down until only about a ton of buoyancy remained (i.e., with about 4½ft of conning tower above water). At a speed of 4 knots with the stern planes up (and well under water) she would descend on an even keel. At 7 knots the boat could dive with 2 tons of reserve buoyancy (i.e., with more than the whole conning tower above water). The position of the conning tower made it possible to limit the area and angle of the forward planes. The conning tower was placed as far aft as possible. To test the new method of diving, DNC suggested fitting a 'B'-class submarine with a second set of fore planes be just abaft the conning tower which would project beyond the largest hull diameter. The modified 'B'-class submarine would test both the use of submerged fore planes and the new diving technique. There was no consideration at all of how quickly the submarine could dive to escape danger, no means of crash diving.

Full-scale experiments were essential because it was impossible to rely on model experiments, for example to give the relationship between the speed, time, diving helm (plane angle) and reserve of buoyancy at which a given submarine would dive. According to a September 1905 note to DNC, 'experience at present seems to show that the full sized boat is rather safer than the model would indicate'.[33] In October 1906 diving trials of *C 1*, which had bow planes, showed that they were quite safe and workable (similar but smaller bow planes had already been tried successfully in *B 4*).[34] As a result of extensive tank tests, the stern was redesigned, the planes were re-sized and relocated and it was proposed to fit two conning towers to equalise total forces on the hydroplanes when diving at level trim.

In October 1911 ICS asked that the remaining 'B' and 'C'-class submarines without bow planes (*B 1*–*B 3*, *B 6*–*B 11*, *C 2*–*C 6*) have their conning tower planes replaced by the bow planes now standard in later 'C' class and in 'D' and 'E'-class submarines.[35] By this time it was accepted that a submarine with bow planes would dive more quickly than one with conning tower planes; that she would take a steady depth more quickly; and that control was far easier (a submarine with bow planes could keep her depth despite considerable negative buoyancy). The last advantage was considered particularly important for submarines operating in deep water, as at Gibraltar. With bow planes a submarine could survive even if she had negative buoyancy due to some mischance or error in trimming calculation. She could hold her depth despite considerable negative buoyancy while buoyancy was corrected. This type of control was also important as a torpedo was fired, changing the boat's trim; and under helm. 'A boat fitted with Conning Tower planes will break surface and would possibly disclose her position.' DNC agreed; all the boats involved had sufficient bow ballast to accommodate the change. He added that in bad weather conning tower planes sometimes threw water up onto the bridge and they caused vibration when pounded by the sea. It would, moreover, be expensive to move the existing conning tower hydrophones up far enough to avoid waves.

Not surprisingly, Controller did not recommend immediately shifting to the new design. On 19 July 1905 he reported that the sub-committee on designs recommended building 'B'-boats (by this time, 'C'-boats) while continuing model experiments and work on the 'D' design. It seemed that a 'B'-boat would cost £50,000; a 'D'-boat would cost £60,000 or more, about as much as a destroyer. Controller therefore wanted some expression of policy for the future. Director of Naval Intelligence (DNI) Captain C L Ottley (in effect chief of the British naval staff) wrote that 'if submarines can be designed that could be safely and easily towed at high speeds and in any weather, without hampering a battle squadron, the tactical possibilities before them can hardly be over-rated, but unless that can be done the policy of spending large sums upon a type of vessel which has very narrow limitations is at least very questionable for a Power which is necessarily always obliged to aim at a wide maritime supremacy as we are'. First Sea Lord (Admiral Fisher) set £60,000 as the current limit.

In a November 1905 note to Controller, ICS (Captain Lees) added to the pressure to build the 'D' prototype.[36] He cited an article in the French *Temps* which named Great Britain as the leading builder of attack submarines, based on the size, speed and seaworthiness of recent boats; ICS had said as much. However, the French 1905–6 submarine programme amounted to thirty-six boats of 400 tons light displacement, which would certainly outclass the British 'B'/'C' class. 'I cannot express too strongly that I feel sure the time has arrived for a further

increase in size, speed, radius of action and armament of the submarine boat.' He had already written as much when advocating the 'D' design. The coming 1906–7 Programme included provision for one experimental boat, which he urged should be the 'D'-boat. It was pointless to wait for hydroplane tests using *B 4*, since the French already used bow planes.

After detailed work by DNC, in November 1905 Controller sent the design back to the submarine committee for further consideration. Tank tests showed that it would take about 900 BHP (rather than the initial 1200 BHP) to drive the submarine at the desired 14 knots on the surface. It seemed likely that the new submarine would need less power because her propellers would be more efficient, as they would turn more slowly.[37] By January 1906 it was clear that there was a weight problem.[38] The designers had allocated 37 tons to main engines, including circulating water and exhaust piping, as well as shafting back to the coupling to the main motors. A pair of gasoline engines would require only 27 tons, but heavy oil engines were a different matter. Initial estimates showed about 44 tons. EinC wrote that he hoped that the oil engine Vickers was then hoping to fit in *A 13* would be much lighter. Presumably this was the Hornsby-Ackroyd engine.

'D' was the first submarine design completed by DNC's Royal Corps of Naval Constructors (RCNC), which had to produce a detailed hull specification as a basis for tenders. DNC also subjected the new design to much more comprehensive tank tests than those conducted for the earlier Vickers boats. They were intended largely to verify the planned plane arrangements. For example, a convenient way to fit diving rudders (i.e., in the propeller stream) in a twin-screw submarine would be to adopt a forked stern. It was understood that this arrangement increased resistance, but the French had adopted it in their Boat X. Tank tests showed how inefficient the proposed form was. DNC therefore reverted to the earlier tapered-stern form, adding a tail frame and diving rudders in the propeller stream. This was even though it was not at all certain that diving rudders were necessary; 'in the absence of experience it is considered that it would be injudicious to dispense with them in the first instance'. The tail frame could be eliminated later.

Because no previous submarine had been modelled for diving tests, it was not possible to compare results with the performance of earlier submarines. The full-scale behaviour of earlier full-scale boats was known, but not the details of forces acting on them. Some conclusions could be drawn, however. Tests showed that with the initially planned plane areas the angles required to dive on a level keel were prohibitive; the planes had to be enlarged. There was not enough power to enable the boat, as originally designed, to dive at 8 knots with her conning tower out of the water. Again, greater plane area could solve the problem. Generally the boat had an undesirable tendency to rise bodily in the water without any reserve buoyancy; but existing submarines seemed to have a similar tendency. The cure might be a modified hull form. When trimmed horizontally, down to the level of the base of the conning tower and driven ahead, the boat did have a tendency to trim by the bow and then to dive; this tendency to incline by the bow disappeared when more of the conning tower rose above water. When moving with 5° inclination, the boat required extreme plane angles to avoid diving deeper. Although she would not normally run this way, Froude pointed out that ships tended to yaw over greater rudder angles and the analogy in depth would be to take up a deeper angle. His cure was to fit diving rudders.

From aft, *D 2* shows her topside rudder and also the fairing for her stern torpedo tube. She is running light, her saddle tank quite visible. (R A Burt)

At this stage the 'D' design showed two conning towers, each with its own periscope. The need for a second periscope had been demonstrated and it seemed that providing a second conning tower would insure against the destruction of one of them.

By the spring of 1906 Vickers seems to have been confident that the 600 BHP diesel it was developing would be satisfactory.[39] It convinced DNC that the new engines would take up less space (and would be no heavier) than the gasoline engines originally planned. The weight otherwise used for a water jacket could go into a thicker pressure hull. Vickers incorporated the diesels in three single-hull designs it offered between 17 April and 4 May 1906 as alternatives to 'D'.[40] DNC preferred 'D', but the Vickers designs were revived later as the basis for proposed improved versions of the 'C' class, offered as alternatives to the more expensive 'D'.

DNC argued that in 'D' he had a true submersible, i.e. a submarine with over 30 per cent reserve buoyancy. Without unduly increasing depth, its increased displacement bought more powerful armament, greater speed, greater crew comfort, greater radius of action and much greater safety than Vickers' designs offered. Beside the advantages DNC claimed for 'D', 'there is the prospective advantage of enlarging our experience by departing from the type hitherto followed'. The single-hull submarines could not grow. Although DNC did not envisage matching reported French designs of 800 to 1200 tons, the saddle-tank 'D' design was well adapted to further growth. Controller asked whether DNC would breach the agreement with Vickers by building at a Royal Dockyard. He was assured that in that case Vickers could collect £2500 if any of its patents was used.

DNC submitted a final *D 1* design to the Admiralty Board on 7 August 1906. By this time the submarine had grown to 160ft x 20ft 7¾in (pressure hull diameter 13ft 4½in) and submerged displacement was given as 578 tons (437 tons surfaced), which was larger than originally planned.[41] Total power, on two engines, was 1200 BHP, with 30 tons of oil fuel. The battery had 210 cells and the motors produced a total of 480 BHP at the one-hour rate (125 BHP for nine hours). Complement was twenty. The submarine would have four torpedo tubes (two forward and two aft) with a total of six torpedoes (reloads forward but not aft). The Board approved the design on 7 August. Vickers would turn this outline design into working drawings. It had to guarantee this entirely novel design and in working out details it increased weight estimates.

Unfortunately, the usual description accompanying the list of data has not survived in the Cover. For example, ultimately the after conning tower was cut down to a watertight trunk inside the hull, although the designation was retained. It is not clear when this change was made; the Cover appears not to mention it (although it does mention the after conning tower). As a remnant of the earlier arrangement, *D 1* had two widely-separated periscopes. In August 1909, when *D 2* was being built, she was ordered modified if possible, with the two periscopes moved near the conning tower and their supports stiffened if possible to reduce vibration.

When it came time to bid (September 1906), Vickers' tender was £84,910, compared to £46,882 for a 'B'-boat (£46,750 for 'C'-boats). The Vickers price included royalty payable to Electric Boat for the use of some of its patents. ICS (Captain Lees) considered the price reasonable, given the difficulties always involved in a new class. Cost per ton was about £143, compared to £141 for the 'B' and 'C' classes. The Admiralty file carries the anonymous comment that this was far more than the price per ton of a normal surface ship and that it seemed excessive even allowing for the costs associated with high test pressure and predominantly curved plating. DNC and EinC asked whether Vickers should be asked to reconsider. Under Admiralty pressure the company returned early in October with a revised price of £79,910. Controller wrote that before preparing to accept the tender, he wanted to be sure that the heavy oil engine worked; if not, what would be involved in changing engines. ICS (Captain Lees) could not guarantee that the oil engine would be ready in time. Petrol engines could be substituted without changing the overall design, except for a rearrangement of the cylinders. However, doubted that a gasoline engine could simply replace the heavy oil engine envisaged.

The engine issue stalled the contract award. In mid-November, Vickers felt compelled to admit that it could not guarantee the planned 1200 BHP in the available space and weight, although it did expect to provide at least 900 BHP. The Admiralty ordered further changes, particularly substitution of one torpedo tube aft for the original two (to make up for weight increases and also in view of the very limited space available) and increased motor power (554 BHP rather than 480 BHP).[42]

As late as November 1908, DNC was asking ICS whether experiments with heavy oil engines were sufficiently advanced to make it possible to advertise for further 'D'-class submarines.[43] ICS (now Captain S S Hall) answered that the results in A 13 had been successful enough to warrant adoption of heavy oil engines; the submarine had run 800nm and the engine had run extensively in the shop at Barrow before installation. However, this was not the diesel contemplated for the 'D' class and at least the original engines built for D 1 failed.[44]

Vickers worked hard to limit the weight of the engine. Because it was designing both engine and submarine, it was able to put some of the required stiffness into the submarine structure under the engine, reducing the structure (hence weight) of the engine itself. The Vickers diesel department later complained that when the Admiralty took over all aspects of submarine design during the First World War, it kept the same Vickers' diesels but its naval constructors ignored the need for stiffness (which added weight) under the engines, with unfortunate consequences.[45]

The great diesel problem was apparently fuel injection. Fuel had to be placed in the cylinder at just the right time for it to burn, as the up-stroke of the piston heated the air. Like other diesel builders, Vickers initially used an air blast. All diesel makers were unhappy with air injection, because the compressors were a constant problem. However, they were reluctant to adopt the alternative of solid injection. In 1910–11 both Vickers and the staff of ICS began experimenting with solid (airless) fuel injection. Vickers patented its first solid injection technique (which proved unsuccessful) on 27 November 1911 and it used airless injection in D 2. That failed, but Vickers ran a successful if unofficial six-hour shop test using solid injection in one engine for D 5. Fuel consumption was slightly higher and exhaust not quite so clear, but installation was approved for one of the two engines of D 6, to give a direct comparison in service. Solid injection saved 4 tons on two engines (no air compressors), improved reliability and reduced maintenance. The engine vibrated less because it was better balanced. In D 6 the two engines ran nearly identically, although air injection produced a clearer

exhaust. Given favourable reports (April 1912), by early 1913 all the class were given solid injection. Other modifications made the engines more flexible. They were incorporated in the next ('E') class, described in the next chapter.

Until Vickers solved the injection problem, its submarine deliveries were so slow that in August 1913 ICS (Captain Roger Keyes) personally complained that deliveries were months late. Without some other builders the Royal Navy would soon be hopelessly behind the Germans. In hopes of solving the problem, EinC (Vice Admiral Sir Henry Oram) on 9 May 1913 personally ordered Engineer Lieutenant Floyd Rabbidge to leave the navy and join Vickers' diesel team. Rabbidge became head of Vickers' diesel development.[46]

Rabbidge focused on the design of the fuel injector nozzle; previously Vickers' diesel team had concentrated on injection pressure. The injectors in different cylinders were working differently, pouring in different amounts of fuel and thus causing the cylinders to fire differently, with different outputs which helped tear the engine apart. Rabbidge conducted numerous experiments which largely solved the problem. The new nozzles were introduced in E 9; their greater efficiency increased the submarine's cruising radius by 200nm. The outbreak of the First World War precluded work on nozzles for larger cylinders, so that Vickers found itself increasing power (as needed) by adding cylinders rather than by enlarging them. It doubled up the earlier six-cylinder engine to double its power to 1200 BHP in some wartime submarines. However, it did succeed in scaling down to an eight-cylinder 450 BHP engine in the 'V'-class coastal submarine. Vickers later complained that the Royal Navy freely distributed the hard-won results of this work.

Even so, Vickers never completely solved the fuel problem. Pouring too much fuel into a cylinder left a residue unburned and that translated into a dark exhaust. The Germans later claimed that during the First World War they could track British submarines by their smoke. Their own engines produced no such residue. All the work done after 1910 did not benefit the 'D' class. In 1913 Commodore (S) wrote that they were always subject to engine trouble after any lengthy period of running.[47] Their crews' solution to the injector problem was to connect all the fuel lines together, in what would later be called a common rail system, so that all shared the same fuel pressure. In theory that should have equalised output per cylinder.

There had never been any question of buying more than the prototype D 1 in the 1906–7 Programme. This submarine programme was also smaller than in previous years; it was reduced to six rather than the previous usual ten submarines, D 1 plus C 11–C 15. In September 1906 Controller wrote that early completion of the large prototype submarine was more important than that of the five smaller 'Cs'.

Chatham received building drawings for a 'C'-class submarine on 29 October 1906, in time for the 1907–8 Programme. A detailed building specification followed in November. Two such submarines were included in the 1907–8 Programme. Given a fixed total amount available, the question for the rest of the programme was how to allocate it between numbers ('C' class) and quality ('D' class). Each 'D'-class submarine had three torpedo tubes and carried six torpedoes; a 'C' had two tubes and carried two torpedoes. For the same amount, 'Ds' would carry more torpedoes to an enemy than the more numerous 'C' class.[48] Controller pointed out that the 'D' class was untried and it might be impossible to order any (based on trial experience) until very late in the 1907–8 financial year, although it was desirable to order all

BRITISH SUBMARINES IN TWO WORLD WARS

the 1907–8 boats in December. Controller therefore suggested ordering three 'C' class from Vickers. On the basis of earlier practice, that would leave either another seven 'C' class or an equivalent in 'D'-class boats. Late in June Controller proposed laying down two 'C' class at Chatham and four 'C' class at Barrow (Vickers) in December, leaving open the question of the 'D' class; First Lord and First Sea Lord (Fisher) agreed. The D 1 trials did not allow for a decision, so the 1907–8 submarines were six 'C' class (C 16–C 21).

After the order for D 1 was placed further model tests showed that a slight change in hull contours would save about 130 BHP at full speed. Once this change was accepted, DNC could make further changes in any follow-on boats. The most important were probably to fit Exide rather than Chloride batteries (at least 110 cells per half-battery) so that the boat could operate at 220 volts; and a separate battery ventilating system, with separate fans. DNC offered two alternatives to the proposed five more 'D' class: a 'C'-boat very slightly altered to take a 600 BHP diesel (like that in the 'D' class) or an enlarged twin-screw 'C' with diesels. The second alternative was close to what Vickers had offered in 1906, at a far more reasonable price than the more radical D 1. At this time Vickers was having engine production problems, due mainly to bad castings.

In December 1908 ICS (Hall) rejected DNC's ideas. 'D' offered overwhelming advantages over 'C' even if the same amount was spent. For Hall the key question was how many torpedoes submarines of a given total price could carry into action. At most a 'C'-class submarine could carry four torpedoes (two tubes); when submerged she would need 3½ minutes to load her third shot and 5 minutes for her fourth. With three tubes, a D could carry eight torpedoes (Hall's estimate) and would probably reload more rapidly. One 'D' would bring as many torpedoes into action as two 'C'-boats, at 2 knots higher speed. She would need two officers and twenty-one men, but the two 'C'-boats would need four officers and twenty-eight men. That was aside from substantially better seakeeping in the larger 'D'-class submarine. Hall also suspected that a 'D'-class submarine would dive more quickly.

The French and the Germans were building submarines larger than the British 'C' class with greater buoyancy; the standard French design displaced about 500 tons submerged and experimental ships displacing 800 to 900 tons were being built. Hall was very anxious to get some 'D'-class submarines, which he could use as flotilla leaders. 'They will be the only class of fighting vessel ever evolved of which it can be said with truth, they can go out and fight at any time, day or night, good weather or bad, against any odds however overwhelming.'

In December 1908 Controller (Jellicoe) proposed that Vickers be asked for four more 'C' class (like C 22–C 30), plus one 'D' class. Reports of experience with D 1 would probably not be available much before March; to await them would badly delay the submarine programme. The submarine had many experimental features: 'all Admiralty experience goes to show that an order placed for a gun, ship or mounting that has not been thoroughly tried leads to endless delays'. Furthermore, numbers mattered. First Lord agreed to defer further 'D'-class submarines.

Any follow-on 'D'-class construction was deferred to 1908–9 or beyond. In 1907 the Board decided to provide £500,000 for 1908–9 Programme submarines, to be divided up as decided. That was equivalent to about ten 'C' class. It paid for nine of them: C 22–C 30. The same amount as in 1908–9 was provided for 1909–10. A substantially modified 'C' class was proposed, but the redesign was dropped as too expensive.[49] It would have incorporated 'D'-class features, such as twin

screws and diesels. Instead a final eight 'C' class were built (C 31–C 38). The most noticeable feature of the later 'C' class (C 21 onwards) was a permanent bridge in place of the earlier collapsible one. It reduced both underwater drag and weight. This feature was first tested in C 13; the new bridge added 0.8 knots underwater. In October 1908 ICS (Captain S S Hall) asked that the bridges of all 'B' and 'C'-class submarines be modified in this way. C 19 and later boats also had a smaller-diameter conning tower.[50]

Following Jellicoe's reasoning, a single follow-on 'D'-class submarine (D 2) was included in the 1909–10 Estimates. The rest of the class was included in the 1910–11 and 1912–13 (last ship) Estimates.[51]

Early in March 1909 the addition of a 12pdr on a retractable mounting was proposed. The submarine would spot a gun target while submerged, pop up using her planes and aim using her rudders and her hydroplanes (the latter for elevation), sights being arranged behind a glass in the conning tower. Since the conning-tower hatch never had to be opened, the whole operation could be very rapid. However, the large waterplane area of the submarine precluded the quick changes of trim envisaged. The gun had to elevate and train normally. In September 1909 Vickers suggested a 12pdr semi-automatic gun, which would not be watertight and it submitted designs for both gun and mounting. The idea was formally approved by Controller in January 1910. Only D 4 was fitted and the installation was apparently not very successful.

A table prepared in 1910 in support of what became the 'E' class showed differences between D 1 and D 3–D 8; it did not include D 2.[52] By this time each diesel in D 1 was rated at 520 BHP at 356 RPM, giving the submarine a maximum speed of 13.8 knots on the surface. With 27 tons of oil, endurance at 10 knots was 240 hours. D 3 was slightly larger, 162½ft rather than 160ft long between perpendiculars and 495 tons rather than 483 tons surfaced, with slightly less beam (20.5ft rather than 20.8ft). Her diesels were rated at 600 BHP at 380 RPM for 14.5 knots; endurance at 10 knots was 300 hours (30 tons of fuel). D 1 had 210 cells, each chloride cell producing 1160 amps for one hour. D 3 had 220 Exide or Tudor cells, each rated at 1800 amps at the one-hour rate. Corresponding motor powers were, respectively, 290 BHP (9.8 knots) and 350 BHP (10.5 knots for 1½ hours). The table did not show that the later 'D' class had special mild steel and a new type of framing and plating, which strengthened their hulls at a small additional cost.

Looking back, the 'D' class was important not so much for its own capability, but because it embodied the saddle-tank configuration which made it possible for the Royal Navy to build the considerably larger 'Overseas' submarines which proved so successful during the First World War, the 'E' and 'L' classes.

The Vickers Monopoly

Vickers had bought rights to all of Holland's patents. In 1905 the Admiralty was negotiating a new agreement with Vickers for future submarine construction. That August Controller (Captain H B Jackson) asked ICS Captain Lees just how limiting that would be.[53] Lees concluded if the Royal Navy secretly patented what mattered before private firms could do so, it could choose its submarine builders. Important features of the 'C' and 'D' designs should be secretly patented. Bacon pointed out that the Admiralty had agreed only not to build or cause to be built by other firms, any boats which were known as 'Holland boats' or were on the general lines of those

D 7 had a much more pronounced humped superstructure than D 2. D 3 through D 6 had shorter bridge fairwaters with a stepped fore side, and their periscopes set back from the fore part of the fairwater. D 7 and D 8 had their fore periscopes at the fore end of the fairwater, as in later British submarines of this era. Surviving units were fitted with steel bridge screens in 1917–18 (right forward in D 7 and D 8, set back in the others). (NHHC)

boats. To Bacon, the only Holland patent 'of the slightest use' was the one dealing with the disposition and shape of the tanks; he had told the previous Controller that he could design a submarine which would not infringe the Holland patents. To that end he began the designs of the 'C' and 'D' classes. When the agreement came up for renewal, the Admiralty had the option of going elsewhere. The real value of the agreement was that the Admiralty gained access to the accumulated experience of American experiments, which it considered more valuable than any patents. It had been the Admiralty's choice to accept the claim that its boats were covered by patents. Once the original agreement lapsed, Vickers should be treated as a manufacturer rather than a patentee. The Admiralty should build in its own yards to provide price comparisons.

Bacon saw no reason to repudiate the Vickers' patents, but also no reason to prevent other firms from doing so. 'We cannot do better than co-operate with Messrs Vickers in building the numbers we want. They have experience which it will take three years for any other firm or the Dockyards to acquire. We will have to pay for this experience in the case of the Yards, but there is no reason that we should do so in the case of private Firms. The division of work between Vickers and

ourselves will provide just sufficient for both.' From the 'Hollands' on, the Royal Navy had been responsible for all development, but 'at the same time remember that the enterprise of the Firm has been invaluable to us in starting and has saved us the years of delay that building experimental boats in the Royal Dockyards would have occasioned and that they have experience and accumulated skill that no Works now beginning will have for three years at least. They have served us right well in the past, let us stick to them in the future, but introduce into the new agreement clauses which are really efficient to check price.'

Chatham Royal Dockyard became the Royal Navy's submarine builder. Controller saw this as the beginning of a move towards giving DNC responsibility for submarine designs, analogous to its role in other warship work. Up to this point Vickers had been design agent. If DNC had to recreate all the relevant calculations for repeat 'C'-class submarines, much of the value of continuing to deal with Vickers would be lost. Vickers was therefore asked for the weight and centre of gravity estimates which DNC would normally have supplied. The company provided the relevant drawings to Chatham.

The new agreement with Vickers (1906) included a key clause that the Royal Navy would not pass Vickers' patents and drawings to any other private yard. In return Vickers agreed not to export its submarines or its designs. The question, raised again and again, was whether Vickers had gained an effective monopoly. By this time the Royal Navy was increasingly interested in trying alternatives to Vickers' designs. British submarine officers sometimes argued that Vickers was too conservative, that it was time to try other designs. In 1910 DNC pointed out that the monopoly was probably no longer of much value to Vickers, because they were already assured of the bulk of Admiralty orders and foreign orders were likely to be far more profitable. An attempt by Vickers to gain permission to sell abroad would effectively cancel the agreement, freeing the Admiralty to send out designs and call for tenders from any other firms.[54]

DNC was certainly well aware of foreign designs; one of the Covers (290A) includes a detailed copy of a 1907 specification for a FIAT San Giorgio (Laurenti) submarine.[55] Several British yards soon had licensing agreements with European builders. Scotts bought a licence from Laurenti, the Italian builder and Thornycroft bought a licence from Lake, Holland's American competitor. Each offered a design to the Admiralty in 1909.[56] Thornycroft had already offered a submarine

design in 1903. Reviewing the Italian designs, DNC thought it might be worthwhile to try the non-circular pressure hulls they used, as experience 'would considerably enlarge the possible variations in design which we could follow without much risk and increase our power of meeting possible future naval requirements'. Thornycroft was actually asked to tender for a Lake design it offered. DNC considered these designs of roughly equal value to Laurenti's.

ICS was less impressed by the Italian design. It was similar to that of the Swedish *Hvalen*, which had visited Portsmouth en route from Italy to Sweden. The boat had suffered numerous breakdowns, probably due to excessive weight-saving and therefore flimsy construction. In ICS's view the fatal defect of the Laurenti design was that it

D 4 was fitted experimentally with a 12pdr deck gun on a retractable mounting, the raised portion of the casing being extended forward. This non-housing gun corroded badly. However, by the time the gun had been tested, space for a gun house (presumably for a retractable gun) had been set aside in the original 'E'-class design. Presumably the gun was the idea of the outgoing Inspector of Submarines; his successor Captain Keyes saw no point in it. The alternative to the open mounting was a watertight housing, but that was impractical (among other reasons, on weight grounds). Keyes would accept only a gun small enough to be carried internally and easily and quickly brought up the conning tower hatch for use. On 19 June 1912 DNC informed the two 'E'-class builders that the superstructure space previously reserved should be constructed like the rest of the superstructure. Guns did not appear on board British submarines until well into the First World War. (NHHC)

could not accommodate beam torpedo tubes; the success of recent trials 'renders *any design* without this feature unworthy of consideration'. Also, the two-cycle heavy oil engine required

> is not yet an accomplished fact, by the time the design was settled and the vessel built and tried she would be of no use in helping us to what ought to be done without delay – i.e. design a submarine with beam discharges. No object is seen in encouraging this firm or any other, over the details of a design with right ahead discharges. Five years ago it might have been, but not now. The results of beam discharges for torpedoes from submarines are considered to be so far reaching and important that as submitted to you [Controller] on 12.11.09 I think it all-important to get out a design to embody this feature. I do not think at this stage that any design without it is worth consideration.

At this point the only submarine designed for beam discharge was Thornycroft's Type A, which had deck tubes – which the company would guarantee only at the slowest controllable speed. They could not be accessed while the submarine was submerged. Nothing was done, but in August 1911 British officers witnessed the trials of the Italian *Velella* and *Medusa* and one such boat ('Submarine X') was ordered from Scotts.

Under the Vickers agreement, either party could terminate with two years' notice. The Admiralty gave this notice on 31 March 1911; in 1913 it would be free to order as it liked.[57] Now the Vickers monopoly issue arose. Vickers immediately charged Scotts with infringing its patents. Scotts stood its ground, but the issue was raised in 1912 when ICS recommended buying foreign designs. The Royal Navy was particularly interested in French Laubeuf submarines, which it planned to buy from Armstrong (EOC).[58]

Given Vickers' warnings to Scotts, the Admiralty was justifiably nervous. In May 1912 First Lord Winston Churchill met with Sir Trevor Dawson of Vickers to warn him that relations with Vickers would suffer if his firm tried to block other builders. Sir Trevor promised not to do so 'in so far as the law allowed', which was clearly not enough. He was later warned of serious trouble if the firm tried to block purchase of new types of boats. The Admiralty view was that there could be no problem with the patents as long as the firms involved *without any Admiralty assistance* could submit designs. However, what would happen when the Admiralty criticised the proffered designs? In effect that would lead to a more-or-less joint design, which would reflect 'the skill and knowledge of Admiralty officers contributing to it, from the experience gained by them from the manufacture and use of boats built to the joint designs of Vickers and ourselves'. This would not contravene the letter of the clause in the agreement that 'the Admiralty will not send drawings or specifications made by them or by Vickers to any Firm other than Vickers for the purpose of inviting tenders'. However, the agreement might be interpreted to cover Admiralty modification of a firm's design for the purpose of accepting their tender.

This question affected the 1912–13 Programme. Initially plans called for including several non-Vickers submarines. It turned out that at no time in previous discussions of the Vickers arrangements had the Treasury Solicitor, the Admiralty's legal advisor, been asked specifically about the question of asking for competitive tenders from other yards. In June 1912 the Solicitor advised the Admiralty that unless it was likely that the whole design offered by a yard was likely to be accepted as offered, it would be better to wait for the agreement with Vickers to expire the following year.

That must have been embarrassing. In June 1912 the 1912–13 Programme was laid out, based on advice from ICS. Vickers would be asked to design a new double-hull overseas submarine not to exceed 1200 tons, as well as two 'E' class; Chatham would also build two 'E' class. The crucial part of the programme was a proposal to 'extend the field of competition' by ordering a small submarine with a large reserve of buoyancy for coastal work, not to exceed 300 tons surfaced. One would be ordered from Armstrong Whitworth to a French Laubeuf design and the other from Vickers of their own design (an early version of the programme showed two Armstrong Whitworth Laubeufs; Vickers would build three 'E' class).[59]

As of January 1913, the 1912–13 Programme consisted of only three submarines, the last 'D' class and the first two 'E' class. None of the experimental submarines survived. To some extent this must have been a change in the way the Admiralty distributed its money, but the absence of the urgently wanted Laubeufs was striking. The 1913–14 Programme initially comprised only 'E'-class submarines and Scotts' 'Submarine X'. As of January 1913, the experimental boats were shifted to the 1914–15 Programme. Presumably tenders could not be requested until the Vickers agreement lapsed. Ultimately the 1912–13 Programme expanded to include 'Submarine X' (the Laurenti-designed *S 1*), the two desired Laubeufs from Armstrong Whitworth (*W 1* and *W 2*) and Vickers' big *Nautilus*, its experimental overseas submarine, as well as Vickers' coastal submarine (*V 1*). The 1913–14 Programme bought two more 'S' class, three more 'V' class, two modified 'W' class and further 'E' class (up through *E 18*), plus the experimental Scotts steam submarine *Swordfish*.

Aftermath

By 1914, the 'A' and 'B'-class submarines were considered obsolete. By 1917 the anti-submarine war was the chief priority and it demanded greater and great numbers of patrol craft. The War Staff asked for a design for a 'B'-class submarine converted into a patrol boat.[60] Half the battery, periscopes, most air bottles, one bilge pump, the hydroplanes, airlocks and other submarine structure would be removed, as none was required for a surface ship. A forecastle carrying a 12pdr gun would be built and 30 tons of pig iron ballast installed. The resulting ship would have about the surfaced performance of a 'B'-boat: about 12 knots with a radius of action of about 1500nm at 9 knots, assuming that the engines were still efficient.

CHAPTER 4
OVERSEAS SUBMARINES

The early British submarines graduated from harbour to coastal defence, but there was little expectation that they could operate instead on an enemy's coast or in support of a deployed fleet. Captain Ottley's question about high-speed towing suggested that more distant deployment, if it proved possible, would be worthwhile. Larger submarines could do better. They were characterised as 'overseas', as opposed to 'coastal', craft. The 'D' class was the first approach to such

a submarine; the follow-on 'E' was always characterised as an overseas submarine.

Later it was said that the larger submarines were conceived due to the perception that the new 'D' class might not be manoeuvrable enough to hit a moving target with her bow tubes. The Royal Navy chose to solve the problem by using broadside tubes in an enlarged 'D'-class submarine, which became the 'E' class, the First World War

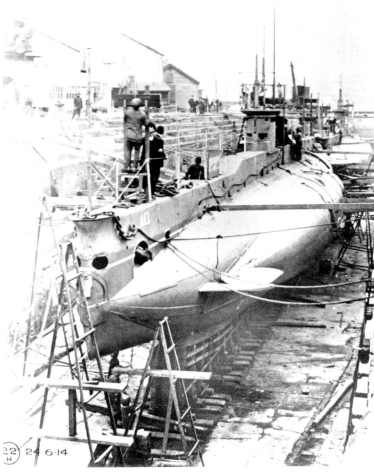

The two Australian 'E'-class submarines *AE 1* and *AE 2* are shown in dry-dock at Cockatoo Island, 1914, after delivery. Note the single bow torpedo tube, standard in the first group of 'E'-class submarines, and the slightly flared stem (which was also in *E 3*, *E 5* and *E 6*; *E 1* and *E 2* had straight bows). These submarines all had large fairwaters and prominent raised decks forward of them. The dark splotch on the side of the saddle tank may be the muzzle of one of the two broadside torpedo tubes, which pointed in opposite directions. Note the bow planes; later 'E'-class submarines housed theirs in slots in the casing. Australia was the only country to receive 'E'-class submarines from the United Kingdom, although Turkey ordered them (they became *E 25* and *E 26*) and Vickers negotiated with Greece to sell them. (RAN Naval Historical Section via Dr Josef Straczek)

The bridge of *AE 1*, the first Australian submarine. She was lost accidentally, having dived off Rabaul, on 19 September 1914. (RAN Naval Historical Section via Dr Josef Straczek)

48

AE 2 being launched on 18 June 1913. The large circular cover is for her starboard broadside torpedo tube. She served in the Dardanelles campaign, successfully penetrating the Straits. She had to be scuttled after suffering gunfire damage from the Turkish torpedo boat *Sultan Hissar* on 30 April 1915. (RAN Naval Historical Section via Dr Josef Straczek)

workhorse. As Commodore (S) Roger Keyes later wrote that he could not exaggerate the value of broadside tubes, particularly when attacking an enemy steaming in a column or in line abreast and approaching to attack through a destroyer screen. The only alternative in foreign submarines was to angle the torpedo gyro, 'which *is not* efficient for accurate shooting as we practice it'.[1]

Although later accounts stressed the idea that that broadside firing was needed to overcome the limited manoeuvrability of a large submarine, that argument does not appear in the early papers in the 'E' Class Cover. It may have been more important that ICS wanted to match the heavier torpedo batteries of foreign submarines (but he may also have thought it the best argument to use). It seems unlikely that anyone thought that four bow tubes could be squeezed into a current submarine; during the design of the 'D' class one of the original pair of stern tubes had been discarded. In the sketch design all ICS got was one additional tube (but of 21in rather than 18in diameter, which was significant).

The manoeuvrability argument is made, however, in an undated and unsigned (but almost certainly DNC) paper on 'New Submarine Boat Designs 1910-1911' in the 'E' Class Cover. It is almost certainly a draft of the paper submitted to the Board for a decision. This paper explained the 'D' design as an attempt to gain (a) greater safety in surface running and seaworthiness; (b) reduced explosion risk; and (c) better manoeuvring power due to twin screws. Other gains included higher surface and submerged speed and the addition of the stern torpedo tube. 'One effect of the increased size, however, has been to depreciate the value of the bow torpedo tubes, on account of the great speed and great diameter of the turning circle of the boat, which increases the danger of firing from the bow at an enemy at close range . . . the stern torpedo discharge, though not open to this objection, is tactically less easy to manage and possibly less accurate . . .' Hence the need for broadside tubes. The smaller of two proposed designs was a slightly enlarged 'D' offering one broadside tube on each side. One bow tube was eliminated in view of the perceived reduced value of bow tubes. Pressure hull diameter had to be increased to accommodate the tubes and their loading arrangements. The pressure hull had to be reinforced around the holes for the tube muzzles and for loading the

tubes. The author, probably DNC, pointed out that the strengthening actually increased test depth, to 200ft (although it was impossible to be quite sure of this depth without actual trial as was done in foreign navies). It would have been even better to adopt a non-circular pressure hull and DNC prepared a tentative design with an elliptical-section hull. It proved unsuited to any engine except perhaps the Sulzer and it probably would not be strong enough.

In November 1909 ICS asked Controller to approve an experimental submarine.[2] He had found that a submarine could fire a torpedo out of an ordinary above-water tube at up to 15 knots and he considered the 'D' class large enough to accommodate a beam tube. He considered broadside firing so important that no experimental submarine without it was worth building. He observed, too, that in torpedo boat development the first step had been to develop beam firing (trainable tubes) 'on account of the undesirability of right-ahead discharge'. ICS (Captain Hall) asked for immediate design of a submarine carrying four beam tubes. The French and the Germans were credited with 800–900-ton submarines carrying seven or nine tubes; 'it is essential for us to put an experimental vessel in hand at once if we are to keep our place in submarine construction'. Large surface ships already fired torpedoes underwater on the broadside, using bars to protect them from the water flowing around the ship. To see what could be done, *Vernon* test-fired some torpedoes from HMS *Furious* without using a bar, as a submarine would do. The cruiser was running at up to 17 knots, far beyond the underwater speed of a submarine, yet the torpedoes generally fired properly. Torpedoes fired without bars did have to be strengthened, but there was no other problem.

DNC found that to fit ship-type broadside tubes with breeches would push up the size of the submarine beyond what might be acceptable – to about 32ft beam and a submerged displacement of at least 1500 tons, at a cost of about £200,000. Side-loading would reduce that to about 1000 tons. Something like a 'D'-class submarine could accommodate training tubes housed in its superstructure, but they could not be reloaded while the submarine remained submerged. Thornycroft had already offered something like that in its Lake A design. However, DNC doubted they were worthwhile; Thornycroft would not guarantee that they could fire at anything more than the lowest controllable speed, probably about 3 knots. Moreover, no such tubes had yet been tested. DNC much preferred tubes low in the boat rather than in the superstructure. Nothing should be done before DNO and *Vernon* had worked out a tube design in conjunction with Portsmouth Royal Dockyard.

The minimum length absorbed by two broadside torpedo tubes would be 10ft. If lengthening were limited to that, the resulting submarine would lose some speed and radius of action, so DNC added another 3.5ft. He could then install more powerful engines (1600 BHP rather than 1200 BHP total), slightly increasing surface speed and also endurance. Although he could not accommodate more battery cells, he could use the slightly heavier 'Neptune' cell, which would offer a submerged endurance of 33 hours at 3 knots (the latest 'D' class had an endurance of about 38 hours). If Exide cells were used instead, endurance would be reduced by about 10 per cent. Surface displacement would increase by 156 tons and submerged displacement by 165 tons; reserve buoyancy would not be affected. The new steel and framing introduced in *D 3–D 8* would be used. DNC also proposed, for the first time, to divide the submarine into compartments (four of them this time) by watertight bulkheads. They would add greatly to its strength, its safety and its habitability. European navies already used such bulkheads; DNC argued that a submarine as long as the proposed one had to have them too. Because the capacity of the forward compartment was less than the reserve buoyancy, the boat would not sink if it were flooded due to a collision. That was not the case with either of the two large compartments containing the battery and the main machinery. A collision bulkhead shut off the after 17ft of the boat. Provision was made to mount a single 12pdr, as in the 'D' class (actually, only in *D 4*).

In January 1910 DNC circulated a sketch of the desired submarine, armed with two 21in broadside torpedo tubes and single 18in bow and stern tubes, with a total of eight 18in torpedoes.[3] This project was apparently not very urgent, as it was not until 2 June that Controller convened a conference between DNC, CinC Home Fleet, DNO and ICS. A design should be prepared for submission to the Board on 11 July, for a modified 'D' 176ft long with two broadside tubes and single

bow and stern tubes. The modified 'D' could be powered by 800 BHP (rather than 600 BHP) Vickers, Sulzer or Nurnberg engines. It would be 176ft long, with a surface displacement of 630 tons (reserve buoyancy 24 per cent compared to 25.5 per cent for *D 3*). Estimated maximum speed would be 15 knots and endurance at 10 knots 378 hours using 40 tons of oil fuel. Using the same batteries as *D 3*, but with a few more cells (224 rather than 220) and 420 BHP motors, it should be able to maintain 10.4 knots submerged for 1⅛ hours. Endurance at half speed would be 15 hours, compared to 16 hours for *D 3* and 10 hours for *D 1*.

There was also a design for a larger 20-knot submarine; initially the 1910–11 Programme was to have comprised six of the modified 'Ds' and one of the larger submarines. The large-submarine design proved more difficult than expected and it was pushed into later programmes. At the time, the estimated contract price of the smaller broadside

AE 2. She is not yet wearing her pennant number, 81. It is not clear how this fit into the Royal Navy series, which did not include 80 but assigned 81 to *E 1*. Her sister is alongside. Note the absence of freeing ports in her casing; in 1914 no one was thinking in terms of crash dives. (RAN Naval Historical Section via Dr Josef Straczek)

The 'E' class was conceived as an ocean-going craft. On 23 August 1915 *E 25*, about to be launched by Beardmore, shows her flared seakeeping bow (later modified to a straight bow) and the indentation (not yet cut away) for one of her two bow torpedo tubes. The large folded object on the side of her casing is a wireless mast (she had another aft). The submarine had been ordered by Turkey and taken over on the outbreak of war. *E 19*, *E 21*, *E 22*, *E 23*, *E 24*, *E 25*, *E 26* and *E 27* were similar. Compared to later boats, they had small bridge fairwaters. (Dr David Stevens)

submarine was £105,000, compared to £179,000 for the large submarine and £89,100 for *D 3*.

All involved were unpleasantly aware of Vickers' diesel problems. Vickers was developing a four-cycle engine; European manufacturers Sulzer and MAN offered two-cycle engines. At the time the Vickers engine was the heaviest of the three. Of the six smaller submarines, two would be built at Chatham with Sulzer engines and four at Vickers with Nurnberg (MAN) or Carels engines. DNC later wrote that the Vickers-built engines (using Vickers detail designs) would probably be

considerably heavier than their foreign prototypes. It might be necessary to accept slightly lower speed to reduce weight and size. The sketch design of the modified 'D'-class submarine was based on a total output of 1600 BHP at 390 RPM; it might have to be modified for alternative engines.

Later accounts of the 1910 proposals mention three alternatives, the modified 'D', an 'Italian' design and a 'French' design. Presumably the 'Italian' design, based on Laurenti concepts, had an elliptical-section pressure hull. The big submarine, which was dropped from the programme, was clearly the 'French' design. The Board seems to have sanctioned further work on both the modified 'D' and the 'French' design, as an assistant constructor submitted calculations for both on 25 October. Two days later Vickers was asked to tender for the modified 'D'. A month later it offered tenders for one, two or three modified 'D'-class submarines powered by Carels engines or for one, two, three, four or five with Vickers diesels. These modified 'D'-class submarines became the 'E' class. On 2 February 1911 the Admiralty accepted the

This stern pre-launch view of *E 25* shows her saddle tank and the bulged stern for her after torpedo tube. These ships had two bow tubes, two broadside tubes and one stern tube. The saddle tank provided the beam required for the broadside tubes. During the First World War several 'E'-boats had these tubes removed to provide space for a long-range Poulsen wireless installation: *E 40*, *E 48*, *E 53* and others. (Dr David Stevens)

tender for submarines powered by Vickers diesels. The 1910–11 Programme bought two from Chatham (*E 1* and *E 2*) and four from Vickers (*E 3* through *E 6*). *E 3* was completed with Belgian Carels diesels, which proved unsuccessful and were replaced with Vickers engines. The 'E' class was the smaller of two proposed alternatives.[4]

During 1911 DNC proposed improvements.[5] If the bow was lengthened by 4ft, two torpedo tubes could be fitted, with much better-protected bow caps (ICS wanted the extra tube). The extra length made it possible to load the tubes without having the torpedo project through the collision bulkhead. It was also possible to lower the tubes and to move the anchor drop weight. DNC was also able to move the diesels forward towards amidships. That changed the shaft lines, inclining them slightly up, which in turn reduced the bow hydroplane angle, which in the 'D' class cost underwater speed. Moving the engines gave much more space for them and the motors. Motor diameter could be increased, an important advantage for the slow-running motors. Moving the engines and motors also cleared more space to work torpedoes (in the existing design the engines were closer together than one torpedo diameter). To do all of this the after watertight bulkhead was moved forward and the quarter-battery formerly forward of the bulkhead was moved aft to between the shafts. With the quarter-battery moved, three-quarters of the battery was in one compartment and a quarter in another, so that flooding one compartment could no longer put the whole battery out of action. Air blowing pumps (tested in *B 4*) would replace centrifugal pumps to empty the main ballast tanks.

Modification of the existing design involved considerable drawing

work, for which Vickers was much better equipped than Chatham. Vickers built the prototypes of the new version of the 'E' class. As formulated in the summer of 1911, the 1911–12 Programme called for six submarines, of which two would be built at Chatham and four under contract.

ICS made his recommendation for the 1911–12 Programme at the end of August 1911.[6] None of the 'E' class had yet been delivered and only two 'D'-class submarines (presumably *D 2* and *D 3*) were in service. They had proven useful seagoing vessels, but given their size ICS did not consider them well suited to coast or harbour work. For that he wanted something more like the 'C' class (300 to 350 tons). Since there were already sixty coast or harbour defence submarines, he saw no point in building more for the moment, though next year at least three should be built to make up for expected attrition. ICS preferred not to proceed with larger submarines until more experience had been gained with the 'D' and 'E' classes.

ICS pointed out that the 'D' and 'E' classes 'could no doubt perform by day many of the duties expected of the Torpedo Boat Destroyer at night'.[7] At this time British destroyers were expected to operate independently of the fleet, attacking surface ships with their torpedoes. They might also prevent German torpedo boats from getting to sea, blockading their bases. However, another role was developing. By 1911 a conventional blockade of German fleet bases seemed less and less practicable in the face of German torpedo craft, including submarines. The alternative was an observational blockade: the blockaders would watch the German fleet emerge, indicating to a British fleet much further offshore its course and speed, so that it could be intercepted. That was just possible using destroyers, the theory being that submarines would find it difficult to torpedo such fast shallow-draft ships. ICS' comment could be read as a suggestion that submarines might replace destroyers in the observational blockade role. That would become important by 1912.

By this time Hall had been replaced as ICS by Captain Roger Keyes, who was soon promoted to Commodore (S). Hall had declared Laurenti's double-hull submarine substantially inferior to the British single-hull type. Keyes felt otherwise, based in part on a new written and verbal report on a recent Laurenti submarine. Scotts of Greenock was still Laurenti's licensee in the United Kingdom and Keyes wanted to buy one of their submarines. He considered it vital to break free of Vickers' monopoly on submarine design and felt similarly about the company's diesels. Hall wrote that Keyes was too ready to abandon know design policies, which were working well enough.

ICS' arguments would have justified construction of six more 'E' class, but he complained that the agreement with Vickers prevented the Royal Navy from offering plans to any competing firm. He seems not to have been aware that by this time the Admiralty had given Vickers notice that the agreement would lapse in two years. As ICS understood the Vickers agreement, the Royal Navy had to order at least half its submarines from the firm; ICS proposed the minimum, three. Another two would be built at Chatham. The sixth should be a new type. The 1911–12 Programme thus provided five 'E'-class submarines (*E 7* through *E 11*) and the special Scott submarine, which became *S 1*. The decision was taken to have Vickers do the detailed redesign; the two 1911–12 Chatham submarines (*E 7* and *E 8*) repeated the earlier design. Vickers' *E 9* was the first of a modified type.

In 1912–14 the blockade role became more and more important, as it was increasingly obvious that nothing but a submarine could remain in sight of a German base. In 1914 First Lord (Winston Churchill) argued that four flotillas, each comprising four groups of

E 4 was one of the original group of 'E'-boats. Note her low bow, without the flare of later boats. She and other 'E'-boats of the original group had only a single bow tube; later units had two. Note also that she had the topside rudder introduced in the 'D' class (it did not last long). It is not visible on her sister *E 5*, as completed, and may have been removed before she entered service. As completed, *E 4* had a unique sloping bow (changed to a conventional one with slight sheer in 1914), and she had a relatively long fairwater. Note also that she lacked the raised deck forward of her fairwater; so did several other Vickers boats: *E 9–E 16* and *E 20*. Her casing extended unusually far aft, all the way to the topside rudder in this photograph. Of the group of similar ships, *E 14–E 16* all had above-water hydroplanes in their bows. This photograph was probably taken on preliminary trials, as she does not show periscopes, and there are numerous civilians aboard. (US Naval Institute)

three submarines each (total forty-eight) were needed.[8] Commodore (S) (Keyes) agreed. The Chief of the War Staff thought that three might be enough. In 1914 there were hardly enough submarines capable of operating on the German coast, causing a crisis in submarine construction. Neither Vickers nor Chatham was building fast enough. Among Admiral Fisher's publicised accomplishments when he returned to the Admiralty in 1914 was a crash programme of 'E'-class construction, described in a later chapter.

The blockade role made wireless particularly important, since the observational blockaders were intended to report that the German fleet was emerging from its base. Wireless would also be useful for coast defence submarines cued by surface scouts. A September 1912 policy summary called for wireless in all 'E'-class (overseas submarines) and in all 'D' class (semi-overseas), plus sets for two 'C'-class submarines in all flotillas, except for four in the 7th Flotilla.[9]

The Big Submarine

In 1910, with the 'E' class in hand, ICS became interested in a larger, faster submarine which could operate with the fleet. Somewhat later this kind of submarine was characterised as an 'ocean' submarine and even later as a fleet submarine. The end result was construction of the 'K' class during the First World War. This evolution began with the large submarine project pursued in parallel to the 'E' class, initially for the 1910–11 Programme.[10] As it became clear how complicated a much larger submarine would be, the project was delayed first to the 1911–12 Programme and then to 1912–13.

DNC sketched a submarine that would make 20 knots, nearly battleship speed. To reach that speed, it would use 2400 BHP Carels (Belgian) diesels and it would be lengthened considerably (to 210ft, 870 tons) to reduce resistance. Armament would be four broadside and two bow tubes plus the stern tube. Greater size (and 65 tons of oil) would buy greater endurance: 1500nm at full speed, 2500nm at 15.25 knots and 4000nm at 13 knots (also given as 4000nm at 10 knots). With 280 battery cells and 450 BHP motors it should make 10.25 knots for one hour submerged. Endurance at half speed would be 13 hours.

DNC considered the larger boat comparable to a new French submarine displacing 800 tons, also using 4800 BHP engines; it was understood that the French boat would be fully seagoing and would be fast enough to keep the sea with the fleet. This seems to have been the

origin of British interest in a fleet submarine, which would operate in direct support of the battle fleet.

During the 1911–12 fiscal year DNC continued work on large submarine designs.[11] Carels failed to produce the 2400 BHP engine, so three smaller engines had to be substituted, increasing total engine weight and requiring a larger submarine. Pressure hull diameter had to be increased to 16ft. To achieve a commensurate increase in surface speed, the submarine had to be lengthened to 230ft. It was also just enough to justify a step up in battery power without changing cell size. The ship would have been 233ft 10in overall, with an extreme beam of 22ft 6½in, as in an 'E'-boat.[12] At half power (16.5 knots) endurance would be 1660nm (it was later given as 1620nm). DNC considered that this combination 'would fit her for cruising with the fleet, to which her high submerged speed and endurance and powerful torpedo armament would render her a formidable auxiliary for offensive purposes'. Estimated cost was £195,000, later cut to £190,000. This submarine was expected to displace 970 tons surfaced (1160 tons submerged). It seemed to be expensive but affordable and it led to a series of further DNC sketch designs. Presumably this design was unacceptable due to its short surface endurance at half power.

A somewhat later version of the design would have displaced 1203 tons surfaced and 1691 tons submerged (reserve buoyancy 34.5 per cent, from 483 tons of main ballast tanks and 96 tons in parts of the superstructure).[13]

By late 1911 three designs had been prepared: one derived from the 'E' class plus 'French' and 'Italian' designs based on Laubeuf and Laurenti practice. As DNC's design evolved, maximum speed (on the expected 4800 BHP) declined, so that in July 1911 it was 19 knots rather than 20 knots. Three 230ft alternative designs were prepared: TG ('E' type enlarged), TJ (partly circular-section pressure hull) and TK (double-bottomed).[14] Each had 23ft beam, compared to 22ft 7in for the 'E' class.[15] Submerged displacements were 1158 tons, 1034 tons and 1301 tons respectively, compared to 790 tons for an 'E' class. The key change was that 2400 BHP diesels were no longer available; these ships would have a total of 3200 BHP (330 RPM). They offered surface speeds of only, respectively, 17.76 knots, 17.5 knots and 17.2 knots, compared to 15 knots for the 'E' class. This was not at all what ICS had in mind for the big new submarine to operate with the fleet. These designs also fell short in endurance: at 11 knots it was 2640nm, 3000nm and 2540nm, compared to 2100nm for the 'E' class.

HM SUBMARINE *E 9* GENERAL ARRANGEMENT. Port elevation. (© National Maritime Museum M1063)

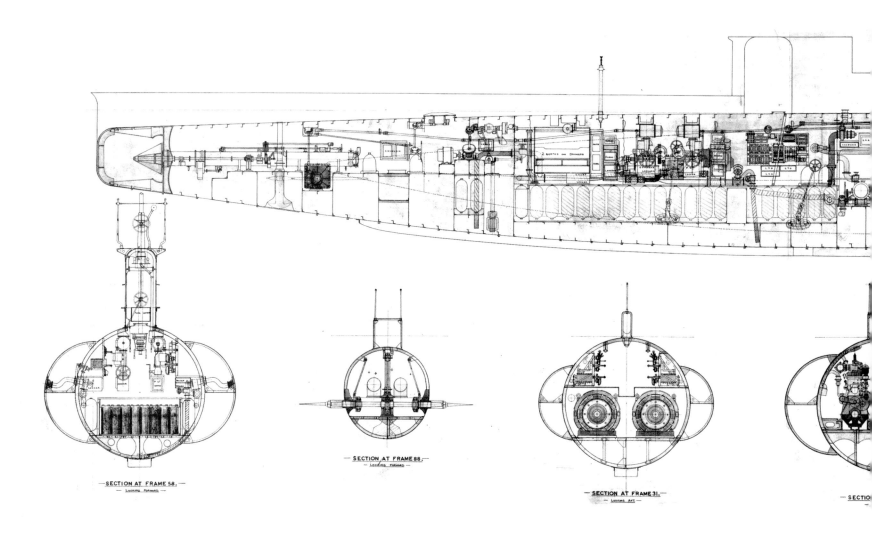

SECTION AT FRAME 58,
— Looking Forward —

SECTION AT FRAME 88,
— Looking Forward —

SECTION AT FRAME 31,
— Looking Aft —

SECTIO

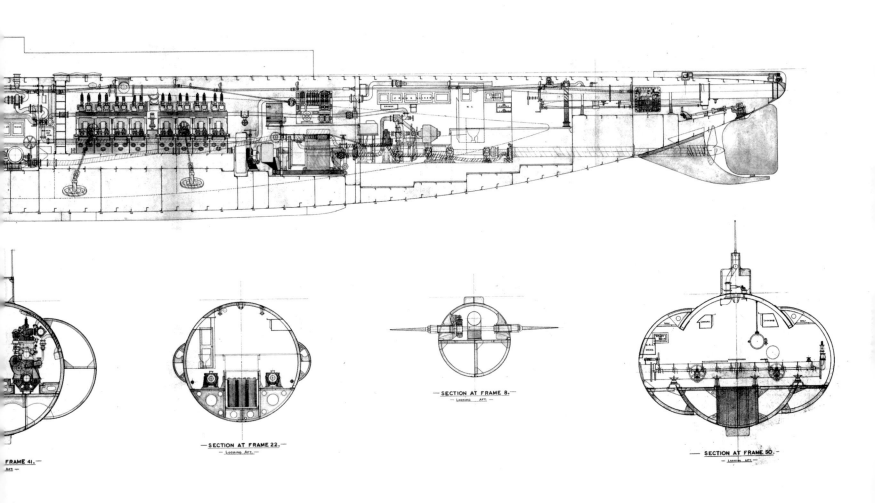

FRAME 41.
Aft

— SECTION AT FRAME 22. —
Looking Aft.

— SECTION AT FRAME 8. —
Looking Aft.

— SECTION AT FRAME 50. —
Looking Aft.

HM SUBMARINE *E 9* GENERAL ARRANGEMENT. Starboard elevation and sections. (© National Maritime Museum M1062)

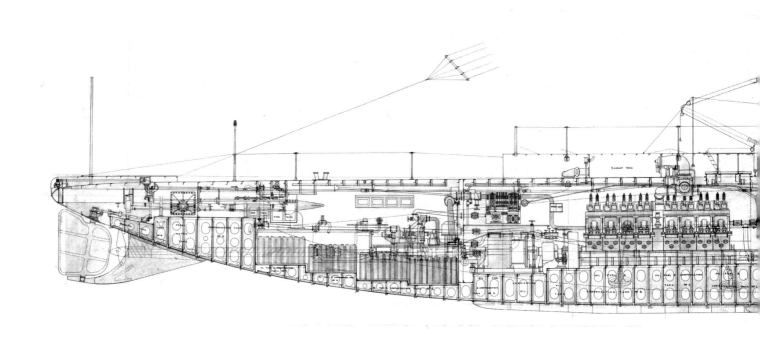

HM SUBMARINE *E 9* GENERAL ARRANGEMENT. Plan and superstructure. (© National Maritime Museum M1064)

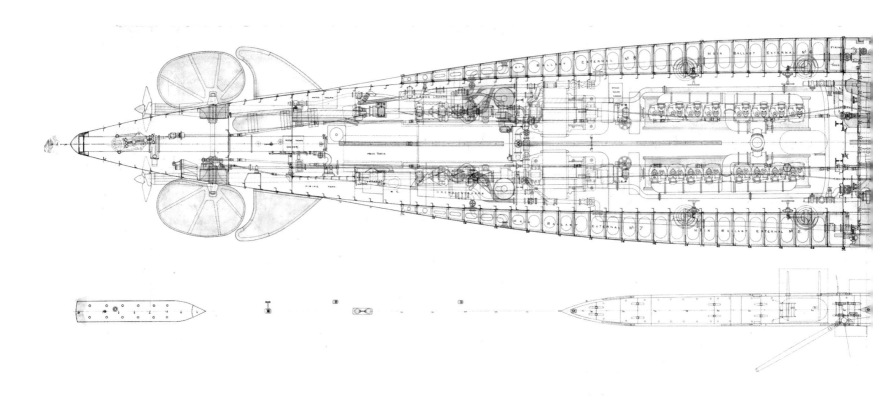

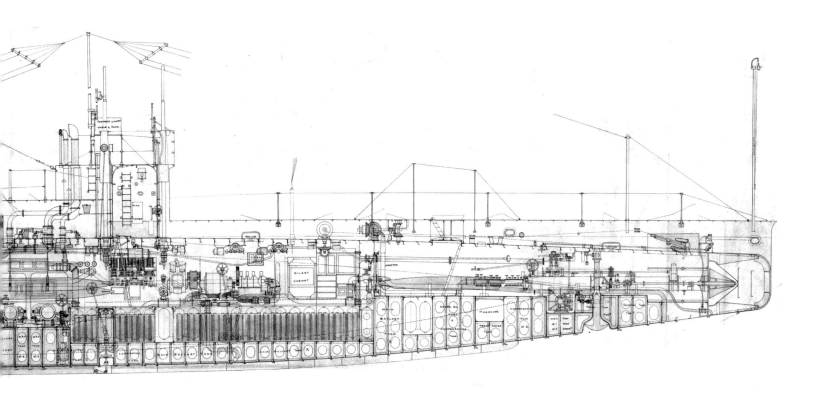

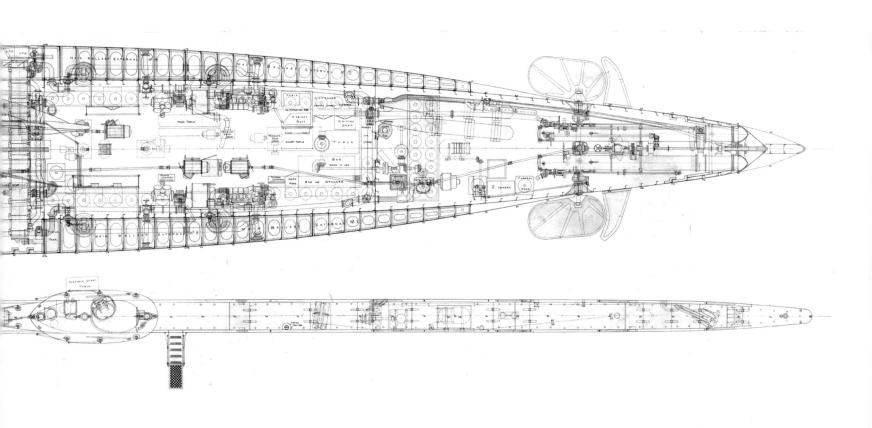

A fourth, completed somewhat later, was a further derivative of the 'E' class with reduced engine and motor power and increased reserve buoyancy.[16] This design was lengthened to 240ft to improve its surface performance.[17] In 1912 DNC's design offered 50 per cent reserve buoyancy, on a surface displacement of 1083 tons (submerged displacement 1595 tons). Surface speed would have been 17.2 knots (14.5 knots at half power). However, with 75 tons of oil the ship would make 2200nm at half power, a considerable improvement. Exclusive of gun and mounting, this submarine would cost £175,000. Space was provided for the 4800 BHP Carels engines envisaged in 1910, in which case surface speed would increase to 18.75 knots; the boat would cost £200,000. In this case the cost of the engine was based on that of the heavy Vickers-Carels engine in *E 3*.

The effort to develop a large submarine must have been encouraged by an article in the 17 November 1911 issue of *Engineering* describing the latest designs advertised by Electric Boat: a 230-footer like the new overseas boats and a 33-ton midget.[18] The outcome of the large-submarine project is described in a later chapter.

Periscopes

ICS and the Admiralty were already unhappy with Vickers' diesels, although the Admiralty did buy them for the new 'E' class. In the case of periscopes, the Admiralty bought foreign prototypes for test and made it clear that it might adopt them (manufactured mainly in the United Kingdom) for future Vickers-built submarines. Up to this point Vickers had been responsible for periscopes as for such other items as the diesel; its periscopes were made by Sir Howard Grubb. ICS pointed out that, in the 'D' class, periscope weight and diameter were considerably increased over those of the 'C' class, to the point that they substantially reduced stability but also required power operation and contributed appreciably to resistance underwater. There was apparently also a strong suspicion that foreign periscope-makers were considerably better than Vickers' contractor. The decision to build submarines at Chatham opened the possibility that they could be fitted with non-Vickers periscopes. ICS sent one of his officers, Commander A P Addison, to visit the major Continental periscope makers: Officine Galileo of Florence (who had a British licensee, Kelvin and James White of Glasgow); Goerz of Berlin, who had a British agent in London; and two French firms, Laccur-Berthiot and J Carpentier. This search continued through early 1914.

Photographed by Cribb off Portsmouth in January 1914, *E 6* demonstrates why the flared bow was needed (but note that it was eliminated in most wartime boats, probably because it took time to fabricate). Note that she is making considerable smoke – a much-disliked feature of the Vickers diesels which powered this class. (US Naval Institute)

All of the foreign manufacturers used non-magnetic nickel steel supplied by Krupp, which was far stiffer than the bronze used by Grubb, hence could be used in a smaller-diameter tube without risking vibration. Officine Galileo came first. As a matter of course it offered fittings Grubb had been unable to supply: internal desiccating tubes, heating and an arrangement of moving wires (a micrometer) to give range. Against that, it used a ground glass (for viewing from a distance) rather than the eyepiece of British periscopes. It offered insufficient light, so that it would be impossible to pick up an approaching ship at anything like the distance possible with an eyepiece. That would be a danger in the face of fast torpedo craft. Officine Galileo also showed a binocular periscope, which was

E 14 shows three torpedo bodies (without warheads, which were normally stowed in a magazine). She seems to be newly completed, perhaps running torpedo trials; she has no canvas 'cheater' to protect her bridge, and her officers are in full uniform. Note her flared bow and the prominent slot for her housing fore plane, just under the forward torpedo body. She was one of a group of very similar submarines: *E 9*–*E 16* and *E 20*, all of which lacked the down-sloped deck forward of the fairwater. They had relatively short casings abaft the fairwater. *E 7* and *E 8* were similar but had straight bows from the outset. Housing planes seem to have been limited to *E 14*, *E 15* and *E 16*. (Dr David Stevens)

The most impressive wartime change was gun armament. At Malta, *E 2* shows her 4in gun on her casing forward of her bridge fairwater. By mid-1915 experience in the Dardanelles had shown that guns were worthwhile. Malta Dockyard mounted 4in BL Mk VIII guns (4in/41.6 intended for destroyers), probably beginning with *E 12* (which was written into the August 1915 gun mounting list [i.e., before the next edition, printed in November], and was the only submarine armed with a 4in gun in the October 1915 list of British ship data). In October 1915 the official list of British ships showed only two other E-class submarines armed with guns: *E 11* and *E 14*, both with 6pdrs. The November 1915 list of British gun mountings showed 4in P III mountings on board *E 2* and *E 21* (*E 12* was crossed out, but was later listed as having this mounting). *E 11*, *E 14*, and *E 25* had 4in P III* mountings. The July and November 1916 lists also showed a P III* mounting on board *E 5* (but apparently not yet fitted). In the July 1917 list *E 2* was crossed out, so that only *E 21* had a P III mounting. *E 5* was still listed for a 4in mounting (but still apparently did not yet have one) and *E 11* was crossed out of the P III* list . In November 1917 *E 14* and *E 25* still had P III* mountings, and *E 5* was still listed but (as before) without any particular mounting indicated. The same list credited *E 25* with the replacement 12pdr 8 cwt gun, but did not give a serial number for the mounting, as it did for other ships. Unfortunately the October 1918 armament list, the first to include submarines, did not include the 'E' or earlier classes. At least a few boats had 12pdr 12 cwt QF guns (3in guns): *E 7* was sunk with one on 4 September 1915, *E 14* was fitted with one as of 28 August 1915, and it appears that in *E 11* this gun was replaced by a 4in gun. However, these weapons appear in neither the August 1915 nor the November 1915 list of gun mountings. The November 1915 list shows the first boats of the 'E' class with the 12pdr 8 cwt gun that was adopted as standard: *E 21*, *E 25*, and *E 29* were printed in, and *E 22*, *E 23*, *E 26*, *E 30*, *E 31* and *E 43* inked in. *G 1* was also inked in. In June 1918 4in Mk IX guns returned by the army were sent out to Malta for installation on board submarines; *E 48* may have been fitted. Some units

had 6pdrs. They were fitted to submarines going to the Baltic, probably beginning with *E 11* (which could not get through) and *E 13* (interned in Denmark); the two submarines sent in 1914 (*E 1* and *E 8*) did not have these weapons. The other Baltic submarines did: *E 9* and *E 19* (according to sketches in the Perkins album, which presumably were made from photographs). A photograph of *E 11* returning from the Dardanelles in 1915 does not show a 6pdr, so presumably by that time it had been landed. These weapons were not in the official list of gun mountings, and presumably other E-boats also had 6pdrs, at least for a time. The July 1916 gun mounting list showed 6pdrs in *E 1*, *E 2* and *E 11*; presumably *E 1*'s had been fitted in Russia (a 1916 photo of *E 8* does not show any gun). By November 1917 at least *E 14* (also in the Mediterranean) had a 6pdr. While in the Baltic, some or all of the E-boats were fitted by the Russians with external Drzewiecki torpedo dropping collars of the type the Russian navy used. According to the early post-war Technical History of alterations to British submarine armament, the initial wartime requirement was for a small HA gun. Several submarines were given 8 cwt or 12 cwt 12pdr (3in) guns while a hundred 2pdr pom-poms were ordered, as these were considered the largest which could easily be mounted and dismounted by hand. None of these guns appears in the official lists of British gun mountings published in November 1914 or in February or May 1915, but that may merely mean that they were part of pools of guns assigned to various bases. The April 1916 mounting list shows pom-poms on board *E 33*, *E 34*, *E 35*, *E 38*, *E 39*, *E 40*, *E 44*, *E 45*, *E 46*, *E 49*, *E 50*, *E 53* and *E 54*, and planned for *F 2* and *F 3* (the July list shows all three 'F'-class and all four 'V'-class with these guns). In October 1916 the 2pdrs were actually on board *E 27*, *E 32-36*, *E 37–E 40*, *E 42*, *E 44*, *E 52* and *E 56* and also *J 1–J 6*; they had not yet been mounted on board the F-boats, and they were planned for *H 5–H 10*. By July 1917 all the 2pdr submarine mountings had been moved ashore; ultimately these guns armed motor launches. (Dr Josef Straczek)

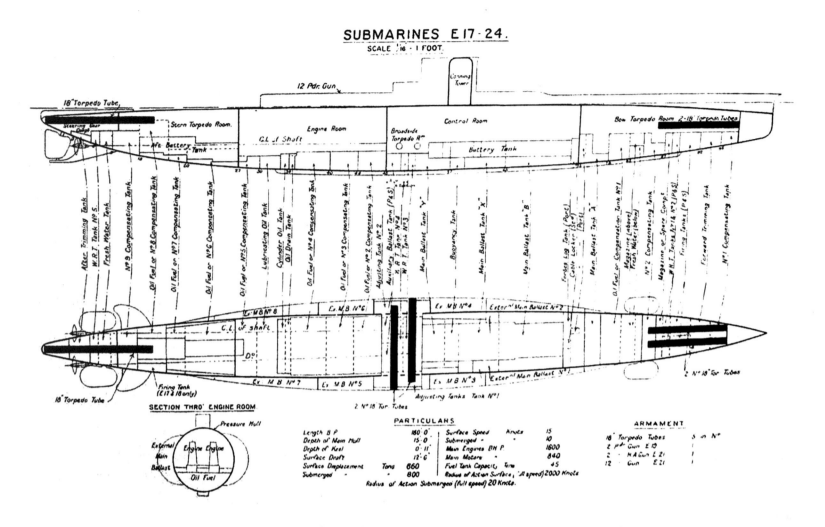

SUBMARINES E 17-24.
SCALE ⅛ = 1 FOOT.

DNC's drawing of the production 'E' class (*E 17–E 24*) from his end-of-war submarine design history. (Author's collection)

pronounced an excellent instrument with, however, too large – hence too visible – a head.

Goerz also offered a ground glass, which Addison wrote was 'evidently a pet device of Opticians, but in the opinion of all users of periscopes it is of little value'. Goerz offered three types of periscope: a simple one similar to that in British service; a 'combined' type (simple plus ground glass); and 'Pancrama', a new type.[19] The Pancrama used a fixed nickel tube, inside which a simple periscope revolved. It was so well fitted that it could revolve at the touch of a finger, giving a quick all-round view. In the view of the British officer, that would make for a better look-out. Inside the tube was erecting gear, so that the object was always seen erect and always (to the viewer) accurate and steady. Presumably that meant that the eyepiece was fixed as the periscope revolved. This was standard for German periscopes. Within the field of view a circular screen showed the bearing of the object. The British officer considered it an advantage that the British periscope operator had to point in the direction of sight, but it was a disadvantage that to take a bearing the operator had to look away from the eyepiece. With the Pancrama, the operator could quickly sweep the horizon, take bearings and return to any particular bearing (e.g., the angle at which a torpedo should be fired) without ever taking his eye from the periscope. Goerz offered an additional marking showing points of the compass placed in the field of view, rotatable until the course of the submarine was opposite the zero on the scale. The pointer would then indicate the compass bearing of any object. The only objection was the

size of the tube, but Goerz considered it possible to neck down the tube at the top, as in British periscopes. The important point was the superior arrangement of lenses and prisms.

Addison saw the French Laccur-Berthiot periscope in 1912.[20] With regard to the definition of objects and light, it was very good. Its inventor stressed what he called the 'anneau oculaire', whose diameter he claimed determined the degree of light and clarity. It was demonstrated using a ground glass held before the eye piece of the periscope, the rays focused on a 4mm ring. The comparable ring for a 'C'-class periscope was less than half as large. The inventor claimed that the large 'anneau oculaire' made it possible to see clearly at dusk and in bad light; that seemed to be proven when the officer looked through the periscope at dusk and again when it was nearly dark.

Although previously only the British had demanded small upper tubes and heads, now they were standard. The outside glass of the French periscope was only 22mm in diameter (less than an inch). Addison thought the French periscope the best in this respect. Moreover, its inventor had managed not to sacrifice light, 'which was the great objection advanced at first'. The eye piece was 'very neat' with a good focusing arrangement. The rangefinding arrangement used a moving wire similar to those in the German and Italian periscopes; Addison preferred the British arrangement of degree divisions in the field of view. He pointed out that the foreign arrangements all required that both hands be used to work the rangefinder, whereas the British mechanism could be read out instantly. Magnification was 1.05 with a field of 50° (the British standard was 45°). Unfortunately, the firm had no British agents or licensees.

By this time Addison was sure that 'we have been putting up with an inferior instrument'. Foreign periscopes should be tested in a 'C'-class submarine. One of the French periscopes was lent to *C 34* for tests. In nine out of ten attacks, the submarine managed to avoid being seen before firing a torpedo and surfacing. Her commander attributed that to some extent to the small top and neat design of the prism and lens box and the very small diameter (2¾in) of the top of the periscope.

E 32 is shown soon after the war (as indicated by the style of the numbers), with her retractable 12pdr erected, and the sides of its platform set up. Most E-class submarines eventually had 12pdr 8 cwt guns (3in/28) as shown, on retractable mountings abaft their bridge structures: *E 21–E 56* (except for *E 28*, not built). The mounting was that designed for 'River'-class destroyers. The weapons were standard boat and landing guns. In 1917 a US officer reported that the Royal Navy preferred the position abaft the bridge because the forward position was too wet; all guns forward of the bridge had been moved back. Two other ships were armed with 12pdrs: *E 3* (fitted about January 1916) and *E 4* (fitted about September 1917). Neither appears in the November 1917 list of British gun mountings; *E 3* is listed as awaiting a 12pdr 8 cwt gun, but *E 4* is not listed at all. The Perkins album shows her with a gun well aft of her bridge fairwater, dated 1915. Presumably the fittings were taken from a pool at one of the bases. (Abrams photo via Dr Josef Straczek)

E 42 runs trials, 26 May 1916; note her crowded bridge. The object which appears to be a partly-retracted gun forward of her bridge is probably the insulator for the vertical element of her wireless antenna, connecting to the horizontal element above. Similar objects appear in photographs of *E 21* and *E 41*. *E 19*, *E 30*, *E 41* and *E 54* were similar to *E 42*, with small bridges and moderately long decks aft. Note the submarine's smoky exhaust, a serious operational problem. (Author's collection)

The picture was 'most brilliant' and free from any chromatic errors, although he could wish for better resolution (detail) and the image did show some parallax towards its edges.

The search for a periscope continued. In February 1914 now-Captain Addison visited the Paris works of Messrs J Carpentier. The company offered three alternatives, a short large-diameter periscope, a main periscope (meeting specifications for 'W'-class submarines) and a Type L periscope. The short periscope was excellent but not suited to British practice. The main periscope was rejected due to its small magnification; it was about as good optically as a standard British periscope, but much better mechanically. The Type L was excellent; Addison told Armstrong (which was building the 'W' class) that he wanted something equally good. He was particularly impressed by the small diameter of the upper tube, as in the Laccur-Berthiot scope. 'I was again struck with the superiority of these foreign periscopes over those manufactured by Sir Howard Grubb and unless he very considerably improves on his present instruments, it will be a question for consideration whether the periscopes for Vickers' boats should not be supplied by the Admiralty and purchased from other makers.' By this time Kelvin and White had reached an agreement to build Goerz periscopes under licence. Presumably Armstrong would buy Carpentier periscopes for their *W 1* and *W 2*.

E 20 is shown newly completed, in August 1915, with a 6in howitzer. She was assigned to the Mediterranean, where she was soon lost. Presumably the gun was intended to bombard Turkish forces defending the Straits (it was described officially as a special fitting for a special operation). This was by far the most powerful gun mounted in any British submarine prior to the advent of the 'M'-class submarine monitors. *E 20* was one of the last six 'E' class built at Barrow, the only ones from that yard to be completed with guns. Of these submarines, *E 19* had only a 2pdr, but *E 21–E 24* got the desired 12pdr 8 cwt. (Dr David Stevens)

When the Germans began attacking Britain with Zeppelins, the Admiralty positioned warships armed with HA guns on the paths they were expected to take. That included submarines, the hope being that they could surprise a relatively low-flying Zeppelin. This is E 4, with a pair of 3in 20 cwt QF Mk I guns fitted in 1916. Early in September 1915 she and E 6 had been fitted with four 6pdrs (two before and two abaft the bridge fairwater), also as Zeppelin traps. The concept proved unsuccessful, but the idea that a submarine could ambush aircraft reappeared much later, during the Cold War. The US Navy considered placing anti-aircraft missiles on board submarines which would fire on command by surface or air units tracking a Soviet bomber force heading out to attack US carriers. Much the same idea was also proposed for surface ships, which would lurk with their radars silent (the tactic was called 'silent SAM'). (R A Burt)

E 55 was photographed on completion. Her wireless masts have been folded down (the after one extends beyond the casing), and the platform for her 12pdr has been folded down. Note her modified stem, nearly without any flare. Some important improvements were invisible: a water jet ('whale spout') for signalling her identity (what appears to be a vertical tube on the fore side of the bridge fairwater is actually the housing for the forward periscope), a Fessenden underwater communication device, a sounding machine, and WCs which could be blown at depth (80 to 100ft), so that the submarine did not have to surface for the crew to use them. According to a 1917 US Navy report on British submarines (by Lieutenant M B Pierce USN), the whale spout was a pipe leading to a nozzle on the bridge, which could blow water up to a height of 30 or 40ft as the submarine came to the surface, so that nearby patrol craft and aircraft would not fire at her. It could even be used to make recognition letters in Morse code. A surfaced submarine normally used a blinker to make recognition signals. The US officer noted some defects: the 'E' class had no heating (other than a two-light electric heater) and no refrigerator (on an eight-day patrol aboard E 34, meat had to be thrown overboard on the third day). (Author's collection)

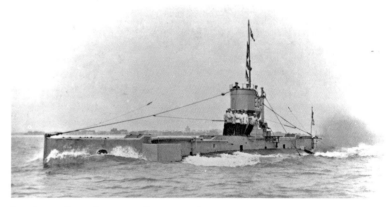

E 32 shows her pair of wireless masts, hinged rather than telescoping, soon after the war (as indicated by the style and position of the numbers on her bridge). According to a 1917 US Navy report, these masts were used for long-range transmission. For short ranges, the submarine had a telescopic mast and used her jumping wire, including the serrated part forward intended to cut nets and mine cables. E 32 shows the important late-war improvement (ca 1917) of a metal shield to the bridge, which otherwise had a canvas 'cheater' for protection. Her 12pdr gun is obscured by the men standing on its platform. E 33–E 36, E 39, E 40, E 50, E 55, and E 56 were very similar. E 41–E 49, E 53, and E 54 were similar but had a longer bridge fairwater and a longer raised casing aft. (John Lambert collection)

Running on the surface soon after the war (as indicated by the style of the number on her bridge), E 54 shows the standard late-war metal bridge screen, folded-down wireless masts fore and aft, and a folded-down gun platform abaft her bridge structure, with the gun barely visible. In these and other wartime British submarines, a relatively large bridge surmounted a small watertight conning tower, which was used only on the surface (it was an excellent heavy-weather steering station). US officers reported that, in contrast to US practice, British conning towers were entirely external to the pressure hull, connected to it by a watertight hatch. In the event of being rammed, the conning tower might be destroyed without flooding the pressure hull. The metal bridge screen was adopted because submarines almost never had time to unrig canvas screens when they had to dive, as they always had to dive quickly. (Dr Josef Straczek).

CHAPTER 5
EXPERIMENTAL COASTAL SUBMARINES

On trials in 1915, the Admiralty coastal *F 2* shows her broad stern, characteristic of Laurenti-type double-hull submarines. (Author's collection)

In 1911 the recently-appointed ICS Roger Keyes suspected that the Royal Navy had erred in deriving its submarines from Holland's prototype. He thought that his predecessor Captain S S Hall had been wrong to reject the Laurenti design in 1909.[1] He sent his assistant Commander A P Addison, DNC's submarine expert H G Williams and Engineer Commander Garwood (EinC's diesel expert) to visit the FIAT San Giorgio yard, which built Laurenti submarines. They unanimously recommended that the Admiralty buy a FIAT boat. Scotts was prepared to guarantee performance in tests more severe than those imposed on Vickers.

The alternative to Laurenti was the French Laubeuf double-hull submarine, which the three Admiralty experts saw at the Schneider yard at Toulon. They considered it too long, too slow and unacceptable because it carried its torpedoes externally, but it was still of considerable interest as an alternative to single-hull Admiralty designs. The only other major foreign builders were Krupp and Electric Boat. Krupp presumably would not have welcomed a visit and Electric Boat, Holland's old company, was not a real alternative to Admiralty designs.

Writing to Hall in October 1911, Keyes described a discussion with DNC and with the three experts on the large submarine he hoped to build.[2] As for the 'E' class,

> I believe that Williams is thoroughly ashamed of that ridiculous saddle tank. He accepted the [double hull] principle worked on by Lauboeuf [*sic*] and Laurenti, but applied it in a grotesque way. He certainly had no intention of repeating it in the larger boats . . . At any rate both he and Sir Philip Watts [DNC] are most keen to have a Fiat or Lauboeuf [*sic*] boat and admit we have a lot to learn from them.

S 1 as completed, presumably on trials (note the rigged lifelines and the lifebuoys, and also the civilians). The very small bridge fairwater was typical of Laurenti but not Royal Navy practice. (R A Burt)

Hall disagreed.[3] Although he and others had considered buying foreign designs, it was much better to maintain a consistent programme offering common training, interchangeability, stores, etc. 'I always advised the Admiralty that simplicity and a homogeneous lot was in my opinion worth more than any possible gain in material.' By this time Keyes was interested in the large long-range submarine and he considered it irrelevant to compare it with the earlier Admiralty coastal designs. Hall had supported an enlarged 'E'-class submarine, which Keyes clearly disliked.

No big Laurenti submarine was on offer and in any case the Royal Navy needed to begin with an existing design. Laurenti was building coastal submarines for the Royal Italian Navy. There were real questions as to whether the complex Laurenti hull could be built in the United Kingdom. EinC noted that Scotts' submarine was to be powered by FIAT engines lighter than those being installed in the 'D' class; he wanted extensive shore tests. This engine had already been installed on board the Italian submarine *Medusa*. Keyes' first step was Scotts' Laurenti-FIAT coastal submarine, initially called 'Submarine X' and then *S 1*.[4]

Once Scotts showed that it could build a Laurenti-type double hull, it was encouraged to shift to something much larger, which became *Swordfish* (see the next chapter). It seems clear that from the outset Keyes and Williams both considered the Laurenti double hull the key to future large submarines. In 1911 there was a theoretical need to replace the ageing 'A'-class coastal submarines, but it seems much more realistic to see the Scotts coastal submarine as the smaller-scale prototype for the much larger overseas and even ocean submarines Keyes envisaged. The wartime 'J' and 'K'-class submarines were of Laurenti type.

The new coastal submarine programme was covered by the February 1912 paper by a committee of submarine officers splitting the force into coastal and overseas submarines. Existing coastal craft did not meet the officers' requirements: more reserve buoyancy, probably requiring a watertight superstructure; a surface displacement between 250 and 300 tons; a partial or complete double hull; internal watertight subdivision; twin screws; speed not less than 14 knots; radius of action not less than 1400nm; good accommodation; two periscopes; two bow tubes and (if possible) a stern tube; and lifting bolts to simplify salvage. It is not clear to what extent this was cover for Keyes' programme of prototypes.

The Visit to FIAT

At FIAT's invitation, a British team led by Commander Addison visited the company and inspected the new Laurenti submarines *Velella* and *Medusa*, broadly comparable to the British 'C' class.[5] Their hulls seemed stronger due to framing between pressure and outer hulls and by keeping all the ballast tanks outside the pressure hull they offered maximum internal space. Addison felt that the main advantage was that each tank could be blown at a high pressure. He considered it an additional advantage that the full volume of the pressure hull could be used for machinery and accommodation. Addison wrote that recent accidents had demonstrated the value of compartmentation, as in Laurenti submarines. Had she been compartmented, the British *C 11* might have been saved; compartmentation had saved the German *U 3*. He particularly liked the 40m (130ft) pressure bulkheads which cut off the part of the boat containing the batteries.

Unlike the British, Laurenti distributed his battery cells around the submarine. The battery was ventilated by the same system as the boat itself. Because the cells were not concentrated, a battery explosion was much less likely. If it did happen, it was well enough contained that a man standing nearby was not injured. Acid would not splash as the cells charged and there was no danger of acid spilling in rough weather. DNC pointed out that the Chloride cells in a 'C'-class submarine were 47 per cent heavier than the Tudor cells in the Italian submarine for less than three-quarters of the power. The lightest cells the British had ever considered, Exide, weighed 34 per cent more for less power. Insisting on Exide batteries in a Laurenti submarine would reduce submerged radius of action by a quarter.

Because the British team could not ride the boat underwater, due to the battery explosion, they could not comment on Laurenti's rather different hydroplane and diving arrangements; his planes were carried well out of the water and could operate either separately or geared together. The British had recently introduced a 'spot of light' instrument to show the angle of the boat; Laurenti used a pendulum. Addison returned in November 1911 to dive on board *Velella*.[6] He found trimming and diving very satisfactory; the boat was clearly easy to handle (the man working the rudders had done so only three times before, but he managed well). Despite its high reserve of buoyancy, it could dive as quickly as a 'C'-boat. Underwater speed was limited to 7 knots because only the two after batteries could be used (there were problems with the forward set). The single-man plane operation was new to the British officer and it seemed that the boat was easily controlled. He thought, however, that in a rougher sea depth-keeping would be improved by working the forward and after planes separately, as in British submarines. Laurenti had no problem providing that capability.

Velella had a German MAN engine, which was not very satisfactory; however, the British officers were impressed that it was reversible. FIAT was marketing its own diesel, which was shown on a test stand. The officers were impressed that the Italians used a variable-pitch propeller, which could be adjusted for both surface and underwater running. The British used a fixed-pitch propeller, which inevitably was a compromise. The Italians also used a different method of compensation as fuel was burned: they simply let water into the tank, the fuel floating on top. Something similar had been tried in the 'Hollands', but never perfected. This technique did away with a large compensating tank and it seemed to be the major reason the Italian boats had so much more internal volume than their British equivalents. DNC pointed out that experience with the 'Hollands' seemed to show that it was impossible to keep fuel and water from mixing; but all foreign navies using heavier oil were using single tanks.

The verdict was obvious: Addison was 'much struck' with the Laurenti submarine and strongly advised that it be purchased. It was entirely different from the British submarines. Probably the best future submarine would be a compromise, but it could be reached only by gaining experience with both types. Examination of the Laurenti submarine also suggested that the British generally erred too much on the side of excess weight in many internal items, such as engines, pumps and air bottles.

The submarine designer, Williams, was more cautious. He agreed that the larger reserve of buoyancy in the Laurenti boat made her safer in a collision or other accident, but doubted that it resulted in greater seaworthiness: the Laurenti boat had a much greater metacentric height, hence would pitch and roll more and more quickly, as the 'D' class did compared to the smaller 'C' class. The deck of the Laurenti boat was only 3in further out of the water; it was more

On the slip, Scotts' *S 2* shows the broad stern characteristic of Laurenti designs. DNC saw this and other double-hull coastals as prototypes for much larger double-hull submarine, the overseas 'G' class and the 'J' and 'K' 'ocean' classes. (Author's Collection)

ought to have a higher surface speed (probably 14 knots, although only 13 knots was guaranteed). There would be little difference in submerged qualities, though the 'C' class would probably be faster with greater endurance. Williams was particularly impressed by the way that the Italians got much the same results as the British on much lighter weights. For example, FIAT saved weight by using two-cycle engines rather than the four-cycle type Vickers used. The British team was also much impressed by the periscope of the Italian submarine; that led to the more general exploration of alternatives to Vickers' periscopes described in the previous chapter.

DNC agreed to buy a Laurenti boat from Scotts for £50,000, but he did not consider Scotts' specification sufficient. He warned that this was fundamentally different from buying an Admiralty-designed submarine from Vickers, in which case the contractor was not responsible for any set trial performance.[7] On 23 January 1912 the Admiralty formally accepted Scotts' 6 September 1911 tender. The projected submarine had been designated 'Submarine X' in December 1911.[8]

In January 1913 it seemed that Scotts had gone far enough to show that it could build a Laurenti-type overseas submarine, which became HMS *Swordfish*. The projected 1913–14 Programme included it and also further Laurenti coastal submarines. The relative importance of the two showed in Controller's reaction when Scotts asked for £75,000 per repeat coastal boat. Presumably this was far too close to what an 'E'-class submarine cost; coastal boats were meant to be cheap. Scotts was told to go ahead with the big submarine but to rethink its bids on the smaller ones.[9]

Armstrong's Laubeuf Boats

The team which had visited FIAT visited two Laubeuf boats built by Schneider at Chalons-sur-Saône and then floated down by barge to Toulon: *Ferré*, built for Peru, and *Delphin*, built for Greece. The party also visited Chalons-sur-Saône to see boats under construction, one on the slip and one ready to go out on the barge. The Peruvian commander of *Ferré* took the Admiralty team to sea in her.[10] Depth-keeping and depth control were excellent. In contrast to British practice, the boat had three sets of planes, each separately controlled. The man on the midships planes gave instructions to those at the ends. Despite the crew's inexperience (this was the first Peruvian submarine), it easily controlled the submarine. With the rudder hard over, the boat showed the same tendency to rise and come up by the bow as British submarines did. However, whereas 'D'-class submarines sometimes got out of control and broached unless their planes were turned hard to dive, *Ferré* stayed down without difficulty. Apparently it was noteworthy that the boat did not have to stop to trim for diving, time from the order to flood main ballast to reaching 7m depth (23ft) was 4 minutes 45 seconds. That included time to let some water into the midships trimming tank, which corresponded to the British auxiliary ballast tank.

The boat was quite dry, but had no conning tower, only a low temporary bridge (*Delphin* had a conning tower, hence was somewhat longer). Eliminating the conning tower reduced underwater resistance, but that did not seem to be worthwhile in terms of surface seakeeping. Laubeuf submarines which did have conning towers had quite small ones. In contrast to British practice prior to the 'E' class, these submarines had a steering position inside their conning towers, a feature Williams much liked; he thought it more than compensated for the smaller and lower bridge.

habitable in rough weather because the Italian submarine had much less tumblehome. DNC credited the lightness and large reserve of buoyancy entirely to the use of a double hull, the outer hull being a 'mere shell', double-bottomed in places, skilfully designed so that the outer hull contributed to the strength of the pressure hull. The weight of a battery tank was saved by carrying cells uncased, each held down only by a light bracket or strap. Fuel was all carried outside the pressure hull.

Williams added that practically all auxiliary machinery and fittings in the Italian submarine could not meet Royal Navy specifications and practices; adopting Royal Navy practices would make it impossible to build a Laurenti submarine. 'It is interesting to compare the six square feet or so of switchboard in the *Velella* with the corresponding arrangements in our boats occupying nearly the whole of both sides of the boat in wake of the battery tank (about 50 sq.ft. in C Class).' The Italians saved considerable weight on their main motors thanks both to the variable-pitch propeller and to accepting high engine revolutions, which reduced the required torque for a given power. The British had tried an apparently similar variable-pitch propeller in *A 1* without success. Laurenti himself did not recommend the variable-pitch propeller except in the lead boat of a class, in which it would be used to establish the best propeller pitch; Williams considered that the Admiralty already had such extensive information that no such experiments were needed.

A Laurenti design could not be built to complete British specifications. The Laurenti hull could conform to British specifications, but then all internal parts would have to be Laurenti's. British experience suggested that the result would be unreliable.

On the whole *Velella* was as efficient as a 'C'-class submarine of similar size and safer. She would probably be more comfortable and

HM SUBMARINE *W 3*. Profile and sections. (© National Maritime Museum M1078)

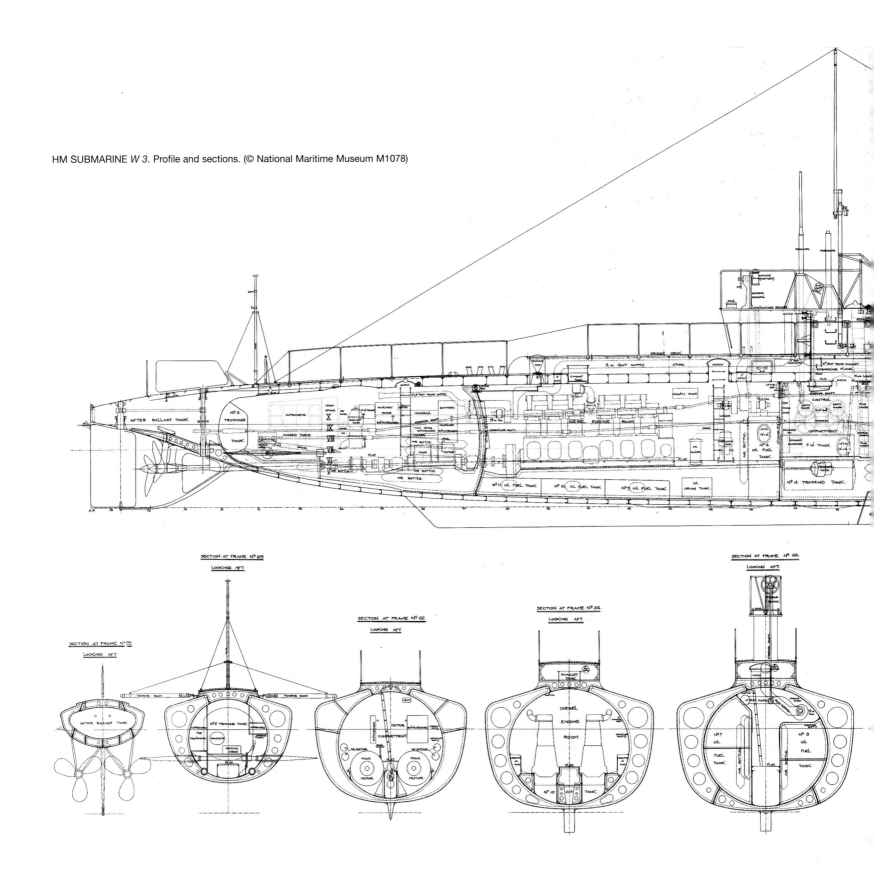

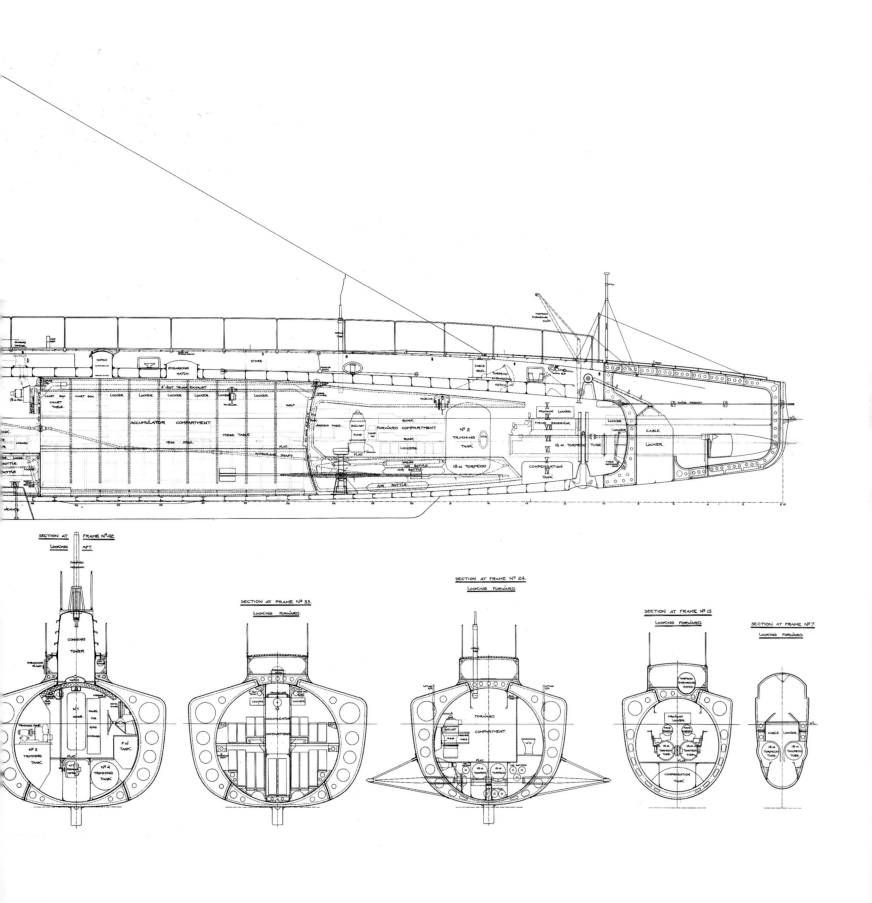

HM SUBMARINE *W 3*. Plan views. (© National Maritime Museum M1079)

NAVIGATING BRIDGE.

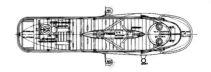

BRIDGE DECK.

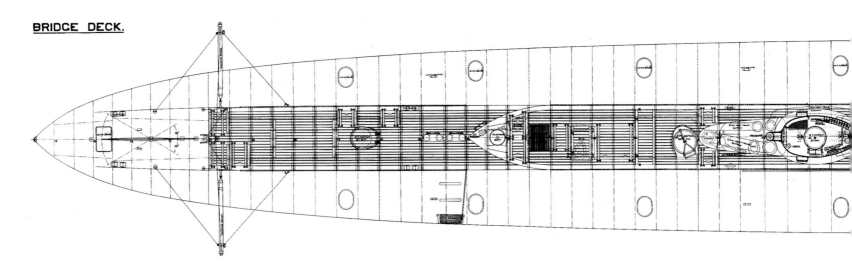

INTERNAL PLAN VIEW.

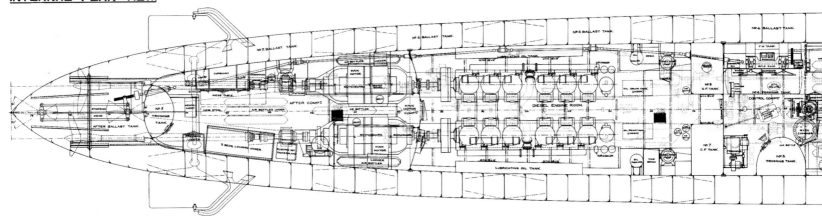

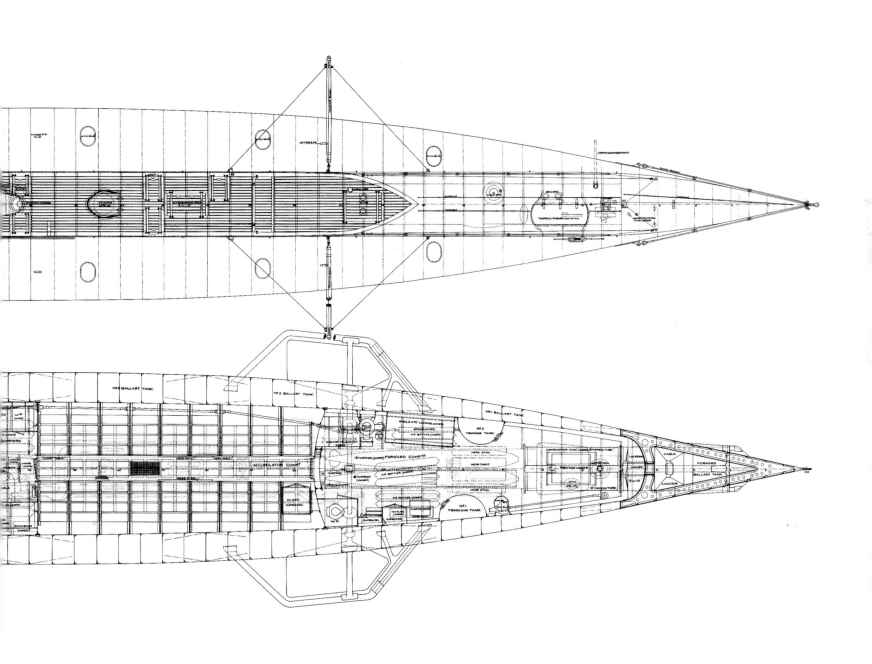

Armstrong based its double-hull submarine on the French Laubeuf design rather than the Laurenti. Commodore (S) Roger Keyes considered the Laurenti much superior, but wanted the insurance of an alternative design. W 2 is shown newly completed, with the incomplete battleship Canada in the background. In 1915 both she and W 1 had a single gun mounted abaft their bridge fairwaters. (Brass Foundry C.33101)

DNC commented that although there was little to choose from between Laurenti and Laubeuf in a small submarine (300 tons), Laubeuf's complete (i.e., full-length) double hull 'will be found better for larger boats and for this reason, as well as on account of the intrinsic merit of the boat and its proved efficiency in the French Navy, it is considered desirable that a boat of this type should be obtained'.[11] Unlike Laurenti, Laubeuf used a circular-section pressure hull, which was inherently stronger than Laurenti's more ship-like form. DNC speculated that the circular-section hull would also be better able to resist longitudinal vibration, although as far as he could tell neither Laubeuf nor Laurenti suffered much in that regard.

DNC compared Laubeuf's *Delphin* to Scotts' 'Submarine X'.[12] The French submarine was longer (162.8ft vs 148.1ft) and heavier (311 tons vs 252.5 tons surfaced, 460 tons vs 372.5 tons submerged), with about the same reserve of buoyancy (48 per cent vs 47.8 per cent). Although it had somewhat less powerful engines (360 BHP vs 400 BHP) it was faster on the surface (13.2 knots vs 13 knots), presumably due to its greater length. Greater size also bought greater endurance, 1800nm at 9 knots vs 1600nm at 8.5 knots (equivalent to about 1440nm at 9 knots). Greater size increased underwater resistance, so the French submarine was somewhat slower (8 knots vs 8.5 knots). The Italian submarine had somewhat greater underwater endurance. The French submarine had one bow tube and four external torpedo ejectors (Drzewiecki frames), compared to the two bow tubes of 'Submarine X'. Both alternatives offered much the same design depth.

Laurenti offered a much broader upper deck, which DNC thought might take more water in a seaway. It had considerably lighter machinery; DNC preferred Laubeuf's battery configuration, all cells being confined to one compartment rather than being spread over two, as that saved length. To do that Laubeuf stowed batteries in tiers with the lightest possible supports and insulation. That was objectionable:

some cells were practically inaccessible and it made for a high centre of gravity for the battery. Length saved went into the engines. Neither design offered access to the back of the engine 'as is necessary with the type of engine used in our boats'. The weight saved in battery stowage went into a heavier drop keel, 40 tons rather than the 20 tons in a 'D'-class boat. Overall, Laubeuf had managed to work a complete double hull by carefully saving weight on the details of his submarine.

The volume of the double hull was set by reserve buoyancy. Had the designer of the 'D' class tried to provide a full double hull, its volume would have been so limited that 'the two skins would have been so close together as to render the work of riveting practically impossible and the space between the skins would have been inaccessible'. Even in a Laubeuf boat, the double bottom was so shallow that it was difficult to get good-enough workmanship building it and it was inaccessible except by opening up the plates; it was therefore filled with cement up to the turn of the bilges. Williams considered that the Royal Navy would have to unrivet the bottom and remove the cement at least once every three years to be sure that the plating was in good condition.

Williams wrote that although there was not much to choose between Laubeuf and Laurenti submarines, 'the Laubeuf boats show evidence of the greater experience of their designer, with the practical requirements of submarine boats and of a little less daring in cutting down the weights and reducing the margin on which durability and safety depend, apart from the qualities which can be expressed in

V 3 was Vickers' version of the double-hull coastal submarine. She and her sisters may have been completed with 12pdr guns. Note the gun pedestal forward of her bridge, and the steering stand visible at the after end of the bridge. At the end of the war all four were given steel bridge screens. (Dock Museum VPA.0001)

figures'. Laubeuf's first boat, *Narval*, had been built in 1900.

Armstrong-Whitworth obtained a licence from Laubeuf, the principal alternative to Laurenti. On 27 September 1911 it received a provisional order for one boat, paralleling the order for *S 1*.[13]

Admiralty requirements were framed around the Laurenti design already accepted. Armstrong pointed out that no Laubeuf design could meet them, partly because they included a desired maximum length and tonnage.[14] The company pointed to essential Laurenti features: end ballast tanks, the separate battery compartment and the long engine.[15] The submarine could not meet the usual length requirement and at the same time the requirements for speed and endurance. To comply with all the conditions the proposed Laubeuf boat would have to be redesigned into something more like a Laurenti submarine, including using two-cycle engines.

As laid out on 8 June 1912 by Controller, the 1912–13 Programme included one Laubeuf submarine.[16] Later a second was added and *W 1* and *W 2* were ordered in January 1913. They were armed with two internal tubes and four Drzewiecki frames, the latter feature objectionable to the Royal Navy as it seemed likely that torpedoes carried externally would deteriorate. That was certainly the case with the external tubes the Royal Navy used during the Second World War, and those tubes were closed at the ends.

For the 1913–14 Programme Laubeuf drastically modified the design to bring it closer to the requirements stated earlier by the Admiralty, shortening it to 149.93ft.[17] Surface displacement was now 320 tons (490 tons submerged). Guaranteed surface speed was 13

knots and guaranteed submerged speed was 8.5 knots. Radius of action on one engine would be 2500nm at 9 knots (1600nm at 10 knots on two). Radius of action submerged was given as 68nm at 5 knots. The submarine would be armed with two bow tubes (no external frames). Two submarines were built to the new design, *W 3* and *W 4*, in the 1913–14 Programme. As of August 1913 the rest of the programme was Scotts' *Swordfish* and three Vickers coastals.

The Vickers Coastals

Vickers' involvement with coastal submarines began when the company's representatives met with Commodore (S) (Keyes) on 1 May 1912 to discuss its Design A for an oversea submarine, which ultimately led to the construction of HMS *Nautilus*.[18] The meeting was attended by submarine officers and by a DNC representative. Vickers' proposed design was not considered suitable, so within a few days the company offered a Design B. At the same meeting it was suggested that Vickers design a coastal submarine. This Design C was forwarded to Keyes on 15 May. He considered it acceptable and DNC evidently agreed. The Vickers coastal design, like its overseas *Nautilus*, can be seen as the company's interpretation of a Laurenti double-hull configuration. Vickers records show a twin-screw Design 618.[19]

On 12 August Controller asked Vickers to tender to build a submarine of this design.[20] He stressed the importance of quick diving, which in 1912 meant that the time should not exceed four minutes (the boat could be rejected if trial diving time exceeded five minutes). Later this would be considered ludicrously slow.

Controller accepted the design but considered Vickers' hull price very excessive. Too, the price of the battery seemed high in comparison to that quoted for 'E'-class submarines. Controller also pointed out that Vickers was giving an endurance of 85nm at economical speed, rather than at the required 6 knots.[21] Vickers stood by its prices. One

Above and below: *F 2* on trials, 1917. By this time a metal screen for the bridge was standard. The double-hull coastals briefly seemed to promise an inexpensive way of maintaining sufficient numbers of submarines near the German coast in wartime, but by late 1913 their proponents had to admit that they lacked the necessary endurance. Note the protuberance for the stern tube. *F 1* could be distinguished from her two sisters in that she had a raised deck fore and aft of her bridge fairwater, but she was lower fore and aft. As completed she also lacked the steel bridge screen which was built onto her two sisters. (Author's collection)

experimental Vickers coastal submarine was included in the 1912–13 Programme: *V 1*.

Vickers apparently offered a modified version about July 1913 for the 1913–14 Programme.[22] It was 3ft 6in longer, 3in narrower and with 5 tons greater surface displacement. The extra length was used to enlarge the battery space. Motor power was increased from 300 BHP to 380 BHP. DNC accepted the lengthening, as that would offer slightly greater surface speed. Presumably at Admiralty request, the company tendered for two or three boats. The 1913–14 Programme showed three of these modified submarines, *V 2* through *V 4*.

Controller asked DNC (now d'Eyncourt) to produce a design. It was designed around the engines Vickers had developed for its own coastal submarine and the same Chloride batteries that Vickers used in both its overseas and coastal submarines. On 900 BHP (surfaced) the submarine would make 14.5 knots; 450 BHP (total) motors would give 9 knots submerged for about 75 minutes. The cross section was much like that of a Laurenti submarine, with a broad upper deck. However, no watertight baling flats were evident. As in Scotts' Laurenti submarine, the hydroplanes would house, reducing resistance both surfaced and (if they were retracted) submerged. They would also solve some of the problems with fins and locking gear which had been experienced in the 'D' and 'E' classes. Commodore (S) had asked for a stern torpedo tube, but to provide it the designer would have had to lengthen the submarine to about 150ft, beyond the 148ft Keyes had specified 'as about the maximum for coastal requirements'. Keyes' assistant Captain Addison had asked for a few more cells than the 120 provided and DNC saw no problem with that. He also mentioned that Chloride was promising a new battery with greater capacity. Keyes discussed the design with the officers of his Submarine Committee, who concurred in its general arrangement and offered no suggestions. However, the Committee unanimously approved the slightly lengthened design with the stern tube, which could be put out to tenders for the coming programme year.[23] A month later Chatham was informed that the design with the stern tube would be substituted for the original design. The design was sent to Commodore (S) on 24 June 1913.[24] It was to be built at Chatham.

There was a real question as to whether this submarine would use Vickers main engines and auxiliaries.[25] Shipbuilder J S White offered an MAN engine, eighty-seven of which had already been supplied to various navies. EinC pointed out that thirty 450 BHP engines were being built by MAN for the US Navy. Denny was approving Burmeister & Wain engines for the submarines it was building in Holland for the Dutch navy. It offered a Sulzer engine which was the lightest alternative, about 4 tons lighter than Vickers'. The Vickers 450 BHP diesels were the firm's first reversible ones, not yet tested in the summer of 1913. This was aside from EinC's desire to widen competition by having Vickers licence its diesel design. That had already been done in the case of Parsons steam turbines.[26] Alternative batteries were also being offered. Cell capacity was far greater than originally envisaged, it might be possible to reduce the total number and to rearrange them.

The Chatham designers forwarded particulars of the new submarine to the Admiral Superintendent on 10 February 1914. Because the Admiralty owned this design, it could put it out to tender. On 29 March 1914 the Admiralty provisionally accepted a tender by J S White of Cowes, using White diesels.[27] Thornycroft also received an order for one submarine. *F 1* was built by Chatham under the 1913–14 Programme. Under the 1914–15 Programme White built *F 2* (with MAN diesels) and Thornycroft built *F 3* (with Vickers diesels).

The End of the Coastals

In effect the 'F' class showed that DNC could now design a Laurenti-type double-hulled submarine; such craft were no longer experimental. The coastals offered considerable range, if not habitability. For example, in July 1913 Captain George Ballard, Chief of the War Staff, wrote that the coastals could really function as overseas submarines operating on the German coast.[28] Each would cost about 75 per cent as much as a destroyer. On 15 August 1913 Keyes wrote that the new coastals were the minimum acceptable.[29] Presumably he meant, along the British coast, as he considered the 'B' and 'C'-class submarines unable to operate far from their bases, particularly in winter, due to their poor habitability and seakeeping (the surviving 'A' class were, in his view, useless for anything beyond harbour defence). Keyes liked the 'E' class for the planned patrol off the Elbe, but cautioned that the minimum depth they needed to dive (7½ fathoms, 44ft) would prevent them from going inside Heligoland. In good weather the Admiralty coastal was quite capable of carrying out patrols off the German coast, but in winter they were too small.

When he laid down a submarine-building policy in August, First Lord Winston Churchill wrote that coastals were for defence and deterrence; only overseas submarines, like the 'E' class, could conduct a blockade. However, when a conference on submarine policy was called in December 1913, the general opinion was that the new coastals were the type suitable to blockade the German coast.[30] It fell to Keyes to disabuse those present of this idea. The coastals could reach the German coast and they could remain at sea for a few days, but a 350-ton submarine with only two officers was hardly suitable to steam 600–700 miles and then keep a close watch in bad weather. Churchill now asked why such large and expensive coastals had been built in the first place; surely it would be better to build much smaller ones. Keyes pointed out that even coastal patrol in British waters required good seakeeping. The poor performance of the 'Cs' and 'Bs' showed that a double hull was needed. Laurenti's submarines were not much smaller than the various coastals.

The 1914–15 Programme already included seven Admiralty coastals.[31] In December 1913, after the conference, Churchill ordered the programme recast to emphasise the overseas submarines ('E' size) which were clearly most useful.[32] As many as possible of the seven Admiralty coastals were to be dropped. It turned out that five contracts could be cancelled, so only *F 2* and *F 3* were built under the 1914–15 Programme.

On 25 October 1915 all three 'S' class were transferred to Italy; although completed in September 1915 *S 3* had never been commissioned into the Royal Navy. The following year all four 'W' class were transferred (*W 4* on 7 August 1916 and the others on 23 August). Arrangements may also have been made to sell 'B'-class submarines to Italy, but that was not done.

The 'G' Class

Although the 'G' class were full-fledged overseas boats, it seems appropriate to include them in a chapter explaining how the Royal Navy came to learn how to design and build double-hull submarines. The class originated in a December 1913 submarine policy conference, at which it was pointed out that although the Germans had spent about as much as the British over the past five years, they had invested that money more effectively by concentrating on overseas submarines. The conference seems to have concluded that the best future British

The 'G' class was in effect a double-hull coastal submarine scaled up to the size of the 'E' class. Without a saddle tank, these submarines needed extra space to accommodate the beam torpedo tubes of the overseas submarines. This bulged hull area shows on board *G 3*, floating high out of the water while fitting out. (R A Burt)

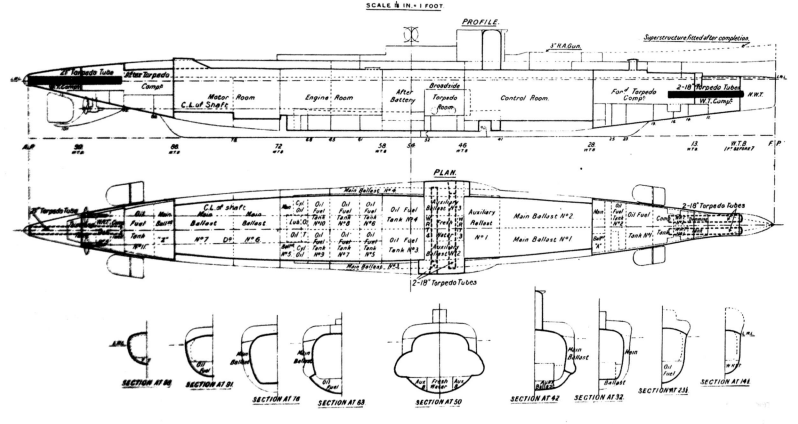

SUBMARINES G 1,2,3,4,5.
GENERAL ARRANGEMENT.
SCALE ⅛ IN. = 1 FOOT

submarine was a double-hulled equivalent to the 'E' class, which was built as the 'G' class, the next in sequence after the 'F'-class Admiralty coastal. By early 1914, plans called for seven of these improved 'E'-class submarines, one of which would be built at Chatham, the others under contract.[33]

On 10 December 1913, the day after the conference, DNC wrote that Controller wanted a design of the size and with the same armament and machinery as the 'E' class, but of the Admiralty coastal form lengthened (i.e., double-hulled). Cost should not exceed that of the 'E' class.[34] Designs were produced by both Vickers and DNC. Neither met Controller's cost limit, both being somewhat larger and presumably more difficult to build. The Board approved the DNC sketch design and in March 1914 Controller asked that invitations to tender be circulated. The design was now called the 'E 1914-15 Design'.

Plans initially called for one Chatham submarine and six contract-built submarines, but when tenders were received the prices were so high that Controller wrote that 'it is evident there is a general feeling with the contractors that we can be squeezed over this very specialised form of construction'.[35] It turned out that Chatham could build four submarines rather than one, at a unit price of less than £110,000 (Chatham was soon allocated a fifth submarine). Armstrong offered the lowest price among the contractors. Earlier the Admiralty had agreed to take a minimum number of submarines in order to tempt Armstrong to build such craft and in 1914 two more had to be ordered to complete that deal. DNC and Controller badly wanted a large yard to compete with Vickers, both to increase production and to hold down cost; none of the other builders was as large. In July Armstrong was provisionally given an order for two boats, one using MAN and the other Sulzer diesels.[36]

DNC's drawing of the 'G' class, from his end-of-war history of British submarine design. Note the 18in tubes forward and amidships, with a single 21in tube – the first in a British submarine – aft. Note, too, the bulge for the amidships torpedo tubes. (Author's collection)

The submarines were redesignated the 'G' class, but it is not clear just when that was done. The pre-war order covered *G 1–G 7*, of which Chatham built *G 1–G 5*. Armstrong built the other two. Neither had the proposed foreign-built diesels, as the war blocked import of either MAN or Sulzer (Swiss) engines. They received Vickers engines instead. Early war experience showed that numbers of torpedoes in a bow salvo was more important than calibre, so two 18in tubes replaced the single bow 21in tube.[37] Plans to fit housing planes were abandoned after *S 1* encountered trouble after her August 1914 delivery. *G 5* was later given a raised bow, which considerably improved her diving qualities.

As launched, *G 4* shows her Laurenti seakeeping hull form, with its flare forward (note the freeing ports on the outer hull), and the blister for the broadside torpedo tube. Note the raised deck forward of the bridge fairwater, which accommodated a retractable gun. (John Lambert collection)

G 3 at the end of the war (note the style of the number and the steel bridge screen). She and others in the class had their bows raised considerably, to the level of the earlier structure forward of the bridge fairwater. (Dr Josef Straczek)

'G'-class submarines were completed with built-up sections of deck forward of their bridge fairwaters to accommodate retractable gun mountings. *G 3* is shown at Scapa Flow, 1916, with wireless masts up and an open bridge. The gun seems to be a 6pdr on a HA retractable mounting. 'G'-class submarines were not listed with this weapon, but it was held in a pool for issue to submarines, and photographic evidence (like this) shows it. She and others (*G 1–G 8*) had smaller bridge fairwaters than the Vickers boats and *G 14*. The *G 1–G 5* group could be distinguished by the vertical pipe just abaft the bridge fairwater, which was absent from *G 6–G 8*. (R A Burt)

She was also much drier on the surface, although pitching increased due to extra buoyancy forward.[38]

In July 1914 Churchill wanted to substitute fifteen Improved 'E'-class submarines ('G' class) for one battleship, making a total of twenty-two, but that was not done. When Churchill wrote, the issue had to be put before the Board and presumably the outbreak of war intervened.[39]

Soon after the outbreak of war Churchill asked Controller for an emergency programme to build more destroyers and submarines; 'the latter should be the maximum which our yards can manage without hampering existing work of an urgent character'.[40] Doubtless he had in mind the urgent need for overseas submarines to blockade the German fleet. Keyes had warned that no very close blockade was yet possible. Submarines so employed would take heavy losses and there were too few to maintain a blockade. Controller answered that any programme depended almost entirely on Vickers' engine production capacity. That made the maximum twelve Improved 'E' (i.e., 'G') -class submarines, of which eight could be ordered at once and four more before the end of the year. Of these, Scotts could probably build two powered by FIAT engines it could make.

The first eight were ordered about the end of September, bringing the class to *G 15*.[41] Of these six were ordered from Vickers (*G 8–G 13*), *G 14* at Scotts and *G 15* at White. Scotts proposed to use FIAT diesels in *G 14* and White licence-built MANs in *G 15*, but the latter was cancelled on 20 April 1915. *G 14* did have FIAT diesels, which apparently gave sufficient trouble that she was assigned to the experimental and trials flotilla at Portsmouth upon completion and stayed there. In a December 1917 note on submarine allocation she was described as unsuitable for patrol; according to another note (November) she would shortly be re-engined. A US officer who visited Portsmouth in January 1918 reported that the FIAT engines were disliked.

G 10, after the war, showing her gun erected and her two hydraulic wireless masts. The similar *G 13* could be distinguished by a prominent platform extending forward from her bridge fairwater, at the bridge level. At the end of the First World War the standard armament for such ships was one 3in 10 cwt gun and one Lewis light machine gun. (Dr Josef Straczek)

G 14 is shown with the fleet in 1918. The gun is a 3in 10 cwt. *G 14* was powered by FIAT diesels, which were apparently unsatisfactory; on completion she joined the trials and training flotilla at Portsmouth and stayed there through the war. (R A Burt)

CHAPTER 6
THE OCEAN SUBMARINE

With the very large overseas submarine now in sight, First Sea Lord ordered a conference of submarine officers chaired by Commodore (S). Looking towards the 1912–13 Programme, it reported on 29 February 1912.[1] For the future, the submarine officers divided craft into overseas and coastal types. Their main recommendation was to lay down 'with as little delay as possible' a large oversea experimental submarine, which should be completed before any further large submarines were built. It should have a surface speed of about 20 knots and should displace about 1000 tons on the surface, with a complete or partial double hull. Maximum submerged speed, maintained for a short time, should be high. Endurance both surfaced and submerged should be high at economical speeds. The submarine should dive in three minutes. It should have good accommodation. Torpedo armament should be two bow, two stern and four broadside tubes.

The submarine officers' report on the big submarine was reflected in requirements circulated by DNC. His sketch designs were apparently considered feasibility studies providing some idea of what the private companies could produce. In contrast to the 'D' and 'E' classes, DNC made no attempt to dictate an outline design.[2] Maximum surface speed should be at least 18 knots and endurance at this speed not less than 90 hours; endurance at half speed should be not less than 500 hours. Maximum submerged speed should be at least 9 knots; endurance at this speed should be stated and guaranteed. The submarine should be capable of being driven submerged at any speed between 3 and 9 knots without varying depth more than 2ft in a one-mile run. Submerged endurance should be not less than 4 hours at 8 knots and not less than 20 hours at 5 knots. The submarine should hold sufficient provisions and means of purifying air to allow the crew to remain submerged for at least 24 hours. Test depth (to the top of the hull) should be not less than 150ft. Diving (and surfacing time) should be no more than five minutes. Reserve buoyancy should be at least 40 per cent.

When running submerged, the submarine should be able to fire at least two torpedoes directly ahead within two minutes; at least two astern within 10 minutes; and at least two on each side of the ship (broadside) within two minutes, in each case without bringing the boat to the surface for reloading or for any other reason.

Potential builders were Vickers, Scotts (Laurenti licensees), Armstrong Whitworth (Laubeuf licensees), Beardmore, Thornycroft and Denny (associated with Whitehead).[3] They were invited to Controller's 8 May 1912 conference at which dates for ordering items in the 1912–13 Programme would be discussed. At this time the contract portion of the 1912–13 Programme consisted of three 'C' class and three 'E' class; Controller had no doubt that the programme would be changed.[4]

Foreign navies favoured double hulls and Controller wanted the Royal Navy to try them, too. Unlike Commodore (S), he wanted to encourage Vickers to design and build a double-hulled submarine while continuing to build overseas ('E' class) submarines. The more promising Laurenti design was still being tried out in miniature in the form of Scotts' 'Submarine X'. At First Lord's direction, ICS submitted a programme. First Lord (Churchill) wanted to increase the amount spent in 1912–13, either by enlarging the programme or front-loading spending. On 19 June 1912 Churchill approved an enlarged programme: one double-hull overseas submarine, to be built by Vickers; five 'E' class (three by Vickers, two by Chatham); and two experimental double-hull coastal submarines (Laubeuf type by Armstrong).

DNC representatives met with representatives of Vickers on 1 May. To reach 20 knots with reasonable power, Vickers needed a long hull, so its Design A was 278ft long, displacing 1203 tons (presumably surfaced). Its double hull extended over most of its length. Even with the great length, it needed considerable power, on three shafts, two of which, with their motors, were inside the double hull. Armament was single bow and stern tubes and two broadside tubes plus two 4in guns.

The 'J'-class were the first attempts at an ocean submarine capable of working directly with a fleet. They were too slow, and never fulfilled that role, but they were very useful pickets off the German fleet base at Wilhelmshaven. Here *J 3* enters Cockatoo Island Dockyard, having been transferred to Australia. Like her sisters, she had been modified with a raised gun platform. (RAN Naval Historical Section via Dr Josef Straczek)

Vickers was told that this submarine was too long and that the single hull in wake of the broadside tubes was a great source of weakness. The torpedo armament was too weak for so large a submarine and the 4in guns too large.

On 15 May Vickers returned with Design B.[5] It was 236ft long, with twin screws. The double hull ran the whole length of the ship and surface displacement increased to 1373 tons. Both guns and the entire superstructure abaft the conning tower were eliminated, but there were four broadside tubes. Watertight subdivision was carried much further than in the previous design; the broadside tubes were in their own compartment, as were the engines, the motors and the storage battery. Vickers claimed a speed of 17 knots and a very large radius of action at cruising speed (5300nm) and the great endurance submerged (72nm at economical speed). Freeboard forward was as in Design A.

ICS (Keyes) wanted the conning tower closer to the point at which the submarine trimmed fore and aft, as in all other current British submarines, as that would considerably simplify trimming; submerged endurance should be greater at economical speed; the boat should have one or two small guns, as simple as possible. Keyes apparently later added that, given the size of the submarine, she should have paired bow and stern tubes. Controller accepted these requests.

Controller considered the surface displacement excessive. Since the cost of the submarine would be roughly proportional to surface displacement, the submarine would probably be too expensive. Whether this was true could be found only by seeking competing designs. Vickers' offer of 12-hour endurance at 6 knots was only about half an hour less than DNC had been able to guarantee with a smaller design

and a larger battery. Controller proposed informing Vickers that Design A was of no further interest. It should modify Design B with two bow and two stern torpedo tubes (two torpedoes per tube) and with one or two small guns, as well as the changes Keyes wanted. Also, 'rapidity of passing from the surface condition to diving condition' was very important and should not exceed four minutes; the boat would not be accepted if it exceeded five minutes.

EinC pointed out that although Vickers was proposing diesels much more powerful than any yet built for submarines, he considered the company capable of building them. Although the submarine's electric motors could be used for reversing, EinC wanted the diesels to be reversible to avoid depleting the battery charge and also to gain greater control when manoeuvring and in emergencies.[6]

On 12 August Vickers was formally asked to submit a design and tender, which were provisionally accepted on 29 October.[7] Modifications included lengthening to 240ft. The design showed the desired pair of 18in stern torpedo tubes, but only a single 21in bow tube. The submarine was laid down in March 1913, a month before she was formally ordered.[8] Named HMS *Nautilus*, she was not completed until October 1917 (as *N 1*) and was never operational.[9] In effect she was Vickers' unlicensed version of a Laurenti submarine.

It must have been no great surprise that Vickers could offer only 17 knots on a displacement which had grown to 1270 tons surfaced and 1694 tons submerged. To achieve that, Vickers needed a new twelve-cylinder 1850 BHP diesel, with more than twice the output of the problematic engine in the 'E' class. In 1912 this was an enormous leap, despite promises some makers (such as Carels) were making for even

Nautilus, soon redesignated *N 1*, was Vickers' pre-war approach to building an ocean submarine. She is shown newly completed, with her 3in 10 cwt gun forward of her bridge fairwater. The deadlights in the fairwater betray her pre-war origin. Once war broke out, she had only a low priority, so she was not completed until October 1917, long after true ocean submarines, the 'Js' and 'Ks', were in service. Although he rejected 12pdrs for the 'E' class, Captain Roger Keyes did accept 12pdrs for the new ocean submarines. A 12pdr on an HA mounting was ready for fitting to *D 7* at the outbreak of war in 1914, but it is not clear whether it was fitted. This mounting was planned for *Nautilus* and *Swordfish* and the 'G' class, but mounting was deferred as the war programme accelerated. Both ships were completed with 3in 10 cwt HA guns in retractable mountings. The single gun in *Nautilus* was forward of her bridge; *Swordfish* had two guns, one atop her forward torpedo room and one atop her engine room, both of them on hydraulic lifts with watertight covers for the guns when retracted. (R A Burt)

more powerful engines. This engine seems not to have been successful, which may well explain why *Nautilus* never really entered service. The engine problem also explains why the only important new wartime Vickers engine was a twelve-cylinder version of the eight-cylinder 800 BHP type.

During construction displacement increased to 1430 to 1440 tons surfaced and 2025 to 2035 tons submerged. Some, but hardly all, of the additional displacement could be attributed to 15ft of added bow, to accommodate two side-by-side 18in torpedo tubes in place of the original single 21in tube.[10] With the two tubes, *Nautilus* met Controller's requirement for two bow and two stern tubes plus four beam tubes. With 98 tons of oil fuel, surface endurance was given as 2000nm at 17 knots but 3400nm at 14 knots and 5300nm at 11 knots, certainly the sort of figure wanted in a fleet submarine. Vickers later quoted a maximum of 4400nm. Designed submerged endurance was 72nm (Vickers later gave the corresponding speed as 9 knots). Designed diving depth was 200ft.

When Vickers received the *Nautilus* contract, DNC asked Laurenti in Italy via its licensee, Scotts, for its own approach to fleet submarine design. On 5 February 1913, with Scotts already authorised to go ahead, he laid down formal requirements: a large reserve of buoyancy, a surface displacement of about 1000 tons (less if possible); length not to exceed 240ft; of Laurenti type; surface speed at least 18 knots; more if possible; submerged speed at least 10 knots; large surface and submerged endurance (surface at least 2500nm); capable of diving in under five minutes; good accommodation; armament one bow tube, four broadside tubes and two stern tubes; to be capable of carrying a gun (not to exceed 12pdr) if required; and two periscopes.[11]

FIAT offered its Project 140, powered by a pair of its new 1650 BHP diesels, then under test.[12] The Laurenti data are not dated, but British accounts suggest that they were offered about September 1912. The sheet in the Cover includes Keyes' requirements pencilled into the description of the 140bis design. Apparently Laurenti himself suggested a steam plant as an alternative to the experimental diesels;

it could easily produce the desired power in the available space. Scotts offered a steam version of 140bis in June 1913 and it was accepted. Reportedly it was criticised for its limited radius of operation and for the delay a steam plant imposed when getting underway. Commodore (S) rejected both arguments, pointing out that given its large reserve buoyancy, such a submarine could carry oil in external tanks otherwise used for ballast water. He rejected the argument about delay getting underway; crash-diving and crash surface running were not yet considered essential. A steam plant might be much less efficient than a diesel, but the technology was mature. Commodore (S) also cited less strain on the engineering personnel and more economical upkeep; the turbine would not vibrate like a diesel.

DNC sometimes commented that Laurenti's submarines were lightly built. Scotts had to beef the submarine up, considerably increasing displacement during construction. That reduced projected surfaced endurance. Guns were added. This submarine, HMS *Swordfish*, was built under the 1913–14 Programme ordered on 18 August 1913. She was not completed until July 1916, in part because Scotts had to solve numerous novel problems connected with a steam plant. The company's solutions were incorporated in the 'K'-class design.

In addition to the innovative steam plant, Scotts introduced telemotors to control valves remotely, a technology which soon spread to all new submarines. DNC wrote in 1919 that 'the hydraulic method of working the vent and flooding valves in a submarine together with the central control of these valves . . . has rendered the control of large submarines when submerging much quicker and easier than with the old hand-worked gear . . .'. Telemotors controlled superstructure vent and flooding valves. All HP air bottle group connections were brought to a master valve box in the control room. The blow valves for all main ballast tanks and compensating tanks were in the control room and these tanks could also be blown from the control room.[13]

Swordfish seems not to have been particularly successful. She was commissioned on 28 April 1916 as tender to HMS *Dolphin*, renamed *S.1* (the previous *S.1* had been sold to Italy in July 1915). She was

Diesels could never provide the desired high speed, so the Admiralty contracted with Scotts to build a steam-powered submarine, *Swordfish* (redesignated *S 1* after the original 'S'-class coastals were transferred to Italy). She was probably shown on trials. Although *Swordfish* was not completed until July 1916, by which time the 'K'-class programme was well underway, in the course of her construction Scotts solved many of the problems the later design entailed. She was far less powerful than the 'K' class, and her performance did not justify the sacrifices steam demanded, so she was soon ordered converted into a surface patrol boat. (R A Burt)

completed in July 1916, but less than a year later (27 June 1917) she was taken in hand at Portsmouth for conversion into a surface patrol ship, reverting to her earlier name of *Swordfish*. She was commissioned as such as tender to HMS *Victory* on 10 August 1917 but not completed until 24 January 1918. She was paid off for sale on 30 October 1918, before the war ended.

On 16 January 1913 Commodore (S) (Roger Keyes) described to Controller a Submarine Committee discussion of the 1913–14 submarine programme. They unanimously agreed that no further submarine of the size of the Vickers Overseas (*Nautilus*) should be built until she was tested. A really large submarine raised new questions, for example of control of the boat. They were not happy that *Swordfish*, which was nearly twice as large as earlier Laurenti submarines, had been ordered before *Nautilus* was tested. They were particularly concerned that First Lord Winston Churchill wanted to build a new class of very large submarines before either *Nautilus* or *Swordfish* could be completed.

The Fast Submarine

In July 1913, First Lord Winston Churchill wrote a Minute introducing a third submarine category, which he called the ocean submarine.[14] The overseas submarine would be an effective blockader, but the ocean submarine would be 'a decisive weapon of battle and as such must count in partial substitution of battleship strength'. Churchill was then finding it more and more difficult to pay for battleships being built to compete with the Germans. He faced further problems as the Germans' ally Austria was beginning a major naval

programme and Italy was nominally also a German ally.[15] Churchill was being forced to pull British battleships out of the Mediterranean to maintain the balance in home waters. He saw big submarines as an affordable way of maintaining British power there.

The ocean submarine had to be fast enough to overhaul a battle fleet so that it could be sure of getting ahead to dive and to attack. He considered 24 knots fast enough. The big submarines would cruise under escort but would fight alone, guided by other ships to the point of attack. Armament would be limited to anti-aircraft guns and torpedoes, including four 21in beam tubes (if possible capable of firing on either side) and at least one bow and one stern tube, with four reloads for each. Churchill imagined organising these craft in flotillas of three or four submarines plus two light cruisers, one set up as a seagoing depot ship and the other carrying three seaplanes for scouting. He wanted four such flotillas created, stationed in the North Sea and in the Mediterranean, the channels from their bases deep enough that they could leave port submerged. Cromarty, Gibraltar and Malta were all suitable. In July, Churchill wrote that one of his flotillas should be considered equal 'as a decisive fighting unit' to a first-class battleship or cruiser. If that were true and if the flotilla was really far less expensive than a battleship, he could have the equivalent of the desired 60 per cent margin over the Germans at an affordable price.

Chief of the War Staff Captain George Ballard, who had to align the fleet and the war plans, disagreed. The first priority was the close blockade of German bases – the overseas 'E' class.[16] Ballard hoped that Admiralty coastal submarines, which cost £75,000 – 20 per cent less than a destroyer – might suffice, although that turned out not to be

The 'J' class ('Reapers') were the first British operational ocean, as opposed to overseas, submarines, designed for high speed. They were assigned to the vital observation role outside the Heligoland Bight, to report the emergence of the High Seas Fleet. Three of the leading Royal Navy submariners were assigned as initial commanding officers: Nasmith (*J 1*), Boyle (*J 5*) and Horton (*J 6*). This is *J 1* as built, with a low bow and a gun on a raised position forward of the bridge. These submarines were initially armed with 12pdr 8 cwt guns, as in the 'E' class. In the July 1916 list of gun mountings this was changed to a 3in 10 cwt gun on a retractable HA mounting (this gun was also in the 'G' class and in *Swordfish*, renamed *S 1*). (RAN Naval Historical Section via Dr Josef Straczek)

HM SUBMARINE *SWORDFISH*. Profile and sections. The forward retractable gun is shown lowered; the after mounting is in the firing position. (© National Maritime Museum J8855)

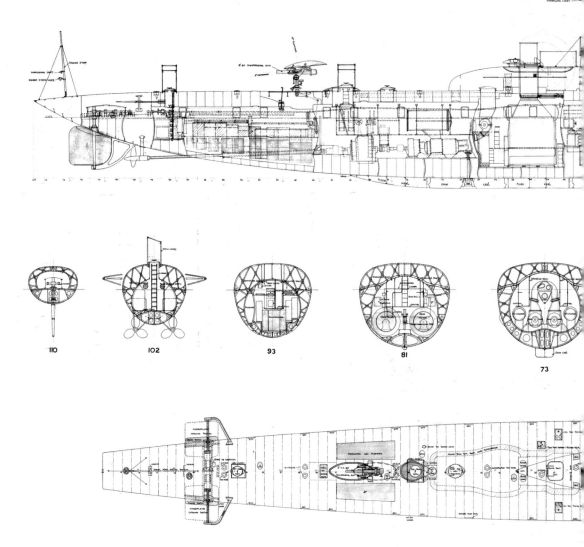

HM SUBMARINE *SWORDFISH*. Deck plans. Again, the retractable guns are shown raised (aft) and lowered (forward) on the superstructure deck view. (© National Maritime Museum J8949)

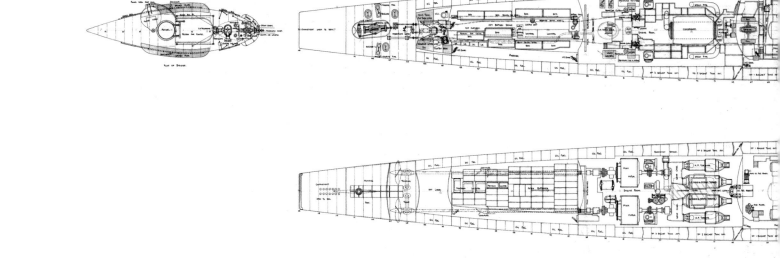

the case. Ballard's second priority was the big overseas submarines, which would watch for hostile squadrons in open water, to some extent taking over from light cruisers. Presumably they would function as fleet scouts. At the currently estimated cost of £200,000 each, three could be built for the cost of two light cruisers. Upkeep would also be considerably less. Moreover, unlike light cruisers, they could threaten enemy forces they spotted. However, they could not assume classic cruiser duties abroad, such as trade protection. Ballard saw them as submersible cruisers, to be distinguished from submersible blockaders and submersible coastals. The price of a flotilla of twenty destroyers would buy twenty blockaders backed by two submersible cruisers. Ballard did not address speed, but scouts typically needed a speed margin over the fleet with which they operated. Writing to Fisher on 13 August, Churchill pointed out that any submarine which was considered a partial substitute for battleship strength had to have sufficient strategic (i.e., sustained) speed to overhaul or evade a battle fleet.[17]

The idea of a very fast submarine was not entirely new. Churchill probably got it from Admiral Fisher, who was his main unofficial naval advisor. Fisher in turn may have had it from Admiral Jellicoe, who by 1911 was espousing what he called a Submarine Destroyer.[18] The name indicated a torpedo craft fast enough to participate in a fleet action, having accompanied the fleet to sea. The usual 20 knots was not enough, because although a submarine might steam with the fleet, it could not manoeuvre into position to attack enemy surface ships. At best it could occupy a position into which the fleet might lead the enemy. Jellicoe's early interest in fleet submarines helps explain his concern after 1914 that the Germans would lead his fleet over their waiting submarines. The idea seems never to have been tested in manoeuvres, although submarines certainly did show that they could engage capital ships.

Recently-appointed DNC Sir Eustace Tennyson d'Eyncourt offered a sketch design.[19] Like *Swordfish*, she would be steam powered, but with 10,000 SHP rather than 3250 SHP turbines. A much longer hull (320ft pp, 338ft overall), was better adapted to high speed. Surface displacement would be 1660 tons (2660 tons submerged). Beam would be 29ft. Maximum surface speed would be 24 knots, as Churchill asked, with a submerged speed of 10 knots. D'Eyncourt

wrote that tank tests confirmed his performance estimates.[20] Steam limited endurance to 1100nm at full speed and 2500nm at cruising speed. Armament would be two bow and two stern tubes plus four broadside tubes, all 21in diameter, and there would be two 3in anti-aircraft guns on retractable mountings. Bow and stern tubes would fire at a slight angle (6° forward and 10° aft) to the centreline, allowing for a better hull form. D'Eyncourt paid special attention to compartmentation and he expected to armour the superstructure lightly in wake of the funnel hatches, engine-room ventilation trunks and gun positions. Estimated cost was £250,000 and estimated building time 21 months. The accompanying sketch showed two low funnels and a low bow.

Commodore (S) (Roger Keyes) agreed that the overseas type envisaged in 1912 was intended to accompany a battle fleet to sea and that it needed the highest possible speed. Without experiments he did not want to exceed the dimensions chosen in 1912, which were about twice existing practice.[21] He later wrote that £80,000 was a lot to pay (in *Nautilus*) for two torpedo tubes and two knots. It was worthwhile only to gain experience with a very large submarine and thus to decide whether to lay down the still larger Vickers ocean submarine. The projected ocean submarine was about three times the displacement of an 'E' class submarine and nearly twice as long. It had a higher percentage of buoyancy, so it had to handle six times the volume of water. To submerge, it would have to shut down and cool a steam plant with three times the power produced by *Swordfish*.

On 10 June 1913 Churchill asked Controller about reaching maximum submarine output and also about the situation in regard to large submarines. He could not spend more than £1½ million in 1914–15, but could reach £2¾ million in 1915–16. The 1914–15 money would buy two large overseas submarines from Vickers plus twenty-five coastal submarines (nine at Vickers, three at Scotts and thirteen at two Royal Dockyards). There must have been no real expectation of building d'Eyncourt's ocean submarine in the near future. On 15 July First Sea Lord and Controller (Third Sea Lord) met to consider whether 'E'-class submarines should be substituted for slightly faster (18-knot) overseas boats.[22] They wrote that 18 knots was not enough. It was faster than needed for ordinary oversea duties but not enough to overhaul an enemy fleet and manoeuvre around it. Until the really fast submarine could be built, it would be best to buy more 'E'-boats while

The 'Js' were initially too wet. As in the 'G' class, their bows were built up (in 1917–18). This is *J 2*. (RAN Naval Historical Service via Dr Josef Straczek)

awaiting completion of the large Vickers and Scotts submarines. Third Sea Lord proposed buying two more big Vickers boats in the 1914–15 Programme, but Commodore (S) rejected them as too slow and too expensive. Churchill rejected them for the same reason; 24 knots was a minimum.

The project was brought up during a conference in Churchill's room at the Admiralty in December 1913.[23] Churchill wanted to lay down a prototype fast submarine. He could not afford to delay ordering more before the first had been tested. Keyes killed the project, pointing out that the submariners still had to learn how to control such long submarines. Adopting new ones had to await experience with *Nautilus*. *Swordfish* would pioneer the necessary steam technology. One prototype of d'Eyncourt's submarine was acceptable, but not a class built without any experience of large submarines. Churchill did not want a prototype, because he needed a way of reining in the cost of the battleship-building race with Germany. The conference agreed to defer further discussion to late 1914, when a fast submarine might be included in the 1914–15 Programme.

Churchill lacked sufficient support within the Admiralty to override Keyes. However, as he began to frame the 1914–15 Estimates, he again saw fast submarines as a solution to the Admiralty's financial problems. In January 1914 he asked Controller for the latest date at which fourteen submarines could be substituted for a battleship to be built at Plymouth, in order that all of them could be completed by June 1917, which is when the battleship would be ready.[24]

Once war broke out, the highest submarine priority was overseas submarines to operate on the German coast. However, Churchill and Fisher retained their interest in the ocean submarine. Late in 1914 it was reported that the Germans had 22-knot submarines. That sort of speed would make it possible for the submarines to accompany the High Seas Fleet. Jellicoe, who had long been interested in the possibilities offered by submarines working directly with a fleet, seems to have assumed that the Germans would not go to sea without their submarines.[25] The report justified immediately ordering fast submarines on an emergency basis. This was about the same time that Fisher ordered the battlecruisers *Renown* and *Repulse* and the 'large light cruisers' *Courageous*, *Furious* and *Glorious*. He may well have seen the door for ordering large ships closing and very fast submarines would need just as much Cabinet approval as the battlecruisers and the 'large lights'. No trace of the 22-knot submarine report has surfaced and it would fit well with Fisher's style to invent such a report to justify an emergency order. He may have seen fast submarines as part of the same programme. From the first they were called 'Reapers', which suggests that they were to reap what the big ships sowed, catching German ships running from the new fast capital ships. The remarkably sparse surviving documentation suggests a very forced programme. The first Folio in the 'J' Class Cover is a 1 April 1915 query to EinC about the planned exhaust tank. Compared to other submarine Covers, this one (and that of the 'K' class) is remarkably innocent of preliminary information, such as a stated requirement or stated characteristics. Much the same can be said of the Covers for Fisher's fast new capital ships. It was later said that no German submarine could exceed 18 knots on the surface.

According to the 1918 DNC history of wartime warship design and construction, upon receiving the report of fast U-boats Fisher directed DNC to look into the fastest possible submarine, but using oil engines (diesels) rather than steam turbines. The DNC history cites

recent experience with the French steam-powered *Archimède*, operating in the North Sea with 'E'-class submarines. She was ordered to dive as German destroyers approached, but a beam sea striking her funnel made it impossible to lower. Clearing the funnel and lowering it took 20 minutes. This would be more convincing had Fisher not ordered the steam-powered 'K' class a few months later. It seems likelier that hulls were ordered based on calculations d'Eyncourt made in 1913, but that when the steam plant was designed it turned out to be too large. According to the DNC history, the design was completed by the end of January 1915 (drawings went to the yards on 29 January 1915). The hull form was the one the test tank had run as UR.[26]

Calculation showed that the UR hull form could be driven at 20 knots with 3500 to 5000 SHP. Vickers was already building 800 BHP engines for the 'E' class and apparently considered it reasonable to add another half-engine (total twelve cylinders) to produce 1200 BHP on one shaft. On that basis three shafts (3600 BHP) would be barely enough. The same shaft bearings were used, high-tensile steel being substituted in the propeller shafts to deal with the 50 per cent increase in torsion. To minimise resistance on the surface, the usual 'drowned' bow planes were replaced by planes which housed when not in use, even though there was a danger that they might jam in the closed position. The stern planes were 'drowned', and the submarine could dive using only them.

The three shafts set the machinery arrangement: two engine rooms, with the motor room between them. As in the earlier submarines, the design showed broadside tubes. The tubes and the engines consumed so much length that not much was left for batteries. The solution was to use higher battery cells than in the 'E' class. The new design showed 232 cells rather than 224, but their increased capacity made it possible for the motors in the new submarines to develop 1400 BHP compared to 840 BHP in the 'E' class. Although specified speed was 20 knots, it appears that the designers did not expect more than 19.5 knots, as quoted in 1918 by DNC; this changed to 'over 19 knots' in 1919.[27] There were four bow tubes (for the first time in a British submarine), two broadside tubes (rather than the four envisaged in 1913) and no stern tubes.

The double hull followed Laurenti practice, accounting for 56 per cent of the ship's length. It had two watertight 'baling flats' between the two hulls just above the waterline, the spaces below being flooded by Kingstons in the bottom. The baling flats were flooded by twenty-four telemotor-operated scoop valves opening forward. Eventually the baling flats were eliminated, the whole side tankage being joined together. On trials it turned out that the big free-flooding space forward flooded in a seaway, bringing the bow down and slowing the submarine considerably. This problem was worst in shallow water. Before boats entered service this space was made watertight (it flooded using telemotor-controlled vents). Once that had been done, the boats could maintain 17 knots even in a heavy sea. The most visible post-completion modification was a raised bow divided into three watertight ballast tanks.

Eight 'J'-class submarines were ordered from Royal Dockyards: four from Portsmouth, two from Devonport and two from Pembroke, but two of the Portsmouth units (*J 3* and *J 4*) were cancelled in April 1915. Because none of the yards had previous submarine experience, DNC's department had to prepare an unusually large volume of detailed drawings. Conning towers duplicated those of the 'E' class and some other components also came from earlier submarine designs. While building *J 7* was drastically redesigned, her control room

moved from just forward of the broadside torpedo tubes to the motor room 60ft further aft; her conning tower and bridge were similarly moved. According to DNC, writing in 1925, this was done to improve seakeeping.[28]

The Admiralty bought some Sulzer diesels during the war and DNC considered a proposal to install two of them in place of the three Vickers diesels.[29] It turned out that for the same total power they required more space and weight and an appreciably larger-diameter pressure hull.

Construction seems to have slowed as soon as the 'K'-class design, which really did offer 24 knots, was ready. The two Portsmouth cancellations seem to have coincided with the early stage of the 'K'-class design.

Looking back, it seems likely that the 'J' class was conceived as a fleet-speed submarine and that as the design developed it became clear that it would not be fast enough. That may mean that the fleet speed requirement had been relaxed to the 20 knots desired earlier or, more probably, that it was turning out that a parallel design for the necessary steam plant could not be accommodated inside the 'J'-class hull. Surviving documentation is far too sparse to say. The d'Eyncourt papers include an undated list of designs in hand, probably from 1916, including a project for a modified 'J'-class submarine with two steam turbines and one internal combustion engine; any space freed would go into habitability and any weight saved into fuel. This note cannot refer to the 'K' class, because the same list includes a cruiser submarine as well as a monitor based on the 'K' class.[30]

As with the 'J' class, the 'K' Class Cover is very thin. According to the 1918 DNC history, some time early in 1915 the Grand Fleet asked for a submarine fast enough to work with it; unfortunately no such note from Admiral Jellicoe or his staff has surfaced. On 15 April 1915 Vickers offered a steam submarine, the design of which can be inter-

J 7 was redesigned, her control room moved aft to be adjacent to the engine room. She alone of the 'J' class was armed with a 3in 20 cwt HA gun, which was mounted well forward, as shown, presumably because its magazine was not moved aft. (RAN Naval Historical Service via Dr Josef Straczek)

J 7 shows her much-modified configuration. The 3in HA gun was later moved aft to just before the bridge, its original place taken by a 4in gun. Both could house. In 1918 she was further modified. (Dr David Stevens)

preted as a calculation of what it would take to turn the 'J' hull into a sufficiently fast boat.[31] Dimensions were somewhat larger, to accommodate 14,000 SHP turbines on wing shafts and a diesel on the centre shaft, offering 23 knots on the surface.[32] According to the 1918 DNC history, DNC then revived his 1913 design, as it was smaller (in displacement, not length) and offered higher speed.

The most important addition to the earlier design was an auxiliary diesel. In his pre-war paper on submarines, Fisher had rejected steam power because the plant required so much time either to start up (after

DNC's drawing of the 'J' class, from his end-of-war submarine design history. (Author's collection)

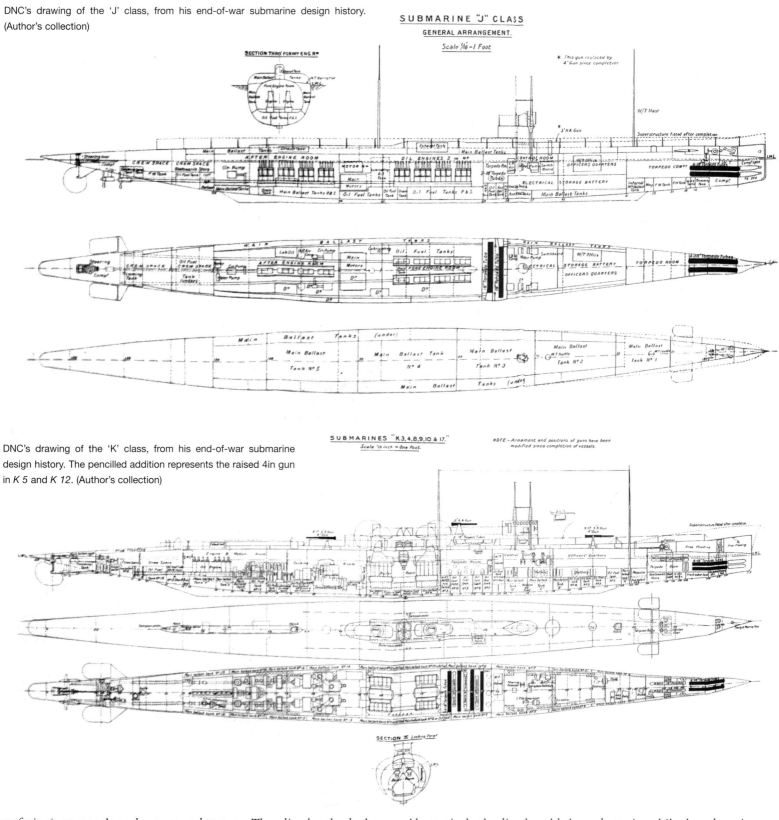

DNC's drawing of the 'K' class, from his end-of-war submarine design history. The pencilled addition represents the raised 4in gun in *K 5* and *K 12*. (Author's collection)

surfacing) or to shut down to submerge. The diesel solved the problem. Also, a steam plant offered limited endurance, but running on the diesel alone the submarine could run a much greater distance.[33] Initially, as in the Vickers design, the diesel would have driven its own shaft. Instead it ran a generator (a standard 'E'-class engine), which could drive the submarine through the motors on the main shafts.

Alternatively the diesel could charge batteries while the submarine ran on her steam turbines. Many of the auxiliaries were electrically driven. Using them could run down the battery, so to top them off a small motor-generator was fitted, driven by the main shaft. *K 3*, the first of class, made 23.8 knots on trials. This performance was particularly impressive because some of her tanks were flooded, making her appre-

A 'K'-class submarine being launched, showing her Laurenti-type hull form and the shutters of two of her four bow tubes. The black holes visible on the side of the hull are two broadside torpedo tube muzzles, giving her a total of eight 18in torpedo tubes. Note the considerable flare of her bow, which was insufficient to deal with rough seas. (John Lambert collection)

K 3 as completed, in a heavy sea, showing why placing her 4in guns on her weather deck was unacceptable. She was the first boat of the class to be completed, one of a pair from Vickers. She was armed with two 4in guns and a 3in 20 cwt HA gun (abaft the forward 4in gun) plus a twin revolving torpedo tube for surface action, carried between bridge and forefunnel, behind superstructure doors. These torpedo tubes were later eliminated. At least some of the boats were completed in this configuration. A sketch in the official DNC history based on the general arrangement drawing for K 3 and K 4 shows an alternative arrangement, which presumably applied to most boats: the 3in gun was on the bridge deck between bridge and forefunnel. A photograph of K 2 as completed shows only one gun, the 3in HA on the bridge deck. Initially all were to have had two 5.5in guns, but an official drawing of K 1–K 14 shows their replacement by 4in guns, leaving the heavier guns still planned for K 15–K 17. Only in K 17 were the 4in guns replaced by 5.5in (but only one was mounted). The 5.5in guns allocated to K 15 and to K 16 seem never to have been mounted. This gun was also intended for the L 50 class, but they were armed instead with 4in guns. (Author's collection)

ciably heavier than her design displacement. In April 1917 K 9 made 23.5 knots at 10,900 BHP although she was drawing a foot deep due to leaky main tank vents.[34]

The main motors were rated at 1440 BHP for 1½ hours and at 2040 BHP for 20 minutes. Submerged speed was 8 knots at normal rating and probably 9 knots at the higher rating. In 1918 endurance was given as 13.5nm at 9 knots (presumably on the assumption that it would be achieved at the 1½-hour rating) and as 83nm at 1.75 knots. DEE later assumed the batteries would sustain 8 knots for only an hour and offered 30nm at 4 knots and 45nm at 1.5 knots.[35]

Many of the novel problems associated with the steam plant had been solved by Scotts in designing Swordfish. That company's solutions were incorporated in the 'K' class. For example, Scotts worked out the method used to close off openings (for the down- and up-takes) using telemotors. The openings were far larger than in previous submarines and they had to be closed down and secured within half a minute. For the funnels, pressure-tight coamings were fitted from the pressure hull to the top of the superstructure, closed at each end by a watertight cover. There were also four smaller openings to lead air into the boiler room fans.

As with the 'J' class, this was a Laurenti-type design with baling flats above free-flooding main ballast tanks. Also as in the 'J' class, this arrangement proved too complex, so in the end the only watertight partition was a centreline bulkhead, leaving ten ballast tanks on each side. That left a very simple venting arrangement, two vents per tank (at its ends), as high as possible. Initially the ballast tanks were flooded through Kingstons, but after the first one or two holes were cut in the bottoms of the tanks to promote faster diving. The four midships tanks were not cut; they could be used for oil fuel.

The 21in tubes projected in 1913 were dropped in favour of 18in bow tubes. Quadruple bow 18in tubes had already been designed for the 'J' class; the only design for a 21in bow tube was for Swordfish. Similarly, 18in tubes were adopted for the broadside mounting because there was no design for a 21in broadside tube. In a 3 May 1915 note Commodore (S) (by this time former ICS S S Hall) proposed adding a twin above-water trainable tube in the superstructure abaft the conning tower. It would enable the submarine to fire on the beam at night to perform destroyer functions; Hall was not at all sure that the broadside tubes could be fired at full speed. He understood, correctly, that the additional tubes would not cause any problems.[36]

Gun armament was two 4in and one 3in high-angle (HA). As completed the 'Ks' had low bows and were often very wet, so they were modified with raised 'swan' bows. Their superstructures were rearranged, a new high steering position being built with a view over the new bow. One 4in gun was eliminated and the other (and the 3in HA gun) moved to the top of the superstructure from the upper deck. The deck torpedo tubes were eliminated as they were considered too close to the waterline to be useful. The last three boats were to have had 5.5in rather than 4in guns, but that appears not to have been done. The original 4in guns were a destroyer type. Post-war surviving 'K'-class submarines received two submarine-type 4in guns (Mk XII on S1 mountings) in place of the single surviving destroyer 4in and the 3in HA gun.

The Cover shows that the submarines were ordered under a cover designation as flotilla leaders; it includes (as Folio 2) the 18 June 1915 acceptance of Vickers' tender for K 3 and K 4.[37] A file on design details shows that as of May 1915 planned power was 10,000 to 12,000 SHP.[38] Vickers produced detailed drawings, the first going to DNC at the end of June 1915. The superstructure, bridge and fairwater were all mocked up and examined at a conference at Vickers on 21 January 1916.[39]

K 1 and *K 2* were ordered from Portsmouth; it is not clear exactly when. Presumably they simply replaced the two cancelled 'J'-class boats. A further batch, *K 5–K 14*, were ordered in August 1915: *K 5* from Portsmouth, *K 6–K 7* from Devonport, *K 8–K 10* from Vickers, *K 11–K 12* from Armstrong, *K 13–K 14* from Fairfield (of which *K 13* was renamed *K 22* after foundering and being raised). *K 15–K 18* were ordered in February 1916, *K 19* in May 1916 and *K 20–K 21* in August 1916. Of these submarines, *K 18–K 21* were all reordered in 1917 as 'M'-class 'submarine monitors' described in the chapter on the First World War. Finally, early in 1918 *K 23–K 28* were ordered to an improved 'K'-class design. Only *K 26* was completed.

The 'K' class have generally been considered grotesque failures, proofs that the very idea of close support by fast submarines was defective. That is probably why Churchill did not take credit for them the way he did for the *Queen Elizabeth*-class battleships and the *Arethusa*-class cruisers in his *The World Crisis*. The great proof of failure is generally taken as the 31 January 1918 'Battle of May Island', a disastrous fleet exercise in which both *K 4* and *K 17* were sunk by collision. As nine 'K'-class submarines proceeded to sea, they encountered minesweepers which had not been informed of the sortie. *K 14* jammed her helm trying to evade and *K 22* rammed her. She was soon rammed by the battlecruiser *Inflexible*. In the confusion which followed, the light cruiser *Fearless* rammed *K 17* and *K 6* rammed *K 4*; *K 4* was rammed again by *K 7*. Not surprisingly, *K 17* and *K 4* sank, although *K 14* survived. The total cost was 103 men. *K 1* was also sunk by collision on 17 November 1917. *K 13* foundered in the Gareloch on 29 January 1917 while running trials.

After the 'Battle of May Island' a wag wrote that the 'K' class had the speed of a destroyer, the turning circle of a battlecruiser and the bridge control facilities of a picket boat. This was exaggerated, but the lack of bridge facilities – which meant means of maintaining situational awareness – was real. The disaster reflected a wider problem. It does not appear that any officers understood just how difficult it would be to manage a complex fleet without constant communication and also without constant verification of where ships were in relation to each other. In many ways Jutland demonstrated the problem, but it was not well understood until after the war. A fleet running at night without lights and with very little inter-communication invited disaster. It was not that the idea of direct support by submarines was disproven, but rather that a great deal had to be done to make it work. Other major navies were also much interested in direct support or at least in using submarines in conjunction with surface forces, but given a combination of poor situational awareness and poor communication that was impossible at the time. Admiral Jellicoe's recurring fear that the Germans would lure him into a submarine ambush was another form of the same idea (and the Germans had much the same fear when confronting the British). Without good communications and good shared situational awareness this too was essentially impossible.

The other major problems of the class were their great length and the potential for mischief in all of the engine-room openings. The 'Ks', like other British submarines, had a designed diving depth of 200ft. With more than 50 per cent greater length, a 'K' diving at too steep an angle could easily put part of herself below rated depth. If enough of the submarine was below rated depth, enough could be crushed open to sink the rest. *K 5* may have been lost in 1921 by diving too

For a time *K 3* apparently had only the after 4in gun. The two forward guns were apparently removed after trials and before commissioning. At least some boats (such as *K 14*) were completed with the 4in gun aft and the 3in HA gun on the bridge deck between bridge and forefunnel. Later the 4in gun was moved up onto the bridge deck and the 3in HA gun also mounted there, between bridge and forefunnel. The 4in guns on the casing may have been in disappearing mounts, which would further complicate interpretation of gun arrangements. The low structure aft, which all the 'K' class had, covered, among other things, the exhaust tank (muffler) for their single diesel engine. (John Lambert collection)

K 3, *K 6* and *K 7* of the 12th Submarine Flotilla alongside, presumably at Scapa Flow. Note the raised funnels on board *K 6*. All have the 4in gun forward of the high-angle gun on their bridge decks, and *K 3* has been given a metal bridge screen in place of the canvas 'cheaters' visible on board the others. The nozzle visible at the after end of the closed bridge of *K 6* may be a whale spout. The submarine in the background is not identified. In addition to *K 6*, *K 15* and *K 16* had raised funnels. *K 15* had a sponson under her bridge fairwater. All surviving units except *K 7* eventually had steel bridge screens, which varied in shape (some were narrow). (John Lambert collection)

K 5 as completed, her gun armament reduced to the single 3in 20 cwt HA gun on her bridge level. Note the opening under it for the twin revolving torpedo tubes. In the background is the large destroyer HMS *Swift*. *K 6* was similarly armed. The 3in 20 cwt HA Mk III mounting was to have armed the 'K' and 'L' classes, and eighty-three were made. In 1918, twenty-one were in the 'K' and 'L' classes, but it had been decided not to mount the gun in the modified 'K' class or in the *L 50* class, and most were mounted in old destroyers and in the 1919 destroyers projected in 1918. (John Lambert collection)

K 6 newly completed, running trials in Plymouth Sound. She shows her low bow and her two high wireless masts. (Author's collection)

K 6 in sea state 3 at 20 knots off Scapa Flow, 4 December 1917, showing that the original bow was inadequate, even with the guns raised to the bridge deck. (Author's collection)

steeply. They also dove slowly because so much had to be closed and the boilers had to shut down. The best time was 3 minutes 25 seconds, but 5 minutes was usual. By way of contrast, a small 'H'-class submarine could dive in 30 seconds. Even with so much time to close a boat down, any obstruction which happened to enter a funnel or ventilator could jam it open, flooding the engine room when the submarine dived. Ventilators jammed on several occasions.

A contemporary view was given by Captain Little, who commanded the 'K'-boats in the Grand Fleet, in 1917 in a discussion with a US submarine officer.[40] Little considered the means of handling funnels and ventilation safe and reliable, 'though it is understood that one submarine of this class sank due to improper closing of some valve'. He considered the boilers and steam plant similar to those of a destroyer, the boilers being enclosed to keep heat from other parts of the boat and also to keep the boiler warm while the submarine submerged, so that as little time as possible would be spent getting up

steam again once the submarine surfaced. In view of the large size (i.e., poor manoeuvrability) of the 'K' class, Little considered it essential that the boat should be heading parallel with the enemy (using her broadside tubes) when within 2000 yards.

The next class of steam submarine (*K 26* class) would have a considerably raised deck forward of the conning tower to improve weatherliness. Little liked the permanent light metal bridge better than a temporary bridge with weather screens; it could be abandoned instantly for a quick dive. The conning tower was very small, the boat being handled from inside.

The Grand Fleet certainly liked the idea of direct support. Fast submarines could, for example, have solved the problem that Admiral Jellicoe encountered at Jutland: if the Germans turned away, what should he do? If he pursued them and the Germans fired torpedoes back, he would be running into their torpedoes. However, if he could project a group of fast submarines beyond the retreating Germans,

K 15 as modified for better seakeeping, with a raised 'swan' bow and guns (4in forward of her forefunnel, 3in HA abaft it) relocated to her bridge deck. It is not known whether the two lost in the 'Battle of May Island' (*K 4* and *K 17*, on 31 January 1918) had received the high bows before their loss. (John Lambert collection)

K 16 shows the modified gun arrangement and the 'swan' bow. It is not clear whether her topside torpedo tubes have been plated in. Both wireless masts have been raised. (Author's collection)

HM SUBMARINES *K 3*, *K 4*, *K 8*, *K 9*, *K 10*, *K 17*. General arrangements and sections. (Drawn by John Lambert)

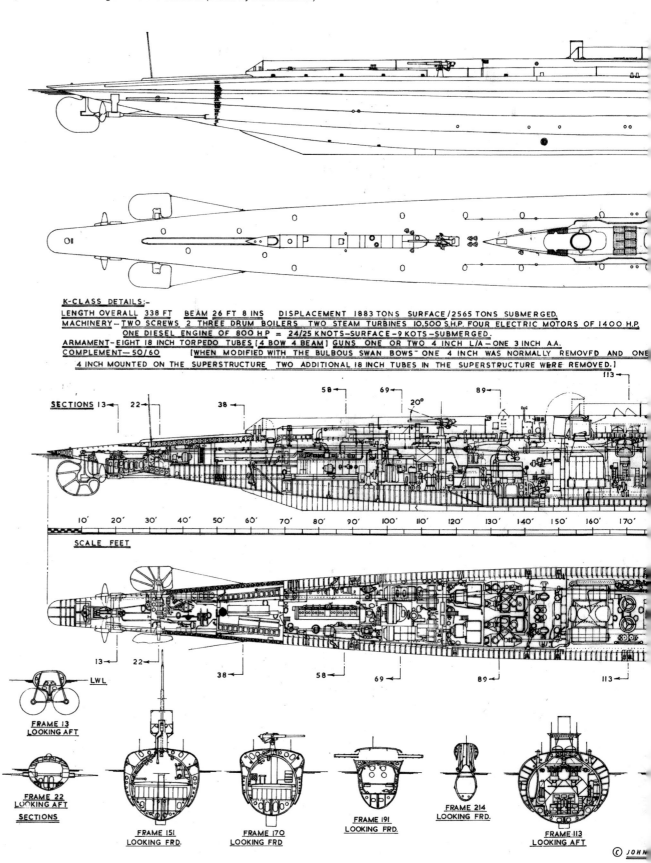

K-CLASS DETAILS:-
LENGTH OVERALL 338 FT   BEAM 26 FT 8 INS   DISPLACEMENT 1883 TONS SURFACE/2565 TONS SUBMERGED.
MACHINERY - TWO SCREWS 2 THREE DRUM BOILERS TWO STEAM TURBINES 10,500 S.H.P. FOUR ELECTRIC MOTORS OF 1400 H.P.
ONE DIESEL ENGINE OF 800 H P = 24/25 KNOTS - SURFACE - 9 KOTS - SUBMERGED.
ARMAMENT - EIGHT 18 INCH TORPEDO TUBES [4 BOW 4 BEAM] GUNS ONE OR TWO 4 INCH L/A - ONE 3 INCH A.A.
COMPLEMENT - 50/60   [WHEN MODIFIED WITH THE BULBOUS SWAN BOWS" ONE 4 INCH WAS NORMALLY REMOVFD AND ONE
4 INCH MOUNTED ON THE SUPERSTRUCTURE TWO ADDITIONAL 18 INCH TUBES IN THE SUPERSTRUCTURE WERE REMOVED.]

SCALE FEET

SECTIONS

FRAME 13
LOOKING AFT

FRAME 22
LOOKING AFT
SECTIONS

FRAME 151
LOOKING FRD.

FRAME 170
LOOKING FRD

FRAME 191
LOOKING FRD.

FRAME 214
LOOKING FRD.

FRAME 113
LOOKING AFT

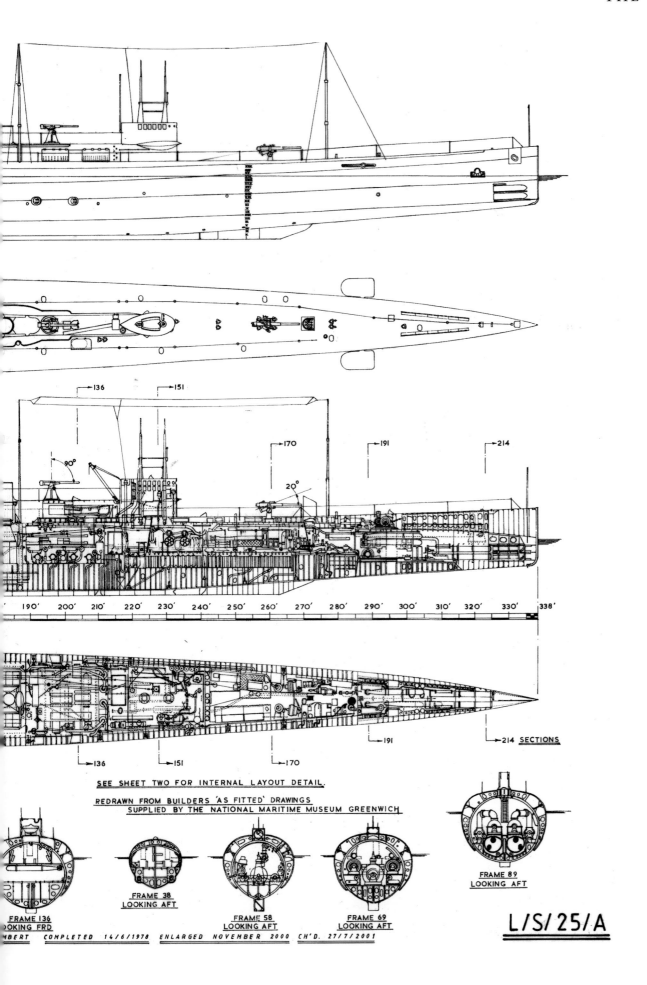

SEE SHEET TWO FOR INTERNAL LAYOUT DETAIL.

REDRAWN FROM BUILDERS 'AS FITTED' DRAWINGS
SUPPLIED BY THE NATIONAL MARITIME MUSEUM GREENWICH

FRAME 89
LOOKING AFT

FRAME 136
LOOKING FRD

FRAME 38
LOOKING AFT

FRAME 58
LOOKING AFT

FRAME 69
LOOKING AFT

...MBERT   COMPLETED 14/6/1978   ENLARGED NOVEMBER 2000   CH'D. 27/7/2001

L/S/25/A

HM SUBMARINES *K 3*, *K 4*, *K 8*, *K 9*, *K 10*, *K 17*. Detail. (Drawn by John Lambert)

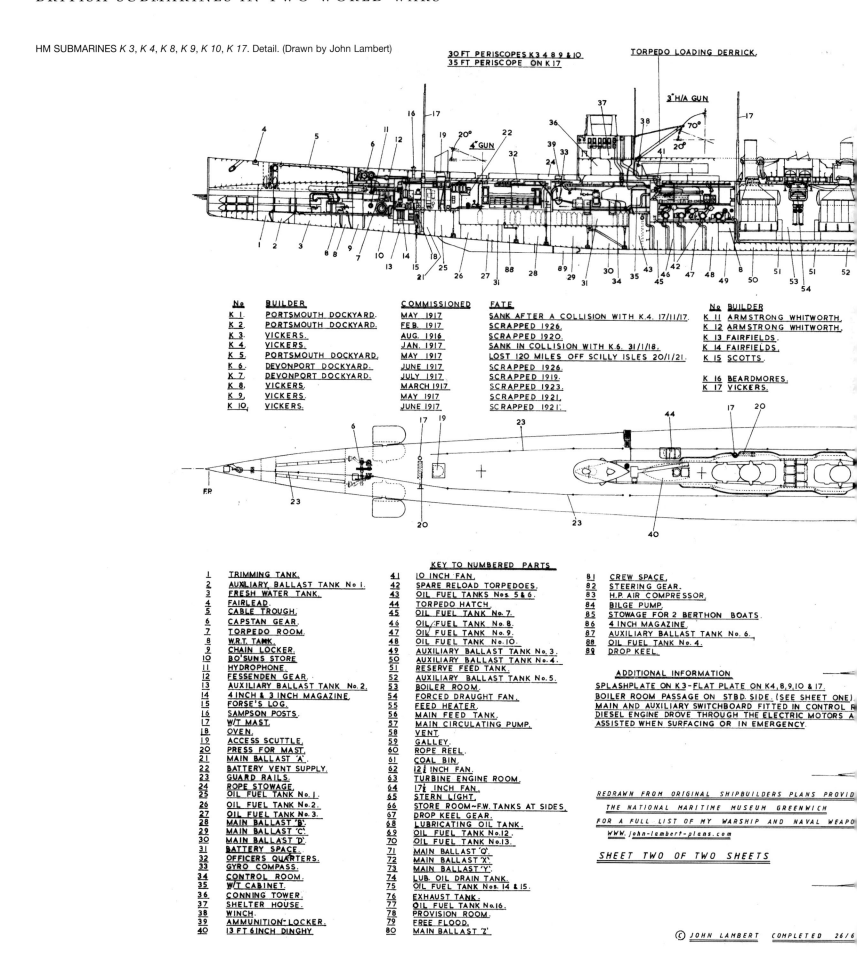

No.	BUILDER	COMMISSIONED	FATE	No	BUILDER
K 1.	PORTSMOUTH DOCKYARD.	MAY 1917	SANK AFTER A COLLISION WITH K.4. 17/11/17.	K 11	ARMSTRONG WHITWORTH,
K 2.	PORTSMOUTH DOCKYARD.	FEB. 1917	SCRAPPED 1926.	K 12	ARMSTRONG WHITWORTH,
K 3.	VICKERS.	AUG. 1916	SCRAPPED 1920.	K 13	FAIRFIELDS.
K 4.	VICKERS.	JAN. 1917	SANK IN COLLISION WITH K.6. 31/1/18.	K 14	FAIRFIELDS.
K 5.	PORTSMOUTH DOCKYARD.	MAY 1917	LOST 120 MILES OFF SCILLY ISLES 20/1/21.	K 15	SCOTTS.
K 6.	DEVONPORT DOCKYARD.	JUNE 1917	SCRAPPED 1926.		
K 7.	DEVONPORT DOCKYARD.	JULY 1917	SCRAPPED 1919.	K 16	BEARDMORES.
K 8.	VICKERS.	MARCH 1917	SCRAPPED 1923.	K 17	VICKERS.
K 9.	VICKERS.	MAY 1917	SCRAPPED 1921.		
K 10.	VICKERS.	JUNE 1917	SCRAPPED 1921.		

KEY TO NUMBERED PARTS

1	TRIMMING TANK.	41	10 INCH FAN.	81	CREW SPACE.
2	AUXILIARY BALLAST TANK No 1.	42	SPARE RELOAD TORPEDOES.	82	STEERING GEAR.
3	FRESH WATER TANK.	43	OIL FUEL TANKS Nos. 5 & 6.	83	H.P. AIR COMPRESSOR.
4	FAIRLEAD.	44	TORPEDO HATCH.	84	BILGE PUMP.
5	CABLE TROUGH.	45	OIL FUEL TANK No. 7.	85	STOWAGE FOR 2 BERTHON BOATS.
6	CAPSTAN GEAR.	46	OIL FUEL TANK No. 8.	86	4 INCH MAGAZINE.
7	TORPEDO ROOM.	47	OIL FUEL TANK No. 9.	87	AUXILIARY BALLAST TANK No. 6.
8	W.R.T. TANK.	48	OIL FUEL TANK No. 10.	88	OIL FUEL TANK No. 4.
9	CHAIN LOCKER.	49	AUXILIARY BALLAST TANK No. 3.	89	DROP KEEL.
10	BO'SUNS STORE	50	AUXILIARY BALLAST TANK No. 4.		
11	HYDROPHONE.	51	RESERVE FEED TANK.		
12	FESSENDEN GEAR.	52	AUXILIARY BALLAST TANK No. 5.		ADDITIONAL INFORMATION
13	AUXILIARY BALLAST TANK No. 2.	53	BOILER ROOM.		SPLASHPLATE ON K3 - FLAT PLATE ON K4,8,9,10 & 17.
14	4 INCH & 3 INCH MAGAZINE.	54	FORCED DRAUGHT FAN.		BOILER ROOM PASSAGE ON STBD. SIDE. (SEE SHEET ONE)
15	FORSE'S LOG.	55	FEED HEATER.		MAIN AND AUXILIARY SWITCHBOARD FITTED IN CONTROL R
16	SAMPSON POSTS.	56	MAIN FEED TANK.		DIESEL ENGINE DROVE THROUGH THE ELECTRIC MOTORS A
17	W/T MAST.	57	MAIN CIRCULATING PUMP.		ASSISTED WHEN SURFACING OR IN EMERGENCY.
18	OVEN.	58	VENT.		
19	ACCESS SCUTTLE.	59	GALLEY.		
20	PRESS FOR MAST.	60	ROPE REEL.		
21	MAIN BALLAST 'A'.	61	COAL BIN.		
22	BATTERY VENT SUPPLY.	62	12½ INCH FAN.		
23	GUARD RAILS.	63	TURBINE ENGINE ROOM.		
24	ROPE STOWAGE.	64	17½ INCH FAN.		
25	OIL FUEL TANK No. 1.	65	STERN LIGHT.		
26	OIL FUEL TANK No. 2.	66	STORE ROOM~F.W. TANKS AT SIDES.		REDRAWN FROM ORIGINAL SHIPBUILDERS PLANS PROVID
27	OIL FUEL TANK No. 3.	67	DROP KEEL GEAR.		THE NATIONAL MARITIME MUSEUM GREENWICH
28	MAIN BALLAST 'B'.	68	LUBRICATING OIL TANK.		FOR A FULL LIST OF MY WARSHIP AND NAVAL WEAPO
29	MAIN BALLAST 'C'.	69	OIL FUEL TANK No. 12.		WWW. john-lambert-plans.com
30	MAIN BALLAST 'D'.	70	OIL FUEL TANK No. 13.		
31	BATTERY SPACE.	71	MAIN BALLAST 'Q'.		SHEET TWO OF TWO SHEETS
32	OFFICERS QUARTERS.	72	MAIN BALLAST 'X'.		
33	GYRO COMPASS.	73	MAIN BALLAST 'Y'.		
34	CONTROL ROOM.	74	LUB. OIL DRAIN TANK.		
35	W/T CABINET.	75	OIL FUEL TANK Nos. 14 & 15.		
36	CONNING TOWER.	76	EXHAUST TANK.		
37	SHELTER HOUSE.	77	OIL FUEL TANK No. 16.		
38	WINCH.	78	PROVISION ROOM.		
39	AMMUNITION LOCKER.	79	FREE FLOOD.		
40	13 FT 6 INCH DINGHY	80	MAIN BALLAST 'Z'.		© JOHN LAMBERT COMPLETED 26/6

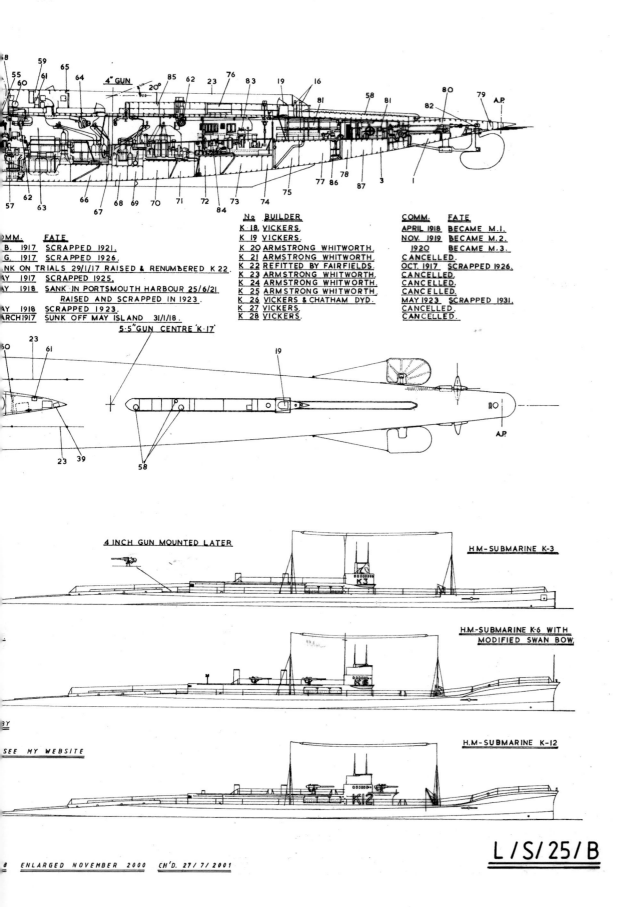

No	BUILDER	COMM.	FATE
K 18	VICKERS.	APRIL 1918	BECAME M.I.
K 19	VICKERS.	NOV. 1919	BECAME M.2.
K 20	ARMSTRONG WHITWORTH.	1920	BECAME M.3.
K 21	ARMSTRONG WHITWORTH.	CANCELLED.	
K 22	REFITTED BY FAIRFIELDS.	OCT. 1917	SCRAPPED 1926.
K 23	ARMSTRONG WHITWORTH.	CANCELLED.	
K 24	ARMSTRONG WHITWORTH.	CANCELLED.	
K 25	ARMSTRONG WHITWORTH.	CANCELLED.	
K 26	VICKERS & CHATHAM DYD.	MAY 1923	SCRAPPED 1931.
K 27	VICKERS.	CANCELLED.	
K 28	VICKERS.	CANCELLED.	

MM.	FATE
B. 1917	SCRAPPED 1921.
G. 1917	SCRAPPED 1926.
NK ON TRIALS 29/1/17	RAISED & RENUMBERED K 22.
AY 1917	SCRAPPED 1925.
AY 1918	SANK IN PORTSMOUTH HARBOUR 25/6/21 RAISED AND SCRAPPED IN 1923.
AY 1918	SCRAPPED 1923.
ARCH 1917	SUNK OFF MAY ISLAND 31/1/18.

5.5" GUN CENTRE 'K.17'

4 INCH GUN MOUNTED LATER

H.M-SUBMARINE K-3

H.M-SUBMARINE K-6 WITH MODIFIED SWAN BOW

SEE MY WEBSITE

H.M-SUBMARINE K-12

L / S / 25 / B

B ENLARGED NOVEMBER 2000 CH'D. 27/7/2001

K 12 shows the late-war armament modification for anti-submarine work, her 4in gun on a raised platform, presumably atop a gun crew trunk, forward of her bridge. *K 5* was similarly modified, but the two could be distinguished by differences in the shape of their bridge screens. (Dr Josef Straczek)

K 22 after the war, with 'swan' bow and both guns on her bridge deck. Note that they appear to be identical, in which case she had two 4in guns rather than the 4in and 3in combination. (RAN Naval Historical Service via Dr Josef Straczek)

they could dive and fire as the Germans approached. In that case the Germans would be caught between the heavy guns of the fleet and a large torpedo salvo.

The October 1921 Admiralty Technical History of British wartime submarines was very complimentary to the 'K' class, pointing out that in September 1918 two 'K'-boats overtook the Grand Fleet, which was hove-to in a heavy north-west gale by the North Dogger Bank. 'The boats are undoubtedly better than their designers expected. In P.Z. exercises with the Grand Fleet . . . they were able each time to close within torpedo range of their objects, showing that an action with the High Seas Fleet would have in all probability given them a great opportunity.' The 'K' class 'showed that we could confidently produce a successful boat of any size and specification asked for and that we have long passed the stage of experimental production'. The requirements quoted were a surface speed of 23 knots, to dive in five minutes, to dive (i.e., to remain submerged) for six hours and to be seaworthy on the high seas. All of these requirements were exceeded.[41]

Repeat 'K' Class

In February 1918 Admiral Beatty asked the Admiralty for more 'K'-class submarines; the three which had been lost should be replaced and the aim should be two flotillas of ten each, so that eight each could be available at any time.[42] 'This should be in addition to the special "K" class', presumably meaning the monitors, which were still designated in the 'K' series at the time. Beatty wrote that experience over the past year had shown that the 'Ks' were an important adjunct to the fleet. 'Their speed and seagoing qualities enable them to conform to Fleet movements and tactical requirements; in consequence they may be confidently expected to arrive at the scene of action at the right time; moreover their speed admits of their being employed to cut off an enemy's retreat at a strategic point. These are great advantages and cannot be over-estimated.' Note that this was after the 'Battle of May Island', which is conventionally taken as proof that the entire 'K' concept was wrong.

On 17 April 1918 the Royal Navy ordered six modified 'K'-class

K 26 was completed after the war to a heavily modified design. She had three 4in guns instead of the single 4in and single 3in guns of the earlier 'K' class. (RAN Naval Historical Service via Dr Josef Straczek)

submarines, *K 23–K 28*. The design seems to have been worked out in response to a 10 March 1918 list of features proposed by the Captain of the 12th Submarine Flotilla, the unit assigned to the Grand Fleet, which operated the 'K' class.[43] Captain C J C Little ended a four-page list of proposals with the comment that 'we [the officers of the flotilla] are all agreed that the present 'K' class design having been carried out without practical trial is a great achievement. The slow flooding of the external ballast tanks due to their disposition is their chief drawback. With the present experience embodied the new type will contain enormous possibilities.' Little's comments give some idea of experience with the 'Ks'.

Little wanted the same high bow as in the modified 'Ks', but he also wanted a cylindrical pressure hull instead of the somewhat irregularly-shaped one in the 'J' and 'K' classes. The ends might not reach as far forward and aft, so that the flat tail would not be part of the pressure hull – it was a source of weakness. Little rejected the Laurenti hull form; he wanted something closer to a saddle-tank design, in which the tops of the external tanks would be awash before the pressure hull itself submerged, 'to keep a "head" on for quick flooding'. Years of war had shown just how important quick diving could be. Little saw no reason the submarine should need more than two minutes to dive; his experience showed that size would not be a problem. On the other hand, Little wanted all the reserve buoyancy of the current 'K' class; he accepted that the hull might have to be filled out. As in smaller submarines, Little wanted a large internal quick-flooding tank amidships to promote fast diving.

The conning tower should be over the control room, as far aft as possible so long as the control room was not next to the boiler room; but Little realised that probably neither control room nor conning tower could be moved much further aft. The control room was to be as quiet as possible, free of auxiliary machinery. The electrical arrangement, with each compartment containing its own switches and fuses, should be like those in the 'L' class.

Little wanted a non-watertight superstructure running between the high bow and the conning tower and from the conning tower and funnel casing aft, for harbour use and to carry boats etc. It would be about a foot higher than the existing upper deck. The funnel casing would also be raised about a foot to allow freer access for boiler room air. The wheelhouse and the bridge above it should be about 2ft 6in higher than the current one. The funnels needed better protection from the sea, perhaps as in *K 5*. Boiler air inlet hatch coamings should be raised 3 or 4ft above the hull. Funnel casings should admit air more freely.

All fuel should be carried externally, to reduce tankage inside the pressure hull and so to provide the crew with more space; Little made habitability his main concern. He pointed out that the war had shown that crews had to live aboard, not only to keep such complex craft operational but also to be at fleet notice.

Armament should be six 21in bow tubes and two 21in broadside tubes. Little argued against any gun larger than 4in unless displacement was considerably increased. This was presumably a reference to the monitors. Gun armament should be three 4in, one forward of the conning tower and two abaft it on the funnel casing level. When on the surface, all guns and torpedoes should be controlled from the bridge as in a light cruiser, though with a simpler arrangement.

Construction at the two private yards was cancelled on 26 November 1918, but the orders were transferred to the Royal Dockyard at Chatham.[44] Ultimately only *K 26* survived. Like the modified earlier 'Ks', she had high bows. Her superstructure was redesigned and raised, this time carrying three 4in guns instead of the earlier two 4in and one 3in HA. The most drastic change was in the bow, which was redesigned to accommodate six 21in torpedo tubes. The 18in broadside tubes remained. Designed surface displacement increased to 2140 tons. Despite this considerable increase, estimated surface speed was still 23.5 knots.[45]

K 26 from astern. Note her shielded gun. She had a much more powerful bow salvo, six 21in rather than four 18in tubes, but retained the four 18in beam tubes of earlier 'K'-class submarines (they were removed about 1929). She could dive more quickly than the other 'Ks', partly because most of her ballast was carried internally (external tanks were mostly filled with fuel oil). (John Lambert collection)

There was some post-war interest in abandoning steam power in favour of three 3000 HP diesels with electric drive.[46] That would have cost 250 tons and at least a knot and it was doubtful that there was enough space. However, there was a feasible alternative. Two engines could drive shafts through clutches, the third driving a 2060 kW generator. Each shaft would carry two motors in tandem, each giving 625 HP on the surface and about 430 HP when submerged. This arrangement would cost 50 tons but that would be balanced by a saving in fuel. At full power the submarine could make 22.6 knots rather than 23.5 knots. With both direct-coupled engines disconnected and only the main generator running, speed would be 15.2 knots. Nothing came of this idea.

CHAPTER 7
SUBMARINE AND ANTI-SUBMARINE: THE RUN-UP TO WAR

Unlike other navies, the Royal Navy bought its first submarines to learn how to neutralise submarines. To do that, it had to learn what the submarines could do, in exercises beginning in 1903. It was soon clear that submarines could be an effective means first of local defence and later of attacking enemy capital ships in waters nominally controlled by the enemy. Conversely, as British submariners learned to attack effectively, they became vital advisors on anti-submarine warfare. It appears that the Royal Navy was far more aware of and interested in, anti-submarine warfare than any other before the First World War.

That did it little good once the Germans began attacking British shipping, however – ASW was then, and remains, extremely difficult.

In May 1903 Bacon produced an initial report on submarine experience, based on almost a year's experience.[1] He was already convinced that it would be very dangerous for ships to pass within about 25nm of a permanent submarine base.

To thoroughly appreciate the value of these boats it is necessary to place oneself in the position of the Captain of a ship in the

In dry-dock, *E 47* shows the impact of pre-war thinking about submarine tactics and ASW, a broadside torpedo tube, the muzzle of one of which is visible. The Royal Navy was very interested in using its overseas submarines against enemy capital ships, which it expected to cruise in columns. A submarine running down a column was well-placed to fire broadside shots, but might find it difficult to turn quickly enough to fire bow-on. It might not even be able to fire until it was too close. A stern shot would not bring the submarine too close, but probably would be less accurate. This is a wartime photograph, as indicated by the style of the number on the submarine's fairwater. Note the standard 12pdr abaft the bridge, the sides of its platform folding down when the gun was retracted. The crewmen cleaning the submarine give a sense of scale. (John Lambert collection)

vicinity of a port known to contain certain boats. My experience at Portsmouth after many attacks leads me to the statement that, on starting to pass near that port I am always confident that one boat at least will successfully approach the ship near enough to attack. However good a lookout may be kept, however practiced and keen the observers, a well handled boat, even in calm weather, will press her attack home without being seen before the attack can be avoided. The risks of allowing a large ship to approach such a port are so great that I unhesitatingly affirm that in war time it should never be allowed.

Even if the captain of the ship spotted a periscope, he would find it difficult to decide what to do; his only choice would be to turn 16 points (180°) and run at maximum speed. He would know that there might be other boats present, whose periscopes had not been seen. Evading one might bring him towards another, which could sink him. Steering directly for the submarine would offer the smallest possible target (Bacon did not envisage ramming), but it would not deal with other boats which might be present. Bacon considered submarines ideal for local defence of Gibraltar and Malta, in the former case controlling the Straits. Submarines might also be a good local defence for Alexandria, from which they could guard much of the Egyptian coast. He proposed a total of eighteen boats for home service and twenty-four for the Mediterranean, all of the current 'A' class. As of 1903, thirteen boats were building. For the future, Bacon envisaged ten each year in 1904, 1905 and 1906, to produce a total of forty-three 'A'-class submarines.

Bacon reported on his first series of twenty exercises early in 1904.[2] By this time his crews had had practically a year to learn how to use their boats before beginning manoeuvres with the fleet. He pointed to the extraordinary reliability the boats had demonstrated. A table showed fifteen successes out of twenty attacks planned, the failures including all cases in which boats were unable to reach their rendezvous owing to the state of the sea, but the figure did not take into account entire days in which the weather would have precluded operations. Most of the attacks were carried out against the torpedo

Many late pre-war exercises tested and demonstrated wireless in the context of fleet battle. Existing short-range sets were valued as a means of coordinating a group of submarines working with a surface ship, which would have both long- and short-range sets. One lesson of the manoeuvres was that submarines needed a dedicated wireless officer, instead of one of the usual two officers, one of whom might be knowledgeable. D 1 shows her wireless installation. The star- and X-shaped objects were spreaders, separating the wires of an inverted-vee antenna. It required the tall supporting mast shown. The radiating element was vertical. (R A Burt)

gunboat *Hazard*, whose crew had been trained to detect the boats and knew where to look for them. Furthermore, during the six months all the boats had changed commanders, their previous more experienced ones going to new 'A'-class boats. Thus performance could not be attributed to crew quality. Experience showed that although submarines could not be the sole defence of an ordinary harbour in all weather, they would still be a very valuable adjunct to the defences and to the defence of a coastline. Practice against moving targets had shown that the combination of an optical tube (periscope) and torpedo director worked. Bacon had avoided actual torpedo shots in the open sea to avoid the delays involved in retrieving the torpedoes afterwards. He argued that shots would have proved nothing.

The next step would be manoeuvres with the Home Fleet.[3] These were undertaken in February and March 1904, followed by exercises with the Portsmouth Flotilla of destroyers in May and June and with the Red and Blue Fleets of the Torpedo Craft Manoeuvres in the Irish Sea. During the partial mobilisation in October, *Hazard* and the 'A'-class submarines went to Dover and *Thames* with the 'Hollands' to Sheerness. 'The question of what is the best defence against or method of attack on Submarines, remains still unsolved' with experiments proceeding at Portsmouth.

The ASW exercises involved visibility trials of submarines and destroyers, duels between submarines and destroyers, gun practice against submarine conning towers, torpedo shots at destroyers and a test to see how well destroyer speed could be estimated using a periscope. On the visibility trials, the approximate direction of approach of the destroyer was known to the submarine, the submarine position being known to the destroyer. Submarine officers could use binoculars when standing on their conning towers, hence could see the destroyer as soon as it came over the horizon. At that time the destroyer could see only the head of the officer atop the conning tower; it seemed that the submarine enjoyed about a 50 per cent advantage. That was enough to allow the submarine to dive out of sight before the destroyer spotted her. A submarine did better keeping her stern to the sun. Generally submarines spotted destroyers about 1.9nm further than destroyers could see them. In one case, however, the submarine was more visible at greater than at less range because her periscope stood out better. Duels were carried out with destroyer and submarine mutually visible at the outset. They were depressing, because as a destroyer approached the submarine could dive. Without any weapon usable against a submerged submarine, the destroyer could do nothing and the submarine could easily pop up again nearby. For example, a destroyer ran in at 15 knots towards the spot where a submarine had dived, then circled. The submarine rose unseen 3 points on the destroyer's bow 300 yds away. Using a pair of destroyers seems not to have helped. On the other hand, in one case the target the destroyer presented was probably too small for the submarine to hit. Gun practice was also disappointing, as a small simulated conning tower proved difficult to hit. The submarines registered eight out of twelve hits on a destroyer target; of three misses, two were due to torpedo failures. This was the first time captains of submarines had been asked to estimate the speed of destroyers using their periscopes. In nearly all cases the errors they made would not have been enough to cause their torpedoes to miss.

ASW was going to be difficult. Nothing a destroyer did could definitely prevent a submarine from getting into attack position and against a destroyer submarines would probably register 70 per cent hits when speed was known approximately. If the submarine com-

manders had to judge target speed, they would still make about 50 per cent hits. If the destroyers tried to evade, that might fall to 25 per cent hits. Submarines would endanger destroyers unless the latter were able to attack them. As yet there was no way for a destroyer to be certain of damaging a submarine. Gunfire did not work. Ramming would be almost impossible, since the submarine could turn away so quickly when it dove. A towed explosive would probably be ineffective, as it was nearly impossible to estimate the exact position of a submarine after she dived. A 60lb guncotton charge exploded 160ft from a submarine would have no effect, but to get even that close seemed nearly impossible. The other proposal was a wire sweep suspended from two destroyers. The manoeuvres showed that the main chance for a destroyer trying to evade a submarine was to turn radically towards or away, which would hardly be possible if she was bound to a second destroyer by a sweep wire. The balance of power was with the submarines.

The manoeuvres tested the ability of submarines to break a close blockade by destroyers. The Royal Navy had been forced to abandon close blockade by heavy ships, but destroyers had been considered an acceptable substitute as they could avoid enemy surface torpedo craft. The 1904 manoeuvres showed that they almost certainly could not evade submarines. Destroyers would be forced to stay well off the entrance to a port at night. Either many more destroyers would be needed or the blockade would leak. Bacon wrote that there should be no difficulty in using three submarines to keep destroyers at least 10 miles out to sea. Destroyers would be unable to keep enemy torpedo craft from escaping.

The Royal Navy was still oriented mainly against France. There was a realistic fear that the French planned to flood the Channel with torpedo craft, which would attack British shipping there. The British planned to use destroyers to blockade the French torpedo boat bases. Bacon had shown how difficult that would be.

Bacon also used his boats to defend Milford against an enemy fleet. To that end he avoiding wearing out his big 'A'-class boats, holding them back against an attack. It turned out, he wrote, that the enemy commander limited himself to steaming back and forth with minimum loss. Bacon would have needed many more than the three he had to infest the area and impose substantial losses on the enemy. As it was, he was impressed by the seakeeping of his 'A'-class submarines. General orders for the manoeuvres envisaged using destroyers to find the submarines before a fleet arrived or to be stationed in front of the fleet to warn of submarines and their periscopes. Once a submarine was seen, the two nearest destroyers should try to close in and follow until the submarine dived, then spread out to try to pick it up again when it surfaced. If the fleet was nearby, it should be assumed that the submarine would steer to gain attack position.

Reporting on the manoeuvres, Bacon concluded that the danger to the battleships made their commanders very cautious. The paucity of submarines, increased caution and the invisibility of the submarines produced false confidence in the Home Fleet, leading to the loss of the cruiser *Juno*. Of fifteen submarines claimed sunk during the manoeuvre, the umpires allowed thirteen, of which three were due to accidents. The others were considered sunk by destroyers. The umpires disallowed all claims by submarines that they had sunk destroyers (in at least seven cases the submarines claimed that they would have sunk the destroyers first). Without submarines, the whole Home Fleet could have anchored daily off the Nab. The presence of the submarines (i) made reconnaissance by more than one ship at a time highly dangerous; (ii) required that ship always be accompanied by a cloud of destroyers; (iii) forced single ships to steam in and out at high speed and not remain off the port; (iv) made blockade impossible, as no ships dared to remain in the offing in daylight; and (v) would have caused considerable losses to destroyers defending ships reconnoitring the port. One large and five small submarines had exerted remarkable leverage. 'Surely no other type of vessel has assumed suddenly so vast an influence on the daytime operations of an enemy.' The umpires concluded that speed and frequent alterations of course were the only reliable defences against submarine attack. For example, the battleship *Resolution* was almost within torpedo range on eight occasions, the submarines being unable to get within range due to her speed and constant alterations of course. The submarines took up the full attention of the enemy fleet, which sometimes risked destruction by coming too close to the guns defending Spithead.

The umpires wrote that

the risk from submarines seems to be undoubtedly very great to a force operating on an enemy's coast or even within 100 miles of it or more . . . we consider that the submarine, used as either an offensive or defensive weapon, has achieved a state of completion and perfection which must render it in naval warfare a continual danger and menace to an enemy in enclosed waters or in any position within its radius of action. Its capabilities in the hands of well-trained and experienced officers are very great and the fear of what it can do renders its strength still greater . . . it is very evident that some means of protecting battleships and cruisers must be devised or some method of construction must be adopted which will render the attack of a modern torpedo less fatal than it now is . . . submarines must be provided for the defence of all our important ports . . .

The 1904 manoeuvres in effect confirmed that British submarines should supplant mines as port defences, as Admiral Fisher argued. At about the same time British attention shifted from France to Germany. The French had invested heavily in submarines, so the 1904 manoeuvres were testing what they could do as well as what the Royal Navy could do. In 1904 Germany was just beginning to buy submarines. *U 1* would not be commissioned until 14 December 1906 and *U 2* not until 18 July 1908. Without numerous submarines, the Germans could not challenge an observational blockade conducted by destroyers. The underwater threat they posed to larger British ships was surface torpedo craft and mines. By 1912, however, the Germans had enough U-boats either built or building that the lessons of the 1904 manoeuvres applied: a destroyer blockade could not be maintained anywhere near the German coast. Hence the British shift to overseas submarines and also the revival of interest in some means of protecting their fleet against U-boat attack.

The next set of ASW experiments was conducted in June and July 1909, supervised by Commodore (S), using HMS *Terpsichore* and eight 'A'-class submarines.[4] The object was to determine whether a submarine could accept or avoid action under various conditions; *Terpsichore* passed through an area containing two or more submarines. Submarine vs submarine encounters were also tried. In that case a submarine could not be sure of the identity of another submarine before closing to within weapons range, so submarines should dive whenever they spotted nearby submarines. A submarine was so much less visible than a surface ship that she could always dive in time to attack once the surface ship was identified as a warship. That might be impossible only if the surface ship were running at high speed, 20 knots or more, in very clear weather. On the other hand, the bow wave of a submarine could be spotted relatively easily, so to reduce visibility a submarine should stop on the surface. It was no easier to see a division of three submarines than a single submarine and the three would keep a better lookout. Conning towers were generally too visible because they were too dark; grey and white checks were better, but trials with various colours were needed. From an attack point of view, a submarine commander could generally estimate the approximate course of an approaching ship by the time he knew she was a warship.

Further trials were proposed. The submarine's ability to cross a patrolled area of 30 to 50nm radius and to find and attack a fleet outside that radius, should be tested. The ability of capital ships to evade torpedoes on seeing their tracks should be tested. Trials should indicate what difficulties a submarine would encounter when attacking a fleet screened by numerous small cruisers (this exercise would also familiarise both the fleet and submarines with attacks against fleet units). The sighting experiments just conducted should be continued in rougher weather. A 'Holland' should be modified with a German-style conning tower as a towed target, her planes adjusted so that she could porpoise while under tow by a destroyer. Machine-gun fire against a periscope should be tried both to see whether it was a good way to get a gunlayer onto the target and to see whether the submarine could be blinded. A further test should be carried out in which a submarine had to dive on recognising a ship or ships as warships.

In March 1910 a Submarine Committee (not to be confused with the submarine design committee created by Keyes in 1912) was appointed to develop ASW methods and weapons. It issued its first report on 20 April 1910. Its first step was to order practical tests of submarine capability; the danger submarines presented 'has not yet been accurately determined and may easily be exaggerated, as the natural fear of fighting an unseen enemy enormously multiplies the actual danger'. At this time it was assumed that the submarine had to keep her periscope up within 1000 to 2000 yds of the target; the committee suspected that it could be seen, at least in smooth water. Much would also depend on how well a submarine could navigate without above-water assistance. If that was possible, the danger of a successful attack well out to sea would be increased. If, however, submarines could not navigate reliably more than 200nm from base without assistance by surface craft, the threat on the high seas was considerably less. In any case, the submarine would try to remain on the surface as long as possible, so that when she did have to dive she would have as much battery charge as possible. If the enemy's ports could be watched by fast craft, enemy submarines might find it impossible to sortie on the surface. That raised the question of what decided underwater endurance – battery capacity, as often stated, or air purification. After an hour or so air might become stale. 'We are thus reduced to the probability that the capabilities of the submarine at sea are far more limited by the human element than they are by the capacity of the boat.' Trials were needed.

Envisaged submarine roles were attack on a battle fleet at sea; harassment of a blockading squadron (or attempted break-outs by the submarines); and attacks on an enemy coast far from a base. Shipping warfare did not figure in the Committee's list, even though it had been a fixture of French naval strategy in the recent past.

D 1 shows her saddle tanks, not broad enough to accommodate broadside torpedo tubes – which were already badly wanted when she was completed in 1909, but had not been conceived when she was designed. Such tubes proved less than successful in wartime, submarine commanders much preferring end-on (usually bow) shots. (NHHC)

The Committee recommended attack at source, but some submarines might get to sea. It seemed unlikely that a submarine with very limited vision could find capital ships at the centre of a moving circle with a radius of 35nm, with cruisers on the circumference and cruiser squadrons sweeping outside the circle, particularly if the fleet was always more than 150nm from the enemy coast. Such a fleet would have destroyers sweeping ahead using explosive sweeps and grapnels.[5] On the outbreak of war, every attempt should be made to blockade the enemy's coast using fast craft, such as destroyers, armed with a rapid explosive sweep and an explosive grapnel. The suggested change from earlier practice was to use a kite to keep the grapnel at a depth of 10 fathoms. The proposed sweep would be used if a periscope was briefly sighted at a range of about 1800 to 2000 yds. 'Destroyers would sweep in such a manner that, in whatever direction the submarine steered below the surface, she would be caught. The grapnel would be a secondary means of dealing with the submarine when the sweep could not be used or was not available.' To deal with possible enemy attacks on British ports, similar ASW craft would patrol their approaches.

Experiments were proposed. A three-submarine division should be taken 100nm into the North Sea with an escort and then ordered to return to base, the escorting ship not assisting but following them. If that succeeded, the distance should be increased to 150nm and then to 200nm. If that worked, a ship representing a fleet should be sent 200nm into the North Sea and her position indicated to a submarine division assigned to find her. These trials would indicate whether submarines were really dangerous to a battle fleet on the high seas. Trials should also be conducted with the sweep which had been designed for fast craft; for development it could be towed by minesweepers. A 'Tribal'-class destroyer should be assigned to test kites and otters to determine the best way for the sweep to hold depth. She would try a kite attached to an explosive grapnel. Other tests should determine the chance of a destroyer torpedoing a submarine at 500 yds or more, the submarine showing only her periscope.

It had been suggested that a submarine could be seen from a balloon, 'on the assumption that the human eye, aided with glasses, would act in a similar capacity to a bird detecting a fish under water'. In June 1912 off Harwich a floatplane tried to detect *C 12* from the air. In one case, with the submarine 18–30ft below the surface and the water smooth, the aircraft could clearly see the hull of the submarine from directly overhead due to the light colour of the paint. The upper deck and track were also visible when the submarine was at 15ft depth, with her periscope up. On another trial, however, when the submarine was in diving trim, with only the conning tower above water, the hull could be seen only from directly overhead. It seemed that in the North Sea a submarine would never be seen at a depth of 30ft. With her periscope up, however, its wake would give her away.

Other suggested tests were firing Lyddite (HE) shell at an abandoned submerged 'Holland' (with 2ft of periscope showing); laying indicating nets when a periscope was sighted; and firing machine guns at periscopes. These were considered less important.

The submariners told the Committee that their endurance was typically a week in summer and three to four days in winter (on board 'C' and earlier submarines), which meant a summer steaming distance of 800nm (600nm in winter) ready to dive if an enemy was sighted. The 200nm navigation was no problem. Long dives did make the crew sleepy, but three or four hours had no appreciable effect.

They agreed that it would be difficult to penetrate to the battle fleet at the core of an extended formation, but it was a misconception that submarines only went out to attack the fleet; any vessel was a good quarry. Any surface ship watching a port would be in danger 'and it is a matter for consideration how long the supply of watchers could be kept up'. The important question was how a ship could protect herself; the battle fleet could be considered later. As for the sweep, for a ship making 15 knots and a submarine making 6 knots, the minimum breadth of sweep would be three-quarters of a mile. Any decrease in speed or increase in numbers of ships in company would grossly increase the breadth of front. For example, at 12 knots it would be a mile. Was it really worth hampering a fleet by using such sweeps? 'It has always been taken as a first principle that ships should have perfect freedom of individual movement to dodge torpedoes, when proceeding in company where submarines may be expected.' That is, the submariners had discovered the concept of limiting lines of approach. A submarine had to be within the limiting lines in order to attack an approaching ship. The faster the ship, the narrower the angle between the lines.

The torpedo gunboats HMS *Speedwell* and *Seagull* were assigned to the Committee. It tried a two-ship sweep, each ship towing a charge. The two ships were connected by two wires, one 30ft above the other, kept in position by 12ft kites. Presumably the wires would snag a submarine and pull the charges together onto it. Meanwhile the navigational trial was carried out by *C 28*, *C 29* and *C 30*, which proved that they could navigate perfectly well out into the North Sea: they could find an enemy fleet if its position were given.

A November 1910 report showed that machine-gun fire was useless. Nor were torpedoes likely to be effective: four torpedoes were fired at an underway submerged submarine at 1000 to 1200 yds range and only one could have hit. Lyddite shells suspended near a submarine had little effect, including a 12in shell exploded 100ft from the submarine. A diving shell with a delayed-action fuze was proposed. In April 1911 there were further tests using 6in diving shells, which sank the submerged submarine but failed to damage its main structure.

That left the sweep as the best of a series of discouraging alternatives. In November 1910 the destroyers *Maori* and *Crusader* were tested with an improved double sweep. It was tested against *A 1*, which had been modified so that it could run automatically underwater and then surface automatically. The double sweep was replaced by a single (ship) sweep, which was the standard British ASW weapon when war broke out. For it to work, the attacking ship had to come within 150 yds of the submarine. Could a submarine that close fire a torpedo effectively at a destroyer?

Meanwhile, on 21 February 1911, six submarines attacked eight Home Fleet battleships proceeding down Channel, the object being both to train the submarines and to obtain reports from the ships of arrangements they had made to sight and locate the submarines. The submarines were told only that a fleet would pass through a certain area between stated hours. Torpedoes were not fired because the weather precluded recovering them. To indicate that they would have been fired, the submarines surfaced. The weather was overcast and misty, visibility varying between five and two miles.

Five of the six submarines were able to attack. Three of the eight ships saw nothing until the submarines surfaced. The other five sighted periscopes, but never for longer than 90 seconds before attacks were delivered. It was recommended that one or more screens of light craft steam ahead of the fleet to force submarines to dive earlier and to upset the nerves of their commanders. They would advance on a broad front with frequent changes of course. Similarly, periscopes should be fired at in order to make attacks more difficult and to unnerve submarine commanders. Because a submarine would attack at 1000 to 1500 yds, the pairs of sweeping ships should be no more than 450 yds apart, the kites at 15ft depth. The fleet should change formation frequently, again to upset the submarine commanders.

The commander of the attacking submarines considered the exercise very valuable and wanted more such exercises. They concluded that they could generally get close to capital ships, which might manoeuvre out of the way. They therefore wanted fast, short-range torpedoes with large warheads.

In May 1914 the Committee listed submarine weaknesses in order of importance: limited battery power, periscope and compass, low speed on the surface and submerged, limited range of vision through the periscope and difficulty in determining the course and speed of the enemy through the periscope. To exploit the first, air and surface patrols should try to keep submarines down, exhausting their batteries or at least limiting their mobility. Ideally submarines should also be prevented from lying on the bottom to conserve their batteries until patrols passed. Flotillas of destroyers should sweep the approaches to bases where submarines might expect to find targets. As soon as there were enough destroyers with sweeps, they should also be assigned to the fleet. Ships themselves should be organised for self-defence. As soon as a periscope was spotted, fire should begin to produce obscuring splashes between it and the ship. Bursts from large-calibre shells near a periscope might damage the submarine. Mining should be revived; shoals not mined should be aggressively patrolled. Channels used by submarines off their own ports should be mined. In future aircraft would accompany the fleet. They should patrol ahead to harry submarines. Submarines would most likely attack within 60 miles of their own coast and within 100 miles of the British coast. The sweep proved useless, but most of the recommendations, particularly mining, proved sound.

Overall, the experiments showed that ASW would be difficult at best. Admiral Wilson, who had commanded the fleet attacked by submarines in 1904, was First Sea Lord in 1911. He was aware of claims that submarines could not operate in shallow water and he probably also knew that torpedoes might be ineffective there – they would sink until they were moving fast enough for their fins to be effective. It happened that by 1911 submarine depth-control was good enough to allow shallow-water operation, although there were still limits on large submarines (the 'E' class was not considered safe in less than 7½ fathoms). That year there was a war scare over a crisis in Morocco and Prime Minister Asquith asked Wilson about war plans. Among other things, Wilson told Asquith that he would begin with an attack against German torpedo craft in their home waters – what would later be called an attack at source. Wilson was not particularly articulate and it did not help that he told Asquith that he had kept his plans secret from the rest of the Royal Navy. Asquith was shocked, either by Wilson's willingness to take what seemed an extreme risk or by his obvious aggressiveness. He appointed Winston Churchill First Lord,

Pre-war exercises emphasised torpedo attack against capital ships. The object of British naval strategy was to force the German fleet out into the North Sea where it could be destroyed. Submarines could enforce the desired observational blockade, and they could attack the German fleet as it came out. It took time for the Royal Navy to appreciate the value of minelaying in a war against U-boats and a fleet-in-being. In April a sunken German UB-type submarine minelayer was examined, inspiring Admiralty interest in a British equivalent. In October 1915 *E 24* and *E 41*, still building, were ordered modified as minelayers. *E 41* is shown running trials on 13 February 1916. The four holes on her saddle tank are the tops of mine chutes, the stowed mines being dropped from their bottoms. They replaced her broadside torpedo tubes. The gun-like object forward of the bridge is the folded-down insulator tube leading down to the wireless cabinet below decks. The two hydraulic wireless masts are raised. *E 41* was ready for minelaying in June 1916, and by 3 August had completed six lays (the first of the minelayers, *E 24*, had been lost on her second operation). The 'E'-class minelayers all operated out of Harwich as part of the 9th Submarine Flotilla, with depot ship *Maidstone*. (Dr David Stevens)

probably with instructions to fire Wilson. However, the reality remained that in 1911 there was little real chance of dealing with German torpedo craft, including U-boats, once they got to sea. That was certainly apparent once war broke out in 1914.

British submarines proved effective in the pre-war fleet exercises. Their mission was obviously to destroy enemy warships, particularly capital ships. That shaped their training and also their weaponry, as will be seen. During a 1912 CID discussion of Mediterranean policy, Admiral Sir John Fisher, former First Sea Lord and permanent member of the CID, told his colleagues that submarines and destroyers would make the North Sea impassable for any large fleet.[6] In wartime the British battle fleet would cruise to the north or west of Scotland or outside the Straits of Dover. If the Germans came out, British submarines and destroyers would attack them. The British fleet would pounce if the Germans chose to come far enough out. The discussion concerned likely reductions in the Mediterranean Fleet. Fisher said that given the power of the submarine, no heavy ship was safe in narrow waters. 'Therefore if we had adequate flotillas of submarines and destroyers at Malta, Gibraltar and Alexandria no battleship could move in the Mediterranean.' Reginald McKenna, who had recently left as First Lord, had asked specifically whether in Fisher's view the North Sea was now unsuitable for battleships. Churchill later proposed stationing a flotilla of 'E'-class submarines at Alexandria specifically to preclude any Turkish seaborne attack on Egypt. The transcript of the 1912 meeting makes no reference to a decision to station 'B'-class submarines at Gibraltar and Malta for local defence, but that seems to have been decided at about this time. Fisher had largely predicted the policy the Admiralty actually adopted when war broke out. The Grand Fleet really did cruise in the north. The Admiralty did form a Channel Fleet, but it consisted of pre-dreadnoughts which might be considered expendable. Without such a fleet and without pre-dreadnoughts assigned to various ports, the British population would have considered itself vulnerable, even if the Admiralty considered coastal submarines its real protection. As it turned out, the 1914 raid on Hartlepool brought Fisher's faith into question.

Submarine operations in the 1913 manoeuvres seem to have been spectacularly successful. The Blue Fleet tried current anti-submarine measures: a double screen of destroyers in the van consisting of a forward screen four to five miles ahead and a rear screen in an irregular formation; high speed; and zigzagging by cruisers (alterations of course four points each way every fifteen minutes).[7] *Neptune* and 1st

Battle Squadron tried these methods when passing through an area in which submarines had been reported. Despite them, with a glassy-smooth sea, *D 8* managed to surface about 1500 yds off the bow of the rear battleship of the starboard section. *Collingwood* was attacked by *E 5* off the Swaarte Bank lightship while steaming at 10.5 knots; the attack was judged successful. At this time explosive sweeps were still experimental, but they seemed unlikely to be effective. Home Fleet CinC Admiral Callaghan wrote that 'I do not know of any case during the manoeuvres were, when a ship was attacked by a submarine, the submarine could have been herself attacked by a destroyer with single sweep in time to be of any use'.

Writing after the 1913 manoeuvres, Rear Admiral Lewis Bayly, commanding one of the battle squadrons, wrote that he had been attacked four times by submarines.[8] In two cases the sea was moderate and attacks were not expected (though lookouts were posted). In one case the ship was altering course four points every fifteen minutes (zigzagging). In each case the lookouts could not see the submarine in time to open fire before she got into attack range (1000 yds), particularly because the periscope was dipped again immediately after it had been seen. Although submariners claimed they could make hits from greater ranges, Bayley doubted that in wartime, given varying weather and ships running at different speeds.

Keyes wrote that too many officers, particularly destroyer commanders, seemed to have only a vague idea of submarine capabilities, their methods of attack and of evading attack ('judging by the claims made against submarines and the manner in which the claims of the latter were often over-ruled').[9] This question had to be faced 'if we are to prepare ourselves to deal with the submarines of the enemy. I am convinced that there will be a very rude awakening if tactics which were common during the recent manoeuvres are repeated in actual warfare.' Despite the real limitations of submarines, 'I think that the battle squadrons of the Home Fleets will concede that submarines' torpedoes run straight and that, given the opportunity, they can be relied upon to deliver a high percentage of successful attacks'. Keyes thought that during the manoeuvre the submarines took practically all the risks they would have taken in wartime. 'Ships altered course frequently at high speed, destroyers and light cruisers rushed full speed at the submarines who, thanks to the training they have received during the last year, have learnt that there is nothing to fear from light draught vessels. The vitals of submarines are at all times below the keels of destroyers and those of the later classes under the keels of light cruisers . . .' It was practically impossible for a light-draught ship to run down or damage any part of a submarine other than her periscope. Diving under a battleship was not so attractive, but submarines had often been saved by doing so; *D 8* deliberately dived to 60 or 70ft on hearing the propellers of battleships, after passing under two destroyer screens.[10] 'It is necessary to know the depth of water you are in and to have at least 10 fathoms for the smaller submarines and 12 for the larger, but given this the operation presents no difficulties . . . The nerve of the captain is of course the all-important factor, but I think it is evident that a well handled submarine is an exceedingly difficult object to ram.'

In Keyes' view gunfire on the surface was the chief threat and the only real risk the manoeuvres could not simulate. However, it was unlikely that a destroyer rushing in at high speed could sink a submarine in two minutes, particularly since the latter's vitals would be submerged. The conning tower was so small that it probably would not be hit at all. The manoeuvre rules, that it was sufficient for a conning tower to be seen for a submarine to be considered out of action, were unrealistic. The value of firing at a periscope had been much exaggerated.

Also entirely unrealistically, many officers seemed to assume that a submarine had to rise to fire torpedoes. On more than one occasion a submarine was counted out of action when rising to claim a hit, on the ground that she had fired out of range. Allowance was rarely made for the deflection necessary to hit a fast ship and also for the fact that it took about a minute for the submarine to surface. She would therefore appear at a very different bearing from the one when she fired.

Keyes later wrote that it would be perfectly feasible for 'E'-class submarines to accompany a fleet to sea.[11] They would be relieved of many of their anxieties, hence could keep the sea for several days.

> They might prove invaluable to an inferior force and might well be placed in a position to do considerable damage to some units of a superior hostile fleet. It is more difficult to see how they could be brought in contact with the enemy, should he be endeavouring to avoid an engagement, but it is conceivable that he might be induced or forced to alter course towards the submarines. I think a good case has been made out for carrying out an exercise on these lines with the fleet.

Keyes pointed out that the usual line-ahead formation of the fleet was inherently dangerous. It lengthened the target. If the submarine could not attack the leading ship, through misjudgement or interference by destroyers, she would still have a good chance to attacking another further down the line. Often a submarine could not attack the leading ship because of the fleet speed or a position too broad on the bow, but she could still easily get into position against one further back. Nor did Keyes think that it was difficult to judge the course of a single-masted ship, as the battleships were so large compared to the craft submarines normally practised against.

British submariners were taught to fire at very close range and would continue to do so wherever possible. However, once they received longer-range (presumably 21in) torpedoes, the fleet would need more extended flank screens to force them back. The Germans were already using larger-diameter (20in) torpedoes.

Admiral of Patrols de Robeck suggested using smoke produced by screening destroyers to blind submarines. In 1918 smoke was an important ASW measure, but it seems to have been rejected in a fleet context for fear of causing collisions. As for cooperation between submarine and the fleet, Callaghan thought it would be governed by W/T performance: if good communication could be obtain by night at up to 60nm on the surface and 20nm submerged in daytime, the Admiral would have some hold over his submarines' actions. At present he had far too little. Callaghan agreed with Keyes' estimate of submarine endurance off the Baltic and asked whether it could be extended by fuelling at sea and by exchanging personnel at sea. Overall, the fleet needed more opportunities to work with the big overseas submarines.

After the manoeuvres, the War Staff laid out wartime submarine functions.[12] The lessons of the manoeuvres had been 'emphasised in frequent War Staff Minutes [now apparently lost] dealing with submarine questions. Very great potentialities appear to lie in this direction.' The Staff did not want money diverted from battleship-building (suggesting that Churchill was already pressing for the 'ocean submarine' as a battleship substitute) because submarines were a special type, suited only to operations within a limited sphere; they

This photo, obtained by the US Office of Naval Intelligence, seems to have been doctored from one of *D 4* to indicate that the Royal Navy had a larger pre-war gun installation programme than it actually did. The 12pdr was probably the most powerful pre-1914 submarine gun, and only one submarine (if any) had a gun. (NHHC)

could not be battleship or cruiser substitutes. However, 'those of the larger type may . . . be legitimately regarded as valuable prospective substitutes for a large proportion of our destroyer force of the future'. The context was the use of destroyers independent of the fleet to maintain an observational blockade of the Heligoland Bight. The Staff had three submarine roles in mind. The most important was watch on enemy harbours, reviving close blockade. Submarines would have to dive in 6 fathoms, due to the shallow depths off the German coast. High surface speed would be unimportant, as submarines would dive to escape attack. The Staff liked the Admiralty Coastal, 80 per cent as expensive as a destroyer. Numbers were essential and the current building capacity was inadequate. The blockading submarine force might have to be backed by a few destroyers acting as scouts.

As such submarines entered service, they should be organised into six- or ten-boat flotillas controlled by Commodore (T), who currently commanded the 1st, 2nd, 3rd and 5th Destroyer Flotillas intended to maintain the observational blockade of Germany. Initially they would work with the 1st Destroyer Flotilla, which they would ultimately replace. During the transition period the two would work together. Because the submarines would hardly be used for coast patrol or local defence, they should no longer be placed under the Admiral of Patrols. In the Mediterranean, the blockade role would be much the same, except that water would be deeper. However, there was no point in designing a special type of submarine for that sea. A gun would be very useful for both blockader and submersible cruiser, to deal not only with hostile surface ships and aircraft, but also with merchant ships in the commercial blockade role. It would not have to be very powerful, because if a merchant ship disregarded a warning shot she would risk being torpedoed.

A second role would be a watch for enemy squadrons known to be at sea, the submarines replacing to some extent light cruisers. Principal requirements would be high surface speed, enabling them to chase an enemy ship before diving to attack. That meant the two big submarines under construction; three could be built for the cost of two 'Town'-class cruisers and they would probably be much cheaper to operate and to maintain. However, outside the North Sea they could hardly fulfil cruiser duties such as trade protection. Probably the proportion between blockading coastals and the larger submarines should be 10 to 1.

A third type would be needed for coastal patrol, as small as possible to obtain maximum numbers. Construction was not yet urgent, given the large number of small submarines already in commission.

The War Staff saw its paper as the basis for future submarine-building programmes. In December the notion that Admiralty Coastals were really overseas submarines was quashed and the 'E' class and its successor came to dominate First World War submarine construction. However, the War Staff paper gives a fair idea of how the Admiralty saw submarines in the summer of 1913. Its remarks and those circulated to the fleet after the 1913 manoeuvres demonstrate that the pre-war Royal Navy hardly showed the disdain for submarines often attributed to it. In any case the enormous effort expended by the Submarine Committee strongly suggests that the fleet took submarines quite seriously. Unfortunately the means developed pre-war did not work. The best of them, a mine offensive, failed because British mines were mediocre; they were not perfected until 1917. Attack at source was impossible, because the German fleet in effect shielded the U-boat bases. Hold-down tactics had to await the growth of patrol forces, particularly aircraft. For some reason depth charges were not conceived before the war. Possibly the explosive sweeps seemed adequate.

The one gap in the pre-war work was detection. It seems to have been assumed that submarines could be seen only when they showed their periscopes.[13]

THE FIRST SUBMARINE WAR

The First World War was the first submarine war. British submarines operated effectively in the North Sea, the Mediterranean and the Baltic. This experience shaped the interwar British submarine fleet. The service grew enormously after 1914.[1] At that time it comprised 62 submarines, with 168 officers and 1250 enlisted men. On 30 June 1916 there were 130 submarines, most of them larger than in 1914 (there were 82 rather than 20 overseas submarines and 14 fleet submarines), manned by 432 officers and 3755 enlisted men, a total of 4187. On 11 November 1918 a total of 133 submarines were in commission, including 6 anti-submarine submarines and the sole 'M'-class monitor. The service had grown to 444 officers and 4196 enlisted men. Many of the officers were reservists; Commodore (S) thought it remarkable that only one of the submarines they navigated, *G 11*, was ever stranded, becoming a total loss on the last patrol of the war.

The coastal patrol submarines functioned largely as a school for those who would operate the overseas submarines which saw most of the action. In mid-1917 Commodore (S) reported that through the first two years of the war (i.e., through August 1917) coastal submarines supplied 130 trained officers and 64 trained crews. Coastal patrol was a valuable test for new officers; fourteen had failed as commanding officers and had reverted to general service. Similarly, during 1917 the coastal submarines provided trained officers for the thirty-five new overseas and fleet submarines commissioned. During this period thirty officers had to revert to general service. Figures were not given for 1918.

The rapid expansion of the wartime submarine service seems to have demonstrated the need for better training for submarine commanders. In the autumn of 1918 the first school for them, the prede-

The 'E' class were the workhorses of the First World War British submarine fleet. Here *E 25* is towed out to sea for trials. The two workmen aft are standing atop her after torpedo tube. A US Navy officer who spent a week in 1917 on a war patrol by *E 34* reported that boats habitually rode their vents, so that they could dive in 30 to 40 seconds – a direct response to wartime surprises, particularly by aircraft. Submarines would crash-dive immediately if anything suspicious was sighted. The standard drill was for the commanding officer to sound the hooter (klaxon) and to close the conning tower hatch himself. Without further orders engines were secured and main ballast vents opened. The Kingstons were typically kept open, but in this class they were too small for rapid diving; note also the few freeing holes in the superstructure, which presumably trapped air during a crash dive. Some later submarines had no Kingstons – the valves in the bottoms of the ballast tanks – at all, as they were habitually left open. To make for faster diving, at night nothing was carried on the bridge except a small flashlight, a torpedo director, night glasses and a Sperry gyro-repeater. Typical periscope procedure was a quick sweep of the horizon followed by a sky sweep and then by a more careful search at high power. US officers generally found British periscopes much superior to their own. The crew immediately went to action stations if anything was spotted, the batteries being thrown into series so that the boat could speed up. Typical night practice was to run one engine to charge the battery, the submarine being propelled by the other. One of the wartime surprises was how long boats remained submerged, as much as 15 to 20 hours. The Royal Navy therefore used an air purifier, a motor-driven fan passing air through a box filled with a regenerating chemical. There were also typically several light fans to keep air circulating, which were considered a great help. US submarines generally remained underwater for so short a time that nothing of this sort was needed. That changed when US submarines were assigned to anti-submarine operations in the Irish Sea. (Author's collection)

Returning home triumphant after penetrating the Dardanelles on 8 August 1915, *E 11* shows few wartime modifications. The Dardanelles operation combined the expected pre-war mission of attacking enemy warships with a new interdiction mission, in this case mounted against Turkish supplies reaching the garrison in the Dardanelles by sea. The vertical object forward of the bridge is an insulator for her wireless, the wire extending vertically to a sloping wire above it. Note the flared bow introduced in this group of ships. (R A Burt)

cessor of the later 'Perisher', opened at a temporary home at Portsmouth. This 'Periscope School' was scheduled to move to Campbeltown, where it would be easier to practice attacks. Some US officers attended. The school first appears in the October 1918 *Navy List*, with the submarines *F 1*, *F 2*, *F 3*, *V 3* and *V 4*, all clearly surplus to operational requirements. The next month's *List* shows the school at its planned location on the Clyde.

The Wartime 'E' Class

The 'E' class became the wartime workhorse. As soon as Admiral Fisher returned to the Admiralty (31 October 1914), Churchill formally asked him to order twenty more submarines. Fisher decided to order engines for twenty-five boats so as to be sure of the twenty. In November he appointed former ICS Captain Hall as Captain Supervising Submarine Construction. Hall soon wrote Controller that all evidence showed that 'E'-class submarines could be built faster than 'G' class. Further production of 'G'-class submarines died in favour of more 'E' class. *E 17* and *E 18* had been ordered from Vickers immediately after war broke out. Submarines were now ordered from Vickers (six), Armstrong (two), Beardmore (two), Yarrow (two), Thornycroft (two), John Brown (two), Fairfield (two), Palmers (two), Cammell Laird (two), Swan Hunter (two), White (one) and Scotts (one), a total of twenty-six. The two from Beardmore (*E 25* and *E 26*) had been ordered by Turkey (subcontracted by Vickers). That brought the class numbering to *E 44*.

On 11 December 1914 Churchill told the Cabinet that the war programme, which replaced the 1914–15 and 1915–16 Programmes, included no fewer than seventy-five submarines.[2] That included the twenty 'H' class ordered in the United States. The approved 1914–15 Programme had included nine submarines and another ten had been planned for 1915–16. Omitting Fisher's twenty-six new 'E' class, the 75-submarine programme should have amounted to twenty-nine new submarines. Presumably that included the last eight 'G' class and the twelve last 'E' class (*E 45*–*E 56*), the latter often lumped with the big November batch. Builders were: Beardmore (two), Scotts (one), John Brown (one), Fairfield (two), Yarrow (one), Cammell Laird (two) and Denny (three). Two of the 'E' class were later cancelled. The remaining eleven were presumably the seven 'J' class and the first four 'K' class, although none was ordered until 1915.

Apart from those built by Vickers, these were repeat *E 12*s. They differed from earlier 'E'-class submarines in having two bow tubes rather than one and unlike the Vickers boats they had the whole battery forward of the engines (Vickers placed a quarter abaft the engine room). To speed production, the Admiralty rather than the builders ordered the main hull castings, conning tower, periscope brackets, periscopes, steering and hydrophone gear, motors, pumps, compressors, air service fittings, Kingstons and other fittings. Engines and main motors were built to Admiralty order by numerous firms. According to the post-war DNC history, these methods made it possible for relatively inexperienced firms to complete submarines in times which compared favourably with the pre-war performance of the two specialist builders. Before the war it took Vickers 30 months to complete *E 14*, but the firm completed *E 19* in eight months (due in part to diversion of engines already built for 'G'-class submarines).

From *E 19* on, all had 'plough' bows for better seakeeping. All 'E'-class submarines had their upper rudders removed in wartime. Wartime additions included a larger W/T installation, large housing W/T masts instead of the original much smaller wooden ones, hydroplane guards, sky searchers in the periscopes, slop chutes, Fessenden sound signalling (S/T) gear, jet signalling gear, and WCs which could be blown at great depth. Guns were fitted (see below). In mid-1917 Commodore (S) also listed among new wartime equipment the gyro compass, hydrophones, the Forbes log (to monitor underwater speed), sounding machines (using wires and weights to sound from inside a submarine), air purifiers and masts worked from inside the boat (for wireless). Limited submarine size made it difficult to add more specialists to maintain and operate the new equipment. Even adding a single wireless operator was a problem.

Some boats operating in the Sea of Marmara had spare torpedoes lashed to their casings. Early in 1916 *E 22* was given a ramp carrying two Sopwith Baby floatplanes, to be flown over the Heligoland Bight, but when it was tried, the aircraft failed to take off. The submarine was soon lost (25 April 1916).

In 1917 the British began to copy the German practice of providing permanent bridge screens rather than canvas 'cheaters' which were rolled down to dive. The screens protected watchkeepers on the bridge and made them safer in bad weather, but the additional 12ft^2 of bluff area facing the stream of water submerged cost some underwater speed. That was accepted (see the figures for the 'L' class).

Six were completed as minelayers, vertical tubes replacing their broadside torpedo tubes: *E 24, E 41, E 34, E 45, E 46* and *E 51*.

Home Waters

In 1914 the submarine force in home waters comprised nine flotillas This organisation had been adopted in May 1912, the flotillas initially being called Sections.[3] As they entered service, the overseas

submarines formed the 8th Flotilla, under the direct control of Commodore (S).[4] Other submarines were under the general control of Commodore (S) but through him under the control of CinCs of Home Ports or, for longer-range coastal submarines, under Admiral of Patrols Rear Admiral John M de Robeck (appointed April 1912). That is why de Robeck was an important commentator on the 1913 manoeuvres. The 8th Flotilla, stationed at Harwich, was earmarked for offensive operations in the Heligoland Bight, in which the German High Seas Fleet was expected to operate. At the outbreak of war Harwich was also the base for a strong destroyer force under Commodore (T), which might act directly against a German force in the North Sea or else might join the Grand Fleet. Of the others, the surviving 'A' class were limited to harbour defence and did not much figure in operational planning.[5] 'B' and 'C'-class submarines were assigned to particular places.[6] In 1913 some 'B' and 'C'-class submarines had been allocated to overseas fleets for the local defence of their main bases: *C 36 –C 38* for the China Fleet (presumably for Hong Kong) and *B 6–B 8* at Gibraltar and *B 9–B 11* to Malta.[7] Through 1916 the 'C'-class submarines assigned to coastal patrol saw little of the war, apart from some assigned to anti-submarine work (see below), two of which had been lost by August 1916. Typically, a portion of each flotilla was at sea every morning at dawn, the others standing by while ready for sea.

At the outbreak of war the British envisaged three probable German courses of action. They might break out of the North Sea to attack British trade. The Grand Fleet at Scapa Flow blocked the Germans at the north end of the North Sea, the Dover Patrol (including 4th and later the 6th Flotillas) at its southern end, at Dover.

During the war, submarines were assigned to Harwich to block the southern end of the North Sea, and to join the Grand Fleet in the event of a fleet action. *D 6* lies alongside two 'E'-class submarines, probably *E 53* (inboard) and *E 32*. Note the 6pdr forward of the bridge of *D 6*. The July 1916 gun mounting list showed *D 3* and *D 7* inked in, meaning that they were fitted some time before the next edition in November 1916. Through November 1917 *D 6* was not listed with such a gun; it may have been a temporary fitting from a base pool. The Harwich flotilla included the 'E'-class minelayers. (John Lambert collection)

The western end of the Channel was blocked by a cruiser force and by some French submarines, which could cooperate with the Channel Fleet. The Germans might raid the East Coast, either on a small scale or as an invasion, which would be blocked by local defence flotillas, including submarines.

The Germans might try to interdict the planned movement of a British army to France by intercepting the transports. The Harwich flotilla (destroyers and overseas submarines) would warn of any German approach to the cross-Channel transports; it was supported by a cruiser force and by the Dover Patrol. When the British Expeditionary Force was sent to France, its cover included the Harwich submarines (8th Flotilla) and the Dover submarines (4th Flotilla).

As an operational commander, Commodore (S) reported directly to CinC Home Fleets, who also commanded the Grand Fleet. Commodore (S) also administered the whole Submarine Service. At the outset, CinC ordered the overseas flotilla used, as far as numbers permitted, for an offensive on the German coast, initially in the Heligoland Bight. Keyes had pointed out earlier that operations so far inshore would be hazardous, so initially he sent only two submarines (*E 6* and *E 8*) to gauge conditions.[8] They spotted many wireless-equipped trawlers, which he considered means of calling in anti-submarine forces. Keyes preferred a watching patrol in the southern North Sea, which could catch the German High Seas Fleet if it tried to break out. To this end he initially sent out two pairs of submarines. Once the British transports were at sea, it seemed likely that the Germans would come out to attack them. Keyes increased his patrol to ten submarines, moving them 15 miles to the south. Another patrol, mounted by the Dover-based 4th Submarine Flotilla, was further south.

Submarines were deployed to support the British offensive into the Heligoland Bight which resulted in a battle later in August. Poor staff work nearly resulted in British submarines attacking some of the British cruisers; the submarine commanders had not been informed of exactly what was planned. This may have been the Royal Navy's first experience of the reality that submariners would find it difficult to recognise ships they spotted. Despite attempts to devise identification signals, it was best to assign submarines to places where they could fire freely. Thus direct support of surface forces, an important wartime theme, turned out to be difficult or impossible.

In December 1914 the British were alerted by signals intelligence when the Germans shelled Yarmouth and Hartlepool. Eight Harwich Force submarines were placed across the route the Germans would take between the southern North Sea and their base at Wilhelmshaven. Due to limited W/T range, Commodore (S) had to gather his submarines together to control them. That kept four of them out of range of the German return track. Only *E 11* found herself in position to fire. Rolling heavily, she missed her two targets even though the range was only 400 yds; the torpedoes went too deep. Her commander could not take the desired third shot because he had to go deep to avoid a collision as the German ship came straight for him. By the time he surfaced, the German ships were gone.[9] Pre-war exercises had not revealed just how complicated it was to link up widely-separated forces and in particular to exploit radio intelligence.

By October 1914, Keyes had eight 'D' class and eleven 'E' class in commission and he expected two more 'E' class by the end of October. That was still not enough to maintain the watch envisaged before the war, but he could keep five or six submarines constantly at sea in the Heligoland Bight. That required twelve or fifteen submarines.[10]

A typical 8th Flotilla patrol lasted seven or eight days, including

Airborne anti-submarine operations during the First World War must have come as a great surprise. Without this threat, a submarine could operate freely on the surface until she spotted enemy ships. With her low silhouette, she would almost always see the enemy before she was seen; she was in danger mainly when deliberately approaching the enemy to attack. Once air patrols became common, submarines were always at risk on the surface. Crash-diving became an essential skill. It also became important to train pilots and air observers to distinguish friendly from enemy submarines. The Royal Navy published a booklet of photos of ships, particularly submarines, as seen from the air. This is *C 20*. (NHHC)

operating close to the German coast.[11] The area involved was so small that the Germans could patrol it thoroughly; the submarines could never risk surfacing in daylight. Because the German surface fleet did not spend much time at sea, opportunities to attack were rare. Writing in 1916, Commodore (S) pointed out that periscopes offered a very limited field of view and that their heads were close to the water. Even so, his submariners managed to make 32.5 per cent hits per shots fired, which he considered the best which could be expected. In one case, an experienced submarine commander lying on the bottom at night off Norderney heard ships passing overhead, but did not rise to attack, because he did not hear them until they were too close and because they were accompanied by escorts using explosive sweeps. He considered the night too dark; had he surfaced he would have been among fast ships and might have been run down. Also, he could not be sure of distinguishing friend from foe. Another submarine arrived near Horns Reef, towards which the High Seas Fleet was steaming, on the morning after Jutland. He was forced down by a Zeppelin and depth-charged. He also heard something being dragged over his submarine. However, he did not hear any ships. Communications were limited; he had no idea that the enemy fleet was at sea. He supposed that he was being hunted by German anti-submarine craft in the usual way. Commodore (S) added that among 370 patrols (1680 days, just over 200,000nm) undertaken by 8th Flotilla, there were only three cases of failure (including the two described) into which he had ever had to inquire closely – and in each case he deemed the conduct involved entirely justified.

In summer submarines off the German coast had to stay down for 19 to 20 hours at a time; but after 12 hours the air was so oppressive (despite the new purifiers) that even the head of a match would not burn. In winter the North Sea weather and cold were similarly punishing. According to Commodore (S), the worst of it was that 'there has been little hope during the last year of any target beyond the extremely difficult one of a submarine . . . the exhilaration of an encounter with the enemy is only very rarely obtained . . . these officers and men [show] 2 o'clock in the morning courage for the whole of the time they are at sea'. As evidence of how wearing patrols were, Commodore (S) cited two US submarine officers who had recently made a week's patrol on board a British submarine and, in their words, were 'all out and fit for nothing' at the end of it, 'though they both had an encounter with the enemy to cheer them up, in one case sinking a German ship and the cruises were not what our officers call trying ones'.

Through the war, one flotilla of overseas submarines was assigned to the Harwich Force; all other overseas submarines in home waters were part of the Grand Fleet. Until flotillas were reorganised in the autumn of 1916, this was the 8th Flotilla. By April 1916, when the Germans raided Lowestoft, the 8th Flotilla included a smaller group at Yarmouth, which cooperated with the Harwich boats. During the 1916 raid on Lowestoft it contributed four submarines (*V 1* and *H 5*, *H 7* and *H 10*). When the Germans attacked Yarmouth, *D3*, *D 5* and *E 10*, lying off Gorleston, were ordered to intercept the Germans off Terschelling as they returned home. They were unsuccessful.

Some of the Harwich overseas submarines went to the Mediterranean to support the fight in the Dardanelles. Coastals replaced them and in turn were replaced by US-built 'H'-boats. The combination of true overseas submarines and Coastals must have been awkward. When the Flotillas were renumbered in September 1916, the overseas submarines were all concentrated in the 9th Flotilla (fourteen 'E' class) and a new 8th Flotilla took up the Coastals which had been in the 8th Flotilla the previous month.[12] This flotilla included destroyers whose main role was to link it with long-range shore wireless. Commodore (S) found it satisfying that on the only three occasions the Germans did come out in 1916–17 (for Jutland and on an abortive sortie in August and in November 1916 to salvage a U-boat) his submarines had successfully attacked.[13] In 1917 the Flotilla began laying mines in German waters, initially using *E 24* and *E 41*, of which the former was lost on her third trip. Since the enemy's surface ships only rarely went to sea, many Harwich patrols were in effect anti-submarine sweeps even before there was any formal policy promoting them.[14]

A third of the overseas submarines had been lost by August 1916, by far the heaviest proportion of any in the British forces, about 10 per cent per year. Commodore (S) had seen no slackening of enthusiasm to go from coastal to overseas boats, but these losses 'bear out my contention that the overseas submarine, particularly those of the Harwich flotilla, are always in action when in enemy waters, though the actions have not been made the subject of despatches and the losses have not been announced'.[15] Up to 4 August 1916, forty-one new overseas submarines had been commissioned, joining twenty-one in commission on 4 August 1914 when the war began. Of these submarines, twenty-two had been lost, fifteen of them with all hands. In another three about a quarter of the crew were saved and in the remaining four the crews were saved and taken prisoner.

Unlike the U-boats, the British submarines were hunting warships and military transports. Traffic in the Heligoland Bight was limited, most German ships being exposed only when in large fast-moving formations heavily escorted by sweepers. In his report for 1914 through

August 1916, Commodore (S) listed enemy warships sunk: two battleships, two armoured cruisers, two light cruisers, seven destroyers, five gunboats, four submarines, one Zeppelin, five armed auxiliaries and an armed trawler; plus unarmed ships: eleven transports, six ammunition/supply ships, two store ships, fifty-three steamships and 197 sailing ships.[16] The cost was 19 per cent of all British submariners.

The other important role of overseas submarines was the observational blockade of the High Seas Fleet. In 1914 it was considered vital, but the overseas submarines were not well equipped for it: they had (if any) only short-range W/T.

The Grand Fleet

Admiral Jellicoe warned the Admiralty in 1914 that he might be unable to pursue a withdrawing High Seas Fleet because it might be leading him into a submarine trap. Somewhat earlier German CinC Admiral Pohl had included just that possibility on the British side in his draft war orders. By October 1914 the Royal Navy had Pohl's orders and Jellicoe and his officers were certainly aware of what Pohl had written.[17] Jellicoe badly wanted submarines of his own, as he supposed that the Germans would bring submarines to sea with their High Seas Fleet. Even if the submarines had limited speed, they still might set up an ambush. Jellicoe also wanted submarines to help block the northern end of the North Sea, which was part of his area of responsibility.

Initially the Admiralty considered overseas submarines in too short supply and also unsuited to the Grand Fleet. However, late in October

Admiral Jellicoe demanded, and got, a flotilla of submarines for indirect support of the Grand Fleet. These 'G'-class submarines were based at Blyth so that they could rendezvous with the fleet in the event of a battle in the southern North Sea. Two are shown alongside their 10th Flotilla depot ship HMS *Lucia* in 1917. *G 8* is outboard (the inboard submarine is probably *G 12*). Note her two guns, both on retractable mountings. The forward gun is a 3in 10 cwt; aft is a 6pdr HA gun. The 'G' class were never assigned 6pdrs, so this one was presumably temporarily provided from a pool of such weapons. Late in the war the pool was just large enough to provide one for each 'G'-class submarine, but it is not clear whether that was done.

J 3 in Australian waters, with the destroyer leader *Anzac* in the background. She shows her short-range wireless antenna, its two wires led up to the spreader above the after part of the bridge fairwater. A higher antenna was fitted for longer-range signalling. The pipe outboard of the fairwater may be part of a whale spout installation. She was probably the last of the 'Js' to be rearmed; one report has her retaining her 3in gun in 1918. (RAN Naval Historical Service via Dr Josef Straczek)

1915 it decided to add an 11th Submarine Flotilla to the Grand Fleet.[18] Ultimately twelve submarines would be attached to the tender *Titania*, initially 'E' class and later 'G', 'J' and 'K' class.[19] In October 1915 three 'C'-class submarines (*C 25*, *C 26* and *C 27*) were assigned to Scapa Flow, to operate with trawlers in an ASW ruse (see the submarine vs submarine section below). Once the 11th Flotilla had been assigned to the Grand Fleet, Jellicoe proposed moving the 'Cs' to Invergordon, to be used against U-boats. The U-boats had just abandoned their anti-shipping offensive and Jellicoe expected them to operate off fleet bases. The Admiralty sent the small submarines to Rosyth instead, as it was more vulnerable to German attack. The following year *C 26* and *C 27* were among the four 'C'-boats shipped to Russia for Baltic operations.

Grand Fleet Battle Orders, as issued early in January 1916, show no direct submarine role; the submarines were in distant support.[20] Formal submarine instructions issued later in the month described the role of the new 11th Submarine Flotilla, then being formed at Blyth. It would be organised in groups of three submarines and one destroyer, the destroyer linking the group to the fleet. The submarines were stationed at Blyth so that they could join the fleet in time to take part in a fleet action in the central or southern North Sea. Taking a shorter route to the expected battle area than the fleet, the submarines could reach it more quickly, the fleet reaching them from astern. Once that happened, a group would form on either bow of the fleet, 10 to 12 miles ahead. If there were three groups, two if possible should be on the eastern and one on the western bow. These stations would allow the submarines to attack when the fleet deployed. The fast 'K' class were not yet in service; when they appeared, they would probably be attached to the battlecruisers.

A group which missed the German battle line would push on towards Heligoland so as to be across the line of retreat of the German fleet. They might surface to follow the Germans, in case they turned away. That would be particularly desirable if the enemy deployed away from Heligoland. In that case the Germans would have to turn away sooner or later, 'and submarines placed so as to intercept this movement should have a good opportunity of attacking'. Submarines following the enemy line might also be able to sink disabled ships. The flotilla would also be employed in the northern North Sea and to assist against a possible raid or invasion north of Flamborough Head.

In August 1916, four submarine flotillas were being organised, the 10th, 11th, 12th and 13th, of which the last two would consist entirely of 'K'-class submarines. They would be based at Scapa Flow with the fleet. The two slower flotillas would be based separately, the 10th at Tees and the 11th at Blyth.[21] Priority now went to detached operations north of 55° North, the flotilla to form a patrol line. Orders divided up the North Sea between the northern area for the Grand Fleet submarines and a southern area in which the flotillas based on Harwich and Yarmouth would generally operate.

Participation by the slow submarines in a fleet action came last in priority because the 'K'-boats would operate in direct support of the fleet. The elaborate new orders may have reflected experience in exercises. When proceeding to the rendezvous, the submarines would first be overhauled by the light cruiser or cruiser screen ahead of the main body. The appearance of these ships would allow the destroyers working with the submarines to ascertain the position, course and speed of the main body and thus to arrange the submarines so that they would be on the bows of the fleet. The submarines needed this information as soon as possible; if necessary the senior officer of the screen would detach a ship to get into close visual touch the destroyer working with the submarines.[22] If the CinC wanted to change course while maintaining W/T silence, he would detach a destroyer to get into visual touch with the destroyers leading the submarines. The battle fleet might be advancing at up to 20 knots 'and it must be the constant endeavour of the officers in command of submarines to keep well ahead and continue pressing on in advance along the route of the fleet, until it is necessary that they should take up their battle stations'. Although the submarines were slower than 20 knots, their initial position well in front of the fleet would give them some time before it caught up.

Post-Jutland Grand Fleet Battle Orders (11 September 1916) included a paragraph warning that the enemy might turn away to draw the fleet over his submarines or mines, which was much what Jellicoe envisaged doing to the Germans. 'It will generally be fairly evident whether the circumstances are such as to render tactical co-operation possible between the enemy's battle fleet and their submarines. When the action commences in waters which can obviously not have been "prepared" by the enemy, either by mines or submarines, the risk of our van leading in, is small.' Jellicoe seems to have had an unrealistic idea of how well he would know where his and the enemy's submarines were, particularly once they submerged. Although the Royal Navy paid far more attention to situational awareness than the Germans, experience at Jutland showed that plotting (its means of maintaining that awareness) was far less effective than it had to be for submarines to operate in close support of a fast-moving fleet.

New orders for the 10th and 11th Flotillas were issued on 14 November 1916, Admiral Beatty having taken over the Grand Fleet. Divisions in a favourable position – on the flank towards which the enemy deployed – were to attack at once, proceeding to their bases once their torpedoes were gone. Those on the quarter of the fleet after it deployed were to surface, following the enemy battle fleet in case it turned away and also to attack disabled enemy ships. Submarines unable to attack the enemy battle line or which could not regain contact with the enemy fleet were to push on towards the enemy's line of retreat. If the submarines missed the place of battle altogether, one division should proceed (without its destroyer) to the Skaw, providing the engagement was north of 55° North. The other would proceed towards Horns Reef, which the Germans would pass going home. If the fleet action was fought further south, half would go towards Horns Reef and the other to a position somewhat further north. CinC could order divisions to proceed to the Skaw or to Horns Reef via the linking destroyers.

Beatty could now look forward to the advent of the 'K' class. These submarines would accompany the battle fleet and would attack at the first opportunity, returning to the disengaged side of the fleet and coming to the surface to await orders. They would probably be detached shortly before dark to operate on the enemy's path back to the Heligoland Bight. 'K'-class orders issued in November 1916 were sketchy because there had not yet been any experience with these craft. These orders give no indication that they would operate in the divisional organisation arranged for the slow submarines. They would, then, operate without attached ships with full plotting (situational awareness) facilities.

New instructions dated 6 October 1917 reflected initial experience with the 'K' class, which was to be organised into two-boat divisions. Orders for the other submarines were radically different than in the past. Should the Grand Fleet proceed to sea to concentrate against the enemy, Grand Fleet submarines on patrol in the North Sea would take up positions 10 miles apart on one or more of four specified patrol lines. The 'J' class would join the fleet; if they missed the rendezvous they would go to the patrol lines. The 'G' and 'E'-class submarines would either take up patrol line positions or proceed direct to the Kattegat to cut off enemy ships; or take up positions to defend the Newcastle, Blyth and Middleborough areas – i.e., against possible enemy raids. In effect the 'J' class replaced the slow submarines included in earlier versions of the orders. The 'K' class would cruise with the fleet.

These instructions were repeated on 16 January 1918. These revised instructions added considerable detail on the 'K' and 'J' classes. Until the enemy heavy ships were sighted, the 'K' class would keep to the rear of the light cruiser screen ahead of the Grand Fleet, falling back if necessary on the battlecruisers, so that enemy light craft would be unable to force them to dive and thus to be, in effect, immobilised. As soon as the enemy heavy ships were sighted, the submarines would press forward, diving about five miles from the enemy fleet (closer in bad visibility). They were to try to avoid being seen, because once they were the enemy might retreat and thus preclude the desired fleet action.

The 'K'-class submarines would place themselves on the far side of the enemy fleet, so that the Germans would be threatened on both sides. Whenever the enemy was nearer its base than the submarine force, the submarine should steer more or less directly for that base, the submarines forming a patrol line spaced about five miles apart, at right

J 4 at sea, showing her high seakeeping freeboard. (Alan C Green via State Library of Victoria)

angles to the bearing of the enemy's base. Having passed the enemy fleet and manoeuvring for position behind them, at least some part of that fleet should be kept in sight, as 'once lost the chances of sighting again are small'. Although it would often be preferable for the submarines to attack later than at the first opportunity, once the main fleets were engaged it would rarely be desirable to wait. The 'J' class would join the submarine flotillas at the rear of the battle fleet if unable to attack immediately on deployment. All of these submarines would follow the British fleet on the surface and be ready to attack the enemy fleet should it turn away. These submarines would also deal with cripples.

Any submarine which lost contact and which still had torpedoes left and any submarine still with the fleet and with torpedoes on board at sunset was to proceed without further orders to a designated patrol line (B). 'Submarines met with should not be attacked unless their enemy character is definitely established . . . Once battle has been joined submarines to act on their own initiative . . .' Minelayers attached to the fleet would lay mines on the enemy's line of retreat inside the submarine patrol lines. Thus the retreating enemy fleet would encounter first mines and then British submarines.

The post-action section was somewhat amplified in the edition dated 30 April 1918. The submarines were going to the patrol lines in hopes of cutting off retreating enemy units. Before the action there would be an attempt to designate the patrol lines and to indicate their order of importance, but that might be impossible. 'It is to be realised that submarines on these patrols are placed with the object of attacking enemy ships. Submarines met with will probably be friendly and should not be attacked unless their enemy character is definitely established.' These instructions were still in force at the end of the war.

Admiral Beatty seems to have seen in the 'K' class a solution to the problem revealed at Jutland: what should the British fleet do if the Germans turned away in their 'battle turn?' His predecessor Admiral Jellicoe feared that he was being led over mines and U-boats. Despite his written claim that he could tell whether that was likely, he reacted almost automatically. Later it was pointed out that as the Grand Fleet moved towards a retreating High Seas Fleet, it might well be running onto torpedoes those ships launched as they fled. If, however, the 'K' class could be inserted between the High Seas Fleet and its base, in turning away from the guns of the Grand Fleet it would be turning towards the torpedoes of the 'K' class.[23] Despite their real limitations, the 'Ks 'were the only available answer to the real tactical problem of a German turn-away and they demonstrated an ability to maintain their speed in weather which much slowed the rest of the fleet. Certainly fleet commanders wanted further fleet submarines post-war, albeit preferably with diesel power plants.

The Mediterranean

In 1912, when reduction of the Mediterranean surface ships was discussed, one issue had been the impact of Turkish hostility on the Muslim population of the Empire; the Sultan of Turkey was the Caliph, nominally the leader of all Muslims. Submarines appealed to First Lord Winston Churchill as an inexpensive alternative to a battle fleet defending Egypt. He proposed stationing a flotilla of 'E'-boats in Alexandria with their tender. Given the more urgent needs of the North Sea, nothing had happened when the Turks declared war on 31 October 1914. The only British submarines in the Mediterranean were six small 'B'-class local defence submarines, three at Gibraltar (not formally part of the Mediterranean Fleet) and three at Malta. B 11 showed what they could do. On 13 December 1914 she penetrated the

Dardanelles and sank the Turkish battleship *Messudiyeh*. She had to stay submerged for nine hours as she returned down the Straits. As an indication of her limitations, by the time she surfaced her air was so foul that it was difficult to start her gasoline engine.

It took time to reinforce the Mediterranean submarine force. The March 1915 *Navy List* shows the three Gibraltar submarines transferred to Mediterranean Fleet control and a single larger one, the Australian *AE 2* (*AE 1* having been lost at Rabaul). When Italy entered the war on the Allied side in April, one of her conditions was that the British and the French directly support the Italian fleet. The six 'B'-boats were based at Venice in October 1915 to help watch the Austrian fleet at Pola.[24] They were assigned to a new British Adriatic Force which included battleships.

By early April 1915 the Royal Navy was preparing to attack the Dardanelles. Five 'E'-boats (*AE 2, E 11, E 15, E 21* and *E 25*) were assigned to the Mediterranean, together with the smaller US-built *H 2*. Now it was essential to operate inside the Dardanelles, since submarines there could interdict supplies for the Turkish army fighting at Gallipoli. Supplies came almost entirely by sea, because roads were limited. British submariners had to contend with density layers created by water flowing out of the Black Sea mixing with Mediterranean water. Initially they found it difficult to keep their submarines trimmed; later they found they could lie atop a density layer as though bottomed. Losses were heavy. *E 15* was stranded almost at the entrance to the straits, off Kephez Point (15 April 1915). *AE 2* was sunk inside the Dardanelles by the Turkish gunboat *Sultanhisar* (30 April 1915). *E 14* succeeded in penetrating and spent the rest of her career in the Mediterranean. *E 11* was the second successful submarine. Two more were soon lost: *E 7* on 5 September 1915 and *E 20* on 5 November. By December 1915 the force had stabilised at six 'E'-class submarines: *E 2, E 11, E 12, E 14, E 21* and *E 25*, backed by more 'H'-class submarines.

In December 1915 the British evacuated Gallipoli. Two of the Mediterranean 'E' class (*E 12* and *E 14*) and two 'H' class were transferred to the Adriatic Force watching the Austrians. The other 'H'-class submarines soon followed, replacing the two larger 'E'-class submarines in the Adriatic. The main role of the remaining Aegean submarines was to watch the mouth of the Dardanelles in case the battlecruiser *Goeben* and the cruiser *Breslau* emerged. When they did so in 1918, mines sank *Breslau* and badly damaged *Goeben*. *E 14* was mined on 27 January 1918 trying to penetrate the Dardanelles to torpedo the stranded *Goeben*.

About December 1917 a new Aegean Squadron was created. By this time the Allies were pressing Greece to enter the war on their side; at the least they wanted to control the sea around Greece. Two of the Mediterranean 'E'-class submarines joined the Aegean force (*E 2* and *E 12*). In January 1918 all of the other Mediterranean submarines were in the Adriatic, partly because the Adriatic was the source of the U-boats infesting the Mediterranean. About May 1918 the minelayer *E 46* joined the Adriatic Force, the only British submarine minelayer to serve outside the North Sea. *E 48* moved from Gibraltar. *H 7* and *H 9* joined the Adriatic Force about September 1918. At the end of the war there were eleven submarines in or near the Adriatic, including *H 7* and *H 9*.

Around January 1918 a new flotilla was created at Gibraltar to deal with long-range German submarines operating near the Azores: *E 35* and *E 48*, joined by *J 1* by March. *E 48* moved to the Aegean about May; she was replaced by *E 54* about September.

The Baltic

Early in the war Keyes placed two submarines in the Kattegat (part of the strait between Denmark and Sweden). Their presence so alarmed the Germans that they stopped all shipping from leaving Lübeck for 24 hours. Keyes concluded that British submarines should operate there continuously. Within a few days this idea had morphed into a plan to station submarines in the Baltic. They could stop the vital iron ore trade between Sweden and Germany. The Baltic submarines also made it difficult for the German High Seas Fleet to exercise freely in the southern Baltic, sinking several German warships. These submarines were attached to the Russian Fleet.[25]

Initially three 'E'-class submarines (*E 1*, *E 9* and *E 11*) were ordered to pass through the straits between Sweden and Germany to operate out of Russian bases. They left Gorleston on 14 October 1914.[26] En route *E 11* was forced back twice and ultimately turned back. She went to the Dardanelles the following year, where she distinguished herself. Initial operations were successful enough to encourage reinforcement. *E 8* and *E 13* were despatched from Harwich, probably on 14 August 1915. *E 13* ran aground off the Danish island of Saltholm. German ships disabled her and she was interned in Denmark on 18 August 1915. The Baltic submarines were all assigned to the Russian fleet and the Russians determined what they would do. They were very successful in 1915, but during 1916 suffered badly from Russian naval politics. They began to operate effectively again late in 1916, but the following year the Revolution made their operations entirely impossible.[27] The Russians were informed on 29 August that two more British submarines were coming.[28] *E 18* and *E 19* left Harwich on 28 August and both got through. *E 18* was mined off Bornholm, 24 May 1916, leaving four 'E'-class submarines in the Baltic through early 1918.

Initial successes in the Baltic led to a 1916 decision to add more submarines, but by that time the Germans had blocked the route through the Danish Straits.[29] The British therefore sent four 'C'-class submarines under tow to Archangel. They were then secured, one each, to barges which were towed via inland waters and canals to Kronstadt: *C 26*, *C 27*, *C 32* and *C 35*, of which *C 32* was stranded in the Gulf of Riga on 24 October 1917. The 'C'-boats were sent without their batteries, to reduce their weight, and the batteries were shipped separately. Apparently they arrived damaged and the boats were not fully operational until 1917. All of the Baltic submarines were destroyed in 1917 to prevent them from falling into German hands due to the Revolution.

Submarines as ASW Weapons

The coastal patrol submarines became involved in the effort to defend against the unrestricted U-boat offensive the Germans announced in February 1915. Early that year U-boat attacks on British fishing vessels in the North Sea intensified. U-boats could not use torpedoes against such shallow-draft craft, so they had to attack on the surface.[30] Seventh Submarine Flotilla (twelve 'C' class) tried having trawlers tow submarines, the two being linked by telephone. On spotting a U-boat the submarine would be slipped to attack. In theory the U-boat would not see the largely-submerged submarine. Towed by the trawler *Taranaki*, *C 24* torpedoed *U 40* on 23 June 1915; towed by *Princess Louise* on 20 July 1915 *C 27* torpedoed *U 23*. However, while under tow by the trawler *Ariadne* on 29 August 1915, *C 29* hit a mine which the trawler cleared due to her shallower draft. Unfortunately prisoners from *U 23* were allowed to mix with German civilians being allowed to return to Germany after internment; their story got out and the ruse was finished. It was revived (without success) in 1916 when the Germans again began attacking the British fishing fleet, using submarines operating from the Humber. There were also a few unsuccessful attempts to use this technique in the Channel.

In 1917, when the submarine force was turned towards ASW, the Q-ship idea was revived, using small 'H'-class submarines that they would tow. Trials were conducted by *Q.12* (*Tulip*-class sloop) and *H 8* in February 1917, using a completely submerged (hence invisible) towing line. *Q.12* was sunk, but other ships were fitted with similar

J 1 shows a variation on the theme, an unshielded gun and a gun platform built out to the sides of the ship. She seems to have been unique. She was the first of the class to be rearmed. (Alan C Green via State Library of Victoria)

submerged towing rigs. However, German documents captured in October 1917 showed that Q-ships were no longer effective lures for U-boats.

Up to the end of 1915 British submarines were generally limited to the North Sea, patrolling mainly off the German North Sea bases and Zeebrugge, the other main German submarine base. Placing submarines on the far side of the North Sea avoided the blue-on-blue problem. British submarines not involved in the trawler operation managed to sink three U-boats on passage to their patrol areas.[31] No special study of submarine vs submarine potential was made until late in 1916, when it became clear that the Germans were about to begin unrestricted submarine warfare early the next year. The Admiralty Anti-Submarine Division was formed. At this time, once clear of the coast and any watching British submarines, a surfaced U-boat could operate freely as long as she avoided patrol craft.

The systematic use of British submarines against U-boats seems to have been conceived by a Submarine Committee created in October 1916 at the request of Admiral Jellicoe, who was still CinC Grand Fleet (he would soon become First Sea Lord).[32] Jellicoe wrote that visits by *U 53* and merchant U-boats to the US east coast showed that German submarines could operate much further afield than had previously been imagined: off the North American coast and in the St. Lawrence. Destroyers lacked the endurance to deal with enemy submarines in such open waters. The Committee considered overseas submarines and decoy (Q) ships were the best answer. Since the 'J' and 'K' class were needed for the Grand Fleet, Jellicoe suggested 'E' and 'G'-class submarines plus any 'H' class which could be built in the United States and assembled in Canada. The committee understood that no 'H'-class submarines could be obtained and that the 'E' and 'G' class were in short supply.

Because the members of the Committee were submariners, they looked at the problem from the point of view of enemy submarine commanders. Canadian trade would probably be fairly safe in the spring and early summer due to fog and ice. Nantucket and Sandy Hook would be more attractive hunting grounds. If British submarines could be deployed to the US coast, they could at least deter U-boats from making close-range surface attacks on merchant ships. If U-boats could be limited to submerged attacks, they would soon run out of torpedoes and they would be far from supplies at home. Decoys and armed merchant ships would help, even if they sank no U-boats. 'The presence or even the suspicion of a hostile submarine in the vicinity in which a submarine is engaged in attempting to deliver surface attacks on trade must unquestionably add greatly to the anxieties of the latter's Captain, who is bound to be subjected to great and continuous strain, while operating at such a distance from home.' Hunting of submarines in the open sea by surface craft *other than decoys* (emphasis in the original) was a waste of time and effort, because a submarine could dive in ample time to avoid them. The combination of a decoy ship and a submarine, which had been tried frequently in the Mediterranean, had possibilities but had not yet succeeded.

However, the committee recommended against basing any British submarines in Canada, particularly since they would have to operate more than 500nm from their base. If submarines did have to be sent, the 'G' class were better than the 'E' class because they were more habitable.

This report seems to have turned Jellicoe towards using submarines for anti-submarine warfare, as a way of keeping U-boats submerged in distant waters. To that end he proposed immediately ordering twelve

more 'H'-class submarines in the United States. The original 'H' class had been built so quickly that it seemed that the repeat 'H' class might be ready by April or May 1917. Once in service, they could release longer-range submarines for the operations the committee envisaged. Jellicoe imagined that they could either be built in sections and assembled in Canada or delivered as unarmed merchant submarines and armed at Halifax. Given President Wilson's reaction to the earlier 'H'-class deal, the Admiralty saw no chance for this one. However, it could assure Jellicoe that orders for many new submarines would soon be placed in the United Kingdom and also that about twenty-five more submarines, already under construction, would be in service by 1 April 1917.

Jellicoe's successor as CinC Grand Fleet, Admiral Beatty, soon wrote to his submarine flotilla commanders, on the Tees and at Blyth, that the German U-boat offensive, which was expected, could be defeated only by underwater weapons, meaning British submarines and mines. He felt that the large British submarine force was doing far too little. Its only offensive operations in home waters were one submarine of the Harwich flotilla patrolling off the Maas, five off Terschelling and four off the Horns Reef and the Skaggerak (from the 10th and 11th Flotillas). Beatty wrote that most of the eighty-six submarines in home waters were reserved to deal with the raid or invasion threat 'which exists only in the imagination'. The Grand Fleet submarines should be used for constant operations in force rather than in ones and twos, submarine divisions proceeding to where German submarines were reported, to 'quickly check enemy activities'. Beatty's concept of mobile groups helped shape the British submarine ASW campaign which soon began.

Beatty wanted flotillas reorganised to give him at least forty boats, to be based on Scapa Flow, Blyth, the Tees and the Humber.[33] The stationary patrols at Yarmouth and Harwich should be reduced to the old 'C' class, as these waters were unsuited to submarine operations. The Dover patrol would remain. Remaining 'E' and 'H'-class submarines should be used for foreign service, based at Halifax, Bermuda and Gibraltar and working on the trade routes. Permanent patrols should work off the entrance to the Sound and Belts (the routes from the North Sea to the Baltic). Effective command and control was essential: 'it is assumed that every British submarine will be fitted as rapidly as possible with Poulsen [long-range W/T], Fessenden [underwater sound communication] and Directional Plates [directional hydrophones]'.

Beatty apparently did not realise how many submarines it took to maintain standing patrols. For example, submarines maintained a continuous patrol at the Horns Reef by relieving each other on station: for three days of each patrol, two submarines were at sea, one either going out to the station or returning from it. As a result, 10th Flotilla averaged 32 per cent of its strength at sea. Owing to fitting long-range radio (Poulsen), directional plates etc and docking and fixing defects, 10th Flotilla submarines averaged 8–9 days out and 7–12 days in harbour. Furthermore, according to the flotilla commander, the five 'J' class 'have not taken their share of patrol' and three 'G' class were often detached to operate in the White Sea. Captain (S) of 10th Flotilla (Tees) considered that at least 40 to 50 per cent of submarines should be allowed as a working margin over those on operations, both to replace losses and to give officers and men the necessary rest. Nor did Beatty appreciate the value of the Patrol Flotillas as a training organisation.

Captain (S) on the Tees (10th Flotilla) proposed that all overseas submarines in the North Sea come under CinC Grand Fleet (Beatty) and that a submarine officer should join Beatty's staff. His proposal that the Grand Fleet oversea submarine flotillas and their destroyers should join in Grand Fleet exercises suggests that had not previously been done. He proposed a North Sea submarine organisation, but went further to suggest that the Mediterranean 'E' class be moved from Mudros to Otranto, the mouth of the Adriatic through which German and Austrian submarines came (this was done). They should be reinforced by six 'C' class to deal with enemy threats from Cattaro. That had been the role of the 'B'-boats in 1915–16. Other 'E'-class submarines should work from Plymouth on the trade routes. As a deterrent against unrestricted German submarine warfare, Captain (S) proposed the threat of unrestricted submarine warfare in the Baltic. He cautioned that submarine vs submarine warfare would be difficult. In winter visual periscope range was no more than half or three-quarters of a mile. A submarine firing entirely on the basis of sound might well hit another British submarine.

Beatty asked the Submarine Committee Jellicoe had appointed the previous October (now including Commander Ernest Leir) to consider reorganising the submarines for ASW. Little pointed out that under favourable conditions, a submarine could deliberately attack an enemy submarine caught unawares. 'It cannot be doubted our submarine officers have had more experience than the Germans and should come off well . . .' Only submarines had any real chance of attacking U-boats during daylight. By the summer the Royal Navy would have seventy-seven of what Little called patrol submarines ('D' and later classes, excluding the 'K' class). Another thirty coastal submarines ('C' class, including the three at Hong Kong) were also available. Little considered them best for ASW due to their small size. The longer-range submarines should block the three exits from German bases: Zeebrugge (a base for small German submarines on the North Sea), the Heligoland Bight and the Skaggerak. He thought that only Zeebrugge could be

completely sealed (as was attempted in the Zeebrugge Raid the following year). Repeated mining to close the Bight would soon begin. A submarine patrol of the Skaggerak was attractive.[34]

The Admiralty was reluctant to give up the anti-raid mission, as the Grand Fleet was so far from possible German targets.[35] However, it accepted the ASW patrol idea, beginning with a patrol off St. Kilda. Once weather moderated, 'C'-class submarines would be based in the Shetlands to attack U-boats on passage. Beatty kept pressing to shift from coast defence to a submarine ASW role, laying out proposed submarine organisation for that purpose. Beatty also wanted submarines assigned to the trade routes. To that end the Admiralty set up its first dedicated submarine ASW flotilla, at Queenstown on the Irish coast, using the tender *Vulcan* and seven overseas submarines (three 'D' and four 'E' class), plus another at Lough Swilly using the Australian tender *Platypus* (three 'D' class and three 'E' class).[36] As of March 1917 plans also called for attaching one 'H'-class submarine to *Vulcan*, to be towed by a Q-ship. These submarines were part of a new Coast of Ireland command.

The Admiralty ordered the Captain (S) at Harwich to assign eight 'C'-class submarines specifically to intercept minelaying U-boats operating out of Zeebrugge; they were drawn from Dover (three), the Nore (three) and the Tyne (two). This reassignment suggests that the Admiralty was much more interested in submarine ASW than its words indicated. Initially performance was poor because the boats' previous coast defence role had worn them and their personnel down and, presumably, much reduced their initiative. However, numerous contacts were made and in April 1917 *C 7* torpedoed *UC 68* in a night attack. Prisoners of war later stated that they understood that a British 'duty submarine' was generally on patrol near the North Hinder Light. That kept them submerged in daylight and thus reduced their mobility.

U-boats from Germany generally passed north of Scotland to run down the West Coast of Ireland towards the trade routes converging

J 7 was given a new raised gun platform on which a 4in gun was mounted (it is barely visible here). The 3in HA gun remained, on a retractable mounting forward, atop the raised structure. (RAN Naval Historical Section via Dr Josef Straczek)

After the United States entered the war, US submarines were assigned to the British ASW operation. USS *L 11* lies alongside the light cruiser *Patrol*, the flagship of the Coast of Ireland Station. To distinguish the US submarines from their British counterparts, an 'A' prefix was painted on their fairwaters – AL 11 in this case. US Navy submarine officers rode British submarines and reported back on British, as compared to American, practices. One of the few areas in which the US Navy seemed more competent was in hovering at zero speed by balancing the submarine to neutral buoyancy. The Royal Navy did not bother with hovering, and indeed considered it nearly impossible; in a course on submarine capabilities for merchant navy officers, Royal Navy instructors said that a submarine could not maintain depth unless she kept moving, with water flowing over her planes. (David C Isby)

south towards the British west coast ports, particularly Liverpool. U-boats also operated in the Irish Sea. Aside from sinking U-boats, anything which hindered their free passage reduced their time on patrol and hence their effectiveness. A U-boat confronted by an aircraft could dive briefly, but an invisible British submarine on patrol could deter it from running on the surface except at night; even then it might be spotted and attacked. Submarine vs submarine operations often relied on signals intelligence. It was not good enough to cue anti-submarine forces, but it was often good enough to place a submerged British submarine within range of a U-boat which could not see it and therefore could not crash-dive to evade it. There was one problem, however. The submarines were controlled by CinC Irish Coast but the Admiralty had the best information on U-boat positions, thanks to special intelligence. It proved necessary to shift operational

control of the submarines to the Admiralty as far as was possible.

A new flotilla, with *Vulcan* as depot ship, was assigned to CinC Queenstown in Ireland. Its submarines – ultimately to be six 'E' class, six 'D' class and two 'H' class – would operate on the West Coast of Ireland to attack U-boats passing down that coast en route to the southern trade route approaches. In March 1917 the *Vulcan* flotilla amounted to *D 3*, *D 7*, *D 8*, *E 32*, *E 54*, *H 5* and *H 8*, the 'D'-class submarines having been taken from 3rd Flotilla. The following month *Platypus* was formally added (the flotilla was now the *Vulcan* and *Platypus* flotillas), with more submarines assigned to ASW: *D 4* and *D 6–D 8* (but not *D 3*) and more E-boats: *E 23*, *E 35* and *E 48*, of which the last would soon be detached to Gibraltar.

At this time merchant ships approaching British waters were given specified routes, which took 10 to 14 days to change. The secret routes, which were also used in the Mediterranean, were betrayed whenever a U-boat happened upon a ship using one; it immediately communicated its information. Routes therefore had to be changed as soon as any submarine was reported – and British submarines were often misreported as hostile. Also, British submarines on passage were at a considerable risk from patrol craft hunting for U-boats. According to the post-war account of this campaign, 'Auxiliary Patrol officers were not so familiar with the respective characteristics of British and German submarines as they were in the last year of the submarine campaign'.

For all of these reasons the initial plan was abandoned in April 1917. Submarines were assigned fixed patrol lines. Surface ships were kept clear. *Vulcan* (which then supported six 'E' class and two 'H' class) moved to Lough Swilly and the second planned depot ship, *Platypus* (six 'D' class), was stationed at Killybegs.[37] While this was being done, *E 54*, which was not initially part of this programme (but became part of the *Vulcan* flotilla), sank *U 81* on 1 May 1918; the U-boat had surfaced after torpedoing a merchant ship.

To deal with U-boats passing north around Scotland, 'G' and 'E'-class submarines were detached from the flotilla in the Tees; almost immediately *G 13* sank *UC 43*. The entire Tees flotilla was then transferred to Scapa Flow and during the summer three 'C'-class submarines were added. During this operation *U 52* sank *C 34*.

Between April and September 1917 the convoy system became effective; successful attacks on Atlantic shipping declined steeply. The Germans concentrated on the approaches to the Irish Sea and to the Channel. To meet this change, the *Vulcan* flotilla moved to Berehaven and new patrol lines were set for the *Platypus* flotilla. Initially there was great reluctance to approve submarine operations in the Channel itself due to the dense traffic, the limited area and the likelihood of attack by British patrol craft and aircraft. However, the initial success of the 'C' class in the North Sea encouraged establishment in May of Channel patrols by two 'C'-class submarines. During the first patrol a 'C'-class submarine made a promising contact, but had to break off when a British seaplane appeared. Even so, the results were good enough to justify adding three more 'C'-class submarines to the flotilla in November.

'C' and 'E'-class submarines patrolled the area north of the net barrage at Dover; on 1 November 1917 *E 52* sank *UC 63* at night near a buoy used by both sides as a navigational mark. Two days later *C 15* sank *UC 65*. This success led to urgent requests for more Channel patrols; two 'F'-class submarines were transferred from Yarmouth and arrangements were made for the 'D' class to be transferred as well as soon as they were relieved by new 'L'-class submarines.[38]

During the winter of 1917–18 the Germans became very active in the Irish Sea, so in December submarine patrols were set up in the southern part of it. In February 1918 *Platypus* and her flotilla moved to Campbeltown, from which they could operate either in the northern part of the Irish Sea or north of Ireland. Dense shipping and patrol activity made the Irish Sea particularly dangerous; *H 5* was rammed and sunk by a merchant ship on 6 March 1918. Meanwhile USS *Bushnell* and a flotilla of seven US 'L'-class submarines (designated the 'AL'-class to avoid confusion with the British 'L' class) arrived at Queenstown to supplement the Irish Sea patrol in the area south of Ireland. *Vulcan* moved to Kingstown with two 'H'-class submarines and a further tender, *Ambrose*, came to Berehaven. She and her flotilla had to move to Portsmouth on an emergency basis at the end of March 1918, as it was feared that to support their offensive on land the Germans would risk sending their surface ships into the Channel to break the Allied lines of communication. *Ambrose* went to Devonport early in October as the situation on the Western Front was no longer considered as desperate.

At about the same time a new flotilla was formed to attack U-boats going to or returning from their patrol areas in the Atlantic. These tracks were affected by the developing Northern Barrage. *Vulcan* moved to Blyth. Her new flotilla comprised ten 'H' class and two 'R' class.

The Germans operated long-range cruiser submarines further out in the Atlantic. At the end of October 1917 *E 35* and *E 48* were sent to Gibraltar to search for the cruiser *U 156*. Presumably on the basis of radio intelligence, *E 48* found her in the Canaries and attacked while submerged. One torpedo hit but did not explode. *U 156* made off on the surface. *E 48* was transferred to the Mediterranean and replaced by the faster *J 1*, which was fitted with depth charges (see below). *E 35* was more successful: on 11 May 1918 she sank *U 154*.[39]

In all, British submarines sank eighteen U-boats and hit another seven without sinking them, largely due to failures of torpedoes to detonate. Post-war analysis indicated that five of the twenty-five attacks were conducted at night. In nine cases the submarine was hit while in her operating area (in sixteen she was on passage). In one case, both the U-boat and the attacker were on passage (*E 34* on 10 May 1918). In all, there were 564 contacts, so there was a ratio of 29.7 contacts to sinkings. Immediately after the First World War it was generally claimed that submarines had sunk more U-boats than any other type of warship; later it turned out that the most successful ASW measure had been mines (forty-eight U-boats sunk).

The Germans were certainly aware of the threat of British submarine attack; for example, they zigzagged while passing through the North Sea and kept a very sharp lookout. Post-war analysis suggested that submarines had been among the most effective anti-U-boat measures, but that was largely because surface ships had virtually no way of detecting submerged submarines. As a consequence, convoying could reduce sinkings of merchant ships but convoys did not become the submarine killing grounds that they were in the Second World War: convoy escorts accounted for only sixteen U-boats. Patrols and hunters sank twenty-eight and another nineteen U-boats were lost to unknown causes. It was impossible to quantify the effect of submarines and other anti-submarine measures which tended largely to inhibit U-boat commanders. This 'moral' effect was, however, well understood.

New ASW Weapons

British submarines only rarely managed to sink U-boats. In July 1917 Commodore (S) issued a memo explaining why.[40] To sink a U-boat, a British submarine had to get within attack distance, estimate enemy course and speed, get into attacking position and fire with the right deflection. The most frequent problem was inability to get into position, the U-boat on the surface being about twice as fast as the submerged hunter. Range-taking was impossible; the only ways to estimate enemy course and speed was a quick plot or the director. Either depended on an estimate of enemy bearing, based on the appearance of his conning tower; the target showed no freeboard, masts or funnels. Commodore (S) described this as one of the insuperable difficulties and the director did not solve it. Probably the only effective attacking position was 6 points off the enemy bow. When sighted the U-boat might be anything up to 180° from the firing course and it would take a submarine three to four minutes to turn as required. At the same time the enemy's bearing had to be obtained quickly and accurately so as to judge his course and speed. At the same time 'the greatest care in manoeuvring is required so that the periscope will not be dipped or the submarine break surface'. Calculations would be thrown off if the enemy altered course – as he did because he zigzagged. Practically all attacks were snap-shots, but at the best target angle the target was small enough that it allowed for an error in direction of one knot at 1000 yds. 'Every known successful attack . . . has been a matter of eye and judgement with a large element of luck and no director has assisted.'

Attempted remedies were submarine-vs-submarine exercises and installation of elaborate attack teachers to give submarine commanders a sense of what they would encounter. Nine types of directors had been tried, of which the standard director and Commander. Nasmith's 'Is-Was' had been supplied to all submarines. Since commanders' preference was personal, they were allowed to have any of the others. Submarines were now firing at ranges of up to 5000 yds, at which hitting 'is a pure fluke and the number of misses inevitably occurring makes it appear that the skill of submarine officers is much less than it is actually believed to be'. That was clear from the anti-ship record. The main remedy proposed was more torpedoes per salvo, perhaps using externally-carried weapons.

The Grand Fleet Submarine Committee proposed some remedies: guns, longer (30ft) periscopes and external torpedoes.[41] The guns should have a wide arc of fire, which would seriously affect underwater speed and stability. Commodore (S) pointed out that the gun would give 'E' and 'G'-class submarines gun armament equal to that of U-boats displacing 500 tons more. The Admiralty was already considering guns, but in the context of surprise attacks: the British submarine would suddenly surface and open fire. That required special trunking to bring up ammunition and a crew as quickly as possible. Only the 'L' class was really suitable.

Although the Operations Committee considered the torpedo the main anti-submarine weapon, it noted occasions when an unsuccessful torpedo attack could have been followed up with a gun. When two submarines sighted each other on the surface, a gun was essential. British submarines were currently outgunned by the Germans. The Committee recommended fitting overseas submarines with high-velocity 4in guns with 10,000 yds range. Some U-boats had shot accurately at this range. As of July 1917 *J 1* was being armed with one 4in gun and one howitzer and *L 3* with a 4in gun at the height of, but before, the conning tower, with special trunking. The trunking was to supply ammunition and to allow the gun crew to man the gun rapidly.

Commodore (S) added that attacks had failed mainly because the attackers had been unable to close rapidly enough; for that reason DNC was currently working on the 'R' class (15 knots underwater).

The matter was referred to the Operations Committee for decision. Issues included a proposal to remove beam tubes from 'J'-class submarines in order to fit depth charges. Should other classes be provided with depth charges? In October, the committee decided that 90° angled gyros should be supplied to all submarines with beam tubes, with priority for ASW submarines.[42] No additional tubes or Drzewiecki frames would be fitted, but 'J'-class submarines would have their beam tubes replaced by depth charges, pending tests on board *J 1*. No other classes should be fitted. Any changes in gun armament should be deferred pending trials of *J 1*, but all 'L'-class submarines should have a 4in gun. *L 50* should have two such guns and

In 1917–18 large British submarines were rearmed with 4in guns specifically so that they could attack surfaced U-boats they came upon suddenly. It was assumed that the U-boat would be spotted on the surface, the British submarine surfacing so quickly to engage it that it could catch the U-boat before it could dive. The guns were given high positions and special watertight gun access trunks were provided. The gun crew entered the trunk before the submarine surfaced, ready to burst out to man the gun almost immediately upon surfacing. Guns were also shielded. The 'E' class were too small for such modifications, but the big 'J' and 'L'-boats were fitted. *J 5* shows the new arrangement. *J 1* was the first to be rearmed, using the same S I mounting as in the 'K' class. This rearmament seems to have been ordered before the rearmament of the 'L' class. This photograph was probably taken when she arrived in Australian waters in 1919. (Alan C Green via State Library of Victoria)

so should the new 'R' class (as high as possible without interfering with underwater speed). Fire-control instruments should not be fitted.

Guns had not previously been very important. They were considered in 1912 but rejected and the 1913 comments by the War Staff did not change that. The post-war British view was that the navy had rejected guns because their main role would have been to attack commerce. The British attributed greater German interest in guns to an interest in attacking merchant ships, although there is little evidence of that.[43] Also, guns ruined streamlining and thus cost underwater speed which British submarines would need in order to close in on fast warships.

Guns were eventually fitted, apparently due to experience in the Sea of Marmara during the Dardanelles campaign. Malta Dockyard fitted a 12pdr to *E 11* and a 4in gun to *E 12*. The builders fitted *E 20* with a 6in howitzer. She was lost so soon after arrival in the Dardanelles that it is not clear how it was to be used. Some North Sea boats received 3in or 12pdr HA guns and some were sent on anti-Zeppelin patrols in hopes of suddenly catching these aircraft overhead. Because aircraft threatened surfaced submarines, by 1917 anti-aircraft guns were common: typically an 'E'-class submarine had a 12pdr 8 cwt gun.

Beside guns, the other new ASW idea was the submarine-borne depth charge. Once a U-boat dived, neither gun nor torpedo was of much use. The first proposal was submitted to CinC Grand Fleet on 24 April 1917.[44] Standing in for the flotilla commander, Commander Max Horton observed that a vertical and horizontal spread was essential. He recalled how often his 11th Flotilla had had opportunities for depth-charge attacks over the past two months – if only the submarines had had depth charges. He proposed four depth-charge throwers abaft the conning tower. In August the Admiralty informed Admiral Beatty that during her forthcoming refit on the Tyne, *J 1* would be fitted with a 7.5in howitzer (to fire depth charges) as well as

a 4in BL Mk XI gun in place of her current 12pdr (the howitzer plan was abandoned about 21 September). Depth charges were a separate idea: in a 27 August 1917 report Captain (S) of 10th Flotilla mentioned plans to replace the beam tubes in 'J'-class submarines with depth charges.[45] *J 1* was given twenty depth charges in vertical tubes closed top and bottom by outer and inner watertight doors. The tubes could train 30° each side from right ahead, which proved inadequate. Internal stowage may have been attractive because it would not subject depth-charge pistols to water pressure when the submarine dived. After 2–10 December trials, it was recommended that charges be set for no less than 150ft and that the submarine should run at 15 knots while firing.[46] Communication between bridge and depth charge compartment proved inadequate. Overall, trials went so well that it was recommended that all the 'J' class be fitted as soon as possible. Director, ASW Division (DASD) suggested detaching *J 1* temporarily from 11th Flotilla to gain sufficient experience to decide whether to modify all the other 'J'-boats. She went to Gibraltar for a special operation to intercept German submarines detected by signals intelligence. It is not clear whether she ever used her weapon and no other 'J'-class submarine was fitted.

There was a separate proposal to arm 'K'-class submarines with depth charges, beginning with a May 1918 proposal.[47] *K 9* reported sighting a U-boat and coming within a thousand yards before the enemy dived. Three other 'K'-boats had had similar experiences. The two 'K'-class flotilla commanders proposed using standard Thornycroft depth-charge throwers; it is not clear whether they were aware of just how extensive modifications to *J 1* had been. The thrower could be installed at the after end of the funnel casing, trained on the quarter. The charge could be set for a minimum depth of 90ft and dropped at a speed of 16 knots to ensure that it would not explode less than 180ft from the submarine. The danger radius of the charge at 90ft was 50ft, but even with a short shot it would explode 135ft from the

The experience of suddenly coming upon a U-boat prompted submarine officers to propose alternative weapons, such as the Thornycroft depth-charge mortar mounted aft on board *K 22*. Her funnels are tilting into their submerged positions as she prepares to dive. Note the freeing ports in the door of her free-flooding torpedo tube space, under the barrel of the 4in gun. (Dr Josef Straczek)

submarine. To protect the submarine while diving, the primer would not be placed in the charge until needed. A spare charge could be lashed down near the muzzle of the thrower. As an initial test, the attached destroyer *Ithuriel* dropped depth charges nearby. A single depth-charge thrower was installed on board *K 6* and trials carried out early in August 1918 (the report is dated 13 August). Shock was acceptable. There was also a proposal to provide 'K'-class submarines with stick bombs similar to those then being carried on board destroyers (there was a fuzing problem); the Board approved trials with a dummy stick bomb. It does not appear that depth-charge throwers were installed on board 'K'-class submarines operationally, nor that stick bombs were issued before the end of the war. The depth-charge idea seems to have died completely after the end of the war. However, the 1921 technical history of British submarines refers to the 'K'-class thrower as though it was a standard installation. That may be no more than sloppiness.

Sound Communication

Submarines had Fessenden (Submarine Signal Company) underwater communication systems called sound telegraphs (S/T) as opposed to wireless telegraphs (W/T: radio).[48] Many surface ships also had S/T, but in 1919 it was ordered removed from all battleships and battle-cruisers except *King George V* and *Emperor of India*. In future S/T would be fitted only to submarines and associated destroyers and cruisers. The current system was designated Type 101. Type 102 was an improved design. Type 103 was a simpler cheaper type (receive only) primarily for communication between a destroyer and a submarine.[49] It was understood that range could be increased considerably by tuning the circuits to the 540 Hz frequency produced by Fessenden Oscillators and that a Note Magnifier (amplifier) would help. By 1921 four sets of Tuned Receivers and Note Magnifiers were being installed in submarines for trials. The Oscillator was very directional, giving the greatest range in the direction in which the diaphragm faced. Receiving stations could take accurate bearings on transmitting ships. As of 1921, under favourable conditions working range was about 20 to 30nm, with both transmitters and receivers in deep water and submerged to at least 10 to 15ft.[50] S/T was later superseded by Asdic communication. The Signal School continued to work with S/T until 1931, when Type 106X was developed specially for new 'S'-class submarines, operating at 1000 Hz, hence less subject to self-noise interference.

Periscopes

In April 1914 Commodore (S) claimed that although periscopes were still made by Vickers' contractor Sir Howard Grubb & Sons Ltd, the threat of foreign competition had much improved his products.[51] At Admiralty request a second firm, Kelvin, Bottomley and Baird (KBB), negotiated a licensing agreement with the German periscope maker Goerz early in 1914. However, because the Admiralty did not let any pre-war contracts to KBB, there was little or no technology transfer. On receiving the Admiralty contracts after war broke out, KBB went to the National Physical Laboratory for the necessary optical calculations. After three months they proved useless. The Admiralty Contracts Department then suggested that two KBB employees go to Carpentier in Paris for technical assistance. However, according to KBB, except for ten periscopes based on Carpentier's, all of theirs were entirely home-grown. KBB's first periscope was a 22ft 6in monocular type with an outer diameter of 150mm (5.9in) and a top of 90mm

(3.5in). Immdium bronze replaced the non-magnetic steel of earlier periscopes. It offered much the same advantages as nickel, but was more easily machined and was more readily obtainable. From the German periscopes KBB adopted the idea of making the ocular box (when stripped of externals) the same diameter as the main periscope tube, for easier installation. The performance of this early periscope was such that KBB received orders for others with double magnification. They were also asked to develop a sky search feature.[52]

Some foreign periscopes, such as the Italian ones, offered two alternative magnifications. Typically that required a change of lenses at the eyepiece, which was inherently unsatisfactory. Furthermore, the more magnified image was smaller. KBB pointed out that to have the exit pupil (the image) retain its size at both magnifications the lenses at the top of the periscope had to change. That was no easy thing in a 3in tube with a sky searcher, particularly when a large field of view and a sharp image were also wanted. KBB solved the problem, evolving two kinds of 30ft periscope, CR (monocular, 2½in diameter at the top) and DR (bi-focal with sky search, with top diameter about 3in).[53] KBB introduced a means of reading off azimuth while looking through its periscope and also of reading off the angle of elevation in the sky search. There were also night eyepieces. Later in the war the company was asked for a 150mm 36ft periscope and somewhat later it was decided that 36ft periscopes should have 7½in diameter (4in at the top). These instruments were to offer two magnifications and sky-search. As of 1921 KBB was working on the design of the instrument.

In 1917 Barr & Stroud, until then a rangefinder and binocular maker, produced its own prototype periscopes.[54] Officers who used the 30ft Barr & Stroud periscope in 1918 considered it far ahead of the average German periscope and slightly better than the enemy's best. New features included an internal focusing lens, which permitted the observer to change focus without removing his eye from the eyepiece. Internal colour glasses replaced the earlier caps fitted over the eyepiece. By turning the handles on the periscope, the observer could change magnification and alter the elevation of the top prism, functions previously done using levers. After 1920 Barr & Stroud offered a range estimator using prisms to measure the angle subtended by the height of the target. A known height gave the range. Barr & Stroud became the standard British periscope supplier after the war.[55]

Torpedoes and Fire Control

The Royal Navy simplified the attack process by limiting itself to straight-running torpedoes, on the grounds that it was difficult to take into account the manoeuvre a torpedo carried out as it turned under gyro control. By 1901, when the 'Hollands' were ordered, the standard Royal Navy torpedo was 18in in diameter. Early British submarines had 18in cold torpedoes, but by 1914 British submarines had 18in Mk VIII torpedoes with a speed of 41 knots for 1500 yds. In April 1914 Commodore (S) wrote that British submarine commanders were trained to attack at short range and high speed, so that short-range torpedoes best fitted their tactics. They were in the tubes of the 'coastals' and in the broadside tubes of the 'overseas' submarines. Typical performance of a short-range (cold) 18in torpedo was 800 yds range at 30 knots. In 1918 the range of a Mk VII** heater torpedo was 5000 yds at 35 knots. These torpedoes could reach 3000 yds at 41 knots. Mk VIII range was 2500 yds at 35 knots.

By this time the Royal Navy was very interested in longer-range 'browning' shots against enemy formations.[56] For submarines, browning shots would be essential if the submarine could not get into close range against fast enemy capital ships. By 1914 long-range heater torpedoes were being supplied for the bow tubes of all 'D', 'E' and later oversea submarines. *Nautilus* and *Swordfish* were armed with 21in torpedoes.[57] Typical performance of the Mk II version was 4200 yds at 44.5 knots (with higher air pressure, 4500 yds). In 1918 the higher-speed setting was being changed to 35 knots (5000 to 6000 yds).

The fire-control problem reduced to leading the target, pointing the submarine so that its periscope pointed to the target at the appropriate director (or deflection) angle (DA). As in the gun fire control problem being attacked at the same time, there were two approaches. The simplest was to rely on what could be seen directly, for example the angular rate at which the target seemed to move. The alternative, which became standard for post-war gunnery, was to deduce the target's course and speed and work from that. The longer the range, the less valid simple deduction was. Deflection rates changed as the target moved across the submarine's line of sight. In effect the submarine commander solved a triangle, the legs of which were the line of sight to the target at the moment of firing, the distance the target moved along the track before the torpedo arrived and the torpedo run.

Initially submarine COs were issued with tables showing range based on masthead height and periscope angle; deflection angles for the two available torpedo speeds (29 and 41 knots); and tables giving time, speed and distance.

The initial step towards using target course and speed as the basis for an attack was taken by Lieutenant Commander Martin E Nasmith (later Dunbar-Nasmith), who had commanded *E 11* in the Dardanelles and thus was a major submarine hero. He was aware of the Dumaresq used by surface gunners to estimate the rate at which range was changing based on assumed target (and own-ship) course and speed. Nasmith invented a submarine torpedo director to find the optimum attack course.[58] It was not widely adopted, but it was the basis for his extremely successful 'Is-Was', first used successfully by Lieutenant Claud Barry to sink *UB 72* in March 1918.[59]

A drawing in the post-war Admiralty Technical History shows how the 'Is-Was' was used. The submarine commander (more likely, his No 1) set it up by entering enemy course relative to the submarine and enemy speed. The 'Is-Was' solved the torpedo firing triangle, indicating the deflection associated with the enemy's speed along the indicated course. The device consisted of a series of concentric circles associated with different target speeds, from 6 to 15 knots. A long own-ship bar was pivoted at its centre. To solve the triangle, it was pointed along the target course, its long end pointing at a series of deflections associated with different target speeds. A shorter enemy bar could be used for higher target speeds. Typically the centre of the device was a gyro compass repeater, so that true (as opposed to relative) courses could be used. Using true courses made it possible for the submarine to manoeuvre without distorting the solution. Thus the example shown in the Technical History had the target course 250°, which was equivalent to a 100° track angle for the submarine. That in turn equated to a target inclination (the angle between target course and line of sight) of 35°, enemy bearing from the submarine being 65°. The innermost circle of the device was set at 35°, a ring further out showing the equivalent 65° bearing from the submarine. The own-ship bar was set along the 100° track angle of the target. Between the two rings was the compass repeater, indicating that 100° was 250° true. The 10-knot ring showed a 16° deflection or director angle.

The outer ring showed that the device could handle track angles

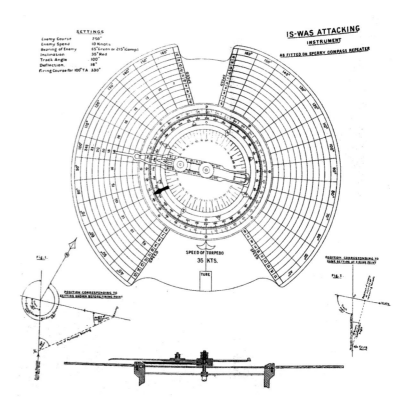

The 'Is-Was,' from the early post-war Admiralty Technical History. (Author's collection)

between 40° and 160° (in 10° increments) on either side. Solutions were approximate; the diagram in the Technical History shows 16° deflection at 10 knots for track angles of 90 to 120°. That made sense: it allowed for the length of the target. The solution was instantaneous; it appeared as soon as the device was set up.

Despite its name, the 'Is-Was' did not show where a target 'is' based on where it 'was', so the operator could not check his estimates of target speed and inclination. He relied on his trained 'eye', glancing very briefly at the target when he raised his periscope. Several officers, including Nasmith, tried to solve this problem after the war, but their instruments were not adopted. However, a plotting board was introduced in June 1927.[60]

Reliance on the submarine commander's eye made practice attacks extremely important, but before the war they could be made only against assigned target ships, giving submarine commanders far too little experience. In 1913 the Gibraltar Flotilla offered an alternative, an Attack Teacher. Production was delayed in the belief that the war would be short, but a production prototype was set up on board the depot ship *Thames* at Sheerness in the spring of 1915. The submarine commander watched target models through a periscope with a voice pipe to a plotting room, in which a 'coxswain' operating a ship's wheel simulated turns by the submarine. The models were pulled across a simulated sea on a carrier, which could be manoeuvred to simulate zigzags, destroyer screens, navigation in shoal waters or near minefields and even ramming by the ship being attacked. The tracks of submarine and target were recorded on a plotting board for post-exercise analysis.

The later Submarine Torpedo Director incorporated a position-keeper which could project ahead target position based on assumed course and speed (and range). That could be checked against what was seen through the periscope and the target data corrected for re-checking.

CHAPTER 9

WAR CONSTRUCTION

The first approach to a repeat war programme seems to have come in June 1915.[1] It included no submarines, because 'it is not foreseen that any further orders for any types below "J" class will be required'. Once the yards had completed the big war order for 'E'-class overseas boats, more 'J' and 'K'-class submarines would be laid down.[2] The Chancellor of the Exchequer approved the programme on 3 July 1915. Late that month the Australians asked for two submarines to replace the two 'E' class they had lost.[3] Nothing happened, because British submarine-building capacity was fully employed. On 22 July Controller recom-

mended new submarine construction.[4] It was now urgent, because unless more submarines were ordered the big engine-building organisation created to build up the 'E' class would run down. Controller considered the number of coastals and overseas submarines adequate (if more of the latter were needed, Controller preferred the 'G' class). That left the fleet submarines, of which only four 'K' class were on order. As for the Australians, in August First Lord (now Balfour, rather than Churchill) affirmed that all submarine output was needed for home waters.

The 'L' class was the only wartime submarine type really suited to post-war conditions. Here *L 26* and *L 27* lie alongside. Note the hump in the casing similar to that in the 'E' class. Both were minelayers, but their tubes are not visible. Only *L 27* shows the top of her saddle tank. Note the insulator at the fore end of her jumping wire, which made it usable as a wireless antenna. (RAN Naval Historical Section via Dr Josef Straczek)

The first new type of submarine ordered in wartime was the US-built 'H' class. *H 4* is shown in Italian waters in 1917–18, with a 6pdr on her foredeck. Note that she does not have the metal bridge shelter installed in many other Royal Navy submarines to facilitate crash-diving. Unlike contemporary Royal Navy submarines, these US-designed craft had folding bow planes, as is evident here. By May 1915 a pool of 6pdrs had been set up for submarines, initially seven and then twelve and thirteen guns (in November 1915 it was fifteen and later seventeen guns). In addition individual submarines were assigned these weapons: the November 1915 gun mounting list showed *E 11* plus *H 2*, *H 3* and *H 4* (i.e., Mediterranean 'H'-boats). *H 1* (the other Mediterranean 'H'-boat) was also to have had a 6pdr, but as of November 1917 it had not been fitted. (R A Burt)

British intelligence was poor; Controller wrote that 'there is no doubt that we are behind the Germans in this type of submarine and as the future of naval submarine warfare will in all probability lie with [the 'K' class] type . . . our numbers should certainly be increased . . . there should be two for each Battle Squadron, with four as spare, i.e., a total of fourteen'. This was the origin of *K 5–K 14*. In fact the Germans had never seriously considered building fleet submarines. The only oversea submarines contemplated at this time were the two which had been suspended, at Yarrow and at Scotts.

The Board approved this programme on 30 July. Controller had already ordered diesel engines so as to avoid running down the existing organisation, but so few were required for the fleet submarines that it is not clear why they were mentioned. The July programme was soon overtaken by growing concern that unless the British pressed submarine development the Germans would leave them far behind. A Submarine Design Committee was formed specifically to decide the best types to be developed. Among its surprise conclusions was that coastal submarines would be well worth building. Unfortunately it is not clear what building programmes were decided later in 1915–16.

Two of an improved 'E' class ('elongated "E" class') were ordered in February 1916, initially as *E 57* and *E 58* and then as *L 1* and *L 2*, the first of a new class. Further boats were soon ordered: *L 3–L 8* in May 1916. *L 9* (ordered August 1916) was the first of a modified class, followed by *L 10–L 33* in December 1916. *L 34–L 35* were ordered from Pembroke. Builders: Vickers (twenty-three), Cammell Laird (two), Swan Hunter (two), Denny (one), Pembroke (one), Fairfield (two) and Beardmore (one). *L 11*, *L 12*, *L 14*, *L 17* and *L 25* (all Vickers) were minelayers. *L 28–L 31* (Vickers) and *L 34–L 35* (both building at Pembroke) were cancelled 12 April 1919. Eight of the Vickers boats had been ordered as minelayers.

L 13 and *L 36–L 49* were not ordered.[5] It is not clear why, but the ordering dates suggest a decision at the end of 1916 to substitute *L 50*-class cruiser submarines. The November 1916 Programme called for twelve 'L-class' submarines, of which six were to have been built instead as *L 50*s. Orders for the new class began early in 1917. Planned initial orders were two from Armstrong and one each from Fairfield and Denny.[6] Initially the new programme would have begun with *L 51*, but apparently *L 13* was ordered to the new design as *L 50*. If, as seems likely, the whole of the November 1916 Programme was replaced by *L 50*s, that would account for twelve of the fourteen missing numbers *L 36–L 49*.

L 50–L 55 were ordered in January–February 1917, before *L 1* had run trials. *L 56–L 58* and *L 67–L 73* were ordered in April 1917 and *L 59–L 66* and *L 74* were ordered in April 1918. Builders: Armstrong (four), Cammell Laird (four), Scotts (four), Denny (three), Fairfield (five), Beardmore (three) and Swan Hunter (two). Cancellations: *L 50–L 51* (Cammell Laird), *L 57–L 58* (Fairfield), *L 59* (Beardmore), *L 60–L 61* (Cammell Laird), *L 62* (Fairfield), *L 63–L 64* (Scotts), *L 65–L 66* (Swan Hunter), *L 67–L 68* (Armstrong), *L 70* (Beardmore), *L 72* (Scotts) and *L 73–L 74* (Denny). Framing for *L 67* and *L 68* were used for the Yugoslav *Hrabri* and *Nebojsa*, completed in 1927.

In January 1918 three alternative 1919 Programmes were being considered: twenty-two 'H' or 'R' class (first delivery June 1919); twenty-two *L 50* class (first delivery October 1919); and five 'K' class (first delivery March 1920) and seventeen *L 50* class (first delivery October 1919).[7] Eight more submarines could be delivered in place of the battlecruiser *Anson*. The initial Operations Committee decision in favour of the combined 'K' and 'L' class programme was reconsidered at a 2 March 1918 meeting. DCNS pointed out that in order to provide two flotillas, each containing ten 'K'-boats, six would have to be included in the 1919 Programme, so it was recast as six 'K' class and sixteen *L 50* class.[8] Orders actually placed in April 1918 were the desired six modified 'K' class and seven 'L' class.[9]

By August 1918, pressure to build ASW vessels and to repair and build merchant ships was forcing cuts in production of larger warships, including submarines. 'It was agreed that the British Navy is better supplied with submarines than with any other class of vessel.' Work on 'H' and 'L-class submarines completing before 1 January 1919 (respectively, eleven and fifty-one) would continue, but further boats would be slowed to reduce the programme to completing two per month of either class after that, with preference for the 'L' class. 'R' and 'K'-class submarines would continue as at present. This proposal stopped work on three of the four *Hood*-class battlecruisers.[10] At this point eighty submarines were on order or building and work on forty-five of them was ordered slowed. All work on the 'M' class was stopped because they had 'no important operational value'.

In addition to all of these large submarines, late in 1916 Admiral Jellicoe pressed hard for twelve more 'H'-class submarines, which he imagined could be built in the United States and delivered without armament, which would be fitted in Canada. The Admiralty informed Jellicoe that it was impossible. Instead the twelve (*H 21–H 32*) were ordered from Vickers in January 1917, Bethlehem Steel providing engines, motors and some fittings.[11] A second batch was ordered in March 1917: six from Cammell Laird, eight from Armstrong Whitworth, four from Beardmore, two from Pembroke and two from Devonport (*H 33–H 54*). Some had British-made engines. Ten (*H 35–H 40, H 45–H 46* and *H 53–H 54*) were cancelled in October 1917 when twelve 'R'-class submarines, many of them with 'H'-class components, were ordered on an urgent basis.[12] Eight of the repeat class were still in service in the Second World War.

'H' Class

The first new British submarines of the First World War were actually an American design.[13] In 1914 Vickers essentially controlled the Electric Boat company in the United States, from which it had licensed the Holland patents.[14] In October, Charles M Schwab, president and chairman of Bethlehem Steel, visited the Admiralty to see what he could sell. Fisher was now First Sea Lord, and determined on a crash submarine programme. Could Schwab deliver submarines in six months, an unheard-of time?[15] Schwab offered to do even better if the price was right. He contracted to build twenty submarines at about twice the normal unit cost. For quick delivery, they would duplicate the 'H' class being built for the US Navy.[16] Although the US government had no problems with exporting weapons or ammunition, whole warships were another matter. Schwab was fortunate that his lawyer visited the State Department for permission while its Secretary William Jennings Bryan – a pacifist who hated all arms exports – was away.

The twenty submarines were built at the two Bethlehem Steel shipyards, Fore River in Massachusetts (twelve submarines) and Union Iron Works in San Francisco (eight). Electric Boat made some patented parts and its subsidiary the New London Ship and Engine Company (NELSECO) built the diesels. The *New York Times* broke the submarine story on 10 November.[17] When Bryan returned to Washington, he challenged the submarine contract, hinting at likely pressure in Congress from the large German-American lobby. Schwab considered the sale integral to his attempt to become the leader in supplying munitions to the Allies, but President Wilson decided to block the sale. Schwab was forced to promise to cancel the order; an attempt to change the President's mind only made Wilson more rigid.

The first ten 'H'-boats were built by Canadian Vickers using parts fabricated in the neutral United States. Determined to maintain neutrality, President Woodrow Wilson was furious, and he stopped the programme. The remaining ten boats were built by US yards and sequestered until the United States entered the war in 1917. Here *H 11*, from the later programme, lies alongside *H 8*, which had been delivered in 1915. They are recognisable by their US-style folding fore hydroplanes. The significance of the striping on the bridge fairwater of *H 8* is unknown. This photograph was taken on 3 June 1918. At that time both were probably in a new four-boat flotilla (with *H 12*; the fourth boat, *H 14*, was soon paid off) with the flagship *Vulcan* (which is not the ship in the picture). The flotilla was part of the anti-submarine force built up along the Irish coast. (David C Isby)

In Canada, Prime Minister Sir Robert Laird Borden saw cancellation as an opportunity; he could build the submarines the Admiralty wanted.[18] That gave Schwab a way out. Early in December he visited Montreal and Canadian Vickers, bringing the chief engineer of the Fore River yard. Canadian Vickers had considerable unused capacity. Despite Schwab's acceptance of Wilson's order, work went ahead at Fore River and at Groton (Electric Boat); US Navy inspectors at both plants reported that instead of being erected on the slip, parts were being shipped to an unknown destination. Schwab offered the Admiralty the submarines if he could have unrestricted use of Canadian Vickers. Little time would be lost.[19] Schwab pointed out that his costs would be considerably higher, so the Admiralty boosted the price per submarine to $600,000, while it halved bonus and penalty clauses. Delivery date was extended several months and the contract was cut to ten submarines. The first keel was laid on 11 January.

Erection of the submarines in Canada was hardly the big munitions contract Borden had envisaged, but he was in no position to complain. In the autumn of 1914 he was concerned largely with Canada's position within the Empire and therefore her voice in Empire strategy. Borden realised that participation in the war was bound up with the large orders he hoped would revive Canadian industry. It helped that only a few Bethlehem workers – highly-skilled specialists – had been brought to Canadian Vickers, while the company had hired large numbers of Canadians. The company itself was unhappy. Also, the submarine programme badly slowed progress on a large icebreaker the Canadians considered essential for winter navigation. They had sold

When numerous submarines were badly needed, the Admiralty duplicated the 'H' class, the main modification being a 21in torpedo armament. By this time the United States was in the war, so there was no problem obtaining components, such as diesels. *H 27* is shown in September 1930. *H 21–H 32* had bow planes similar to those of the earlier 'H'-boats, except that they were not tipped up.

H 28 shows the chariot bridge screen of a British-built 'H'-class submarine. Note also the windscreen and the wireless insulator (actually, a stack of insulators) at the after end of the bridge fairwater. All units of the class had the torpedo loading derrick, visible here, forward of the bridge. 'H'-class submarines from different builders could be identified by the shape of the bridge screen and by the big slots in the casing alongside the bridge fairwater in *H 43* and *H 44*. (RAN Historical Section via Dr Josef Straczek)

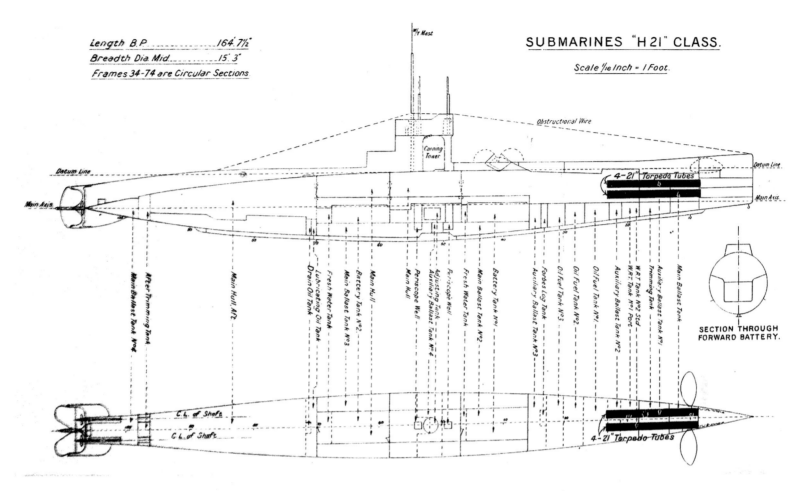

Length B.P. .... 164'.7½'
Breadth Dia Mid. .... 15'. 3'
Frames 34-74 are Circular Sections

SUBMARINES "H 21" CLASS.

Scale ⁹/₁₆ Inch = 1 Foot.

SECTION THROUGH FORWARD BATTERY.

DNC's drawing of the *H 21* class, from the end-of-war DNC history of Royal Navy submarine construction. (Author's collection)

their previous icebreaker to Russia on a war emergency basis and had justified that sale by progress on the new one. Moreover, there could be no follow-on submarine work. An attempt to promote surface warship construction fell flat, as did a Canadian proposal to build merchant ships to make up for British losses. By this time, too, Fisher's project to accelerate production of 'E'-class submarines had made Canadian-built ones far less valuable to the Admiralty. The Admiralty made no effort to gain control of the second ten submarines, but given Wilson's opposition that would surely have been hopeless.

The first of the submarines, *H 1* through *H 10*, was launched late in April, nearly four months ahead of schedule.[20] *H 1* through *H 4* went directly to the Dardanelles, the others to the coastal patrol and the North Sea.[21] They seem to have been the first submarines to have crossed the Atlantic, a year before the German cargo submarine *Deutschland* visited Baltimore to be proclaimed as the first across.

The second series (*H 11–H 20*) remained at Fore River until the United States entered the First World War. To ensure that they could not escape, US naval officers were aboard during their sea trials in September 1915. Ultimately the Royal Navy received only *H 11*, *H 12*, *H 14* and *H 15*. The other six went to Chile in payment for various ships taken over by the Royal Navy.[22] After the war, *H 14* and *H 15* went to Canada, which redesignated them *CH 14* and *CH 15*. Others were exported after Bryan resigned in June 1915 to be replaced by his pro-Ally deputy Robert Lansing.[23]

Unlike the British coastals, the 'H' class had single hulls. They were 150ft 3½in long, displacing 359 tons surfaced and 467 tons submerged. On the surface they were somewhat slower than their

British equivalents: 480 BHP for 13 knots, but faster submerged (620 BHP for 11 knots at the 1-hour rate, 320 BHP for 5 knots submerged for 6 hours). Estimated endurance was 2000nm at 13 knots and 2800nm at 11 knots. The Royal Navy found these submarines such excellent underwater craft that their stern form was adopted for the later 'L' class.[24] The main early modification in British service seems to have been to add wireless.[25]

Repeat 'H'-class submarines were ordered in 1917. The most important change was to substitute four 21in bow tubes for the

H 33 shows the revised bow planes fitted to later units of the 'H' class. The hump aft is the escape hatch for the Davis Submarine Escape Apparatus (DSEA), fitted in 1933–4. (Silberstein via US Naval Institute)

original four 18in. The boats had to be lengthened by 15ft and their surface displacement increased to 440 tons (500 tons submerged). Vickers boats used engines (two 240 BHP), motors and some fittings supplied by Bethlehem Steel. The repeat boats had machinery made in England, the engines being of US design. Their motors were slightly different (310 BHP for one hour, 160 BHP continuously, fed by two 55-cell batteries).

Submarine Design Committee

In 1915, with a large submarine programme underway, a Submarine Design Committee was convened to decide future policy.[26] The first meeting (8 September 1915) considered six alternative types: (1) coastal, (2) patrol, (3) fleet submarine, (4) cruiser submarine, (5) minelayer, and (6) monitor. The first two already existed and the value of (3) would be gauged after the first-of-class (*K 3*) trials. Two 'E-boats were already being converted to minelayers.[27] The cruiser (4) was considered feasible, but it would have few targets. A long-range submarine of this basic type would, however, be invaluable in connection with a blockade.

That left only (6), the monitor, for near-term construction. It would mount a single 12in gun, in effect substituting for torpedoes. It would be used for surprise attack, the submarine popping up and firing. It may be considered the very distant ancestor of submarine-launched anti-ship missiles. During 1915 British submarines sometimes missed attacks as the enemy suddenly changed course.[28] According to the 1921 Admiralty Technical History, 'it is a debatable point whether a spread salvo of four torpedoes fired on the beam of an enemy ship will be more likely to give better results than a heavy shell fired as the attacker rises in the wake of the target – a shell fired at close range and with no deflection'.

A monitor submarine could also shell places inaccessible to British surface ships. Unfortunately only in one place along the German coast was it possible to submerge within range of Heligoland. At the distance at which 12in fire would be effective, it would be relatively easy for the shore defences to put the boat out of action. 'On the other

Lying alongside *L 23* and an 'S'-class submarine, *H 33* and *H 49* show how much smaller the 'H' class was. (John Lambert collection)

hand, it is quite possible that the Germans are working on this problem and, unless something is done towards getting a design ready, we may find ourselves thus placed at a disadvantage.' The Committee rejected a 12in gun in favour of a good 7.5in gun (with air spotting) with a range of 7,000 to 8,000 yds. It envisaged two alternatives: (a) with a low-velocity gun firing a high-capacity shell and (b) high velocity gun (projectile about 200lbs), two guns to be carried with armour. Once these drawings were ready it would be possible to consider how the boat could be used.

The Committee envisaged a continuous demand for coastal submarines after the war, as they were the answer to the threat of enemy bombardment and raiding. They would also protect bases abroad. Large numbers would be needed, their size held down to limit their cost. The Committee asked DNC to prepare a design which could replace 'C'-class submarines. It would be about the size of the current coastals (about 500 tons), with a surface speed of 13 to 14 knots, a single hull (for low cost and ease of construction) and a 12pdr. No design survives.

The Committee divided patrol (formerly called overseas) submarines into slow ('E' and 'G' classes) and fast ('J' class) types, the latter being held in harbour until needed at a strategical position. Designs for both should be prepared. Again, these designs appear not to have survived, but the 'L' class seems to be the slower patrol submarine envisaged.

The cruiser submarine was more threat than promise: if the enemy had a few with good habitability and long endurance, he could do much harm in such places as the River Plate, interfering with meat and grain ships. Guns on board merchant ships would not solve the problem, because guns without highly trained crews would achieve little. DNC pointed out that if the speed of a 'K'-class submarine were cut by 4 knots, the hull might be expanded considerably (without adding length, hence without costing handiness), making for better habitability and greater endurance. The current 5000nm endurance at 10 knots could be doubled. DNC was asked for a design with sufficient battery power for 24 hours submerged (and for fair speed for 12 hours), with good habitability, with two bow and four broadside torpedo tubes (but more torpedoes per tube than a 'K') and with maximum possible gun armament. Gun alternatives would be (a) large-calibre lightweight gun, (b) 6in ordinary-velocity gun and (c) 6in low-velocity gun.

DNC d'Eyncourt's papers include an undated summary of designs in hand, which seems to have been prepared for the Committee.[29] DNC began with a 500-ton coastal submarine which would be similar to the 'H' class, with a single hull and light superstructure. 'Commodore (S) wishes the form of "H" preserved as far as possible as it frees itself so quickly of the seas. Although the form is not quite so good for surface speed it is probably somewhat better for underwater speed. These vessels are to be armed with a 12pdr.'

A second new design was a modified 'G'-class submarine made more habitable, the stern tube being eliminated; the submarine would have four rather than two bow tubes. 'A proposal was discussed with Commodore (S) to do away with the broadside tubes as this would leave more room for accommodation but it was decided to retain them in view of their great military value and if the accommodation cannot otherwise be improved the vessel is to be somewhat lengthened.' Although DNC was referring to the 'G' rather than to the 'E' class, this seems to be the origin of the 'L' ('elongated E') class.

A third was a 'J'-class submarine modified for steam power (two

steam engines and one diesel). Any space saved would go into habitability; any weight saved would go into fuel. Nothing seems to have come of this project.

A fourth was a cruiser submarine based on the 'K' design, with reduced steam power but increased motor power for higher submerged speed. As a cruiser, this submarine would need a more powerful gun armament (DNC suggested two 6in).[30] Nothing came of this project, but it seems clear that the cruiser idea survived (see below). The idea probably explains the decision to arm 'K'-class submarines with 5.5in guns.

Fifth was the monitor, described in greater detail than the others because it was of more immediate interest. DNC wanted to hold to 'K'-class length (320ft) but to increase beam to 40ft and draft to 15ft. Displacement would be 2500 to 3000 tons surfaced and 4000 tons submerged. DNC expected to retain steam power but to reduce it to 5000 SHP on two shafts (plus a 1000 BHP diesel on the centre shaft). That would give 19 to 20 knots. Submerged speed would be 9 to 10 knots (2000 BHP). Armament would be either two 7.5in guns or one 12in gun forward and one 4in or 6in gun aft, plus four bow torpedo tubes. 'This latter design will take more time owing to the difficulty of getting a satisfactory arrangement for the armament which is greatly in excess of anything that has hitherto been fitted in a submarine.' This was clearly the beginning of the 'M' class, but the design changed considerably before it was completed.

On 18 October the Committee met again to examine DNC's sketch designs.[31] It recommended approval of the coastal design, which was powered by two six-cylinder Vickers diesels. The cruiser was based on the 'K' class, but reduced to 20 knots; it was armed with two 6in 'wet' guns and four bow and four broadside torpedo tubes. Like the 'K', it had steam machinery, but in this case only one boiler (but two turbines) producing 5500 SHP. Battery power would be a third greater than in the 'K' class. Surface radius would be 2700nm at 15 knots and 10,000nm at 10 knots. There was no armour other than an inch on the conning tower. A proposal for a more powerful gun was rejected. However, the Committee wanted greater elevation (the full 30° vice 15°) and more ammunition (100 vice 50 rounds per gun).

The Committee also saw no point in retaining a steam plant; if possible it wanted the twelve-cylinder 'J'-class engine instead. The monitor showed a 12in/25 gun rather than the 7.5in the Committee had favoured. There was no general agreement as to functions. Commodore (S) favoured the heavier gun DNC was asked for two alternative designs, one with a single 12in gun and one with two, fore and aft.[32]

Somewhat later DNC proposed a 30-knot cruiser.[33] Commodore (S) wrote on 16 May 1916 that this type of ship had been discussed by the Committee, which was loath to jump to such dimensions before the 'K' class had been tested. The submariners needed experience with handling the long 'K'-boats. DNC answered that the control of the 'J' class had been most encouraging, but inevitably there would be surprises.

By late 1916 the Committee had morphed into the Submarine Development Committee, which reported on DNC's 'L'-class cruiser (see below). Unfortunately its papers appear to have been lost.

'L' Class

It is not clear when the decision was taken to redesign the 'E' class as the 'Elongated "E" Class', soon to be renamed the 'L' class.[34] The first two were ordered from Vickers in February 1916 as *E 57* and *E 58*, which were soon renamed *L 1* and *L 2*. They had much the same

The 'L' class was conceived as an improved 'E'. Photographed in December 1917, *L 2* shows her 3in 20 cwt HA gun forward (on a wet rather than a retractable mounting). Submarines of this class were soon fitted with gun access trunks and with raised 4in guns specifically to attack surfaced U-boats, but *L 2* and *L 7* seem not to have been modified until after the war. The 3in guns were apparently mounted on board *L 1–L 16* (as late as November 1917, *L 10* had no gun at all, the minelayer *L 14* had no gun, and there was no *L 13*). (Dr David Stevens)

L 5 photographed before her 3in gun was mounted. The white stripes fore and aft were presumably an air recognition marking. (RAN Naval Historical Service via Dr Josef Straczek)

saddle-tank hull form as the 'E' class, with a wedge-shaped stern like that of the 'H' class.[35] Planes and rudders aft were abaft the propellers. The two forward planes were of the drowned type. All vent valves were telemotor-controlled from the control room. Subdivision was much better than in the 'E' class: nine rather than three main bulkheads. Later boats had an additional bulkhead abaft the bow tubes to protect against mines. Accommodation was much better than in the 'E' class, the longer (higher-capacity) battery having a much longer accommo-

dation space above it. Twelve-cylinder diesels (as in the 'J' class) replaced the eight-cylinder diesels of the 'E' class. According to the DNC history, this change was suggested by Third Sea Lord Admiral Tudor. The battery was also enlarged, to 50 per cent larger than in an 'E'-class submarine (336 cells) and the motors enlarged to 1600 BHP rather than 840 BHP. To increase underwater endurance, a 20 BHP 'creep' motor was placed to drive each shaft via gearing.

Initially the torpedo battery doubled the bow battery of the 'E'

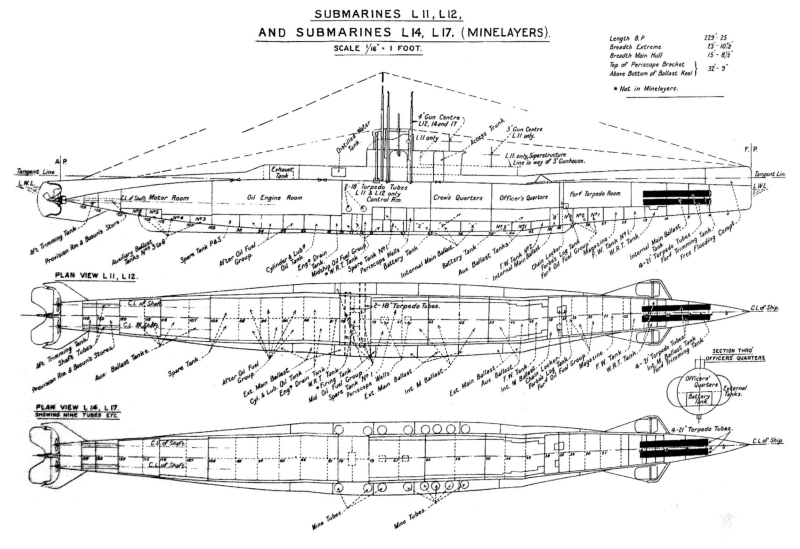

SUBMARINES L II, L I2,
AND SUBMARINES L I4, L I7. (MINELAYERS).
SCALE 1/16" = 1 FOOT.

Length B.P	229'·25
Breadth Extreme	23'·10½'
Breadth Main Hull	15'·8½'
Top of Periscope Bracket	
Above Bottom of Ballast Keel	32'·9'

* Not in Minelayers.

DNC's drawing of some 'L'-class submarines, from the end-of-war DNC history of Royal Navy submarine development. (Author's collection)

class (to four 18in) and omitted the single stern tube, for a total of six torpedo tubes. After the first eight, the bow tubes were made 21in, the boats being lengthened by 8ft. Gun armament was to have been two 3in 12 cwt, which was replaced by one 3in HA gun in a retractable mounting. After trials these weapons were given up in favour of a 4in gun at the bridge level in front of the bridge screen, with an access trunk for quick manning.

On December 1917 trials the lead boat made 17.2 knots rather than the 16.5 to 17 knots expected, although submerged speed was 10.8 knots compared to the expected 11 to 11.5 knots. DNC attributed the lower submerged speed to the presence of a fixed bridge screen about 5½ft high, which was not in the original design. The boat could crash dive to 30ft when running at 10 knots in 1½ minutes. Large planes made it possible to maintain full submerged control at 1.5 knots. An accidental deep (300ft) dive by *L 2* caused few problems. DNC d'Eyncourt's submarine file included a note showing how rugged *L 2* was.[36]

According to the Admiralty Technical History (1921), the 'L' class was 'certainly the best type of patrol submarine in existence'.[37] When he wrote to Admiral Beatty asking for 'L'-class submarines, Captain (S) of 10th Flotilla argued that their higher speed of 17 knots would be of

great value in getting them to the scene of a fleet action, whether at base or on patrol, particularly the latter; they should prove good for patrol work in deep water and in the open sea; they would have the advantage of four bow tubes for ASW or anti-fleet work. Given their speed, they could run down enemy submarines. Their size would make it possible for them to maintain their speed in bad weather.[38] On 15 November 1917 the Admiralty wrote Beatty that the 'L' class joining the Grand Fleet would form a new flotilla intended specifically for the submarine patrols in the North Sea. The Grand Fleet would receive the boats with 21in bow tubes.

When Controller met CinC Grand Fleet (Jellicoe) at Scapa Flow on 12 October 1916, he said that Board policy was to lay down long-range 'cruiser' submarines after completing the current 'L' class. They would be armed with two 5.5in guns and be capable of operating in distant seas.[39] They would take 18 months to build. Jellicoe was interested but objected that submarines were needed now, not in mid-1918. Controller also told Jellicoe that 'E'-class submarines were being converted into minelayers capable of operating near U-boat bases: *E 45* and *E 46* were in commission and *E 51* was due in December 1916, to be followed by *E 34* in February 1917 and *E 44* probably in April. However, the 'E' class was somewhat 'extravagant', as it carried so few

L 1 had the raised 4in gun without the bulwark erected around it in most 'L'-boats. The structure below the gun contained a watertight access trunk, through which the gun crew could rapidly climb as a submarine surfaced, for a quick attack on a surfaced U-boat caught, it was hoped, by surprise. Removal of 3in guns from *L 1* and *L 2* (and replacement by 4in guns) was ordered late in 1917, and the remainder (except *L 7*, *L 10* [which was soon sunk], *L 12*, and *L 14*) on 18 February 1918. The rest of the class amounted to *L 17–L 27* and *L 33*, of which the minelayers (*L 17*, *L 24–L 27*) initially had no guns. Of these, *L 14* and *L 17* were given guns and raised platforms as part of the anti-submarine programme, but *L 24* and *L 25* retained their original bridge fairwaters. *L 26* and *L 27* had (and retained through their careers) 4in guns on raised gun platforms with bulwarks. Others in similar configuration to *L 1* were *L 3*, *L 6*, *L 9*, *L 10* and *L 15*. *L 6* was later fitted with a shield revolving with the gun. *L 14* and *L 17* had gun shields with sloping backs, turning with the gun (their guns were removed altogether in 1920 and 1920–1, respectively). In 1924 *L 1* was modified with the fixed gun shield standard on most 'L'-boats. (Abrahams photo via Dr Josef Straczek)

L 15 was similar to *L 9* shown opposite. (Abrahams of Devonport via Dr Josef Straczek)

L 22 shows the standard anti-submarine modification, in which a 4in gun was raised to bridge level and protected by a fixed bulwark. Only *L 24* and *L 25* (minelayers) never had 4in guns. (Dr David Stevens)

mines per ton; the 'L' class would be even worse. Chief of Staff wrote in November 1916 that unless submarine minelayers suffered heavy losses, the numbers already available should be enough. 'What is wanted is not more minelayers but more places to lay mines.'[40]

D'Eyncourt's design notebook shows the original cruiser design.[41] His papers include a 24 November 1916 paper on an alternative: an 'L'-class submarine cruiser designed at Controller's request.[42] It introduced a duck-tail stern (as in the 'J' and 'K' classes), adding some reserve buoyancy and reducing resistance at 18 knots by about 400 BHP. Shaft lines were lowered to provide mess space over the motors and also a mess space aft. For better immersion, the propellers were supported by shaft brackets, as in a surface ship. The run aft was finer. The improved habitability would have been important in a long-endurance cruiser. The bow matched that of the existing 'L' class, with four 21in tubes. Broadside tubes were eliminated. Gun armament increased to two 5.5in guns rather than the single 3in HA gun of the original 'L' class. D'Eyncourt proposed to boost the twelve-cylinder 'L'-class engine to 1600 BHP by adopting lightweight pistons. Estimated cost was £200,000 (as for an 'L') and building time was 12–15 months. D'Eyncourt proposed to substitute the new type for six projected repeat 'K' class. This paper was the origin of the *L 50* class, which did have two guns (4in rather than 5.5in), the new stern and no broadside tubes, but also had additional bow tubes.

The 'L'-class cruiser was reviewed at a 29 November 1916 meeting of the Submarine Development Committee.[43] The Committee concurred with the design except that Commodore (S) strongly wanted six rather than four bow tubes (DNC was to provide at least five, if could not provide the desired six) and the proposed two 5.5in guns. The Committee wanted a more flexible design which could accommodate alternative batteries: one 5.5in and one 3in HA gun or the original two 5.5in. If possible, the packing rings (on which guns were mounted) should be arranged to take either 5.5in or 3in guns. The

L 9 shows her two wireless masts, her raised night periscope and her open 4in mounting. The visible wire aft is the stay to the mast; the aerial strung between the masts is nearly invisible, except for the insulators at its ends near the masts. The short mast is a signal mast, forward of the three periscopes. (Abrahams of Devonport via Dr Josef Straczek)

Committee also considered the 5000nm radius of action insufficient, but that could be more than doubled by using ballast tanks for fuel. It was not considered necessary to fit long-range (Poulsen) W/T, as these ships would not work with the fleet. The first would be *L 51*. DNC submitted the six-tube sketch design on 9 December 1916; it had six spare 21in torpedoes as well as those in the tubes. To accommodate the two extra tubes the submarine had to grow by about 20 tons. The main complication in the modified design was that provisions to load the two lower tubes and the stowage of their reloads made it difficult to provide shell stowage and a magazine for the forward gun. DNC

L 27 shows a voice pipe connecting her gun with her bridge, a characteristic feature of British interwar and Second World War submarines. Its downward extension was a flexible pipe with a head piece. The continuation of the jumping wire can be seen above it. The raised mast is both signal and wireless mast (by this time this submarine, at least, no longer had two separate wireless masts fore and aft). At sea the jumping wires and the rather elaborate loop above the bridge fairwater were the wireless antennas; in harbour a higher antenna could be strung from the signal mast. This photograph was taken in 1926. She and *L 26*, both minelayers, were recognisable by the large sponsons under their bridges. (RAN Naval Historical Section via Dr Josef Straczek)

As completed, *L 69* shows the pair of 4in guns of the *L 50* class, at both ends of an enlarged bridge fairwater. In five ships the after gun was later replaced by a sonar dome. In 1927, of seven *L 50*-class submarines in service, only *L 52* and *L 53* still had both guns. *L 53* lost one of hers in 1935, *L 52* having been scrapped that year. (RAN Naval Historical Section via Dr Josef Straczek)

pointed out that his problem would be much simplified if the forward position carried a retractable 3in HA gun, the after one carrying the 5.5in. The axis of the 3in gun would be about 5ft above that of the earlier 5.5in and it could therefore operate in rougher seas. Chief of Staff liked the new design; 'beam tubes . . . have not proved so generally useful as those in the bow and on the whole the addition of two 21in bow tubes . . . is considered more than compensation for the sacrifice of two 18in beam tubes . . . A great gain is made in accommodation'. He was also willing to sacrifice one of the two 5.5in guns,

as 'there is no evidence at present to call imperatively for two 5.5in guns and the want of a HA gun *has* been experienced'.

The new class was much what D'Eyncourt had offered the previous autumn, except that two more 21in tubes were added in the bow and the gun armament was two 4in. These boats had eleven main transverse bulkheads. Engines, motors and the battery were as in the earlier 'L' class – the boosted twelve-cylinder engine had not materialised. However, there was provision for carrying extra oil fuel in some of the main ballast tanks, for a total of 100 tons rather than 80 tons.

M 3 shows her huge 12in gun and her 3in HA gun aft. (RAN Naval Historical Section via Dr Josef Straczek)

A loose sheet in the d'Eyncourt file was probably prepared in 1917. Qualities of what appears to have been *L 50* were long range (10,000nm) for reconnaissance, a speed of 15 knots if armed with torpedoes and 12 knots if with mines, a communications mast for 500nm W/T range, a 4in gun and tropical accommodation. The approximate date is given by a note mentioning the 'R' class, as a fast underwater type.

US submarine designer E S Land, later Chief of the Bureau of Construction and Repair and then chief of the Maritime Administration, said immediately after the war that 'boat for boat I consider the *L 50* class of the British design to be the equal if not the superior of the U-boat. If the engines of the two were traded, the British boat would completely outclass the German boat. The British boats are better designs so far as the design of submarines is concerned.'[44]

'M' Class

The 'M'-class submarine monitor seems to have been the first fruit of the Submarine Design Committee. Armament was one 12in/40 Mk IX gun (taken from an old battleship), one 3in HA gun and four torpedo tubes. The big gun could elevate to 20° and could train 20° (10° on either bow). Its muzzle carried a watertight tampion controlled from the loading chamber. Like a torpedo tube, it would be aimed using the whole submarine, although in this case training offered some degree of correction. The gun was 'wet', and it could fire properly after a week on patrol, when the submarine sometimes dived to 100ft. After seeing a target at periscope depth (28ft), the submarine could reach the surface in 25 seconds, fire and return to periscope depth in 15 seconds. One of the two main periscopes incorporated a rangefinder and in addition to the usual pair of periscopes a third was for gun control with its eyepiece in a compartment behind the loading chamber. Surface seakeeping was particularly important, as was handiness (the gun could not traverse very far).[45] Fear that the shock of firing would damage batteries proved groundless.

To insure against the possible failure of the gun, the ship had to be adapted to patrol work. Apart from the gun, the submarine had good underwater qualities. *M 1* could dive in 90 seconds, which was considered quick for so large a boat. To do that, she had remote-controlled scoop valves in her main ballast tanks just below the waterline, as well as additional Kingstons. Construction was similar to that of the 'J' class and the power plant was that of the 'L' class, with the same auxiliary motors geared to the shafts.

The design may have been begun in November 1915; it was essentially complete about June 1916.[46] Ordered beginning in February 1916, the monitors were initially referred to as the Special 'K' class and were designated *K 18–K 21*. They were renamed *M 1–M 4* on 17

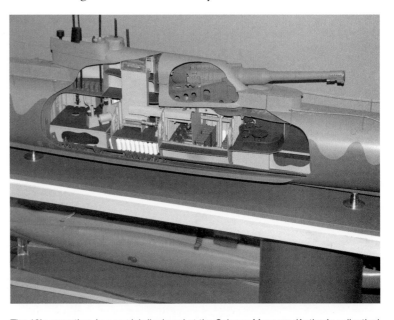

The 12in mounting, in a model displayed at the Science Museum. (Author's collection)

M 1 in camouflage, as delivered. The 3in HA gun abaft her bridge has been retracted into the casing. (John Lambert collection)

DNC's drawing of the 'M' class, from his end-of-war history of Royal Navy submarine development. (Author's collection)

April 1918. The first pair were designed with 18in torpedo tubes, the second pair with 21in. The first two had open bridges, but *M 3* had a cab bridge giving greater shelter.

Construction was initially delayed for fear that the Germans would build their own submarine monitors, which would do far more damage to the British than the British could inflict. However, construction was later accelerated and *M 1* entered service in mid-1918. Trial speed was initially 14.7 knots, but the measured mile involved (Stokes Bay) was shallow for this size ship and with new propellers 16 knots was expected.

The gun was never used operationally and any idea of using a gun as a torpedo substitute died after the war. However, large submarines with good underwater qualities proved useful, because they could usefully be converted for other test purposes – *M 2* became in effect a submersible aircraft carrier and *M 3* a minelayer.

'R' Class

The one wartime type not considered by the Submarine Design Committee was one specialised for attacking submarines. In May 1917 DNC proposed a special ASW submarine with a high submerged speed. His design showed four 18in bow tubes and an underwater speed of 13.5–14 knots; it was rejected. However, Commodore (S) was interested and DNC continued to develop the design. On 28 August 1917 DASD passed a proposal for an anti-submarine submarine to ACNS.[47] Its author, Commander George B Lewis, was then commanding the 5th Flotilla of coastal patrol submarines. He argued that high surface speed and long-range guns were not very useful against U-boats. Instead he wanted high underwater speed (12–15 knots) backed by a large battery and a low-powered cruising motor to give large submerged endurance at low, quiet speed. Eight 14in bow tubes capable of nearly simultaneous discharge should be backed if possible by two tubes on each broadside. A single quick-manning 4in semi-automatic gun should

fold down underwater to minimise underwater resistance. Listening gear would comprise a complete outfit of plate hydrophones, a directional hydrophone in a streamline casing well forward and a Nash 'Fish' hydrophone of directional type towed astern, capable of being retracted into a casing aft when submerged. Engines should be able to charge the big battery in six hours. The hydrophones would indicate not only the direction of a target but also would permit a good estimate of range if the target was nearby. The submarine would use her high burst speed to get close enough to fire a torpedo salvo. Then she would quietly surface and open gunfire. If the enemy chose to dive, the submarine would try to stay in touch using her hydrophones,

possibly obtaining opportunities for ramming or torpedoing him whilst submerged. A comparatively light blow on the stern of a submarine has a very good chance of damaging his hydroplane or vertical rudders and thus put him out of action as a submarine . . . a case actually occurred of one of our 'E' class, whilst diving, firing a torpedo at and missing a submarine of the early UB type and then overtaking it submerged and successfully torpedoing it. The submarine was on passage and her speed estimated at 6 to 7 knots.

Commodore (S) Hall wrote on 3 September that saw no point in a new 12-knot submarine armed with 14in torpedoes because all current submarines could already make 10–12 knots submerged and were armed with 21in torpedoes. However, 14–15 knots would be quite worthwhile. He had been working with DNC for some time on such a vessel, which very nearly met Commander Lewis' requirements. It had six 14in bow tubes, but could not accommodate any beam tubes. It also had two quick-manning 4in guns. This submarine was about 160ft long, with a single 300 BHP engine and two electric motors totalling 1200 HP submerged. DNC hoped for 14 knots and a tank

The anti-submarine submarine *R 7* as completed. The structure forward of the tall bridge fairwater was to have supported a 4in gun, which was never fitted. (John Lambert collection)

trial was scheduled for that week; DNC was currently trying to get 15 knots.

Submerged speed depended heavily on minimising wetted surface. Putting too much into the design – beam tubes, Poulsen W/T, etc – would push up the length and cut speed, to the point where it would be an uncomfortable 'H'-boat. It had to be a very simple, cheap vessel, hence probably quicker to build than any previous submarine. To do that it had to accept low surface speed and poor charging qualities – if six hours' charging time was vital, it would need a more powerful engine or even two engines and would become too large. 'If the vessel is worth while at all as an anti-submarine one, *everything* should be sacrificed to the qualities that will bring success in anti-submarine attack.' Hall wanted two guns because when dashing in at high underwater speed the boat would be unable to use her periscope; if she had only one gun it might not bear when the submarine burst through the surface. A four-torpedo salvo might be enough – the rationale for six was hitting at greater range.

A design was submitted to the Board on 27 September.[48] It showed six 14in torpedo tubes and two 4in guns, as proposed slightly earlier. Commodore (S) wrote that if better results were to be obtained in submarine vs submarine warfare, this design was the best means of gaining them. According to CNS (First Sea Lord), the Naval Staff considered 15 knots submerged speed of the greatest value, 'which will be increased immensely if the boat could be built within a year . . . it may be possible to alter some of the later "H" class to this design'. Controller told the Board that if the single-engine design was adhered to, if there was no delay in producing the design of the new torpedo tubes and if the submarine had priority over the cruiser *Hawkins* building at Chatham, ten could be delivered within twelve months of the decision being given. To do that, eight 'H'-class boats had to be cancelled and eight of the new type substituted; another four would be built at Chatham. By early October the twelve submarines had been ordered.[49] An account of a 2 October Admiralty Conference shows that by this time the 14in torpedoes had been abandoned in favour of 18in (which eliminated the problem of a new torpedo tube design); gun armament was 'two 4in guns (probably)'. Other details matched those given to the Board the previous week.

Admiral Sims, the US Navy commander in European waters, who had good access to the Admiralty, reported home that statistics showed that British submarines had accounted for as many enemy submarines as any other type of ship engaged in ASW.[50] Submarine attacks on U-boats usually failed because the attacker was too close when the U-boat was spotted. Since the U-boat often made 10 to 12 knots on the surface, the submerged attacker generally could not hit unless she was

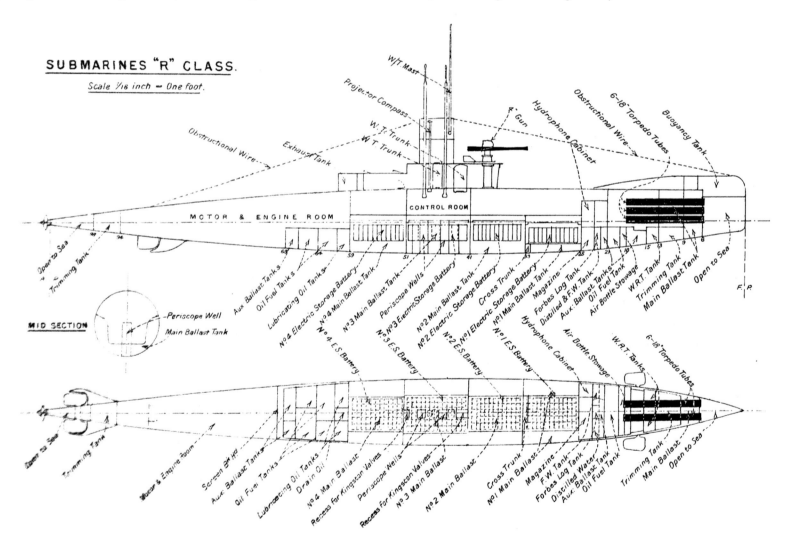

DNC's drawing of the 'R' class, from his end-of-war history of British submarine development. Note the 4in gun and the extra batteries. (Author's collection)

almost directly on the enemy's track. Once the ASW submarine spotted a target, she had to reach an attacking position as quickly as possible. To hit, she needed the widest possible torpedo spread. To assist in her submerged attack, she needed the most complete possible hydrophone array. She might even rely entirely on her hydrophones, so that she would not have to show a telltale periscope. Each of the 4in guns would have a special watertight trunk nearby accommodating its two-man gun crew. As soon as the U-boat was sighted through the periscope, the men would go into the tubes, so that they could jump to the guns as soon as the submarine broke the surface; saving even a few seconds was considered vital in such a surprise attack.

The underwater speed attained was unequalled in the Royal Navy until after the Second World War. Model tests had shown that for minimum underwater resistance the submarine had to have what Sims called a fish-shaped form, with maximum beam about one-third of the length from the bow. From there the lines tapered to a very small diameter at the stern, so the hull could not accommodate motors of the necessary size on two shafts. To reduce underwater drag there was no superstructure abaft the bridge and what might later be called the sail itself was minimised. Shaft brackets and similar sources of resistance were eliminated, the propeller simply emerging from the after end of the pressure hull, as in the 'H' and 'L' classes.[51] Hence the choice of a single shaft driven by two motors in tandem. Model tests also showed that there was considerably less resistance when the boat submerged to 16ft than to only 10ft (it was a little over 500 EHP at 16ft but 70 EHP more at 10ft). To make that possible the submarine had abnormally long periscopes, much of whose length inevitably was

above the superstructure. Experiments having shown that the periscope would vibrate badly with an unsupported length over 8ft 6in, the submarines had a fairwater, about 10 or 12ft high, surrounding its periscopes. For better seakeeping, there was a high false bow. There was practically no bridge. Initially it was assumed that the submarine would have only a small steering wheel or steering stand in the open on the superstructure.

In addition to the usual planes, these submarines had a set of emergency planes amidships, which could bring the boat level should it dive at a steep angle while submerged. The foreplanes were non-housing.

Model tests showed that the submarine required about the same power for 15 knots surfaced or submerged, but she had only a small diesel (as in the 'H' class, 240 BHP) and two large (600 BHP each) electric motors. On diesel power she would make 9.5 to 10 knots (she could make 15 knots on the surface on batteries, but full battery power was for only one hour). The big motors were supplied by oversized 'J'-class cells (220 of them). There was also a 30 BHP creep motor abaft the two main motors. It was fitted directly on the shaft rather than geared to it, as in the 'L', L 50 and 'M' classes. Not surprisingly, at a 2 October 1917 builders' conference, Vickers was told that these submarines should have precedence over 'L'-class submarines not yet laid down and should be completed within eight months.

The only submarine of this type to meet a U-boat was R 7. She closed at full speed for 20 minutes at 60ft and attained the ideal firing position right ahead of the target, but at the last minute the U-boat changed course to avoid a steamer.[52]

R 4 in July 1929. The dome forward of the bridge on the gun support is a directional hydrophone. (US Naval Institute)

HM SUBMARINES *M 1* AND *M 2*. (Drawn by John Lambert)

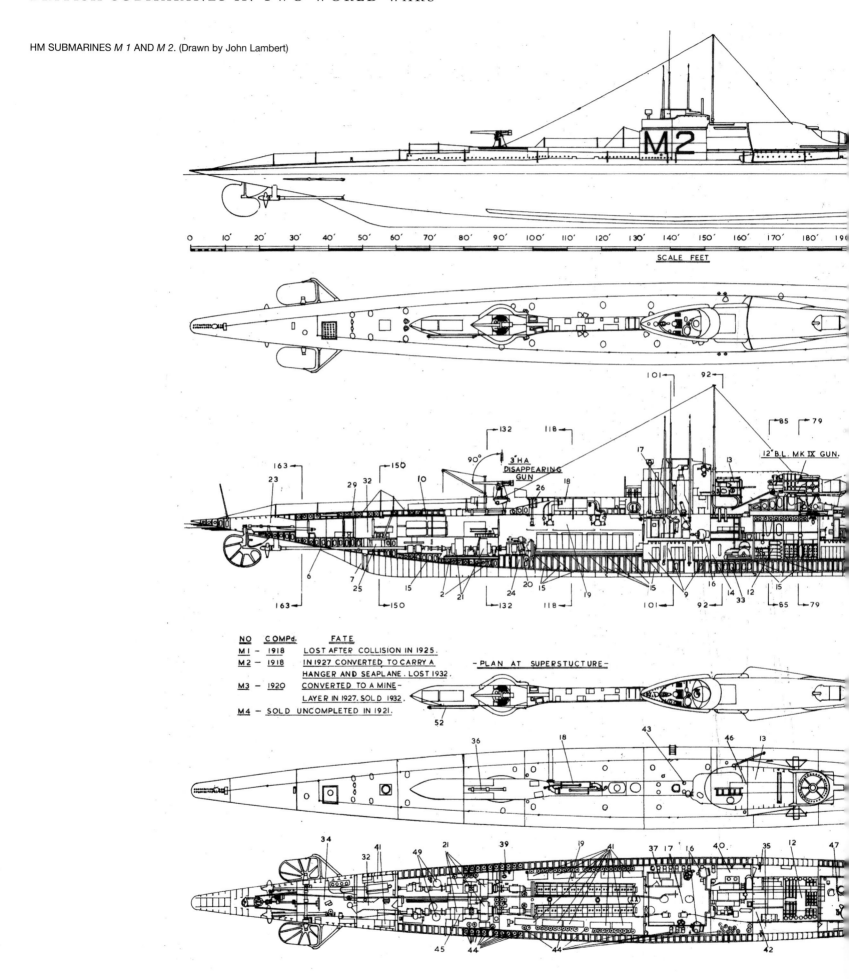

SCALE FEET

3"HA
DISAPPEARING
GUN

90°

12"B.L. MK IX GUN.

NO	COMPd.	FATE
M1 –	1918	LOST AFTER COLLISION IN 1925.
M2 –	1918	IN 1927 CONVERTED TO CARRY A HANGER AND SEAPLANE. LOST 1932.
M3 –	1920	CONVERTED TO A MINE-LAYER IN 1927. SOLD 1932.
M4 –		SOLD UNCOMPLETED IN 1921.

—PLAN AT SUPERSTUCTURE—

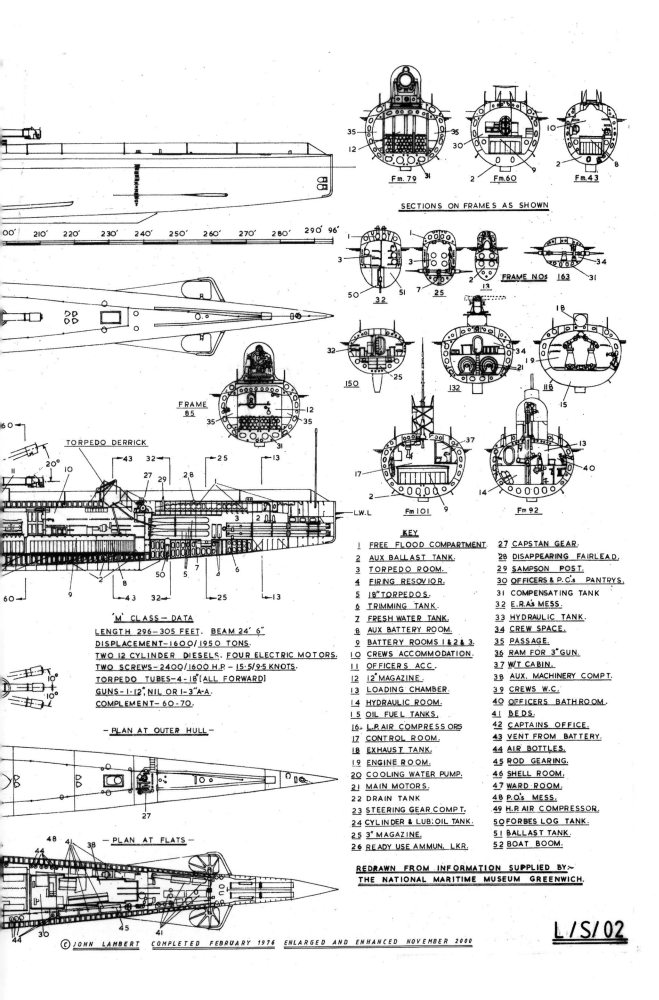

Fm.79   Fm.60   Fm.43

SECTIONS ON FRAMES AS SHOWN

FRAME NOS 163

FRAME 85

TORPEDO DERRICK

Fm 101   Fm 92

L.W.L

KEY

1	FREE FLOOD COMPARTMENT.	27	CAPSTAN GEAR.
2	AUX BALLAST TANK.	28	DISAPPEARING FAIRLEAD.
3	TORPEDO ROOM.	29	SAMPSON POST.
4	FIRING RESOVIOR.	30	OFFICERS & P.C's PANTRYS.
5	18"TORPEDOS.	31	COMPENSATING TANK
6	TRIMMING TANK.	32	E.R.A's MESS.
7	FRESH WATER TANK.	33	HYDRAULIC TANK.
8	AUX BATTERY ROOM.	34	CREW SPACE.
9	BATTERY ROOMS 1 & 2 & 3.	35	PASSAGE.
10	CREWS ACCOMMODATION.	36	RAM FOR 3" GUN.
11	OFFICERS ACC.	37	W/T CABIN.
12	12" MAGAZINE.	38	AUX. MACHINERY COMPT.
13	LOADING CHAMBER.	39	CREWS W.C.
14	HYDRAULIC ROOM.	40	OFFICERS BATHROOM.
15	OIL FUEL TANKS.	41	BEDS.
16	L.P. AIR COMPRESSORS	42	CAPTAINS OFFICE.
17	CONTROL ROOM.	43	VENT FROM BATTERY.
18	EXHAUST TANK.	44	AIR BOTTLES.
19	ENGINE ROOM.	45	ROD GEARING.
20	COOLING WATER PUMP.	46	SHELL ROOM.
21	MAIN MOTORS.	47	WARD ROOM.
22	DRAIN TANK.	48	P.O's MESS.
23	STEERING GEAR COMPT.	49	H.P AIR COMPRESSOR.
24	CYLINDER & LUB. OIL TANK.	50	FORBES LOG TANK.
25	3" MAGAZINE.	51	BALLAST TANK.
26	READY USE AMMUN. LKR.	52	BOAT BOOM.

'M' CLASS — DATA

LENGTH 296-305 FEET. BEAM 24' 6"
DISPLACEMENT-1600/1950 TONS.
TWO 12 CYLINDER DIESELS. FOUR ELECTRIC MOTORS.
TWO SCREWS-2400/1600 H.P - 15·5/9·5 KNOTS.
TORPEDO TUBES-4-18"[ALL FORWARD]
GUNS-1-12", NIL OR 1-3"A·A.
COMPLEMENT-60-70.

— PLAN AT OUTER HULL —

— PLAN AT FLATS —

REDRAWN FROM INFORMATION SUPPLIED BY:-
THE NATIONAL MARITIME MUSEUM GREENWICH.

L/S/02

© JOHN LAMBERT COMPLETED FEBRUARY 1976 ENLARGED AND ENHANCED NOVEMBER 2000

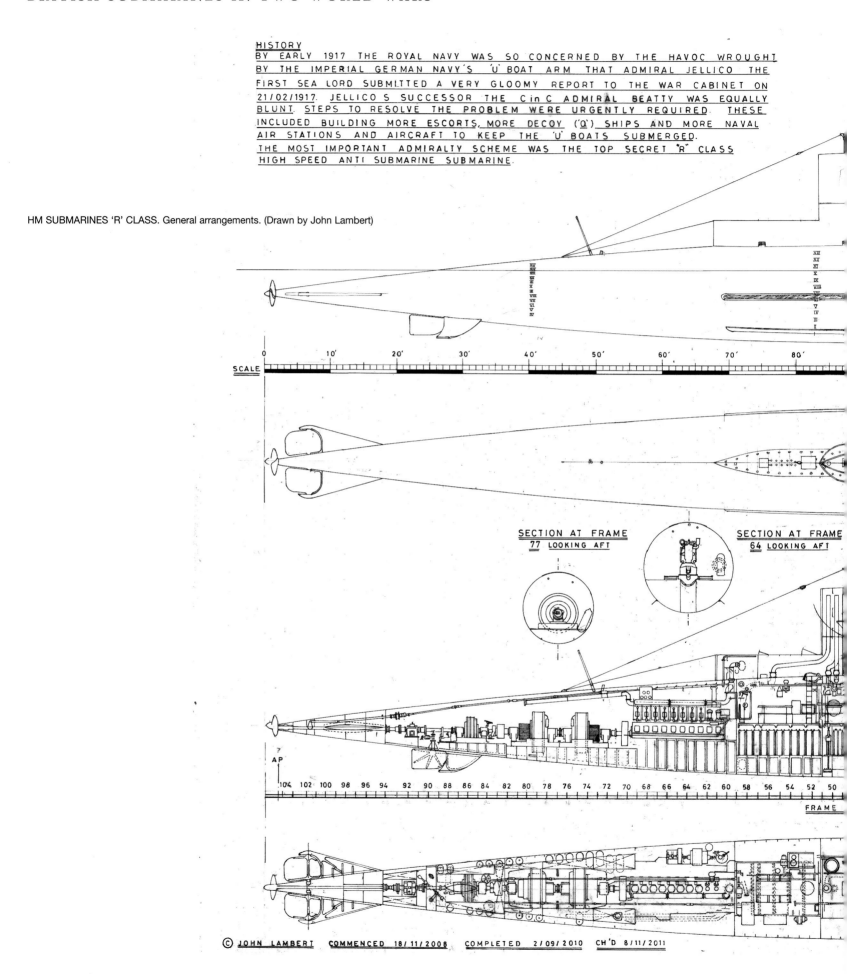

HISTORY
BY EARLY 1917 THE ROYAL NAVY WAS SO CONCERNED BY THE HAVOC WROUGHT
BY THE IMPERIAL GERMAN NAVY'S 'U' BOAT ARM THAT ADMIRAL JELLICO THE
FIRST SEA LORD SUBMITTED A VERY GLOOMY REPORT TO THE WAR CABINET ON
21/02/1917. JELLICO'S SUCCESSOR THE C in C ADMIRAL BEATTY WAS EQUALLY
BLUNT. STEPS TO RESOLVE THE PROBLEM WERE URGENTLY REQUIRED. THESE
INCLUDED BUILDING MORE ESCORTS, MORE DECOY ('Q') SHIPS AND MORE NAVAL
AIR STATIONS AND AIRCRAFT TO KEEP THE 'U' BOATS SUBMERGED.
THE MOST IMPORTANT ADMIRALTY SCHEME WAS THE TOP SECRET 'R' CLASS
HIGH SPEED ANTI SUBMARINE SUBMARINE.

HM SUBMARINES 'R' CLASS. General arrangements. (Drawn by John Lambert)

SCALE

0   10'   20'   30'   40'   50'   60'   70'   80'

SECTION AT FRAME
77 LOOKING AFT

SECTION AT FRAME
64 LOOKING AFT

AP

104 102 100 98 96 94 92 90 88 86 84 82 80 78 76 74 72 70 68 66 64 62 60 58 56 54 52 50

FRAME

© JOHN LAMBERT COMMENCED 18/11/2008 COMPLETED 2/09/2010 CH'D 8/11/2011

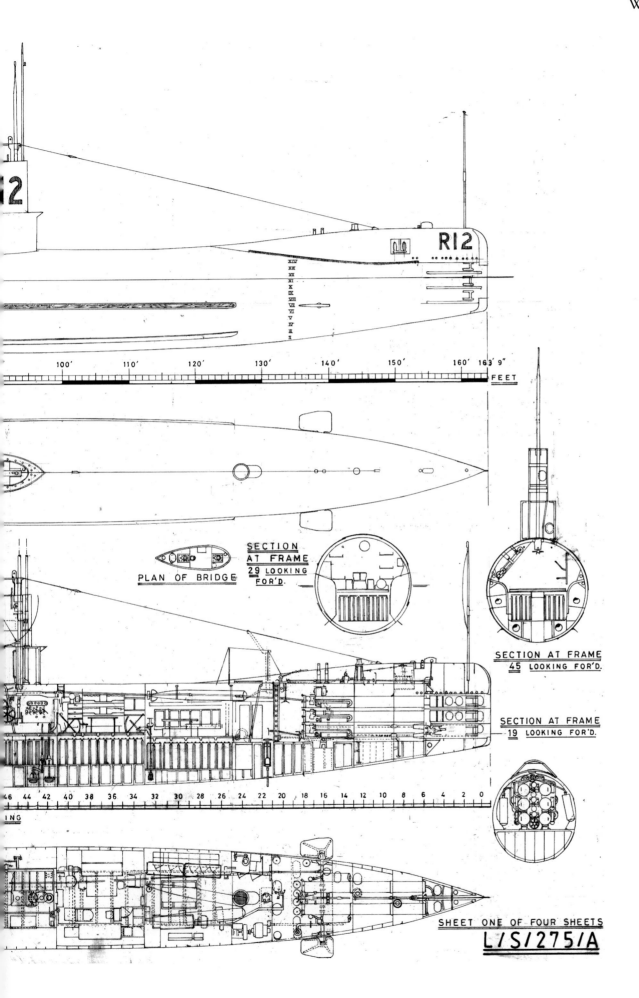

R12

100' 110' 120' 130' 140' 150' 160' 163'9" FEET

PLAN OF BRIDGE

SECTION AT FRAME 29 LOOKING FOR'D.

SECTION AT FRAME 45 LOOKING FOR'D.

SECTION AT FRAME 19 LOOKING FOR'D.

46 44 42 40 38 36 34 32 30 28 26 24 22 20 18 16 14 12 10 8 6 4 2 0

ING

SHEET ONE OF FOUR SHEETS
L/S12751A

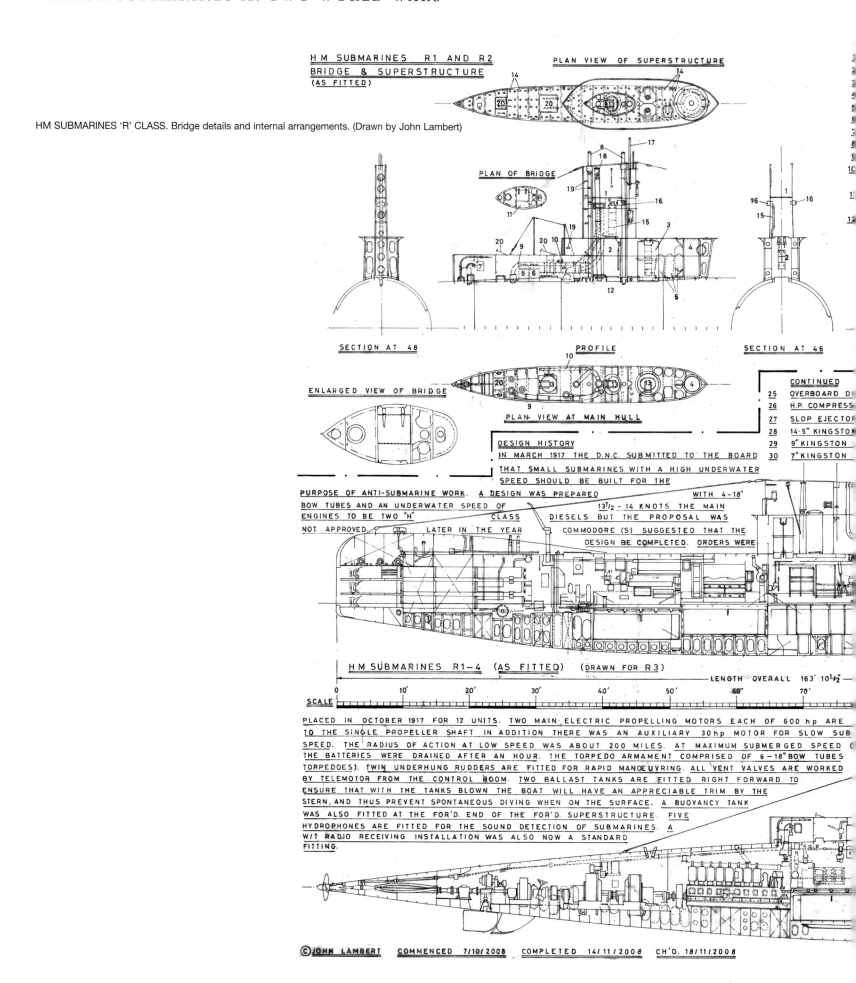

HM SUBMARINES 'R' CLASS. Bridge details and internal arrangements. (Drawn by John Lambert)

HM SUBMARINES R1 AND R2
BRIDGE & SUPERSTRUCTURE
(AS FITTED)

PLAN VIEW OF SUPERSTRUCTURE

PLAN OF BRIDGE

SECTION AT 48

PROFILE

SECTION AT 46

ENLARGED VIEW OF BRIDGE

PLAN VIEW AT MAIN HULL

CONTINUED
25 OVERBOARD D
26 H.P. COMPRESS
27 SLOP EJECTOR
28 14·5" KINGSTO
29 9" KINGSTON
30 7" KINGSTON

DESIGN HISTORY
IN MARCH 1917 THE D.N.C. SUBMITTED TO THE BOARD
THAT SMALL SUBMARINES WITH A HIGH UNDERWATER
SPEED SHOULD BE BUILT FOR THE
PURPOSE OF ANTI-SUBMARINE WORK. A DESIGN WAS PREPARED WITH 4-18"
BOW TUBES AND AN UNDERWATER SPEED OF 13½ - 14 KNOTS THE MAIN
ENGINES TO BE TWO "H" CLASS DIESELS BUT THE PROPOSAL WAS
NOT APPROVED. LATER IN THE YEAR COMMODORE (S) SUGGESTED THAT THE
DESIGN BE COMPLETED. ORDERS WERE

HM SUBMARINES R1-4 (AS FITTED) (DRAWN FOR R3)

LENGTH OVERALL 163' 10½

SCALE 0 10' 20' 30' 40' 50' 60' 70'

PLACED IN OCTOBER 1917 FOR 12 UNITS. TWO MAIN ELECTRIC PROPELLING MOTORS EACH OF 600 hp ARE
TO THE SINGLE PROPELLER SHAFT IN ADDITION THERE WAS AN AUXILIARY 30hp MOTOR FOR SLOW SUB
SPEED. THE RADIUS OF ACTION AT LOW SPEED WAS ABOUT 200 MILES. AT MAXIMUM SUBMERGED SPEED
THE BATTERIES WERE DRAINED AFTER AN HOUR. THE TORPEDO ARMAMENT COMPRISED OF 6-18" BOW TUBES
TORPEDOES). TWIN UNDERHUNG RUDDERS ARE FITTED FOR RAPID MANOEUVRING. ALL VENT VALVES ARE WORKED
BY TELEMOTOR FROM THE CONTROL ROOM. TWO BALLAST TANKS ARE FITTED RIGHT FORWARD TO
ENSURE THAT WITH THE TANKS BLOWN THE BOAT WILL HAVE AN APPRECIABLE TRIM BY THE
STERN, AND THUS PREVENT SPONTANEOUS DIVING WHEN ON THE SURFACE. A BUOYANCY TANK
WAS ALSO FITTED AT THE FOR'D END OF THE FOR'D SUPERSTRUCTURE. FIVE
HYDROPHONES ARE FITTED FOR THE SOUND DETECTION OF SUBMARINES. A
W/T RADIO RECEIVING INSTALLATION WAS ALSO NOW A STANDARD
FITTING.

© JOHN LAMBERT COMMENCED 7/10/2008 COMPLETED 14/11/2008 CH'D. 18/11/2008

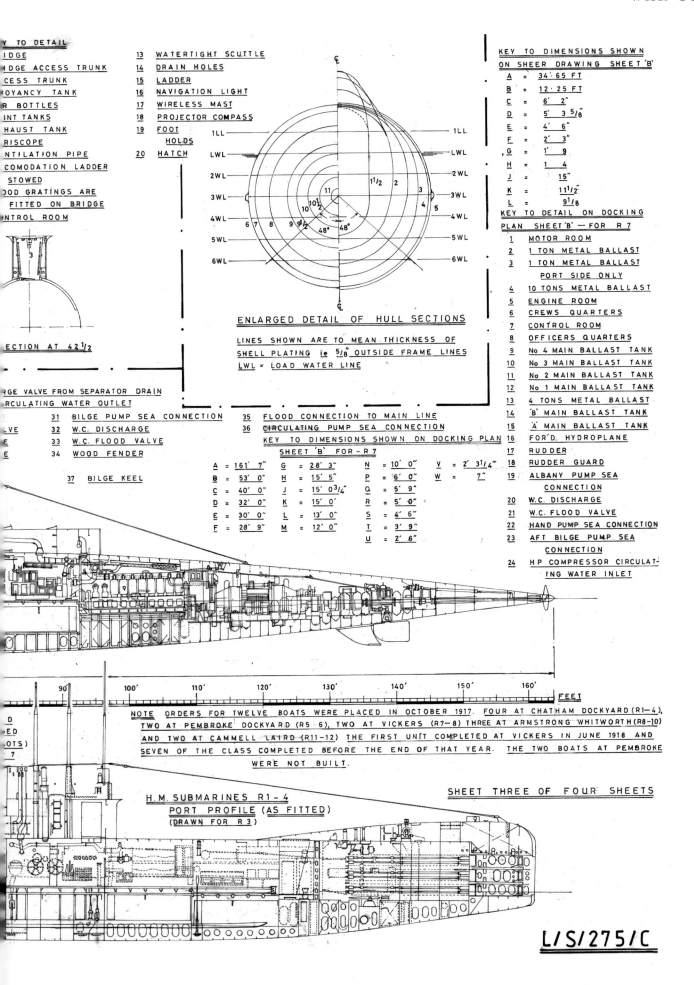

Y TO DETAIL
IDGE
IDGE ACCESS TRUNK
CESS TRUNK
OYANCY TANK
R BOTTLES
INT TANKS
HAUST TANK
RISCOPE
NTILATION PIPE
COMODATION LADDER
STOWED
OD GRATINGS ARE
FITTED ON BRIDGE
NTROL ROOM

13 WATERTIGHT SCUTTLE
14 DRAIN HOLES
15 LADDER
16 NAVIGATION LIGHT
17 WIRELESS MAST
18 PROJECTOR COMPASS
19 FOOT HOLDS
20 HATCH

ECTION AT 42½

GE VALVE FROM SEPARATOR DRAIN
RCULATING WATER OUTLET

31 BILGE PUMP SEA CONNECTION
32 W.C. DISCHARGE
33 W.C. FLOOD VALVE
34 WOOD FENDER

37 BILGE KEEL

35 FLOOD CONNECTION TO MAIN LINE
36 CIRCULATING PUMP SEA CONNECTION

ENLARGED DETAIL OF HULL SECTIONS

LINES SHOWN ARE TO MEAN THICKNESS OF
SHELL PLATING i.e. ⅝" OUTSIDE FRAME LINES
LWL = LOAD WATER LINE

KEY TO DIMENSIONS SHOWN
ON SHEER DRAWING SHEET 'B'

A = 34·65 FT
B = 12·25 FT
C = 6' 2"
D = 5' 3⅝"
E = 4' 6"
F = 2' 3"
G = 1' 9
H = 1 4
J = 15"
K = 11½"
L = 9⅛"

KEY TO DETAIL ON DOCKING
PLAN SHEET 'B' — FOR R 7

1 MOTOR ROOM
2 1 TON METAL BALLAST
3 1 TON METAL BALLAST PORT SIDE ONLY
4 10 TONS METAL BALLAST
5 ENGINE ROOM
6 CREWS QUARTERS
7 CONTROL ROOM
8 OFFICERS QUARTERS
9 No 4 MAIN BALLAST TANK
10 No 3 MAIN BALLAST TANK
11 No 2 MAIN BALLAST TANK
12 No 1 MAIN BALLAST TANK
13 4 TONS METAL BALLAST
14 'B' MAIN BALLAST TANK
15 'A' MAIN BALLAST TANK
16 FOR'D. HYDROPLANE
17 RUDDER
18 RUDDER GUARD
19 ALBANY PUMP SEA CONNECTION
20 W.C. DISCHARGE
21 W.C. FLOOD VALVE
22 HAND PUMP SEA CONNECTION
23 AFT BILGE PUMP SEA CONNECTION
24 HP COMPRESSOR CIRCULATING WATER INLET

KEY TO DIMENSIONS SHOWN ON DOCKING PLAN
SHEET 'B' FOR R7

A = 161' 7"   G = 28' 3"   N = 10' 0"   V = 2' 3¼"
B = 53' 0"   H = 15' 5"   P = 6' 0"   W = 7"
C = 40' 0"   J = 15' 0¾"   Q = 5' 9"
D = 32' 0"   K = 15' 0"   R = 5' 0"
E = 30' 0"   L = 13' 0"   S = 4' 6"
F = 28' 9"   M = 12' 0"   T = 3' 9"
                               U = 2' 6"

NOTE ORDERS FOR TWELVE BOATS WERE PLACED IN OCTOBER 1917. FOUR AT CHATHAM DOCKYARD (R1-4),
TWO AT PEMBROKE DOCKYARD (R5-6), TWO AT VICKERS (R7-8) THREE AT ARMSTRONG WHITWORTH (R8-10)
AND TWO AT CAMMELL LAIRD (R11-12) THE FIRST UNIT COMPLETED AT VICKERS IN JUNE 1918 AND
SEVEN OF THE CLASS COMPLETED BEFORE THE END OF THAT YEAR. THE TWO BOATS AT PEMBROKE
WERE NOT BUILT.

SHEET THREE OF FOUR SHEETS

H.M. SUBMARINES R1-4
PORT PROFILE (AS FITTED)
(DRAWN FOR R3)

L/S/275/C

145

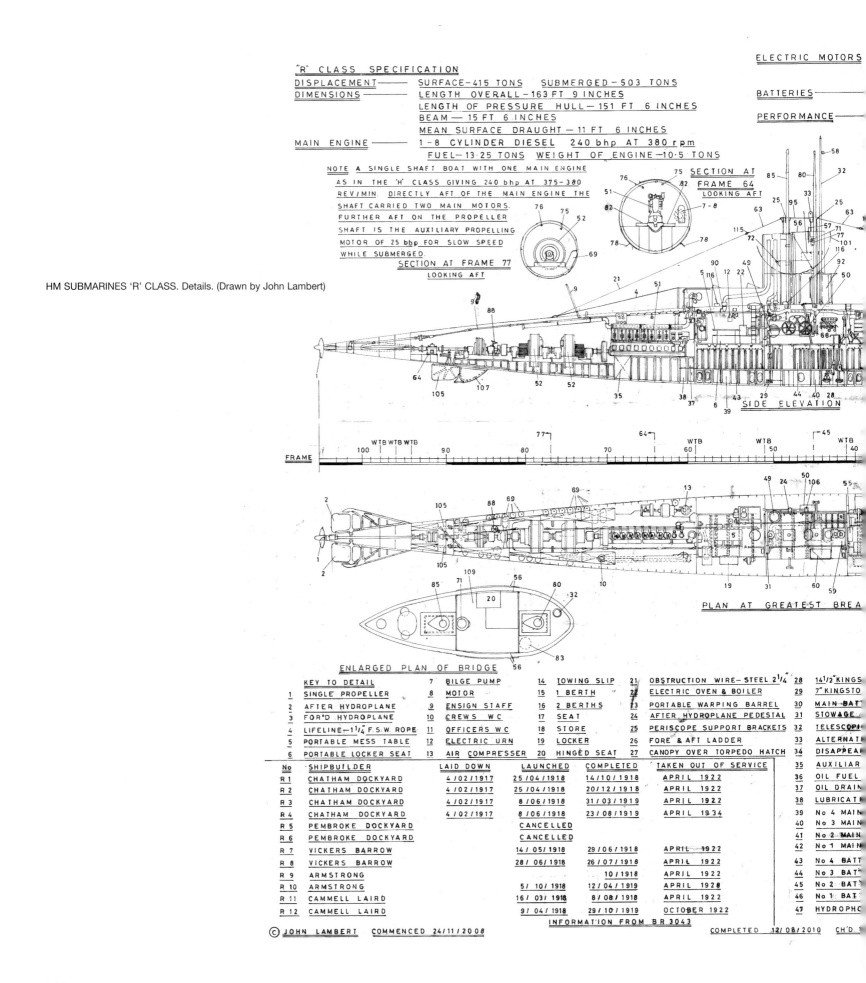

"R" CLASS SPECIFICATION

DISPLACEMENT —— SURFACE—415 TONS   SUBMERGED—503 TONS
DIMENSIONS —— LENGTH OVERALL—163 FT 9 INCHES
LENGTH OF PRESSURE HULL— 151 FT 6 INCHES
BEAM — 15 FT 6 INCHES
MEAN SURFACE DRAUGHT — 11 FT 6 INCHES
MAIN ENGINE —— 1 - 8 CYLINDER DIESEL 240 bhp AT 380 rpm
FUEL—13·25 TONS WEIGHT OF ENGINE—10·5 TONS

NOTE A SINGLE SHAFT BOAT WITH ONE MAIN ENGINE
AS IN THE 'H' CLASS GIVING 240 bhp AT 375-380
REV/MIN. DIRECTLY AFT OF THE MAIN ENGINE THE
SHAFT CARRIED TWO MAIN MOTORS.
FURTHER AFT ON THE PROPELLER
SHAFT IS THE AUXILIARY PROPELLING
MOTOR OF 25 bhp FOR SLOW SPEED
WHILE SUBMERGED.

SECTION AT FRAME 77
LOOKING AFT

SECTION AT FRAME 64
LOOKING AFT

ELECTRIC MOTORS

BATTERIES

PERFORMANCE

HM SUBMARINES 'R' CLASS. Details. (Drawn by John Lambert)

SIDE ELEVATION

FRAME

PLAN AT GREATEST BREA

ENLARGED PLAN OF BRIDGE

	KEY TO DETAIL									
1	SINGLE PROPELLER	7	BILGE PUMP	14	TOWING SLIP	21	OBSTRUCTION WIRE—STEEL 2¼"	28	14½"KINGS
2	AFTER HYDROPLANE	8	MOTOR	15	1 BERTH	22	ELECTRIC OVEN & BOILER	29	7"KINGSTO
3	FOR'D HYDROPLANE	9	ENSIGN STAFF	16	2 BERTHS	23	PORTABLE WARPING BARREL	30	MAIN BAT
4	LIFELINE—1¼" F.S.W. ROPE	10	CREWS WC	17	SEAT	24	AFTER HYDROPLANE PEDESTAL	31	STOWAGE
5	PORTABLE MESS TABLE	11	OFFICERS WC	18	STORE	25	PERISCOPE SUPPORT BRACKETS	32	TELESCOP
6	PORTABLE LOCKER SEAT	12	ELECTRIC URN	19	LOCKER	26	FORE & AFT LADDER	33	ALTERNAT
		13	AIR COMPRESSER	20	HINGED SEAT	27	CANOPY OVER TORPEDO HATCH	34	DISAPPEAI

No	SHIPBUILDER	LAID DOWN	LAUNCHED	COMPLETED	TAKEN OUT OF SERVICE		
R1	CHATHAM DOCKYARD	4/02/1917	25/04/1918	14/10/1918	APRIL 1922	35	AUXILIAR
R2	CHATHAM DOCKYARD	4/02/1917	25/04/1918	20/12/1918	APRIL 1922	36	OIL FUEL
R3	CHATHAM DOCKYARD	4/02/1917	8/06/1918	31/03/1919	APRIL 1922	37	OIL DRAIN
R4	CHATHAM DOCKYARD	4/02/1917	8/06/1918	23/08/1919	APRIL 1934	38	LUBRICAT
R5	PEMBROKE DOCKYARD		CANCELLED			39	No 4 MAIN
R6	PEMBROKE DOCKYARD		CANCELLED			40	No 3 MAIN
R7	VICKERS BARROW		14/05/1918	29/06/1918	APRIL 1922	41	No 2 MAIN
R8	VICKERS BARROW		28/06/1918	26/07/1918	APRIL 1922	42	No 1 MAIN
R9	ARMSTRONG			10/1918	APRIL 1922	43	No 4 BATT
R10	ARMSTRONG		5/10/1918	12/04/1919	APRIL 1928	44	No 3 BAT
R11	CAMMELL LAIRD		16/03/1918	8/08/1918	APRIL 1922	45	No 2 BAT
R12	CAMMELL LAIRD		9/04/1918	29/10/1919	OCTOBER 1922	46	No 1 BAT
						47	HYDROPH

INFORMATION FROM BR 3043

© JOHN LAMBERT COMMENCED 24/11/2008

COMPLETED 12/08/2010 CH'D

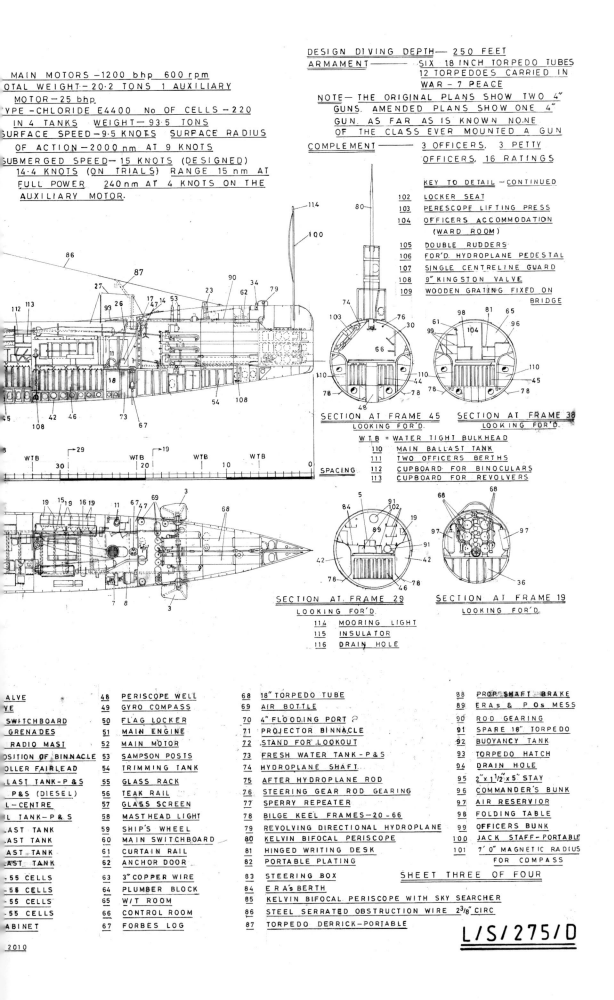

MAIN MOTORS —1200 bhp 600 rpm
TOTAL WEIGHT—20·2 TONS 1 AUXILIARY
MOTOR—25 bhp.
TYPE —CHLORIDE E4400 No OF CELLS —220
IN 4 TANKS WEIGHT—93·5 TONS
SURFACE SPEED—9·5 KNOTS SURFACE RADIUS
OF ACTION —2000 nm AT 9 KNOTS
SUBMERGED SPEED— 15 KNOTS (DESIGNED)
14·4 KNOTS (ON TRIALS) RANGE 15 nm AT
FULL POWER 240 nm AT 4 KNOTS ON THE
AUXILIARY MOTOR.

DESIGN DIVING DEPTH— 250 FEET
ARMAMENT——— SIX 18 INCH TORPEDO TUBES
12 TORPEDOES CARRIED IN
WAR - 7 PEACE
NOTE— THE ORIGINAL PLANS SHOW TWO 4″
GUNS. AMENDED PLANS SHOW ONE 4″
GUN. AS FAR AS IS KNOWN NO.NE
OF THE CLASS EVER MOUNTED A GUN
COMPLEMENT——— 3 OFFICERS, 3 PETTY
OFFICERS, 16 RATINGS

KEY TO DETAIL —CONTINUED
102 LOCKER SEAT
103 PERESCOPE LIFTING PRESS
104 OFFICERS ACCOMMODATION
(WARD ROOM)
105 DOUBLE RUDDERS
106 FOR'D. HYDROPLANE PEDESTAL
107 SINGLE CENTRELINE GUARD
108 9″ KINGSTON VALVE
109 WOODEN GRATING FIXED ON
BRIDGE

SECTION AT FRAME 45
LOOKING FOR'D.

SECTION AT FRAME 38
LOOKING FOR'D.

W.T.B = WATER TIGHT BULKHEAD
110 MAIN BALLAST TANK
111 TWO OFFICERS BERTHS
112 CUPBOARD FOR BINOCULARS
113 CUPBOARD FOR REVOLVERS

SPACING

SECTION AT FRAME 29
LOOKING FOR'D.

SECTION AT FRAME 19
LOOKING FOR'D.

114 MOORING LIGHT
115 INSULATOR
116 DRAIN HOLE

ALVE	48	PERISCOPE WELL	68	18″ TORPEDO TUBE	88	PROP SHAFT BRAKE
VE	49	GYRO COMPASS	69	AIR BOTTLE	89	ERAs & P Os MESS
SWITCHBOARD	50	FLAG LOCKER	70	4″ FLOODING PORT ?	90	ROD GEARING
GRENADES	51	MAIN ENGINE	71	PROJECTOR BINNACLE	91	SPARE 18″ TORPEDO
RADIO MAST	52	MAIN MOTOR	72	STAND FOR LOOKOUT	92	BUOYANCY TANK
OSITION OF BINNACLE	53	SAMPSON POSTS	73	FRESH WATER TANK—P&S	93	TORPEDO HATCH
OLLER FAIRLEAD	54	TRIMMING TANK	74	HYDROPLANE SHAFT	94	DRAIN HOLE
LAST TANK—P&S	55	GLASS RACK	75	AFTER HYDROPLANE ROD	95	2″x 1½″x5″ STAY
P&S (DIESEL)	56	TEAK RAIL	76	STEERING GEAR ROD GEARING	96	COMMANDER'S BUNK
L—CENTRE	57	GLASS SCREEN	77	SPERRY REPEATER	97	AIR RESERVOIR
L TANK—P&S	58	MASTHEAD LIGHT	78	BILGE KEEL FRAMES—20-66	98	FOLDING TABLE
AST TANK	59	SHIP'S WHEEL	79	REVOLVING DIRECTIONAL HYDROPLANE	99	OFFICERS BUNK
AST TANK	60	MAIN SWITCHBOARD	80	KELVIN BIFOCAL PERISCOPE	100	JACK STAFF—PORTABLE
AST TANK	61	CURTAIN RAIL	81	HINGED WRITING DESK	101	7′ 0″ MAGNETIC RADIUS
AST TANK	62	ANCHOR DOOR	82	PORTABLE PLATING		FOR COMPASS
55 CELLS	63	3″ COPPER WIRE	83	STEERING BOX		
55 CELLS	64	PLUMBER BLOCK	84	ERA's BERTH	SHEET THREE OF FOUR	
55 CELLS	65	W/T ROOM	85	KELVIN BIFOCAL PERISCOPE WITH SKY SEARCHER		
AST TANK	66	CONTROL ROOM	86	STEEL SERRATED OBSTRUCTION WIRE 2⅜″ CIRC		
ABINET	67	FORBES LOG	87	TORPEDO DERRICK—PORTABLE		

2010

L/S/275/D

HM SUBMARINE *L 5*. General arrangements. Plan and sections. (© National Maritime Museum M1065)

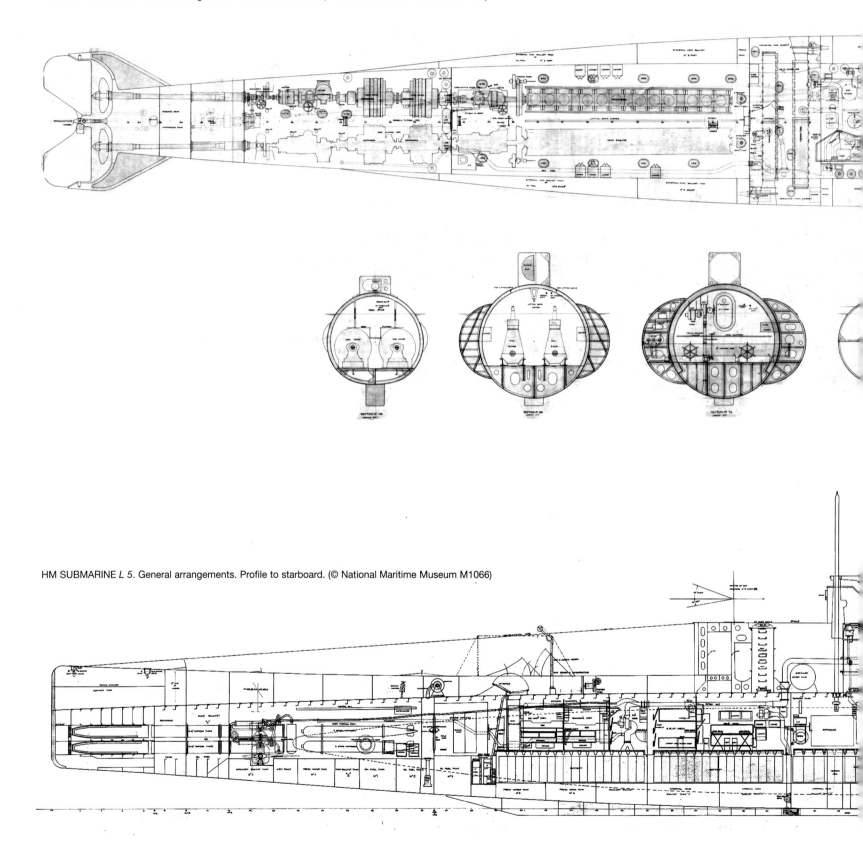

HM SUBMARINE *L 5*. General arrangements. Profile to starboard. (© National Maritime Museum M1066)

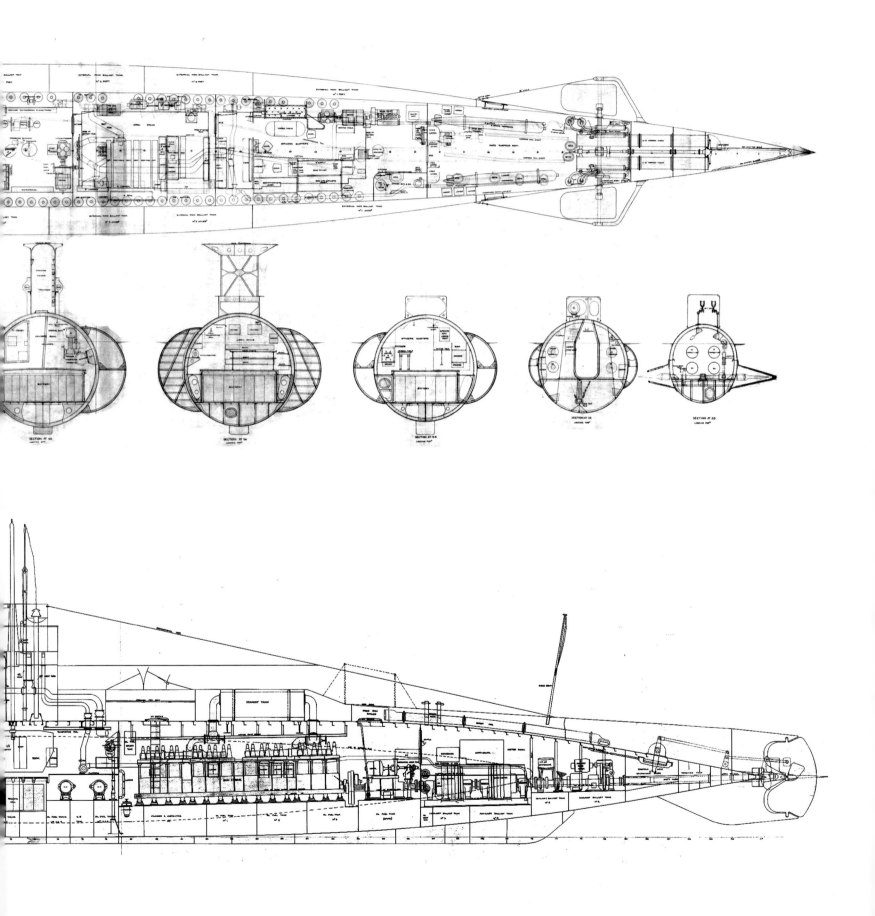

CHAPTER 10
WAR EXPERIENCE AND NEW TECHNOLOGY

Evaluating Wartime Submarines

The Naval Staff formed a Post-war Questions Committee in 1919 to gather wartime lessons.[1] The war had proven the military value of submarines, although torpedo failures had limited their effectiveness against enemy warships. Also, wartime submarines had been effective against slow and damaged ships, but seldom against fast and well-screened ones, 'though the moral effect of the submarine menace was very great'. Although results attained were limited, 'we do not consider they can be taken as a fair criterion of the submarine's military value, which your Committee assess at a higher figure for the future'. Submarines were, moreover, inexpensive, with long service lives. 'No Fleet is complete without submarines of a surface speed at least equal to that of the Battle Fleet trained to work as an integral part of that Fleet to attack enemy heavy ships.' However, the steam plants of wartime fleet submarines were unsuitable; 'when the diesel engine can develop the necessary power . . . this type will be valuable'. The future unit battleship force (ten ships) should operate with fourteen submarines, so as to ensure having two flotillas (six each) always fit for service. That would be far more than the desired wartime proportion of 'K'-class submarines to capital ships.

In anti-submarine warfare, the submarine uniquely could operate unseen 'on equal terms with their quarry'. The proof was that the U-boats had felt compelled to zigzag when on the surface in the North Sea. Future submarine minelayers should carry their forty to fifty mines internally, as otherwise they could not dive deep. The Committee saw no need for the wartime monitors.

The one type the wartime Royal Navy had not built was the long-range cruiser. In 1918 German U-cruisers had made an enormous impression, because they could carry the submarine war across the Atlantic and thus force considerable diversion of effort. The combination of high surface speed and heavy gun armament could enable a U-cruiser to destroy convoy escorts and then convoys with near-impunity. Guns were a far more efficient way of doing so than torpedoes, as two German cruisers had demonstrated when they massacred a Scandinavian convoy in November 1917. Unlike a conventional submarine, moreover, it could fight effectively within the laws of trade warfare – it would not have to pursue a dangerous unrestricted submarine warfare policy.

The German initiative raised considerable interest in the Royal Navy, to the point that DNC produced a design for a large cruiser around the beginning of 1918. Although a submarine cruiser might displace as much as 4000 tons, in 1919 it appeared that 2000 tons was best. A cruiser of that size would be habitable enough for long cruises and could be heavily armed; the Committee envisaged guns firing 100lb shells and a small torpedo armament, with an endurance of about 15,000nm and a surface speed of 16 knots.

The Post-war Questions Committee asked whether the big submarine monitors were needed in the future fleet. *M 3* runs at speed, October 1924. The object atop her after periscope was probably a frame coil for wireless reception at shallow depth. (Dr David Stevens)

On the basis of evidence given by veteran submarine officers, the Committee recommended that sketch designs be prepared for five types of submarine:[2]

- A submarine combining some of the qualities of the 'H' and 'R' classes, which the Committee characterised as coastal patrol craft, operating in the approaches to the coast, ports, channels and the approaches to overseas bases; with high underwater speed they could be used effectively to attack the larger enemy submarines.
- An improved 'L' class.
- A submarine minelayer.
- An improved 'K' class.
- A cruiser or, more correctly, an 'overseas submarine'.

Commander R H T Raikes emphasised handiness. The British were ahead of the Germans in main principles of construction, handiness submerged and general working, as well as in initiative of design. U-boats were not as handy underwater and their diving qualities not so good, although they got underwater more quickly. Other British advantages were the extensive use of telemotor (remote-control) gear for operating vents, bow torpedo caps and periscopes. DNC's representative attributed the inferiority of U-boats to less longitudinal stability, a different hull shape and smaller planes. He said that the hulls of ordinary U-boats were weaker than those of British submarines due to the absence of flats inside the boat and wider frame spacing. However, the big U-cruisers (*U 140* class) had thicker pressure hulls and were stronger. DNC also considered it a marked advantage for British submarines that they had so many small tanks rather than a few larger ones; they could survive grounding much better. The British had not much improved habitability, but now submarines for the Mediterranean and China were being fitted with cooling apparatus 'as an established principle'. The one important area of German superiority was their simpler and more efficient diesels.

Raikes disliked the steam plants of the 'K' class because it was difficult to close and raise funnels, because they were too hot inside and because boiler fires could be put out by water coming down the funnel. The high bow of the modified 'K' made them too visible, but it was worthwhile for seakeeping.

Raikes badly wanted to angle torpedoes, because beam shots were the easiest form of attack. The Germans did angle theirs and their method had been adopted in the 'K' class. The breech of the tube had a plug handle with a pointer on it, the handle being pulled and turned to 90° or more. The main problem, which had been raised before the war, was that aiming had to take into account the turn after the torpedo left the tube. Raikes also recalled reliability problems: in seven cases he had hit U-boats but the torpedo had not exploded. Too often 18in Mk VII torpedoes had broken the surface either on being fired or during their runs. There were few complaints about the replacement Mk VIII.

S/T worked well only when the submarine was not moving. Instead of the 30nm or more achieved with a static submarine, at high speed a 'K'-boat would not exceed 800 yds when signalling right ahead. Asdic promised much more.

Asked what type of submarine he would lay down to fight Japan in five years, Raikes said that depended on how important commerce warfare would be. If it was not to be German-style unrestricted warfare, a submersible cruiser would be best. It would also be best for watching the Japanese coast (although for closer work smaller sub-marines would be wanted) and to support convoys to Australia. Raikes envisaged a 2000 to 4000-ton cruiser submarine mounting six 6in guns with a speed of 20 to 25 knots and a radius of action of 10,000 or 20,000nm.

Lieutenant Commander Stoker had been the first British submarine commander to penetrate the Dardanelles, although ultimately his submarine had been sunk (he and his crew became PoWs). The Committee asked what had gone wrong, both with his submarine *AE 2* and with her torpedoes (only one of seven shots was successful). Without any previous experience, Stoker had to find his own way through shallows and strong currents, diving through Turkish mine-fields. He grounded, with enough of the boat above water to attract heavy, if ineffective, gunfire. Repeated bumping opened leaks in the submarine, flooding engine and motor bilges aft. They could not be pumped out because they contained oil, which would have given away his position. Once he found himself unable to dive because he could not trim his boat. He managed to remain in the Dardanelles for six days. When sunk, *AE 2* was absolutely out of trim and Stoker could not say why; *E 11* had previously suffered a trim problem while being chased by German destroyers in the North Sea. Suddenly her bow came up and she started making for the surface near the destroyers. Her commander flooded all his tanks and went to the (shallow) bottom, coming back up at night. Detailed examination in a yard failed to explain what had gone wrong. Commodore (S) Hall attributed these problems to peculiar density levels, as shown by density charts. Overall Stoker considered the 'E' class the easiest type to handle underwater.

Two of Stoker's misses might have failed due to pressure when the submarine grounded. One of the torpedoes did not start, coming to the surface. A DTM representative stated that there had never been proper facilities for torpedo trials as each new class of submarine entered service. Torpedo problems became a major theme in evaluating wartime submarine operations.[3] With their very fine bows, the 'K' class presented particular problems in torpedo firing. A torpedo had to travel about 16ft before getting clear of the hull and bow shutters; during that passage it rubbed against the side of the ship's structure and its tail could be damaged, particularly at the 29-knot setting (it was better at 35 knots and 44.5 knots). Unfortunately the 29-knot (long-range) setting was needed for fleet actions. No solution had yet been found. The former Assistant Director of Torpedoes (ADT), an experienced submarine officer, had argued for a bluffer bow more like that in a U-boat.

The DTM representative stated that British torpedo detonators were not good; there was reason to doubt that the pistol would properly transmit detonation to the detonator and then to the main charge. Also, the pistols were designed to strike at a set limiting angle. That might explain failures against U-boats with rounded hulls.

Wartime Commodore (S) Hall had been responsible for all the wartime designs. He doubted that so many different types were needed and wanted to abolish coastal and purely defensive submarines. The minelaying and patrol types should merge. Hall recalled that the submarine cruiser considered by the Submarine Development Committee had not been adopted because it was essential a commerce destroyer, but it would be worthwhile if the British had to attack enemy commerce. He argued that had the Germans built U-cruisers early on they could have wiped out all of the British ASW craft and conducted perfectly legitimate commerce warfare without risking US intervention. To succeed such a cruiser had to be designed around her gun armament (which he felt *M 1* was not) and needed great habitability. It needed good seakeeping and endurance, not high speed. Hall considered 2000 tons a natural limit because it would be difficult to find captains for much larger craft. He found plenty of suitable captains for 'K'-boats, but overall it was 'very difficult to get Captains certain to rise superior to their materiel, whom you can rely upon as thrusters to make most of an opportunity. These vessels are such a large and complicated machine for one man to manage, that you could get better value if you restricted the Cruisers to 2000 tons.' Hall had never gone into cruiser characteristics in detail, but he envisaged an endurance of 10,000 to 12,000nm, using two standard engines to make about 16 knots surfaced with four 5.5in guns on turntables each with a hatch so that it could be quickly manned. Torpedo tubes should be reduced to a minimum; a commerce destroyer would need plenty of room for prize crews.

Hall considered the monitor the 'most successful submarine we have ever had; has a very large radius of action, can send her 10,000 miles; extraordinarily good under water; good torpedo armament and gun does not restrict her in any way. She is large, but for a spread-out Empire like ours is a most valuable vessel; is a very comfortable ship, no difficulty in crew living in her for a year so she could be self contained for very long cruises.' He explained the monitor as a counter to German light cruisers, which were nearly impossible to torpedo when zigzagging at high speed. The monitor would be difficult to see or to hit and her gun was operated entirely from inside. However, the monitor could not stop battlecruisers raiding commerce; her gun was not powerful enough.

Although submarines had been successfully converted into minelayers, specialised ones would be needed for a war against America or Japan, as laying only sixteen mines at a time would hardly be worthwhile.

Old submarines were worth retaining because they could never become truly obsolescent; Hall mentioned the wartime successes of the 'C' class against U-boats. These would become obsolescent only if some new type of power plant usable underwater appeared.

Hall testified that submarine officers were generally unhappy with the torpedoes they were given. Before the war they had asked for a fast short-range torpedo, which they were given in the form of the Mk VIII. Hall considered it exceedingly good, but it was not what early war experience showed was wanted. The officers found that they wanted greater range, so they were given Mk VIIs. Submarine officers 'expected that what they did want could be produced in a week'.

Hall thought that the U-boats had been designed from the outset only to attack merchant ships, hence that underwater speed had been relatively unimportant.[4] They were very uncomfortable, crowded with all sorts of superfluous equipment (such as elaborate means of purifying and re-oxygenating air). Access to gear was poor and repairs surely took a long time. The mass of deck fittings in the U-cruisers created too much underwater resistance. Hydroplanes were small and U-boats steered poorly. That underwater control was poor was borne out by the testimony of a torpedoed U-boat officer. He said that they had been 'steeple chasing' fore and aft even when attacking. Hall said that the British had had similar experience of the 'F' and 'G' classes, which were of German shape; their hydroplanes had to be enlarged. Overall, the U-boats showed no original features. German hull construction was very fine, better than British, but Hall did not think it differed materially from British submarines. Overall, Hall saw nothing new or original in the U-boats.

Like Raikes, Hall was very impressed by German diesels. He would

not say they were better than British, because he suspected that they needed a good deal of repair after a cruise. However, for silence and smokelessness and ease of handling and reversing, they were better made than the British engines and they developed more power per cylinder.

Torpedo expert Captain Candy saw nothing to choose between British and German torpedoes. German torpedoes looked simpler; 'but their men are not allowed to play with them so much as ours are, which is quite wrong'. He doubted that so complex a weapon could ever be made foolproof. Rushed wartime training might have been part of the problem. The British might have gone too far with safety arrangements. Candy liked the torpedo tubes of later German submarines, which he thought should be copied. The muzzles were not flush with the sides of their submarines: the Germans had accepted reduced speed 'rather than have any doubt about efficiency of torpedo'.[5] Paired torpedo tubes were in steps, rather than one over the other as in British submarines. That made for much better access to the lower tubes (not always the case in British submarines) and allowed a man to stand between the lower tubes and work easily on top of both lower and upper tubes because there was more space between the two upper ones than the two lower ones. German torpedo gear was very simply constructed and worked easily, even in a surrendered boat that had been at Harwich for over six months without overhaul.

Candy thought the many protrusions in U-boats' outer skins showed a lack of interest in high underwater speed – which was natural if the targets were slow merchant ships. German hydroplanes were very small for the size of their submarines. They also had fewer (but larger) tanks and larger vents, simplifying operation. DNC's representative said that it took a month to find the best diving angle for the captured *U 86* (between two and three degrees by the bow). That submarine took 80 seconds to dive with full buoyancy, compared to 86 seconds for an 'L'-boat with smaller vents and flooding valves.

Candy considered the 'H' class 'a very fine design for a small boat. As it came over from America it had ample room and boat was evidently designed by a syndicate of experts to put on market and sell well.'[6] It was faster underwater than British submarines due both to its hull form and to its higher-powered motors. Because motor power was about equal to that of the diesels, the designers could choose a very efficient propeller rather than a compromise. Candy much preferred the original 'H' class to the new ones (*H 21* class) because in the original arrangement all four bow tubes could be placed 'right up in the snout'. The bow cap revolved so that only two tubes could fire at the same time. As modified, all four tubes could be opened and fired at once. Compared to British boats, the 'H' class had bluffer bows and finer tails.

Commander Brodie thought that the 'K' class could be handled safely with a battle squadron, if they were drilled continuously. They were no more difficult to combine with the battleships than destroyers, but 'they need more signalmen . . . if they are to be used with Fleet'. Brodie considered beam torpedo tubes best for attack against a fleet, but it would be better if the same shots could be made by angling torpedoes. Angling would also be useful for other submarines.

Brodie thought that at the end of the war British submarines were distinctly superior to U-boats, although the Germans might have been better during the winter of 1915–16. Their engines were certainly better at the time and up to the end they were quieter. Their periscopes were better for a time, but no longer. Their torpedoes were more destructive and were better depth-keepers. The Germans had paid more attention to hull watertightness because they were more

The 'H' class were well-liked but too small. Onlookers on the swing bridge give an idea of scale. (RAN Naval Historical Section via Dr Josef Straczek)

concerned to be able to go deep – over 200ft – but overall they were no stronger. Subdivision was more complete, but ventilation and accessibility – which were more important – were inferior. Observers might exaggerate their quickness of diving because they would see how quickly the conning tower disappeared. That was only the final plunge in a dive.

Endurance would take on a different meaning in the vast spaces of the Far East. Wartime endurance in the Dardanelles had been measured not in miles but in what personnel could take and, in the first few cases, fresh water. If a submarine could bottom, that would greatly increase both personnel endurance and the endurance of the battery. 'The strain on commanding officers on a patrol on which they sighted nothing and were constantly searching horizon with periscopes was surprisingly great; in contrast to [the Sea of] Marmara, where actual danger very much greater and prospect of an increasingly difficult passage back always at the back of their minds, they seemed to feel strain less than one would expect. Excitement a considerable tonic and something being in sight, even land, all the time.' Brodie pointed to the unique experience of lying on a density layer 80 or 90ft down in the Sea of Marmara. There was a similar situation in the Baltic, but it was less consistent.

In the Adriatic Brodie had encountered Austrian, French and Italian submarines. He had no experience of Austrian as distinct from

German submarines 'but we had a moderate opinion of Austrian personnel'. He liked Italian coastal submarines 'but difficult to say whether their continual breakdowns mainly due to materiel or personnel. French boats rather complicated and of such varying types, but certainly superior to Italians. In number of patrols kept per boat: may have been largely due to personnel, excellent in French boats.' As to the two types of British submarines mainly employed, Brodie preferred the 'H' to the 'E' class because the latter required much more repair work and general upkeep and was less economical in men. However, in open heavy weather the 'E' was superior. The 'C' class was a very satisfactory coastal submarine, handy and excellent for submerged attack, although slow with bad limited seakeeping. As for upkeep they were excellent. He saw little point in the 'M' class.

Captain Nasmith envisaged five types for the future: a fleet submarine, a cruiser, an improved 'L', an improved 'H' (coast defence and watching enemy harbours, plus ASW if necessary) and a minelayer. The fleet submarine should make at least 25 knots and should have six 21in bow tubes and as many beam tubes as possible. If it could have 21in beam tubes, the bow tubes might be given up, provided that there were no fewer than six beam tubes on each side. Hopefully improved diesels could supersede wartime steam plants. Nasmith wanted the cruiser submarine to be as large as possible; he imagined arming it with 7.5in or even 9.2in guns and giving it an endurance of 40,000 or 50,000nm. It could stand up to conventional surface craft. It would be armoured. The improved 'L' would be a fleet scout and would operate on an enemy's coast. Nasmith wanted a surface speed of 18 knots and an endurance of 5000nm at 9 knots. The minelayer should have longer endurance (8000nm at 8 knots) and should carry fifty dry mines (the big German minelayers carried forty-two).

Both British and German torpedo-firing gear could be improved and bubbles created by firing eliminated. Nasmith considered German torpedo-angling gear better than British. Their double-hull construction resisted depth-charging better than British single or double hulls. The Germans had better engines and clutches; better electrical installations; better trimming pumps; and better telegraphs and helm indicators. German engines were more powerful than their British counterparts, did not vibrate as much (hence did not break their bolts) and did not shake loose on their beds as did the British engines. Nasmith attributed German superiority to their use of air injection.

When hunted by aircraft, the maximum depth at which Nasmith's submarine could be seen depended entirely on the clarity of the water. 'When once completely submerged I considered they had lost sight of me altogether. In clear water, however, necessary to go to 60 or 100ft to avoid detection.'

Rear Admiral Dent, a non-submariner, was Hall's successor.[7] In a 29 October 1919 letter to the Secretary of the Admiralty he called for sketch designs of five types of submarine: (i) a combination of the 'H' and 'R' classes for patrols within medium distance of base and with high underwater speed; (ii) an improved 'L' class for patrols far from a base; (iii) a submarine minelayer with internal stowage; (iv) an improved fleet submarine with higher surface speed and, if possible, endurance; and (v) a cruiser submarine. Given sketch designs, the submarine service would be able to discuss future policy with the Naval Staff. These sketches would be a basis for discussion, not finished designs. Classes (ii), (iii) and (v) and possibly (iv) should be able to operate in the tropics. That would require a CO_2 (i.e., refrigeration) plant to cool the batteries. Also, because the water was so clear, the submarines would have to dive much more deeply. The determining factor in these designs would be the diesel and after that an improved battery. Dent planned to commission *U 135* in 2nd Flotilla to test her alongside an 'L' boat.

Commander Bower had taught at the submarine school. He felt that before the war the Royal Navy had far better and more complete training than the Germans and a larger reserve of officers to fill up new boats as built, but towards the end the percentage of contacts to hits showed that only experience and the very best training could ensure that a boat was really dangerous to the enemy. During the war British submarines were able to attack and hit fast enemy ships when zigzagging, but on occasion enemy ships zigzagging at speed could defeat attack, particularly by inexperienced captains.

Bower visited Germany after the Armistice. The Germans talked freely, although it is not clear that they were particularly forthright. They said that late in the war it had been difficult to man their submarines. U-boat officers had received very poor training. The German submarine staff had discounted the value of a large percentage of their boats due to the lack of training of their commanding officers. During the last two years of the war, according to his sources, only certain more experienced captains were really working against shipping. U-boats were told not to attack warships unless it was a safe shot; commerce was always a preferable target. Experienced senior officers were allowed to use their discretion. This was in 1917–18.

German officers told Bower that they knew that for every boat they had on patrol in the Atlantic, the British had a submarine waiting for them. This was entirely untrue, but it appears that German intelligence was very poor. German Commander Jees, who worked in the Irish Sea, told Bower that he was most afraid of aircraft. He did not fear direct attack, but he felt that his position was constantly being reported, so he would never be left in peace at night. Traffic was constantly being diverted. Thinking it over later, Jees doubted that he was always seen, since he usually saw aircraft before they saw him, but he always had to act as though he had been seen. British boats in the Heligoland Bight had had much the same reaction. There had also been design problems: the latest German U-cruisers were delayed by nine or ten months owing to miscalculation of their metacentric heights.[8]

Bower pointed out that 'K'-class submarines were practically invisible at night, making very little wash even at high speed. In that sense they were better than destroyers for torpedo attack. On two occasions in 1918 'K'-boats on patrol kept station within 2000 yds on British light cruisers passing through their patrol areas, observing them until satisfied that they were British, at a speed of 22 knots. On another occasion 13th Submarine Flotilla was leading the Grand Fleet back to Rosyth when *K 9* broke down and fell out of line. The Grand Fleet passed her at 9 knots in two divisions, the nearest destroyers

Fleet submarines were valued, but the steam-powered 'K' class were too short-legged for the Far East. Hence the pressure for high-powered diesels. This is *K 12*, before her bow was raised. (Dr David Stevens)

The emergency programme to fit submarines with 4in guns and access trunks was undertaken without any proof that the guns would be effective. Post-war test firing against *UB 21* and *U 141* showed that short-range hits were unlikely to penetrate a submarine's pressure hull; they would mostly glance off. In 1924 RA(S)' Newsletter cautioned that it had to be accepted that a 4in gun fired from inside 6000 yds would probably not inflict vital damage. This perception may explain the need for a voice pipe to pass data to a gun crew; those on the bridge could probably estimate the range to the target. This is *L 54*, with voice pipe installed (leading visibly to the forward gun; the pipe also ran aft to the after one). (RAN Naval Historical Section via Dr Josef Straczek)

being two cables (400 yds) from *K 9*. The submarine did not challenge them and the whole fleet passed within half an hour without seeing her. This was about midnight.

However, night conditions could vary radically. On one occasion in 1917 Bower tried to attack German destroyers by moonlight when they were against the moon. He was going slow at less than half buoyancy. They opened fire at him at 1800 yds, made good shooting and turned to ram. On the other hand, with full buoyancy, he once passed a German torpedo boat at less than a cable (200 yds) and was not seen even though he turned in to fire torpedoes. The chief wartime torpedo lesson was that a very much larger charge was wanted to get definite results.

Bower considered the cruiser the most necessary future type. It could replace both the monitor and possibly the overseas patrol type (modified 'L'). He envisaged a submarine which could leave England for the Pacific and remain on patrol for three months before returning. Speed would be at least 20 knots and armament would include at least four power-loaded guns larger than 6in with director firing. She would also have four bow tubes and two on each beam. She would have 2in armour along the top strakes of her hull. Displacement should be at least 4000 tons and length no more than 400ft. Bower emphasised the impact of the cruiser on ASW forces. Instead of small, inexpensive craft the enemy would need light cruisers. That might be impossible: war experience indicated a ratio of forty hunters to one hunted. When faced by strong enemy ships, the cruiser could simply dive out of the way. Probably the best antidote would be an ASW submarine like the 'R' class. Other submarines would need intermediate bases.

The future ASW weapon would be 'a long-range, slow speed, hydrophone torpedo launched in the direction of submarines. Depth charges now used with hydrophones is a very primitive method of combining search and attack. You could fire a torpedo in direction of periscope and steam away and leave torpedo to do its work for next quarter of an hour in looking for enemy. Not practicable at present,

but might have it in five years' time.' No other witness before the Committee suggested anything similar and nothing came of this proposal.

Engines

Engines were the one weakness of wartime British submarines. When war broke out, Vickers had just solved most of the problems of its eight-cylinder four-cycle engine and the design was frozen.[9] In the 'J' and 'L' classes it was expanded by adding more cylinders, but output per cylinder hardly changed.[10] Nor did Vickers' solid fuel injection, which was practically unique among submarine diesel builders of the time. British officers blamed it for excessive smoking (i.e., incomplete combustion).[11] Smoky exhaust had made British submarines far too conspicuous on the surface. British officers also found Vickers engines too loud. They vibrated too badly, breaking bolts in their structures.

EinC was well aware that the 'E' class had insufficient foundations for its engines and that something more was needed to handle their vibration.[12] All submarines with twelve-cylinder Vickers engines had very strong, heavy girders fitted under them. They amounted to 15 tons in an 'L'-class submarine, adding 14lbs per BHP. The Germans did much better, the U-shaped structure surrounding their crank shafts adding considerable rigidity. In a 3000 BHP engine this casing was about 4ft deep. The supports to the cylinders were strong castings well connected together and to the bottom framing. This continuous framing took up all internal forces which the engine might generate. In a German engine additional stiffening amounted to not more than 5lbs per BHP, partly due to the shorter length of the engines (16ft vs 29½ft for 1200 BHP) and partly because so much of the stiffening was integral with the engine. Forces generated by the engine were taken up by its framing and not by the hull structure, so that the girders only had to support the engine weight. DNC cited a lack of homogeneity and strength in British engine framing, presumably worsened in the 'J' and 'L' classes by the addition of four cylinders to the original eight.

Running in the fleet anchorage, *K 6* shows smoky exhaust from her Vickers diesel, used at low speeds. Such smoking was a considerable operational danger, as it allowed a British submarine to be spotted from a distance. Smoking led to the Admiralty programme for in-house diesel development. Smoking is relatively rare in photographs of British submarines of this era, perhaps because exhausts were generally underwater (drowned). (US Naval Institute)

Running in Grand Harbour, Malta, probably in the early 1930s, *L 26* shows only white exhaust aft. The carrier is *Glorious* or *Courageous*. (Dr Josef Straczek)

EinC added that on recent trials with *U 135*, with her engines working at full power, there was almost no vibration. With the engine running, notes could be written clearly and legibly in a book resting on the engine framing. Vibration in a British engine would have made that entirely impossible. DNC quoted 54lbs/BHP for the German 1200 BHP engine, plus 5lbs/BHP of girders, for a total of 59lbs/BHP. The Vickers 1200 BHP engine weighed 64lbs/BHP, to which its

foundation added 14lbs, for a total of 78lbs/BHP.

Allied personnel who operated U-boats after the Armistice all commented on the reliability of German engines, even on board submarines where inexperienced crews were operating engines which had not been maintained for six months. Much of this was down to quality control and extraordinary skill with complicated steel castings, to a degree unavailable outside Germany.

By this time all concerned were well aware that engine-shaft combinations had critical speeds at which torsional vibration peaked and became intolerable. At full power British submarine engines ran at about 390 to 400 RPM, which was well above the critical speeds. For example, for the 'L' class the critical range was 240–260 RPM; for the 'E' class it was 230–285 RPM.[13] The Germans managed to move the critical speed to one through which the engine quickly passed as the submarine operated.[14]

As Commodore (S), Roger Keyes had attacked Vickers' engine monopoly before the war. The wartime Admiralty hoped that competition would provide it with better post-war engines. In 1917 it created the Admiralty Engineering Laboratory (AEL), which was intended to perform basic research.[15] Its mandate was to develop more powerful but lighter engines, so it tried double-acting engines and two-cycle operation. In the end, however, it focused on the same single-acting four-cycle type the Royal Navy was already using, although it abandoned solid injection in favour of air injection. AEL's first experimental unit was a single-cylinder engine of standard Vickers type built in 1916 by Ruston & Hornsby and set up at AEL in September 1917. Initially the object was to increase output by increasing both engine speed and mean pressure. To increase speed AEL adopted lighter-weight (aluminium pistons). Vickers had spent heavily to perfect its diesel and it was furious that AEL published its discoveries.

By this time the Germans had an operational engine producing 300 BHP per cylinder; at the end of the war the British obtained a German ten-cylinder 3000 BHP engine, which was the most powerful submarine engine in the world. This output became AEL's target.[16] AEL also wanted smokeless exhaust, so it adopted air injection, which

On completion, *X 1* was the largest submarine in the world. She was inspired by the wartime German U-cruisers, and several British submarine officers told the Post-war Questions Committee that cruisers would be ideal in a war against a distant enemy, such as Japan or the United States. Later it was claimed that clauses in the Washington Naval Treaty prohibiting unrestricted submarine warfare made all submarine commerce warfare illegal, and hence that no further cruisers should be built – but such large submarines with heavy gun batteries were ideal for exactly the sort of commerce warfare which was still legal. *X 1* is shown at Malta during her 1930 Mediterranean deployment. Her lower hull was painted black, as here, from 1928 on. (US Naval Institute)

AEL claimed made it possible to achieve greater power. The 300 BHP single-cylinder prototype ('Digit' as compared to the 100 BHP 'unit') had 20in bore and stroke and ran at 300 RPM.[17] Drawings were released in May 1918, construction began that autumn and the engine first ran in November 1919. EinC considered 'Digit' the appropriate basis for a multi-cylinder engine. However, AEL also tried alternatives developed by various British firms.[18]

The Admiralty kept AEL alive after the war because it saw no commercial future for the sort of compact lightweight diesels needed for submarines. Private companies would not invest in such engines and the submarine market was not, in the Admiralty's view, large enough to support private development.[19] Late in 1920 AEL's 3000 BHP design for *X 1* (390 RPM, bore and stroke 21½in) was chosen by EinC in the face of competition by five leading British firms as well as by Sulzer and MAN. AEL's was considered the best possible combination of minimum weight and space with reliability and ease of access (for maintenance). EinC wrote that it was beyond question that the *X 1* engines were lighter per BHP and required less space than either Sulzer or MAN. They completed bench trials in May 1923. The multi-cylinder Admiralty diesels in the *Oberon* and her successors were derived from this engine. At the same time EinC ordered the development of a two-stroke double-acting engine for a future fleet submarine (the test unit, presumably a single cylinder, was to produce 1000 BHP). As of November 1925, this engine was expected to power a fleet submarine in the 1929–30 Programme.

In October 1925, while *X 1* was being built (two years later than planned), RA(S) complained that engine development was hardly satisfactory.[20] Naval Intelligence had just reported that in Switzerland Sulzer was producing a 7000 BHP engine. What had gone wrong? EinC answered that RA(S) did not understand what had happened. *X 1* had the highest-powered diesels afloat and AEL was testing a two-stroke double-acting engine which would exceed anything under test anywhere. No one else had commissioned a submarine with a 3000 BHP engine. Sulzer was testing a 6000 BHP engine, but it needed a second powerful engine to drive its auxiliaries. If the engine drove its own auxiliaries, its output would be only 4800 BHP.[21] An *X 1* type engine could produce that much power in a smaller-diameter hull and a shorter engine room. Britain was leading, not following.

As with many contemporary submarine diesels, *X 1*'s suffered badly from torsional vibration. In the case of *X 1* the critical speeds were just below 200 RPM and about 300 RPM; the diesel had to operate between 200 and 280 RPM, well below its maximum output rate. Torsional vibration at the high end of this range was described as 'fantastically severe', so bad that camshaft wheels broke. On trials, at about 19 knots (critical speed) the shaft coupling between one of the engines and its motor-generator began to heat, the paint turning black. Given the torsional problem, effective maximum output was about 2700 BHP.

For the *Oberon*s AEL designed a six-cylinder four-stroke engine rated at 1350 BHP at 400 RPM (bore and stroke 18½in).[22] This engine had to be derated in 1936 to 1160 BHP due to recurring seizures of the aluminium pistons.[23] Similar engines powered the two *Otway*s for Australia, but they were rated at 1500 BHP with slightly larger bore and stroke (19¼in). They experienced considerable service problems, *Otway* being re-engined. As in the transition from the 'D' to the 'E' class, the later patrol submarines had eight-cylinder versions of the same engine (2200 BHP, 20in bore and stroke). They were considered reliable except that they suffered cracks in their piston crowns.

'River'-class fleet submarines had an enlarged ten-cylinder version (21in bore and stroke) rated at 4000 BHP (350 RPM) or 5000 BHP with a supercharger. They were derated in 1936 to 3000/4000 BHP. The contemporary minelayers had six-cylinder engines rated at 1650 BHP (20in bore and stroke) at 400 RPM; they were reliable enough that they were never derated. AEL also produced the smaller engines in the 'S' class and in some of the 'T' class.

In addition to conventional diesels, the Royal Navy was still interested in alternative forms of submarine propulsion, which might offer high underwater power. RA(S) considered any method which would do away with delicate and costly secondary machinery (the electric plant) very desirable. The two alternatives were the 'soda boiler' and what would now be called a closed-cycle diesel. In 1916 the Board of Invention and Research (BIR) considered but rejected closed-cycle propulsion in favour of the 'soda' or 'caustic' boiler. EinC later recalled numerous futile experiments. The French had already tried the 'soda' boiler unsuccessfully. The British experimenters found it difficult to obtain materials which could resist the concentrated caustic solutions involved. Preliminary experiments were not completed until the end of 1917. The next step, building an experimental boiler, was abandoned because the special steel involved could not be obtained in wartime. In 1926, when there was interest in closed-cycle diesels, EinC wrote that under current conditions it would be impossible to develop a soda boiler. RA(S) thought that the wartime project showed that the soda boiler had distinct promise. In August 1926 Controller (Chatfield) asked EinC what he meant. EinC replied that the soda boiler was associated with a steam plant, which probably would not come back; the soda boiler had been tried because the 'K' class was being built. The current focus on tropical water made storing energy thermally a problem. Development had gone only to the laboratory stage, in which the chemical side had been explored. RA(S) backed off, but wanted NID to monitor developments abroad. He was also unwilling to abandon steam power, which still seemed to be the only way to attain high surface speed. EinC replied that considerable progress had been made with diesels; he was confident that 450 BHP per cylinder could be attained. Soon there would be double-acting diesels suitable for fleet submarines. Chatfield closed the soda boiler discussion.

The closed-cycle alternative arose in a 1924 proposal rejected as impractical, but still apparently promising enough to end up in the miscellaneous submarine Cover.[24] The idea was reviewed in May 1926 when such a system was reportedly provided by Germans to Japan. DNC wrote at the time that several closed-cycle diesels had been proposed and that an American was said to have built a small submarine using a closed-cycle engine and to have remained submerged for several hours. 'The American Naval Authorities are understood to be sceptical as to the claims the inventor has made, but for several years an item has appeared in the US Naval appropriations to provide for the building of a submarine on this principle.'

British work on alternative forms of propulsion seems to have re-started in 1936, apparently prompted by a report that the Germans had perfected a single power plant (Erren) usable submerged as well as surfaced and that it was operational. The Admiralty formed a Submarine Propulsion Committee (1936–9).[25] In retrospect it seems that the Germans floated the Erren story at least partly as cover for their real work on hydrogen peroxide submarines. Engine power was applied to an electrolyser, which broke down water into hydrogen and oxygen. These gases were stored to feed the same engine underwater.

K 26 tested the suitability of steam fleet submarines in the tropics, sailing from England on 2 January 1924, arriving at Singapore on 14 May and leaving there on 10 June. Operation were feasible if somewhat difficult, as conditions were 'very arduous'. Like other steam ships, she lost speed in hot weather due, for example, to heating in her condensers. On a full-speed run in the Malacca Strait, her maximum was 17 knots rather than 20 knots, although she could have maintained a higher speed without risking damage (and she had a dirty bottom). Her CO reported in the RA(S) Submarine Newsletter that on passage, with two boilers lit, boiler and evaporator room watches had to be shortened to two hours. The heat in these spaces did not dissipate when the submarine dived, so that boiler and engine rooms were accessible for only a few minutes at a time when diving. After diving from full speed (two boilers lit) it was impossible to enter the boiler room at all. The motor room was also excessively hot. Steam could not be raised immediately upon surfacing, as entry into the boiler room had to be delayed as much as 17 minutes. The crew needed a special diet. A passage from Bombay to Colombo (25–28 April) was particularly bad; two stoker petty officers (boiler room watchkeepers) had to be relieved due to giddiness and weakness. One stoker had to be turned in suffering from violent diarrhoea, headaches and weakness. With the entire engine room staff disabled, the ship had to lie to 10 miles off the Indian coast, giving all hands a rest except for the officer of the watch and the quartermasters. The sea temperature rose to 85° F. Locals considered the east coast of India almost unbearable at this time of year. Then the monsoon broke, and conditions improved. The submarine ran into the full force of the monsoon during her run from Bombay to Aden (28 June–8 July), proving an excellent seaboat. Waves were 25 to 30ft high, very steep and short (approximately 300ft). She lifted into the air, her bows unsupported, then slammed down and passed through the next wave instead of lifting again. Her new-pattern superstructure kept her boiler rooms absolutely dry. Her ends worked considerably, and her rivets would have slackened more had she been running at higher speed. As it was, the crankshaft of her diesel broke while she charged her batteries in heavy weather. The heavy weather reduced her endurance dramatically; she barely reached Aden on fuel which should have sufficed for a 35 per cent margin (it should have been good for 2245nm). Losing the diesel cost her another 650nm of margin. During this cruise, dives showed that the problems of underwater control in earlier 'K'-class boats had been eliminated. The average time from surface to just under periscope depth was 2 minutes. (Dr David Stevens)

The system operated on mixtures of recirculated exhaust steam with oxygen and hydrogen produced by electrolysis of water under pressure.

By July 1938 the Committee realised that the Erren system was useless. Its high-pressure electrolyser was unsuitable for a submarine and no alternative was in sight. In an ocean-going submarine, the oxygen-hydrogen combination would offer less underwater performance than the current electrical system. In a coastal submarine, it might add performance, particularly if the gases could be stowed outside the pressure hull. The Committee considered the risks unacceptable. Before the oxygen-hydrogen mixture was dropped, an experimental oxy-hydrogen engine was installed at the Beardmore yard. Estimates were made of an oxy-hydrogen diesel to replace the existing propulsion system of a 'T'-class submarine.[26] The Erren story survived at least as late as 1944.

Closed-cycle propulsion was still interesting, so the Committee considered a diesel plant using stored oxygen. The exhaust normally consisted of steam, carbon dioxide (soluble in water) and nitrogen from the inlet air. If something condensable or water-soluble could be substituted for nitrogen, much of the problem of disposing of the exhaust would be solved. One possibility was to feed the engine with oxygen and carbon dioxide, the oxygen being carried in pressure bottles. The exhaust would be cooled and some of the carbon dioxide scrubbed out. What was left would be mixed with fresh oxygen and sent back into the engine. Calculations involving a 'U'-class submarine indicated that this technique offered enough advantages to justify experiments.[27] A contract was let to the Ricardo company. The final paper in the Committee file (dated 30 October 1939) was an account of tests of a diesel engine fed with mixtures of carbon dioxide and oxygen or carbon dioxide, oxygen and argon rather than air. The CO_2-oxygen mixture would correspond to what the engine would be fed if running on a closed-cycle basis. The Committee also considered and rejected two novel steam generators; only a diesel of some sort was worth pursuing.

Not surprisingly, this long-range project died on the outbreak of war, but the US Navy continued to pursue it. Nowhere in the Committee's papers was there any indication of interest in HTP (high-test peroxide), which was the oxidizer of greatest interest to the wartime Germans.

Asdic

Post-war submarine development was profoundly affected by the advent of active sonar, which the Royal Navy called Asdic.[28] It offered submarines much improved target detection, including detection of surface ships. It also offered far better, longer-ranged and more reliable underwater communication, the Asdic pinger being used as a form of telegraph. It seemed likely that eventually all major navies would adopt Asdic and therefore that submarines would lose some of their First World War effectiveness. None of these expectations turned out to be quite accurate, but it is fair to say that Asdic made it far more dangerous for submarines to attack convoys. In the Second World War Asdic helped turn North Atlantic convoys into killing grounds for U-boats.

Once the First World War broke out, the Submarine Committee began work on submarine detection.[29] At least through 1916 that meant using hydrophones, which would later be called passive sonar, working at audible frequencies. Their operators listened for sounds produced by submarines, both by their machinery and by the water flowing over their hulls. Their ears were considered far more sensitive (and far better at recognition) than any alternative. The detector had to filter out noises created by the sea and by the weather; it was generally useless if the ship or submarine mounting it was moving.[30] It was also entirely useless against a stopped submarine, particularly one lying on the bottom.

The standard wartime British submarine installation was a pair of listening plates, typically in hull tanks forward. They compared favourably with hydrophones taken from captured German submarines. In theory they could indicate whether a sound came from port or starboard. Experiments using the submarine *B 3* began in February 1916.[31] She managed to fire torpedoes entirely on sound information, as accurately as with her periscope. The first thirty installations were ordered in April 1916, fittings beginning the following year.[32] As of October 1918, about ninety sets of Mk IV plate hydrophone receivers had been fitted to British submarines in commission. These plates often picked up ships 20nm away.

At the end of the First World War the standard British submarine installation was plates plus a directional hydrophone.[33] By 1918,

H 34 shows the dome of a directional hydrophone, added at the bows of these boats in 1923, and suppressed in 1926 when the hydrophone was moved into a bow tank. (John Lambert collection)

L 56 shows the sonar dome of her Type 113 Asdic, which replaced her after 4in gun. (US Naval Institute Fahey Collection)

nineteen submarines had the new Mk II revolving directional hydrophone (RDH), with about two-thirds the range of the plates.[34] At reasonable ranges RDH could determine the bearing of a target within 2° either way. Its remote control handles, pointers, dial, etc. were in the forward torpedo flat, which was the quietest part of the submarine apart from the silent cabinet used for wireless reception. The operator could listen to the Mk IV plates from the same position. It would have been preferable to listen from inside the silent cabinet, but there was insufficient space. At this time RDH was to be fitted as quickly as possible to submarines in commission. Typically operators used the plates for initial detection and then scanned the directional hydrophone to get a bearing on a target. The standard post-war arrangement was two plates in the pressure hull plus an RDH on the extreme stern, either on the superstructure plating or on a streamlined stool or inside the bow buoyancy tank. The hydrophone operator had a headset and an extension headset was fitted in the control room for the captain.[35] The 1924 submarine hydrophone manual claimed an accuracy of 5° in direction out to 5000 yds. After the war these hydrophones were relocated to positions atop the casing forward of the bridge.

The North Sea was so shallow that U-boats could often bottom. It was soon understood that only an active pinger could detect them. Although a pinger had been patented immediately after the *Titanic* sank, it was abandoned as impractical.[36] The first wartime proposals were submitted to the French government in February 1915 and prominent French physicist Paul Langevin began work on supersonics (i.e., on signals with frequencies above the usual human hearing limit of about 20 kHz) in March.[37] By April 1916 Langevin had a workable scheme; he was given two vessels for his experiments (one to send, the other to receive). He was able to send a signal 3km and to detect a large iron plate at a range of 100m using a 100 kHz signal. Langevin's breakthrough was to use a quartz transducer, which could create the sharp pulse he needed. He first tried it in February 1917. In February 1918 his mature system could signal at a range of 8km and for the first time it produced clear echoes of a submarine. By May 1918 Langevin had a practical device, operating at 40 kHz, producing a beam 15 to 20° wide. Tests in June and July 1918 gave a maximum range of

1500m. Langevin thought he could do better at a lower frequency. Langevin led because vacuum-tube amplifiers were so important: they were necessary to pick up weak echoes. France led in 1916 because French vacuum tubes were superior (the United States also led in this technology). Thus in 1918 Langevin was using an eight-stage amplifier to produce the outgoing ping and a nine-stage amplifier coupled to the quartz to receive its echo.

Maurice de Broglie, who worked with Langevin, visited the BIR experimental site at Hawkcraig in May 1916 and invited British scientists to Langevin's laboratory. Two BIR members received full details of Langevin's work at an Allied conference on submarine detection in Washington in the late spring of 1917. On their return BIR formed two teams to develop a Langevin-type system: one for quartz transmitters, one for tube amplifiers.[38] The quartz came from France. By the end of October 1917 the BIR team was matching Langevin's performance, initially at 75 kHz. They obtained their first submarine echoes in March 1918 at 500 yds. They also found that signals could penetrate the same kind of canvas-covered dome used for directional hydrophones on board submarines. Its advantage was that it surrounded the transducer with still water, shielding it from water flow noise. The first ship with an inboard Asdic (Type 111) was the trawler *Ebro II*; installation was completed by 16 November. She received echoes at a range of 600 yds. Meanwhile twenty sets had been ordered in June 1918, the first warship fitted being one of twelve 'P'-boats: *P 59*. She had he first inboard installation, the set being standardised post-war as Type 112. There were no plans to mount the devices on board British submarines.

The Americans asked the French for full information on the Langevin device, together with examples, arguing that they could supplement limited French research facilities.[39] The French responded by calling an inter-Allied conference on supersonics, which met in Paris, 19–22 October 1918. Both the British and the French developers described their work and their plans. Representatives of the French, Italian, Royal and US navies attended, of which all but the Italians were actively pursuing supersonics research.[40] The French developers may have seen the conference as a means of exerting pressure on their own government to pursue the project. The conference recommended formation of a permanent inter-Allied Commission for the Development of Supersonic Methods, but the war ended before that could be done.

HM SUBMARINE *X 1*. As fitted. Profile. (© National Maritime Museum M0246)

PROFILE

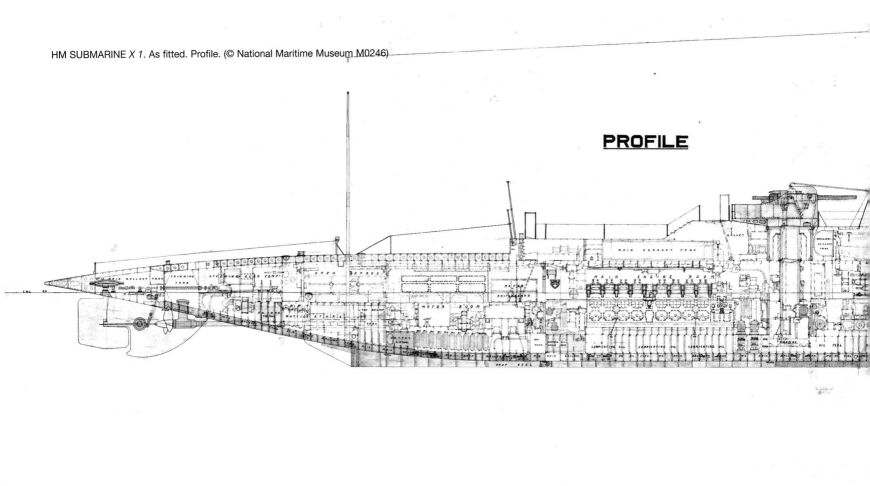

HM SUBMARINE *X 1*. As fitted. Plan views. (© National Maritime Museum M0248)

SUPERSTRUCTURE

SCALE ¼" = I FOOT.

OUTER HULL

INNER HULL

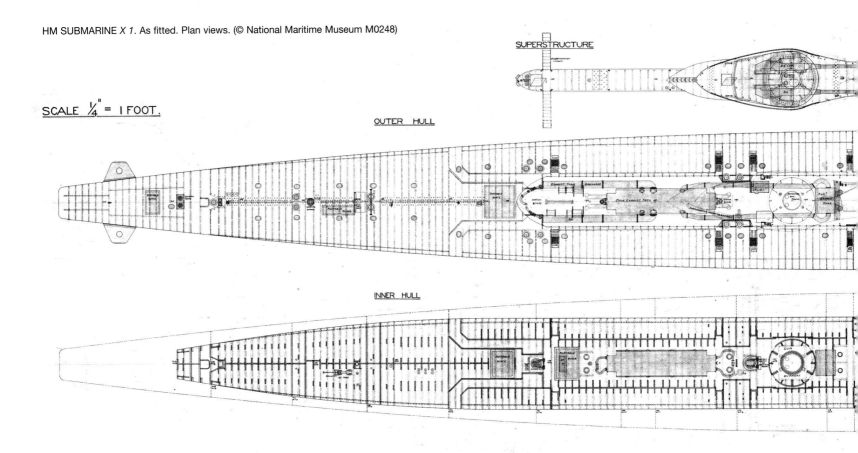

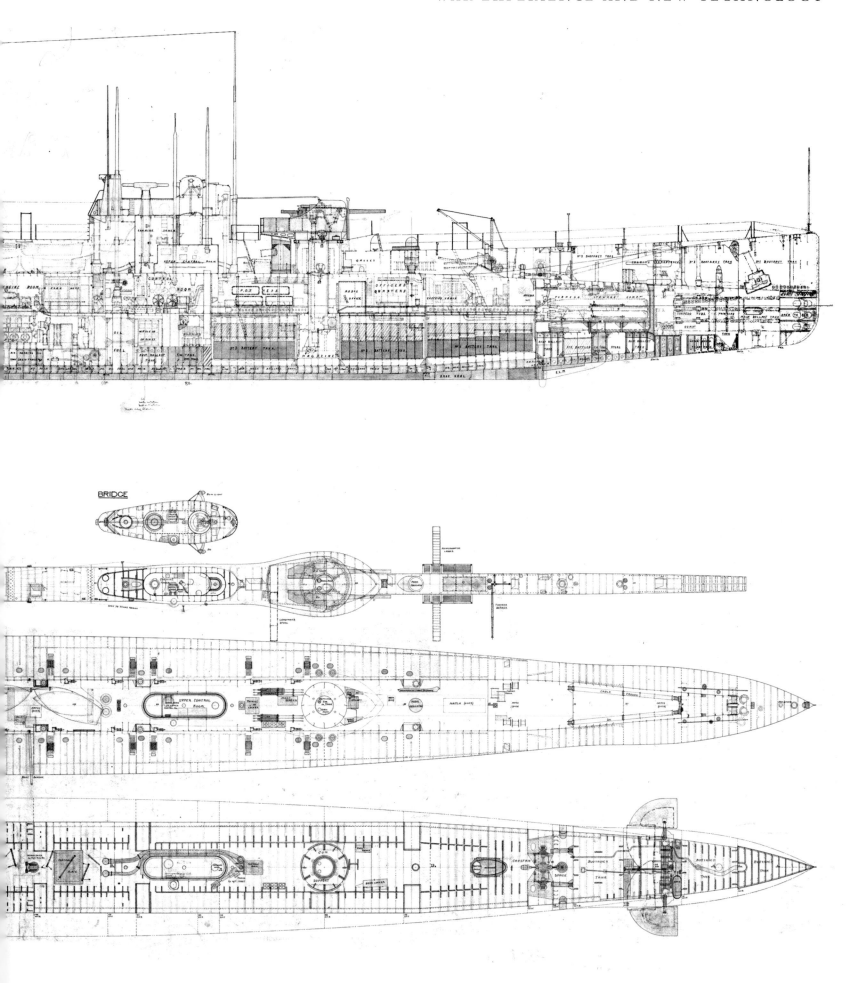

HM SUBMARINE *X 1*. As fitted. Sections. (© National Maritime Museum M0250)

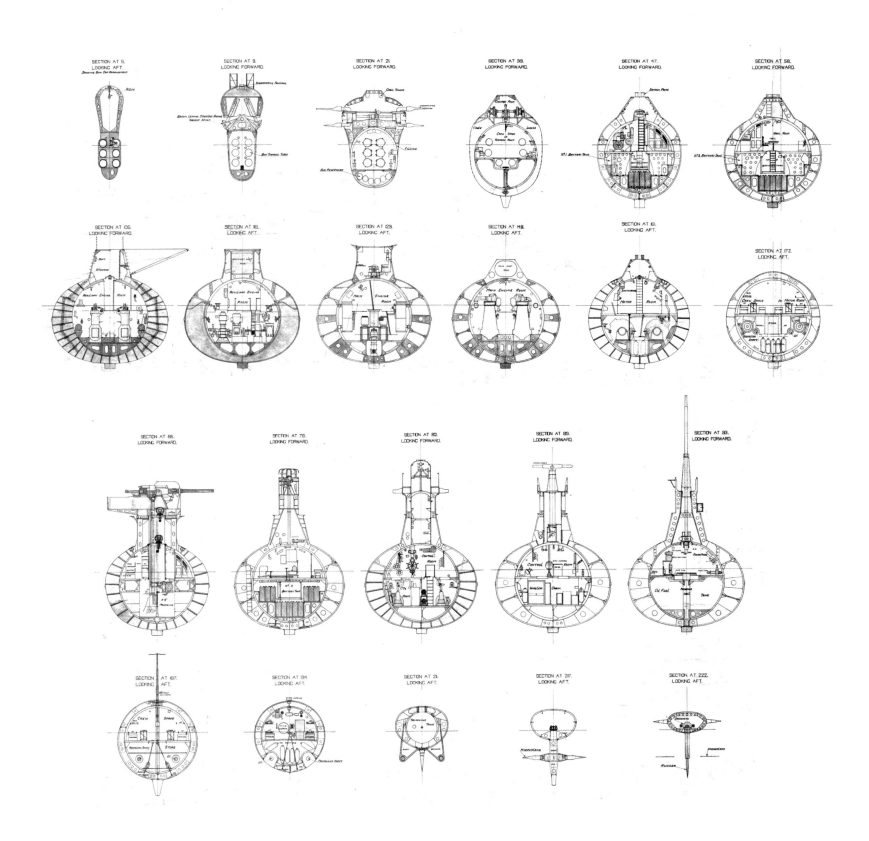

All of this discussion with the Allies (not to mention the French work) suggested that, however effective it might be, Asdic would hardly remain secret for long.[41] Among the major naval allies, only the Japanese had not been invited to the 1918 conference. Since for much of the interwar period the Royal Navy focused on a possible future war against Japan, the presence or absence of Japanese Asdic would profoundly influence British submarine operations. According to post-war report on Japanese sonars, pre-war effort went mainly into hydrophones.[42] Remarkably, the Germans seem to have been unaware of the nature of Asdic.[43] They invented their sonar independently.

When the war ended, the Royal Navy abandoned its twelve-ship programme. Instead it fitted experimental Asdic sets to the old armoured cruiser *Antrim* as well as to the submarine *H 32*. A November 1921 report showed that Asdic was fulfilling its promise.[44] In fine weather, with sea state 2 or less (perhaps less than 3) and with the submarine position known at the outset, up to a range of 1500 yds or even 2000 yds, two Asdic vessels would generally be able to maintain contact and attain a depth-charge attack position. However, that was with highly-trained operators. Furthermore, the submarine did not employ the best escape tactics and was reluctant to use full speed. It appeared that mass-trained operators would attain about 70 per cent efficiency. The submarine commander in the Asdic experiments emphasised that a ship gaining an attacking position over the submarine would not necessarily be able to kill her. Wartime experience (and experiments using ex-German submarines) and the reality that the submarine might be anywhere from 40 to 180ft below the surface (with a greater range in future) showed that depth-charge attacks would be anything but easy. Very large numbers of depth charges would be needed.

Experiments using one to three ships screened by two Asdic ships showed that the odds favoured the Asdic ships detecting an attacking submarine in time for the targets to evade attack and maintaining contact until the submarine had completed her own attack, assuming that in her attack the submarine would pass within 800 yds of the screen.

Against all of this, the experiments showed numerous false echoes and contacts. It was still difficult to say how well Asdic would work in practice. Maximum range for practical purposes was 2000 yds or less and as fitted in 'P'-boats it was of little value in sea state 3 or above. It was not yet clear why bad weather was such a problem. Efficiency did decrease considerably over 12 knots and Asdic operators seemed to lose their edge after four hours. It was essential that Asdic be fitted in new submarines. Although if used as a transmitter it would give away the position of the submarine, as a receiver it would enable the hunted submarine to obtain accurate bearings of the hunters and thus to evade them. The study of Asdic countermeasures had just begun.

For security, Asdic sets were coded in the same Type 100 series as the Fessenden S/T sets, the experimental submarine set used in 1921 being Type 113X (the surface ships had Type 112X). These sets used retractable canvas domes and they were not roll-stabilised; the operator manually compensated for roll and pitch by following indicators. The first destroyer set was Type 114 (1922), its successor being Type 115 (aboard 2nd Destroyer Flotilla in the Mediterranean). Type 113A was fitted first to *H 32* and then to 'L'-class submarines; there were seven in all.[45] Early trials justified a policy that all post-1928 submarines be equipped with Asdic.[46] *L 27*, which was joining 1st Submarine Flotilla, was also fitted. Hydrophones and echo-sounders were designated in a 700 series. By 1929 Type 709 had been designed for the 'P'

class. It used microphones without the earlier rotating element. Trials were proceeding with a 7in Asdic oscillator to replace the earlier PDH in non-Asdic submarines.

It was soon decided that submarines needed Asdic both above and below their hulls. Type 116 had a tube passing through the hull. A pulse sent into the tube could be reflected by a mirror either above or below; unfortunately the tube leaked. Also, the transducer had to tilt; this was considered undesirable. Most submarines had only the bottom element. Type 116 introduced a loudspeaker, as in surface ships.[47] Introduced in 1926, it was superseded in 1928 by the single-dome Type 118, which survived into the Second World War.[48] It survived until 1937. Its very similar successor was Type 120 ('River' and early 'S' class).[49] The main difference was that the Type 120 transducer was remote-controlled, so that its operator did not have to be directly above or below it. The Asdic cabinet could be moved back to a position adjacent to the W/T cabinet, the ultimate object being to merge the two. This arrangement was tested in the large submarine *Thames*. New formal Asdic requirements were stated in 1935.[50] The final interwar set was Type 129, initially in 'T' and 'U'-class submarines. With a transducer in a strengthened cage forward, it could be used surfaced or submerged or bottomed. It was electrically steered and gyro-stabilised.[51]

The Royal Navy became interested in anti-Asdic measures, including jamming.[52] By 1931 there was increasing interest in whether Asdic emissions, either from surface ships or submarines, could be detected during an attack. Because the Royal Navy operated in such a wide variety of places, it was well aware of adverse Asdic conditions such as adverse temperature gradients (layering). Exercises showed that diving deep, which would protect a submarine against air observation, would help an Asdic hunter. The following year continuing experiments showed that the best measures were to use very slow speed or even to stop with holding trim; and to present an end-on target. *H 32* carried out jamming trials in July 1932. Under some conditions she could certainly jam surface Asdics, but how well she could do so depended on how efficient the surface ship's operators were. Indiscriminate emissions would help the surface hunters. If three surface ships hunted together, a submarine could not evade by jamming. In 1934 it was stated that jamming seemed likely to be less and less effective. Trials showed that Asdic offered about 1¼ minutes' warning of an impending attack, although it was difficult for a submarine to deduce what was happening when three hunters worked together. By 1935 tests confirmed reports that newer, smaller, submarines were more difficult to detect by Asdic. In theory echo strength should depend on the reflecting area at right angles to the Asdic beam; it turned out to increase in the ratio of the square root of displacement. Interest in estimating enemy speed continued. In addition to Doppler, it might be obtained by a turn count (but that required detailed knowledge of the enemy ship) and by combining rate of change of range with rate of change of bearing. Further evasion trials described in 1936 showed a distinct difference between a submarine at dead slow speed and one with motors stopped. At 'dead slow' contact could be established or regained using echoes, but with motors stopped it was either never established or was lost. Work continued on exploiting enemy Asdic: in 1938 it was estimated that listening for enemy pings would give a submarine about a minute's warning.

Trials described in 1936 showed that the danger that a submarine Asdic ping could be detected and exploited was 'appreciably less than was at one time anticipated' as long as submarines showed reasonable discretion. However, exercises in China revealed errors which suggested that attacks could not be made based entirely on Asdic data. This problem was solved the following year: sixteen of twenty-nine Asdic-aimed attacks succeeded. Using 10 kHz oscillators, submarines detected surfaced submarines running at 10–15 knots at 3400 yds by echo and at 5300 yds passively. Destroyers at 8–24 knots could be detected at 3500 yds actively and at 6500 yds passively. Trials against submerged submarines had only been conducted using the older 20 kHz oscillators. A 1–4 knot target could be detected passively at 1400 yds and actively at 1300 yds. Reports in 1938 were that further tests showed how superior the 10 kHz Asdic was: all Asdic-fitted submarines of the 1st, 2nd and 6th Flotillas had now been fitted, with the 4th and 5th shortly to be fitted.

On the other hand, the lower frequency made it more difficult to determine target speed. As of 1936, attention was shifting to turn counts and efforts were being made to collect foreign speed-revolution data. The turn count technique was standard in 1937. If speed-revolution data were known, 98 per cent of attacks showed an error of 1 knot or less in enemy speed.[53]

Asdic also became the standard means of submarine-to-submarine signalling.[54] Initially the frequency was 20 kHz, but it was reduced to 10 kHz to meet RA(S)' 20nm range requirement to replace the earlier S/T (Asdic signalling was often called S/S/T, the two S's indicating super-sonic). Submarine Asdics had their oscillators tuned to 10 kHz rather than to the usual higher frequency specifically to support communication. Trials reported in 1937 showed that, using the new oscillator and knowing their relative bearings, two submarines could pass an enemy report an average range of 14,400 yds (maximum 25,000 yds). The average for all signals was 19,300 yds, the maximum range recorded being 42,000 yds – just over RA(S)' requirement. With bearing unknown, the maximum range was 25,000 yds, the average being 13,200 yds. In 1938, maximum reported full-power SS/T range was 44,000 yds (the average was 14,600 yds). In 1939 the maximum range was 43,700 yds (as recorded in 1938–9).

As submarines began to use their Asdics passively, the Royal Navy

became interested in silencing.[55] In 1934 it stated a new design requirement that auxiliary machinery be quieted, since the Asdic-frequency sound it produced could be detected at up to 4000 yds, even though submarines at 3 knots were rarely detected by their audible sound. In 1935 the Royal Navy tested (but apparently did not adopt) the 'Gill' shrouded propeller to reduce noise at speeds below 7 knots. Trials had shown that propeller noise generated by a diving submarine at 4 knots and above could be heard by enemy ASW craft and also interfered with the submarine's own Asdic reception. In 1936 it was announced that all submarines would undergo noise trials when submerged. The Germans already subjected U-boats to 'silence tests' before accepting them.

In 1938 the Director of Scientific Research announced a formal noise measurement programme; all auxiliary machinery would be subject to 'noise measurement' before and after installation and external noises would be measured at Portland.

Noise measurements disclosed two other sources of underwater noise: The Royal Navy had also discovered two other sources of submarine noise, the 'whistle effect' and the 'rattle'. The whistle was attributed to insufficiently lubricated parts of hydroplane mechanism. Lubricating oil could escape into the water, to be an even surer indication of the submarine. Since the sound could be heard only when a submarine dived at sea, it would take time to find a cure. Further work showed that 'whistles' might be present even without a submarine, apparently due to shoals of large fish such as dolphins and porpoises. It was hoped that improved lubrication would solve the problem.

The rattle was characteristic of the first four *Swordfish*-class submarines; its cause was not known as of 1936. Soon it was associated with propeller action, but exactly how was unclear. Further investigation suggested that the rattle in the 'S' class was linked to hull vibration aft, though the source was unknown. With smaller, faster-running propellers *Sunfish* seemed to show less rattle than her sisters. Blanking plates fitted to the after free-flooding spaces of *Snapper* and *Sunfish* offered no advantages and interfered with submarine trim while diving, so they were removed. In 1939 rattle was still a puzzle,

X 1 as completed, showing the 9ft rangefinder atop her bridge abaft the DCT. Both could be raised for use, the DCT by 2ft and the rangefinder by 8ft. Forward of the tower was a fire-control periscope, the eyepiece of which was in an upper control tower. Just abaft it was No 1 periscope, the eyepiece of which was in the control room. The eyepieces of the big rangefinder were in the conning tower which, in contrast to the ones in most British submarines, was quite large. The wireless cabinet was below the control room. The Asdic office was on the deck forward of the forward gun mounting. The guns were a unique 5.2in/42, firing a 70lb shell, the only interwar British naval gun which did not survive into the Second World War. (Author's collection)

X 1 shortly after completion. She had enormous freeboard and reserve buoyancy, far more than in any other British submarine, since she was expected to spend much of her time on the surface, hunting merchant ships like a conventional commerce-raiding cruiser. Note the open-backed 5.2in mountings and the single stowable bow plane. Her single wireless mast is raised; note the spreader immediately forward of her after twin mounting. The same stub standard houses a periscope. The projecting object just abaft her bridge windows is the control periscope for her guns. She also had a periscope just abaft it, but that is not visible here. The forward periscope passed through the upper control room (fire-control room). The curved structure visible is the director, which was raised for use. Note an Asdic dome on deck just forward of the forward gun mounting; another was in the drop keel slightly further forward. (NARA)

but it was known to coincide with intense propeller noise. Stiffening of the tail of *Spearfish* had not helped, though hull vibration had been reduced. The outbreak of war seems to have stopped work.

The Experimental Submarine: *X 1*

Like other navies, the Royal Navy was much impressed by the large long-range cruiser submarines the Germans introduced late in the First World War. Grand Fleet CinC Admiral Beatty apparently personally requested that DNC design one and in a 22 January 1918 letter he proposed construction.[56] That was impossible due to urgent wartime needs, but the idea resurfaced in December 1918. It made sense: a war against Japan would necessarily involve an attack on Japanese merchant shipping. Questions asked by the Post-war Questions Committee testify to continued interest. Initially a British version of the wartime German cruiser, using captured German engines, seems to have been planned, but the project morphed. There was no question of ordering a prototype cruiser in 1919, not only because there was no money but also because the Board proposed that at the Versailles Conference the British Government should propose a ban on further submarine construction. The project came to life once that initiative had failed: design work was underway by 1920.[57] The Admiralty seems to have accepted the need for a big experimental submarine to test new technology. This role may explain the designation *X 1* applied to the new submarine.

As drafted in 1920, there were no submarines at all in the projected five-year programme (1921–2 through 1925–6). By July 1921,

however, the new submarine had been inserted.[58] Note that this was well before the drastic cuts in the programme due to the Washington Conference, which had not yet met.

DNC had already proposed that sketches be prepared as a basis for future decisions. By the autumn of 1920 the combination power plant the Germans had introduced in their *U 139*-class cruisers had been adopted. The Germans retained the usual direct-drive diesels but added dedicated diesel generators which could charge batteries while the main engines ran at full speed. Alternatively, they could drive the propellers if the generators they drove were connected to the motors. This arrangement was later called diesel-electric as opposed to direct drive. For maximum surface speed the submarine would run her main diesels and her auxiliary diesels, the latter driving the electric motors.

Initially the British expected to use captured German 3000 BHP diesels as the main engines of the new submarine, supplemented by the usual 1200 BHP German submarine engines as generators. It helped DNC considerably that the size and weight of the German engines were known. However, once the cruiser was seen as an experimental submarine, she became the test bed for the new Admiralty 3000 BHP diesels (that had not yet been settled as of January 1921). German generator engines were still used, presumably because there was no new Admiralty engine in that power range. Although the generator diesels were rated at 1200 BHP, they could not feed more than 1000 BHP worth of electricity into the motors (on batteries the motors were rated at 1200 BHP each).

In January 1921 RA(S) proposed beginning detailed design.[59] It

This view from aft shows the open backs of the twin 5.2in mountings, which were unarmoured. (NARA)

must soon have been clear that the experimental submarine would be the largest yet built. The initial sketch design seems to have called for a surface displacement of 2300 tons.[60] Undated detailed design data, probably compiled late in 1920, showed a surface displacement of 2680 tons, which compared to 2130 tons for the largest late-war German U-cruisers (the abortive *U 183* class) and 1600 tons for the 'M' class.[61] Beam torpedo tubes were omitted because it was assumed that those in bow tubes could be angled. The three 4in guns would have been on individual turntables and the submarine would have had a 9ft rangefinder and a director control tower (DCT). The upper part of the pressure hull plating would be strengthened as in the German U-cruisers (total thickness 1in). Initially DNC planned to use 448 cells, a third more than in the largest British submarines, to attain a submerged speed of 10 knots, but DEE wanted to cut back to 336 to simplify electrical arrangements, using larger cells. Director of Gunnery Division (DGD) wanted 6in guns in spray shields, but RA(S) preferred 4in. By March 1921 DGD had been argued back down to a twin experimental 5in gun, DNC asking that the diameter of trunk it required not exceed that necessary for a twin 4.7in (which had presumably been designed, although no such gun yet existed). DNO wanted a HA gun, but DNC considered it of little value and it was never included in the design. RA(S) feared that DGD was trying to turn the big submarine into a gunnery experiment, a very secondary matter. He was willing to accept 5in guns. EOC and Vickers were asked for gun designs.[62]

DNC emphasised the need for submerged control, quick diving and underwater endurance (i.e., limited resistance underwater). Habitability would be vital for a submarine with such long range. ACNS wrote that no one could say what the future of the large submarine was, whether it would be the fleet submarine or the cruiser. The design should not be spoiled by trying for too much. He agreed with RA(S) on the 5in gun. The new boat should be called an Experimental Large Submarine. Externally, her striking features were her massive bridge structure, carrying two twin 5.2in mountings and gun controls including a rangefinder and a DCT.

Surface displacement did not change as the design developed, although there were other significant changes, such as adoption of four larger-calibre guns in a pair of power-worked mountings. By this time the overall configuration of the ship had been chosen, with a nearly complete double hull covering most of her length. The outer hull extended around the pressure hull to meet the top of the pressure hull near the centreline. The space between the outer and pressure hulls contained the main ballast tanks. Fuel was stowed atop main tanks amidships, with four oil fuel compensating tanks amidships. Initially the design called for 500ft maximum depth (as in the later *Oberon* and the reconnaissance submarines), but during design that was reduced to 350ft. Intended operating depth was 200ft. The Board Stamp was applied to the building drawings on 9 May 1923.

Construction took much longer than expected. *X 1* was laid down on 2 November 1921 and commissioned in December 1925. She ran successful full-power trials in March 1926 and was then accepted for service. She was then the largest submarine in the world. She was considered a good seaboat and handled well surfaced and submerged. However, she suffered from crippling engine trouble due to torsional vibration. Her critical range of revolutions (RPM) was unfortunately near that required to make full speed. Once completed, she was sent to Gibraltar, but suffered serious engine trouble going out and returning. She was then returned to dockyard hands. She joined the Mediterranean Fleet in 1927 after a successful full-power trial, but she suffered further engine trouble after a near-full-power trial in January 1928. Although she was repaired at Malta, she suffered further trouble

on her passage home in April 1928. She also experienced trouble with her auxiliary engines and with her HP air compressors, after which she spent most of her time in dockyards.[63] In 1933 the Board decided that in view of her age and her limited operational value she was no longer worth keeping active. In December of that year she was placed under dockyard control and her main Kingstons were blanked off. Her main impact on the British fleet at this point was that she accounted for an unusually large fraction of the total allowed submarine tonnage. Under the 1930 London treaty, she could not be scrapped until she was overage. In 1936 she was deleted from the list and she was scrapped in 1937, the London Naval Treaty having lapsed by that time.

X 1 in her final configuration, with the two bow planes and the additional wireless masts. The short periscope near her DCT is for the fire-control compartment below it. (Dr Josef Straczek)

CHAPTER 11
A NEW SUBMARINE FOR A NEW KIND OF WAR

A Post-war Fleet

By the end of the First World War, British finances were in ruins. The War Cabinet adopted what was later called the Ten Year Rule: the assumption that the British Empire would not be engaged in a major war for the coming decade. The Ten Year Rule was repeated year after year; it was made self-perpetuating in 1928. To the Admiralty of the 1920s, it provided a target for modernisation: the fleet had to be ready to fight the war which might come after a decade. Modernisation was urgent not only because the recent war had produced a great deal of new technology, but more importantly because the existing fleet – including submarines – lacked the endurance to fight an oceanic rather than a North Sea war.

The Royal Navy faced two major sea powers, the United States and Japan. War against the United States was considered impossible, but it was essential to balance growing US naval strength in order to preclude undue US pressure on the Empire. That required that Britain maintain a capital ship fleet at least as strong as the US fleet. The cost of that fleet might preclude some other naval projects.[1]

Japan was different: although she was bound to the British by an alliance, the Dominion governments in the East were already nervous: in wartime Japan had backed anti-British movements as support for

Otway and Osiris lie alongside, probably at Chatham, 1932. They were very similar, but Otway had been built to a slightly different design for the Royal Australian Navy (although later taken over by the Royal Navy). Note that Osiris has folded fore planes; those of Otway must have been below water (drowned). Both had the cab (streamlined) bridges and gun shields then standard. (RAN Naval Historical Section via Dr Josef Straczek)

'Asia for the Asians'. When the Dominion governments asked Admiral Jellicoe to advise them about naval defence, he pointed to the potential Japanese threat. The Admiralty played that down for the time being, but even in 1919 the Committee on Post-war Questions kept asking witnesses what they would need to fight Japan. The alliance was terminated as a result of the 1921 Washington Naval Conference, which produced a Five-Power Treaty intended to stabilise the Far East. British realists saw nothing of the sort. Through at least the mid-1930s the potential shape of a Japanese war dominated British naval thinking. Even after the British faced the Germans and the Italians in Europe, they were uncomfortably aware that much of the economic power of their Empire lay in the East, where Japan could threaten it.

Distances in the Far East dwarfed those in the North Sea. Of the war-built submarines, only the *L 50* class approached the required endurance, 10,000nm with some ballast tanks filled with oil fuel. It was not, moreover, obvious what sort of submarines were wanted for the new kind of war. A planned 1 October 1921 staff conference on this subject was deferred due to the Washington Conference, but it set the agenda for later discussions.[2] The types of submarines on offer were a patrol or reconnaissance submarine and a fleet submarine. CinC Atlantic Fleet (at the time the main fleet) asked whether an overseas patrol boat of moderate displacement could have 1000nm wireless (necessary to connect a submarine off Japan with Hong Kong), better endurance than an 'L'-class submarine and as good armament? What might have to be sacrificed to attain the desired wireless range? Could it be incorporated in an 'L'-class submarine?

What should be the characteristics of a fleet submarine, if it should be perpetuated at all? Was the 'K' class satisfactory? Given tight finances, should the surviving 'Ks' be considered a dispensable luxury? Other types to be considered were cruiser submarines, local defence submarines, minelaying submarines and anti-submarine submarines. What should the building programme be? CinC Atlantic Fleet, Director of Plans and Director of Tactical Division (DTD) all put forward proposals.[3]

War in the East

Far more than any other country, Japan depended on imports. The mainstream view was that Japan would be defeated by strangulation: blockade. That would begin with blockage of the straits leading from the Indian Ocean into the South China Sea. British cruisers off the US coast would block imports from the United States. The British fleet would move north to one or more advanced bases from which Japanese ports could be blockaded more and more effectively.[4] As during the First World War, a British fleet would shield the lighter ships carrying out the blockade. The Royal Navy had learned from the war that it did not want to deal with an enemy fleet in being. It hoped that the Japanese would feel compelled to fight to break the blockade.

Despite the accent on strangulation, the British had no intention of fighting an unrestricted submarine war against Japanese shipping. They were determined to revive the pre-war cruiser rules for commerce warfare: ships had to be searched for contraband before they could be seized or sunk. That was vital for British survival in the face of anyone else's blockade. Also, the unrestricted U-boat war had proven disastrous for Germany because it had brought the United States into the war.[5] The post-war United States was determinedly neutral and the British hardly wanted to risk bringing the country into war against them.

It did not help that no large British fleet could be maintained in the East in peacetime, even if sufficient infrastructure was built up at Singapore. Planners had to take account of the real possibility that the Japanese would try to seize the fleet's base before it could arrive. Whatever was on station at the outbreak of war would have to keep the Japanese from doing so. Once the fleet arrived, it would need to know when the Japanese fleet sortied and where it was going. During the war, much of that had been done by signals intelligence, but once that had been publicised it was unlikely that the Japanese would allow a repeat performance. In 1920 the only of British warships which could survive near Japanese naval bases were submarines.

The Post-war Submarine Fleet

Planning the post-war fleet began in the spring of 1918. An Atlantic Fleet (essentially the wartime Grand Fleet) would be backed by a semi-active Home Fleet, with a much smaller fleet in the Mediterranean and one in China. The initial plan called for eighty submarines ('E', 'G', H 21, 'J', 'K', 'L', 'M' and 'R' classes) in the Atlantic Fleet and fourteen in the Home Fleet ('D' class, 'R', H 21, 'L' and 'E' classes).[6] None was included in the Reserve Fleet, on the theory that to keep submarines effective they had to have full crews on board. A February 1919 plan envisaged four Atlantic Fleet submarine flotillas (as in the wartime Grand Fleet) backed by a fifth available for foreign service. Two of the four Atlantic flotillas would consist of 'K'-class fleet submarines.[7] A revived Mediterranean Fleet would have its own 5th Submarine Flotilla (six 'G' class, to be replaced by 'J' class if not wanted by Australia, the monitor M 1, three 'E' class and two 'E'-class minelayers). The China Fleet would have the 4th Submarine Flotilla (ten 'L' class and two 'L'-class minelayers). In addition, six submarines would

The new Far East patrol submarines dwarfed their predecessors. Here an 'O'-class submarine lies alongside M 2, L 25 and H 32, in descending size, with other 'O'-class submarines forward of her. Note the stub wireless mast at the after end of the casing on both the 'O' boat and M 2. (John Lambert collection)

be attached to torpedo schools, four (plus three more if available) for ASW training and seven for submarine training.

Reality soon asserted itself: the September 1919 force was all of forty-four active submarines. The foreign service flotilla and the Mediterranean flotilla were eliminated. As a hedge against a future emergency, fifty-three submarines would be kept in reserve.[8] The only submarine force not cut was the big China Fleet flotilla. It was kept at full strength throughout the interwar period as insurance against a sudden Japanese attack on Singapore or Hong Kong. Initially it was backed by seven 'J'-class submarines given to the Royal Australian Navy in 1919.

Through the 1920s the Royal Navy submarine force generally comprised two seven-submarine flotillas with the main fleet (1st at Chatham, 2nd at Portsmouth in 1923, of which the 1st consisted of four 'K' class and the three 'M' class; 2nd had seven 'L' class, two of them of the *L 50* type), one other seven-boat flotilla in home waters (3rd at Devonport in 1923, with seven *H 21* class), the more powerful flotilla in the China Fleet (4th) and about thirteen attached to schools (in 1923, the Submarine School at Portsmouth [six *H 21* class, the target ship *E 48* and four submarines in reserve] and the Periscope School at Portland [six *H 21* class and *R 4*, plus seven submarines in reserve]). The most important change was a shift from the Atlantic to the Mediterranean Fleet as the principal naval formation, submarines moving there. Thus in January 1928 the Mediterranean Fleet included 1st Submarine Flotilla (*X 1*, *K 26* and five 'L' class). Other submarines were based in home waters: 2nd Flotilla at Devonport (under RA(S): six 'L' class), 5th at Portsmouth (a training half-flotilla of seven *H 21* class; an experimental half-flotilla of *H 43*, two 'L' class and two 'M' class; and a reserve half-flotilla of five 'L' class); and 16th Flotilla at

Portland (six *H 21* class, *R 4* and *R 10* in full commission and three *H 21* class in reserve). Presumably the Portland flotilla supported training and experimental ASW work.

A Prototype Patrol Submarine: *Oberon*

In February 1922 RA(S) proposed an Admiralty conference to discuss the type of submarine to be built in the event of war.[9] Chaired by ACNS and held on 2 May, it concluded that the most important requirement was for distant patrol. Main requirements, probably in order of priority, were a wireless range of at least 500nm and preferably 1000nm; a surface displacement of about 1200 tons; endurance at economical speed of 10,000nm; a maximum surface speed of 15 knots (12 knots cruising speed); a minimum submerged speed of 9 knots; a gun armament of one 4in (fifty rounds) and one pom-pom or, alternatively, one 4.7in and two Lewis guns; six 21in bow tubes; and habitability and internal arrangements suitable to the tropics. DNC was to examine the effect on the design of accepting a surface speed of 13 knots and a cruising speed of 10 knots. DCNS supposed that surface speed had been traded off for habitability, 'a matter which is likely to be of vital importance in any future war'. In a recent exercise (XA) during the 1922 spring cruise of the Atlantic Fleet, *K 2* shadowed a convoy for 48 hours and at the end of that time, despite heavy weather, carried out unseen an attack on HMS *Queen Elizabeth*, which had been escorting the convoy. The exercise showed the value of submarines for reconnaissance and shadowing. Speed mattered for shadowing. CinC Atlantic Fleet wrote that cruising speed should be no less than 12 knots and that submerged speed should be at least 10 knots, with sufficient battery capacity for good submerged endurance.

The chief function of the proposed submarine was reconnaissance,

Early in her career, *Oberon* shows stub wireless masts fore and aft. They were removed in 1935 and the wireless mast modified. (Dr Josef Straczek)

An 'O'-class submarine in dry-dock at Cockatoo Island, Sydney, in the late 1920s shows her two after torpedo tubes, a new feature in the big patrol submarines. (Navy League of Australia via Dr Josef Straczek)

which made wireless the key issue and a driver for more internal space. As of 1922, 1000nm range had not yet been achieved in battleships. Yet it was a minimum if a submarine patrolling off a Japanese base was to communicate directly with Hong Kong or Singapore.[10] In effect wireless was the primary weapon of a reconnaissance submarine. In November 1922, DNC offered a 10ft section of the submarine for a W/T room and even that was considered so small that the alternators (AC generators) powering the radio would have to be outside the W/T room. Part of the aerial inductance had to be outside the pressure hull. DNC placed the W/T compartment forward of the control room, leaving the engine room adjacent to the control room. That was

desirable for command of the submarine, but not for wireless operation; the best place for the tube connecting the transmitter to the aerial was at the after end of the bridge structure. Wireless range was so important that the wireless room was relocated to a position abaft the control room.[11]

The conference decided that a design should be pursued at once and, having been approved, be built as soon as possible. A special minelayer should also be designed. CinC Atlantic Fleet strongly favoured fleet submarines, which he considered should have a speed of at least 18 knots, to be used not only for torpedo attack but also for fleet reconnaissance. However, the conference considered them of secondary importance, at least for the present, to the overseas patrol submarine. Similarly, the conference rejected calls for special designs for local defence and ASW submarines, arguing that these roles could be carried out by the overseas patrol submarine (CinC Atlantic Fleet wanted an ASW submarine designed). Nothing should be done about fleet or cruiser submarines pending experience with *K 26* and *X 1*. However, it was understood that the Washington Conference had banned commerce destruction, which had been the whole point of cruiser submarines.

DNC wanted the shortest possible engine room. That ruled out the twelve-cylinder Vickers engine of the 'L' class. EinC chose the new AEL engine, which twice the power per cylinder.[12] Both 1000 BHP and 1200 BHP engines were considered. *Oberon* was powered by a pair of six-cylinder Admiralty diesels rated at 1350 BHP (400 RPM); later they were uprated to 1475 BHP. She had three sets of 112 battery cells each. The twin-armature motors were considered a considerable advance in that they were fully enclosed, hence did not produce dangerous sparks. To save space and weight, a higher pressure for compressed air was adopted (3500 psi rather than 2500 psi).

RA(S) wanted more space around and between torpedo tubes so that full advantage could be taken of external fittings to adjust torpedo speed, depth and angle.[13] A 24.5in torpedo was being developed and RA(S) thought it might turn out to be more desirable than the standard 21in weapon (DNC developed alternative bow arrangements for six 21in or four 24.5in tubes). In December the submarine grew

Oberon as modified with additional freeing ports in her bridge fairwater, to speed diving. Note also the absence of the stub wireless masts fore and aft, and the modified wireless mast with its light element at the top, as modified in 1935. (RAN Naval Historical Section via Dr Josef Straczek)

further when two stern torpedo tubes were added.[14] A later RA(S) requested for a heavier gun armament was rejected.[15]

The bow buoyancy tank was modified, compared to earlier submarines, by moving its flooding holes to the keel. In previous submarines the free-flooding holes had been above the surface, so when riding the vents the tank did not contribute buoyancy until the bow had descended into the sea. Thus opening the vents in the bow buoyancy tanks of the 'H' and 'L' classes made little difference in their behaviour in a seaway. Compared to previous classes, the pressure hull was strengthened to withstand depth charges or to allow deeper diving to minimise the risk of depth-charging.[16]

DNC submitted the sketch design on 22 January 1923, the Board approving it on 15 February.[17] The prototype patrol submarine *O 1* (later *Oberon*) was included in the 1923–4 Programme.

At this stage surface speed was 15 knots and submerged speed 9.5 knots. As DNC developed the design, it proved necessary to add 15ft to accommodate the enlarged wireless system and the projected Asdic. The added length also provided more space for accommodation (specifically for operation in tropical waters) and cooling for both the battery and the crew spaces.[18] The Board approved. A detailed Legend was submitted on 6 May 1924 together with a general arrangement drawing.

Legend speeds were 15 knots surfaced (on 2700 BHP rather than 2400 BHP) and 9 knots submerged (1300 BHP). On trials *Oberon* reached only 13.74 knots on 2950 BHP at 1598 tons. Model tests suggested that the ship would not reach 8 knots underwater on 1300 BHP. As completed *Oberon*'s motors were rated at 1350 BHP. On trial she made only 6.89 knots at 1250 BHP, equivalent to about 7.1 knots at 1350 BHP. At the one-hour rate she might have made 7.5 knots. It did not help that during design topside fittings grew enormously, with considerable impact on submerged speed. *Oberon* was later cleaned up to some extent, but she could not have made the desired 9 knots.

Legend endurance was 5000nm at full speed and 12,000nm at 8 knots. Submerged endurance was 60nm at 4 knots (15 hours). The speed and endurance figures were based on the 1480-ton design displacement, which was considerably exceeded (1598 tons). After completion *Oberon* was credited with 11,400nm at 8 knots with 186 tons of fuel; later she was credited with 6800nm at 10 knots. By 1938 fuel had been cut to 160 tons, giving 10,800nm at economical speed under trial conditions, but an operational endurance of 8150nm at 8 knots.

Follow-Ons

On 13 December 1923 First Sea Lord Admiral Beatty asked for a Naval Staff study of the use of submarines in a war against Japan. He assumed that fleet and reconnaissance submarines would be needed. The fleet submarines would help bring the enemy battle fleet to action and to destroy it. 'The reconnaissance submarines must play a vital part in Eastern Waters where distances are so great and where the CinC will necessarily have to depend on reconnaissance units of great endurance and ability to protect themselves without support. Ability to obtain and report information is the primary qualification. The carrying of aircraft and a large W/T installation is indicated.' Beatty added that although these were the two main types, he would be glad to consider other types. He mentioned minelayers and he asked whether a type might be developed specifically to penetrate enemy bases to attack the fleet there, surmounting booms and other defences.[19]

The Staff concentrated on reconnaissance and attack. Due to

Asdic, reconnaissance submarines would have to keep out of range of local ASW defences: more were needed to cover the approaches to any particular port. However, Asdic most affected the submarines' ability to deliver torpedo attacks, greatly reducing the chance of success by a submerged submarine using short-range torpedoes; 'in future it is doubtful whether this form of attack will hold out sufficient chance of success to make it a profitable form of warfare'. A browning attack at moderate range would be a different matter. Attack on a convoy would be browning with torpedoes or gunnery. ASW development would also make minelaying more difficult, particularly in waters in which it was most valuable, such as heavily used channels and harbour entrances. ASW developments would have the least impact on submarines working with the main fleet. Once the enemy fleet deployed, its CinC would have to choose between keeping destroyers close as an ASW screen or using them offensively against the British fleet. After action the enemy would have far fewer light craft to screen him. A flotilla of fleet submarines would likely be quite effective. Asdic would make submarines far less effective than surface ships for ASW.

Submarines might be the only useful means of reconnaissance.[20] They might have to reconnoitre Japanese ports from Singapore, a 4600nm round trip. Allowing for that amount of fuel for emergencies and auxiliary services, the 10,000nm endurance required for *Oberon* should suffice. A wireless range of 1500nm would be satisfactory. Without it submarines or surface craft would be needed as links.

How many reconnaissance submarines were needed depended on how far they could see. *O 1* (*Oberon*) was being given a crow's-nest which would extend the submarine's horizon to slightly more than 8nm. To do much better the submarine needed an aircraft or at the least a manned kite. This seems to have been the origin of experiments with *M 2*. The *Oberon* Cover includes details of a German proposal for a containerised floatplane to operate from a U-boat. The idea of providing a reconnaissance submarine with an aircraft suggests current ideas of using unmanned vehicles to extend submarine footprints. The Royal Navy and the US Navy both experimented with submarine-based airplanes, but only the Imperial Japanese Navy used them operationally.

Because reconnaissance was primary, torpedo armament could be reduced. Underwater endurance was essential because the submarine would be operating near enemy bases and might have to evade strong local ASW defence forces. Similarly, deep diving might be essential. Because reconnaissance required multiple submarines, good submarine-to-submarine communication would be valuable.

The Staff envisaged a minelayer derived from the reconnaissance submarine, torpedo armament being sacrificed for mines. She would perform reconnaissance as well as minelaying duties.

Priority would go to the reconnaissance submarine, followed by the minelayer and then by the fleet submarines, with other roles (including base attack) following. Fourth came a cruiser, a submarine with heavy gun armament, which could approach enemy light forces unseen (submerged) and then suddenly surface to attack when within decisive range. Working together as a division, such submarines would make it difficult for the enemy to maintain patrols and they might force him to disperse his destroyers.

To estimate required numbers, the Staff considered two contingencies. In one, Japan was engaged in land operations in North China. The Japanese held Hong Kong, with the main British fleet at Singapore. The British would want to maintain a patrol of three sub-

Oxley shows the upper dome of her Type 116 Asdic; a companion dome was in her keel. Submarines without the upper dome had Type 118. The upper sonar dome was removed in 1931. The wireless stub masts were removed in 1936, and a voice pipe was installed connecting bridge and gun. Note the multi-line wireless aerial extending from the after stub mast to a stub on the bridge fairwater. Pendant numbers were painted up on the bridge fairwater in 1939. (NARA)

marines in each of the Formosa (Taiwan) Channel, the waters south of Formosa and off Hong Kong, plus two W/T links. Counting submarines transiting to and from each patrol area, the three patrols required a total of fifty submarines plus six for links.[21] Another twelve cruiser submarines would be used against Japanese communications and patrols and the fleet would require nine fleet submarines.

A second contingency envisaged a British fleet based at Hong Kong intending to establish a base closer to Japan, which controlled the Pescadores and Formosa. Japanese naval bases had four exits, so the British had to maintain eight submarines there at all times. In addition, they would maintain two off the Pescadores. The bases were about as far from Hong Kong as Singapore was from the patrol areas in the first case, so unsurprisingly a total of forty-two was required, plus seven for the Pescadores. As before, two more were needed for W/T links. The total needed was fifty-five rather than fifty-six reconnaissance submarines.

A year later the Admiralty was seeking Cabinet approval for a ten-year building programme. A Staff conference held on 13 February 1925 to decide the type and design of the submarines in the 1925–6 section of the programme was followed by a wider conference on 19 February.[22] Both agreed that the 1925–6 building programme should be confined to reconnaissance (patrol) submarines, the most urgently-needed type. So many were needed that there was no point in building fleet submarines. The 10,000nm endurance of the *Oberon* was confirmed, but higher speed was wanted; 17 knots on 13 February. At the later meeting RA(S) asked for more: the US *T 1* was credited with 20 knots on 1120 tons. ADNC thought such speed would require a

much larger submarine and rightly doubted the report.[23] Director of Plans pointed out that given the relatively small number of submarines which might be available early in a Far Eastern war, reconnaissance submarines also had to be able to shadow enemy forces for several days. The 17 knots was considered necessary to ensure that the submarine could shadow a fast convoy, that it be able to concentrate rapidly and also to allow for a slight difference between designed and actual speed.[24]

Increased power offered another advantage. A submarine making a fast transit should be able to keep her batteries fully charged against the possibility that she would have to dive, but even 3000 BHP would not be enough for that; it would not offer sufficient margin. To provide sufficient auxiliary power while charging at the fullest possible rate would require 1250 BHP, the other engine propelling the ship at a moderate speed; this was an economical load for a 2000 BHP engine.

The desirability of stern torpedo tubes was confirmed but the 19 February conference recommended deleting them if by that means an extra 2 knots could be gained (that turned out not to be the case). This conference considered the 4.7in gun the most suitable. A larger gun would cost too much in submerged capabilities.

Omitting a fleet submarine from the 1925–6 Programme was acceptable because it would not sacrifice continuity of design and handling; the 19 February conference suggested including a fleet submarine in the 1926–7 Programme instead of the cruiser provisionally included in it. Construction of another cruiser should await experience with *X 1*. Although a committee of submarine officers considered a harbour attack submarine, no decision was reached. CinC Atlantic, RA(S) and Plans Division agreed on the rough proportion of types: for ten reconnaissance submarines they would buy two fleet and two cruiser and two minelaying submarines.

For the reconnaissance submarine, CinC Atlantic Fleet, who would command the main fleet in a Far Eastern war, wanted a wireless range of at least 2000nm and considered an aircraft essential (a man-lifting kite would be useful).

HM SUBMARINE *OSIRIS*. As fitted. Port elevation. (© National Maritime Museum J9695)

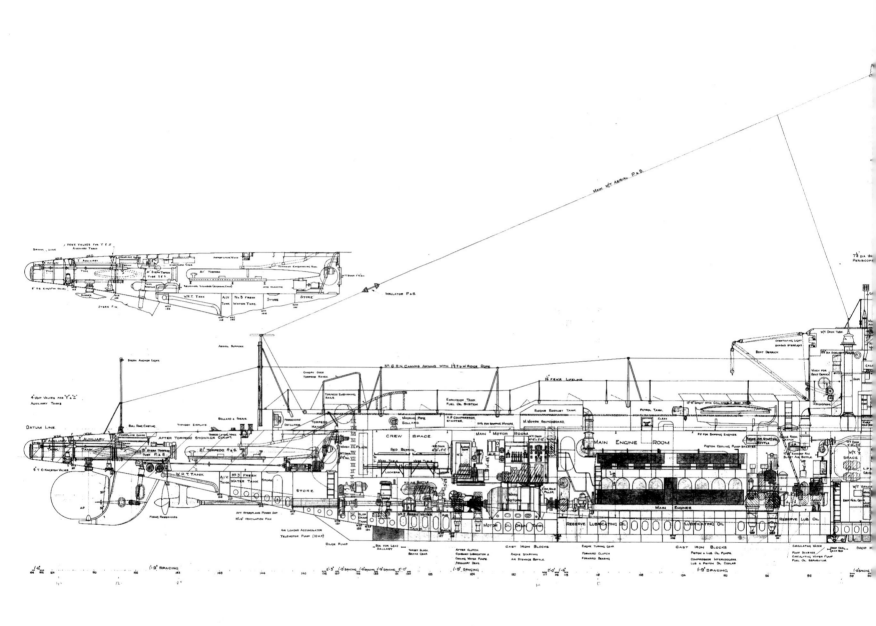

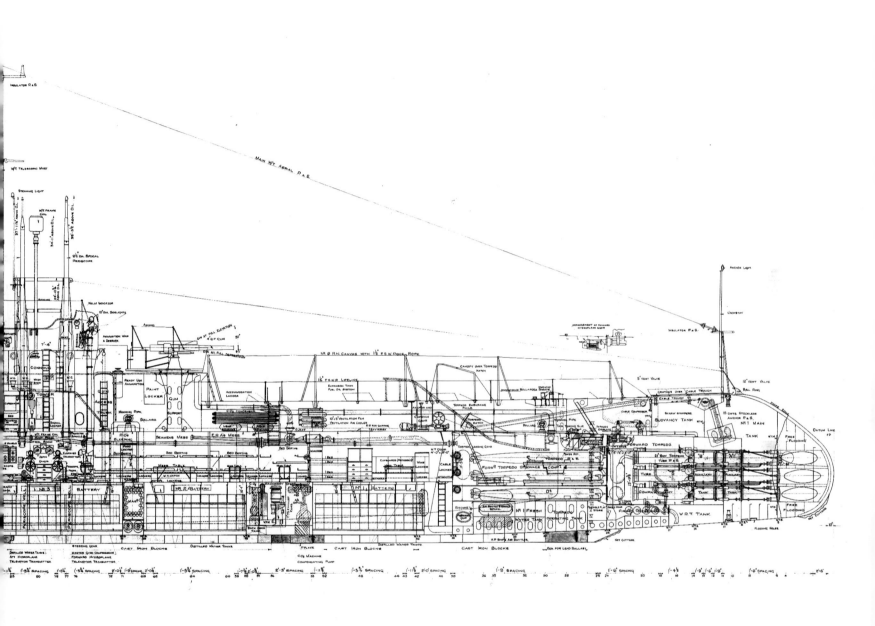

HM SUBMARINE *OSIRIS*. As fitted. Starboard elevation and sections. (© National Maritime Museum J9697)

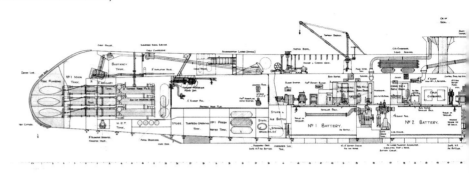

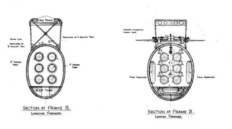

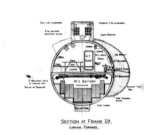

HM SUBMARINE *OSIRIS*. As fitted. Plan views. (© National Maritime Museum J9698)

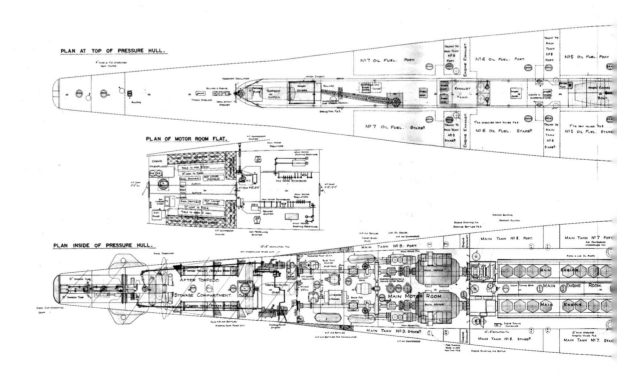

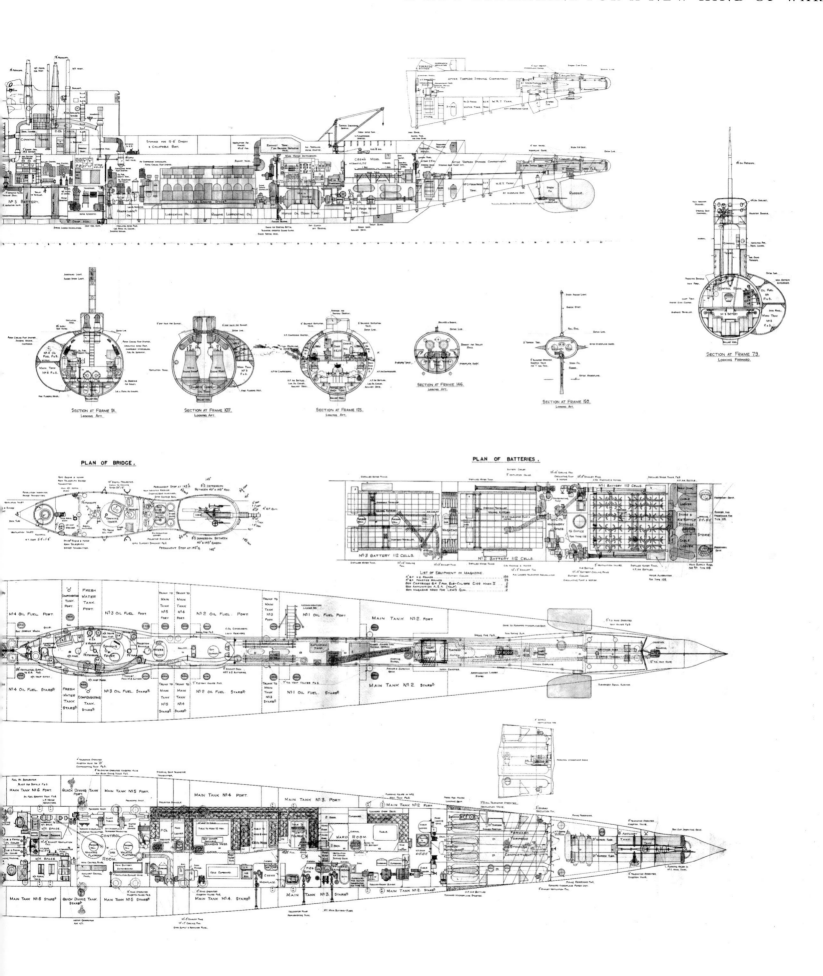

Otway as built. The object between the two periscopes is a frame coil, which could be rotated as a radio direction-finder (note the circular fitting in the beam connecting the periscope standards. (NARA)

CinC China (Rear Admiral A C Leveson), who might have to hold off the Japanese until the main fleet arrived, had little use for the reconnaissance submarine. During the war, it had been vital to know what the High Seas Fleet was doing, because it was only 24 hours away. In the Far East, it was days away. Moreover, merely to spot an emerging enemy fleet was not enough; the submarine had to be fast enough to keep up with it to see where it was going on its long run south. Submarines were inherently limited both in what they could see and how well they could communicate it. The real wartime lesson was that submarines had not been a tenth as useful as the Intelligence Department (presumably meaning signals intelligence). The Admiralty was paying far too little attention the really urgent task, defending Singapore and Hong Kong against a surprise attack. Submarines designed for his station had to cope with its two main features, very long distances and difficult, variable and bad weather – monsoon half the year, typhoon the other and a few good days between. Leveson's view of the weather on his station probably explains why he doubted that a submarine aircraft would be of much use. Moreover, the Japanese would inevitably get Asdic and that would reduce the invisibility which made reconnaissance submarines effective. British submarines on peacetime patrols would know as much, because they would hear Japanese pinging. For their part the submarines would learn to counter Asdic; they were hardly finished.

Nor did Leveson value fleet submarines. Even in the North Sea the

'K' class had only been barely habitable; their boiler heat would be horrific at any time off Singapore and between April and October off Hong Kong. Monsoon seas would severely restrict their speed and efficiency, particularly north of Hong Kong. At this time the Royal Navy was experimenting with the 'K' class in the East, learning that even if they could be made habitable, high sea temperatures would drastically reduce their speed. Leveson argued that they could not carry out their main function of forcing an enemy away from an area into the teeth of the fleet. Submarines lying in wait would probably be spotted by enemy ships or aircraft, forced down and then kept out of the battle by quickly-laid smoke. They would be unable to keep up with a rapidly-manoeuvring enemy fleet. It would be better to spend the money on the battle fleet.

Leveson wrote that 'until I have got a great number of destroyers on the station, I would not spend a shilling on submarines . . . the nearer you approach a destroyer type the better . . . This is high speed with good endurance . . . ' He was not particularly confident of submarine torpedoes, except against what he called a 'patient sheep' – an unarmed merchant ship. He did value what he called creating a funk: 'if submarines are well distributed and they appear all over the place, the enemy *for a certain time* can never feel comfortably safe about them. After a bit, the enemy will locate every one of them and the fright will diminish.' He wanted to try mixed units of one destroyer and one submarine, but doubted that anything could be done as long as there were separate destroyer and submarine organisations. In any new submarines he wanted high surface speed, good endurance and a heavier gun. He would settle for four torpedo tubes.

CinC East Indies (Rear Admiral Richmond) also saw no point in long-range reconnaissance, as it gave him information on which he could not act. The submarines should concentrate closer to the main fleet. He would accept a radius of action of no more than 1500nm and a wireless range of no more than 1000nm. Unlike other flag officers, he considered torpedoes secondary, to be carried only in such quantities as would not impair submarines' value as scouts or increase their size. The others considered the torpedo the chief weapon of the reconnaissance submarine.

RA(S) pointed out that torpedo armament had little impact on submarine size, since the space was not useful for other purposes. He wanted an *Oberon* capable of 17 knots.

Captain S.4 (China submarine squadron) also had little faith in submarine reconnaissance. He wanted deadlier torpedoes and sufficient endurance to reach the enemy. The 'L' class was good enough.

The Staff pointed out that it was 1500nm from Hong Kong to the mouth of the Inland Sea. An 'L'-class submarine could maintain a seven-day patrol off the Inland Sea on an endurance of 5000nm, but would have only 15 per cent of fuel in hand. That would be too small a margin for shadowing, attacking and taking up a position on an enemy's probable line of retreat. Moreover, until the fleet could operate from Hong Kong or a more advanced base, a 5000nm submarine would be of little value.

A recent strategical game at the RN Staff College showed that long range wireless was essential in the opening phase of a Far East war. DSD wanted two 100ft masts 200ft apart to obtain the desired 1500nm wireless range; DNC said that would require another 18 to 20ft of submarine length and another 50 to 60 tons, bringing displacement to about 1600 tons. The Staff did not want to increase displacement and hence unit cost, as numbers were vital. It would accept a guaranteed 1500nm using a kite aerial, but hoped DSD could do better. DSD referred to current experiments, which probably meant HF radio – which indeed offered that sort of range in a much smaller package.

Most of the flag officers badly wanted minelayers, but CinC Mediterranean considered their value doubtful and CinC East Indies wrote that in a war with Japan they would be a waste of money without any specific object.

This discussion was affected by the design of two modified *Oberon*s for the Royal Australian Navy (initially *O 2* and *O 3*, later named *Otway* and *Oxley*).[25] Experience building *Oberon* revealed the need for modifications. 'Circumstances not contemplated in the original design' ran up the size and weight of the main motor switchgear, congesting the motor room. It proved difficult to accommodate the Asdic and the battery cooling plant.[26] A conference concluded that the submarine should be lengthened by 4½ft, 2½ft of which should go into the motor and engine rooms. One foot would go into battery cooling and another into accommodation. Displacement would increase 25 tons. To maintain the 15 to 15.5 knot speed, engine power had to increase from 2700 BHP to 3000 BHP. The conference also decided to simplify the switchgear and to investigate the addition of

Otway about 1930, showing her deck Asdic dome. (Navy League of Australia via Dr Josef Straczek)

an auxiliary motor (for minimum submerged speed) using a silent worm drive to connect to either shaft.

Very shortly after this DNE wrote that RA(S) was seeking to increase speed by 2 knots, which would require still more length. Should the Australians be told? They had already received tenders for a repeat *Oberon*; they would have to request new ones. They did not press for higher speed. Vickers received the contract. Engine power was increased from 2700 BHP to 3000 BHP. On this basis the Australian submarines would be 275ft long, compared to 269ft 8in for *Oberon*, with beam reduced from 28ft to 27ft 7in.[27] Designed load displacement was 1540 tons rather than 1480 tons, but both classes grew while being built. In the Australian submarines emergency oil fuel stowage was reduced from 84 tons to 82 tons. As completed *Oberon* displaced 1598 tons, due mainly to an additional 74 tons of oil. *Oxley* and *Otway* increased to 1636 tons, the additional growth due mainly to 19 tons of additional hull and equipment, 9 tons of oil and 16 tons of ballast keel. On the other hand, compensating and trimming water was reduced by 28 tons.[28]

As built, *Oxley* and *Otway* could be distinguished from *Oberon* by their receding stems, which were intended to accommodate net cutters. They also had higher periscope standards. Vickers made considerable efforts to clean up their hulls, perhaps based in part on work already done to modify the *L 50* design for the Yugoslavs. The Vickers diesels were rated at 1500 BHP (on trials one of the Australian submarines developed 3170 BHP total at 1636 tons). However, like *Oberon*, these submarines did not meet their Legend performance. Instead of 15.5 knots, rated speed in 1938 was 13.74 knots. Hull modifications did improve underwater performance; Vickers claimed a speed of 8.5 knots.[29] As built, *Oxley* was rated at 14,000nm at 8 knots with 195 tons of oil fuel; in 1930 she was credited with an endurance of 8450nm at 10 knots on 201 tons of oil.

Production Submarines

After the end of the 1923 Imperial Conference Naval Staff proposals for the 1923–4 Programme included seven patrol submarines.[30] However, the 'emergency' programme (to relieve unemployment) the Board approved on 21 November showed only three. The Tory Government fell before the programme could be approved, leaving its Labour successor to rethink. The Board continued to press a ten-year

Odin shows the additional freeing ports and also the elimination of the deck Asdic dome. (RAN Naval Historical Section via Dr Josef Straczek)

programme it had previously developed; a revised version was formulated by Director of Plans in March 1924.[31]

The Admiralty pointed to the need for a 'general transformation' because the existing fleet had been built to fight in the North Sea, but in future it would have to be ready to work under oceanic conditions 'for which great endurance and mobility are necessary and little dependence can be placed on shore facilities'. Submarines were important enough to be Part 3 of the Admiralty plan, after light cruisers and destroyers but before minelayers and carriers (and, for that matter, ASW craft). The Admiralty stated that studies of requirements for war against either Japan or France (the latter to conceal Admiralty concentration on Japan) showed that about the same number of submarines were needed in each case: sixty overseas patrol type and twelve cruisers.[32] Priority would go to patrol submarines: fleet submarine construction should be deferred until at least eight patrol (reconnaissance) submarines had been laid down, but (presumably due to ageing 'K'-boats) it would be 'absolutely necessary' to lay down (probably in 1926–7) a group of four fleet submarines. The target number of fleet submarine was two three-boat divisions plus a margin of two to allow for refits, a total of eight. This seemed to be a bare minimum. With any fewer, it would be impossible to justify the expense of maintaining a special type of submarine. That meant eighty submarines in all: sixty patrol, twelve cruiser, eight fleet.[33] An eighty-submarine target and a ten-year lifetime implied an eight-submarine annual programme.

The Labour Government rejected the submarines and hoped to cut costs by extending Washington Treaty limits to lesser ships. In April the Cabinet asked Admiral Beatty for new treaty proposals. ACNS suggested limiting fleet submarines to 2000 tons and patrol submarines to 1500 tons.[34]

After Labour lost the October election, the Admiralty's situation did not much improve. The new Chancellor of the Exchequer was

Winston Churchill, strongly opposed to spending, including naval spending. His initial manoeuvre was to separate the 1925–6 naval construction programme from the basic Estimates, so that it could receive special Cabinet review. The Admiralty now suggested that new-construction submarines might last fifteen years, in which case only $5\frac{1}{3}$ might have to be built annually to maintain an eighty-submarine fleet. The Admiralty presented a new programme dated 6 March 1925.[35] It was compelled to cut costs, although an 18 June version still showed eight submarines per year (but only one fleet submarine, in 1928–9). Cruiser submarines were eliminated altogether, in line with the ongoing analysis of submarine needs. The programme was revised again to come within a £13.5 million annual ceiling (the Admiralty accepted a £51 million cut in construction over the six years 1925–6 through 1930–1). This 1 July version was cut to six submarines per year between 1925–6 and 1930–1.[36] At some point submarines were eliminated altogether from the 1925–6 Programme.

Six submarines per year meant sixty in ten years and a twelve-year lifetime would justify a total of seventy-two. This was not too far from what the Board had requested. The 1926–7 Programme comprised the annual allotment of six submarines tentatively designated *O 2* through *O 7*; they became the *Odin* class. By this time the need for higher speed was definitely appreciated.

As designed in February 1925, the modified 'O' class was 14ft 9in longer than *Oberon* (using a parallel mid-body added), with a modified stern. For model tests, the range of surface speeds would be 9 to 19 knots.[37] It was assumed that 4000 BHP would be needed to achieve the desired 17 knots.[38] In December 1924 DNC suggested that adding two cylinders to each engine would increase total power to 4000 BHP, which would give 16.5 to 17 knots. Length would have to

Oberon shows standard wartime modifications, January 1943: the antenna of a Type 291W air-warning radar antenna atop her periscope standards (rather than, as in many submarines, in place of her wireless mast) and a 20mm anti-aircraft gun on an extended bridge fairwater abaft her original fairwater (with its after side opened up for access). The wire surrounding the 20mm gun is a pipe rack to prevent the gun from firing into the submarine while its operator concentrated on an air target. The wireless stub masts fore and aft were removed before the war, the voice pipe to the gun being fitted in 1936–7.

increase another 5½ft. EinC pointed out that running a 2000 BHP engine to charge batteries was uneconomical. Adding a 300 BHP charging engine would prolong the life of the main engines and also improve economy. If the auxiliary generator was set athwartships, the total increase in length might not have to exceed 5ft, for a total increase in machinery length of 12ft 6in over *O 1*. RA(S) considered the extra engine a luxury best avoided. Standard practice when running on the surface was to take a small charge off one motor while the same engine propelled the ship. With more powerful (hence heavier) machinery, the engine and motor rooms had to be moved forward 10ft to maintain trim. The ERA and stokers' messes were therefore moved to the after end of the motor room.[39] DNC admitted that this was a disadvantage compared to the accommodation in *Oberon*, but it could not be avoided. Length had to grow to 273ft (pp) or 281ft 3in overall (excluding the stern cap for the torpedo tubes) and displacement to 1620 tons surfaced (1970 tons submerged).[40] That compared to 269ft 8in overall for *Oberon*.

Design for the tropics meant providing a carbon-dioxide cooling plant for both the batteries and for internal spaces.[41] About 1930 the commanding officers of the four submarines thus far completed all recommended supplying cooled air to the control room; *Odin* recommended that this be extended to the engine room. The cooler substantially reduced humidity in the submarine.

At this time it was assumed that the submarines would be included in the 1925–6 Programme. In June 1925 Controller (Admiral Chatfield) circulated the Board decision on the type and design of 1925–6 submarines as a matter of urgency, since the design had to be prepared quickly for tendering during the Financial Year. This decision was based on the conclusions of the 19 February 1925 conference described above, which confirmed that the submarine should have a speed of 17 knots with full reserve fuel tanks. DNC promised to have a design ready for the Board in July 1925. The design showed the desired 4.7in gun and the auxiliary 50 HP motor introduced in the *Oxley*s. The top of the bridge was raised 2ft to clear the new gun.

RA(S) rejected several suggestions from *Oberon*, most prominently that for more free-flooding living space to be used on cruises that might last as much as three months. To provide this space, the upper deck casing would be enlarged; the submarine's captain suggested raising the upper deck by about 2ft along its whole length.[42] The casing should also be widened. RA(S) wrote that no commanding officer would use the enlarged casing for living space at sea or be justified in doing so in wartime. The enlarged casing would add both top weight and visibility, neither of which were desirable. There was one habitability improvement, however; based on experience in *Oberon*, the flats in some spaces over batteries were lowered 6in. It was accepted that cells could no longer be passed over each other, but that was considered far less important than improving crew spaces. The Fessenden (sonic signalling) gear was moved out of the crew spaces, where it took up considerable space. Since its equipment was remote-controlled, it could be placed below the flat near the oscillators.

About the time of the Board submission, submarines were eliminated altogether from the 1925–6 Programme and the six improved *Oberon*s became the 1926–7 submarines. The Legend was dated 9 August 1926; the design received the Board stamp on 12 November.[43]

The *Odin* class repeated the unusual bow form of the *Oxley*s; at full speed it created a considerable bow wave. Later experiments showed that a more conventional bow could support an effective net-cutter and the two later reconnaissance submarine classes were redesigned accordingly. Tank tests showed that in calm water the unconventional above-water bow had no effect on speed. Trials showed that the desired 17 knot speed could be reached: *Osiris* reached 17.630 knots at 395.75 RPM.[44]

Orpheus was the prototype for the Vulcan (hydraulic) clutch employed in the two later classes. It was intended to reduce torsional vibration by isolating the engine from the rest of the power train.[45] Oil in the clutch transmitted engine rotation to the shaft connected to the motor, with a slip of only about 2 per cent at full power and 8 to 10 per cent when charging and operating at low power; the average efficiency of energy transmission was about 97 per cent. The clutch disengaged as oil was drained. There was no need to stop the engine in

order to engage or disengage the clutch, as there was with a conventional cone clutch. Draining took only about a minute and a half. To accommodate the new clutch, the after engine room bulkhead was moved 3ft 9in further aft and the auxiliary machinery compartment rearranged to suit; the main motors had to be moved aft and the pressure hull filled out to accommodate them. The hope was that the destructive torsional frequencies were due to the combination of engine and drive train, including the propeller shaft. Unfortunately that was not the case; engines continued to suffer at critical frequencies at which they had to operate. Vickers produced a successful torsion damper, which could be installed at the fore end of the engine.[46]

Unfortunately these large submarines dived slowly. In April 1927 *Oberon* took 3 minutes 10 seconds to reach a depth of 25ft.[47] Retested in October 1927 after holes were cut in the superstructure, *Oberon* took 1 minute 50 seconds to reach 25ft. *Oxley* was slightly faster, reaching

Otway is shown in late-war camouflage (white, blue and purple-blue on her pressure hull), with a 20mm gun on the after side of her bridge fairwater, but apparently without radar. The prominent objects on her periscope standard are insulators for her two pairs of aerials, her jumping wires and the thinner pairs of wires below them. At this time (as indicated by the camouflage) she was training ASW escorts. That she had been doing so since 1941 may explain her lack of radar. (John Lambert collection)

25ft in 1 minute 43 seconds. These submarines seemed to hang before continuing to dive, so further holes were cut. With superstructure hatches open, it took *Oberon* an average of 1 minute 22 seconds to reach 24ft (the best time was 1 minute 11 seconds). She did not do as well with superstructure hatches closed, showing that there were still pockets of air in the casing. Further holes were cut during a Chatham refit. In *Oberon*, most of the main tanks flooded in 17 to 32 seconds, but four of them took 38 to 50 seconds, because they extended above the normal waterline. In the *Odin* design the main tanks were terminated below the waterline: average time to flood main tanks in *Osiris* was 23 seconds (maximum 30 seconds). In March 1929 diving trials *Osiris* reached 25ft in 2 minutes 5 seconds. She hung briefly at 12–24ft depth, probably due to air pockets in way of the gun platform, bridge (particularly at the after end of the bridge in way of the aerial load). Additional flooding holes were cut during a Chatham refit. All of these times, moreover, were reached without using the quick-diving tank. *Otway* initially needed about 3 minutes to reach 40ft without using these tanks, but 1½ minutes with them.

Six *Parthian* ('P') class originally called the 1927 'O' Class, followed in the 1927–8 Programme: they were similar enough that DNC planned to issue the sheer draught of the *Odin* class for tendering. The dimensions and form were nearly the same.[48] They incorporated the two main changes made to the *Odin*s after Board approval, an enlarged lower conning tower and above-water forward planes. The important difference was the use of Vulcan clutches abaft the main engines. The engines were more powerful (4640 BHP) but the clutches somewhat less efficient, so that power actually delivered

to the propellers was the same. The machinery spaces had to be considerably rearranged, the engine rooms lengthened from 45ft 3in to 50ft and the other machinery compartments shortened (from 36ft 9in to 34ft 9in); total machinery length increased by 2ft 9in. It was gained by rearranging the battery spaces (1ft) and by shortening the stern torpedo compartment (1ft 9in), in the latter case by eliminating power loading and spare stern torpedoes. Accommodation forward had to be shortened by a foot. The after crew spaces would be shorter and less habitable, the motor and auxiliary machinery spaces somewhat congested. Also, the motors were about a foot longer due to electrical equipment changes. Trials data suggested that more oil fuel was needed to achieve the desired 10,000nm endurance, so arrangements were made to carry oil fuel in some of the main ballast tanks: normal capacity was 136 tons (compared to 145 tons in *Odin*), but with oil in No 7 main ballast tanks it was 175 tons. This modification was extended to the *Odin* class. With a useful capacity of 130 tons of oil (95 per cent capacity) endurance was 9060nm at 8 knots (allowing 5 gallons/hr for battery charging); with the additional 36 tons it was 11,500nm at 8 knots.[49]

After tenders had been submitted but before they were approved, DNC considered modifying the stern of the new submarine; possibilities included eliminating the stern tubes and rearranging them to lie vertically over each other rather than horizontally. In November 1927 RA(S) pointed out that the main requirements for the reconnaissance mission were wireless, endurance and habitability; the submarines' patrols might last six weeks or longer – which might be compared to the one-week patrols of 'E'-class submarines during the war. RA(S) was

Pandora and other 'P'-class submarines could be distinguished from the 'O' class by their different bows, much more conventionally shaped. The object between the periscopes was a frame coil (DF and underwater wireless reception). The wireless mast was shortened in 1933–4. (RAN Naval Historical Section via Dr Josef Straczek)

Perseus shows her 4.7in gun and her big housed frame coil, the housing including the periscope standards. Ships were completed with the smaller frame coil and then refitted. Note also the extra freeing ports in her bridge fairwater. (RAN Naval Historical Section via Dr Josef Straczek)

Parthian, *Perseus* and *Proteus* all had 4.7in/40 guns instead of the earlier 4in; they could be distinguished by their hooded gun shields. Here *Proteus*, *Pandora*, *Poseidon* and *Perseus* lie alongside each other in 1930. (RAN Naval Historical Section via Dr Josef Straczek)

willing to eliminate stern tubes to hold down displacement. Surely with the advent of 90° angling it was less important to provide a submarine with another chance to fire if a bow attack at close quarters was frustrated. RA(S) also hoped that a new stern shape would increase underwater speed. Model tests showed, perhaps surprisingly, that little if anything would be gained. The proposal was rejected on the ground that the small increase in habitability did not justify so large a reduction in armament.

However, the bow above water was modified. By early 1928 it appeared that the bow introduced in *Oxley* was not the best for cutting a net; DNC developed a new form. In addition to improving net-cutting, it was intended to improve seakeeping by lifting the bow. The 1927 submarines could be modified without any additional cost and that was done. In service, the 1927 submarines dove somewhat more slowly than the *Odin*s.[50]

The *Odin* and *Parthian*-class submarines were all to be armed with 4in guns pending planned rearmament with 4.7in guns. *Perseus* alone was completed with a 4.7in gun for tests.[51] Money seems to have been too tight to rearm the 'O' and 'P' classes.

Another six reconnaissance submarines were included in the 1928–9 Programme: the 'R' (*Rainbow*) class. However, two of them were cancelled in July 1929, presumably as part of the run-up to the 1930 London Naval Arms Control Conference.

The 'R' class had to be designed before the 'P' class were completed, so modifications to the basic design were based largely on experience with the 'O' class. The main issue was underwater speed.[52]

Pandora shows her cab bridge during a Puget Sound Navy Yard refit, 1941. (NARA)

DEE offered a higher motor output of 1600 BHP. With all topside fittings in place, *Osiris* made 7.729 knots at 1388 BHP. If as many as possible were removed she made 8.346 knots with 1395 BHP. The gun was a major source of resistance. DNC offered two alternatives. One was to cover the gun with a canopy and fair the gun platform into the bridge. The bridge was lowered 1ft 6in and the insulator for the main aerial was dropped. The alternative was to drop the gun platform 3ft 5in and to completely cover it. With 1320 BHP the first offered a speed of 8.65 knots; with 1600 BHP the submarine would make 9.22 knots submerged. With the second modification the speeds would be 8.81 knots and 9.40 knots, respectively. If the stump wireless masts fore and aft had to be kept rigged while diving and the main wireless mast raised to its diving position (with aerials and insulators rigged), but topside fittings removed and the second modification made, the submarine would make 8.50 knots at 1320 BHP and 9.12 knots at 1600 BHP, compared to 7.90 knots and 8.40 knots for *Oswald*. For the new class DNC proposed the more drastic modification, applying the less drastic one to existing 'O' and 'P'-class submarines. At an Admiralty meeting, DNO rejected the more drastic modification on the ground that a completely closed-in shield would be impracticable because the increased weight of the shield would make it prohibitively difficult to train the gun. Instead a modified version of the simpler modification was adopted, with some additional improvements such as a slight lowering of the gun and shaping of the fore end of the bridge canopy. The bridge would be dropped 1ft 6in compared to *Odin*. RA(S) was willing to go further if that would reduce resistance, but the consensus at an Admiralty meeting was that dropping it further would be undesirable. This bridge would be a foot higher than that in *Oberon*, which had complained about the effects of spray on the bridge.

The modified bridge could be fitted in *Rainbow*, because work on her superstructure in wake of the bridge and gun had been held up. The bridge flat was dropped from 13ft to 11ft 6in above the pressure hull and the gun platform from 9ft 6in to 6ft 4in above the pressure hull. The bridge structure itself was cut down. That not only reduced underwater resistance, it also reduced the silhouette. The diameter of the upper conning tower was reduced from 5ft 3in to 4ft and the commanding officer's cabin was moved from the after side to the fore side of the conning tower. The bridge was given a streamline shape quite different from that in the 'O' and 'P' classes. A canopy was built over the gun. Bridge structures were already complete in the *Odin*s, so no action was possible. In the *Parthian* class work in wake of the gun could be carried out but the bridge could not be changed. Thus a canopy was fitted over the fore end of the gun in *Perseus*, *Proteus* and *Parthian*. Another possibility in the *Rainbow*s was to shorten the wireless mast when retracted, so that it and its cross stay would be completely housed below the bridge bulwark. That was impossible because it would have required the mast to be cut from 56ft 6in to 44ft 6in above the waterline when erected, reducing wireless range by about 20 per cent.

To improve manoeuvring, the diesel starting platform and controls were moved to the after end of the engine room near the switchboard controlling the motors. The engines themselves were moved forward; the change made it possible to shorten the engine room by 2ft.[53] This reduction applied to the hull as a whole.

Initially all the *Rainbow*s were to have had 4.7in guns, but it turned out that under conditions of low buoyancy they were not sufficiently stable.[54] The main cure was to replace the heavier gun by a 4in gun, as in the 'O' and 'P' classes. Two buoyancy chambers were fitted in the

Rover was externally very similar to the 'P' class; of this series only *Rainbow* had a 4in gun. She is shown in 1931. The hoods to the shields were soon removed. (RAN Naval Historical Section via Dr Josef Straczek)

Rainbow shows her 4in gun. (RAN Naval Historical Section via Dr Josef Straczek)

superstructure. This decision was taken in 1931, not long after the submarines were completed (it received Board approval on 5 March 1931). It applied to *Rainbow* and *Regulus*, the others not yet having been completed.

The first twelve patrol submarines were all allocated to the China Fleet, but as of 1928 plans called for the six 1928–9 submarines ('R' class) to go to the Mediterranean and the 1929–30 submarines (five patrol plus one new type) to go to the Atlantic Fleet. Construction of further patrol submarines ended in favour of the faster 'G' class described in the next chapter.

By 1939 these submarines were fairly old and unsurprisingly they

and their engines severely strained the depot ships maintaining them.[55] Often replacement parts had to be made, since the engines were long out of production. However, they were considered valuable and they were particularly well remembered for their trips carrying essential supplies (including gasoline) to Malta during its long siege.

Derating and careful routine maintenance kept the engines reasonably reliable. The post-war official technical history notes particularly that Severn and Clyde (faster versions of the basic patrol submarine) gave little trouble running at about two-thirds power (340 RPM) unsupercharged. There was insufficient British production capacity to modify or redesign the machinery.

Rover, with *Regulus* inboard, on the China Station alongside a 'County'-class cruiser. Both were armed with 4.7in guns, whose hoods had been removed. (Silberstein via Blumenfield courtesy of Naval Institute)

Aircraft

If it could be accommodated, an aircraft would greatly extend the vision of a patrol submarine; it was a natural match. Not surprisingly, in July 1923 CinC Atlantic Fleet proposed development. He recalled the abortive wartime project abandoned because existing submarines were too small and a more recent discussion by the committee on aviation arrangements in HM ships.[56] 'The more the probable conditions of a possible future war are studied, the more obvious it becomes that greatly increased reliance, in comparison with the late war, must be placed on submarines and aircraft for early information of enemy's movements.' This was much the argument behind the patrol submarine itself. In this case, CinC seems to have envisaged a flotilla of aircraft-carrying submarines attached to his fleet as scouts. He proposed modifying an 'M'-class submarine for tests, as it 'presents advantages which can only be described as peculiarly fortunate'. It was well known to have better diving qualities than any other type of similar size and one could easily be spared from the Atlantic Fleet, to be replaced by the nearly-complete *K 26*. The pressure-proof hangar would replace the existing 12in gun.

Directors of Plans and of Operations liked the idea and DNC's submarine expert considered it feasible. The aircraft would have to fly off forward with the submarine making a good speed into the wind. In that case there seemed to be sufficient take-off space. Naval Air Section wanted a two-seat reconnaissance type and suggested that a catapult would be needed. The aircraft would return to land on the water. The Air Ministry would have to order a special type of aircraft. DNC offered alternative plans, one involving a 'K'-class submarine with a cylindrical hangar, the others the 'M' class with a hangar in place of the 12in gun. In the 'K' class the seaplane would be carried disassembled and assembled on deck, with the stern of the submarine dipped so that it could float off. 'The United States have recently been carrying out experiments with such an arrangement and it is understood that the Japanese are doing the same.' In the 'M' class, as suggested, a small hangar would replace the gun and turret, leading to a flying deck with a catapult. The larger the hangar opening, the greater the design problem, so the seaplane had to be as small as possible. RA(S) had wanted a higher-performance land plane, but it could not have returned to the submarine to fly again. The proposed 'K'-class cylinder could be fitted to the new 'O'-class patrol submarine. A submarine required to have the same W/T performance as the 'O' class plus a hangar would have to be considerably larger.

Controller saw no point in going further until the Air Ministry could definitely say that it could supply a suitable aircraft, which would have an endurance of no less than 1¼ hours and a 50nm wireless set.[57] The Air Ministry considered the project feasible and it went ahead. Money for the submarine modification – to *M 2* – was provided

The Royal Navy became interested in using small submarine-launched aircraft to extend the reach of its patrol submarines, in much the way current submariners are interested in using UAVs. To that end it converted the 'monitor' *M 2*, replacing her 12in gun and turret with a hangar and catapult. (John Lambert collection)

M 2 dives. Her loss coincided roughly with the London Naval Treaty (1930) and with severe financial problems which ended construction of large patrol submarines and thus also ended Royal Navy interest in aircraft they might carry. The US Navy also experimented with, and abandoned, submarine-borne aircraft, but the Imperial Japanese Navy persisted. It saw such aircraft as scouts for groups of submarines controlled by a large cruiser submarine equipped with a catapult. Ultimately the Japanese became interested in submarine-borne strike aircraft. (John Lambert collection)

in the 1925–6 Estimates. The Air Ministry pointed out that anything short of a catapult would limit the aircraft to very low performance and would also require considerable wind over the deck – for a 50ft run, typically 26 knots, far beyond submarine performance. Nor would it be wise to re-embark the aircraft by floating it on board. As a fallback, *M 2* could use her crane to place the seaplane in the water so that it could take off under its own power.

The Air Ministry went ahead with two Parnell Peto two-seaters. As the first attempt to produce a small folding seaplane for submarine stowage, their design was experimental and they proved to be over 200lbs overweight. Even so, to save weight it had been made rather flimsy, limiting the maximum acceleration the catapult could provide. That complicated catapult design, as from a ship point of view catapult length was limited to that needed to accelerate the aircraft to 45mph – an increase in length from about 50ft to 72ft or 56ft would be difficult. Increased acceleration might also be undesirable. The Naval Staff had to accept that the aircraft could not be launched in still air. That was acceptable with a purely experimental aircraft.

Completion of the conversion was initially set for May 1926, but problems with the catapult and with delivery of the hangar door frame casting delayed it. The latter was delayed by ongoing coal strikes. If the catapult could not be delivered, the submarine would suffer further delays due to further structural modifications. By mid-November 1927 the design of the catapult was nearly complete, material had been ordered and work was finally in hand. Objections by the ship's prospective commanding officer, who wanted a different type of catapult, were rejected. Work extended into 1928; working-up trials began only in April. *M 2* commissioned on 8 October. On trials in December 1928 *M 2* achieved about 12.5 knots, about a knot less than her sisters before conversion.

M 2 foundered on 26 January 1932.[58] She sank stern first and was found on the seabed with her hangar door and also the access hatch between hangar and submarine open. This combination of facts was inconsistent; if *M 2* had flooded through her hangar, she should have sunk bow first. DNC concluded that there had been a substantial loss of buoyancy aft, which would have been more than enough to counteract the trim by the bow due to water ordinarily allowed in the hangar. That most likely was due to valves to the after ballast tank being inadvertently left open, the tanks filling after the submarine surfaced with her tanks blown. That would cause a bodily sinkage which would have brought the sill of the hangar door below water. Typically about a foot of water was allowed in the hangar above the floorboards, which was a foot below water level. This free surface would have surged aft as the submarine trimmed by the stern. The access hatch was level with a foot of water over the floor boards. A 4° trim by the stern would have brought the top of the coaming 6in below water, not allowing for any surge. 'There is little doubt that to provide against such a contingency the order book directed that the hatch should be closed when the hangar was manned.' In this case it was open and water could get through. The bodily sinkage of the submarine due to a loss of buoyancy aft would have brought in more water through the hangar and worsened the situation. DNC suspected that, had the hatch been shut, the submarine would have survived. Normally the submarine CO stood atop the hangar when the submarine had surfaced and was preparing to fly off its aircraft. That the hatch was open indicated that he had proceeded there and it seemed to DNC reasonable to suppose that, on realising there was a problem, he went below. He was too late to have the vents closed; the open conning tower hatches 'facilitated the sinking by providing a ready vent to the air from the compartments which flooded with an ever-increasing rate through the hangar access hatch as the bow sank'.

By this time tonnage restrictions made it impossible for the Royal Navy to consider building any further aircraft-carrying submarines. However, a 1935 report on experiments with aircraft-carrying submarines carried a comment that consideration had been given to stowing a dismantled seaplane in a pressure-tight hangar on board an 'R'-class submarine.

HM SUBMARINE *M 2*. Catapult for aircraft. (© National Maritime Museum J9713)

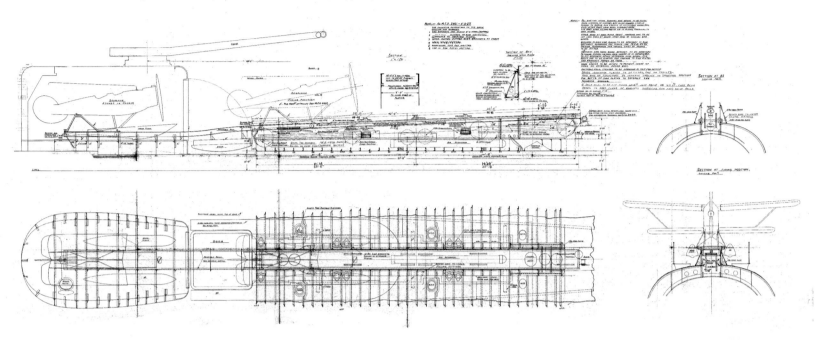

HM SUBMARINE *M 2*. Sections. (© National Maritime Museum J9717)

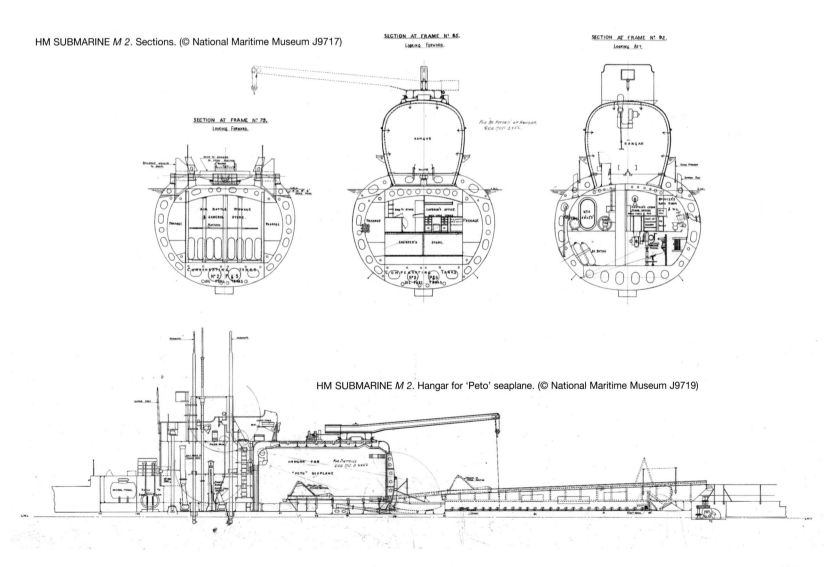

HM SUBMARINE *M 2*. Hangar for 'Peto' seaplane. (© National Maritime Museum J9719)

CHAPTER 12
FLEET SUBMARINES AND MINELAYERS

Reconsideration

On 9 July 1926 the Sea Lords met to discuss the submarine programme. Although the requirement for sixty patrol submarines seemed to be set by operational requirement, the 72-boat total was no more than an affordability figure, so details of the remaining twelve submarines were not at all settled. Thus the conference did not change the 1928–9 Programme (six repeat 'P' class). These remaining submarines became the smaller 'S' class described in the next chapter.

When the submarine programme was reviewed in June 1928,

Cachalot was one of six submarine minelayers built in the 1930s, recognisable by their raised after casings containing mines outside their pressure hulls. (RAN Naval Historical Section via Dr Josef Straczek)

Plans Division set war requirements at sixty-four large and fifteen small submarines.[1] Australia had bought two 'O'-boats and was expected (wrongly) to buy two more, consistent with a Royal Navy requirement for sixty large submarines – five per year. Estimating that two small submarines would be no costlier than one large one, Plans Division proposed building five large and one small submarine in the 1929–30 Programme and then five large and two small ones in 1930–1 and later Programmes. By this time DNC had designed the quasi-fleet submarine (G type) described in this chapter, which superseded the big patrol submarines. The Staff wanted four in each of the 1929–1 Programme years. Although each cost more than a patrol submarine, four of them plus two small submarines would cost less than five patrols and one small submarine.

Given badly-strained British finances, in 1928 Churchill demanded deeper cuts. When the Board protested that its planned force was needed to face Japan, Churchill extracted a Foreign Office statement that hostilities there were most unlikely. The Admiralty was reduced to justifying its fleet on the basis of British commitments elsewhere, particularly those imposed by the Treaty of Locarno, which guaranteed German frontiers.[2] That particularly undermined the case for the big patrol or G-type submarine. In 1929 two of the six patrol submarines of the 1928–9 Programme were suspended.[3]

In October 1929 the Board proposed a 1929–30 Programme including the six submarines of the earlier five-year programme. By this time it seemed likely that the next arms control treaty would set submarine lifetime at thirteen rather than twelve years. The Board considered the current rate of construction (six per year) a bare minimum, only enough to maintain an underage fleet of fifty-five submarines (due to scrapping of older overage submarines). Given great pressure to cut costs, the proposed 1929–30 Programme was set at two G (fleet) type and four small submarines (the 'S' class; see Chapter 13), rather than the earlier four G type and two small submarines. This was cut further to three submarines (one rather than two G type) and in March 1929 the British government suspended all three pending the outcome of the London Naval Conference, given its professed desire to abolish submarines altogether.

The submarine programme was revived when the conference limited total submarine tonnage (to 52,700 tons) rather than banning new construction. It bought the prototype G- type submarine *Thames* and two small submarines. In May 1930 Director of Plans laid out a long-term programme. The new London Naval Treaty would expire on 31 December 1936. It embodied a thirteen-year submarine lifetime. On expiration 34,009 tons of underage submarines would be left, so 18,691 tons could be laid down under the 1929 through 1933 Programmes. An annual average of 3700 tons would suffice for only one large and two small submarines. Target strength would be twenty fast patrol submarines (Design G), twelve small patrol submarines (about 650 tons each) and six minelayers (1480 tons each), adding up to 52,680 tons.[4]

The 1930–1 Programme was the prototype minelayer (*Porpoise*) and two small submarines. For 1931–2 the Board wanted two large submarines (a minelayer and a G type [*Severn*]) and one small one, but to cut costs it agreed to substitute a small submarine for the minelayer. In December 1931, the Board approved a 1932–3 Programme including one G-type submarine (*Clyde*) and one minelayer plus one small submarine. Early the following year the Cabinet approved the programme, but it failed to provide sufficient money to continue the 1931–2 Programme already underway. The projected 1933–4 Programme (as of December 1932) included one minelayer (*Grampus*) and two small submarines.[5] Apparently the 1932–3 minelayer was held over to 1933–4, as two minelayers are listed in that programme (*Grampus* and *Narwhal*). A similar programme was offered for 1934–5 (as of November 1933), the minelayer being *Rorqual*. Two more minelayers completed the planned sextet: *Cachalot* in the 1935–6 Programme and *Seal* in the 1936–7 Programme.

Fleet Submarines

Royal Navy interest in fleet submarines continued after 1918, although steam was increasingly seen as a dead end. Requirements for a fleet submarine were formulated in 1921.[6] She should be 10 per cent faster than the fleet in order to obtain the necessary tactical freedom,

be a good seakeeper, have a heavy torpedo armament, good diving qualities and submerged control and at least the endurance of a destroyer, with a light gun armament. It was understood that there was no immediate way to obtain the desired speed except by using steam power, as in the 'K' class. Unfortunately steam could not offer the desired endurance; the Staff wanted 4000 to 5000nm for a war against Japan. It added that the fleet submarines should be able to lay a gas or smoke cloud. CinC Atlantic formulated requirements, including a speed of 25 knots, as part of his 1924 Battle Instructions.[7]

In June 1925 Vickers offered the Admiralty a diesel alternative, proposing a submarine about the size of *K 26*, with slightly greater internal diameter.[8] Guaranteed speed was 23 knots for about 1600nm, 20 knots for about 3200nm and 9 knots for about 6000–7000nm. Each of two shafts was driven by two engines in tandem, with clutches between them, giving a total of 12,000 BHP. Main electric motors were slightly more powerful than in *K 26*. Armament was six 21in bow tubes, two 4.7in guns and one 40mm anti-aircraft gun.

Vickers was actually advertising much more powerful diesel engines as its alternative to AEL's. The proposed engines were so interesting that RA(S) wanted them to power at least one of the repeat 'O'-class patrol submarines. Could Vickers actually develop 500 BHP per

Thames was the first of three diesel-powered fleet submarines. Although she generated roughly the same power as a 'K'-class steam fleet submarine, she was larger and hence somewhat slower. British submarine designers were never able to build diesel boats which could manoeuvre relative to the battle fleet, which even in the 1920s required a minimum of 25 knots. The requirements of high speed show in the high seakeeping bow. Alone of the three, this boat had a 4.7in gun in a bulbous shield. (RAN Naval Historical Service via Dr Josef Straczek)

cylinder? In a joint 31 July 1925 report EinC and DNC concluded that even more would actually be needed.

The largest cylinder unit Vickers had produced to date, for the minelayer *Adventure*, had developed 375 BHP. This engine was still under test. Vickers was proposing the same type of engine (four-cylinder solid-injection, trunk type) but with higher mean effective pressure (MEP), 70 psi rather than 50 psi. EinC doubted that the company could produce it. At the least it should complete an experimental unit first. During brake trials the *Adventure* engine had smoked, hence would have been unacceptable in a submarine. Even if the engine could be built, Vickers was mounting it in tandem units 62ft long. EinC pointed out that as the hull worked, the units would get out of alignment and the coupling between their engines would become unreliable. In all previous cases (e.g., in the *Blake*-class cruisers of the nineteenth century) tandem engines had been unsatisfactory. The permanently-coupled units would have to run at very low output to charge batteries. The motors would also be in tandem, clutched together, adding more problems. For cruising, Vickers envisaged running the engines at 400 BHP to drive the forward motor as a generator, the after motor driving the propeller shafts. This arrangement would be uneconomical, giving poor endurance at low speed – yet with the shift to the Far East endurance was more and more essential.

Presumably Vickers hoped that the Admiralty would finance development of its new engine. Admiralty policy, however, was to encourage private firms to develop engine designs on their own initiative by asking for alternative designs when calling for tenders. Thus Vickers had recently offered is own solid-injection diesel design as an alternative to the Admiralty design (employed in the 'O' class) and both Denny and Armstrong submitted designs employing Sulzer diesels (the Admiralty engine was chosen). This and the detailed objections by DNC and EinC, killed the project, which was formally rejected in September 1925.

As part of the discussion looking towards the 1925–6 Programme, in February 1925 CinCs were asked about fleet submarines.[9] CinC Atlantic Fleet wanted good submerged submarine-to-submarine communication and good habitability. CinC Mediterranean Fleet did not consider them essential, but felt that they should be integral with the main fleet; stopping development of fast submarines would hamper the natural evolution of submarines. He emphasised high surface speed and fast diving and would accept smaller endurance. CinC China considered that general service submarines were good enough (his submarine flotilla commander did not consider them worth their cost) and CinC East Indies considered them a luxury. RA(S) considered fleet submarines essential; he wanted an endurance of 5000nm at fleet cruising speed.

The long-term programme set in July 1925 showed a prototype fleet submarine (and five reconnaissance submarines) in the 1929–30 Programme. The key question was how fast this submarine had to be. The Staff retreated from 25 knots to 22 knots, seeing the new type more as a fast general-purpose submarine. It wanted the endurance of a patrol submarine, 10,000nm at 8 knots. That alone ruled out steam, which consumed about four times the fuel for the same output. Controller pointed out that the heat of a steam plant ruled it out for the tropics. EinC held out hope that the machinery problem might be solved by new double-acting two-cycle diesels – which never actually materialised. To gain some speed on a reasonable displacement, the Staff was willing to omit stern torpedo tubes, but it wanted a heavier gun battery (two 4.7in). As with the patrol submarine, desired wireless range was 1500nm.[10]

DNC could offer only 20 knots on two 4500 BHP engines, which did not yet exist (the most powerful in British service was the 3000 BHP engine in *X 1*). DTD commented that current diesel technology indicated that 20 knots was the effective speed limit; he was impressed by the enormous jump in power required to increase speed by only 2.5 knots over that of the patrol submarines. Surface displacement would be 3000 tons (standard displacement 2700 tons, compared to 1700 tons for an 'O'-boat).[11] Director of Tactical Section considered that too much for a submarine which could not manoeuvre relative to the fleet, as the 'K'-boats had been expected to do.

Overall, DNC saw something like *X 1* as an ideal fleet submarine in view of her seaworthiness (due to great surface buoyancy) and her diving capabilities. A twelve-cylinder version of the *X 1* engine would produce 4500 BHP; speed would be 20 knots. The fleet submarine version of *X 1* would do away with her heavy guns (which were expensive and added about 100 tons high in the ship). This ship would have two engine rooms, one with two and the other with one 4500 BHP engines. The pressure hull would be somewhat thinner, the outer hull somewhat stronger. This submarine would displace about 3000 tons and would make about 20 knots surfaced. This was still prohibitively expensive and it seemed to offer very little speed advantage on its huge tonnage: 3000 tons surfaced (2700 tons standard). RA(S) pointed out that the main features of a fleet submarine were speed and torpedo firepower. He wanted a minimum of 22 knots in main ballast trim and if possible 25 knots, with the endurance of a *Nelson*-class battleship (which was less than 10,000nm). Such a ship would not need long-distance wireless: 200nm (50nm submerged) would do.

In mid-December DNE suggested relaxing requirements for guns, wireless and endurance. In January 1927 DNC's submarine expert A W Johns suggested cleaning up (and shrinking) the basic design, for example by using bow shutters to streamline the hull, omitting power-loading torpedo gear (which added length), simplifying towing arrangements and reducing auxiliary power (compared to *X 1*). Clearly nervous about the non-existent 4500 BHP engine, in February 1927 DNC proposed using a pair of *X 1* engines (total 7540 BHP). The two *X 1* auxiliary engines might be replaced by a single 1500 BHP engine, freeing some space. RA(S) considered power torpedo loading too valuable to abandon.

Further discussion was suspended pending a Preliminary Conference on Cruiser and Fleet Submarines. It met on 22 February 1927. It adjourned until 2 November to await the outcome of what turned out to be an abortive naval arms conference in Geneva.[12] The British Government had proposed an 1800-ton limit, which was applied to the design even though no international agreement had been signed. The conference changed the definition of a fleet submarine. It should be able to transit with the fleet, but no higher speed was necessary if it pushed the design towards undue specialisation. Higher speed would naturally help the submarine when she attacked the enemy battle fleet, but 'experience in exercises shows that the tactical development of the battle is generally the deciding factor for all forces'. If really high speed (25 knots) was impractical the submarine needed only to be slightly faster than the maximum battle

fleet speed. Maximum fleet speed was 21 knots and the fleet typically steamed more slowly so that ships could manoeuvre. CinC Atlantic Fleet observed that in a recent exercise (JD) demonstrated the value of 'submarines with a speed equivalent to the speed of the Fleet'. This time wireless range was set at 300 to 500nm, with the ability to receive wireless messages while submerged. EinC offered a new 3000 BHP engine (with a potential to reach 4000 BHP) which could be accommodated within a 20ft diameter hull. The submarine would have a three-shaft power plant.

Cutting back on some 'O'-class features – stern tubes and 500ft depth – might increase speed. The 500ft depth had been chosen both to give submarines a better chance of evading depth-charging and to strengthen their hulls against it. Submariners did not expect to dive that deep (depth was 200ft), although they welcomed insurance against an involuntary deep dive; 300ft might be enough. Moreover, depth calculations were imprecise, so a submarine designed for 300ft would be able to dive deeper. For example, on one occasion *E 40*, which had been designed for 200ft, dove to 340ft and recovered safely.

As new staff requirements were being framed, RA(S) asked in February 1928 for a rated speed of 23–24 knots to ensure 21 knots operationally. It was difficult to see how that could be attained within the 1800-ton limit. EinC and DNC were willing to give a rated speed of 21 knots if the 500ft diving limit was waived. At this time higher speed was definitely wanted for the six 1928–9 submarines ('R' class), tentatively allocated to the Mediterranean Fleet. Director of Plans offered a new set of staff requirements in a 13 April 1928 memo. A rated speed of 21–22 knots would ensure 18–19kts under all circumstances, which should be enough. Diving depth would be reduced to 300ft and stern torpedo tubes abandoned. Otherwise the fleet submarine should match the patrol submarines, including their 4.7in guns.

The six 1928–9 submarines had to be ordered in March 1929. In May 1928 DNC offered a series of sketch designs, in each case with six 21in bow torpedo tubes, one 4in HA gun, a displacement of 1800 tons or less, a diving depth of 200ft and 2640 BHP main motors. Endurance was set at 8500nm at 12 knots, which was presumably more than equivalent to 10,000nm at 8 knots. High-powered engines on offer were EinC's double-acting Cygnet (3000 BHP at 350 RPM, probably 4000 BHP at 400 RPM), a 4300 BHP AEL engine and ten-

Clyde from aft, 20 May 1937, presumably at that year's Coronation Review. (© National Maritime Museum N10024)

cylinder versions of the *X 1* engine and the *Odin* engine. Yet another possibility was to couple pairs of *Odin* engines in tandem. Cygnet required a 20ft 4in diameter pressure hull; the AEL engine (with more cylinders) required a considerably longer pressure hull. Given the displacement limit, greater pressure hull diameter had to paid for with shorter overall length, which in turn increased resistance and required more power for a given speed.

Design H, with the long 4300 BHP engine, was ruled out due to its excessive length. Designs A and C used Cygnet; Designs B and B1 used ten-cylinder versions of the *X 1* engine; Designs D, G and J used the *Odin* engine (with triple shafts in J and G, J having a ten-cylinder version and D two sets of tandem *Odin* engines [an arrangement offered by DNC but clearly rejected by EinC]). Designs A, C and D had additional engines to charge batteries or to drive various auxiliaries to the main engines. None of the sketch designs offered more than 22 knots. If that were the minimum, J could be adopted. However, G (21 knots) seems to have been clearly preferable. All were expensive: DNC estimated that Design G would cost £460,000 compared to £392,000 for an *Odin* built under contract.

So much for what British engineering could do, but it was suggested that foreign submarines were faster. It is not altogether clear which submarines EinC had in mind; the highest rated speeds were about 20 knots. EinC told a 9 July 1928 Sea Lords conference that nothing more could be achieved with the direct-coupled engines the Royal Navy was using; to get more power would require more engines and propellers. How much was enough? RA(S) argued that operational speed was generally 2 knots less than rated speed. On this basis the 'O' class were good for 15 knots, which was not enough for shadowing, distant screening or rapid runs to get into attacking positions; these submarines 'were practically reduced to taking up the role of floating wireless stations'. Exercises in the Mediterranean had revealed the possibilities of shadowing work. Operational speed should be 18–19 knots.

An 18 June 1928 staff conference considered whether to replace the patrol submarines with the new type, which could take over their mission. Director of Plans brought up a substantially smaller type, which could be built alongside the larger ones. An all-G programme was rejected as unaffordable because a fleet of them would cost £3.5 million

more than a comparable fleet of patrol submarines. ACNS argued that the fleet would need one division of fast submarines (three each) on each flank of the 'A-K' line of cruisers in the van and another in the centre of that line. A total of twelve would give the desired 25 per cent reserve. The Far Eastern war would require forty-eight patrol submarines; ACNS also wanted twelve smaller ones, already proposed in 1926, for training (they became the 'S' class). The staff had already decided on twelve fast submarines (guaranteed speed 19 knots), forty-eight improved 'O' class (17 knots) and twelve small class. DCNS put the staff view that not even the G design would be fast enough.

ACNS agreed that there was a strong case for a submarine which could accompany the fleet, but 'in these days of small fleets of quick manoeuvre' it was not clear that submarines could be used tactically. Was the cost of a new type justified when it was not certain that it could carry out its missions? A true fleet submarine should make 25 knots; the proposed Design G (19 knots) was not a true fleet submarine. The Mediterranean Fleet had found that once it was known that submarines were nearby their threat could be reduced greatly by air and surface screening. The G type would be capable of shadowing an enemy transport force. Should the special submarine envisaged in the 1929–30 Programme be the G? First Sea Lord was unwilling to accept a G in the 1929–30 Programme. The discussion was referred to the fleet commanders.

The CinCs distinguished between a fleet submarine fast enough to accompany the fleet and a 'battle submarine' intended to act in tactical cooperation with the fleet in battle. Atlantic Fleet manoeuvring orders already took into account the possibility that submarines would occupy the wings of the 'A-K' line in the van of the fleet. They had to be in the van because they were so slow once forced to dive. It seemed unlikely that the submarines' moral effect would help bring the enemy fleet to action. They offered other possibilities. For example, once the CinC knew where they enemy fleet was, they could be placed where the enemy might have to pass or stationed on his likely line of retreat. By night they could shadow and attack an enemy force. CinC Atlantic considered the 19 knots on well worthwhile. He proposed to measure the excess speed required for shadowing in a January 1929 exercise. He was much less impressed with the 15-knot operational speed of the

Severn was a sister to *Clyde*. The derrick abaft the bridge fairwater was for her boat. (© National Maritime Museum N3597)

patrol submarines. The best choice would be Design G, the combination fleet and patrol submarine. All concerned agreed that the battle submarine could not be built. Even if it could be, it would be difficult to employ during a fleet action, because just when they most needed their speed to gain a favourable position they would have to dive and thus nearly immobilise themselves. If they remained on the surface (hence fast) they would lose their element of surprise. In effect they would be nothing more than slow destroyers.

CinC Mediterranean Fleet generally echoed the views of CinC Atlantic Fleet. The battle submarine was pointless. Even if in theory it was fast enough to reach a tactically useful position, in reality it would lose much of its mobility as enemy surface ships and aircraft forced it down. The patrol submarines were too slow. It was impossible to separate the patrol and fleet functions, since 'operations of a patrol and/or reconnaissance nature will, either as a result of a fleet action or from information received from the CinC, probably result from having been in company with the fleet'. CinC Mediterranean favoured Design G.

In March 1929 DCNS summed up.[13] With only one or two dissenters, those at sea favoured G, but it would take a much faster submarine to get into a useful tactical position to attack an enemy battle fleet. On the other hand, the 18–19-knot G would be of undoubted value during the ocean passage by the fleet. 'My opinion is that unless the G type has got a reasonable chance of attacking the enemy's Battle Fleet in a day action its raison d'être largely disappears. Because I think it has this possibility I am in favour of the type being built.' DCNS proposed an annual programme of four G and two small submarines for the next three years, which would cost less than the current annual policy of building six patrol submarines. ACNS (Dudley Pound) and Controller (Admiral Backhouse) agreed.

Would the G submarine be manoeuvrable enough? Her length would be closer to that of X 1 than to the 'O' class.[14] Published data were unreliable. For example, the submarine handbook credited X 1 with a tactical diameter (submerged) of 460 yds at 25° helm, although it would more likely approximate the 600 yds credited to K 26. None of the 'O' class had yet been tested, but DNC considered 450 yds likely and the 'G'-class would probably have a submerged tactical diameter of 560 yds. As for the vertical plane, the handbook tabulated times to dive from 35ft to 70ft: 1 minute 25 seconds for X 1, 40 seconds for K 26 and 35 seconds for the 'L' class. The G design was closer to X 1 in length, but closer to the 'O' class in submerged displacement, hence ought to be able to approximate 'O'-class performance in changing depth.

The Sea Lords held a formal conference on 25 April 1929 to discuss the new designs, both G and the projected small submarine (*Swordfish*, see Chapter 13).[15] RA(S) said the 200ft designed diving depth of the 'G' class was enough, but 300ft would be better. ACNS considered 300ft necessary for a submarine this long (345ft); it was adopted, if necessary at the cost of speed. which Controller thought DNC's single 4in gun too weak; the submarine should have more gun power than patrol vessels she might meet. RA(S) considered 4in enough, but ACNS agreed with Controller that 4.7in was better for fire control. Their view carried. DSD explained the need to fit both long- and short-wave wireless sets. DNC said the arrangements would match those of the 'O' and 'P' classes. RA(S) wanted some reduction in wireless requirement, which affected both internal space and underwater speed (due to masts etc); RA(S) hoped for some reduction. The conference was unwilling to cut back DSD's proposed installation, but DSD would try to do so. Pending that the wireless installation would match that of the 1928–9 submarines.

EinC said that he could guarantee the desired speed using the engines of the 1928–9 submarines, on three shafts. DNC liked a three-shaft design from the point of view of hull form. EinC argued that it was too complicated, requiring more maintenance and more personnel. The three-shaft 'J' class had not been a success and officers with wartime experience of them agreed. EinC asked for more time to consider a two-shaft alternative.

Controller suggested an underwater speed of 10 knots. DNC pointed out that 10 knots was beyond what he had provided and that he envisaged 7 to 7.5 knots. RA(S) wanted 9 knots, which he thought the highest currently practicable. The general feeling was that high submerged speed was extremely important. It would mean larger batteries and heavier motors. Although it was unlikely that 9 knots would be exceeded, to some extent underwater resistance could be reduced by shrinking the conning tower and also by reducing hull excrescences. The meeting proposed that this be tried and that DNC investigate what would be required for 10 knots. The desired surface endurance of 10,000nm at 8 knots was endorsed. Submerged endurance was set at 30 hours at 3 knots and/or 1¼ hours at full speed.

The conference agreed to delete stern torpedo tubes, retaining the six bow tubes and six reloads previously accepted. RA(S) pointed out that given torpedo angling stern tubes were no longer needed. DTM resisted any change in the bow shape, because that would require a new tube design, which in turn would delay design.

DNC now sketched alternative two- and three-shaft designs (the two-shaft version of G was G.2). To get enough power on two shafts, EinC supercharged his diesels. In that respect the design was largely experimental. The motors were too large to move well aft, so the superchargers had to be abaft the motors. The prototype engine was built to an AEL design, with detailed design by Vickers.[16] At about this time AEL was promising a much more powerful engine, which could make a real fleet submarine possible, in two to three years; a submarine so powered might be bought in five years.

When the conference asked for higher underwater speed it was asking not only for larger motors but also for a lot more battery capacity, to meet the 1¼-hour underwater maximum speed endurance. As DNC developed the two-shaft design, it grew because it had to accommodate heavier batteries and motors than previously expected. Early in June 1929, the required power grew to 7750 BHP (for 21 knots).[17] DNC asked EinC whether he could fit powerful enough machinery in the available space.

DNC submitted a sketch design and Legend in June 1929.[18] He offered the desired 21 knots on 1760 tons Geneva displacement, i.e., according to the rules proposed at the abortive Geneva conference. As desired, endurance would be 10,000nm at 8 knots, wireless and Asdic would be as in the 1928 patrol submarines and diving depth would be 300ft. This was the two-shaft design preferred by the April conference; DNC understood that EinC could guarantee the required 7750 BHP within the available space and weight, although some further trials were needed before the engine could be adopted.[19] The battery would use X 1 cells. The bridge structure would be specially streamlined, as had already been proposed for the 'O' class, to reduce resistance. It turned out that the full 30 hours submerged at 3 knots could be achieved, but only one hour at full speed. Adding another quarter-hour at full speed would complicate battery arrangement and require considerably greater displacement. A 29 July 1929 Sea Lords meeting recommended that two G boats be included in the 1929 and 1930 Programmes. The other submarines in these programmes would be either two 'S' and two 'P' (patrol type) or four 'S'.

BRITISH SUBMARINES IN TWO WORLD WARS

HMS *THAMES*. General arrangement. Starboard elevation and sections. (© National Maritime Museum M1074)

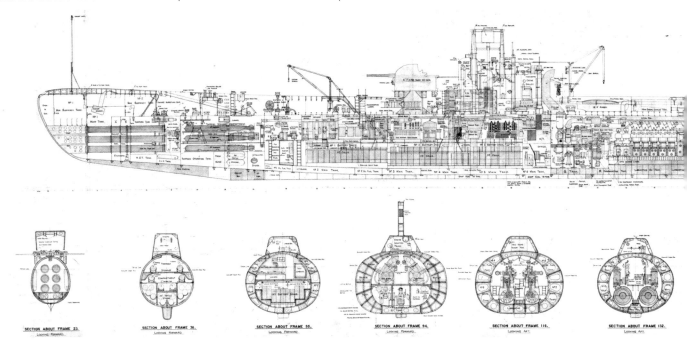

HMS *THAMES*. General arrangement. Plan view. (© National Maritime Museum M1076)

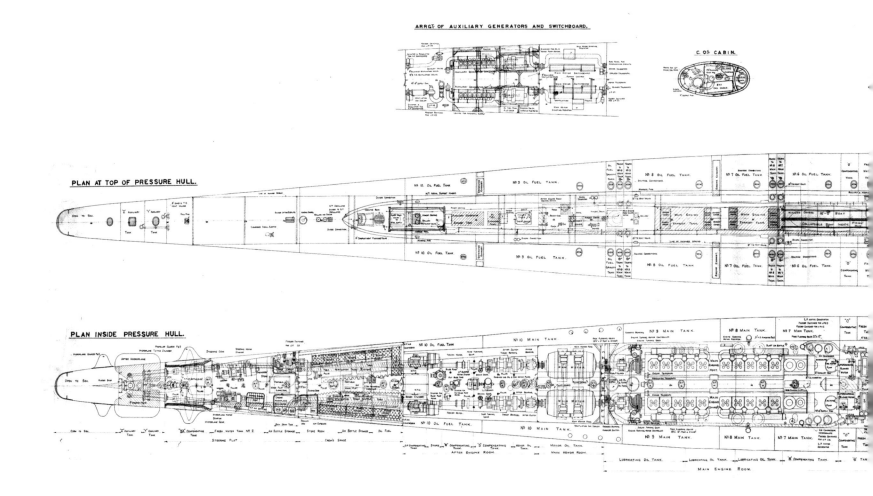

198

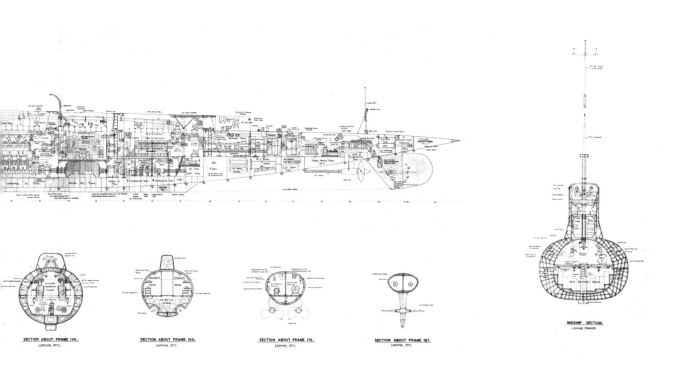

SECTION ABOUT FRAME 146.
LOOKING AFT.

SECTION ABOUT FRAME 160.
LOOKING AFT.

SECTION ABOUT FRAME 175.
LOOKING AFT.

SECTION ABOUT FRAME 187.
LOOKING AFT.

MIDSHIP SECTION.
LOOKING FORWARD.

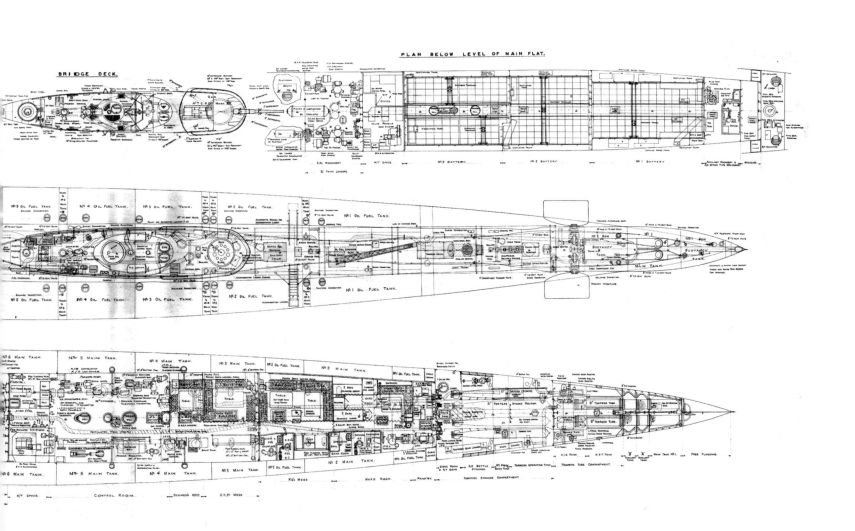

BRIDGE DECK.

PLAN BELOW LEVEL OF MAIN FLAT.

Severn in 1941, camouflaged, with extra freeing holes in her bridge fairwater. This Admiralty photograph was given to the US Navy at the time. She was then in the Mediterranean. (US Navy)

It seemed inevitable that the coming London Naval Conference would set a limit on total British submarine tonnage, as indeed it did.[20] The Royal Navy had to choose numbers or size. RA(S) wanted the G type to be the future patrol submarine. Because the G design was experimental, it was unwise to begin building in quantity before the prototype had been tested and proven. At this point the planned 1929–30 submarine programme was four G type and two 'S' class. Somewhat later Controller pointed out that it would be extremely difficult to include two 'R' class (repeats) in the 1929 Programme because two had just been cancelled. It would be better to order four 'S' class. It soon seemed likely that the Royal Navy would be getting only four submarines per year. Both the G type and the small 'S' class seemed important; the Staff Requirement was twelve fleet-capable submarines. That equated to an annual programme of two Gs and two 'S' class. In October First Sea Lord proposed substituting the cancelled (but partly-built) *Royalist* for one of the 1929–30 G type, making the programme two large submarines and four 'S' class. That would have saved about £80,000, but it was not done.

The London Naval Conference set the British submarine tonnage allocation at 52,700, well below what anyone had expected in 1929, but it set a 2000-ton rather than 1800-ton limit on individual submarines. Any hope of building forty to fifty large submarines died. Director of Plans laid out a new long-term programme: twenty fast patrol submarines (Design G), six minelayers and twelve small submarines. Minelayers were considered viable alternatives to patrol submarines.

By May 1930 the 1929–30 Programme had been cut to one G-type submarine and two small 'S' class. The annual programme was cut to three submarines per year. From a programmatic point of view, the alternatives in any one year were a cruiser or a minelayer.

Thames was built under the 1929–30 Programme. On the measured mile (Skelmorlie) she made 22.57 knots on 9960 SHP, far beyond her original rated power, at 405.5 RPM.[21] Her commanding officer reported a transit from Portsmouth to Venice in July 1933 through heavy seas in the Bay of Biscay.[22] She managed an average of 17.32 knots over 2745nm, having to reduce speed by 3 knots in some of the head seas. Despite them, she took only spray over her bridge. To the boat's captain, the run demonstrated that she could, as advertised, accompany the fleet on a long wartime run. This run was succeeded by a test in the Red and Arabian Seas in October–November 1933. In effect it tested the boat in the tropics, meaning the Far East in wartime. The captain wrote that the crew's health had remained excellent, apart from one case of heat exhaustion aggravated by a knock on the head. On the other hand, the bottom fouled badly, so that although only four months out of dock she had already lost 1.5 knots when making revolutions which would normally drive her at 16 knots.

At this speed she suffered 30 per cent increased fuel consumption. It seemed that the Royal Navy's anti-fouling paint was no good. When *Thames* arrived in Venice, having left Portsmouth with a clean bottom, she already had considerable weed on her starboard side. A Yugoslav submarine visited at Biograde, which had been out of dock for five months, showed practically none. With water temperatures as great as 90° F, internal conditions were tolerable despite the humidity. Diving would have been unbearable without the ship's efficient ventilation-circulation and cooling. The open type of cooling for the main motors made their compartment the coolest place in the boat when submerged. In earlier submarines it had been one of the hottest in the boat. The electric bulbs fitted were too hot. The captain referred to the CO_2 plant, which ran the cold and cool food stores and also two ventilation coolers. It could have run all three coolers had the cold and cool rooms been better insulated.

Thames was followed by *Severn* (1931–2 Programme) and *Clyde* (1932–3). Construction of fleet submarines then lapsed in favour of the 'T' class described in a later chapter. The two later fleet submarines were very similar to *Thames*, but their design was modified after HMS *Poseidon* was sunk by collision while surfaced. In June 1931 Controller asked whether these big submarines were sufficiently subdivided.[23] RA(S) rejected further bulkheading (for a one-compartment standard) on the ground that additional bulkheads might make it more difficult to pass commands from one compartment to another and that they would almost certainly increase tonnage (hence cut numbers, given treaty requirements). In order to submerge a submarine had to sacrifice some surface safety and buoyancy; 'this fact is recognised in the shape of extra pay to officers and ratings'. DNC stated that as designed *Thames* would float and be stable if any compartment except the main engine room was flooded, together with the two main ballast tanks abreast it on one side. Flooding the main engine room and the two adjacent ballast tanks on one side would bring the submarine down by the stern, ultimately on end and then sunk. The main engine room could not be subdivided without adding considerable length and displacement. RA(S) wanted the bulkheads around the main engine room strengthened; the meeting agreed that this should be studied.

Controller (Rear Admiral Backhouse) asked whether the pressure hull plating over the larger compartments could be thickened. That might help in a collision and would also offer some protection against shellfire. The bulkheads at the ends of the larger compartments should be specially strong. DNC doubted that a thicker pressure hull would protect against collision. *Poseidon* had been holed by a small ship despite having 35lb plating (the G design showed 25lbs); 40lbs was unlikely to do any better. Bringing the G design up to the standard of the patrol submarines would cost 78 tons; going to 40lbs would cost 120 tons. If the extra plating were to be confined to the nearly vertical sides of the engine room, the one space which, if flooded, would sink the submarine, the extra weight would be 18 tons. It might be better to add stiffening to the external plating where beam was greatest, as a buffer against gun or depth charge attack. *Thames* was already only 195 tons below the limit laid down in the London Naval Conference. DNC offered 50 tons of extra strength: thicker nearly vertical sides to the engine room, a redesigned non-watertight flat amidships turned into a girder. Remote-controlled Kingstons would also be fitted. Submerged buoyancy would have to increase to carry the additional weight. That could buy improved accommodation. Standard displacement would be 1850 tons rather than 1805 tons; surface displacement would be 2210 tons rather than 2165 tons and submerged displacement would be 2725 tons rather than 2680 tons. Surface speed would be reduced by 0.2 knots and surface endurance by about 2.5 per cent, to 9750nm at 8 knots. Controller chose less drastic action: increased stiffening to external plating, strengthened main bulkheads, but no Kingstons. *Thames* was too far advanced to be modified, but the 1931–2 submarine (*Severn*) was built to the altered design.

Thames turned out to be faster than expected; as a result of her trials the Legend of the 1931–2 submarine was altered, the maximum surface speed increased from 21.5 knots to 22.25 knots and the endurance at 8 knots increased to 12,500nm. W/T aerials were changed. The main aerial, now to be called the diving aerial, was attached to a fixed point amidships. The former W/T mast would now carry a rod (whip) antenna only. Where *Thames* had a combined periscope aerial and direction-finding (D/F) installation, the new submarine would have only a D/F installation on her periscope. She was also rearranged internally, the Asdic office being placed adjacent to her W/T office. The Board approved the new Legend and drawings on 19 July 1932.

As a result of the *Thames* trials, DEE proposed a revised battery arrangement. In *Thames* batteries were grouped to provide 330 volts for maximum power; otherwise the submarine operated at 220 volts. Shifting from one setting to the other took time. Standardising on one voltage simplified the use of the auxiliary generators and increased battery charging current from the main motor-generators by about 50 per cent, drastically shortening charging time. Control of the super-charging motor was much simplified. In both designs, as in the patrol submarines, each motor had two armatures in tandem (in effect was two motors in tandem). As redesigned the submarine always operated at 220 volts, the armatures being either in series or in parallel. On the surface, the battery powered the supercharger blower. The change required 9½ tons of weight and a minimum increase in the motor room of 10½in. DNC proposed lengthening the submarine by 2ft to gain sufficient extra buoyancy. Standard displacement would grow from the 1835 tons approved by the Board to 1850 tons. DNC was told to incorporate the improved electrical arrangements without, if possible, increasing length or tonnage. To that end it might be possible to combine the W/T and Asdic offices and to reduce fuel capacity (as the expected endurance exceeded requirements). If these changes were not enough, a 4in gun might replace the planned 4.7in.

DNC tried to reduce the size of the bridge; a Haslar tank test suggested that the submarine might gain as much as a quarter-knot of submerged speed. It helped that EinC was willing to accept a reduced

induction trunk (air intake for the diesels) at the after end of the bridge. DNE wrote that what counted was a reduction in underwater resistance, which would increase submerged endurance by cutting the need for power. RA(S) wrote that 'the aspect of the forward end of the Gun Canopy and breakwater and of the bridge are of equal importance to a submarine, as the shape of the bow below water is to a surface ship and progress in design of this part of the structure is therefore desirable'. He would accept a slight increase in silhouette due to a larger gun canopy, given the much larger structure towering above it.

On the measured mile at Skelmorlie, *Severn* made 22.146 knots at full power on 6 October 1934. She took over five hours to work up to full power and during this period her draft increased by about 5in, as water was taken into her main ballast tanks owing to bad weather. She had been out of dock for 29 days. The DNC representative estimated that the ship would have slightly exceeded her designed speed of 22.25 knots had she been run under conditions similar to those for *Thames*. The 1932–3 fleet submarine (*Clyde*) was a repeat *Severn*.

In 1936 the possibility of fitting external torpedo tubes to the older submarines was raised. That could not easily be done in *Thames* for stability reasons, but no great difficulty was expected in the other two.[24] Two tubes could be fitted, but that was never done.

Minelayers

During the war, the British converted 'E' and 'L'-class submarines to carry mines in vertical tubes in their saddle tanks. They may have been inspired by discovery of minelaying tubes on board one or more sunken 'UC'-boats.[25] The six 'E'-class minelayers carried twenty vertical tubes (ten each side) in place of their broadside tubes. 'L'-class minelayers had only fourteen tubes, because their diameter was considerably greater. In both cases the tubes were open to the sea, mines being loaded before the submarine left port. Mines were also designed for launching from existing torpedo tubes (Type I from 18in tubes, Type II from 21in tubes). Both used mechanical (external lever) pistols, which the British favoured in the early part of the war but then considered unreliable. They also lacked any automatic depth-taking mechanism. Submarine-laid mines benefitted from the wider revolution in British mine design in 1916, in which mines were provided with horns as their contact mechanism and also with automatic depth-taking. Submarine versions of existing mines were designed, beginning with the S.IV for 21in tubes. The limitation in diameter made for a long narrow mine case which was poorly adapted for standing up in a tideway. However, S.IV became standard for 'E' class minelayers and it was also laid from some coastal motor boats (CMBs). A further S.V was better shaped: 31in in diameter and 5ft 9in long including its sinker. It was delivered by 'L'-class minelayers. Compared to S.IV, S.V was more reliable and was better adapted to laying in a tideway due to its better shape. In 1920 the British considered it superior to wartime German submarine-laid mines.

The Germans also built numerous minelayers with external tubes, but they also built minelayers carrying mines internally. The *U 117* class had two minelaying tubes aft. In 1920 DNC was asked for particulars as a preliminary to designing an equivalent submarine.[26] Deputy Director of Plans argued that submarine minelayers could go where surface ships could not; their main disadvantage was the small number of mines they could carry, at most (for the Germans) 42 compared to 300 for a surface ship. Typically submarines did not carry the full mine complement. Mines were arranged in three tiers in the after part of the submarine, loaded three at a time into the two minelaying tubes. The tubes were flooded only just before beginning to lay, just as with torpedoes. The German design seemed superior; in 1920 the captured *U 126* was attached to the Mining School for trials. If the British could design an internal minelayer, they might be able to use the same mines for both surface and submarine laying, a considerable advantage (sinkers and other auxiliaries would be a different proposition, however).

In February 1920 it was decided that the design of a specialised British minelaying submarine should be pursued and Plans Division soon asked DNC to summarise the pros and cons of external vs internal mine stowage. In July DTM asked for staff requirements. Plans Division called for speed comparable to that of other submarines, which eventually meant comparable to patrol submarines.[27] Endurance should be 7000nm (the 10,000nm endurance of the patrol submarines had not yet been chosen). The important clause was that the submarine employ the same type of mines as surface minelayers. Mines should be laid either surfaced or submerged; the submarine should be able to lay all of her mines in a continuous line, at intervals which would protect them from counter-mining each other when they exploded. The submarine should be able to lay mines at any speed up to her full speed. The minelayer should be able to dive in 10 fathoms (60ft), so that she could operate in shallow water suitable for mining. The mine load should be no fewer than forty, backed by six bow torpedo tubes (one reload each). The powerful torpedo battery made the minelayer an effective conventional submarine after she laid her mines. Plans wanted two 4in guns (the Germans had had one 5.9in); DNC soon argued that gun armament should be minimised to limit underwater resistance (he favoured a 3in gun on a retractable mount).

As the Far Eastern war plan developed, minelaying was important, so formal requirements were formulated. Requirements for a new submarine mine, formulated at a June 1923 conference, were that it be suited to laying in depths up to 140 fathoms (existing submarine mines were limited to 60 fathoms). Mines should be adjustable (e.g. for depth setting) until the time of laying, which implied that they would be stowed internally. They would be laid in groups of not fewer than ten, with a spacing of 150ft, at any speed from lowest up to 8 knots. They could be laid when the submarine was either surfaced or submerged. Apparently the 1920 requirements resulted in sketch designs with excessive displacement, so new ones were drafted. Like the patrol submarine, the minelayer should have a diving depth of 500ft, the mine tubes capable of withstanding water pressure down to 200ft. Mine capacity should be at least thirty-six, ideally forty. Submerged displacement should not exceed 2500 tons. Ideally endurance should be 10,000nm at cruising speed (not less than 7,000nm). The conference agreed to recommend that a design with a mining compartment amidships should proceed, so that a minelaying submarine could be included in the 1924–5 Programme.

As of 1923 Superintendent of Mining had produced two schemes for internal minelaying, K and L, but neither met the requirements. A new scheme (N) used two horizontal tubes taking five mines each. Mines were stowed above the tubes. To lay mines, the tubes were flooded, with inboard and outboard doors closed. Five mines were then fed into each tube, the water displaced going into the trough down which the mines had been fed. Once the tube was full, its outer door could be opened and the mines dropped. Once all the mines were gone, the process could be repeated. A drawing of Type N showed three rails abreast over a pair of horizontal mine tubes. The two mine tubes were nearly rectangular in section, their sides slightly curved for strength. An accompanying drawing of a German internal minelayer (*U 123*) showed a mine tube opening into the stern of the submarine, fed by mines stowed forward of it. Mines were stowed on three levels, moved to the tube by a chain run from a wheel. The mines were loaded into the submarine via a hatch forward of the mine stowage. A prototype

Roughly parallel to the diesel fleet submarines was a series of minelayers, designed after tests with the rebuilt *M 3*. The key feature was external mine stowage, in her case in the considerably built-up casing fore and aft. It was chosen in preference to the internal stowage the Germans had adopted in their big wartime U-minelayers. Note that the mine stowage stopped short of the bow; the boat is heading to the left. (NHHC)

Porpoise was the first of the purpose-built minelayers of the 1930s. She is shown as built, with her 4.7in gun in a bulbous shield. (RAN Naval Historical Section via Dr Josef Straczek)

mining tube for a large minelaying submarine was built, with mine rails running into it.[28]

Director of Plans (Dudley Pound) pointed out that although no provision had been made for a minelaying submarine in the 'programme of construction and reconstruction' (P.D. 01813/23) under consideration by the Board, such a design could certainly be included if it was ready in time. This programme called for beginning submarine construction in 1925–6. DNE commented that it should have taken three months rather than three years to arrive at these conclusions, in which case sketch designs would have been available.

In January 1924 DTM wrote that he doubted that minelaying arrangements would be anything like as simple as had been imagined. Current surface minelayers used tiers of mines on rails, which were hauled aft by machinery. Individual mines were pulled from the face of the tier and then thrust into the discharge trap by hand. There they remained until the appropriate interval had elapsed. In a submarine the whole sequence would have to be automatic. Surely extensive design and experimental work were needed. Moreover, existing mines were unlikely to be suitable; at the least the sinkers would have to be redesigned. The sinkers were not watertight. If they were exposed to

the sea, they would all fill and empty each time the submarine dove and surfaced. The mines in 'L'-class minelayers were always waterborne as soon as they were loaded, but the proposed minelayer would be rather different. DTM asked whether it was much more than an inferior surface minelayer capable of submerging.

By June 1924 the contemplated mine compartment of the internal minelayer was 60ft 6in long, mines being carried on rails as in a surface minelayer (this length soon grew slightly).

Meanwhile work proceeded on an external minelayer, to carry more mines than the wartime 'E' and 'L'-class conversions. Because the internal system was more complex, it was described in greater detail. RA(S) preferred the external approach because it would not require so large a submarine. Such a submarine might also be effective in other roles: reconnaissance and attack.

A submarine minelayer design was begun in 1924.[29] It was soon clear that the minelayer could not possibly be ordered under the 1924–5 Programme; as of December 1925 work on designs for both internal and external mine layers was only at the stage of sketching mine arrangements. Drawings and estimates for the minelaying tube for the internal minelayer had been submitted to the Admiralty. Once they had been approved it would take seven more months to complete the experimental tube. For the external minelayer, a single section of rails 100ft long (capacity twenty-five mines) would be ready in January 1926.

HM SUBMARINE *M 3*. Profile and topsides, as fitted. (© National Maritime Museum M1071)

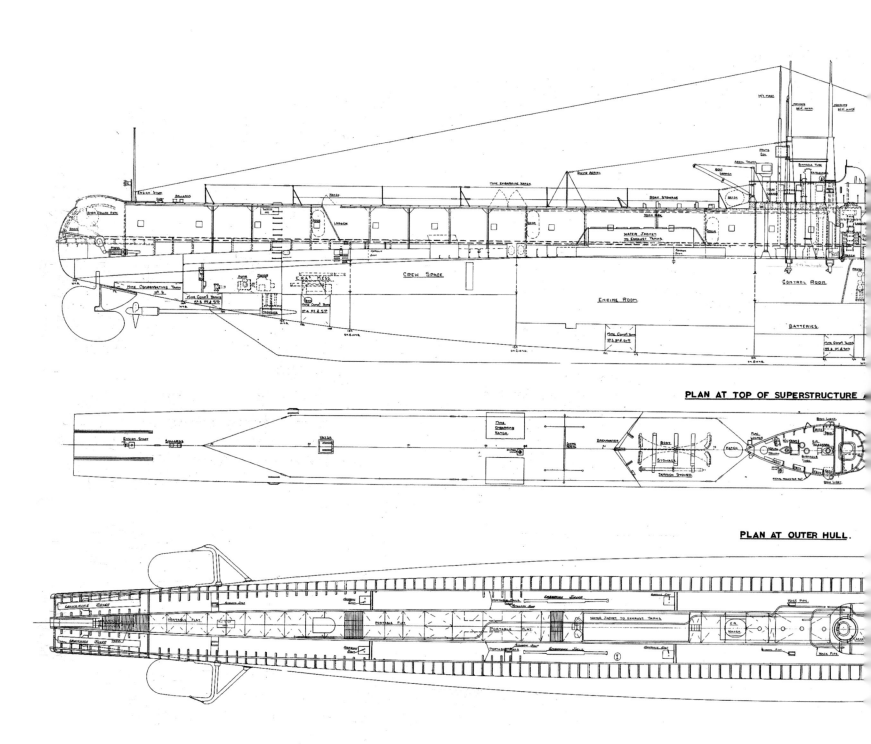

PLAN AT TOP OF SUPERSTRUCTURE

PLAN AT OUTER HULL.

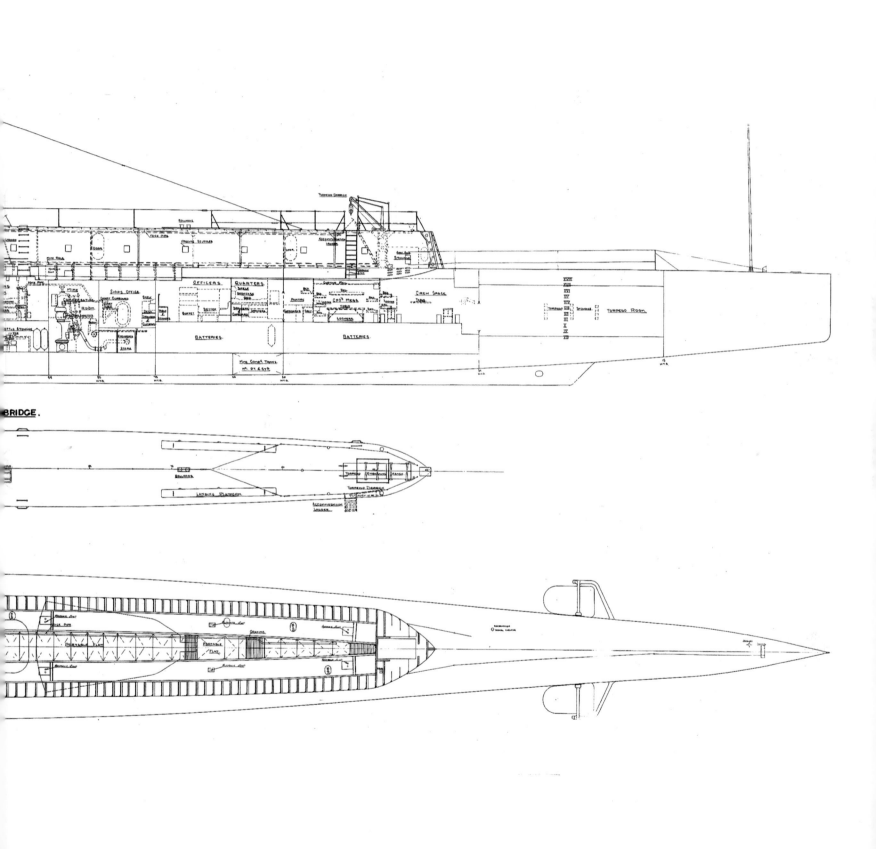

Meanwhile the big submarine *M 3* was ordered converted into an external minelayer, i.e., with mines stowed outside her pressure hull. It was impossible to convert her into an internal minelayer, because her pressure hull was not large enough. Given her large superstructure, she was fitted with two mine rails, the mines being moved down the rails by 'hydraulic jiggers'. The alternative was a chain-and-rack system. The idea was first raised in 1923 by Captain Max Horton (1st Submarine Flotilla) and was warmly supported by RA(S), who gained approval despite objections from the technical departments.[30] Once it had been approved, work on the internal minelayer was officially abandoned (1925).

RA(S) claimed various advantages for an external minelayer: smaller surface displacement (1600 tons vs 2500 tons), more mines (100 vs 40), no sacrifice of internal space for mines, maximum speed of laying to obtain 150ft spacing (15 knots vs 8 knots), higher minimum speed (2.5 knots vs 3.5 knots, due to smaller size), smaller compensating tanks and no cooling plant (required for mines carried internally). DTD objected to some of these claims, such as the great number of mines (although the external minelayer would always carry more than the internal) and the greater internal space (the external type required considerable space for mining machinery and compensating gear). Disadvantages *not* mentioned by RA(S) were slow diving due to the large free-flooding superstructure; larger silhouette; continuously-immersed mines and sinkers which could not be maintained on passage, hence not as reliable as those kept internally; greater vulnerability of mines to depth-charging; inability to clear a jam without surfacing; and limited mine depth (80 fathoms; a 200-fathom design could not be laid externally).

Given experience with the prototype minelaying device, a conference on minelaying submarines was held on 2 November 1927.[31] It was to decide whether a design for an internal minelayer should be investigated now; if the *M 3* trials proved unsuccessful, 'we shall be left in the air at the end of 1928'. Similarly, on what lines should the design of an external minelayer proceed, assuming the *M 3* trials succeeded? What was the maximum acceptable size of such a submarine?

About this time Plans Division formalised requirements for the Far East war.[32] The submarine would operate from Hong Kong, about 1500nm from the most distant of the twenty-two places to be mined. Ten ability mines per month would be laid off fourteen important points and five mines per month off eight less important ports, a total of 100 per month. This paper called for a total of six submarines, each carrying forty mines. Fewer submarines of greater capacity would find it difficult to cover all the places involved. Preferably the submarine should carry more mines.

Director of Plans told the November 1927 conference that the first priority was to provide enough overseas patrol submarines. He did not want to lay down any other kind of submarine until that had been done. RA(S) did not want submarines larger than the *Odin*s. No 'internal' minelayer could combine minelaying and patrol functions in the size of an *Odin*. Further work on internal minelayers should be postponed until after the *M 3* trials. If they succeeded and a satisfactory combination of minelaying and patrol functions could be provided, Director of Plans was willing to lay down a minelayer in the 1929–30 and later Programmes, subject to the tentative programme of six submarines per year being approved. The *Odin* displacement (1710 tons) and a capacity of forty mines were taken as basic requirements, possible trade-offs being diving depth (300ft vs 500ft), the two stern

tubes, power loading gear for torpedoes, gun armament and Asdics.

RA(S) pressed the case for the external minelayer, which could probably retain some or all of the main features of the *Odin* class and thus could be available for reconnaissance after laying its mines. An internal minelayer, if limited in size, would be of little use for anything else. Controller (Chatfield) asked whether it was time to begin a sketch design. In March 1928 DNC pointed to the heavy workload of his submarine section, which by this time included the conversion of *M 3* into a minelayer. The staff requirements laid down by the 1927 conference were practicable and by the end of 1928 he expected to have sufficient time available to develop a sketch design. By that time, too, experience would have been gained with the *M 3* conversion.

In December, Chatham reported that it could not take *M 3* in hand for conversion until early February 1929, because of delays in the design of the minelaying gear. Director of Plans wrote that unless the international situation demanded the construction of a minelayer in 1929, it would be better to wait until *M 3* had been completed and tested. ACNS and First Sea Lord (Admiral Madden) agreed. In June 1930 First Sea Lord, DCNS, Controller, ACNS, Vice Admiral Dreyer, RA(S) and Director of Plans met to discuss the 1930–1 Programme. One G type and two 'S' class, all experimental, were already on order or to be ordered. A second G should not be ordered until its high-powered engines had been thoroughly tested in the shop. No more patrol submarines were wanted. It already seemed that the Australians would be turning over their two *Odin*s if they found maintaining them unaffordable, as turned out to be the case. The group considered replacing the G type with a minelayer. Including one large submarine in the 1930 Programme was preferable to building three small ones, since in that case three large submarines might have to be built in 1931, at prohibitive cost. That settled the issue; a prototype minelayer was included in the 1930–1 Programme. No more would be built until it had been tested. Controller wrote DNC that he had assumed that the design could be completed in time, if not by March 1931 (the end of the 1930–1 fiscal year) then not too long afterwards. CNS was willing to accept some delay because it was important to get on with this type. If it were not in the 1930 Programme, there would be a year's delay.

DNC immediately produced a rough sketch of an external minelaying submarine. It seemed possible that a 1500-ton external minelayer could carry forty mines, but a 1500-ton internal minelayer could not carry more than twenty at most; to carry forty or fifty mines she would have to displace 300 to 400 tons more. That was very important given the new treaty limit on total submarine tonnage.

The chief question was probably whether mines would survive exposure over an extended mission. For her final test, *M 3* spent thirty-three days, including some severe weather, at sea and then laid mines both surfaced and submerged. The test proved that her special minelaying equipment and mines and sinkers could stand up to extended wartime missions. Some problems with depth taking were attributed to minor design flaws in the mines. Controller described *M 3* as a 'good minelayer but a bad submarine'; the future minelaying submarine also had to be a good submarine.[33]

When it came to a decision on the 1930 minelayer, all recent experience had been with the external minelayer *M 3*. A 26 June 1930 conference met to decide what kind of minelaying submarine to build. The internal minelayer could not quickly lay a field. She had to limit herself to groups of three or four depending on the size of the mining chamber in the stern (the midships chamber had been abandoned). After discharging its load of mines, it had to be reloaded. The tonnage issue was decisive. Also, the Royal Navy had no experience with internal minelaying. Controller (Admiral Backhouse) wrote that the issue might be reconsidered after DNC had completed a sketch design, 'but [these factors] are mentioned here to indicate the line that is being followed'. DNC did continue with an internal design, assuming that the best arrangement would be horizontal stowage with discharge through horizontal tubes at the stern, as the Germans had done.

In proposing staff requirements late in June 1930, DTD observed that submarine mining was to follow a monthly cycle, so endurance should suffice to get the boat to its operating area, keep it there for two to three weeks and return. Since the submarine would spend much of its time in transit, it needed a reasonably high cruising speed: DTD recommended 6000nm at 12kts. Underwater endurance should be 20 hours at 2–3 knots, which was presumably typical. Neither high surface nor underwater speed was necessary, although the latter might be important when attacking enemy ships with torpedoes. DTD suggested a maximum surface speed of 15 knots (12 knots cruising) and an underwater speed of 8 knots, the latter roughly what the big patrol submarines were then developing. A complete Asdic installation was essential, because the minelayer would spend much of her time on the surface in transit, open to attack by enemy submarines. By this time, too, Asdic was proving a valuable aid to navigation; *H 32* had managed to pass through the Dardanelles guided solely by her Asdic. Examining DNC's sketch designs, DTD considered their silhouettes excessive for a submarine spending so much of her time on the surface: 7ft or more above water over about two-thirds of the length.

The *M 3* trials convinced RA(S) that for good diving qualities the future external minelayer should have a single row of mines in a greatly-reduced casing, given that great attention was paid to the shape of the casing, especially its after end. The silhouette should be as low as possible. Surface speed need not exceed 15 knots. Six bow torpedo tubes were desirable, but four could be accepted. Asdics and good W/T were definite requirements, but a gun was not.

The Royal Navy had only four minelaying submarines: *M 3* and three 'L' class. Under the rules of the London Treaty, two of the 'L' (*L 14* and *L 17*) should be scrapped in 1931 and *M 3* in 1933. *M 3* was so poor a submarine that in 1930 DNC proposed to alter her bow to improve her diving qualities. That was approved provided it could be done within the next refit at a moderate cost.

DNC offered Design A, a 1505-ton external minelayer on a *Rainbow* hull, with the same characteristics except that there was no stern tube, no power loading and 300ft diving depth. She would carry forty mines in a streamlined casing about half the size of that in *M 3*. The conning tower, bridge and gun were moved 42ft forward to correct the balance upon diving with mines on board. RA(S) killed the design on the ground that the bridge was too far forward for good sea-keeping.

Design B, 1750 tons, carried forty mines externally as in Design A but another forty in three rows in a watertight box at the fore end of the casing. The box corrected the balance of the design, so the conning tower and bridge could be amidships. Reserve mines would be transferred aft on the surface after the first forty had been laid. This design was dropped both because there was insufficient tonnage under the treaty, but also because it was essential to cut down the size of a submarine operating in enemy waters. The reserve mine box gave the

superstructure of the submarine a bad shape and too large a silhouette. If the box was reduced, there were hardly enough mines left for a useful second lay. However, some form of watertight box was needed for balance, if the bridge was to be amidships.

DNC offered a compromise. Speed was cut from 17 knots (in Design A) to 15 knots and a watertight box built onto the bow forming part of the ship structure and streamlined, containing no mines but available for any other purpose. On this basis the submarine might not exceed 1500 tons and her bridge could be amidships. She would probably carry more than forty mines. The conference liked this option. The internal minelayer was dropped because it could not be built on 1500 tons with a reasonable mine load.

The hydraulic jigger used to move mines aft in *M 3* was rejected because it needed too much upkeep; the new minelayer would use a chain-and-rack system.

The internal minelayer did not quite die; in July 1930 Director of Torpedo Division asked DNC to develop a design for comparison with the external type when a future programme was discussed. DNC's sketch showed German-type mining tubes aft. Superintendent of Mining Dept was still interested in discharging mines amidships, but DNC pointed out that would make little difference. The German arrangement had already been tested. It could discharge six mines at a time, whereas DTM's current arrangement would lay four mines (from four tubes) at a time.[34]

DNC submitted new designs in September 1930, Designs A and B having been rejected. Design C was a 1490-ton external minelayer carrying fifty mines, as suggested by the 26 June 1930 conference. Design D was the alternative internal minelayer: 1500 tons with forty mines, the minimum acceptable.

Design C was a modified *Rainbow*-class submarine, weight having been saved by reducing power (six vs eight cylinders, for 15 knots rather than 17.5 knots). Endurance would be unchanged, 10,000nm at 8 knots and as in the *Rainbow* class, there would be Vulcan (hydraulic) clutches. Batteries and motors were as in the *Rainbow* class, but the 4.7in gun was omitted. The W/T and Asdic sets were also the same. Diving depth was reduced from 500ft to 300ft. Mines were carried on a single line of rails on the centreline, extending about three-quarters the length of the submarine. They passed under the bridge, which was amidships, the conning tower and periscopes being moved to one side. Given the unfortunate experience with *M 3*, DNC proposed to solve the three key problems: (i) the position of the buoyancy of the mines, which caused the stern of the submarine to sink rapidly initially, making it difficult to submerge; (ii) the size and to some extent the shape of the superstructure over the mines (gross free-flooding capacity above water in *M 3* had increased from 160 tons to 770 tons on conversion); and (iii) the large increase in overall submerged displacement without a corresponding increase in hydroplane area. To deal with (i) DNC provided a pressure-tight bow buoyancy tank which ensured that the ship would dive by the bow whatever mine load was on board. DNC expected this feature alone to greatly improve submerging. Although the new minelayer would have 480 tons of free-flooding space above her waterline compared to 240 tons in *Rainbow*, the percentage (compared to surface displacement) was similar to that in *X 1* and *K 26*, both of which were considered good divers. Changes in the shape of the casing might, DNC wrote, be of some value in rough weather. The stern planes would be placed to take advantage of the stream of water from the screws, as in the latest submarines. This was not the case in *M 3*.

HM SUBMARINE *GRAMPUS*. Port profile, as fitted. (© National Maritime Museum M1083)

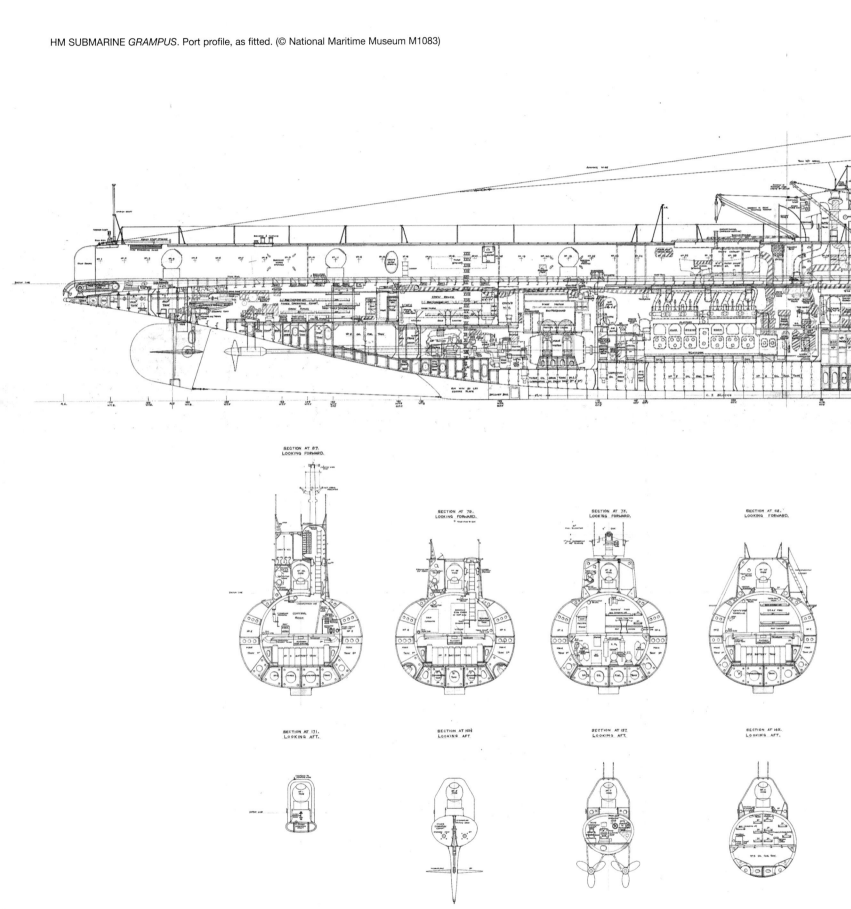

HM SUBMARINE *GRAMPUS*. Sections, as fitted. (© National Maritime Museum M1087)

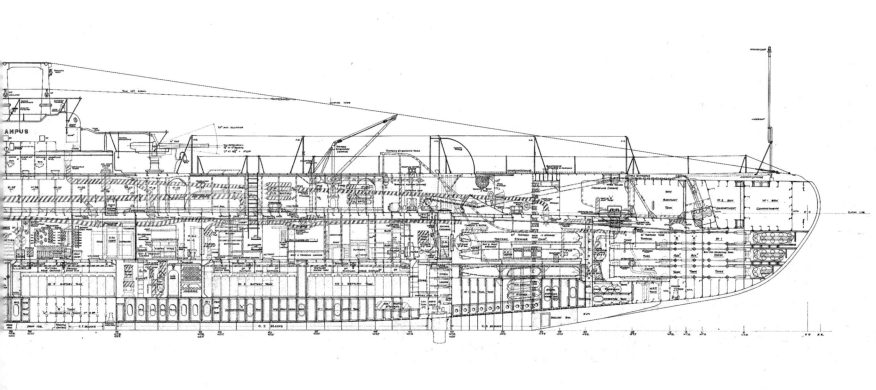

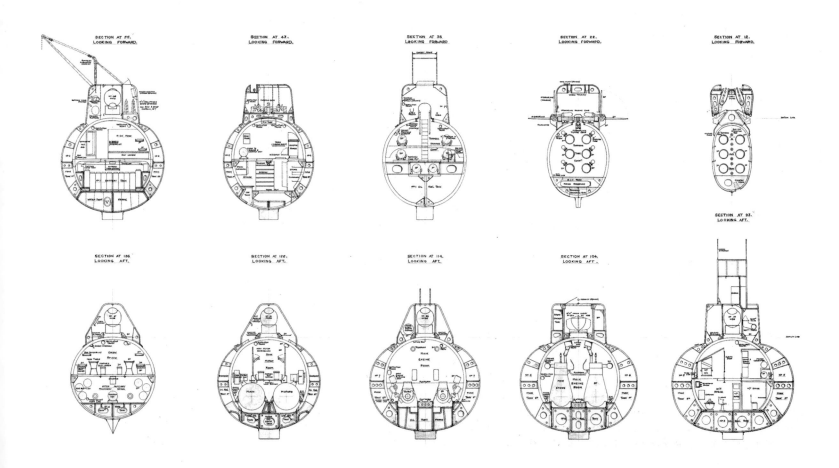

Porpoise with the gun shield and also the frame coil removed. (RAN Naval Historical Section via Dr Josef Straczek)

In the internal design, although the mines themselves weighed only 30 tons, they and their laying gear accounted for 300 tons and as a result the internal minelayer would have only 83 per cent of the buoyancy of the external one. The only available compensations were the engines, the motors and the battery. In Design D the batteries were unchanged but the engines and the main motors were cut (engines were as in the new 'S' class). In an alternative Design E, the batteries were cut. As a result, Design D (1500 tons) would make only 11.5 knots surfaced and 8 knots rather than 8.75 knots submerged; Design E would make 14 knots surfaced but 7.5 knots submerged. The reduced battery in Design E would provide 25 hours rather than 40 hours submerged at 2 knots. Both Designs D and E would displace 1500 tons standard. A Legend showing details of Designs C and D was produced in September 1930 (another sheet compared both with the German *U 124* and with *M 3* as a minelayer). On 7 October 1930 the Board approved Design C, the only change being addition of a 4.7in gun.[35] Adding the gun (and other minor changes) raised standard displacement to 1505 tons. DNC said that the design could be completed for tendering by March 1931 and the first boat ordered in June. A Legend was dated 24 February 1931. The Board approved the Legend and drawings on 5 March.

The submarine built under the 1930–1 Programme was HMS *Porpoise*. She and the other minelayers could be recognised by their raised, angled casings, which housed the mine track above the pressure hull. A second minelayer (*Grampus*) was included in the 1932–3 Programme (the large submarine in the 1931–2 Programme was a G-type fleet submarine). Unlike the 1930–1 and 1931–2 Programmes, this one initially included two large submarines, one G type and a minelayer, with only one small 'S'-class submarine. Up to that point the average submarine tonnage (3700 tons) since the London Treaty had been insufficient to maintain Treaty strength in submarines and the situation had been worsened by the losses of *Poseidon* and *M 2*. An 11 November 1932 memo from First Sea Lord, who was leaving office, called for laying down 7176 tons in 1933.

Grampus was conceived as a slightly modified *Porpoise*.[36] When Controller balked at adding 35 tons for what seemed to be minor advantages, DNC reinvestigated the design. It was already desirable to increase compressed air stowage, because so much air was needed to

surface with a full load of mines on board. Sea experience showed that at low buoyancy *Porpoise* was not stable enough; more displacement would solve the problem. Controller was willing to accept growth for such purposes. If adding length was not enough, ACNS suggested landing the gun when mines were embarked, as was already done in minelaying sloops and destroyers. RA(S) noted that the thin plating covering fuel stowed externally would probably leak if a depth charge exploded less than 30ft away, betraying the submarine. All oil should be stowed internally. Further design work showed that the forward airlock could be fitted without adding length or tonnage if the mine load was reduced from fifty to forty-eight, a slight congestion in accommodation was accepted (and a more serious congestion in store spaces) and the number of air bottles reduced from twenty-three to twenty-two.[37]

The shift to internal oil stowage required considerable rearrangement; the Board decided to shift *Grampus* to the 1933–4 Programme. In the original design all of the internal tankage was used for trimming and compensating water for diving the boat, for compensation for mines and for fresh water and lubricating oil. The pressure hull would have to be lengthened considerably (length overall would grow from 292ft 6in to 317ft 6in and standard displacement from 1535 tons to 1565 tons). To minimise additional length, the oil could be stowed in a block filling the pressure hull completely over a limited length, with a gangway through it. DNC proposed reducing oil fuel capacity (from 155 tons to 110 tons) by accepting an endurance of 8000nm at 8 knots, compared to the original 11,500nm.

On 12 June 1933 the Board ordered *Grampus* replaced by a repeat 'S'-class submarine, to be built at Chatham. Using a Royal Dockyard avoided any problem involving a contract change. The 1933–4 Programme was revised to consist of *Grampus*, a repeat *Grampus* (*Narwhal*) and an 'S'-class submarine. Internal oil stowage was approved.[38] A Legend dated 28 July 1933 showed *Grampus* as approved on MF 0786/33 (i.e., a repeat *Porpoise*) and two sets of sketch designs (A/B and C). Design A had her oil fuel in the block occupying the whole cross section of the pressure hull. In Design B the oil was

Narwhal was one of five sister minelayers armed with 4in guns. She is shown in May 1938. (John Lambert collection)

stowed instead below the flat deck, space being cleared by moving the CO_2 machinery and the W/T and Asdic to positions above the flat. In Design C, length between perpendiculars was reduced to that originally planned (271ft 6in) by making the pressure hull deeper along the centreline, the oil being stowed in tanks at the bottom of the pressure hull. The original *Grampus* had displaced 1535 tons (standard). Designs A/B were lengthened to 296ft 6in (1565 tons). Design C was reduced back to the original length and actually displaced less (1510 tons). The modified designs all had their endurance reduced to 8000nm at 8 knots. All designs showed fifty mines. An attached note

indicated that by using the after external tanks for fuel, another 25 tons could be carried and endurance increased to 10,000nm.[39] A conference on gunnery requirements for submarines held in June 1933 helped by recommending replacement of the 4.7in gun by a 4in gun. That would improve stability but it would not affect standard displacement. Controller recommended Design C. ACNS wrote that the desired 10,000nm requirement was adequately met by provision to use the after main ballast tanks for fuel; 'it is preferred not to lengthen the hull to obtain the extra stowage which probably would only be required on rare occasions'. First Sea Lord (Admiral Chatfield)

Photographed from aft, *Rorqual* shows her long mine stowage space aft. During the Second World War this space was used to transport supplies to Malta in special cylindrical containers. This is a wartime photograph; the X-shaped antenna of a Type 291W air-warning radar is visible abaft the periscope shears. Note that the other main wartime improvement, a 20mm anti-aircraft gun, is not visible at all. *Rorqual* was the only one of the class to survive the war (*Seal* was captured, the others sunk). (US Naval Institute)

approved Design C on 3 August 1933. The Board formally approved the sketch design on 1 November. The hull form was somewhat revised after tank tests, estimated surface speed increasing from 15.5 knots to 16 knots.[40]

The financial crisis made it impossible to ask for more than three submarines in 1933/34. The Board found itself balancing the desire to complete a flotilla of the G type against the shortage of minelayers. A third minelayer was more important than the G-type flotilla. RA(S) pointed to the shortage of submarines and wanted two additional 'S' class in the 1933–4 Programme (Controller offered one). Given the financial situation and therefore the undesirability of asking for more than the usual three submarines per year, the Board deferred the

Seal is shown before the war. She had the misfortune to be captured by the Germans after laying mines off the Kattegat; she was commissioned by the Germans as *U B* and used for training and trials, being decommissioned in 1943 and scuttled on 3 May 1945. The objects on the periscope shears are aerial insulators for wire aerials running up and around the shears. The forward (search) periscope was 9½in in diameter, the after (attack) one 7½in. (RAN Naval Historical Service via Dr Josef Straczek)

G-type submarine planned for 1933 and instead asked for one minelayer and two 'S' class, a total of 2780 tons. The second *Grampus* in the 1933–4 Programme was *Narwhal*. The 1934–5 Programme included a contract-built repeat *Grampus*, *Rorqual*. The 1935–6 minelayer was *Cachalot* and the final unit of the class was *Seal* (1936–7).

CHAPTER 13
ARMS CONTROL

Attempts at arms control were an almost constant feature of British naval reality between 1921 and 1936. Successive British governments saw arms control as a way of limiting expenditure, hence pressed the Admiralty for proposals to cut back the size of all classes of warships, including submarines. Although the 'S' class was never explicitly associated with arms control, it fits the idea of limiting size to limit expenditure. Another constant theme was the total abolition of submarines, given the evil the U-boats had done during the First World War. Abolition was particularly championed by King George V. It was

never accepted, but the British (and the Americans) did convince governments to sign a pledge against the sort of unrestricted (sink on sight) warfare the U-boats had waged. This agreement, which collapsed in stages during the Second World War, convinced interwar Royal Navy submariners to concentrate on attacking enemy warships, as they had before and during most of the First World War.

Once it had rejected abolition, the 1921 Washington Naval Conference went on to consider limiting total submarine tonnage, as it had limited capital ships. The French made that impossible: they

Sealion and *Shark* alongside before the war, showing the tops of their saddle tanks. (John Lambert collection)

Swordfish as completed, with her 3in HA gun atop a structure into which it could retract for streamlining. *Sturgeon* also had this structure. The other two units of the original 'S' class, *Seahorse* and *Starfish*, were completed with 3in guns mounted permanently on their casings. These and the other pre-war 'S' class were all completed with semi-enclosed 'cab' bridges. (RAN Naval Historical Section via Dr Josef Straczek)

demanded at least 90,000 tons of submarines.[1] Applying the ratios already accepted for capital ships would have allowed the three major sea powers effectively unlimited submarine fleets (257,000 tons). All of the other powers were willing to accept a quota of 90,000 tons for the United States and the British Empire. The conference also failed to limit total tonnage of lesser surface ships, such as cruisers and destroyers.

After the 1923 general election, the incoming Labour Government badly wanted to limit naval spending. It hoped that the sizes, hence the costs, of a wide variety of warships – including submarines – could be cut back by negotiation. In the spring of 1924 the Cabinet asked the Board to propose new naval arms control measures.[2] Work on this study continued after the Labour Government fell, as the incoming Tories were also determined to cut defence costs. DNC suggested splitting submarines into fleet and patrol categories, with tonnage limits of, respectively, 2500 tons and 1500 tons (Controller considered such a split unwise). Controller wrote in 1925 that any smaller nation with whom the British were likely to go to war (which mainly meant Japan at this time) 'will [only] . . . consent to a limit in numbers and size provided she is left with a force capable of striking effectively at our vulnerable lines of communication'. The Royal Navy had to maintain a sufficient anti-submarine force, which meant a reserve of older destroyers and sloops.[3]

DTD later opposed any attempt at abolition, as 'we know now how best the submarine can be combated tactically and strategically and are almost certainly the most advanced of any nation in technical means for its location and destruction'. He was presumably referring to Asdic. No matter what was agreed, some country might secretly build submarines and the Royal Navy would have to maintain its ASW edge. That would be difficult without British submarines against which to

experiment. Given a limit on total tonnage, it might be best to allow other countries to spend heavily on large, expensive submarines like X 1 and thus to limit numbers.

Even so, when the Admiralty proposed future arms-control polity to the Cabinet in September 1925 it argued that total abolition was very much in the interest of the Empire and that it should continue to be British policy. The Versailles Treaty ban on German submarine construction might help. The Board pointed out that the chance of achieving abolition was small, leaving a strict limit on total tonnage as the most realistic option.

To a Royal Navy focused on war in the Far East, anything which precluded Japanese construction of big long-range submarines was attractive, even if that precluded British construction of long-range patrol submarines. Moreover, if some future treaty limited total submarine tonnage, the only way the Royal Navy could gain numbers would be by building much smaller short-range submarines. Although arms control was never mentioned in the context of the 670-ton *Swordfish* class, it was conceived at a time of maximum British Government interest in, and hopes for, naval arms control. By 1926 the British were trying to exclude small submarines (defined as 600 tons or less) from any future naval arms control agreement; unsurprisingly the small type was defined as a 600-tonner.[4]

The small submarine was brought up during the 1926 discussion

Sturgeon with her gun retracted. (Dr Josef Straczek)

of future types. RA(S) and the staff both liked the idea. They argued that there were important wartime roles, such as patrols off Singapore and Hong Kong, which would not require large boats. CinC Atlantic emphasised the training role. A smaller, hence more manoeuvrable, submarine would be a better trainer for the rapidly-expanding submarine force which would be needed in an emergency, since 'the standard required is not so high as for the larger types'. Rapid wartime production would be an important advantage. The small submarine might be powered by lightweight aircraft diesels then being developed. The 550-ton Dutch *K 'V'* class had an endurance of 5500nm at 11 knots, which was not so much less than the 6220 miles achieved by *Oberon* at that speed. Displacement should probably be about 700 tons. DCNS was ordered to include the smaller submarine in future programmes.

In October 1926 RA(S) proposed a new type of submarine to be included in the 1930 Programme.[5] The big 'O' class was too large to fulfil many submarine functions: defence of fleet bases, coastal patrol, W/T link near bases, nearer patrols at sea and training. 'Moreover, in operations in a very wide area such as a war in the Far East large total numbers will be required and more duties which can be assigned to the smaller type of submarine, the fewer it will be necessary to provide of the larger type.' All of the existing small submarines of the 'H', 'R' and 'E' classes would be gone by 1932 (based on ten-year lives). Seven of the remaining 'L' class would be gone by 1936–7, leaving only two of them beside the 'O' class. RA(S) envisaged a 700-ton submarine capable of 12 knots, with an endurance of 3500nm at 8 knots, taking into account fuel used to charge the battery. Armament would be four 21in bow tubes and two Lewis machine guns. Communications would be by Asdic and W/T. Underwater speed and endurance would be roughly that of the 'L' class. Hull form would be as in the 'O' class,

with a maximum diving depth of 300ft. Ordered in batches, such submarines would cost about half as much as an 'O' class patrol submarine. Complement would be about thirty, compared to fifty-three for the large submarine. Refitting two would cost slightly more than refitting one patrol submarine.

The current building rate of six per year implied a target force of seventy-two, of which sixty were to be long-range patrol submarines.[6] Of the remaining twelve, six fleet submarines were wanted, plus minelayers. In December 1926 RA(S) pointed out that no provision had been made for training. All of the planned submarines were too large and using them for training would be wasteful. Two small submarines could be built for the price of one large one. From 1930 on, the annual programme should be five large and two small submarines, providing twelve small submarines by 1937 – when all existing small submarines would be gone. The twelve could provide training, experimental and ASW training services.

RA(S) strongly supported the argument by Director of Operations Division (DOD) for wartime operational value: the small submarine was much handier when submerged, hence far better suited to shallow water. The Far East was not the only possible future theatre of war and in important places elsewhere water was shallow and sea room limited. RA(S) pointed to European waters and also to waters near major British bases. When torpedo attack was the main object, where high speed and great endurance bought little and the elaborate W/T installation involved in the patrol mission unnecessary, the small submarine would be very useful. The German *Marine Rundschau* had just made a convincing case for a small submarine.

In January 1927 both ACNS and DCNS approved the idea. Controller (Admiral Chatfield) added that 'if we are to build all submarines (and I may add destroyers as well) of the largest type, we shall have to face a maintenance bill which we may be unable to afford'. A paper on the characteristics of the small submarine should be started

215

in April 1928, two years before the earliest date when a small submarine could be laid down.

In 1927 US President Calvin Coolidge called a conference at Geneva to extend the Washington Treaty limits to smaller warships.[7] When it approached this conference in the spring of 1927, the Admiralty proposed dividing submarines into a large offensive type (up to 1600 tons, later up to 1800 tons) and a smaller defensive type (600 tons or less).[8] The Admiralty clearly saw the projected small submarine as defensive, hence attractive to advocates of arms control within the British Government. The offensive submarines should be limited in number (the British proposed sixty or even fewer); the defensive ones need not be limited at all. The Japanese wanted 600-ton submarines exempt from limitation; the British later said that they needed about forty-five large submarines and fifteen small ones.[9] Nothing was agreed; the two European powers with large submarine fleets, France and Italy, both refused to attend.

DNC began work on a small submarine in 1928, for the 1929–30 rather than the 1930–1 Programme.[10] He offered three alternative small submarines (S1, S2 and S3) alongside the big G design fleet submarine. Characteristics were:

	New G	S1	S2	S3
LOA (ft-in)	345-0	177-6	186-0	190-0
B (outer hull) (ft-in)	28-0	–	–	–
B (pressure hull) (ft-in)	17-4	15-0	15-0	15-0
Depth (pressure hull) (ft-in)	14-6	15-0	15-0	15-0
Dispt (Geneva) (tons)	1640	604	703	635
Dispt (tons)	1950	690	800	722
Dispt (submerged) (tons)	2300	abt 800	abt 920	abt 835
BHP6960	1450	1650	1550	
BHP (motors)	1320	840	1000	1300
Motors	4	2	2	2
Surface speed (knots)	20.5–21	14	14	14
Submerged speed (knots)	–	9	9	10
Oil fuel	200	52	60	52
Cells	336	224	336	224 HC Type
Surface endurance (nm/knots)	8500/12	3250/8	3250/9	3250/9
Submerged endurance (nm/knots)	40/4	50/4	75/4	90/3
Gun (1)	4in	3in HA	3in HA	3in HA
Torpedo Tubes (21in bow)	6	4	6	6
Torpedoes	12	8	12	12
Complement	–	———— Assumed 33 ————		
W/T range (nm)	500	W/T as L 50, S/F and S/T as Odin		
Max diving depth (ft)	200	300	300	300

	G1 Design	S Design
LOA (ft-in)	345-0	187-6
B (outer hull) (ft-in)	28-0	24-0
B (pressure hull) (ft-in)	17-10	15-0
Depth (pressure hull) (ft-in)	15-6	11-3 FP/12-8 AP
Dispt (Geneva) (tons)	1760	642
Dispt (surface) (tons)	2070	735
Dispt (submerged) (tons)	2400	930
BHP7750	1550	
BHP (motors)	2600	1300
Motors	4	2
Surface speed (knots)	21	13.75
Submerged speed (knots)	10	10
Oil fuel (tons)	200	52
Cells	336 (X 1)	224
Surface endurance (nm/knots)	10,000/8	3250/9
Submerged endurance (nm/knots)	90/3	1/10, 36/2
Gun (1)	4.7in	3in HA
Torpedo Tubes (21in bow)	6	6
Torpedoes	2	12
Complement	–	33
W/T range I (nm)	–	–
Max diving depth (ft)	300	300

Sturgeon as modified with her 3in/45 QF gun mounted directly on deck. Note the gun platform extending over the side, and the voice pipe to the gun, absent in *Swordfish* when she carried the retractable mounting. As in earlier boats, *Sturgeon* had the standard periscope arrangement of one 9½in periscope forward and one 7½in periscope abaft it. The tall telescopic wireless mast visible abaft the periscopes was used only when surfaced, and it carried the harbour aerial; at sea submarines used lower wires as their wireless aerials. Both the heavy jumping wires and a set of lighter lower wires were used; the forward periscope housing carries insulators supporting both. The vertical wire visible near the after end of the bridge fairwater carried the signal to the jumping wire; it ran through a heavy insulator in the fairwater. The object visible near the after end of the fairwater is probably the reel for the kite aerial. The object visible on the after side of the forward periscope housing is the steaming light. Not visible are two Lewis gun mountings, standard in British submarines of this era. (RAN Naval Historical Section via Dr Josef Straczek)

Geneva displacement was the tonnage specified in the recent abortive negotiations; it was not quite the standard displacement specified at Washington in 1921. The Board voted for a design with four bow torpedo tubes.[11]

In August 1928 the Board sketched staff requirements so that it could ask the Atlantic and Mediterranean fleet commanders for comments: an endurance of 3000nm at 9 knots (including battery charging and a week on patrol, equivalent to say 4500nm at 9 knots), a surface speed of at least 17 knots (more if possible), a submerged endurance like that of the existing 'L' class, a W/T range of at least 600nm (Gulf of Finland to the Skaw), a maximum diving depth of perhaps 200ft, four bow torpedo tubes, one 3in HA gun if possible and a standard tonnage of 600 if possible 'being the tonnage suggested by Great Britain at the late Geneva Naval Conference for the smaller type of submarine (no agreement proved likely upon this figure, however)'.

RA(S) later set 760 tons ('L'-class displacement) as a maximum figure, based on Baltic requirements.[12] The two main factors in deciding displacement were (a) the maximum size to enter the Baltic when passage was opposed, and (b) habitability and seakeeping. RA(S) wanted something smaller provided attacking qualities were not sacrificed. As for short-range patrols, RA(S) had in mind operations within

500 miles of a base, lasting ten days (fifteen days total at sea, including transits). He later argued that in narrow waters offensive power should be more important than surfaced speed, but that the small submarine should be able to overtake an average merchant ship (meaning a speed of 14 knots). He thought a 600-ton submarine would suffice, armed with six bow tubes (later he wrote that any smaller submarine would have an inadequate torpedo armament and endurance). Two stern tubes were desirable but not vital. He wanted a 3in HA gun and two machine guns to defend against aircraft and, possibly, to use against shore targets. Diving depth should be the 300ft accepted for the new patrol submarine in 1928. Submerged endurance should be about that of the 'L' class. Since the submarine would probably be operating close to enemy bases, it should have the smallest possible silhouette. DTD outlined requirements in a 16 February 1929 paper based on RA(S)'s arguments.[13]

DTD considered 760 tons needlessly large for training and short-range patrols near bases. Both he and RA(S) looked to the 600-ton limit proposed at Geneva.[14] Director of Plans doubted that the base would always be within 500 miles; he considered 1200 to 1300 miles more realistic. If the submarine remained on patrol for eight days, it would spend a total of twenty days at sea. A small submarine should be able to remain at sea for three weeks. RA(S) also mentioned a W/T range of 500nm (the original staff proposal was 600nm). This was apart from short wave, which should give 2000nm range. Sketch designs should be prepared for a range between 600nm and 760nm. In each case an eight-day patrol and a twelve-day passage at about 9 knots should be assumed. Allowing for battery charging, etc., that equated to an endurance of 4500nm at 9 knots.

DNC produced two sketch designs (I and II) to explore what was possible, one of 600 tons and one of 760 tons. The staff discussed them on 25 April.[15] Both had power-loaded torpedoes, as in the larger submarines. Sacrifices included battery cooling. The designers discovered that the desired endurance required relatively little oil, because on patrol a submarine expended relatively little. DNC based his oil fuel estimate on 'L'-class experience (1.7 tons/day on periscope patrol). On that basis the best he could do was 3250nm at 9 knots. Submerged

endurance was 50 hours at 4 knots submerged in the smaller submarine, 75 hours in the larger one (the small submarine had 224 battery cells, the larger one 336).[16] Surface speed was 14 knots (9 knots submerged). Diving depth was the desired 300ft. The most important difference was in armament: four torpedo tubes in the small submarine, six in the larger Design II. Both had 3in guns. Estimated displacements were 604 tons and 703 tons. Design I could have six tubes at a cost of 17 tons; submerged endurance would be reduced. Stern tubes had not been considered because the distribution of weight and buoyancy did not lend itself to such an installation. Adding them would entail considerably greater length and another 30 to 40 tons. DNC's submarine designer thought an ideal small submarine could be designed on the lines of Design I modified with six bow tubes, displacing 650 tons. For increased endurance, oil could be carried externally. Design I would gain 61 tons and Design II 71 tons; these changes would apply to the surface and Geneva displacements.

RA(S) pressed for the small design, because he wanted the submarine to operate within the 10-fathom line. He considered fuel excessive and was willing to retreat to 12 knots surface speed, but he wanted the six bow tubes. ACNS pointed out that a 12-knot submarine could not catch up with even relatively slow ships. EinC could provide power for 14 knots in nearly the same space as for 12 knots. Submerged speed was actually increased to 10 knots. Underwater endurance was now fixed at 30 hours at 3 knots and/or at least 1 hour at full submerged speed, which was rather different from what DNC offered. As for armament, the question was whether the four-tube submarine could have twelve torpedoes, as in the larger one, but it became clear that this would not appreciably help DNC hold down size. DNC pointed out that adding Asdic would add 4ft 6in to the length of the submarine, but submarine officers argued emphatically that it could not be omitted. DNC ended up saying that the requirements demanded something like the 760-tonner.

DNC's submarine designer produced Design S.3 (I and II were also called S.1 and S.2), a six-tube version of his preferred S.1. It was lengthened 12ft 6in, but 9ft 6in of that was an extension of the after free-flooding space, which gave a better arrangement of steering and

Seahorse shows the straight after side of the bridge fairwater in the first group of 'S'-class submarines. Note that she has no gun in this 1937 photograph. She could be distinguished from her sisters by her broken superstructure right aft. (RAN Naval Historical Section via Dr Josef Straczek)

hydroplane gear. As in S.1, she would have 224 high-capacity batteries, offering 1305 BHP at the one-hour rate (1143 BHP for 1¼ hours), allowing for auxiliary load. For surface power the submarine would need 1550 BHP per shaft; EinC could offer either a six-cylinder 1450 BHP engine or an eight-cylinder 1650 BHP engine. If the flat in the engine room were dropped, the engine could have a longer stroke; DNC's submarine designer thought a six-cylinder engine could develop the desired 1550 BHP. This submarine would be 190ft long and would have a Geneva displacement of 635 tons (722 tons surfaced, 835 tons submerged). Submerged endurance would be 90nm at 3 knots. Estimated cost was £210,000, compared to the initial estimate that a small submarine would cost £175,000.

A 25 May 1929 conference accepted the S.3 design and DNC submitted a sketch and Legend. On 6 June Controller presented S.3 to the Sea Lords.[17] First Sea Lord pointed out that the object of seeking a size limit at Geneva had been to ensure that submarines could not go far and so could operate only in home waters; but this submarine had a radius of action of 3000nm. Was it really 'defensive'? Could its tonnage be reduced? Controller considered it important to preserve underwater speed. Director of Plans wanted to hold tonnage to 600 tons, as the British had proposed at Geneva and as they hoped to propose at the coming London Conference. Size was due to large battery power (for underwater endurance) and Asdic. Since Asdic could not be eliminated, First Sea Lord suggested cutting W/T. ACNS said that the Staff view was that a submarine without the best communications would lose much of her value. It was difficult to forecast the role of the new submarine. If radio range were reduced, it might not be possible to make use of information possessed by a submarine 400nm away.

First Sea Lord decided to call another meeting to find sacrifices which would bring displacement down to 600 tons. Because submarines had to be ordered in February or March, it was impossible to

Shark shows the longer bridge fairwater, with a rounded after side, of the second group of the 'S' class (*Shark* class). *Salmon*, *Sealion*, and *Shark* were completed without guns; all others in the class had them on completion. This photograph was taken in January 1935. (John Lambert collection)

make further cuts; the design was approved. Controller told First Sea Lord that every effort had already been made to cut its cost. The design was forwarded to the Board on 13 June 1929. It exceeded the 600-ton Geneva limit, but no other country favoured that limit anyway. The design received the Board Stamp on 27 June, two 'S'-class submarines being included in the 1929–30 Programme. Attempts to enlarge the submarine substantially were rebuffed.[18] Length overall grew 1ft 6in due to a slight change in the shape of the bow for better net cutting. To reduce underwater resistance (given the priority of underwater speed), the 3in gun was placed on a retractable mounting in a housing extending forward of the bridge fairwater, in view of the priority given to underwater speed. At this time the only other such mounting on board a British submarine was on board *M 2*. The first two submarines were completed without guns, pending trials with *Swordfish* to see whether the added topweight would affect surfacing. It would not and she and her 1929 sister *Sturgeon* were fitted with the guns during 1936 refits. The retractable mounting was later removed and replaced by a simple mounting bolted to the top of the pressure hull. The two 1930–1 boats were completed in this form. With the gun lowered, the top of the bridge fairwater could also be lowered, reducing underwater resistance.[19]

It turned out that the definition of Geneva displacement had been somewhat ambiguous. The Geneva displacement of the completed design was given as 642.5 tons, with the note that it would have been 650.5 tons had not 8 tons of trimming water (which did not count)

been included instead of a 68-ton ballast keel (the ballast keel was 20 tons). The Geneva figure included 4.4 tons of water round torpedoes (WRT), but it was not definite whether that should be included.[20] This was much the sort of ambiguity which was discussed at enormous length for surface warships in connection with Washington and London Treaty limits. There also were further weight-saving possibilities. Calculated submerged endurance exceeded the requirement (36.5 vs 31.6 hours): some battery cells could be omitted. Machinery weight was slightly less than in original estimates because there was no auxiliary motor.

Building drawings were submitted to the Board on 25 November 1929, receiving the Board Stamp on 28 November. The design was somewhat simplified after a 27 February 1930 conference at the submarine headquarters Fort Blockhouse; for example, one HP air compressor was eliminated. The main engines were moved slightly forward, so that the bulkhead could be moved to between engines and motors. There was pressure to improve habitability. DNC listed several possibilities, including eliminating a pair of torpedo tubes and their reloads and eliminating power torpedo loading. RA(S) was unhappy with oil stowage under the batteries, citing problems in the 'G' class, but no complaints were known in *L 50*-class submarines. DNC's representative pointed out that oil fuel had been stowed internally because of objections to external stowage (leakage which gave the submarine away) and because stowing oil fuel externally would increase Geneva displacement – which had to be held down. RA(S) agreed that external stowage was unacceptable. A submarine designed for minimum Geneva displacement could not afford to waste any space, even abreast and under the main batteries. RA(S) offered various possibilities, including welding the battery tanks (but there was little experience of such welding as yet).

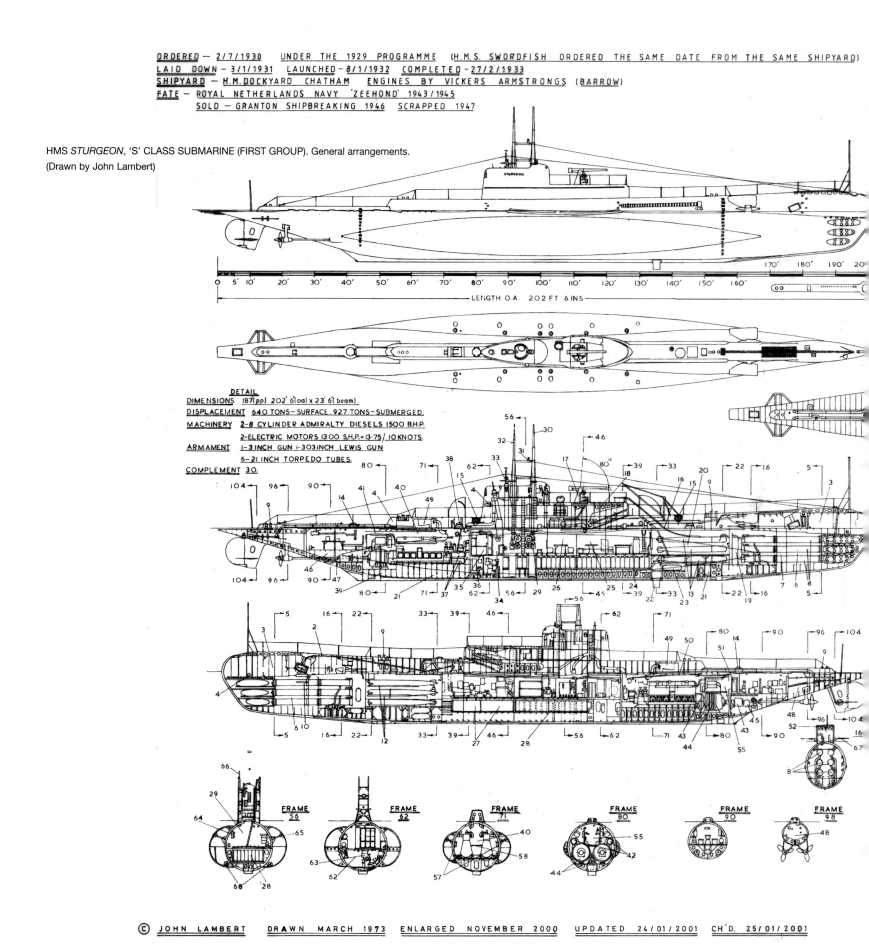

ORDERED — 2/7/1930   UNDER THE 1929 PROGRAMME   (H.M.S. SWORDFISH ORDERED THE SAME DATE FROM THE SAME SHIPYARD)
LAID DOWN — 3/1/1931   LAUNCHED — 8/1/1932   COMPLETED — 27/2/1933
SHIPYARD — H.M.DOCKYARD CHATHAM   ENGINES BY VICKERS ARMSTRONGS (BARROW)
FATE — ROYAL NETHERLANDS NAVY 'ZEEHOND' 1943/1945
        SOLD — GRANTON SHIPBREAKING 1946   SCRAPPED 1947

HMS *STURGEON*, 'S' CLASS SUBMARINE (FIRST GROUP). General arrangements.
(Drawn by John Lambert)

LENGTH O.A. 202 FT 6 INS

DETAIL
DIMENSIONS 187'(pp) 202' 6'(oa) x 23' 6' beam)
DISPLACEMENT 640 TONS — SURFACE. 927 TONS — SUBMERGED.
MACHINERY 2-8 CYLINDER ADMIRALTY DIESELS 1500 B.H.P.
          2-ELECTRIC MOTORS 1300 S.H.P.=13·75/10 KNOTS.
ARMAMENT 1-3 INCH GUN 1-303 INCH LEWIS GUN
          6-21 INCH TORPEDO TUBES.
COMPLEMENT 30.

FRAME 56   FRAME 62   FRAME 71   FRAME 80   FRAME 90   FRAME 98

© JOHN LAMBERT   DRAWN MARCH 1973   ENLARGED NOVEMBER 2000   UPDATED 24/01/2001   CH'D. 25/01/2001

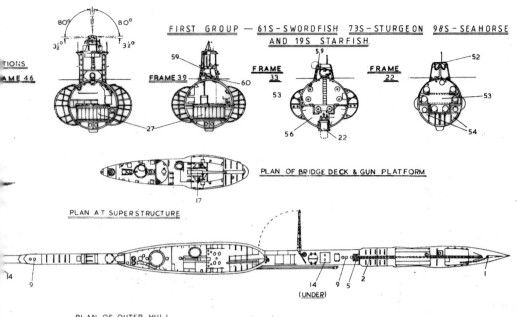

FIRST GROUP — 61S-SWORDFISH 73S-STURGEON 98S-SEAHORSE AND 19S STARFISH.

SECTIONS
FRAME 46

FRAME 39

FRAME 33

FRAME 22

PLAN OF BRIDGE DECK & GUN PLATFORM

PLAN AT SUPERSTRUCTURE

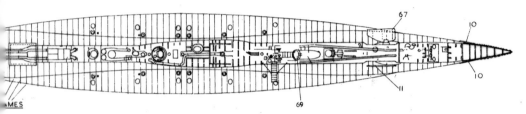

(UNDER)

PLAN OF OUTER HULL

KEY TO DETAIL

1	BULL RING.	37	OIL COOLERS.
2	4 INCH DIA CABLE.	38	ENGINE ROOM HATCH.
3	BOW BOUYANCY TANK.	39	LUBRICATING OIL DRAIN TANK.
4	HYDROPHONE.	40	ENGINE ROOM.
5	GRATING.	41	SWITCHBOARD.
6	No.1 MAIN TANK.	42	MAIN MOTOR COOLER.
7	'A' AUXILIARY TANK.	43	CLUTCH.
8	21 INCH TORPEDO TUBES.	44	MAIN MOTOR.
9	DISAPPEARING FAIRLEAD & BOLLARDS.	45	THRUST BLOCK.
		46	STORE.
10	FENDER.	47	STERN GLAND.
11	HYDROPLANE (FOLDED).	48	'Z' AUXILIARY TANK.
12	TORPEDO LOADING RAIL.	49	ENGINE EXHAUST TANK.
13	Mk VIII 21 INCH TORPEDOES.	50	HYDROPLANE CONTROL SHAFTING.
14	DAVIS ESCAPE HATCH.	51	CREWS W.C.
15	INDICATOR BOUY.	52	TOWLINE TROUGH.
16	TORPEDO EMBARKING RAIL.	53	TORPEDO STOWAGE COMPARTMENT.
17	3 INCH Q.F. H/A Mk X GUN.	54	COMPENSATING TANK.
18	GUN TROUGH.	55	MOTOR ROOM.
19	FIRING RESERVOIR	56	COX'NS STORE.
20	SEAMENS MESS.	57	OIL STRAINER.
21	OIL FUEL TANK.	58	WALKING PLATFORM
22	TYPE 120 OSCILLATOR (ASDIC).	59	TORPEDO DERRICK (STOWED).
23	AIR BOTTLE STOWAGE.	60	TORPEDO DERRICK WINCH.
24	WARD ROOM.	61	FRESH WATER TANK
25	P.O's MESS.	62	MACHINERY SPACE.
26	E.R.A's MESS.	63	SLUDGE PUMP.
27	No.1 BATTERY TANK. (112 CELLS)	64	TELEMOTOR PANEL.
28	No.2 BATTERY TANK (112 CELLS)	65	CHART TABLE.
29	CONTROL ROOM.	66	LEWIS GUN MOUNTING.
30	9.5 INCH PERISCOPE.	67	HYDROPLANE.
31	STEAMING LIGHT.	68	KINGSTON VALVE.
32	7.5 INCH PERISCOPE.	69	TORPEDO LOADING HATCH.
33	MAIN W/T MAST.		
34	W/T OFFICE.		
35	W/T SILENT CABINET		
36	TYPE 120 CABINET		

SECTIONS

FRAME 104

Without her gun, *Shark* shows another characteristic feature of the second series of 'S'-class boats, the stepped structure forward of her bridge containing a gun access trunk. (RAN Naval Historical Section via Dr Josef Straczek)

DNC had estimated fuel requirements based on experience with the 'E', 'H' and 'L' classes, all of which had relatively inefficient diesels. A lot had happened since: efficiency was now much better. DNC was forced to admit that the 52 tons he wanted were far more than needed; 38 tons might suffice. Increasing displacement very slightly (to 648 tons) would make it unnecessary to stow oil under the battery. Oil stowage was linked with the need for continual compensation: a surfaced submarine burning oil always had to be ready to dive. Early submarines led water into compensating tanks as they burned oil, but eventually there was no space: 'K', 'L' and later submarines piped compensating water into the oil tanks, the remaining oil floating on the sea water. Since sea water was about 17 per cent heavier than oil, a further compensating tank of sea water had to be emptied as the water filled the fuel tanks. Some oil tanks were not compensated, water going instead into trimming tanks.

To hold down displacement in the 'S' class, the special oil fuel compensating tank was eliminated. Tanks were grouped in threes: when the two end ones were filled with water and the middle one emptied, the weight would be the same as when all three were filled with oil. In effect this was halfway between completely compensated and completely non-compensated arrangements. It became possible to place oil fuel anywhere desired along the length of the submarine, since each group of tanks was self-contained.

Omitting quick-diving tanks (Q tanks), as RA(S) suggested, would cut Geneva displacement back to 642 tons. RA(S) wanted the tanks to function as either Q tanks or as compensating tanks. If compensation was their main function they could be eliminated altogether to save 4½ to 5 tons in Geneva tonnage. DNC considered it unjustified for a submarine designed specially for limited tonnage to spend 4½ tons on Q tanks, which had to have unusually strong structure (3½ tons). As a whole the 'S' class had an unusually large water tank capacity, including 23 tons of auxiliary and compensating water, none of which was needed to compensate for oil fuel: 3.2 per cent of surface displacement, about twice that in an *Odin*-class submarine. DNC accepted RA(S)'s proposal to eliminate power reloading, which would free space for better habitability and also for better arrangement of auxiliaries.

RA(S) also wanted to drive as many auxiliaries as possible directly from the main engines; that too would save space. A June 1930 conference agreed that RA(S)'s proposals had been met as far as possible.

In the attempt to shave weight down as far as possible (or conceivable), the ballast keel was virtually eliminated. It weighed only 18 tons, of which only 6 tons was in cast-iron blocks and lead. Even to get that 6 tons of moveable weight the drop weight had been reduced from 8 tons to 5 tons. Like any other submarine, the 'S' class had to balance weight and volume very precisely; in earlier designs the lead in the ballast keel provided a margin against errors and changes. This time it was nearly gone. That made weight control during construction even more important than usual.[21] The 1929–30 Programme was set at one G-type submarine (*Thames*) and two of the new 'S' class, both of the latter to be built at Chatham Royal Dockyard: *Swordfish* and *Sturgeon*.

During the run-up to the next naval arms control conference (London in 1930) British Prime Minister Ramsay MacDonald, a strong advocate of disarmament, announced that talks with the Americans had been so successful that he could delete ships, including two submarines, from the building programme.[22] As usual, the Admiralty advised the Government as to the terms it should seek. It was willing to trade destroyer tonnage for deep cuts in submarines, on the theory that much of the British destroyer force was retained for wartime ASW.[23] As before, the official British position was that submarines should be abolished, apparently dictated by King George V, who was personally horrified by what his country had experienced during the World War. The British knew that other powers would block that. The United States, France and Japan had the largest submarine fleets.[24] The United States, Italy, Japan and the United Kingdom were all willing to accept a 2000-ton limit, but France wanted a limited number of 3000-ton submarines (such as her big *Surcouf*). Similarly, all but the French were willing to accept an upper limit for submarine guns of 5in (the French wanted 6in). Ultimately the French and the Italians withdrew.

To the Admiralty's horror, the British Government cut its destroyer force without achieving any deep reduction in foreign submarine strength. All three signatories (the United States, the United Kingdom and Japan) were allowed the same 52,700 tons of modern submarines. Maximum tonnage was set at 2000 tons, with an exception for larger existing submarines such as *X 1*. Maximum gun calibre was set at 6.1in. The British Empire had 43,331 tons of submarines built and another 26,110 tons building, so to get down to the allowed figure 17,040 tons of submarines (seventeen boats) had to be scrapped. The proposal that submarines of 600 tons and less should not be limited at all died (but a similar non-limitation clause for surface torpedo craft survived). However, the overall tonnage limit favoured the small submarine, which could be built in greater numbers.

The submarine-destroyer agreement was only one of several which infuriated the Admiralty Board; it was far angrier over an agreement to slash cruiser numbers. A disgusted Board asked the Foreign Office when it might be free of the burden of the Ten Year Rule.[25] Probably to its considerable surprise, Permanent Under-Secretary Sir Robert Vansittart answered that the Continent was

riddled with pre-war thought . . . whilst it would be to our interests and policy to maintain the League [of Nations] and all it stands for, the Old Man Adam [i.e., the propensity for war] still remains and our difficulties and dangers will be enormously increased if by undue and premature enfeeblement economically or navally or by the loss of imperial solidarity, we led him to think that we are living at tea time. Our assumption of a 10 years' period of peace rests, it would appear, on slender foundations.

Vansittart was writing well before Hitler gained power, but the Germans were already attacking the arms-control system, demanding equality with the other powers in return for participating in a proposed general arms-control treaty.

The Far East did not figure in Vansittart's remarks, but in 1930 Japanese politics turned radically towards expansionism and a policy of ejecting the West from Asia. That particularly threatened the British formal and informal empires. Japanese occupation of Manchuria in 1931 showed that the League of Nations was incapable of deterring aggression. The Royal Navy was too weak to carry out its Far East war plan, particularly since its planned primary base at Singapore had not been completed.[26]

None of this was a call for many more submarines; the Board accepted the rate of three per year (cruisers were the main issue at the time). The 1930–1 Programme bought *Seahorse* and *Starfish*, which were repeats of the 1929–30 submarines. The 1931–2 pair (*Sealion* and *Shark*) were modified. Controversy over what could or should be done shows just how badly the Royal Navy wanted to hold down tonnage so that it could build a maximum submarine force within the London Treaty limit.

At a February 1932 conference DNC was asked to strengthen bulkheads and to fit internal airlocks (for escape hatches).[27] The bulkheads should be strong enough to resist 70 psi pressure (160ft depth) and not leak badly at less than 87.5 psi (200ft). That required 2ft more of length (657 tons rather than 648 tons standard). RA(S) wanted the stronger bulkheads, but he wanted to minimise any growth. Airlocks had already been approved for the *Thames* class. Given an internal airlock, an entire compartment would not have to be flooded before the airlock could be used for escape. Men would spend much less time standing in cold water waiting to leave the submarine. DNC estimated that two such airlocks would lengthen a submarine by 5ft; standard displacement would rise to 670 tons.

Starfish shows the gun access trunk, with its hatch, without the surrounding structure evident in other units of the class. (RAN Naval Historical Section via Dr Josef Straczek)

Spearfish was completed with an open rather than a cab bridge, a feature which became standard in wartime. She is shown in April 1937. *Sterlet* and *Sunfish* were also built with open bridges. They were the last three units of the class. The only difference from wartime practice was that in wartime wind deflectors were built around the lip of the bridge screen. (RAN Naval Historical Service via Dr Josef Straczek)

RA(S) wanted the airlocks placed in the main ballast tanks (to avoid any lengthening) but that was impossible. It did turn out that the after airlock could go in 'Z' auxiliary tank, which saved length. DNC welcomed extra length, as it would relieve congestion and would make for a more convenient arrangement of fittings. On his calculation, both improvements would cost 7ft more length and would increase standard displacement to 679 tons. That would cost a quarter knot surfaced and submerged. Adopting the airlock in 'Z' tank made it possible to DNC to provide the airlocks and the stronger bulkheads at minimal cost: 2ft of length and 10 tons in standard displacement. With the airlock inside, 'Z' tank still had enough trimming capacity trimming under all standard conditions. RA(S) wanted another high-pressure compressor, because without it there was no means of compressing the air when submerged to relieve excess pressure due to firing a salvo of torpedoes, venting tanks inboard or to air leaks. Some improvements in internal arrangement were foregone; RA(S) accepted that in the interest of holding down any growth.[28] Four main ballast tanks replaced the six of the earlier submarines. The W/T outfit was simplified and the retractable gun replaced by a gun on a fixed mounting. The Board approved the revised design on 9 May 1932. It was planned for both the 1931 and 1932 (*Salmon* and *Snapper*) groups of 'S'-class submarines.

RA(S) took this opportunity to point out that the single motor on each side, which DNC had demanded in 1929–31, required considerable extra cabling to group the batteries. He wanted to substitute two smaller motors per shaft, one of which would suffice to charge batteries (operating as a generator). The increased length would be balanced by reduced motor diameter and also be reduced cabling. He suggested that it would be possible to reduce the diameter of the hull aft, improving hull form and reducing resistance. It would also be possible to revert to the previous practice of driving the auxiliaries (such as air compressors and pumps) from the propeller shafts, eliminating the extra power units adopted since the 'E' and 'H' classes. DEE agreed; the rearrangement might be so useful that it might be well to defer asking for tenders until the submarine had been redesigned. Controller and ACNS agreed. Two alternative designs were produced: Scheme 1 with the twin motors and compressors driven off the main shaft (208ft 8in, 669 tons standard) and Scheme 2 with extra length reduced by staggering bulkheads (207ft 2in, 664 tons).[29] The 1931–2 submarines were 208ft 8in long overall and displaced 675 tons (standard). Rated surface speed was 13.75 knots and endurance at 9 knots was 3800nm. These submarines had RA(S)'s two motors per shaft. The Board approved the Legend and drawings on 19 July 1932.

A new design cycle was occasioned by the discovery, based on trials, that *Swordfish* had an endurance of 55½ hours submerged at 2 knots instead of the required 36 hours. Battery capacity could be considerably reduced.[30] Now the diesels were rethought. Solid (airless) injection had been abandoned because wartime Vickers diesels smoked badly, but newer diesels would operate more cleanly. They would not need air compressors to blast fuel into their cylinders, so engine rooms could shrink. The new engines would not be as powerful, so some surface speed would be lost.[31] RA(S) favoured the new engines. EinC thought new diesels could achieve 1380 BHP, particularly if DNC accepted higher revs. DNC offered Design A, with the same 224 cells as the earlier 'S' class and Design B with 112 individually larger cells of *Thames* type. Both were the same length as the 1931–2 submarines. RA(S) credited the 224-cell battery with an endurance of 69 hours at 2.5 knots, far beyond the original requirement. Both A and B had 1375 BHP solid-injection diesels instead of the 1550 BHP plant in the 1931–2 submarines. That reduced the length of the engine room by 3½ft. Space saved would go into the auxiliary machinery compartment, which was also used to stow air bottles. Additional length above the flat made it possible to arrange the Asdic and W/T cabinets side by side. Surface speed was cut to 13.5 knots. Design A had the same 1300 BHP motors as the 1931–2 submarines, for 10 knots submerged. Surface endurance at 9 knots would be 3800nm, as in the 1931–2 submarines. Standard displacement would be 664 tons rather than 675 tons. Design B had 900 BHP motors, reducing her submerged speed to 8.75 knots. Surface endurance would be 4600nm, because she had more space for fuel. Standard displacement would be 656 tons. DNC argued that adopting a different cell size for patrol submarines would require forward bases to maintain two sizes of spares. EinC cautioned that it might be impossible to save 3½ft on the length of the engine room.

DNE liked the solid-injection engines because they would be easier to maintain, even if they were slightly smokier, but not reductions in surfaced and submerged speed. Available engine room space should go higher power for higher surfaced speed.[32] DTD wanted to know how long the submarine could run at 5 knots at the beginning of a day's diving patrol, if she had to spend the next 15 hours submerged at 2.5 knots. Similarly, he wanted the endurance at 5 knots after 15 hours at 2.5 knots. With 224 cells (4750 amp-hrs capacity), Design A could run for 45 hours at 2.5 knots or for 9 hours at 5 knots before the 2.5-knot patrol or for 8½ hours at 5 knots after the 2.5 knot patrol. With lower-capacity cells (3700 amp-hrs) the figures were 34 hours, 5½ hours and 5 hours. DTD had asked how many minutes the submarine could run at 5 knots, so these were clearly surprising figures. He asked similar questions for Design B (112 cells, 6300 amp-hrs each): 30 hours, 3½ hours and 3 hours. All were based on trials figures for *Swordfish*. Figures for B showed that too much submerged endurance was lost for the gain in surfaced endurance.

DTD could accept airless injection, but it was a definite requirement that the engine be smokeless at operational speed. He emphasised the need for reliability in hot climates, which suggests that the emphasis on the Baltic had been abandoned. In 1934 hot climates meant the Far East. RA(S) doubted that the current high-capacity batteries would be suitable for diving patrols of up to 7 days in hot climates; he wanted trials in the Mediterranean in 1934 or 1935. RA(S) therefore wanted to repeat the 1931–2 design (*Shark*). DNE pointed out that the case against the high-capacity battery was based on very limited experience. DEE strongly defended the high-capacity batteries already planned for *Shark*, *Sealion*, *Salmon*, *Snapper* and *Seawolf*, the submarines of the 1931–2 through 1933–4 Programmes.

By this time, according to DNE, the existing 'S'-class design had

been considerably simplified – RA(S) had listed excessive equipment he wanted to eliminate – and the submarines were considered popular with officers and crews. Some additional changes had been made in the 1931–2 group. It would be undesirable to redesign the ships before the improved version had been completed. However, airless diesels were definitely worth fitting. RA(S) agreed that the 1934–5 submarines should be repeats of the 1931–2 design but with airless injection diesels. He could see no reason why such engines should be any less powerful than air-injection ones. The Board decided that the airless-injection engines should be of the same or greater power than in the 1931–2 'S' class, so EinC expected to need eight rather than six cylinders; no engine room length would be saved, but the submarine would not have to be lengthened, either. Invitations to tender reflected RA(S)'s decision. DNC prepared new sketch plans accordingly.[33]

These decisions applied to the rest of the class: one in 1933–4 (*Seawolf*), two in 1934–5 (*Spearfish* and *Sunfish*) and a final unit in 1935–6 (*Sterlet*). By 1935 a new larger submarine, the 'T' class, was in production.

Further Attempts at Limitation

While the naval conferences proceeded, the League of Nations prepared for an ambitious general disarmament conference, which opened in February 1932 at Geneva. By this time the Japanese had invaded and taken over Manchuria and were bombing Chinese cities and prospects for general disarmament must have been less than encouraging. The major delegations all called for deep cuts in armaments, but it is difficult to imagine that any expected them to be approved. There were calls for particular limits on 'offensive' weapons, including submarines. This time the US delegation joined the British in calling for abolition of submarines.[34] The Japanese countered that although aircraft carriers were offensive, submarines were defensive and should be retained. The French agreed. The British then proposed limiting submarines to 250 tons (previously the British had agreed with the Americans that small submarines were against both their interests, presumably because they would be useful mainly to the Japanese in the event of a major Pacific war). This idea went nowhere and the conference itself collapsed. The Japanese withdrew in February 1933 (they left the League in 1935).

DNC had approached the minimum submarine problem by asking how much the patrol submarine could be scaled down if sustained surface speed was not critical. Operating from Hong Kong, it would have to conduct a reconnaissance patrol in hot weather in the Sea of Japan.[35] A 5000nm endurance, half that of the big patrol submarines, would support a 23-day patrol: 8 days to get to the Sea of Japan at 8 knots (and 8 days back), plus a 2-day patrol, with allowance for bad weather. Speed could be cut to 12 knots if the submarine did not have to shadow fast forces. W/T range was still vital: it could be 1500nm if a kite aerial was used. Ideally the submarine would retain her six bow tubes and six reload torpedoes. For habitability, which had to be good, she needed a cooling plant. This represented a cut of 5000nm of endurance, 6 knots in surface speed and two stern torpedo tubes; the 4in gun of the big submarines would be replaced by a 3in HA gun. Size might be cut even further if an 18in torpedo as destructive as the current 21in type could be developed. Range would be sacrificed (it could be cut to 4000 yds).

DNC wrote that a patrol submarine could meet these requirements on 770 to 790 tons, the larger tonnage providing for airlocks, which were under consideration for new submarines for life-saving. He

HM SUBMARINE *SEAWOLF*. Starboard profile, as fitted. (© National Maritime Museum M1094)

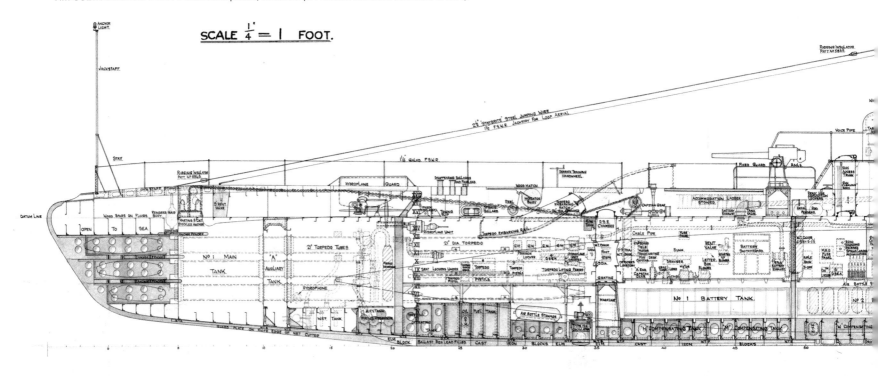

HM SUBMARINE *SEAWOLF*. Plan of outer hull, superstructure and bridge, as fitted. Note: bow to the right. (© National Maritime Museum M1095)

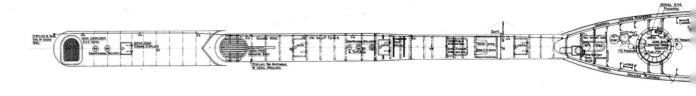

PLAN AT SUPERST

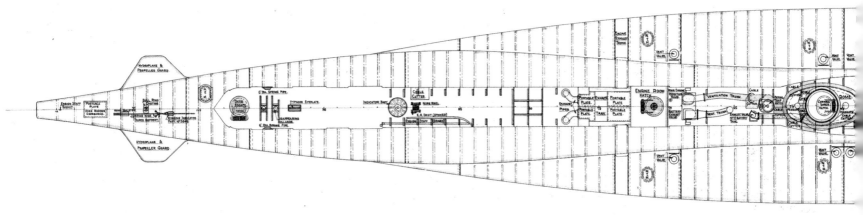

PLAN AT OUTER H

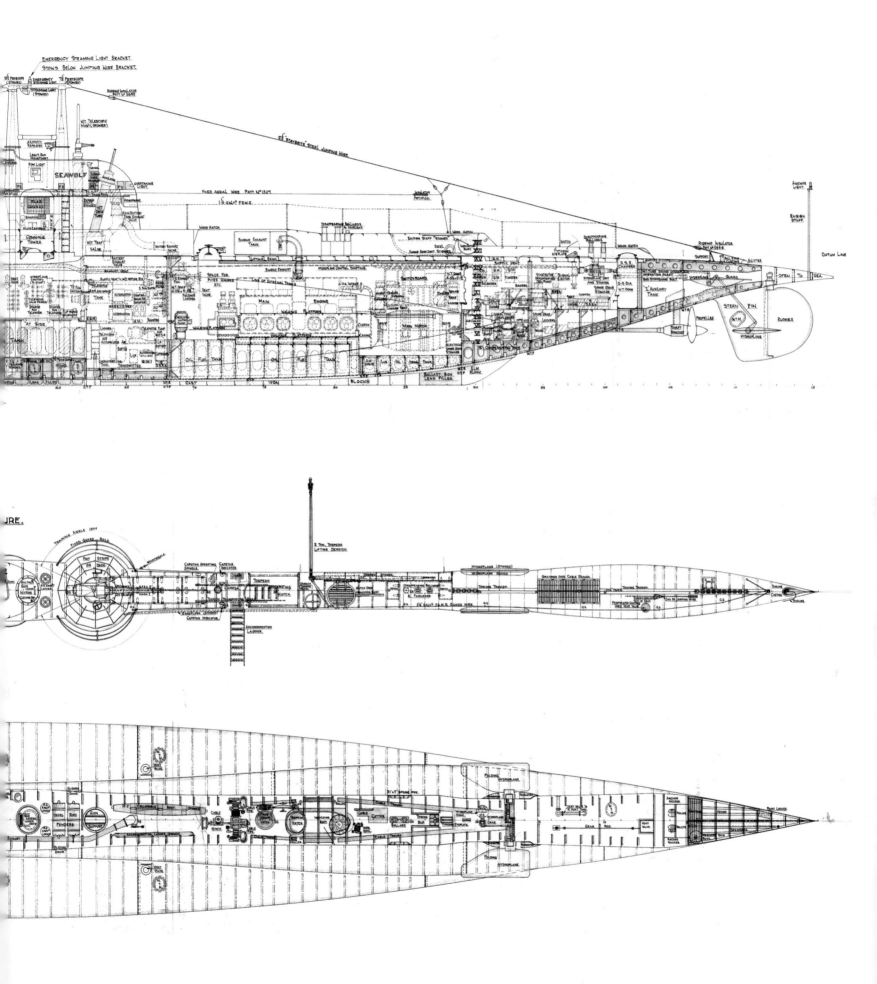

envisaged 21in torpedo tubes, since DTM could not give the length of an 18in torpedo with the same destructive power. Using the current 18in torpedo would save 15 tons, but DNC would prefer to put any displacement saved into habitability. Details offered by DNC were:

LOA (ft-in)	213-0	209-0
Beam (ft-in)	26-0	26-0
Beam of PH (ft-in)	16-3	16-3
Dispt (surfaced) (tons)	900	870
Dispt (standard) (tons)	785	765
Dispt (submerged) (tons)	1130	1100
Surface speed (knots)	12	12
Endurance (nm @ 8 knots)	5000	5000
Fuel (tons)	55	53
Cells	224	224
Motor BHP	1300	1300
Submerged speed (knots)	9.5	9.5 knots
Submerged endurance	¾ hr at 8.5 knots	¾ hr at 9.5 knots
	35 hr at 2 knots	35 hr at 2 knots
Diving depth (ft)	300	300

Both versions had six bow tubes and twelve torpedoes, with one 3in HA gun.

These submarines were hardly the minimum the British felt they had to offer. DNC offered an anti-submarine submarine similar to the 'R' class but with a standard displacement of 250 tons rather than 385 tons:

	New	'R' class of 1918
Dispt (standard) (tons)	250	385
Dispt (surface) (tons)	278	420
Dispt (submerged) (tons)	328	510
Length (ft)	126	163
Mean diameter (ft)	13	15
Batteries	2 x 35 HC cells	4 x 55 cells
BHP (surface)	180	240
Surface speed (knots)	8.5	9.5
Motor BHP	650	1200
Submerged speed (knots)	12	15
Torpedo tubes	4 x 18in	6 x 18in bow
Torpedoes	1 spare	1 spare
Fuel (tons)	12	12–13 tons
Surface endurance (nm/knots)	2400/8.5	2200/9.5
Submerged endurance (hrs/knots)	12/12	15/15
	130/4	240/4

DNC was also asked for a more conventional 250-ton submarine. An undated Legend (1932) compared it with the old 'C' class and with the 'H' class, which were the closest equivalents. Armament would be four 21in torpedo tubes, with one reload each, plus the same single 3in HA gun adopted for the 'S' class a few years earlier. Surface speed would be only 10 knots, using a 240 BHP engine and endurance would have been 3450nm at 8 knots.[36] DNC estimated that the minimum standard displacement of a submarine armed with six 21in bow tubes of current British type would be 450 tons (submerged displacement 600 tons). That would allow for a surface speed of 11 knots (endurance 3000nm at 8 knots, allowing for battery charging) and a submerged speed of 9 knots (endurance 44nm at 2 knots).

Eliminating two of the tubes would cut displacement to 435 tons and would slightly increase speed.

DNC was now asked to design a 600-ton submarine.[37] At the other end of the scale, DNC sketched a 1200 ton submarine, which was closer to what the Royal Navy was soon building.[38]

The Geneva Conference collapsed, but a new purely naval conference had to be held in 1935 to find a replacement for the London Treaty, which would expire on 31 December 1936. Meanwhile Hitler came to power and began to rearm. His delegates withdrew from the Geneva Conference (and the League of Nations) in October 1933. The British now had to face resumption of German capital ship and U-boat construction. Both were serious problems. If the British battleship fleet had to balance a German battle fleet in European waters, the strategy of sending a fleet to the Far East could be compromised, since what was left might not be superior to the Japanese fleet. Moreover, in 1934 the Japanese announced that they were withdrawing from Washington and London Treaty limitations. Although the British were building escorts, they would not welcome a resumption of First World War submarine warfare, just having agreed to scrap so many of their older destroyers. In April 1935 the Germans announced that they were building twelve U-boats. The British had already suggested to Hitler that talks on Anglo-German naval questions should be held in London and Hitler had accepted.[39]

The initial British position for the 1935 conference was once again total abolition and, as a fallback, limitation to 250 tons.[40] The Japanese soon withdrew from the conference, dooming the total tonnage limits enshrined in the 1921 and 1930 treaties. All that was left was limits on the tonnage of individual ships, including submarines.

The British found German rearmament particularly ominous, so they decided to negotiate a separate naval limitation agreement with the Germans. The French, who were not consulted, were furious, but in the end they did not break with the British. The Anglo-German Naval Treaty was signed on 18 June 1935. The Germans were allowed up to 35 per cent of total British surface ship tonnage and up to 45 per cent of British submarine tonnage. The treaty included a clause allowing the Germans to escalate to 100 per cent 'in the event of a situation arising which, in their opinion, makes it necessary for Germany to avail itself of her right'. The Germans said that if submarines could not be abolished, they might accept a limit of 500 to 600 tons, as they were already building 250-tonners. Soon their negotiator admitted that the Germans were already building two 750-ton prototypes (of the Type VII, the standard Second World War U-boat). The Germans soon announced 17,500 tons of submarines as part of their 1937–42 Programme.

The most important submarine consequence of the 1935 agreement was that once the Germans announced on 13 December 1938 that they were building up to 100 per cent of British submarine tonnage, the British had to ask whether new submarines were worth the additional U-boat threat they were incurring. This was so close to the outbreak of the Second World War that it had only minimal effect on British construction; it was presumably responsible for the curtailment of the 1939–40 submarine programme.

Comparisons

The 'S' class was about the size of the standard German wartime Type VII U-boat. British files contain comparisons with a German-built Spanish submarine and one with the captured Type VIIC U-boat *U 570*, which became HMS *Graph*. Another comparison was with an

Salmon comes alongside, December 1939. Note her early-war pennant number, 65S, with the flag superior (the letter) after rather than before the numerals. (John Lambert collection)

Italian submarine offered by Cantieri Monfalcone, presumably the Italian *Argo* class bought by Portugal in 1931 but then cancelled in favour of the British-built Vickers boats.

The British NID report refers to the Spanish submarine as *C 3*, but it was actually *E 1*, built in Spain from parts produced in the Netherlands (*C 3* was an Electric Boat submarine built in Cartagena and she did not resemble the German-designed submarine, with her sharply raked bow). Delivery was cancelled due to the fall of the Spanish monarchy in 1932.[41] After several attempts to sell the submarine to other navies, it ended up as the Turkish *Gur*. It seems to have been the German Type I design. She had four bow and two stern torpedo tubes, rather than the six bow tubes of *Swordfish*; limiting the number of bow tubes made for a better hull form and made the submarine substantially faster. *Swordfish* required 1530 BHP to make 13.75 knots and the reported 2800 BHP of the Spanish submarine would have given 17 knots with the same hull form. The Germans reportedly made 19 knots and their submarine may have touched 20.17 knots on overload power. The reported 1000 BHP submerged would have driven *Swordfish* at 8.75 knots; the quoted 9.25 knots of the Spanish submarine was almost certainly an overestimate.

According to the report, the Spanish did not consider the submarine roomy enough. The only crew accommodation was in the torpedo compartments fore and aft; in wartime all bunks would be removed except in the CO's cabin and the wardroom. 'The vessel has therefore been designed without consideration of crew accommodation and this of course greatly assists in obtaining a very efficient layout of gear.' No spare torpedoes were carried in peacetime and there seemed to be no racks or trays. Loading gear was a single horizontal overhead rail, which limited loading to one torpedo at a time. Reload time had to be considerably longer than in British submarines.

The pressure hull had circular sections throughout, for strength. That was possible because the submarine had only four bow tubes; it would have been impossible with six, as in *Swordfish*. Fore and aft bulkheads were about 1in thick, compared to ⅜in in *Swordfish*. It was unlikely that, as claimed, the remaining bulkheads were as strong as the pressure hull unless they were very heavily stiffened. Chatham was currently testing a curved bulkhead for comparison with the usual flat British bulkheads.

There were only two ventilating fans, compared with five ship ventilation and four battery ventilation fans in *Swordfish*:

It is considered that ventilation in these vessels will be bad and also dangerous, as the fans are used for exhausting the batteries as well as the ship. This is the exact opposite of our principle of having entirely separate ship and battery ventilation systems. The leads taken from outboard to just forward of the engines are similar to our engine outboard induction except that pipes do not connect with the engines. The ventilation of the ship by the main engines has been found objectionable in practice because of discomfort to personnel in the engine room.

There were no LP blowers. Instead, tanks were first blown by HP air and then by exhaust from the main engines. 'This is novel in as far as it dispenses with the LP blowers, but the tanks cannot be blown unless main engines are running without using HP air for the entire operation. This is undesirable.'

There were two periscopes, without brackets; the longer one was 30ft long. 'The arrangement and collection separately of fittings under the controls of the CO is ideal in this case where the CO concentrates on attack and the Engineer Officer dives and controls the vessel.' The conning tower contained all indicators and telegraphs. That made for a large tower, contrary to British practice. The raised gun platform was fitted forward of the bridge, served via the conning tower hatch. Unlike British submarines, this one had no separate gun access trunk, making for slow manning of the gun.

Swordfish was compared to an Italian submarine bought by the Portuguese but cancelled.[42] The Italian submarine was slightly larger (758 tons vs 735 tons surfaced, 678 tons vs 640 tons standard, 980 tons vs 935 tons submerged) and slightly faster on the surface (16.5 knots vs 14.3 knots, on 2300 BHP [2530 BHP maximum] rather than 1550 BHP). Submerged speed was lower, 9.25 knots rather than 10 knots (1100 BHP vs 1300 BHP motors), but submerged endurance was comparable (100nm vs 101nm at 4 knots). Where *Swordfish* had six bow torpedo tubes, the Italians had four bow and two stern tubes, with the same total number of torpedoes (twelve). The British constructor pointed out that by reducing the number of tubes forward, the Italians had gained a much better hull shape and they had also been able to continue the circular section of their pressure hull all the way forward, the ship-shaped hull being wrapped around it. They had also been able to reduce their silhouette, the superstructure being cut down to a minimum of 2ft amidships, compared to 4ft in *Swordfish*. The deciding factors in *Swordfish* were the hydroplanes, capstan and anchor gear etc. forward. In the Italian boat they were much lower thanks to the omission of two torpedo tubes forward. The six-torpedo salvo had been a key factor in British design, apparently not demanded by the Portuguese who ordered the Italian submarine.

In the Italian submarine, spare torpedoes were stowed low down atop the torpedo compensating tank, no attempt having been made to get them into position for quick reloading. Loading was by hand from overhead steel rails. Compensating-tank capacity seemed inadequate.[43] The Italian submarine had a 4in gun where the British had a 3in gun. Placing the gun on the deck cut down the profile considerably. The Italian superstructure was flat-topped throughout, wider than in *Swordfish*. The W/T mast was 40ft high rather than 50ft in *Swordfish* and was of the Admiralty telescopic type. W/T and hydrophone offices had about two-thirds the volume of the corresponding spaces in *Swordfish*.

The Italians used a double hull, the pressure hull of circular-section throughout, closed with curved bulkheads. The outer hull could then be shaped to give a good ship form. Considerable length was saved by omitting the bulkhead the British required between the torpedo tubes and torpedo stowage (aside from the 'S' class, of smaller British submarines only the 'L' class had this bulkhead). The bulkhead did ensure against flooding through damaged torpedo tubes, but it was inconven-

ient for torpedo handling. By omitting end auxiliary tanks the Italians saved two heavy bulkheads. By stowing all oil fuel externally and lowering shaft lines the Italians gained a good arrangement of engines and motors for space, the motors being entirely below the flat.

The Italian submarine was built of Nickel steel whose strength was comparable to the HST of the *Swordfish* (30–34 tons/in^2). The Italians used a comparable slightly stronger steel (35–38 tons/in^2) for their pressure hull framing (the British used a 37–40 tons/in^2 steel). All of the internal bulkheads were corrugated and were considered strong enough to withstand 142 psi pressure. The end dome bulkheads were heavier than in the 'S' class (32lbs vs 26lbs). Fuel and lubricating oil were carried externally. Rated diving depth was 300ft, with a safety factor of at least 3 at this depth; fittings were generally designed to 300ft depth, except for a vent to the auxiliary ballast tank tested to 492ft (214 psi); in the 'S' class all fittings were tested to 225 psi. In the 'S' class the main compartments of the pressure hull were tested to 70 psi (71 psi in the Italian submarine), but auxiliary ballast tanks and adjusting tanks were tested to 100 psi (71 psi in the Italian submarine). The battery in the Italian submarine used fewer (180 vs 224) but individually heavier (1685lbs vs 950lbs) cells; for space and weight the 'S' arrangement was better. The Italian battery took up more space than necessary due to wasted space under and at the sides of the wells.

The Royal Navy captured *U 570* (renamed HMS *Graph*) on 27 August 1941.[44] A stick of four 250lb depth bombs had exploded close alongside, causing a 3in split in the pressure hull on the port side, cracking 90 per cent of the battery containers, slightly buckling the bulkhead between the battery tanks and internal oil tanks, breaking one of two pairs of 500-amp fuse holders (this caused the loss of all lighting and of power to auxiliaries), jumping the battery supply switches to the main motor switchboards but not damaging them and breaking several gauge glasses, lights, porcelain fuses and minor bracket welds.

Graph was slightly larger than *Swordfish*, displacing 784 tons surfaced, including about 42 tons of oil. Submerged displacement was 883 tons. She was somewhat longer than Swordfish (220ft). Maximum surface speed was 17.8 knots. Maximum fuel capacity was 109 tons, 55 per cent of that inside the pressure hull. Surface endurance (presumably including external fuel) was 7500nm at 10 knots on both engines. Submerged speed, 8 knots, was slightly less than for British submarines. Like the Spanish submarine, this one had a circular-section pressure hull, in this case 0.88in thick amidships, nearly completely welded. One large ballast tank was inside the pressure hull, which the British considered a bad feature. All other ballast was external, either in saddle tanks or in the ends. As in the Spanish submarine, limiting the bow battery to four tubes made for a good bow form. Planes extended further than in British submarines. Control while dived was considered good. Details of the planes, guards and jumping wires suggested that passage through submarine nets was not considered important.

There were four bow and one stern tube plus seven internal and two external reloads. 'Gyro angling gear is more complicated than ours but permits application of very accurate angling up to the last minute of the attack.' That is, German torpedo fire control was more like that of the US Torpedo Data Computer (TDC). Unfortunately the fire-control mechanism had been smashed before the submarine surrendered. The instrument was in the conning tower near the attack periscope and was described as considerably more elaborate than the British Submarine

A pre-war photograph of *Seawolf* shows the modified bow fitted in 1936. It probably housed an experimental net-cutter, and it did not last long. (John Lambert collection)

Torpedo Director (STD), with 'a large number of dials' but not giving a clear picture of the relative position of own and enemy ships as did the British instrument. That could also have been said of the TDC. Outputs were director angle, with torpedo speed hand-set and initial inclination hand-set and then corrected automatically; calculation of gyro angle (with range hand-set); and calculation of spread angle. The generated gyro angle was shown on the face of the instrument and transmitted to receivers at the tubes through a selector panel. Gyro angle was normally set either by hand or directly from the calculator. The British credited the German approach with the ability to manoeuvre freely before firing and also with the ability to fire snap shots without altering course. British torpedoes could angle only at 90° and to do that they had to be set manually. They argued that their method was simpler and saved weight and maintenance. However, at about the same time the *Graph* report was being written, the British were trying to acquire the similar US TDC. The Germans spread their salvoes by applying corrections to the mean gyro angle, which allowed them to fire a salvo in minimum time, all the torpedoes reaching the target at the same time, hence difficult to evade. The British varied the firing interval, which was simpler and lighter, but made for large firing intervals against slow targets and torpedoes easier to avoid.

The Germans used a steel disc, driven by air behind it, to push their torpedoes out of the tubes; discharge was splashless. This was simpler than the British approach, in which discharge air was vented inboard but could leak out the muzzle of the tube. However, the British tube automatically compensated after a torpedo was fired. To accommodate the single internal torpedo tube aft, the submarine was given double rudders; they did not give her a smaller turning circle than an 'S'-class submarine.

The British were impressed by the elaborate acoustic system, including a 48-element array hydrophone (GHG) which had no British equivalent.[45] A circular blank flange in the hull seemed to be intended for an Asdic, which had not been fitted. A supersonic (15 kHz) short-pulse mine detector (AEG gear) was mounted at the stern; it had a range of 500m. There was an underwater sonic telegraph

(called UT gear). There was also an echo-sounder.

Space allocated to W/T in a British 'U'-class submarine (i.e., smaller than an 'S') was somewhat larger than in *Graph*. The British Type 55 transmitter had an output of about 2 kW and covered 3–18 MHz; MF output was about 5 or 6 kW over 100 to 1400 kHz. *Graph* had two HF transmitters: 200 W for 3.5–15 MHz and 40 W for 5–16 MHz, plus an MF transmitter (150 W at 300–600 kHz). British policy was to rely almost entirely on HF for long range, with MF a short-range fall back, but German policy was to use practically equal power for each, about a tenth that of Type 55. The HF receiver in *Graph* was badly damaged, but examination of Dutch receivers of similar types showed that it offered only moderate performance. It is not clear how mediocre W/T performance was acceptable in the context of the German strategy of centrally-directed U-boat operations. In this context two-way communication was essential, since U-boats functioned as scouts and had to send their reports all the way home. Moreover, the Germans followed normal European practice in using their jumping wires as aerials, which would offer much worse performance than British insulated aerials with the submarine awash. The rotating-coil DF aerials were similar to those fitted earlier in British submarines and then abandoned for policy reasons. *Graph* also had a VHF transceiver (41.5–45.7 kHz) which the British assumed was for bridge-to-bridge communication on the surface, with a range of up to 10nm (presumably it was equivalent to Talk Between Ships). At this time the British had nothing similar in their submarines.

Special efforts had been made to reduce silhouette. The fixed-eyepiece periscopes were worked from the conning tower rather than the control room, so they could be shorter than in British practice. These periscopes were arranged so that the operator could use them in any vertical position, so that they did not have to be raised completely for use. That was done by splitting the periscope between an upper movable part and a fixed lower part, with moveable prisms. Reserve buoyancy was low when carrying fuel in ballast tanks, further reducing silhouette, but also making the bridge extremely wet in a short sea. Though *Graph* rode comfortably in a heavy swell, speed had to be reduced considerably.

Vents, bow caps and torpedo transport were all hand-worked and *Graph* lacked many fittings standard in British submarines – she was designed for mass production. As in the Spanish submarine, she had no LP blowers. Without these omissions, 'hopeless congestion would arise. As it is, congestion is serious in the forward and after ends and living quarters are very cramped.' A small refrigerator, little food stowage and a small galley 'reduce living conditions below the British standard'. When *U 570* was captured, it turned out that her crew's head had been used to stow food; 'overturned buckets of excrement added to the general noisome conditions'. She was not far into her patrol and she was crammed with food which 'formed a revolting morass that in places was knee deep' due to some flooding.

The engines were as large as could be fitted in the available space with a fairly low shaft line. They were four-stroke reversible with engine-driven superchargers. Electrical arrangement was similar to that in modern British submarines, with a 124-cell battery in two sections and tandem motors on each shaft. Batteries and motors could be grouped in parallel or series. In comparison with British cells, the Germans had about 45 per cent greater output per weight at all rates of discharge. They were expected to be less durable. Life probably would not exceed 2 to 2½ years, due to the use of numerous thin plates (but

in 1943 those in *Graph* were still giving good service after 2½ years and were expected to last 3 to 3½ years).[46] Gas was produced at about three to four times the British rate. Control equipment was semi-automatic and was designed so that operators needed relatively little training. Little had been done to protect against magnetic mines: the submarine had not been 'wiped' or 'flashed', but might have been 'de-permed'.

Graph was clearly built for offensive action. 'The centralisation of most controls and the number of automatic and semi-automatic fittings make it obvious that she had been designed to be run by an inexperienced crew with the minimum of experienced ratings. She was not captured through any serious defect of material, but as a result of being poorly manned.'

Commenting on a paper describing British wartime submarine development, Sir Stanley Goodall, who was DNC when *U 570* was captured, said that her examination dispelled current ideas that U-boats were superior. Prime Minister Churchill had complained that German submarine steel was better than British, but that was definitely not the case; Goodall also described the German steel as dirty, presumably meaning impure.

Sturgeon deploys a boat, using the collapsible boat crane visible here. Note the insulators hung from the jumping wire to support the two lighter aerials below it. The wire to the two-wire antenna is visible rising from the after part of the bridge fairwater. The ship's wireless mast is raised, and the associated wire antenna is barely visible both at its high end and at the end connected (by insulator) to the jumping cable aft. The photograph is dated to late 1944 or 1945 by the camouflage (Scheme H), announced officially in December 1944 but probably used somewhat earlier. This Home Waters scheme (sometimes described in publications as a Far East pattern) combined white areas with blue ones (b30), the pressure hull and saddle tanks being painted purple-blue (pb10). A photo of *Sealion* shows her in a somewhat similar scheme, but with patches of an additional colour. Of the twelve pre-war 'S' class, by 1941 only *Sturgeon* remained of the first four, and only *Sealion*, *Seawolf* and *Sunfish* (transferred to the Soviets in 1944 and sunk in error by a Coastal Command aircraft) of the modified *Shark* class, had survived. *Sunfish* could be distinguished from the others by her open bridge. None of the four was fitted with an Oerlikon gun, and it appears that only *Sunfish* was ever fitted with radar. The photograph is somewhat puzzling, as *Sturgeon* was transferred to the Royal Netherlands Navy (albeit under Royal Navy operational control) in 1943; however, this ship is flying a Union Jack on her jackstaff, and seems to be flying the White Ensign. The ship may therefore actually be *Sealion* or *Seawolf*. All were credited with two Lewis guns. A photo of *Sealion* shows one of them on a pedestal abaft the bridge fairwater. Note that a camouflage scheme for foreign stations comparable to H was later issued as Scheme J, using white, green (g45), blue (b20) and black. Very few Royal Navy submarines wore either scheme. (Silberstein via Blumenfield courtesy of Naval Institute)

CHAPTER 14

REARMAMENT

By 1932 it was clear that the era of peace and goodwill of the 1920s was over; the Japanese were on the march in the Far East and Europe was bubbling with nationalism. The end of the Ten Year Rule was postponed only because Prime Minister Ramsay McDonald, who had recently triumphed (as he saw it) at the London Naval Conference, was unwilling to embarrass the big League of Nations general disarmament conference in Geneva. Symbolically, the committee formed to frame British proposals at Geneva became the Defence Requirements Committee (DRC).[1] The British naval focus returned to the Far East.

Looking ahead to the end of the London Naval Treaty, Director of Plans reviewed submarine-building policy in December 1933.[2] By this time the big patrol submarines were in service. DTD wrote that in recent exercises the large submarines were too easily detected by aircraft and by Asdic. Their poor manoeuvrability often ruined attacks. The ability to attack undetected was so important that it might be worthwhile to reduce offensive power to cut size. He wanted a submarine of something less than 1000 tons with sufficient endurance to maintain the observation patrols envisaged for the patrol sub-

Trident comes alongside her depot ship in the Holy Loch, March 1942 following a deployment to the Arctic. She was unmodified, with a bulbous bow carrying a pair of external tubes, and the midships external tubes firing forward, for a ten-torpedo salvo. (John Lambert collection)

marines. DOD strongly agreed, although he also pointed out that to be effective on observation patrol a submarine had to be relatively fast, so as not to waste too much time on passage. Patrol submarine design unduly emphasised speed. This was a dramatic reversal of the demands for a faster patrol submarine which had resulted in the three fleet submarines. DOD defined endurance as miles on the surface plus days on diving patrol, e.g. 6000nm at 12 knots and 28 days on diving patrol. The earlier requirement for so many miles at 8 knots seemed meaningless.

Although it was impossible to calculate the number of patrol submarines needed to fight a Far Eastern war, it would take twenty submarines (forty was pencilled in) to maintain eight continuously on patrol 1000nm from a fleet base. This was a very different calculation from that which had justified about fifty big patrol submarines operating much further afield. These submarines would lie in wait for an approaching enemy fleet rather than reporting its sortie from a base in Japanese waters. It appears that plans now called for submarines to occupy choke points between Japan and Hong Kong and Singapore. The shift was an inescapable consequence of the limit embodied in the London Naval Treaty, but it may have been justified by the rise of air reconnaissance by RAF flying boats based at Singapore.[3] Note that in effect the twenty P submarines simply replaced the twenty G-type fleet submarines in the fleet projected in May 1930.

The minelayer programme remained unchanged and twelve 'S' class were still planned, a total of thirty-eight submarines. Director of Plans later argued in addition for six smaller submarines (no larger than the 'H' class) for Asdic training, a total of forty-four. For the coming London Naval Conference, he proposed demanding at least forty-five submarines. Given treaty rules, nothing could be done very quickly. The first three big patrol submarines would not be overage (i.e., replaceable) until 1940, their replacements included in the 1937 Programme. Director of Plans argued that at least sixteen 'S' class were needed in peacetime, to provide submarine and anti-submarine training (RA(S)'s proposal for a much smaller training submarine, which became the 'U' class, came later). They were larger than the 'E' class which had been suitable for patrol service in European waters and especially in restricted areas for which large submarines were unsuited. Sixteen such submarines plus the minelayers would leave 32,000 tons for other types – at most 1600 tons for each of the twenty long-range submarines. Twenty was a bare minimum, so as long as the treaty system remained it was vital to hold down tonnage. Director of Plans envisaged a 1200-tonner. In that case the fleet could ultimately comprise one three-submarine unit of the G type, six minelayers, twenty new patrol submarines (1200 tons each) and about twenty 'S' class (say 670 tons), adding up to 52,230 tons.

RA(S) wrote in February 1934 that 1200 tons was far too much. Small size could buy vital numbers. Fleet submarines were pointless because, as the enemy wore down the British force, no fleet commander could afford to tie them down to his heavy ships, 'waiting for a contact with the enemy fleet which may never take place'. They would soon revert to patrol and attack, for which they were ill-suited. The question was how small a submarine could accommodate what British submarines needed: good W/T and a powerful torpedo salvo.[4] Exercises showed that it was increasingly difficult for a submarine to penetrate an Asdic screen; future submarines would need larger salvoes so that they could get sufficient hits from greater ranges. Probably no more than six tubes could be accommodated internally, so it was time to investigate external tubes. To evade hunters, the submarine should

Triton as completed, in 1939, showing her sharply cut-up bridge bulwark. (John Lambert collection)

be as small as possible, for maximum manoeuvrability. The new submarine was tentatively designated the P (patrol) type. It became the 'T' class (the next class after the small 'S' class).

In contrast to past practice, there was no attempt to poll fleet CinCs as to what they might need. Past experience, particularly the bitter experience at the 1930 conference, must have convinced the staff that politics would dominate: the navy would have to look at what it could get the Government to accept. It was widely accepted in Whitehall that arms control was nearly dead and that war might well be approaching, but that was not accepted outside Government and the public view limited what any British government could do in the way of spending more on defence. Governments therefore continued to see naval arms control as the best of a series of bad alternatives, a way of limiting the threat they faced.

In October 1935, looking towards the outcome of the next arms control conference, Director of Plans called a conference on submarine policy.[5] RA(S) summarised total war requirements: thirty-eight patrol types, twelve 'S' class, nine minelayers, six G type, six 'replace "H"' class (i.e., the new small submarine which became the 'U' class) and six overage. Director of Plans argued that it would still be worth building the new small submarines if treaty limits on totals were removed. The smaller submarine might be preferred for its handiness and relative immunity from detection. The 'S' class was too small. Even in the Mediterranean its short endurance was proving a nuisance. RA(S) now considered the 'S' class a poor compromise between what he now wanted, with its greater endurance and the small 'replace "H"' class. Even an improved 'repeat S' would lack important features for long patrols, such as air-conditioning and distilled water for batteries. The 'replace "H"' should be given sufficient endurance and habitability for a 1000nm patrol and a speed of 12 knots (10 knots at cruising speed). It would take about 18 months to build.

Before the 1936 London Naval Treaty eliminated total tonnage limits, the formal Admiralty paper prepared for the Naval Conference stated a requirement for six minelayers, three G type, twenty replacement patrol submarines (P type), twelve 'S' class and six 'replace "H"' type.[6] RA(S) wanted no more G-type submarines; the focus should be on numbers. DNC thought the 'T' class could be placed in production without waiting for tests of a prototype.[7] However, the 'replace H' required more experimental equipment, as a lot had to be packed into a very small submarine. A prototype was needed. The conference proposed as the 1936–7 Programme a 'T', a 'replace "H"', and a minelayer. Since it would take 18 months to finish the prototype 'replace H', it could not be included in the following year's programme, which should consist instead of three 'T' class. The 1938–9 Programme could then be four 'replace "H"'. By this time some emergency was entirely possible; DNC's representative said that from a production point of view it was undesirable to have a gap year in which no 'T'-class submarines were built.

Production of the 'T' class was moved up. The 1935–6 Programme included the last 'S'-class submarine, the prototype 'T' class (*Thetis*) and a minelayer (*Cachalot*). For 1936–7 the Admiralty proposed a second 'T'-class submarine, a minelayer and two (rather than one) prototype 'replace "H" class' submarines (the first of the 'U' class). By February 1936 Government policy was to offer a supplemental budget after a White Paper on defence had been presented to Parliament. A 23 June 1936 Board memo on acceleration of the naval programme called for building seven rather than three submarines in each of the next three years, adding four submarines to the projected 1936–7 Programme. Construction of existing ships would also be accelerated. The proposed additions were three 'T' class and one small submarine.

The 1936–7 Programme ended up, then, with four 'T' class, the last minelayer (*Seal*) and three prototype 'U' class. As rearmament accelerated, the 1937–8 Programme included another seven 'T' class. Another six were included in the 1938–9 Programme. As of February 1938, however, that programme was to have comprised three 'T' class and three 'U' class. As an economy measure the Government reduced the 1938–9 Programme by, among other vessels, the three 'U'-class submarines, which were understood to have been deferred rather than cancelled. They were revived after the outbreak of war, but as 'T' rather than 'U'-class submarines (numerous 'U'-class submarines were also ordered at this time). Because of the Admiralty understanding of the 1938 cuts, they are generally counted as part of the 1938–9 Programme and not of the initial war programme.

From 1936 on, the limiting factor in production was yard capacity, submarines being built by Vickers Armstrong, Cammell Laird and Chatham Royal Dockyard (one of the 1937–8 boats was built by Scotts).

As of December 1938, the proposed 1939–40 Programme included two 'S'-class patrol submarines and two minelayers of a new design. That it was so much smaller than the earlier programmes seems to have been due to shipyard congestion.[8] Before the programme was

When raised, *Thetis* was renamed *Thunderbolt*. Her bulbous upper bow and its two external torpedo tubes were removed in response to criticism by submarine chief Admiral Max Horton, but she retained her midships forward-firing external tubes. Note her cab bridge. She is shown in January 1941. *Thunderbolt* was later fitted with two cylinders to carry Chariots, as was *P 311*; *Trooper* had three such cylinders. (R A Burt)

approved, the minelayers were replaced by another pair of improved 'S'-class submarines: the 1939 Patrol and Minelaying Submarine, essentially an 'S'-class hull with vertical external mine tubes. This design was never built, but its development influenced that of the 1940 'S' class, which certainly was built in numbers.

The 'T' Class

In a 21 February 1934 paper RA(S) described an 800-ton (standard) submarine scaled up from the 'S' class, not down from the patrol or fleet submarine, enlarged as necessary to fight in the Far East.[9] Surface displacement would be about 960 tons (1200 tons submerged) on an overall length of about 250ft, suited to a 42-day patrol. Diving depth should be the 300ft of the fleet submarines and minelayers. Wireless would be as in *Thames* (at present the most powerful in a submarine). The torpedo battery would be six internal and four external tubes, with one reload for each bow tube.[10] RA(S) was particularly concerned that the external tubes be side by side, not superimposed. He was willing to accept a broad upper deck to cover them, noting that the trials of the Vickers-built Portuguese *Golfinho* showed that such a deck did not affect submerged control.[11] There would be a single 3in gun. RA(S) expected a surface speed of 14.5 knots, with a surface endurance of 6000nm at 11 knots or 10,000 at 8 knots. Submerged speed would be 9 knots (1 hour rate), with an endurance of 60 to 70 hours at 2 knots. He thus hoped for the endurance of the big submarines but expected that cutting their speed drastically would make it possible roughly to halve their size.[12]

The 4in gun on board *Thunderbolt*, showing how the shield revolved with the gun. (John Lambert collection)

The displacement limit was soon stretched to 1000 tons (standard). DNC produced alternative designs A and B using the *Grampus* midship section, which stowed oil fuel inside the pressure hull using tankage slung below the midships part of ship, in the bottom of what was called a keyhole shape.[13] There were major disadvantages, beginning with added weight (about 20 tons on a 260ft submarine). The transitions to a smoothly curved cross section towards each end created major structural problems. The bottom of the keyhole would take up space normally used for ballast tanks, so the tanks would have to be spread towards the ends, increasing the prismatic coefficient, which would increase resistance. Enlarging the tanks amidships to regain necessary ballast would enlarge the submarine's silhouette on the surface.

To achieve the desired low-speed submerged endurance would require 336 *Swordfish*-type battery cells (Design A). So large a battery would be out of proportion to the motors required to provide the desired 9-knot submerged speed; DEE would probably want more powerful motors to reduce charging time (when they would run as generators). The alternative (Design B) was a two-battery (224-cell) arrangement which could drive the ship submerged at 1.5 knots, based on *Swordfish* trial figures. On that basis it would be possible to guarantee 55 hours at 1.5 knots (RA(S) would accept this lower submerged speed). The 336-cell submarine would somewhat exceed the desired 1000 tons; the 224-cell submarine would be somewhat smaller. In Design C, 250ft long, standard displacement was held down to 1000 tons but submerged low-speed endurance was extended beyond that in B. To do that, the battery arrangement in A was used, machinery space being shrunk by adopting airless injection diesels (as in the 1934–5 'S' class). Surface speed would be reduced to 14.5 knots and surface endurance to 8600nm at 8 knots.[14]

In these sketch designs the external tubes were set at a 10° angle to the centreline; they could be fired on the surface without fouling the hull and submerged without fouling the hydroplanes (the torpedoes would turn away from the hull).

A Staff Requirement apparently framed on the basis of Designs A and B, but demanding much greater endurance, 4000nm at 11 knots plus fuel for a 28-day patrol and a 30 per cent allowance for a foul bottom. DNC estimated that these figures would have required 200 tons of fuel, far too much on 1000 tons.[15] He adopted an alternative proposed by RA(S): 3000nm at 11 knots (bottom dirty) plus 16½ days at 8 knots (bottom dirty) plus 10 per cent, amounting to the 135 tons. Because all of the oil fuel was stowed internally (DNC assumed external stowage was not acceptable), the submarine had to be about as long as the big 'O', 'P' and 'R'-class reconnaissance submarines, although standard displacement was only 1075 tons, 75 tons above the Staff Requirement. To cut back to 1000 tons DNC would have shortened the submarine by 13ft and cut endurance to 2400nm at operational speed and 14 days at economical speed, rather than the 3000nm and 16½ days wanted by RA(S). The shorter submarine would be more manoeuvrable, a quality emphasised by the Staff and by RA(S). The superstructure was cut down and the bridge shortened to reduce silhouette. The gun would be a 4in, rather than the 3in specified in the Staff Requirement. Since the external torpedo tube had not yet been completely designed, it was understood that at least the first few units would not have it as completed. DNC's submission was dated 23 April 1935. This was Design D.

Controller held a meeting on 1 May to review the design.[16] RA(S) wanted length cut by about 30ft, by placing some fuel in a pressure-

proof external tank. Whatever was done to shorten the submarine, RA(S) rejected any reduction in the battery. RA(S) and the Staff noted that size made for easier detection: the big *Thames* was about 60 per cent easier to detect than the 'H' class used for Asdic training. Even *Swordfish* was much easier to detect.

The submarine could also be cut back by reducing trimming tanks, which in turn would reduce the range of water density (specific gravity) in which she could dive. Changing from 1010 (as in the Baltic) to 1020 (salt water) would make it possible to add 13 tons of oil when the boat was in salt water, equivalent to 500nm at 11 knots. Endurance would then be 5000nm in salt water and 4500nm in fresh. In the interest of compactness, EinC wanted to use airless injection diesels and he suggested eliminating reversing, which RA(S) considered a luxury. Adopting high-capacity batteries would save 4½ tons (low-capacity cells barely gave the desired endurance). Using an auxiliary motor would reduce the battery load at low speed. In the past such motors had been noisy; this time using chain instead of gear drive might work. Controller approved further investigation. EinC also suggested putting the hydroplanes on rubber bearings to eliminate squeaking. ACNS was willing to reduce minimum submerged speed to 1 knot. Bow shutters, proposed by RA(S), would increase submerged speed.

The Staff set 30 seconds diving time because it would take 20 seconds for personnel to get down from the bridge. An officer alone could get down in 15 seconds, so the Staff proposed 20 seconds for diving from half buoyancy. ACNS accepted that the submarine would take 60 seconds to dive from full buoyancy and 30 seconds from 20 per cent buoyancy, but wanted the Staff requirement kept at half these figures. Size could also be cut by adopting Italian-type airlocks forward (with British ones aft).

That this was an attack rather than a patrol submarine (despite its

A Vickers gas-operated 0.303in machine gun on the bridge of *Truant*. British submarines typically had two posts on which such portable guns could be mounted (the pre-war standard was the Lewis gun). In effect they were superseded by the 20mm Oerlikon. (John Lambert collection)

designation) is shown by RA(S)'s W/T requirement stated in March 1935: medium-power high-frequency, capable of transmitting submerged to 100nm, but reception at all frequencies and submerged reception. That suggests that he envisaged other forces transmitting an enemy warning to the submarine so that she could attack. She would not generally be able to transmit back an enemy report at long range. This seems to have been a considerable break from past practice. RA(S) was quite happy to dispense with D/F, but ACNS wanted it to D/F an enemy when lying off Japan, for example. Controller decided to omit it for the moment.

Within a few weeks, DNC had his staff sketch a 260ft (overall) design, displacing 1250 tons surfaced.[17] It could make 14.5 knots on 2100 BHP with bow shutters (2300 BHP without) or 15.5 knots on 2700 BHP with bow shutters. To have an endurance of 3000nm at 11 knots (6 months out of dock in the tropics) plus 16½ days on patrol at 8 knots, it would need 135 tons of oil with shutters and 150 tons without. This was apparently unsatisfactory (it had only two external tubes), so a 276ft 6in submarine was sketched, with its pressure hull extended right aft for maximum volume. It did have the desired four external tubes. Speed would be 15.5 knots surfaced (2500 BHP) and 9.5 knots submerged; endurance would be 4500nm at 11 knots with

a foul bottom and 10 per cent fuel reserve. At a meeting with Controller, this design was accepted because it offered improved manoeuvrability and also because it seemed to improve the submarine's ability to evade Asdic (DNC's note-taker pointed out that experts said that length made no difference to Asdic). Oil fuel could not be reduced. A Legend showed this design with a standard displacement of 1075 tons. It also showed that on a length of 260ft or 265ft overall only two external tubes could be accommodated.

DNC reconsidered the requirement that all oil fuel should be carried inside the pressure hull to avoid any risk of leakage under depth-charge attack.[18] DNC pointed out that this view might be justified in boats with thick pressure hulls (35lbs in the 'O', 'P' and 'R' group), but when the pressure hull was thin (17lbs in 'S' class) it would be preferable to put the oil in external welded tanks rather than in the riveted pressure hull. The P type as now proposed would have 20lb plating, thin enough to make it desirable to carry oil externally. For stability, it would be preferable to carry fuel low in the hull. The circular cross section now desired would have to be enlarged to provide enough volume. This oversized pressure hull would add weight. The alternative keyhole hull would need large flat surfaces specially stiffened against diving pressure, plus structural discontinuities.

Taku at Malta in wartime, with *Una* (left) and *Unrivalled* in the background. (John Lambert collection)

Truant shows a slightly modified bow with one tube visible. She has returned to Holy Loch, 3 December 1942.

Alternatively curved tankage could be added to the lower part of the circular-section pressure hull. That might provide stowage space for a longer periscope, a welcome improvement, but it would also require considerable deadwood fore and aft, which would make turning sluggish unless the rudder were enlarged. Yet another possibility was a figure-eight extension below the pressure hull. DNC's submarine designer thought the simplest and best solution was fuel tankage outside and below the pressure hull.

As submitted in July 1935 the design had all oil fuel stowed inside the pressure hull. Although the weight of the fuel did not figure in standard displacement, the extra structure involved certainly did. By this time it seemed clear that midships external tubes could not be fired when the submarine was surfaced, as they would foul the saddle tanks.

On 1 August 1935 the Board approved the sketch design. As submitted it would displace 1090 tons rather than 1000 tons, but the any reduction would cut performance and there was no objection from the point of view of international agreements. Of four external tubes, the two in the bow could be fired surfaced or submerged, the two abreast the bridge structure only when submerged. This was a Far East submarine with an air-conditioning plant both to cool and to dehumidify.[19] The Legend and building drawings were submitted on 12 February 1936. By this time standard displacement was 1095 tons and overall length had grown to 277ft (265ft between perpendiculars); surface displacement was 1300 tons and submerged displacement 1595 tons.

Successful experience with Vickers solid-injection engines in *Sunfish* justified the use of a variety of solid-injection engines in the new class: a new AEL design, a Vickers engine and foreign-designed engines from Cammell-Laird (Sulzer) and Scotts (MAN). Vickers used a single fuel pump for the whole engine; AEL used one pump per cylinder, which had to be individually adjusted. The Vickers diesels were considered simple and reliable; a cylinder which failed could be disconnected while the engine kept running. The AEL engine was considered somewhat more complex but also reliable.[20] Initial trials on board HMS *Triton* showed the need for a balanced crankshaft. There were also fuel pump problems (a new pump was introduced in 1945–6). A post-war official evaluation was that the design was 'perhaps just adequate with good workmanship', but the quality of workmanship declined through the war. Enlarged supercharged versions of the Vickers and AEL engines were used in the follow-on 'A' class.[21]

The two-stroke Sulzer engine, a modified version of the firm's commercial QD 6, was popular and initially reliable. However, beginning in 1941 these engines began to suffer cracks in their cast-iron engine blocks. The problem was attributed to a combination of poor design and poor castings.[22] The MAN was a failure, probably because it required steel castings of a complexity unknown to the manufacturers. Thus at the outset they had blow-holes and cracks in their cast steel frames.[23]

As built, the 'T' class had four external torpedo tubes: two in the bow and two amidships, firing forward. Early war experience emphasised the need for an ability to fire astern.[24] Later units had their midships tubes pointed aft. A single stern tube was added to production boats beginning in 1940 and eight earlier ones were fitted with it: *Taku, Thunderbolt, Tigris, Torbay, Tribune, Trident, Truant* and *Tuna*.

The 1939 Patrol and Minelaying Submarine[25]

As offered to the Board late in 1938, the 1939 minelayer would have been a modified *Cachalot* using high-capacity battery cells (as in the 'T' class) to gain endurance. It would also have differed from *Cachalot* in having a circular-section pressure hull and in incorporating the lessons of initial underwater tests (Job 81). The design summary was dated 19 December 1938.[26]

HM SUBMARINE *TARPON*. Starboard profile, as fitted. This is the original design with external torpedo tubes. (© National Maritime Museum J9619)

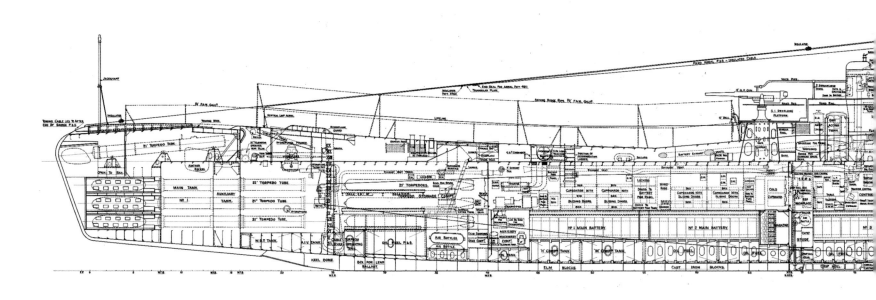

HM SUBMARINE *TARPON*. Port profile, as fitted. (© National Maritime Museum J9620)

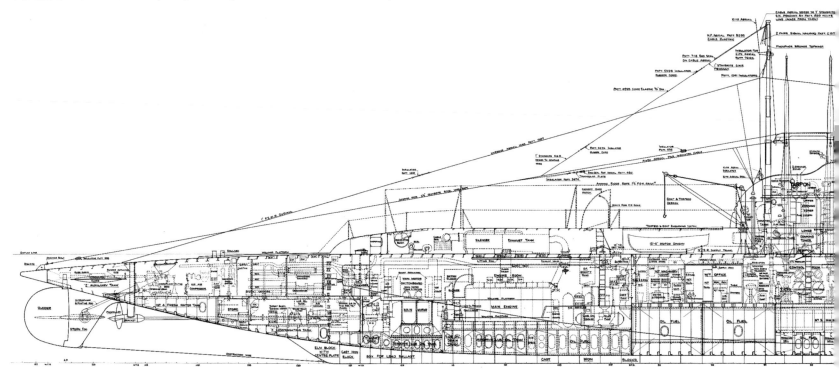

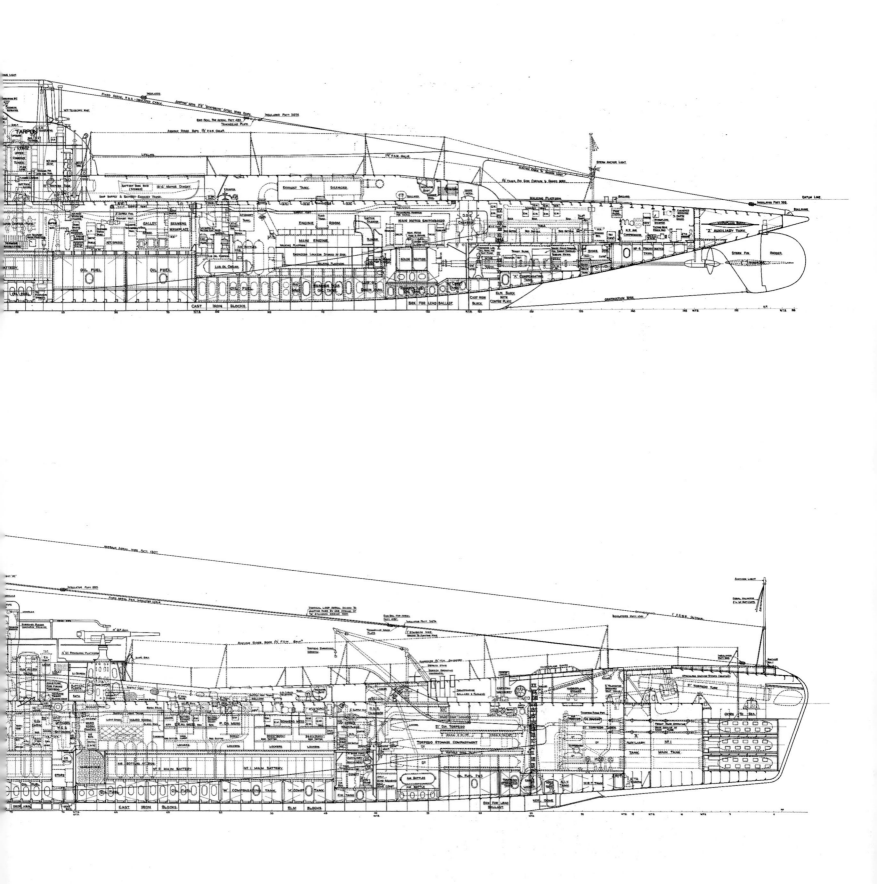

HM SUBMARINE *THUNDERBOLT*. Starboard elevation, as fitted. This depicts the initial modification
of the class with the external tubes removed. (© National Maritime Museum J9700)

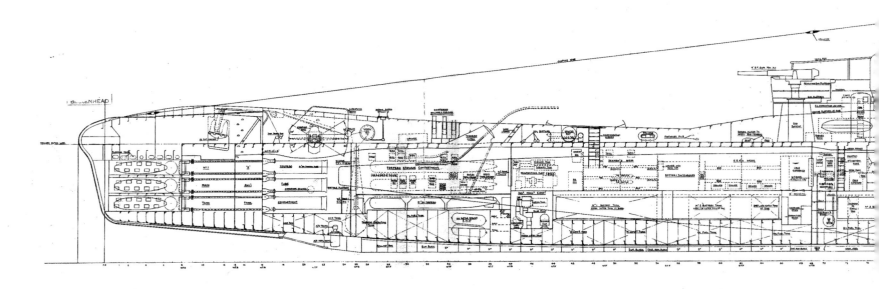

HM SUBMARINE *THUNDERBOLT*. Plan of superstructure, as fitted. Note: bow to the right. (© National Maritime Museum J9699)

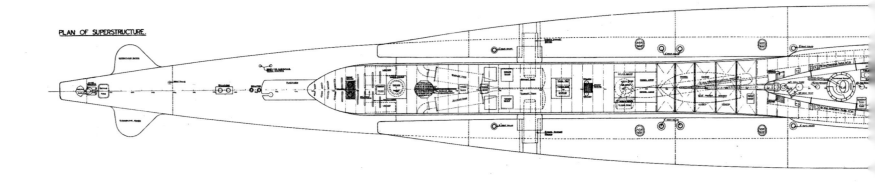

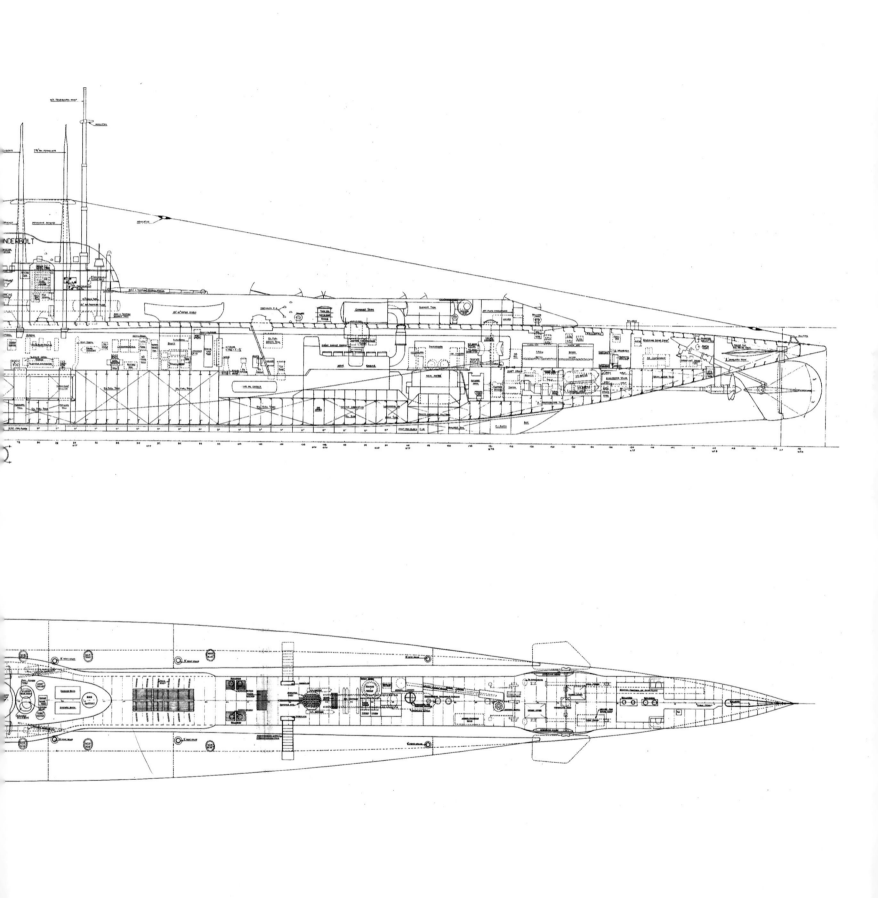

Talisman on 22 March 1942. (John Lambert collection)

The 1939 Programme included two 'S'-class submarines. In December 1938 RA(S) laid out the improvements he wanted.[27] He wanted the rattle eliminated (but its cause was still being investigated). Diving should be faster; he wanted special attention paid to the placing and size of Kingstons, free-flooding holes and vents, trunking up the vents to the top of the superstructure and quick flooding and venting of the bridge and superstructure. If the same engines were to be used as in *Sunfish*, their higher power should be used to gain speed, the stern being altered if necessary. Surface endurance was inadequate; it should be 4000nm at 11 knots with a clean bottom. All oil fuel should be stowed inside the pressure hull. Submerged speed was extremely important, so RA(S) wanted bridge resistance reduced, if possible by introducing a cab bridge. Would a revolving streamlined shield and platform for the gun help? Should the size and shape of the casing be changed? Did the gap between the lower edge of the casing and the hull add resistance? The existing plane control gear was too stiff and too noisy. RA(S) wanted at least one external tube. It might even be that adding two at the bow would not cost much underwater speed or surface displacement.

CNS (First Sea Lord) proposed a minelayer/patrol submarine in a 17 December 1938 memo. It could be substantially smaller than the big minelayers, because it need not carry as many mines: twenty-four or thirty might be enough. During the last war many German submarines carrying far fewer gave the British much trouble. Director of Plans saw a requirement for minelayers to operate in the North Sea in a European war: twenty mines might be enough. DOD agreed with the others that the Estonian *Kalev* class, which Vickers had built, showed what could be obtained in a reasonable size. An entirely new design might be too late for the 1939 Programme, but an existing one might be adapted. DTD considered it possible to design a submarine minelayer on the displacement of the 'T' class.

First Sea Lord called a meeting to discuss submarine design, particularly the minelayer, on 20 January 1939.[28] In a general policy discussion, First Lord characterised the 'T' class as replacements for the big patrol submarines and the 'S' class as a good intermediate type. RA(S) said that for offensive action close to the coast the new 'U' class were easy to handle and to operate and very good boats. They were relatively invulnerable to depth-charging because their Kingstons could be closed when they dove. The 'U' class might be a standard small type for the future, but nothing definite was said about including them in future programmes.

Diesels were a problem. Except for the 'U' class (see below), running at full rating taxed current engines too highly. The *Sunfish* engine was not as reliable as RA(S) wished; he liked diesel-electric propulsion as in the new 'U' class and wanted it adopted for all British submarines. EinC cautioned against scaling it up due to space and weight problems. EinC said that he was pinched for space; to gain reliability he wanted a greater reserve of power than in the past. RA(S) pointed out that where in 1918 there had been two types of engine, now there were eleven. If staff requirements could be kept stable for a decade, the navy could adopt a single proven engine. DNC pointed out that the modified 'S' class already provided the desired 14 knots with 11 knots operational speed. To get higher speed, the submarine would have to be lengthened to take advantage of the higher power of a seven-cylinder version of the *Sunfish* engine. The conference agreed on a maximum surface speed of 14 knots (11 knots operational) using, as in the improved 'S' class, the enlarged *Sunfish* engine, which provided 300 to 350 more BHP than required (the ship would not be lengthened to take advantage of the extra power). The engine would be derated from about 1850 BHP to about 1550 BHP. Fuel would be increased to get the desired 4000nm at 10 knots. There would be no external torpedo tubes. Engine power was redefined, the submarine being required to charge batteries while proceeding at operational speed (11 knots).

As for minelayers, First Sea Lord rejected a repeat *Grampus* (too large to work in the Heligoland Bight) and also the large 1939 minelayer (unable to lay mines in less than 15 fathoms).[29] RA(S) would accept a small mine load: the object was to keep the enemy constantly on the alert, sweeping everywhere. About a dozen mines per submarine would suffice. Every submarine should carry a few mines. DNC thought as many as eight might be accommodated in the saddle tanks of existing 'S'-class submarines. Superstructure stowage (as in *Grampus*) would require an unacceptably larger submarine. After a long discussion, First Sea Lord decided to adopt the saddle-tank stowage as it would limit size, visibility from the air and unit cost.

DNC gave particulars of a modified *Sunfish*: 725 tons standard, 14 knots surface speed (3500nm at 10 knots), 9.5 knots submerged, six torpedo tubes, one 3in gun and twenty-four mines. RA(S) thought twenty-four mines excessive; DNC offered two per tube. He could reduce size by reducing to four torpedo tubes, but that was unacceptable. After some discussion, 4000nm at 10 knots was considered sufficient for the North Sea and the Mediterranean.

The 1939 patrol and minelaying submarine designs merged in the form of a modified 'S'-class submarine carrying a few mines internally, without the external torpedo tubes envisaged for the earlier 1939 'S' class.[30] This follow-on design was sometimes described as a repeat 'S'. By March it had been decided that mines would be stowed in open wells rather than in the tubes used during the First World War. There would be three mine openings on each side (six were initially planned).

The sketch design incorporated the solid (airless) injection engine used in *Sunfish*, the last 'S'-class submarine, eight to twelve mines in the saddle tanks, endurance increased to 4000nm at 10 knots and a maximum speed of 14 knots. External tubes would be omitted. According to the DNC history, First Sea Lord recommended that these ships replace the two 1939 minelayers. Approved Staff Requirements were for minelayers suited to the North Sea, the Baltic and the Mediterranean, capable of laying mines in water 12 fathoms deep. Surface speed was specified as the maximum available with the *Sunfish* engine, but operation was to be absolutely reliable at 11 knots. Maximum submerged speed was 9 knots. The sketch design showed

Some of the original 'T'-class submarines, like this unidentified one, were modified with aft-firing midships tubes. (NHHC)

length between perpendiculars of 188ft (overall of 221ft 6in), displacement 730 tons standard and 820 tons surfaced (1030 submerged), diving depth 300ft, surface speed 14 knots (endurance 4100nm at 10 knots) and submerged endurance 120nm at 3 knots. There would be six bow torpedo tubes (with six reloads) and twelve mines.[31] Tenders were invited, but Controller dropped the project in view of the 1939 crisis which led to war.

Initial design work on a modified 'S' class for 1939 would seem to explain why DNC could offer a fresh design instead of a simple repeat 'S' class in January 1940. However, note that very soon they were replaced by a minelaying design. Note that the 1939 Patrol and Minelaying Cover includes a discussion of the control room planned for the 1940 'S' class.

To increase minelaying capacity, tubes for six to eight mines were proposed for the saddle tanks of the three 1938 'T' class (*Tetrarch*, *Talisman* and *Torbay*). The mine was that designed by Vickers for submarines it built for Estonia. The wells carried six mines on each side.

Trials in *Tetrach* were not entirely successful (comments in the Cover are more acid) and when carrying mines 1.5 knots was lost. This speed could nearly be eliminated if the minelaying ports were blanked off, a drydock job.[32] Only *Tetrarch* was tested with mines and none was ever carried operationally. In March 1940 it was decided that the seven War Programme 'T' class would not have mine wells in their saddle tanks.

The 'U' Class

In 1933 RA(S) pointed to the need for submarines for anti-submarine training 'which is already becoming difficult and will in the future be more so'. Each of six planned Asdic-equipped destroyer flotillas would need at least one training submarine. The Anti-Submarine School needed at least five more. The surviving 'H'-class submarines had proven ideal, but were nearing the end of their lives. RA(S) wanted something even simpler and cheaper. It should have a good torpedo armament for short-range patrols, presumably in the context of a European war.

'U' CLASS SUBMARINES (FIRST GROUP) HMSs *UNDINE, UNITY* AND *URSULA*. General arrangements. (Drawn by John Lambert)

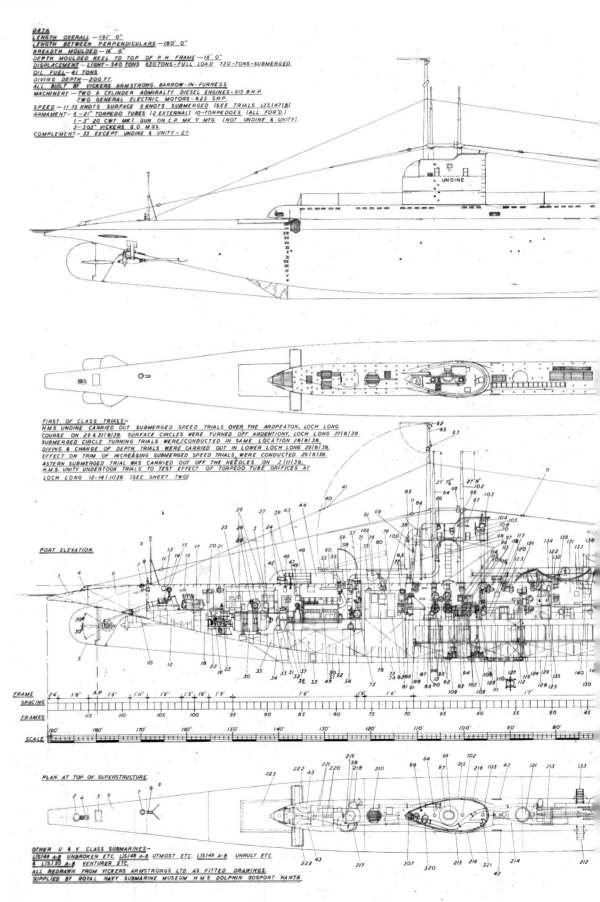

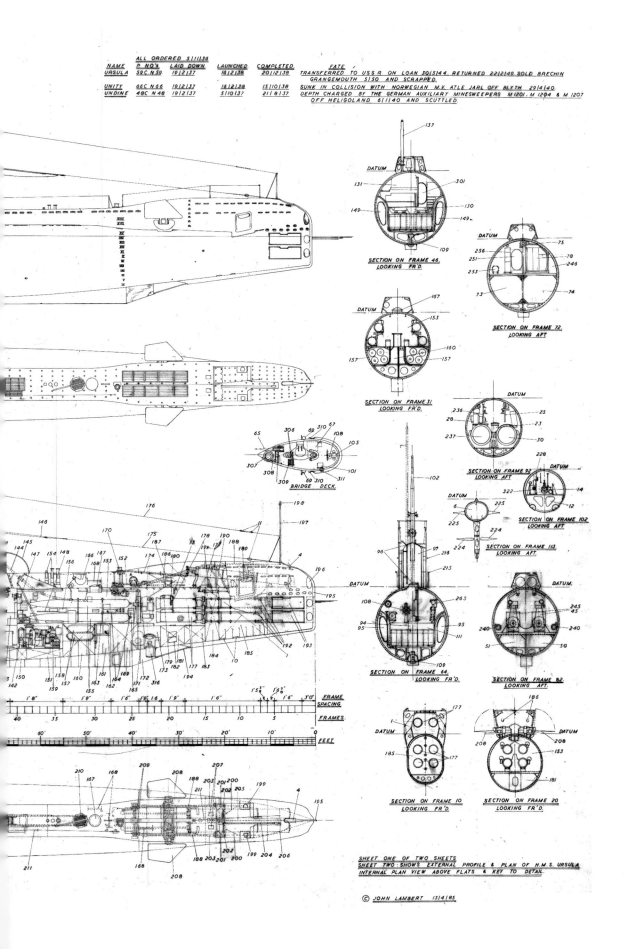

NAME	ALL ORDERED 5/11/36 P. NO's	LAID DOWN	LAUNCHED	COMPLETED	FATE
URSULA	59C N59	19/2/37	16/2/38	20/12/38	TRANSFERRED TO USSR ON LOAN 30/5/44. RETURNED 22/2/49. SOLD BRECHIN GRANGEMOUTH 5/50 AND SCRAPPED.
UNITY	66C N66	19/2/37	16/2/38	15/10/38	SUNK IN COLLISION WITH NORWEGIAN M.V. ATLE JARL OFF BLYTH 29/4/40.
UNDINE	48C N48	19/2/37	5/10/37	21/8/37	DEPTH CHARGED BY THE GERMAN AUXILIARY MINESWEEPERS M1201, M1204 & M1207 OFF HELIGOLAND 6/1/40 AND SCUTTLED.

SECTION ON FRAME 46. LOOKING FR'D.

SECTION ON FRAME 72. LOOKING AFT

SECTION ON FRAME 31 LOOKING FR'D.

SECTION ON FRAME 92. LOOKING AFT

SECTION ON FRAME 102 LOOKING AFT

SECTION ON FRAME 113. LOOKING AFT.

BRIDGE DECK.

SECTION ON FRAME 64. LOOKING FR'D.

SECTION ON FRAME 82. LOOKING AFT.

SECTION ON FRAME 10 LOOKING FR'D.

SECTION ON FRAME 20 LOOKING FR'D.

FRAME SPACING
FRAMES.
FEET

SHEET ONE OF TWO SHEETS
SHEET TWO SHOWS EXTERNAL PROFILE & PLAN OF H.M.S. URSULA INTERNAL PLAN VIEW ABOVE FLATS & KEY TO DETAIL.

© JOHN LAMBERT 15/4/85

247

'U' CLASS SUBMARINES (FIRST GROUP) HMSs *UNDINE*, *UNITY* AND *URSULA*. Detail. (Drawn by John Lambert)

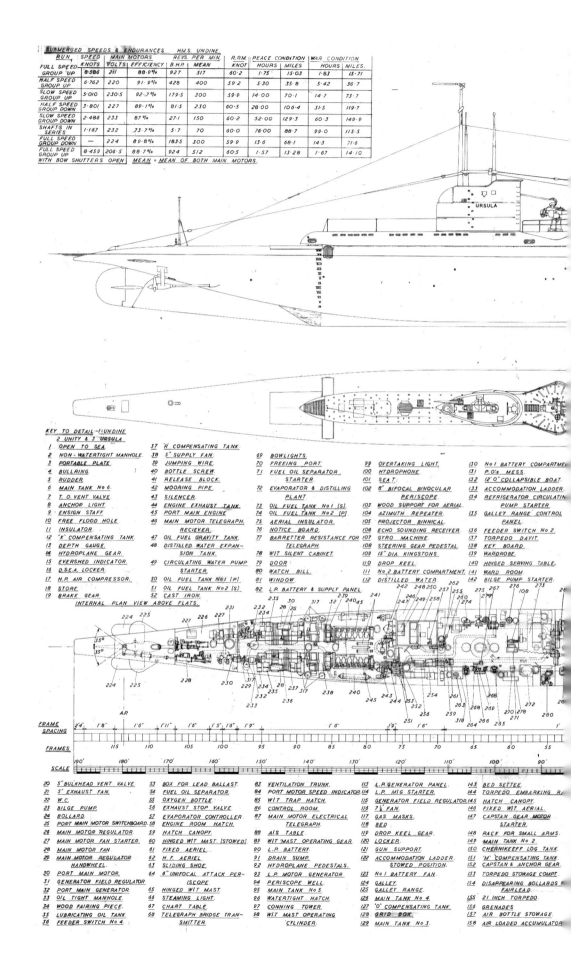

SUBMERGED SPEEDS & ENDURANCES			HMS. UNDINE.							
RUN.	SPEED	MAIN MOTORS		REVS. PER MIN.		R.P.M.	PEACE CONDITION		WAR CONDITION	
	KNOTS	VOLTS	EFFICIENCY	B.H.P	MEAN	KNOT	HOURS	MILES	HOURS	MILES.
FULL SPEED GROUP UP	8·586	211	88·9%	927	517	60·2	1·75	15·03	1·83	15·71
HALF SPEED GROUP UP	6·762	220	91·9%	428	400	59·2	5·30	35·8	5·42	36·7
SLOW SPEED GROUP UP	5·010	230·5	92·7%	179·5	300	59·9	14·00	70·1	14·7	73·7
HALF SPEED GROUP DOWN	3·801	227	89·1%	81·5	230	60·5	28·00	106·4	31·5	119·7
SLOW SPEED GROUP DOWN	2·486	233	87%	27·1	150	60·2	52·00	129·3	60·3	149·9
SHAFTS IN SERIES	1·167	232	73·7%	5·7	70	60·0	76·00	88·7	99·0	115·5
FULL SPEED GROUP DOWN	—	224	89·8%	183·5	300	59·9	13·6	68·1	14·3	71·6
FULL SPEED GROUP UP WITH BOW SHUTTERS OPEN	8·459	206·5	88·7%	924	512	60·5	1·57	13·28	1·67	14·10

MEAN = MEAN OF BOTH MAIN MOTORS.

KEY TO DETAIL ~1= UNDINE
2 UNITY & 3 URSULA

1 OPEN TO SEA.
2 NON-WATERTIGHT MANHOLE.
3 PORTABLE PLATE.
4 BULLRING.
5 RUDDER.
6 MAIN TANK No 6.
7 T.O. VENT VALVE.
8 ANCHOR LIGHT.
9 ENSIGN STAFF.
10 FREE FLOOD HOLE.
11 INSULATOR.
12 'X' COMPENSATING TANK.
13 DEPTH GAUGE.
14 HYDROPLANE GEAR.
15 EVERSHED INDICATOR.
16 D.S.E.A. LOCKER.
17 H.P. AIR COMPRESSOR.
18 STORE.
19 BRAKE GEAR.

37 'R' COMPENSATING TANK.
38 5" SUPPLY FAN.
39 JUMPING WIRE.
40 BOTTLE SCREW.
41 RELEASE BLOCK.
42 MOORING PIPE.
43 SILENCER.
44 ENGINE EXHAUST TANK.
45 PORT MAIN ENGINE.
46 MAIN MOTOR TELEGRAPH. RECIEVER.
47 OIL FUEL GRAVITY TANK.
48 DISTILLED WATER EXPANSION TANK.
49 CIRCULATING WATER PUMP. STARTER.
50 OIL FUEL TANK No 1 [P].
51 OIL FUEL TANK No 2 [S].
52 CAST IRON.
INTERNAL PLAN VIEW ABOVE FLATS.

69 BOWLIGHTS.
70 FREEING PORT.
71 FUEL OIL SEPARATOR. STARTER.
72 EVAPORATOR & DISTILLING PLANT.
73 OIL FUEL TANK No 1 [S].
74 OIL FUEL TANK No 2 [P].
75 AERIAL INSULATOR.
76 NOTICE BOARD.
77 BARRETTER RESISTANCE FOR TELEGRAPH.
78 WIT SILENT CABINET.
79 DOOR.
80 WATCH BILL.
81 WINDOW.
82 L.P. BATTERY & SUPPLY PANEL.

99 OVERTAKING LIGHT.
100 HYDROPHONE.
101 SEAT.
102 8" BIFOCAL BINOCULAR PERISCOPE.
103 WOOD SUPPORT FOR AERIAL.
104 AZIMUTH REPEATER.
105 PROJECTOR BINNICAL.
106 ECHO SOUNDING RECEIVER.
107 GYRO MACHINE.
108 STEERING GEAR PEDESTAL.
109 15" DIA. KINGSTONS.
110 DROP KEEL.
111 No 2 BATTERY COMPARTMENT.
112 DISTILLED WATER.

130 No 1 BATTERY COMPARTMENT
131 P.O's. MESS.
132 12' 0" COLLAPSIBLE BOAT.
133 ACCOMMODATION LADDER.
134 REFRIGERATOR CIRCULATING PUMP STARTER.
135 GALLEY RANGE CONTROL PANEL.
136 FEEDER SWITCH No 2.
137 TORPEDO DAVIT.
138 KEY BOARD.
139 WARDROBE.
140 HINGED SERVING TABLE.
141 WARD ROOM.
142 BILGE PUMP STARTER.

20 5" BULKHEAD VENT VALVE.
21 5" EXHAUST FAN.
22 W.C.
23 BILGE PUMP.
24 BOLLARD.
25 PORT MAIN MOTOR SWITCHBOARD.
26 MAIN MOTOR REGULATOR.
27 MAIN MOTOR FAN STARTER.
28 MAIN MOTOR FAN.
29 MAIN MOTOR REGULATOR HANDWHEEL.
30 PORT MAIN MOTOR.
31 GENERATOR FIELD REGULATOR.
32 PORT MAIN GENERATOR.
33 OIL TIGHT MANHOLE.
34 WOOD FAIRING PIECE.
35 LUBRICATING OIL TANK.
36 FEEDER SWITCH No 4.

53 BOX FOR LEAD BALLAST.
54 FUEL OIL SEPARATOR.
55 OXYGEN BOTTLE.
56 EXHAUST STOP VALVE.
57 EVAPORATOR CONTROLLER.
58 ENGINE ROOM HATCH.
59 HATCH CANOPY.
60 HINGED WIT MAST [STOWED].
61 FIXED AERIAL.
62 H.F. AERIEL.
63 SLIDING SHOE.
64 6" UNIFOCAL ATTACK PERISCOPE.
65 HINGED WIT MAST.
66 STEAMING LIGHT.
67 CHART TABLE.
68 TELEGRAPH BRIDGE TRANSMITTER.

83 VENTILATION TRUNK.
84 PORT MOTOR SPEED INDICATOR.
85 WIT TRAP HATCH.
86 CONTROL ROOM.
87 MAIN MOTOR ELECTRICAL TELEGRAPH.
88 AIS TABLE.
89 WIT 'MAST OPERATING GEAR.
90 L.P. BATTERY.
91 DRAIN SUMP.
92 HYDROPLANE PEDESTALS.
93 L.P. MOTOR GENERATOR.
94 PERISCOPE WELL.
95 MAIN TANK No 5.
96 WATERTIGHT HATCH.
97 CONNING TOWER.
98 WIT MAST OPERATING CYLINDER.

113 L.P. GENERATOR PANEL.
114 L.P. M/G STARTER.
115 GENERATOR FIELD REGULATOR.
116 7½" FAN.
117 GAS MASKS.
118 BED.
119 DROP KEEL GEAR.
120 LOCKER.
121 GUN SUPPORT.
122 ACCOMMODATION LADDER. STOWED POSITION.
123 No 1 BATTERY FAN.
124 GALLEY.
125 GALLEY RANGE.
126 MAIN TANK No 4.
127 'O' COMPENSATING TANK.
128 GRID BOX.
129 MAIN TANK No 3.

143 BED SETTEE.
144 TORPEDO EMBARKING RA
145 HATCH CANOPY.
146 FIXED WIT AERIAL.
147 CAPSTAN GEAR MOTOR STARTER.
148 RACK FOR SMALL ARMS.
149 MAIN TANK No 2.
150 CHERNIKEEFF LOG TANK.
151 'M' COMPENSATING TANK.
152 CAPSTAN & ANCHOR GEAR.
153 TORPEDO STOWAGE COMPT.
154 DISAPPEARING BOLLARDS FAIRLEAD.
155 21 INCH TORPEDO.
156 GRENADES.
157 AIR BOTTLE STOWAGE.
158 AIR LOADED ACCUMULATOR

FRAME SPACING
FRAMES
SCALE

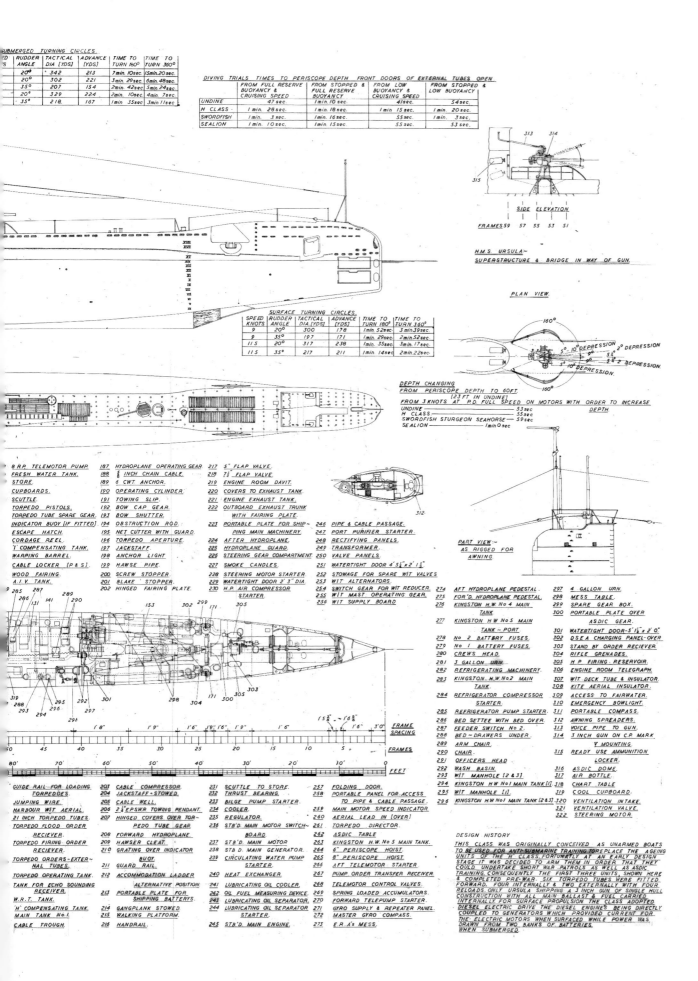

SUBMERGED TURNING CIRCLES.

SPEED	RUDDER ANGLE	TACTICAL DIA [YDS]	ADVANCE [YDS]	TIME TO TURN 180°	TIME TO TURN 360°
	20°	342	213	7min. 10sec	15min. 20 sec.
	20°	302	221	3min. 29sec	6min. 48sec.
	35°	207	154	2min. 42sec	5min. 24sec.
	20°	329	224	2min. 10sec	4min. 7sec.
	35°	218	167	1min 35sec	3min 11sec.

DIVING TRIALS TIMES TO PERISCOPE DEPTH FRONT DOORS OF EXTERNAL TUBES OPEN

	FROM FULL RESERVE BUOYANCY & CRUISING SPEED	FROM STOPPED & FULL RESERVE BUOYANCY	FROM LOW BUOYANCY & CRUISING SPEED	FROM STOPPED & LOW BUOYANCY
UNDINE	47 sec.	1min. 10 sec.	41sec.	54sec.
H CLASS	1 min. 28sec.	1min. 18sec.	1min 15 sec.	1min. 20 sec.
SWORDFISH	1min. 3sec.	1min. 16 sec.	1min. 3 sec.	1min. 3 sec.
SEALION	1min. 10 sec.	1min. 15 sec.	55 sec.	53 sec.

SIDE ELEVATION

FRAMES 59 57 55 53 51

H.M.S. URSULA~

SUPERSTRUCTURE & BRIDGE IN WAY OF GUN.

PLAN VIEW.

SURFACE TURNING CIRCLES.

SPEED KNOTS	RUDDER ANGLE	TACTICAL DIA.[YDS]	ADVANCE [YDS]	TIME TO TURN 180°	TIME TO TURN 360°
9	20°	300	178	1min. 52sec.	3min 39sec.
9	35°	197	171	1min. 29sec.	2min 52sec.
11.5	20°	317	238	1min. 35sec.	3min. 17sec.
11.5	35°	217	211	1min. 14sec	2min. 22sec.

160°

5° 10° DEPRESSION
5½° 2° DEPRESSION
5½° 2° DEPRESSION
5° 10° DEPRESSION

160°

DEPTH CHANGING

FROM PERISCOPE DEPTH TO 60FT.
[23 FT IN UNDINE]
FROM 3 KNOTS AT P.D. FULL SPEED ON MOTORS WITH ORDER TO INCREASE DEPTH.

UNDINE — 53sec
H CLASS — 55sec
SWORDFISH STURGEON SEAHORSE — 59 sec
SEALION — 1min 0 sec

PART VIEW~
AS RIGGED FOR
AWNING

No.	Description	No.	Description
	8 H.P. TELEMOTOR PUMP.	187	HYDROPLANE OPERATING GEAR
	FRESH WATER TANK.	188	⅝ INCH CHAIN CABLE.
	STORE.	189	6 CWT. ANCHOR.
	CUPBOARDS.	190	OPERATING CYLINDER.
	SCUTTLE.	191	TOWING SLIP.
	TORPEDO PISTOLS.	192	BOW CAP GEAR.
	TORPEDO TUBE SPARE GEAR.	193	BOW SHUTTER.
	INDICATOR BUOY [IF FITTED]	194	OBSTRUCTION ROD.
	ESCAPE HATCH.	195	NET CUTTER WITH GUARD.
	CORDAGE REEL.	196	TORPEDO APERTURE.
	'I' COMPENSATING TANK.	197	JACKSTAFF.
	WARPING BARREL.	198	ANCHOR LIGHT.
	CABLE LOCKER [P & S].	199	HAWSE PIPE.
	WOOD FAIRING.	200	SCREW STOPPER.
	A.I.V. TANK.	201	BLAKE' STOPPER.
		202	HINGED FAIRING PLATE.

217	5" FLAP VALVE.
218	7½" FLAP VALVE.
219	ENGINE ROOM DAVIT.
220	COVERS TO EXHAUST TANK.
221	ENGINE EXHAUST TANK.
222	OUTBOARD EXHAUST TRUNK WITH FAIRING PLATE.
223	PORTABLE PLATE FOR SHIPPING MAIN MACHINERY.
224	AFTER HYDROPLANE.
225	HYDROPLANE GUARD.
226	STEERING GEAR COMPARTMENT
227	SMOKE CANDLES.
228	STEERING MOTOR STARTER.
229	WATERTIGHT DOOR 2' 3" DIA.
230	H.P. AIR COMPRESSOR STARTER.

246	PIPE & CABLE PASSAGE.
247	PORT PURIFIER STARTER.
248	RECTIFYING PANELS.
249	TRANSFORMER.
250	VALVE PANELS.
251	WATERTIGHT DOOR 4' 5½" x 2' 1½".
252	STOWAGE FOR SPARE WIT VALVES
253	WIT ALTERNATORS.
254	SWITCH GEAR FOR WIT REDUCER.
255	WIT MAST OPERATING GEAR.
256	WIT SUPPLY BOARD.

No.	Description	No.	Description
274	AFT HYDROPLANE PEDESTAL.	297	4 GALLON URN.
275	FOR'D. HYDROPLANE PEDESTAL.	298	MESS TABLE.
276	KINGSTON H.W. No 4 MAIN TANK.	299	SPARE GEAR BOX.
277	KINGSTON H.W No 5 MAIN TANK ~ PORT.	300	PORTABLE PLATE OVER ASDIC GEAR.
278	No 2 BATTERY FUSES.	301	WATERTIGHT DOOR-5' 1½" x 2' 0".
279	No 1 BATTERY FUSES.	302	D.S.E.A. CHARGING PANEL- OVER
280	CREWS HEAD.	303	STAND BY ORDER RECIEVER.
281	3 GALLON URN.	304	RIFLE GRENADES.
282	REFRIGERATING MACHINERY.	305	H P FIRING RESERVOIR.
283	KINGSTON H.W.No2 MAIN TANK.	306	ENGINE ROOM TELEGRAPH.
284	REFRIGERATOR COMPRESSOR STARTER.	307	WIT DECK TUBE & INSULATOR.
285	REFRIGERATOR PUMP STARTER.	308	KITE AERIAL INSULATOR.
286	BED SETTEE WITH BED OVER.	309	ACCESS TO FAIRWATER.
287	FEEDER SWITCH No 2.	310	EMERGENCY BOWLIGHT.
288	BED~DRAWERS UNDER.	311	PORTABLE COMPASS.
289	ARM CHAIR.	312	AWNING SPREADERS.
290	CHAIR.	313	VOICE PIPE TO GUN.
291	OFFICERS HEAD	314	3 INCH GUN ON C.P. MARK V MOUNTING
292	WASH BASIN.	315	READY USE AMMUNITION LOCKER.
293	WIT MANHOLE [2 & 3]	316	ASDIC DOME.
294	KINGSTON HW No1 MAIN TANK [1]	317	AIR BOTTLE.
295	WIT MANHOLE [1].	318	CHART TABLE
296	KINGSTON HW No1 MAIN TANK [2 & 3]	319	COOL CUPBOARD.
		320	VENTILATION INTAKE.
		321	VENTILATION VALVE.
		322	STEERING MOTOR.

No.	Description	No.	Description
	GUIDE RAIL FOR LOADING TORPEDOES.	203	CABLE COMPRESSOR.
	JUMPING WIRE.	204	JACKSTAFF~STOWED.
	HARBOUR WIT AERIAL.	205	CABLE WELL.
	21 INCH TORPEDO TUBES.	206	2½ EPSWR TOWING PENDANT.
	TORPEDO FLOOD ORDER RECIEVER.	207	HINGED COVERS OVER TORPEDO TUBE GEAR.
	TORPEDO FIRING ORDER RECIEVER.	208	FORWARD HYDROPLANE.
	TORPEDO ORDERS~EXTERNAL TUBES.	209	HAWSER CLEAT.
	TORPEDO OPERATING TANK.	210	GRATING OVER INDICATOR BUOY.
	TANK FOR ECHO SOUNDING RECEIVER.	211	GUARD RAIL.
	W.R.T. TANK.	212	ACCOMMODATION LADDER ALTERNATIVE POSITION.
	'H' COMPENSATING TANK.	213	PORTABLE PLATE FOR SHIPPING BATTERIES.
	MAIN TANK No. 1.	214	GANGPLANK STOWED.
	CABLE TROUGH.	215	WALKING PLATFORM.
		216	HANDRAIL.

231	SCUTTLE TO STORE.
232	THRUST BEARING.
233	BILGE PUMP STARTER.
234	COOLER.
235	REGULATOR.
236	STB'D. MAIN MOTOR SWITCH~ BOARD.
237	STB'D. MAIN MOTOR.
238	STB D. MAIN GENERATOR.
239	CIRCULATING WATER PUMP STARTER.
240	HEAT EXCHANGER.
241	LUBRICATING OIL COOLER.
242	OIL FUEL MEASURING DEVICE.
243	LUBRICATING OIL SEPARATOR.
244	LUBRICATING OIL SEPARATOR STARTER.
245	STB'D. MAIN ENGINE.

257	FOLDING DOOR.
258	PORTABLE PANEL FOR ACCESS TO PIPE & CABLE PASSAGE.
259	MAIN MOTOR SPEED INDICATOR
260	AERIAL LEAD IN [OVER]
261	TORPEDO DIRECTOR.
262	ASDIC TABLE.
263	KINGSTON H.W. No 5 MAIN TANK.
264	6" PERISCOPE HOIST.
265	8" PERISCOPE HOIST.
266	AFT TELEMOTOR STARTER.
267	PUMP ORDER TRANSFER RECEIVER.
268	TELEMOTOR CONTROL VALVES.
269	SPRING LOADED ACCUMULATORS.
270	FORWARD TELEPUMP STARTER.
271	GYRO SUPPLY & REPEATER PANEL.
272	MASTER GYRO COMPASS.
273	E.R.A's MESS.

DESIGN HISTORY

THIS CLASS WAS ORIGINALLY CONCEIVED AS UNARMED BOATS TO BE USED FOR ANTI-SUBMARINE TRAINING TO REPLACE THE AGEING UNITS OF THE H CLASS. FORTUNATELY AT AN EARLY DESIGN STAGE IT WAS DECIDED TO ARM THEM IN ORDER THAT THEY COULD UNDERTAKE SHORT WAR PATROLS AS WELL AS ASDIC TRAINING. CONSEQUENTLY THE FIRST THREE UNITS, SHOWN HERE & COMPLETED PRE-WAR, SIX TORPEDO TUBES WERE FITTED FORWARD, FOUR INTERNALLY & TWO EXTERNALLY WITH FOUR RELOADS. ONLY URSULA SHIPPING A 3 INCH GUN OF SINGLE HULL CONSTRUCTION WITH ALL MAIN BALLAST & FUEL CARRIED INTERNALLY FOR SURFACE PROPULSION THE CLASS ADOPTED DIESEL ELECTRIC DRIVE THE DIESEL ENGINES BEING DIRECTLY COUPLED TO GENERATORS WHICH PROVIDED CURRENT FOR THE ELECTRIC MOTORS WHEN SURFACED WHILE POWER WAS DRAWN FROM TWO BANKS OF BATTERIES WHEN SUBMERGED.

Undine was the first 'U'-class submarine to be completed. The bulbous upper bow, which contained two torpedo tubes, was considered objectionable once boats were in service, as it made depth-keeping difficult. Later submarines built under the war programmes had fined bows. She is shown in November 1938. (John Lambert collection)

A formal proposal submitted in March 1934 by RA(S) presumably described a DNC sketch design: a single-hulled submarine (as in the 'H' class) displacing about 410 tons (standard) with a diving depth of at least 150ft.[33] She would have four 21in bow torpedo tubes, with two spares to be carried only in war, as they would constrict crew space. Gun armament would be two Lewis guns. She would have twin screws and simple low-rated machinery (total 480 BHP) for 11.5 knots (10 knots cruising), with a surface endurance of 2000nm at 10 knots. Submerged speed (periscopes lowered) would be 9 knots (1 hour rate), with an endurance of not less than 40 hours at minimum speed. All fittings would be as simple as possible, e.g. hand-worked vents and Kingstons and uncooled main motors. The submarine would have escape hatches, not airlocks. Space and weight for wireless would be no more than in the 'H' class, something like Type 51 (M/F and H/F). Asdic would be essential, because a submarine without one would be useless for instructing submarine personnel in the submarine use of Asdic, which would be part of the function of the class. The submarine should be able to listen and communicate when bottomed. Complement would be two officers and twenty-one ratings (three officers in war). A Legend was dated 19 April.[34]

DNC forwarded details of a sketch design at the same time as he forwarded Designs A and B for what became the 'T' class. He had met RA(S)'s requirements except for a speed of 11.25 knots rather than 11.5 knots and he had been able to provide airlocks without lengthening the submarine. Once engine and motor details had been settled, standard displacement might be reduced to 400 tons. The lightest engine was the fastest-running, so the lightest alternative was to gear it down to propeller revs. DNC cautioned that the gearing might cause vibration at a critical frequency in the machinery. Direct drive

was used in existing submarines. The simplest but heaviest alternative was electric drive. The submarine could gain a bit more surface speed by adding electric power from the batteries to that supplied directly by the engines, driving the generators. Because it was heaviest, electric drive was used to estimate the engine weight in the Legend.

Compared to the 'H' class, the main improvements DNC could offer would be a smaller and lighter main engine (saving about 5 tons and considerable space), Asdic, stronger internal main ballast tanks and longer periscopes. Advantages of his new design, which should be retained in any 'replace "H"', would be the new stern shape (good for passage through nets and also for leaving the bottom), more modern planes, an internal trimming system (with small submarines it was essential that trim when dived not be disturbed by taking in or ejecting water from and to the sea), modern main motors and the current methods of working vents, blows, Kingstons, planes and steering gear. Principal differences from the 'H' design were (i) raised stern, with a stern fin and after hydroplanes as in other recent designs; and (ii) omission of bow torpedo tube shutters. The raised stern was intended to improve surfaced stability; it was also preferred for steering and planes and it shortened shafting. As for speed, DNC noted that although some 'H'-class submarines reached about 11.5 knots, it would be safer to credit them with 10.5 to 11 knots, with which RA(S) was perfectly satisfied.

In May Director of Plans defined the alternative wartime mission. A 10-day patrol out to 500nm from her base should suffice for any European war outside the Mediterranean. She should therefore be able to transmit and receive W/T reliably out to 500 miles. That was interpreted to mean 400 to 500nm on medium frequency (M/F) using a kite aerial and 100nm using her standing aerial. She would also have

H/F. There was no need for any D/F capability. It turned out that the set meeting these requirements would not fit in the available space; the submarine had to grow. Space for Asdic (Type 120 and a Type 710 hydrophone) would be tight. No S/T installation could be accommodated (it was not yet clear that Asdic was a good substitute). Looking towards the 1935 London Naval Conference, DCNS found the RA(S) proposal 'irresistible'. The submarine should be of about 400 tons.

In December 1934 Captain Barry, who was Chief of Staff to RA(S), suggested an entirely new design, in effect an update of the 'R' rather than the 'H' class. It was discussed at a meeting in DTSD's room.[35] In wartime the new small submarine would conduct defensive patrols around the British Isles and overseas bases, mostly against enemy submarines. Possible wartime operating areas would be the Channel and approaches, Gibraltar, the Suez Canal and Singapore and Hong Kong. Barry argued that the new submarine would always be operating in waters under British control, so she would not have to contend with hostile aircraft and ASW ships. She might be subject to sporadic attack by enemy screening ships and aircraft, but they probably would not be detached to conduct sustained searches and hunts. This submarine needed high submerged speed (about 12 knots) and endurance; ease of control and manoeuvre submerged; quick diving; the smallest possible silhouette (but good lookout facilities when surfaced); and a heavy torpedo armament. All of this would cost surface qualities such as speed, endurance, seakeeping in heavy weather and communications. Any such sacrifice would be more than offset by better submerged performance, which would be useful not only against enemy submarines but also against enemy surface ships. Increased battery power could probably be obtained by placing a third battery in the control room bilge space, space and weight being saved by cutting engine power and W/T installation. A surface speed of 10 knots would be enough and engine power should be set by the need to charge batteries quickly.

A single engine might well be better than the usual two, but in that case the usual clutched direct drive would be unacceptable: the sole engine would be unclutched while charging batteries. Diesel-electric drive would solve that problem. The engine could be mounted lower in the submarine, giving it a longer stroke and hence greater power output without adding much volume. It would always run at its optimum speed, saving the usual wear and tear due to changes in speed. It also seemed that using separate generator and motor would add efficiency. The motor and propeller shaft could be more in line with the centre of resistance, improving submerged control. If the small pressure hull could not accommodate more than four 21in tubes, then two more might be added externally, as in the 'T' class then being designed.

Barry offered an alternative (Scheme B, A being the original one) for a two-shaft submarine with diesel-electric drive, capable of 12 knots for one hour submerged and 10 knots surfaced. The battery should be charged from half-discharged state in no more than 8 hours (4½ hours had been crossed out). The submarine would be able to keep the sea for 14 days (7 had been crossed out). It would have six torpedo tubes, but no reloads. The six-torpedo salvo was needed both to deliver an effective blow against large surface ships and to improve the chance of hitting small targets such as submarines. It seemed unlikely that the submarine would encounter a second target on the same day; she would be able to return to base to reload. That in turn would reduce space, weight and torpedo personnel; Vernon claimed that it had a torpedo which could remain in a tube for weeks without servicing. Diving depth was given as 200ft.

After the meeting, Barry produced a Scheme C in which he reduced minimum acceptable underwater speed to 10 knots for 3 hours. Time to charge a half-charged battery was reduced to 6 hours. A single screw would be acceptable, but twin-screw propulsion was preferable if practicable. The submarine should be able to keep the sea for 15 days. The

Seen from ahead, *Unity* shows her two upper torpedo tubes. (John Lambert collection)

Ursula was given a 3in/45 gun at the expense of two reload torpedoes. (RAN Naval Historical Section via Dr Josef Straczek)

200ft diving depth was justified on the ground that the submarine's great submerged mobility and small size would make her more immune from depth-charging than larger submarines. 'In any case an increase of hull strength to withstand depths below 200ft is not practicable without undue complication to the design.'

It turned out that the requirement to be able to charge the battery (from half-charged condition) in 6 hours while cruising at 5 knots was particularly difficult. For example, it would take 430 SHP (without allowing for battery charging at full speed) to drive a submarine at 10 knots. However, to meet the 6-hour requirement the submarine would need 900 BHP, 800 BHP of which would be devoted to charging. With the usual two-shaft direct drive plant, either engine would have to be available to charge the battery. It would have to develop about 650 BHP, of which 150 BHP would be needed to make up the 800 BHP charging load. However, a diesel-electric plant would need only 900 BHP altogether, since both engines could charge batteries while residual battery power drove the submarine at 5 knots. Allowing even a slightly slower charging rate would greatly reduce required charging power. For 6¼ hours, for example, only 600 BHP would be needed, so the direct drive installation could be reduced to 1000 BHP and the diesel-electric to 700 BHP. Either could fit in a 44ft machinery space, the diesel-electric version weighing 31 tons and the direct-drive 29 tons.

Meanwhile Director of Plans and DTD laid out requirements of both a Far Eastern and a European war; this must have been one of the earliest references to European requirements.[36] 'Owing to the ability of submarines to operate in waters controlled by the enemy, it appears that conditions in the Far East before the arrival of our Main Fleet will be particularly suitable for their employment in defence of harbours and bases . . . there will shortly be a requirement for new local defence submarines for use in the Far East. The number necessary has been stated as 10.' The 'L' and 'S' class boats used for local defence in the Far East were unsatisfactory, the 'Ls' rapidly becoming obsolete and the 'S' class due to their poor habitability.

In a European sund/or Near Eastern war, British submarines would blockade numerous ports which could be used by enemy commerce

raiders. Some of them would be so close to British waters that small submarines might suffice. The two Directors doubted that these submarines would be employed in ASW, because with the advent of Asdic that would be done by hunting flotillas and by air patrols.

The DNC design offered acceptable size and surface speed, but not the desired 10-day patrol 500nm from base (which would require an endurance of 3160nm at 9 knots). However, if the desired patrol was reduced to 7 days, that would equate to 2512nm at 9 knots, which was attainable. The design was deficient in underwater speed and endurance, which were important since she would be operating in the face of intense enemy ASW. Six bow tubes were very desirable, but the gun could be eliminated. A maximum diving depth of 200ft was acceptable. The Signal Division had proposed a 500nm M/F set using a kite aerial, but owing to the danger that the submarine could be D/F'd the new submarine should rely entirely on HF transmission in war.

This paper was referred to RA(S), newly in office early in 1935. He generally concurred with Director of Plans and DTD. They both rejected ACNS' preference for something more like a *Swordfish*: unless size was held down submarines could never be built in sufficient numbers. Also, RA(S) argued in March 1935 that operating inshore the submarine would face heavy enemy ASW: she should be no larger than 450 tons (standard). Six torpedo tubes were desirable, but five would be acceptable if four were internal. He accepted diesel-electric drive, the key argument (already made by Barry) being that it could be used with efficient fast-running engines, which would save space and simplify upkeep. Holding down engine size would make it possible to fit larger batteries. RA(S) thought 14-day patrols too long for a very small submarine and suggested 10 (but 14 for a particular mission); diving patrol should not exceed 7 days. Surface endurance should be 2200nm at 10 knots, which would make it possible to maintain a 2-day diving patrol 900nm from base of a 7-day diving patrol 320nm from base, allowing for 9 knots on passage. Submerged speed should be as high as possible, not less than 12.5 knots with periscopes down; minimum submerged speed should be no more than 2 knots with periscopes raised. The submarine should be able to accelerate and decelerate quickly.

The submarine should be able to dive from cruising speed on the surface at full buoyancy to periscope depth in not more than 60 seconds without using her Q tank. Underwater she should be able to accelerate over her full speed range without changing depth, to put the rudder hard over without having to shift water ballast and to turn 360° in 4 minutes. She should have a main ballast tank at each end, capable of withstanding full water pressure, fitted with HP blowers to be used for surfacing. The other main tanks would be tested to 100ft and fitted with hand-worked Kingstons. All of these details were new.

DNC started a new design. As a first cut, requirements were a 450-ton submarine with habitability for 10 days but water and stores for 14 days, could make 10 knots surfaced with a clean bottom and 12.5 knots submerged as desired (1-hour rate); it would be able to charge batteries from half-charged state in 6 hours with the ship moving at 5 knots. Surface endurance would be 2200nm at 10 knots. The submarine would have twin-shaft diesel-electric propulsion.[37] The submarine would be able to dive in water with specific gravity between 1010 and 1030. If in less than 1010 (fresher water), a main tank would be used as a compensating tank. There would be no escape chambers, to hold down size. Barry told DNC's submarine designer that RA(S) wanted 224 battery cells on the assumption that they would provide a submerged speed of not less than 12 knots for one hour, with periscopes housed, which he preferred to the stated 10 knots for 3 hours. DNC's submarine designer rejected the first cut at a hull form, which 'cocked up' the bow too much to allow for increased

battery weight well forward and torpedoes to be loaded into tubes above the level of the battery. He feared that this hull form would affect submerged control.

Calculation showed that it would take a lot more power to make 12.5 knots underwater: 1600 BHP compared to 750 BHP for 10 knots (later somewhat reduced). On that basis the 10-knot submarine would require enough battery power to maintain 9.5 knots for 3 hours. The 12.5-knot submarine (for one hour) would require more than twice the battery power, 6020 Watts per cell compared to 2870. Existing batteries could maintain that level of output for 20 minutes. By mid-June 1935 DEE was reporting serious problems with a motor to produce enough power for 12.5 knots, while meeting the other requirements.[38] That seems to have killed the 12.5-knot submarine. British submarine designers would not be interested in that sort of speed for nearly a decade and then in connection with reports of fast German submarines. Even with the reduction to 10 knots, DEE reported that he could not meet the 2-knots submerged high-endurance (80 hours) requirement with a single shaft. DNC wanted to increase propeller revs considerably, as that would reduce main motor weight and size.

As the design proceeded, some of the early requirements were relaxed. In September, Captain Barry agreed to accept 6¾ hours to charge from half to full charge, rather than the original 6 hours. By this time a new Asdic set, to be concentrated forward, was being proposed, but if it did not materialise, the W/T and Asdic offices could be combined. Reload torpedoes (two if possible) were now wanted and two torpedo tubes would be external, as in the 'T' class. Each external tube was considered preferable to two reloads.[39] The submarine began to expand, diameter amidships increasing to 15ft 9in (615 tons submerged without appendages).

Ursula in 1942. The object protruding from her bridge fairwater is a folded-down wireless mast. (John Lambert collection)

HM SUBMARINES *UNDINE*, *UNITY* AND *URSULA*. General arrangement. Starboard elevation and sections. The drawing shows the revised bow shape, both superimposed on the original elevation and as a separate sketch. The section about frame 64, cropped out of this plan, is reproduced on the first colour page, facing page 256. (© National Maritime Museum M1094)

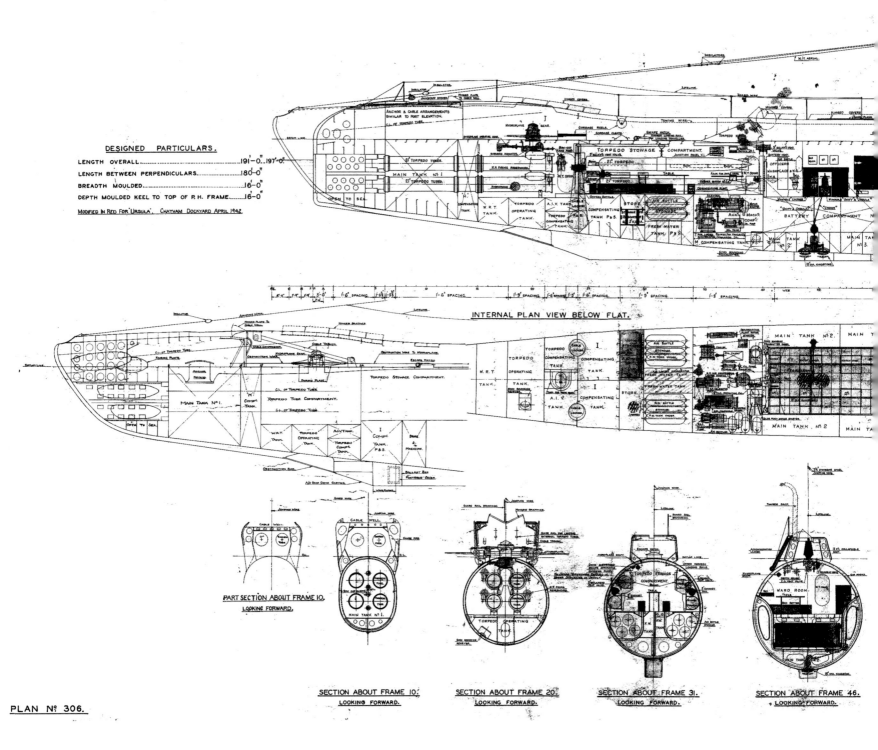

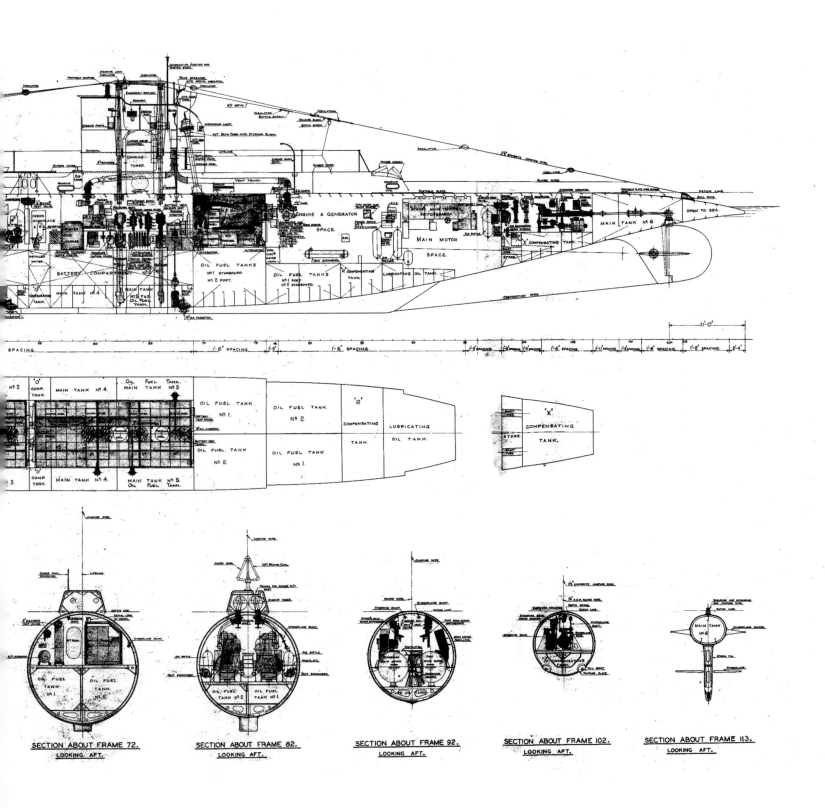

SECTION ABOUT FRAME 72.
LOOKING AFT.

SECTION ABOUT FRAME 82.
LOOKING AFT.

SECTION ABOUT FRAME 92.
LOOKING AFT.

SECTION ABOUT FRAME 102.
LOOKING AFT.

SECTION ABOUT FRAME 113.
LOOKING AFT.

Neither the Admiralty nor any private company had been designing suitable low-powered high-performance diesels, so in mid-October an alternative was suggested: eight 87.5 BHP bus engines, for a total of 700 BHP. That must have been rejected very soon. The submarine ended up with a small commercial Paxman 6 RXS four-stroke six-cylinder diesel producing 400 BHP at 825 RPM. It was reportedly among the most reliable Royal Navy diesels.[40]

Captain Barry reviewed the design on 23 October 1935.[41] By this time he wanted much the same endurance as in the 'S' class, 4500nm at 8 knots, equivalent to about 3000nm at 10 knots. With increased endurance spare torpedoes were necessary; Barry wanted four of them. The submarine should be able to dive in fresh water at the beginning of a patrol and also after a third of her fuel had been used. Some form of cooling was desirable, since the submarine might be at sea for 23 days. Twin shafts were preferable for manoeuvring and also if one motor broke down. Up to this point a single screw had been considered acceptable if not as good as twin screws. A submerged speed of 10 knots was sufficient.

As of early November 1935, expected displacement was about 500 tons. Controller pointed out to ACNS at the end of February 1936 that 'the original intention . . . for training only, has developed into a useful offensive submarine as well at the cost of 50 tons and an extra £25,000'. At the end of March ACNS wrote that the surface endurance requirement had been more than met: in the North Sea or Mediterranean six months out of dock and in sea state 3 or 4 the submarine could carry out a 7-day diving patrol 600nm from base (where 400nm had been required). In good weather the patrol could be 1000nm from base instead of the 800nm required. The extra endurance had been achieved not by enlarging the submarine but rather by making full use of space for fuel after the size had been set by requirements for armament, machinery and stability. Higher underwater speed might have been desirable, but it had proven too expensive and 10 knots was acceptable. Unlike

other submarines, this ones could sustain maximum underwater speed for two hours.

In February 1936 diesel-electric drive was selected, the associated risk (dependence on main motors for all propulsion) being deemed acceptable.[42] The Board approved the sketch design on 14 May and the Legend and drawings received the Board Stamp on 24 July 1936. By that time DNE had proposed that instead of being called the 'replace "H" class' the new submarines be designated the 'U' class; RA(S) wanted them referred to by the name of the first boat to avoid having them called U-boats.

The Staff Requirement was amended: the design should be suitable for quick installation of a deck gun; weight and stability compensation would be to land the two external torpedoes. In February 1937 DNC found that the cost of a 3in gun and fifty rounds of ammunition would be the two external torpedoes and one reload.[43] The external tubes seem not to have been considered worthwhile. In response to complaints of poor handling in rough weather, a 5 April 1940 meeting in the office of VA(S) recommended urgently that the bow casing be fined by removing them from *Unity* as well as from all 'U'-class submarines under construction.[44] A proposal to move the external tubes back to amidships was rejected because it would have reduced submerged speed and endurance.

The new submarines exceeded their designed surface speed using only their main engines, with no additional energy from their batteries. However, they were slower than expected underwater, *Unity* making 8.8 knots (9 knots with her external tubes blanked off).[45] It was not immediately clear what had gone wrong. Futhermore, when firing a salvo the submarines tended to become too light. Repeat boats had a Q tank forward of amidships to counteract this and also for quick depth-changing.

The three prototype 'U' class were included in the 1936–7 Programme: *Undine*, *Unity* and *Ursula*; for a time they were known as the *Unity* class. Twelve more were ordered under the initial war programme (ordered 4 September 1939).

Ursula was given a fined-down bow with considerable rake in 1942; as in modified 'T'-class submarines, her two external bow tubes were moved back. (John Lambert collection)

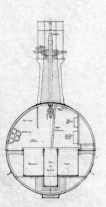

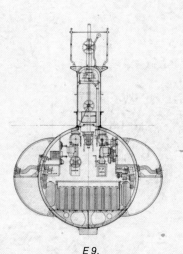

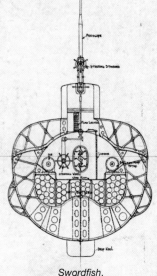

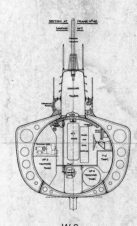

C 19 and *C 20*.
(© National Maritime
Museum, Part of M1060)

E 9.
© National Maritime
Museum, Part of M1062)

Swordfish.
(© National Maritime
Museum, Part of J8855)

W 3.
(© National Maritime
Museum, Part of M1078)

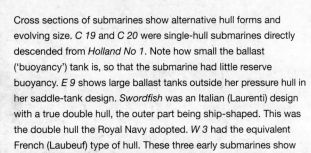

Cross sections of submarines show alternative hull forms and evolving size. *C 19* and *C 20* were single-hull submarines directly descended from *Holland No 1*. Note how small the ballast ('buoyancy') tank is, so that the submarine had little reserve buoyancy. *E 9* shows large ballast tanks outside her pressure hull in her saddle-tank design. *Swordfish* was an Italian (Laurenti) design with a true double hull, the outer part being ship-shaped. This was the double hull the Royal Navy adopted. *W 3* had the equivalent French (Laubeuf) type of hull. These three early submarines show the three alternatives designers tried. *Thames* was a double-hulled long-range submarine using some of her external tankage for oil fuel, a practice later disliked because oil could leak out and disclose her position. *Grampus* was a minelayer carrying her mines externally, above her pressure hull; note how her conning tower had to be offset. *Seawolf* reverted to saddle-tank configuration, to cut her size. Finally, *Undine* shows that to make a submarine really small it had to revert to single-hull configuration. Note that her wireless mast is offset from her centreline periscope.

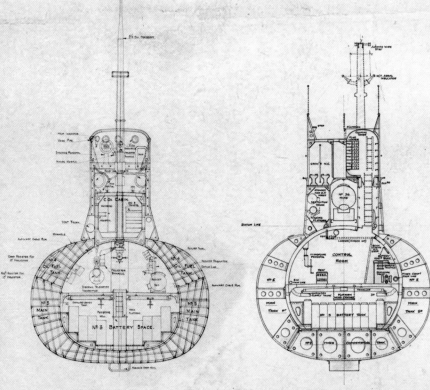

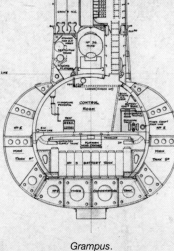

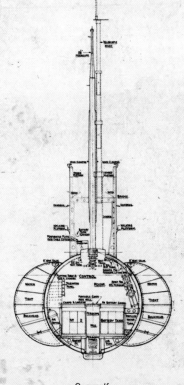

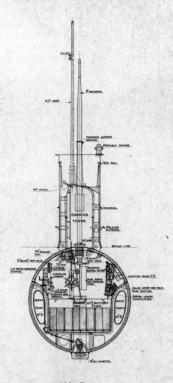

Thames.
(© National Maritime
Museum, Part of M1074)

Grampus.
(© National Maritime
Museum, Part of M1087)

Seawolf.
(© National Maritime
Museum, Part of M1091)

Undine.
(© National Maritime
Museum, Part of M1108)

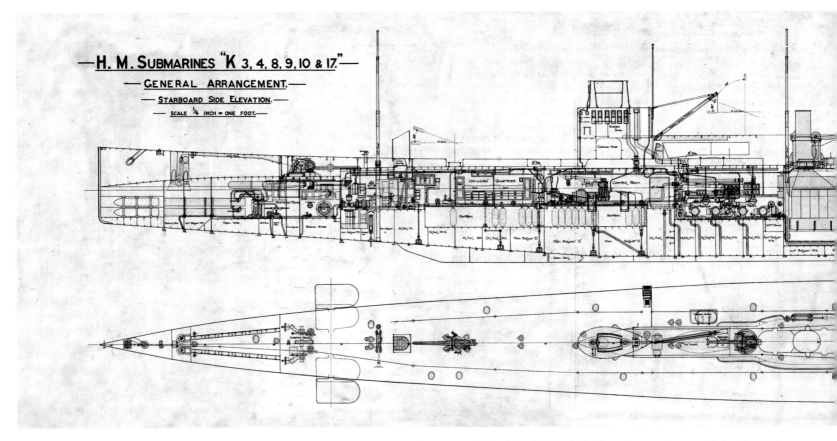

This is the configuration of the 'K'-class steam submarines as built. The deck view under the port profile gives a sense of how much of the submarine was taken up by her three separate power plants (steam, diesel, electric motor). The athwartships torpedo tubes are not visible, although athwartships torpedoes are shown as dashed lines in the torpedo room forward of the boilers.
(© National Maritime Museum J8698 and J8699)

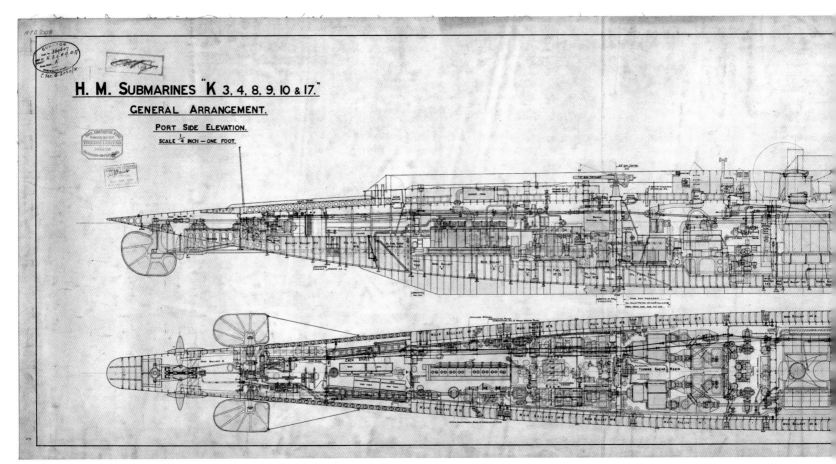

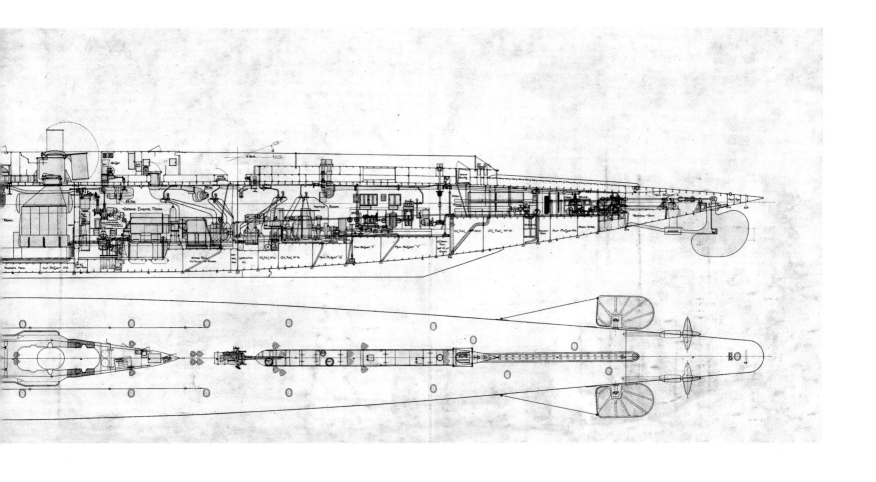

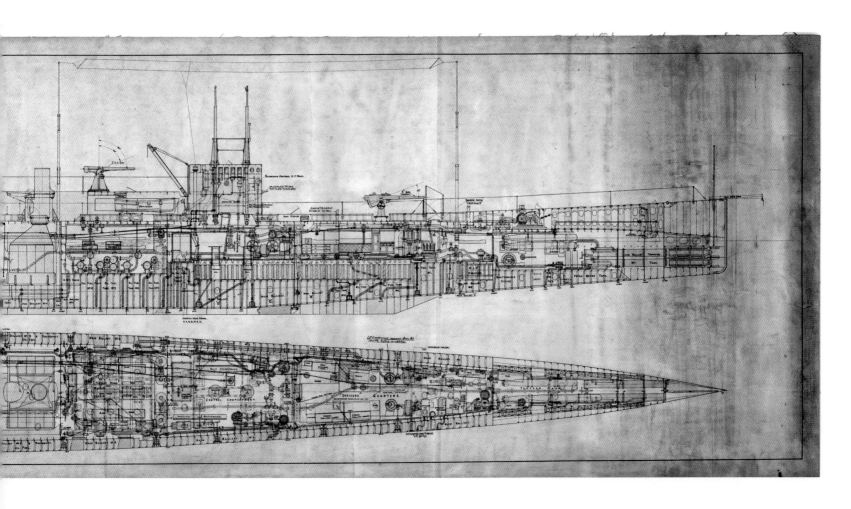

H.M. SUBMARINE "L 52".

PROFILE AND TOPSIDES. (AS FITTED)

SCALE ¼ INCH – 1 FOOT.

L 52 was the ultimate development of First World War patrol submarines, modified with a heavy gun battery (two 4in) for sudden attacks against U-boats. Note the watertight access trunks near the guns, in which their crews could wait as the submarine surfaced rapidly.
(© National Maritime Museum M1069)

PROFILE

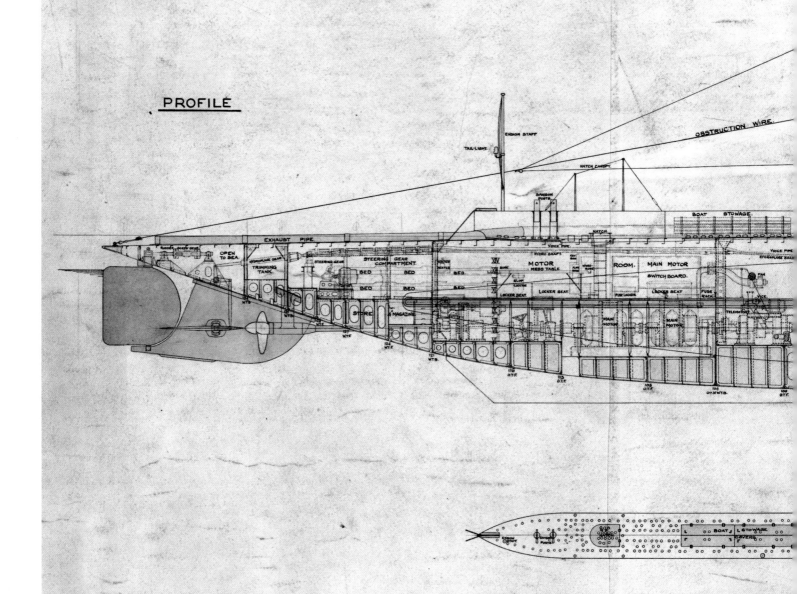

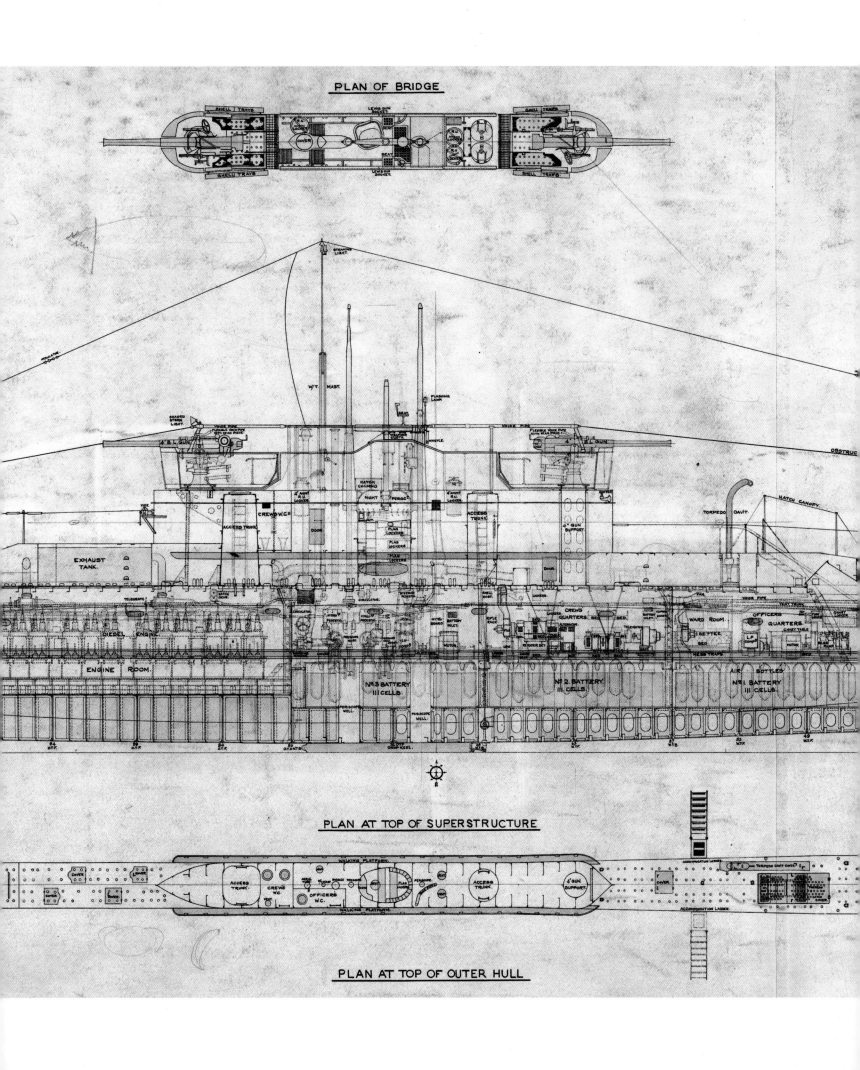

PLAN OF BRIDGE

PLAN AT TOP OF SUPERSTRUCTURE

PLAN AT TOP OF OUTER HULL

As a diesel fleet submarine, *Thames* needed massive supercharged diesel engines, the superchargers being driven by motors powered indirectly by a separate diesel generator abaft her main motors. This was the sort of space a 'K'-class submarine devoted to her steam plant. The ship's Type 120A Asdic transducer is barely visible under her torpedo room forward. (© National Maritime Museum M1075)

H. M. S. "THAMES."
GENERAL ARRANGEMENT.

PORT ELEVATION.

SCALE ¼ INCH = ONE FOOT.

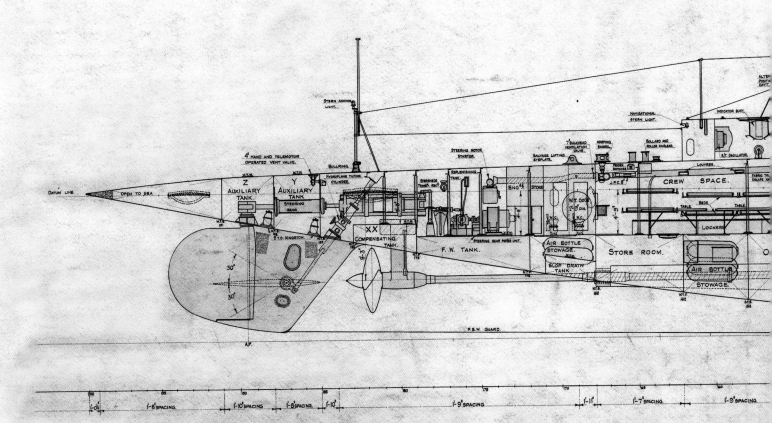

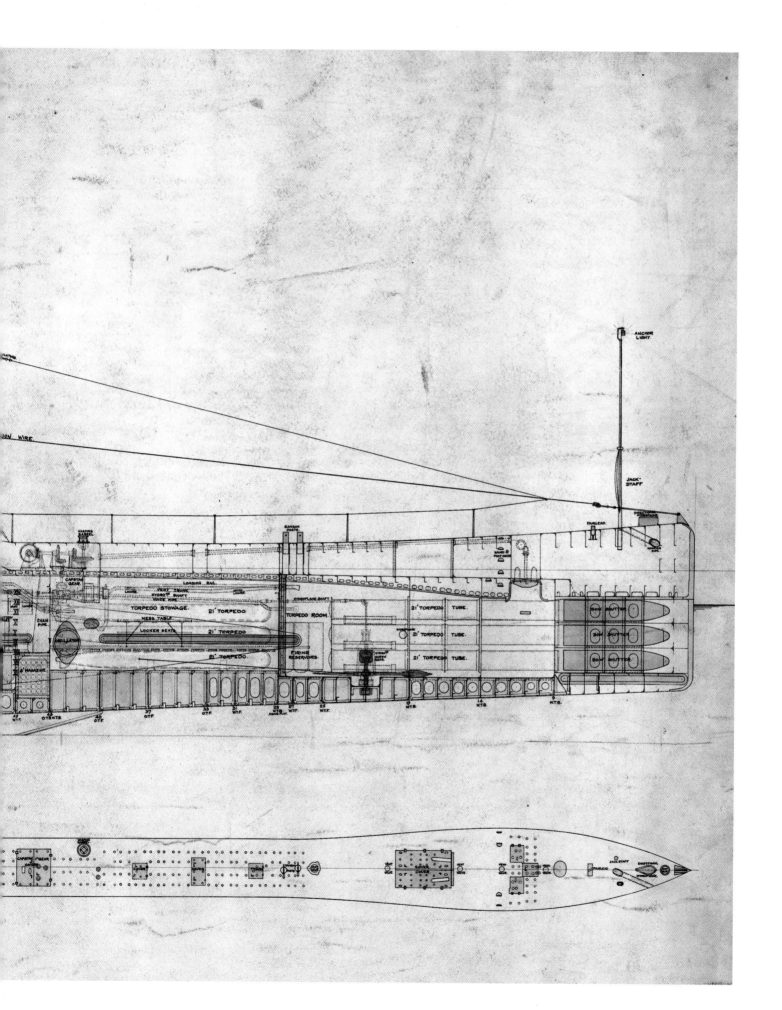

H. M. SUBMARINE "SEAWOLF".
PORT PROFILE.
(AS FITTED.)
SCALE $\frac{1}{4}" = 1$ FOOT.

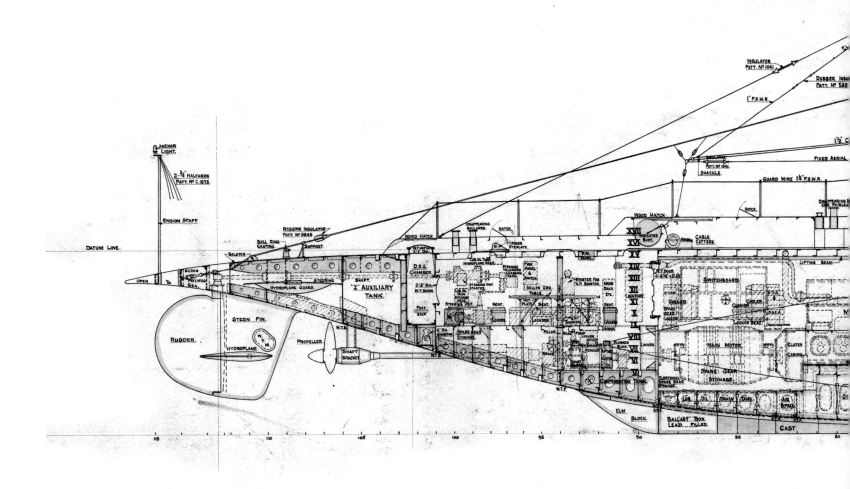

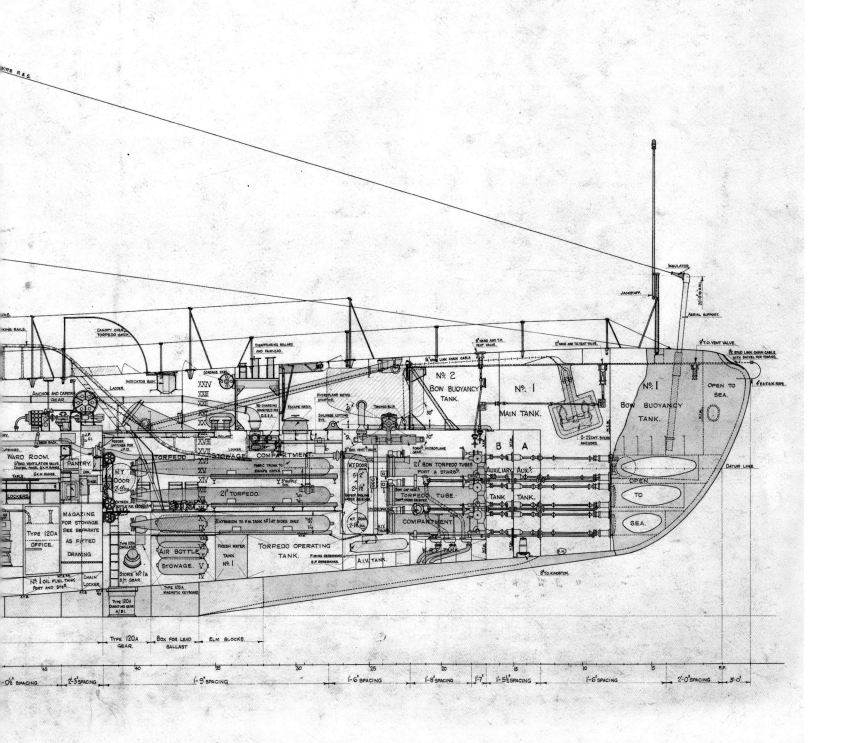

WIRE P.&S.

KING RAILS.

CANOPY OVER
TORPEDO HATCH.

No. 2
BOW BUOYANCY
TANK.

No. 1
MAIN TANK.

No. 1
BOW BUOYANCY
TANK.

OPEN TO
SEA.

JACKSTAFF.

INSULATOR.

AERIAL SUPPORT.

8" STUD LINK CHAIN CABLE
WITH SWIVEL FOR TOWING.

4" E.S.F.& W. ROPE.

6" T.O. VENT VALVE.

4" STUD LINK CHAIN CABLE.

6" HAND AND T.O.
VENT VALVE.

12" HAND AND T.O. VENT VALVE.

6" BKHD. VENTILATION VALVE.

DISAPPEARING BOLLARD
AND FAIRLEAD.

INDICATOR BUOY.

ANCHOR AND CAPSTAN
GEAR.

LADDER.

CORDAGE REEL.

RE-CHARGING
MANIFOLD FOR
D.S.E.A.

ESCAPE HATCH.

HYDROPLANE MOTOR
STARTER.

SALVAGE LIFTING
EYE.

TOWING SLIP.

2-22CWT. BYERS
ANCHORS.

DATUM LINE.

OPEN
TO
SEA.

WARD ROOM.
6" BKHD. VENTILATION VALVE
CONTROL PANEL & G.K.M. RANGE

PANTRY.

G.K.M. RANGE.

TABLE

LOCKERS

MAGAZINE
FOR STOWAGE
SEE SEPARATE
AS FITTED
DRAWING

TORPEDO STOWAGE COMPARTMENT

W.T.
DOOR
2'-9¾"

21" TORPEDO.

FABRIC TRUNK TO
ESCAPE HATCH.

S'PPLY
TANK.

W.T. DOOR
5'-½"

BKHD. VENT VALVE.

TORPEDO EMBARKING GEAR.

21" BOW TORPEDO TUBES
PORT & STARB⁰.

FORW⁰. HYDROPLANE
GEAR.

B
TANK.

A
TANK.

AUXILIARY AUX².
TANK.

BOW CAP HDLG.
GEAR.

TORPEDO TUBE.
TORP. CROSS RECEIVER

HYDROPHONE.

N.R.F. TANK.

TYPE 120A
OFFICE.

AIR BOTTLE
STOWAGE.

FRESH WATER
TANK
No. 1

TORPEDO OPERATING
TANK.

FIRING RESERVOIR.
B.P. RESERVOIR.

A.I.V. TANK.

No. 1 OIL FUEL TANK
PORT AND STB⁰.

CHAIN
LOCKER.

STORE No. 1 &
S/T. GEAR.

TYPE 105A
MAGNETIC KEYBOARD

TYPE 120A
DIRECTING GEAR
A/S.L.

8" TO KINGSTON.

TYPE 120A
GEAR.

BOX FOR LEAD
BALLAST.

ELM BLOCKS.

48   40   35   30   25   20   17 15   10   5   F.P.

0'½" SPACING   2'-3" SPACING   1'-9" SPACING   1'-6" SPACING   1'-8" SPACING   1'-7" 1'-5½" SPACING   1'-6" SPACING   2'-0" SPACING   3'-0"

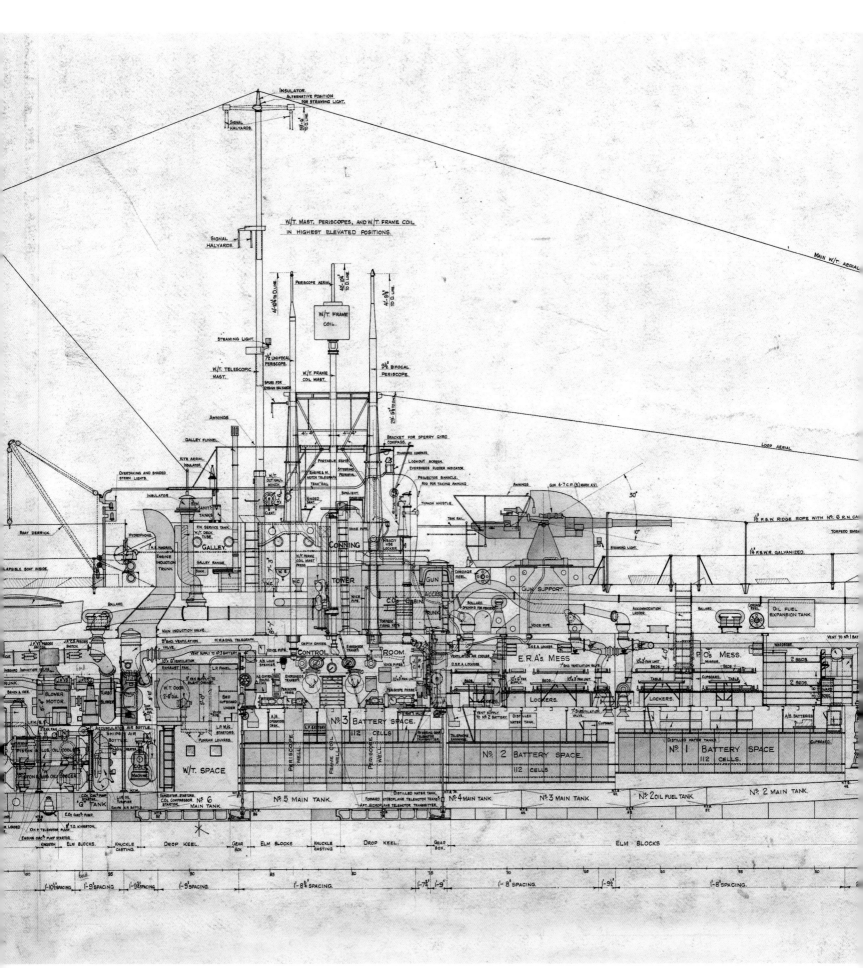

W/T MAST, PERISCOPES, AND W/T FRAME COIL
IN HIGHEST ELEVATED POSITIONS.

The much smaller *Seawolf* offered the same torpedo salvo as the huge
Thames, but she had nothing like the same speed or endurance.
(© National Maritime Museum M1093)

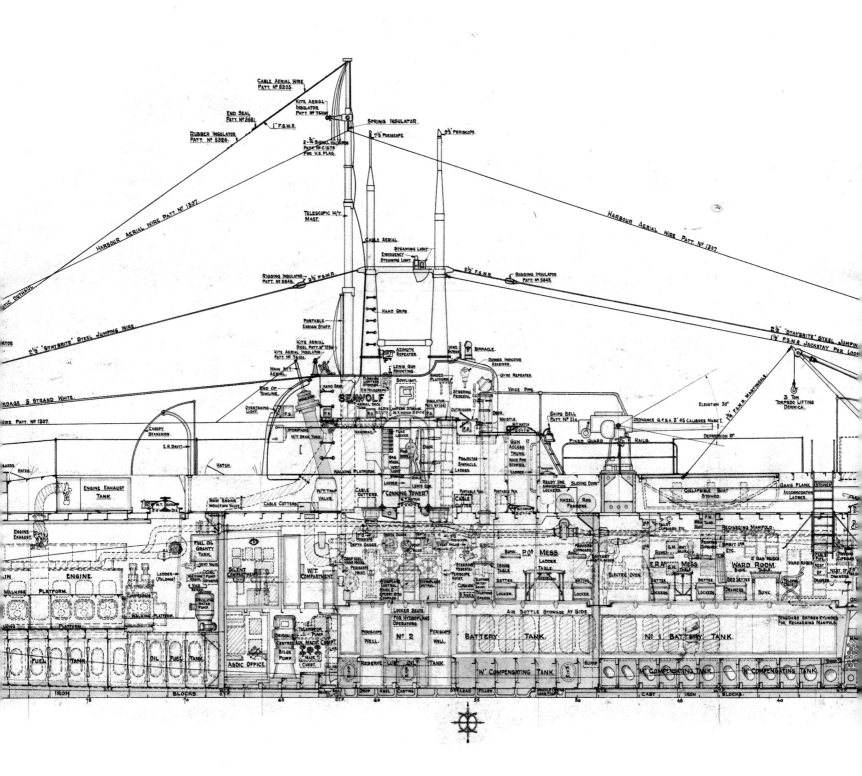

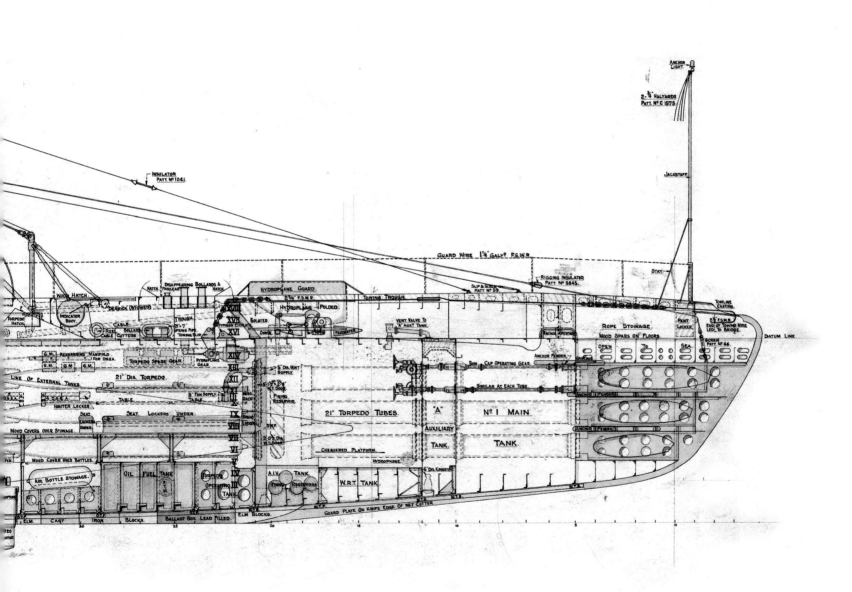

ANCHOR
LIGHT.

2-¾" HALYARDS
PATT. N° C 1575

JACKSTAFF

INSULATOR
PATT. N° 1041.

GUARD WIRE 1¼" GALV° F.S.W.R.

RIGGING INSULATOR
PATT. N° 5845.

STAY.

Slip & Screw
Patt N° 59

TOWLINE
CASTING

DISAPPEARING BOLLARDS &
HATCH

HYDROPLANE. GUARD.

TOWING TROUGH.

WOOD HATCH

2¾" F.S.W.R.

2¾ F.S.W.R.
END OF TOWING WIRE
LED TO BRIDGE

DERRICK (STOWED)

HYDROPLANE FOLDED

ROPE STOWAGE

PAINT
LOCKER

DATUM LINE

INDICATOR
BUOY

HATCH

BOLSTER

TYPHOON EYEPLATE

VENT VALVE TO
"A" AUXT TANK.

WOOD SPARS ON FLOORS

SCREW
PATT. N° 66.

TORPEDO
HATCH

CABLE
BOLLARD & HATCH

TROUGH

FAIRWATER

OPEN

TO

SEA

FREE
CABLE

SPRING PIPE
TOWING SLIP

CUTTERS

ANCHOR APERTURE

RECHARGING MANIFOLD
FOR D.S.E.A.

TORPEDO SPARE GEAR.

HYDROPLANE
GEAR.

BON CAP OPERATING GEAR.

ANCHOR FENDER

G.M.

G.M.

5" DIA VENT
SUPPLY.

LINE OF EXTERNAL TANKS

21" DIA TORPEDO.

5"-½"x 2¼"
W.T. DOOR.

SIMILAR AT EACH TUBE.

ANCHOR (FENDER)

IGNITER LOCKER

5" FAN SUPPLY
TABLE

FIRING
RESERVOIR.

TABLE

MESS
RACK

SEAT
LOCKER

SEAT LOCKERS UNDER.

BREAD
LOCKER

21" TORPEDO TUBES.

"A"

N° 1 MAIN

ANCHOR (FENDER)

WOOD COVERS OVER STOWAGE.

2-0½ DIA
W.T.DOOR.

AUXILIARY

TANK.

CHEQUERED PLATFORM.

HYDROPHONE.

TANK.

WOOD COVER OVER BOTTLES.

AIR BOTTLE STOWAGE.

OIL FUEL TANK

O.M.

TORPEDO
OPERATING
TANK

A.I.V. TANK

FIRING
RESERVOIRS

W.R.T. TANK.

6" DIA KINGSTON

ELM.

CAST

IRON

BLOCKS.

BALLAST BOX LEAD FILLED.

ELM BLOCKS.

GUARD PLATE ON KNIFE EDGE OF NET CUTTER

PLAN Nº 305.

H. M. S. "UNBROKEN", "UNISON", "UNITED", "UNRUFFLED", "UNRIVALLED", "UNSHAKEN", "P 48", "UNSEEN".

GENERAL ARRANGEMENT. (AS FITTED.)

PORT ELEVATION AND PLAN VIEWS.

SCALE. ¼ INCH = ONE FOOT.

Conceived for training, the small 'U'-class submarines proved extremely successful in European waters. *Unbroken* is shown as built, before radar was installed; note her tall wireless mast and its stowage position folded down abaft her bridge fairwater. She lacks the three machine guns later installed. Propulsion was diesel-electric, which meant that the dynamo (generator) driven by the diesel was separate from the electric motor driving the propellers. That is more evident in the plan view than in the inboard profile. (© National Maritime Museum M1105)

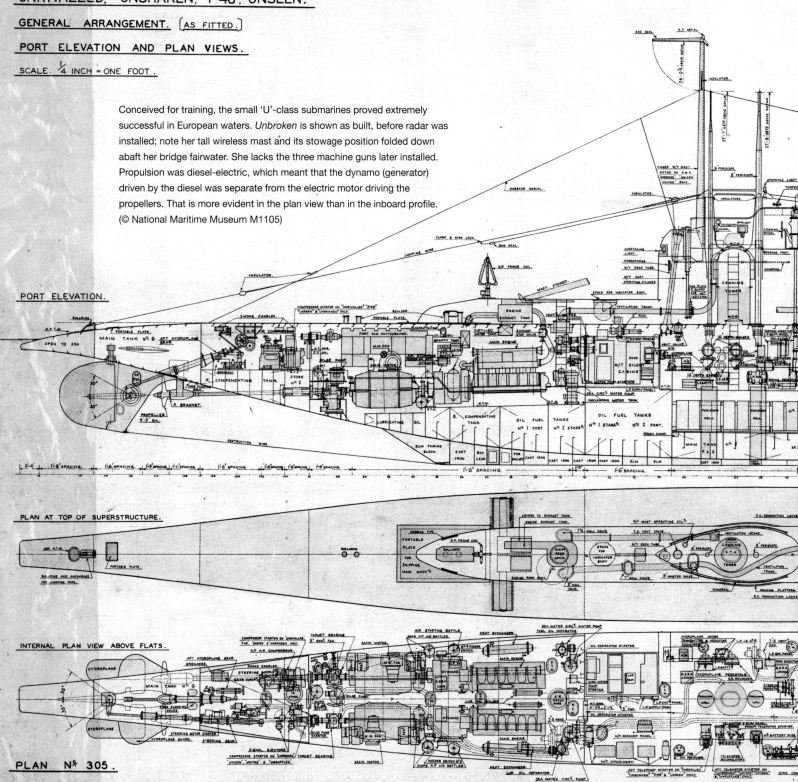

PORT ELEVATION.

PLAN AT TOP OF SUPERSTRUCTURE.

INTERNAL PLAN VIEW ABOVE FLATS.

PLAN Nº 305.

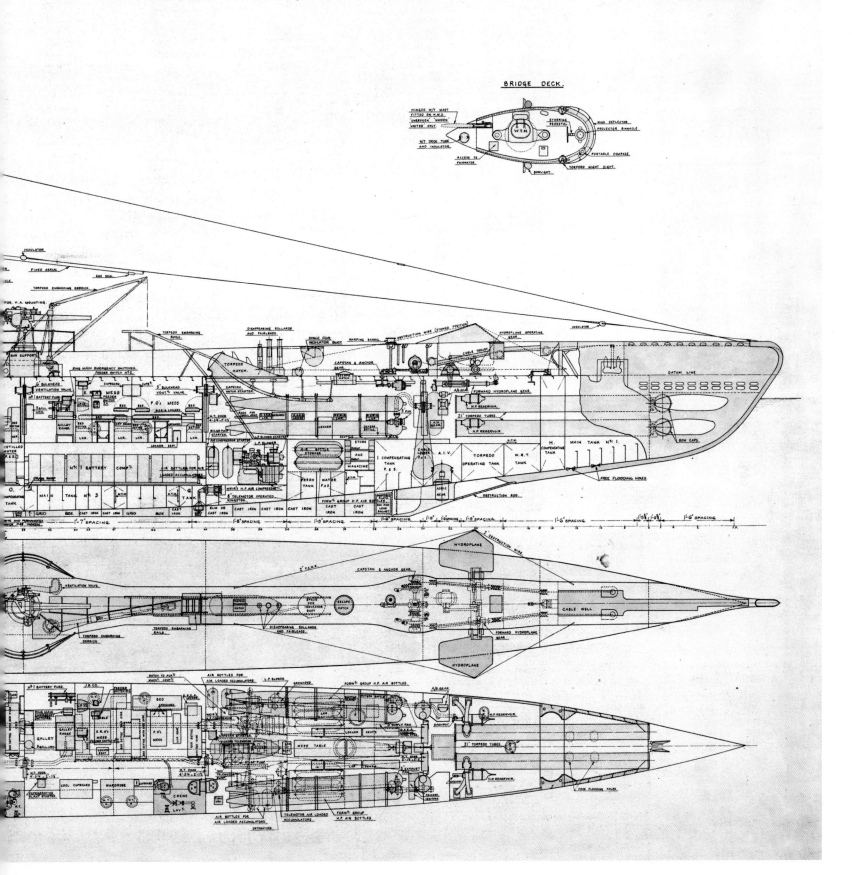

BRIDGE DECK.

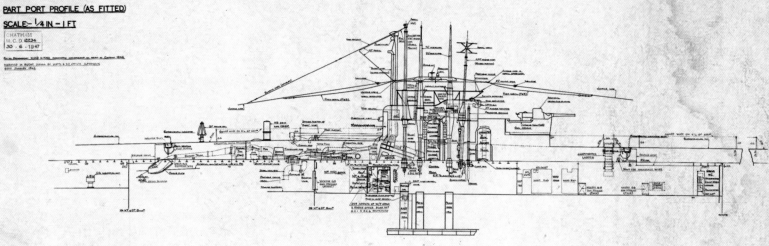

H. M. S. "THULE"
PART PORT PROFILE (AS FITTED)
SCALE:- 1/4 IN = 1 FT

H. M. S. "THULE"
PART PLAN OF FLAT (AS FITTED)
SCALE:- 1/4 IN = 1 FT

H.M.S "THULE"
PART STARBOARD PROFILE (AS FITTED)
SCALE:-1/4" = 1FOOT

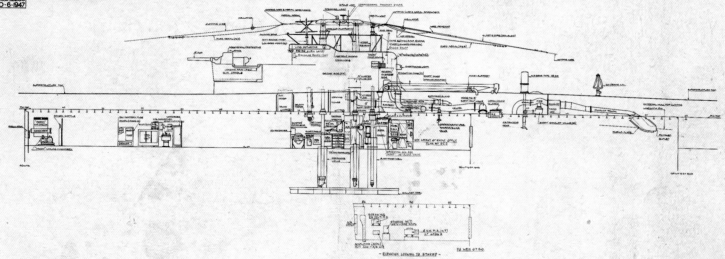

Thule shows the snorkel ('snort') conversion applied to British 'T'-class submarines soon after the Second World War. It was far more extensive than its US counterpart. These drawings also show the radar arrangement applied late in the war, with the X-shaped air-warning antenna moved to the fore end of the bridge fairwater (the antenna at the after end was for surface search). Cross-hatched lines show how the induction and exhaust piping of the main engines had to be altered, the 8in induction pipe passing up through the new snort mast instead of up the after end of the fairwater. (© National Maritime Museum M1102, M1103 and M1104)

CHAPTER 15
THE SECOND WORLD WAR

British submarines fought in every theatre of the Second World War, from the Arctic to the tropics. The British submarine service fought a very intense war; it lost many more submarines than the much larger US submarine force, which even so lost a higher percentage of its personnel than any other US Navy branch. Its greatest protracted struggle against shipping, which might be compared to the Battle of the Atlantic or to the US-led attack on Japanese shipping, was the fight to cut the supply lines across the Mediterranean to Italian and German troops in North Africa. The British anti-shipping campaign

was credited with starving Rommel and thus stopping his 1942 offensive. Compared to the Japanese, the Royal Italian Navy was a much more effective anti-submarine force, and the cost of success was high. In all, seventy-six British submarines were lost during the war. The loss figure includes British-built ships manned by Allied crews under British operational control.

After the first nineteen War Programme submarines it was decided not to name any more, referring to them instead by their pennant numbers, all of which began with the letter P. The first boat of the

The wartime Royal Navy: from left to right these are a pre-war 'S'-class submarine (identifiable by her saddle tanks), a 'U' class, a wartime 'S' class (note the stern torpedo tube), and two more 'U' class. None has either of the two major wartime modifications, radar and 20mm guns. Note too that not all have D/F antennas, and that none has the standard wartime Type 138 Asdic aft. The boat on the far right is HMS *Unison*, completed in February 1942. (John Lambert collection)

second Vickers batch of 'U' class, originally to have been *Ullswater*, was changed to *P 31*, further boats following in sequence omitting numbers containing a zero. The first of the repeat 'S' class was initially *P 61*, but this was later changed to *P 211* (*P 213* was omitted); the first of the next batch of 'T' class was *P 311*, and the first of the new minelayers (later cancelled) would have been *P 411*. Numbers were also applied to US submarines acquired for training under Lend-Lease. In December 1942 Churchill demanded that submarines be named, for morale purposes; that finally happened on 1 February 1943.

Torpedoes and Their Control[1]

In 1939 there were too few modern torpedoes, and production was limited. There was an insufficient reserve of the current Mk VIII* and -*E, and the follow-on Mk VIII** had not yet passed its sea trials. Some submarines were still using the previous standard Mk IV, which had been introduced for both surface ships and submarines in 1917. Because so many remained in 1939, during the torpedo famine it was used by some newer submarines. It could not stand pressure below 100ft. The warhead was 515lbs of TNT. It normally ran at 40 knots (5000 yds). The Mk IV* SL surface-ship version was used by some submarines during the torpedo famine. Its running depth could not be altered once it was loaded. Speed was 35 knots (7000 yds). Mk II was an even older wet heater torpedo, typically used only for practice in the 1930s, but fired by some submarines during the 1940–1 torpedo famine. It carried 228lbs of dry guncotton explosive. Original performance was 5000 yds at 40 knots.

To carry a heavier warhead (750lbs), Mk VIII used a more efficient burner (semi-diesel) propulsion cycle.[2] It could stand 300ft depth. Depth could be set at 8ft to 44ft. When fired by a deeply submerged submarine, it typically required 350 yds to come up to set depth. Like Mk IV, it had a range of 5000 yds at 40 knots, but it would keep running at decreasing speed out to 9000 yds. Mk VIII*E, introduced in 1943, had a stronger air vessel (3000 psi vs 2500 psi); range at 40 knots increased to 7000 yds (over-run to 11,500 yds). Mk VIII**, introduced just before the end of the war, had an alternative 45-knot rating (5000 yds, over-run 10,000 yds). During the war, TNT warheads were replaced by Torpex, which was 25 per cent more powerful. After the war, Mk VIII was retained because the new homing torpedoes were not designed to deal with surface targets; this torpedo sank the Argentine cruiser *General Belgrano* in 1982.

British submarine torpedoes could be angled to turn 90° after firing (90-0-90 gear), but attacks using this equipment tended to be inaccurate because the turning circles of different torpedoes varied. This feature was ordered inactivated in 1945. Very limited angling may have improved reliability.[3] However, British submarine commanders missed many shots because they could not turn onto the right track in time, and as they became increasingly aware of German and American methods of control, they demanded the ability to do the same thing.[4]

In 1939 production shifted from the Mk 3 contact exploder to the Duplex (contact and magnetic) pistol. The non-contact element imposed an unacceptable limitation on the submarine. However, with stocks of Mk 3 running down, the Duplex had to be issued in 1941 with only the impact element activated. A successor CCR (contact/non-contact) was accepted for service before the usual sea trials could be carried out. It was urgently wanted to deal with German heavy ships in Norwegian waters. After some successes in July 1942, CCR was put into limited service in the Mediterranean, where

it promised to deal with shallow-draft targets such as escorts. As with the US magnetic torpedo pistol, there were prematures, but they were attributed to minor insulation problems. Operational trials continued, and CCR pistols were issued to the 10th Submarine Flotilla in the Mediterranean in April 1944 and also to MTBs. CCRs were also issued to the Eastern Fleet, which was seeing large numbers of shallow-draft Japanese targets. The pistol did not stand up to tropical conditions, primarily due to moisture in its vacuum tubes. In January 1945 captains were ordered to set pistols to contact only unless needed for special targets, and in March the Admiralty ordered the non-contact (magnetic) feature inactivated.

The Submarine Torpedo Director (STD) Mk I equipped British Second World War submarines. The bottom dial represented the submarine, the upper one the target, the line connecting them representing the periscope line of sight. True bearing rings around each dial were fed by the gyro compass. Director Angle was displayed by the pointer on the submarine dial. Cranks on the right input, top to bottom, enemy course, enemy speed, enemy length, and range. Cranks on the left input target height and target vertical angle (as seen in the periscope) to calculate current target range. The small windows at the top for closing speed, time before firing, and distance for the submarine to run before firing, seemed reminiscent of those of a gambling 'fruit machine,' hence the nickname (the operator could set desired closing speed and firing range). This one is at the Royal Navy Submarine Museum, Gosport. (John Gourley)

The pre-war Royal Navy had few aids to fire control: the 'Is-Was', a slide rule to convert observed masthead angle into range, and 90° tables to assist in firing angled shots. The slide rule could provide estimated inclination and distance off track, plus the distance the target would cover in a given time. The first submarine automatic plots (dead-reckoning tracers) were installed in the 'River' class; it was also approved for the minelayers, but only one was installed. Other submarines used hand plots to create a picture of a tactical situation. War experience showed that an automatic plot was essential, and a new one suited to all submarines appeared in 1945. The British generally turned the submarine in the direction of fire. This was called 'catching the DA [director angle]'. It took time. The British hitting rate was about the same as the American, suggesting that better manoeuvrability made up for a more primitive system.

Hugh Clausen, who had worked on the big Admiralty fire-control computers, began work on a submarine torpedo director (STD) in 1932, based on a 1929 proposal by Captain G W Wadham, who was then at Fort Blockhouse.[5] Wadham envisaged something like the B Sight then being installed on board cruisers. A demonstration model was produced in 1934, and a production prototype in 1936. The main problem it solved was to compensate for the turn a torpedo made when angled 90° (for a time continuous angling was contemplated, but it was rejected). Total production for the Royal Navy was just under 300, plus 80 made in the United States for the Soviet Navy.

In effect the STD was a much better equivalent of the 'Is-Was'. Inputs were own course (from gyro), range, current enemy bearing (from the periscope), estimated enemy course and desired track angle (angle between torpedo and enemy course). Unlike fire-control computers, the STD did not embody a model of the tactical situation (a position-keeper); its solution depended on what could be seen from the periscope at the moment of firing. Its most important feature was correction for both the distance from periscope to torpedo tube muzzle and for torpedo turning circle in the case of angled shots. The face of the STD showed two dials, one for enemy and one for own ship. Enemy course was entered using a handle; own course was automatically entered. Range was entered using a handle. Range could be computed automatically from mast height. The line connecting the two dials represented the line between the submarine and the target; the enemy-ship dial could be rotated to bring the own-ship dial to the present periscope angle. When that was done, a red pointer showed the calculated required director angle, taking into account convergence (the angle between the line of sight and the required path of the torpedo). This was called the 'should' pointer, as it indicated the course on which a torpedo 'should' be fired to hit. The own-ship dial carried four torpedo pointers indicating the four possible torpedo paths: directly from the bow or stern tubes, and at 90° and 180° angles. They were the 'can' pointers, showing what could be done. Track angle pointers rotating with the own-ship dial worked over the enemy dial to show the track angles which the four shots would make. Shots could be made when the 'should' and 'can' pointers lined up. When they did not line up, the future DA could be read off, for example after the submarine altered course. The STD was called the 'fruit machine' in analogy to one-armed bandit gambling machines.

In May 1934 a hand-worked model was installed in the Submarine Attack Teacher at Fort Blockhouse. It demonstrated that, with some modifications, it could solve all the problems currently solved using the 'Is-Was', the Combined Slide Rule, the Periscope Angle Tables and the Asdic Torpedo Correction Tables. Two STDs were ordered for

trials.[6] The production prototype was completed about mid-1937 and was initially retained by the manufacturer, Evershed. It was installed in *Sunfish* and was initially used by the CO Qualifying Course.[7] Initial deliveries planned for May 1938 were delayed. STD was in all Royal Navy submarines by 1940.

The Royal Navy encountered the US Torpedo Data Computer (TDC) when the fleet submarines of SubRon 50 arrived in 1942. Unlike the STD, the TDC incorporated a position-keeper, in effect a model of the engagement. The submarine commander estimated enemy course and speed; the position-keeper predicted enemy position (hence periscope angle). The submarine commander could correct estimated enemy course and speed until prediction matched reality. After that the TDC kept predicting (generating) enemy course and speed, which were fed into a triangle-solver roughly equivalent to the STD. The difference was that the solver allowed for continuously adjusting torpedo angle to hit the target, where the STD (and the Royal Navy) allowed for only straight and 90° or 180° angled shots. This combination allowed the submarine commander greater freedom of action. It also kept supplying current information so that a salvo could be fired at any time, even without using the periscope.[8]

The British decided that they wanted continuous angling, which they introduced in a new Mk VIII** Mod 2 in 1944.[9] In 1944 the US Navy agreed to supply twenty-four TDCs under Lend-Lease. With the end of the war in Europe, this was cut to six, one of which was installed on board HMS *Alcide*; another was set up in the Attack Teacher at Fort Blockhouse. An improved STD Mk II provided periscope angles for gyro angling in 10° steps up to 50° each way. It could handle longer-range torpedoes and could set torpedo speed. It was installed in the new 'A' class.[10]

When the British captured the German *U 570* (which became HMS *Graph*) they acquired German G7E electric torpedoes, which they copied as the 21in Type Y (later Mk 11). Initially Mk 11 was to have been used by MTBs, but after surface-firing trials failed it was offered to the submarine service. Mediterranean submarines urgently wanted a wakeless torpedo, as air escorts seeing torpedo tracks had often frustrated attacks. Mk 11 could fit a standard British torpedo tube, but it was too long to be stowed, hence had to be redesigned with a shorter warhead. Sea trials proved lengthy, and these torpedoes were not ready until the end of the war. The US Navy developed its own copy of the German electric torpedo, but it was not ready in time for the Mediterranean submarine campaign. British submarines fired 5121 torpedoes in 1671 attacks, of which 46.4 per cent were considered successful.[11]

In addition to torpedoes, some submarines carried tube-laid ground mines: thirteen 'T' class (twelve each) and three 'S' class (eight each).[12] Initial laying trials were carried out by *Tigris* and *Talisman* in 1940; mines could be laid from the internal bow tubes at speeds up to 8 knots. On this basis, on 25 September 1940 VA(S) ordered 'T'-class submarines fitted to lay mines. Problems of trim after laying were solved only after March 1941 trials by *Torbay*, and the first field laid was by *Trespasser*, off the coast of Sumatra, on 14 March 1944.

Guns

Guns were important, particularly when submarines encountered small targets. On the outbreak of war the 'T' class had 4in guns on special submarine mountings which had originally been designed for the First World War classes; work on a new mounting did not begin until 1943, mainly due to the intense pressure of other work. In the

tropics this S I mounting proved less and less satisfactory because it was more difficult to maintain, inaccurate at short ranges and slow to open fire. It also suffered from rapid corrosion. The other new submarines had smaller guns, 3in in the 'S' class (on a mounting designed in 1935) and in *Ursula*. The last seventeen 'S'-class submarines were given 4in guns at the expense of their stern torpedo tubes. As for the 'U' class, when the external tubes were eliminated a 3in gun became standard. During the war designs for new 3.5in and 4in guns were pursued, but none was mounted during the war (the new 4in gun armed submarines from 1946 on). Early in 1942 a Staff Requirement was raised to fit all new submarines with 20mm Oerlikons, mostly of a special Mk 2A type.

Major Wartime Modifications[13]

At the outbreak of war there was considerable interest in streamlining bridges to reduce underwater resistance. Cab (largely enclosed) bridges helped, but by 1941 open bridges were demanded for their better view. They were fitted with wind deflectors, which were never completely successful, partly because the rounded fore end of the bridge

Sceptre and *Volatile*, 1944. *Sceptre* shows the voice pipe to her 3in gun, and also the decking above the gun access trunk. She also shows her 20mm gun. *Volatile* shows the cylindrical dome of her Type 138 Asdic, abaft her bridge fairwater. The two circular objects visible abaft her 3in gun are ready-use ammunition lockers let into the casing above her pressure hull. (John Lambert collection)

was considered the worst shape for wind deflection. Nearby shielded 4in guns did not help. To gain space, particularly for radar masts, the bridge steering position was removed from 'S' and 'T'-class submarine and omitted from the new 'A' class.

When they went to sea in wartime, submarines generally carried far more stores than had been envisaged in their design, so that early in the war they were typically 12 to 16 tons heavy, and had difficulty trimming themselves.

Ventilation and air-conditioning proved inadequate, particularly in the Far East; one submarine had to withdraw from patrol because all personnel were exhausted from the heat. Two 55,000 BTU Freon air-conditioners were fitted to all 'S' and 'T'-class submarines. Cooled air was led to all mess spaces W/T, and radar offices. The W/T and radar panels

Sahib in May 1942 was typical of the 1940 'S' class. Note her cab bridge and the loop in her aerial wires abaft her periscopes. *Saracen* was similar. *Sea Dog* also had a cab bridge, as did others. (NHHC)

were separately cooled. All submarines were fitted with distillers. The 'A'-class staff requirement framed on the basis of this experience demanded particularly good habitability. Long periods dived fouled the air in a submarine, so air purification became important. Initially that meant spreading CO_2 absorbent and releasing bottled oxygen, but the chemicals involved were not very efficient. By the end of the war a sound-insulated blower blew air through canisters loaded with CO_2-absorbing material, while a burning cartridge in a generator released oxygen.

Endurance was inadequate, particularly in the Far East. Main ballast tanks were converted to fuel tanks to extend range, typically a pair of main tanks in 'U' and 'S'-class submarines, and two pairs in the 'T' class. Other internal tanks had to be converted to stow additional fresh water and lubricating oil.

Despite considerable interest in quieting before the war (which seems not to have been matched by other navies), the British considered their submarines too noisy at the outbreak of war. Early in 1940 reports suggested that starting up auxiliary machinery often triggered accurate hunts by an enemy relying mainly on hydrophones. A noise range was set up, based on the depot ship *Forth* in the Holy Loch. A permanent noise range was later set up at Loch Goil. Because the Mediterranean submarines also suspected that they were being hunted passively, measurement gear was set up at Alexandria and later at Malta. Most self-noise measured at this time came from propellers. That decreased with speed, so that motor sound predominated at lower speeds (it decreased as the submarine ran faster). At a critical speed, total sound was minimised. Beyond a few hundred feet, a submarine running at minimum speed was inaudible.[14] Efforts to reduce propeller singing led to the adoption of much quieter cast-iron pro-

pellers. Machinery was increasingly sound-mounted, and flexible piping was introduced. Machinery itself was silenced, particularly in respect to bearings and gears, the magnetic hum of motors, water noises, etc. For example, in 1940 the standard ballast pump could be heard at 10,000 yds, but in 1945 the ballast pump of the 'A' class was intended not to be heard beyond 500 yds in a flat calm. The initial post-war target was to be noiseless out to 100 yds. Officers were made 'self-noise' conscious, and care and maintenance of machinery began to take quietness into account. However, ships' companies too often jammed machinery in with stores and spare gear, so that the only sound insulation measure left was the flexible piping. Builders, too, sometimes ruined silencing measures.

Shock-proofing was also inadequate. Shock trials showed that pressure hulls tended to tear at 'hard spots' such as the ends of bulkhead stiffeners and brackets. Submarines were fitted with steel pads at such spots to spread out the stress. Similarly, they were fitted where lines of welding occurred exactly opposite one another on the pressure hull, one inside and one outside. The pressure hull structure was considerably simplified in the 'A' class, but that could not be applied to the earlier designs.

Trials against a full-scale submarine section (Job 81) showed that welded T-bar frames were better than the Z-bar frames previously used. Hence early war construction 'T' and 'S'-class submarines had welded T frames but riveted plating. In 1941 all 'T' and 'S'-class submarines were ordered built of a new 'S' quality steel and completely welded; they became the first major British warships to be completely welded.[15] Welding saved enough weight to thicken the pressure hulls and thus to increase diving depth (and, therefore, resistance to depth-charging). With all-welded pressure hulls, the diving depth of the 'S' and 'T' classes was increased to 350ft, and that of the 'U' class to 300ft. A higher-strength steel was developed, but welding and working procedures had not been completed by the end of the war.

Submarines were tested to greater than rated depths: to 350ft (300ft rated) for the riveted 'S' class, 400ft (350ft) for the welded 'S' class, 400ft (350ft) for the welded 'T' class, and 600ft (500ft) for the late-war 'A' class.

Engines typically ran 4000 to 5000 hours between refits, which might be 18 months apart. This was a great improvement over the 2000 to 3000-hour pre-war standard. The Vickers 'T'-class engine was considered good for up to 5000 to 6000 hours, although after 4000 hours many engines suffered from serious defects. The British used drowned (underwater) exhausts despite back pressure (from the sea) as great as 6 psi, and also despite difficulties with exhaust springs. They considered US exhausts into the air too noisy.[16]

At the outbreak of war the standard submarine radio transmitter was Type 55, designed to a 1937 RA(S) requirements. It was a high-power HF transmitter with a low-power MF attachment intended mainly for communication with merchant ships. The MF part was of little value, and in 1944 Type 55 was superseded by a version which omitted it. Submarines had HF and LF receivers, the latter allowing them to receive signals while submerged. They were considered obsolescent. Two of them employed an external oscillator (which unfortunately produced detectable signals) to receive continuous wave signals. They were superseded in 1940 by a US all-wave superheterodyne receiver, which in turn was replaced by a British set in 1942.

All submarines had four aerials: a fixed aerial for surface HF or MF transmission or reception; an HF aerial for surface or periscope-depth HF; a kite aerial for long-range MF; and a loop aerial for submerged LF reception.[17] There was also a harbour aerial for use if the submarine was W/T guard ship in harbour. Earlier large submarines also had frame D/F antennas. Masts carried their HF aerials, either hinged (in the 'U' class) or telescopic. When it became clear that submarines would do very little MF transmitting, the kite aerial was abandoned. Once radar was introduced in mid-1941, the W/T mast had to give way to a radar mast. It was accepted that HF could not be transmitted or received at periscope depth. The aerial which had been used for that purpose was connected to the after jumping wire to become the Emergency Aerial.

Submarines typically received their traffic on VLF (16 kHz) from Rugby, which initially repeated messages every four hours until traffic was cleared. That imposed an unacceptable limit on urgent operational traffic, so from 1940 on urgent message traffic was inserted in the last five minutes of each hour (increased to 20 minutes in 1943). Three were also two long series of messages each night.

When submarines went to the Far East in 1944, W/T silence seemed less and less important. Like the US Navy, the Royal Navy formed wolf packs coordinated by voice radio: both a low-power HF radio telephone and Type 86M VHF (between submarines 10nm apart and to aircraft up to 50nm away at 5000ft). Type 86 was the standard British bridge-to-bridge tactical radio, equivalent to the US TBS. Without a VLF station to support them, Far East submarines relied on HF, and were given HF aerials usable at periscope depth. The aerial lead-in was modified to receive HF at periscope depth; another aerial was led to the radar mast. Early war patrols revealed the need for an MF/DF set; FM 4 was introduced in 1940, and later superseded by FM 11.

The standard submarine Asdic in 1939 was Type 129, which was later supplied to French, Dutch, Russian, and Turkish submarines and also to British submarines transferred to Allied navies. It was intended to operate mainly as a hydrophone on the surface and also for supersonic telegraphy (S/T) communication. When submerged it could also be used for echo ranging, for sonar interception, and as a highly directional hydrophone when firing from deep, using its 10 kHz oscillator at 50 kHz.[18] Fitted with a chemical recorder and a short-pulse unit, Type 129 also proved useful for locating enemy minefields. Submarines typically used it passively, so they were silenced to improve performance. When listening while surfaced 'U'-class submarines suffered from airborne diesel noise, so an additional remote listening position was provided forward; similar positions were later installed in 'S' and 'T'-class submarines. Asdic communication, which had been developed before the war, was used in European waters, e.g., so that a submarine out of range of a target could tip off a submarine which was likely to be in range when the target appeared. In the Far East it supported wolf pack tactics.

Submarines also had Type 710 plate hydrophones as a secondary

Photographed in 1946, *Sturdy* shows the cylindrical dome of the Type 138 Asdic fitted to British submarines at the end of the war. Photos of such boats taken in 1944 do not show it. She has the full Type 267PW radar, incorporating a microwave surface-search set. The air-warning component (Type 291W) has been relocated to a position forward of the periscopes. The microwave surface element (Type 267W) is on a new mast abaft the after periscope standard; its antenna is visible above the wireless aerials. Late-war and post-war 'T'-class submarines had similar radar arrangements, the 'T'-class operations room being rearranged drastically to suit the new equipment. (RAN Naval Historical Section via Dr Josef Straczek)

The amidships part of *Turpin* (1945) shows the initial radar arrangement: a microwave surface-search set forward of the search periscope, and the Type 291W air-search set on a telescoping mast abaft the attack periscope. The mast of the surface-search set did not telescope, so the radar could not be used while the submarine was submerged. The ultimate arrangement was to place the air-search antenna forward of the periscopes and to provide a telescoping mast abaft them for the surface-search element. (Alan C Green via State Library of Victoria)

means of listening, but they were not considered reliable and range was not good. Reports of grunts and groans heard in the North Sea prompted installation of an amplifier, to detect possible enemy sonar pulses. It was fitted to *Sturgeon* and *Tuna*. Special amplifiers were fitted to *Tigris* and *Tuna*. Tested on board HMS *Graph*, a new amplifier gave results comparable to those the Germans were getting with their array hydrophones.

A secondary Asdic was wanted to cover the blind arc astern, to listen when the submarine was bottomed, to listen when Type 129 was out of action, and to listen to a second target or an escort. This was Type 138, introduced in 1944. Its oscillator was mounted on the after casing, trained by hand from the engine room. It had no transmitter. It was widely used in the Far East, and was modified so that it could be power-trained and controlled from the control room.

The main new wartime sensor was radar, beginning with Type 286PW in 1941. The first installation, on board HMS *Proteus*, was completed in July 1941, using the existing W/T mast. Although performance was erratic, on one occasion excellent range and bearing of an enemy convoy were obtained. Meanwhile the much more powerful Type 291, using the same antenna, was being developed. It became the

standard wartime British submarine radar, the main problem being to find enough internal space. Nearly all British submarines had it by 1944.[19] German radar detectors at Stadlandet and Obrestad in Norway could and did detect British submarines, but British fears that such devices would be more widely installed proved unfounded. No German aircraft seem to have homed in on British submarine radar beams.

Some British submarines in the Far East were fitted with US SJ microwave surface radars.[20] By late in the war there was a British equivalent, incorporated in a new standard Type 267PW radar, which combined Type 291 with a new surface-search element. Initial installations (267W) had a mast fitted immediately forward of the forward periscope, the mast rotating but not capable of being raised. Later (267MW), the aircraft-warning component was moved forward and a new telescoping mast added abaft the periscopes for the surface warning component.

War Service

In 1939 the Royal Navy had five submarine flotillas: one with each major fleet (1st with the Mediterranean Fleet, 2nd with Home Fleet, and 4th with the China Fleet) plus 5th Flotilla at Portsmouth (training, trials, and running reserve) and 6th at Portland (Asdic training and experiments and three reserve submarines).

Plans for a European war emphasised the threat of the German surface fleet: it would have been covered by 3rd Flotilla in the Heligoland Bight and 2nd in the Skagerrak or Kattegat.[21] They would be under the operational control of RA(S). Two minelayers would have operated in the in the estuaries of the Elbe and the Weser. The post-

Transfers were the quickest way to make up for wartime submarine losses. The initial spring 1941 British request for US warships (to be provided under Lend-Lease) included forty submarines as an urgent item. The United States transferred nine: six 'S' class (which broadly approximated the First World War 'L' class) and three smaller single-hull 'R' class. *P 511*, shown on 16 February 1943, was the former *R 3*. All were used mainly for training, but occasionally as convoy escorts. The first to be transferred were *R 3* and *S 25* (which became *P 551*), on 4 November 1941. At that time the US Navy had nineteen 'R'-class and thirty-eight 'S'-class submarines on hand, but it is not clear whether the British were hoping for something more modern. All other transfers were made in wartime. Just before the outbreak of war the US Navy offered eighteen submarines (apparently six 'S' and twelve 'R' class) including the two already transferred, subject to reconsideration if the United States entered the war, as it did. At that time it was agreed that if the United States entered the war before transferring half the agreed submarines, old US-manned submarines would be based at the Gareloch (the rest of the planned eighteen) and at Gibraltar (ten 'S' class). The British hoped that some of the US submarines operating on the East Coast and in the Caribbean could be sent as Task Forces to work from Gibraltar and the UK, as had been previously intended. Presumably the detachment of a squadron of modern US fleet submarines (SubRon 50) to British waters in 1942 reflected this policy (the US Navy also detached large surface ships to supplement the Home Fleet at Scapa Flow). In December 1941 the British Admiralty Delegation was asking for the remaining twenty-two submarines under the proposed Third Lend-Lease Appropriation Act, but it was aware that none was likely to be provided out of US production; US capacity was barely enough to meet US programme requirements, which amounted to eighty-three submarines by 1944. The Admiralty Delegation had drawn up a list of deficiencies in British warship numbers due to the outbreak of war with Japan, showing an immediate need for thirty-five more submarines, and an expected deficiency of fifty-five as of January 1944. In this series of charts, the requirement for submarines to be laid down in 1942 was thirty-eight, to be completed by January 1944. Ultimately no modern US submarines were transferred to the Royal Navy.

Munich mobilisation included an enormous increase in anti-submarine ships and craft, all of which needed training by 'tame' submarines. New war plans for war against Germany and Italy were issued early in 1939, assuming France would be an ally. The Mediterranean Fleet would move to Alexandria, because Malta was considered too vulnerable to air attack. Due to the threat of air attack, shipping would be routed around the Cape. However, Malta was retained as an air and submarine base.

It seems to have been obvious as early as July 1939 that war was imminent. Manning of reserve submarines began about 3 July. On 31 August a patrol line was set up to intercept German ships and U-boats sailing before war broke out, but the Germans had already gone to sea.[22] Once the Italians announced that they would not enter the war, the Mediterranean submarines were nearly all moved into home waters, where they were urgently needed, particularly as the Home Fleet submarines took early losses. Thus by March 1940 only three 'O'-boats were left at Malta.[23]

In the run-up to war in Europe, attention was still being paid to possible war in the Far East. In that case the bulk of the Mediterranean Fleet would have formed a War Fleet despatched to Singapore. The Mediterranean Fleet therefore included the three 'River' (G)-class fast submarines. Three of the minelayers were assigned to the Home Fleet, and two more to the China Fleet. The latter included all thirteen of the 'O', 'P', and 'R' classes.[24] Just before war broke out, the Committee on Imperial Defence wanted more submarines sent there to deter the Japanese from further aggression in China.

When war broke out in Europe the Royal Navy valued its submarines mainly for reconnaissance – the important First World War role of watching enemy bases. In 1939–40 the British had nothing like the advantage of code-breaking they had enjoyed in the previous war. Air reconnaissance was often hindered by weather. Submarine commanders were generally discouraged from attacking major enemy ships they saw, because an attack would prompt a counter-attack which would hold the submarine down and preclude reporting. The main exception to reconnaissance was the assignment of big patrol submarines to the Atlantic on anti-raider patrols.[25]

As the war progressed, submarine commanders were allowed to sink shipping on sight in wider and wider areas, beginning with a portion of the Skagerrak during the Norwegian campaign.[26] Other areas were later opened up. Initially, too, as in the First World War, British submarines were assigned to attack U-boats. As early as September 1940 there were day submerged attacks on U-boats using Asdic, but they were unsuccessful.[27]

There was a running debate over whether submarines could or should escort convoys, as a deterrent to surface attack. For example, the idea was raised (again) after the 'pocket battleship' *Admiral Scheer* attacked Convoy HX 84. VA(S) generally opposed it, because the escorting submarine might easily be mistaken for a U-boat and sunk by other convoy escorts. In 1940–1 VA(S) consented reluctantly on the grounds that trade protection was a crucial Royal Navy task. No convoy escorted by a submarine in the Atlantic was attacked, but that

does not prove that the idea was wrong; the French in particular advocated submarine escorts for their deterrent effect on surface raiders.[28] Even minor damage would force a major German warship home, because repair facilities were so limited; for example, *Bismarck* had to turn towards the French coast after taking a hit in a fuel tank. Submarine escorts were particularly common in Arctic convoys threatened by major German surface ships.

When it became clear that Italy was about to enter the war (about May 1940), the only source of reinforcement submarines was the fifteen large patrol submarines of the China Fleet. The war plan against Italy required thirteen British submarines, even though the French had fifty-three of their own in the Mediterranean. Japan was not then showing any aggressiveness. Initially the depot ship *Medway* and five submarines were sent from Singapore. By mid-May 1940 there were twelve large submarines at Alexandria along with the depot ship. Six of these submarines were sent to Malta, including two minelayers (the mines on the station were all at Malta). Italy declared war on 10 June, but on 25 June France declared an armistice with Germany, transforming the situation in the Mediterranean.

Up to that point, the substantial Italian army in Libya had been only a limited threat to Egypt and the Suez Canal, because in the west it faced a large French army in Tunisia, backed by more troops in Algeria. Freed from that threat, it could move east. Its logistical support defined the rest of the submarine war in the Mediterranean: it depended on supplies sent from Italy, and also on coastal shipping to distribute them. Since the success of the Italian convoys largely determined whether the army in Africa could attack (or even survive), ultimately the convoy war against the Italians largely decided what would happen to Egypt.[29] Conversely, because the attacks on the convoys would have been ineffective without Malta, the fight to keep the island alive became crucial to the British. Brutal losses to British convoys eventually forced, among other things, the use of submarines to bring in vital supplies.

As in the Battle of the Atlantic, submarine operations against this shipping depended on intelligence. Unfortunately the Italians changed their ciphers on the outbreak of war, for a time denying the British signals intelligence. The Italians began air raids against Malta, the vital submarine base athwart their convoy routes, for a time forcing the submarines there to retire to Alexandria.

Due to their state of completion, some of the 1940–1 'U' class had to retain more or less bulbous bows, although their external tubes were eliminated. This is *Upholder*, the top-scoring British submarine. Others with this type of bow were *Unique*, *Upright*, *Usk*, *Utmost* and *Unbroken*. (John Lambert collection)

HM SUBMARINES *STURDY* AND *STYGIAN*. General arrangements. A 1940 'S' class with stern torpedo tube. (© National Maritime Museum J8948)

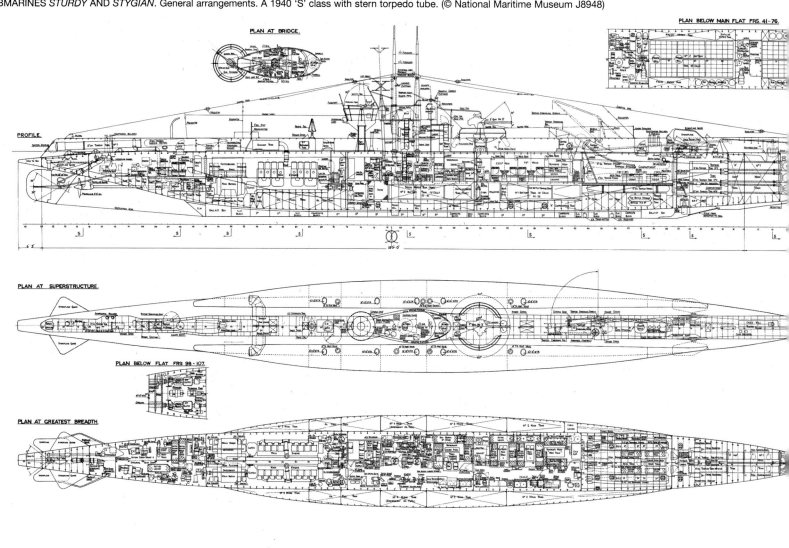

HM SUBMARINES *STURDY* AND *STYGIAN*. Port profile. (© National Maritime Museum J9033)

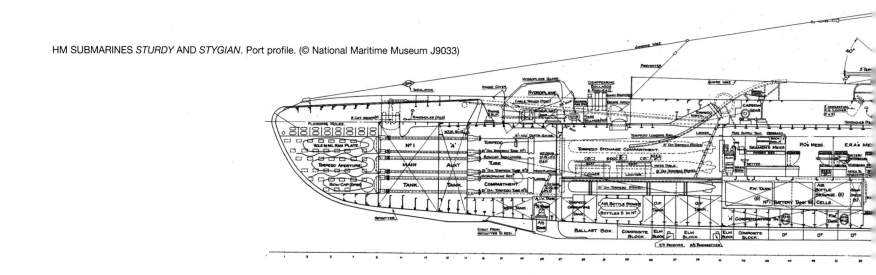

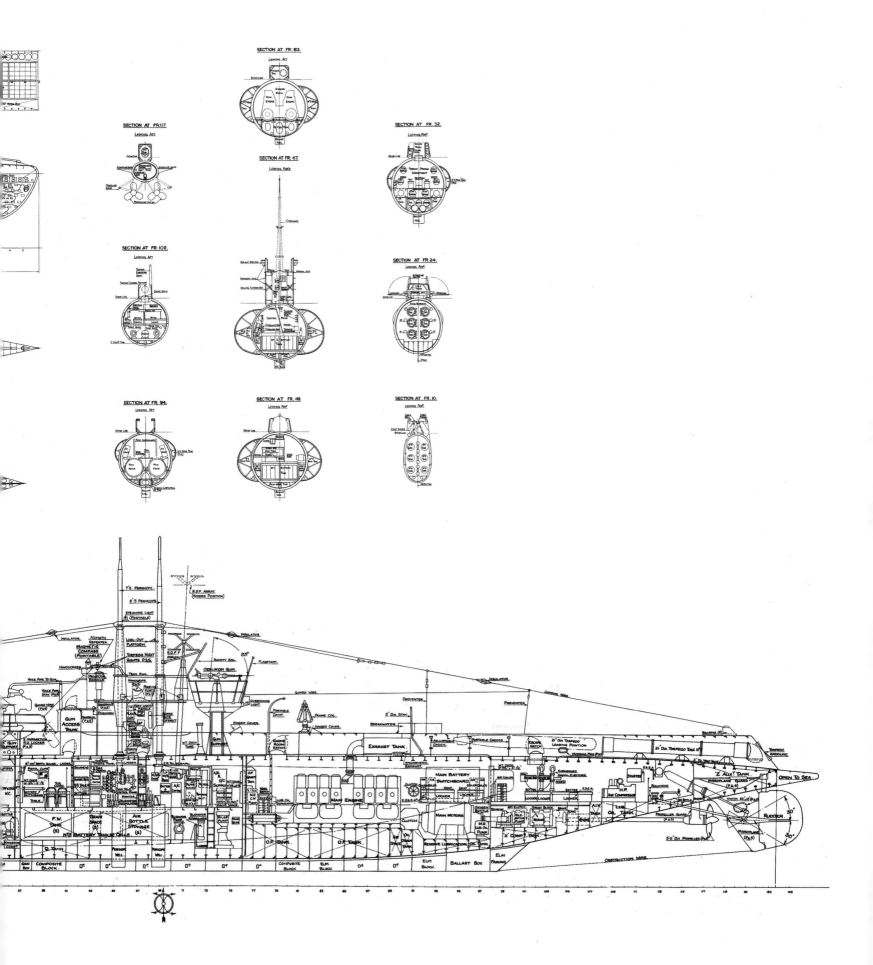

Shakespeare shows typical wartime modifications: Type 291W air-warning radar (the X-shaped antenna abaft the periscopes) and a 20mm gun on a platform at the after end of the bridge fairwater. *Seraph* was similar.

For submarines, the Mediterranean was a very different theatre to the North Sea. The North Sea was relatively shallow and relatively opaque. Shallowness meant both that submarines could bottom if they had to, and that minefields could be laid almost everywhere. The British submarine force suffered badly from mines in 1939–40. The Mediterranean was generally deep (below test depth) but its waters were usually so clear that submarines could be seen from the air down to about 60ft. On the other hand, the deep areas could not be mined (but elsewhere mines claimed several submarines, and Malta was mined from the air). The Far Eastern patrol submarines which had reinforced the Mediterranean Fleet were all large, with silhouettes which made them too visible.[30] All had external fuel tanks which could leak under depth-charging, and all had long (40ft) periscopes. 'T'-class submarines better adapted to the Mediterranean began to arrive in September 1940. The first 'U'-class submarines arrived in November. It became possible to withdraw the surviving large submarines for operations in the Atlantic.

With territory on both sides of the Mediterranean, the Italians had built up an extensive and efficient D/F network, which often made it possible for them to locate British submarines sending sighting reports.[31] Despite their First World War connection with the Allied supersonics programme, the Italians had nothing like Asdic, only hydrophones and their eyes.[32] They did experiment with sonar, and about mid-1941 they found that the Germans had achieved much the same level of development, except that they had placed their device in production. The Italians ordered about sixty of the German sonars and laid down a new class of ASW corvettes.[33] By mid-1941 the Mediterranean was becoming the most active operational theatre for British submarines in terms of numbers and importance.

This was a see-saw war. Initially, the British army drove the Italians back well over the border with Libya and the Greeks drove the Italians back into Albania. The British Mediterranean Fleet seemed to control the Mediterranean, able to run convoys freely into Malta. Then the Germans entered the fight. In January 1941 their dive bombers seriously damaged the carrier HMS *Illustrious*, whose presence had been so important. Stung by their losses in Libya, the Italians moved an armoured division (Ariete) and a motorised division (Torino) to North Africa. Soon they would be joined by the German Afrika Korps and

Rommel. To make matters more difficult, in the spring of 1941 Malta was suffering a serious torpedo shortage. Many of the torpedoes there had gone with the submarines withdrawn to home waters in 1939. The situation was so bad that Malta had to convert destroyer torpedoes for submarine use. In the first half of 1941 the average reserve was three torpedoes per submarine, rather than the 100 per cent contemplated before the war.

Thanks largely to RAF air reconnaissance out of Malta using Maryland aircraft, the British finally became aware of the main Italian convoy route. Air operations from Malta were severely limited by heavy air attacks, but at the end of May the formidable German Fliegerkorps X was moved to Greece to prepare for the attack against Russia. Even so, during the first half of 1941 the Italians moved 82,491 men to North Africa, losing only 5.1 per cent, and 447,815 tons of supplies, losing only 6.6 per cent. The main barrier to German operations was lack of trucks to carry supplies from port to army. Submarines were responsible for most of the German and Italian ships sunk.

As in the Battle of the Atlantic, code-breaking provided critical convoy intelligence, sometimes giving convoy routes and composition and timing. To avoid compromising code-breaking, intelligence was not passed directly to submarines at sea. Instead it was used to direct reconnaissance aircraft, which spotted and reported the convoys. In May 1941 the German naval cipher was being broken within four to six hours, and the Italian naval cipher machine began to be broken.

The Italians later called the second half of 1941 the 'First Battle of the Convoys', the first period when the Axis powers became really concerned with attacks on the route from Italy to Libya. They were apparently unaware that the British were reading their codes.[34] Submarines were not of course the only threat, but they could operate despite heavy damage inflicted on Malta, which could deny it as an air and surface ship base. During September 1941, 29 per cent of military cargo and 24 per cent of fuel sent from Italy was lost, and no British submarines sunk in the process. Sinkings forced the Italians to use destroyers rather than large liners to carry troops to North Africa, in turn helping immobilise their battle fleet. They even had to use submarines to carry supplies. The German Mediterranean commander Admiral Weichold reported that the submarine was the most dangerous

Allied weapon. In September 1941, of thirty-six submarine attacks, nineteen succeeded; eight ships were sunk just outside Axis harbours. They could not be replaced. In November, the Axis armies in North Africa were receiving less than half of the tonnage they needed. The Italian navy began running as many small convoys as possible, keeping them widely separated. During the seven-month 'First Battle of the Convoys' supplies landed in North Africa fell from 125,076 tons in June to 39,000 in December. The Italian Navy did manage to land just enough to avoid total defeat. The Italians lost sixty-two ships (270,386 tons), of which twenty-eight (108,820 tons) were sunk by submarines.[35] The small 'U'-class submarines were concentrated at Malta, the larger ones at Alexandria. At the end of 1941 there were nineteen efficient Allied submarines in the Mediterranean.

Japan entered the war in December 1941. The China Station had been stripped of its submarines the previous year, and none had returned as the Japanese began to move south. The only British submarine at Singapore was *Rover*, brought there for repairs after Crete; all of her main machinery had been removed (she escaped with only one engine complete, and her refit at Bombay was not completed until December 1944). Two new 'T'-class submarines were now sent. From February 1941 on, there was some joint planning for a possible Far Eastern war, both with the Dutch (who had fifteen submarines in the Netherlands East Indies) and with the Americans (for whom twenty-nine submarines were the primary defence of the Philippines). The two 'T'-class submarines had to withdraw to Colombo for repairs, where they were joined by four Dutch submarines to form an East Indies Fleet submarine force.[36]

The Indian Ocean was not as clear as the Mediterranean, so submerged submarines were effectively invisible from the air. That made passage by day safe, as submarines could dive in time to avoid air attack. On the other hand, the heat was considered unbearable without air-conditioning. Many commanders of 'T'-class submarines considered their air-conditioning too noisy.[37]

Meanwhile, the Germans moved an air force (Fliegerkorps II) to Sicily. It resumed heavy attacks on Malta. Quite aside from direct damage to submarines, these attacks frustrated their convoy-attack mission. For example, British code-breakers became aware of a large January 1942 convoy, but air attacks prevented air reconnaissance from Malta, which could not sight the convoy until it was near its destination. It was therefore impossible to base submarine attacks on air reconnaissance, as in the past, to protect code-breaking successes. Submarines alone could not break the Italian convoys: in January 1942 the Italians managed to get 43,328 tons of supplies and equipment and 22,842 tons of fuel to North Africa, losing only 9 per cent. That was enough to support the offensive which recaptured Benghazi. According to the official Italian naval history, most of the ships the submarines sank in January were empty, headed back to Italy. Their loss did not directly affect the supply situation in North Africa. In March the submarines' situation worsened, as the Germans began to concentrate on bombing the submarine base at Malta. Submarines had to stay out of the harbour, submerged, during the day, and ultimately they left altogether. The Italians were able to run convoys more effectively, delivering a record tonnage to North Africa in April: 150,389 tons (including 48,031 tons of fuel), losing less than 1 per cent. This tonnage (and that delivered in May) powered a successful offensive by the Afrika Korps and its Italian allies. The British were compelled to withdraw their submarine base from Alexandria to Haifa. In the process a U-boat sank the depot ship *Medway*. Until Haifa was fully operational, the only effective British submarine base in the Mediterranean was at Gibraltar. The British soon began to use the existing French submarine base at Beirut.

The Italian official historian considered July through October 1942 the 'Second Battle of the Convoys'. Fuelled by the convoy successes of the previous months, the Germans and Italians advanced towards Egypt. They were stopped at El Alamein only on 3 July. The front was now far from the ports at which supplies had piled up.

Spiteful was a typical 1940 'S' with an external stern tube and an open bridge. Her air-warning radar antenna is barely visible abaft her periscope standards. She was photographed on 21 September 1943.

Coastal traffic became more important to the Germans and the Italians. Fliegerkorps II had to be withdrawn to fight in Russia, relaxing air pressure on Malta. German plans to seize the island were cancelled after Hitler declared it neutralised; he needed his forces elsewhere. The British submarines were able to return, much closer to the Italian convoy routes.

In August the submarines and the RAF managed to destroy 25 per cent of general military cargo and 41 per cent of the fuel sent to North Africa. Rommel's desert army began to run out of supplies, and British code-breakers knew as much. By early September the supply situation was worsening; Vice Admiral Weichold said that if the losses imposed in August continued, there would be a crisis. Rommel attributed the failure of his last offensive to lack of supplies. According to the Italian official history, the Royal Italian Navy was bleeding away in the attempt to continue to supply Libya.[38] Although it might have been most profitable for British submarines to have concentrated on the

convoys, they were spread over a greater area to force the Italians to spread their escorts thinly, and so to make it easier to attack the crucial convoys. In September the Italians lost 20 per cent of what they shipped to Africa. Sinkings were not enough in themselves to win the war in North Africa, but they made it impossible for Rommel ever to resume the offensive after El Alamein.[39]

By the end of October 1942, the total volume of shipping available to the Axis in the Mediterranean had been roughly halved; 1.1 million tons had been sunk. The replacement building programme amounted to only about 300,000 tons; the seizure or purchase of foreign ships added another 500,000 tons. About 200,000 tons had been damaged and was being repaired. The 1.6 million tons available was about enough, but ships were being sunk at the rate of 500,000 tons per year, so that available tonnage would be halved in eighteen months. The situation was so bad that negotiations began to have the French Vichy government turn over 120,000 tons. However, these ships had been

Thorn, shown in 1941, was typical of early wartime 'T'-class submarines (Group II), with a fined bow (and protruding torpedo tube muzzles) and aft-firing midships tubes. She was one of the first group of seven war programme 'T'-boats. Note her cab bridge, which was unusual. Others with such bridges included *Traveller* and *Trooper*. All three were completed without provision for a 20mm gun. *Thorn* was sunk by an Italian torpedo boat off Tobruk. It was often said that the 'T' class, which suffered heavily there, were too large for the Mediterranean. Recent research published in the *Naval Review* indicates that these large submarines suffered heavily because their considerable endurance made it possible to send them to more distant, and more dangerous, waters, including areas beyond heavily-mined straits. The Italian convoys which Mediterranean submarines attacked were heavily escorted, sometimes with more escorts than ships escorted. The Italians used First World War escort tactics: they ran down torpedo tracks and peppered the point at which they originated with large numbers of depth charges. Their experienced escort commanders had to guess which way an attacking British submarine would turn to evade after firing, because without Asdic they could not maintain contact with their targets. (John Lambert collection)

laid up and would have to be refitted before they were sent to sea.

In November Allied armies landed in North Africa.[40] Squeezed between the British coming from Egypt and Allied armies coming from the west, the Germans moved troops and materiel into Tunisia. The supply route from Sicily was now the critical one, but it was much shorter than the run to Libya. Passage might take only a night, while submarines lying along it were surfaced charging their batteries. The area involved was bordered by minefields, and only the agile 'U' class were considered suitable. This operation was not particularly successful, aircraft and surface ships causing more Axis losses. Submarines were withdrawn from this battle in January 1943 to patrol the Tyrrhenian Sea, the north coast of Sicily and the east coast of Tunisia. The Italian naval historians called their operations the 'Third Battle of the Convoys', January–May 1943, culminating in the defeat of the Axis army in North Africa. In July, of fifty-one ships that sailed, twenty-four were sunk and seven more seriously damaged. This was a higher casualty rate than in any month in 1942.[41] By the beginning of February, Italian escort forces were reduced to nine torpedo boats and one destroyer; eight destroyers were being used to ferry personnel. Fuel was so short that battleships were emptied to supply escorts. At times the convoy ports simply ran out of fuel.

Once the North African campaign and the invasion of Sicily were over, the large submarine force in the Mediterranean was free to interdict the other important supply line, to the big Italian army (thirty divisions) in the Balkans. This route ran across the Adriatic to the coasts of Yugoslavia and Greece. However, no submarines were involved in attempts to prevent the German army in Sicily from evacuating to the Italian mainland.

Meanwhile the most important submarine role in home waters was watching heavy German ships in case they broke out either into the Atlantic or to attack convoys to Russia. As the Battle of the Atlantic intensified, however, submarines were assigned to patrol lines straddling U-boat routes from the North Sea to the Atlantic. Nothing came of this, largely due to German code-breaking.[42] British submarines supported midget submarine attacks, most notably against the *Tirpitz*. By the end of 1943 *Tirpitz* had been disabled, *Scharnhorst* had been sunk, and the other heavy German ships were no longer considered as threatening to the Russian convoys. Thus in the spring of 1944 submarines in home waters were employed mainly against German coastal trade, which supplied Germany with iron ore from Sweden and supplied German troops in Norway. This relatively minor operation employed on average half a dozen submarines.[43] It was possible because the British were now well aware of the positions of the minefields the Germans had laid to protect their coastal traffic. As before,

HMS *Trenchant* in 1945 returning from the Far East deployment in which she sank the Japanese cruiser *Ashigara*. Note the camouflage carried in that theatre. (John Lambert collection)

some submarines stood anti-U-boat patrols; during the spring of 1944 they sank two U-boats. The coastal traffic around Norway became more important in the autumn of 1944, as the Germans were now fighting actively on a new Finnish front (supplied from Norway) and as the Swedes were refusing to ship iron ore across the Baltic because so many of their ships had been sunk by air-laid mines there. In addition to submarines, there were strikes by the Fleet Air Arm, by RAF Coastal Command and by British MTBs; a major issue was how to avoid interference between these forces.[44]

Although this effort did not concentrate on German U-boats, HMS *Venturer* had an extraordinary success. On 9 February 1945, submerged, she heard a U-boat on her Asdic, then spotted a periscope on the indicated bearing. She stalked the U-boat for an hour, plotting her course and speed, and spotting the periscope from time to time. She then fired four torpedoes, set to run at 30ft and 36ft, at a deduced range of 2000 yds. One of them hit, sinking *U 864*.[45] No other submerged submarine was sunk by another submarine during the Second World War.

With Italy out of the war, in September the Admiralty decided that all new and refitted 'T' and 'S'-class submarines would go to the Far East. The 'U' class were too small. By the end of 1943 five 'T'-class submarines were standing offensive patrols in the Japanese-held Malacca Strait. Plans to send 'S'-class submarines out from the Mediterranean were suspended due to a growing crisis in the Aegean, where the Germans had taken over Italian-held islands. They managed to eject or defeat British troops who had landed on some of the islands; British submarines had to run in supplies in some cases. The Germans also occupied much of the Italian mainland. Given limits of the Italian road and rail systems, they required a considerable tonnage of coastal shipping, which could be attacked by British submarines. The Royal Navy therefore set up a forward submarine base at Maddalena, which opened in December 1943.

Early in 1944 the British East Indies Fleet was rebuilt to the point where it could begin an offensive against the Japanese in the Indian Ocean, to turn them out of Burma and Malaya which they had seized in 1942. In addition to the five 'T'-boats, another two were en route, together with four 'S' class. In February, after the US Navy began its central Pacific offensive, the Japanese withdrew their fleet to a new base at Lingga Roads, south of Singapore. The Japanese fleet had raided the Indian Ocean effectively in 1942, and the British wondered whether this indicated a new raid on a larger scale. The Japanese fleet at Lingga Roads was considerably more powerful than the British East Indies Fleet, so it became vital for the newly-enlarged East Indies Fleet submarine force to watch the Malacca and Sunda Straits through which the Japanese might come. The area east of Singapore and the Malay Peninsula fell within the South West Pacific area under US control, but it was the best place to watch the Japanese fleet at Lingga Roads. In theory US fleet submarines should have operated there, but the area was shallow, and at least the British considered their smaller submarines better adapted to this task.[46] Later it became clear that the Japanese were withdrawing out of range of immediate US attack in the expectation that they might soon fight a fleet action – the battles of the Philippine Sea and Leyte Gulf were coming.

From 1943 on, the British planned to deploy a Pacific Fleet to work with the US fleet. The submarine element appeared first: the depot ship HMS *Wolfe* arrived in Australia in August 1944. A flotilla would operate out of Fremantle, alongside the US submarines there, under the operational control of Commander Submarines US Seventh Fleet, to limit any interference between submarines. When the US submarines moved up to Subic Bay in the Philippines, the British submarines in Fremantle went there and the submarines at Ceylon moved to Fremantle. A new flotilla would operate out of Ceylon. By this time the Japanese had very few merchant ships left, so sinkings were limited.[47]

After the war, a veteran submarine officer compared British and US submarines, based heavily on reports from his Pacific Fleet liaison officer, Lieutenant Commander R B Lakin, who had served in British submarines and had made war patrols in their US counterparts.[48]

Whilst appreciating [the] good points [of US submarines] I feel absolutely certain that they would not have done for our submarine war as they would have been a damn nuisance in the Med, or off Burma, or off Norway. They were designed for their purpose and did it magnificently, though I am unconvinced that a fleet of German 740 tonners [Type VIIC] would not have done it just as well and far more economically. The Hun managed to operate 500 tonners in the Gulf of Mexico, each S/M using about half the crew of an American Fleet S/M . . . one must remember that they [US fleet boats] employ about 3 times as many people servicing them as we do, and they are better placed for stores. For instance, the only thing which gives trouble in the Admiralty S or T engine is the vertical drive. Instead of laboriously refitting and patching up these after every 2 or 3 patrols, if only we could produce them, we could slip in a new vertical drive (it drives the camshaft and a few auxiliaries) and be OK again. *Trenchant* has just done 15,000 miles with negligible defects, with 82 of 94 days at sea. With our air-conditioning plants even the 'S' class are entirely habitable, and the Freon acts as a distiller to provide washing water.

Also, perhaps just a coincidence but at any rate significant, the Americans have recently lost 3 boats doing just the same as our boats, with certainly no more enterprise, whilst we have lost none. Our shallow periscope depth and smaller size is an advantage. It is a mathematical certainty that the smaller target has a better chance against torpedo, mine, or D/C attack. I do not say our boats are first class, but they have served their purpose *economically* and well. We have never had need of vast endurance, and I think that, except in electronics, we have more to learn from the Hun than the Americans.

I have been round the logger head, and the cleanliness and neatness and comfort of the boats is magnificent. The extraordinary thing is that in their frigates and CVE (the only American-built ships I have any knowledge of) the Americans are Spartan to a degree which fills our personnel with gloom. Yet in their submarines they have gone to the other extreme, and I am certain that it is wrong, and that their sailors like the Germans and British can take it.

Now the pros and cons.

Engines: our boats are hopelessly under engined, particularly the T. But we could barely supply our S/Ms with two engines apiece – let alone 4 [as in US submarines]. I do not like electric drive, though now that the Americans are eliminating gearing, it seems to lose much of its disadvantage. The 1600 HP high-speed American submarine diesel is, I think, streets ahead of our engine, and worth accepting electric drive to have. However, the Germans may have a better direct drive engine.

Tantivy displays standard late-war camouflage on her return to Portsmouth, 17 April 1945. This is probably the foreign stations version (Scheme J) in which the panels alternating with white ones are green (g 45) and the pressure hull is blue (b20) and black. Horizontal surfaces were black in both this and the corresponding home stations scheme (H). Schemes H and J were the first standard disruptive schemes announced for British submarines. Earlier standard schemes were overall pb 10 (purple-blue) for the Mediterranean and MS 3 (overall green with a black casing and saddle tanks). Surviving photographs indicate that submarine camouflage was extremely rare, nearly all submarines being painted in standard light grey with dark horizontal surfaces. (John Lambert collection)

Range and Habitability: I do not think we have a requirement for such great range. The German 740 tonner was as fast as the Americans, and seemed to stay at sea for ages (165 days I know was done by one).

Torpedo Control: Good, but by no means the answer to everything. Given the American radar periscope, I reckon we could have put up a staggering performance with submerged attack. The data computer was by no means infallible until fed by a radar range. I would rather ask less of the torpedo, and economise on the attack team – our manpower situation was acute . . . I got 21 hits out of 51 torpedoes in *Safari* . . .

Periscopes: I prefer our bifocal. The ST radar [US periscope ranging radar] however is, I think, the answer to a submariner's prayer.

Radio: the Americans streets ahead. Type 55 is the most b—y awful botch up inflicted on a long suffering sailor. On the other hand, I am not in love with 'voice,' and I think the Americans make too much noise on the ether.

Radar: Americans several laps ahead, except that our 291 is a damn good set, better than SD.

Asdic: We are well ahead here, but need a sonic band detector. Our SS/T signalling is V.G.

Night Sight: I have tried for years to get a decent torpedo night sight. The Americans have in stream. We should have copied *Graph*'s years ago, instead – production of course comes

in – we have suffered from abortions.

Electrics: Apart from the 'U' class, our Main Motors and general 220 volt systems have been excellent.

Telemotor: though cursed with troubles, we were ahead here.

Torpedoes: the Cutey [US homing torpedo] is miles ahead of us, but otherwise our Mk VIII** is I think the best torpedo in the world. God knows what slaughter the Germans could have done on big convoys with it and its 10,000 yd range. The trouble is we kept the poor thing flooded, week in week out, which no one else (except possibly the Jap, I don't know) would have dreamt of doing.

Gunnery: A late starter, the Americans are catching us up. Our 4in gun and gun tower is still ahead, though. *Trenchant* shot down 5 sub chasers, 3 of them single handed. Our radar gun control will be good I think, in fact is good. With a single or twin mounting there is no point in a director. Cut out the intermediate and get your sight on the gun. I have no brief for our Victorian telescope, P.T.; binocular sights are the answer – but production has beaten us here, not neglecting to ask for it. Our boats shoot better than anyone else's. Accuracy is what counts, that means training. The 40mm is a damn good choice I think, with a decent LA sight. The 20mm is too short range. I have no use for rockets and other inaccurate missiles.

Kiosks: I have always been in favour of these to date, but I think we are getting too many gadgets to fit in. the American kiosk has not enough room to use the periscope decently, and they use theirs carelessly. The German fixed eyepiece periscope should go with a kiosk. Personally, I am now in favour of banishing all the submarine control (planes, blows, pumps, etc) from the CR [control room] and use the CR as an attack chamber, rather than having a kiosk.

Technique: The Americans copied the German 1939-42 technique of surface night attack, but by using radar made it far more deadly. The point is they had the ocean convoys to use it on, and furthermore were never subjected to the same opposition as the Germans or us. For years we had a solid block of opposition from some of our submariners to night shadowing. I started it (night shadowing) in the 3rd Flotilla as soon as I arrived ex *Safari*, and it was months before we finally broke down the prejudice. Then people went haywire, as if it – as practiced by the Germans in 1914-18 war – was the only method of attack. Our boats were ill-equipped for it, but the 8th Flotilla, our predecessors here, tried to concentrate on this technique, instead of the inshore technique which the British have developed and for which their boats were suited. A S/M should be able to vary its tactics to the need of the moment. My flotilla have applied British technique, and dare I think very much better than the 8th, though I think the S, particularly the 4in S, is a faster and better boat than the T for the job.

Armour: the Americans, Germans, and Dutch are well ahead of us in this. Being thousands of miles from DNC, we have got a bit of extra armour on our boats, but not enough, by private enterprise.

General: the American is a magnificent boat to suit a particular need, and made possible by large resources of men and materiel. It is uneconomical by comparison with German and British boats, and defensively inferior owing to its size and unsuitability for inshore work against keen opposition. It is a submersible rather than a submarine. I would liken it to the Packard staff car and our boats to the jeep. The jeep is more use in congested combat areas.

Future: Our A boat is better than a T, but only has a blown [supercharged] T boat engine with a couple of extra parts. It handles much better than a T, dives easily to 600ft test depth, and I should say 800ft is within its limits. It is undergunned – it should have a twin 4in and a 40mm. In order to get speed without engine power (again engine production our bottleneck) the torpedo rooms fore and aft have been fined to uncomfortable limits. It has 2 externals, and 4 dry internals forward with six reloads; and 2 externals and 2 internal stern tubes with 4 reloads. It is 30 tons more displacement, thinner and longer than a T. The radar periscope, which you can't see through, it being a Type 267 (a sort of 3 cm ST) reflector on a periscope tube, gives you range and bearing, and draws out on a PPI. It has troubles but a future. The A is a wartime design to utilize existing and available material. It is not an outstanding new design at all. It looks rather like a German U-boat with standards for the 40ft sticks (T boat = S boat = 34ft). The control room is a fair compromise – a brilliant brain having had some say! – but not ideal. All the CO's stuff is on the starboard side, and all the submarining stuff on the port side so that you don't have the 1st Lieutenant talking to the outside ERA across

the Captain talking to his fruit machine.

It was hoped to put in American Data Computer and angling, but this has not yet arrived, and anyhow there is not enough room . . . for some of it. I do not know if it will turn out well, but it seemed to handle nicely submerged, and is singularly free from vibration.

However, future designs will evolve around closed-cycle propulsion, intelligent torpedoes, submerged endurance etc in the submarine; with a future – I amongst few think – for the dual purpose submersible as well . . .

Don't think that I am too proud to learn from the Americans, who are the most charming people to work under, and do not suffer from our equipment troubles. But our boats do not compare badly as fighting machines, and I know which I would rather have taken into the Inland Sea. Actually I reckon that the outstanding S/M of this war is the German 500 tonner. Top of the sinking tonnage, too, and fought to the last.

Further evaluations were offered in the discussion following a paper delivered by DNC's submarine designer A J Sims to the Institution of Naval Architects in 1947. Captain Lord Ashbourne DSO, who had served as Chief Staff Officer (Operations) for A(S), compared British to German and US submarines. The Germans needed high surface speed to intercept convoys, and the Americans needed it to get to the Far East quickly enough from Hawaii. The later U-boats were also deeper-diving. The Germans had had to give up battery capacity and the Americans built unduly large submarines. Ashbourne argued that both navies designed for particular areas, whereas the British had to operate everywhere, from the Arctic to the equator, mainly on offensive patrol. They were completely unsupported, often near the enemy's coast. Large battery power and long underwater endurance were absolutely essential.

Ashbourne pointed to two other differences: the position of the captain and the position of the gun. British captains were in the control room, 'in the very closest contact with the first lieutenant and the men under him who are responsible for diving the submarine'. Typical foreign practice had the captain in an enlarged conning tower, with attack instruments. That separated him and the attack team from the rest of the submarine, and also made for deeper periscope depth, as the eyepiece was in the conning tower. 'I am quite sure that our arrangement suits our temperament better.'

Foreign guns were typically on the casing, but the Royal Navy placed them higher up if possible, sometimes even at the level of the bridge. The gun could be manned much more quickly on surfacing, and it could be fought in much rougher weather.

FOSM's representative pointed to cases of severe damage which British submarines had survived:

- *Spearfish* survived heavy depth-charging, some of the charges coming practically into contact with her hull.
- *Triumph* had her fore-end blown off and her torpedo tube compartment flooded by mining.
- *Tally-Ho* had all her main tanks on one side ripped open by a Japanese destroyer.
- *Terrapin* was so badly depth-charged that her side was pushed up against her torpedo tubes.
- *Stubborn* and *Ultimatum* were forced to twice their designed depths by depth-charging.

War Programmes

The changing war programme reflected the perceived needs of a changing submarine strategy. When war broke out on 3 September 1939, the Royal Navy was building the big 'T' class and the small 'U' class. A quickly-assembled emergency war programme included seven 'T' class and twelve 'U' class, all of which were ordered on 4 September 1939. In January 1940, five 'S' class replaced five 'T' class which had just been ordered as additions to the initial seven.[49] The initial War Programme 'T' class included the three deferred in 1938, which were sometimes counted as part of the 1938 Programme.

The 1940–1 Programme was initially specified simply as sixteen submarines of unspecified types. As of March 1940, ten 'U'-class submarines had been ordered and 'S'-class submarines were planned. By September 1940, Treasury permission had been granted to order five 'T', seven 'S' and twelve 'U'-class submarines. In addition, three 'T' class and eleven 'S' class were due to be ordered in March 1941. As of

April 1941 the Supplemental 1940–1 Programme was modified to three 'T' class, eight 'S' class and three minelayers, nominally repeat *Cachalots*. They had been requested by VA(S) in October 1940 to replace earlier minelayers lost in action, but they were not built.[50] Actual figures were six 'S' class and ten 'U' class in the 1940–1 Programme (ordered, respectively, in April and March 1940) plus nine 'T' class (five ordered in September and four in November 1940), seven 'S' class (another seven were transferred to the 1941–2 Programme in January 1941), and twelve 'U' class (ordered August 1940), for a total of twenty-two 'U' class.

Meanwhile the 1941–2 Programme was drafted. Initially it included either eighteen 'T' class and nineteen 'S' class or twenty 'T' class, sixteen 'S' class, and two minelayers (the latter was chosen, but the minelayers were never built). On 14 June 1941, however, Churchill personally pressed for maximum submarine production over the next year, citing the needs of the Mediterranean. The combination

Safari and *P 222* were unique among the 'S'-class submarines ordered in 1939 in having no stern torpedo tube, i.e., in being simple repeat 'S'. The others ordered at this time were *Sahib*, *Saracen*, *Satyr*, and *Sceptre*. *Safari* is shown on her return to Portsmouth from the Mediterranean, 8 September 1943. Note her cab rather than open bridge. Within a year *Safari* had a stern tube, probably fitted during a September 1943–January 1944 refit at Troon. After that she was used mainly for training, except for participation in Operation 'Foremost' (March 1944), a deployment against a possible movement of the German battleship *Tirpitz* back to Germany for repairs. (US Naval Institute)

UNITED (ex-P44)
Gr. Britain - SS
(UNITY Class)
Feb. 1944

United was one of the second series of 'U'-class submarines, with low flat bows and four torpedo tubes. She shows her Type 291W air-warning radar. These submarines were never fitted with 20mm anti-aircraft guns; instead they had three 0.303in machine guns (Lewis or Vickers). The cage protected the Type 291W antenna as it retracted. *United* is shown in February 1944. At the end of the war all 'U'-class submarines were either scrapped, transferred to Allied navies, or retained in Category C reserve earmarked for shock trials. *United* was broken up in 1946.

of the 1941 and Supplemental Programmes called for twenty-seven 'T' class, thirty 'S' class, and five minelayers. Due to attacks on British yards and industry, however, current capacity could provide only sixty-three submarines: nineteen 'T' class, twenty-seven 'S' class, twelve 'U' class, and the minelayers. The main pool of additional industrial capacity was on the Tyne, where 'U'-class submarines could be built. The programme was rewritten, the minelayers being eliminated; it now comprised thirty 'T' class, twenty-seven 'S' class, and twelve 'U' class. That would cost somewhat less than the earlier programme, but the money would be spent more quickly – and the submarines would be completed more quickly. Plans initially called for building more of the smaller 'S' class than of the larger 'Ts', but fewer yards had the expertise to build the smaller 'S' class; hence the larger number of 'Ts'. Ultimately the 1941 Programme included seventeen 'T'-class submarines (eighteen authorised, increased to twenty-one in June 1941, but cut back to seventeen in July; the cancelled four were replaced by 'U'-class submarines), twenty-three 'S' class (reduced to fifteen in July 1941), and twenty 'U' class.

When the 1942–3 Programme was being framed early in 1942 the Naval Staff asked for twenty-four more 'T'-class submarines, but Controller could find building capacity for only fourteen. Against a request for nine 'S' class, only seven could be built. However, there was capacity for sixteen 'U' class, against a request for twelve. Soon the number of 'T'-class submarines was increased to sixteen and 'S' class to eight. VA(S) (Admiral Max Horton) considered the proposed programme totally inadequate, but no change (except some acceleration) was possible. On 22 October 1941, however, there were some additions: four 'S' and eight 'U' class. This resulted from greater

capacity offered by Cammell Laird ('S' class) and Vickers Tyne ('U' class). Ultimately the 1942–3 Programme included sixteen 'T'-class submarines, four of which were reordered as 'A' class, and two of which were later cancelled (two were not ordered, but HMS *Spearfish* was built instead). It also included thirteen 'S' class (eight ordered October 1942, four in November, and one in April 1943) and twenty-four 'U' class (of which ten were cancelled).

By early 1943 the British were beginning to think through the requirements of a return to the Far East. A new large submarine, which became the 'A' class, was designed. In effect it replaced the 'T' class. Initially the draft 1943 Programme included twenty-two 'U' class, but their numbers were drastically cut because these submarines were clearly unsuited to the vast distances of the Far East.[51] As initially approved the 1943–4 Programme included thirty-six 'A' class, four 'S' class, and ten 'U' class. Four of the 1942–3 'T' class would be reordered as 'A' class. Late in 1943 it was proposed that six 'A' class be added and all ten 'U' class deleted. Two of the 'U' class were actually ordered in April 1943, but they were replaced by an 'A'-class submarine in November. Another eight were cancelled in July 1943 in favour of five 'A' class. In addition, four 'T' class of the 1942–3 Programme were reordered as 'A'-class submarines, for a total of forty-six rather than the original thirty-six. In addition, the 1943–4 Programme included four 'S' class (another five were cancelled).

By this time plans were well advanced to move British submarines to the Far East; at the end of 1943 A(S) told the Admiralty that at the beginning of 1945 the Royal Navy could deploy forty operational submarines there. To maintain that force would require a total of eighty, counting time lost in refits in the United Kingdom, trials, working-up and passage. Another 15 per cent should be added for losses and wastage. By this time the Royal Navy had a huge ASW force. Its training and submarine training would require another fifty submarines – a total of 130. Most training submarines would be the 'U' type. Another twenty-four elderly submarines would become redundant, given current building programmes; they could be scrapped or used as bottom targets for ASW training. Numbers on order were still excessive. A(S) proposed cancelling sixteen 'S', 'U', and 'V'-class submarines not yet ordered, substituting twenty more 'A' class in the 1944–5 War Programme. Admiralty discussions of the programme showed no realisation that Britain was quickly running out of naval manpower. The programme was personally backed by First Sea Lord, who appreciated the value of submarines which could operate in nominally enemy-dominated waters – which in the spring of 1944 meant much of the Far East. The twenty new 'A' class and the disposal of older submarines were approved, and in August 1944 the forty-submarine Far East force was also approved, subject to manpower. By this time large numbers of French and Italian submarines were being used for ASW training, but they were not included in the force projections. Using them saved considerable British naval manpower. On the other hand, transfers of new 'U' and 'V'-class submarines to allies (such as four to the Soviet Union in 1944) made it necessary to keep some older submarines running.

The 1944–5 Programme was offered to the Cabinet on 1 May 1944, much later than would usually have been the case (the financial year began on 1 April). Looking towards the Pacific, and a war which was expected to continue into 1946 or 1947, this programme included twenty of the new 'A' class but no smaller submarines. By the autumn of 1944, the Royal Navy was well aware of the new German U-boats, which would make the 'A' class obsolete, so cancellations began: twenty in October 1944 and another ten in October 1945. Of the 1944–5 'A' class, seventeen were cancelled on 22 November 1944 and the other three were cancelled but then reinstated in the projected 1945–6 Programme. The 1944 units were apparently to have had 'B' names.

A 1945–6 Programme described in a 29 June 1945 Cabinet memo was never formally discussed or approved. It included three improved 'A'-class submarines and one experimental submarine intended to embody the radical advances in submarine design the Germans had developed.[52]

War Construction: 'T' Class

As designed, the 'T' class had four external tubes firing forward, two in the bow and two amidships. By the end of 1939 there was a demand for stern fire. All new 'T'-class submarines were therefore given a stern tube, and the two midships external tubes were set to fire aft. The stern tube was first fired successfully in trials using HMS *Thrasher* in 1941.[53] Two external stern tubes were fitted to the earlier large submarines *Severn* and *Clyde* in 1942.

Turpin in Australia (probably Melbourne), 1945. (Alan C Green via State Library of Victoria)

HM SUBMARINES *TUDOR* AND *THULE*. Port profile, as fitted 1944. This has been amended to show the 1949 modifications, which did not include the fitting of snort. (© National Maritime Museum M1096)

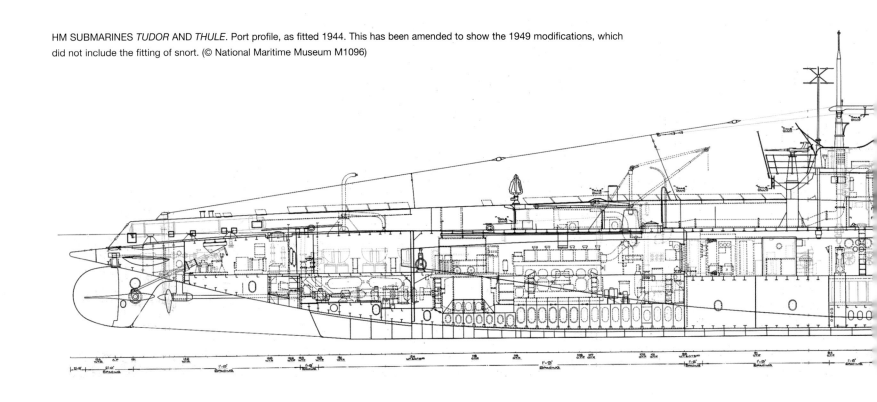

HM SUBMARINES *TUDOR* AND *THULE*. Starboard profile, as fitted 1944. (© National Maritime Museum M1097)

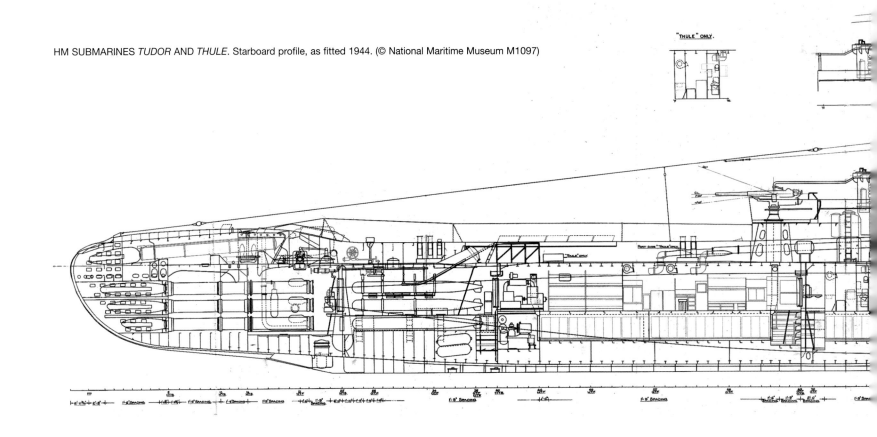

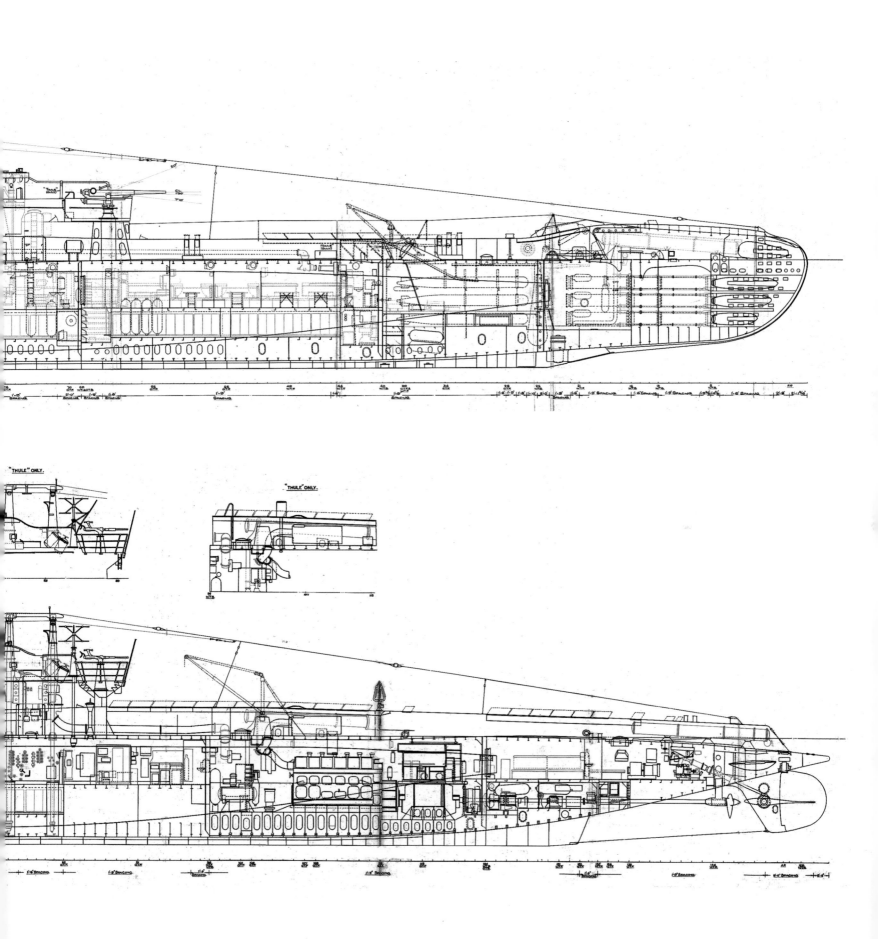

"THULE" ONLY.

"THULE" ONLY.

A December 1939 conference had already recommended measures to reduce bridge wetness. The 1938–9 'T' class and War Programme 'T' class were all to have cab rather than open bridges; in addition *Tarpon* and *Tuna* would be fitted providing that did not delay their completion. *Triumph*, which was being rebuilt, would get a cab, and so would *Thunderbolt* (*Thetis*, which had been lost and raised), again if it did not delay her. Experiments would be conducted with a collar (splash plates) around the bridge to reduce wetness.

Submarine designs were reviewed at a 22 January 1940 meeting presided over by VA(S) Vice Admiral Max Horton. The blunt bow form of the 'T' class, adopted to accommodate the external bow tubes, cost them considerable speed in rough weather. Later it was said that they were proving singularly difficult to handle at periscope depth in rough weather. Their bridges were wet. After some discussion a proposal to surrender the two bow tubes was dropped for the present, but *Triumph* was to be rebuilt without bow tubes as a test. *Thunderbolt* would be reconditioned similarly. Further data on speed loss would be collected. DNC would investigate an alternative finer bow form which would retain the two external tubes.

About April 1940 DNC proposed moving the bow external tubes of the War Programme 'T' class back 7ft, making it possible to fine the bow considerably and eliminate the troublesome flare. VA(S) was unimpressed, so DNC offered something more: to move the tubes further back although they stuck out of the casing. His representative thought that would be unacceptable because it would cost submerged speed (and would make it more difficult to penetrate nets), but VA(S) concentrated on the finer bow, since 'to be able to keep a periscope watch in bad weather was an overriding requirement'. DNC also considered enlarging the forward planes because the 'T' class seemed sluggish in answering their plane helm. At about this time it was also decided that the midships external tubes should point aft rather than forward, to give a total of three aft-looking tubes.

The modified submarines were generally called Group Two.[54] They had cab bridges. In *Thresher*, *Thorn*, *Trusty*, *Turbulent*, and *Tempest* the midships tubes were angled 10° off the centreline to avoid fouling the saddle tanks, but that required an unusually large area of flat casing which affected depth-keeping. *Trooper* and *Traveller* therefore had their tubes angled 7°. All Group Two boats went to the Mediterranean, but *Thresher* and *Trusty* returned home for extensive refits in which their cab bridges were eliminated, and radar and a 20mm Oerlikon installed. Later boats (Group Three) had further fined bows (apparent in the above-water bulges of their external bow tubes). Of this group only *P 311* and *Trespasser* were completed without Oerlikons. The casing around their conning towers was flattened down, and they were built with open bridges. Some were partially welded (*P 311*, *Trespasser*, *Taurus*, *Tactician*, *Truculent*, *Templar*, *Tally-Ho*, *Tantalus*, *Tradewind*, *Trenchant*, *Thule*, *Tudor*, *Zwaardvis*, *Terrapin*, and *Thorough*); others were fully welded (*Tiptoe*, *Trump*, *Tactician*, *Tapir*, *Tigerhaai*, *Talent*, *Teredo*, *Tabard*, *Totem*, *Truncheon*, *Turpin*, and *Thermopylae*). All-welded boats used thicker steel in their pressure hulls (30lb vs 25lb, 'S' quality

Tantalus illustrates the standard configuration of wartime 'T'-class submarines, with their three aft-firing external torpedo tubes.

rather than HTS), and were rated at 350ft diving depth (*Tiptoe* dived satisfactorily to 400ft). Fuel could now be carried in external ballast tanks. Riveted boats intended for the Far East had their external tanks welded up to avoid leakage.

As modified for Far Eastern operations 'T'-class submarines had two main ballast tanks modified to stow an additional 80 tons of oil (for a total of 215 tons), giving them an endurance of 11,100nm. In riveted submarines, tanks were welded up to avoid telltale leakage, but the working of the structure could still produce small leaks. Small suction pumps were installed to keep the oil in. Fresh water stowage was increased, and two 55,000 BTU Freon air-conditioners installed, with a distiller to increase their water supply. Although endurance was now six weeks, typical patrols from Ceylon into the Malacca Strait lasted three.

The Repeat 'S' Class[55]

At the 22 January 1940 meeting on the submarine programme RA(S) said that the 'T' class were too large, and the 'U' class too small, for the North Sea. He wanted repeat 'S'-class submarines. Five recently-ordered 'T' class were cancelled in favour of 'S'-class boats. Although RA(S) wanted simply to repeat the existing design, DNC's representative pointed out that it was already nearly a decade old, and that it did not take into account the recent underwater explosion tests (Job 81). The 17lb pressure hull was too thin and the stern should be redesigned to solve the rattle problem. Diving depth should be 300ft and endurance 4000nm at 10 knots with a clean bottom. No mines would be carried. The wardroom would be next to the control room, for ready access. The weight of the casing should be reduced if possible. A simple form of radio D/F should be provided. The battery tanks should have steel tops. Planes should be operated from rods geared from the control room, with a greater range of angles than at present to take account of mis-alignment. Periscopes would match those in the 'S' class, but should house in the keel. A cab bridge was wanted. The dehumidifier could be omitted, as these boats would not

fight in the tropics. The engine should be a type adapted to rapid production, of an approved design. It should meet the requirement, raised during the design of the 1939 patrol and minelaying submarine, that the submarine be able charge batteries while proceeding on the surface at operational speed (in this case, 11 knots), six months out of dock. The new requirement was based on experience running *Shark* at operational speed but at full power to charge batteries. The power actually needed for charging would depend on how long that was allowed to take.[56] That would normally be done in darkness, and in summer the North Sea nights were very short. A 30 January 1940 conference discussed the requirement, including absolute reliability at 11 knots (raised in connection with the previous year's patrol and minelaying submarine). By this time 'S'-class submarines were having piston problems due, it seemed, to the wartime need to operate them at maximum power.

DNC refused to provide the extra power unless the Staff Requirement was formally changed, as he had to justify the greater length involved. As of 16 February 1940 it was assumed that the repeat 'S' class would be considerably larger than the original: 185ft rather than 163ft between perpendiculars (217ft rather than 208ft 8in overall), displacing 716 tons rather than 670 tons standard, 804 tons rather than 771 tons surfaced, and 975 tons rather than 961 tons submerged. The 1900 BHP plant would be derated to 1500 BHP to leave a margin for charging. To ensure a sufficient reserve of power at operational speed, the propellers would be suited only to the 1500 BHP at 14 knots. With a clean bottom, endurance would be 4000nm rather than 4500nm at 9 knots on slightly more fuel (44 tons rather than 40 tons). The Legend approved by Controller in April 1940 showed a surfaced endurance of 3800nm at 10 knots with a clean bottom, even though oil fuel had been increased to 45 tons.

After a March 1940 meeting Assistant Controller confirmed the need for reserve power, as without it the desired operational speed could not be provided: it was always essential that a submarine arrive in the operational area with a fully-charged battery. Submarines

Surf was a typical 1940 'S' with an open bridge and a stern tube. Her air-warning radar mast is raised. It replaced the telescoping wireless mast of earlier submarines. She is shown at Liverpool in March 1943. She was part of a massive building programme that, even so, did not approach what the Naval Staff wanted. Late in 1942 the target strength of the British submarine force in an ideal future fleet (as given in a report for First Sea Lord by the Naval Staff), was 300 submarines – which was wildly above anything attainable. At this time it was assumed that production would be limited to the 'S', 'T' and 'U' classes. Projected programmes through 1943 (conceived at that time as twenty-two 'U' class, fifteen 'S' class and fourteen 'T' class) would produce enough submarines to give the Royal Navy an estimated 192 on 1 January 1946 (it is not clear what losses were envisaged), leaving a deficit of 108 submarines.

without reserve power had to run their engines at full power for long periods, a practice which probably accounted for some of the existing engine problems. ACNS and Controller agreed.

When production of the 'S' class resumed in 1940, three alternative engines were offered: the Admiralty engine (with solid injection) employed in *Sunfish* in 1934, a seven-cylinder Vickers engine adapted from one they had used in a Portuguese submarine, and a five-cylinder version of the Sulzer engine used in Cammell Laird 'T'-class submarines.[57] For production reasons, the Sulzer engine was not adopted, and after three submarines the Vickers engine was dropped so that Vickers could concentrate on the 'T' class. A proposed Admiralty 'Revised S' seven-cylinder engine was also dropped. Modifications to the *Sunfish* engine included strengthening the top member of the engine frame and fitting a torsional vibration damper. These engines

Photographed on 23 February 1944, *Stygian* shows her Type 291W antenna fully raised. She was one of three 1942–3 boats with a stern tube and a 3in gun, the others being *Sturdy* and *Subtle*. All of the others had the 4in gun and omitted the stern tube. (NHHC)

were initially successful, but they encountered serious problems in their vertical drive and camshaft late in 1943 (the 'T' class encountered vertical drive problems in January 1945).

Late in June 1941 VA(S) asked for new submarine designs which would be considerably faster so that they could better attack merchant ships: 17 knots (15 knots cruising).[58] Existing engines would be used, so as not to upset production. The submarine should have four bow tubes and one stern tube. Three alternative designs were developed: A, C, and D (there is no mention of B).[59] Of these, A used the 'U'-class

Late 'S'-class submarines had a 4in rather than a 3in gun, in the usual elaborate mounting. As weight compensation they surrendered the single external stern tube. *Sea Devil* was photographed on 28 April 1945. She shows the Type 138 Asdic dome right aft. Her Type 291W antenna is retracted abaft her periscope housings, and her 20mm gun is not visible (its pipe rack is). (RAN Naval Historical Section via Dr Josef Straczek)

Above and below: Photographed on 7 February 1950, *Seneschal* showed a more elaborate gun shield and a Type 291W radar, but no snorkel, despite the elimination of any 20mm anti-aircraft gun.

engine, C used the *Sunfish* engine, and D used the 'T'-class Sulzer engine. C and D were based on the 1940 'S'-class design, but had different torpedo batteries. The structure was substantially simplified by omitting some bulkheads and the flats beneath the battery, admittedly at the expense of safety when surfaced 'which it is suggested is more important in peace than in war'. Hull diameter was also reduced to minimise displacement and maximise diving strength. VA(S) saw little advantage over the 1940 'S' class, particularly since a new design could not be built any more rapidly. He opted to keep building the 1940 'S' class, except with a single external tube added aft. It would impose little delay, so it was adopted for 1941 'S'-class submarines.[60] Soon a heavier (4in) gun was also wanted. Stability precluded fitting both. The gun won out.[61]

The Repeat 'U' Class

At a 22 January 1940 meeting on the submarine programme, it was stated that the 'U' class were difficult to handle near the surface and when firing a six-torpedo salvo, and had main tank Kingstons that difficult to operate.[62] They had no gun, and they sweated when submerged. The external bow tubes were surrendered so that an HA gun (alternatively, an Oerlikon) could be fitted, and the 10 per cent larger bow planes already incorporated into War Programme 'U'-class submarines accepted. Pillars and curtains would be substituted for bulkheads between messes. VA(S) Admiral Horton was convinced that the original voluminous bow made for poor handling, having decided much earlier that the First World War 'M' class handled particularly well submerged because of its fine deck lines.[63] The first repeat 'U'

Una was a 1940–1 'U'-class submarine. In these boats the two external torpedo tubes were removed altogether so that the bow could be lengthened, flattened, fined, and sharply raked. *Una* is returning to port flying a 'Jolly Roger' on which horizontal stripes indicate ships torpedoed. *Umpire* also had this bow. It was probably also in *Unbeaten*, *Undaunted*, *Union*, *Urchin* and *Urge*.

class (*Utmost* and the *Usk* group) did not have the external bow tubes, but their bows were larger than desired because it was necessary to fair over their bow plane operating gear. Later units had finer bow lines, the plane operating gear being housed in an excrescence. All of the repeat 'U' class had deck guns, either a 3in or 12pdr.

Very early in 1940 the first 'U'-class submarines reported occasional whistles ('singing') from their propellers. Although the first repeat 'U'-class submarine did not report this problem, it was quite evident in the next ship, and trials with four different propellers did not cure it. Several remedies failed. Work at Haslar produced a solution: the propellers needed a much better finish, but Haslar also found that the hull form around the propeller (nearby planes and cut-up) were a problem. Unfortunately the special edge shape, virtually a knife edge, was quickly damaged in service, singing recurring. When the third group of 'U'-class submarines were redesigned, it was possible to revert to the earlier stronger propeller shape.

The reports of singing in the 'U' class caused greater attention to propeller noise in other classes, which were subject to special noise trials. It was soon clear that the 'S' and 'T' classes also suffered, their problems being cured by improving propeller finish.

About 1942 two main ballast tanks were converted for oil fuel to extend range. Other wartime improvements included movement of the wardroom from forward over No 1 battery (in the first fifteen) to adjacent to the control room (as required by war experience), better shock resistance for the battery containers, sound insulation of

In 1942 *Unique* (shown) and *Unbroken* were given flush bows identical to those in *Una* and in the next group of boats. They were also given 3in 20 cwt QF guns instead of the earlier 12pdr 12 cwt, and were fitted with Type 291W air-warning radar. (John Lambert collection)

auxiliary machinery, omission of the starboard anchor, and addition of a single Oerlikon gun.

In 1941 it was decided to redesign the class and at the same time to cure 'singing' by fining the stern. The bow was further fined, overall length increasing to 204ft 6in.[64] Pressure hull plating was thickened (25lbs vice 20lbs), S quality steel was introduced, and welded tee-bar framing and welded pressure-hull butts introduced. Welding saved weight that went into the thicker hull. Displacement increased to 658 tons (surface) and 740 tons (submerged); diving depth increased from 200ft to 300ft. Later units of the class were given 'V' names.

On 26 June 1941 Controller asked DNC for designs of single-purpose anti-invasion submarines. EinC suggested using the engine Vickers had employed in its Estonian and Turkish submarines. Using the 'U'-class engine would cost 1.5 knots. Hydroplanes and vents would all be hand-operated, and structure would be drastically simplified. The design could be complete in 2–3 months, and once that was done submarines could be built in about 8 months. At the 18 July 1941 conference on submarine policy, VA(S) rejected the anti-invasion

submarines; production and manning should not be tied up for a special type at the expense of general-purpose submarines. Controller agreed.[65]

The 'A' Class[66]

In effect the abortive 1941 minelaying submarine showed what could be done with greater displacement than the 'T' class. The most interesting features were probably its high-capacity battery cells and its new engines (eight-cylinder versions of the six-cylinder 'T'-class type) totalling 3300 BHP, far beyond the output of the current production submarines. Given its substantial size (1737 tons surfaced, 2085 tons submerged), it took powerful engines to drive the minelayer at 15.75 knots; it had enough fuel (140 tons) to make 11,000nm at 8 knots. Submerged endurance would be 50 hours at 2 knots (maximum submerged speed on 1630 BHP was 8.75 knots). As in previous minelayers, this one would have six bow torpedo tubes (one reload each) and would carry fifty mines. The submarine would be 298ft long overall.[67] No sketch design was prepared, on the grounds that this was

The end-of-war 'A' class embodied wartime experience. *Aeneas* is shown in July 1946. Note her high seakeeping bow and her shielded 4in gun. She had the end-of-war radar arrangement with her air-warning antenna forward and a telescoping mast at the after end of the periscope standards for her surface-search antenna. (NHHC)

only a slightly modified version of the approved 1939 minelayer. The Board approved Legend and building drawings in April 1941. Submarines were ordered from Scotts, but they were never built.

At the 18 July 1941 meeting on submarine policy, VA(S) asked that a submarine be designed using the 3300 BHP pair of diesels planned for the abortive minelayers. The alternative, a supercharged diesel, actually was adopted for the next-generation submarine.[68] This would seem to have been the origin of the 'A'-class design. A January 1942 conference decided to get a supercharged engine into service as quickly as possible by seeking minimum modifications to an 'S'-class hull.[69] If that worked, the modification might be introduced into a production 'S'-class hull, to be ordered later. A modified 'S'-class submarine would have the lightest possible high-capacity battery in a lightweight container, and it would have a supercharged 'S' or 'T'-class engine. The new engine could also be used in a modified 'T'-class submarine with two rather than three battery sections, using the new high-capacity cells. No such submarine was built, however.

In February 1942, not long after war broke out in the Far East, VA(S) observed that, given the short endurance of 'S'-class submarines, some form of replenishment submarine would be valuable. In effect he merged this new requirement with that of the abortive minelayer. DNC agreed to sketch a dual-purpose minelayer and cargo carrier, of about 'T' size, intended mainly for minelaying. It would stow 120 tons of avgas in external tanks for and be able to carry thirty-six torpedoes in containers in the casing. Speed would have been 18.5 knots.[70] The combination of avgas and torpedoes suggests the needs of Malta, to fuel aircraft and to resupply the submarine base with weapons. Staff requirements were framed in the autumn of 1942.[71]

Another possibility was to provide substantially more cargo fuel, 600 tons, plus spare torpedoes and mines. One battery would be omitted. Due to shortage of staff Vickers was asked to produce a pre-liminary design. Meanwhile it was clear that no new design could enter production in Britain, so an abortive attempt was made to have it built in the United States. A Vickers design submitted in March 1943 was huge: 2494 tons surfaced, 2914 tons submerged, and 289ft 2in long on the waterline, but it offered stowage for only 430 tons of oil, 130 tons of stores, twenty-four torpedoes, and 150 rounds of gun ammunition.

Staff requirements for a new design, designated the 'A' class, were framed in October 1942.[72] It would have higher surface speed, greater endurance, and improved habitability to operate in the Far East.[73] It was also be specially designed for welded construction.[74] Work on this design seems to have begun in mid-1942. From the outset it had a circular-section pressure hull, for greater strength: cylindrical amidships, with conical ends. The fore end could not accommodate the six tubes of a 'T'-class submarine, so all versions of the design showed four internal tubes forward plus two external. All showed two internal tubes aft, the earliest showing a single external tube (soon replaced by a pair of such tubes). These early designs also showed two reloads aft.[75]

A sketch design was completed in February 1943.[76] It generally met the draft Staff Requirement, except that at A(S) request endurance was increased from 8000nm at 10 knots to 12,200nm at 10 knots and to 15,200nm at 10 knots if fuel was carried in two external main ballast tanks. Endurance would be reduced by about 25 per cent if the ship was 4 months out of dock facing Sea State 3 on passage. This was the first class of British submarines with a fully circular-section pressure hull (for strength). That precluded the deep bow torpedo compartment of earlier submarines, so to get the desired six-tube bow

salvo it had two external bow tubes. There were also two external stern tubes. As in the 'T' class, they had a 4in gun.

The Legend compared the new submarine with the current 'T' class. The pressure hull was shorter (222ft vs 244ft) but the submarine was longer, 277ft 9in vs 273ft 6in overall and slimmer (beam extreme was 22ft 3in vs 26ft 6in). Standard displacement would be 1120 tons rather than 1090 tons (surfaced 1360 tons vs 1325 tons, submerged 1590 tons vs 1575 tons). The new design also had more powerful engines. Options were six or eight cylinders with superchargers, producing a total of 3600 BHP or 4300 BHP, for either 18 or 19 knots surfaced. The 'T' class produced 2500 BHP (15.75 knots). Submerged power was reduced from 1450 BHP to 1250 BHP, so submerged speed was down a knot, to 8 knots. With a smaller battery (224 high-capacity vs 336 cells), underwater endurance at 4 knots would be 20 hours rather than 21 hours. Diving depth would be 500ft rather than 300ft. To avoid production problems, four of the class would have the six-cylinder Admiralty diesel of the 'T' class. Presumably they would have been the four built instead of four 1942 'T'-class submarines.

The British were aware of Dutch work on snorkels, so the staff

requirements called for the ability to charge batteries submerged.[77] Based on Dutch experience, it was suggested that auxiliary diesel generators should be used. However, the idea was dropped on the ground that 'submerged dieseling' had no operational value to British submarines, presumably because neither the Germans nor the Japanese had effective airborne sea-search radars to threaten submarines at night. Late in the war the idea was revived, and plans were made for depot ships in the Far East to fit snorkels ('snorts' in British parlance) if necessary. Initial trials showed that with supercharger at full power, the engines were extremely loud. There were also reports of main crank pin bearing problems.[78]

Initial operations by the prototype HMS *Amphion* showed disappointing seakeeping.[79] On passage to Bermuda, with a Force 5 wind on her quarter, she rolled so heavily (up to 50°) that the sea came up over the weather side of the bridge. When she proceeded with her head to the sea, in a Force 9 gale, acid spilled out of her batteries. Her commanding officer wrote that he would have been quite anxious had his boat encountered a hurricane or typhoon. The bridge was wet unless the wind was blowing less than Force 4, and there was no swell; or

unless the wind and sea were within 30° of right astern and did not exceed Force 5. Otherwise any attempt to maintain 12 knots on the surface would bring water constantly onto the bridge and down the conning tower hatch. After two hours in a sea exceeding Sea State 4, 60 to 70 tons of water was shipped into the main ballast tanks; the boat's commander thought its free surface was largely responsible or the lack of stability. He wanted the main tanks partitioned to prevent this free water from flowing from side to side as the boat rolled. Even in a moderate sea, the space above the pressure hull between the ballast tanks was constantly full of water, which never had time to drain; it added considerable topweight. Buoyancy forward was insufficient; even with a blower running, the main tank forward tended to fill, and to bring the bridge down. That made the bridge wet and it also reduced speed substantially.

Alcide shows her two external stern torpedo tubes and her twin 20mm anti-aircraft gun, March 1947. (NHHC)

'S' CLASS SUBMARINES (EARLY THIRD GROUP) *SERAPH*, *SHAKESPEARE* AND *P 222*. General arrangements. (Drawn by John Lambert)

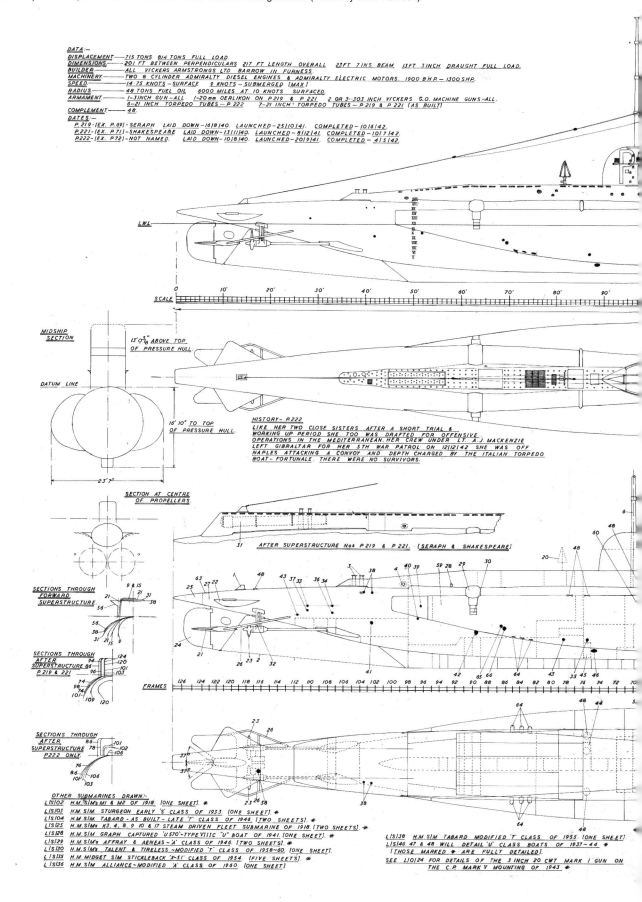

DATA:-
DISPLACEMENT—715 TONS 814 TONS FULL LOAD.
DIMENSIONS:—201 FT BETWEEN PERPENDICULARS 217 FT LENGTH OVERALL 23FT 7INS BEAM 13FT 3INCH DRAUGHT FULL LOAD.
BUILDER:—ALL VICKERS ARMSTRONGS LTD BARROW IN FURNESS.
MACHINERY:—TWO 8 CYLINDER ADMIRALTY DIESEL ENGINES & ADMIRALTY ELECTRIC MOTORS. 1900 BHP—1300 SHP.
SPEED:—14.75 KNOTS—SURFACE 9 KNOTS—SUBMERGED [MAX]
RADIUS:—48 TONS FUEL OIL 6000 MILES AT 10 KNOTS SURFACED.
ARMAMENT:—1-3INCH GUN—ALL 1-20mm OERLIKON ON P 219 & P 221 2 OR 3-303 INCH VICKERS G.O. MACHINE GUNS-ALL.
6-21 INCH TORPEDO TUBES – P 222   7-21 INCH TORPEDO TUBES – P 219 & P 221 [AS BUILT]
COMPLEMENT:—48.
DATES:-
P.219-[EX. P.69]-SERAPH LAID DOWN-16|8|40. LAUNCHED-25|10|41. COMPLETED-10|6|42.
P.221-[EX. P.71]-SHAKESPEARE LAID DOWN-13|11|40. LAUNCHED-8|12|41. COMPLETED-10|7|42.
P.222-[EX. P.72]-NOT NAMED. LAID DOWN-10|8|40. LAUNCHED-20|9|41. COMPLETED-4|5|42.

LWL

SCALE

MIDSHIP SECTION

13'0 1/8" ABOVE TOP OF PRESSURE HULL.

DATUM LINE

16' 10" TO TOP OF PRESSURE HULL.

23' 7"

SECTION AT CENTRE OF PROPELLERS.

HISTORY- P222
LIKE HER TWO CLOSE SISTERS AFTER A SHORT TRIAL & WORKING UP PERIOD SHE TOO WAS DRAFTED FOR OFFENSIVE OPERATIONS IN THE MEDITERRANEAN. HER CREW UNDER LT. A.J. MACKENZIE LEFT GIBRALTAR FOR HER 5TH WAR PATROL ON 12|12|42 SHE WAS OFF NAPLES ATTACKING A CONVOY AND DEPTH CHARGED BY THE ITALIAN TORPEDO BOAT- FORTUNALE. THERE WERE NO SURVIVORS.

SECTIONS THROUGH FORWARD SUPERSTRUCTURE

SECTIONS THROUGH AFTER SUPERSTRUCTURE P 219 & 221

AFTER SUPERSTRUCTURE Nos P 219 & P 221. [SERAPH & SHAKESPEARE]

FRAMES

SECTIONS THROUGH AFTER SUPERSTRUCTURE P222 ONLY.

OTHER SUBMARINES DRAWN:-
L|S|02 H.M.S|M's M1 & M2 OF 1918. [ONE SHEET]. *
L|S|03 H.M.S|M. STURGEON EARLY 'S' CLASS OF 1933. [ONE SHEET]. *
L|S|04 H.M.S|M. TABARD - AS BUILT - LATE 'T' CLASS OF 1946. [TWO SHEETS]. *
L|S|25 H.M.S|Ms K3, 4, 8, 9, 10 & 17 STEAM DRIVEN FLEET SUBMARINE OF 1918. [TWO SHEETS]. *
L|S|28 H.M.S|M GRAPH CAPTURED 'U570'-TYPE VIIIC 'U' BOAT OF 1941. [ONE SHEET]. *
L|S|29 H.M.S|M's AFFRAY & AENEAS ~ 'A' CLASS OF 1946. [TWO SHEETS]. *
L|S|30 H.M.S|Ms TALENT & TIRELESS ~ MODIFIED 'T' CLASS OF 1958~60. [ONE SHEET].
L|S|35 H.M. MIDGET S|M STICKLEBACK 'X-51' CLASS OF 1954. [FIVE SHEETS]. *
L|S|36 H.M.S|M ALLIANCE ~ MODIFIED 'A' CLASS OF 1960. [ONE SHEET]

L|S|38 H.M.S|M TABARD MODIFIED 'T' CLASS OF 1955. [ONE SHEET].
L|S|46 47 & 48 WILL DETAIL 'U' CLASS BOATS OF 1937~44. *
[THOSE MARKED * ARE FULLY DETAILED].
SEE L|0|24 FOR DETAILS OF THE 3 INCH 20 CWT MARK I GUN ON THE C.P. MARK V MOUNTING OF 1943. *

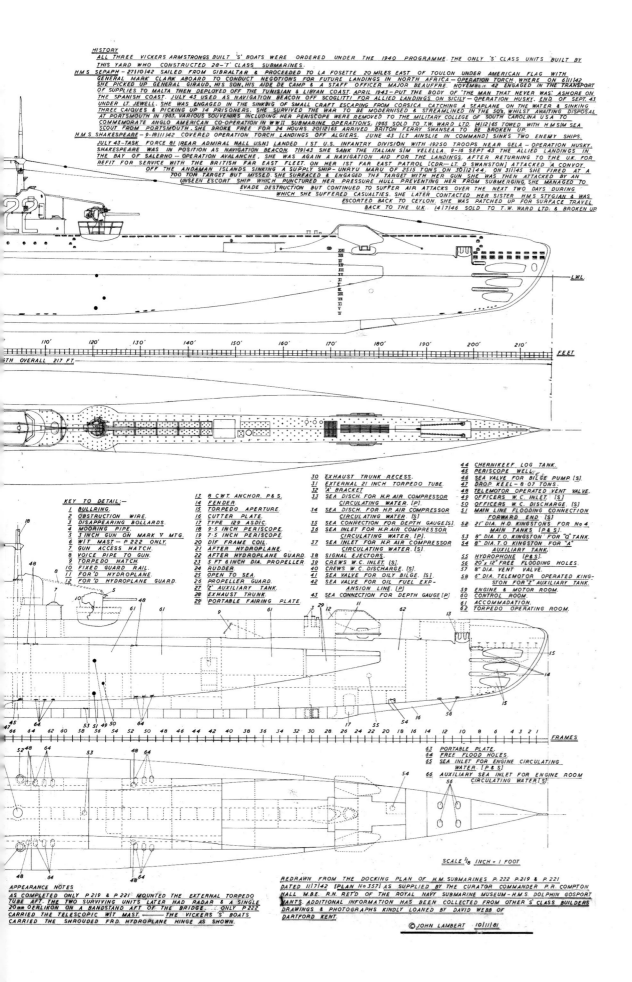

HISTORY

ALL THREE VICKERS ARMSTRONGS BUILT 'S' BOATS WERE ORDERED UNDER THE 1940 PROGRAMME. THE ONLY 'S' CLASS UNITS BUILT BY THIS YARD WHO CONSTRUCTED 28-'T' CLASS SUBMARINES.

HMS SERAPH - 27|10|42 SAILED FROM GIBRALTAR & PROCEEDED TO LA FOSETTE 20 MILES EAST OF TOULON UNDER AMERICAN FLAG WITH GENERAL MARK CLARK ABOARD TO CONDUCT NEGOTIONS FOR FUTURE LANDINGS IN NORTH AFRICA - OPERATION TORCH, WHERE ON 6|11|42 SHE PICKED UP GENERAL GIRAUD, HIS SON, HIS AIDE DE CAMP & A STAFF OFFICER MAJOR BEAUFRE. NOVEMBER 42 ENGAGED IN THE TRANSPORT OF SUPPLIES TO MALTA THEN DEPLOYED OFF THE TUNISIAN & LIBYAN COAST. APRIL 1943 - PUT THE BODY OF 'THE MAN THAT NEVER WAS' ASHORE ON THE SPANISH COAST. JULY 43 USED AS NAVIGATION BEACON OFF SCOGLITTI FOR ALLIED LANDINGS ON SICILY - OPERATION HUSKY. END. OF SEPT. 43 UNDER LT. JEWELL. SHE WAS ENGAGED IN THE SINKING OF SMALL CRAFT ESCAPING FROM CORSICA CATCHING A SEAPLANE ON THE WATER & SINKING THREE CAIQUES & PICKING UP 14 PRISONERS. SHE SURVIVED THE WAR TO BE MODERNISED & STREAMLINED IN THE 50's, WHILST AWAITING DISPOSAL AT PORTSMOUTH IN 1963, VARIOUS SOUVENIRS INCLUDING HER PERISCOPE WERE REMOVED TO THE MILITARY COLLEGE OF SOUTH CAROLINA USA TO COMMEMORATE ANGLO AMERICAN CO-OPERATION IN WWII SUBMARINE OPERATIONS. 1965 SOLD TO T.W. WARD LTD. 14|12|65 TOWED WITH HMSIM SEA SCOUT FROM PORTSMOUTH. SHE BROKE FREE FOR 24 HOURS. 20|12|65 ARRIVED BRITON FERRY SWANSEA TO BE BROKEN UP.

HMS SHAKESPEARE - 9-18|11|42 COVERED OPERATION TORCH LANDINGS OFF ALGIERS. JUNE 43 [LT AINSLIE IN COMMAND] SINKS TWO ENEMY SHIPS. JULY 43 - TASK FORCE 81 [REAR ADMIRAL HALL USN] LANDED 1ST U.S. INFANTRY DIVISION WITH 19250 TROOPS NEAR GELA - OPERATION HUSKY. SHAKESPEARE WAS IN POSITION AS NAVIGATION BEACON. 7|9|43 SHE SANK THE ITALIAN SIM VELELLA. 9-16 SEPT 43 THE ALLIED LANDINGS IN THE BAY OF SALERNO - OPERATION AVALANCHE. SHE WAS AGAIN A NAVIGATION AID FOR THE LANDINGS. AFTER RETURNING TO THE U.K. FOR REFIT FOR SERVICE WITH THE BRITISH FAR EAST FLEET. ON HER 1ST FAR EAST PATROL [CDR- LT. D SWANSTON] ATTACKED A CONVOY OFF THE ANDAMAN ISLANDS SINKING A SUPPLY SHIP- UNRYU MARU OF 2515 TONS ON 30|12|44. ON 3|1|45 SHE FIRED AT A 700 TON TARGET BUT MISSED. SHE SURFACED & ENGAGED THE TARGET WITH HER GUN SHE WAS THEN ATTACKED BY AN UNSEEN ESCORT SHIP WHICH PUNCTURED HER PRESSURE HULL PREVENTING HER FROM SUBMERGING. SHE MANAGED TO EVADE DESTRUCTION BUT CONTINUED TO SUFFER AIR ATTACKS OVER THE NEXT TWO DAYS DURING WHICH SHE SUFFERED CASUALTIES. SHE LATER CONTACTED HER SISTER HMS STYGIAN & WAS ESCORTED BACK TO CEYLON. SHE WAS PATCHED UP FOR SURFACE TRAVEL BACK TO THE U.K. 14|7|46 SOLD TO T.W. WARD LTD. & BROKEN UP

LWL.

110' 120' 130' 140' 150' 160' 170' 180' 190' 200' 210'   FEET

(LENG)TH OVERALL 217 FT.

KEY TO DETAIL:-

1 BULLRING.
2 OBSTRUCTION WIRE.
3 DISAPPEARING BOLLARDS.
4 MOORING PIPE.
5 3 INCH GUN ON MARK Y MTG.
6 W/T MAST - P 222 ONLY.
7 GUN ACCESS HATCH.
8 VOICE PIPE TO GUN.
9 TORPEDO HATCH.
10 FIXED GUARD RAIL.
11 FOR'D HYDROPLANE.
12 FOR'D HYDROPLANE GUARD.

13 8 CWT. ANCHOR. P&S.
14 FENDER.
15 TORPEDO APERTURE.
16 CUTTER PLATE.
17 TYPE 129 ASDIC.
18 9.5 INCH PERISCOPE.
19 7.5 INCH PERISCOPE.
20 DIF FRAME COIL.
21 AFTER HYDROPLANE.
22 AFTER HYDROPLANE GUARD.
23 5 FT 6 INCH DIA. PROPELLER.
24 RUDDER.
25 OPEN TO SEA.
26 PROPELLER GUARD.
27 'Z' AUXILIARY TANK.
28 EXHAUST TRUNK.
29 PORTABLE FAIRING PLATE.

30 EXHAUST TRUNK RECESS.
31 EXTERNAL 21 INCH TORPEDO TUBE.
32 'A' BRACKET.
33 SEA DISCH. FOR H.P. AIR COMPRESSOR CIRCULATING WATER. [P].
34 SEA DISCH. FOR H.P. AIR COMPRESSOR CIRCULATING WATER [S].
35 SEA CONNECTION FOR DEPTH GAUGE[S].
36 SEA INLET FOR H.P. AIR COMPRESSOR CIRCULATING WATER. [P].
37 SEA INLET FOR H.P. AIR COMPRESSOR CIRCULATING WATER. [S].
38 SIGNAL EJECTORS.
39 CREWS W.C. INLET. [S].
40 CREWS W.C. DISCHARGE. [S].
41 SEA VALVE FOR OILY BILGE. [S].
42 SEA VALVE FOR OIL FUEL EXPANSION LINE. [P]
43 SEA CONNECTION FOR DEPTH GAUGE [P]

44 CHERNIKEEF LOG TANK.
45 PERISCOPE WELL.
46 SEA VALVE FOR BILGE PUMP. [S].
47 DROP KEEL - 8.07 TONS.
48 TELEMOTOR OPERATED VENT VALVE.
49 OFFICERS W.C. INLET. [S]
50 OFFICERS W.C. DISCHARGE. [S]
51 MAIN LINE FLOODING CONNECTION FORWARD END [S]
52 21" DIA. H.O. KINGSTONS FOR No 4 MAIN TANKS [P & S.]
53 8" DIA. T.O. KINGSTON FOR "Q" TANK.
54 8" DIA. T.O. KINGSTON FOR "A" AUXILIARY TANK.
55 HYDROPHONE [P&S].
56 20" x 12" FREE FLOODING HOLES.
57 8" DIA. VENT VALVE.
58 6" DIA. TELEMOTOR OPERATED KINGSTON FOR 'Z' AUXILIARY TANK.
59 ENGINE & MOTOR ROOM.
60 CONTROL ROOM.
61 ACCOMMADATION.
62 TORPEDO OPERATING ROOM.

FRAMES

63 PORTABLE PLATE.
64 FREE FLOOD HOLES.
65 SEA INLET FOR ENGINE CIRCULATING WATER. [P & S]
66 AUXILIARY SEA INLET FOR ENGINE ROOM CIRCULATING WATER. [S]

SCALE 1/8 INCH = 1 FOOT

REDRAWN FROM THE DOCKING PLAN OF H.M. SUBMARINES P.222 P.219 & P.221 DATED 11|7|42 [PLAN No 357] AS SUPPLIED BY THE CURATOR COMMANDER P.R. COMPTON HALL M.B.E. R.N. RET'D OF THE ROYAL NAVY SUBMARINE MUSEUM - H.M.S. DOLPHIN GOSPORT HANTS. ADDITIONAL INFORMATION HAS BEEN COLLECTED FROM OTHER 'S' CLASS BUILDERS DRAWINGS & PHOTOGRAPHS KINDLY LOANED BY DAVID WEBB OF DARTFORD KENT.

© JOHN LAMBERT 10|11|81

APPEARANCE NOTES
AS COMPLETED ONLY P 219 & P 221 MOUNTED THE EXTERNAL TORPEDO TUBE AFT. THE TWO SURVIVING UNITS LATER HAD RADAR & A SINGLE 20mm OERLIKON ON A BANDSTAND AFT OF THE BRIDGE. ONLY P 222 CARRIED THE TELESCOPIC W/T MAST. — THE VICKERS 'S' BOATS CARRIED THE SHROUDED FRD. HYDROPLANE HINGE AS SHOWN.

'T' CLASS SUBMARINES (THIRD GROUP) *TABARD*. (Drawn by John Lambert)

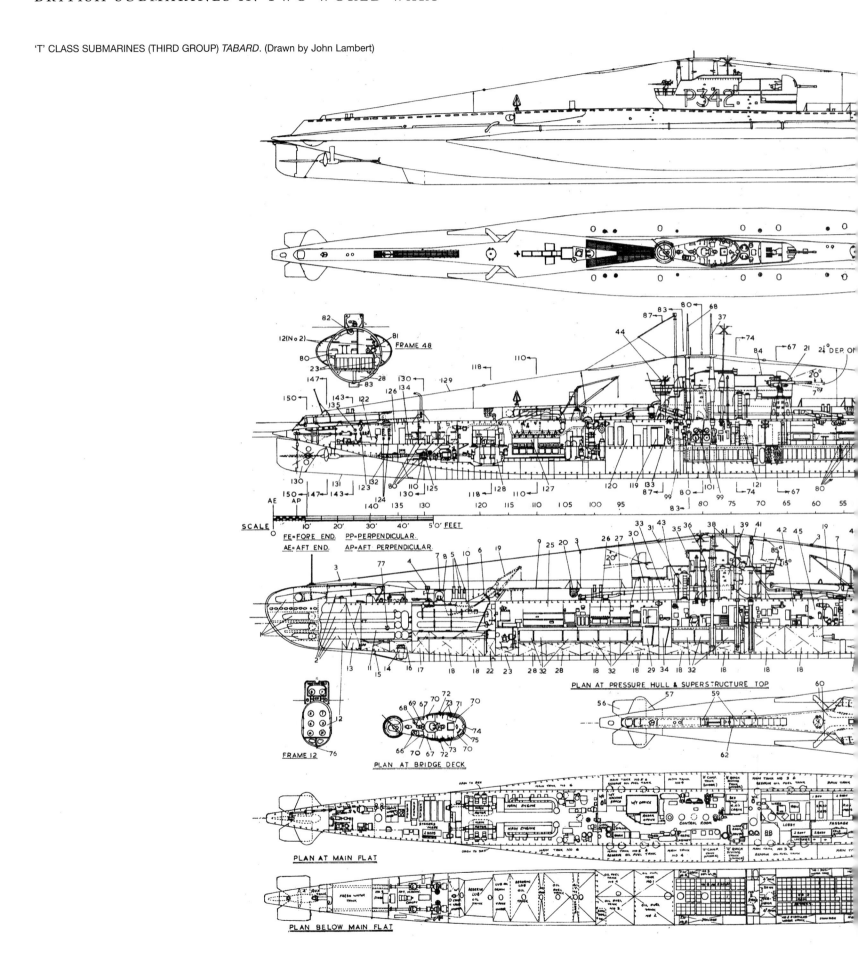

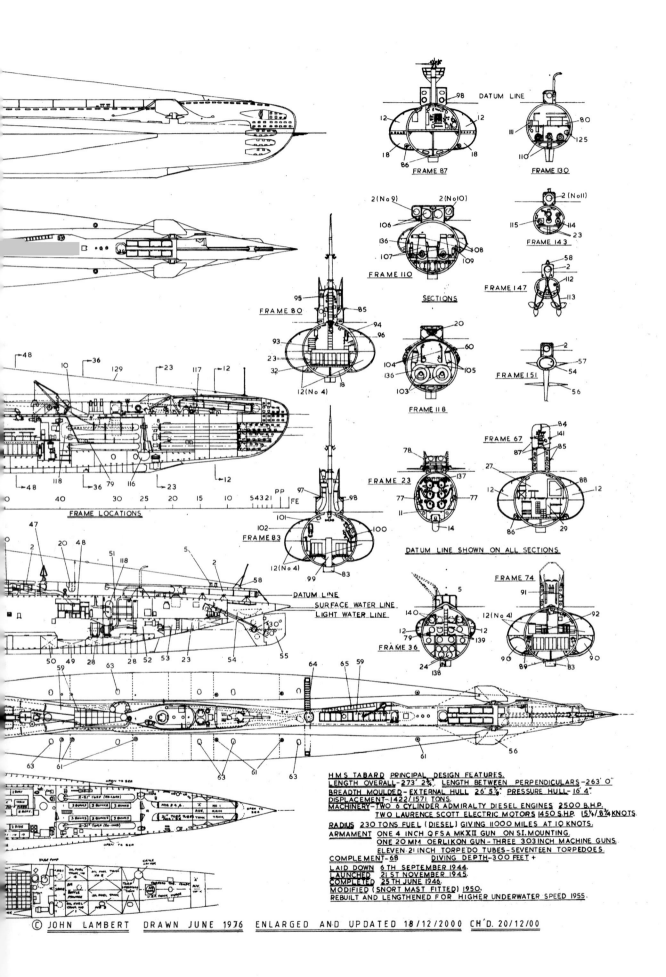

FRAME 87

FRAME 130

DATUM LINE

FRAME 110

FRAME 143

SECTIONS

FRAME 80

FRAME 147

FRAME 118

FRAME 151

FRAME LOCATIONS

FRAME 67

FRAME 23

FRAME 83

DATUM LINE SHOWN ON ALL SECTIONS

FRAME 74

DATUM LINE
SURFACE WATER LINE
LIGHT WATER LINE

FRAME 36

H.M.S. TABARD PRINCIPAL DESIGN FEATURES.
LENGTH OVERALL- 273' 2¾". LENGTH BETWEEN PERPENDICULARS- 263' 0".
BREADTH MOULDED - EXTERNAL HULL 26' 5½". PRESSURE HULL- 16' 4".
DISPLACEMENT- 1422/1571 TONS.
MACHINERY- TWO 6 CYLINDER ADMIRALTY DIESEL ENGINES 2500 B.H.P.
TWO LAURENCE SCOTT ELECTRIC MOTORS 1450 S.H.P. 15⅛/8¾ KNOTS.
RADIUS 230 TONS FUEL (DIESEL) GIVING 11000 MILES AT 10 KNOTS.
ARMAMENT ONE 4 INCH QFSA MKXII GUN ON S1.MOUNTING.
ONE 20 MM OERLIKON GUN - THREE 303 INCH MACHINE GUNS.
ELEVEN 21 INCH TORPEDO TUBES - SEVENTEEN TORPEDOES.
COMPLEMENT- 68   DIVING DEPTH- 300 FEET +
LAID DOWN 6TH SEPTEMBER 1944.
LAUNCHED 21ST NOVEMBER 1945.
COMPLETED 25TH JUNE 1946.
MODIFIED (SNORT MAST FITTED) 1950.
REBUILT AND LENGTHENED FOR HIGHER UNDERWATER SPEED 1955.

© JOHN LAMBERT DRAWN JUNE 1976 ENLARGED AND UPDATED 18/12/2000 CH'D. 20/12/00

'U' CLASS SUBMARINES *UTMOST*, *UPRIGHT*, *UNIQUE*, *USK*, *UPHOLDER* AND *UNBEATEN*. General arrangements. (Drawn by John Lambert)

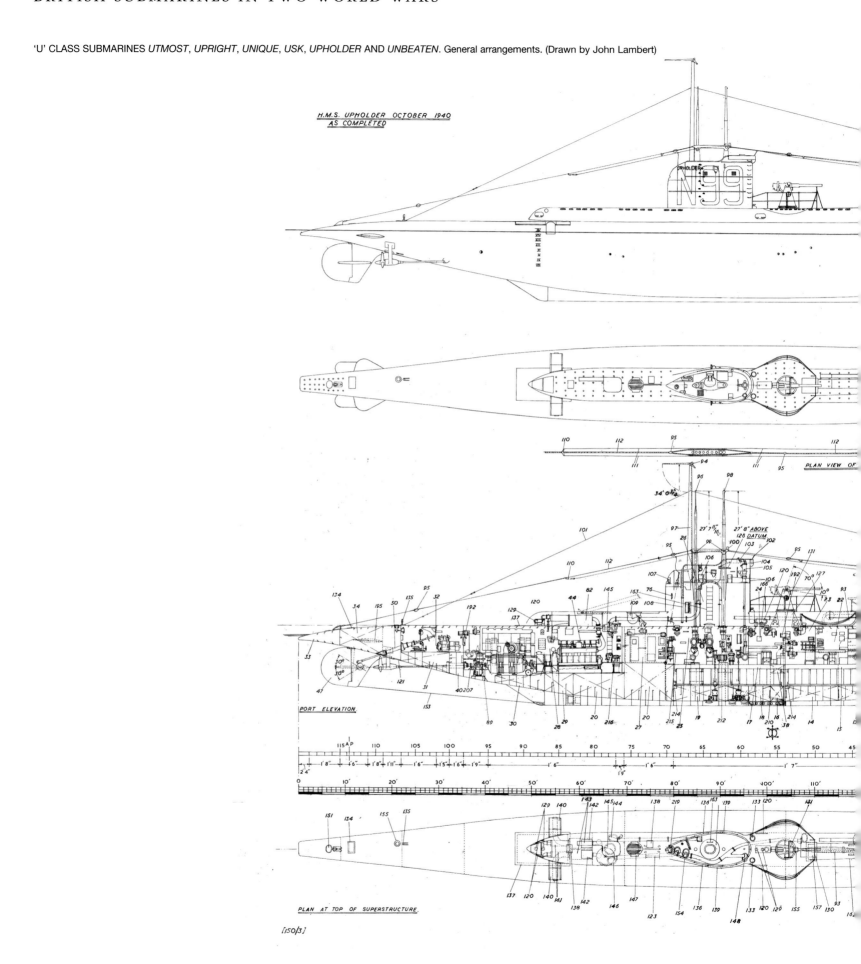

H.M.S. UPHOLDER OCTOBER 1940
AS COMPLETED

PLAN VIEW OF

PORT ELEVATION.

PLAN AT TOP OF SUPERSTRUCTURE.

[150/3]

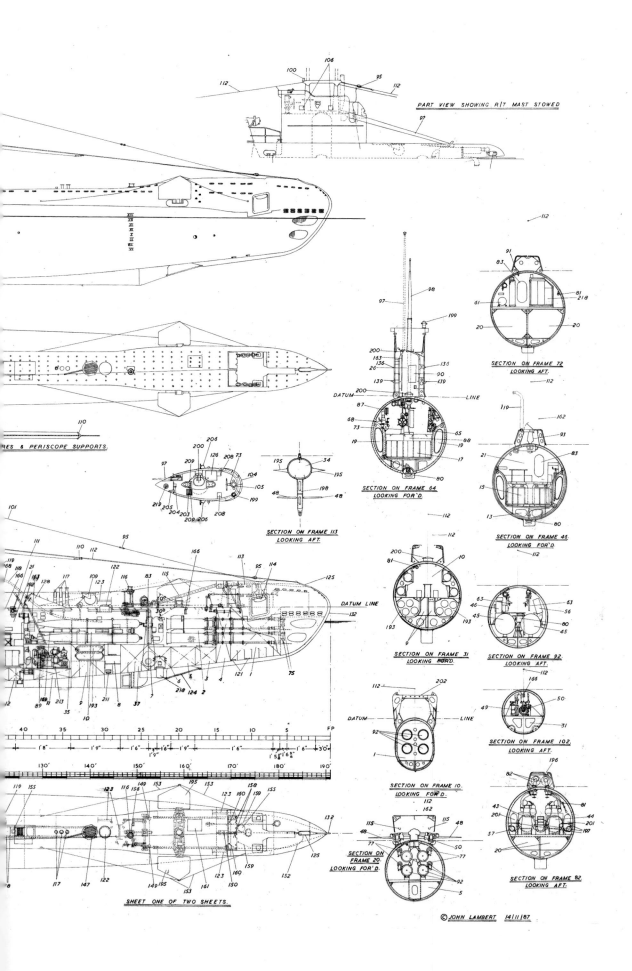

PART VIEW SHOWING R/T MAST STOWED

SECTION ON FRAME 72
LOOKING AFT.

SECTION ON FRAME 64
LOOKING FOR'D.

SECTION ON FRAME 46
LOOKING FOR'D.

SECTION ON FRAME 113
LOOKING AFT.

SECTION ON FRAME 31
LOOKING FOR'D.

SECTION ON FRAME 92
LOOKING AFT.

SECTION ON FRAME 10
LOOKING FOR'D.

SECTION ON FRAME 102
LOOKING AFT.

SECTION ON
FRAME 20
LOOKING FOR'D.

SECTION ON FRAME 82
LOOKING AFT.

RES & PERISCOPE SUPPORTS.

DATUM LINE

DATUM LINE

SHEET ONE OF TWO SHEETS.

© JOHN LAMBERT 14/11/87

293

'U' CLASS SUBMARINES *UTMOST, UPRIGHT, UNIQUE, USK, UPHOLDER* AND *UNBEATEN*. Internal details. (Drawn by John Lambert)

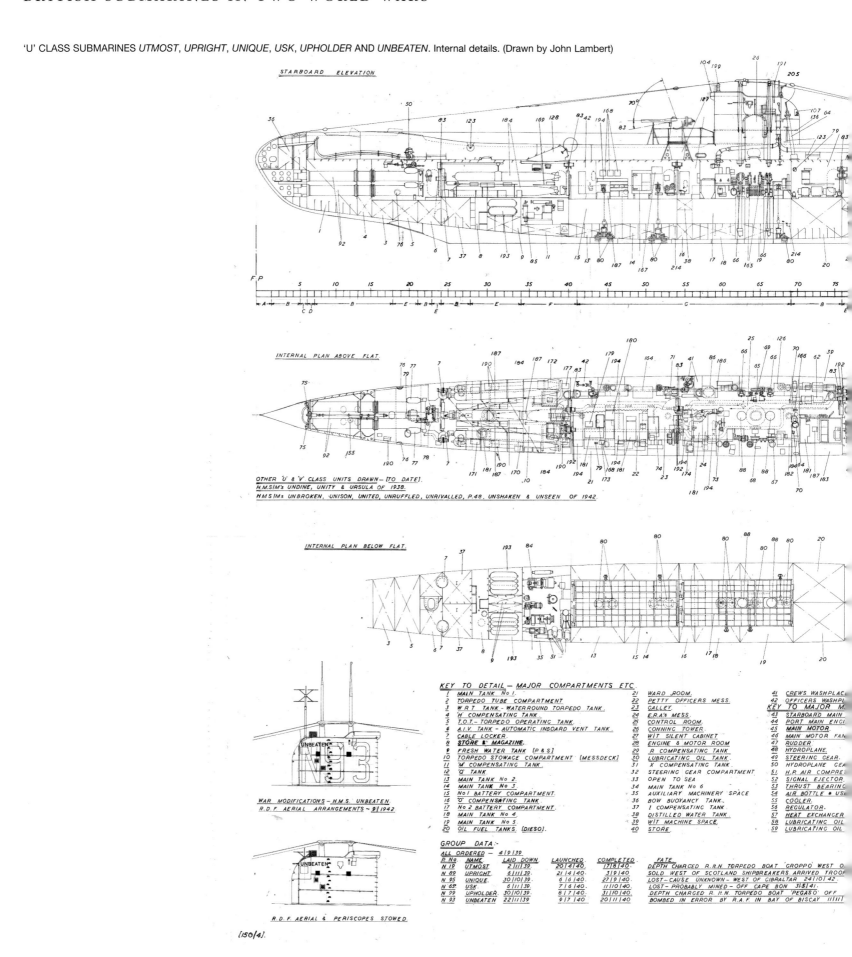

STARBOARD ELEVATION

INTERNAL PLAN ABOVE FLAT.

OTHER 'U' & 'V' CLASS UNITS DRAWN - [TO DATE].
H.M.SIM's UNDINE, UNITY & URSULA OF 1938.
H.M.SIMs UNBROKEN, UNISON, UNITED, UNRUFFLED, UNRIVALLED, P.48, UNSHAKEN & UNSEEN OF 1942.

INTERNAL PLAN BELOW FLAT.

WAR MODIFICATIONS - H.M.S. UNBEATEN.
R.D.F. AERIAL ARRANGEMENTS ~ 9/1942.

R.D.F. AERIAL & PERISCOPES STOWED.

[150/4].

KEY TO DETAIL - MAJOR COMPARTMENTS ETC.

1	MAIN TANK No 1.	21	WARD ROOM.	41	CREWS WASHPLAC
2	TORPEDO TUBE COMPARTMENT	22	PETTY OFFICERS MESS	42	OFFICERS WASHPL
3	W.R.T. TANK - WATERROUND TORPEDO TANK.	23	GALLEY.		KEY TO MAJOR M.
4	'H' COMPENSATING TANK	24	E.R.A's MESS.	43	STARBOARD MAIN
5	T.O.T.- TORPEDO OPERATING TANK.	25	CONTROL ROOM.	44	PORT MAIN ENGI
6	A.I.V. TANK - AUTOMATIC INBOARD VENT TANK.	26	CONNING TOWER.	45	MAIN MOTOR
7	CABLE LOCKER.	27	W/T SILENT CABINET	46	MAIN MOTOR FAN
8	STORE & MAGAZINE.	28	ENGINE & MOTOR ROOM	47	RUDDER
9	FRESH WATER TANK [P & S]	29	R COMPENSATING TANK	48	HYDROPLANE.
10	TORPEDO STOWAGE COMPARTMENT [MESSDECK]	30	LUBRICATING OIL TANK.	49	STEERING GEAR.
11	'M' COMPENSATING TANK.	31	X COMPENSATING TANK.	50	HYDROPLANE GEA
12	'Q' TANK.	32	STEERING GEAR COMPARTMENT.	51	H.P. AIR COMPRES
13	MAIN TANK No 2.	33	OPEN TO SEA	52	SIGNAL EJECTOR.
14	MAIN TANK No 3	34	MAIN TANK No 6	53	THRUST BEARING
15	No1 BATTERY COMPARTMENT.	35	AUXILIARY MACHINERY SPACE	54	AIR BOTTLE & US
16	'O' COMPENSATING TANK.	36	BOW BUOYANCY TANK.	55	COOLER.
17	No2 BATTERY COMPARTMENT.	37	I COMPENSATING TANK.	56	REGULATOR.
18	MAIN TANK No 4.	38	DISTILLED WATER TANK.	57	HEAT EXCHANGER
19	MAIN TANK No 5	39	W/T MACHINE SPACE.	58	LUBRICATING OIL
20	OIL FUEL TANKS [DIESO]	40	STORE.	59	LUBRICATING OIL

GROUP DATA:-

ALL ORDERED - 4/9/39.

P.No.	NAME	LAID DOWN	LAUNCHED	COMPLETED	FATE
N 19	UTMOST	2/11/39.	20/4/40.	17/8/40.	DEPTH CHARGED R.H.N TORPEDO BOAT 'GROPPO' WEST O.
N 89	UPRIGHT	8/11/39.	21/4/40.	3/9/40	SOLD WEST OF SCOTLAND SHIPBREAKERS. ARRIVED TROO
N 95	UNIQUE.	30/10/39.	6/6/40.	27/9/40.	LOST - CAUSE UNKNOWN - WEST OF GIBRALTAR 24/10/42.
N 65	USK.	6/11/39.	7/6/40.	11/10/40.	LOST - PROBABLY MINED - OFF CAPE BON 3/5/41.
N 99	UPHOLDER.	30/10/39.	8/7/40.	31/10/40.	DEPTH CHARGED R.I.N. TORPEDO BOAT 'PEGASO' OFF
N 93	UNBEATEN	22/11/39	9/7/40	20/11/40	BOMBED IN ERROR BY R.A.F IN BAY OF BISCAY 11/11/

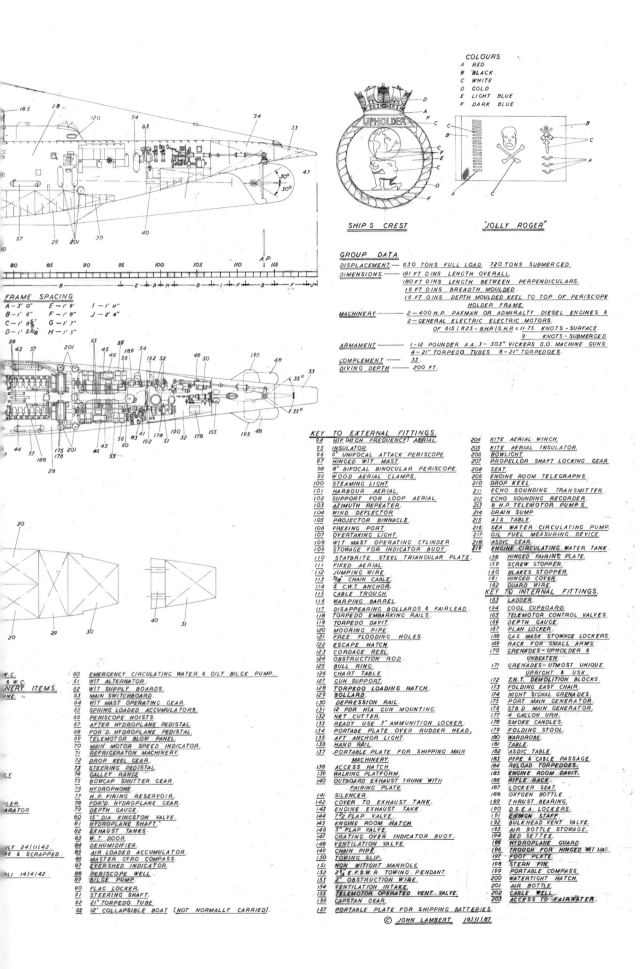

COLOURS
A RED
B BLACK
C WHITE
D GOLD
E LIGHT BLUE
F DARK BLUE

UPHOLDER

SHIP'S CREST

"JOLLY ROGER"

GROUP DATA

DISPLACEMENT.— 630 TONS FULL LOAD. 720 TONS SUBMERGED.
DIMENSIONS.— 191 FT 0 INS LENGTH OVERALL.
        180 FT 0 INS LENGTH BETWEEN PERPENDICULARS.
        16 FT 0 INS BREADTH MOULDED.
        16 FT 0 INS DEPTH MOULDED KEEL TO TOP OF PERISCOPE
        HOLDER FRAME.
MACHINERY.— 2—400 H.P. PAXMAN OR ADMIRALTY DIESEL ENGINES &
        2—GENERAL ELECTRIC ELECTRIC MOTORS.
        OF 615/825—B.H.P./S.H.P = 11.75 KNOTS - SURFACE.
                    9 KNOTS - SUBMERGED.
ARMAMENT — 1-12 POUNDER A.A. 3-303" VICKERS G.O. MACHINE GUNS.
        4-21" TORPEDO TUBES 8-21" TORPEDOES.
COMPLEMENT — 33.
DIVING DEPTH — 200 FT.

FRAME SPACING
A - 3' 0"   E - 1' 9"   I - 1' 11"
B - 1' 6"   F - 1' 8"   J - 2' 4"
C - 1' 6⅝" G - 1' 7"
D - 1' 5⅜" H - 1' 5"

KEY TO EXTERNAL FITTINGS.
94 HIF (HIGH FREQUENCY) AERIAL.
95 INSULATOR.
96 6" UNIFOCAL ATTACK PERISCOPE.
97 HINGED W/T MAST.
98 8" BIFOCAL BINOCULAR PERISCOPE.
99 WOOD AERIAL CLAMPS.
100 STEAMING LIGHT.
101 HARBOUR AERIAL.
102 SUPPORT FOR LOOP AERIAL.
103 AZIMUTH REPEATER.
104 WIND DEFLECTOR.
105 PROJECTOR BINNACLE.
106 FREEING PORT.
107 OVERTAKING LIGHT.
108 W/T MAST OPERATING CYLINDER.
109 STOWAGE FOR INDICATOR BUOY.
110 STAYBRITE STEEL TRIANGULAR PLATE.
111 FIXED AERIAL.
112 JUMPING WIRE.
113 5/8 CHAIN CABLE.
114 6 C.W.T. ANCHOR.
115 CABLE TROUGH.
116 WARPING BARREL.
117 DISAPPEARING BOLLARDS & FAIRLEAD.
118 TORPEDO EMBARKING RAILS.
119 TORPEDO DAVIT.
120 MOORING PIPE.
121 FREE FLOODING HOLES.
122 ESCAPE HATCH.
123 CORDAGE REEL.
124 OBSTRUCTION ROD.
125 BULL RING.
126 CHART TABLE.
127 GUN SUPPORT.
128 TORPEDO LOADING HATCH.
129 BOLLARD.
130 DEPRESSION RAIL.
131 12 PDR H/A GUN MOUNTING.
132 NET CUTTER.
133 READY USE 3" AMMUNITION LOCKER.
134 PORTABLE PLATE OVER RUDDER HEAD.
135 AFT ANCHOR LIGHT.
136 HAND RAIL.
137 PORTABLE PLATE FOR SHIPPING MAIN MACHINERY.
138 ACCESS HATCH.
139 WALKING PLATFORM.
140 OUTBOARD EXHAUST TRUNK WITH FAIRING PLATE.
141 SILENCER.
142 COVER TO EXHAUST TANK.
143 ENGINE EXHAUST TANK.
144 7½ FLAP VALVE.
145 ENGINE ROOM HATCH.
146 3" FLAP VALVE.
147 GRATING OVER INDICATOR BUOY.
148 VENTILATION VALVE.
149 CHAIN PIPE.
150 TOWING SLIP.
151 NON W/TIGHT MANHOLE.
152 2½ E.F.S.W.R. TOWING PENDANT.
153 2" OBSTRUCTION WIRE.
154 VENTILATION INTAKE.
155 TELEMOTOR OPERATED VENT VALVE.
156 CAPSTAN GEAR.
157 PORTABLE PLATE FOR SHIPPING BATTERIES.

204 KITE AERIAL WINCH.
205 KITE AERIAL INSULATOR.
206 BOWLIGHT.
207 PROPELLOR SHAFT LOCKING GEAR.
208 SEAT.
209 ENGINE ROOM TELEGRAPHS.
210 DROP KEEL.
211 ECHO SOUNDING TRANSMITTER.
212 ECHO SOUNDING RECORDER.
213 8 H.P. TELEMOTOR PUMPS.
214 DRAIN SUMP.
215 A/S TABLE.
216 SEA WATER CIRCULATING PUMP.
217 OIL FUEL MEASURING DEVICE.
218 ASDIC GEAR.
219 ENGINE CIRCULATING WATER TANK.

158 HINGED FAIRING PLATE.
159 SCREW STOPPER.
160 BLAKES STOPPER.
161 HINGED COVER.
162 GUARD WIRE.
KEY TO INTERNAL FITTINGS.
163 LADDER.
164 COOL CUPBOARD.
165 TELEMOTOR CONTROL VALVES.
166 DEPTH GAUGE.
167 PLAN LOCKER.
168 GAS MASK STOWAGE LOCKERS.
169 RACK FOR SMALL ARMS.
170 GRENADES - UPHOLDER & UNBEATEN.
171 GRENADES - UTMOST UNIQUE UPRIGHT & USK.
172 T.N.T. DEMOLITION BLOCKS.
173 FOLDING EASY CHAIR.
174 NIGHT SIGNAL GRENADES.
175 PORT MAIN GENERATOR.
176 STB'D MAIN GENERATOR.
177 4 GALLON URN.
178 SMOKE CANDLES.
179 FOLDING STOOL.
180 WARDROBE.
181 TABLE.
182 ASDIC TABLE.
183 PIPE & CABLE PASSAGE.
184 RELOAD TORPEDOES.
185 ENGINE ROOM DAVIT.
186 RIFLE RACK.
187 LOCKER SEAT.
188 OXYGEN BOTTLE.
189 THRUST BEARING.
190 D.S.E.A. LOCKERS.
191 ENSIGN STAFF.
192 BULKHEAD VENT VALVE.
193 AIR BOTTLE STOWAGE.
194 BED SETTEE.
195 HYDROPLANE GUARD.
196 TROUGH FOR HINGED W/T MAS.
197 FOOT PLATE.
198 STERN FIN.
199 PORTABLE COMPASS.
200 WATERTIGHT HATCH.
201 AIR BOTTLE.
202 CABLE WELL.
203 ACCESS TO FAIRWATER.

MACHINERY ITEMS.
60 EMERGENCY CIRCULATING WATER & OILY BILGE PUMP.
61 W/T ALTERNATOR.
62 W/T SUPPLY BOARDS.
63 MAIN SWITCHBOARD.
64 W/T MAST OPERATING GEAR.
65 SPRING LOADED ACCUMULATORS.
66 PERISCOPE HOISTS.
67 AFTER HYDROPLANE PEDISTAL.
68 FOR'D. HYDROPLANE PEDISTAL.
69 TELEMOTOR BLOW PANEL.
70 MAIN MOTOR SPEED INDICATOR.
71 REFRIGERATON MACHINERY.
72 DROP KEEL GEAR.
73 STEERING PEDISTAL.
74 GALLEY RANGE.
75 BOWCAP SHUTTER GEAR.
76 HYDROPHONE.
77 H.P. FIRING RESERVOIR.
78 FOR'D. HYDROPLANE GEAR.
79 DEPTH GAUGE.
80 15" DIA KINGSTON VALVE.
81 HYDROPLANE SHAFT.
82 EXHAUST TANKS.
83 W.T. DOOR.
84 DEHUMIDIFIER.
85 AIR LOADED ACCUMULATOR.
86 MASTER GYRO COMPASS.
87 EVERSHED INDICATOR.
88 PERISCOPE WELL.
89 BILGE PUMP.
90 FLAG LOCKER.
91 STEERING SHAFT.
92 21" TORPEDO TUBE.
93 12' COLLAPSIBLE BOAT [NOT NORMALLY CARRIED].

© JOHN LAMBERT 18/11/87

'U' CLASS SUBMARINES *UNBROKEN*, *UNISON*, *UNITED*, *UNRUFFLED*, *UNRIVALLED*, *P 48*, *UNSHAKEN* AND *UNSEEN*. General arrangements. (Drawn by John Lambert)

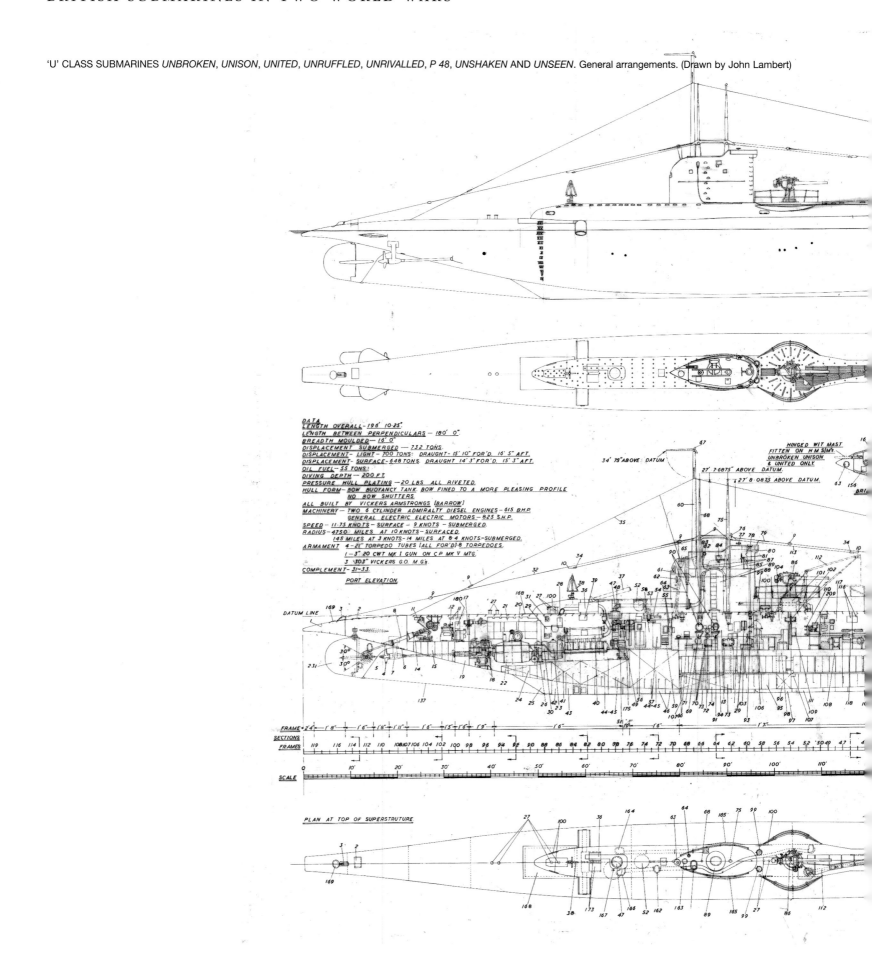

DATA

LENGTH OVERALL - 196' 10.25".
LENGTH BETWEEN PERPENDICULARS - 180' 0".
BREADTH MOULDED - 16' 0".
DISPLACEMENT SUBMERGED — 732 TONS.
DISPLACEMENT- LIGHT - 700 TONS. DRAUGHT-15' 10" FOR'D. 16' 5" AFT.
DISPLACEMENT- SURFACE-648 TONS. DRAUGHT 14' 3" FOR'D. 15' 3" AFT.
OIL FUEL- 55 TONS.
DIVING DEPTH - 200 FT.
PRESSURE HULL PLATING - 20 LBS ALL RIVETED.
HULL FORM- BOW BUOYANCY TANK. BOW FINED TO A MORE PLEASING PROFILE
　　　　　　NO BOW SHUTTERS.
ALL BUILT BY VICKERS ARMSTRONGS (BARROW)
MACHINERY — TWO 6 CYLINDER ADMIRALTY DIESEL ENGINES - 615 B.H.P.
　　　　　　GENERAL ELECTRIC ELECTRIC MOTORS - 825 S.H.P.
SPEED - 11.75 KNOTS - SURFACE - 9 KNOTS - SUBMERGED.
RADIUS - 4750 MILES AT 10 KNOTS - SURFACED.
　　　　　145 MILES AT 3 KNOTS-14 MILES AT 8.4 KNOTS-SUBMERGED.
ARMAMENT 4-21" TORPEDO TUBES (ALL FOR'D) 8 TORPEDOES.
　　　　　1 - 3" 20 CWT MK I GUN ON C P MK V MTG.
　　　　　3 .303" VICKERS G.O. M.G's.
COMPLEMENT- 31-33.

PORT ELEVATION.

PLAN AT TOP OF SUPERSTRUTURE

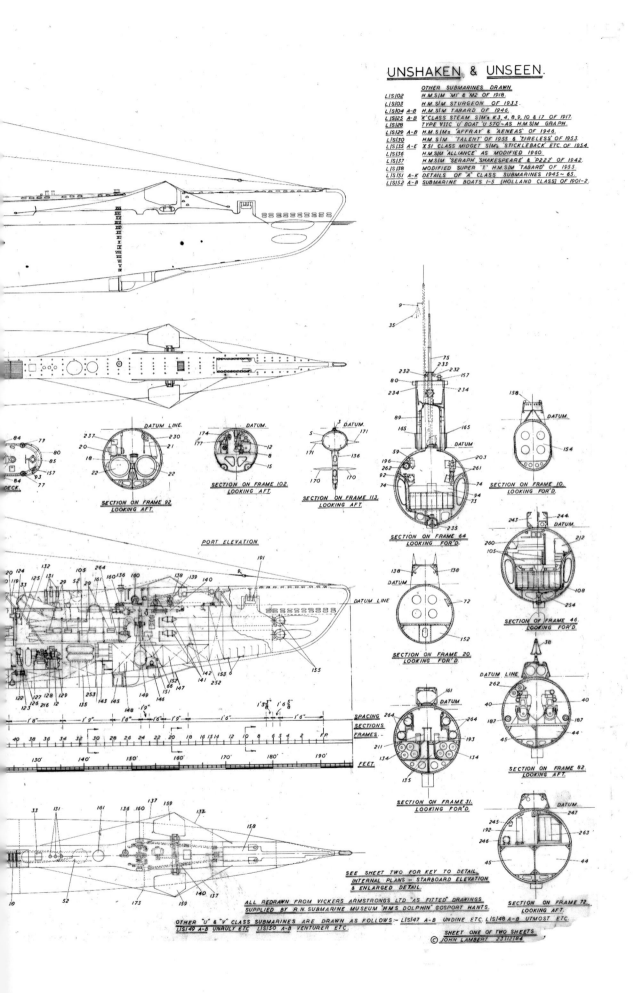

UNSHAKEN & UNSEEN.

OTHER SUBMARINES DRAWN
LISIO2	H.M.S/M 'MI' & 'M2' OF 1918.
LISIO3	H.M.S/M STURGEON OF 1933.
LISIO4 A-B	H.M.S/M TABARD OF 1946.
LISI25 A-B	'K'CLASS STEAM S/M's K3,4,8,9,10 & 17 OF 1917.
LISI28	TYPE VIIC 'U' BOAT 'U 570'~AS H.M.S/M GRAPH.
LISI29 A-B	H.M.S/Ms 'AFFRAY' & 'AENEAS' OF 1946.
LISI30	H.M.S/M 'TALENT' OF 1955 & 'TIRELESS' OF 1953.
LISI35 A-E	X5I CLASS MIDGET S/M's 'STICKLEBACK' ETC. OF 1954.
LISI36	H.M.S/M 'ALLIANCE' AS MODIFIED 1960.
LISI37	H.M.S/M 'SERAPH', 'SHAKESPEARE' & 'P222' OF 1942.
LISI38	MODIFIED SUPER 'T' H.M.S/M 'TABARD' OF 1955.
LISI5I A-K	DETAILS OF 'A' CLASS SUBMARINES 1945~65.
LISI52 A-B	SUBMARINE BOATS I-5 (HOLLAND CLASS) OF 1901-2.

SEE SHEET TWO FOR KEY TO DETAIL
INTERNAL PLANS ~ STARBOARD ELEVATION
& ENLARGED DETAIL.

ALL REDRAWN FROM VICKERS ARMSTRONGS LTD 'AS FITTED' DRAWINGS
SUPPLIED BY R.N. SUBMARINE MUSEUM 'HMS DOLPHIN' GOSPORT HANTS.
OTHER 'U' & 'V' CLASS SUBMARINES ARE DRAWN AS FOLLOWS:~ LISI47 A-B UNDINE ETC. LISI48 A-B UTMOST ETC.
LISI49 A-B UNRULY ETC LISI50 A-B VENTURER ETC.

SHEET ONE OF TWO SHEETS
© JOHN LAMBERT 23/12/84

'U' CLASS SUBMARINES *UNBROKEN*, *UNISON*, *UNITED*, *UNRUFFLED*, *UNRIVALLED*, *P 48*, *UNSHAKEN* AND *UNSEEN*. Internal details. (Drawn by John Lambert)

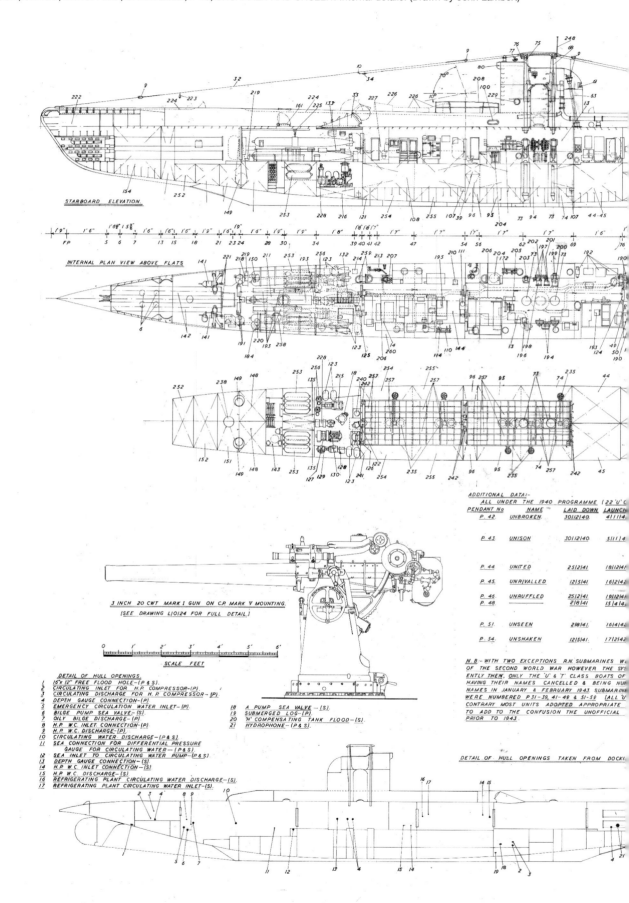

STARBOARD ELEVATION.

INTERNAL PLAN VIEW ABOVE FLATS

3 INCH 20 CWT MARK I GUN ON C.P. MARK V MOUNTING.
[SEE DRAWING L10124 FOR FULL DETAIL.]

SCALE FEET

DETAIL OF HULL OPENINGS.
1   15"x 12" FREE FLOOD HOLE-(P&S).
2   CIRCULATING INLET FOR H.P. COMPRESSOR-(P).
3   CIRCULATING DISCHARGE FOR H.P. COMPRESSOR-(P).
4   DEPTH GAUGE CONNECTION-(P).
5   EMERGENCY CIRCULATION WATER INLET-(P).
6   BILGE PUMP SEA VALVE-(S).
7   OILY BILGE DISCHARGE-(P).
8   H.P. W.C. INLET CONNECTION-(P).
9   H.P. W.C. DISCHARGE-(P).
10 CIRCULATING WATER DISCHARGE-(P & S).
11 SEA CONNECTION FOR DIFFERENTIAL PRESSURE
       GAUGE FOR CIRCULATING WATER-(P & S).
12 SEA INLET TO CIRCULATING WATER PUMP-(P&S).
13 DEPTH GAUGE CONNECTION-(S).
14 H.P W.C. INLET CONNECTION-(S).
15 H.P W.C. DISCHARGE-(S).
16 REFRIGERATING PLANT CIRCULATING WATER DISCHARGE-(S).
17 REFRIGERATING PLANT CIRCULATING WATER INLET-(S).

18 A PUMP SEA VALVE - (S).
19 SUBMERGED LOG-(P).
20 'H' COMPENSATING TANK FLOOD-(S).
21 HYDROPHONE- (P & S).

ADDITIONAL DATA:-
ALL UNDER THE 1940 PROGRAMME [22 'U' C
PENDANT No   NAME   LAID DOWN   LAUNCH
P. 42.   UNBROKEN.   30.12.40.   4.11.4.
P. 43.   UNISON.   30.12.40.   5.11.4
P. 44.   UNITED.   25.12.41.   18.11.41
P. 45.   UNRIVALLED. 12.5.41.   16.2.42
P. 46.   UNRUFFLED.   25.12.41.   19.12.41
P. 48.   ————   2.8.41.   15.4.4.
P. 51.   UNSEEN.   2.8.41.   16.4.42
P. 54.   UNSHAKEN.   12.5.41.   17.2.42

N.B - WITH TWO EXCEPTIONS R.N. SUBMARINES W
OF THE SECOND WORLD WAR HOWEVER THE SYS
ENTLY THEN, ONLY THE 'U' & 'T' CLASS BOATS OF
HAVING THEIR NAMES CANCELLED & BEING NU
NAMES IN JANUARY & FEBRUARY 1943. SUBMARINE
WERE NUMBERED P 31-39, 41-49 & 51-59 [ALL 'V
CONTRARY MOST UNITS ADOPTED APPROPRIATE
TO ADD TO THE CONFUSION THE UNOFFICIAL
PRIOR TO 1943.

DETAIL OF HULL OPENINGS TAKEN FROM DOCK

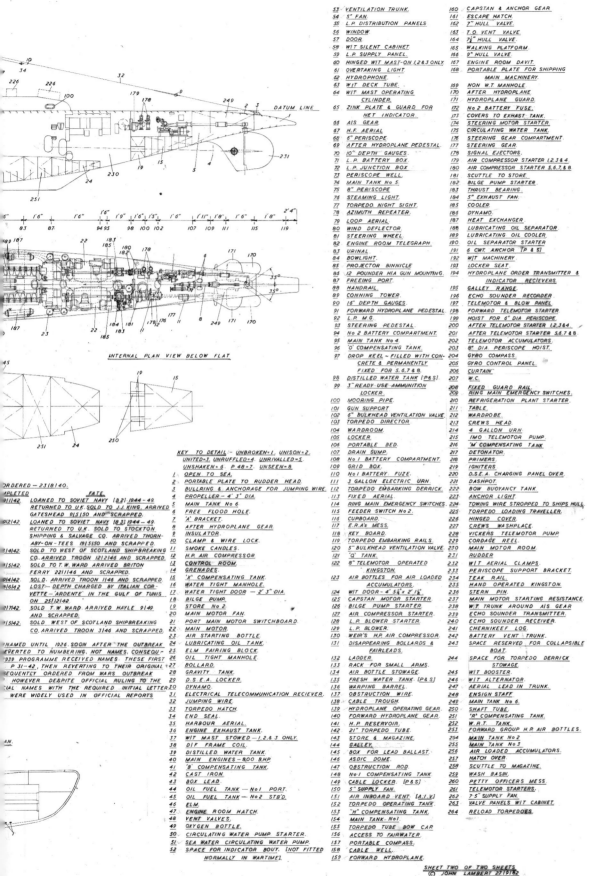

INTERNAL PLAN VIEW BELOW FLAT

KEY TO DETAIL:- UNBROKEN=1, UNISON=2, UNITED=3, UNRUFFLED=4, UNRIVALLED=5, UNSHAKEN=6, P 48=7, UNSEEN=8.

1 OPEN TO SEA.
2 PORTABLE PLATE TO RUDDER HEAD.
3 BULLRING & ANCHORAGE FOR JUMPING WIRE.
4 PROPELLER - 4' 3" DIA.
5 MAIN TANK No 6.
6 FREE FLOOD HOLE.
7 'A' BRACKET.
8 AFTER HYDROPLANE GEAR.
9 INSULATOR.
10 CLAMP & WIRE LOCK.
11 SMOKE CANDLES.
12 H.P. AIR COMPRESSOR.
13 CONTROL ROOM.
14 GRENADES.
15 'X' COMPENSATING TANK.
16 WATER TIGHT MANHOLE.
17 WATER TIGHT DOOR - 2' 3" DIA.
18 BILGE PUMP.
19 STORE No 2.
20 MAIN MOTOR FAN.
21 PORT MAIN MOTOR SWITCHBOARD.
22 MAIN MOTOR.
23 AIR STARTING BOTTLE.
24 LUBRICATING OIL TANK.
25 ELM FAIRING BLOCK.
26 OIL TIGHT MANHOLE.
27 BOLLARD.
28 GRAVITY TANK.
29 D.S.E.A. LOCKER.
30 DYNAMO.
31 ELECTRICAL TELECOMMUNICATION RECIEVER.
32 JUMPING WIRE.
33 TORPEDO HATCH.
34 END SEAL.
35 HARBOUR AERIAL.
36 ENGINE EXHAUST TANK.
37 WIT MAST STOWED - 1,2,& 3 ONLY.
38 DIF FRAME COIL.
39 DISTILLED WATER TANK.
40 MAIN ENGINES - 800 B.H.P.
41 'B' COMPENSATING TANK.
42 CAST IRON.
43 BOX LEAD.
44 OIL FUEL TANK - No1 PORT.
45 OIL FUEL TANK - No2 STB'D.
46 ELM.
47 ENGINE ROOM HATCH.
48 VENT VALVES.
49 OXYGEN BOTTLE.
50 CIRCULATING WATER PUMP STARTER.
51 SEA WATER CIRCULATING WATER PUMP.
52 SPACE FOR INDICATOR BOUY. (NOT FITTED NORMALLY IN WARTIME).

53 VENTILATION TRUNK.
54 5" FAN.
55 L.P. DISTRIBUTION PANELS.
56 WINDOW.
57 DOOR.
58 WIT SILENT CABINET.
59 L.P. SUPPLY PANEL.
60 HINGED WIT MAST-ON 1,2&3 ONLY.
61 OVERTAKING LIGHT.
62 HYDROPHONE.
63 WIT DECK TUBE.
64 WIT MAST OPERATING CYLINDER.
65 ZINK PLATE & GUARD FOR NET INDICATOR.
66 AIS GEAR.
67 H.F. AERIAL.
68 6" PERISCOPE.
69 AFTER HYDROPLANE PEDESTAL.
70 10" DEPTH GAUGES.
71 L.P. BATTERY BOX.
72 L.P. JUNCTION BOX.
73 PERISCOPE WELL.
74 MAIN TANK No 5.
75 8" PERISCOPE.
76 STEAMING LIGHT.
77 TORPEDO NIGHT SIGHT.
78 AZIMUTH REPEATER.
79 LOOP AERIAL.
80 WIND DEFLECTOR.
81 STEERING WHEEL.
82 ENGINE ROOM TELEGRAPH.
83 URINAL.
84 BOWLIGHT.
85 PROJECTOR BINNICLE.
86 12 POUNDER HIA GUN MOUNTING.
87 FREEING PORT.
88 HANDRAIL.
89 CONNING TOWER.
90 16" DEPTH GAUGES.
91 FORWARD HYDROPLANE PEDESTAL.
92 L.P. M.G.
93 STEERING PEDESTAL.
94 No 2 BATTERY COMPARTMENT.
95 MAIN TANK No 4.
96 'O' COMPENSATING TANK.
97 DROP KEEL - FILLED WITH CONCRETE & PERMANENTLY FIXED FOR 5,6,7 & 8.
98 DISTILLED WATER TANK (P&S).
99 3" READY USE AMMUNITION LOCKER.
100 MOORING PIPE.
101 GUN SUPPORT.
102 6" BULKHEAD VENTILATION VALVE.
103 TORPEDO DIRECTOR.
104 WARDROOM.
105 LOCKER.
106 PORTABLE BED.
107 DRAIN SUMP.
108 No 1 BATTERY COMPARTMENT.
109 GRID BOX.
110 No 1 BATTERY FUZE.
111 3 GALLON ELECTRIC URN.
112 TORPEDO EMBARKING DERRICK.
113 FIXED AERIAL.
114 RING MAIN EMERGENCY SWITCHES.
115 FEEDER SWITCH No 2.
116 CUPBOARD.
117 E.R.A's MESS.
118 KEY BOARD.
119 TORPEDO EMBARKING RAILS.
120 5" BULKHEAD VENTILATION VALVE.
121 'Q' TANK.
122 8" TELEMOTOR OPERATED KINGSTON.
123 AIR BOTTLES FOR AIR LOADED ACCUMULATORS.
124 WIT DOOR - 4' 5¼" x 2' 1½".
125 CAPSTAN MOTOR STARTER.
126 BILGE PUMP STARTER.
127 AIR COMPRESSOR STARTER.
128 L.P. BLOWER STARTER.
129 L.P. BLOWER.
130 WEIR'S H.P. AIR COMPRESSOR.
131 DISAPPEARING BOLLARDS & FAIRLEADS.
132 LADDER.
133 RACK FOR SMALL ARMS.
134 AIR BOTTLE STOWAGE.
135 FRESH WATER TANK (P&S).
136 WARPING BARREL.
137 OBSTRUCTION WIRE.
138 CABLE TROUGH.
139 HYDROPLANE OPERATING GEAR.
140 FORWARD HYDROPLANE GEAR.
141 H.P. RESERVOIR.
142 21" TORPEDO TUBE.
143 STORE & MAGAZINE.
144 GALLEY.
145 BOX FOR LEAD BALLAST.
146 ASDIC DOME.
147 OBSTRUCTION ROD.
148 No 1 COMPENSATING TANK.
149 CABLE LOCKER. (P&S)
150 5" SUPPLY FAN.
151 AIR INBOARD VENT. (A.I.V.)
152 TORPEDO OPERATING TANK.
153 "H" COMPENSATING TANK.
154 MAIN TANK No 1.
155 TORPEDO TUBE BOW CAP.
156 ACCESS TO FAIRWATER.
157 PORTABLE COMPASS.
158 CABLE WELL.
159 FORWARD HYDROPLANE.

160 CAPSTAN & ANCHOR GEAR.
161 ESCAPE HATCH.
162 7" HULL VALVE.
163 T.O. VENT VALVE.
164 7½" HULL VALVE.
165 WALKING PLATFORM.
166 9" HULL VALVE.
167 ENGINE ROOM DAVIT.
168 PORTABLE PLATE FOR SHIPPING MAIN MACHINERY.
169 NON W.T. MANHOLE.
170 AFTER HYDROPLANE.
171 HYDROPLANE GUARD.
172 No 2 BATTERY FUSE.
173 COVERS TO EXHAUST TANK.
174 STEERING MOTOR STARTER.
175 CIRCULATING WATER TANK.
176 STEERING GEAR COMPARTMENT.
177 STEERING GEAR.
178 SIGNAL EJECTORS.
179 AIR COMPRESSOR STARTER 1,2,3 & 4.
180 AIR COMPRESSOR STARTER 5,6,7, & 8.
181 SCUTTLE TO STORE.
182 BILGE PUMP STARTER.
183 THRUST BEARING.
184 5" EXHAUST FAN.
185 COOLER.
186 DYNAMO.
187 HEAT EXCHANGER.
188 LUBRICATING OIL SEPARATOR.
189 LUBRICATING OIL COOLER.
190 OIL SEPARATOR STARTER.
191 6 CWT. ANCHOR (P & S)
192 WIT MACHINERY.
193 LOCKER SEAT.
194 HYDROPLANE ORDER TRANSMITTER & INDICATOR RECIEVERS.
195 GALLEY RANGE.
196 ECHO SOUNDER RECORDER.
197 TELEMOTOR & BLOW PANEL.
198 FORWARD TELEMOTOR STARTER.
199 HOIST FOR 6" DIA PERISCOPE.
200 AFTER TELEMOTOR STARTER 1,2,3 & 4.
201 AFTER TELEMOTOR STARTER 5,6,7 & 8.
202 TELEMOTOR ACCUMULATORS.
203 8" DIA. PERISCOPE HOIST.
204 GYRO COMPASS.
205 GYRO CONTROL PANEL.
206 CURTAIN.
207 W.C.
208 FIXED GUARD RAIL.
209 RING MAIN EMERGENCY SWITCHES.
210 REFRIGERATION PLANT STARTER.
211 TABLE.
212 WARDROBE.
213 CREWS HEAD.
214 4 GALLON URN.
215 IMO TELEMOTOR PUMP.
216 'M' COMPENSATING TANK.
217 DETONATOR.
218 PRIMERS.
219 IGNITERS.
220 D.S.E.A. CHARGING PANEL OVER.
221 DASHPOT.
222 BOW BUOYANCY TANK.
223 ANCHOR LIGHT.
224 TOWING WIRE STROPPED TO SHIPS HULL.
225 TORPEDO LOADING TRAVELLER.
226 HINGED COVER.
227 CREWS WASHPLACE.
228 VICKERS TELEMOTOR PUMP.
229 CORDAGE REEL.
230 MAIN MOTOR ROOM.
231 RUDDER.
232 WIT AERIAL CLAMPS.
233 PERISCOPE SUPPORT BRACKET.
234 TEAK RAIL.
235 HAND OPERATED KINGSTON.
236 STERN PIN.
237 MAIN MOTOR STARTING RESISTANCE.
238 W.T. TRUNK AROUND AIS GEAR.
239 ECHO SOUNDER TRANSMITTER.
240 ECHO SOUNDER RECEIVER.
241 CHERNIKEEF LOG.
242 BATTERY VENT TRUNK.
243 SPACE RESERVED FOR COLLAPSIBLE BOAT.
244 SPACE FOR TORPEDO DERRICK STOWAGE.
245 WIT BOOSTER.
246 WIT ALTERNATOR.
247 AERIAL LEAD IN TRUNK.
248 ENSIGN STAFF.
249 MAIN TANK No 6.
250 SHAFT TUBE.
251 'R' COMPENSATING TANK.
252 W.R.T. TANK.
253 FORWARD GROUP H.P. AIR BOTTLES.
254 MAIN TANK No 2.
255 MAIN TANK No 3.
256 AIR LOADED ACCUMULATORS.
257 HATCH OVER.
258 SCUTTLE TO MAGAZINE.
259 WASH BASIN.
260 PETTY OFFICERS MESS.
261 TELEMOTOR STARTERS.
262 7.5" SUPPLY FAN.
263 VALVE PANELS WIT CABINET.
264 RELOAD TORPEDOES.

SHEET TWO OF TWO SHEETS
© JOHN LAMBERT 27|9|82

ORDERED — 23|8|40.

PLETED	FATE.
11|42.	LOANED TO SOVIET NAVY (8.2) 1944 - 49. RETURNED TO U.K. SOLD TO J.J. KING. ARRIVED GATESHEAD 9|5|50 AND SCRAPPED.
12|42.	LOANED TO SOVIET NAVY (8.3) 1944 - 49. RETURNED TO U.K. SOLD TO STOCKTON SHIPPING & SALVAGE CO. ARRIVED THORNABY-ON-TEES 19|5|50 AND SCRAPPED.
14|42.	SOLD TO WEST OF SCOTLAND SHIPBREAKING CO. ARRIVED TROON 12|1|46 AND SCRAPPED.
15|42.	SOLD TO T.W.WARD ARRIVED BRITON FERRY 22|11|46 AND SCRAPPED.
14|42.	SOLD. ARRIVED TROON 11|46 AND SCRAPPED.
16|42.	LOST:- DEPTH CHARGED BY ITALIAN CORVETTE 'ARDENTE' IN THE GULF OF TUNIS ON 25|12|42.
17|42.	SOLD T.W.WARD. ARRIVED HAYLE 9|46 AND SCRAPPED.
15|42.	SOLD WEST OF SCOTLAND SHIPBREAKING CO. ARRIVED TROON 3|46 AND SCRAPPED.

NAMED UNTIL 1926. SOON AFTER THE OUTBREAK EVERTED TO NUMBERING, NOT NAMES, CONSEQU-1939 PROGRAMME RECEIVED NAMES. THESE FIRST P 31-42, THEN REVERTING TO THEIR ORIGINAL SEQUENTLY ORDERED FROM WARS OUTBREAK HOWEVER DESPITE OFFICIAL RULING TO THE IAL NAMES WITH THE REQUIRED INITIAL LETTER WERE WIDELY USED IN OFFICIAL REPORTS

'A' CLASS SUBMARINES *AFFRAY* AND *AENEAS*. General arrangements. (Drawn by John Lambert)

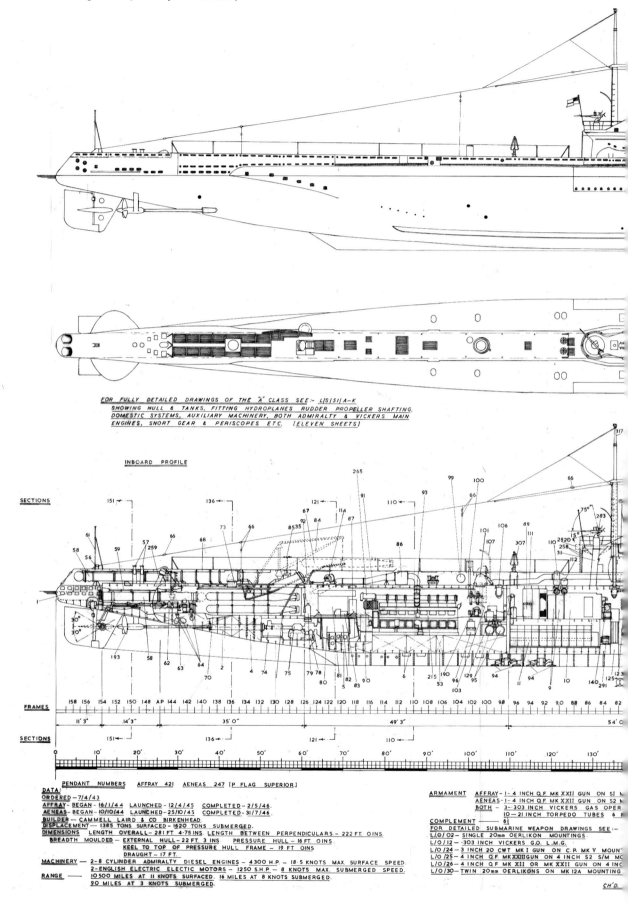

FOR FULLY DETAILED DRAWINGS OF THE 'A' CLASS SEE:- L|S|S| A-K
SHOWING HULL & TANKS, FITTING HYDROPLANES RUDDER PROPELLER SHAFTING,
DOMESTIC SYSTEMS, AUXILIARY MACHINERY, BOTH ADMIRALTY & VICKERS MAIN
ENGINES, SNORT GEAR & PERISCOPES ETC. [ELEVEN SHEETS]

INBOARD PROFILE

SECTIONS

FRAMES

SECTIONS

PENDANT NUMBERS AFFRAY 421 AENEAS 247 [P FLAG SUPERIOR]
DATA:
ORDERED - 7/4/43
AFFRAY - BEGAN - 16/1/44 LAUNCHED - 12/4/45 COMPLETED - 2/5/46.
AENEAS - BEGAN - 10/10/44 LAUNCHED - 25/10/45 COMPLETED - 31/7/46.
BUILDER - CAMMELL LAIRD & CO BIRKENHEAD.
DISPLACEMENT - 1385 TONS SURFACED - 1620 TONS SUBMERGED.
DIMENSIONS LENGTH OVERALL - 281 FT. 4·75 INS. LENGTH BETWEEN PERPENDICULARS - 222 FT. OINS.
BREADTH MOULDED - EXTERNAL HULL - 22 FT. 3 INS. PRESSURE HULL - 16 FT. OINS
                  KEEL TO TOP OF PRESSURE HULL FRAME - 19 FT OINS
                  DRAUGHT - 17 FT.
MACHINERY - 2-8 CYLINDER ADMIRALTY DIESEL ENGINES - 4300 H.P. - 18·5 KNOTS MAX. SURFACE SPEED.
            2-ENGLISH ELECTRIC ELECTIC MOTORS - 1250 S.H.P. - 8 KNOTS MAX. SUBMERGED SPEED.
RANGE - 10 500 MILES AT 11 KNOTS SURFACED. 16 MILES AT 8 KNOTS SUBMERGED.
        90 MILES AT 3 KNOTS SUBMERGED.

ARMAMENT AFFRAY - 1- 4 INCH Q.F. MK XXII GUN ON SI M
          AENEAS - 1- 4 INCH Q.F. MK XXII GUN ON S2 M
          BOTH - 3- ·303 INCH VICKERS GAS OPER.
                 10 - 21 INCH TORPEDO TUBES 6 F
COMPLEMENT - 61
FOR DETAILED SUBMARINE WEAPON DRAWINGS SEE:-
L/O/ 02 - SINGLE 20mm OERLIKON MOUNTINGS.
L/O/ 12 - ·303 INCH VICKERS G.O. L.M.G.
L/O/ 24 - 3 INCH 20 CWT MK I GUN ON C.P. MK V MOUN
L/O/ 25 - 4 INCH Q.F. MK XXIII GUN ON 4 INCH S2 S/M MC
L/O/ 26 - 4 INCH Q.F. MK XII OR MK XXII GUN ON 4 INC
L/O/ 30 - TWIN 20mm OERLIKONS ON MK 12A MOUNTING

CH'D.

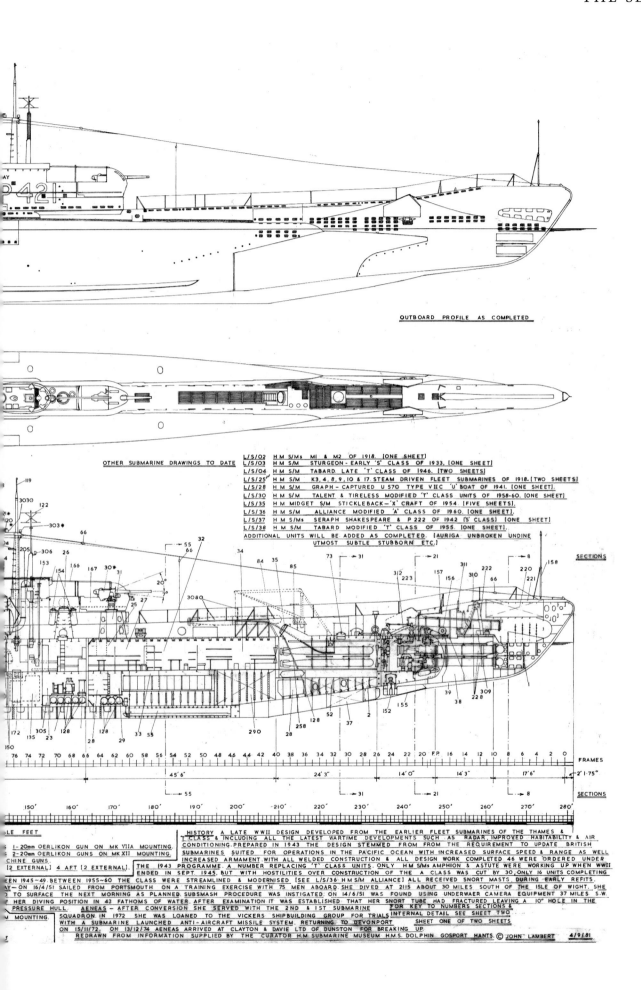

OUTBOARD PROFILE AS COMPLETED

OTHER SUBMARINE DRAWINGS TO DATE

L/S/02 H M S/Ms M1 & M2 OF 1918. [ONE SHEET]
L/S/03 H M S/M STURGEON - EARLY 'S' CLASS OF 1933. [ONE SHEET]
L/S/04 H M S/M TABARD LATE 'T' CLASS OF 1946. [TWO SHEETS]
L/S/25 H M S/M K3, 4, 8, 9, 10 & 17. STEAM DRIVEN FLEET SUBMARINES OF 1918. [TWO SHEETS]
L/S/28 H M S/M GRAPH - CAPTURED U 570 TYPE VIIC 'U' BOAT OF 1941. [ONE SHEET].
L/S/30 H M S/M TALENT & TIRELESS MODIFIED 'T' CLASS UNITS OF 1958-60. [ONE SHEET]
L/S/35 H M MIDGET S/M STICKLEBACK - 'X' CRAFT OF 1954. [FIVE SHEETS].
L/S/36 H M S/M ALLIANCE MODIFIED 'A' CLASS OF 1960. [ONE SHEET].
L/S/37 H M S/Ms SERAPH SHAKESPEARE & P 222 OF 1942 [S' CLASS] [ONE SHEET]
L/S/38 H M S/M TABARD MODIFIED 'T' CLASS OF 1955. [ONE SHEET].
ADDITIONAL UNITS WILL BE ADDED AS COMPLETED. [AURIGA UNBROKEN UNDINE
UTMOST SUBTLE STUBBORN ETC.]

SECTIONS

FRAMES

SECTIONS

SCALE FEET

1-20mm OERLIKON GUN ON MK VIIA MOUNTING.
2-20mm OERLIKON GUNS ON MK XII MOUNTING.
CHINE GUNS.
[2 EXTERNAL] 4 AFT [2 EXTERNAL].

HISTORY A LATE WWII DESIGN DEVELOPED FROM THE EARLIER FLEET SUBMARINES OF THE THAMES &
T CLASS & INCLUDING ALL THE LATEST WARTIME DEVELOPMENTS SUCH AS RADAR, IMPROVED HABITABILITY & AIR
CONDITIONING. PREPARED IN 1943 THE DESIGN STEMMED FROM FROM THE REQUIREMENT TO UPDATE BRITISH
SUBMARINES SUITED FOR OPERATIONS IN THE PACIFIC OCEAN WITH INCREASED SURFACE SPEED & RANGE AS WELL
INCREASED ARMAMENT WITH ALL WELDED CONSTRUCTION & ALL DESIGN WORK COMPLETED 46 WERE ORDERED UNDER
THE 1943 PROGRAMME. A NUMBER REPLACING 'T' CLASS UNITS. ONLY HM S/Ms AMPHION & ASTUTE WERE WORKING UP WHEN WWII
ENDED IN SEPT. 1945. BUT WITH HOSTILITIES OVER CONSTRUCTION OF THE A CLASS WAS CUT BY 30, ONLY 16 UNITS COMPLETING
BETWEEN 1945~49. BETWEEN 1955~60 THE CLASS WERE STREAMLINED & MODERNISED [SEE L/S/36 H M S/M ALLIANCE] ALL RECEIVED SNORT MASTS DURING EARLY REFITS.
ON 16/4/51 SAILED FROM PORTSMOUTH ON A TRAINING EXERCISE WITH 75 MEN ABOARD. SHE DIVED AT 2115 ABOUT 30 MILES SOUTH OF THE ISLE OF WIGHT. SHE
TO SURFACE THE NEXT MORNING AS PLANNED. SUBSMASH PROCEDURE WAS INSTIGATED. ON 14/6/51 WAS FOUND USING UNDERWAER CAMERA EQUIPMENT 37 MILES S.W.
HER DIVING POSITION IN 43 FATHOMS OF WATER. AFTER EXAMINATION IT WAS ESTABLISHED THAT HER SNORT TUBE HAD FRACTURED LEAVING A 10" HOLE IN THE
PRESSURE HULL. AENEAS - AFTER CONVERSION SHE SERVED WITH THE 2ND & 1ST SUBMARINE FOR KEY TO NUMBERS SECTIONS &
MOUNTING. SQUADRON. IN 1972 SHE WAS LOANED TO THE VICKERS SHIPBUILDING GROUP FOR TRIALS INTERNAL DETAIL SEE SHEET TWO.
WITH A SUBMARINE LAUNCHED ANTI-AIRCRAFT MISSILE SYSTEM. RETURNING TO DEVONPORT SHEET ONE OF TWO SHEETS
ON 15/11/72. ON 13/12/74 AENEAS ARRIVED AT CLAYTON & DAVIE LTD OF DUNSTON FOR BREAKING UP.
REDRAWN FROM INFORMATION SUPPLIED BY THE CURATOR H.M SUBMARINE MUSEUM H.M.S. DOLPHIN GOSPORT HANTS. © JOHN LAMBERT 4/9/81

'A' CLASS SUBMARINES *AFFRAY* AND *AENEAS*. Detail. (Drawn by John Lambert)

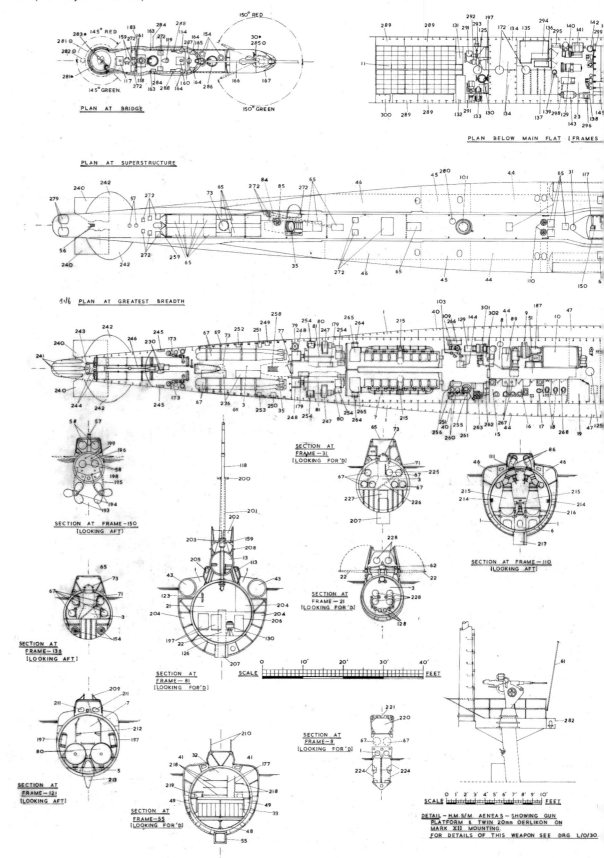

KEY TO DETAIL CONTINUED

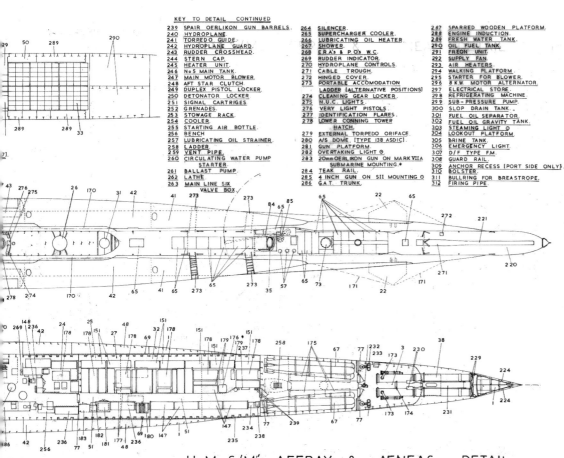

239	SPAIR OERLIKON GUN BARRELS.
240	HYDROPLANE.
241	TORPEDO GUIDE.
242	HYDROPLANE GUARD.
243	RUDDER CROSSHEAD.
244	STERN CAP.
245	HEATER UNIT.
246	No 5 MAIN TANK.
247	MAIN MOTOR BLOWER.
248	AFT STAR CLUTCH.
249	DUPLEX PISTOL LOCKER.
250	DETONATOR LOCKER.
251	SIGNAL CARTRIGES.
252	GRENADES.
253	STOWAGE RACK.
254	COOLER.
255	STARTING AIR BOTTLE.
256	BENCH.
257	LUBRICATING OIL STRAINER.
258	LADDER.
259	VENT PIPE.
260	CIRCULATING WATER PUMP STARTER.
261	BALLAST PUMP.
262	LATHE.
263	MAIN LINE SIX VALVE BOX.
264	SILENCER.
265	SUPERCHARGER COOLER.
266	LUBRICATING OIL HEATER.
267	SHOWER.
268	E.R.A's & P.O's W.C.
269	RUDDER INDICATOR.
270	HYDROPLANE CONTROLS.
271	CABLE TROUGH.
272	HINGED COVER.
273	PORTABLE ACCOMODATION LADDER (ALTERNATIVE POSITIONS)
274	CLEANING GEAR LOCKER.
275	N.U.C. LIGHTS.
276	VERY LIGHT PISTOLS.
277	IDENTIFICATION FLARES.
278	LOWER CONNING TOWER HATCH.
279	EXTERNAL TORPEDO ORIFACE.
280	A/S DOME. (TYPE 138 ASDIC)
281	GUN PLATFORM.
282	OVERTAKING LIGHT ⊘
283	20mm OERLIKON GUN ON MARK VIIA SUBMARINE MOUNTING.*
284	TEAK RAIL.
285	4 INCH GUN ON S11 MOUNTING ⊘
286	G.A.T. TRUNK.
287	SPARRED WOODEN PLATFORM.
288	ENGINE INDUCTION.
289	FRESH WATER TANK.
290	OIL FUEL TANK.
291	FREON UNIT.
292	SUPPLY FAN.
293	AIR HEATERS.
294	WALKING PLATFORM.
295	STARTER FOR BLOWER.
296	8 K.W. MOTOR ALTERNATOR.
297	ELECTRICAL STORE.
298	REFRIGERATING MACHINE.
299	SUB-PRESSURE PUMP.
300	SLOP DRAIN TANK.
301	FUEL OIL SEPARATOR.
302	FUEL OIL GRAVITY TANK.
303	STEAMING LIGHT ⊘
304	LOOKOUT PLATFORM.
305	BRINE TANK.
306	EMERGENCY LIGHT.
307	D/F TYPE F.M.
308	GUARD RAIL.
309	ANCHOR RECESS (PORT SIDE ONLY).
310	BOLSTER.
311	BULLRING FOR BREASTROPE.
312	FIRING PIPE.

H.M. S/M's AFFRAY & AENEAS ~ DETAIL.

KEY TO DETAIL.

1	OPEN TO SEA.
2	TORPEDO OPERATING TANK.
3	TORPEDO FIRING & STOWAGE.
4	AFT TRIM TANK. (COMPARTMENT.
5	LUBRICATING OIL DRAIN TANK.
6	LUBRICATING OIL TANK.
7	MAIN ENGINE & MOTOR ROOM.
8	GALLEY.
9	W/T MACHINEY.
10	W/T OFFICE.
11	No 2 BATTERY COMPARTMENT.
12	AIR CONDITIONING COMPARTMENT.
13	C.O's CABIN.
14	CONNING TOWER.
15	CREWS WASHPLACE.
16	P.O's & E.R.A's WASHPLACE.
17	OFFICERS WASHPLACE.
18	CREWS W.C.
19	RADAR OFFICE.
20	A/S OFFICE.
21	CONTROL ROOM.
22	HYDROPLANE IN WORKING POSITION.
23	AUXILIARY MACHINERY COMPARTMENT.
24	WARD ROOM.
25	E.R.A's MESS.
26	GUN ACCESS TRUNK.
27	PETTY OFFICERS MESS.
28	COXSWAINS STORE.
29	ENGINEERS STORE.
30	4 INCH GUN ON SI MOUNTING. *
31	GUN SUPPORT.
32	STOKERS MESS.
33	No 1 BATTERY COMPARTMENT.
34	SEAMENS MESS.
35	TORPEDO HATCH.
36	TORPEDO TUBE COMPARTMENT.
37	BALLAST BOX.
38	CABLE LOCKER.
39	NET CUTTER.
40	No 3 OIL FUEL TANK.
41	No 1 EXTERNAL OIL FUEL TANK.
42	No 2 MAIN TANK.
43	'Q' COMPENSATING TANK.
44	No 4 MAIN TANK.
45	No 3 OIL FUEL TANK.
46	No 4 EXTERNAL OIL FUEL TANK.
47	MAIN TANK No 3.
48	No 2 OIL FUEL TANK.
49	LOCKERS.
50	DISTILLED WATER TANK.
51	PASSAGE WAY.
52	TRIM TANK.
53	AIR SPACE.
54	W/T DECK TUBE.
55	Q TANK.
56	BULLRING.
57	DISAPPEARING BOLLARD.
58	21 INCH DIA. TORPEDO TUBE.
59	STERN CAP OPERATING GEAR.
60	RUDDER OPERATING SHAFT.
61	ENSIGN STAFF.
62	HYDROPLANE GEAR.
63	A.I.V. TANK (AUTOMATIC INBOARD VENT)
64	FIRING BOTTLES.
65	PORTABLE GRATINGS.
66	INSULATOR.
67	21 INCH DIA. MARK XI TORPEDO.
68	PORTABLE CENTRE GIRDER.
69	WOOD LINING.
70	D.S.E.A. TWILL TRUNK.
71	OVERHEAD CARRIAGE.
72	ESCAPE HATCH.
73	STEERING GEAR POWER UNIT.
74	THRUST BLOCK.
75	AFT CLUTCH CASING.
76	W/T DOOR.
77	OILY BILGE PUMP.
78	AIR LOADED ACCUMULATOR.
79	MAIN MOTOR.
80	SWITCHBOARD.
81	FAN.
82	FAN MOTOR.
83	TORPEDO DERRICK.
84	TORPEDO DERRICK TRAINING.
85	EXHAUST TANK (HANDWHEEL.
86	REGULATOR.
87	MAIN ENGINE SUPERCHARGER.
88	GALLEY RANGE.
89	ENGINE CLUTCH.
90	LIFTING BEAM.
91	PORTABLE TORPEDO EMBARKING.
92	INBOARD EXHAUST VALVE. (RAIL.
93	24 INCH DIA. H.O. KINGSTONE VALVE.
94	OIL COOLER.
95	PORT CIRCULATING PUMP.
96	BOLLARDS.
97	MOORING PIPE.
98	OIL FUEL EXPANSION TANK.
99	TYPE 138 B ASDIC.
100	ENGINE ROOM HATCH.
101	VENTILATING VALVE.
102	SIGNAL EJECTORS.
103	AIR COMPRESSER.
104	OIL FUEL GRAVITY TANK.
105	ENGINE INDUCTION VALVE.
106	ENGINE ROOM DAVIT (PORTABLE).
107	LUB. OIL PUMP STARTER.
108	TYPE F.M.1 DIRECTION FINDER.
109	No 4 MAIN TANK VENT.
110	VENTILATION ENGINE.
111	No 3 MAIN TANK VENT (INDUCTION.
112	BATTERY VENT.
113	TORPEDO DERRICK WINCH.
114	ENGINE TELEGRAPH.
115	SANITARY TANK.
116	A.N.F. RADAR MAST.
117	9.5 INCH DIA. PERISCOPE.
118	7.5 INCH DIA. PERISCOPE.
119	TYPE 253 MW. RADAR.
120	TYPE 86M RADAR.
121	TYPE 267MW. RADAR ARRAY.
122	TELEMOTOR CONTROL PANEL.
123	TRIM PUMP MOTOR.
124	RADAR MAST WELL.
125	WASHING WATER TANK.
126	10 GALLON WATER HEATER.
127	AIR BOTTLES.
128	H.P. AIR COMPRESSOR.
129	GYRO COMPASS.
130	TELEMOTOR OIL STORAGE TANK.
131	SEWAGE TANK.
132	RADAR MAST HOIST.
133	'R' COMPENSATING TANK.
134	MAIN COLD ROOM.
135	READY USE COLD ROOM.
136	MAGAZINE.
137	DISTILLER.
138	OLEO PRESS.
139	TELEMOTOR PUMP.
140	L.P. ROTARY BLOWER.
141	TELEMOTOR ACCUMULATOR.
142	4 OR 5 K.W. MACHINE.
143	DESK.
144	WARD ROOM WINE CUPBOARD.
145	RUM CUPBOARD.
146	3 HINGED BEDS.
147	STEERING WHEEL.
148	HYDROPLANE INDICATOR.
149	DEPTH GAUGE.
150	BED- LOCKERS UNDER- HINGED BED
151	TYPE 128A ASDIC. (OVER.
152	BRIDGE SEAT.
153	4 INCH READY USE AMMUNITION LOCKER.
154	STAY.
155	CAPSTAN UNIT.
156	TWIN TOWING SLIP.
157	JACKSTAFF.
158	20 mm READY USE AMMUNITION LOCKERS.
159	PORTABLE WOOD SEAT.
160	STEP.
161	BOW LIGHT.
162	SOCKET FOR .303 INCH GAS OPERATED MACHINE GUN.
163	NIGHT SIGHTS.
164	AZIMUTH REPEATER.
165	VOICE PIPE.
166	REVOLVING GUN PLATFORM.
167	H/F AERIAL.
168	WASH BASIN.
169	GUARD WIRE.
170	WALKING FLAT.
171	PERISCOPE WELL.
172	FIRING GEAR.
173	FIRING PANEL.
174	HINGED BED.
175	C O² ABSORBTION UNIT. *
176	CURTAIN.
177	TABLE.
178	SEAT LOCKER.
179	No 1 BATTERY FUSE PANEL.
180	ICE CHEST.
181	LETTER BOX.
182	URINAL.
183	WARD ROOM PANTRY.
184	GYRO ANGLE TRANSMITTER.
185	CHART TABLE.
186	IMO PUMP.
187	CIRCULATING WATER PUMP STARTER.
188	LUBRICATING OIL HEATER.
189	LUBRICATING OIL SEPARATOR.
190	LUBRICATING OIL PUMP STARTER.
191	BALLAST PUMP.
192	5 FT 9 INCH DIA. PPOPELLER.
193	PROPELLER SHAFT.
194	SHAFT BRACKET.
195	No 5 MAIN TANK.
196	AIR COOLER.
197	STEERING GEAR SHAFTS.
198	TORPEDO BOW CAP SHAFTS.
199	JUMPING WIRE STAY.
200	PERISCOPE SUPPORT BRACKET.
201	BREAKWATER.
202	BRIDGE DECK.
203	No 3 MAIN TANK.
204	ENGINE INDUCTION TRUNK.
205	GYRO PANEL.
206	BALLAST KEEL.
207	BRIDGE HANDRAIL.
208	TORPEDO EMBARKING RAILS.
209	PORTABLE GUARDRAILS.
210	EXHUST TRUNK.
211	HANDRAIL.
212	CAST IRON BLOCK.
213	MAIN CABLES.
214	MAIN ENGINES - 8 CYL ADMIRALTY DIESEL.
215	ENGINE TURNING GEAR.
216	BALLAST KEEL.
217	HINGED BED.
218	SEAT LOCKER.
219	BOW BUOYANCY TANK.
220	TOWING TROUGH.
221	HAWSE PIPE.
222	HYDROPLANE GUARD PLATE.
223	BOW SHUTTER.
224	TORPEDO IN LOADING POSITION.
225	PORTABLE RAMP.
226	TROUGH.
227	TORPEDO TUBE.
228	BOW CAP.
229	BOW CAP OPERATING GEAR.
230	No 1 MAIN TANK.
231	EXTERNAL FIRING GEAR.
232	A/S UNIT.
233	HOT CUPBOARDS.
234	WOOD LINING.
235	2 HINGED BEDS.
236	FIRST AID CUPBOARD.
237	4 GALLON URN.

* FITTED IN THIS POSITION 'AFFRAY' ONLY.
⊘ FITTED IN THIS POSITION 'AENEAS' ONLY.

SHEET TWO OF TWO SHEETS.

22/8/81   © JOHN LAMBERT

CHAPTER 16
A GLIMPSE OF THE FUTURE

Throughout the Second World War, the Royal Navy concentrated heavily on the Battle of the Atlantic. Its submarines had a dual role. They fought the Germans and their allies directly, but they also provided the anti-submarine force with a sense of what enemy submarines could be expected to do. When the Allies became aware that the Germans were turning to radical new types of submarines, the British, who were already short of resources, nonetheless converted submarines to simulate the new German types. They provided the Royal Navy and the US Navy with their first glimpse of what future submarine warfare might mean. For the Royal Navy, too, this glimpse led to plans for new types of submarines. The US Navy did not take this step until well after the war had ended.

Truant with her prototype snort, 1945. Note that in addition to the exhaust on her snort mast, she has a secondary exhaust (visible on the right) lower down, to see whether back pressure at greater depth was prohibitive. A deeper exhaust would have been more difficult to detect. In this form *Truant* made a submerged run to and from Gibraltar. On the way out, she remained submerged except for surfacing each day at noon to check her position (by sighting) and report it. On the way back, she remained submerged for ten days but then had to surface due to an engine failure. (Dock Museum Photo VPA 0073)

For the Germans, at least initially the driving force was radar. Effective surface-search radar on board escorts, which was operational as early as 1941, made it impossible for the Germans to continue their earlier tactics of surface attack at night. Effective aircraft radar, which entered service by 1942, denied U-boats the ability to charge their batteries at night on the surface. To a limited extent the Germans were able to mitigate this latter threat by using radar warning receivers, and the Allies were forced to adopt new airborne radars. The Germans never solved the problem the X-band radars presented.

The initial German solution was the schnorchel (snorkel, snort in British parlance). It was a pair of tubes extending above the surface of the water. Using a snorkel, the engine in a submerged U-boat could breathe and exhaust. A U-boat could run her diesels when submerged, although she could not make very high speed. The snorkel did not completely solve the problem, because X-band air radar could often detect a snorkel head, and the exhaust could be detected, but it made anti-submarine warfare far more difficult.

The other German approach was more revolutionary: a submarine which could sustain high underwater speed for a protracted period. It might outrun many escorts. The most extreme version used high-test (hydrogen) peroxide (HTP) for several hours of very high speed. The HTP engine turned out to be difficult to develop, so the Germans tried the alternative of adding batteries and using higher-powered motors. This fast battery submarine became the standard after the war; its existence demanded revolutionary approaches to anti-submarine warfare. The great question, raised even before the war ended, was how close the higher-performance HTP submarine was to practicality.

The Royal Navy had several sources of information. One was prisoners of war. As the U-boats suffered from improved Allied measures, their chief Admiral Dönitz tried to keep morale up by assuring his officers that revolutionary new weapons would soon save them. He had to say a good deal about what he had in mind, and some U-boat prisoners of war told their interrogators about them – not least as a boast that the Royal Navy would soon be losing.

A second source was code-breaking. The Japanese ambassador to Germany, General Ōshima, was a favourite of senior Nazis, who provided him with detailed information. Lacking any land line back to Japan, he transmitted copious coded messages. The Allies broke his machine code early in 1944.[1] He was an excellent reporter, with good connections in Germany. His 30 May 1944 message described German submarine policy and gave details of the new Types XXI and XXIII. It summarised a meeting between Admiral Dönitz, the attaché, and Admiral Abe, head of the Japanese naval mission in Berlin. Others present were the Chief of German Naval Operations and the Chief Constructor. The Japanese had asked specifically for details of the new fast U-boats, with which Dönitz hoped to resume the Battle of the Atlantic in 1944.

More conventional sources included air reconnaissance, captured documents and, presumably, agents. For example, a trove of about 5000 documents covering the period between October 1943 and

October 1944 captured at the Hermann Göring Werke at Strassburg referred to the construction of Type XXI U-boats. Although the plant was only a sub-contractor, it must have provided considerable insight into the German prefabrication programme.

The Snorkel[2]

Initially the Royal Navy was apparently unaware of German interest in the snorkel. The Most Secret appreciation of the U-boat situation issued on 2 August 1943 listed likely German countermeasures to increasingly successful ASW measures.[3] Probably in order of likelihood they were better anti-aircraft weapons; efficient radar; efficient search receivers to deal with air radar; realistic radar decoys; and hulls strengthened for deeper diving. Further analysis pointed out that U-boat radar was in its infancy, and that Allied aircraft could home on it; that measures already in development should destroy German faith in search receivers; that the Allies were already testing radar decoys to learn how to disregard them; and that deeper diving would require a completely new U-boat design.

The 'child's guide' to U-boats of 29 November 1943, intended as the first periodic summary of what was known about them, mentioned many reports of experiments intended to produce a U-boat driven by the same engine submerged as on the surface.[4] The two types cited were the closed-cycle Erren diesel the British had considered before the war and a gas-driven turbine 'considered to be the more probable development'. The latter was the Walter (HTP) submarine. Both engines were expected to give higher underwater speed. The schnorchel was not mentioned.

By February 1944, the German word 'Schnorchel' was turning up in their radio traffic; as of 3 February two U-boats were said to have been fitted with it. NID 0568 of 11 February stated correctly that it almost certainly meant diesel propulsion submerged, although evidence was not yet conclusive as to whether the means was closed-cycle operation or protruded exhaust and inlet trunks.[5] German messages had said that 'schnorchel' was unprotected against enemy location, but it was not clear what sort of location was meant. Nor was there evidence as to whether it was successful, nor on the rate at which

it was being fitted. The subject was vital because U-boats would be used to resist the D-Day invasion. The nature of the 'schnorchel' must have been clear by July 1944, when a summary of future German U-boats mentioned it in passing; the main news was the new Types XXI and XXIII.[6]

A British 1942–3 project to fit a snorkel in a 'U'-class submarine as an experiment was cancelled before the design was complete.[7] It seems to have been inspired by knowledge of Dutch submarines using air intakes to run their engines submerged; such submarines had escaped to England in 1940 when the Netherlands was overrun by the Germans.[8] The British were unaware of the German work; this project was probably connected with the early design stage of the 'A' class.

We now know that the first experimental German snorkels were installed on board the small Type II U-boats *U 57* and *U 58* in 1943, the tube replacing one periscope. They were inspected on 30 July 1943 and completed their trials on 24 August 1943. It proved possible to snorkel at 3.5 knots while charging the battery at maximum rate (6.5 knots without charging at all). Radar measurements showed that the boat could not be detected beyond ¼ to 1nm, compared to 3.5 to 4nm when the boat was surfaced. At full charging rate, propeller noise was louder than engine noise. However, the CO of *U 58* pointed to problems. Due to increased back pressure, exhaust joints leaked into the boat. Maximum snorkel speed was limited by lack of air, causing a smoky exhaust. The snorkel head blocked the periscope. The German naval staff continued to resist adopting the new device, and plans called for fitting it to only ten operational submarines (Type VIIC) by February 1944. Even then the staff requirement provided for only enough air capacity to charge batteries; not until the summer of 1944 was it realised that a submarine could use her snorkel to proceed submerged. By that time the decision had been taken to fit snorkels to all U-boats. All operational snorkel masts were folded down on deck when not in use; they did not telescope like periscopes. Typically they were mounted on one side, forward of the conning tower.

On 1 November 1944 FOSM wrote the Admiralty that he wanted snorkels for British submarines; using them, the Germans had gained respite from air attack. In future British submarines might come under

Before the Royal Navy put snorkels on board its own submarines, it produced dummy snorkels to help train ASW forces to deal with German snorkel U-boats. *United* was the first British submarine so fitted. It is the tall pipe mast which replaced her attack periscope. Alongside is *Upright*, which had not been modified. Other 'U'/'V'-class submarines with dummy snorkels included *Vulpine*. In addition, a dummy snorkel was installed on board at least one of the Italian submarines which was stationed at Key West to assist in ASW training (and to release Royal Navy submarines for combat). (RAN Naval Historical Section via Dr Josef Straczek)

heavy attack from radar-equipped aircraft, 'particularly as their characteristics are favourable for their employment in shallow, confined, and coastal waters, when compared with their much larger [US] counterparts'. However, it was not at all certain that the snorkel had come to stay. Its weaknesses included its demand for space and weight inside and outside the submarine, inability to operate in rough weather and considerable discomfort 'not uncoupled with danger to personnel'. FOSM suspected, too, that by increasing a submarine's chance of survival, the snorkel would tend to make submarine commanders feel unsafe when it was not being used. Submarines would be encouraged to remain submerged even when they did not have to do so, and thus 'decreasing their mobility . . . their offensive spirit and power to inflict damage. Results to date seem to indicate this state of affairs.'

Moreover, snorkelling was noisy. All three Axis navies had relied on sonic hydrophones; even when they acquired echo-ranging, they retained the earlier devices. 'The extent of this weakness will doubtless be proved in our own efforts to subdue the German U-boats should they operate in confined waters.' A snorkel submarine would need radar and probably a search receiver to warn it of the approach of ships and aircraft, to avoid being surprised at snorkel depth. The noise of the main engines would reduce the effectiveness of the submarine's own Asdic.

Given the weaknesses, the Royal Navy should not fit snorkels wholesale until either they were necessary operationally or experience had been accumulated. Therefore a snorkel should be fitted in one of each of the current submarine classes, 'U', 'S', 'T' and 'A', as soon as possible for experiments. If they succeeded, the Royal Navy should if practicable fit all operational submarines so that they could be equipped at short notice by depot ships or shore bases. *Amphion* was not to be fitted because she was urgently needed for first of class trials. The device should have a British name: FOSM proposed 'snort', which was soon adopted.

Details were settled at a 28 November 1944 meeting at Warminster, attended by A(S) as well as DNC and EinC.[9] A(S) wanted a snorting submarine to develop 40 per cent of maximum engine power, for a speed of 6.5 knots with a margin to drive auxiliaries (he would use one engine running at 80 per cent power). This engine would drive a charging generator, the battery driving the motors propelling the boat. DNC and EinC both liked this 'semi-electric' form of propulsion, which DNC argued gave the most horsepower per cubic foot of air taken through the snort. After some discussion A(S) was willing to settle for a submerged speed of at least 5.75 knots while snorting, taking account of the auxiliary load, with the submarine at periscope depth. A(S) defined that as the depth at which the periscope could look out over the snort to give an all-round view. No firm requirement was stated as to the time to charge batteries. The sea state in which snorting was possible would be fixed by experience. A radar antenna would be mounted atop the snort. The key requirement was that the snort be suitable to be fitted readily by the staff of a depot ship in the event installation became necessary.

DNC offered three alternatives. One was a German-style snort mounted forward of the bridge. A second was a modified German type mounted abaft the bridge; the third was a periscope induction plus some form of exhaust. The first was rejected because it would require the surrender of the 4in gun. Difficulty was expected with the ship's compass, and the exhaust trunking would be long. The advantages were the use of the bridge structure to support the snort mast, and the likelihood that air brought down could be used to clear the control room. Mounting the snort abaft the bridge would require surrender of the Oerlikon anti-aircraft gun. The midships tubes in the 'T' class would present some problems, and there would be problems with engine rooms in all classes. The periscopic induction offered better flow and better water separation, but in existing submarines one periscope would probably have to be surrendered. That ruled it out. After some discussion, the arrangement abaft the bridge was chosen; DNC and EinC were told to produce a set of equipment for each of the 'U', 'S', 'T' and 'A' classes, based on German designs. Surrendering the Oerlikon was far more acceptable than surrendering the 4in gun, and DNC pointed out that some surrender was inevitable as weight compensation.

Vickers would produce designs for the 'T' and 'U' classes, and Chatham for the 'S' class. By this time some snorkel components had fallen into Allied hands at Toulon, and A(S) asked NID for details. *Truant* was chosen as the 'T'-class prototype. The other choices made at this time were *Surf* at Chatham and *Universal* or *Varangian* at Blyth. Only *Truant* survived.

On 13 December 1944 the Board approved the prototype programme. Installations in *Truant* and *Una* were soon approved, followed in May 1945 by *Sirdar* (the 'A'-class submarine was not yet chosen).[10] The *Truant* tests culminated in an all-snorting run to Gibraltar and back, after which she was scrapped and her snort removed for examination. The next experimental installation (post-war) was on board *Sirdar*. Snorkels were never fitted to *Una*, or any other British 'U'/'V'-class submarine, although several were fitted with dummy snorkels to simulate snorkel U-boats for detection trials and for training (some units transferred to other navies later got snorkels). During 1946 the first production installations were made (eight 'T'-class and 'A'-class submarines not yet completed).

Meanwhile, on 29 November 1944 Director of Anti-U-Boat Warfare wrote that 'The Schnorkel has [altered] the whole character of the U-boat war . . . in the enemy's favour. He has managed to penetrate to and remain on our convoy routes in focal areas with impunity in spite of intensive air and surface patrols. With more experience and training and with the confidence engendered by his present impunity from air, and often from surface attack, he is likely, in the future, to do us more real harm than he has up to the present.'[11]

The HTP Submarine

By 1944 the British were aware that the German were developing a 'Walterboote' (W-Boat) but, as with the snorkel, they did not quite know what it was.[12] Initially the British associated the W-Boat with another project, for an 'underwater S-boat' (i.e., an underwater motor torpedo boat). They guessed that it would be only about 90ft long, normally lying in wait with only its conning tower out of the water. They thought correctly that it would use the same engines for both surfaced and submerged cruising, but erred in thinking that they would operate on a closed cycle. Speed might be as high as 40 knots surfaced and 30 knots submerged, endurance would be 500 to 600nm on the surface (50–60 hours submerged). Diving depth was thought to be 30m (100ft). There was some doubt as to whether the craft would have a periscope; if it lacked one, it would probably use its high underwater speed mainly to escape after striking. Armament would be twin torpedo tubes forward. Such craft would do what S-boats did: they could attack coastal convoys or ships in open anchorages, as well as defended harbours, anywhere between Flamborough Head and the Bristol Channel. Director, Scientific Research (DSR) assumed that the W-boat was a single-purpose craft intended for sorties rather than cruises. Thus its torpedoes would be loaded at its base, minimising the space they required.

DSR speculated that the noise generated by such a craft might be its greatest vulnerability; he wanted DNC to estimate the characteristics of suitable propellers. He also speculated that a really fast sub-

Sirdar was the second British submarine, after *Truant*, to be fitted with an operational snort. She was followed by eight 'T'-class conversions and by 'A'-class submarines fitted with snorts before completion. *Sirdar* is shown in 1946, with the new standard radar outfit (air-warning forward of the periscopes, surface-warning abaft them). Her snort mast is folded down abaft her bridge fairwater. The mast was a copy of the wartime German mast, but the Germans placed theirs forward of their bridges. The snort was presumably installed during a long refit at Chatham, 26 June 1945 through early March 1946. Wartime plans also called for snort installation in a 'U'-class submarine, but that was never done. (RAN Naval Historical Section via Dr Josef Straczek)

mersible could not have large planes, hence might have to move at no less than half speed to maintain underwater control. The craft would probably displace about 125 tons submerged and could run at about 25 knots on 3500 SHP; it might use a small creep motor for low speed. Submerged endurance would probably be 4 to 5 hours at full speed (say 100nm). Maximum range would probably entail an hour at full speed and 12 to 16 hours at half-speed, in all 200 to 250nm. Anything more would be at slow speed either surfaced or submerged. DSR assumed the boat would use a lightweight high-duty engine, probably a turbine, 'using an oxygen-bearing fuel such as hydrogen peroxide . . . the oxygen released is then combusted with a normal hydrocarbon fuel . . . exhaust gases may be dispersed into the wake or recycled'. DSR chose hydrogen peroxide because the Germans apparently already used it in various power plants. The British had not yet considered its use in underwater propulsion. DNC thought the craft would probably displace 140 to 150 tons, with a length of 85 to 100ft, using a motorboat bow extending well aft. On 4000 SHP such a craft, if perfectly streamlined, might reach 25 knots. It would have to sacrifice surfaced speed, because the best hull form for submerged performance was poorly adapted to surface running.

This was the beginning of the Royal Navy's romance with HTP power plants for submarines, although that was not yet obvious. It was also a good illustration of the strength and weakness of signals intelligence. Professor Walter's name had cropped up in connection with a wide range of submarine innovations, but no one yet knew that he was concerned mainly with exploiting HTP in various ways, and certainly not in a closed-cycle engine. The official appreciation confused the Walter boat, not yet mature enough for service, with a substantial programme of mature midget submarine development. None of the midgets had the sort of performance HTP offered.

We now know that Professor Helmuth Walter had suggested as early as 1933 that a submarine could use HTP to supply oxygen for high underwater speed.[13] Initially he envisaged a closed-cycle diesel. At the end of 1933 Walter was allowed to sketch a 300-ton submarine, which received the official designation Type V. By this time Walter had found that when really concentrated HTP disintegrated to yield oxygen, the reaction created considerable heat. That reduced diesel efficiency, but a hot air-water (and steam) mixture could be used efficiently in a turbine. In 1936 a 4000 SHP Walter turbine ran successful tests. Walter established his own firm to exploit HTP. At the

Taciturn was an early 'T'-class snort conversion. The snort in effect replaced her 20mm gun, and she was given the modernised radar suite in which the air-search antenna was forward of her periscopes. The 20mm gun would have interfered with the snort, but it could also be argued that it was not needed if the submarine could operate entirely submerged. Note also the much-enlarged 4in gun shield. In boats built by the Royal Dockyards the snort added excessive topweight, and in March 1949 it was decided to remove the 4in guns as weight compensation (not all boats were so modified). The alternative, removing the two external bow tubes, was rejected, though later on that was done to allow submarines to retain both gun and snort. *Taciturn* was photographed on 1 November 1946. Between 29 April and 26 May 1947 she made a prolonged snort patrol in the Atlantic, snorting by day and diving deep at night, not surfacing at all to show that prolonged all-submerged operation was practicable using the snort. Maximum rate of advance was 130nm per day (average 5.4 knots), but her commanding officer considered that this could not be maintained for more than 48 hours due to the strain on the Officer of the Watch and the planesmen, who had to maintain periscope depth (for snorkelling) in rough weather.

beginning of 1939 he received a contract for an 80-ton test submarine, *V 80* (V for *Versuchs*, test) to explore the problems of high underwater speed. Secret trials began in April 1940. In deep water *V 80* achieved 28.1 knots. Walter offered an alternative 'hot' version of his HTP power plant burning fuel in the oxygen liberated from the HTP. It became the basis for all later developments.

After the spectacular success of *V 80*, the German navy ordered a 'hot' version. Walter's patron in the German navy construction office proposed immediately building six small Walter boats (at the cost of twelve conventional submarines) to gain sufficient experience to produce operational submarines within a few years. However, the U-boat war was going well; long-range projects were discouraged. The new type of engine should prove itself in a land test bed. Only a single test boat (*V 300*) was envisaged, initially a 320-tonner driven by two turbines (total 4000 SHP) for 25 knots submerged. As the design developed, it grew, so that in the final version (September 1941) it displaced 600 tons. Since turbine power did not increase, maximum speed was expected to be 19 knots. A contract for *U 791* was let on 18 February 1942. Meanwhile Walter proposed a much smaller (220-ton) boat using two 2500 SHP turbines to reach 26 knots. Walter went around the back of the unenthusiastic German Admiralty to Dönitz, who strongly supported the project. Different versions were designed by Germania (Krupp) and Blohm & Voss (Types XVIIG and XVIIB,

Taciturn shows her enlarged gun shield, 1 November 1946, as initially converted. *Thule* (photographed 22 October 1946) had a similar shield.

respectively). The only Walter boats ever completed were *U 792–U 795* and *U 1405–U 1409*. Of the Type XVIIBs (*U 1405–U 1409*), *U 1407* became the post-war British Walter test bed. These were single-screw submarines with two turbines. Construction began in December 1942 at Blohm & Voss and early in February 1943 at Germania.

The Germans tried to keep their new submarines secret from their Japanese allies, but in December 1943 a Japanese engineer visiting a German yard saw a Type XVIIB submarine and correctly reported its high underwater speed. He did not understand that it used a radical power plant. When the message was translated in June 1944, it did not alert the Allies to the Walter programme.[14]

Dönitz was more interested in a long-range Walter boat suited to the Atlantic, which was designated Type XVIII. The project was important enough for Hitler to attend a meeting about it on 28 September 1942. Two boats (*U 796* and *U 797*) were ordered on 4 January 1943. Their power plant was two 7500 SHP turbines, and submerged speed was expected to be 24 knots. The main perceived design problem storing the mass of unstable HTP. The solution was a figure-eight pressure hull, the lower lobe of which would be devoted to HTP and fuel. HTP propulsion proved difficult to perfect, so the figure-eight hull was retained in the more conventional Type XXI submarine, the lower lobe being filled with batteries. Type XVIII was not built, but in 1945 its turbine (Type 18X) was nearly complete.

In the autumn of 1943 the main German hope to resume the Battle of the Atlantic was the new generation of fast battery submarines, particularly the big Type XXI. Admiral Abe described the two new conventional submarines in detail to his navy (and, unknowingly, to Allied code-breakers) on 31 May 1944. An initial Japanese message mentioned Type XVIIB, but its nature apparently was not understood. Dönitz considered Type XXI too large and hence not a suitable replacement for the mass-produced Type VIIC, which had fought most of the convoy battles. Walter was encouraged to upgrade the small Type XVII for action around the British Isles. The official designers produced a parallel design, originally to have displaced less than 1000 tons. It became Type XXVI, powered by a single 7500 SHP turbine of the type developed for Type XVIII. All of this was very much 'the best is the enemy of the good enough'. The contract for the two Type XVIII

was cancelled in favour of Type XXVI on 28 March 1944. Plans called for 100 Type XXVIs (*U 4501–U 4600*), but sections of the first four were only being fabricated at the end of the war.

In February 1945, the Japanese naval attaché provided full details of Type XXVI.[15] Given the Japanese reports, at the end of February 1945, NID reported that the Germans had completed at least three Type XVIIBs and were building five more; they would soon be building Type XXVI. To avoid mentioning signals intelligence, the official story was that the secret of the Walter engine was not really understood until British Assault Teams entered Germany.[16] The research establishments and personnel were immediately placed under British control. HTP was an Anglo-American secret: when a British delegation negotiated the division of the German fleet with the Russians, it was told not to discuss HTP facilities (the Russians found out anyway). When Captain Roberts RN visited Germany to investigate German submarine tactics shortly after the war ended, he spent about a fifth of his time looking for Type XVIIs, which had been scuttled contrary to the surrender terms. He questioned the Germans on tactics they had planned to use with the bigger Type XXVI.

The British raised *U 793* for trials, but soon discarded it.[17] Initially they planned to refit *U 1407*, raised in June 1945, in Kiel, but in mid-July ordered it brought to England together with the Type 18X turbine (once bench-tested) and Professor Walter and his team. The submarine was sealed up and towed to Barrow in August 1945, becoming HMS *Meteorite* (*U 1406* was taken to the United States). The British tried to order a large HTP submarine from Blohm & Voss, the builders – only to find out that much of it existed only on paper.

The 'Elektro' Submarine and Fast Targets

When the Walter programme ran into trouble, the Germans shifted to U-boats with high underwater speed gained by increasing motor and battery power: the big Type XXI and the coastal Type XXIII, which they called 'Elektro' submarines. A message the Japanese naval attaché sent on 30 May 1944 described both types in some detail, although it did not refer to them by Type numbers.[18] The larger type was intended for the Atlantic, and perhaps later for the Indian Ocean; the smaller one was for the Mediterranean. The Germans told the Japanese that until the Allies had had time to develop new countermeasures, these submarines could operate virtually unopposed. Secrecy was therefore essential. The British already assumed that the Germans were building U-boats with much higher underwater speed, as an obvious counter to existing ASW methods.[19]

Early in June 1944 NID stated that the Germans were concentrating on building three types of submarines, one with a speed of 16 knots submerged (1200 tons), a second smaller type having a speed of 12 knots submerged, and also a deep-diving type. At a 6 June 1944 meeting DNC and DNE queried the 16 knots because it was far beyond anything the British could achieve, and also far beyond anything the Germans had done previously. DNI's representative stated that these data had been reported consistently from various sources. Diving depth was said to be less than in previous submarines. Really fast submarines would require new countermeasures. To develop them the British needed their own high-speed submarine. It did not have to be operational, only a target which could be pursued. DASW wanted a fast target by the autumn of 1944. In October 1943 NID had already asked DNC to investigate the possibility of producing a fast underwater target which would simulate such a submarine. He concluded that by streamlining the hull and removing all appendages an existing British submarine could achieve 13 knots for 20 minutes.

Candidates for conversion were the 'U' and 'S' classes, neither of which was well suited to the Far East. An additional battery could replace the torpedoes and tubes of a 'U'-class boat. Engines and main motors could be replaced by 'T'-class motors and two 100 kW diesel generators. For 20 minutes such a submarine could run at 12 knots submerged. If the bridge were cut down to 4ft width, and the ship stripped and her torpedo tubes blanked off, that might be increased to 13 knots or even 14 knots. Propellers would be changed and planes cut down. The main bottleneck would be design and production of new telemotor equipment to operate the planes. That this project would take five months even at high priority was not acceptable.

Alternatively, by redesigning the bridge of an existing 'S' or 'U'-class submarine and overloading the motors using the existing batteries, speed might be increased to, respectively, 11.5 knots and 11 knots for half an hour. Plane area would have to be reduced, and that

would require some work in the test tank at Haslar to ensure that control would still be adequate.

A discussion showed that although the staff wanted at least 12 knots, even 11 knots would provide very useful information, since the fastest speed used by current training submarine was 5 to 6 knots. To some extent the effect of much higher speeds could be estimated. The 6 June meeting offered three alternatives: simple stripping of a 'U' or 'S'-class submarine, or more extensive stripping of a 'U'-class submarine fitted with increased batteries, or the same in slower time so as not to delay the 'A' class.

For a time DNC concentrated on the 'U'-class option. To achieve 12 knots such a submarine needed 3000 BHP total; motors from cancelled 'T'-class submarines would give 3160 BHP at 490 RPM. They could be accommodated if engines and generators were removed (enough space would remain for a small generator). A third set of cells could replace the torpedo stowage forward, giving 3160 BHP for half an hour. The torpedo tube compartment would be converted into a mess space to replace that formerly in the torpedo stowage. Redesigning the bridge, removing the gun, and streamlining the hull would reduce resistance about 10 per cent, but that would add only about 3 per cent speed. DNC thought the modified ship would be ready in about 5½ months.

DNE held a meeting on 13 June to consider the design. The key requirement was speed: 15 knots was desirable, but 10 knots would be acceptable. Submerged endurance should be 90 minutes, with a burst of top speed for 30 minutes. The submarine must be able to keep her depth at any depth down to 150ft. If possible the hull form should simulate that of the new U-boats, to avoid making an unrealistic wake. The submarine would not have to operate in anything but fair weather, and she could charge her batteries alongside. Only one target was wanted immediately, although more might be wanted later. Because it was larger, the 'S' class was considered a better prospect. *Seraph*, at Devonport for repairs after a diving accident but not yet in hand, was a possibility. At this stage the main planned modification was streamlining: covering apertures and providing a new cab-type bridge. The

Taciturn shows the later version of the enlarged gun shield. Her snort mast is raised. The exhaust outlet is the lower element about three-quarters up the mast, facing aft. That the Admiralty was willing to convert eight 'T'-class submarines immediately, despite serious financial problems, testifies to the importance the Royal Navy attached to the snort programme. According to the 1949 edition of the Admiralty's *Progress in Underwater Warfare*, 'no British submarine is now considered operational unless snort fitted'. Ultimately all surviving 'T'-class submarines were converted. In 1948 the Admiralty approved conversion of two 'T'-class submarines for high underwater speed, the first being *Taciturn*. Plans called for conversion of all remaining welded-hull 'T'-class submarines by 1956, amounting to eight (nine if the Dutch returned *Tapir*). This rough equivalent to the US 'Guppy' conversion is to be covered in the subsequent volume on post-1945 British submarines. (Alan C Green via State Library of Victoria)

Not all the initial 'T'-class snort conversions were given the enlarged gun shields. *Thorough* was photographed late in December 1949. *Telemachus* and *Truncheon* were similar at the same time. The earliest photographs of the conversion are dated November 1946. By 1957 *Thorough* had the enlarged gun shield. *Thorough* and *Tactician* were lent to the Royal Australian Navy. (Alan C Green via State Library of Victoria)

torpedo tubes would be blanked off, although not removed. The planes would be cut down, the forward ones fixed in the 'out' position. A high-capacity battery would be fitted. The motors would be modified to run faster, using redesigned propellers.[20] With existing propellers she might make 11 knots; with new propellers that could be increased to 11.5 knots. As long as no extensive alterations to the hydroplane operating gear were needed, she could be completed, as desired, by the end of August 1944. Because she would be faster than existing British submarines, submerged control experiments would have to be carried out, possibly entailing major modifications to hydroplane gearing (for faster response).

Seraph was ready as planned, at the end of August 1944. She ran trials in September and then carried out Asdic and tactical trials. This was well before any Type XXI made an operational cruise. Streamlining substantially reduced the submarine's echo strength when she was end-on, although at high speed the submarine's Doppler helped operators distinguish her echo. At low speed the more efficient propellers fitted to *Seraph* turned more slowly and hence were quieter, but she was easily detected by her propeller noise (hydrophone effect [HE]) above 6 knots. As a result, initial suggestions as to how to counter the new submarines emphasised their HE. However, it was suspected that a Type XXI could markedly reduce her HE by diving deeper. Post-war trials showed that the Germans had been well aware of this possibility, and that they had effectively silenced the Type XXI propellers. Once trials were complete, *Seraph* was used to train ASW groups as part of the Western Approaches Tactical Unit (WATU).

Based on trials with *Sahib*, which made 8.82 knots submerged, Haslar estimated that with underwater resistance reduced by 45 per cent, *Seraph* would make 11.7 knots with existing motors and batteries overloaded, each motor producing 1600 BHP rather than 1460 BHP. If BHP per motor could be increased to 4000, estimated speed would be 15.2 knots (14.2 knots with 3000 BHP). Initial trials were inconclusive because it excessive periscope vibration made it difficult to get cuts on the marks defining the measured mile. Speed may have been as great as 12.8 knots. Summary trial data credited *Seraph* with just over 12.5 knots at 1647 BHP. The increase in underwater speed

exceeded expectations. Without any streamlining it would have taken 4000 BHP to give that speed; the difference showed the price a modern conventional submarine paid for her many excrescences. The main improvement was the drastically reduced bridge structure, although blanking off holes contributed substantially. The effect of changing propellers and plane settings was relatively minor.

The conversion was considered successful, and during 1944 *Satyr* and *Sceptre* were also converted. Conversions continued after the war: *Solent* and *Statesman* were converted in 1946, and *Selene* and *Sleuth* in 1947. A more ambitious programme produced the Super-*Seraph* *Scotsman*, intended to exceed 15 knots submerged. She will be described in the volume on the post-1945 British submarine programme.

The British told the US Navy that in addition to their target function, they wanted the high-speed conversions to determine the limiting possibilities of obtaining high underwater speed using conventional machinery.[21] In August 1946 DNC's chief submarine designer A J Sims told US officers that with some overload on her main motors one of these submarines could make 13 to 14 knots running below periscope depth.[22]

The fast targets were a remarkable achievement, particularly since British submarine construction resources were stretched so badly by 1944. It helped the Royal Navy learn how to counter the Type XXI submarine – which, fortunately, entered service only at the very end of the war.

Captured U-Boats

In October 1944 FOSM wanted enough Type XXIs to maintain two operational, plus two Type XXIII (one to commission, one to cannibalise).[23] During the summer of 1945 British crews manned *U 2502* and the Type XXIII *U 2326* for trials.[24] *U 2502* was the oldest of the class and suffered considerable mechanical defects.[25] She was therefore discarded having suffered a wrecked motor on passage, scuttled and replaced by *U 3017*. The Admiralty acted as caretaker of surrendered U-boats for the Allies, so it was essential that no damage be caused during any trials.

The British planned thirty-day trials of one Type XXI and one Type XXIII against a frigate force. Similar trials had been carried out against *Seraph* in the Western Approaches late in 1944.[26] The Type XXI and XXIII were to carry out standard 'first of class' trials. The Type XXI would be run over a sound range and also subjected to thermal detection tests. Sonar target strength would be measured. Under an Anglo-American agreement, the two navies exchanged data

on the tactical trials they conducted with captured U-boats. At the outset Type XXIII trials may have been considered particularly urgent because the British expected to encounter similar submarines in Japanese coastal waters, the Germans having provided the Japanese with considerable information.[27]

Type XXIII had been designed for a maximum submerged speed of 12.5 knots for one hour. Captured documents showed that *U 2321* attained 10.35 knots at periscope depth and 11.20 knots at 20m depth; with an enclosed bridge and many flooding holes blanked off she might make 12.665 knots at 20m on 665 BHP. On trial *U 2326* actually attained 9.69 knots with 502 BHP and 11.143 knots on 600 BHP, both at periscope depth. At 600 BHP she burned out a large percentage of her main motor brushes. The British figures implied a speed of 10.2 knots with 550 BHP, similar to German figures. That the Germans actually attained a knot or two less than design figures made claims for other classes (Types XVII, XXI, and XXVI) suspect. DNC saw no evidence that the hull forms used in later German designs were any better than the converted *Seraph*. Designed endurance was 43nm at 10 knots, 70nm at 8 knots, and 175nm at 4 knots; trials indicated that actual endurance at these speeds would be, respectively, 17nm, 32nm, and 163nm. DNC pointed out that a 'U'-class submarine had an endurance of 22nm at 8 knots and 107nm at 4 knots at periscope depth.

Designed surface speed was 9.75 knots (630 BHP), and 9.82 knots was attained. Manoeuvrability was poor. On the surface *U 2326* had a larger turning circle than HMS *Venturer* of about three times the displacement. Much the same was true submerged. At 8.3 knots with her rudder 35° over *Venturer* had a tactical diameter of 235 yds. With her rudder 25° over at 8 knots, *U 2326* had a tactical diameter of 182 yds.

U 2326 could dive slightly faster than British submarines when the latter were not using their Q tanks. However, she tended to 'hang' early in the dive because her after planes were brought back too early and then put back to dive, to level her out. Overall, control was comparable to British standards. Plane operation was wearing on the operators, and the controls became stiff below 100ft.

The submarine could not use passive sonar above half speed. She could not, for example, keep station under a convoy running at any speed above 7 knots. In an exercise, a simulated convoy had to slow down so that the submarine could remain under it for safety. To some extent the problem may have been the very poor condition of the hydrophones. Compared to the array in a Type VIIC, Type XXIII had twenty-two rather than forty-eight units, with consequently poorer performance.

Tactical trials showed that the Type XXIII was a good echo target even when crawling, and at her maximum effective speed (9 knots) she

Tradewind was converted at Chatham between 6 September 1945 and September 1946 for experimental acoustic work; at least initially she might have been considered the Asdic equivalent of the fast 'S'-boats. She was given the two main Asdics of the German Type XXI submarine. A German Balkon low-frequency passive array (GHG) in place of the Type 129 at the fore end of her ballast keel. A 'Niebelung' (SU) was faired into the fore end of her bridge. It had been conceived as a blind-fire fire-control sonar, providing a passive target track and then using up to three pings to obtain target range. A plot of range and bearing would give target course, speed, and bearing, and could be the basis for firing acoustic homing torpedoes. All gun armament and external torpedo tubes were removed, and four of the six bow torpedo tubes blanked off. The superstructure and bridge plating were faired, all gratings being removed and plating fitted instead. As modified *Tradewind* ran first-of-class trials in September 1946. She attained 9.142 knots submerged (equivalent endurance was 1.31 hours). *Tradewind* is shown on 29 January 1952, a snorkel having been added, with the sonar dome of a Type 120 Asdic on her foredeck, and Type 138 aft. She is credited with having run silencing experiments with the snort, leading to the very quiet *Porpoise* and *Oberon* classes. (US Naval Institute)

was quite noisy. The CO of the submarine wrote that she was a better Asdic target than a larger British submarine. That was the great surprise. On one occasion contact was held beyond 4800 yds. As might be imagined, she offered her poorest sonar target end-on. The British concluded that no special tactics were needed to deal with this type of submarine. Director of Torpedo, Anti-Submarine and Mine Warfare (DTASW) thought, however, that if intelligently handled Type XXIII might be more difficult. If she could run 5 knots faster, which would be possible even with batteries, she would be a more difficult problem. The CO of the submarine wrote that he had been unable to evade hunting vessels in any orthodox way, so he tried to confuse the hunters. He did a full turn (360°) at 6 knots under full rudder and then bottomed under the resulting confused water in 140ft. That finally worked, but since the exercise ended soon afterwards he could not be sure how long immunity would have lasted. The surface ships stated that the situation did become obscure after the turn, because the wake reflected pings. The CO concluded that it was no easier to evade in a Type XXIII than in a British submarine.

Against a simulated coastal convoy, *U 2326* was 'no better or worse than another submarine'. After making an undetected attack at 900 yds, she went under the convoy to hide. In the confusion of wakes and sound, escorts which came quite close did not identify the submarine, and she escaped.

The submarine was well adapted to evade ahead-thrown weapons (Hedgehogs and Squids) because she had a small turning circle and turned so fast (180° in 2 minutes 4 seconds with slow group down).

However, the CO doubted that evasion could be maintained during a hunt to exhaustion.

Type XXI showed what the British called admirable conception but poor execution, partly due to over-engineering (which the US Navy also noticed) and partly because by this time non-ferrous metals such as copper were in very short supply; steel valve spindles and similar gear often seized up.[28] Detail design was poor; the Germans had increased diving depth not by improving their structures but by reducing their safety factors. Although rated collapse depth was 300m (975ft), the boat could not submerge below 180m (585ft), and even then local structural weaknesses were evident.

Through the summer of 1945 the Type XXIs in British hands began to experience problems, some quite dangerous. Experience with Type XXIII must have raised questions about their supposed 15-knot underwater speed. The main point of the trials would have been to evaluate ASW capability against a really fast target, but if the 15 knots could not be attained, the existing fast targets were good enough.[29] Selected for trials, *U 2502* she needed shipyard work, and she broke down badly en route to Cammell Laird. Instead of repairing her, without any guarantee that she would not break down again, *U 3017* was taken from the mass of surrendered submarines. An August 1945 battery explosion put her out of commission. The court of inquiry found that this had probably been due to adoption of German rather than British practices; a German engineer officer recalled four battery explosions in Type XXIs. The problem seems to have been poorly-insulated main electrical cables run in the bilges under the battery. Bilge water caused arcing, and when the battery was charged it produced hydrogen. Hydrogen explosions had always been a danger to submarines, but it seemed that extensive shipyard work would be needed before a Type XXI was safe enough to operate. British submarine refit capacity was limited. The Germans had not made their own Type XXIs operational. Trials were cancelled on 14 October 1945 and the two in British hands were reduced to care and maintenance status. Unlike the US and Soviet navies, the Royal Navy did not retain any Type XXIs in service. *U 2518* and the Type XXIII (*U 2326*) were lent to France. For data on Type XXI the Royal Navy relied on US trials.

To the extent that the Royal Navy wanted a Type XXI mainly to

'A'-class submarines under construction were completed with snorts. In Long Island Sound, 18 March 1953, *Andrew* shows one version. Her snort exhaust pipe is mounted on the radar mast supporting her surface-warning set; her snort induction pipe is folded down on her port side. Other 'A'-class submarines in this configuration were *Alcide*, *Alliance*, *Ambush*, *Amphion*, *Anchorite*, *Astute*, *Aurica* and *Aurochs*. *Andrew* had previously had a combined induction and exhaust mast and a modified gun shield. *Ambush*, *Alliance* and *Anchorite* also had folding combined snort masts. They also retained twin 20mm guns.

learn how to fight a 15-knot submarine, it was enough to produce the super-fast target *Scotsman*, which presented far fewer problems.

The 1944–5 Programmes

On 11 January 1945 A(S) held a meeting at his headquarters to discuss future submarine designs.[30] He laid out three alternatives for future submarine designers. They could try for maximum surface speed, endurance, and armament with the best submerged performance that allowed. Alternatively, they could try for maximum underwater performance (including endurance) and the best surface performance that allowed. The third alternative was a compromise. Maximum underwater performance seemed to be the best alternative, and certainly the British design target. Such a submarine needed sufficient diving depth to guarantee safe control at all speeds; automatic control might be desirable but would not be essential. The submarine should embody maximum resistance to underwater weapons. The use of a fuel containing oxygen, or with a means of producing oxygen to feed the power plant would mitigate, but not necessarily solve, the key requirement of sustained underwater operation. Highly efficient air-conditioning and air purification were essential.

It might be several years before an appropriate power plant could be produced. Meanwhile work should proceed on an efficient hull form. Existing motors and batteries had to be used. A(S) envisaged a series of experimental submarines, each an improvement on its predecessor in offensive power, as an extension of the trials already underway with *Seraph*. They showed that it was already possible to build a submarine with a special hull form, much greater battery capacity and high-power motors, with increased diving depth and specially-designed control gear. Such a hybrid could not closely approach the high requirements of the future submarine, but trials using it would save considerable time and labour. They would largely solve the problems of hull form, control at high speed, and human endurance.

Meanwhile work would have to proceed on the current type of submersible, in the form of the 'A' class and an improved version. A(S) thought the Germans were doing much the same thing by developing their standard submersible into a long-endurance, high submerged speed submarine by using snorkels and high-powered motors. Note that this was before details of the German HTP programme emerged.

The future submarine would need new kinds of weapons, both projectiles (presumably missiles) and torpedoes, which could be fired at reasonable depths, based on attack instruments capable of predicting the range, bearing, and possible speed of the target. Missiles ('bombing projectiles') would have to be suitable for firing from torpedo tubes. Submerged shore-ship communication and navigational fixing would have to be developed. Submerged ship-ship communication out to 50nm or more was desirable. Preferably all forms of submerged communication and navigational fixing should be possible at maximum diving depth.

A(S) asked the Board to approve construction of an intermediate hull form as the basis for future development; the 1945–6 Programme was then being framed. A(S) would ask for one experimental boat and three of an improved 'A'-class design.

Writing on 3 February, DNC agreed. Although a next-generation power plant might not be available for some time, enough battery power could probably be packed into an 'A' class-size hull to manage short 20-knot bursts. That would be enough to investigate the problem of control at various depths, and should lead to an optimum hull form, having regard to underwater resistance and diving depth. A

Initially no 'S'-class submarines were included in the snort programme, but by 1949 DNC had a design for modernisation including a snort and Type 267 surface/air-warning radar, at the cost of a smaller W/T office and a slight reduction in transmitter power. Guns were landed. The first 'S'-class submarine was to be taken in hand in 1950. This is *Scorcher*, 17 June 1953.

sketch design (A) for a test submarine similar in concept to *Seraph* showed the 'A'-class pressure hull, with sufficient power for brief bursts of very high underwater speed.[31] DNC estimated that he would need 8000 BHP for 20 knots. That would have taken too massive a battery. The A design had 560 batteries (five sections) to power two main motors with a total of 5750 BHP, sufficient for 18 knots. Endurance would have been 20 minutes. As in *Seraph*, engine power was insufficient to keep the battery charged up. In this case it would have been a pair of Muscovic diesel generator sets (2000 SHP). Surface speed would have been 15 knots, and there would have been a single periscope and no armament whatever.

By later in February 1945 two torpedo tubes forward and one aft had been added so that high-speed firing trials could be carried out.[32] This was not an offensive submarine, however; the object was to produce a hull form suited to high speed. The experimental submarine would have no engine for propulsion either surfaced or submerged, her batteries charged from the shore or by a depot ship. Dispensing with the engine would make it possible to use six batteries (131 cells each) of 'A'-class type, forced to give high power for maximum speed. Short battery life would be accepted. Symmetry of form would be desirable, although the stern torpedo tube would cause problems. By this time plans called for two motors geared down to 300 RPM. The first requirement as always was to accommodate the main batteries, to which end circular cross sections had been drawn for 18ft, 19ft and 24ft diameter, plus a pear shape 17ft wide and 23ft deep. The initial outline drawing showed the 24ft hull with two types of stern: twin rudders and hydroplanes in the propeller stream, or a single centreline rudder. The first would offer a kind of symmetry, the other being more conventional. One periscope would suffice. Ballast tankage would suffice only for harbour navigation; the submarine would have one main tank at each end plus one internal tank amidships. The bridge would be based on that of *Seraph*, with space for only two men. Its shape would be chosen after model experiments. Diving depth should be as great as possible, 700ft or more. By late October 1945 there were four parallel designs for an experimental submarine, presumably employing the four alternative cross sections.

Meanwhile the improved 'A'-class design was pursued. New features might be a telescopic (rather than folding) snort, variable-pitch propellers, greater diving depth through the use of a better steel, and some adjustment of the fore and aft ends of the pressure hull for better access. The control room would be enlarged to accommodate an Action Information Organisation (AIO – the British equivalent of the US Combat Information Centre).[33] It turned out that operationally acceptable reduction in appendages would not be enough to increase underwater speed materially. This was still essentially a submersible surface ship. Work continued at least through May 1945.[34]

By this time information was continually being received describing German designs for high underwater speed using snorts, HTP and closed-cycle diesels. Work on the modified 'A' class was abandoned. On 17 July 1945 Controller called a meeting to discuss policy.[35] A(S) repeated that the aim should be a 'true submarine', which would spend an entire patrol submerged. He was no longer interested in a more conventional submarine. Experimental design work should continue on a hull form suited to high underwater speed. The three 1945 submarines should be a radical break with the past, something like Type XXI. However, in FOSM's view the Germans had compromised by beginning with a submersible and modifying it for high submerged performance. The British should start by emphasising underwater performance. He asked whether starting a new design could be justified before more was known about the Walter engine. In notes for this conference, FOSM wrote that it would be impossible to incorporate Walter features for a long time. Afterwards he suggested leaving space for later installation by sacrificing batteries and by adopting smaller motors. It was assumed that no submarine could have everything: Walter, large batteries, and a 'super Snort' (presumably meaning a telescopic one).

The designers substituted two new design projects: a Future Submarine (24ft diameter pressure hull, 20 knots submerged) and a 'B' class (displacement about as 'A' class, 19ft diameter pressure hull, snubbed bow, special snort arrangements, minimum appendages, etc.). The object in both cases was to enable Haslar to make models with different hull forms.

The Walter power plant must have seemed quite close. In August 1945 A(S) understood that trials of the 6000 SHP version were to have been completed at Kiel in November 1945. If the trials succeeded, the engine should be reproduced in the United Kingdom and incorporated in the 1945 submarine. If the Walter unit was not ready in time, the new submarine should provide space for later installation. The Royal Navy should proceed with one experimental 'true submarine' and the three operational submarines of the 1945 Programme.

Tentative Staff Requirements for the operational submarine included the ability to charge batteries *completely* (emphasis in the original) in reasonable time while submerged; provision had to be made to dispose of the battery gas generated late in the charging cycle. The design should incorporate a Walter engine with maximum fuel for a long burst of high submerged speed. Torpedo armament should be the maximum possible, with at least a six-torpedo bow salvo of (all reloadable if possible). A stern salvo was desirable but not so essential, and the tubes did not have to be internal. Detectability by radar, Asdic and magnetic equipment (presumably MAD and detection loops) should be minimised. The communication and navigational requirements A(S) had set were repeated.

Late in October DNC prepared a pair of preliminary designs for the operational submarine, which he designated BI and BII, both providing space for a Walter engine.[36] Each had two sections of 112 cells each, of 'S' size in BI and of 'A' size in BII. DEE was working on a higher-

Sleuth as a fast target ('slippery S' conversion), March 1947, with the original minimal open bridge (note the hatches which could be closed to streamline the bridge fairwater). Note the streamlined housing for the single periscope. (R A Burt)

capacity cell, which might provide enough energy for 20 minutes. Before a further meeting on the design, scheduled for early November, some propulsion questions had to be decided. In their large Walter submarine (Type XVIII) the Germans had accepted high RPM (700) for the turbine, gearing motors and diesels to the propeller shaft. For silent running they had used a creep motor driving the shaft via a belt. High RPM made for small propellers, but DNC much preferred lower RPM (300–400) and larger more efficient propellers, with direct drive. Diesel-electric drive (as in the 'U' class) might also be worth considering.

A meeting on the B design was held on 27 November 1945.[37] Should all surface qualities be sacrificed? It was now clear that no anti-radar coating could make it possible for submarines to operate freely on the surface in the face of aircraft, and that non-radar detection (IR) was coming. Conventional submarines were finished.

It seemed likely that snorting range would be far less than surfaced range. Snorting speed might be increased to 10 to 12 knots in good weather, but in rougher seas snorting depended not so much on the size of the induction and exhaust as on the pulsation of air in the submarine if waves frequently opened and closed the induction valve. In that case snorting speed would probably be limited to about 5 knots. Unless passage was partly made on the surface, average speed might be limited to 7 to 8 knots. Air cover might make it possible to proceed 300 to 500 miles from base on the surface.

Studies to date showed that for a given overall 'form' displacement, a submarine designed for high underwater speed would need about 50 per cent more fuel to achieve a snorting endurance equal to what a conventional submarine might achieve on the surface. In a conventional submarine, surface endurance would be about four times snorting endurance at the same speed. On the other hand, a surfaced submarine would lose range by zigzagging.

Photographed on 20 June 1953, *Selene* shows her open bridge. Note the hinged covers for her port anchor, to cover its recess in her hull.

Sleuth is shown on 16 May 1956.

No one could say that the Walter turbine would succeed; the Germans themselves had had mixed views, and no Walter submarine had become operational. 'Apart from the development position of the turbine itself, and of safe handling of the fuel, there is no experience of its operation under tropical conditions or whether its effect on habitability would be appreciable.' EinC saw no fundamental difficulties, although he knew that he would have to improve auxiliaries and the combustion system. He thought it would take 18 months to make *U 1407* operational without major improvements. The operational British submarine would have twin 6250 SHP Walter turbines. EinC thought that it would take 3½ to 4 years to design and produce the first plant. No accurate figures could be provided until the 18X unit was running. EinC also pointed out that the Walter plant lost power with depth: 12,500 SHP at periscope depth would be 9300 SHP at 100ft. He hoped to reduce this loss. FOSM was willing to accept 100ft as the depth for maximum speed with 'trackless' running.

DNE was less optimistic. Instead of jumping immediately to a high-powered Walter submarine, he would begin with the high battery capacity submarine the Royal Navy could have at once, with a speed of about 18 knots, to gain experience of high underwater speed. It could be followed by two small submarines with *U 1407* power plants, to gain experience before building a full-scale HTP submarine. A(S) disagreed. He wanted the three fast 1944 submarines, with full operational capacity and habitability at least as good as in the 'A' class. EinC agreed with DNE that the quickest way to provide a prototype Walter submarine was to use the existing low-powered turbines, perhaps even a single turbine in a smaller hull. It would probably take two years to make this turbine suitable for installation. However, an attempt to duplicate the *U 1407* engine might preclude trials with the only HTP submarine the Royal Navy had.

EinC much preferred diesel-electric to the usual direct drive, despite the extra space and weight involved, because it would eliminate two of the three clutches per shaft. Machinery design could be standardised and the diesel generators sound-insulated (a point DTASW liked). Electric losses would increase specific fuel consumption by about 9 per cent, but the more favourable generator location would probably buy about 15 tons more fuel. DNC's B designs had 6–10ft longer engine rooms whatever type of diesel drive they used. DTASW emphasised the value of silencing while snorting; the Staff wanted the new submarine to be able to listen through her own engine noises.

Plans called for complete drawings to be sent to yards by the autumn of 1946, so that a keel could be laid early in 1947 for completion in mid-1948. Would the Walter turbine be ready in time? Would its advantages last for long, and would they be worth having once the submarine was built? All navies were competing to build fast underwater submarines. The Walter turbine would be useful only between half and full speed. If beaten in that range it would be useless for silent

propulsion. A Walter submarine could not be fully converted into a battery design. HTP would be stored at the expense of oil fuel, so snorting endurance would be reduced. The stern would inevitably be congested, because it would need fine lines for high speed. That would congest the rest of the submarine. Stern tubes would probably be impossible to fit. Complement would have to increase because specially trained personnel would be needed. Docking draft would probably be greater. DNC cautioned that the Walter turbine probably would not be ready for adoption until 1949; even then it was not certain that it would be adopted. Large-battery submarines could be built at once.

It seemed unlikely that the Germans would have achieved their 25-knot goal; generally the speed of their submarines dropped as design progressed. They had also accepted greater congestion than the British found acceptable. A submarine with accommodation and control room comparable to that of the 'A' class, powered by two 7500 SHP Walter turbines, would be unlikely to exceed 20 knots. Would more be needed or wanted?[38] Space available for propulsion in a submarine of about 'A'-class size could not exceed that in Type XVIII. It might be possible to save space and weight by adopting a single shaft, but two shafts were much preferred not only for greater reliability, but also for greater manoeuvrability. Should a silent creep motor should be provided, or would the main motors be able to run at quiet low speed? Adopting diesel-electric propulsion would simplify layout and probably would reduce noise when snorting, but fuel consumption would increase. A Walter submarine would be heavy aft, so it would be important to save propulsion weight.

A submarine displacing about as much as the 'A' class could accommodate about 11,000ft³ of liquid fuel and HTP. The latter required about 33½ft³ to the ton, compared to 42½ft³ for oil. Type XVIII had enough HTP for 5 to 6 hours at full speed. With that much HTP, the submarine could not have the snorting endurance of the 'A' class. With 166 tons of oil fuel, the 'A' class had a 10,000nm endurance at 10 knots (7850nm at 12 knots). The B 1 design (147 tons oil fuel) offered 8000nm at 10 knots (5500nm if snorting) and 6250nm at 12 knots (4250nm if snorting) plus 6 hours (nominal) at 21 knots on HTP. Adding 300 tons of form displacement would increase snorting endurance to 6500nm at 10 knots or 5000nm at 11.25 knots (maximum speed with 2500 BHP engines), but such figures would depend on what other claims on space were made. Speed on turbines would be reduced from 21 knots to 20 knots. FOSM wanted the snort endurance at 10 knots to be at least that the 'A' class maintained on the surface at 12 knots. He did not want the size of the submarine

Solent, 4 February 1953.

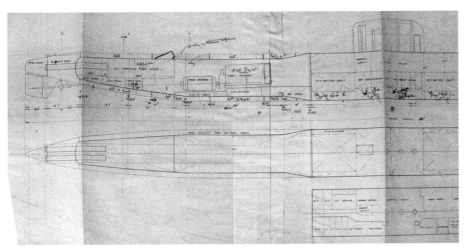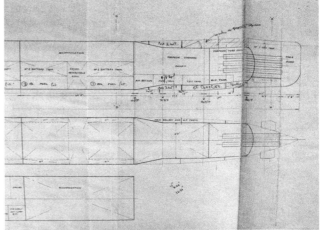

Design B-4, 1945, the 'improved "A" class' as sketched by British designers. This drawing was in several designers' notebooks. (Author's collection)

increased if that cost underwater speed. The loss of endurance made fuelling at sea an important issue.

The alternative to the Walter submarine would be increased battery power, as in Type XXI. Maximum submerged speed for a battery submarine would probably be about 18 knots. The hull form of such a submarine would be fundamentally different from that of a Walter submarine (probably meaning provision for HTP stowage). It might be well to design the 'B' class as a diesel-battery submarine and to develop a separate Walter 'C' class. It had been assumed that the submarine would be of about 'A'-class size, which offered good ocean-going qualities. If the submarine would operate only submerged, did it have to be that large? If surface qualities could be sacrificed and a bluffer bow accepted, a submarine could have six bow tubes and as many as ten reloads. Stern tubes would be impractical, and external tubes would add too much underwater resistance.

The conference recommended a size about like that of the B 1 design: form displacement 1770 tons. DNC thought he could provide 21 knots in an 1800-ton (form) submarine if it had very low appendage resistance and size was held down. He doubted the German claims for the Type XVIII design.

The large experimental submarine was no longer important, because and it could not be built much faster than the operational submarine, and it could not reach anything like the same speed. DTASW wanted a much faster target submarine (16–18 knots) to support development of new-generation sonars. That led DNC to work on an improved *Seraph* with greater battery power, with a hull more completely stripped, and without main engines and oil fuel.[39] One possibility was to install a third battery, which would increase power to 2400 BHP. Four 'S'-class batteries could drive two 'S'-class motors per shaft (3200 BHP), but space would be insufficient. Alternatively four 'S'-class batteries could drive two 'T'-class motors (6in greater diameter than 'S' class); to make space the motors would be moved 5ft forward. DNC found this possibility attractive. Maximum RPM would be 520. The 'T'-class motors could run instead at higher speed (650 RPM), and they could be geared to the shafts. Alternatively, 'A'-class cells could be used. The first scheme was the simplest and could be realised in the least time. Speed with three battery sections would be 15.5 knots, with four it might be 17 knots. DNC considered the extra 1.5 knots hardly worth the additional complexity. The new 'S'-class conversion emerged later as *Scotsman*, described in the post-1945 volume. As the meeting ended, A(S) suggested that steam propulsion might be a viable alternative to Walter. EinC said that was already under consideration. Such a plant could use normal air when snorkelling.

When DNC reviewed the situation in December 1945, he concluded that the Walter engine was only way to reach really high underwater speed, at least over 20 knots.[40] Even if future alternatives were better, a Walter submarine would give the best experience of what high-speed submarines needed. However, it was unproven and its snorting endurance would be limited. It would be difficult to produce in any quantity in an emergency until after 1950, because it would take firms time to master production of the new kind of power plant. The entire building programme would be badly delayed. Additional battery power could, however, quickly be incorporated into a submarine which could be built rapidly in an emergency. Maximum submerged speed would be only about 13–14 knots, well short of what an HTP submarine could achieve, and submerged endurance would be appreciably less. DNC strongly supported A(S)'s push for HTP as the highest submarine priority, but EinC pointed out that it was a long-term project. Meanwhile 'there was something to be said' for making one of the 1944 submarines a large-capacity battery type with 2½ to 3 times the submerged endurance of a conventional submarine, capable of bursts of submerged speed.

The experimental 1945 submarine should be the smallest possible, for maximum performance with either the 7500 BHP Walter turbine being brought to the UK or two 2500 BHP units reproduced from those in the captured *U 1407*. Although these engines had passed the research stage in Germany, much ashore testing would be needed in the UK. The *U 1407* refit would not be complete in much less than 18 months (from January 1946). Its engine could be copied immediately, albeit probably at some expense to the refit. The experimental 7500 SHP (Type 18X) unit would need considerable design and development. Current British design resources and workloads seriously limited capacity to develop the engine very quickly. Also, large-scale production and storage of HTP had to be developed. By the summer of 1946, any hope of immediately building an operational Walter submarine was dead. A pair of experimental Walter submarines emerged much later as *Explorer* and *Excalibur*. The stories of the Royal Navy HTP submarine and of its fast battery alternative are told in the subsequent volume on post-1945 developments.

RADIO (W/T) AND SUBMARINES

Wireless (W/T) was so important to British submarines that it seems best to bring together its history, rather than spread it through the text.

Radio exploits the fact that any varying electric current creates waves which spread outward. We do not sense very low-frequency waves, such as those created by 60 cycle current, because they are weak and because their wavelengths are so long (in this case, 5000 km). The earliest Royal Navy radios worked at low frequency (LF), typically defined as 30 to 300 kHz (1 kHz is a thousand cycles per second), with wavelengths between 1km and 10km. As technology developed, W/T could operate at medium frequency (MF), 300 to 3000 kHz (wavelengths down to 100m) and then at HF (3000 to 30,000 kHz, typically written as 3 to 30 MHz, with wavelengths down to 30m. Technology determined what could be done and how well W/T could work at these frequencies. It also determined the impact of W/T installation on submarines.

All radio transmits both a ground wave, following the surface of the earth, and a sky wave going up at an angle. LF and MF work mainly by ground wave, transmitted power determining the range. HF is different. Its ground wave does not extend far – perhaps 180nm at most – but its sky wave bounces off the ionosphere. The bounces offer remarkable range, but between bounces nothing can be heard. Moreover, the ionosphere moves up and down both with the time of day and with the season. At different times and different seasons different frequencies are more or less useful. That is why, although the promise of HF was obvious in the early 1920s, it took a long time for the Royal Navy to abandon its earlier techniques.

B 4 shows an early wireless antenna installation, usable only when she was surfaced. The wires themselves are hardly visible, but the spreaders between them are evident. As in later installations, the ends of the bundles of wires are connected to the ship's structure (in this case her guard rails and her yardarm) by insulators. This photograph was presumably taken at the time of the 1910 trials, when she and *D 1* were fitted with wireless; *B 4* had the transmitter and *D 1* the receiver. The instruments were all borrowed from HMS *Vernon*, the torpedo and electrical school. Although the transmitter in *B 4* was not particularly successful, *D 1* received signals in Torbay until she entered the Needles Channel. The receiver was on deck, the operator being the ship's CO. Commodore (S) suggested that even better results could have been attained using a below-decks silent cabinet and a better-qualified operator. DNO, who was responsible for wireless at the time (because it was being developed by *Vernon*), strongly endorsed installation of wireless in submarines. Work on a set, with a range of 30nm, was ordered. (NHHC)

AE 1 shows the original wireless configuration of the 'E' class. A multi-element aerial was strung from the yardarm visible atop her wireless mast. It did not telescope; instead it unfolded in multiple throws. The vertical element of the antenna emerged from the vertical tube visible forward of her bridge. It led into a silent cabinet below decks. Antenna efficiency depended on the height of the 'roof' (in this case an inverted-vee) and the number of wires in it. Hence the elaborate pre-war bundles of wires with their insulators – which could not possibly be rigged quickly enough for wartime use. (RAN Naval Historical Section via Dr Josef Straczek)

The other side of the story was the changing demand for W/T capability. Short-range W/T (tens of miles) could make it possible for submarines to work with surface ships, typically using a linking ship to connect them with longer-range command from a fleet flagship or a shore command station. That was the expectation before and early in the First World War. However, as submarines operated more and more in denied areas such as the Heligoland Bight, linking ships were impractical. During the war British submarines were employed mainly as scouts in the Bight, watching for the High Seas Fleet to emerge. To do that they had to be able to reach back hundreds of miles to the Admiralty via stations in the UK. That required a new type of radio, the Poulsen.

The change to emphasis on the Far East required a further leap, as a submarine on patrol off Japan would probably be more than a thousand miles from base. The main interwar radio theme was the attempt to reach greater ranges. That often seemed to require more and more elaborate antennas and from the mid-1930s on it was understood that it might be impossible to use them in wartime. Large antennas had been tolerated during the First World War, because a submarine could remain reasonably securely on the surface at night or even when she was well outside normal operating areas. During the interwar period aircraft were increasingly a factor and anything precluding a crash dive was less and less tolerable.

Transmitters

A radio transmitter has three main elements: a power source, a transducer which converts that power into higher-frequency electric oscillations and an antenna coupled to the transducer, which sends out the W/T waves. There is also a key which somehow interrupts or modifies what goes out to produce intelligible signals. The power source and transducer are separate because there was never a power source which by itself could produce high enough frequencies. It is one thing for a generator to produce 60-cycle or even 400-cycle power and quite another to produce what might amount to 30,000 cycle power.[1]

The first widely-used transmitters, as in pre-war British submarines, had DC on-board power, converted into AC by a motor-generator. AC was needed to raise voltage to the point where a spark could be created between the power circuit and the transducer circuit. The latter was tuned to the desired frequency. It can be thought of as an electronic bell, rung by the spark. This bell in turn was linked to the antenna. The resonant (ringing) frequency of the transducer was limited by existing components (condensers and capacitors and inductances). Closing the sending key closed the circuit which energised the spark and thus indirectly created a W/T signal. This technique had the important merit of simplicity, but it had important drawbacks. First, only a fraction of the energy in the spark was converted into radio energy, so range was relatively limited. Second, the impulse delivered by the spark had to be quenched quickly, so the 'ringing' soon tailed off. That decay mixed a range of frequencies into the signal which went out, making it difficult to split off different channels. On the other hand, whenever the key was not pressed, the operator could listen for other signals.

In 1902 Valdemar Poulsen invented an alternative which sent out its signals continuously. He found that a carbon arc connected to a tuned (resonant) circuit could oscillate at radio frequency, up to 200 kHz, above the frequency of a spark transmitter. As in a spark set, the character of the resonant circuit set the frequency which came out. The arc itself was the oscillator linked to the aerial. Since the signal was continuous, it had a pure frequency (it did include harmonics – multiples of the basic frequency – but they are not relevant here). Because the arc took time to start and to stabilise, there was no question of keying by turning it on and off. However, it was possible to change output frequency by 1 to 5 per cent by adjusting the resonant circuit, typically where it sent power into the antenna. In effect this was what would later be called frequency-shift keying. Some low-power Poulsens later turned the arc on and off or else connected and disconnected it from the antenna.

The situation was transformed with the appearance of reliable vacuum tubes (valves in British parlance). A circuit employing tubes could generate signals of the desired frequency and other tubes could amplify it as desired. Both Poulsen and spark transmitters were discarded after the First World War.[2]

Early antennas consisted of wires strung between masts, the wire from the transmitter going vertically to connect with them. The signal is radiated by the vertical element, the horizontal wire (a 'roof' or 'flat top') adding capacitance to increase electrical height. The higher the 'roof' or 'flat top', the more efficient the antenna. The combination transmits and detects vertically-polarised signals, which travel much further than horizontally-polarised ones. From a submarine point of view, unfortunately height means long masts.

Beginnings

Initial submarine wireless experiments seem to have been made in July 1910, the torpedo gunboat *Skipjack* and *B 3* communicating at up to 35nm, the submarine stopped with her receiver on the bridge in the open. With her engine running, the submarine could receive signals at 20nm in fine weather. Given this success, ICS had three sets of receiving gear put together, using a tuned 70ft wire strung between two 20ft masts, the latter hinged to fall quickly as needed. They were used during the 1910 manoeuvres. Installations were ordered the following year for all 'B', 'C' and 'D'-class submarines. Maximum receiving range was reportedly 50nm, but sending range was shorter. ICS proposed fitting one boat in three, but in March 1911 DNI (in effect chief of the naval staff) called for all submarines to be fitted, at the least all new boats and all 'D' class.[3]

In April 1911 HMS *Defiance* (the W/T development organisation) reported that under ordinary conditions unskilled operators could exchange signals between two submarines at 35nm and skilled operators could easily read at 55nm. As of November 1911 the 1912–13 sketch Estimates included provision for fitting six boats; Keyes wanted eight, to provide him with two in each of the four seagoing flotillas attached to the mother ships *Vulcan*, *Thames*, *Bonaventure* and *Arrogant*. The remaining mother ship, *Forth*, had only a five-boat flotilla. Keyes chose *B 5* as the first. She completed at Devonport in June 1912. Tests were successful enough that *B 10* and *B 11*, based at Malta and thus not in Keyes' initial programme, were added.

The initial Type X (later Type 10) test set was standard at the

outbreak of war.[4] According to the 1912 *Vernon* W/T Appendix, it was broadly similar to current destroyer sets. In 1913 Type X was being modified for the 'B', 'C', 'D', 'E' and 'X' (*Swordfish*) classes, boats being fitted as they came into dockyard hands. Plans called for installation by April 1914 on board one 'B', eleven 'C', all eight 'D', seven 'E', two Commonwealth (the Australian *AE 1* and *AE 2*) boats and one 'X'-class submarine (*Swordfish*), plus one set for *Vernon*. The 1914–15 Estimates called for installations in all new boats, in all 'B' and later-class submarines not yet fitted, plus sets for the Torpedo Schools and Portsmouth Signal School, a total of sixty sets.

Tests using the tender *Forth* showed a maximum range of 25nm, less than expected. For the best performance a submarine needed two masts, but they would be difficult to lower quickly. The single mast of *B 5* could be lowered much more quickly in order to dive. Initially the mast fitted to many submarines proved unsatisfactory because it could not be raised and lowered quickly enough in a seaway.[5] Two new types (telescopic and collapsible) were made for trials. A collapsible mast gave good results on board *D 2*. It had to be short enough when collapsed not to interfere with the periscope, but in some submarines (mainly 'C' class) that limited its height when erected to less than the desired 30ft. The proposed solution was a three- rather than two-part collapsible mast. Submarine W/T figured for the first time in the 1913 manoeuvres, when numerous submarines were given temporary sets.[6]

By April 1915 W/T communication with the Harwich oversea submarines operating in the Heligoland Bight was a high priority; the Ipswich W/T station was ordered devoted entirely to this purpose.[7] Submarines used D wave (213m: 1400 kHz), which they could reliably receive at 50nm.[8] Given pre-war estimates, it is surprising to read that submarines were expected to receive signals from Ipswich (on the longer S wave, 1000m: 300 kHz) at 150nm by day and 250nm by night. Sending was much more difficult: reliable range was given as 30nm by day and 50nm by night, although a Type 10 did once send 100nm in daytime. The high W/T masts required by the submarines was a particular problem.

Assistant DNO for Torpedoes (in effect the Admiralty's submarine expert) considered it 'vitally necessary' that the oversea submarines be able to receive signals, repeated at prearranged times, both by night and by day, at a distance of 300 miles maximum' – on the other side of the North Sea. 'It is also desirable that they should be able to send this distance by night.' He had what he considered conclusive proof that the Germans could send and receive over this distance under normal night conditions.

Assistant Director of Signals Philip Dumas replied that the British W/T system had been designed on the assumption that British submarines would always work with linking ships. The Germans seemed to use their whole wireless organisation to get signals to their submarines. However, Dumas doubted that U-boats communicated back to Germany at any great distance, except by using linking ships or else exploiting freak conditions at night (destroyers in the Mediterranean were often heard in the Channel at such times). 'It would never be safe to assume that a message sent by wireless from an English shore station reached a submarine unless it were sent on several different occasions.' Dumas doubted that U-boat W/T ranges were much better than British, since their destroyer W/T range was no better than British. Examination of a captured German U-boat set in 1917 indicated that it would outrange Type 10 but would not have nearly the range of the Poulsen Type 14 installed for long-range communication from the Bight.

The subsequent meeting decided to devote Ipswich entirely to submarine signalling, tuned to R wave (794m) for maximum range. A submarine should be sent out to find out at what range she could receive Ipswich and at what range, day and night, she could contact it.[9] An 'E'-class submarine received signals up to about 100nm and her signals were received at Ipswich, Dover and Newhaven up to about 50nm. Since the linking destroyers could have no idea of whether the submarine was submerged and hence could not receive, the submarine would have to query them for any information to be passed from shore. That opened the submarine to interception, but it was considered far better than holding her to a rigid receiving schedule.

Only a Poulsen arc, incompatible with all tactical spark sets, offered the desired 300nm range.[10] Its aerial had to be strung between two masts, special deck tubes for the wiring and rearranged internal fittings. As an interim step, given how important the look-out in the Bight was, four destroyers and six submarines were fitted with Poulsen sets.[11] An 'E'-class submarine probably could not accommodate both Type 10 and a Poulsen set, but submarines could probably have Poulsen receivers in addition to their Type 10s. Ideally the submarine should have a full Poulsen set and a spark receiver (but not transmitter). A destroyer could send and receive on both systems, although switching between might not be very quick. Since the submarine could not transmit on spark, she would have to call up a destroyer on Poulsen (V wave); both submarine and destroyer could transmit to Ipswich using V wave (otherwise used for communication between medium power stations in the British Isles and Whitehall: 1729m: 174 kHz). However, a destroyer using her Poulsen would be unable to communicate with other destroyers using spark sets. Both destroyer and submarine would be using far too much power, hence their signals would be intercepted much further away than if they were using spark sets. The scheme was approved and also installation of Poulsen sets on submarines, but that required further trials.

Once Poulsen equipment had been demonstrated successfully on board Harwich submarines, attention shifted to the Grand Fleet. The Aberdeen radio station, like Ipswich, was converted to Poulsen and as an initial measure, by October 1916 the submarine tenders *Lucia* (10th Flotilla) and *Titania* (11th Flotilla) had Poulsen installations. By November 1916, all 'G' and later submarines in home waters, as well as all battleships, battlecruisers and light cruisers in home waters, were being given Poulsen installations. A third shore station, Pembroke, was being added.

At the end of the war, in good weather, with good aerial insulation, a Poulsen set (Type 14) might transmit to 350 to 400nm, but range could be cut short in worse weather.[12] Under moderate conditions (aerial and feeder not enveloped by spray, but general dampness reduced insulation resistance) range might not exceed 250nm. Under bad conditions, with aerial and feeder enveloped by spray, 150nm would be an excellent performance. The arc, which burned in the aerial, might be put out altogether, making signalling impossible.

Several submarines could receive signals while submerged using two fixed-frame coils built into the superstructure (Model SA), using a high-power tube amplifier and a tuning circuit. Under normal con-

E 56 shows shows a standard First World War wireless mast installation. The two masts folded up in sections and were erected hydraulically. The horizontal element of a 'flat top' antenna was strung between them, with a vertical element down to the wireless transmitter below decks. Also prominent are the jumping wires extending from the bridge structure to the ends of the ship, and the telescoping signal mast abaft the two periscopes. Rigging all of these wires took far too long, so that by the end of the war submarines were generally using parts of their jumping wires as antennas. Later submarines generally retained the wireless mast near their two periscopes, but not the two antennas fore and aft. Note also the 12pdr gun abaft the bridge fairwater, on a folded-out platform, and the white air recognition stripe forward of the bridge. (Author's collection)

ditions a submarine could receive signals from a suitable shore station at 400 to 500nm or even more depending on the power of the station. A ship could be received at 30 to 40nm.[13] Unfortunately it was often more important for the submarine to be able to send than to receive messages. In a 1922 test, *L 12* had four frame coils, two forward and two aft angled 90°, on her conning tower. At periscope depth, with the coils 20ft below the surface, signal strength was little less than on the surface. She received shore stations quite strongly – Eiffel Tower, Horsea and Leafield – but lost most signal strength at 30 to 35ft. The frame coils were also effective for D/F, the set being little inferior to that in surface ships. For comparison, a loop aerial was fitted along the jumping wire. It gave even better results, Leafield being heard at 45ft. By mid-1923 there was considerable interest in an antenna on a paravane a submarine could tow at a fixed depth, allowing her to communicate while more deeply submerged. A conference on board the fleet flagship *Queen Elizabeth* on 30 April 1924, attended by RA(S), recommended that all submarines should have a non-directional frame coil or electrode on a telescopic mounting, to receive W/T at periscope depth; that all but fleet submarines should have the paravane receiver; and that all but fleet submarines should have DF antennas (but for surface use only).[14] Initial fittings of SA coils were suspended pending further work by the Signal School.

By this time there was also interest in using a kite or a kite balloon to carry a long vertical antenna aloft, a theme which persisted through the interwar period. If the submarine had to crash-dive, she could simply release the kite, which was much simpler than collapsing one or two masts. Both fair- and foul-weather kites were developed and tested extensively.[15]

Interwar

The important new post-war technology was high-frequency radio (HF), work on which began under the cover name of 'natural waves'. It enabled a relatively weak signal to travel extraordinary distances. Moreover, because the wavelength was relatively short, in the tens of metres, a high-gain antenna did not have to be very large. Operating at 28m wavelength (about 10 MHz), *H 43* was able to transmit from Spithead to Aden.[16] At sea she managed brief communication with Matara in Ceylon (Sri Lanka). She did not do so well when transmitting alongside a destroyer in Dartmouth harbour.

H 43 also tried to transmit at periscope depth using a three-quarter wave aerial at 12m wavelength. By January 1925 she had a three-quarters wave antenna suspended from her periscope. A surface ship received her signals at 45nm and aircraft up to 20nm. Although this was short of the 50nm desired by CinC Atlantic Fleet, the Admiralty Board doubted that more could be done.[17] It considered fitting submarines with short masts for submerged HF transmission. For submerged reception the ship tried a horizontal coil consisting of ten turns of rubber-covered cable on a 2ft x 2ft wooden former fixed to the night periscope. With 3–5ft of water above the coil, *H 43* could receive signals on 2000m wavelength.

This work continued as late as 1929. At that time *H 43* had a periscope aerial and another was being fitted to an 'L'-class submarine in the Mediterranean. Initially she used an improvised wire lashed to a periscope, but by 1929 she had a 10ft periscope aerial. During Exercise AP, she was able to communicate with nearby ships (surface wave) out to 50nm and to 800 to 1000nm (sky wave) using a periscope aerial showing only 5ft above water, with a special receiver from the Signal School. By January 1930 *H 43* was using her periscope antenna

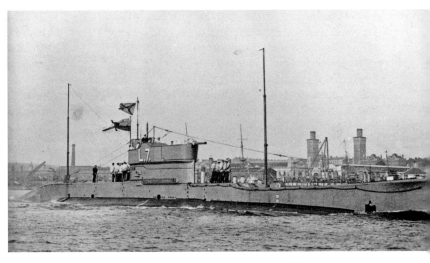

L 7 shows her two tall wireless masts soon after the First World War. Her periscopes have been retracted; the only really visible one is the night periscope between them. Abaft her after periscope is her wireless mast, which was generally used to support an inverted-vee antenna. It is inside the fairwater which protected the deck tube through which the vertical element of her wireless antenna passed. This vertical element was strung to the top of the wireless mast. It passed down to the control room. Most 'L'-class submarines probably lacked the two additional vertical masts altogether; for example, they do not feature in the official plans of *L 6*, dated 3 December 1918. (Dr Josef Straczek)

to communicate with a Fairey IIIF floatplane, as a test of what a patrol submarine could do with an embarked aircraft.[18] She could receive from the aircraft at least out to 33nm (she did not try longer range). In a related trial (6 November 1929), *H 43* could be heard by HMS *Iron Duke* at 50nm.

There was some hope that jumping wires could be turned into antennas, but in 1924 they were ordered abolished, as they became too slack with age to help a submarine pass through a net. Later, tests with booms showed that even in good conditions jumping wires were of limited value.[19]

The two taller masts planned for *Oberon* were too cumbersome, so the Staff opted for maximum W/T range with 50ft masts (which it considered the practical limit for a submarine), plus a kite for longer distances. A 19 February 1925 meeting substituted one 60ft mast for the two 50ft masts chosen earlier, as it would give better results.

As of late 1925 all submarines were to have transmitters operating at three wavelengths: (a) 10 to 15m; (b) 23 to 50m; and (c) 400 to 3000m. (a) was for short-range submerged transmission using a periscope aerial (40–50nm); (b) was for long-range work on the surface; (c) was for normal work by arc and spark sets, now being replaced. The new set, which used tubes, was designated Type 46, the first being fitted to *L 26* and to *H 43*.[20] The set in *L 26* was considered very successful.[21] Because there was not enough space in her W/T office for sufficiently powerful transformers and transmitting tubes, her W/T range on long waves was reduced to half to two-thirds that of her earlier arc set, with the same power input, but that was more than balanced by the short-wave set effective to a thousand miles or more. When submerged she could transmit on 12m to about 25nm. Operation was also much quicker than with earlier sets. New 'L'-class sets would replace the broadside torpedo tubes in that class. They would be much more powerful, with much greater range.

As of 1927, 'O'-class submarines had no fewer than seven aerials, using three separate masts (a tall one plus stumps fore and aft) plus a signal mast. In addition to aerials slung from extendable masts, they had a diving antenna, which was kept rigged when they dived. This combination offered a range of 400 to 450nm with the diving aerial, 1200nm with the kite and 800 to 1200nm with the main aerial on masts. Estimated ranges for submarine-to-submarine communication using identical aerial systems were 100 to 150nm with improved diving aerials, 1200nm with kite aerials and 800 to 1200nm with the existing main aerials. RA(S) wanted to eliminate the main aerial and the special wireless mast, relying for transmission entirely on the diving (i.e., permanent) aerial and the kite. The mast supporting the main aerial caused interfered badly with the ship's compass. The submariners badly wanted to reduce the cumbersome rig, ideally improving the *Oberon* diving antenna so that it could replace the main mast and aerial.

When the 'P' class was designed, the major issue was how to use the new HF technology to achieve the desired wireless range.[22] The Signal School considered 1200nm the greatest range which could be guaranteed, but submarines often did much better. They were given short HF antennas for submarine-to-ship communication at periscope depth, which CinC Atlantic Fleet considered essential for cooperation with the fleet. Unfortunately that seemed to require a 30ft collapsible mast, which interfered with the existing W/T rig.

At a May 1927 conference the submariners proposed abandoning the paravane antenna (for submerged long-range reception) and not fitting the periscope aerial (for HF) in patrol submarines until it offered much greater range than its present 40nm. A diving aerial

lengthened by about 50 per cent could extend from the superstructure to the after end of the upper deck casing. Using it, a submarine could transmit to 1300 to 2000nm on HF. Maximum transmission range on long wavelengths (2800m) would be about 400nm. Alternatively, a double aerial could be carried on a spreader across the bridge, providing space for the kite. Another possibility was a bare wire extending the full length of the submarine. It would offer a range of 700nm in good weather, but in a heavy sea it would probably be less satisfactory.

Oberon tested three rigs: a combined main and diving aerial; a kite; and a half diving aerial. [23] With the combined aerials, she communicated at 950nm. Using the combination as a diving aerial, she managed 410nm at 2800m by day and 950nm at 2400m at night. There was some trouble with insulators breaking down. This combination proved easy to handle, changing from one aerial to the other. The kite took longer to get up. The half aerial was rejected for poor radiating properties. HF trials in *Oberon* continued until she was withdrawn for an extended refit, after which *M 2* was given an improvised HF set.[24] It gave up to 600nm range during the fleet's spring cruise.

A modified *Oberon* rig was tested on board *Phoenix* about the summer of 1931, between her position near the Scilly Isles and Fort Blockhouse.[25] Yards on the fore and aft stump masts were eliminated, the aerial outhauls being brought together at the after stump mast. There was no difference between the two rigs, so the modified rig was proposed for all patrol submarines. The search for a suitable periscope-depth antenna continued. *Regulus* tried a cab-tyre aerial (several turns of insulated wire) on her W/T mast. The top throw of the mast was

L 53 shows her wireless aerials, May 1931. Her wireless mast is raised, supporting the vertical (actually slanted) parts of an inverted-vee antenna. The vertical element was strung from the after arm of the inverted-vee, meeting a tube in the bridge fairwater. The objects visible on the two arms of the inverted-vee are insulators. The installation was relatively inefficient in wireless terms, because the arms were short and consisted of a pair of single wires. Surface ships typically used bundles of horizontal wires, but submarines could not. Below the antenna wires were the jumping wires, which were not used for wireless at this time. (John Lambert collection)

Wireless was a key element of the big interwar patrol submarines; *Otus* is shown. She shows the stub masts fore and aft used to raise the ends of her inverted-vee wireless antenna, which was supported amidships by the telescoping wireless mast shown. The vertical element was strung from the after leg of the vee, meeting an insulated tube in the after part of the bridge fairwater. Between the two periscopes (forward bifocal, 9½in diameter, after 7½in unifocal [attack] periscope) was a frame coil which could be used for underwater reception and for radio direction-finding. Here its housing is faired into the standards of the periscopes (the top of the attack periscope is barely visible). The wireless mast has a yardarm for signal flags, but the upper yardarm is insulated to take the two wires of the inverted-vee. The object visible abaft the bridge fairwater is a boat derrick, the ship's boat being stowed in a recess in the casing below it. Note also the two windscreens. (RAN Naval Historical Section via Dr Josef Straczek)

reduced in cross section and streamlined and the W/T yard moved down to the top of the second throw. Lowering the yard cost MF range and by early 1932 trials were ongoing to see whether the arrangement met the MF and HF requirements.[26] While on passage from England to Malta with this rig, *Regulus* obtained a range of about 900nm on MF (107 and 115 kHz). She was then fitted with a rigid 'periscope' or rod aerial at the top throw of her mast.[27]

By the spring of 1932 submarine W/T rigs were again being reviewed. In wartime in enemy waters the complicated W/T masts could not be used, leaving only kites for MF signalling beyond the range of the diving aerial (500nm). Submarines had to spend more of their time practicing with kites, in all weathers day and night. A few months later the reported average time from surfacing to passing a message via a kite was 11 minutes. In an exercise submarines off Oban, 400nm from Fort Blockhouse, sent seventy-eight messages, only one of which failed (and that only through interference at Fort Blockhouse). As yet there was little experience in using HF as an alternative.[28] However, it was increasingly evident that any submarine signalling on MF was likely to be found by radio direction-finding (D/F'd). There was some hope that a submarine using HF might be immune.[29]

In April 1932 RA(S) proposed an ideal W/T rig. It was approved by the Board and promulgated at a 29 September 1932 conference.[30] At this point RA(S) would settle for a reliable 400nm range and as much more as possible up to 800nm, far short of earlier requirements. This had to be achieved without adding projections which could foul nets and also if possible without placing outhaul winches on the bride. Arrangements agreed at the conference would not prejudice the staff requirement. With the aerial in the fixed position 400nm should be attainable on MF under normal conditions and much greater under

The fleet submarine *Thames* shows a hinged wireless support aft and the usual high wireless mast amidships abaft her two periscopes, with a frame coil housed between them. Although the frame coil is integral with the periscope standards, it has its own mast leading its output down into the control room. The more-or-less vertical elements of the main aerial are led down into tubes in the after part of the bridge fairwater through insulators. In contrast to earlier practice, another forward wire is used as a secondary (loop) aerial, remaining rigged when the submarine dived. Forward there is an aerial support just forward of the jackstaff, although it is not as prominent as in the 'O' class. *Thames* shows the prominent shield of her 4.7in gun, not supplicated in her sisters (it was removed in 1935, replaced by a 4in gun). (© National Maritime Museum G.10147)

Clyde shows her prominent bow aerial support, its antenna evident by the insulator visible abaft her jackstaff. Also very visible is the loop antenna stretching up from the deck forward. That it is not really a jumping wire is evident from the presence of the stub bow aerial support mast. The ship's DF loop is visible between her periscope supports. *Clyde* was photographed in 1935–6. The torpedo derrick has been erected forward. (© National Maritime Museum N21226)

good conditions. The kite aerial should offer 1000nm under normal conditions. RA(S)'s representative suggested that now that the kite was the main means of obtaining really long range, it should be called the main aerial and the fixed aerial the diving aerial. However, the conference rejected this terminology; there would be kite and diving aerials. Also, it was agreed that the proposed rig would not be suited to a submarine penetrating defences, meaning nets; 'very special arrangements' would be needed for that. Even so, the rig would avoid any projections which would foul anti-submarine nets. Fouling light indicator nets was unavoidable (eventually the solution adopted was a light jumping cable to sense the net, activating an electric cutter). The aerial had to be as high as possible, for range. Stump masts fore and aft would have to allow the centre of the aerial to be fixed, eliminating the need for winches to tighten it. Insulators would be arranged to guarantee the safety of personnel on the bridge, which mean that they would be either on the periscope standards or on the fixed support to the W/T mast.

The high W/T mast could not be extended in wartime, when a submarine always had to be ready to crash-dive. For MF beyond the range of the fixed aerial, submarines would rely on kites. Trials in *Rainbow* justified replacing the top section of the mast with a rod aerial, its top 6ft above the tops of the periscopes when they were raised. RA(S) was willing to accept 4 or 5ft if necessary. Trials showed that the existing mast could stand up to the pressure of water flowing past it at maximum submerged speed. Note that this mast folded up in sections; it did not telescope. China submarines would be fitted first. Mediterranean submarines (1st Flotilla) were already to be fitted with temporary cable aerials secured to their periscopes. The new arrangement was being tested on board *Regulus* and *Rainbow*. The

In an undated photo, *Clyde* shows an experimental antenna, probably an HF whip, atop her wireless mast. The short yardarm mounted on the mast supported the ship's main long-wire antenna. Note too the short whip atop the periscope standards and the circular DF antenna between the periscope standards. That probably dates the photograph to about 1937. (RAN Naval Historical Section via Dr Josef Straczek)

patrol submarines would all be fitted, as would be *Porpoise*. The new rig would also go on board the 'S' class. However, the first three 'O' class (*Oberon* and the *Otways*) were a more difficult problem, owing to their design. *Thames* already had a rod aerial and she would not be refitted with a new arrangement. The square DF coils in submarines would be eliminated, as this would reduce their silhouette and save weight. The horizontal coils used for submerged MF reception would also be eliminated, loop (wires forward of the conning tower) or rod aerials being used instead. Trials on board *Rainbow* showed that she could receive MF and LF submerged satisfactorily on a rod aerial. New submarines would have telescopic masts fore and aft to raise the insulators there at least 8ft above deck. Kites would be flown from an outhaul carried on the mast or, in older classes, the periscope, to raise the kite clear of eddies formed by bridge structure.

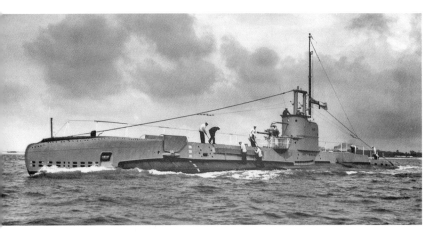

Sunfish shows her open bridge and most of her wireless aerials. The heavy wires extending fore and aft from her periscope standards are jumping wires, to get her through nets. Insulators connect the jumping wires fore and aft to loop antennas to be used at sea. The higher wire rigged to the wireless mast is a harbour aerial. A forward element is not rigged. At least some boats of this type also had a horizontal fixed wire antenna extending aft from the bridge fairwater above the life lines visible here. It connected to an angled element which in turn connected to the tube bringing wireless signals into the submarine. Note that the DF loop of earlier submarines is absent.

Using a rod antenna, *Rainbow* received MF and LF at periscope depth, Malta transmitting at 44.5kHz at range 1100nm, Blockhouse 156 kHz at 50nm, and Cleethorpes 90.2 kHz at 180nm. Reception of HF was also satisfactory. Using the rod for both transmission and reception, at moderate HF frequency (5 MHz), *Rainbow* managed communications at 1000nm while en route to China.[31] She was surfaced at the time. Trials at higher frequency with Fort Blockhouse were unsatisfactory; at 43.6 MHz she managed to hear Fort Blockhouse at 22nm, not the desired 50nm. She did much better on Mediterranean HF (5 or 6.45 MHz), contacting Malta at either 2000 or midnight and once more at 0800, at a range of 1000 to 1180nm.[32] She also managed to contact Fort Blockhouse at ranges up to 950nm. RA(S) concluded that there were distinct possibilities for HF at periscope depth, provided frequency was selected to suit the time of day and the distance. MF data on this cruise was insufficient (the best range was 450nm), but LF was very satisfactory, the best performance being contact with Malta at 2000nm (at 44.8 kHz). With the diving aerial occasional communication was possible up to 950nm (at 107 kHz).

In September 1933 the Admiralty ordered trials of rod aerials using *Porpoise*, *Starfish* and *Seahorse*.[33] On 18–25 MHz the ground wave faded at about 70nm and when surfaced reliable results could not be achieved beyond about 25nm. Results when submerged were even less

Supreme was photographed at Liverpool, 13 May 1944, with a typical late-war wireless antenna outfit. She had no wireless mast (hence no harbour aerial), her air-search antenna (for Type 291W) having replaced it. She had a loop aerial forward and her main aerial aft, in both cases strung from jumping wires. The loop antenna abaft her bridge fairwater was a standard wartime installation, the earlier frame coil between the periscope shears having been abandoned. Note the pipe rack to prevent the 20mm gun from firing into the ship. (NHHC)

Early 'U'-class submarines had hinged, rather than telescoping, wireless masts, set into the port side of their bridge fairwaters. Photographed in October 1938, *Unity* has her mast extended, with its characteristic folding horizontal section at the top. It supported the usual harbour aerial. The mast retracted by folding down at an angle to the upper-deck. A fixed aerial was connected to the jumping wire. Ultimately (about 1942–3) the folding wireless mast was replaced by a radar mast carrying the antenna of a Type 291W air-search radar. (RAN Naval Historical Section via Dr Josef Straczek)

reliable and frequencies about 13 MHz did little better. However, results were considerably better at lower frequencies (5 MHz, 6.45 MHz and 12.85 MHz), so it seemed that about 8 MHz should be adopted as the frequency for shadowing submarines, the D/F risk being accepted. Reports from China and the Mediterranean gave similar results, although China preferred 12.3 to 12.85 MHz. The important conclusion was that the rod was not as efficient as a cable aerial attached to the hull, which was cheaper and more easily fitted and maintained.

The small new submarines of the 'S' class had insufficient space between deck and pressure hull to house the full height of the stump masts fore and aft, so they were fitted in two sections and erected by telemotor. RA(S) pointed out that the masts were very expensive to make and unduly complicated the telemotor system. Its piping outside the hull was dangerous, since breaks would leak oil betraying the submarine. Were the stump masts worth keeping? They did raise the aerial clear of sea and spray.

A July 1934 Admiralty conference recommended replacing rod with cable aerials on all submarines from *Oberon* on.[34] Of submarine building, only *Severn* and *Clyde* would retain their rods until they needed replacement. Meanwhile 4th Submarine Flotilla tried out some further rig ideas. The best was a 'roof' led from the top throw of the mast 16ft aft along a jackstay. The conference also reviewed stump masts in the 'S' class, taking into account that in war jumping wires would be fitted fore and aft – not to penetrate nets, but to ward off explosive sweeps that the Italians were known to use.[35] Further trials were wanted with jumping wires in place and fixed diving aerials rigged: (a) parallel to the jumping wires and suspended from the fore periscope standard and brought to a fixed point on each side of the casing below the jumping wire with insulators 5ft above the casing; and with the fore and aft legs shortened about 20ft as in *Seahorse* trials;

and (b) with the ends of the aerial outhauls raised to 5ft above the casing, the insulators about 8ft above casings fore and aft. This trial assumed that some simple form of mechanically-operated stump mast would be fitted. A third variation would have a single aerial wire carried at the top of the second throw of the wireless mast, its ends fixed to suitable blocks carried in the jumping wires. The last would be adopted if the fixed aerial gave insufficient range.

Trials carried out by *Porpoise* at the end of August 1934 compared the kite to a single-wire aerial raised on a telescopic masts.[36] Its efficiency was 11.1 per cent. The efficiency of an aerial lying entirely under the jackstays was 5.5 per cent if they were insulated and 3.1 per cent otherwise. If fitted to the periscope brackets and raised above the jackstays by stumps, efficiency was 7.2 per cent and 6.0 per cent, respectively. The Signal School concluded that the effective heights of the normal diving aerial and of the special aerial were very poor whether the jackstay was earthed or insulated. Even the single wire aerial connected to the W/T mast had a small effective height.

Trials in *Swordfish* showed that the most efficient HF antenna was the 'roof' about 9ft long at an angle of 45° or less to the horizontal. Off Portsmouth on average it tripled signal strength.[37] The cable forming the roof would be secured to the casing or some other point aft by rubber cord, to take up the slack when the mast was lowered. It was now necessary to fit the fixed aerial below the level of the deck insulator, i.e., at a 'negative height'. In theory, the greater the negative height, the more efficient the aerial. However, the lower the aerial, the more liable it was to push down. It was also liable to losses due to the proximity of the casing. Calculated ranges for the aerial 5ft above the casing were 160nm for an aerial running forward and aft, and 95nm for one running aft only. In practice the full-length aerial gave 130 to 350nm depending on weather. The frequency was 155 kHz; ranges would be greater at higher frequency. By late 1935 telescopic stump

Photographed on 10 January 1954 with her deck gun and DF loop gone, *Upstart* shows the pipe racks fitted to keep anti-aircraft gunners from firing into the bridge or into her (retracted) radar mast. 'U' and 'V'-class submarines were too small to accommodate 20mm guns, so they made do with three light machine guns atop their bridge fairwaters. *Upstart* shows the usual multi-wire aerials fore and aft of her bridge, with vertical elements leading up to them.

masts had been abolished; they would gradually be removed from new submarines.

New Type 54 and 55 transmitters for submarines were announced in 1938, of which only Type 55 survived.[38] Type 54 was a high-power master-controlled HF transmitter with coupled aerial circuits, for 3 to 20 MHz, with an associated low-power MF element. Type 55 was an analogous medium-power set for 3 to 18 MHz, with a low-power element for 100 to 1400 kHz. By 1944 the standard sets were Types 55M and 55MR, the modification being removal of the MF panel and extension of HF coverage to include port waves (frequencies). Older submarines were refitted as opportunity offered. VLF signals could be read on the D/F receiver.[39] According to the post-war Admiralty technical history of W/T, the aerial rig proved satisfactory. The telescopic aerial, originally fitted to give short-range HF communication with a few feet of aerial showing, was removed to save space and weight. Kites fitted before the war were given up, as experience showed they could not be used. A diagram comparing outfits in 1939 and 1945 shows limited changes. In both a loop aerial was strung from conning tower to bow and the main aerial was strung aft. In 1939 there were also a telescopic aerial and a DF aerial. In 1945 the telescopic aerial was gone. In 1939 the submarine had one high-powered HF transmitter and one low-powered MF; in 1945 there was also a low-powered VHF transmitter to support wolf-pack operations and there were two HF receivers rather than one HF and one LF (the 1945 receivers could also receive LF).

APPENDIX B
MIDGET SUBMARINES

During the Second World War the Royal Navy operated both midget submarines and manned torpedoes (Chariots), as well as smaller clandestine submersibles. Because the latter were never part of the mainstream of development, they are not included here.

Midget submarines were one of several responses to a problem raised by the First World War: an enemy fleet in a defended harbour. Prior to the advent of submarines, bottling up an enemy fleet solved the threat to sea power, and was considered quite sufficient. The First World War showed that even a bottled-up enemy fleet could shield submarines to some extent, since it could preclude attacks on submarine bases. Probably the most damning criticism of Admiral Jellicoe's failure to destroy the High Seas Fleet at Jutland was that it precluded the attack at source which might have ended the U-boat problem. In the 1920s the Royal Navy formed a Harbour Attack Committee, and it supported work on an explosive-laden semi-submersible which might be sent into a harbour, guided by an aircraft overhead. Midget submarines were an alternative, as demonstrated by their effective attack on the *Tirpitz* in 1943.

By late 1939 the British were receiving reports (which were false) that the Germans were building midget submarine. The reports had never been substantiated, but it seemed that such craft would have advantages over conventional submarines in attacks on ships in harbour; they might well be able to penetrate the usual defences. DNC was asked what they might be like.[1] In December 1939 he offered three possibili-

ties, on approximate displacements of 25, 50, and 100 tons. The smallest (23 tons surfaced, 26 tons submerged) was 33ft long, carrying 1800lbs of explosive. It might use a 22 BHP motor to make 7 knots submerged. To sink a battleship it would probably have to destroy itself when attacking. Such a submarine would cross the North Sea either in a carrier (perhaps a converted whale factory ship) or under tow. The next size up (48/53 tons, 54ft 3in x 8ft 6in) would have a 100 BHP engine for surface running and a 60 BHP motor, for 8.5 knots on the surface and 7 knots submerged. It could be armed with two 18in torpedoes, and endurance would be 750nm at 8.5 knots or 1200nm at 7 knots. Finally the large midget (96/106 tons, 77ft x 9ft 6in) would be armed with two 18in tubes and would carry two reloads; on 200 BHP it could make 9.5 knots surfaced (90 BHP for 7 knots submerged). Endurance would be 750nm at 9.5 knots or, submerged, 3 hours at 7 knots, 15 hours at 5 knots or 60 hours at 2 knots. These possible threats were taken seriously: for example, the mesh in anti-submarine nets was being reduced. Detection, either by the usual magnetic loops or by Asdic, would be much more difficult than for conventional submarines, so the defence would rely heavily on anti-submarine booms. Patrols would help; a very small submarine trying to enter a harbour would probably rely heavily on her periscope. She would be more likely to broach than a conventional submarine if there was eddying in the tidal stream. The Admiralty issued these data to CinCs in January 1940. DNC's estimates were not too far off for the X-craft the Royal Navy actually built.

A model of a typical British midget, *X 24*, at the Royal Navy Submarine Museum, Gosport. In the foreground is a model of its weapon, the big side charge. The forward mast is the diesel induction, which could be tipped back at an angle. Abaft it is the periscope. Between the two is the short night periscope. The after side of the diesel induction mast carried a wireless aerial. The hatch forward covered a wet and dry compartment a diver could use. (John Gourley)

X-Craft

The beginning of the X-craft project seems to have been a British Army proposal for a 'submersible tank' which could swim down the Rhine attacking river installations such as bridges.[2] It was conceived by Major (later Brigadier) M R Jeffries. This sort of attack became impossible when the Germans overran France, but the idea was taken up by VA(S) Max Horton. He had Jeffries lent to the Admiralty. The initial naval operational requirement was to lay a magnetic mine in coastal shipping routes. Retired Commander C H Varley RN, who had his own Varley Marine Engineering Works near Southampton, was responsible for the design and production of a prototype. It was very different from the original army design.

These submarines were initially designated Job 82, but they were soon known as an X-craft. The designations *X 1* and *X 2* already having been used for submarines, the prototypes became *X 3* and *X 4*.[3] *X 3* was designed and built by Varley near Southampton; *X 4* was completed at Portsmouth. *X 3* was ready for trials in March 1942. *X 4* was slightly modified; it was ready in October 1942. These proto-

An X-craft at sea, the officer in the hatch giving an idea of its tiny scale. This is one of the *X 20–X 25* series. The diesel induction mast has been tipped back. (© National Maritime Museum P39656)

types were discarded in shock trials in 1944. They were built in three sections and were designed to dive to 200ft. Their weapon was a pair of side charges (2 tons of explosive each), which could be released from within the submarine. In addition, the submarines had a wet and dry chamber through which a diver could swim to attach a magnetic limpet mine (150lbs) to the target; this requirement was later dropped. Without the side cargo, surface speed was 6 knots (5.5 knots with the cargo) and endurance was 1400nm (1100nm) at 4.5 knots or 650nm at 6 knots (550nm at 5 knots). Submerged endurance was 85nm at 2 knots.[4] Special equipment included a trailing arm for accurately navigating along the bottom of a channel. Varley proposed a further version, which might have a conning tower; it was not built. Alternative armaments were (i) eight charges (150lbs each) plus two torpedoes (in tubes or dropping gear) and two ¾-ton depth charges; or (ii) as (i) but with two Chariots rather than torpedoes; or (iii) eight charges plus four 1-ton depth charges. Depth charges would be laid on the bottom or could float up under the target. This version was intended to offer greater surface endurance (4600nm at 7 knots, 8000nm at 6 knots) as well as the alternative armaments. Surface displacement would have been 46.4 tons (60ft x 8ft). The power plant would have been two Gardner 42 HP engines or one Gardner 85 HP engine plus one Gardner 20 HP engine. This midget would have had an air-cooler and dehumidifier.

The Vickers production version was *X 5* through *X 10*, which were intended specifically to attack German heavy ships in Norwegian waters. They were armed with two 4-ton side charges. Surface speed was to be 6 knots (endurance 1200nm at 4 knots) and submerged speed 5 knots (80nm at 2 knots submerged), with a crew of three. Initial plans to bring them near the target on board a suitable surface ship were discarded. A new design, which could be towed into place, was prepared by Vickers. It was adopted in preference to a design offered by Varley, presumably the one described above. Twelve were ordered in July 1942, the object being for six of them (12th Submarine Flotilla) to carry out an operation in the spring of 1943. Six were ordered from Vickers and six from the Broadbent Group. The last of the initial order for six (*X 10*) was delivered on 16 January 1943.

The weapon was a side cargo charge weighing 4 tons in air and carrying 2 tons of explosive, released from inside the submarine. As of November 1943 a new design was being developed with a detachable explosive chamber. Without the side cargo in place, surface displacement was 27 tons (51ft 7in x 5ft 9½in [8ft 6in with cargo]). Diving depth increased to 300ft. Surface speed with cargo in place was 6.5 knots; endurance in that condition was 1320nm at 6.5 knots. Submerged speed with cargo on board was 5 knots (endurance 80nm at 2 knots). Human endurance was given as 7–10 days in home waters. The main engine was rated at 42 HP.

Although Varley had initially envisaged an operation in which the X-craft went all the way to the target under their own power, by 1943 it was accepted that they should be towed most of the way. Initially they were to have been towed by SOE fishing boats, but it turned out that the boats were not powerful enough (or reliable enough). When *Tirpitz* moved to north Norway, moreover, she was out of their range. The X-craft training organisation proposed that they be towed by submarines. Towing reduced the endurance of a 'T'-class submarine by 5½ per cent at 10 knots, and of an 'S'-class submarine by 30 per cent at 10 knots. Accidents with *X 3* and *X 4* made it impossible to make the desired attack during the autumn of 1942. Vickers was also experiencing teething problems with the production X-craft (the six operational

X 10 underway about 1943. She seems to have a rudimentary conning tower instead of a periscope. Development of X-craft showed that they badly needed sensors, among other things to determine when they had passed under a target ship. Initially a higher-frequency passive version of the standard submarine Type 129 Asdic was tried, mounted on the night periscope, but it was soon clear that it would be confused by small craft operating near a target. That led developers back to active sonar; they chose a very high frequency (300 kHz), ten times that of any known enemy sonar. The beam of this Type 151 Asdic (target indicator) was so narrow that interception was considered most unlikely. It was first tested on board *X 8* in June 1943. The oscillator was mounted flush with the casing, on top, with a second oscillator looking down as a depth finder. X-craft also had a Type 156 underwater telegraph set, its oscillator in the forward ballast tank, to communicate with, for example, the mother ship towing the submarine. (© National Maritime Museum N6797)

craft were delivered during January 1943). The operation was postponed to March 1943, but early in February it became clear that teething troubles would preclude that; the operation had to be postponed to the autumn. The first full exercise (PBX 4) was conducted between 26 March and 2 April 1943, using *X 5*, *X 6*, and *X 7*.[5] They demonstrated their seakeeping, navigational and attacking qualities. *X 5* and *X 6* were towed through heavy seas and high winds. Because the distance was less than 80nm, they kept their operational crews on board throughout (on a longer operation, passage crews would have been on board until the craft neared the target area). *X 6* was towed by a motor fishing vessel, a form of camouflage considered for the attacks. Probably the main lessons were that *X 5* and *X 6* would have been quite effective in attacking, and that they were never seen by patrols, lookouts ashore and observers from the target ship. *X 7* was also effective, but was too late to be towed all the way to the operational area, hence attacked alone from closer in. The exercise did display a variety of problems, some of which recurred during the attack on *Tirpitz*.

On 11 and 12 September 1943 the six left Loch Cairnbawn, towed by submarines. One was lost on passage, and one had to be scuttled as her side charges flooded. Three which reached Kaa Fjord were destroyed close to their target, one and a half crews being lost. At least two completed their attacks and seriously damaged *Tirpitz*, and a sixth failed to complete her mission owing to electrical defects and had to be scuttled.

X 23 at anchor, 16 March 1944. The pipe abaft the flagstaff carries a compass clear of the magnetic field of the electric motor. Its image was projected down onto a screen in front of the helmsman. Initially X-craft had only gyro compasses; the magnetic compass was added because there were so many gyro failures. The binnacle with the magnetic compass could be raised or lowered. The magnetic compass did not really solve the problem, both because its raised binnacle would foul anti-submarine nets and because it was badly affected by the magnetic mass of the target. Raising and lowering it in the event of gyro failure were also too slow. As a substitute for both it and the gyro compass, craft were fitted with aircraft-type direction indicators intended to maintain a steady course for a limited time; but on one occasion the indicator also failed, turning an X-craft back the way it had come. (© National Maritime Museum 8993-5)

HM SUBMARINES *X 5 TO X 10*. General arrangement. Looking to port. (© National Maritime Museum M1109)

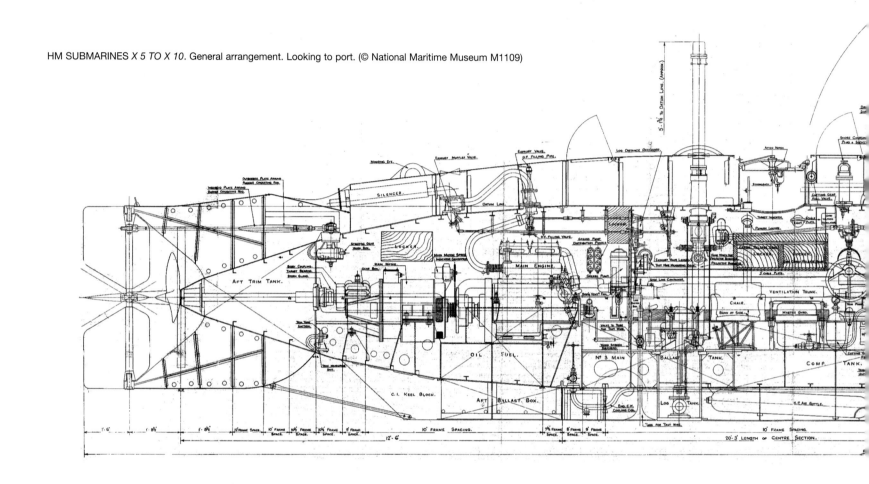

HM SUBMARINES *X 5 TO X 10*. General arrangement. Plan of interior. (© National Maritime Museum M1110)

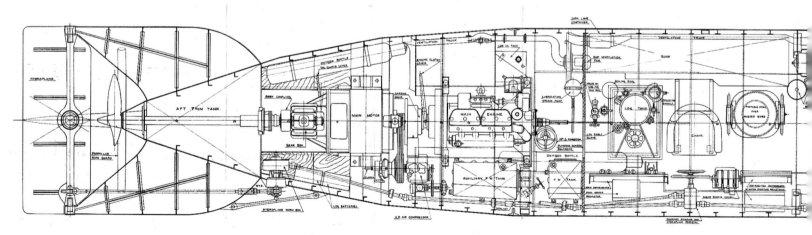

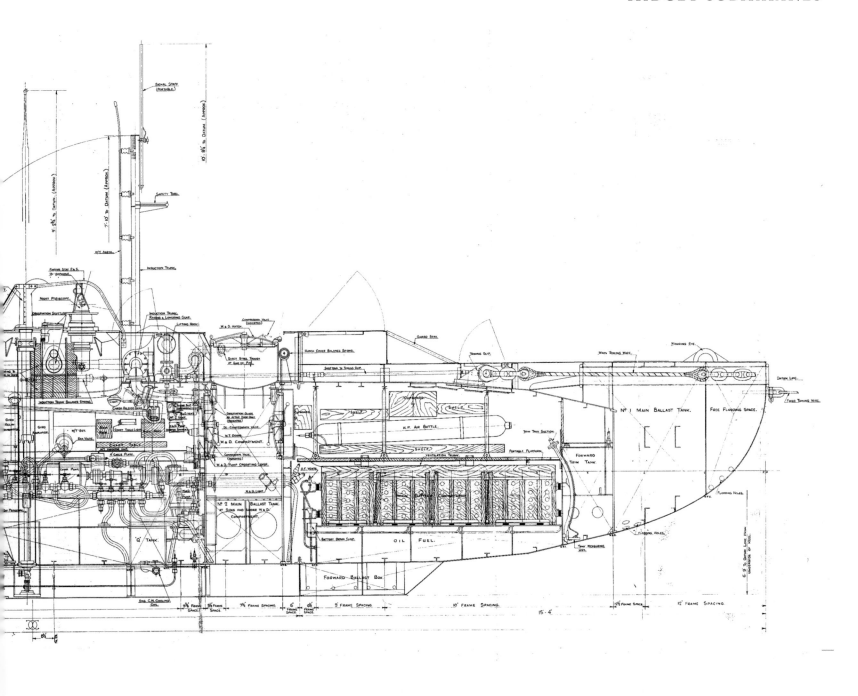

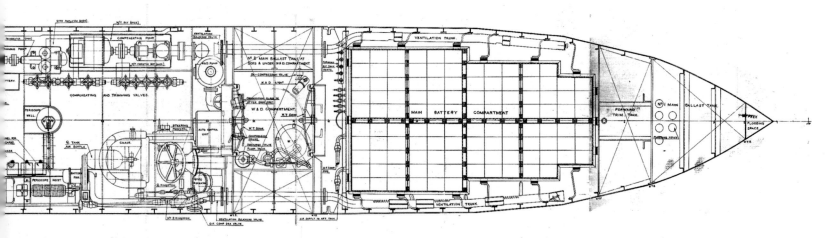

HM SUBMARINES *X 5 TO X 10*. General arrangement. Plan of outer hull and superstructure. (© National Maritime Museum M1112)

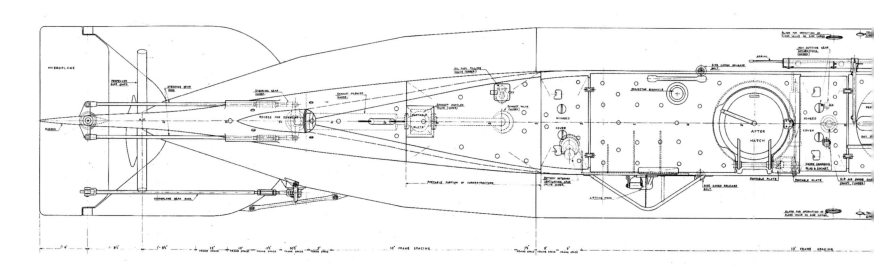

HM SUBMARINES *X 5 TO X 10*. General arrangement. Sections. (© National Maritime Museum M1113)

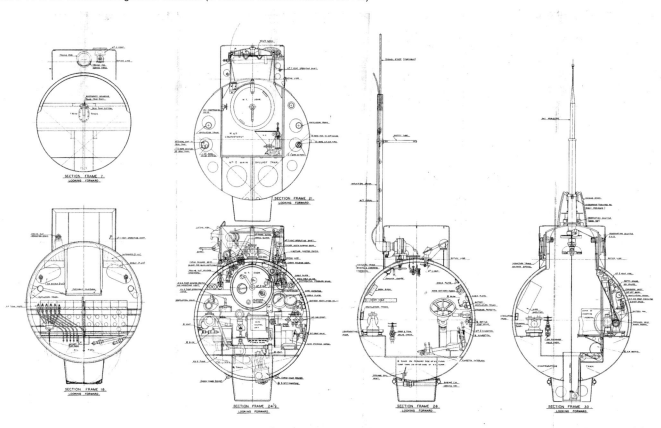

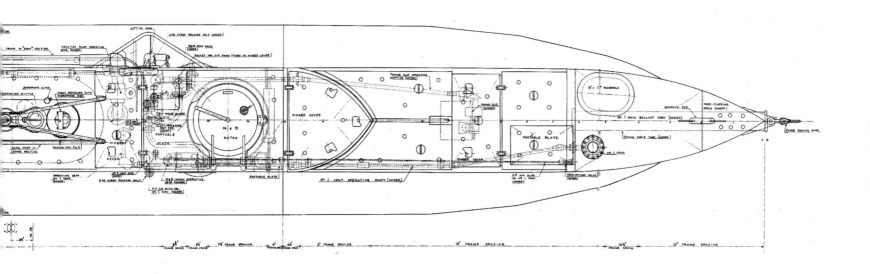

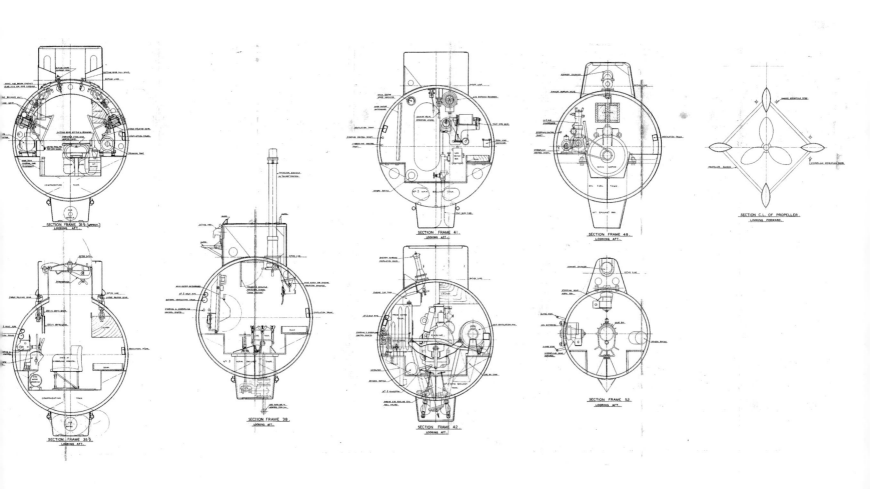

The X-craft weapon: the side charge of the restored *X 24* at the Royal Navy Submarine Museum, Gosport. The tube above is part of the diesel induction; most of the induction tube has been removed. (John Gourley)

Night and attack periscopes on board the restored *X 24*. Not all X-craft had the protective piping. (John Gourley)

The six Broadbent craft were *X 20* through *X 25*. Their design was slightly modified to reflect operational experience with the Vickers craft, so they were delivered between November 1943 and April 1944. *X 24* carried out two attacks on the German base at Bergen, in one of which (in September) a large floating drydock was destroyed. Two of them served as beacons for landing craft on D-Day. Their main role was to train crews for planned Far Eastern operations. In this role *X 22* was lost with all hands.

After these craft had been ordered, A(S) asked for a non-operational version which might be used as an ASW training target, relieving full-size submarines in that role. Initially they were called Z-Craft, but later they were designated XT-craft. In May 1943 six were ordered from Vickers and twelve from Broadbent. These craft were similar in all respects to the X-craft, but were simplified: side cargo release gear, auto-helmsman and night periscope were not fitted. The day periscope, projector compass, and engine induction trunk were all fixed in the up position. Fuel capacity was for 500nm at 4 knots.

The Vickers craft were delivered by March 1944; they helped train light forces defending invasion beaches against German midget submarines. X-craft acted as navigational beacons off the Normandy beaches, using telescopic masts fitted with signal lamps. The first six Broadbent boats were built more slowly; they were cancelled in March 1944 and XE-craft ordered instead. The other six XT-craft were cancelled in September 1944, as there was no further requirement for such targets.

The next series were designated XE-craft, for the Far East. They were air-conditioned and better insulated against humidity. Their improved electrical equipment proved much more reliable than that of the original X-craft. Eighteen were ordered early in 1944: the first six from Vickers and the rest from Broadbent (the designation *XE-13* was not used). At the end of 1944 the first six formed the 14th Submarine Flotilla, leaving for the Far East in February 1945 aboard the depot ship *Bonaventure*. Initially all twelve were to have operated from *Bonaventure*, but by April 1945 it was not even clear that the first six would be used.[6] In May 1945 Director of Plans wrote that if there was no operational employment for X-craft in the Pacific, the XE-craft should be scrapped in Australia and their depot ship used by the Fleet Train on that station. In this area the US Navy was the lead submarine service. It found no use for the XE-craft in the south-west Pacific, but the XE commander hoped for some useful role further north.

Initially the US fleet did not want them, and for a time they were simply to have been scrapped in Australia. However, their commander persuaded that command to allow them to be used. Two of them penetrated the Japanese anchorage in the Johore Strait to sink the damaged cruiser *Takao*. The damaged *Myoko* was also a target, but it turned out that she could not be attacked. It was not known whether the cruisers were operational, but she was considered a threat to the projected British landings in Malaya. Two other XE-craft cut the Saigon/Hong Kong and Singapore/Saigon cables, forcing the Japanese to use radio, which could be intercepted and decrypted.[7] All six were scrapped in Australia at the end of the war. By that time five of the Broadbent craft had been delivered, the rest being cancelled. Four of them were transferred to the 5th Submarine Flotilla at Portsmouth in the spring of 1945 to form a nucleus of trained personnel, and also to test harbour defence equipment.

Chariots

The Italians used manned low-speed torpedo-like devices, which they called *Maiale* (Pigs). Although they began operations as early as August 1940, their attacks do not seem to have impressed the British high command until they damaged the battleships *Queen Elizabeth* and *Valiant* in Alexandria harbour in December 1941.[8] The *Maiale* were electrically powered, the operators riding atop them. When they reached their target, they would detach the warhead and leave it on the seabed underneath. In theory the operators could escape aboard what was left of the *Maiale*. The key technology was the self-contained breathing apparatus used by the operators, since without it they could not have functioned. It had to be self-contained, because otherwise a submerged device would have given itself away by the stream of bubbles produced by its operators. Speed was limited because it increased pressure on the divers' chests; beyond a low speed they could not breathe. Italian work on such devices began in 1935, based on the Davis Submerged Escape Apparatus (DSEA) developed for submarines. It included a small oxygen cylinder and a canister to absorb carbon dioxide from the user. The Italians added two oxygen cylinders sufficient for six hours, the gas passing through a reducing valve on the operator's chest.

In January 1942 Prime Minister Churchill asked what the navy was doing to develop something similar.[9] By that time one of the Italian craft had been salvaged, and was being copied as what the British called a Chariot. The British developed their own breathing apparatus; it is not clear to what extent it was derived from a captured Italian one.[10] On 24 January 1942 an initial order was let to Messrs. Stodart and Pitt, crane manufacturers of Bath. The resulting Chariot Mk I carried a 600lb warhead in its nose and was powered by a 2 HP electric motor. As of April 1942 it was credited with an endurance of 5½ hours at 2.8 knots; it weighed 1½ tons and had a diving limit of 50ft.[11] The body was steel, but the superstructure was wood covered by metal, to add buoyancy. The floodable buoyancy (ballast) tank was between the two operators. The British operators rode the torpedo upright (the Italians crouched atop the torpedo body, like jockeys), shielded by the superstructure.

As of April 1942 estimated Chariot production was two for completion during June 1942, a total of six by July, eighteen by August, and twenty-six by September, with twelve to be ready operationally in September 1942.[12] A total of thirty-four Mk I Chariots was produced.[13] All were designated by Roman numbers.

Because they were simpler than X-craft, Chariots developed more rapidly. At the end of June 1942 a plan evolved for SOE, which used motor fishing vessels to bring agents into and out of Norway, to tow two Chariots there to attack the *Tirpitz*. That aborted when *Tirpitz* left her anchorage at Trondheim for Alten Fjord and then Narvik; when she returned in October, the plan was reactivated. Two Chariots with their crews left the Shetlands on 26 October, and they were hoisted out as planned on the 30th.[14] They were to be towed submerged, so that the fishing vessel could pass through port defences. That worked, but in a heavy sea in the open fjord the towing wires of the Chariots parted, the Chariots being lost almost in sight of their target. The fishing boat had to be scuttled, unfortunately in shallow water. The Germans salvaged the boat and the technique was compromised.

By this time the Admiralty considered the Mediterranean a much more promising venue for Chariots. Like the Italians with their human torpedoes, the Royal Navy would carry them into range on board submarines. Moreover, it was considered essential to overcome the numerical superiority of the Italian battle fleet, particularly before the Italian landings.[15] Three Chariot-carrying submarines arrived in the

The engine room of *X 24*, in the Royal Navy Submarine Museum. In the foreground is her Gardner diesel, the type used at the time in London buses. Further aft is the pump, with the motor/generator in line with the diesel. The X-craft programme included a very aggressive attempt at noise reduction, the boats ultimately being rated as detectable only inside 500 yds. Rafting (placing the diesel and the motor on a rigid sound-insulated bed) was tested in *XT 5* and applied to the final XE version of the craft. They may have had the first submarine application of this method, which became extremely important after the war. Propellers were modified to reduce cavitation, thrash, and 'singing'. Pump noise, however, was a continuing problem. All X-craft were degaussed and were painted in non-magnetic paint to counter magnetic indicators and harbour defence loops. (John Gourley)

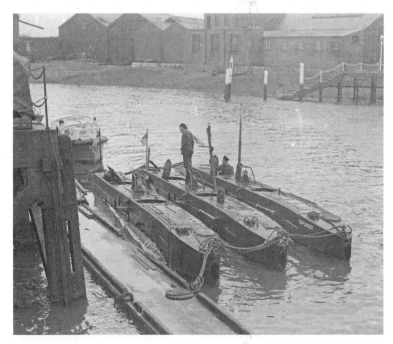

XE craft intended to operate in the Far East were the final wartime version of the X-craft, although the idea was developed further after the war. Here *XE 7, 8, 9,* and *12* are moored post-war. In these craft the characteristic step on the casing was removed, possibly because it formed a corner which made it a particularly strong radar target. Similarly, the bow and stern were rounded. (© National Maritime Museum N22277)

An XE-craft shows its rounded hull. The officer is gripping the diesel induction mast. It incorporated a safety rail for the officer of the watch.

Mediterranean in November 1942 with nine Chariots (one had been brought out for trials on board *P 247* during October). They were to attack the three Italian *Littorio*-class battleships in Taranto, but before any attack could be carried out the Italian ships left for Naples. Nevertheless preliminary reconnaissance was ordered, using *Traveller* – which was lost in the process, probably mined. Attack timing depended on the phase of the moon. A submarine launching Chariots had to lie surfaced with her hatches open and numerous personnel on deck; she could not crash-dive. She had to be within about 8 miles of the target base. The charioteers needed moonlight to see to attack, but it was better for the parent submarine to launch without any moon. By this time there was some question as to whether it was so important to attack the battleships, which had achieved very little so far. Captain (S) 10 argued for alternative targets: cruisers at La Maddalena and merchant ships supplying Tunisia, which lay at Palermo and Cagliari. The next favourable time was January 1943. The target areas were reconnoitred to make sure that patrol activity was light enough that submarines could indeed launch their Chariots. *P 311* (Chariots *X* and *XVIII*) attacked La Maddalena, *Trooper* (Chariots *XVI*, *XX* and *XXIII*) attacked Palermo and *Thunderbolt* (Chariots *XV* and *XXII*) attacked Cagliari. The Chariot submarines were considered too vulnerable to wait for the Chariots to return, so two 'U'-class submarines were assigned as recovery ships, *P 37* at Cagliari, *P 43* at La Maddalena and *P 46* at Palermo. Reconnaissance confirmed that two cruisers were still at La Maddalena, and a cruiser and considerable shipping at Palermo, but only a few ships at Cagliari, so that attack was cancelled. *P 311* was lost, probably mined but possibly due to an accident with her Chariots on deck. The other two attacked Palermo. One badly damaged the liner *Viminale*, others sinking the new cruiser *Ulpio Traiano* and attaching limpet mines to three destroyers – which the Italians unfortunately found and removed. All seven Chariots were lost, six of their crew were killed, six were taken prisoner, and only two were rescued.

Trooper had her containers removed, but *Thunderbolt* retained hers. She embarked two of the remaining Chariots (XII and XIII) to sink blockships with which the Italians hoped to disable the port of Tripoli, which the Eighth Army was rapidly approaching. One was lost, and the other entered the harbour just as its blockship target sank. He sank an alternate target. When *Thunderbolt* returned to Malta, her containers were also removed.

For the preparation for the Sicilian landings in March 1943, submarines landed survey parties (Combined Operations Pilotage Parties – COPPs), which used small folbots (folding canoes). Many of them were lost, so Chariots, which remained at Malta, were considered an alternative. They were much more robust, but the driver had to be Chariot-trained and was not a COPP, whereas the passenger was a COPP unfamiliar with Chariots. For this operation Chariots were carried on chocks on the decks of 'U'-class submarines; that worked as long as the submarine did not dive below Chariot limits.

Even though the Italian battle fleet had not interfered with the landings in Sicily, it was thought that they might intervene when the Allies landed on the Italian mainland. An attack on the battleships *Doria* and *Duilio* was planned, using Chariots carried by *Ultor* and *Unrivalled*; dummy attacks were made on the battleship *Rodney* in Malta. The operation was cancelled on 26 August, with the submarines already at sea, because by that time the Italians were negotiating the surrender of their fleet.

The final Mediterranean Chariot operation was mounted in cooperation with the Italians, now co-belligerents. Two were launched by Italian MTBs off La Spezia on 21 June 1944 to attack the cruisers *Bolzano* and *Gorizia*, which were being prepared for use as blockships. *Bolzano* was sunk (capsized), but defects prevented the other from attacking *Gorizia*. The other European operation was an abortive attempt to attack shipping in Norway in November 1943, the Chariots being transported by an MTB.

Five Sunderland flying boats were adapted to carry Chariots on their fuselages under their wings. This method of delivery was dropped because it could never be clandestine, and also because it was unlikely that the Sunderland could retrieve the operators after an attack.

Commander (E) S M Terry RN proposed a Mk II Chariot in October 1942, and thirty were made. Its two operators sat back-to-back in cockpits inside rather than astride the torpedo body with more than twice the weight of explosive (1000lbs). The operators had a detachable Perspex hood covering them. Mk II was faster than Mk I, and had twice the range (4.5 knots, range 5–6 hours at full speed). However, the depth limit was reduced to 30ft.[16] It was designed to be carried on chocks on the saddle tanks of large submarines.

Early in 1944 the depot ship *Wolfe* carried seven Mk II Chariots to the Indian Ocean. The intended target was the Japanese battle fleet at Lingga Roads south of Singapore. The initial operation was an attack in October by two Chariots, carried by *Trenchant*, against merchant ships under repair at Phuket. Both targets were sunk, and the Chariots recovered and scuttled. By this time the Japanese fleet had left Lingga Roads. Since it did not return, the Chariot organisation was disbanded at the end of 1944.[17] That was not quite the end of the story, since at least some Mk IIs were retained at the end of the war, and used after the war for trials of seaward defence against sneak craft.

In October 1943 A(S) asked for (and received) permission to have the submarine depot ship HMS *Titania* construct a prototype Mk III, intended to be similar to Mk II but smaller (5ft shorter, 3in smaller diameter).[18] It is not clear whether this device was built. There may also have been a one-man Chariot carrying lobster-pot charges.[19]

In April 1942 VA(S) suggested a joint X-craft/Chariot policy with the US Navy; cooperation was essential to avoid giving away the existence of these craft before they could be used in a concentrated way, in all theatres, simultaneously. Admiral Horton understood that the US Navy was also interested in midget submarines; he wanted the earliest possible exchange of data.[20] If the US Navy was not develop-

A British Chariot Mk I, awash, carries its two operators. The buoyancy of the submerged hull was just enough to balance the weight of the two men. They are wearing Sladen Mk I ('clammy death') diving suits, recognisable by the single eyepiece (Mk II had goggles, so that the operators could use binoculars). The driver has the usual oxygen container strapped to his back. The back-seat man is opening a small locker placed above the single ballast tank amidships. This locker also functioned as a backrest for the pilot in the front seat. The pilot controlled the 'Chariot' using a joystick; he also had a ballast pump control. Both the Chariot and the earlier Italian *Maiale* handled notoriously badly and somewhat unpredictably. The prototype wooden Chariot was ready for trials in June 1942. (US Naval Institute)

ing Chariots, Horton proposed supplying them with nine for use in the Far East, using either British personnel or Americans trained in the UK. Meanwhile Chariots should be supplied to submarines operating in the Far East, and a maximum number should be supplied to the Mediterranean Submarine Flotilla for use against Italian capital ships. Although X craft were not as limited as Chariots, they did need calm

water. Horten hoped that the US Navy would build X-craft of its own or, failing that, would cooperate with the Royal Navy in training and manning. The US Navy did test a Mk II in 1945.[21]

In addition to Chariots there was a menagerie of much smaller submersibles which the British called clandestine craft, including the one-man Welman submarine, 100 of which were made.[22]

EXPORT SUBMARINES[1]

Vickers (and then Vickers-Armstrong) was the only British export submarine builder. Before 1913 its monopoly agreement with the Admiralty barred nearly all export sales, the exceptions apparently being two 'C'-class submarines for Japan under the Japanese 1904 Programme (built 1907) and two of a modified version under the Japanese 1910 Programme. Vickers presumably supplied the design for the Japanese-built Vickers-Kawasaki submarine No 13, also built under the Japanese 1910 Programme. These sales were probably acceptable because of the Anglo-Japanese alliance then in force. During the First World War Vickers produced a design similar to that

of the 'L' class for Japan (late 1917 contract) which the Japanese designated L 1. The Japanese may have imported the diesels for the first of two built by Mitsubishi (building contract March 1918). Four of a slightly modified L 2 type were built under the Japanese 1918 Programme; they lacked the beam torpedo tubes of the L 1 type. Three of a further improved L 3 type roughly equivalent to the *L 50* class followed, a minelaying version having been planned but not built. The final L 4 version was built under the 1921–8 Programme (nine boats).

The Thurston notebook of early Vickers designs shows that versions of both the original Vickers coastal submarine (Design 618)

P 614 was the ex-Turkish *Burak Reis*, taken over in September 1939 with her sister ex-*Uluc Ali Reis*. She was roughly equivalent to an 'S'-class submarine, but was a separate Vickers design. Note the relatively low enclosure to her gun (the 'S' class had no enclosure at all), the relatively high forebridge and the absence of the usual connection from the bridge to the 4in gun. She also lacks the usual Oerlikon at the after end of her bridge structure. Displacement was 687/856 tons (624 standard); dimensions were 210ft 7in (overall) x 22ft 4in x 11ft 10in. She had four bow tubes (one reload each) and one stern tube (no reload). Speed was 13.75 knots surfaced and 9 knots submerged. Rated range was 2500nm at 10 knots, far short of the 7500nm at 10 knots of a late 'S'-class submarine. Two other sisters were commissioned as *P 611* and *P 612* only for delivery trips to Turkey. *P 615* was torpedoed and sunk in British service. Returned to Turkey on 17 January 1946, she resumed her original name.

and its original overseas submarine (619, which became *Nautilus*) were considered as possibilities to offer Japan (as Designs 620 and 621), but were not offered. A 20-knot Design 622 was rejected under discussion.[2]

By 1913 Vickers badly wanted export sales to supplement the limited income from Admiralty sales. It tried to sell 'E'-class submarines to Greece. The Admiralty vetoed the sale by pointing to its ownership of key patents. First Lord Churchill raised the question of secrecy regarding broadside tubes. The veto may have been intended to protect an arrangement in which the French and the British divided up Greek naval business. Greece ordered two Laubeuf submarines in France in 1912 (they were taken over by the French navy after war broke out in 1914). The firm did sell 'E'-class submarines to Turkey (order dated 29 April 1914), presumably as part of the deal which included the battleship *Erin*. On the outbreak of war the Royal Navy took them over as *E 25* and *E 26*. At this time the Italians and the French were far more successful submarine exporters.

Denny designed several submarines for the Royal Netherlands Navy, but did not build any of its own design at home, either for the Royal Navy or for export.

Post-war British export success was limited. Vickers' records show that the company competed for most of the available orders, to the extent that its papers give a good idea of what various countries were trying to obtain at the time. Vickers built submarines approximating the 'S' class for both Portugal and Turkey, and it sold small minelaying submarines to Estonia.

Most interwar export sales went to France and Italy (whose government subsidised naval exports in the 1920s). The Dutch also entered the export market, selling to the Polish Navy. Sweden and Denmark designed and built their own submarines. The Japanese built the two submarines Thailand (Siam) bought. The Germans built submarines clandestinely in other countries, such as Spain. By the early 1930s German involvement must have been an open secret – *E 1* was advertised for sale as a German submarine – and observers must have realised that official U-boat production was not far off. Finland was a customer.

Vickers was more successful with its engines, built both by itself and under licence by Normand in France and by Kawasaki in Japan. Vickers' engines powered Spanish submarines, which were designed by Vickers' under a Vickers-Armstrong agreement to revitalise the Spanish shipbuilding industry. The initial licence-built engines were based on Vickers First World War types. Normand was the first European licensee; its engine was based on the 800 BHP engine (100 BHP/cylinder) of the *G 13*. Normand built a six-cylinder version; it managed to add another 50 BHP per cylinder. Later it offered a 900 BHP eight-cylinder version, which powered the Polish *Wilk* class. Beside its own Portuguese and Turkish boats, both of which approximated the 'S' class, Vickers provided engines for Spanish and Estonian submarines. The 1000 BHP engine used in Spanish 'C'-class submarines had some similarities, particularly in the drive for the fuel pump. Vickers developed a new eight-cylinder 1150 BHP design for the Portuguese *Delfim* class. It introduced new features (a new type of framing and a low mid-engine driven camshaft) characteristic of later Vickers diesels through those in the 'A' class. For Estonia Vickers built six-cylinder 600 BHP engines; the Turkish submarines had 775 BHP engines. This business kept Vickers' diesel division alive, and that made it possible for the company to offer new engines for the 'T' class in 1935.

Europe

The First World War created new states which saw submarines as an equaliser to deal with much more powerful neighbours: Estonia, Latvia, Finland and Poland.

Estonia was offered a modified 'H'-class submarine (Design 846) in August 1923. Dimensions were 150ft x 15ft 3in, for a surface displacement of 365 tons. Armament would have been four 18in torpedo tubes (four reloads) forward and a 2pdr anti-aircraft gun. Design 1053 (18 August 1923) was even smaller: 130/235 tons, 135ft/130ft pp x 12ft 6in mld/13ft ext, 235/276 tons, draft 10ft 9in, 10.5 knots surfaced, 8 knots submerged, 1000nm at 10 knots surfaced, 45nm at 5 knots submerged, complement 5 officers and 45 men. Armament was four 18in tubes, all forward, and one Lewis gun. Nothing came of these projects.

Vickers built two *Kalev*-class minelaying submarines for Estonia. Like the First World War 'E' and 'L'-class minelayers, they had external mine tubes in their saddle tanks. This example was significant in Royal Navy discussions of new minelaying submarines in 1938–9. *Lembit* is shown. (Dock Museum photo VPA 0044)

MINELAYING SUBMARINES FOR THE ESTONIAN GOVERNMENT. General arrangement. Vickers-Armstrongs Ltd. The external mine tubes either side of the conning tower are evident in the plan views. (© National Maritime Museum M1058)

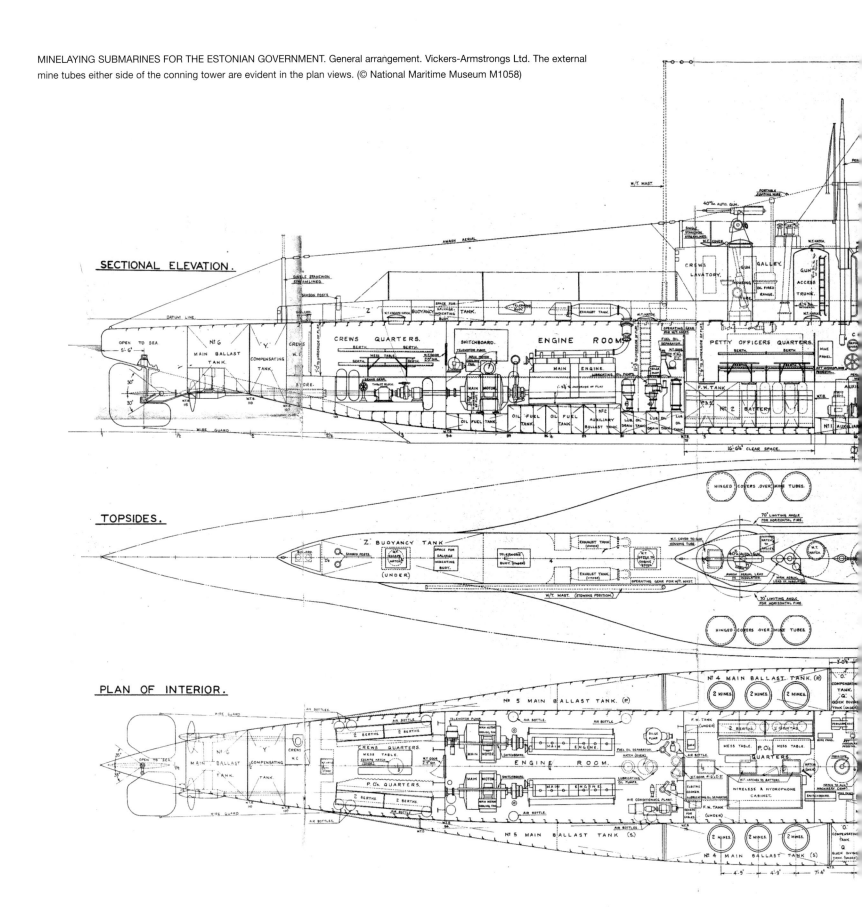

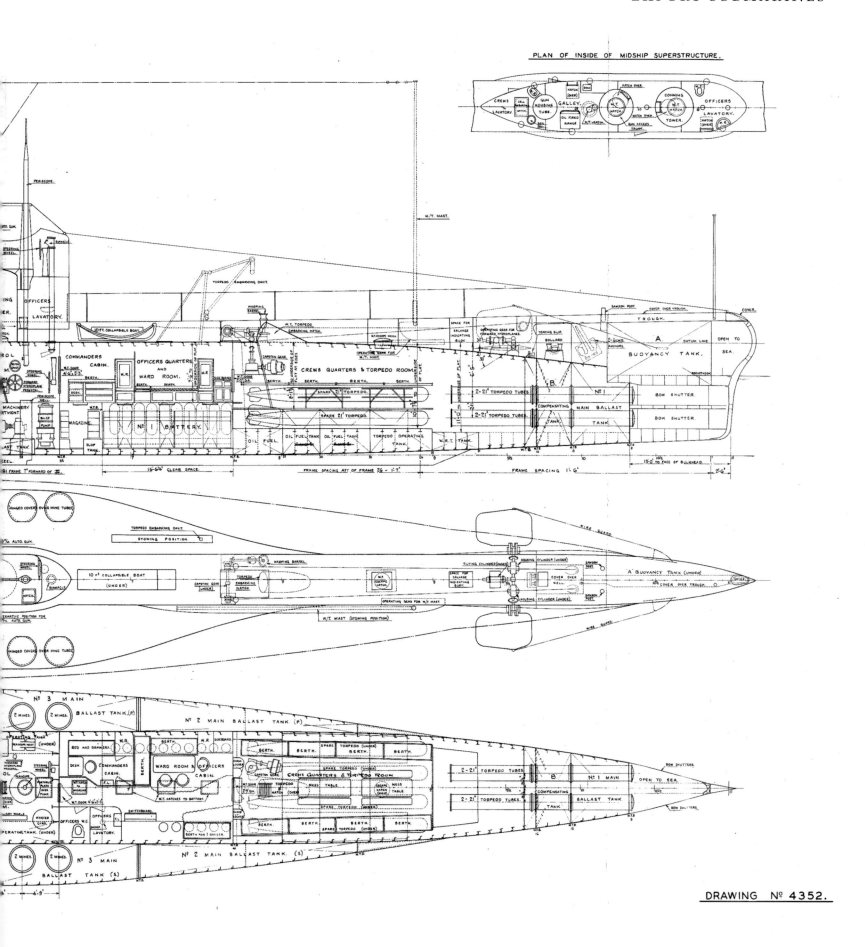

PLAN OF INSIDE OF MIDSHIP SUPERSTRUCTURE.

DRAWING Nº 4352.

MINELAYING SUBMARINES FOR THE ESTONIAN GOVERNMENT. Arrangement sections and plan under main flat. Vickers-Armstrongs Ltd. The external mine tubes can be seen either side of the conning tower in the 'Section about Station 5¼'. (© National Maritime Museum M1059)

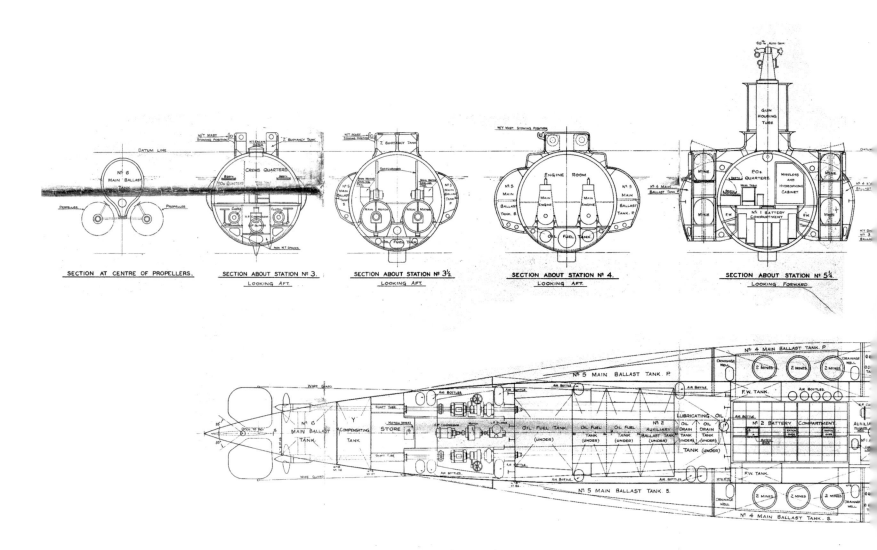

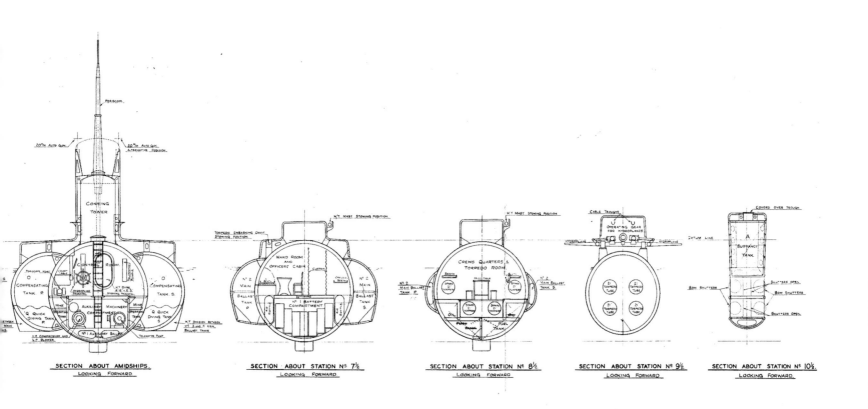

SECTION ABOUT AMIDSHIPS.
LOOKING FORWARD.

SECTION ABOUT STATION Nº 7½
LOOKING FORWARD.

SECTION ABOUT STATION Nº 8½
LOOKING FORWARD.

SECTION ABOUT STATION Nº 9½
LOOKING FORWARD.

SECTION ABOUT STATION Nº 10½.
LOOKING FORWARD.

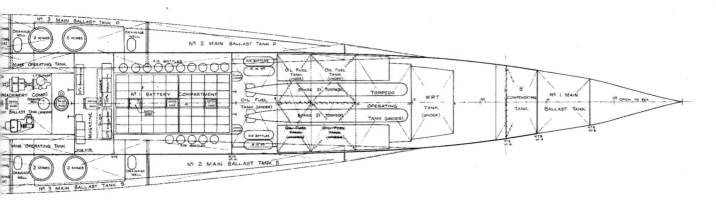

The Estonians were back on the market in 1933; a Vickers' design book shows two designs dated September 1933: 1048 and 1050, the latter described as an alternative. Design 1048A was a submarine minelayer, 182ft 9in (overall) 179ft 6in (between perpendiculars) x 13ft 9in x 10ft 7in (ready to dive), 579/760 tons. Design 1050 was 181ft 3in (wl) 178ft 9in (pp) x 24ft (pressure hull diameter 13ft 3in) x 10ft over the keel, with a total immersed volume of about 550 tons. Design 1051 was slightly smaller (174ft 3in [oa] 171ft 9in [wl] 171 [pp] x 24 x 10ft 1in over keel), displacing about 530 tons submerged. There was also a Design 1064. An undated (but slightly later) powering calculation simply marked 'Estonian Submarine' refers to a larger boat: 193ft (wl) 192ft (pp) x 24ft 6in x 10.15ft, displacing 685 tons surfaced and 1010 tons submerged. Vickers built the two Estonian minelaying submarines *Kalev* and *Lembit*. Unlike contemporary British submarines, they were apparently completely welded. They were somewhat smaller than the 'S' class, 621 tons standard, 193ft (wl) x 24ft 8⅝in x 11ft.[3] Presumably to accommodate their minelaying tubes, their saddle tanks had unusual flattened tops over part of their length. These submarines were significant for the Royal Navy because they provided the experience reflected in the attempt to provide minelaying capability to the 1938 'T' class.

In addition to normal submarines which could operate in the Baltic, Finland was interested in extremely small submarines to operate on Lake Ladoga: the treaty (1920) limit on their tonnage was 100 tons. Vickers offered designs to meet both requirement, both dated 19 February 1924. The small one was Design 1101: 113/133 tons (hence slightly too large), 92ft 6in (oa) 87ft 6in (pp) x 10ft x 10ft depth x 9ft draft, with a speed of 9/6.5 knots, Endurance would have been 1750nm at 7.5 knots surfaced and 50nm at 4 knots submerged. Armament was one 18in torpedo tube (three torpedoes) and two machine guns capable of anti-aircraft fire. The larger submarine (a design also offered to Turkey: Design 1107) would have displaced 470/554 tons (177ft [oa] x 15ft 3in x 15ft 3in x 12ft 4in). Speed would have been 13.25/8.5 knots and surface endurance 3000nm at 9 knots (submerged 60nm at 5 knots). Armament would have been four bow 18in torpedo tubes (two torpedoes per tube), two 3in HA guns and two machine guns. Vickers books show a further Design 1220 dated 29 December 1925 (without any data), showing that the company was still hoping for an order at that time. Finland ended up buying German-designed submarines about 1930. They were part of the clandestine U-boat development programme.

The earliest post-war design offered to Greece seems to have been Design 1077 (7 January 1924), a 600-ton submarine: 208ft/206ft x 19ft 3in mld/19ft 9in ext x 12ft 9in; 700/850 tons, 13.75 knots surfaced, 9 knots submerged, 2000nm at 10 knots surfaced, 100nm at 4.75 knots submerged, one 3in AA, one MG and four 21in bow tubes, plus four 18in in the superstructure, two forward and two aft. There were apparently two 21in reloads, but none for the superstructure tubes. Design 783 (February 1924) was a more conventional design without the superstructure tubes, but with a 4in QF gun and a 2pdr (pom-pom) anti-aircraft gun: 648 tons surfaced. This design does not appear in any of the Vickers design books. A Vickers list in the Brass Foundry also shows Design 788 for Greece.[4] Greece was also offered Design 833, which was also offered to Argentina.

Design 850, a coastal submarine, was offered to Latvia in December 1923: 445/505 tons, 164ft 7½in/171ft 4in x 15ft 4in x 12ft 6in, 200ft diving depth, 14.5/9 knots, 1300nm at 14.5 knots surfaced or 2400nm at 10 knots submerged. Armament was four 18in torpedo tubes (four

reloads) and a 75mm gun. Latvia ordered two French submarines in 1925. However, the Vickers estimate book shows figures for Latvia (labelled 'approximate only', without any design number) dated 27 March 1929, for a saddle-tank submarine of about the same size, with two 600 BHP engines, displacing 450/580 tons (165ft [pp] 172ft [oa] x 20ft 6in [13ft 9in pressure hull] x 11ft 9in), armed with four 18in bow tubes and two orientable 18in tubes in the superstructure (total ten torpedoes), plus one 75mm gun and three machine guns. It would have two 600 BHP engines for a speed of 14.5 knots (9 knots submerged). Latvia ordered no further submarines between the wars.

Just after the First World War Vickers offered the Dutch Design 766, armed with a 6in/45 gun, a 3in/45 anti-aircraft gun forward and four 21in torpedo tubes. It did not correspond to anything the Dutch built.[5] A Vickers list in the Brass Foundry includes a Design 774 offered to the Netherlands in November 1920, when the Dutch were designing their *K XI* class. The 'K' designation indicated an ocean-going type intended for the Netherlands East Indies; other Dutch submarines ('O' series) were coastal.

The Vickers Estimate Book shows Design 949 (estimate dated 1 September 1928) for the Dutch Government: 230ft 9in (oa) x 20ft 9in (pressure hull 13ft 9in) x 13ft 4in (820/1020 tons), with a slightly larger alternative 949A (891/1099 tons). The power plant would have been two Spanish-type (as in the 'C' class) engines (2000 BHP) for 16 knots surfaced (9 knots submerged). The enlarged 949A would have had 2600 BHP engines, for 17 knots surfaced. Armament would have been the usual four bow and two stern 21in tubes plus two revolving tubes in the superstructure (fourteen torpedoes), plus one 8.8cm/50 gun and two 40mm anti-aircraft guns. The table in the Estimate Book does not show endurance. These were rather larger than the submarines the Dutch were then building, and presumably they were intended for overseas use. The Dutch were still designing their own submarines, by this time probably with German help.

Vickers offered Design 1023 to Norway. A calculation sheet dated 11 July 1931 shows a displacement of 560/750 tons (excluding superstructure, say 850 tons total) with dimensions 195ft (waterline) x 18ft 6in x 11ft 7in to bottom of keel. Designed surface speed seems to have been 20 knots. Other details were not given (this was a sheet of propeller calculations). Design 1023B was similar but had a twin 18in torpedo tube built into its casing. Design 1024 covered two alternatives, a 540-ton submarine and a 580-ton minelayer. The Vickers plan does not show the intended buyer, but that it was consecutive suggests that it was an alternative for Norway. Norway did not buy any new submarines, having built some Electric Boat-designed craft in the 1920s.

In 1934 Vickers offered Poland Design 1077.[6] This was *not* the Design 1077 offered to Greece (it was presumably in a different Barrow series). Dimensions: 290ft (wl) x 23ft 6in (pressure hull 15ft 3in) x 15ft 3in to bottom of keel, 1380 tons London Treaty displacement (1450 tons when ready to dive with normal fuel, 1550 tons with maximum fuel, 1856 tons submerged). Designed test depth was 80m (the Poles initially wanted at least 80m, and then 80m with a factor of safety of 2). The Poles asked for two-cycle reversible diesels sufficient for 20 knots at a maximum of 400 RPM; Vickers offered two four-cycle engines producing a total of 5000 BHP using exhaust-drive superchargers at 500 RPM. They would provide the desired surface speed of 20 knots (given as a minimum). Total motor BHP was 1450, for 9 knots (the minimum required) submerged. Estimated diving time was 70 seconds (45 seconds required). The Poles required that the submarine use their standard Tudor PM.25 batteries. Vickers met the endurance requirement of 3500nm at 10kts on normal fuel, and on maximum fuel offered 8000nm at 10 knots (vs required 7000nm). Submerged endurance was 100nm at 4.5 knots (the requirement was 100nm at 5 knots, later cut back to 100 at 4.5 knots). The submarine was required to fire both 550mm (21.7in) and 533mm (21in) torpedoes, as the Poles had previously bought French submarines. Initially they wanted four tubes forward and four aft plus two twin rotating tubes; later that changed to six forward and two aft plus the rotating tubes. Vickers offered the desired hull tubes plus one twin fixed external mounting. Required torpedo capacity was one per tube plus eight spares, a total of twenty, later changed to ten spares (total twenty); Vickers offered the twenty. Vickers met the requirement for one 100mm/46 gun, but in addition it offered one twin and two single Hotchkiss 13.2mm machine guns rather than the desired two twins. The company met the requirement to be able to flood main ballast tanks in 30 seconds. A list of problems in meeting the Polish requirements (possibly produced by DNC) showed that the desired 5-knot submerged endurance speed could not be met, that orientable tubes were disliked (and could not meet the splashless discharge requirement), and that the Polish requirement to angle torpedoes in 3° increments (unlike 1°, as in French submarines) would ruin accuracy. The Poles wanted supersonic equipment (possibly for communication rather than Asdic) which would require too much space. Reserve buoyancy seems to have been a problem, the Poles initially asking for 33 per cent and then backing down to 23 per cent. They apparently wanted excessive GM (60cm on the surface, cut back to 50cm, and 25cm submerged, cut to 22.5cm). In view of the size of the conning tower, that would require 212 tons of lead in the keel, which prejudiced the whole design and pushed up the size of the submarine. Penalties for failing to meet the original requirements would add up to £5,000 per ship.

Vickers lost this competition to the Dutch, who built the Polish *Orzel* class. It came closer to the desired size (1100/1473 tons) and it

met the speed requirements; it also had the desired four tubes fore and aft plus two trainable twin tubes. These two submarines were reportedly ordered on 29 January 1935, which considerably predated the DNC evaluation (presumably in connection with a protest). DNC was asked to compare the Vickers submission with Polish requirements, which were described as severe, and generally far beyond those demanded of British submarines of about 1000 tons (presumably the 'T' class), the size the Poles had in mind. Polish requirements, including a crew of fifty-five, were all much in excess of what the British hoped to get on that tonnage. For example, the Poles wanted a tank capacity of 33 per cent (presumably reserve buoyancy), which was later reduced to 25 per cent (360 tons); Vickers offered 28 per cent, more than in British submarines. The Dutch offered 60 tons, a very considerable cut which would leave the submarines, in the British view, with very inferior seagoing capability. In DNC's view, Vickers generally met the requirements, and it was difficult to see how size and cost could be cut appreciably.

Portugal was offered Design 902 in 1926 (the estimate is dated 12 February 1926): 230ft (pp) 234ft 6in (oa) x 22ft 6in (pressure hull 15ft) x 12ft 3in; displacement 840/1120 tons. Safety depth was 250ft. There were apparently alternative eight- and twelve-cylinder diesels. With the eight-cylinder engines, speed was 16.5/8 knots. The twelve-cylinder engines were rated at a total of 2600 BHP. Surface endurance was 1000nm at 16 knots or 2100nm at 9.5 knots (but with extra fuel, 4200nm at 9.5 knots). Underwater endurance was 12nm at 8 knots or 80nm at 4 knots. Armament was four bow and two stern 21in torpedo tubes and two 3in/45 HA guns. Nothing came of this, but the Portuguese were still interested, so in June 1930 Vickers offered Design 1004, which was somewhat larger (250ft [pp] 257ft [oa] x 24ft [pressure hull 15ft 3in], 1021/1260 tons, with the same torpedo battery (ten torpedoes) but one 4in/45 and one 0.5in machine gun. On 2660 BHP this submarine would make 16 knots surfaced (10 knots submerged).

Vickers built three *Delfim*-class submarines for Portugal in 1934. They occasioned work on a new diesel which the company later proposed for 'S'-class submarines of about the same size. This is the name ship. Note her First World War-style wireless masts and her nearly-enclosed gun, not at all characteristic of contemporary Royal Navy practice. (Dock Museum photo VPA 0018)

347

PORTUGUESE SUBMARINES *DELFIM*, *ESPADARTE* AND *GOLFINHO*. Longitudinal section (looking to port) and plan views. (© National Maritime Museum M1080)

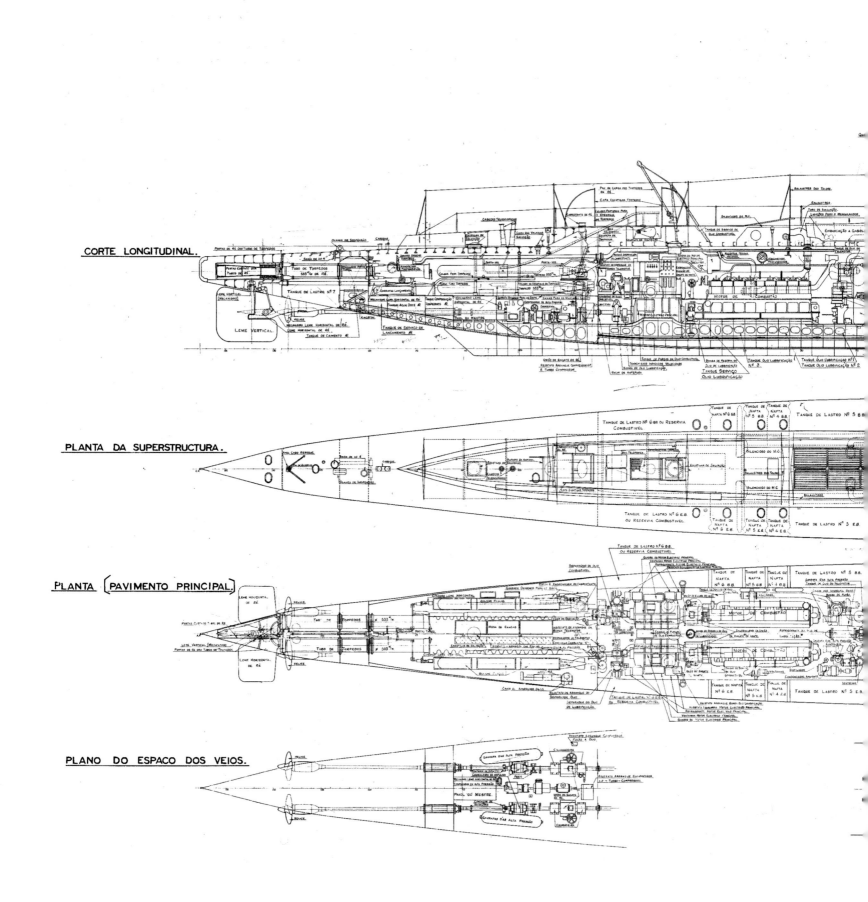

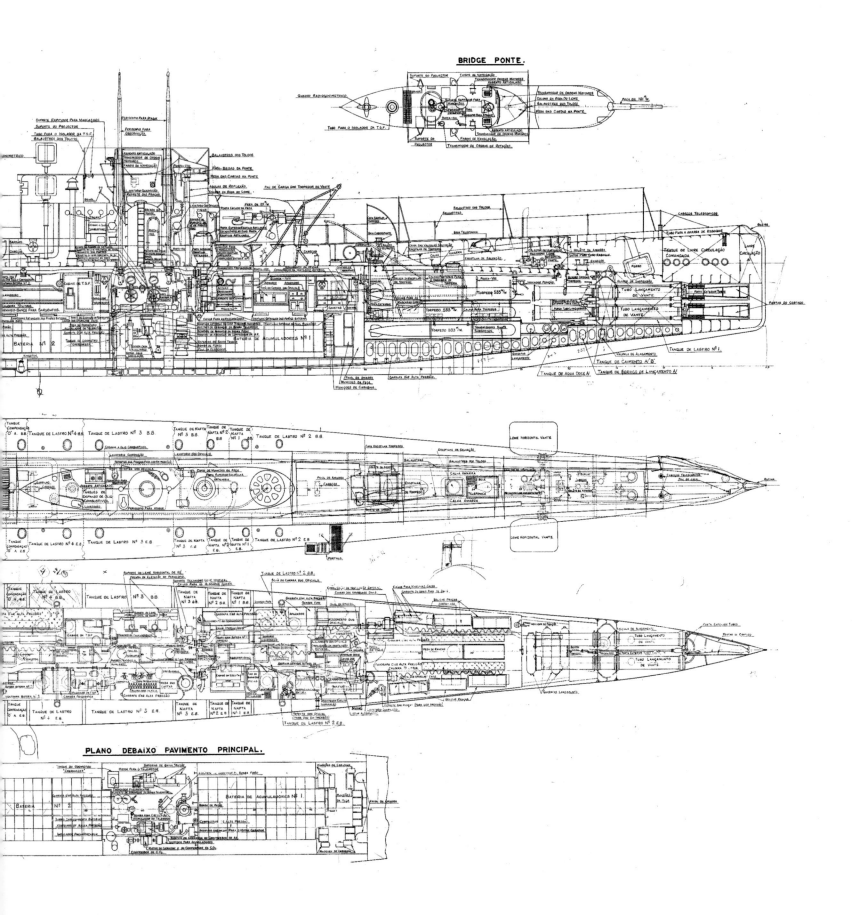

BRIDGE PONTE.

PLANO DEBAIXO PAVIMENTO PRINCIPAL.

PORTUGUESE SUBMARINES *DELFIM*, *ESPADARTE* AND *GOLFINHO*. Longitudinal section (looking to starboard) and sections. (© National Maritime Museum M1081)

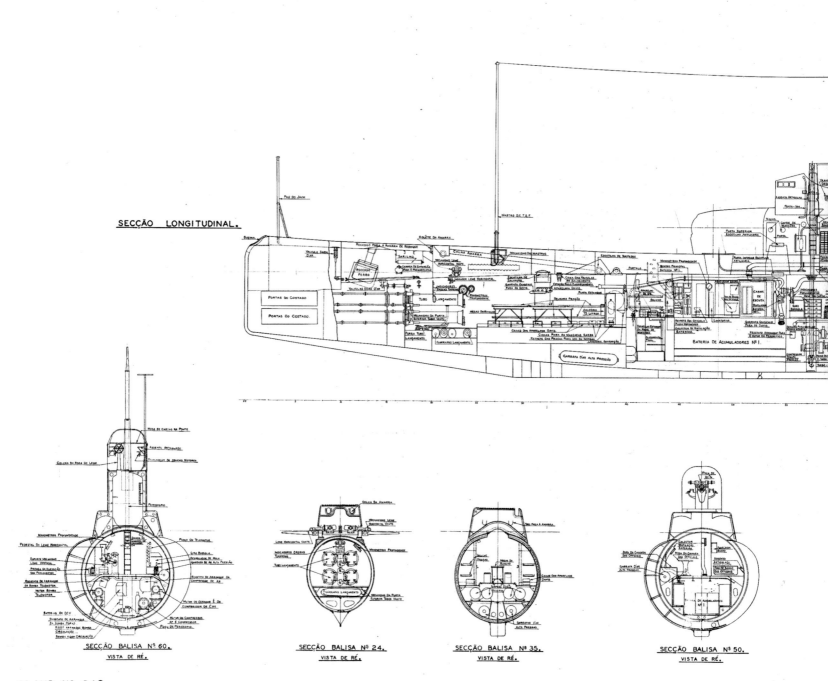

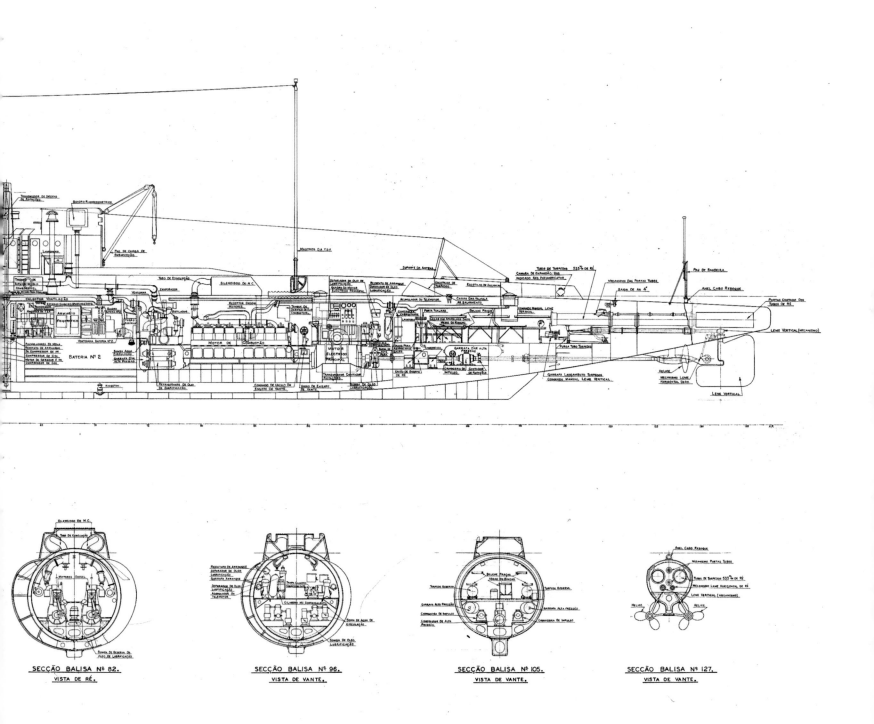

SECÇÃO BALISA Nº 82.
VISTA DE RÉ.

SECÇÃO BALISA Nº 96.
VISTA DE VANTE.

SECÇÃO BALISA Nº 105.
VISTA DE VANTE.

SECÇÃO BALISA Nº 127.
VISTA DE VANTE.

Vickers seems to have renewed its campaign in June 1930 with Design 1004 of about 1050 tons. That seems to have elicited as formal Portuguese specification, for which Vickers offered Designs 1013 and 1014 in January 1931 According to the Vickers' design notebook, the Portuguese asked for two submarines of about 750 tons, reserve buoyancy 25 to 30 per cent, strength of hull 100m (328ft), diving time not more than 1 minute. Surface GM was to be 50–60cm (20–24in), and submerged GM 20cm (7.9in). Surface speed not less than 14.5 knots, submerged speed not less than 9 knots. Radius on surface at economical speed not less than 6000nm at 10 knots. Submerged radius at economical speed not less than 110nm. Periscopes were to include a rangefinder with a horizontal base of not less than 1.5in. Armament was to be six 21in torpedo tubes, four forward and two aft, with a total of ten to twelve torpedoes, plus one 4in/40 and one 25mm pom-pom. Provisions should suffice for 5 weeks. The initial estimate was 226ft x 22ft x 11ft (pressure hull diameter 13ft 6in) for a surface displacement of 700 tons (880 submerged). Portuguese submarine design 1014 was 953A modified with a six-cylinder engine, fore planes above water, and increased submergence (presumably meaning diving depth). Length would have been 230ft on the waterline x 22ft to 25ft beam x 12ft 3in draft, for a light displacement of 790 tons. A table showed 230ft x 22ft 3in (pressure hull 14ft 6in) x 12ft 3in (light), with displacements of 800 tons light, 815 tons when trimmed in light surface condition, 754.5 tons 'Geneva', and 1000 tons submerged. Designed diving depth was 170m (test depth 100m). Main engines would be two 750 HP diesels, for a guaranteed surface speed in light condition of 14.5 knots (radius 1300nm at 14.5 knots with normal fuel, 2000nm at 10 knots; 6000nm at 10 knots with maximum fuel). Submerged speed would be 9.5 knots (two 450 BHP motors). Submerged endurance was 1½ hours at 9.5 knots or 110nm at economical speed (not given). Diving time (1 minute) was from 10 knots on the surface to going completely under water. At this time the Portuguese were also interested in buying a seaplane carrier (called an aircraft carrier in Vickers' records, as it had a 60ft flying-off deck). Vickers lost this contest to Italy (CRDA Monfalcone), but the Portuguese cancelled their two Italian submarines (which went to the Italian navy) in favour of Vickers. The three Vickers' submarines (the Portuguese *Delfim* class) were built to Design 1035. These submarines were broadly comparable to the British 'S' class.[7] In December 1939 Vickers offered Portugal a submarine based on the 'T' class (Design 1108A).

Vickers offered Romania Design 885 in 1925 (the cost estimate sheet is dated 7 April): 195ft 3in (oa) x 21ft (14ft 3in pressure hull diameter) x 12ft, displacement 600/759 tons, with a surface speed of 14 knots (1200 BHP) and a submerged speed of 9 knots. Armament was unusual: in addition to the usual four bow and one stern 21in tubes there were two 21in tubes in a deck turntable. A total of eleven torpedoes would have been carried. The submarine would also have been armed with one 4in and one anti-aircraft machine gun. Vickers also offered Design 1168 (and 1168A and 1168B); unfortunately no details have survived. The Romanians bought one submarine from Italy during the interwar period, *Delfinul*. She was completed in 1931 but not accepted until about 1934, by which time she had been heavily modified, apparently partly to increase her endurance. She presumably corresponded to the requirement Vickers was meeting, since she had four bow and two stern tubes plus two external tubes in her after superstructure.

Spain built her first class of interwar submarines under licence from Electric Boat. That was remarkable because at the time Vickers and Armstrong controlled the Spanish shipbuilding industry, and Vickers designed all major Spanish surface warships.[8] Although the Spanish planned twelve such submarines, they built only six, and the follow-on 'D' class was badly delayed by the turmoil following the overthrow of the monarchy in 1932 (and then by the Civil War).

Before work began on the 'C' class, Vickers offered Spain a small submarine (Design 1038, 20 June 1923): 170ft, 470/560 tons, 177ft oa x 15ft 3in x 15ft 3in depth to main hull x 12ft 4in surface draught, 11.75 knots surfaced, 9.25 knots submerged.

Vickers maintained a drawing office at the Cartagena yard in Spain, and a Vickers' design notebook includes details of a submarine it designed under the designation E (unfortunately undated). E.I was 70m (229.6ft) x 5.98m (19.62ft) x 3.82m (12.53ft), 647.7 tons surfaced, with a speed of 17 knots. E.II was 267.8ft x 22.38ft max x 12.52ft mean draft to bottom of keel; 1009/1284 tons, 21 knots for 4 hours surfaced, 20 knots for 24 hours, 10 knots submerged. E.II seems to correspond to the 'D' class (1065/1480 tons), which was subjected to considerable modification during its lengthy gestation. It looked somewhat British, with a gun on a raised structure forward of the conning tower, although the conning tower itself looked German. The Vickers Estimate Book includes Electric Boat's Design 1052A (17 November 1930) for a large fast submarine: 273ft (oa) x 21ft 4in x 13ft 6in, 1020/1300 tons, with a test depth of 80m (262ft) and a speed of 20.5 knots (guaranteed 20 knots for 24-hour trial) on 3900 BHP (submerged speed 9 knots). Armament was six bow and two stern tubes (sixteen torpedoes) plus one 4.7in/40 gun and two 0.50-calibre machine guns. There was a companion 600-ton submarine, Electric Boat 1056A (Vickers Estimate Book date 22 December 1930): 230ft x 19ft 1in x 12ft 5in, 680/850 tons, with the same four bow and two stern tubes plus one 4in/40 and one machine gun, making 16.75 knots (16 guaranteed on 24-hour trial) on 1600 BHP (9 knots submerged). As with the larger submarine, test depth was 80m. Vickers' role was probably to review the design.

The first Vickers design offered to Turkey may have been No. 1125 (26 July 1924), a small 330/495-ton (192ft x 15ft 5in x 10ft 8in x 8ft 10⅞in) submarine capable of 13/8.5 knots, with an endurance of 2500nm at 9 knots surfaced and 65nm at 5 knots submerged. Armament was four bow and two stern tubes, of which two bow and two stern tubes were above water. There would also be a single machine gun. Vickers also offered Design 869 (about 1924–5), an even smaller small single-hulled coastal submarine: 260/305 tons (135ft/142ft 6in x 13ft 6in x 11ft), capable of diving safely to 50m (about 164ft), with a surface endurance of 1600nm at 10 knots or 2300nm at 7 knots; submerged endurance was 28nm at 7 knots or 80nm at 4 or 4.5 knots. The power plant was a single Vickers HO diesel, BHP not given. Armament was two 18in bow tubes and one 2pdr anti-aircraft gun. The Turks bought a pair of Dutch-built (German-designed) coastal submarines instead. They were about twice the size of the Vickers design, and more heavily armed.

In 1928 Vickers offered Turkey Design 953 and a companion minelayer Design 954 (estimate dated 20 October 1928). Dimensions: 215ft (pp) 216ft 6in (oa) x 22ft 3in (14ft 6in pressure hull) x 12ft (750/915 tons); the minelayer had a beam of 26ft to accommodate mines in her saddle tanks. She would have displaced 788/975 tons. The submarine was armed with the usual four bow and two stern 21in tubes (ten torpedoes) plus one 4in/45 QF gun and one 0.50-calibre machine gun. The minelayer had only the two bow tubes (six

Builders left with cancelled incomplete 'L'-class hulls were allowed to buy them so that they could be completed and sold. Armstrong was the only successful seller, to Yugoslavia. *Hrabri* (ex *L 67*) is outboard, *Nebrojsa* (ex *L 68*) inboard. They lay at Elswick until 1926, when they were towed to High Walker, hauled up (as shown here) and reconditioned and completed. They are shown before after torpedo tubes were added. They were relaunched on, respectively, 15 June and 15 July 1927. (© National Maritime Museum PM2199-13)

torpedoes), but she also carried forty 440lb mines. Engines were two 800 BHP diesels, for 14.5 knots (14 knots for the minelayer); submerged speed was 9.5 (9) knots. Turkey was then offered a slightly enlarged Design 953A (estimate date 8 April 1929). The Turks bought two Italian submarines instead.

Turkey approached Vickers in March 1938. She was originally offered Design 1092, which seems to have been similar to the 'U' class. Turkey was then offered Design 1101, which was probably similar to the 'S' class; by September 1938 that had been superseded by Design 1103, which the Turks bought as part of larger deal (including destroyers and coast defence guns) brokered by the Admiralty.[9] Of four Design 1103A submarines building at Barrow in 1939, two were taken over by the Royal Navy and two delivered to Turkey. At about the same time Turkey bought three German-designed submarines (two built in Germany), having already bought the German-designed *Gur*, which had been built in Spain to conceal its origins.

Yugoslavia bought two 'L'-class submarines from Armstrong. They had been cancelled at the end of the war. Apart from some cleaning up to gain speed, they were unmodified (the Yugoslavs wanted stern torpedo tubes, but found that they would be far too expensive). According to a November 1929 Admiralty report on the French-built Greek *Katsonis*, the Yugoslavs and the Greeks considered their British-built submarines far superior.[10]

Vickers had probably already offered Yugoslavia its Design 860; later it offered Design 913 (Estimate book, 2 December 1926). Dimensions: 190ft (pp) 202ft (oa) x 20ft 6in (12ft 6in pressure hull diameter) x 11ft 6in, 600/750 tons. Two Vickers six-cylinder diesels would have provided 1300 BHP for 14.5 knots (9 knots submerged). Armament would have been the usual four bow and two stern 21in tubes (twelve torpedoes) plus one 3in/45 and one 0.50-calibre machine gun. A parallel Design 916 was slightly larger: 199ft (pp) 211ft (oa) x 21ft 6in x 11ft 9in, 650 tons surfaced, with a 4in/45 instead of the 3in gun. There would have been eight-cylinder diesels (total 1600 BHP) for 15.5 knots surfaced and 9 knots submerged. Yugoslavia was also offered Design 953B: 221ft (oa) 220ft (pp and wl) x 22ft 3in x 12ft 3in, displacement 790/967 tons. Designed surface speed seems to have been 15.5 knots. Designed submerged speed was 9.5 knots. About 1930 Vickers offered Yugoslavia a further Design 1028; later it offered Design 1031. The Yugoslavs did not buy any further submarines during the interwar period.

The Far East

Vickers' only export success in the Far East was its sale of two modified 'O'-class submarines to Australia under the designation Design 1148: *Otway* and *Oxley*. Australia had bought its two pre-war submarines, *AE 1* and *AE 2*, from Vickers, though as Empire products of the sole British commercial builder they could hardly be considered competitive exports.

The Japanese bought several other types of European submarines alongside their Vickers boats, but the German U-cruisers turned over after the First World War had the greatest impact. They seem to have inspired the cruiser submarines which followed. Vickers tried to hold the Japanese market for a time, and the company's records show several designs for Japan. Vickers tried to hang on: its Design 842 (July 1923) was offered to Mitsubishi as No 2. This was a big cruiser intended to compete with the German U-cruisers: a large conventional submarine, 300ft pp 306ft oa x 27ft (pressure hull diameter 19ft 6in) x 16ft 3in (normal surface displacement 1708 tons, 2242 tons submerged). She would be driven by two-shaft diesels (6400 BHP) at 20 to 20.5 knots on the surface and by motors at 8.5 knots submerged (one-hour rate). Radius with maximum fuel would have been 3440nm at 20.5 knots (10,000nm at 10.5 knots). Armament would have been six bow and two stern 21in tubes, plus one 4.7in/45 and one machine gun. Design 844 was an alternative using Vickers vertical (presumably opposed-piston) diesels (also 6400 BHP): 310ft pp x 27ft, 1800/2350 tons, 20 knots surfaced and 8.5 knots submerged, endurance on maximum fuel 1900nm at 20 knots and 10,000 at 10.5 knots. Gun armament would have been two 5.2in and one 4in HA.

Later the Chinese government sought a variety of equalisers against Japan, both submarines and motor torpedo boats. Vickers offered China Designs 1067 and 1068, the latter a minelayer. The minelayer's dimensions were: 181ft (wl) x 24ft 4in x 10ft (excluding keel), 600/907 tons (excluding superstructure) tons. Designed surface speed was 12.25 knots. Test depth was 75m (246ft). The collection of Vickers plans shows an un-numbered design for a minelayer, which appears to be a slightly expanded version of 1068; the design number and the prospective customer have been redacted by cutting them off. The Chinese submarine contract went to Germany. After Japan attacked, these submarines were not deliverable, and the Germans took them over as *U 25* and *U 26* (Type IA).[11]

Vickers offered Siam its Design 1074: 151ft (pp) x 20ft 6in (pressure hull diameter 13ft 6in), 405/550 tons. A later estimate, with beam reduced to 20ft, was 426/560 tons. Surface speed was 12.25 knots. Siam bought two Japanese submarines instead.

Latin America

Vickers records show that it courted both Argentina and Brazil. In October 1921 Vickers offered Argentina a version of its Design 851: 197ft pp x 21ft 6in (pressure hull diameter 14ft 6in), displacing 640 tons surfaced and 777 tons submerged. It had one 4in gun. There were four 21in bow tubes and, apparently, four trainable 21in tubes. There was one 4in gun. A slightly different version was credited with 14 knots on 1200 BHP (1200nm at 14 knots, 4300nm at 10 knots with extra fuel). Vickers designs for large and small submarines for Argentina (1086 and 1087) are dated 7 March 1924. The small one (1086) would have displaced 610/745 tons (200ft [oa] x 18ft 6in mld x 12ft 3in) and would have been armed with five 21in torpedo tubes (one reload each, one aft), one 4in gun, and two machine guns. Speed would have been 14/8 knots; surface endurance would have been

8000nm at 8 knots (submerged, 75nm at 4 knots). The large submarine would have displaced 910/1100 tons (226ft x 21ft 3in). Speed would have been 16/8 knots, and armament would have matched that of the smaller one. A companion minelayer (Design 1088) would have displaced 1200/1550 tons (260ft x 24ft mld x 18ft 6in hull depth to main hull x 14ft 9in). Speed would have been 15/7 knots and surface endurance 10,000nm at 8 knots. The submarine would have had four bow 21in torpedo tubes and two mine ejectors aft, as in wartime German minelayers, with forty mines. In addition she would have had one 4in and two machine guns capable of HA fire. Slightly later Vickers offered Design 941 (21 December 1921). No details were given, but a list of armament plans shows 6in guns and 21in bow and stern tubes, with some protection. A Vickers design list shows Design 1011, a 740-ton 205ft submarine armed with two 3in guns and six 18in torpedo tubes – something like an 'L'-class – offered to Brazil in 1923.

Design 855 was offered to Argentina, probably about 1924–5. It was 656/913 tons, 200/204ft 6in x 21ft 6in (14ft 6in pressure hull diameter) x 12ft, with HO engines developing 1600 BHP (14.5 knots) and a submerged speed of 8 knots. Endurance on normal fuel was 1360nm at 14.5 knots; on maximum fuel it was 8800nm at 8 knots. Submerged endurance was 80nm at 4 knots. Armament was four 21in bow tubes and two stern tubes, plus one 4in/45 gun and two machine guns. Maximum safe depth was 250ft.

The Vickers Estimate Book shows (as its No 2916) a submarine of *L 11* type for Argentina (22 September 1926) without any Vickers design number. This may have been a proposal to complete a cancelled submarine. This submarine would have been somewhat larger than Design 855. Other designs offered to Argentina, for which details are missing, were Nos 783 (minelayer), 831 and 833 (also offered to Brazil and to Greece).[12] Argentina bought three 775-ton Italian-built submarines about 1930 in return for an agreement to buy agricultural products; the Argentines cancelled a French order. Vickers seems to have offered a later submarine minelayer design (Design 1084), as well as a conventional submarine (Design 1125, probably not the 1125 offered to Greece).

In 1919 Brazil already had Italian-built submarines. Vickers offered Brazil its Design 784 in November 1921: 740 tons surfaced, 205ft x 23ft 6in, armed with six 21in torpedo tubes, one 4in/45 gun, and one 1½pdr anti-aircraft gun. On 10 January 1923 Vickers offered Brazil two alternative submarine designs (1011 and 1012), both armed with four bow and two stern torpedo tubes. No. 1011 would have displaced 740 tons surfaced and 963 tons submerged, with diesels developing 1800 BHP (14.5 knots) and motors for 9 knots submerged. Endurance would have been 3200nm at 10 knots and, submerged, 55nm at 5 knots. No 1012 was smaller, 185ft rather than 205ft long, displacing 690 tons surfaced and 800 tons submerged, with the same speed and power surfaced but 10 knots submerged. Endurance would have been reduced to 1100nm at 10 knots surfaced but 70nm at 5 knots submerged. Armament would have included two 3in HA guns. There was also a Design 1153 dated 20 December 1924, details of which have not survived.

In the other series, Brazil was offered Design 879 about February 1925.[13] Dimensions were 270ft 9in (pp) 280ft 9in (oa) x 25ft (pressure hull diameter 17ft 3in); displacement was not given. Armament was four bow and two stern 21in torpedo tubes (total ten torpedoes) and one 4in/50 plus four machine guns. Surface speed would have been 18 knots (3800 BHP), and submerged speed 9.5 knots. This is probably

Many governments were glad to buy ships more or less identical to those bought by the Royal Navy. Chile bought three *Capitan O'Brien*-class submarines, essentially the 'O' class, from Vickers. This is the name ship. (NHHC)

the design which lost out to the Italians (the submarine was *Humaita*). It is not certain why it alone in the Thurston notebook is described as a twin-screw submarine, since that was nearly universal for Vickers submarines at this time.

By 1932 Brazil was back on the market; the Vickers design calculation book shows a minelaying submarine (Design 1061), detailed strength calculations for which were dated 4 November 1932. There was also a Design 1060. Its dimensions were 262ft x 22.5ft x 15.92ft (depth); maximum surface speed would have been 18 knots. There was also a Design 1062 covering several alternatives. Vickers' effort failed; Brazil bought three more Italian submarines (transferred directly from the Italian navy) about 1936.

Vickers' only Latin American success was with Chile, which eventually bought three modified 'O'-class submarines. This was a comedown from the country's immediate post-First World War plan. By November 1919, the long-range Chilean naval plan envisaged six 2000-ton submarines and fourteen small coastal units, but that was never affordable.[14] The Chilean contract must have been negotiated in 1926; British files include a 17 July 1926 letter to Vickers stating that there was no objection to their submitting the 'O'-class design provided some sensitive items were omitted, including the underwater recognition signal ejector, automatic inboard venting gear, 40ft periscopes, the latest revolving hydrophone, the W/T inductance space and closed inductance to the main engine. Vickers agreed to keep maximum diving depth secret, and to impress on the Chileans that it had to be kept secret.[15]

The formal proposal may have been Design 833 (26 January 1926), for which the Vickers data book is empty. On the same date Chile was offered two alternative submarine minelayers (Designs 857 and 874). In the Thurston notebook, Design 857 displaced 880/1165 tons (235ft 9in [pp] 240ft 3in [oa] x 15ft x 22ft 6in x 12ft) and had two Vickers HO engines (1600 BHP) to drive her at 14 knots (8 knots submerged); endurance was 1500nm at 14 knots and (with maximum fuel) 8000nm at 8 knots; submerged endurance was 12nm at 8 knots or 80nm at 4 knots. She had four bow 21in torpedo tubes and, apparently, German-style minelaying tubes aft for thirty-six mines (220lbs each). Gun armament was one 4in/45 and one 2pdr HA, and safe diving depth was 250ft. Design 874 was a smaller minelayer (630/830 tons, 198ft 6in/200ft 6in x 20ft 6 [13ft 6in pressure hull] x 11ft 9in), powered by two six-cylinder Vickers engines (1200 BHP, 14 knots), capable of 8.5 knots submerged. Endurance was 1100nm at 14 knots on normal fuel, and 3000nm at 10 knots on maximum fuel; submerged endurance was 12nm at 8 knots or 65nm at 4.5 knots. As in Design 857, instead of after torpedo tubes this submarine would have two mine discharge tubes, in this case sufficient for eighteen Vickers mines. Gun armament would be cut to one 3in. Chile was offered another submarine (perhaps the final version of the *Oberon* she received) dated 1 April 1927 (Design 1298). In 1939 Chile was offered Design 1112 (230ft 6in x 14ft dia x 21ft 9in x 13ft 9in, 923/1126 tons). The first was in the Walker series, the second in the Barrow series.

Peru, the only other Latin American submarine buyer, is not represented at all in surviving Vickers submarine files. It bought submarines from Electric Boat, saving that firm. Vickers' plan files show Design 1032 (260 tons) for Colombia, which bought no submarines during the interwar period.

NOTES

Chapter 1: The Royal Navy and the Submarine, 1901–1945

1. Nicholas Lambert, *The Submarine Service 1900-1918* (Aldershot: Navy Records Society, 2001), p 21, quotes a 21 January 1901 memo by Controller (Wilson) describing the previous policy of trying to delay submarine development by rejecting proposals. 'A very well thought out design for a submarine boat was brought to my notice while Commander of the *Vernon* about 1879, which only required one small addition which any torpedo Officer could have supplied to make it efficient. Experiments . . . proved the practicability of the one point in this invention which was novel and the inventor was given no further encouragement . . . Each design has been carefully examined and sufficient experiment has been made in each case to ascertain its probable value. It has then been quietly dropped with the result of delaying the development of the submarine boat for about 20 years.' Now that the French had produced a practical submarine, such tactics were no longer possible. It was still wise to avoid assisting in the improvement of the submarine 'in order that our means of trapping and destroying it may develop at a greater rate than the submarine boats themselves'. Hence Wilson's unwillingness to encourage British submarine designers. British attaché files in ADM 1 (PRO) include considerable material on John Holland's *Fenian Ram* of 1880, mainly because it was to have been used by Irish revolutionaries against the Royal Navy. The Royal Navy took this submarine seriously enough that British diplomats expended considerable effort to keep it out of British waters.

2. The naval attaché in Paris, Captain Henry Jackson, reported in 1899 that the French finally had a reliable submarine which could manoeuvre underwater and fire torpedoes: Lambert, *Submarine Service*, p ix. Jackson was later Controller (1905–8) and First Sea Lord (1915–16). In February 1900 the NID was ordered to investigate French submarine progress and in April the Admiralty authorised the use of contact (rather than controlled) mines as an ASW weapon, since they did not require an observer to see the target. The torpedo school (and underwater R&D organisation) HMS *Vernon* was ordered to begin work on ASW. Its captain answered in May 1900 that he could not begin until he knew more about submarine capabilities. That triggered British submarine acquisition. In May Controller Rear Admiral Sir A K Wilson recommended purchase of a single submarine for ASW experiments. According to Lambert, Wilson was torn between the need to develop countermeasures to foreign submarines and the fear that public acceptance of submarines by the Royal Navy would encourage foreign navies to buy their own submarines. He wanted to keep the British programme secret. In 1901 Vickers summarised French submarines for the Admiralty (ADM 1/7522, file dated 22 June 1901). The first really successful French submarine (submersible) was the 270-ton *Gustav Zédé*, powered by two 720 HP motors and designed to achieve 14 knots (but was limited to 8 knots due to bad batteries). She had one torpedo tube forward (three torpedoes). She was entirely electrically powered. *Narval*, the other successful French boat, was a 106-ton submersible (200 tons submerged), in effect a torpedo boat hull wrapped around a pressure hull. She was powered on the surface by a 250 HP triple-expansion steam engine fed by an oil-burning boiler and was credited with an endurance of 252nm at 11 knots (624nm at 8 knots); under water she could run 25nm at 8 knots or 70nm at 5 knots. She carried four torpedoes launched from Drzewiecki drop frames outside her pressure hull. Another eight submersibles were included in the 1901 budget.

3. Lambert, *Submarine Service*, pp xiii–xvii. Balfour's committee became the CID in 1904.

4. According to Lambert, *Submarine Service*, p xvi, Fisher beat off attempts to slant the exercise rules to favour battleships and prevented Admiral Wilson from using the accidental loss of HMS *A 1* to show that submarines had failed.

5. Non-submarine heads of the submarine service were Rear Admirals Douglas Dent (1919–21), Hugh Sinclair (1921–3), Wilmot Nicholson (1923–5, a Vice Admiral), Vernon Haggard (1925–7) and Henry Grace (1927–9). RA(S) were Martin Dunbar-Nasmith (1929–31), Charles Little (1931–2), Noel Laurence (1932–4), Cecil Talbot (1934–6), Robert Raikes (1936–8) and Bertram Watson (1938–40), followed by Vice Admiral Sir Max Horton (1940–2) and then by Rear Admiral Claud Barry (1942–4). The first officer formally designated FOSM was Rear Admiral George Creasy (1944–6).

6. Cover 306 (*Nautilus*) Folio 1 is the 9 March 1912 report on immediate future submarine construction submitted to Controller; according to it Controller had ordered formation of the committee on 29 February. Members were Keyes, Commander A P Addison (Assistant ICS), Lieutenant C J C Little and Lieutenant C W Craven (Secretary). Representatives of DNC and EinC and Engineer Officers of the Submarine Service participated. 'Tiny' Little had joined the Submarine Service in 1903 and commanded *D 1* in 1908–11. He was FOSM 1931–2, DCNS in 1932, CinC China in 1936–8, Second Sea Lord 1938–41 and head of the British Admiralty Delegation in Washington 1941–2.

7. As described in the report on submarines (TH 21) in the Admiralty First World War technical history series: *Submarine Administration, Training and Construction*, TH 21 in the Technical History and Index, a series of histories of Admiralty Technical Departments (October 1921); it was published as CB 1515(21). Copy in Admiralty Library. 'The whole worked well and in its centralisation, economy and saving of time was undoubtedly the ideal way in which the Submarine Service ought to be run in war. Suggestions or requests were negatived or approved without delay and as access to the Commodore and his staff was easy and even encouraged, the personnel were able to get their wishes and their desire for information met whenever this was practicable. An officer building a new boat could choose his crew at Fort Blockhouse, having already been allowed to draw some men from his last command as a backbone for his new complement. He could arrange personally with the Commodore's Assistant Commander for the appointment of his chosen officers. He could, while building his boat, obtain support from the office for improvements or alterations, which seemed advisable on his recommendation. And, on putting to sea, he could find nobody but himself to blame if he was not satisfied with the boat and crew under him.' In 1918 Hall's tiny staff sufficed to run 135 submarines.

8. This account of the changes in the Staff are based on BR 1875 (originally CB 3613), *Naval Staff Monograph (Historical): The Naval Staff of the Admiralty: Its Work and Development* (September 1929), ADM 234/434.

9. US naval officers claimed that formation of the Plans Division was inspired by their own planning work in London and that this division had little impact during the war. Later it was quite important, as references to Director of Plans show.

Chapter 2: Making Submarines Work

1. Details of British submarine practice are from the 1943 version of the *Handbook of Submarines* Vol I (CB 1795A, ADM 239/45).

2. The important exception is that the submarine may come to rest on a layer of greater density. That was particularly the case when lighter fresh water flowed into the sea from large rivers. The main cases in point were the Danish straits (Skaggerak and Kattegat), the Dardanelles and the China seas. Density layers also create major sonar problems.

3. Captain Bacon, the first British Inspector of Submarines, used exactly this analogy. Admiral Sir Reginald Bacon, *From 1900 Onward* (London: Hutchinson, 1940), pp 51–2.

4. Holland patented the idea of diving with full ballast tanks. The Electric Boat Company, which bought up Holland's patents, survived the immediate post-First World War depression in submarine construction partly by dunning every navy which operated or had operated submarines for patent royalties.

5. According to the 1927 edition of the *Handbook of Submarines* Vol II (in the RN Submarine Museum) typical maximum pressure in a two-stroke engine was 450 psi (500 psi in a two-stroke engine). The temperature reached at 500 psi was about 1000° F. The limit on compression was set both by the load on the piston head (and other parts) which had to resist pressure on the up-stroke, wear and tear on the engine compressor and valves for air blast injection and increased wear on the cylinder liners.

6. Photographs of collapsed test sections are in the Brass Foundry, in an un-numbered Cover created about 1939.

7. D K Brown, 'Submarine Pressure Hull Design & Diving Depths Between the Wars' *Warship International* No 3 (1987), pp 279–6. In Brown's view, the advent of Asdic made it necessary for designers to seek greater depths. It can equally be argued that the shift to the Pacific forced British designers to contemplate deeper diving.

8. Brown, 'Submarine Pressure Hull Design'. Stress was set at pressure x hull radius/thickness, for a circular hull section. Local discontinuities such as hatches were typically over-designed, although, according to Brown, the torpedo loading hatch was often the beginning of fatal stresses. Deep diving trials measured the deflection of oval hull sections, e.g. at bow and stern, as a guide to the safety of the boat. Another indicator was paint cracking on the webs of pressure hull frames as they compressed. A safety factor was applied to the boiler formula to make up for its inadequacies. Brown wrote that interwar design practices are still not entirely understood and that much depended on comparison with previous successful designs. *L 2* had dived successfully to 300ft, which was twice its designed operating depth. Brown's own later calculation suggests that her collapse depth was 500ft, which was not realised at the time. Brown also wrote that the boiler formula was typically used as a basis for comparison rather than as a design criterion; through the 1920s the rule seems to have been to keep stresses in plating and framing to about those in the 'E' class. Brown wrote that by 1929 J H B Chapman had collected considerable theoretical and empirical data on stiffened cylinders, which he then related to the successful 300ft dive by *L 2*. They were used in the design of *Sunfish* and probably *Thames*. After the war, several British submarines were tested to collapse by lowering them into deep water. Brown compared the predicted collapse depth (aft) according to the boiler formula with actual collapse. The two were fairly close: for *Stoic* the prediction was 534ft and collapse occurred between 527ft and 537ft. For *Supreme* (S quality steel) the prediction was 700ft and collapse was at 647ft; *Varne* collapsed at 576ft (prediction was 614ft). The partly-completed hull of *Achates* collapsed at 877ft (860ft predicted). During the Second World War, *Stubborn* survived a dive to 540ft, which was greater than the depth at which her sister *Stoic* collapsed.

9. Paper read before the 7 April 1933 meeting of the Institution of Naval Architects, Folio 21 in General Submarine Cover (185C). Payne was a member of the RCNC working for DNC on submarines. Payne assumed that the ratio of frame spacing to diameter would be about 0.10 to 0.15 and the ratio of thickness to diameter would be about 0.0025 to 0.0045. He wrote that late pre-war practice had been to envisage the hull as a series of rings, each a short cylinder stiffened by a frame. Its collapse formula was well-known. It was assumed that the effect of bulkheads would be local.

10. General Submarine Cover (185C), Folio 35, dated 4 April 1934 referring to RA(S) submission of a design by Captain Villars, who wanted both a much heavier torpedo armament and better protection. The test was made against the light cruiser *Falmouth* (test 5, described in CB 1622/22). In this case the space between hulls was filled with water and the inner hull failed first. DNC considered this an isolated case. The framing was between the two hulls and the inner hull tore away from it. The water backing always limited damage to the outer hull and the inner hull invariably took greater damage when the space was filled than when it was empty. Although a thin inner hull would fail before a thick outer one, all experimental evidence showed that if the plates were of about the same thickness, the outer one would fail first. The Villars design, which is included in the Cover, showed angled external torpedo tubes mounted around the base of the conning tower, two forward and two aft, plus eight internal bow tubes, on a standard displacement of 876 tons (compared to 1475 tons for *Odin*). Folio 37 is the formal DNC paper dated 9.1.34 (presumably meaning 1 September). It mentions the 1000-ton submarine with four external tubes (which became the 'T' class) dated 19 April 1934.

11. D K Brown, *Nelson to Vanguard* (London: Chatham Publishing, 2000), p 119. This was work on land-based pressure vessels and thus on stress working outward, but it might be analogised to reliance on the boiler formula; it was published too late to affect wartime 'S', 'T' and 'U'-class submarines.

Chapter 3: Beginnings

1. Lambert, *Submarine Service*, Document 7. Rice had American financier August Belmont write to Nathaniel Rothschild, the British banker, asking for a letter of introduction to the Admiralty for Rice. Holland became Rice's employee, a position he found increasingly onerous, as Electric Boat did not accept his ideas for new submarine concepts. By 1914, when he died, Holland had been shut out altogether. The full correspondence is in ADM 1/7515, including a file ('Admiralty 15/1/1901') titled 'Holland' type submarines 1900–1901. Its Appreciation of Submarine Boats and Warfare, circulated to the Board, seems not to have survived.

2. Lambert, *Submarine Service*, Document 8, Controller Minute 3 August 1900.

3. Lambert, *Submarine Service*, pp 14–15, minute dated 8 October 1900 (1901 as printed, but context indicates the correct date); p 16 is the precis of Rice's proposal to the Admiralty dated 19 October 1900. According to a draft letter from Controller to the Treasury (22 October 1900, Lambert Document 10), Rice was unwilling to sell a single submarine without a guarantee that the Admiralty

would buy ten more over the next five years or pay a royalty of £10,000 on each of twenty boats built or purchased elsewhere. Controller considered five 'the least number of boats that would enable experiments, instruction and practice in meeting the attacks of these boats to be efficiently carried out'. Lambert includes a 24 October 1900 minute by First Lord: the boats should not be bought only for ASW experiments, as they might be very useful to defend places like Hong Kong. Senior Naval Lord agreed.

4. DNC had already pointed out that this seemed high for the dimensions, as larger French submarines reportedly cost £24,000 to £26,000.

5. Bacon seems to have requested the periscopes, which may have been inspired by one seen on the Italian *Delfino* (reported in ADM 1/7618). He explained to Vickers' representative how the tube was to be installed; he asked for drawings and cost estimates. Folio 9 of the General Submarine Cover (185) is Bacon's 20 June 1901 note to Controller concerning manufacture of these optical tubes, referring to Controller's minute of 8 June (not quoted).

6. Bacon memo dated 30 July 1901 in General Submarine Cover (185), folio 6. It includes a detailed analysis of forces involved; Bacon wrote that with fore and aft planes the submarine could submerge on an even keel. In his view that was needed to counteract the force of buoyancy (which Holland considered a safety feature) which could awkwardly accelerate the boat – for example, cause it to broach.

7. Described in Cover 212, Folios 64 and 75.

8. ADM 1/7725, enclosure to letter from Bacon dated 3 June 1903. Copy courtesy Royal Navy Submarine Museum. Bacon noted that as they submerged boats were apt to roll badly, because their waterplane area was vanishing. He had therefore ordered the boats to keep their head to the sea if they found themselves rolling while trimming down to dive. He hoped that bilge keels would largely solve the problem.

9. In *From 1900 Onwards*, pp 61–2, Bacon wrote that he had foreseen serious shortcomings in the 'Hollands' before they had been completed; they were too small for seagoing work. 'If submarines were to become vessels of practical value, their size and speed above and below water and also their seagoing qualities, would have to be increased. These could only be obtained by an increase in tonnage. Therefore, before the first of the Holland boats had been completed, I obtained the sanction of the Controller of the Navy to start the design and manufacture of a larger vessel.' He was given the services of a drawing office at Vickers Barrow and decided to install a 500 HP engine and a battery of twice the earlier capacity. 'Probably the greatest of all the improvements was the raising of the conning tower to some six feet above the deck. This gave a fairly high position from which to navigate the boat. It raised the officer in control well above the seas which constantly washed over the boat when under way; so that both in fine weather, when the hatch fitted on the top could be opened and in bad weather, when closed down, it provided a reasonably high position from which to navigate . . . the periscope could pass up through it. This not only supported the tube against vibration, but also gave a greater length of tube above the hull, thus increasing the efficiency. In addition it allowed the periscope to be dropped vertically when being housed instead of using the rather clumsy arrangement of the ball-and-socket joint.'

10. 'Holland', 'A', 'B' and 'C' Class Cover (290), Folio 3, CN 10940/05, Inspecting Captain of Submarines (Lee) to Controller, 24 June 1905, concerning repairs to *No 2* when her battery was replaced. The top of the main ballast tank had deteriorated; Lees wanted a thorough refit. He also wanted to test a higher conning tower, like the 4ft 6in high one Holland was providing in Japanese and Russian boats; the original low towers were too low to be safe in a seaway. It suggested fitting one to *No 2* during her overhaul. The 'A' and 'B' classes already had high conning towers, with watertight shutters at their bases to protect them in the event the conning tower was shot away.

11. BR 3043, A N Harrison, *The Development of H.M. Submarines from Holland No. 1 (1901) to Porpoise (1930)*, published by MoD as BR 3043 January 1979. Harrison was a veteran submarine designer and DNC 1961–6. He does not give his source.

12. Bacon summarised engine development in 1903, in connection with Vickers comments (Cover 185, Folio 35). When *A 1* was ordered, the most powerful existing gasoline engine (in the 'Hollands') developed 160 BHP. In consultation with Vickers, Bacon decided to press for 600 BHP, which he considered the most desirable power output for such a boat. He did not set a definite output in the contract because it was unlikely that his target power would be attained initially. This the initial small engine eventually produced about 400 BHP. The question was whether to tinker with this engine or to install it to gain experience in fitting the exhaust, circulating water and gasoline systems. He told Controller that the Royal Navy had no experience as to which engine of the desired power could be fitted in the small available space without, for example, disabling the crew by leaking exhaust gas or risking a gasoline vapour explosion.

'I am only too glad this engine was installed as it has taken six months hard work to overcome all these difficulties and the experience gained can now be applied to the larger engines in the "A" class.' The new 600 BHP engine was double the weight of the earlier one. Bacon wrote that accepting the smaller engine was definitely to the navy's advantage, but at the same time it was accepted only because Vickers had done the best they could in so large a departure from previous practice. He did not like Vickers' 'tone of self-satisfied complacency . . . hinting broadly that they were mainly responsible for and had met with uniform success in developing the submarine and based claims on these fictitious merits. I thought it as well to remind them in answer to their grasping financial claims that the Admiralty has been fair and reasonable . . .' A table in the 'Holland' and 'A', 'B' and 'C' classes Submarines Cover (290), folio 19, giving the submarine situation as of 31 March 1906, credits the *A 1* engine with 350 HP compared to 150 HP for the 'Hollands'; *A 2–A 4* were credited with 450 HP and *A 5* through *A 12* with 600 HP. The 750 HP figure is from notes Bacon made to explain why he wanted to make the next step to *B 1*. Corresponding surface speeds were 9 knots for *A 1*, 10.5 knots for *A 2* and 11.5 knots for *A 5*. *A 13* was rated at 550 HP (11.5 knots). The 'B' class had the 600 HP gasoline engine used in the *A 5* class. Submerged output of the 'A' class was 160 HP for 7 knots, compared to 60 HP (7 knots) in the 'Hollands'.

13. Admiralty letter to Vickers dated 29 June 1903 in Cover 185, Folio 35 (which also contains the discussion of buying more submarines to cut unit cost). Desired changes in *A 5* on were a slight increase in hull diameter (9–10in, without increasing displacement), a stiffer battery tank bottom, heavier and larger seating for the motor, a water space surrounding the gasoline tank, elimination of extra flats in the ballast tanks (which added weight) and the larger engine (the smaller engine in *A 1* had been accepted 'in consideration of the experimental work that you [Vickers] had carried out in connection with the engines'). This applied to nine submarines from *A 5* on. Their gasoline engine had enlarged cylinders and stroke (12in cylinders with 12in stroke rather than 8½in diameter and 10in stroke). The main motors were enlarged and the boats had two rather than one bilge pumps (the earlier ones had one auxiliary pump). Vickers objected that the changes would be expensive, particularly working the 3in layer of water around the gasoline stowage.

14. Figures from BR 3043, detailed sources not given. In 1912 DNC gave other figures: 8.5 knots on 280 BHP for *A 1* (suggesting that the small gas engine had been overrated), 10.5 knots on 450 BHP for *A 2* and 11 knots on 600 BHP for *A 12*. BR 3043 quotes surface endurance as 600nm at 11.5 knots, which the author considered optimistic. In 1912 DNC credited *A 1* with 540nm at half power; at half power stated endurances of *A 2* and *A 5* were 530nm. The 1914 data list (CB 1815) credited *A 5* with 400nm at full power and 650nm at 8.5 knots. Later Vickers figures for *A 1* were 489nm at full power, 735nm at half power; for *A 2*, 325nm and 490nm and for *A 5*, 325nm and 490nm. Legend submerged speed was 7 knots at 160 BHP (4.5 knots at 80 BHP was also given, but the author of BR 3043 doubted the submarine would be controllable at that speed). He also doubted that they could exceed 130 BHP submerged. Many years later submerged speed was given as 6 knots, which the author considered reasonable. Full battery discharge was at the 4-hour rate, so submerged endurance was probably 20 to 24nm at full speed.

15. Cover 185, Folio 35, letter to Vickers dated 21 May 1903.

16. 'The Development of British Submarines', circulated by Commodore (S) in November 1914. Copy in ADM 137/2067.

17. Engineer-in-Chief first mooted the heavy oil engine for submarines in a 29 May 1903 memo (General Submarine Cover [185] folio 34). The Hornsby tender was formally accepted in September 1903 (Cover 185). Gasoline offered great power on limited weight because it was easy to vaporise – which also made it dangerous. He wanted Vickers to use petroleum with a flashpoint of at least 100° F, if that could be done without delaying completion. Bacon divided petroleum oils into those having a flashpoint over 110° F, those with a flashpoint of 77° F and those under 77° F. Only oil with a high flashpoint was absolutely safe. Submarines in the tropics might easily be heated to 80 or 90° F. A House of Commons Select Committee divided safe and dangerous oils at 100° F. Bacon asked whether crews should regard any oil as fully safe – conditions in home waters were not those of Malta or Singapore. He considered gasoline no more dangerous than coal gas in a room, which had a flashpoint hundreds of degrees below zero. The difference between gas at home and gasoline in a submarine was nothing more than the way it was stored. In later submarines the gasoline tank was completely surrounded by water. Its pipes were far more secure than in a home on shore. 'No smell of gasoline is allowed in a boat', and it could not burn without air. There was certainly a danger of flashback from a light held near the vent, but vents were being covered with gauze to prevent that. There was no point in adopting oil equally dangerous in the tropics. Gasoline engines were, moreover, much simpler than oil engines whose fuel had

to be vaporised or sprayed. EinC replied that submarine fuel was very different from coal gas in a home. As soon as a little escaped from a leaky joint, it was smelled and measures taken, but a few drops of gasoline would vaporise to form a large explosive volume in the confined space of the submarine. EinC also doubted that all engines were necessarily so heavy.

18. This was a non-diesel engine made by Hornsby; Ackroyd was the inventor. It burned heavy (non-volatile) oil, but not by compression and therefore was presumably much less efficient than a diesel. It had a hot bulb let into the side of each cylinder. Oil was sprayed into the bulb, the mixture there normally being too rich to ignite (i.e., it was mixed with too little air). Air pumped into the cylinder on the up-stroke changed the mixture and the heat of the cylinder sufficed to ignite it, creating the hot gas which pushed the piston back down. This four-cylinder 550 BHP engine was expected to produce 600 BHP for brief periods. Controller's formal decision to use this engine in one of the 1903–4 boats (*A 13*) was on S.15438/3 dated 24 August 1903. General Submarine Cover (185) folio 33. In fact it was not used.

19. ADM 1/8678/69, which includes a 1925 Admiralty history of British submarine engine development.

20. Report by ICS for Controller, on a run from Barrow to Portsmouth, 1 July 1908, in 'Holland', 'A', 'B' and 'C' Class Cover (290), Folio 107. The 'A'-class submarine was designed to be powered by a horizontal gasoline engine. To install the vertical heavy oil engine one of the two fuel tanks had to be removed, halving fuel supply. The propeller shaft had to be tilted up, causing problems when the submarine was submerged. ICS (S S Hall) wanted her fitted with bow hydroplanes to balance the downward thrust of the tilted propeller. The submarine commander reported that the engine compared very favourably with the usual 'A'-class gasoline engine. Unlike a gasoline engine, it relied heavily on its air compressor. For most of the run it operated on only four of its six cylinders, one having had its connecting rod slightly bent. According to the 1925 Admiralty report on submarine engine development, the *A 13* engine was rated at 500 BHP (380 RPM), with 13in x 14in cylinders and a weight of 81lb/BHP, compared to the 500 BHP horizontal gasoline engine of contemporary 'C'-class submarines, which ran at 400 RPM (sixteen 11¼in x 12in cylinders, 66lb/BHP).

21. Cover 185, Folio 31. Vickers was formally asked to produce a general design by a 15 January 1904 memo, which indicated a length of 135ft rather than 100ft and a displacement of 300 tons rather than 200 tons; battery capacity would be 200 HP for four hours instead of 150 HP for four hours. Motors were to be capable of working at 300 HP when desired. 'It is very important that the Boat should be laid down this financial year [ending on 30 April] and therefore dispatch is necessary.' Vickers answered on 22 January, noting that Bacon had carefully considered whether the boat should be 125ft or 135ft long; the company offered a 125-footer. The increase in price would be £7786 (an 'A'-boat cost £40,215). A 135-footer would cost an additional £882.

22. A modern formulation would be that resistance underwater is mainly frictional, varying with the surface area of the submarine (i.e., rising more slowly than displacement). In Bacon's formulation, if a 200-ton boat required 150 HP to get 8 knots for four hours, a 300-ton boat would need 225 HP. He claimed further that hull weight was generally 35 per cent of the displacement; battery weight was about the same. That would leave 30 per cent for anything else. On this basis, increasing displacement 100 tons would leave 30 tons for everything but hull and batteries; little of that could go for increased underwater speed. It was also desirable to avoid much increase in the number of batteries.

23. Bacon estimated that of the 100 additional tons, 35 tons would go into the hull, 10 tons into extra oil, 3 tons into extra motor power, 18 tons into extra water ballast, 10 tons into extra battery power and 1½ tons into the gun and its mounting and ammunition. That would leave 22½ tons for ballasting and increased metacentric height. He estimated that all of this would entail an additional cost of £6100 (plus the gun) over the current figure of £41,000 for an 'A'-class submarine.

24. H S. Deadman, 9 December 1903, stamped approved by DNC Philip Watts.

25. Controller's draft letter dated 12 March 1903, folio 35 of General Submarine Cover (185). Initially the 1903–4 Programme envisaged five repeat 'A' class, to be designated *A 5–A 9*. Ship Branch noted that under the Vickers agreement the Royal Navy would get a discount if it could order seven boats or more at the same time: each would cost £37,000 rather than £41,000 (Cover 185, Folio 35, same date). Bacon agreed, proposing that the first five be completed during the 1903-4 financial year and the others during the next, which would suit planned spending. According to ADM 1/24200, the New Supplemental Programme for 1903–4 (dated 20 January 1903) included ten submarines. Provided trials with *A 1* were successful, nine repeats plus one experimental submarine (*B 1*) were to be built. At that time the submarine programme amounted to three boats built, four building and four more approved but not yet laid down, i.e., to six sub-

marines beyond the five 'Hollands'. CAB 37/63 No. 142 (1902, actually 17 October 1901) The Cabinet approved a building programme in the autumn of 1902 and as of 4 January 1904 (CAB 37/67 No 90) the 1904–5 Programme called for ten submarines (*B 2* through *B 11*).

26. 'Holland', 'A', 'B' and 'C' Class Cover (290), Folio 14, CN1 1906/06 of 20 January 1906. The 'C' class designation seems to have been introduced at this point, 'so preserving the continuity to the D Class now being tried in the tank at Haslar'. Dimensions and displacement matched those of the 'B' class (*B 2* through *B 11*): 135ft x 13.5ft, 313 tons (120-ton hull), with the same 600 BHP Vickers gas (petrol) engine and the same 15 tons of fuel and with the same 210 HP motor (7 knots submerged). Like the 'A' and 'B' classes, these boats were described as modified versions of the Holland design.

27. Figures and notes on improvements in the 'C' class are from BR 3043.

28. Folio 1 of the 'Holland', 'A', 'B' and 'C' Class Cover (290) is the account of this 23 June 1905 meeting compiled for Controller (who attended). The submariners were represented by Captain Bacon, who had just completed his tour as Inspecting Captain and by his successor Captain Lees. The technical authorities were DNC and EinC. Folio 2 of the 'D' Class Cover (212) is the design report submitted to DNC on 15 May, including a discussion of the method of diving.

29. Lambert, *Submarine Service*, Document 75, from Keyes Papers, British Library. The report was submitted by the submarine depot ship *Vulcan*; Hall wrote that it generally confirmed what was already known, but probably this knowledge had not previously been widely disseminated within the Admiralty The Swedes claimed that *Hvalen*, which was about the same size, was much superior to a 'C'-class submarine. In Hall's view, existing British submarines had extraordinary seagoing capabilities, equalled (if at all) only by US boats designed on similar lines (i.e., derived from Holland's original submarine). The captain of the low-reserve buoyancy French *Emeraude* considered his ship at all times steadier and more comfortable than the double-hulled Laubeufs. All he wanted was about twice the reserve buoyancy – about 10 per cent, not far from the 12 per cent of the 'C' class. Hall argued that the crew gained nothing from a hull projecting much further above the surface because they were still confined inside. Submerged performance was much more important. The captain of the Swedish submarine told Hall that he could make 6.5 knots submerged. Hall suspected that was due in part to the mass of obstructions covering the submarine, which he associated with her high surface speed. Until much more was understood of submarine tactics, it was best to follow his predecessor's (Bacon's) advice, not emphasising one characteristic (surface speed) at the expense of another (submerged speed). DNI (actually Deputy Director, Captain Thomas Jackson) was sceptical; the French had abandoned low-reserve buoyancy submarines well before the trials Hall mentioned and in October 1909 one of their Laubeuf-type submersibles, *Papin*, had established a world record by running from Rochefort to Oran (1200nm) in five days (Hall argued that it was unrepresentative of realistic conditions). He challenged Hall's priorities and pointed to the relatively high maximum submerged speed of the French craft. DNC suspected that *Hvalen* was lightly built, based on how much had been achieved in so little tonnage (185 tons surfaced and 300 submerged, compared to 291 tons and 320 tons in a 'C'-class submarine).

30. The gasoline explosion hazard was dramatised on board *A 5* at Queenstown early in 1905. Her leaking gasoline pump let in free gasoline, which quickly vaporised inside the boat, creating a foul vapour. To clear the boat of fumes, the main motor was started. It would turn over the engine, which was expected to suck the fumes out of the body of the boat. Sparks from the motor's brushes caused the vapour to explode.

31. EinC's remarks appended to the account of the 23 June 1905 meeting in the 'D' Class Cover (212). Conversion of existing submarines to heavy oil was being considered, but nothing seems to have come of that.

32. 'Holland', 'A', 'B' and 'C' Class Cover (290), Folio 11, July 1905.

33. 'Holland', 'A', 'B' and 'C' Class Cover (290), Folio 12. The diving issue appears to have arisen after the loss of *A 8*. It seemed that a surfaced submarine running at high speed might accidentally dive. Afterwards standing orders limited surface speed and required all submarines to maintain full buoyancy when running on their gasoline engines. Later it was not clear whether *A 8* had been driven under by a loss of buoyancy and trim (bow down) owing to entry of water or due to fast running at a deep trim. A model test indicated that with a buoyancy of 6 tons the model would not dive with a trim of 2° by the bow at a speed of 10.3 knots. With 10 tons buoyancy the boat was stable at 11 knots. The trials were interpreted to show that at a small buoyancy (6 tons) 10 knots was too high a speed for safety under all conditions. The stern planes could do very little to prevent diving if her trim and speed were such as to make diving likely and could even be dangerous. DNC modified the proposed 'D'-class hull form and bow planes were added.

34. 'Holland', 'A', 'B' and 'C' Class Cover (290), Folio 33. Bad weather limited the value of these trials.

35. Cover 290A, Folio 98, 16 October 1911.

36. Cover 212, Folio 12, dated 16 November 1905 Lees later wrote that the French 1905 programme included eighteen large submarines, followed by twenty more in 1906. He the experimental submarine built at Barrow even though the new agreement with Vickers had not yet been signed. Bacon disagreed.

37. Froude estimated that efficiency would be a third better (40 per cent) – meaning a third less horsepower required. Hence the 900 BHP estimate. Froude could not predict underwater speed, as previous models either had not been run or had been run without conning towers. The EHP required to drive the conning tower through the water seemed to be as great as that for the whole hull when submerged. Froude suggested two conning towers of elliptical or oval cross-section instead of a single conning tower.

38. Cover 212, Folio 17, reference sheet dated 8 January 1906.

39. According to C Lyle Cummins, *Diesels for the First Stealth Weapon: Submarine Power 1902-1945* (Wilsonville OR: Carnot Press, 2007), Vickers had formed a diesel development group at Barrow after the failure of the Hornsby-Ackroyd engine. The *D 1* engine was 10lb/BHP heavier than the gasoline engines it replaced; it was nearly 2ft longer than a gasoline engine (overall length was 17ft including a flywheel).

40. Cover 212, Folio 22, dated July 1906. The three designs were submitted on 17 April, 30 April and 4 May and sent jointly by DNC and EinC to Controller. Vickers called these its 'E' designs. 'E1' was a 'B lengthened by 13 per cent (to 152.5ft) and with 9.2 per cent greater maximum diameter (14.75ft). With the same lines as a 'B', displacement would increase to 422 tons and main ballast to 37.8 tons, but the lines were somewhat filled out to give a displacement of 437 tons; if the increase were devoted to ballast, that would give 52.8 tons; surface displacement would be 384.2 tons. 'E2' was larger (155ft x 15.3ft), again roughly an enlarged 'B' (enlarged by 14.8 per cent in both length and diameter) with its lines somewhat filled out to give 482 tons submerged displacement (415 tons surfaced). At this time the submerged displacement of 'D' was 535 tons. Both Vickers designs could be described as 'B' hull forms run light on the surface with very slightly filled-out lines. DNC estimated that the boats would make 14.15 knots on 1200 BHP, slightly less than 'D' and 13.63 knots and 13.62 knots, respectively, on 900 BHP ('D' was expected to make 13.88 knots at this point). DNC also pointed out that the apparently minor changes from the 'B' hull form would make considerable differences in diving performance. It seemed likely that either 'E' design would dive easily and run horizontally under hydroplane control. Since the predicted surface speeds were higher than the maximum speed of a 'B'-class submarine, it was not certain that either would be safe from spontaneously diving. As the single-hull submarines had grown, their metacentric height had decreased, largely because the nature of the design demanded that several heavy weights be kept at about the same vertical distance from the centreline of the hull: battery, engines, motors, torpedo tubes and permanent heavy weights. The limit might already have been reached in the 'C' class, whose surface metacentric height was only 4½in in load surface condition (for 'D' it was 21in). Combining increased diameter with vertical engines would reduce metacentric height further unless the submarines were given considerable permanent ballast. Also, to maximise main ballast tanks, the 'E' designs had no separate compensating tanks to be used as fuel was burned. Instead, Vickers proposed to let water into the fuel tanks. EinC considered that undesirable, as it might cause engine trouble. After DNC prepared this analysis, Vickers offered a third design, with 3in greater maximum diameter (15ft 9in) in hopes of regaining stability; it would displace 495 tons submerged. The upper ballast tanks of the earlier designs could be eliminated, lowering the centre of gravity and improving internal arrangement at the cost of speed. Vickers also offered a superstructure, which would make its 'E3' design somewhat similar to the 'C2' design considered and rejected in 1905 due to its comparatively great diameter (19ft) and draft. Vickers re-submitted its May design in August 1906 (Folio 33) and it was again rejected.

41. The decision to add 10ft of parallel mid-body seems to have been taken just before the data were sent to the Board, as it is the subject of a 7 August 1906 note to the test tank at Haslar, asking for a new estimate of diving qualities (Cover 212, Folio 28A).

42. Cover 212, Folio 35, undated memo from Controller, C.N.2467/07. Under the terms of the five-year Vickers agreement, the company had to fulfil the stated requirements. They were allowed a considerable margin in a submarine of entirely new design. Hence a considerable increase in estimated weight, particularly of the hull. Vickers offered a modified bow torpedo tube ('tandem') arrangement which, according to DNC, 'would go far towards the solution of one of the difficulties in the design of submarines, viz., the provision of adequate armament for large boats as they are increased in size to meet the demand for greater speed and seaworthiness'. A second boat could easily be built with four bow tubes in the 'tandem' arrangement. As the submarine hull was laid off at

Barrow displacement had to be increased from the original 578 tons to 585¾ tons, which DNC considered acceptable. DNC asked for a definite decision as to the modified bow arrangement.

43. Cover 212, Folio 43, query dated 10 November 1908.

44. Cummins, *Diesels*, p 180. According to Cummins, although the Admiralty ordered diesels in 1906, it took seven years (to 1913) to make them reliable enough for service use.

45. Cummins, *Diesels*, based on comments by Vickers engine designers. Apparently the 'L' class suffered particularly badly. The specific weight of the Vickers engine, not including shafting, was 69lb/BHP.

46. This account is from Cummins, *Diesels*.

47. ADM 137/1946 p 437, notes by Admiral of Patrols (de Robeck) dated 29 August 1913, describing ASW and related lessons from the 1913 manoeuvres. Commodore (S) commented that if the Admiral commanding the fleet had reliable W/T communication at night up to 60nm on the surface and 20nm in day when submerged, he could integrate submarines with his force; but neither condition was anywhere near being satisfied. Commenting on Commodore (S)'s estimate that a submarine could spend three days on blockade duty, De Robeck wrote that 'the entrance to the Baltic other than by the Canal would be made very dangerous to an enemy, provided that we can keep our submarines in the locality'.

48. DNO 25 April 1907 paper on 'Torpedoes for Submarines', Folio 85 of the 'Holland', 'A', 'B' and 'C' Class Cover (290). At this time the greatest number on board any British submarine was three, in *D 1*. Orders had just been given to carry six. The proposed scale of reloads was six for a three-tube submarine and possibly eight for four tubes.

49. 'Holland', 'A', 'B' and 'C' Class Cover (290), folio 108, June 1908. The boat would be lengthened by about 7¼ft and her lines modified, but the maximum diameter and general shape of the 'C' class were maintained except at the after end, where the ship would be modified to take twin screws. Total displacement would increase by about 54 tons (36 tons on the surface). They would have heavy oil rather than gasoline engines and a greater reserve of surface buoyancy. Controller expected that with twin screws about 12 or 13 per cent more of the total power delivered would be available at the propeller. The submarine would also gain somewhat from her greater length. Considerably more fuel could be carried in the available space. Controller expected that at least 700 BHP (380 RPM) would be attained in the available space and weight, compared to 600 BHP for the single-screw submarine (estimated surface speed was 13.25 knots rather than 12.25 knots). The twin-shaft electric motors were arranged to develop 500 BHP (together) at 270 RPM, using new more efficient propellers. For better seakeeping, the boat had been redesigned to trim by the stern. The internal main ballast tanks were enlarged (to 11.25 per cent [41 tons] rather than 8.5 per cent of the volume of the main hull) and as much as possible of the superstructure was made watertight (to gain another 8 or 9 tons of reserve buoyancy). These tanks would drain automatically when the boat surfaced. Controller offered a spare ballast tank (3½ tons) if any weight could be saved on his estimates. Rearranging the hull for twin screws made it possible to improve the arrangement of steering and diving rudders (stern planes) which would reduce resistance and also reduce the tendency to heel when turning submerged. The new boats would have the same Exide battery as *C 21*, but with 166 rather than 160 cells. Estimated cost was £52,000, compared to £48,229 for *C 21–C 30*. On 20 August 1908 Controller (Rear Admiral Jackson) suggested to First Sea Lord that if the price of the twin-screw 'C' class was so high that it would be better to repeat the single-screw *C 21–C 30*. After that the only remaining question was whether to repeat the Exide battery of *C 21* or the Chloride batteries of *C 22–C 30*.

50. Folio 116, Cover 290. The Cover refers to the existing *C 1* through *C 16* and the future *C 19* through *C 30*, omitting *C 17* and *C 18*, building at Chatham.

51. Based on a list of submarines built under various Estimates in a paper prepared in January 1913 for First Lord Winston Churchill (Cover 290B, no Folio given). The request to Vickers to tender for *D 2* was dated 13 January 1909, which would apply to the 1909–10 Programme, since the order would not be let before 30 March 1909. However, the 'D' Class Cover includes a 13 July 1909 note from Controller to First Sea Lord, First Lord and Financial Secretary proposing that the 1909–10 boats be of the 'D' class, at a unit cost of £84,000 compared to £48,000 for a 'C'-class boat. Admiral Fisher (First Sea Lord) and Reginald McKenna (First Lord) agreed and Controller (Jellicoe) wrote that Chatham should be informed, as it might build some of the boats.

52. Cover 291, Folio 3, not dated but presumably 1910.

53. 'Holland', 'A', 'B' and 'C' Class Cover (290), Folio 4, request by Jackson dated 7 August 1905. Lees considered four patents crucial: Nos 15816, 15819, 16351 and 8009. He considered it unlikely that the first two would stand in court, as they claimed as original 'a common practice of ventilation'. Nothing in 16351

was essential; the only item in the patent which the Royal Navy used was the arrangement of ballast tanks. It was convenient but not necessary. 'No 8009 is a shadowy claim that could not be substantiated. Both as regards our later submarines and the batteries they carry, the patents that really stand in the way of firms wishing to copy them are the joint secret patents taken out by Messrs Vickers and the Admiralty and vested in the Secretary of State for War.' A later summary of the secret patents (Folio 25) listed No. 17319 of 1902, No. 16686 of 1904 and No. 29332 of 1904. No. 17319 was a fairly detailed description of *A 1* (except for its engine) with some added features (such as a feathering propeller and an auxiliary gas engine for the air compressor and main bilge pump) not ultimately adopted. The patent was undermined by a statement that the Patentees did not claim rights to any of the elements of the submarine but rather that the combination of features was patentable. The key claim was that the boat 'is controlled by water ballast so that it can be caused to sink or descend vertically to a level where it will have a predetermined buoyancy and can then be caused to dive – by suitable propelling and steering mechanism'. DNC pointed out that this description included nearly all modern submarines and did not define any particular type for which rights could be claimed; this patent was no more valid than one on a surface ship would have been.

54. Folio 39, Cover 290A. Vickers was apparently seeking permission to sell submarines abroad. The discussion is mainly about the Vickers patents and whether the Admiralty gained advantages from their secrecy. Some of the patents were licensed by Electric Boat on a 25-year basis, but the main agreement with Vickers had a much shorter term.

55. Folio 73 in the 'Holland', 'A', 'B' and 'C' Class Cover (290). This specification dated 25 April 1907 was provided by the British naval attaché in La Spezia, Captain Roger Keyes, who was later ICS. Displacement was given as 175 tons surfaced and 235 tons submerged (metric tons), which was considerably less than a 'B'-boat; dimensions were 42.48m overall x 4.28m x 2.10m when fully surfaced, equating to a length of 140.3ft. The submarine would have three shafts, each driven by two electric motors developing 730 BHP for a maximum speed of 15 knots surfaced, well above that of contemporary British submarines. Submerged with its deck 3m (10ft) below the surface, the boat was to make not less than 7 knots. Of the three shafts, the centreline one would be driven by a gas engine, the two outer ones by 70 kW electric motors. Maximum submerged depth was given as 40m (131ft).

56. Folio 40 of Cover 290A; Scott and Constructor Major Boselli (formerly of the Italian Navy) visited the Admiralty on 4 November 1909. Thornycroft had already offered two designs prepared by Lake. A table in the Cover showed the Fiat 48m design and two designs each from Scott (described as San Giorgio, meaning Laurenti) and from Thornycroft, compared to the Admiralty's *D 1*:

	Fiat 48m	Scott 'A'	Scott 'B'	Thornycroft 'A'	Thornycroft 'B'	D 1
Length OA	157.5	148	148	161	161	163
Beam	17.4	13.8	13.8	13	13	30.5
Surfaced	380	245	245	425	425	480
Internal Main Ballast	101	56	56	17	17	14
External Main Ballast	97	79	79	83	33	100
Submerged	558	380	380	525	475	594
Test Depth	200	130	130	200	200	–
Fixed TT	4	2	2	4	4	3
Training TT	0	0	0	2	0	0
Torpedoes	8	4	4	6	8	6
Total BHP (2 shafts)	1000	400	300	1200	1200	1200
(all heavy oil except Fiat 48 m design)						
Max Speed	14	12.5	10.5	14	14	14.7
Fuel 17	5	6 ¾	38	38	27	
Cells 80	240	240	120	120	210	
Electric BHP	–	–	–	600	600	600
Submerged	9.5	8	7.5	9.5	9.5	9.5
Endurance 4 knots	80	75	80	abt 96	abt 96	abt 120
Compressed Air	190	116	116	100	100	184

(at 2100lbs in Fiat and Scott, 2500lbs in *D1*)

Of the two Scott (Italian) designs, 'B' had 300 BHP motors rather than 400 BHP ones as in 'A so as to increase the number of battery cells. This seems to have had no effect on the claimed underwater speed and endurance and the number of cells was taken from the drawing. In the Admiralty and Lake designs some sacrifices (for example in machinery installation) were made to maintain a circular-section pressure hull. In the Italian designs (Scotts) the pressure hull was shaped for convenience of stowage and for high surface speed. The Italian designs gained their strength from deep framing; the test depth was the same as that offered by Lake; but DNC was certain 'that on anything like the same weight of hull both the Admiralty and Lake designs are stronger than the Italian'. The surface speeds given for the Italian designs were inconsistent with the stated horsepower (either 400 BHP would not suffice for 12.5 knots or 300 BHP would give more than 10.5 knots). Laurenti had failed to take full advantage of his flexibility in hull form. Lake had made no attempt to reduce surface resistance, endurance being obtained by carrying more fuel. Both Lake and the Italians had adopted large conning towers which added considerable underwater resistance, using higher-capacity batteries than in British practice. DNC liked Lake's willingness to disperse his battery cells. He also liked the division into watertight compartments in the Italian and Lake designs. The bulkheads would strengthen the boat, although British officers felt that such division would weaken the control of the officers over the crew, primarily in emergencies. The Italian hydroplane arrangement was similar to that in British submarines and much superior to Lake's. Laurenti offered a higher reserve of buoyancy than the others. It might not necessarily provide greater seaworthiness, as such a boat would probably roll and pitch more in a moderate sea. 'The French, who have debated and experimented on the question of reserve of buoyancy probably more than anyone else, appear to have come to the conclusion that about 25 to 30 per cent of the surface displacement, as in our *D 1*, is the most practically serviceable figure. This is amply sufficient to prevent any tendency of the boat to dive when at the surface with conning tower open, which is one of the dangers of the French "submarine" type and of our earlier boats.' DNC found it remarkable that despite their considerably greater size the Italian designs were no faster or longer-legged than the similar *Glauco* and *Squalo* of only 180 tons (42.5m long).

57. According to the printed account of pre-war submarine development issued by Commodore (S) in November 1914, in ADM 137/2067, the restrictions became intolerable when it became clear both that Vickers would be unable to meet expected British requirements and were suffering serious delays fulfilling current orders. None of the memoranda on Vickers' monopoly position in Cover 290B mentions termination, although they certainly indicate gross dissatisfaction with Vickers' behaviour.
58. Cover 290B, Folio 34, a file on procedure for future submarine construction.
59. Cover 290B gives various forms of the 1912–13 Programme, including a 16 January 1913 summary for First Lord, which shows the drastic change and the 1913–14 Programme as then planned. In this summary, the 1911–12 Programme bought *D 3–D 5*, *D 7* and *D 8*. The 1912–13 submarines were *D 6* and *E 1* and *E 4*. The 1913–14 Programme bought *E 2–E 3*, *E 5–E 11*, *E 14*, *AE 1–AE 2* and Scotts' 'Submarine X'. At this time the projected 1914–15 submarines were *E 12–E 16*, the Vickers Oversea, the Vickers Coastal and two Laubeuf from EOC.
60. Cover 290A, Folio 104, signed by DNC 24 January 1917. By this time the British expected the Germans to begin unrestricted submarine warfare at the beginning of February. An attached memo from the head of the War Staff (Admiral H F Oliver) to First Sea Lord (25 January) reported that twenty armed trawlers were needed for the Otranto Barrage across the mouth of the Adriatic. Six 'B'-class submarines had been paid off as obsolete and were at Malta. Oliver wrote that each submarine could be converted for about £3,000 in about six weeks: six conversions would cost less than two trawlers. After conversion the ships would retain their two bow torpedo tubes. In addition to their 12pdr ideally they would also have a 2pdr (pom-pom) anti-aircraft gun 'which is desirable in view of air craft attacking drifters'. The project was approved on 27 January, to be carried out 'with the greatest possible rapidity'.

Chapter 4: Overseas Submarines

1. Keyes papers, British Library, dated 22 December 1913.
2. Cover 291 ('E' Class), Folio 1, CN0936/09 of 12 November 1909. He imagined that it had been standard practice in the past to lay down one experimental submarine each year and that this practice had ended with the 'D' class, probably because she and her diesel engine represented so great an advance. In fact the only experimental submarine prior to *D 1* was *B 1*. DNC's answer was dated 6 January 1910.
3. Cover 291, Folio 2; the date in January is difficult to read. It would be 172ft long (beam was not given), displacing 620 tons surfaced and 770 tons submerged. Surface speed would be 15 knots (endurance 95 hours) and submerged speed 10.5 knots; endurance submerged would be 8 hours at maximum speed and 15 hours at about 5 knots. To develop the design further, DNC urgently needed a rough torpedo tube design.
4. Letter from departing ICS (Captain S S Hall) to Controller, 7 February 1911, enclosure to Hall's letter to his successor Roger Keyes, Document 76 (from Keyes Papers) in Lambert, *Submarine Service*. Hall refers to two alternative designs, for 800 tons and 1000 tons. Although Lambert identifies the 1000-tonner as the precursor of the later 'L' class, context suggests that it was the projected large overseas submarine. Hall considered the 800-tonner, presumably the 'E' class, too small to have good enough seakeeping qualities. If a sufficiently powerful engine could be obtained, Hall preferred the thousand-tonner. He was willing to give up bow tubes to improve crew accommodation. Otherwise he suggested that either the bow or stern tube be given up in the 800-tonner to improve accommodation. Hall wanted a thousand-tonner built as an experimental submarine; with two guns she might make an interesting comparison with a destroyer. He wanted the submarine built at Chatham to use an engine from a Continental firm in order to motivate Vickers to improve its own engines.
5. Cover 291, Folio 41. The memo is undated.
6. Cover 291, Folio 17. This was due to a combination of increased diameter and length, the former presumably to maintain sufficient stiffness. The *C 1–C 11* periscope was built up of 4in tubes, the object glass being 7ft 1in above the top of the supporting bracket. In *C 12* to *C 16* the main part of the tube was increased to 5¾in to allow for a stereo arrangement. When that failed and the periscopes were converted back to monocular, diameter was not reduced; it became standard. In *D 3* to *D 8*, when fully raised the periscopes projected 8ft 11½in above the supporting bracket, of which the upper 3ft 10¾in was 3½in tube and the rest was 5⅞in tube. In *D 3* the projecting part of the tube was estimated to absorb nearly 50 BHP at 8 knots (about 100 amps on each main motor).
7. For years submarines had been described as 'day torpedo boats', conventional torpedo craft being limited to night operations. ICS expected the big submarines to cruise in wartime trimmed to dive but with ballast tanks empty. He expected them to dive within five minutes, which he considered sufficient to protect them from any surface ships they might spot. Presumably the key change which made crash-diving important during the First World War was the threat of air attack, not yet envisaged in 1911.
8. Keyes papers, British Library, recounting a 15 July memo which began with the question of whether a new 18 knot submarine should replace the 'E' class. At this time twenty-eight large submarines had been ordered through the 1913–14 Programme, including Scotts' 'S' class and the 'V' and 'W' classes. If the last three were excluded as really coastal rather than ocean-going, the total fell to twenty-one. Third Sea Lord was proposing a 25-submarine programme, giving a total of forty-six ocean-going submarines, including the 'D' class. Unfortunately it was not clear how affordable this programme could be, as it amounted to £312,000 in the 1914–15 financial year (the total cost was about £2.5 million). In a 20 July 1913 memo (in file DEY/31 of the D'Eyncourt papers, National Maritime Museum) Churchill estimated that a submarine blockading the Adriatic from Malta would spend three days on station, three coming and going and six resting or twelve days per submarine. 'To maintain an overseas blockade of the Adriatic *or the Elbe* [italics added] flotillas in 4 reliefs will be needed: one on watch, one in transit, two resting.' This was the basis of Churchill's estimate that forty-eight overseas boats would be required to maintain a continuous blockade of the German rivers in four flotillas of three boats each. 'This force could be created largely at the expense of the destroyers.'
9. Cover 290B, Folio 25. Installation of twenty-nine sets, in addition to those already installed, was given by DNO on 2 October 1912. A total of thirty-seven was envisaged. The standard set was Type 15.
10. As reported in the statement for the First Lord's presentation of the 1911–12 Estimates, in Cover 290A, Folio 92. The equivalent 1911 report stated that designs for larger boats had been prepared. 'One of these, for a boat of about 650 tons surface displacement, has been approved by the Board and preliminary work on the construction of two boats to this design has been taken in hand at Chatham . . . Another and still larger design of about 970 tons has been prepared and is to be brought up again for consideration in May next'. The 650-tonner was the 'E' class.
11. Cover 290B, Folio 31 gives details. Dimensions were 230ft pp/233ft 10in (overall) x 23ft 6½in x 25ft 4in (hull depth) x 13ft (fully loaded). Given a maximum total BHP of 4800 at 360 RPM, surface speed would be 19 knots (at half power, 16.5 knots). On 60 tons of oil, endurance at half power would be 1620nm. This large submarine would accommodate 320 battery cells, giving 1350 BHP for 1⅓ hours at 225 RPM (11 knots). Lowest controllable speed would be 3 knots. At that speed endurance would be 48 hours. The design showed two bow tubes, one stern tube and four broadside tubes, with a total of fourteen torpedoes. There would also be two 12pdr QF guns.
12. Cover 291 ('E' class), Folio 12. Expected price was £190,000, compared to £105,000 for an E-boat, the price of the larger submarine predicated on a guaranteed 18.5 knots on trial.
13. These designations were those of the relevant towing-tank models. The relevant Haslar report book (ADM 226/116) shows a series of T models, including TB (May 1910), TD (23 June 1910), TE (230ft submarine, report requested 27 June

1910), TG (5 March 1911 and later) and TJ and TK (both compared with TG in a report dated 14 August 1911). TB was compared with the earlier model SV, presumably an 'E' class or modified 'E'-class hull. Work continued at least through December, as on 6 December there was a report on a redesigned TK hull. TE was a 230ft submarine and TS was also a submarine. Non-submarines were included in the T series.

14. The 'E'-class submarine was 176ft long. Maximum (1 hour) submerged speed was 9.3 knots for TG, 9.6 knots for TJ and 9.3 knots for TK, compared to 10.2 knots for 1.05 hours in the 'E' class. Endurance at 5 knots submerged with the Mercury cell was 12, 11 and 10 hours, compared to 33 hours at 2 knots with the Neptune cell. According to the November 1914 report by ICS on British submarine design (in ADM 137/2067), TJ was presumably the 'French' design, derived from a Laubeuf design 'which had passed through DNC's hands in connection with a Chilean order in which he was interested'. TK was presumably the 'Italian' design. DNC's fourth design was a further elaboration of the 'E' class. Cover 290B Folio 33 (empty) was a comparison of TJ, TG and TK with the 'E' class, presumably corresponding to the data given.

15. Lambert, *Submarine Service*, Document 77, memorandum from Constructor H G Williams to Controller, 1 September 1911.

16. Cover 290B Folio 26 is a drawing showing space available for a heavy oil engine in this submarine, now 240ft long. At this time DNC asked EinC for the maximum BHP, revs and weight of engines proposed. This design is described in Cover 290B, Folio 32. Dimensions would have been 240ft (pp and oa) x 24ft 5¼in x 28ft 9in hull depth. She would have 320 battery cells, with 1240 BHP submerged for 10 knots for 1 hour. Minimum controllable speed would be 3 knots (endurance 45 hours). She would have two bow, two stern and four broadside tubes (twenty torpedoes), and one 12pdr.

17. Keyes papers, British Library, 22 November 1911 memo by Constructor H.G. Williams to Commodore (S) (Keyes). This is Document 78 in Lambert, *Submarine Service*. Williams pointed out that he was handicapped by the need for a large cross section to accommodate broadside tubes. That increased resistance, so the British boats needed more power and more fuel. That in turn left less of the submerged displacement for ballast and therefore less reserve buoyancy. Nothing could be gained until the British could obtain lighter engines. To Williams the main point of dealing with Laurenti and the FIAT firm was that the Italians could supply lighter-weight diesels.

18. Cover 290A, Folio 96, ICS memo dated 4 September 1911. The simple Goerz periscope offered 1.5x magnification and a 42° visual field. The Pancrama offered the same magnification and a 40° field. It incorporated a telemeter plate for rangefinding, with vertical and horizontal scales (the company offered to graduate them in yards). Goerz was unhappy that after the War Office tested a Pancrama (binocular) sight, it drew up a specification describing it in minute detail and circulated it to British firms for bids. The Admiralty planned to ask Goerz to tender for three Pancrama periscopes and eight simple periscopes. Periscope length was set at 7m for the 'E' class.

19. Cover 290B, Folio 12, an undated memo from ICS (Roger Keyes). The detailed report on the periscope examined in Paris is dated 4 March 1912. It was proposed to buy one for trials in a 'C'-boat. The periscope was somewhat narrower than that in a 'C'-boat (4.646in vs 5.625in diameter) and also somewhat shorter (15.24ft vs 16.5ft, main tube but total length between eyepiece and centre of upper prism was 21.32ft rather than 21.04ft). It was somewhat heavier than that of a 'C'-boat (617lbs) but not as heavy as that in a 'D'-boat, which required power lifting gear. Like the Italian periscopes, this one was made of Krupp non-magnetic steel.

20. Cover 290B, Folio 15a. The report was dated 27 April 1914. The rangefinder in the eyepiece employed two horizontal cross wires, on two glass surfaces sliding over each other near the vertical face of the bottom prism. The lines could be placed over any point in the field of vision to measure the angle subtended by an object. Indicated range (good to 1000 yds) was based on known masthead height.

Chapter 5. Experimental Coastal Submarines

1. Folio 1 in the 'S' Class Cover (289A) is the 1909 comparison between the Laurenti and Lake designs offered, respectively, by Scotts and by Thornycroft.

2. Keyes papers, Document 80 in Lambert, *Submarine Service*. The letter is dated 11 October 1911.

3. Keyes papers, British Library; this is Document 80 in Lambert, *Submarine Service*. Hall's letter is Document 79 in this collection. Keyes saw very little commonality between the 'A', 'B' and 'C' classes and the saddle-tank 'D' and 'E' classes.

4. Cover 289A, Folio 2 is the description of the Fiat San Giorgio submarine Scotts offered, dated 8 September 1911. Scotts asked for a free hand in building its submarine; 'only such alterations which are considered to be necessary for the safety of the vessel and crew should be put forward'. This small submarine

displaced only 249 tons surfaced and 304 tons submerged and was only about 148ft overall. Guaranteed surface speed was 13 knots and radius of action was to be 1800nm at 8.5 knots. Maximum submerged speed would be 8.5 knots and endurance submerged 75nm at 4–5 knots.

5. Cover 289A, Folio 6 is a September 1911 report from Commander Addison, a submarine officer, on the submarines at La Spezia. In a cover letter, ICS (Keyes) pointed to an urgent need to replace the old coastal submarines and also to develop fast seagoing submarines, which was probably the main reason to experiment with Laurenti submarines. The Scotts submarine would be 'a first step towards terminating Messrs. Vickers' monopoly which as far as our type of submarine is concerned, binds us until March 1912'. First Lord concurred. Addison visited Spezia with H C Williams, DNC's submarine expert and with Engineer Commander Garwood. Unfortunately the boat they visited, *Velella*, could not dive because it had recently suffered a battery explosion and would take at least three weeks to repair. Italian submarine officers seemed very pleased with earlier FIAT submarines. Evidence of Italian satisfaction was that eight more were under construction.

6. Cover 289A, Folio 8. In *Velella* the forward and after planes were controlled by concentric wheels, which could be linked as desired. Typically when diving the two sets of planes were set at opposite angles.

7. Cover 289A, Folio 3.

8. Cover 289A, Folio 9, 10 December 1911 notice to offices.

9. Cover 289A, Folio 12, account of meeting dated 29 January 1913, as reported by DNC's representative A W Johns, a future DNC. The meeting covered both the two repeat boats and the large overseas boat which became HMS *Swordfish*. Scotts' representatives had previously met with First Lord Churchill. Scotts complained that they were losing money on 'Submarine X'. The price may have risen because Scotts had to build the engines of any new submarines, although the engine of 'Submarine X' had come from FIAT in Turin.

10. This report is Cover 307, Folio 4. A table compared *Delphin* with a larger boat on order for Japan and with the 'D' class. The Japanese boat had a surface displacement of 457 tons, compared to 490 tons for a 'D' and was considerably longer (187ft vs 162.5ft). Reserve buoyancy was 208 tons compared to 130 tons for the 'D'-class submarine. The Japanese boat developed 2200 BHP, compared to 1200 BHP for the British submarine, hence was much faster on the surface: 17 knots vs 14.5 knots, with an endurance of 1000nm at 13 knots compared to 3000nm at 10 knots for the 'D'-class submarine. Submerged speed was 10 knots, probably for half an hour and endurance was given as 100nm at 4 knots, compared to 120nm for the British submarine. The Japanese boat had two bow tubes and four external torpedo launchers (Drzewiecki frames). *Delphin* carried a lot less compressed air: 38ft^3 compared to 184ft^3 in the 'D' class; compressed air cost about 236lbs per ft^3 in British submarines. Williams pointed to the extra weight of internal torpedo tubes, about 10 tons including torpedoes and compensating water, not counting indirect costs. Laubeuf had not provided detailed weights, but the approximate weights provided showed that battery and main engines were lighter per unit power. He also pointed to lighter hull structure, auxiliary machinery, pumping, flooding and blowing arrangements and a lighter method of battery stowage (which did not incorporate the heavy battery deck of British submarines). He noted far lighter and less bulky electric controlling gear for the motors, light high-RPM centrifugal pumps rather than the usual British reciprocating ones and by eliminating the whole of the LP air service, HP lines being connected directly to the tanks. Thus the difference from British submarines was much more in detail design than in overall configuration 'or any discovery of a principle or patentable arrangement of structure or machinery'.

11. Cover 307 Folio 2, DNC remarks dated 4 June 1912.

12. Cover 307 Folio 3 is Williams' comparison dated 4 June 1912. The French submarine had 192 Fulmen cells, giving 830 amps for two hours. The 240 Tudor cells of 'Submarine X' would give 710 amps for two hours. The French submarine was rated at 75nm at 4.5 knots, equivalent to 81nm at 5 knots. The Italian submarine was rated at 75nm at 5 knots, equivalent to about 92nm at 4.5 knots.

13. Cover 307 (W Class), Folio 1.

14. Cover 307, Folio 5 tabulates requirements against Armstrong's proposal. Length was to be no more than 148ft (Armstrong offered 171.92ft), draft not more than 11ft (Armstrong offered 7.85ft over the main body and 8.66ft over the keel but 9.35ft aft), displacement not more than 360 tons (378 tons), reserve buoyancy less than 40 per cent (48 per cent), speed not less than 13 knots (14 knots if practicable – Armstrong offered 13 knots), radius of action 2600nm at 9 knots (Armstrong offered 2600nm at 9 knots on one engine and 1600nm at 10 knots on two; with additional oil tanks it offered 4500nm at 9 knots on one engine and 3000nm at 10 knots on two), minimum metacentric height submerged 6in (5½in); speed not less than 8 knots submerged (Armstrong offered 8.5 knots); and radius of action 76nm at 5 knots (68nm at 5 knots). The table in the Folio

compares the Armstrong tender with Design X, with a Vickers Coastal ('V' class) and with Design Z. The latter was 176ft x 22.75ft x 13ft 7in with a surface displacement of 482 tons (reserve buoyancy 22 per cent), submerged displacement 807 tons, surface speed 15 knots on the surface (1600 BHP), radius 2800nm at half power, submerged speed 10.25 knots (840 BHP), submerged endurance 99nm at 3 knots

15. As Armstrong explained it in a 23 October 1912 letter justifying its divergence from set requirements (Cover 307, Folio 6a), Schneider's engine owed its reliability and unusually smooth running to its use of numerous small cylinders, each producing low power, in this case eight of them for 360 BHP. That cost space and weight. Stated requirements are in Folio 6b.

16. Cover 307, Folio 5B. DNC asked whether anyone but Armstrong should be asked to tender. In its October 1912 letter Armstrong offered to build two submarines for £84,500 each.

17. A pencilled description dated 29 July 1913 is Cover 307, Folio 10. Armstrong had forwarded a general arrangement drawing and a statement of dimensions etc, without detailed specifications. The firm stated that it would work to the specifications of *W 1* and *W 2*. It now met the Admiralty requirements, except that length was 150ft rather than 148ft and radius of action submerged was 68nm at 5 knots rather than 75nm. Since the underwater radius had already been accepted for *W 1* and *W 2*, that seemed acceptable. The other main change was elimination of the Drzewiecki frames. DNC noted that the calculated surface radius did not allow for charging batteries on passage. He considered the quoted total price per boat (£78,500) high; it was £3000 more than Vickers was charging for each of two coastals (which were a knot faster on the surface and half a knot faster submerged). However, it was £6000 less than for the first two and the engines were more powerful. DNC considered the funnel shown in the general arrangement objectionable.

18. Cover 306, Folio 4, Keyes memo on the three Vickers designs, which had been submitted directly to him.

19. From the Thurston notebook, courtesy of Steve McLaughlin. Unfortunately this entry is undated. The notebook entry shows dimensions of 144ft x 18ft 6in x 10ft 11in, displacements of 364/453 tons and a surface speed of 14 knots using two four-cylinder diesels, 450 BHP each at 450 RPM, with 10¾in diameter (13in stroke) diesels; maximum submerged speed was given as 9 knots (endurance 25nm) using two 150 BHP motors. Surface endurance was given as 1200nm at full speed, 2000nm at 12 knots and 3000nm at 9 knots. A parallel Design 620 was designed for Japan but not put forward (Design 618 was *Nautilus* and Design 622 its export version for Japan). The 'V' Class Cover (Folio 2) shows a beam of 16ft 6in but the same displacements and other data.

20. Cover 289, Folio 4. Vickers offered three designs, of which 'A' and 'B' were overseas submarines. The letter is in Cover 306 (*Nautilus*), Folio 2 (also in Folio 4, 3 August 1912). Design C was 139ft long, with a surface displacement of 298 tons and a surface speed of 14 knots. Vickers stated that it was specially designed to work in shallow water, its double hull covering only the midships part and extending over the top of the pressure hull. 'Great care has been paid to the watertight subdivision', the engines and the electric motors being in separate compartments. Radius of action was 3000nm at cruising speed on the surface and 85nm at economical speed submerged. Armament was two 18in bow tubes.

21. Cover 289, Folio 8, undated letter.

22. Cover 289, Folio 12, apparently dated 22 July, marked CP 0621/13. Cover 289, Folio 2, which lists characteristics of the original design, has the modified ones written in: 147ft 6in (ext) x 16ft 3in x 10ft 11in, 369/497 tons, with the same surface performance but submerged endurance 74nm at 5 knots. No maximum submerged speed associated with the more powerful motors is given.

23. Cover 354, Folio 1a, dated 26 June 1913. The letter informing Chatham of the change (Folio 2) is dated 23 July 1913. Folio 43 summarises the design as of February 1914: 150ft x 16ft x 10ft 4in, 360/530 tons, surface endurance 3000nm at 9 knots, submerged speed 8.5 knots (1 hour rate), endurance 75nm at 5 knots, complement 18.

24. Cover 354 ('F' Class), Folio 1a; Folio 1 is a series of tank capacity charts. Dimensions were 145ft 6in x 16ft x 10ft 9in, for displacements of 345/490 tons.

25. Cover 354, Folio 10.

26. Attachment to Cover 354, Folio 10, undated. Estimated cost of dockyard work was £50,000.

27. Cover 354, Folio 16.

28. Lambert, *Submarine Service*, Document 90 (ADM 1/8331) dated 14 July 1913. He envisaged a unit cost of £75,000.

29. Lambert, *Submarine Service*, Document 91, from d'Eyncourt papers [DEY/31].

30. Lambert, *Submarine Service*, Document 98, from Keyes papers. These are Keyes' notes on the meeting held in First Lord's room on 9 December 1913.

31. The December meeting seems to have initiated action on a double-hulled follow-on to the 'E' class, initially called the double-hulled 'E' and later the 'G'

class. According to Lambert, *Submarine Service*, p 236, probably continuing the account of the 9 December conference, the decision was to build three such submarines, one at Chatham and two at Vickers. Another large overseas boat was wanted, but *Nautilus* was not reproduced because Vickers would better be employed building the new 'E'-class successor. Instead, a repeat *Swordfish* was planned.

32. Lambert, *Submarine Service*, Document 101, a memo Churchill circulated together with Fisher's essay on submarines. It is dated 25 December 1914, but its content and its placement in the book indicate that it should be dated December 1913. Lambert's Document 103 is a February 1914 memo by Keyes on problems in increasing submarine production, pointing out that nearly the whole of the 1914-15 Programme has been devoted to double-hull 'E'-class submarines, which meant production by Vickers. Keyes refers to Vickers' attempt to build 'E'-class submarine for Greece.

33. Originally the 1914-15 Programme had been seven Admiralty coastals, a repeat *Swordfish* and three modified 'E'-class submarines, one by Chatham and two by Vickers.

34. Cover 330 (G Class), Folio 1. The two designs are described in Folio 3, dated 6 March 1914:

	Later 'E' Class	Vickers	Admiralty
Length (ft)	181	185	185
Main hull breadth (ft-in)	18-1½	22-6	19-0
Beam over side tanks (ft-in)	22-9	22-6	22-6
Draft (ft-in)	12-7	14-0	13-2
Surface disp. (tons)	662	780	685
Submerged disp. (tons)	807	1090	1000
Freeboard (ft-in)	5-1	6-0	4-3
	--- Vickers Engines, 1600 BHP ---		
Speed surfaced (knots)	15.25	15	15.5-16
Battery cells	224	224	200
Type	Neptune, Mercury	3400 Chloride	Latest Chloride
Motor BHP	----- 840 -----		
Submerged speed (knots)	10.25 for 1½hr	9 for 1hr	9.25 for 1hr
Surface Endurance (nm/kts)	3000/10	2600/10	Expect more than Vickers
Submerged Endurance (nm/knots) 99/3		70/5	II
Cost	Vickers abt £110,000	£140,000	Vickers £125,000
	Chatham abt £80,000	-	Chatham £100,000

All of the designs showed one 21in bow tube instead of the two 18in bow tubes of the 'E' class; the Admiralty design also showed a 21in stern tube. Both of the new designs showed single 12pdr guns (the 'E' had none). Folio 26 tabulates data corresponding to the Admiralty design. Like the table above, it does not give endurance figures. However, Folio 30 is a July 1914 tabulation, showing a calculated endurance of 2400nm at 12.5 knots and a submerged endurance of 90nm at 3 knots. Surface speed was given as 15.5 knots and submerged speed as 9.5 knots for 1 hour.

35. Cover 330, Folio 24, CP 01265/14, 18 June 1914. The original estimated price for contract construction was £140,000. The lowest contract tender (from Armstrong) for each of two submarines was £127,460 excluding torpedo tubes. Scotts asked for £135,000 and Vickers wanted £140,000. It was accepted that Armstrong could not be pressed much further because it had to pay royalties to both Schneider and Vickers.

36. Cover 330, Folio 19, 4 July 1914.

37. As noted in the DNC submarine history, p 5, but not in the Cover. The same is true of the deletion of housing planes.

38. Cover 330, report dated 30 August 1917. The boat would not break surface while at a depth of 20ft at slow speed (both motors grouped down) under sea conditions which previously would have made her broach or else considerably increase speed to increase the force exerted by the planes. Time to dive was not affected.

39. Lambert, *Submarine Service*, Document 109.

40. Churchill's 10 August request is Lambert, *Submarine Service*, Document 130, which is ADM 1/8390/256. Controller (Tudor)'s reply is the next document, dated 11 August.

41. This order is sometimes dated to 24 November, but that is impossible. On 10 November Churchill wrote about a programme in addition to the eight boats ordered ten weeks before. The crash programme was twenty-six rather than the twenty-five submarines Fisher initially envisaged. All were in addition to the 1914-15 Programme of ten submarines (three 'F' and seven 'G'). With twenty 'H' class coming from the United States (albeit many were not delivered until much later), Churchill counted a total of sixty-four submarines on stream. The big war programme was decided at an 11 November 1914 conference with rep-

resentatives of shipyards. The 1918 DNC history (p 3) claims that thirty-eight 'E' class were ordered at this time: Vickers (six), Beardmore (four), Fairfield (four), Brown (three), Scott (one), Armstrong (two), Swan Hunter (three), Palmer (two), Laird (four), White (one), Thornycroft (two) and Yarrow (four); it adds an order for two from Denny on 20 November. Two of the Beardmore boats were taken over from a Turkish order. The 26-submarine order is from Lambert and it coincides with various comments made by Fisher, so it is entirely credible. Probably the figures given in the DNC history include later orders. According to this history, one of the Yarrow boats was later cancelled and two more were transferred, one to Scotts and one to Denny, on 3 March 1915. When the crash programme began, Vickers had already received a contract for engines for four Chatham-built 'G'-class submarines and they were diverted to some of the Vickers repeat 'E'-class submarines (*E 19–E 24*). That allowed for quick completion of the 'E'-class submarines, but delayed the 'Gs'.

Chapter 6: The Ocean Submarine

1. This report is appended to the Commodore (S) printed report on British submarine design in ADM 137/2067 dated 6 April 1914. A more complete copy is ADM 1/8374/93. It is reproduced in Lambert, *Submarine Service,* pp 178–80.
2. Cover 290B, Folio 27.
3. Whitehead, which was based at Fiume, had an Electric Boat license. Marley F Hay of Denny was its designer; several Hay-Denny submarines were built in the Netherlands. Other Dutch submarines were designed by Electric Boat.
4. Cover 290B, Folio 30. In his 1914 history, ICS wrote that 'it was felt by submarine officers that our "E" design, although a good one in many ways, could not by any means be regarded as the last word, especially as it does not lend itself to further development. It was thought that we should extend the principle of high buoyancy, applying it in a more ship-shape way than the saddle tanks. It was also considered most necessary to increase the percentage of buoyancy to counteract the tendency to dive when running on the surface. An extension of the "E" class could not be driven at a higher speed than about 15 knots without considerable risk of diving, but the French and Italian types could be driven safely at considerably higher speeds.'
5. Cover 306, Folio 2. The letter enclosed three designs, of which C was for a coastal submarine discussed in the previous chapter. The designs are described, but full particulars of Design A are not enclosed. Folio 3 is particulars of Design B, which was to have two 1600 BHP diesels. Dimensions were 236ft extreme x 27ft 9in x 21ft 3in (diameter of main hull) x 16ft 6in with displacements of 1373/1851 tons; reserve buoyancy was 48 per cent of submerged displacement. Surface endurance was 2000nm at 17 knots, 3400nm at 14 knots and 5300nm at 11 knots. Total BHP of the main motors was 1000 BHP for a maximum submerged speed of 10 knots (endurance 17.5nm); endurance at 6 knots would be 72nm. A total of thirteen torpedoes would be carried. The 15 May note in the Cover is written as though Designs A and B were being submitted as alternatives, but the later submission by Keyes shows otherwise.
6. Cover 306, Folio 6, 21 June 1912.
7. Undated particulars are in Cover 306, Folio 15. Dimensions were now 240ft (LBP, not extreme) x 26ft; draft was not given; displacements were 1270/1694 tons. Surface BHP was 3700 (reversible engines, 17in diameter x 19in stroke, 340 RPM) for a surface speed of 17 knots. These engines would weigh 120 tons. Endurance was given as 2000nm at full speed, 3400nm at 14 knots and 5300nm at 11 knots, as before. Main motor power was the same 1000 BHP for 10 knots and underwater endurance was unchanged, except that it was 72nm at economical speed (not specified). These specifications showed two 18in stern tubes but one 21in bow tube instead of the two 18in previously desired. There were four 18in broadside tubes. Price was given as £203,850 (Folio 16, a handwritten summary by DNC).
8. According to BR 3043, the boat was not formally ordered until 23 April 1913. Although she was launched in 1914, work slowed once war began and other orders were far more urgent. She was completed in October 1917 and was apparently used mainly or completely as a depot ship for instructional purposes before being taken out of service in July 1919. As an indication that she never operated, there were no recorded trials figures.
9. *Nautilus* was Vickers' Design 619, described in the Thurston notebook (document courtesy of Steve McLaughlin). The notebook gives design displacement (1270/1694 tons) and dimensions (240ft x 26ft x 13ft 4½in); full speed is given as 17 knots and full submerged speed as 10 knots (endurance 17.5nm at this speed). The diesels were credited with a cylinder diameter of 17in and a 19in stroke (340 RPM), compared to 13⅞in diameter (bore) and a 15in stroke (380 RPM) for the four- and six-cylinder engines in the 'D' and 'E' classes.
10. Folio 24 of Cover 306 is the 19 April 1916 order approving the change, referring to a Vickers letter dated 14 March 1916. At the same time the external ballast tanks were to be modified to the system adopted in the 'K' class. The bow extension left the lengths of the pressure hull and of the outer hull unchanged. It may have been accepted because the ship was heavy aft, presumably due partly to overweight diesels. Even with the extension, the outer hull had to be redesigned; according to BR 3043 it was changed from a Laurenti to a Laubeuf type. Controlled free-flooding spaces were deleted and some buoyancy spaces added aft. The ship was designed with 424 tons of main ballast tanking and 63 tons of controlling free-flooding spaces, but as completed she had 585 tons of main ballast plus 11 tons of firing tanks as designed, plus (as completed) 56 tons of buoyancy tanks, 48 tons of oil fuel tanks and 9 tons of auxiliary ballast tanks. Stated submerged displacements suggest, according to BR 3043, that *Nautilus* had about 320 tons of controlled flooding space, which could not be carried in the double hull. A Vickers reference gave 415 tons of main ballast tankage and 314 tons of watertight superstructure, which together would give 58.5 per cent reserve buoyancy.
11. Cover 289A, Folio 14. Scotts' records were destroyed in a 1941 air raid.
12. Projects 140 and 140B, attributed to FIAT San Giorgio, are from Cover 289A ('S' Class), Folio 13. Data for Scotts' modified 140bis with steam turbines, dated June 1913 and Folio 13a. Unfortunately the *Swordfish* Cover (322) includes no early design information at all, only material on the ship as it was being built.

	140	140bis	140bis Modified
Displacement Surfaced (tons)	1032	820	856
Displacement Submerged (tons)	1570	1230	1024
Length Overall (ft-in)	240	224	231-1¾
Beam maximum (ft-in)	22-8¹¹⁄₁₆	23-3	23-0 (21-1⅞ mld)
Maximum draft (ft-in)	12-10¼	13-9	14-1
Freeboard (ft-in)	6-0	5-8	6-1½
Hull Depth (ft-in)	19-0	17-0	18-3⅝
Reserve of Buoyancy	50	50	50
Surface Speed (knots)	18	18.5	18
Radius/18 knots (nm)	1525	1560	N/A
Radius/10 knots (nm)	3500	3600	3000/8.5
BHP	3250	3250	N/A
Submerged Speed (knots)	10	10	10
Radius/10 knots	1 hr	1 hr	1 hr
Radius/6 knots	12 hr	12 hr	10 hr
21in bow tubes	1	2	2
18in stern tubes	2	None	None
18in broadside tubes	4	4	4

13. Cover 185A, Folio 1. The telemotors, made by McTaggart Scott, were the subject of a post-war claim to the Royal Commission on Awards to Inventors. In the 'K' class telemotors also controlled various items connected with the steam plant, such as the funnel gear and the boiler room vent. The company's tabulation showed a partial installation (9in vents) in the 'F' class and fuller installations beginning with *Swordfish* (scoops and vents) and continuing in *Nautilus* (scoops and vent valves). The 'G' class added flood valves. *J 7* had remote-controlled forward hydroplanes as well as valves. McTaggert Scott also claimed for hydraulic periscope controls.
14. D'Eyncourt papers, National Maritime Museum (DEY/31) dated 20 July 1913.
15. In October 1912 Churchill had already written to Prime Minister Asquith that 'our best and cheapest – perhaps our only – way of meeting this [Austrian fleet threat] will be by a large submarine and torpedo development supported by a fast squadron'. Hence his interest in a submarine blockade of the mouth of the Adriatic, which would keep the Austrian fleet home. Lambert, *Submarine Service*, Document 89, dated 22 October 1912.
16. ADM 1/8331, reproduced as Document 90 in Lambert, *Submarine Service*. It is dated 14 July 1914. The initial sentences in this paragraph, rejecting the ocean submarine, are from the Keyes papers in the British Library.
17. Churchill to Fisher, in Fisher papers; Document 93 in Lambert, *Submarine Service*.
18. In his October 1911 letter to Hall Keyes wrote that it was Jellicoe's dream and that it would come, but certainly not by evolving out of the current saddle-tank designs. As Controller between July 1908 and December 1910 Jellicoe was presumably well aware of the status of British submarine development. In December 1910 he took command of the Atlantic Fleet and became responsible for tactical experiments. In January 1911 Fisher wrote to Jellicoe discussing the wartime role of the Atlantic Fleet and pointing out that 'hardly anyone but yourself . . . clearly realises the immense alteration in both tactics and strategy which the development of the submarine now causes'. A Temple Patterson, *The Jellicoe Papers* (Naval Records Society, 1966) I, p 20, document 14, letter dated 10 January 1911. Fisher pointedly wrote that Admiral Sir A K Wilson, who had

just succeeded him as First Sea Lord, did not understand the implications of the submarine. The *Jellicoe Papers* include as Document 27 extracts from a long memo Fisher sent to Jellicoe in January 1914. He pressed the importance of what he called ocean submarines (actually overseas submarines) to enforce the necessary blockade of Germany, but apparently did not discuss submarines in the context of a fleet action. By 1914 Fisher was using the term 'submarine destroyer' to indicate an ASW unit, commenting that there was no thought of submarine fighting submarine. However, he continued strongly to support the idea of a fast submarine for use in a fleet action. It appears in the essay on 'The Oil Engine and the Submarine', which he circulated during 1914. The 5th edition (May 1914) is Document 96 in Lambert, *Submarine Service 1900-1918*; among the three submarine roles the fleet submarine comes first. Fisher also wrote that the problems of building and operating a large steam submarine (diesels could not generate enough power) were formidable and thus might preclude construction.

19. D'Eyncourt papers, National Maritime Museum (DEY/31), undated; NMM manuscript MS72/030. The *Swordfish* power plant was rated at 4000 SHP; the 3250 BHP figure took losses in gearing into account.

20. The hull design seems to have been tested as model UR, which provided the form for both the 'J' and the 'K' classes, according to D K Brown in *The Grand Fleet: Warship Design and Development 1906-1922* (London: Chatham Publishing, 1999), pp 124–5. The preliminary report on form UR was dated 12 April 1913, which fits with d'Eyncourt's statements on the fast submarine. However, the PRO list of Haslar reports includes a preliminary EHP curve for model VZ for the 'J' class (25 January 1915), with work on screw dimension curves dated April 1915. The final report on model experiments for this class was dated 15 June 1915. The chronology suggests that it took some time to realise that the 'J' class would have to make do with diesel power. The list of Haslar model reports in PRO does not include any for the 'K' class, although there are many for modified 'E'-class submarines, for the elongated 'E' class and also for the modified 'L' class (in 1916). That makes sense; the 'K' class could share the twin-screw hull form of the 1913 design, but the 'J' class had three shafts, hence had a different stern. Of the U-series, UY was another new submarine design of May 1913. Model tests of the new May 1913 submarine design continued at least to July 1914. Presumably this was the 'G' class.

21. Keyes papers, British Library; Keyes' Minute was dated 16 August 1913 and can be read as a comment on Churchill's interest in a larger steam submarine.

22. Keyes papers, British Library.

23. Minutes in Keyes papers; Document 99 in Lambert, *Submarine Service*, dated 9 December 1913. Much of the conference was devoted to the submarine blockade of German ports. The meeting confirmed First Lord's call for four flotillas (twelve boats each) for the blockade. Controller said that he wanted a second *Swordfish* in the 1914–15 Programme, but not a second *Nautilus* – Vickers would be better occupied in building double-hull 'E' class overseas boats (the 'G' class). The rest of the proposed 1914–15 submarine programme was two Vickers double-hull 'E' class, one dockyard double-hull 'E' class and seven Admiralty coastals.

24. Churchill Minutes II, 16, Naval Historical Branch Library; Minute dated 22 January 1914. The next day he asked about the 1915–16 Programme, which he hoped would include about £1 million for submarines, as well as four battleships. Churchill revived this idea in June 1914, as noted in CAB 1/34, reproduced in Lambert, *Submarine Service* as his Document 109. Churchill was reminding Lord Battenberg, then First Sea Lord, of changes he wanted in the 1914–15 Programme. One was to substitute fifteen improved 'E'-class submarines for one of the battleships (*Resistance*); another was to substitute six torpedo cruisers (*Polyphemus* type) for a second battleship (*Agincourt*). Four light cruisers could be substituted for ten planned destroyers or, alternatively, four extra flotilla leaders and four more improved 'Es' could replace these destroyers. Substitution was tricky because at the same time Churchill was pressing Canadian Prime Minister Borden for money to build several battleships. Borden promised the money but was unable to deliver; in a 13 July 1914 letter (Lambert, *Submarine Service*, Document 110) Churchill pointed to the need for early decisions 'in regard to the substitution of submarines and other vessels for a portion of the battleship programme'. . Lambert, *Submarine Service*, Document 112 is an extract from Churchill's draft manuscript history of the First World War, probably written in 1918, in which he explains his apparent shifts between a large battleship programme and a large submarine programme. He argues that throughout he considered the battleships units of power equivalent to particular numbers of submarines. As soon as he secured Cabinet approval for four battleships (March 1914), he converted two of them into submarines and smaller craft. First Sea Lord (Battenberg) fully supported him. He wanted to delay any announcement until after the Germans were entirely committed to their own 1914 battleship programme. Accordingly it was decided not to lay down the

last two battleships until the last moment. Churchill informed only Asquith and Chancellor of the Exchequer Lloyd George. Unfortunately by the time he wrote, Churchill might well have wanted to show how well he understood the coming importance of submarines. Churchill's memoir extract ends with the line that First Sea Lord was sent to persuade the rest of the Board and the technical departments began work on various novel projects. That may be a reference to the 'J'/'K' class.

25. For example, after the 'J' and 'K'-class submarines had been ordered, Jellicoe wrote on 8 November 1915 that 'it is quite certain that the German battle fleet will be accompanied by submarines and that we shall be at a great disadvantage if our own submarines are not in a position to take offensive action against the German battle front'. ADM 137/1926, Document 151 in Lambert, *Submarine Service*. His certainty is somewhat surprising, because the British already had a copy of the German fleet orders. They made no provision for integrating submarines into the High Seas Fleet. The British were probably aware that U-boats had participated successfully in the last pre-war German fleet exercises, but it now appears that the Germans always envisaged a distant support role for U-boats in fleet actions. Jellicoe wanted 'E'-class submarines assigned directly to him even though current plans called for British submarines to attack the High Seas Fleet as it left port or returned to it.

26. ADM 1/8547/340, dated 31 December 1918. The account refers to the UR hull form as intended for certain light cruisers and other vessels, but the list of Haslar reports associates it only with the 1913 submarine.

27. BR 3043.

28. DNC note about submarine seakeeping, Cover 185A, Folio 157. DNC was answering a paper written by Captain Max Horton, at the time Captain (S) of 5th Submarine Flotilla. Horton contrasted the behaviour of the 'J' class in a seaway with the steadiness of the 'M' class.

29. Cover 185A, Folio near the end of the Cover, S.O. 4865/25, a paper on a proposal to buy Sulzer diesels, presumably for repeat *X 1*s.

30. Paper coded MS 72/030 in DEY/31, National Maritime Museum.

31. DNC 1918 history, 9. The 'K' Class Cover does *not* include this design. The DNC history suggests that as Vickers was building 'J'-class diesels, the company became aware that they offered only limited surface speed. BR 3043 attributes the project to Vickers' usual foresight, but the whole history of British submarine design over the previous few years could be read as proof that was lacking.

32. Dimensions were 280ft x 28ft x 23ft hull depth, 2000 tons surfaced and 2760 tons submerged. Armament would have been four bow and four broadside tubes, all 18in, plus one 4in gun and one 12pdr.

33. According to BR 3043, with 197 tons of oil endurance was 800nm at 24 knots. With emergency fuel (oil in some main ballast tanks), endurance at that speed was 1200nm. By way of contrast, with the diesel endurance was 12,700nm at 10 knots and over 19,000nm with emergency fuel. Some years after completion DNC gave a figure of 12,500nm with normal fuel.

34. A 'K'-class Legend produced on 13 November 1925 (in Cover 353A, Folio 7) for the surviving units showed speeds of 24 knots surfaced and 9.5kts submerged; but it may have been a simple reproduction of an earlier, lost, Legend. It also showed as armament two 4in guns and two Lewis guns plus the torpedo tubes. This Legend covered the surviving units: *K 2*, *K 6*, *K 12*, *K 14* and *K 22*.

35. Figures from BR 3043.

36. 'K' Class Cover, Folio 4.

37. According to the 1918 DNC history, Vickers was invited to tender on 4 May 1915. The Cover gives no indication at all of when design work began or of what the stated requirements were.

38. Cover 353 ('K' Class), Folio 4, 'Submarine, Design of', appears to show that the sketch design submitted by DNC and Commodore (S) was approved by Controller on 3 May 1915; details of machinery were to be decided as soon as possible by DNC, EinC and DEE. DNC's submission of draught and general arrangement plus particulars was dated 21 April 1915. At this point four submarines were planned. DNC proposed forwarding the drawings to Vickers and inviting them to tender for two. By this time the gun armament had been set at two 4in guns and one 3in HA gun; DNO wrote that separate action would be taken to obtain the desired 4in mounting. Tabulated particulars showed four bow and four broadside tubes, length between perpendiculars of 320ft (beam 26ft 6in), displacement 1650 to 1700 tons surfaced and 2650 tons submerged, speed 24 knots surfaced (on 10,000 to 12,000 SHP) and 9 to 9.5 knots submerged (two 750 BHP motors). Endurance was given as 1100nm at 24 knots, 3000nm at cruising speed and 55nm submerged. In addition to the two steam turbines, the ship would have an 800 BHP diesel, which would give a speed of 10.25 knots.

39. Cover 353, Folio 29.

40. Folder C-84-30 to 84-89, US Confidential OpNav records 1917-19, National Archives. This paper is dated 10 December 1917 and it was sent by the CinC US Atlantic Fleet to CNO.

41. On one occasion (unofficial figures) *K 8* submerged in 3 minutes 25 seconds; good diving time was 4 minutes 15 seconds. Surface speed was 24.2 knots (*K 12* on a 72-mile run). In calm weather submerged endurance was about 10 hours. Admiralty Technical History and Index, TH 21 (submarines), October 1921.

42. ADM 137/1946, letter to Admiralty dated 24 February 1918, referring to their M.02224 of 13 February 1918.

43. Cover 409 (Modified 'K' Class), Folio 21.

44. Cover 409 Folio 46 is a 15 December 1918 order to transfer three submarines from private yards to Chatham Royal Dockyard. Armstrong's *K 24* and *K 25* and Vickers' *K 26*. However, *K 26* remained at Vickers, having been too far advanced to move. Folio 49 is a 16 January 1919 letter from Vickers concerning machinery for *K 28* originally ordered from them and now assigned to Chatham. A Board Minute dated 11 March 1919 called for cancellation of eighteen submarines (three 'K', two 'H' and thirteen 'L'). An order dated 10 June 1919 cancelled *K 28* but ordered *K 26* launched at Vickers and then towed to Chatham for completion, ensuring continuity of work there. This avoided the loss entailed in scrapping *K 26*.

45. *K 26* Legend dated 16 February 1923, Cover 409, Folio 157. Speed submerged was given as 9 knots and endurance as 80nm at 1.75 knots. Surface endurance was given as 900nm at full speed and 7500nm at 12 knots with 285 tons of oil fuel.

46. Cover 409, unfortunately without a Folio number, mentioning a reference sheet dated 1 April 1919. Presumably the 3000 BHP engines were the ones later used in *X 1*. This project was mentioned in connection with one of the modified 'K's, so presumably others than *K 26* were then still being built. The letter was signed by A D Constable of DEE, 2 April 1919.

Chapter 7: Submarine and Anti-Submarine: the Run-Up to War

1. ADM 1/7725, dated 31 May 1903 for the Board. This paper seems to have been written to support the argument that submarines were a preferable substitute for the mine defence of ports. Bacon's paper was not too different from contemporary US comments about the value of submarines for port defence.

2. 'Tactical and other Exercises of Submarine Boats, 1 June to 31 December 1903', ADM 1/7719 (a typed copy with further papers is in ADM 1/7725). Bacon wrote that he had 'never anticipated that the engines, batteries and motors would have behaved so uniformly satisfactorily during such continuous use'. Repairs had been carried out almost entirely by the crews. Because his readers were unlikely to have any idea of submarine operations, Bacon felt obliged to discuss weather limitations. 'In plain words, is a Holland Boat useless because normally she cannot operate in the open sea in weather usually associated with a force of wind of 6 or more? Mind I am only discussing Holland Boats and our new type ['A' class] should be far more sea worthy.' Bacon distinguished absolute reliability under all conditions from utility as an adjunct to other defences. The other harbour defences were gunfire, mines and torpedo craft, the latter to keep an enemy's ships at a distance at night, when gunners would be handicapped. Submarines would assist gunfire in moderate weather, rendering destruction of a ship certain if it came too close. Submarines could also help defend unguarded stretches of the coast, by operating offensively. They could work under every kind of weather in waters where minefields were currently laid. A sea that would handicap a 'Holland' boat would also preclude any attempted landing. Moreover, Bacon had not yet tried a boat in a wind above Force 6. The great limit in such a sea was the low conning tower, limiting view to the periscope. In misty weather it was difficult to pick up an object, though it could be kept in view. Exercises were: (A) attacking the torpedo gunboat *Hazard* while steaming along a channel 25nm long and 3 wide; (B) attacking *Hazard* while she maintained a position within a predetermined area of 100nm²; (C) defending Sandown against bombardment by using Sandown Bay as a base and attacking *Hazard* as she approached from seaward; and (D) at a greater distance from the base, holding a line and attacking *Hazard* if she tried to cross in any direction. Numbers of attacks, with successful/unsuccessful/doubtful in parentheses, were: 6 A (5/1/0), 2 B (2/0/0), 9 C (6/3/0) and 3 D (2/0/1).

3. Second Annual Report of the submarine flotilla, ADM 1/7795, marked A.861/1905.The comments on ASW are by ICS Bacon. Vice Admiral A K Wilson formulated destroyer (and other) instructions for the attacking fleet. ASW weapons were a hand charge, a towing charge, an indicating net and a lasso net with a charge. The first two were to be used when the periscope could be seen, the latter two when the submarine was completely submerged. The hand charge was an 18½lb guncotton tin attached to a short line with a running noose; it was to be put over the periscope using a long light boathook staff. The towing charge was similar, with a grapnel to catch the periscope. It could be

fired by the destroyer. The indicating net was 120 fathoms (720ft) long and 6 fathoms deep, each mesh about 2 fathoms square, each vertical line being weighted at the bottom. It would be laid across the probable track of a dived submarine. The net carried a buoy with a flag, the idea being that a submarine caught in the net would cause the flag to turn in the appropriate direction. Unfortunately the problem of laying the net very rapidly had not yet been solved. The lasso net was intended to destroy a submarine which had been caught in the indicator net; it used a shorter net (8 x 6 fathoms, with the charge at one end); it would be dropped ahead of a submarine whose approximate position and course had been given by the buoy of the indicator net. When the submarine was caught in it and the wire hauled in, the running noose would be rounded up and the charge brought into position. There was also a preliminary experiment with a combined net and towing charge. These weapons were not too different from those available in 1914. Wilson successfully revived the indicator net at that time. In theory, when the two closest destroyers tried to close in on a submarine they had spotted, one would turn onto the course of the submarine to give it only an end-on shot. The other would turn up under the submarine's stern, trying to use the hand charge and then the towing charge. If the submarine dived, the first destroyer would be in a good position to spread the indicating net in her path. Picket boats but not destroyers could use hand charges, destroyers simulating their use. Although it would be helpful to run down the submarine periscope in wartime, in the manoeuvres that had to be avoided. Before the manoeuvres, Bacon wrote about the constant anxiety his boats would cause in an enemy fleet. Bacon's detailed orders show that post-attack escape was a new concept; it would be best to take a long 'dive' in an unexpected direction, with periscope down (a drawing showed a 25° turn away from the direction in which a torpedo had been fired). Sketches showed that it was safe to fire from abaft the beam, dangerous to fire from ahead of the beam, because in that case the submarine's turn away would not take her far enough from the target ship. Early in the manoeuvre the destroyer *Hasty* managed to get *Holland No 1* in her indicating net, just missed with her lasso net and caught her with her towing grapnel. The submarine repeatedly dived but had to surface and surrender to avoid damage to her periscope. *Holland No 2* surrendered after she lost her bearings while submerged for 1¾ hours. Before that she managed to torpedo the battleship *Royal Oak*. On another day *Holland No 4* put up her periscope so close to the destroyer *Hardy* that she could have been attacked with a hand charge; she later surfaced and would have been destroyed by gunfire. *Holland No 1* managed to rise under a destroyer, breaking her periscope; she was ruled sunk by gunfire after she surfaced nearby. A destroyer managed to follow the line of bubbles left when *Holland No 2* dived, putting her out of action when she suddenly surfaced nearby.

4. Admiralty Technical History and Index TH 40, 'Anti-Submarine Development and Experiments Prior to December 1916' (September 1920), OU 6171/23, formerly CB 1515(40), 8. Copies in RN Historical Branch and also PRO ADM 275/20. Initially the Submarine Committee consisted of a flag officer, a captain, a commander and a secretary. Quite soon it included submarine officers. This paper includes the 20 April 1910 report of the Submarine Committee. The quotations are from the submariners' answer, presumably provided by ICS. Cover 290B Folio 39 summarises the work of the Submarine Committee between 1910 and 1912, but TH 40 carries the story through 1914. The 1910–12 summary was signed by Rear Admiral B Currey and by Rear Admiral W Tupper, who was President of the Committee.

5. This seems a rather odd view of normal fleet cruising disposition, which would be much more concentrated. Integration of destroyers with the battle fleet was just being discussed and limited destroyer endurance made it difficult. Presumably the sweeps and grapnels were those tried in 1904.

6. ADM 116/3493. Fisher's remarks are in the discussion on 4 July 1912, p 14. According to the CID index for the period 1906–12, this was the first occasion on which it discussed the defensive impact of submarines.

7. ADM 137/1926, p 415. The outer screen consisted of destroyers five cables apart. The rear screen was 1500 to 2500 yds ahead of the fleet.

8. ADM 137/1926, p 409, dated 29 July 1913, addressed to CinC Home Fleets. Bayly's suggested defences were light cruisers about two miles from the battle fleet, on bearings from before the beam to right ahead; aircraft patrol the approaches to bases up to about 30nm to sea; the use of high speed (at night) by ships arriving at or leaving their coaling bases; specially trained lookouts; and the use of only a single mast, to make it more difficult for the submarine to estimate a ship's course. He doubted that destroyers would be useful escorts.

9. ADM 137/1926, p 420, 10 August 1913.

10. After further investigation Keyes wrote that due to abnormal water conditions, *D 8* heard the propellers at a much greater distance than normal, giving her CO the impression that the fleet had altered course and was passing over his head. 'The plot on his mooring [plotting] board was apparently very correct and he

reports that if he had not heard the propellers so distinctly, he would, after passing under the inner screen, have come up in a position to attack the first or second ship. As it was, he waited until he was clear of the last ship and then came up to find himself in a position to attack the rear ship of the line at a range of 600 yds (taken from his periscope scale). He reports that three minutes after he was in a position to fire and while on the surface he fixed his position by sextant angle as 1400 yds on the quarter of the last ship': ADM 137/1926, p 432.

11. ADM 137/1926, p 431, part of a follow-on report dated 21 August 1913. This report included Keyes' argument that submarines not be sent into the Heligoland Bight and his estimate that a submarine blockading the German coast would spend three days on station, three days on passage there and back and six days resting and making good defects; hence four flotillas would be needed in winter. Keyes argued that losses in the Heligoland Bight would be heavy, at least early in a war. Apart from the risk of being caught on the surface in hazy weather and destroyed by gunfire, there would be a risk of being stalked on the surface and sunk by U-boats.

12. ADM 1/8331, dated 14 July 1913. According to this paper, experience to date had shown that a maximum of three submarines would be the most effective unit; on this basis open-sea submarines should be organised in three to four such subdivisions. Of each pair, one could be at sea while the other rested. It appears that the War Staff referred to the 1913 manoeuvres as last (fiscal) year's manoeuvres; the account of the 1912 manoeuvres certainly does not emphasise the submarine role.

13. According to Willem Hackmann, *Seek & Strike: Sonar, Anti-Submarine Warfare and the Royal Navy 1914-1954* (London: HMSO, 1984), p 9, the Submarine Committee never considered sound detection, although beginning in 1909 the Royal Navy considered and then adopted sound signalling. The two alternative detectors were single microphones (in port and starboard tanks) advocated by the American Submarine Signal Company and multiple microphones attached directly to the hull (developed by John Gardner, of the British Submarine Signal Co.). To overcome extraneous noise, Gardner tuned his microphones to the frequency of the bells used for signalling. Lieutenant R G Hervey improved this technique by cutting a small hole in the hull, closing it with a diaphragm tuned to 1024 Hz and placing the hydrophone in the centre. The entire device was enclosed in a small steel trunk. By 1911 the Royal Navy had four ships and a submarine fitted with the Hervey-Gardner microphone. It turned out to be unsuited to sound telegraphy (it was conceived to hear navigational bell signals), but in 1915 it was the only shipboard device which could detect noisy U-boats.

Chapter 8: The First Submarine War

1. From 1914–16, 1917, January–June 1918 and July–December 1918 reports by Commodore (S), ADM 137/2077.
2. CAB 37/122.
3. Cover 185, Folio 2, Admiralty order of 29 March 1912. The reorganisation took effect on 1 May 1912. Nine Sections were defined, with peacetime headquarters: 1st (Devonport: *A 7–A 9*), 2nd (Portsmouth: *A 5–A 6, A 13, B 1*), 3rd (Devonport: *B 3–B 5, C 14–C 15*), 4th (Portsmouth, to Dover when that harbour was completed: *C 16–C 18, C 31–C 35*), 5th (Harwich: *C 1–C 6*), 6th (Harwich: *C 7–C 10, C 12–C 13*), 7th (Dundee, until Rosyth was ready: *C 19–C 30*), 8th (Portsmouth: *D 1–D 8*) and 9th (Lamlash: *A 10–A 12*).
4. Soon after the outbreak of war a Captain (S) was appointed to command the Harwich submarines, Commodore (S) taking over administration of the service as a whole.
5. Of ten 'A'-class submarines still existing in 1914, *A 13* was laid up in October 1914, presumably because of its unique engine. *A 2* and *A 4* were on harbour service at Portsmouth, *A 5* and *A 6* were in the 2nd Flotilla at Portsmouth, *A 8* and *A 9* were in the 1st Flotilla at Devonport and *A 10–A 12* were in the 9th Flotilla at Ardrossan (in 1915–16 *A 10* and *A 12* were in the 4th Flotilla at Dover). By 1918 surviving units were being used for training.
6. The test of submarine coastal defence was the Hartlepool Raid of December 1914. *C 9* was in the harbour when the Germans appeared. Their shellfire forced her to dive. Unfortunately she grounded and she could not get off in time to attack the Germans. In September 1914, sixteen submarines were assigned to local defence flotillas and thirty-two to four patrol flotillas. Local defence flotillas were the 1st at Devonport (two 'A' class), 2nd at Portsmouth (*B 1* and three 'A' class including *A 13*), 5th at the Nore (six 'C' class) and 9th at Ardrossan (one destroyer, three 'A' class, formerly the Ardrossan Flotilla). Patrol flotillas were 3rd at Devonport (three 'B' class plus three 'C' class detailed to Dover), 4th at Dover (seven 'C' class plus *D 1* and *S 1*), 6th on the Humber (six 'C' class) and 7th on the Forth (twelve 'C' class). The 4th Flotilla was the submarine arm of the Dover Patrol. The July 1915 *Navy List* showed two patrol flotillas, 6th on the Tyne (eight 'C' class) and 10th on the Humber (four 'C' class,

W 1 and *W 2*), renumbered in September 1916 as the 2nd and 3rd. As of January 1916 local defence forces were 1st Flotilla in Devonport (*A 8* and *A 9*), 2nd Flotilla in Portsmouth (two 'A' class, two 'B' class and the new *G 1*), 5th Flotilla in The Nore at Sheerness (the Thames Estuary: six 'C' class), 7th Flotilla in the Firth of Forth and 9th Flotilla on the Clyde (two 'A' class and *B 4*). The presence of *G 1* in the Portsmouth Flotilla indicated that it was more a training and trials organisation than a true local defence force; that would be obvious later. The local defence flotillas were renumbered in September 1916, the Portsmouth Flotilla (6th) becoming more obviously the trials and training organisation. Thus on completion *N 1* (ex-*Nautilus*) was assigned to the 6th Flotilla as a training ship. She was never fully operational. It must have become evident through 1917 that invasion was less and less likely. The two surviving coastal flotillas were training organisations: *B 3* at Rosyth, the fleet base in the Firth of Forth, as an ASW training submarine (comprising the whole of the 7th Flotilla) and a mixed group at Portsmouth (*C 4, C 20, C 28, F 1, F 2, N 1* and the new *L 1*).

7. It is not clear when the Mediterranean force was formed. The January 1912 list showed *B 9*, but not the others, in Section 1 in home waters. Through 1913 local defence submarines were not included in the *Navy List*, but *B 6–B 11* were not listed among the flotillas in home waters. Nor were *C 36–C 38*. These submarines appear in the September 1914 *Navy List*, which was presumably updated to August. In January 1915 *B 6–B 8* were still assigned to Gibraltar and not to the Mediterranean Fleet.
8. Lambert, *Submarine Service*, Document 113 from ADM 137/1926. Keyes planned to have the submarines towed much of the way by, respectively, the cruiser *Amethyst* and a destroyer from the Harwich Force. Tows would be slipped off Terschelling Light on the Dutch coast. Submarines would remain in the Heligoland Bight no more than three days (two if they did not find themselves well placed for offensive operations).
9. Admiralty Staff Monograph 8 in Admiralty Staff Monographs (Fleet Issue) Vol II (July 1921), *Naval Operations Connected with the Raid on the North-East Coast. December 16th, 1914*.
10. Lambert, *Submarine Service*, Document 122, Keyes to Jellicoe, 10 October, from ADM 137/1926, laying out the condition of the submarine flotilla (presumably the one at Harwich) and some plans.
11. ADM 137/2077, summary reports by Commodore (S) for 1914–16, 1916–17, January–June 1918 and July–December 1918. This volume includes reports by British submarines operating in the Dardanelles and in the Baltic.
12. Renumbering was ordered on 8 August 1916 and became effective on 20 August: ADM 137/1926.
13. He cited torpedoing of the cruiser *München* and the battleships *Westfalen*, *Kronprinz* and *Grosser Kurfürst*. *Grosser Kurfürst* and *Kronprinz* were both torpedoed by *J 1* on 5 November 1916. *Westfalen* was torpedoed by *E 23* on 19 August 1916. The claim about *München* seems to have been erroneous. Commodore (S) claimed seven U-boats sunk.
14. Commodore (S) wrote off submarine vs submarine as 'providing [only] a sporting chance of destroying the enemy . . . an attack is most difficult and hits are seldom obtained owing to the difficulty of estimating one submarine's course and speed through the periscope of another'. However, anti-submarine patrols had a definite moral effect on the enemy.
15. Commodore (S) followed with a series of requests for commendations for particular officers. He proposed a DSCO for Commander Ernest W Leir, who had made seventeen cruises into the Heligoland Bight, during which he was repeatedly in action.
16. The Turkish battleship *Messudieh* was torpedoed on 13 December 1914 by *B 8*. The Turkish battleship *Barbarossa* was sunk on 8 August 1915 by *E 11*. The armoured cruiser was the German *Prinz Adalbert*, torpedoed on 23 October 1915 in the Baltic by *E 8*. It is not clear which other ship was meant in the British mid-1917 report. In his December 1916 report Commodore (S) claimed two battleships sunk and four hit; two battlecruisers hit; one cruiser sunk (*Prinz Adalbert*); two light cruisers sunk (*Hela* was torpedoed by *E 9* on 13 September 1914 and *Undine* was torpedoed by *E 19* on 7 November 1915) and two hit; six destroyers sunk and two hit; four gun vessels sunk and one hit; twenty submarines sunk and one hit; seven armed auxiliaries sunk and three captured; eighteen transports/unarmed auxiliaries sunk and four hit; fifty merchant steamers sunk and four captured; and 207 sailing ships sunk.
17. An English translation of the draft orders dated January 1914 was printed in a small bound volume dated that October. The orders may have been obtained when the German cruiser *Magdeburg* grounded in the Baltic on 26 August 1914; she was supposedly the source of German codebooks. A copy of these orders appears in the collection of German tactical publications in NHB. A copy of the bound October 1914 version is in PRO.
18. Lambert, *Submarine Service*, Document 152 (from ADM 137/1926) is a 17

November 1915 Admiralty message to Jellicoe informing him that the 11th Submarine Flotilla was being formed to support the Grand Fleet, roughly analogous to the role of the Harwich submarines (8th Flotilla). Its phrasing ('it was always intended that the 11th Flotilla should co-operate with the Grand Fleet') suggests much earlier planning. The North Sea was divided into zones in which the 11th and 8th Flotillas could operate to avoid blue-on-blue. Based on Blyth, the Flotilla would also be responsible for defence north of Flamborough Head; its Captain (S) would cooperate with the Rear Admiral Commanding East Coast. The line dividing the two areas of Flotilla responsibility was repeated in Grand Fleet Orders; submarines could cross it only under direct Admiralty control.

19. Letter from Admiral Jellicoe to Admiralty, 29 October 1915, in ADM 137/1926. The 'C' class had been assigned to Scapa over the winter. A 4 November 1915 letter to Jellicoe reminds him that the 'E' class are too slow to accompany the Fleet; 'J' and 'K'-class submarines would be allocated but they would not be available for quite some time. The four ex-Turkish destroyers of the *Talisman* class were allocated to work with the Grand Fleet submarines, reinforcing the *Firedrake* and *Lurcher* already assigned. Such linking ships were necessary until submarines received long-range W/T from 1916 on. The 8 November letter from Jellicoe to the Board pressing for submarines was a reply to this one, i.e., to the Admiralty's delay in forming the promised 11th Flotilla. The Admiralty reminded Jellicoe that the 'C'-boats had been lent to him only for use with trawlers. Since this ruse was now known to the enemy (see the discussion on submarine vs submarine), they would be returned to their original base at Rosyth.

20. ADM 137/289, a collection of Grand Fleet Battle Orders dated 17 January 1916 through 16 January 1918. Fleet cruising speed was 16 knots, which was faster than the 'E' and 'G' classes. Maximum and sea speeds for the various classes were given in March 1916 Grand Fleet submarine orders as: 'D' class 13/11 knots, 'E' and 'G' classes 14/12 knots and 'J' class 19.5/16 knots. The 'E' and 'G' classes would remain in 11th Flotilla only until the 'J' class were available. Jellicoe to Admiralty, 3 February 1916 in ADM 137/1926 describes a meeting with Commodore (S) to discuss 11th Flotilla. Hall approved the submarine tactics now embodied in the Grand Fleet Battle Orders and also the routes laid down for the rendezvous between the submarines at Blyth and the fleet. Future composition would be six 'G' and six 'J'-class submarines and four *Talisman*-class destroyers. 'D', 'E' and 'H'-class submarines assigned to the Flotilla would return to Harwich as soon as the 'G' and 'J'-class submarines arrived. Jellicoe also laid down the organisation he wanted once 'K'-class submarines arrived. Their crews would live on board, like those of destroyers, and the flotilla would have a leader (like a destroyer flotilla) but no depot ship. The leader would accommodate Captain (S) and his staff. Jellicoe assumed that the 'J' and 'K'-class submarines would be delivered with Poulsen (i.e., long-range) W/T. As soon as the 'Js' and the four destroyers detailed as leaders had been fitted with Poulsens, the *Iron Duke* and the flagships of the 1st, 2nd and 4th Battle Squadrons and the Battlecruiser Fleet should be fitted with them, in that order, so that they could communicate with the fleet submarines (instead the Admiralty authorised a Poulsen station at Wick or on board the old battleship *Victorious*). Jellicoe also pointed out that for submarines operating with the fleet to 'brown' the enemy's battle line they needed long-range torpedoes. Commodore (S) agreed; these submarines should have torpedoes with ranges of 7000 to 8000 yds. At this time the Admiralty was considering Jellicoe's request for much longer-range torpedoes for his battleships. It seemed that the Germans were now using their submarines to attack at night and Jellicoe and Commodore (S) wanted the same capacity for British submarines, which in February 1916 were expected to wait until daylight to attack.

21. From a substitute Grand Fleet Battle Orders p 46 dated 22 August 1916. The envisaged compositions of the Flotillas was: 10th: *G 7–G 14, E 39, E 40, E 44, E 49*; 11th: *G 1–G 6, J 1–J 6*; 12th: *K 1–K 8* (or first eight delivered); 13th: *K 9–K 14* (or next six delivered). In fact as of September 1916 only the first two flotillas existed. The 10th was now roughly what the 11th had been, with *E 44* and six 'G'-boats (*G 7–G 12*). The 11th had the rest of the 'G' and 'J' classes: *G 1–G 6* and *J 1–J 6*. Presumably the decision had been made to concentrate all the 'G' class in one place, leaving the earlier 'E' class in Harwich. In December 1916 another two submarines were added to the 10th Flotilla: *E 44* and *G 13*. Now the fast steam-powered 'K' class began to enter service. A 12th Flotilla was added: in April 1917 it comprised *K 1–K 4, K 6–K 8* and *K 11*. In June another K-boat flotilla was added (13th), initially with *K 9, K 11* and *K 14*. The Grand Fleet now had two slow and two fast submarine flotillas. New slow submarines such as the 'L' class joined the 10th and 11th Flotillas. In October 1918 the 11th Flotilla consisted of 'G' and 'L'-class submarines plus, temporarily, the prototype submarine monitor *M 1*.

22. Given their very limited plotting facilities, even surfaced submarines would be

unable to work out the correct path for cooperation. 'A close study should be made of the silhouettes of the destroyers attached to submarine divisions, so that they may not be attacked and the submarines forced to dive thus losing valuable time.' Once the opposing light cruiser screens were in contact and W/T silence was no longer being maintained, 'the positions of our own and enemy ships must be plotted by the destroyers leading the submarines and a study of the movements of the various forces combined with a thorough acquaintance with the Grand Fleet Battle Orders should give a good indication of the approximate time and direction, etc. of deployment'. Beatty's 14 November orders (page 46a in the updated Grand Fleet Battle Orders) make it clear that it was up to the linking destroyers to make sense of complex navigational orders. The orders included details of patrol lines to be set up in hopes the Germans could not pass without being attacked.

23. In his post-war War College lectures on the development of Grand Fleet tactics, Thursfield did not mention this idea; instead he pointed to the turn-away as a continuing problem. The lectures survive at the National Maritime Museum.

24. According to the British Staff Monograph on the Mediterranean 1914–1915, the Italians claimed a shortage of submarines. The six 'B' class were offered; 'they had been found of little use in wide areas, though their small radius of action would be less disadvantage in the narrow waters of the northern Adriatic'. They were refitting at Malta in September 1915. According to this history, the British submarines withstood the rough sea better than the Italians – in effect a comment on Laurenti vs single-hull British designs. However, on 15 November only four of the six were fit for sea and the local British commander asked for 'C'-boats. He did not get them. *B 10* was sunk in dock by an Austrian air raid on 9 August 1916, becoming probably the first submarine ever sunk by air attack. She was salvaged but burned during repairs. The other five were withdrawn in October 1916 and converted into surface patrol craft for the Otranto Barrage.

25. Lambert, *Submarine Service*, Document 125 is Keyes' telegram to Jellicoe dated 13 October 1914: submarines *E 1, E 9* and *E 11* would leave for the Baltic the following day. They would be based at Libau.

26. Lambert, *Submarine Service*, Document 125 is the telegram Keyes sent to Jellicoe on 13 October; he had suggested this operations some weeks earlier and the submarines were leaving the following afternoon. Document 126 is a 25 October telegram from Keyes reporting to Jellicoe that the Admiralty had decided to keep the three submarines in the Baltic, 'which is certainly a more likely field for them than in the Heligoland Bight, which is boycotted by larger ships'. When they arrived, the Russian CinC complained that he had had no notice of their detailed route and that when he heard they were in the Baltic he had been compelled to cancel a large minelaying operation.

27. Lambert, *Submarine Service*, Document 148, Commander Francis Cromie (Commander, Baltic Submarine Flotilla 1916–18) to Commodore (S), 10 October 1917. By this time the developing revolution had badly sapped the Russian Baltic submarines; Cromie wrote that of seventeen boats, only five were usable and that they were being reserved against an expected German naval offensive. Cromie's submarines were being used for important missions, presumably for intelligence-gathering. Few German steamers were risking the open sea, where they could be attacked, and the lack of spares was crippling the British force. Cromie pointed out that although in theory he was subordinate to the Russian Admiral (S), he had a right of direct access to the naval commander in chief; but that post had already changed four times. Cromie wrote about his repeated requests to be allowed to carry out anti-submarine patrols. For a time in 1917 he was held back pending a planned large Russian landing in the Gulf of Riga, which was never carried out.

28. ADM 137/500, a compilation of policy papers kept by Vice Admiral Sir Henry Oliver, collected when he was Chief of Staff 1914–17. This telegram is p 100. These two submarines arrived 12 September (telegram, p 107). On 4 September Commander Lawrence RN in Petrograd asked Commodore (S) for more submarines, but nothing could be done until the next summer, when the four 'C' class were sent.

29. ADM 137/1247 includes the decision to deploy and also the report of proceedings describing the passage from Chatham to Petrograd.

30. The German official history of the war at sea refers several times to a belief that radio-equipped trawlers had betrayed the movements of the High Seas Fleet. This entirely false belief probably explains attacks on trawlers. The British were unaware of it when the submarine vs submarine account was written.

31. *U 6* on 15 September 1915 by *E 16*; *U 51* on 14 July 1916 by *H 5*; and *UC 7* on 21 August 1916 by *E 54*. This account of submarine vs submarine operations is taken largely from Admiralty Technical History TH 1, *Submarine v. Submarine* (March 1919); it was Vol 1 Pt 1 of the 'Technical History and Index'. Copy in Admiralty Library.

32. Lambert, *Submarine Service*, Document 153 is the 14 October 1916 memo; the

members were Captain Keyes, former Commodore (S), Captain Algernon H C Candy and Commander Charles J C Little, who commanded the new Grand Fleet flotilla of 'K' boats. Candy had taken over the Portsmouth submarine flotilla in 1914 and would become Assistant DNO for Torpedoes in 1918. Little had commanded the Dover Patrol submarines in 1914–15, having become commander of the 4th Flotilla in 1911; in 1915–16 he was on the staff of Commodore (S). He was FOSM in 1931–2. The committee report is Document 154, from ADM 137/1926.

33. ADM 137/1926, his HF 0022/527.

34. ADM 137/1926 also contains a more elaborate report dated the next day (2 February). Little's initial report, dated 18 January, is Lambert, *Submarine Service*, Document 156. The 2 February version is Document 158, signed by Keyes. It mentions several encounters with enemy submarines early in the war. Upon sighting each other more or less simultaneously, both submarines dived to preclude being hit. In one or two cases early in the war attacks by submerged submarines failed because they were delivered so close to the enemy that the torpedo did not have enough time to come up to running depth to hit so shallow a draft as a submarine's. Later both sides achieved successes, which made submarine commanders very wary of remaining on the surface near enemy ports. Attack opportunities became increasingly rare. This report emphasised the danger imposed on overseas submarines in the Bight, which 'suffer losses out of all proportion to the military results it is possible for them to attain under the new conditions [of intensified enemy ASW]'. As 'amply proved' by pre-war exercises, the anti-invasion role could be dismissed, because 'no reliance can be placed in submarines employed on such services, since the enemy will naturally not elect to arrive at an hour favourable for submarine attack or choose a locality in the vicinity of our submarine bases. Moreover the number available is quite insufficient to guard every likely landing place or to inflict any appreciable loss on a determined attempt at invasion.' Submarines had probably been assigned to coast defence as part of an 'ancient undertaking' to substitute them for the army's controlled coastal mines. Surely it was time to abrogate the agreement. A submarine in port was a useful deterrent, but when they shelled Hartlepool in 1914 the Germans were probably unaware of a submarine that it had arrived only a few days previously. The enemy withdrew as soon as the submarine dived; presumably, also, the bombardment of Lowestoft had been brief because of the presence of a submarine. Submarines on trade routes would 'add enormously to the anxieties and difficulties of the enemy and will tend to limit his vision to the range of a field of his periscope and his offense to the torpedo'. British submarine activity in the Marmora (near Gallipoli) had been limited by the arrival of U-boats. 'The advantage is all with the hunter . . .'

35. An Admiralty letter dated 23 March 1917 pointed out that with the Grand Fleet at Scapa, much of the East Coast, particularly the part south of Lowestoft, was open to bombardment or invasion; submarines in southern waters offered the only chance of damaging or sinking German ships attacking there. Less than a year ago German battlecruisers had shelled Lowestoft. Thus the Admiralty refused to reduce Harwich below twelve 'E' class (plus minelayers). 'Moreover, a very large portion of the German submarines which go to sea take the Southern route and there is also always a large submarine flotilla based upon Zeebrugge.' U-boats on passage through the middle and southern North Sea were very much aware of the danger of submarine attack, 'and never relax a most vigilant lookout when on the surface.'

36. The *Platypus* boats were taken from Harwich. Under this plan, dated 21 March 1917, two 'C' class taken from the Tyne would be allocated to the defence of the Humber. This allocation was far below Beatty's proposal that twenty-nine patrol submarines operate on trade routes. Also, the Admiralty allocated 'J'-class submarines to Blyth instead of the 'E' class Beatty wanted there. Harwich received twice as many 'E' class as Beatty proposed. The 'C'-class submarines there would carry out ASW patrols

37. In July 1917, *Vulcan* was at Rathmullen in southern Ireland with *E 23*, *E 32*, *E 35*, *E 48*, *E 54*, *E 56*, *H 5* and *H 8*. *Platypus* was at Killybegs in the north with all six surviving 'D'-class submarines.

38. The December 1917 *Navy List* shows the *Vulcan* flotilla reduced to five submarines: *E 23*, *E 32*, *E 54*, *H 5* and *H 8*. *E 48* had been transferred to Gibraltar. The *Platypus* division was now six submarines as well: *D 3*, *D 4*, *D 6*, *D 7*, *D 8* and *E 38*. In January, Vulcan had been relieved as depot ship but her flotilla grew, with new 'L'-class submarines: *L 1*, *L 2* and *L 7*. *D 3* and *D 4* were withdrawn from the *Platypus* group and moved to Portsmouth. *L 4* was added to the former *Vulcan* flotilla in February 1918. German activity in the North Sea was increasing, so a new East Coast Forces command was activated, including a new Local Defence and Escort Flotillas organisation. By April 1918 the southern Irish command had grown; *H 21* replaced the sunken *H 5* and it included *L 1–L 8*. The May 1918 *Navy List* shows only *H 8* in the southern Irish flotilla. It included a new relocatable flotilla using the depot ship *Ambrose*, with sub-

marines formerly in the southern Irish flotilla: *E 43* (paid off), *E 54* and *L 1–L 8*. As the U-boat war kept moving, in June 1918 *Vulcan* was servicing four 'H'-class submarines (*H 8*, *H 11*, *H 12* and *H 14*). *H 14* paid off in July. That month the *Platypus* flotilla now grew to *D 7–D 8*, *E 23*, *E 38*, *E 32* and the new ASW submarine *R 7*. In August, two more 'R' class were added: *R 8* and *R 11*. In September 1918 the *Ambrose* flotilla was at Portsmouth with eight 'L'-class submarines (*L 1–L 8*). In October *R 1* was at Portsmouth, presumably for training. The November 1918 *Navy List* showed a final new 14th Flotilla at Blyth, with *Vulcan* as depot ship, with a combination of small submarines: eight 'H' class (*H 8*, *H 11*, *H 12*, *H 23*, *H 24*, *H 25*, *H 26* and *H 41*) and three 'R' class (*R 1*, *R 2* and *R 9*). *Platypus* had retired from the Coast of Ireland command (she was still there in October 1918). The *Ambrose* Flotilla was at Devonport.

39. According to the Technical History, she was 'apparently waiting to communicate with another U boat'; probably that means that she was caught using signals intelligence, much as many supply U-boats were wiped out in 1943. During the First World War the Royal Navy did not hesitate to take action on such information, apparently not fearing that the Germans would realise that their communications had been compromised. There is every evidence that they were right to do so.

40. ADM 137/834, Operations Committee Minutes and Memoranda, September 1917 – December 1918, p 15. This paper listed recent anti-submarine shots. *C 7* hit at 400 yds, but when *E 42* fired from 7 points on the bow at a *UC*-class submarine at that range, one torpedo passed under the cut-away of the submarine, which presented a target only 80 to 90ft long. Similarly, *E 47* fired from 6 points on the bow of a *UC* type submarine at 400 yds and missed just ahead, the submarine having stopped after steaming in circles. *E 43* fired from 2 points abaft the bow at 1000 yds. *V 1* fired from 2 points abaft at 800 yds; the enemy just evaded by turning away. *E 47* fired from 7 points abaft at 850 yds, *E 33* from 4 points abaft at 1200 yds and *E 46* fired from 4 points abaft at 1200 yds. One suggestion was to increase the number of torpedoes per submarine. There was insufficient capacity to make more torpedo tubes, but it was possible to add external Drzewiecki frames, which the French used (and could supply). Typically four frames could be added to existing overseas submarines and two to coastals. Torpedoes in beam tubes could be supplied with 90° angled gyros to add to bow fire. The main objection to the frames was the loss of underwater speed, but the frames could be streamlined (as in *W 1* and *W 2*, which had them when completed). To some extent the extra drag could be compensated for by removing the 3in HA gun, which was apparently of little use. At this time work was already underway on a submarine with high underwater speed, the 'R' class. The Sub-Committee on Torpedo and Gun Armament in Submarines (p 32: Third Sea Lord, Controller, Commodore (S) and DNC) recommended against the frames, arguing that the Royal Navy had little experience of them, apart from some fitted to E-boats in the Baltic; the frames on *W 1* and *W 2* had been of French type and would have to be obtained there, introducing difficulties. The system used in the Baltic was judged not completely suitable for open waters; much trial and alteration would be needed. Manoeuvring and diving would be affected and torpedoes might be damaged in deep dives. Certainly underwater speed would be considerably reduced. It had already been much affected by wartime alterations such as installation of W/T. 'It is not practicable to convert by any means submarines designed six to ten years ago into the most modern types.' By way of contrast, it would be easy to increase ahead firing by modifying torpedo gyros to turn broadside torpedoes 90° upon firing.

41. The paper from the Grand Fleet Committee has not surfaced, but its content is clear from the remarks by Commodore (S) in the Operations Committee file. Currently the 'C' class had no gun at all; it should have a Lewis gun. Larger submarines should have the 4in gun (coastals would get 3in guns). At present the 'E' class had 12pdr 8 cwt guns, the 'G' class 3in HA and some 'H' class had 6pdr HA guns. The 'J' class and the 'K' class had 3in HA guns. Commodore (S) pointed out that this was an entirely new idea; 4in guns had not yet been tested on board *J 1* and *L 3* and the vital rapid-manning provision had been dropped. The Admiralty had initially concentrated on gaining surprise in any gun attack. There had been no instance of one submarine hitting another with gunfire and the U-boats had been given good guns to deal with unarmed merchant ships, not submarines. When merchant ships were given more guns, the Germans took to torpedo attacks. 'It is considered incredible that German submarines sent out to attack commerce will have instructions admitting of their conducting surface gun actions with our submarines.' Guns would be useful only in surprise attacks, hence the installation proposed for the 'L' class.

42. Operations Committee Minutes of 17 October 1917, p 29 in ADM 137/834.

43. Admiralty Technical History and Index, TH 21 (submarines), October 1921, p 7.

44. ADM 137/1946, p 514. The proposal was dated 21 April 1917. It was from Lieutenant Commander R L Ramsay of *J 6*.

45. ADM 137/1946, p 544.
46. ADM 137/1946, pp 567–9.
47. ADM 137/1946, p 589.
48. Report of Signal School dated 1917 (issued 1919), ADM 186/753. These sets operated at sonic frequencies rather than at the higher (supersonic) frequencies of Asdics (sonars). Fessenden equipment was widely used at the time. S/T died as Asdic was developed; Asdic always included a signalling function
49. Hackmann, *Seek & Strike*, p 74 writes that Types 102 and 103 were conceived about 1917, both using Fessenden's 1913 oscillator operating at sonic frequency.
50. Data mostly from Admiralty Technical History and Index, TH 21 (submarines), October 1921, p 17.
51. Writing after the war, Grubb described a pre-war unifocal instrument with a 3⅜in diameter upper head with a 48° field of view. During the war, the upper tube was reduced to 2in diameter (2½in head) with a 40° field of view. The pre-war bifocal had a 3⅜in diameter head and a 50° field (length was 24ft 3in); there was also a 30ft bifocal periscope with a 4in head. Wartime development produced a bifocal periscope with a 2¾in upper tube (3¼in head), 24ft 3in long. The bifocal version had a sky-watch element, one handle controlling both sky watch and change of power. Grubb noted that during the war it had redesigned the breech pieces so that they did not have to be removed when the periscope was shipped, a very useful improvement according to the technical historian. The historian also considered the improved definition of these periscopes an important feature, although improved clarity and elimination of (spurious) colour was not so marked. A drawing in the 1921 Technical History shows a Grubb Mk XXV 30ft bifocal sky-searcher.
52. The requirement was not new, but the method was. Previously a large prism had been required outside the periscope tube, to direct the image of the sky into the periscope. KBB substituted an internal tilting prism, using a handle or lever. The double-magnification periscopes then in hand were completed with the sky-search feature as monocular ones.
53. According to a footnote in the Technical History, KBB offered excellent clarity and an absence of spurious colour, but definition could have been improved. Later periscopes by the company had better focusing arrangements. Their method of focusing, developed during the war, was also used by Barr & Stroud. Focusing involved moving the whole eyepiece system with respect to the telescope carrying light down from the window atop the periscope. That was difficult; KBB and Barr & Stroud instead moved the lower lens of the telescope up and down.
54. Based on the 1921 Technical History, which contains accounts written by the three manufacturers, not by the Admiralty.
55. Michael Moss and Iain Russell, *Range and Vision: the First Hundred Years of Barr & Stroud* (Edinburgh: Mainstream Publishing, 1988), p 112. Barr & Stroud delivered four CH 3 and three CH 4 periscopes to Portland in 1921 and a CH 7 in 1923. A binocular periscope (CK 1) ordered in 1924 (delivered 1925) offered stereo performance. The company's inclusion in the 1921 Technical History, which describes wartime developments, suggests that the company delivered at least prototypes before the Armistice. The Technical History makes it clear that by 1918 Barr & Stroud's were the best of the British periscopes. It may be describing the 1921 periscopes when it says that the company had recently produced a periscope using eight (rather than thirteen) high-power lenses and ten (rather than fourteen) for low magnification; cutting the number of lenses drastically reduced the loss of light in the tube and greatly improved definition. In the US Navy and in some other navies, the height estimator was a stadimeter. Barr & Stroud offered a 1m base length. This seems to have been unique at the time. Illustrations in the 1921 Technical History show Barr & Stroud CH 2 and CH 5 periscopes, both with 1½ x and 6 x magnification with fields of, respectively, 40° and 10°.
56. 'Browning' was an army term meaning a shot 'into the brown', i.e., a shot into the mass of the enemy. In a fleet engagement the logic of the 'browning' shot was that ships accounted for a large percentage of the total length of a battle line, so that the probability of a hit would be high. The browning concept made it possible for destroyers to attack from outside effective enemy anti-destroyer gun range. That turned out not to work, not least because torpedoes often did not run as straight as expected.
57. Included in 'Development of British Submarines', a printed paper produced by Commodore (S), in ADM 137/2067, dated 6 April 1914.
58. The director was a scale model of the attack, its three bars corresponding to the three legs of the triangle. The enemy bar had gradations indicating speed. A second bar, representing the line of sight to the target at the moment of firing, was clamped to the enemy bar at the estimated enemy speed. This bar was pointed in the direction in which the target would be seen at the moment of firing. The torpedo bar connected the enemy and submarine bars. Its angle indicated the angle at which the submarine had to be pointed when firing, the

director angle (DA). In effect Nasmith shifted attention from the line of sight to the target to the desired torpedo course. The director could be set up for bow, stern or broadside tubes. This description of the initial version of the submarine torpedo director is from a drawing in the 1915 *Vernon* (torpedo school) annual report.
59. The two sources for this discussion are a lengthy paper on British submarine command (including fire control) systems by Commander. David Parry RN on the web-site of the Barrow Submariners Association and the Admiralty Technical History (submarines), pp 20–1. Parry relied heavily on material held by the RN Submarine Museum and illustrated a number of key attack aids used early in the First World War. He collected his information to support an ongoing thesis project on the history of the 'Perisher' submarine command course. The Technical History contains a drawing of an 'Is-Was' set up for an attack, hence indicating how it was used.
60. According to Parry, it was first proposed in 1925 by Lieutenant Commander Alistair S Cumming, at that time on the staff course at Greenwich. He saw an experimental surface ship plotting board in action and suggested a circular one for submarines. It had a revolving circular surface, its circumference marked in degrees. A plotting officer could record target bearing and range; multiple plots gave target speed and course. The board was tested aboard *H 32* and *L 56* and in the attack teacher at Fort Blockhouse. In June 1927 RA(S) ordered it installed in all submarines from the 'L' class onwards. Parry considered it part of the first submarine command system, the others being the 'Is-Was', the combined slide rule, the periscope rangefinder and the patent log. In this system the plot offered situational awareness. The combined slide rule (1924) replaced and simplified earlier slide rules, but it is not clear how widely it was used. As an example of simplification, Parry cites the ability to read off range and distance off track on one rather than two slides. An earlier (1921) slide rule had five scales and multiple functions: range from masthead height; distance off track from range and inclination; speed, time, distance; speed of enemy when closing on a steady bearing; speed of enemy from range and change of bearing; and inclination of enemy based on vertical and horizontal angle.

Chapter 9: War Construction

1. ADM 1/8424/171.
2. No further 'J' class were ordered after July 1915, but twelve 'K' class were ordered in August 1915 (*K 3–K 4* were ordered in June 1915), *K 15–K 18* in February 1916, *K 19* in May 1916 and *K 20–K 21* in August 1916. Unfortunately these dates do not necessarily reflect programming.
3. ADM 137/1098 (Policy 1915, 2nd part), p 473, in the historical section summary. This section includes a summary of work to paint submarines to make them less visible from the air, in response to a Zeppelin attack on *E 18* on 14 July 1915 (the submarine was then submerged at 80 to 100ft).
4. ADM 1/8478/209. A summary showed sixty-nine submarines then under construction: thirty-four 'E' class, three 'F' class, fourteen 'G' class, six 'J' class, four 'K' class, one 'S' class, three 'V' class, two 'W' class, and *Nautilus* and *Swordfish*. This list did not include any submarines at Yarrow. It did show, for each yard, the number of destroyers under construction, since to an extent destroyers competed with submarines for slips. The 82-submarine figure for oversea submarines would be reached in July 1916. The coastal figure (sixty-seven in July 1916) omitted eight 'A' class shortly to be paid off. Another table showed approximate costs to build 'G' and 'K'-class submarines by contract under peacetime and wartime conditions. A 'G'-class submarine would cost £130,000 in peacetime, but £173,400 in wartime. A 'K'-class submarine which would cost £250,000 in peacetime would cost £333,400 under war conditions.
5. The post-war DNC history does not mention the missing numbers in the 'L' class.
6. The *L 50* Cover includes a 7 February 1917 Admiralty note designating the two submarines just ordered from Cammell Laird as *L 50* and *L 51*. Folio 4 is a 19 February 1917 statement of the four planned orders. In fact Armstrong only built one of them. The twelve-boat November 1916 programme is from the *L 50* Cover.
7. ADM 137/834 (Operations Committee), pp 161–2.
8. ADM 137/834, p 173.
9. Modified 'K' Class Cover, Folio 2.
10. ADM 137/834, p 246.
11. Vickers tendered on 30 January and the Admiralty accepted on 14 February (Cover 368, Folio 13). The *L 50* Cover includes a 7 February 1917 Admiralty order to Ship Branch stating that the twelve submarines recently ordered from Vickers were to be designated *H 21* through *H 32*.
12. *H 21–H 32* were ordered January–February 1917 and *H 33–H 54* in June–July 1917, but a fleet order of 20 November 1917 announced cancellation of *H 35–H 40* (Cammell Laird), *H 45–H 46* (Armstrong) and *H 53–H 54* (Devonport).

Note that papers for the 'R' class generally stated that eight 'H'-boats had to be cancelled in favour of eight 'R' class.

13. The political background is from Gaddis Smith, *Britain's Clandestine Submarines 1914-1915* (Archon Books, 1975; reprint of 1964 book from Yale University Press in a series of Yale historical publications). Canada obtained two submarines building at the Seattle Construction & Drydock Company for Chile: *Iquique* and *Antofagasta*. After receiving a warning from the Admiralty that a German cruiser was operating offshore, Sir Richard McBride, the premier of British Columbia, bought the two submarines, which had not been paid for. They arrived just before a US cruiser could intercept them as non-neutral. Both were of Electric Boat design (Electric Boat designed submarines but subcontracted construction, modified versions of the US Navy's 'E' class [designs EB 19B and 19E], but with a stern torpedo tube). They were designated *C-1* and *C-2*. These events prefigured the much larger controversy over US neutrality and the H-boats. Smith, *Britain's Clandestine Submarines*, pp 20–1.

14. Electric Boat had limited success exporting its submarines and it was in financial trouble by about 1903. Vickers began buying Electric Boat stock in 1902; by the end of 1903 Vickers and Isaac Rice together had a majority interest (Smith, *Britain's Clandestine Submarines*, p 11). By 1907 Electric Boat was borrowing heavily from Vickers. Vickers had to sell its interest in Electric Boat once war broke out.

15. Smith, *Britain's Clandestine Submarines*, p 30.

16. The 'H'-class submarines were the last built for the US Navy under contracts which allowed plans to be offered directly to foreign governments. That is why Electric Boat offered the 'H' class rather than the more modern 'K' or 'L' class. The 'H' class was Electric Boat's EB 26 design, three being built for the US Navy under the FY10 programme.

17. Smith, *Britain's Clandestine Submarines*, p 38. The $10 million order was equal to 25 per cent of all orders received by Bethlehem Steel during 1913. The schedule called for the first four submarines to be delivered by 24 April (5½ months), the next six by 10 July (8 months) and the last ten by 10 September 1915 (10 months). For every week in advance of the planned delivery date, Bethlehem would be paid £2000 per boat; for every week of delay, it would pay £1000 per week (the pound was then worth nearly $5.00). Bethlehem would be paid full costs plus 20 per cent in the event that the contract had to be terminated if unusual circumstances such as the end of the war or diplomatic considerations made it unnecessary or impractical to proceed.

18. Smith, *Britain's Clandestine Submarines*, p 52, reports that the companies offering to build submarines were Canadian Vickers of Montreal, the Canada Ship Building Company at Niagara and the Western Dry Dock Company of Port Arthur. Exactly how these completely inexperienced companies expected instantly to build complex submarines is unclear. Part of the background was Canadian anger that large munitions orders had gone to the United States, although some of them could be filled by Canada, which was in a depression. Canadian Vickers had been incorporated in 1911 largely in hopes that Canada would begin building warships as part of the empire naval policy then being promoted by the Admiralty. The victory of the Conservatives in the September 1911 Canadian election wrecked the Canadian naval plan; the new government was more interested in financing battleships to be built in Britain. It fell afoul of Senate opposition. Borden himself came to see construction of smaller warships in Canada for the Royal Navy as an essential element in any naval plan. After war broke out, the Canadian government asked Canadian Vickers to tender for light cruisers, destroyers and submarines for Canada (Smith, *Britain's Clandestine Submarines*, p 76) but the quoted prices were too high and the idea collapsed.

19. According to Smith, *Britain's Clandestine Submarines*, p 81, the Canadian Vickers operation was managed by the vice-president of the Union Iron Works. As a cover story, Bethlehem said that it was supplying structural steel for bridges which had to be replaced in Europe. Smith, *Britain's Clandestine Submarines*, pp 83–4, points out that Bryan was hardly fooled and his assistant Robert Lansing, who had considered the deal legitimate in the first place, was aware that the Bethlehem submarine programme was an open secret. He did propose amending the Neutrality Act to cover construction of parts of warships for export. In Smith's view, Lansing did not want to reinforce the Royal Navy at a time when the United States was claiming that the British blockade of Germany violated its neutral rights. US Navy inspectors monitored the progress of the work, e.g., of the forty NELSECO diesels for the twenty submarines. At Union Iron Works 90 per cent of the labour force was working on the submarines; the work was half finished as of 4 February. As information was widely available, the Austrian and German ambassadors lodged formal protests. Schwab's loophole was to claim that submarines were being built in Canada from materials (not parts, because they required further work) supplied from the United States. Schwab also stated that ten submarines being built at Fore River would not be delivered

to a belligerent during the war, but that they were being completed because so much had already been invested in them. These were actually the second ten submarines. Smith, *Britain's Clandestine Submarines*, p 90, reports that only the Canadian government did not realise what was happening. It had never been consulted. The submarine work not only delayed Canadian work (on the icebreaker), but the mass importation of American specialist workers violated the Canadian Alien Labour Act. That mattered because the current Canadian government had won the September 1911 election on what amounted to a nationalist platform, rejecting a reciprocal trade agreement with the United States.

20. Cover 185A, Folio 75 is a 9 June 1915 letter to Canadian Vickers from constructor C A Campbell in Montreal recounting problems encountered running these boats on trials. The first ran aground when running full speed ahead submerged. *H 2* had one of her engines wrecked when about to be delivered. All of the boats were sent for trials too soon; it turned out that they had to submerge several times before they were watertight in their upper parts. In *H 3* the diving gear gave out while running 11 knots submerged and those on board had a bad time until her main motors could reverse. As it was, she took a down angle of 10° and was rapidly going down before she could be stopped; it turned out that the connections involved had been made carelessly. She went down below 190ft, but showed signs of strain below 150ft; 'experience with the other boats has shown me that the boat is rather harmed/strained if put lower than the latter depth, so I have adopted that as the limit'. Once defects had been cured, the boats were 'very good and useful . . . They run very steadily submerged, have high submerged speed, are very rapidly submerged for diving, are fairly good weather boats and are very roomy inside. Also they carry four torpedo tubes and their engines are very easy to handle and are exceedingly reliable.' By this time they had been earmarked for the Dardanelles. *H 5* and *H 6* had now passed their trials, *H 7* was about to start, *H 8* would leave the next day for the trial ground and *H 9* and *H 10* within a week. In the first four boats the finish 'is only just sufficient to enable them to be serviceable and the boats' artificers will find plenty to do for a while. The labour available latterly has been very indifferent and in regard to many items we have felt it hopeless to try to get the work well finished off.' Later boats would be better finished.

21. According to Smith, *Britain's Clandestine Submarines*, p 131, the decision to send the four to the Dardanelles was made at a 7 June 1915 meeting of the Dardanelles Committee (he quotes a manuscript in the Asquith collection). The commander of *H 1* claimed that his was the first submarine in history to bombard a place on shore under fire; he even shelled a railway and destroyed two troop trains.

22. According to Smith, *Britain's Clandestine Submarines*, p 133, the submarines could be delivered to Chile because that country was neutral. Five of them were offered in September 1916 as a gift; Chile asked to buy a sixth. For a time there was a problem because Secretary of State Lansing feared that the transfer was a ruse to gain control of the submarines; he caved in to Chilean protests. The Chileans were willing to pledge that they would not transfer their new submarines to any of the belligerents. The Canadians received their two submarines, as a gift, in June 1919.

23. Italy approached Electric Boat and Bethlehem Steel to buy 'H'-class submarines; eight were completed during 1916 by Canadian Vickers. Russia bought this type as its AG (Amerikanskij Golland = American Holland) class under its 1915 Emergency Programme. Probably the class was numbered from *AG 11* on because there was also a *G 1–G 10* class of Holland design, built in Russia. They were shipped to Petrograd and Nikolaev (for the Baltic and Black Sea Fleets) and assembled there. *AG 11–AG 15* were completed during the autumn and winter of 1916. *AG 17–AG 20* were undeliverable due to the Revolution. Electric Boat tried to sell them to Norway, but they were taken over by the US Navy. The missing *AG 16* was *AG 13*, accidentally lost, raised and renamed. Of the Black Sea boats (*AG 21* on), *AG 21 –AG 26* were delivered. *AG 27* and *AG 28* were taken over by the US Navy as *H 4* and *H 9*.

24. Cover 185A, Folio 157, DNC's reply to comments about submarine seakeeping by Captain Max Horton, 19 January 1925. Horton argued that the key to surface seakeeping was the distribution of waterplane area. DNC pointed out that this was set by, among other things, the arrangement of propellers. In the 'E' class, which Horton considered an excellent seakeeper, the stern was elongated to provide space for a stern tube, the shafts and propellers being set underneath. The elongated stern offered greater waterplane area further aft and as a result the 'E'-class submarines were not as easily pooped by a following sea as the 'H', 'L' and 'R' classes.

25. Folio 2 of the 'H' Class Cover (368) is a 7 October 1915 notice that *H 6* had been fitted with Type 10 W/T. Reviewing the design, DNC expected that two Admiralty-type torpedo tubes would have to replace the four of US type in the bow, but that was not done. DEY/16 series in NMM, 1914–15 series, 6 November 1914.

26. The Minutes of the first two meetings are in the October 1921 Technical History, pp 10–11. I have not found other copies in the ADM series. The committee consisted of Controller (presiding), Chief of War Staff, DNO, EinC, Commodore (S), DNC and A W Johns, DNC's submarine specialist. DNC's 19 August 1915 memo leading to the formation of the committee is in Policy Vol 2 (July–December 1915), ADM 137/1098. DNC wrote that it was important to formulate a future submarine programme, but that before that could be done 'we must know our limitations'. He was responding to a note from Chief of (War) Staff. The latter apparently saw British submarines as the natural counters to U-boats. DNC wrote that the best way to defeat the U-boats was to design ships which could float despite being torpedoed, which was entirely possible (the Allies made considerable efforts in this direction, in a somewhat later coordinated programme). Commodore (S) wrote that 'now is a critical time in what may be called the staff work of submarine design . . . if we neglect it, we shall rapidly be left behind in a form of warfare which is of particular interest to Germany and almost sure to be under earnest investigation and development'. Tudor listed as the main types to be investigated Submarine Minelayers, Submarine Monitors and Submarine Patrol Vessels. Commodore (S) proposed both fast and slow minelayers suitable to lay connected (presumably meaning moored) mines. His patrol vessels would have long endurance, with long-range W/T, but not very fast either surfaced or submerged. Chief of War Staff (Admiral H F Oliver) agreed. He saw a great need for a large habitable submarine for use all over the world; 'the first nation which develops these and builds 20 or 30 of them will have command of the sea. If the war drags on long enough for the Germans to develop and produce them first we shall lose command of the sea.' On 19 August DNC wrote that he fully agreed with the extreme importance of developing submarine design, which 'has been fully realised and receives constant consideration in my Department'. He cited the 'J' and 'K' classes and referred to still larger boats still in the preliminary stage. He had recently submitted a minelaying version of the 'E' class.
27. The 1921 Technical History dismissed the minelayer as a special type in limited demand.
28. The 1921 report also states that 'to provide a secondary means of attack, if torpedoes failed and to keep abreast of what appeared to be an expected development and to afford the means of surprise for use at night' it was decided to develop a monitor submarine.
29. DEY/31 MS72/030.
30. Cruiser operations would involve stopping and searching merchant ships and also probably engaging surface ships escorting them.
31. Unfortunately no details seem to have survived in the miscellaneous submarine Covers.
32. Commodore (S) pointed out that within the displacement of a 'K'-class submarine a cruiser could be armed with two 6in guns. The 7.5in gun was closer to the 6in than some of the committee realised; a 7.5in-gun monitor would be little different from the cruiser submarine. Commodore (S) argued that the heavier gun was a good replacement for torpedoes which were less and less effective due to high speed and zigzagging by the enemy and also to the comparatively low speed of the torpedo. In effect the gun would replace the beam torpedo tubes. It should be used by day, when bow attack was not reasonably certain and in place of night torpedo attack. On sighting an enemy ship the submarine would close as for a torpedo attack. If that was not possible because of enemy zigzagging or should the torpedo be evaded, the submarine would break surface and fire.
33. This proposal has not surfaced either. Commodore (S) did admit that the trials of S 1 (Swordfish) had shown that the difficulty of raising steam after surfacing had been overestimated. If the funnels and air intakes could be made watertight quickly enough on diving suddenly 'the road seems clear'. Even so, the trials of the 'K' class might be surprising. For example, was the diesel in the 'K' class a necessity or a luxury? Nor was it certain that high submarine speed would always confer tactical advantages. Such speed could bring a fleeing enemy to action or could allow the submarine to avoid action, aside from the value to bringing the submarine to a desired point in time to use her tactical advantage. However, a 28-knot submarine cruiser would always be at a gunnery disadvantage compared to a 28-knot cruiser due to fire-control issues. For a submarine, the most important virtue was the ability to submerge at will. Commodore (S) did allow that a faster submarine might be a better fleet scout. She might not see as well as a light cruiser, but she could dive if threatened by the enemy's battlecruisers and thus could push through the enemy's screen. High speed might also place the submarine in a better position for a torpedo attack without being seen. Against all of that were unhandiness and even danger in the face of enemy mines.
34. Board Minutes for 4 February 1916 show an entry for approval of a new submarine design, but unfortunately no details (detailed Minutes began the

following year). This was almost certainly the 'L' class. Minutes for 13 June 1916 show approval of two new submarine designs, probably the 'M' class and the H 21 class. Again, no details were given. The Minutes mention approval of the building programme (e.g., 2 October 1916), but give no details. ADM 167/50. Although the d'Eyncourt memo on future designs (presumably 1915) refers to the 'G' class, it seems likely that he had to use the 'E' class as basis because by late 1914 it was already accepted that the 'G' class could not be built quickly enough. Hence the 'L' was an elongated 'E' rather than an elongated 'G'. DNC files do not appear to indicate when the lengthened Vickers diesels were proposed or accepted.
35. Following a suggestion by Commodore (S), made during the design period. Unfortunately the Cover for the 'L' class has not survived and is not even listed in the Brass Foundry (the only Cover is for the L 50 class). In his rejoinder to Captain Horton, DNC claimed that the 'L' class with the 'H'-type stern 'was understood to be the best underwater craft in the British Navy and this is principally due to the shape of the stern and the fitting of the hydroplane immediately abaft the propellers'. He admitted that seakeeping in a following sea had been sacrificed.
36. This note by DNC's submarine expert A W Johns was marked 6 March 1918. While on patrol off the Irish coast, L 2 sighted three destroyers (which turned out to be American) about six miles away and dived to 90ft. The destroyers attacked with depth charges, starting a leak in the buoyancy tank. L 2 sank to the bottom in 300ft of water, blew tanks and came to the surface to be fired at from short range (1000 yds). A 3in shell dented but did not penetrate her pressure hull. She then fired recognition signals and the three destroyers apparently realised their mistake.
37. Admiralty Technical History and Index, Vol 3 Part 21, *Submarine Administration, Training and Construction* (October 1921) in Admiralty Library; also in ADM 275/19.
38. ADM 137/1946, letter dated 19 October 1917, repeated a 20 September request.
39. ADM 1/8470/236.
40. The file on the conference includes a handwritten note that 'L'-class submarines could be adapted for minelaying; if approved it would be preferable to fit 'L'-boats other than those at Vickers, since the ones building by other firms and by Pembroke were slightly larger.
41. The D'Eyncourt design notebook in the National Maritime Museum includes (p 50) a comparison between the 1915 cruiser design and L 50:

	Cruiser	L 50
LOA (ft-in)	234-4 ½	235-3
LBP (ft-in)	229-6	230-4
B mld (ft-in)	23-7	23-6
Draft mean (ft-in)	13	13-3
Surface dispt (tons)	927	961
Submerged (tons)	1122	1150
SHP surface	3200	2800
Speed (knots)	18.25	17.5
Submerged SHP	––	1600
Submerged speed (knots)	––	11
5.5in guns	2	1
3in HA	––	1
21in bow TT	4	6

In L 50, the 5.5in gun is at the after end of a raised superstructure. The 3in gun is in a retractable mount forward of the conning tower.
42. DEY/31 MS72/030, National Maritime Museum. A manuscript copy is Folio 3 in the L 50 Cover, as S.02028/16. Controller submitted the design 'in accordance with Their Lordships decision on S.01676'. He wrote that 'these should prove a very useful type of vessel: the armament need not of course be carried [meaning the 5.5in guns] but if it is, she should be able to make a very good defence against a destroyer should she be prevented from submerging owing to damage'. He proposed that the last six 'L' class should be ordered instead to this design, to be built by Vickers (two), Armstrong (two) and Cammell Laird (two). The two Vickers boats were taken from orders planned for Denny and Fairfield. On 8 December Controller wrote that since he had written, a further report showed that the six bow tubes would entail a slight speed reduction and that the alternative armament of one 5.5in gun and one 3in HA gun would be more convenient.
43. L 50 Cover, Folio 3, which is a compilation of papers beginning with DNC's proposal. An attached table showed that all 'L'-class submarines were credited with a radius of action of 3000nm at 12.5 knots, the 'L' cruiser also being credited with 5000nm at 10 knots (but presumably earlier 'Ls' would have the

same endurance). Speed on the surface was given as 17.75 knots (2800 BHP) compared to 16.5 to 17 knots for the original 'L' class. The Submarine Development Committee report is dated 6 December 1916. Chief of Staff remarks were dated 8 December 1916.

44. Comment on A W Johns paper on German submarines in *Transactions* of the Institution of Naval Architects, 1920, p 32. Land wrote that Johns 'might have been more severely critical of German submarine construction for two reasons. One is that the Germans waited while the British, French, Italians and Americans developed their submarines and then they either begged, borrowed, bought or stole everything they wanted. They then went ahead with their design and construction and the world proclaimed them as wonderful designers! Thus they obtained a credit which they did not and do not deserve.' Land went on to say that Johns should have said much more about the relative qualities of British submarines and went on to read an extract of a report he had written on board HMS *Hercules* in Kiel in December 1918. This was the source of the *L 50* statement. As for engines, he pointed out that the Germans had managed to obtain greater output per cylinder than any others.

45. The emphasis on surface steadiness is from the 1925 DNC paper on surface sea-keeping and submarine hull form; the handiness of the 'M' class is from a variety of sources.

46. Folio 7 is a 1 May 1916 list of weights from Vickers for a 12in Mk IX gun on an open mounting, which is what armed the 'M' class. A statement of the submerged buoyancy of *K 18* (which became *M 1*) was dated 26 June 1916. Folio 12 is the letter transmitting an outline general arrangement drawing, dated 29 April 1916. A handwritten Legend (1 June 1916) is Folio 15. At this point gun armament was one 12in/40 and one 3in HA. The surface plant was specified as 12-cylinder Vickers diesels on two shafts, which is the way the ship was built. The 'M' class (as *K 18/19*) is the first submarine entry in the D'Eyncourt design notebook; there is a separate entry for the 'L' class alongside. It shows Legends signed by DNC (for both?) on 1 June 1916 and a Board Stamp on 13 June 1916.

47. Policy 1917 Vol VII, ADM 137/1332, file beginning p 58. The paper describing the proposal is a copy of an original given to ACNS; it was retained by DASD. It is signed by Commander Lewis.

48. Board Minutes and Memos, August–December 1917, ADM 167/54. The design was an additional agenda item.

49. Conference at Admiralty, 2 October 1917, in 'R' Class Cover (292). Nothing in the Cover explains the shift from 14in to 18in torpedoes.

50. This is from Sims' account; this logic does not appear in British documents. His report inspired US interest in ASW submarines. US National Archives, file OpNav C-84-18 to 84-29 (OpNav classified correspondence 1917–19).

51. The account of the elimination of sources of underwater resistance is taken partly from a 1925 DNC paper on submarine hull forms and seakeeping, Cover 185A, Folio 157. DNC pointed out that placing the maximum beam well forward of mid-length exaggerated the uneven longitudinal distribution of waterplane area and thus sacrificed surface seakeeping.

52. This is the account in the Technical History.

Chapter 10: War Experience and New Technology

1. The Committee was formed in response to an Admiralty letter dated 16 June 1919; its president was Vice Admiral Richard F Phillimore. Its final report is in ADM 1/8586/70. It considered the uses and values of different types of warships in view of wartime experience and the proportions they should form of the future fleet. It was also to advise on the ship characteristics. The printed final report (CB 01557) was dated 27 March 1920.

2. ADM 116/2060, pp 706 and beyond. Evidence was dated July, September and December 1919 and January and February 1920. The witnesses, in order of appearance, were Commander Robert H T Raikes DSO, Lieutenant Commander H G D Stoker DSO, Commodore Sydney S Hall CB, Captain Algernon H C Candy CBE, Commander Charles G Brodie, Captain Martin E Nasmith VC, Rear Admiral Douglas L Dent CB, CMG and Commander John G Bower DSO. As commanding officer of *E 54*, Raikes managed to sink two U-boats, *UC 10* on 21 August 1916 and *U 81* on 1 May 1917. On 9 September 1918 he was appointed to the staff of Commodore (S). He was RA(S) December 1936–December 1938. As commanding officer of *AE 2*, Stoker made the first successful penetration of the Dardanelles, although his submarine was sunk there. He had previously taken his submarine 13,000nm from Britain to Australia and in January 1915 he had been sole escort for the second Australian troop convoy. Hall was wartime Commodore (S). Candy had served before the war on the Committee on Submarines (1913). He was Captain (S) of 2nd Submarine Flotilla January 1914–September 1916 and Assistant Director of Torpedoes between 8 February 1917 and 1 March 1919, becoming Captain (S) of 3rd Submarine Flotilla 1 March 1919–8 August 1919. Brodie had been one

of three survivors of the sinking of *C 11* (July 1909); his brother was lost in the Dardanelles on board *E 15*. He commanded submarine flotillas in wartime as CO of the tenders *Thames* (January 1913–January 1914), *Adamant* (August 1915–March 1917) and *Platypus* (March 1917–October 1918), followed by *K 14* (October 1918–July 1919). Nasmith was famous as the first British submarine commander to penetrate the Dardanelles and return. He had been assistant to Commodore (S) 1912–14, commander of *E 11* 1914–16, commander of the *Ambrose* flotilla (West Coast of Ireland) 1917–18; he was RA(S) 1929–31. Dent was Chief of the Submarine Service in August 1919 (succeeding Hall) and then DNE May 1922–May 1924. Bower was commander of *E 42* on 27 April 1917 when she hit *UB 23* with a torpedo (which turned out to be a dud). In August 1919 he was appointed commanding officer of *Arrogant* as a submarine tender. He served in the Naval Section at the Washington Naval Conference.

3. Records for the Sea of Marmara were unreliable owing to submarine losses and other factors. The Turks recovered numerous failed British torpedoes. Because there were no records of expenditure by *E 7* and *E 12* the number of their torpedoes was unknown. *E 11* expended ten torpedoes on her first trip into the Dardanelles, of which nine exploded. Between 27 April and 4 August 1915 *E 14* fired seventeen torpedoes, nine of which did not hit. Between 14 August and 14 September 1915, *E 2* fired seven torpedoes, all of which apparently hit. The Turks recovered fifteen torpedoes, mostly Mk Vs and Mk VIIs, with a few Mk VIs. Torpedo expert Captain Candy remarked that one of the *AE 2* failures was due to firing at too short a range; 'torpedoes will always go under if you fire very close'. Generally a torpedo needed a 250 yd run to pick up her depth. Some torpedoes might have failed due to flooding in tubes left open for some time while the submarine was bottomed. Many wartime torpedoes, particularly 18in Mk VIIs, had broached; the problem had been solved by introducing the Greenock Depth Gear. In some cases, the torpedo tube had been inclined.

4. This seems not to have been true.

5. In a British submarine, after it left the support of the tube, a torpedo passed through dead water, water carried along with the submarine between the internal hull and the outer skin. Then it passed through an aperture previously covered by a swinging shutter, which was opened by the same motion as the bow cap. Candy wanted tubes lengthened to project quite clear of any hull plating, despite the submarine speed penalty involved.

6. In fact the 'H' was simply a standard US Navy design.

7. Dent was accompanied by Commander G Layton DSO and by Engineer Commander P Stocker.

8. According to Bower, when the first of the class, *U 140*, ran trials, on surfacing she heeled 40° to starboard because her port tanks blew first. Acid spilled out of her battery. The whole class was then delayed so that wood fillings could be put in the tops of the external tanks to raise their metacentric height. Armour was moved from the top strakes. The large *U 118* class minelayers had similar problems. Ordered to mine Brest, the first of the class found herself so unstable crossing the North Sea that she had to eject ten of her forty-two mines before she got there. Armour (1.3in thick) was part of the problem, but stability was still insufficient after it had been removed.

9. Vickers did produce one more powerful engine, for HMS *Nautilus*, with twelve cylinders and a rating of 1830 BHP rather than the 1200 BHP of a twelve-cylinder engine in the 'L' class. This engine was unusually long; when completed during the First World War, it suffered from vibration (it had to be down-rated from 340 RPM to 300 RPM) and from poor combustion. As a consequence, it required 0.55lbs of fuel per BHP per hour, compared to 0.47lbs for the engines in the 'E' class and as little 0.381lbs in the 'L' class. It also had piston and liner problems.

10. Cummins, *Diesels*, p 548, attributes this to the way in which Vickers had solved the problem of its fuel injector nozzle. It conducted numerous experiments until its diesel team hit on a successful design – which was adapted to the particular cylinder size used in the 'D' and 'E' classes. These experiments did not provide any basis for scaling the nozzle up for larger cylinders and further work had to stop in wartime.

11. Cummins, *Diesels*, pp 205–6, claims that smoking could be attributed to the unusual flexibility of the Vickers engine structures. Prior to the 'E' class, Vickers was responsible for hull structure as well as for the engine and to reduce overall weight it put much of the necessary rigidity into the hull. When it designed the 'E' class, DNC ignored the company's advice to reinforce the hull. It mounted the engine atop the lubricating oil tank. Vickers was not allowed to redesign its engine, possibly because of the need to limit weight. Fuel supply was regulated by overhead camshafts which quickly lost their alignment as engines flexed. Vickers' diesel expert William F Rabbidge repeatedly but unsuccessfully urged the Admiralty to provide more rigid engine mounts; he said that as a result the engines were in effect slung from their exhaust manifolds. In the interest of production, the Admiralty also refused to allow Vickers to redesign the engines. In

Rabbidge's view smoking, which he did not consider Vickers' fault, was the Admiralty's excuse for dropping solid injection in favour of air injection between wars.

12. *L 50* class Second Cover (588B), Folio 43, which opens with a request by Controller (20 February 1920) for data on the weights of engine foundations of British vs German engines to make it possible to compare the two.

13. *L 50* class Second Cover, document dated 6 October 1920 (G.4487/20). Folio not known, but it is immediately after Folio 43. Other critical speeds were 250 RPM for *M 2* and 240–260 RPM for *M 3*; 250–270 RPM for the 'G' class and 120–150 RPM for the 'H' class. Typical maximum engine speed was about 400 RPM.

14. Cummins, *Diesels*, p 261, quotes a US officer on board the captured *U 117*. There was a 'tremendous racket' at the critical speed, but the engine soon passed it to a rate at which it did not vibrate. Cummins appears to say that the Royal Navy first encountered critical torsional vibration when it operated high-powered diesels in *X 1*. The US Navy seems to have encountered the problem for the first time in the 'S' class, which was also considerably more powerful than earlier US submarines.

15. According to an Admiralty history of submarine diesels (ADM 1/8678/69), a 29 November 1915 joint meeting of the Marine Engineering and Internal Combustion Engineering sub-committees of the Board of Invention and Research unanimously proposed immediate establishment of an Admiralty experimental station for research in naval engineering. It felt that total reliance on private firms had failed: the British were falling behind the Germans in submarine diesels. The station would supplement rather than replace the private firms. AEL was formed on 6 January 1917. In Cummins' view AEL designs often failed because it refused contact with experienced diesel designers (which in 1919 meant the Vickers team) or experienced submariners.

16. This was the MAN S10V 53/53, using the same 300 BHP cylinder as the six-cylinder S6V 53/53. The post-war US Navy copied the smaller MAN S6V 45/42. MAN produced the great bulk of wartime U-boat engines (416; Körting, with 115, was next). The figures were, respectively, bore and stroke in cm. The six-cylinder 45/42 engine was rated at 1200 BHP at 450 RPM. Work on the six-cylinder 53/53 engine began in May 1916, the first being delivered in June 1917, with a rating of 1750 BHP at 390 RPM (292 BHP per cylinder). Twelve engines went to Britain under the Versailles Treaty. Four of the ten-cylinder engines were delivered in January 1918, but the boats in which they were to have been installed were not finished by the end of the war. In 1917 the U-boat Inspectorate ordered MAN to produce a 4000 BHP six-cylinder engine, S6V 50/40. MAN found that it had to adopt two-cycle operation to obtain about 700 BHP per cylinder at 450 RPM. A two-cylinder experimental engine ran on 21 December 1918, but produced only 515 BHP per cylinder due to vibration problems.

17. Cummins, *Diesels*, p 550, points out that the AEL engine was limited to 300 RPM and below because it vibrated badly above that speed. Maximum output would have been at 390 RPM.

18. In 1919 AEL contracted with White to build a 400 BHP two-cycle engine of that company's modified MAN type; it was erected at AEL in September 1921. Experience with it helped AEL conclude that such engines were not suitable for submarines (among other things, it was difficult to start). However, a two-stroke double-acting engine would be far more compact than the usual four-cycle type, so AEL produced a preliminary design for such an engine early in 1919, to produce 1000/1200 BHP. It was deliberately made larger than might be acceptable in a submarine on the theory that it would be easier to scale down than up. Work on this 'Datic' engine overlapped with that on the *X 1* engine (transferred to a commercial firm, it was delivered in March 1924). As of 1925 a third design was in hand. In 1917–19 AEL also approached major British firms to produce high-powered single-cylinder engines: Cammell Laird, Beardmore, Vickers and Mirrlees. Mirrlees was dropped because its progress was too slow and its final design was not considered practicable. Cammell Laird had offered a two-stroke opposed-piston engine before the war. Tested in March 1917, it was not considered suitable for submarines. However, the company was told that if trials with an improved unit were successful orders would follow for two 1700 BHP engines. Each unit comprised two cylinder liners and four pistons; six would generate the 1700 BHP. Satisfactory trials were run in December 1918 and further trials using Texas Oil in 1919, but with the end of the war the 1700 BHP engine was no longer wanted and the project ended. Beardmore offered a two-cylinder vee engine producing 500 BHP. It failed to produce its rated power and its exhaust was unacceptably smoky. That left Vickers, which offered a solid-injection engine derived from its standard type. A single 340 BHP cylinder was ordered in April 1918. One of the contract conditions was that if trials were satisfactory the Admiralty would order two 2400 BHP engines. Trials began in 1920, the final full-power trial following in January 1921. This unit was satis-

factory, except that its exhaust was not always clear. The contract for the two engines (3000 BHP each) for the minelayer HMS *Adventure* was placed early in 1922 .These were essentially submarine engines, but their exhaust was too smoky for submarine use. Protracted shop trials were not completed until October 1924.

19. Dent testimony to the Post-war Questions Committee. It may have been a self-serving attack on Vickers. Foreign companies such as Sulzer certainly did keep developing submarine diesels. In 1925 the Admiralty found itself claiming that their products were inferior to AEL's. However, in the 1930s the Royal Navy found itself buying some of their engines. The US Navy went furthest in this direction. When it needed a new-generation engine for the 1930s, it deliberately chose characteristics which would make it suitable for railway diesels. General Motors was interested in such products at the time and the US reasoning was that the company would find itself not only perfecting the engines but also creating a maintenance base. Railway dieselisation was a distant prospect in the early 1920s and British railways had a good supply of coal, so this possibility does not figure in surviving Admiralty papers.

20. ADM 1/8678/69, containing engine papers dated 1924–1926. This file includes a lengthy history of the submarine engine intended to support EinC's claims regarding AEL and alternative engine suppliers.

21. Before 1918 Sulzer built two-stroke rather than four-stroke diesels, supplying designs for French and Italian submarines (the engines were built under licence). It also made engines for the Royal Netherlands Navy. Between the wars Sulzer supplied ten navies, including the Japanese and the French (under licence). In 1925 Sulzer had a 6000 BHP engine under test. To produce this spectacular output the engine required a separate 1200 BHP engine – about a fifth of total output – to drive its auxiliaries, including its scavenge blower and the blast injection air compressors. Sulzer's 6000 BHP monster was a relatively slow-running (280 RPM, hence massive) eight-cylinder single-acting two (rather than four) stroke engine. Compared to the *X 1* engine, it had greater height to accommodate a longer stroke, hence needed a larger-diameter pressure hull. *X 1* could pack 4000 BHP per shaft into 89ft x 19½ft. Sulzer needed greater hull diameter (23ft) and much more length (110ft). Using the main engines to drive all auxiliaries would shrink the length to 98ft, but output would then be 5250 BHP. Sulzer offered 7000 BHP for one hour at 292 RPM. It was understood that the submarines of the French 1926 programme would be powered by nine-cylinder 3000 BHP Sulzers, the main engines driving all auxiliaries; the additional cylinder had been added to provide sufficient power for the scavenge blower. Many later units had 3000 BHP Schneider (i.e., French-designed) diesels.

22. During the Post-war Questions Discussion with Admiral Dent, EinC's representative Commander Stocker said that six cylinders was the minimum for smooth running, because they could be reasonably balanced.

23. Cummins, *Diesels*, p 555: derating referred to performance required in periodic tests. The engine could still produce its designed output because it still had its original fuel setting.

24. Cover 185A, Folio 137.

25. Cover 185A, Folio 118. The Germans were Herr Oswald Flamm and Herr Julius Mugler. Mugler claimed that he had been chief designer of all German submarines between 1907 and 1918, which was enough to impress DNI. Flamm had worked for Blohm & Voss, which had built both many of the smaller classes (twenty-six *UB* and forty *UC*) and the larger minelayers (*U 117* class). Mugler offered a steam submarine, the heat of whose boilers would be retained in 'accumulators' when it submerged. DNC pointed out that this idea had been embodied in the Nordenfelt submarine as long ago as 1887. He was rather cagy, hoping that the British would hire him to discover more. 'He had a tabulated statement in which were given the main features of these various [steam submarine] designs, but he appeared to resent any attempt to examine this statement too closely.' His 2700-ton boat used 24,000 SHP turbines, for which he claimed a speed of 27 knots. The claimed tonnage did not include 500 tons of boiler fuel and 150 tons of diesel fuel. Steam pressure was 19 atmospheres (280 psi). Flamm, who had first written to the Admiralty in August 1922, was selling an alternative pressure hull configuration employing three intersecting cylinders, two above and one below, the cross section being roughly heart-shaped. He claimed that in effect his smaller-diameter hull could be built of thinner steel. The intersections of the cylinders formed an inherently rigid triangle, which was built out of heavy girders. The constructor saw the girders as an undesirable complication. Each lobe accommodated one 5000 BHP ten-cylinder diesel engine and one 5000 BHP motor-generator. Running engines and motors, the submarine would generate 30,000 BHP and would attain 22–23 knots. Flamm claimed that MAN had successfully tested one cylinder. He had been turned down, but DNE became interested in the German proposals in the autumn of 1923 and that October DNI wrote to the Naval Inter-Allied

Control Commission in Germany that he was impressed. DNI cited evidence of recent Japanese interest in cruiser submarines. He also cited letters from Sefton Delmer (presumably from SIS, later involved in disinformation against the Germans) and from Lord d'Abernon (ambassador to Germany). Director of Plans (Dudley Pound), ACNS and DCNS (Roger Keyes) all agreed; Controller asked that the constructor (Assistant Constructor Kennett) sent to Berlin be accompanied by a submarine officer. DNC and EinC had already rejected Flamm's ideas, which he had been pushing for years.

26. The Erren system was well publicised, to the extent that a wartime US Navy report on German means of running diesels underwater (which actually involved snorkels) referred to it. The papers of the Submarine Propulsion Committee are in ADM 1/15182 and in ADM 1/15114 (work through July 1938). Progress was summarised in ADM 213/424, written in 1945 by J McAulay, who had been associated with the work. The Committee file includes an 11 May 1935 letter from EinC's department laying out questions about the Erren system, using sketches. The file includes a 13 May 1935 letter from Erren Inventions Ltd in London to Engineer-Commander D J Hoare of the EinC department. Sketches showed operation submerged, on the surface and when charging. In each case engines were driven by a mixture of oxygen and hydrogen. The engine exhausted into a water tank. When charging, the engine ran a generator which in turn drove an electrolyser fed by the water tank, producing more oxygen and hydrogen. The committee papers include a detailed account of a 5 July 1937 visit to the Wanne Eickel plant in Germany, which had an example of the compact electrolyser. It used four tubes to produce 300m^3 of oxygen per day. The Germans wanted customers for the tubes. Representatives of the British Oxygen Co., who visited Wanne Eickel, had the only low-pressure electrolyser in the United Kingdom and it suffered from rapid degeneration of the electrolyte and corrosion of the electrodes due to accumulation of CO_2 and chlorine (introduced in minute quantities in the feed water). That seemed to be a problem of the British climate, irrelevant in central Germany. To some extent the Committee used work done by the Torpedo Propulsion Sub-Committee, which was already considering the use of exotic fuel. Vickers Armstrong was in contact with the German Erren Company. The Committee file includes a copy of a 31 October 1936 Vickers letter to the Barrow (submarine) works claiming that 'the German hydrogen-driven boats are purely for coastal defence. They . . . are charged with gas in harbour'. Actually there never were German hydrogen-driven submarines. The same papers include a page from the 26 September 1936 *Illustrated London News* with drawings of the purported German system as revealed by Hector C Bywater, at that time the highly-respected naval correspondent of the *Daily Telegraph* (the article from the *Telegraph* is not included).

27. Work obtainable from the combustion of the right oxy-hydrogen mixture would be 25 per cent of the heat content of hydrogen. Full diesel power would be needed for 6½ hours to store gases corresponding to 1812 HP-hours (the existing battery capacity, equivalent to 1¼ hours submerged at maximum speed). That did not include the half-hour needed to bring the electrolyser up to full working pressure. The proposed installation offered no advantage in submerged endurance or performance. Submerged endurance would probably be reduced. In a 'U'-class submarine with gas stored at 4000 psi, there would be little change in underwater endurance, but endurance at full power might increase to 7.5 to 9 hours or 3.6 to 4.4 hours (and four 1-hour dives) if one battery section and one motor were retained. If gas were stored at 5000 psi and battery and motor eliminated altogether, underwater endurance might increase to as much as 12 hours.

28. This was not, as often claimed, an acronym for Allied Anti-Submarine Investigation Committee Device. Rather, the wartime Royal Navy used the symbol A/S to indicate all methods of submarine detection (which were pursued by its A/S Division). Asdic turned A/S Division (ASD) into a pronounceable name. Only well after the Second World War would the Royal Navy adopt the US name for acoustic detectors, Sonar. The word Asdics appears as the current term for supersonic echo-ranging in the 31 December 1918 BIR report, p 16. According to George Franklin, *Britain's Anti-Submarine Capability 1919-1939* (London: Frank Cass, 2003), p 57, after Churchill (as First Lord) used the term in the House of Commons the compilers of the *Oxford English Dictionary* asked him for its origin; he made up an answer. The explanation here is the one used in the 1924 Portland report, as quoted by Franklin.

29. Initial British work is summarised in 'Anti-Submarine Development and Experiments Prior to December 1916', (September 1920), Part 40 of the 'Technical History and Index' (CB 1515(40), later OU 6171/23), held by PRO (ADM 275/19) and by the Admiralty Library. British work on anti-submarine hydrophones was due largely to the efforts of Commander C P Ryan RN, formerly a wireless specialist and then employed by Marconi. He returned to active service on the outbreak of war and in the autumn of 1914 began working on submarine detection by hydrophone. On 31 January 1915 a prototype over-

the-side hydrophone was being made. Ryan was given the drifter *Tarlair* for sea trials. Ryan's non-directional hydrophone was installed on board ships as the 'drifter' or Portable General Service (PGS) set, which was lowered over the side. Beginning late in 1915, 4534 were made, production continuing to the end of the war. His Hawkcraig base became the main British A/S detection establishment. Ryan's hydrophone was initially intended for use with indicator nets, but as of April 1916, portable hydrophones were being supplied to drifters. The Admiralty formed a Board of Invention and Research (BIR) in July 1915 to harness civilian experimenters and firms. Admiralty hydrophone development was taken over by the Anti-Submarine Division (ASD) formed in December 1916. By 1917 hydrophone research centres were: Parkeston Quay (BIR), Hawkcraig (ASD), Portland (ASD), Cardiff (ASD) and Portsmouth (ASD). In 1916 Hawkcraig developed a Portable Directional Hydrophone (PDH). It entered service in 1917 in two versions, Mk I (844 made) and Mk II (2586 made). By April 1917, about fifty Mk II were in service and on 22 May the Admiralty ordered 1500 of each of the two types. By February 1918 the consensus was apparently that these devices were good in a smooth sea but practically useless as soon as there were waves. The British agreed that they were much inferior to the US C-tube.

30. The wartime Royal Navy did not adopt any equivalent of the array hydrophone both the US Navy and the German Imperial Navy developed to filter out extraneous noises by forming beams.

31. Hackmann, *Seek & Strike*, p 49 and Technical History and Index, Anti-Submarine Division, p 36. According to Hackmann, the two 5in diameter diaphragms were tuned to about 900 Hz. Each was secured in a stout metal ring, in a hole cut into the hull. The operator compared sound intensity in his two headphones. The devices were inspired by the Hervey hydrophone developed before the war by the Submarine Signal Company. In effect the submarine screened between port and starboard hydrophones. They were intended primarily for submarines. According to Vice Admiral Arthur Hezlet, *Electronics and Sea Power* (New York: Stein and Day, 1975), p 148, *B 3* obtained bearings of propeller noises within 2° by pointing her bow towards the target and comparing noise strength in the two plates. According to the ASD history, German hydrophones lacked the heavy ring mounting adopted by the British, hence could be used only with engines stopped. The British mounting was developed based on experience with heavy mountings of buoyed and portable hydrophones.

32. A/S Division History (in Admiralty Technical Histories). A table of service hydrophones and magnetophones developed by Hawkcraig and adopted for service (p 45) shows directional plates ordered in March 1916: 20 sets of Mk I, 235 of Mk II and 130 of Mk IV. The Mk IV version had a diaphragm acoustically isolated from the hull. This was considered the best of the wartime British hydrophones. There were also two versions of the revolving directional hydrophone for submarines. The table shows orders in August 1917 for ninety-two hydrophones and eighty sets of telemotors to rotate them. These are the only submarine hydrophones listed. The plates appear in the 25 December 1917 report of a US hydrophone mission to England (NARA RG 38 ONI series, P-10-f Register No. 9644-C), with the comment that although there had been no systematic attempt to obtain range data, their range with the boat underway was about the same as that of a US C-tube projecting through a submarine hull and possibly greater than that of the S.C. (sub-chaser) type C-tube when the submarine was bottomed in quiet water. The plates could not be used at all when the submarine was surfaced due to water noises; US experience had been similar. Details of Mk IV plates appear in a report dated 1 May 1918, ADM 137/1929, pp 274–6. It was a modification of Mks II and III, which do not appear in ADM 137/1929 at all. The main change seems to have been a smaller thinner diaphragm, 3in rather than 5in in diameter and 0.04in rather than ⅛in thick. The microphone inside was of the same type as before. A large lead ring and a moulded rubber ring were intended to insulate the plate from all sounds from inside the submarine. The area of the outboard surface of the diaphragm was a quarter of that of the Mk II and Mk III, to reduce water noises. All three were tested on board the submarine *B 3*, Mk IV proving by far the most sensitive, with the greatest range. It could be fitted directly on the existing steel saddles fitted and riveted in submarine hulls for Mks II and III. Seven submarines in commission had recently been fitted with Mk IV.

33. Work conducted after December 1916 by the new A/S Division is summarised in Part 7 of the Technical History and Index, 'The Anti-Submarine Division of the Naval Staff, December 1916 – November 1918' (July 1919), CB 1515(7). A list of hydrophones (p 45) developed at Hawkcraig during the war shows a revolving directional type (ninety-two made), dated August 1917 directed by a telemotor (eighty made). It shows three types of directional plates for submarines, dated March 1916: Mk I (20 sets), Mk II (235 sets) and Mk IV (130 sets). The US OpNav/CN'O' classified folder C-26-118 to C-26-120 (RG 38,

NARA) includes a 24 January 1918 report by Admiral Sims on a test of detection devices on board the British submarine *C 23* (identified in a 25 January 1918 report in another file): the submarine plate (on either bow, 26ft abaft the bow and 3ft below the surface in surface trim); the 'clock' (on either bow, 36ft 6in abaft the bow, 3ft 6in below water) in a streamlined wooden chock outside the hull; and the US-supplied C-tube, projecting through the hull with a guard, 32ft abaft the bow, 3ft 9in above the waterline. In a standard installation the plates had their receiving surfaces (diaphragms) insulated from hull noises by a rubber washer, the diaphragm being in contact with the water. The 'clock' had its diaphragm insulated from hull noises by a rubber washer in the hydrophone, the whole hydrophone being carried on a rubber membrane, without any solid contact between hydrophone and hull. The hydrophone was completely surrounded by the water. It was shielded from moving water by an outer ('sea') diaphragm forming part of the streamline surface, 2in from the hydrophone diaphragm. The space between the diaphragms was completely filled with dead water. The receivers of the C-tube were insulated from hull noise by washers, the copper tubes leading from them being carried through rubber tubing. The receiving spheres were in direct contact with moving water, but they were protected from damage by an open streamlined guard. This was apparently a test installation; the January 1918 paper described a two-day test of the C-tube. The tests showed that the sea diaphragm fitted to the 'clock' usefully reduced sea noise. Dead water surrounding the hydrophone apparently made it more sensitive. This was probably the origin of the later water-filled sonar dome. The fore deck of the superstructure was not an ideal location for hydrophones due to the rattling of loose gear in the superstructure, which was considered almost inevitable. Rattling was practically inaudible in the rubber-suspended 'clocks'. As for direction, other than port vs starboard, fixed hydrophones were useless. Although the C-tube was excellent for cancelling out hull and water noise and gave good directivity (binaural effect), it was considerably outranged by the ordinary hydrophones. The submarine hull was an effective screen against the ship's own propeller noise. In July 1918 a US officer reported on a British rotating hydrophone being installed on board some submarines at Harwich (the BIR experimental station, as opposed to the A/S Division station at Hawkcraig), consisting of a directional hydrophone mounted at right angles to a non-directional one, both on a shaft ending in a graduated hand wheel; the operator used a telephone head set. Typically he listened on the non-directional hydrophone. Upon hearing a sound, he cut out the non-directional phone and turned the directional one until the sound was at maximum. The device was in a streamlined case. This report was made by Captain S S Robison USN and is in the NARA OpNav/CN'O' classified file (C26-251, stamped 25 July 1918, folder C6-251 to -258). No designation was given and it seems not to match the Mk II directional hydrophone, which had a pair of diaphragms pointing in the same direction. The reports in ADM 137/1929 are from Hawkcraig rather than Harwich. Note that because Harwich was not an Admiralty station, it does not figure in the report on the A/S Division in the Technical History and Index.

34. As of December 1917 some submarines were just being equipped with Mk I rotatable devices in streamlined enclosures atop the hull. The conning tower screened the hydrophone from own engines and noise from astern: in trials the submarine's own engines could not be heard up to 3.5 to 4 knots and interference from water noises was 'inconsiderable'. Performance is given in ADM 137/1929, p 458, in a report on hydrophone progress during September 1918 (the report is dated early October).

35. *Handbook of Hydrophones in Submarines*, CB 1664, ADM 186/440 (1924 edition), describes Mk II (obsolete) and Mk IV and Mk V (presumably post-war) plates. Mk II used a 5in diameter mild steel diaphragm mounted on a heavy cast-iron ring secured to the pressure hull. The microphone was mounted in the centre of the diaphragm. Most submarines had Mk IV, whose microphone was secured by a moulded rubber ring carried by a mild steel ring fastened in turn to a heavy lead ring. The lead ring and the rubber ring were intended to shield the microphone from sound and vibration from inside the submarine. Mk V was equivalent acoustically but could withstand greater water pressure, down to 300 psi (675ft depth). The principal RDH, Mk VI, a pair of diaphragms whose centres were rigidly connected by a light stiff rod. In the centre was a microphone. There was also a rubber eel towed from the bridge bulkhead on a 150ft reeled cable. It was not directional. All hydrophone-equipped submarines were to have it. It would be suspended beneath the submarine, to be used on a sprint-and-drift basis. It was gone from the 1926 manual (CB 1757, ADM 186/450). Somewhat later submarines were fitted with a third plate hydrophone facing aft, both to give all-round communication cover and to fill the usual deaf arc right aft. It also appears that the RDH was sometimes placed inside the casing in a tank. According to the 1926 edition the plates had superseded the usual Fessenden receivers because their microphones used far less power. Also, the

same operator could monitor Fessenden signals and propeller noises. This edition discussed S/T rangefinding, which submarines used to measure their distance apart using what was later called Distance Measuring Equipment (DME). Both submarines used stop watches, Submarine No 1 sending the letter P and Submarine No 2 answering with the letter F. No 1 would stop his watch on receiving the first short pulse of No 2's F and then repeat it back. No 2 would stop his watch on receiving the first short pulse of No 2's F. No 1 would then signal the range he had measured, No 2 sending back his own measured range. Distance would be calculated based on average sound speed (0.4 x time in seconds) or, more accurately, using a sound velocity table (at 45° F, 4860ft/sec). S/T could also be used for direction-finding, the submarines using their rotating hydrophones and plates in combination.

36. A British patent application was submitted the day after *Titanic* sank envisaged producing the necessary signals mechanically, using bells and whistles; trials were fruitless. Langevin lecture, 1918, at the Inter-Allied Conference.

37. This account is based on Langevin's extensive lecture at the October 1918 inter-Allied conference, the transcript of which is in a US compilation on active sonar produced in November (NARA CNO/SecNav classified papers, C26-333). Because it used radio-type amplifiers, the French system was sometimes called 'underwater radio'. Boyle gave a presentation on his own work, but unfortunately no transcript was included in the US file. Its absence suggest that the US representatives considered Langevin's work far more important and mature.

38. Hackmann, *Seek & Strike*, pp 84–8.

39. By this time the United States was the leading developer of hydrophones, despite having begun ASW research so recently. The key was the massive US telephone and electronics industry, the two great experts being Reginald Fessenden, responsible pre-war for underwater acoustic signalling, and Thomas Edison. Once the Germans declared unrestricted submarine warfare (and before the United States entered the war), the US Navy created a Special Board on Submarine Devices. Its public face was a Naval Consulting Board chaired by Edison. President Wilson also convened a National Research Council. An Anglo-French naval scientific mission visiting the United States between 19 May and 9 July 1917 found little of material significance, but it 'was strongly of opinion that the organisation of the scientific resources of the American nation . . . should produce results at an early date of great value'. US resources existed 'to an extent at present quite unobtainable in England or France'. By this time the Americans had reached the point the British and French had reached a year or eighteen months ago (i.e., about January or June 1916), although many the report's authors thought they were already ahead. Lengthy conferences helped US developers avoid errors made by Allied developers, saving considerable time. In this sense US devices may be considered as having evolved from the British and French devices at the design stage in mid-1917. ADM 116/1430. Submarine Signal Co. (Fessenden), Western Electric (Bell Telephone) and GE pooled their efforts at a new experimental station at Nahant. Initial meetings between US, British and French scientists were held in late May through early July 1917. The Anglo-French scientific mission helped convince the US Navy to finance its own Naval Experimental Station at New London. Within a few months US hydrophones were in service in all three navies. Reports of European supersonic work sent to the United States at this time included a description of the Langevin device, a description of the British method of cutting and testing quartz for supersonic apparatus (identified as Asdic gear) and a set of plans of the British device (not included in the US file). The US Navy asked for a complete set of through-the-hull Asdic gear and to the French for a similar complete set of Langevin gear.

40. The transcript of the papers in the US file includes an account of US work, which began about April 1917 with Professors Pupin and Wills at Columbia University, privately funded. Western Electric provided the Rochelle salt initially used, which that company used as a receptor for low-frequency sound waves. They found that it worked well as an emitter for high-frequency sound. Hearing about Langevin's work with quartz, they tried that as well. The US file includes a strong recommendation by Admiral Sims, commanding US naval forces in Europe: the United States should pursue this technology, both for submarine detection and as a means of silent signalling. It could also be used to measure the speed of a ship and for navigation at sea.

41. According to Hackmann, *Seek & Strike*, p 126, there was disagreement as to whether to disclose Asdic. Although it was suggested that leaking the secret might induce other powers to agree to abolish submarines, NID argued that it would be better to let other powers continue to waste money on submarines. In July 1929 Director of Plans argued that during the forthcoming London Conference the Admiralty should emphasise the increasing power of ASW, not the submarine threat. The term 'Asdic' was declassified that year, although its meaning certainly was not; all information about installations was still secret. Asdic instruments on ships' bridges were to be covered when foreign visitors

were on board. In 1938 submarine commanders were cautioned not to ping near foreign warships.

42. Unfortunately no history of Japanese sonar exists, at least in English. US Naval Technical Mission to Japan (NavTechJap) report E-10, December 1945 claims that this was one of the few fields in which generous use was made of German assistance; the Japanese also benefitted from British equipment they captured, notably in adopting streamlined sonar domes and the chemical recorder (but without the attack-computing feature). According to the report, the Japanese wartime sonar (Type 3, development of which began in 1942) was a copied German type. However, at the outbreak of war the Japanese had a Type 93 sonar, work on which began in 1931 (the first model was produced in 1933, hence the designation).

43. The second post-war edition of the Admiralty publication *Progress in Underwater Warfare* (1947) included extracts from a German War Diary summarising the state of Enemy ASW as of May 1944: 'hydrophone gear is still the principal method of establishing the presence and rough position of a submerged submarine . . . Search gear (Asdic) Probably installed in all anti-submarine units, range slight, normally from 200 – 3000 m; under favourable conditions up to 5000 m; Supersonic location gear: according to a great number of press and spy reports, this American discovery is installed on all American anti-submarine units and, since January 1944, on English units, too.' The editor thought his readers would find all of this amusing. ADM 239/421. According to Hackmann, *Seek & Strike*, pp 194–5, the Germans began sonar development for the U-boats they began openly building in 1935. Their initial set was based on echo-sounding technology, operating at 15 kHz. This set was disliked by the Germans, so it went to foreign navies, including those of Holland, Denmark, Sweden and Finland. The replacement new S-Anlage became the basis of wartime developments.

44. Cover 185A (Submarines, General) Folio 38, enclosing a report on Asdic from Commander (S) at HMS *Vulcan*, with remarks by the Captain of the Signal School which was developing Asdic. *H 32* had a cabinet 9ft long and 3ft wide, extending from the battery boards to the top of the boat. It could not be used for anything else; the question was whether it could be combined with the W/T or hydrophone cabinets. The writer was Commander (S) R. H T Raikes, who had recently given evidence to the Post-war Questions Committee.

45. Hezlet, *Electronics and Seapower*, pp 166–7. In these submarines the Asdic dome was on top rather than on the bottom, as the submarine was expected to use Asdic to support underwater attack. According to Franklin, *Britain's Anti-Submarine Capability*, p 63, Type 113 was essentially Type 112 inverted, the transducer protruding from the top of the hull. Unfortunately it took 30 minutes in the water for the original canvas dome to become transparent to sound. It was replaced by a metal dome, initially of copper, which was unpopular because it had to be polished, and then by staybrite steel. According to the 1924 edition of *Progress in Torpedo, Mining, Anti-Submarine and Allied Subjects* (ADM 186/444: April 1925) streamlined domes made it possible to achieve the same performance at 14 knots as when a ship was stopped; range was 80 per cent at 16 knots and 30 per cent at 20 knots. Range accuracy was 50 yds using what amounted to a stop-watch and it seemed that 10 yds was attainable. Initially Asdics used a 5° beam. The operator had to listen before turning the beam, so that a full circuit took about two minutes; a submarine could pass through the arc between intervals of detection. A broader beam tried in Type 115 but it turned out not to be effective. At this stage one experimental submarine (*H 32*) had an Asdic and Asdic was being fitted to the big new experimental submarine *X 1*. According to the 1926 edition of *Progress in Torpedo etc* (ADM 186/457), Asdic was fitted on board *X 1*, *Oberon*, *H 32*, *L 54*, *L 56*, *L 69*, *L 71* and HMAS *Otway* and *Oxley*. It was assumed that a submarine using her Asdic actively would give herself away. The 1927 edition (ADM 186/461) mentioned the two-dome Type 118 in *Oberon* and the two Australian submarines. Future submarines would have only one (underneath) dome, which would considerably simplify installation, particularly as it would not require that the oscillator be elevatable.

46. The 1928 edition of *Progress in Torpedo etc* (ADM 186/468) mentioned initial development of anti-Asdic tactics for submarines. Submarines were connecting their hydrophones to a W/T receiving circuit. They could now receive pings and judge whether A/S craft were in contact. Three anti-Asdic tactics were described: (i) keeping bow or stern on and proceeding slowly to present a minimum target; (ii) proceeding with bursts of high speed and large alterations of course to create wakes which would return echoes; and (iii) submarines trying to stop holding trim under or near an Asdic ship so that any echo off the submarine would be confused with that from the ship.

47. Commander David Parry, 'The History of British Submarine Sonars', on the website of the Barrow Submariners Association, states that only *Oberon*'s set could be used on the surface, i.e., had a bottom dome. Like its predecessors, this

set used a Morse key to transmit, but it also had a timer, started electromagnetically, for ranging. It introduced a heterodyne amplifier so that returning pings could be heard on earphones (or on the loudspeaker). The conical reflectors, top and bottom, were intended to provide all-round detection, but they dramatically reduced range and were scrapped along with the upper transducer. Parry states that operating frequency was shifted to 10 kHz, but that may have come later with the tests of supersonic signalling described in *Progress in Torpedo etc*. Parry describes Type 118 as a Type 116 with cleaned-up electronics and a staybrite dome.

48. *Progress in Torpedo etc* 1929 (ADM 189/106) announced that Type 118 had been fitted to *Odin* and to *K 26*. The 1930 edition (ADM 189/107) announced that Type 118 had now been fitted to four 'O'-class submarines, five 'P'-class submarines and *K 26*; *Phoenix*, *Olympus*, *Orpheus* and *L 27* would all be fitted early in 1931. The 'R' class would have Type 118A, with an improved amplifier. Type 709 had been fitted to all 'P' and 'R'-class submarines. The earlier tactic of a divisional attack by two or more submerged submarines manoeuvred by the Senior Officer had been abandoned as fundamentally unsound; a more elastic approach was being developed. However, there was still intense interest in underwater signalling using Asdic (SS/T rather than the earlier S/T); trials using the Type 118 set pairing *Otus* and *Oswald* and then *Perseus* and *Proteus* showed that maximum range varied between 6nm and 13nm. RA(S) wanted 20nm. The 1931 edition (ADM 189/108) reported a test installation of a target-speed indicator, which compared received echoes with an artificial echo generated by the signal injector. Presumably it used target Doppler. Trials in *L 27* proved disappointing, but that might have been due to special features of that particular installation; further tests were planned for a *Swordfish*-class submarine. At this point, with the most favourable water conditions, a submarine could detect echoes from a large surface ship at up to 6600 yds and from a surfaced submarine at 7600 yds. An 18-knot destroyer could be detected passively at 8400 yds.

49. The 1932 edition of *Progress in Torpedoes etc* (ADM 189/109) reported new Type 120 Asdic installations in *Thames*, *Porpoise*, *Swordfish* and *Sturgeon* similar to those in 'D' class destroyers. In *Thames* the Asdic office had been made adjacent to the W/T office, the aim being ultimately to combine the two to simplify watch-standing.

50. *Progress in Torpedoes etc* 1935 (ADM 189/112). They included communication (mainly with other submarines) and navigation. Although it might be dangerous for a submarine to use her Asdic actively, when enemy ships were pinging they would find it difficult to distinguish submarine pings from interference caused by other surface ships. Even so, the extent to which Asdic interception could be dangerous was unknown. 'To avoid any premature prohibition being placed upon submarines . . . instructions have been given that transmissions are to be made whenever they will serve any useful purpose.' 1st Submarine Flotilla tried attacks based entirely on passive Asdic bearings, making five hits out of nine against the destroyer leader *Douglas*. The new submarine torpedo director would include a separate pointer to show the Asdic bearing of the stern of the enemy at the moment of firing, greatly simplifying such attacks. Instructions for Asdic evasion had just been issued.

51. The 1936 edition of Progress in Torpedoes etc (ADM 189/113) announced that Type 129X, incorporating a fixed dome, would be tested on board HMS *Seawolf*. This set did not require an Asdic cabinet. It proved quite successful and was the standard set in new-construction submarines. Its electric motor was in a watertight tank inside the pressure hull, into which the oscillator could be pulled for repair. Ranging was initially by the same type of electromagnetic timer (chronoscope) introduced in Type 116, but sets soon had range recorders. German hydrophones could detect the alternator used to produce current to step up for pinging, so a new alternator was installed (Type 129K) and tested against the German hydrophone array in HMS *Graph* (ex-*U 570*). Wartime modifications include the Mine Detection Unit (MDU) tested on board HMS *Triad* in 1940. Several wartime commanders used the MDU operationally.

52. The 1931 edition of *Progress in Torpedoes etc* 1931 (ADM 189/108). References to 1932 and 1934 are to those years' editions.

53. *Progress in Torpedoes etc* 1937 (ADM 189/114).

54. According to the 1931 edition of *Progress in Torpedoes etc* (ADM 189/108), reliable communication ranges at 20 kHz were 5nm on the surface and 8nm submerged. The 1932 edition reported that at 10 kHz submarines could receive sounds at greater ranges, so submarine Asdics were converted to operate at the lower frequency. As of 1932 reliable signalling ranges of up to 10nm had been measured. The 1935 edition announced that SS/T would now completely replace the lower-frequency S/T, though the relevant existing hydrophone fittings would not be removed. New submarines would have 10 kHz rather than 20 kHz oscillators for their Asdics, 'in order, amongst other things, to obtain longer signalling ranges'. The 1936 edition (ADM 189/113) announced that conversion of all submarines to 10 kHz oscillators would be completed in 1937–8.

Submarines were using Asdic beacons for navigation; on one occasion a submarine 20nm from a beacon submarine was ordered to take a berth 5 and 10 cables away and managed to arrive within 350 and 200 yds respectively.

55. *Progress in Torpedoes etc* 1934 (ADM 189/111).

56. Minutes of the Operations Committee for 28 January 1918 mention that Admiral Beatty had proposed construction in a 22 January letter; the Committee rejected the idea for the present, on the ground that there was no apparent current need. One could be built only at the expense of more urgent submarine construction (the 1919 Programme was then being framed). ADM 137/834, p 120. Beatty's letter, covering both the new light cruiser ('E' class) and the submarine, is pp 123–4. It seems to continue earlier correspondence and it refers to the new German U-cruisers: 'we cannot afford to lag behind in the development of this area of the service. Cruiser submarines, with a large radius of action and small complement, have great possibilities.' Beatty considered the proposed 20-knot speed inadequate; he wanted at least 32 knots so that the submarine could work with the new *Hood*. Submerged speed should also be increased. He also wanted bow torpedo armament increased, to eight 21in tubes. The submarine should have a third 6in gun and one 3in HA gun. Beatty also wanted the funnels raised, as otherwise a wind from ahead would render all but the foremost gun unusable. DNC's sketch design is not in this file. The large submarine was discussed again on 2 February 1918 (p 125). Director of Plans had pointed out that to justify construction of a new type of ship at the present stage of the war it would be necessary to show that it would offer great advantages, as building it would sacrifice other ships; the large submarine would not have any ASW value, either in direct offensive action or in operations against submarine bases or in escort. Any advantage she would offer the fleet would be largely negated by the great time she would require to submerge. In a 31 January memo (pp 130–1) Director of Plans also strongly opposed the project.

57. The first substantive paper in the *X 1* Cover (Folio 3) is a 2 November 1920 note from EinC giving the shaft speed (390 RPM) to be adopted with either British or German engines, the basic arrangement already being fixed. He asked for surface speeds expected for 8000 BHP (engines plus auxiliaries), 6000 BHP (main diesels only), 4000 BHP and 2000 BHP. DNC's estimated speeds were, respectively, 21.75 knots, 20 knots, 17.5 knots and 14 knots. By this time there was already a sketch design. Note that, unlike the usual Cover, this one does not include either a set of design requirements or an account of the initial design. An attached note dated 14 August discusses weights of alternative 850 kW generators (equivalent to 1133 BHP). Both would be run by 1200 BHP diesels. On 26 August A W Johns, DNC's submarine designer, had asked for approximate dimensions of a motor to develop 1000 BHP continuously and 1300 BHP for one hour.

58. ADM 167/62, Board Minutes and Memos for 1920 includes a description of the programme, which emphasised the four projected new capital ships (the 'G 3' battlecruisers). The 1921 and 1922 Board Minutes make almost no reference to a new submarine and the Memoranda do not show submission of the usual sketch design; the first submarine sketch design in Board papers is that for the patrol submarine in 1923. Inclusion in the 1921–2 Programme is indicated by Folio 27 in the *X-1* Cover, a reference sheet on machinery arrangement EinC sent DNC, headed 'New Submarine 1921-22 Programme' dated 15 July 1921. The Cover shows no separate paper announcing inclusion in that programme. Building it at the Royal Dockyard which specialised in submarines (Chatham) avoided any tendering process and also any problems with late changes. As of August 1921 plans called for laying the submarine down on 1 December 1921 and launching her the first week of March 1923, beginning trials at the end of August 1923.

59. Paper by ACNS (Chatfield) dated 24 January 1921, referring to RA(S) proposal to begin detailed design.

60. DNC paper, undated, attached to the ACNS paper. The initial design had been developed in consultation with RA(S) and with DNE(S). A date scrawled on the bottom of the page is difficult to read, but is probably 31 January 1921. However, a second paper on the armament of the new submarine is marked 'continued after DNC's Minute dated 9 March 1921'.

61. *X 1* Cover, Folio 12, a table of comparative data. It showed the diesels as finally chosen, with 336 cells and a normal capacity of 200 tons of oil (450 tons capacity). At this stage motor power was 1300 BHP each. Dimensions were given as 369ft x 29ft and gun armament as two pairs of 4in, with six 21in bow torpedo tubes. The German *U 183* had three 5.9in guns and four bow and two stern tubes (all 20in), apparently with more reloads (twenty in the chart in the Cover). Estimated speed of the new submarine, not yet named, was 21.5 knots surfaced and 9.5 knots submerged, compared to 18 knots and 8.5 knots for the German cruiser. Endurance was given as 16,000nm at 10 knots and 20,000nm at 8 knots, compared to 20,000nm at 6 knots for the German boat. The 8 knots endurance entailed running one 1200 BHP engine at half power. A later

undated legend (Folio 106 in the Cover) gives dimensions as 363ft 6in (between perpendiculars) x 29ft 10in x 17ft (mean) and surface displacement as 2780 tons (3600 tons submerged). Surface speed was given as 19.5 to 20 knots and the number of cells as 330, with four motors (total 2600 BHP) for a submerged speed of 9.5 knots. Endurance was given as 10,000nm at 8 knots or 20,000nm at 8 knots with emergency fuel (450 tons rather than 220 tons). This was not quite the final design; the guns were listed as twin 5in rather than the 5.2in ultimately adopted. Folio 25 in the second *X 1* Cover gives amended figures, beam increasing to 29ft 10¼in. Displacement was the same, but guns were given as 5.2in calibre. The battery had 336 cells and fuel stowage was 219 tons (442 tons emergency). Endurance with full fuel stowage was given as 16,000nm at 10 knots and 20,000nm at 8 knots (one 1200 BHP generator engine at half power). This Cover includes a Legend dated 9 May 1923, which was submitted to the Board. It received the Board Stamp on 31 May 1923. The Legend gave length between perpendiculars as 350ft and length overall as 363ft 6in. Beam was 29ft 10in (pressure hull beam 19ft 9½in). Fuel stowage was given as 220 tons normal and 450 tons emergency. Surface displacement was given as 2780 tons. As completed surface displacement was 2759 tons (reserve buoyancy was 34.7 per cent). Designed surface endurance was 14,500nm at economical speed. In 1930 operational figures were given as (according to BR 3043) 5300nm at 18 knots and 16,200nm at 10 knots using 95 per cent of the maximum stowage of 452 tons of oil. As completed rated underwater speed was 9 knots, but this was not achieved; the maximum was apparently 7.5 to 8 knots. It also appears that the planned submerged endurance (50nm at 4 knots) was not approached, the official figure being only 18nm at 4 knots. The author of BR 3043 thought the stated endurance figures (31nm at 2.5 knots and 20nm at 1.5 knots) were too low. Given the critical vibration problem, *X 1* was re-rated to 7000 BHP rather than 8000 BHP; on trials she attained 19.5 knots on 7135 BHP at 2780 tons. In 1930 speed with a reasonably clean bottom was 18.6 knots using new propellers at 3048 tons. Folio 1 of the third *X 1* Cover discusses the projected replacement propeller. It gives trial results with various propellers: 16.45 knots on 4552 BHP at 2846 tons (not officially reported), 18.5 knots on 7441 BHP at 2854 tons (by log) and 18.6 knots on 7180 BHP at 2900 tons (by log). At this time the design figure was 19.5 knots on 8000 BHP at 2780 tons.

62. Submarine design required strict weight control; the revolving weight of twin guns and mounting was not to exceed 24 tons. The gun would fire a 70lb shell at about 2400ft/sec, although a lower velocity could be accepted if necessary to reduce weight. The design should be suitable for a 75lb shell later on. Elevation limits would be +40° and -5°, the gun elevating by hand but trained by a hand-controlled power mechanism. 'X' Class Cover, Folio 18, dated 16 April 1921. DNO signed these requirements on 18 April.

63. Evaluation and account of engine problems are from BR 3043. So are the discussion of hull structure and the statement about diving depth.

Chapter 11: A New Submarine for a New Kind of War

1. CinC Atlantic and Home Fleets (Admiral Madden) wrote in 1919 that Japan was not a serious rival at sea, although the distance between Japan and the centre of British naval power increased the value of her fleet. He expected that in a serious dispute with the United States Japan would probably side with the British. Madden's strategic calculation is pp 227–9 of ADM 1/8549/18. It included the suggestion that British superiority in battlecruisers be used to keep the US fleet divided, by presenting some to Australia, New Zealand and India (and perhaps Canada) to form a fast Pacific Squadron. This revived a pre-war proposal intended mainly to deter Japan. Because war against the United States was not contemplated and because the British did not intend to try a German-style offensive against US shipping, submarines did not figure in Madden's arguments. Madden's comments make the China Fleet submarines and the questions asked in 1919–20 all the more striking.

2. *Oberon* Cover (424), Folio 1, paper designated M.0935/21. This list of questions was posed by Plans Division, dated 8 October 1921.

3. In the Cover, these are mentioned in the account of the May 1922 conference, but all seem to be dated 1921. Although the account of the conference is included in the *Oberon* Cover, the three papers attached to it are not and they do not seem to be in any Admiralty file in the PRO. Those attending the conference were RA(S), a representative of CinC Atlantic Fleet, Director of Plans, Director of Gunnery Division, Director of Torpedo Division, DNC, Director of Naval Equipment (S), Head of Tactical Section and a representative of Director of Signal Division. The conference report was dated 19 May. An undated paper headed 'Agenda Notes' called for a 30-knot fleet submarine, capable of diving in two minutes and keeping depth in North Atlantic conditions. It stated that the fleet was short of seven oversea patrol submarines, four internal minelayers (i.e., minelayers with internal mine stowage), four submarine cruisers and seven fleet submarines; minelayers and cruisers were given priority. The unnamed

author (probably from Atlantic Fleet) wrote that the cruiser submarine would increase in importance. 'If detection devices improve, the cruiser submarine will be fairly immune from attack. *X 1* is a good cruiser. We can improve on her when we have tried her.' The author may have been Max Horton.

4. This war plan is outlined in Andrew Field, *Royal Navy Strategy in the Far East 1919-1939* (London: Frank Cass, 2004). On p 65 Field shows a generic map of the war plan as understood in 1924–31. Phase One would be the movement of the fleet to Singapore. Singapore was far enough from any Japanese territory that it could be attacked only by sea and defended accordingly. In Phase Two the fleet would advance to Hong Kong, placing it near Japanese bases. In Phase Three the fleet would seize an advanced base or bases, probably in the Ryukyus, and bring the Japanese fleet to action. This was not too different from the contemporary US plan, in which the US fleet would steam to the Philippines. Either en route or after it arrived, it would fight a decisive action, after which island bases closer to Japan could be seized as the basis for a close blockade. Field sees the establishment of blockade bases close to Japan as a trigger for the emergence of the Japanese battle fleet. As CinC East Indies in the early 1920s, Rear Admiral Sir Herbert Richmond objected that no British blockade could cut the Japanese off from resources in China, but the war plan survived his comments.

5. At about the same time, arguments by US submariners that they could strangle Japan (which was considered the most likely future US enemy) were rejected by the US naval leadership for fear that an unrestricted submarine campaign would sink many British merchant ships and so bring Britain, which had been allied with Japan in the past, into the war. US war games played in the late 1930s showed that submarines prosecuting an anti-shipping campaign under the accepted cruiser rules would be unacceptably vulnerable; presumably the Royal Navy reached the same conclusion.

6. ADM 1/8549/18, 'Post War Fleet'. Of the 'C' class, *C 4* would be retained temporarily for trials with the Edison battery.

7. Each of 1st and 2nd Submarine Flotillas consisted of seven 'K' class. 3rd Flotilla was eight 'E' class, one 'E'-class minelayer and three *H 21* class; 4th was eight *H 21* class and four 'R' class. 7th Flotilla, available for foreign service, was six 'L' class and six 'E' class, a total of fifty submarines. Admiral Beatty was willing to make do with only one flotilla of 'K'-boats and with half the submarines offered in the other three flotillas.

8. The Atlantic Fleet was reduced to three flotillas: seven 'K', seven 'L' and seven 'H' class. The Mediterranean flotilla was eliminated altogether. The China Station was allocated twelve 'L' class, an indication of future practice. Schools and experimental work were allocated one 'R' class, one 'M' class, one 'L' class and eight 'H' class. The submarine school would remain at Portsmouth, the periscope school to move to Portland as soon as possible. Submarines in reserve would be either in basins or on the mud. In basins would be seven 'K' class, two 'L' class and two 'M' class. On the mud would be nineteen 'E' class, six 'G' class, eight 'H' class and eleven 'R' class.

9. *Oberon* Cover Folio 1, immediately after the October 1921 paper; it was dated 17 March 1923.

10. CinC Atlantic Fleet produced a list of wireless ranges required for submarines operating off various ports trying to communicate with British bases. A submarine off Nagasaki was 1056nm from Hong Kong and 2413nm from Singapore. One off Yokohama was 1564nm from Hong Kong and 2888nm from Singapore. The situation in the Atlantic was considerably better. For example, a submarine off New York was only 500nm from Halifax and only 693nm from Bermuda. Without linking ships, 500nm was too little; Atlantic Fleet considered 1500nm a more reasonable minimum and 1000 to 2000nm a reasonable target. An oversea patrol submarine with no very pronounced qualities of any other kind should be able to afford the space for a large, powerful wireless installation. Providing a sufficient aerial would admittedly be a problem, but surely it could be solved. DSD wrote that experimental work on a long-range submarine wireless would begin after the design of a new destroyer set had been completed. He expected that more space would be needed than in *X 1* and that much would be learned from the set now being designed specially for *X 1*. Director of Plans (Dudley Pound) pointed out that the requirement levied was actually 100 per cent efficiency at 1000nm; he understood that on this basis, under normal conditions, the same transmitter could operate satisfactorily at considerably greater range. He agreed with CinC Atlantic Fleet that it would be most desirable (if feasible) to provide 100 per cent efficiency at 1500nm. DSD replied that the Signal School had carefully considered the question of maximum submarine wireless range. He noted that a submarine set was less efficient than the corresponding battleship type because the aerial was so much closer to the sea. He could design a submarine set with a guaranteed range of 1200nm and possibly 1500nm. It would need 85 kW from the ship's own power supply and an aerial consisting of three wires slung between two 100ft masts, 200ft apart. It would operate at a wavelength of 2000m (150 kHz), chosen to avoid interfer-

ence due to atmospherics and also to enable a tube (valve) transmitter to work under favourable conditions. The submarine might also use a vertical aerial carried aloft by a kite balloon 800ft above the sea. Range under normal conditions would be not less than 1700nm (guaranteed range would be 1500nm). DNE pointed out that *X 1* had 50ft masts. At the May conference, DSD offered a guaranteed range of 500nm and an 80 per cent range of 1000nm using 68ft masts spread 150ft apart. In all of these cases, guaranteed range meant range under bad conditions. There was insufficient space in the design for the guaranteed 1500nm set, but under fair-conditions the 500nm set could reach 1500nm. To some extent space could be gained by placing components outside the wireless room

11. DSD's submission (28 December 1922) is Folio 12 in the *Oberon* Cover. The wireless cabinet was in a compartment below deck level, to leave a gangway above it; the operators would enter the operating space from above. The rest of the wireless gear would be fitted on the deck. Positioning of the two masts was also somewhat difficult, as they had to be 150ft apart in a 250ft submarine. DSD was also concerned with Asdic and sonic signalling (S/T). Each required a separate equipment cabinet.

12. EinC wrote that this was the best that could be done, short of some unexpected revolutionary improvement. He offered a 37-ton 37ft 1200 BHP engine. RA(S) wrote that surely he could do better: the Germans achieved that output in 29 tons in a 30ft engine room. EinC produced a new sketch of a six-cylinder 1200 BHP engine 23ft long (including a 3ft air compressor at one end), unfortunately undated. Initially the submarine was to have had special low-speed motors geared to the shafts in addition to her normal motors. It proved possible to provide equivalent low-speed economy (in terms of how quickly battery charge was used up) by adding windings to the main motors. Eliminating the cruise motors also eliminated their gearing as a source of noise and, therefore, detectability.

13. No gears for depth and gyro setting etc had been fitted to earlier British submarine torpedo tubes. There were small access plugs, but torpedoes had to be withdrawn from their tubes for adjustment. The first external gyro angling gear (for *X 1*) was worked from the rear of the tube. There was insufficient space in that submarine for depth and speed adjustment. DNC wrote that the need for greater spacing between tubes had been lost sight of during the *X 1* design. *Oberon* Cover, Folio 13.

14. This change seems to have been made at a November 1922 Admiralty conference, which dealt with overall configuration (*Oberon* Cover Folio 13 begins with DTM's complaint that he had not been represented there). Most of the Folio is reactions to DTM's demand that torpedo tubes be more widely spaced. The Cover includes a 5 December 1922 submission by RA(S) proposing the stern tubes, with the note that he had not asked for stern tubes at the original May conference on characteristics because 'it was supposed that it would introduce too many difficulties'. Now RA(S) understood that he had been wrong and that stern tubes could be added to the design without risking any delays or any substantial change to the form of the stern. 'The stern tube possesses many invaluable tactical advantages, with either straight or angled torpedoes.'

15. Submission by DNC, 29 October 1923.

16. *Oberon* second Cover (424A), Folio 6, consisting of information for CB 01534. *X 1* had been similarly strengthened. The basic Cover does not mention the increased diving depth. It is generally given as 500ft, with an operating depth of 200ft. The 500ft figure was crush depth.

17. ADM 167/66, undated but keyed to Board Minute 1586 dated 15 February 1923. 'It is . . . urgently necessary to complete and thoroughly test at least one overseas patrol submarine of up-to-date design, so as to have a standard design of proved suitability available for rapid reproduction if required.' RA(S) wanted to be able to build large numbers of patrol submarines in the event of war. The corresponding Minutes are ADM 167/67. The relevant Minute repeated the figures in the memo and added costs; 'it was explained to the Board that if a commencement was made in 1923/24 the Dockyard Staff at present employed on Submarine *X 1* could, when that vessel is finished, be at once employed on the new submarine instead of being dispersed'. Alternatively, work could be delayed until completion of War Programme ships in the Dockyards next year (1924), when it could help balance the sudden drop in work; but planned reconstruction would actually increase the workload at that time. The Board approved construction (for 1923–4) subject to Cabinet approval.

18. Submarine Newsletter No 1 (October 1922) shows why air-conditioning was essential. It described a three-day patrol in the Malacca Strait by the China Flotilla. Temperature on board varied from 90° F in officers' quarters to 140° F in the motor room, the wet bulb thermometer varying between 90° and 124° F during the patrol and was 85° F in port at Penang. Radical improvement in ventilation was necessary. 'A 3 days' diving patrol with present submarines and existing ventilation arrangements is the most that could be carried out; and

crews would require to spend at least twice as much time in harbour as at sea, with complete rest.' Battery temperature was not allowed to go above 100° F, but it fell little below that. No one could say how such temperature affected battery life. File A1922/5, Submarine Museum.

19. ADM 116/3164, covering 1924–5, is a collection of responses to Beatty's request. The formal report began with a summary of the conclusions of the 2 May 1922 conference. It mentioned *Oberon*, five wartime submarines still completing (three 'L' class and two *L 50* class), *K 26* (completed, carrying out trials abroad) and *X 1* (commissioned for trials).

20. There was no mention of signals intelligence. Instead, the report ruled out conventional espionage, on the grounds that Japan had no land frontiers across which information could leak. Europeans in Japan were unlikely to be able to send anything and secret agents were unlikely to be effective.

21. These figures assumed a submarine continuously on station. They took into account time spent going to and from the patrol position. For the three south of Formosa (2200nm from Singapore) the total requirement was sixteen submarines, something over five per station; for the three in the Formosa Straits and off Hong Kong (2400nm and 2250nm, respectively), seventeen were required (something more than six per station). The link ships did not require such allowances: three per link station sufficed. In the second scenario, eight stations at an average distance of 2500nm required forty-two submarines (something over five each) and two off the Pescadores (600nm) required seven (something more than three each).

22. DCNS presided at the 13 February meeting. Present were Controller, ACNS, Director Operations Division (DOD), Director of Torpedo Division (DTD), Director Trade Division (DTD), Director of Plans, Head of Naval Air Section, Director Signals Division (DSD) and Assistant DNC (ADNC). DCNS presided at the 19 February meeting. Present were Controller, ACNS, RA(S), Director of Plans, DOD, DTD, Director Signals Division (DSD), ADNC, Captain Max Horton (submariner, staff of Atlantic Fleet), Captain G Layton, Commander C Cantlie (representing DNE).

23. Rated speed was indeed 20 knots, but the engines were extremely unreliable and the Bureau of Engineering considered derating these submarines to 17–18 knots. They were considered entirely unsuccessful.

24. RA(S) was adamant about the extra speed, which he understood could be gained by a slight increase in size and horsepower (actually about a 70 per cent increase over the original 1200 BHP figure). In December 1924 he wrote that 'in ocean warfare it will be insufficient for a submarine on reconnaissance patrol merely to report the passing of an enemy force. She must follow and shadow the force, both to obtain detailed information of its composition and to report its further movements . . . it appears almost impossible during the dark hours for a submarine to form an accurate estimate of the composition of a force which merely passes through her position and which she cannot follow.' Submarines might be the only effective offensive force in the Far East before the main fleet arrived and they would have to protect Singapore and Hong Kong. They had to be able to concentrate where they were needed as quickly as possible; a landing operation had to be met before troops got to their anchorage. It was not only the higher maximum speed, but also the expected increase in cruising speed from 12 to 14 knots which might be crucial in shadowing an enemy force. Later RA(S) derided slow reconnaissance submarines as nothing more than 'floating wireless stations'.

25. In effect they replaced the two 'E'-boats bought before the First World War and lost in 1914–15; they would supersede the 'J'-class submarines given to Australia in 1919. The Oxley Cover refers to them as *O 2* and *O 3*, but the second *Oberon* Cover calls them *AO 1* and *AO 2*.

26. *Oxley* Cover, Folio 2, marked '*O 1* Mod'. The memo describing these changes was dated 22 December 1924.

27. According to BR 3043, model tests showed that the greater length would improve surface speed, but it appears that the submarines were lengthened to provide required space and then additionally lengthened to accept larger engines.

28. Weights as built from BR 3043.

29. The clean-up and rated speeds are from BR 3043, not the Cover.

30. Stephen Roskill, *Naval Policy Between the Wars* (London: Collins, 1968 and 1976), I, p. 412.

31. ADM 1/8672/230, dated 11 March 1924.

32. No contemporary studies of war against France have surfaced. Another Admiralty paper of about this date pointed to Japan as the sole basis for fleet composition, with the warning that the Prime Minister must not be told as much. The fleet plan paper was designed for consumption outside the Naval Staff. Note that all studies of patrol submarines were based on the need for range for a Far Eastern war and that the numbers developed were a consequence of the vast distances involved.

33. Roskill, *Naval Policy*, I, p 416. The programme included four carriers.

34. Roskill, *Naval Policy*, I, pp 428–9.

35. ADM 116/3441, Case 11446 Vol 3 (Cabinet papers on naval building programme, 1925), pp 102–7. This is the original Plans Division paper, marked PD 02171/25. Page 167 is a table of over- and under-age submarines through 1936–7. The other two volumes in ADM 116 cover later discussions, mainly of cruiser construction.

36. ADM 116/3441, pp 198–9. This programme still showed a carrier in the 1928–9 Programme, later deferred (she became HMS *Ark Royal*). This programme showed six rather than five submarines, all 'O' type, in 1925–6. The most striking feature was a dramatic reduction in the building programme in 1925–6, balanced by increases in 1927–8 and beyond. The published five-year programme (27 July 1925) showed no submarines at all in 1925–6, construction of six per year beginning in the next year (1926–7).

37. Cover 445 (New 'O' Class), Folio 2. Instructions to Haslar (model test tank). Model tests conducted with and without stern tubes showed no advantage in surface speed gained by cutting off the after end of the ship. Folio 21 (9 July 1926) is information from Haslar. At 17 knots the new hull form at 1659.5 tons required 1472 EHP, compared to 1625 EHP for *Oberon* at 1630 tons. At 19 knots the new form required 1985 EHP. If 1472 EHP equated to 4000 BHP, at 19 knots the new submarine would need about 5400 BHP.

38. In February 1926 EinC pointed out that he could provide engines with longer stroke (which might mean more power) if DNC could accept a slight distortion in the circular shape of the pressure hull. In the end the pressure hull shape was formed around a 9in x 9in square, the ends of the square forming the centres of 8ft radii. This was not quite circular; it was 16ft 9in across and deep. Apparently a suggestion to use triple shafts (for more speed) had been considered and rejected. This is evident only from RA(S)'s reply to a suggestion from *Oberon*.

39. That might seem to be a minor change, but it eliminated space which had been used for ballast pumps near amidships (in April 1923 it had been decided that no pumps should be in the control room). The pumps could not be put in the big wireless room. That left the forward end of the engine room (another pump was in the CO_2 machinery compartment and another in the motor room). EinC disliked the engine room location.

40. Cover 445, Folio 5. The increase in length between perpendiculars of 13ft was made up of 1ft for the CO_2 compartment, 1ft in the magazine, 2ft 6in in the motor room for the auxiliary motor (all three already in the *Oxley* class), 1ft in the forward torpedo tube compartment to accommodate a lengthened tube for splashless discharge and 7ft 6in in the engine room (for the 2000 BHP diesels). Accommodation space forward was lengthened by 3ft. To maintain stability, the moulded diameter of the pressure hull was increased from 16ft (width in *Oberon*) to 16ft 9in. In February 1926 EinC asked that 9in be moved from the motor room to the engine room, citing experience with the Australian submarine design showing that this length, which had been moved from the engine room in their design, was not really needed. As approved, the engine room was 45ft 3in long compared to 37ft in *Oberon*.

41. The presence of the cooling plant is indicated by the reference to a CO_2 space in the *Oxley* class. The August 1930 report on cooling is in Cover 445A, Folio 54. The control room had not been ventilated directly; it relied on air flowing in and out of other compartments. It was relatively easy to extend the ventilation supply trunk from the forward cooler so that it could discharge into the control room; this was done in all three classes of reconnaissance submarines. There was also a trunk from the forward end leading to the fan in the engine room, passing though the control room; it was given sliding louvres in the control room. The engine room had fans at either end to stir up the air when the submarine was submerged. Space was insufficient for a separate cooler and fan to supply the engine room.

42. New *Oberon* Cover, Folio 14, March 1926.

43. The copy of the Legend and tracings of the general arrangement were submitted on 30 July. This Legend was approved on 12 August. The Legend shows slightly greater length, 283ft 6in overall (273ft between perpendiculars) and an output of 4400 BHP rather than the earlier 4000 BHP, for a speed of 17 to 17.5 knots. Endurance was given as 10,000nm at 8 knots on 145 tons of oil. Submerged speed would be about 9 knots. Actual surface displacement, used as a basis for standard displacement, was 1724 tons. On this basis standard displacement, calculated about 1930, was 1563 tons (deducting 137 tons of oil fuel and 24.2 tons of compensating water). Cover 445A, Folio 11. Figures were also given for the *Parthian* and *Rainbow* classes.

44. *Oberon* Cover 445A, Folio 9. A report of the trials of HMS *Olympus* (Folio 34) dated 17 February 1930 showed that she developed only 4145 BHP, at which output she made 17.25 knots; at 4350 BHP on the Arran mile she made 17.40 knots. She had last been docked (i.e., her hull cleaned) in September 1929. At this time she had not yet undergone diving trials.

45. Submarine Newsletter No 28 (July 1929) and 31 (May 1930).
46. Submarine Newsletter No 42 (February 1933). The damper was first fitted on board HMS *Thames*, in a separate casing outside the engine. It was a flywheel which was freed from the crankshaft as torsional vibration increased, thus changing the frequency of the system and neutralising the effect at the critical speed. Using the damper, *Thames* ran at a critical speed without noticeable trouble.
47. New *Oberon* Cover (445), Folio 173.
48. 'P' Class Cover, Folio 10. Although according to the DNC memo on the new design dated 28 September 1927 the form would be the same, a later tabulation of changes showed the main motors 3ft 9in further aft than in *Odin*, requiring a slight change in the shape of the pressure hull. Due to the Vulcan clutches main machinery weight was 5 tons greater and simplification of the main motors and the electrical system added another 6 tons. Moving the forward planes above water made it possible to improve the arrangement of tankage forward. Later in 1927 larger-diameter shafting was approved.
49. 'P' Class Cover, Folio 15, notes on oil fuel stowage. When the *Odin*s were designed, ballast tank stowage had been avoided because once a tank was used for oil it was impractical to use it for ballast: every time the tank was blown a film of oil came out. A tank intended for oil was not painted, but instead was coated with oil; when it was used for ballast, it corroded. This was evident in *Oberon*. Unfortunately it took 151 tons of oil to reach 10,000nm, but as drawn the plans offered only 137½ tons. DNC proposed gaining the required oil by making the main ballast vent trunks one rather than two frame lengths.
50. 'P' Class Cover, Folio 116, report from RA(S) dated 23 February 1932. Other factors were more holes in the superstructure and bridge casing of the *Odin* class and a larger volume of flooding space in the 'P'-class bow. RA(S) considered the bow form the main reason why the 'P' class took longer to dive from periscope depth to 80ft. The best time for an *Odin* to reach periscope depth from full buoyancy at cruising speed was 1 minute 5 seconds, compared to 1 minute 23 seconds for the 'P' class. With Q tanks, these figures were reduced to 1 minute and 1 minute 6 seconds, respectively. When running at reduced buoyancy, the dive to periscope depth too, respectively, 50 and 59 seconds, with Q tanks, 37½ and 52 seconds). DNC pointed out that the 'P' class had larger tanks (13 of them, compared to 17 in the 'O' class). Flooding holes were increased by about 30 per cent in the 'P' class to correspond to the larger tanks, but the size of vents was not increased. Moreover, to permit air at the end of the tanks, far from the vent, to escape, sloping pipes were fitted through the oil-fuel tanks above the main tanks to the trunks; in the 'P' class they were longer than in the 'O' class. Not surprisingly, it took longer to flood the main tanks in the 'P' class: on trials *Odin* took 65 seconds but *Parthian* took 85 to 95 seconds. DNC also pointed to the position of the centre of the reserve of buoyancy. The higher that centre, the further into the water the submarine would quickly sink as the reserve of buoyancy was eliminated by flooding tanks. In the 'O' class the centre was appreciably higher than in the 'P' class. RA(S) also claimed that slow diving was due in part to the modified bow form, but DNC seems to have rejected that argument outright.
51. 'P' Class Cover, Folio 120, October 1931. Earlier discussions had brought out the superiority of the 4.7in gun and the preference for an LA rather than an HA version. In 1931 the two available 4.7in mountings were CP(S) Mk XV (maximum elevation 50°, 9 tons 13 cwt) and CP(S) Mk XVI (30°, 8 tons 13 cwt) carrying, respectively Mk X and Mk IX* guns. The latter had a higher muzzle velocity (2650ft/sec vs 2400ft/sec) and therefore a larger danger space at 4000 yds (175 yds vs 127 yds), meaning a better chance of hitting. *Perseus* had a Mk X gun on a CP(S) Mk XV mounting. This was apparently a relatively complicated mounting. DNO proposed that existing 4in QF Mk IV guns on P.IX mountings in 'O' and 'P'-class submarines be replaced by 4in QF Mk XII guns on S.I (submarine) mountings, twenty-three of which were available at Home Dockyards. A change to 4.7in guns would be made if sea experience with the LA gun in the larger submarine *Thames* proved it desirable.
52. 'R' Class Cover, Folios 21, 27 (for the meeting held by Controller on which modification to accept) and 28 (wireless mast). The object was to measure additional speed which could be obtained if topside fittings as well as wireless masts and gantries were removed. Designed BHP of the main motors was 1350. DEE expected to obtain 1600 by using a 'diverter', but the highest power reached was 1395 BHP. Estimated speeds with 1600 BHP would have been 8.1 knots and 8.68 knots. The Admiralty meeting was held on 19 June 1929.
53. 'R' Class Cover, Folio 46 is a comparative table. It shows length between perpendiculars of 271ft rather than 273ft. Overall length is given as 283ft 6in for the *Odin*s, 289ft 2in for the *Parthian*s and 287ft 2in for the *Rainbow*s. The increased overall length was due to the modified bow shape. Surface displacement is given as 1740 tons, compared to 1738 tons for *Odin* and 1760 tons for *Parthian*. In this table all classes were credited with 4.7in guns.

54. R Class Cover, Folio 64.
55. This section is based largely on CB 3210 (ADM 239/414), *H.M. Submarines*, a 1954 Admiralty Technical Staff Monographs; the section on engine experience in pre-war submarines is on p 18.
56. ADM 1/8724/90. CinC Atlantic Fleet also mentioned a 30 January 1923 submission, which is not in this file.
57. Controller remarks dated 11 February 1924 in ADM 1/8724/90, incorporating DNC on alternatives.
58. 'M' Class Second Cover (674A), Folio 11.

Chapter 12: Fleet Submarines and Minelayers
1. ADM 116/2522, p 53. The twelve-year lifetime may have been new; it did not turn up in earlier discussions of the building programme. It and the six per year construction rate appear in the summary of Admiralty policy 1925–9 approved by the Board on 3 June 1929 (ADM 167/79). Plans Division's totals seem to have been in P.D. 02998/28, whose Appendix I is attached to the First Sea Lord's paper in ADM 116/2522, as p 54.
2. Churchill's use of the Foreign Office to negate Royal Navy arguments about Japan is in Roskill, *Naval Policy*, I, p 556. On p 558 Roskill refers to Churchill's attack on the Admiralty's requirement for seventy cruisers, which had been justified by the needs of a war with Japan. The Admiralty was ordered to concentrate on a Locarno war, but it continued to concentrate on a possible Far Eastern war. If the possibility of war with Japan was dismissed at Cabinet level, the only remaining contingency seemed to be a Locarno war against France or Italy in defence of a largely-disarmed Germany, the point of the Locarno treaty being to reassure the Germans so that they would not rearm. Contemporary Admiralty papers include analyses of the vulnerability of France and Italy to British naval pressure.
3. At the 27 June 1929 Board meeting First Lord A V Alexander told the Board that any orders for the 1928–9 Programme which had not yet been placed would be suspended, the question to be referred to the new Committee on the Fighting Services. That committee had asked about the effect, financially and on employment, of total cancellation of the 1928–9 Programme. *Royalist* had already been laid down by Beardmore on 10 June; she and her sister *Rupert* were both cancelled in July. In October 1929 the Board decided that as *Royalist* was already well advanced, she should replace one of the two projected G-type submarines of the 1929–30 Programme. Presumably the initial cut in the 1929–30 Programme from two to one big submarines finally killed *Royalist*.
4. ADM 1/9728, a collection of papers on the submarine building programme assembled in 1938.
5. The April 1938 handbook of British and foreign warships (CB 1815) credits both the minelayers *Grampus* and *Narwhal* to the 1933–4 Programme. Copy in NARA II RG 38 (files taken from Naval History and Heritage Command [NHHC]).
6. Presumably as input to the abortive October 1921 conference; unfortunately this paper has not surfaced.
7. As RA(S) listed them in his July 1924 Submarine Newsletter (in Submarine Museum A1922/5), they were: (a) full surface speed as much in excess of fleet speed as possible; (b) minimum of 25 knots in good weather is considered essential; (c) surface endurance at least equal to that of the battle fleet; (d) ability to dive from full speed on surface to periscope depth in no more than 3 minutes is desirable; (e) powerful torpedo battery; (f) gun armament not essential, but should offer minimum target to gunfire; (g) full submerged speed of 10 knots for one hour desirable; (h) inter-communication between surface units and submerged fleet submarines is most desirable. Two main issues were endurance and surface speed. RA(S) thought the submarine would need diesels for endurance and might have a combined steam and diesel power, with steam for full speed.
8. ADM 1/8675/21 (S.09239/25). A representative of RA(S) visited Vickers House at their invitation on 22 June 1925 to view the design. Each engine produced 3000 BHP with six cylinders (500 BHP per cylinder). As submitted to DNC, the Vickers boat had the same dimensions as *K 26* (351ft x 28ft; draft was not stated); displacement was 2300 tons surfaced (160 tons more than *K 26*). DNC considered the claimed speed of 23.5 knots high for 12,000 BHP and wrote that the claimed 9 knots submerged could not be obtained with the 1600 BHP of motor power. The design showed eight 21in bow tubes, six of them as in later British submarines and the other two high in the bow superstructure. DNC considered this a poor arrangement (it had been adopted only by the French). He noted that no beam tubes were envisaged. The fore and after parts of the submarine were as in *K 26*, the control and wireless spaces were based on the 'O' class and the engine and motor rooms were arranged to suit the engines and motors proposed. The 336-cell battery had six more cells than in the 'O' class. The arrangement of ballast and fuel tanks was poor and the submarine would

dive slowly; they would have to be rearranged completely to match the diving rate of the big *X 1*. Designed diving depth was 300ft compared to 500ft for *X 1* and *O 1*; it should be greater to deal with the danger of depth-charging. Vickers gave no weights other than 308 tons of oil fuel, which compared to 300 tons in *K 26* and about 460 tons in *X 1*. 'A complete redrafting [of internal arrangements] would be required to raise it to the standard of the latest submarine designs'.

9. ADM 116/2522, Future Submarines and Submarine Depot Ships – Provisions as to Types to Be Built, 1926-1929.

10. As given in the Torpedo Division paper dated November 1926 which opens ADM 116/2522.

11. DTD's 27 November 1926 paper commenting on the design is Folio 1 of the *Thames* Cover.

12. Intended attendees were RA(S), Director of Plans, Tactical Section, DNC, EinC and DNE. As held the conference was presided over by DTD. DNC's representative was his submarine designer (and later DNC himself) A W Johns. Presumably the February conference was adjourned pending the outcome of the 1927 Geneva Conference, then resumed when that conference collapsed.

13. *Thames* Cover, Folio 6, remarks by DCNS W W Fisher dated 7 March 1929.

14. *Thames* Cover, Folio 21, Torpedo Division (TD) remarks dated 12 February 1929.

15. *Thames* Cover, Folio 7. Present were Controller (in the chair), ACNS (Pound), RA(S), DNC (Berry), EinC, Director of Dockyards (D of D), DDNE, DEE, Deputy Director of Operations Division (DDOD) Captain Layton), DTM, DSD and Captain R R Turner (Captain (S)) and other members of the departments involved.

16. Vickers built HMS *Thames*. Its claim of responsibility for detail engine design is from the firm's commemorative booklet, Folio 18 in the second *Thames* Cover (458A). The ten-cylinder four-cycle engine had 21in bore and stroke. A pair of Vickers-Ricardo 400 BHP (900 RPM) eight-cylinder auxiliary engines drove generators. The centrifugal supercharging fans were electrically driven directly by these generators; otherwise they charged the battery. On trials, the engines developed 5000 BHP, considerably more than EinC had expected, at 400 RPM and 4506 BHP at 385 RPM. Vickers claimed that at 10,000 RPM the submarine was rated at 22.5 knots.

17. An undated sheet gave BHP estimates for 20.5 knots and 21 knots based on trials of HMS *Oswald* (*Thames* Cover, Folio 12):

Displacement (tons)	BHP for 20.5 knots	BHP for 21 knots
1950	6970	7510
2000	7100	7650
2030	7175	7730

18. *Thames* Cover, Folio 15, dated 20 June 1929.This was the G 1 design, presumably derived from the two-shaft G 2. A Legend was dated June 1929 and the design received the Board Stamp on 11 October 1929.

19. *Thames* Cover, Folio 28 contains EinC's comments on the engine arrangement, dated mid-November 1929. Although triple shafts would not have required much greater individual engine power than in the past, it was a worse arrangement than twin screws, it would have been heavier, it would have required more battery power and it would have reduced underwater speed. To get increased power, EinC had to increase cylinder dimensions slightly, add more cylinders and adopt supercharging. Supercharging could boost peak power at a minimum cost in weight. Alternatively EinC could add more cylinders, at a considerable weight cost. Final supercharging trials were imminent. In the course of design, the hydraulic clutches (Vulcan clutches) used in the patrol submarines were eliminated, with some saving in space and weight (20 tons). By this time the torsional vibration problem was better understood; in October 1930 EinC wrote (Folio 82) that in order to obtain a satisfactory frequency for the system (i.e., to move the critical speed away from any speed the submarine might typically use) he had increased the diameter of the forward intermediate shaft (engine to motor-generator) to 15in.

20. *Thames* Cover, Folio 28, Controller remarks dated 1 July 1929, but marked 'received 19 November 1929', as they included remarks by EinC (dated 25 June).

21. Second *Thames* Cover (458A), Folio 1. Trials were carried out on 17 and 22 July 1932. Displacement was 2200 tons based on her draft marks. At 7030 SHP (375 RPM) she made 21.67kts. She was running in main ballast trim and had just been undocked. A May 1933 report of submerged trials with the ship fifty days out of dock gave 10.85 knots at 2500 BHP with both periscopes retracted and 10.5 knots at 2500 BHP with both raised. Submerged endurance under war condition (170 amps auxiliary load) were 68 hours at 2 knots on one shaft and 38 hours at 3.37 knots on two shafts. Under peace conditions (280 amps

auxiliary load) they would be 52 hours at 2kts one shaft and 33 hours at 3.3 knots on two shafts (Folio 16).

22. Second *Thames* Cover (458A), Folio 19.

23. *Severn/Clyde* Cover (503), Folio 1. All types were to be investigated, beginning with the G type, as further ships of the class were planned. The conference was held on 9 July 1931.

24. *Severn/Clyde* second Cover (503A), Folio 11. This is a March 1939 discussion, referring to the 1936 proposal. It involved a new design for an external tube. The proposal had been deferred pending trials of external tubes in *Triton*. External tubes had also been tested in the 'U' class.

25. Cover 185A (General), Folio 12. Cover 290B contains Folio 78 (M.06114/15), a detailed description of a sunken U-boat minelayer dated 8 August 1915, including seven vertical tubes forward of the conning tower. She was off Lowestoft and mines were still in the three foremost tubes. It is not clear which U-boat this was: according to Groener none of the *UC I*-type minelayers in the North Sea was lost before October 1915. All such submarines had six tubes. Inaccuracies may have been due to examination by divers working under poorly-lit bottom conditions.

26. RA(S) endorsed the idea in a paper written on 29 January 1920, pointing out that the 'E' and 'L'-class minelayers had been extemporised; 'it is not recommended that the methods adopted in them should be continued'. The basic paper was written by Deputy Director of Plans, dated 11 February 1920. DNC's 1920 notes are in Cover 185A (miscellaneous submarine material), Folio 12, beginning with a request for information on tubes for laying mines (18 March 1920), which in turn referred to an Admiralty paper.

27. Cover 185A, Folio 24, dated 30 July 1920.

28. An undated table of proposed British internal minelayers listed Types A through N by the number of tubes and their capacity (Types L and M had previously been rejected). Types A and B used two tubes (three mines each); Type A had them vertical, B horizontal. C and D had six mines for each of two tubes, again vertical and horizontal. Types E and F had four five-mine tubes, vertical and horizontal, respectively. Types G and J had one tube carrying forty mines, G having its axis vertical and H horizontal (it is not clear what a vertical forty-mine tube would look like). Type J had two tubes (twenty mines each), Type K had two vertical tubes (two mines each) and Type N had two tubes (five mines each) amidships. Two photographs are in the Cover for the 1924 minelaying submarine.

29. Cover 438.

30. Appendix II to DTD paper, 'Submarine Minelayers – History' in Cover 491, Folio 8. The internal design was revived in 1926 after NID reported a remarkable German design for an internal layer carrying 104 mines on 1330 tons. DNC criticised it severely, but most of his arguments could be met. For example, speed was only 14.7 knots rather than the 17 knots claimed for the British minelayer, but in DTD's view that was excessive anyway. Diving depth was 250ft rather than 500ft, but again this might be accepted. DNC argued that the British would require cooling machinery to operate in the tropics, but DTD claimed that the value of CO_2 machinery for battery cooling was very controversial. The Germans had 248 battery cells against 336 for the British patrol submarine, but DTD was willing to accept reduced submerged endurance. This design was why the November 1927 conference considered the internal minelayer; it rejected a minelayer which did not meet the standards of a patrol submarine. A survey of foreign submarine minelayers showed the French building an external one but the Italians building only internal minelayers. The US *V-4* was a German-type internal minelayer.

31. Cover on Minelaying Submarines (491), the opening page of which notes that papers leading up to the conference were with NID 0267/26, which discussed features of a German internal minelayer.

32. Cover 491, Folio 8, a paper written by DTD for ACNS, quoting P.D. 02780/27, which laid out submarine mining requirements. No date is given, but the '/27' indicates the year. The TD paper dated 25 June 1930 summarised proposed staff requirements for the minelaying submarine.

33. Cover 491 includes a 14 May 1930 paper submitted by RA(S) describing the peculiarities of *M 3*. With no mines on board, minimum diving time was 3 minutes in calm weather and 8 minutes in rough weather. With mines on board, she flooded all tanks except Nos 8 and 9, which were not flooded until the submarine took a down angle of at least 1° (about 3 minutes). Minimum time to submerge was 5 minutes in calm weather and 13 minutes in rough weather. In rough weather the submarine had to be dived head on to the sea until the casing (600 tons of water) was full, after which she turned beam-on. In any swell she would not dive except beam-on to the sea and at not less than 5° bow down angle. There was no way to correct a list while the main ballast tanks flooded. In calm weather, while diving, although slow to turn the submarine maintained good diving qualities, but diving speed could not be reduced below 2.5 knots (slow grouper down both motors). In Sea State 3 she was still in good control if

beam-on to the sea, but bow-on or stern-on required grouper up on the motors. Diving with 2° bow down was found to be the best angle for maintaining control. In anything over Sea State 3 or in any considerable swell, *M 3* was unreliable at periscope depth (33ft). She had to be trimmed heavy and when below 35ft she sank bodily. Above 30ft she automatically surfaced with an angle of about 4° bow down. The only way to re-submerge was to turn beam-on to the sea, proceed at 6 knots or more and give the submarine negative buoyancy if the sea was really rough. The pivoting point of the submarine seemed to be very far aft, so the after planes had very little effect and were easily overridden by the fore planes in correcting the submarine's angle. The fore planes were used to maintain depth and angle. It seemed that the flat upper deck of the mine casing caused considerable suction aft. The large square stern created dead water aft. The modification for minelaying left the submarine with a large casing at the after end, adding considerable water without any proportionate increase in the power of the stern planes. The distribution of weight and buoyancy was faulty. To RA(S) was 'at present *M 3* is not efficient or reliable as a submarine and could not with safety be used in war'.

34. A sketch (in Cover 491) showed a line of mines above two vertical tubes, mines being launched after they were deposited in the tubes. The drawing showed three lines of mines in parallel, the two outer ones dropping their mines into the tubes. Mines were all on one level and the space below them could be devoted to batteries or to additional mines.

35. Before this, on 29 September Controller (Admiral Backhouse) met with the heads of technical departments (Cover 491, Folio 32). Backhouse recommended the external minelayer for the 1930 Programme after being told that it would take much longer to design an internal minelayer, which would probably have to await trials of its novel equipment. A second issue was the drastic reduction in diving depth, which DNC argued was necessary to save weight. He could produce a lighter structure based on experience gained with the 'O' and 'P' classes. RA(S) considered 300ft sufficient and DTM pointed out that the mine cases were designed for a maximum of 80 fathoms (480ft). To Controller war experience showed that a gun was essential. It would be better to provide it at the outset rather than add it later. The 4.7in gun offered the greatest hitting power with the least weight, compared with the 3in HA and a combined HA/LA 4in gun. At about the same time DNC asked EinC whether the Vulcan clutch could be omitted. The engine room could be shortened and the design significantly improved. EinC agreed that mechanical clutches would suffice and the Vulcan was also omitted from other designs.

36. Cover 523, Folio 10 (February 1933) mentions two changes which were to be adopted across the submarine programme. One was to increase the strength of all main bulkheads to stand 70 psi. The other was to fit permanent one-man airlocks for escape in place of the existing twill trunks. These new airlocks were already being fitted to *Severn*, *Clyde*, *Shark*, *Sealion* and *Salmon*. In *Porpoise* the escape positions were forward in the torpedo stowage compartment and aft, in the after crew space, with a permanent skirt below the pressure hull hatch. The main advantage of the new type of airlock was that men waiting to escape could remain in the dry until their turn to escape came. The line of mines down the centreline of the submarine made it impossible to fit such airlocks on the centreline, the forward one requiring an increase in length of 4ft 6in (35 tons more displacement). The problem was that the only practicable position for the airlock would have been covered by the capstan gear, which had to be moved aft, blocking some of the previous mine stowage. DNC admitted that this was a considerable price (it would cost speed), but 'if decided upon, it furnishes a solution to certain other points that have arisen, although possibly each not in themselves sufficiently important to justify a modified design'. One was a request by RA(S) that in future submarines the CO's cabin be adjacent to the control room. Another was the desire to have the W/T and Asdic offices adjacent, as in *Severn* and *Clyde*. The magazine was to be enlarged to hold six torpedo warheads in peacetime, together with the gun ammunition already there. The extra tonnage would amount to 175 tons over the projected five additional minelayers. However, when the London Naval Treaty expired on 31 December 1936, the Royal Navy would have only 48,300 tons of underage submarines completed, so that was no great problem. Director of Plans did point to a general tendency for ships to grow; for example the 'O'–'P' class patrol submarines started at 1311 tons but had increased to 1475 tons by the end and the G type had begun at 1800 tons but had ended up at 1850 tons. Controller did not consider the claimed advantage worth the extra 35 tons.

37. Cover 523, Folio 10, dated 12 May 1933. Presumably this meant not lengthening the *Porpoise* design. There was no reference to RA(S)'s interest in stowing oil fuel internally, which was mentioned in a handwritten note to a sheet dated 22 May (authorisation for DNC to prepare a new legend and drawings).

38. Typewritten copy of Board Minute in Cover 523, Folio 10 dated 22 June 1933, following a 12 June memo which attributed the change to a discussion among Chief, Controller, DCNS and ACNS. First Lord had given verbal approval. The

1932–3 Programme was to have consisted of *Clyde*, *Grampus* and *Salmon* ('S' class). Now it would consist of *Clyde* and two 'S' class (*Snapper* and *Salmon*). The 1933–4 Programme was to have consisted of one *Porpoise* class and two 'S' class; now it would be two *Porpoise* (*Grampus* and one to be built under contract) and one 'S' class.

39. Legend dated 28 July 1933. Lengths overall were 292ft 6in for the original design and for C and 317ft 6in for Designs A/B. There was a current proposal to retain the oil fuel at the top of the main tanks as in *Porpoise* and to increase scantlings so as virtually to make these tanks into pressure hull, but DNC disliked the effect on stability, preferring Design C, which added weight in the form of stiffer tanks low down in the submarine where their weight helped stability. Design C was soon modified to add 6 more tons of oil fuel (which would not affect standard displacement), increasing endurance at 12 knots from 5700nm to 6000nm. A handwritten note reads: 'Instructions from DDNC: The extra 6 tons of oil fuel within the Pressure Hull is not asked for, but we must provide it in accordance with our promise to Controller' (dated 3 August 1933).

40. A note on the new Legend is dated 7 February 1936; the Legend itself is undated. It is Folio 26 in Cover 523. Standard displacement was 1520 tons, the figure which had previously been accepted.

Chapter 13: Arms Control

1. The French incorporated this tonnage in their 1925 Naval Law defining target numbers.

2. ADM 1/8683/131, Naval Disarmament Conferences 1924-25. The memo by Director of Plans responded to a 23 April 1924 memo from First Sea Lord, who was responding to a Cabinet request for a memo on further arms control.

3. On 26 June 1925 DTD wrote that 'owing to the general superiority of British workmanship in the shipbuilding and engineering industries over that of other nations, a safe line to take in the interests of economy and one which should leave us with an advantage in war, would be to further extend the life of the various classes of ship, to the maximum feasible, when this life is limited by agreement with other nations'.

4. In a 28 June 1928 memo on future building programmes, First Sea Lord gave characteristics of the small submarine: 600 tons, at least 17 knots, four torpedo tubes, one 3in gun, 4500nm at 9 knots (compared to 10,000nm at 8 knots for the 'O' class) and a diving depth of 200ft.

5. This 9 October 1926 paper from RA(S) seems to have been the beginning of the 'S' class design. Cover 185B, Folio 29, not separately numbered, but bound in after the December 1926 paper.

6. Miscellaneous Submarine Cover (185B), Folio 29, paper dated 9 December 1926. Proposed numbers were given in comments by Director of Plans, 13 November 1926.

7. This was a long-standing US goal. A December 1922 amendment to the US naval authorisation bill requested the President to call for a conference extending limitation to classes of ships not limited at Washington; this provision was repeated in naval acts of January 1923, May 1924 and February 1925. The December 1924 bill authorising eight cruisers carried a clause cancelling them in the event of a successful agreement. L H Douglas, *Submarine Disarmament 1919-1936*, PhD thesis for Syracuse University, 1970, p 154. US Submarines under construction in 1927 had been authorised in 1916 and would not have been stopped based on any agreement at Geneva.

8. ADM 1/8715/188, 'Naval Disarmament 1927'. Plans Division memo, May 1927.

9. Statements before the Technical Committee drawing up treaty terms, from Douglas, *Submarine Disarmament*, p 165. The Japanese wanted a 2000-ton limit on large submarines. Later they agreed to include all submarines in total tonnage in exchange for 'special consideration' in total tonnage allocation. Later they asked for 70,000 tons of submarines; they were willing to cut that to 60,000 tons if the 10,000-ton difference was applied to surface craft. It appears that British Admiral Field proposed that all three powers have the same total submarine tonnage (Douglas, *Submarine Disarmament*, p 168). This presumably led to the agreement on submarine clauses in the 1930 treaty.

10. Miscellaneous submarine Cover (185B), Folio 60, 'Design of Small Type Submarine, Construction Programme 1929'. The collection of papers on future submarine policy (ADM 116/2522) does not include any formal proposal for a new small submarine. It was considered at the 18 June 1928 meeting on future submarine policy, attended by Director of Plans, Director of Torpedo Division and Head of Tactical Section; it was held by DCNS and ACNS.

11. DTM paper in Folio 60 regarding requirements for his design section, 13 November 1928. It refers to the 'R' class, which places it about 1928–9.

12. In February 1929 RA(S) (Edgar Grace) wrote that the 'O' class and G type exemplified what was needed in the Far East, but that they would be too large for the Baltic unless conditions there made it impossible to use a base within 500nm.

Grace had not been involved directly in Baltic submarine operations (he was a wartime cruiser commander), but as CO of HMS *Vindictive* he served there in 1918–19, receiving a Mention in Despatches. Presumably his experience suggested to him that at some future time the Royal Navy might well be returning to the Baltic in the face of a hostile Soviet Union. His remarks suggest that he was recalling conditions at the time; he also cited the 'E' class when discussing habitability. If the submarine had to approach through a narrow channel, the 'O' class would require 43ft to submerge her periscope supports (standards), whereas a 600-ton submarine would require only about 30ft. If passage had to be forced at night, the larger submarine would suffer due to her greater visibility. On patrol in confined waters 'such as the Gulf of Finland', a small submarine might surface to charge batteries at night, but a larger one would have to go the more open waters of the Baltic every night. The 'O' class and G types could have forced an entrance to the Baltic under conditions prevailing at the beginning of the war, but enemy ASW forces would have made that quite dangerous and certainly the larger submarine would not have been able to maintain a close patrol on the surface as well as a smaller one.

13. Cover 480 (*Swordfish*), Folio 1.

14. RA(S) observed that the 'H'-class submarines were limited to five- or six-day patrols in the latter part of the war, 'presumably on account of the hardship entailed in a patrol of longer duration'.

15. Cover 480, Folio 2. Design I would have been 177ft 6in long, Design II 196ft. Pressure hull diameter was 15ft. Displacements given were Geneva figures. Surface/submerged figures were 690/800 tons and 800/920 tons. Main engine BHP was, respectively, 1450 and 1650. Oil fuel capacity was 52 tons and 60 tons.

16. A 22 June 1929 Tactical Division paper on underwater speed and endurance (T.D. 2635/29 in Cover 480) argued for high underwater speed and endurance, although it admitted that to some extent one had to be bought at the expense of the other. For example, large motors for high underwater speed would cost battery weight. The Tactical Division argued that a submarine should be able to carry out a diving patrol during daylight at minimum controllable speed, about 2 knots, plus one high-speed attack during this period. High submerged speed would do little good when the submarine was being hunted, because her enemies were so much faster (14 to 100 knots, the latter meaning aircraft). During an attack, the submarine would show a periscope about once every 5 minutes, at which time she could not exceed 5 knots when the enemy was more than 10,000 yds away and about 3 knots closer in. An officer would not use full speed during the attack, because it would take two to three minutes to reach it, after which the boat would have slow almost at once for the next periscope observation. Even a boat designed for 15 knots underwater would gain only 2000 yds on a 10-knot boat during a half-hour attack. To get that 15 knots the boat would be a 'freak type' consisting of noting but battery and motors, with perhaps one tube in the bow. On the other hand, a boat receiving an enemy report might run in at maximum speed to get into a favourable position ahead of the enemy. The Staff concluded that above about 9–10 knots underwater speed was too expensive. It asked for a submerged endurance of 18½ hours at 2 knots, 1½ hours at 6 knots (attack) and a 20 per cent reserve of battery power, all of which could be expressed as mileage at 2 knots. DNC confirmed that the battery power required would suffice for 10 knots for 1½ hours. DEE calculated that the Tactical Division requirements equated to about 31 hours at 2 knots; the 'S'-class battery would suffice for 36 hours. Maximum speed could be sustained for an hour. For the G-type submarine the period was about 34 hours, but using her auxiliary motor a G-type submarine could run for about 45 hours at 2 knots. The 'S' class could have run longer with an auxiliary motor, but there was no space for it and by this time the noise associated with gearing the auxiliary motor to main propeller shafts was unacceptable.

17. Those present were 1st Sea Lord, 2nd Sea Lord, Controller (3rd Sea Lord), 4th Sea Lord, ACNS, RA(S), DNC, EinC, DNE, Director of Plans and DTD. This is Cover 480, Folio 17. S.3 was describe as halfway between the two original designs.

18. The Cover shows two of them. It was inefficient for a high-powered motor to charge the batteries (as generator), so DEE wanted two-armature motors, one armature being used for charging. They did not fit the existing space. Since the bulkhead involved could not be moved, the submarine would have been lengthened at a cost of 30 tons (Geneva displacement 650 tons). DEE backed down. Model tests showed that on the available 1550 BHP the submarine would make 13.75 knots rather than 14 knots. To be sure of getting 14 knots it would need 1750 BHP (lengthened by 6ft to 202ft at a cost of 30 tons, for a Geneva displacement of about 660 tons). Again, nothing was done. It happened that the hull form adopted was about 12 per cent less resistful at 14 knots, so estimated speed with 1550 BHP was 14.5 knots. When the design was submitted to the Board, DNC explained that the torpedo battery forward and the main motor

compartment aft were almost identical with those of the much larger *Rainbow* class (1474 tons), hence required large cross section which precluded a hull form well adapted to surface propulsion. The reduced speed was formally approved to avoid enlarging the submarine.

19. This sequence apparently does *not* appear in the Covers.

20. Cover 480, Folio 55, attached to weights provided to the Board, 18 November 1929.

21. The new Legend dated 23 July 1930 is Folio 96 in Cover 480. Length was 187ft rather than 183ft 9in between perpendiculars (overall length 202ft 2in rather than 197ft 6in). Standard displacement was 648 tons rather than 642 tons, surfaced displacement being unchanged at 735 tons (but 935 tons rather than 930 tons submerged). Oil fuel stowage was increased from 39½ tons to 44½ tons, giving an endurance of 3800nm at 9 knots. The 44½ tons of oil fuel and the greater endurance are in red ink.

22. This announcement was made on 24 July 1929. Douglas, *Submarine Disarmament*, p 182. They were two 'R'-class patrol submarines of the 1928–9 Programme, as noted in the previous chapter. Two cruisers were also dropped. Because (US) naval officers had effectively killed the 1927 Geneva conference, they were largely excluded from this one, making it easier for the British Government to contravene its agreement with the Admiralty.

23. According to the draft Interwar Staff History, the British argued that submarines were offensive rather than defensive (as the French claimed); they had tried and failed to use submarines defensively in 1914–15. Submarines were, moreover, inhumane, as the World War had shown. The United States supported the British position, but the French rejected it. They pointed out that far from being useful only against merchant ships, submarines had been quite effective against warships, accounting for three-quarters of the total French naval losses and one-third of those suffered by the Royal Navy. The French also pointed to the value of submarines as scouts. Italy was willing to abolish submarines, but the Japanese were not. All participants were willing to outlaw unrestricted submarine warfare of the kind the Germans had employed during the First World War.

24. Tonnages: 60,284 British; 82,582 US; 78,497 Japanese; 81,761 French; and 37,085 Italian, as given in the draft Interwar Staff History, Chapter 12: The First London Conference (NHB). In 1930 the British had 63 submarines (built and building) under 13 years of age, compared to 110 for the United States, 71 for Japan, 91 for France and 57 for Italy.

25. Board Minutes, 27 May 1930 (ADM 167/81), p 169, note by First Sea Lord in connection with New Construction Programme, 1930. The influential Sir Maurice Hankey backed the Admiralty demand for a review of the Ten Year Rule and on 15 July 1931 the Cabinet formally decided that the rule should be re-examined in 1932.

26. Roskill, *Naval Policy*, II, p 144 points to looming trouble with Italy in the Mediterranean. Italian expansionist policies were already evident and the Germans were determined to rearm well before Hitler became Chancellor.

27. Cover 510, Folio 10, dated 24 March.

28. DNC later wrote that the 7ft increase was calculated as 5ft for the airlocks and 13in for the stronger bulkheads, adding up to 6ft 1in. Since frames were 21in apart, this required four frame spaces (84in rather than the 73in calculated). In the improved design the minimum space was taken for the forward airlock, which had to stand between the bulkhead and the battery top (18¼in) plus minimum space for stiffeners in way of battery cells. Elsewhere deeper stiffeners would be used without increasing length; in one case the presence of engine bearers helped. That reduced the extra length to 24in: 18¼in for the forward airlock and bulkhead and 5¼in for the bulkhead adjacent to the after battery compartment.

29. Cover 480A, Folio 3, copied from the 1931 'S' Class Cover.

30. Cover 514A (*Sunfish*, 1934 Programme), Folio 1, notes by DNE, 8 November 1933.

31. Cover 514A, Folio 2, 21 July 1933.

32. DNE and EinC comments were dated, respectively, 25 April and 10 April 1934, which seems a long time after the July 1933 proposals.

33. In Scheme 1, the length of the engine room was reduced 3ft and its door placed on the centreline. That made it possible to bring the gun, gun access trunk and magazine aft, giving much better access from magazine to gun and also clearing the fore part of the superstructure and improving the habitability of the bridge, reducing underwater resistance. A rearrangement of the W/T office would add a foot to the control room, which was considered desirable. Fuel stowage would be increased slightly. Schemes 2 and 3 envisaged a reduction of one frame space (20in or 21in), the door being retained just clear of the WT cabinet to starboard of the centreline. This frame space could go into either the after compartment or the torpedo stowage compartment; there would be no additional fuel oil. DNC asked EinC just how much length could be saved in the engine room. This was dated 28 January 1935.

34. Douglas, *Submarine Disarmament*, p 223.

35. Undated single sheet in the miscellaneous submarine Cover (185B), Folio 98. Attached to it is M.0460/32, a paper submitted by DNC referring to the queries shown. It is dated 15 March 1932.

36. On 25 May 1932 the UK delegation requested data on a 250-ton submarine. Dimensions were 135ft (between perpendiculars) x 14ft; surface displacement would have been 275 tons and submerged displacement 325 tons. Legend in Folio 100. The same day the chief British naval delegate, Vice Admiral Dudley Pound, wrote from Geneva that several countries favoured limiting submarine size, but were not willing to go below 500 to 600 tons. 'It is believed that the capabilities of submarines of 600 tons for extended operations is not generally understood by foreign delegations and the opinion is widely held that a submarine of 250 tons would not be able to perform coastal duties efficiently, undertake ocean passages to colonies or afford reasonable safety and comfort to the crew.' He asked for a technical memorandum. DNC wrote on 2 June that it was impracticable to fit 21in torpedo tubes in so small a submarine, although she could have four 18in tubes with a reload each. Two 180 BHP engines would give a surface speed of about 10.5 knots and two 300 BHP motors would give a submerged speed of 11.5 knots. DNC considered it desirable for motor power to exceed engine power in a small vessel in which the battery acted as ballast, as excessive use of solid ballast (such as pig iron or lead) could be avoided. 'Moreover, a defensive submarine should possess good underwater endurance and the relatively large battery would facilitate this being obtained.' About 15 tons of oil would give an endurance of 5000nm at 6 knots, without any allowance for battery charging. Habitability would 'not be too good'. DNC pointed out that the 262-ton submarines completed by Italy in 1919 (N.3, 4 and 5) offered an alternative solution to the small-submarine problem.

37. Cover 185B, Folio 100, 30 May 1932. DNC scaled down the 650-ton 'S' class to estimate characteristics. Endurance would be about 3000nm at 8 knots; surface speed would be 12 knots, submerged speed 8 knots. The submarine would have six bow torpedo tubes but ten rather than twelve torpedoes. Habitability would not be good, but would suffice for extended patrols in European waters. It would not be suited to the tropics, i.e., to the Far East. Seakeeping would be good. DNC estimated that in non-tropical waters the submarine could carry out a diving patrol 1200nm from base. He pointed out that time spent on such a patrol would depend not on the size of the submarine but on the extent of enemy anti-submarine measures she would face. 'Experience in the last war showed that in order to maintain maximum efficiency a diving patrol in enemy waters should be limited to 7-10 days.' On that basis it could be assumed that a patrol would last about 21 days. If operations did not entail protracted time submerged (e.g., operations on trade routes), the submarine might be able to operate for as much as six weeks away from her base (as far as her personnel were concerned). In that case endurance would be limited by the fuel supply. A Legend form compared the 600-tonner to *Swordfish* (648 tons standard). *Swordfish* was 187ft (pp) 202ft 6in (oa) x 24ft 4in; the new design was 177ft (pp) 192ft 6in (oa) x 24ft 4in. The new submarine would displace 685 tons surfaced (vs 735 tons) and 870 tons (vs 935 tons) submerged. Engine power would be reduced from 1550 BHP to 1050 BHP, cutting surface speed from 13.75 knots to 12 knots. Endurance would be reduced from 3800nm at 9 knots to 3000nm at 8 knots. Submerged speed would be 8–9 knots rather than 10 knots and endurance at 2 knots would be 30nm rather than 36nm. Diving depth would remain the same, 300ft. The 600-ton design did not offer battery cooling or airlocks, the former being essential in the tropics. Adding them would require greater diameter in way of the batteries and also extra length (7ft for cooling and 7ft for an airlock); the engine room could but cut back 1ft 9in, but that still lengthened an 'S'-class submarine by 12ft 3in to 210ft. Surface displacement would then be 900 rather than 738 tons (submerged, 1130 tons rather than 933 tons). Compensation would be to cut power from 1550 BHP to 1350 BHP, for a speed of 12 knots rather than 13.75 knots. Endurance with the less powerful engine might be 5000nm at 8 knots rather than 3800nm at 9 knots.

38. Surface displacement would be 1400 tons and submerged would be 1635 tons; length overall would be 255ft and pressure hull diameter 16ft. With 3300 BHP this submarine would make 12 knots surfaced. Oil capacity would be 115 tons. Motors would produce 1320 BHP (no submerged speed was given).

39. Roskill, *Naval Policy*, II, p 302; this was in March 1935. At this point the Germans said they were willing to support British efforts to abolish submarines. However, they also promised agreement to the 'cruiser rules' (no sink on sight) for submarine warfare, which had been incorporated in the 1930 London Treaty. The Germans seem to have introduced the 35 per cent surface tonnage ratio at this point. German Foreign Minister Ribbentrop emphasised that the 35 per cent was not negotiable and the British seem to have rushed into agreement for fear that the Germans would demand more. It is not clear when the 45 per cent submarine ratio

was introduced. Roskill, *Naval Policy*, II, p 306 comments that the fact that many important points were discussed after the agreement had been signed confirms that the Germans used rush tactics to get what they wanted.

40. Roskill, *Naval Policy*, II, p 286, describing a paper written in March 1934 by First Sea Lord Chatfield. Among other things, he repeated an earlier British proposal that future battleships be limited to 25,000 tons with 12in guns, which the US rejected. Slightly later the British told the French that they wanted to bring the Germans into the treaty system, with an allowance of five capital ships (including the three 'pocket battleships'), one carrier, seven light cruisers, twenty-five destroyers and 5000 tons of submarines (Roskill, *Naval Policy*, II, p 292). In Roskill's view, the interwar Admiralty took a wholly unrealistic view of submarines due in part to the submariners' reluctance to talk about their craft and also the limited number of submariners on the Naval Staff.

41. Cover 439, Folios 21 and 21A, referring to the 'German-built Spanish submarine referred to in NID 841/32'. According to Eberhard Rössler, *The U Boat: The Evolution and Technical History of German Submarines* (London: Arms and Armour, 1981), p 91, Spanish industrialist Echevarrieta was willing to build submarines as soon as the Spanish navy gave him a contract, under a considerable German subsidy. His submarine was a test boat, the design having been developed by the German (officially Dutch) IvS firm based on the wartime UG (Project 51a). The project began in 1926. The Spanish initially wanted a larger submarine. The sections of the submarine were built by Fijenoord in the Netherlands and assembled by Echevarrieta's small yard in Cadiz. Work began in 1928, by which time this was a rather larger double-hulled submarine with a surface displacement of 745 tons. The submarine, which the yard called *E 1*, was laid down in February 1929. Engines and other equipment came directly from Germany. The submarine was launched on 22 October 1930 and ran trials between May and 4 July 1931. According to the British report, *C 3* displaced 762 tons surfaced (*Swordfish*: 735 tons) and 950 tons (935 tons) submerged; she was 238ft long overall compared to 202ft 6in for *Swordfish*.

42. The report on the Monfalcone design is Folio 26 of Cover 439 on foreign submarines. Like E 1, it was explicitly compared to *Swordfish*. The report sometimes refers to the specifications, but it seems clear that the submarine actually existed at the time of the report. This report was signed by A N Harrison, a senior submarine designer, on 28 March 1933. Folio 28 is a report on torpedo arrangements in the Portuguese submarines dated 1933, presumably referring to the Vickers design.

43. In the 'S' class, the relevant WRT and TOT (tube operating tank) were provided solely for torpedo operation, with sufficient capacity to drain the tubes after firing. In the Italian submarine the torpedo compensating tank was used to compensate for spare torpedoes when they were not on board. It had too little capacity to handle water drained from the tubes, some of which had to go into a trimming tank. This arrangement was definitely inferior to the British one, as it reduced the capacity of the only end tank available for ordinary trimming. The WRT water was classed as trimming water, hence was not included in standard displacement; the British included WRT water in armament weight. The Italian torpedoes were a foot longer than the British, but weights were similar.

44. *Report on "U 570"* (HMS *"Graph"*), January 1943 (CB 4318R); my copy is from the British material in the RG 38 NHHC file, NARA II. US intelligence files contain other information from British analysis of this submarine. P-10-j Register O8/130-A (Confidential series) is the voluminous initial British report dated 28 September 1941. 'The radio direction finder, the echo-ranging equipment and the 48-spot hydrophone all give additional offensive characteristics . . . In general this submarine has much more equipment to give it stronger offensive characteristics than any submarine of comparable size in either our Navy or the British Navy . . . The only outstanding defensive characteristic of this submarine worthy of mention is its hull strength. The 20mm anti-aircraft gun gives this submarine better defensive characteristics against aircraft than machine guns mounted in British and American submarines.' The US writer considered the German torpedo data computer markedly superior to the British STD but definitely inferior to the US TDC, 'into which all argument for the complete solution of the torpedo fire control problem except angle on the bow and range are automatically introduced'. The night torpedo director on the bridge was considered extremely valuable and 'very definitely superior to corresponding British equipment . . . primarily because binocular sights are definitely superior to the open sights fitted on the British instrument'. The large size of the ballast tank vents, the narrow superstructure deck and power-operated friction-type engine clutches all indicated to the US author that the submarine would be a quick diver.

45. The report dismisses GHG as differing only in detail from multi-unit hydrophones used by most navies, but Hackmann, *Seek & Strike*, says that it made a huge impression. This type of device was copied after the war.

46. According to a post-war British account, the estimated lifetime of the German cells was only 18 months, compared to the British standard of three to four years. According to an 8 August 1942 paper by DEE on battery cells (Cover 483B Folio 35), at that time the typical 5-hour rate of a British cell was 4410 amp-hr. Spurred partly by the German example, at the end of the war it was typically 5350 amp-hr, cell life having been reduced from eight to five years. Based on trials with *P 212*, the new cell would drive a submarine for 1.7 hours at 8 knots, compared to 1.4 hours for the old one. Overall the new cell offered substantially greater endurance at all speeds and it would also save weight. Compared to current cells, the new one would require 1400 amps rather than 1000 amps for initial charging after discharge at the 5-hour rate. It would produce 40 per cent more hydrogen at the end of the charge. DEE badly wanted it and it was soon placed in production. According to a US Navy report of a visit to DEE dated November 1944, the roughly 10 per cent improvement in battery capacity was achieved by using thinner and more numerous plates. The US writer considered British battery jars, which had been developed through lengthy shock testing, superior to US ones. The latest British jar was made out of three layers of a neoprene ebonite with asbestos cloth insertions between the layers. Compared to US jars, it was lighter. Previous British jars had been made of Bakelite (plastic)-bound plywood with a rubber inner lining. This type of jar tended to fail at the dovetail joints of the plywood. The larger cells in the 'A' class had a capacity of 6630 amp-hrs at the 5-hour rate.

Chapter 14: Rearmament

1. Roskill, *Naval Policy*, II, p 146 points out that the Cabinet did not formally state that the Rule was finished.
2. ADM 1/9728.
3. I am grateful to Rear Admiral James Goldrick RAN (Ret) for this account of the changed Far Eastern war plan. It may be significant that the long-range flying boat the RAF put into service about this time was the Short Singapore. The RAF itself seems to have admitted that its long-range aircraft base at Singapore would have more a reconnaissance than an attack (i.e., navy replacement) role.
4. RA(S) remarks in ADM 1/9728, dated 21 February 1934.
5. Cover 548, Folio 21; the conference was on 16 October 1935. Although the note on it is in the 'U'-Class Cover, it ranged much more widely. It seems to have been the only expression of total submarine requirements, as compared to what could be extracted from various treaties and Cabinet agreements. Those present were Director of Plans (Captain Phillips), Assistant Director of Plans (Captain Danckwerts), Deputy Director of Operations (Captain Blacklock), DTD (Captain Boyd), Captain Brind, Commander Halahan, RA(S) with Captain Barry, Commander Hughes Hallett and DNC's reporter.
6. As given in a Board paper on the 1936 Programme, dated 16 November 1935, in the 1935 Board Minutes. Objectives given by First Sea Lord (Admiral Chatfield) were, first, to maintain the strength aimed at in recent years; second to replace the battle fleet as rapidly as possible; and thirdly to increase the rate of cruiser replacements. By this time it was clear that there would be no further limitation of total tonnage in any category. The target submarine strength was taken from paragraph 137 of the Board paper prepared for the 1935 conference. Of the total, five minelayers, three G type, twelve 'S' class and one 1000-ton patrol submarine ('T' type) had been provided for in previous programmes. This paper proposed a 1936–7 submarine programme comprising one minelayer, two new small submarines (which would become the first 'U' class) and one 'T' type submarine. Note that at the time the target strength of the fleet was given as fifteen capital ships, seventy cruisers (ten could be overage) and sixteen destroyer flotillas (four could be overage), without mentioning submarines or, for that matter, aircraft carriers (the Fleet Air Arm, however, did figure).
7. In 1934 Director of Operations had proposed that one of the new patrol submarines be included in the 1935–6 Programme, laid down in March 1936 and ready in December 1937. Experience could be gained before new submarines were laid down in March 1938. This idea died by 1935.
8. Details of the 1938–9 and 1939–40 Programmes as understood in 1938 are from Board Minutes for 1938. The replacement of the minelayers by 'S'-class submarines is from George Moore, *Building for Victory: The Warship-Building Programmes of the Royal Navy 1939-1945* (Gravesend: World Ship Society, n.d.), p 13.
9. Cover 542, Folio 1. Displacement would be 960 tons surfaced and 1200 submerged. Surface endurance would be 6000nm at 11 knots or 10,000 at 8 knots. Submerged endurance would be 1 hour at 9 knots or 60–70 hours at 2 knots. Surface speed would be 14.5 knots. In this paper RA(S) also pressed for a replacement 'H'-class submarine specifically for Asdic training; this proposal led to construction of the 'U' class.
10. The Staff Requirement listed (along with RA(S) requirements and the initial DNC design in Cover 542 Folio 9) for the 1000-tonner seems to have been for

two external torpedo tubes, but RA(S) doubled that to four. The Staff Requirement for 15 hours submerged at 2 knots plus 8 hours at 5 knots was kept. Minimum speed submerged was 2 knots. An undated Legend shows length between perpendiculars increased from 250ft to 275ft, length overall increasing from 266ft to 291ft 2in. Surface displacement would have been 1290 tons rather than 1172 tons and submerged displacement 1560 tons rather than 1450 tons. Surface endurance was given as 4500nm at 11 knots with a foul bottom, compared to 3750nm at 10.5 knots (with 108 rather than 135 tons of oil) for the 1000 tonner. Submerged endurance was the same, 55 hours at 2 knots or 8 hours at 5 knots after 15 hours at 2 knots. This Legend shows two external tubes in the 1000 ton design.

11. Cover 542, Folio 11, 15 March 1935.
12. Paul J Kemp, *The T Class Submarine: The Classic British Design* (Annapolis: Naval Institute Press, 1990), p 10 notes that RA(S) Rear Admiral Sir Noel Laurence, pressed for a double-hull design, the ballast tanks of which would have flooded through a duct keel. He argued that it would protect better against depth-charging. DNC argued that the extra weight involved should be used instead to strengthen a single-hull structure. Kemp points out that during the First World War Laurence had been involved in the controversy over single- vs double-hull overseas boats ('E' vs G type), the submariners preferring the double hull and then disliking it in practice because it required more power.
13. The original 800-ton estimate was presumably based on some sort of DNC sketch. The Cover does not include any indication of why the displacement was pushed up to 1000 tons; DNC's two sketch designs are in Cover 542, Folio 2, a report to DNC by the constructor involved. Details of the two designs, dated April 1934, are in Folio 3. They were:

	A	B
Length overall (ft-in)	260-0	250-0
Beam extreme (ft-in)	22-0	22-0
Mean surface draft in diving trim (ft-in)	15-6	15-7
Surface displacement (tons)	1260	1195
Standard displacement (tons)	1045	990
Submerged displacement (tons)	1540	1455
BHP of engines	2500	2500
Speed surfaced (knots)	14.8	15.0
Endurance at 8 knots (nm)	9500	11,000
Endurance at 11 knots (nm)	6000	7200
Oil fuel (tons)	99	109
Battery cells	336	224
BHP of motors	1300	1300
Submerged speed (knots)	9	9
Endurance at 9 knots (hrs)	2½	1
Endurance at 1.5 knots (hrs)	60	55
Endurance at 2 knots (hrs)	64	48

14. Kemp, *T Class*, p 11, points out that battery capacity could not be reduced because these submarines would operate in northern latitudes where summer nights would be short and the submarine would not have much time to charge at night.
15. DNC's submission is Cover 542, Folio 12. The attached Legend shows alternatives displacing 1059 tons, 1090 tons and 1108 tons, with 2500 BHP, 2000 BHP and 2400 BHP engines. A sheet dated 9 May is a set of calculations for a 275-footer which could carry 125 rather than 135 tons of fuel.
16. Cover 542, Folio 13. Attendees were ACNS, RA(S), DNC, DEinC, DEE, DNE, D of TD and representatives of Staff Divisions. Folio 14 is a summary transcript.
17. Cover 542, Folio 15, sheet showing that these figures were given to Mr Goodall (who was in charge of the design) about 16 May 1935. BHP for motors for 9 knots would be 1350 with bow shutters and 1400 without. Submerged displacement was 1520 tons.
18. Cover 542, Folio 18, 12 March 1935.
19. Details from Board Minutes for 1935.
20. As described by Kemp, *T Class*, p 28.
21. CB 3210 (ADM 239/414), *H.M. Submarines* (1954), in the series of Admiralty Technical Staff Monographs, p 16. Cummins attributes the variety of diesels tried to the inability of AEL to produce a suitable engine quickly enough.
22. According to Kemp, *T Class*, p 30, service opinion was divided. Powered by them, *Thrasher* had few mechanical problems and served in all three theatres. Her CO 'thought they were super. They didn't give much trouble and were much quieter. They purred like a sewing machine as opposed to clattering like a bus. They seemed to make less noise and were smoother running.' Others found the engines over-rated (in rated power) and with insufficient margins of power at full speed. Cylinder rings and then cylinder blocks cracked. The CO of

Taku, in the Mediterranean, said that in every 1000nm of running at least one engine would be unavailable because his engineers were lifting a piston. She returned to the UK with two pistons slung. *Trident*, the third Sulzer boat, had similar problems and had to return home after a patrol off Sumatra.

23. Kemp, *T Class*, p 28, describes how *Tribune* lost her securing bolts and returned to the UK from Canada with her cylinders held down by pit props. By 1943 only she and *Tuna* survived of the MAN boats and both were used for trials and training. When it was proposed to send *Tuna* to the Far East in 1944, A(S) declined: 'she is fitted with a foreign engine which we do not trust far from home'.

24. Kemp, *T Class*, p 19, cites the experience of HMS *Triad*, which could not attack two German destroyers passing aft in moonlight in April 1940. In March 1942 *Torbay* was caught on the surface while turning to bring her bow tubes to bear.

25. Cover 603.

26. ADM 1/24219. This submarine would have been slightly longer (273ft between perpendiculars) and would have displaced 1755 tons rather than 1745 tons surfaced, in the case of *Grampus* without external oil fuel. Standard and submerged displacements would have been the same, 1520 tons and 2100 tons. Oil would have been carried internally (140 tons compared to 118 tons internally and 17 tons externally in the earlier submarine). Endurance would have increased to 11,000nm.

27. Comments on what could be done in the repeat 'S' class are in the Patrol and Minelaying Cover (602), Folio 2.

28. In the run-up to the meeting, RA(S) circulated a memo: CNS (First Sea Lord) had stated that although he hoped to carry through the proposed programmes, regardless of German demands, he was not averse to scrapping older submarines earlier than planned; it would be wrong to use them in war if they were not entirely efficient. RA(S) himself wanted to discuss engine reliability (should it be more important than performance?) and simplification. Could a standard submarine be designed that would be suitable for both patrol and minelaying?

29. Cover 603, Folio 66, reproduced as the introduction to a discussion of the design, including a summary of points raised at the 20 January 1939 meeting. In shallow water such as the North Sea minimum safe depth mattered. Maximum draft at periscope depth was 48ft for the 'S' class, 49ft for the 'T' class – and 55ft for the *Porpoise* class minelayer. For the latter, the minimum depth of water to avoid hitting (with periscopes down) a large ship drawing 33ft was 77ft; to allow a safety margin to avoid hitting the bottom and bouncing and to allow for angle of dive, these submarines should never operate in less than 120ft (20 fathoms), the safe depth given in CB 4000. These large minelayers also put too many eggs in one basket; each was 16 per cent of the Royal Navy submarine minelaying force. DTD considered twenty mines an acceptable minimum. However, according to Goodall's notes, at this meeting First Sea Lord reserved decision as to whether to proceed with the big 1939 minelayer.

30. Cover 602, Folio 3. Notes on the meeting are in Folio 65. Placing mines in the superstructure, as in the previous minelayers, was discussed. Pros were that mines would be more accessible, that the submarine could carry more of them and that mine spacing might be better; the mines were also less subject to damage while lying alongside. Cons were greater visibility (larger profile) and the fact that the nature of the submarine would immediately be obvious; also that the ship would have to be larger, with a larger complement. DNC was asked to estimate the size of an 'S'-class submarine with twenty-four mines carried either in the superstructure or in the side tanks. If the ship was to be small, DNC suggested four bow torpedo tubes, no gun and mines in side tanks. Endurance should be 3500nm at 10 knots. Surface speed should be 13.5 to 14 knots (9 knots submerged). Diving depth was to be given based on 20lb plating and 6in tee frames. Reserve of buoyancy was to be 15 per cent. Before the meeting, DNC (Goodall) wrote to RA(S) that he would welcome any special views, which would enable him to rough out a design before the meeting. If the submarine had to be built in numbers, special questions were the minimum number of torpedo tubes, guns if any, endurance, speed and anything else such as diving depth. The list above seems to have been Goodall's. RA(S) marked up Goodall's questions: he wanted six internal torpedo tubes, a 3in gun which might be surrendered when carrying mines, performance as in the Improved 'S' (i.e., the 1939 'S' class: 4000nm at 11 knots with a clean bottom) and 300ft diving depth. A table was drawn up giving particulars of the 'L' and 'E'-class minelayers, of the German minelayer design for Turkey (*Batiray*) and of the Vickers design for Estonia (*Kalev* class). They were compared with a modified 'S' class which would carry thirty mines internally. The German design was credited with forty mines and the Vickers' one with twenty. Both used minelaying tubes in external tanks. With thirty mines the 'S'-class submarine would be 245ft long (overall) and would displace 975 tons surfaced and 1175 tons submerged.

31. An initial version had no escape chambers; it would have been 185ft long

between perpendiculars (218ft overall), displacing 727 tons standard (815 tons surfaced, 1025 tons submerged). The copy in the Cover (Folio 68) is dated February 1939. The Legend for the version incorporating the escape chamber is dated July 1939. Details of the 1940 'S' class are pencilled in. This is the version described in the text. DNC had written to Controller that he had omitted escape chambers because he could not spare the space required; RA(S) had asked that they be omitted because of the congestion they would cause.

32. D K Brown (ed), *The Design and Construction of British Warships 1939-1945* (London: Conway Maritime Press, 1996) II, p 27.

33. This memo appears in several Covers; in the 'U' Class Cover (548) it is Folio 2. It is marked 'RA(S) proposals for *original* sketch design'.

34. Cover 548, Folio 5, marked 'Small Submarine (to replace H Class)'. The new design was comparable to the 'H' class, with standard displacement 420 rather than 410 tons and surface displacement 460 tons rather than 448 tons, 153ft 6in between perpendiculars rather than 164ft 7½in and 166ft 6in overall rather than 171ft). BHP would be 525 rather than 480, for 11.25 knots rather than 11.4 knots on the surface; endurance at 10 knots would be 2000nm rather than 1600nm. Armament was the same, four 21in tubes and two reloads. This submarine would use 112 high-capacity battery cells rather than the 120 standard cells of the 'H' class. It would be faster underwater, 9 knots rather than 7.5 to 8 knots using a 450 BHP motor. Given higher capacity, endurance at 2 knots would be 40 hours rather than 35 hours. Diving depth would be the same 150ft.

35. Cover 548, Folio 11, with a pencilled note that a revised paper was produced at the 5 December 1934 meeting.

36. Cover 548, Folio 13, a handwritten paper marked M.F.04047/34, dated 12 December 1934

37. Requirements received by phone from Harrison (DNC's submarine designer) on 28 February 1935, as proposed at Fort Blockhouse subject to RA(S) approval. Cover 548, Folio 15.

38. Cover 548, Folio 19, 13 June 1935.

39. The reference to an external tube being preferable to two reloads is dated 30 October 1935 paper, but it in turn refers to a 9 September 1935 visit by RA(S) and Captain Barry.

40. Cummins, *Diesels*, p 568. If a generator failed, the engine could be connected directly to a shaft using a standard emergency coupling between generator and motor. This was installed after *Spearfish* suffered an electrical failure under attack off Norway. The Paxman was unusual in that fuel was injected not directly into the cylinder but instead into a spherical prechamber, where it began to burn. The burning charge was injected into the main chamber (the cylinder head) at high velocity, which imparted a strong swirl. That made for quieter combustion and lower peak pressure, which probably improved reliability. Compression pressure was 530 psi (peak pressure was 760 psi).

41. Cover 548, Folio 21. Barry and RA(S) again reviewed the design on 12 November. RA(S) pointed out that the submarine might have to operate in the tropics, so she needed some form of air cooling and drying. RA(S) wanted a higher bridge (for seaworthiness) and longer periscopes (for better control at periscope depth).

42. The US Navy was adopting diesel-electric propulsion for its larger submarines at about the same time, the main consideration being that compact efficient high-speed diesels could be used. In both navies the issue of possible flooding was raised. In the British case the main motors were made watertight up to shaft level (a proposal to make them completely watertight was dropped). In the British case a key argument was that whether or not the submarine used electric drive, she was so dependent on her battery that any electrical disaster would disable her. If she was unable to recharge her battery (due to a flooded generator), she could not maintain her auxiliary services while running on the surface for more than three days.

43. Cover 548, Folio 62. *Ursula* was fitted with a 3in gun. In 1938 RA(S) asked whether that could be reduced to just the external torpedoes, as it had turned out that a 2pdr anti-tank gun could be fitted without any loss of torpedoes.

44. Cover 548, Folio 76. DNC's representative noted that removal had previously been approved. VA(S) considered the 'U' class were proving difficult to handle at periscope depth in rough weather. Fining the bow would reduce the mass of water set in motion when the boat trimmed. However, the original bows of 'U'-class submarines under construction, except for the first six, were not too different from the satisfactory ones of 'S'-class submarines. VA(S) pointed out that the 'S' class had 34ft periscopes, the 'U' class only 30ft ones. To avoid upsetting production at Vickers-Armstrong a less fine bow was accepted in the first six ships than in the next six of the first batch of twelve and a less fine bow in these six than in the ten of the second Vickers Armstrong batch. Even that would not quite fit VA(S)'s idea of sufficient fineness; he asked that the bow of the last ten be reconsidered and its width drastically reduced. That was done.

VA(S) accepted the modification to the first six Vickers Armstrong submarines to avoid delay, but wanted greater reduction in the next six (the DNC representative did not hold out much hope). He wanted the bow of the last ten built into *Unity* when she came in hand for refit in the first week of June 1940.

45. Cover 548, Folio 66, undated.

Chapter 15: The Second World War

1. Data on torpedo performance are mainly from Vice Admiral Sir Arthur Hezlet, *British and Allied Submarine Operations in World War II* (Gosport: Royal Navy Submarine Museum, 2001), II, p 81.

2. Successive editions of the *Vernon* annual report and of the RA(S) Submarine Newsletter (in the RN Submarine Museum) tell its story. In the 1928 *Vernon* report (ADM 189/48) it was the new Type 'G', a submarine torpedo being developed alongside 'enriched air' (oxygen) surface weapons. Since 'enriched air' was unacceptable in a submarine torpedo, the new torpedo burned fuel using a semi-diesel cycle. Like earlier steam torpedoes, it burned fuel in a 'generator' to heat air, but unlike them it injected additional fuel into the cylinders of its engine. There the air-fuel mixture came into contact with hot gas from the 'generator' and burned, making the engine a semi-diesel. Heat loss was much reduced because most of the fuel was burned in the cylinders. Only about a third was burned in the generator, to keep the generator alight and to keep the temperature of the gas supply to the cylinders high enough to ignite the combustion fuel. The usual water of a wet heater or steam torpedo was not present. This cycle was also used in surface-ship torpedoes. There does not seem to have been any foreign equivalent. Initially three alternative engine-generator combinations were tried, a straight conversion of the existing Mk IV engine (B), a conversion of an 18in engine (BB), and a complete redesign, using a Ring Generator. Initially the BB engine was most successful, offering a range of 11,500 to 12,000 yds at 35 knots compared to 8000 yds with the exiting wet-heater engine. The most promising version, the Ring Generator, had failed completely and was redesigned. Desired speed was 40 knots, and the Superintendent of the RN Torpedo Factory told the Torpedo Design Committee that the BB engine was close to its limit at 40 knots. Submarines did not need the additional range; they needed higher speed, preferably 45 knots. It was decided (according to Newsletter No 24 [July 1928]) to use the added efficiency to enlarge the warhead (to 700lbs and then to 750lbs) by shrinking the air flask, retaining ranges of 5000 yds at 40 knots and 9,000 yds at 30 knots, (Mk IV was rated at 6000 yds at 40 knots and 9500 yds at 30 knots, but carried only a 500lb warhead). If necessary the submariners were willing to accept a modified low speed, say 7000 yds at 35 knots. Engine problems delayed initial production a year. As of mid-1928 the B engine, which promised a reliable speed of 40 knots, was not yet in sight, and a single-speed torpedo using the BB engine had been proposed. A peculiarity of the B engine was that they had a long over-run at declining speed after they finished their full-speed run. For example, estimated performance of a BB engine at 37-knot setting (6000 yds) would include a 2500 yd overrun at an average speed of 35 knots (at 8500 yds the torpedo would be running at 20 knots). These torpedoes were also intended to angle (90° turns only) at full speed, but that was proving difficult, and accepting a reduction to 37 knots would help. A 19 July 1928 Admiralty letter to RA(S) suggested an interim solution. Initial Type G torpedoes would have BB engines, and while they were tested work would go on to develop higher-performance engines. RA(S) agreed. Newsletter No 26 (January 1929) reported that the first six Type G torpedoes were being made for summer 1929 trials, the engine not yet having been selected; with more satisfactory trials of a more powerful engine, it would be possible to reach 40 knots, and Mk IVs were now satisfactorily angling at that speed. According to the 1929 *Vernon* report (ADM 189/49), initial problems had been overcome, and all 'G' torpedoes were to use the Brotherhood 'ring engine'. Performance: 5000 yds at 40 knots, 6000 yds at 39 knots, 7000 yds at 37 knots, and 8000 yds at 34 knots; *Osiris* fired test shots that year at Loch Long. The 'G' torpedo was designated Mk VIII in 1930, set for a single speed (40 knots). Newsletter No. 37 (November 1931) mentions initial satisfactory trials at Loch Long, followed by current extended trials at Portsmouth. These torpedoes had a single-speed setting of 5500 yds at 40 knots and would over-run to 8000 yds at an average speed of 40 knots. They could stand 300ft pressure.

3. The US Mk 14 could be set to turn to any desired angle. It did so by turning its rudder back and forth almost continuously; unfortunately the rudder could apparently jam. To exploit angling, the US Navy used an elaborate torpedo fire-control computer (TDC). Pre-war discussions show that angling was expected to make up for the limited manoeuvrability of large US submarines; they would manoeuvre the torpedo rather than themselves. US retired Commander John Alden showed that about eight US submarines whose loss had been unexplained almost certainly fell victim to circular runs due to gyro failures (others known circular runs). In his Second World War history, Hezlet mentions some

circular runs, but they seem not to have been fatal; he was able to identify nearly all causes of wartime submarine losses.

4. According to CB 03203, *Torpedoes*, an Admiralty Staff Monograph issued in 1948; my copy was in the NHHC (RG 38) collection at NARA II.

5. This account is based on ADM 1/24278, a file on the Admiralty award to Wadham's widow, which includes a detailed description of the STD Mk 1 (not a full handbook) dated October 1937. Commander Geoffrey Wyndham Wadham wrote to Clausen when on the RA(S) staff in 1929 (his letter is included in the file). He wanted a device which did not require the little bars and pointers of the earlier directors and also did not require reference to tables. The machine had to take the torpedo turn onto its track course into account. Wadham suggested something like the existing torpedo sight, and indeed the prototype was considered comparable to the new night surface torpedo sight. Terry D Lindell, 'The Development of Torpedo Fire Control Computers in the Royal Navy', in Martin Edmonds (ed), *100 Years of 'The Trade'* (Lancaster University: Centre for Defence and International Security Studies, 2001) states that STD was delayed by Clausen's work on other systems; overwork helped give him a nervous breakdown in 1933.

6. Submarine Newsletter No 47 (October 1934) and No 48 (April 1935), the latter describing the manual prototype.

7. Prototype completion announced in Submarine Newsletter No 52 (July 1937) and *Sunfish* installation in No 53 (October 1938). There were two versions: Mk I for 'S' and 'U'-class submarines, and Mk Ix for larger submarines.

8. Comments from the post-war staff history, p 57, presumably quoting a contemporary report (not referenced). The relevant correspondence is in ADM 199/1890, papers of A(S). This file begins with a 5 August 1943 paper by DNO describing the torpedo problem and explaining that the TDC solves it (it responds to an earlier DTSD paper, not included). DNO estimated that development of a British equivalent would take at least 2½ years from receipt of drawings. Redesign of the STD to solve triangles for torpedoes which could be angled continuously, and to transmit angles electrically to the tubes, would take as long, and even without a position-keeper the result would be so massive and so complex as to raise serious production problems. No satisfactory form of control for continuous gyro angling could be provided until computers embodying the performance of British torpedoes (their 'torpedo ballistics') were produced, either in Britain or in the United States. This issue of redesign presumably explains why so few TDCs were provided to the Royal Navy. DNO offered an interim solution, a gyro angle scale engraved on the own-ship dial of the STD for bow and stern tubes. On this scale the angular difference between 'can' and 'should' pointers could be read, giving the gyro angle which could be set at the tubes (neglecting convergence, a negligible correction for small angles). This solution would be good for angles up to about 20° (at this angle neglecting convergence would equate to an error of only about 25 yds at the target). A(S) convened a meeting at his headquarters, Northways, three days later. One possible alternative was DNO's simple solution, for angles of at least 30° (up to a maximum convergence error of 100ft). Including a repeat-back from the tubes, it could be implemented within four months. A second possibility (B) would be a somewhat more elaborate version for angles up to 55° (it was rejected). A third (C) was a new STD. A(S) decided that C should be pursued with maximum priority, with the sort of continuous automatic angling the TDC provided. An automatic plot was wanted to support the new STD, compact enough to fit in a 'U' or 'S'-class submarine. A 13 January 1944 meeting at the Admiralty reviewed the situation. Adjustments and limitations of the TDC were considered in detail. The TDC would reject any solution requiring a torpedo running time of over 240 seconds, but British torpedoes might exceed this given their long range; Vernon said that the British required 5½ minutes (330 seconds) and, if overrun was to be taken into account, 10 minutes (600 seconds). To handle longer running time submarines might need STDs in addition to TDCs, or the American 'banjo' (equivalent to the 'Is-Was'). The Americans should be asked about longer running time, at least 5½ minutes (10 minutes was less important). The TDC allowed for a target speed of up to 40 knots, own-ship speed 0 to 25 knots, periscope parallax up to 100 yds, and sonar parallax of up to 30 yds, all of which were acceptable. Its maximum torpedo range was 8000 yds; the British would prefer 15,000 yds. Minimum range was believed to be 500 yds, which would be acceptable if confirmed. The TDC would require some minor modifications, including input by British synchros ('M type' motors). To be fitted in the first 'A'-class submarine, the first TDC would have to be delivered in July 1944, the others at a rate of 3½ per month beginning in March 1945. It seemed likely that the first submarine would be missed, and the desired twenty-four would be delivered at a rate of two per month beginning in October 1944. The conference agreed to ask the Americans to accelerate delivery so that all 'A'-class submarines could be fitted, and meanwhile to allow an order to STD Mk II* computers to stand as insurance

against late deliveries. Three additional TDCs were wanted as shore trainers. US modification and supply were plausible in view of the successful British attempt to obtain US Mk 37 fire-control systems for anti-aircraft guns. In February 1944 the British Admiralty Delegation in Washington informed DNO that the changes in torpedo range and running time could not be carried out in the United States. Six TDC Mk I were expected in six months, to be followed by Mk IIIs (at this time the standard US type). By this time it was clear that some 'A'-class submarines would have STD Mk IIs.

9. HMS *Vernon* 1944 annual report (ADM 189/64), 41 and 49; angling limits were 135° right and left, with an accuracy of a quarter-degree. Sea acceptance tests of the gyroscope (A.B. Mk III) were scheduled for the first 'A'-class submarine. In submarines whose tubes did not have angling gear, the angle would be preset before the torpedo was loaded. According to the 1946 edition, two sets of hand-operated angling gear were made for fitting in HMS *Alcide* for trials.

10. The Staff History, p 57, refers to gyro angling, but in 'The Development of Torpedo Fire Control Computers in the Royal Navy', Lindell writes only that it had a slightly different face than STD Mk I showing DA in increments of 10°. He also writes that torpedo angles had to be set it manually, not continuously, as with the TDC. According to Parry, DNO realised in August 1943 that the Royal Navy probably would not be able to acquire sufficient TDCs, so in September he offered three alternatives: a simple modification to allow angling up to 30° (A); a more elaborate version for angles up to 55° (B); and an entirely new device (C). A(S) wanted to press for C at highest priority, but it was delayed while there was still hope of acquiring TDCs. A became STD Mk IIx and then the post-war TCSS 2*. The difference was apparently an adjunct to transmit desired gyro angles to the torpedoes in the tubes.

11. These figures are from the 1954 technical history, which was apparently written immediately after the war. Hezlet, *British and Allied Submarine Operations in World War II* , I, p 354, quotes a post-war account by the Director of Operational Analysis covering only 1941–5, covering 1732 torpedo attacks against a total of 1893 including the other two years. In the attacks analysed, 4913 torpedoes were fired, most often in four-torpedo salvoes. Two-torpedo salvoes predominated in 1941, which Hezlet calls the year of torpedo famine. Of the 1732 attacks, 1044 missed altogether. The analysis shows a 12 per cent drop in performance after fourteen days at sea. During the famine, submarines often had to fire old torpedoes, which were not as reliable as the later Mk VIII. Some attacks failed because torpedoes broke surface or sank to the shallow bottom, but in 1505 cases torpedoes ran normally. Thus the rate of defects was lower than in peacetime firing. In a few cases, too, torpedoes ran under targets.

12. According to the official minelaying history (BR 1736 (56)(1)), 788, the 'T'-class submarines were *Tactician, Tally Ho, Tantalus, Tantivy, Taurus, Templar, Thorough, Thule, Tradewind, Trenchant, Tresspasser, Truculent* and *Tudor*. The 'S' class were *Sea Rover, Stoic* and *Surf*. In addition, the Dutch *O 19* and the French *Rubis* laid moored mines under RN operational control. The purpose-built minelayers could also lay ground mines through their torpedo tubes (twelve each). Dates of trials are from Kemp, *T Class*, p 48. VA(S) ordered that fitting for minelaying not delay completion, so *Thunderbolt, Trusty* and *Turbulent* were not fitted. According to Kemp, 'T'-class submarines could carry eighteen mines, but in practice never carried more than twelve; presumably the eighteen would include one in each torpedo tube. Mines were ejected by air pressure, like torpedoes, with a minimum spacing of 400ft and a firing delay of 4 hours to protect the submarine. According to Kemp, *T Class*, p 49, *Tetrarch* was the last British submarine fitted to lay mines. Kemp does not note the limited number of 'T'-class submarines actually fitted as minelayers, as listed in the official history. The official list may be limited to submarines which actually laid mines.

13. This section is based largely on CB 3210, *H.M. Submarines*, in the series of Technical Staff Monographs produced by the Admiralty after the war (this one is dated 1954); it is ADM 239/414. Despite its date, this book is written as though at the end of the war, with many references to work in progress which would have been dated by 1954.

14. As reported by US Naval Attache London 24 July 1942, in a collection of ONI reports on British Submarines (General Notes including Armament) dated 1941-42-43 in RG 38, NARA II. The first report in the jacket, which presumably determined its location in the file, is 7489 P-10-H. It is graded Confidential. It includes data for *P 219*. Her critical speed was between 140 and 200 RPM, corresponding to a speed of 2 to 2.5 knots. Another report in the same jacket described the sound range at Loch Goil.

15. The standard STS steel in use in 1940 had a strength (yield point) of 17 tons/in²; the wartime 'S' steel was 18.5 tons/in², but according to Brown there were worries about the consistency of its quality.

16. US Naval Attache report, 20 November 1940, in 'British Submarines: General Notes Various 1939-40-41-42' coded 7489-A P-10-N Secret in RG 38, NARA II.

17. According to a US report dated 20 November 1940, one of the US assistant naval attaches had witnessed radio reception 425nm from the transmitter using a loop antenna, the submarine being 10ft and more below the surface. Report in jacket marked 'British Submarines: General Notes Various 1939-40-41-42' coded 7489-A P-10-N Secret in RG 38, NARA II. A 24 October 1940 report in the same jacket mentioned that with the loop 5m below water and directed to within 40° of Rugby, that station could be received in the Mediterranean. A 15 September report of a visit to VA(S) at Northways included the claim that British submarines on the China station using a loop antenna had been able to receive signals from Rugby in England. 'Since this is by far the most important information gleaned as yet in connection with submarines it will be followed up in more detail.' The report also mentioned that the US attaché had been allowed to read British Secret publications at submarine headquarters, an indication of how open the Royal Navy already was to US observers. A 2 December 1940 report described the observer's experience of a war (anti-submarine) patrol on board *Cachalot*. The British were tracking U-boats using D/F and intercepts 'and the Germans very definitely have not profited from the lessons of the last war in regard to the use of radio'. The observer was Commander Fife, USN. The only items withheld from him were the British magnetic mine and the ship's radio D/F device.

18. It turned out that the W/T motor alternator which powered the amplifier used when listening at 50 kHz was unacceptably noisy, so it was eliminated in favour of battery operation.

19. According to the post-war technical history, Type 291 could typically detect a battleship at 18,000 yds and a submarine at 4500 yds, or an aircraft at 5000ft at 50,000 yds (at 500ft, at 20,000 yds). In a calm sea, a submarine could submerge until the base of the aerial was 3ft above water, and obtain about 30 per cent of this performance.

20. Installations seem to have been made at Fremantle. The first was *Tiptoe*, which used it on her first patrol from that base, 6 May – 17 June 1945. *Trump* was also fitted, a third set being retained for instruction and later fitted to *Truculent* after she returned from the Far East.

21. According to Hezlet, *British and Allied Submarine Operations*, I, p 5, reserve submarines were recommissioned. The Home Fleet flotilla went to Aberdeen, reinforced by the 3rd Flotilla from Portland (at Blyth); the two minelaying submarines went to Blyth. They were replaced by three S and two 'H'-class submarines from 5th and 6th Flotillas. 5th Flotilla at Gosport took over all other submarines in home waters; those commissioned from reserve were used mainly for training. Hezlet points out that the rules allowed for immediate attack on naval auxiliaries and transports, but that submarine commanders were aware that they might be difficult to distinguish.

22. Fourteen U-boats left for patrol stations west of the British Isles on 19 August (with two more on 22–23 August) and two 'pocket battleships' left on 21 and 24 August, with their supply tankers.

23. Hezlet, *British and Allied Submarine Operations*, I, p 44.

24. This represented a recent reorganisation. When the Abyssinian crisis came in 1935, the 1st Flotilla in the Mediterranean consisted of the three fleet submarines and two 'S' class; it was reinforced by three more 'S' class from home and two of the large submarines from the Far East. The 2nd Flotilla (four 'L' class) was sent to Aden. A new 3rd Flotilla (3 'S' class and a minelayer) was formed to go to Gibraltar. After the crisis CinC Mediterranean wanted twenty-one submarines, but no more than thirteen were available: Hezlet, *British and Allied Submarine Operations in World War II*, I, p 5. I have relied heavily on Hezlet because he was both a submarine officer during the Second World War (in command for five years) and a post-war FOSM. He had full access to records, including the three Staff Histories of wartime submarine operations, and his account includes considerable reference to code-breaking, a key factor in submarine warfare. Hezlet had previously written a book on the impact of submarines on sea power, as well as volumes on the impact of aircraft and of electronics.

25. ADM 1/10171 is a memo by Plans Division. It explains that the projected disposition was not a direct attack on fast German warships, but instead was intended to threaten the supply ships on which raiders (including U-boats) would depend. Just before war broke out RA(S) argued that the plan was unlikely to succeed, because it was unlikely that the two submarines which would be maintained at all times would find a raider and its supply ship. Because, in his view, British submarines were the only counter to enemy submarines, that should be their sole shipping protection role. RA(S) wanted to form U-boat hunting groups, each with its own supply ship, a step Director of Plans rejected because, among other things, RA(S) had not explained how the hunting group would find U-boats in the open Atlantic. Beginning about a year earlier (August 1938) large German warships had made extended cruises to the South Atlantic, supported by tankers. These exercises seemed to foreshadow

wartime raiding. Hence the formation of a flotilla of patrol submarines. It did not help that the area in which the hunters were to operate would be under French operational control in war, according to pre-war plans.

26. Hezlet, *British and Allied Submarine Operations*, I, p 27. Some ships were not attacked because they were believed to be neutral.

27. Hezlet, *British and Allied Submarine Operations*, I, p 53, recounts an attack by *Tuna*, probably against *U 59*, on 5 September 1940; she fired three torpedoes and missed, and a torpedo from the U-boat missed her by 200 yds. The next day *Tribune* fired two torpedoes by Asdic at a submerged U-boat at a range of 700 yds and heard an explosion, but no U-boat was sunk that day.

28. Hezlet, *British and Allied Submarine Operations*, I, p 70, points out that German signals intelligence concerning convoys was excellent at this time, so they presumably knew which convoys had submarine escorts; in his view the lack of attacks should be counted a victory. Submarines were no more successful in offensive patrols against major German units, which tended to appear where there were no British submarines. There was no question, in his view, that submarines were too often in the wrong place; 'their strategic handling must be open to question'. German signals intelligence, in his view, was not a sufficient explanation. Submarines were not sufficiently concentrated against the few German major units.

29. This phase of the war began with preparations for an attack on Egypt in August 1940. On 13 September the Italian army advanced into Egypt, taking Sidi Barrani on the 16th. Meanwhile the Italians were moving troops to Albania to prepare for their attack on Greece. Convoy activity increased proportionally. The British were supplying their own army in Egypt from outside the Mediterranean. Initial British attacks on the Italian convoys were ineffective; the Italians managed to ship so much to Tripoli that they had to suspend shipments while the port was cleared. Even so, the need to provide escorts diverted a third of the Italian destroyer force from the fleet and, at least in theory, made fleet operations more difficult. According to Hezlet, *British and Allied Submarine Operations*, I, p 62, initially British submarines largely failed to attack the Italian convoys because it was not understood that the convoy route was west of Malta. Between June and December 1940 the Italians sent 690,000 tons of shipping to North Africa and lost only 1 per cent. As of January 1941, 47,000 troops had been landed without loss, and 350,000 tons of supplies with a loss of only 2.3 per cent. Convoys to Albania at this time carried 623,000 troops (loss 0.05 per cent) and 704,000 tons of supplies (loss 0.2 per cent). Hezlet attributes this failure mainly to misplacement of the submarines and the fact that for much of the time they were not deployed against the Libyan traffic at all. Those based in Alexandria were too far from the convoy routes, and the policy never to surface by day slowed their transit. In any case, despite the success of the convoys, the Italian army in Libya was doing poorly against the British army coming from Egypt.

30. Hezlet, *British and Allied Submarine Operations*, I, p 47. The best colour for the Mediterranean was royal blue, but the big submarines were all painted dark blue; according to Hezlet they were probably more visible at night than Italian destroyers painted light grey. Hezlet considers that long patrols against raiders in the Far East had worn them out, they had carried out few exercises, and they had been cut off from the experience of operations in Home Waters in 1939–40. Many of their crews were overdue for relief.

31. By late July the British had lost five submarines, all to Italian destroyers or torpedo boats, which spotted them at night (Hezlet blames the undue visibility of the big British submarines), typically by running down D/F fixes using patrol lines. In the case of HMS *Oswald*, the last of the five, that was five Italian destroyers running four miles apart.

32. Hezlet's account of German ASW successes in 1939–40 suggests that they had no equivalent. The Germans relied heavily on hydrophones and sprint-and-drift tactics, although they were credited with a few primitive sonars. Presumably German hydrophones were substantially better than their First World War equivalents because they employed vacuum tube amplifiers.

33. Hezlet, *British and Allied Submarine Operations*, I, p 84. On p 157 Hezlet describes the German sonar (SH Mob 5) as a hand-trained magnetostriction device which gave relative bearing, an associated hydrophone being used to give an accurate bearing. It could be used only at slow speed, and was typically trained on a contact previously made by hydrophone. Italian operators were trained in Germany.

34. Hezlet, *British and Allied Submarine Operations*, I, p 83. On p 110 Hezlet points out that thanks to their higher speed ships and aircraft could often make better use of code-breaking. For example, in one night Force 'K' based at Malta managed to sink seven ships and one escort; submarines sank three ships in the same period.

35. According to Hezlet, *British and Allied Submarine Operations*, I, p 116, at the outbreak of war the Italians had 548 ships of over 500 tons (1,749,441 tons);

there were also fifty-six German ships in their ports (203,512 tons). By the end of 1941 they had lost 779,409 tons (201 ships), and few were being built. By this time German mines laid by Italian cruisers had destroyed Force 'K'. Hezlet, *British and Allied Submarine Operations*, I, p 239 states that at the outbreak of war Italy had 786 ships (3,318,129 tons), but 212 of them (1,216,637 tons) were outside the Mediterranean at the outbreak of war and were therefore either seized by the Allies or laid up in neutral ports. Another twenty-six (352,051 tons) were unusable or were hospital ships. Hence the 548-ship figure he uses. Among other things, the Italians needed ships to bring oil from Romania via the Dardanelles, even though there was a rail link; it had insufficient capacity and there were too few tank cars. Up to the end of 1940, Italy lost forty-five ships (161,423 tons), at about twice the rate at which new ships were being built. Axis losses during the first convoy battle were 156 ships (617,986 tons); during the second convoy battle another 138 ships (480,652 tons) were lost. Italian measures to gain shipping during 1942 were procurement from Greece and Yugoslavia, charter from Spain, but mainly an attempt to use laid-up French ships. These means gained 126 ships; another thirty (150,000 tons) were built (in 1941 the figure had been twenty-eight ships totalling about 140,000 tons). The Germans built or captured another 124 ships (378,784 tons). Losses in the third convoy battle were so bad that a shipping crisis was expected in the summer of 1943. During that year, up to the surrender of Italy in September, losses amounted to 226 ships (758,555 tons). At that time the Axis still had 373 ships (1,158,817 tons) in the Mediterranean, but 101 ships (410,239 tons) were being repaired. The Italian official naval historian gave total losses of Axis shipping in the Mediterranean up to the Italian armistice as 565 ships of over 500 tons (2,018,616 tons) plus another 759 small ships (87,905 tons). Submarines were responsible for 43 per cent of the tonnage sunk (44 per cent of the number). Of the 114 British and Allied submarines involved, forty-five were lost, thirty-five with all hands. Another twenty-seven submarines were lost in British home waters at the same time. Hezlet, *British and Allied Submarine Operations*, I, p 241, notes that, surprisingly, despite the clarity of Mediterranean water, only one submarine (if that) seems to have been lost at sea to air attack. Bombers sank four during the assaults on Malta. Convoy escorts sank twenty-two submarines, eight of them before the Italians acquired German Asdics. The number mined is unknown, since in many cases submarines were lost with all hands. Hezlet also points out that a submarine which lost control could easily dive beneath her test depth in very deep water.

36. Reviewing the limited results achieved by Allied submarines between late 1941 and mid-1942, Hezlet, *British and Allied Submarine Operations*, I, p 125, concludes that even had US torpedoes been effective and had the interwar British submarine force been present, the Japanese move south to the Philippines, Malaya and the Netherlands East Indies would not have been much delayed, let alone stopped. Nor could the delay have sufficed to enable the US fleet to carry out its pre-war plan to advance to the Philippines. Hezlet seems not to have been aware that this plan had been abandoned some time before in favour of a step-by-step advance across the Pacific; the hope was that the twenty-nine submarines (and other US naval forces) in the Philippines would impose attrition which would help later on.

37. Hezlet, *British and Allied Submarine Operations*, I, p 123.

38. As quoted by Hezlet, *British and Allied Submarine Operations*, I, p 164.

39. As assessed by Hezlet, *British and Allied Submarine Operations*, I, p 170. He argues that the figures show that a general attack on Axis shipping in the Mediterranean could have won in the end. The alternative, to concentrate on cargoes en route to North Africa, had achieved an average success rate of 14 per cent, although at times it reached 40 per cent. It had been insufficient to win on its own, but clearly made an essential contribution to Rommel's defeat at El Alamein, and to his inability to go back on the offensive, as he had previously been able to do. The submarines operating out of Malta (10th Flotilla) had accounted for about half a million tons of Axis shipping (and damaged another quarter million tons) and had sunk four cruisers, eight destroyers, and eight submarines; they had also damaged a battleship and five more cruisers. On 21 January 1943 the Admiralty stated that British and Allied submarines in the Mediterranean had sunk a million tons of Axis shipping, but that was an overestimate.

40. The North African ('Torch') landings featured the first large-scale use of submarines as navigational beacons. Submarines were also deployed to help defend the landing forces, but the expected Italian and Vichy French threats did not materialise. The Allies were willing to land despite their apparent inferiority in capital ships. The Italian surface threat had to be taken seriously at the time of the landing in Sicily ('Husky') in July 1943 because although it was plausible that they would not come out beyond fighter range to defend the Axis position in North Africa, a landing on Italian soil was expected to be a different proposition. For this and other landings submarines landed parties which reconnoitred

beaches. For 'Husky' the submarine missions were to land commandos; to protect against the largely intact Italian surface fleet; and to isolate Sicily from reinforcement.

41. Hezlet, *British and Allied Submarine Operations*, I, p 201, does not give the totals lost, but does show how meagre the supplies which got through were: 17,600 tons of fuel, 1700 vehicles, 50 tanks, and 214 guns; only 15,000 men came by sea, supplemented by 14,500 by air. These supplies were intended both for the Axis army in Tunisia and for the Afrika Korps, which by March was at the border of Tunisia, having retreated westward. The proportion sunk, presumably in January, by submarines was 40,120 tons (thirteen ships), by aircraft 41,088 tons (nine ships), and by surface ships 7757 tons (four ships). Half of the ships sunk by aircraft were bombed in harbour. Five ships were expended by the enemy as blockships. Half of the losses to submarines were not on the runs to North Africa, but they worsened the tight Italian shipping situation. This was aside from successes achieved with Chariots (manned torpedoes). According to Hezlet, *British and Allied Submarine Operations*, I, p 213, during this campaign 119 convoys and 578 individual voyages by small units (including landing craft) landed 72,246 men and 306,721 tons of equipment, fuel, and supplies. Destroyers landed another 52,000 men and aircraft 65,000. Submarines had attacked sixty-four of the convoys; 164 suffered air attacks. That was apart from 273 air raids on ports into which the ships had sailed. Losses amounted to 23 destroyers and other escorts, 151 cargo ships, and 92 small ships. Losses of cargo amounted to 23 per cent in December, January, and February, rising to 41.5 per cent in March and April and 77 per cent in May. British official figures credited aircraft with the greatest proportion of ships bound to and from Tunisia, a total of ninety-six ships (324,723 tons) compared to fifty ships (155,067 tons) by submarines and eleven (18,011 tons) by surface craft, with four ships (18,011 tons) shared, three (12,502 tons) by mines and fourteen (37,967 tons) by miscellaneous causes (mainly accident and capture). All of these figures are for the Tunisian route. During the same period submarines sank a total of eighty-eight ships (234,368 tons); Hezlet points out that even if they were not headed for Tunisia, they were certainly indirectly supporting that campaign.

42. According to Hezlet, *British and Allied Submarine Operations*, I, p 193, the plan was compromised by a message (which the Germans read) setting up no-bomb areas in which the submarines would operate. This was not realised at the time by the Admiralty.

43. Hezlet, *British and Allied Submarine Operations*, I, p 271, gives results. The submarines sank eighteen ships (60,724 tons) and damaged another seven (28,474 tons). One of the ships was sunk in a midget submarine attack and another by gunfire. During the same campaign, Bomber Command laid 9637 mines which sank seventy-nine ships (61,541 tons) and damaged another fifteen (28,134 tons), losing forty-eight aircraft. Coastal Command anti-shipping strikes sank thirty-six ships (48,007 tons) and damaged seven (29,729 tons), losing fifty-five aircraft. The Fleet Air Arm sank eight ships (30,027 tons) and damaged eleven (33,428 tons), losing six aircraft. The Dover coastal battery sank two ships (11,948 tons). Attacks by destroyers and MTBs on German coastal convoys generally sank escorts rather than the merchant ships. By May 1944 German iron ore imports (on a yearly basis) had fallen from 1,306,800 tons to 420,000 tons.

44. Hezlet, *British and Allied Submarine Operations*, I, p 311, points out that carrier aircraft were not a problem, since they laid their mines inside the leads where submarines could not go. Coastal Command had to accept no-bomb areas, and because navigation was difficult they had to be rather large.

45. Although *Venturer* never spotted a snorkel, the noise the U-boat was making suggests that she was snorkelling. Hezlet suspects that the periscope was spotted so often because it was generally freely used when snorkelling, and also that it had to be high out of the water to look over the snorkel head. Hezlet, *British and Allied Submarine Operations*, I, p 313.

46. According to Hezlet, *British and Allied Submarine Operations*, I, p 326, when the use of British submarines in the Pacific was first suggested in January 1943, US Admiral King particularly welcomed the 'S' class, which he considered ideal for the shallow Java Sea. He wanted to operate the 'T' class in the South China Sea or as far north as they could go.

47. Hezlet, *British and Allied Submarine Operations*, I, p 346. Although the British were prepared to operate to their limits in shallow water, the Americans were uneasy in less than 100 fathoms, and felt vulnerable in less than 30 fathoms. Hezlet cites cases in which British submarines ran aground while attacking at periscope depth; many attacks were in water less than 20 fathoms deep. He cites the successful attack on the Japanese cruiser *Ashigara* as an example. Hezlet also argues that the British gun arrangement, with its quick-manning hatches, was better than its US counterpart, an important point in shallow water against small targets. Hezlet doubted that the Americans could have done as well as they did in the Pacific with British submarines, but the British could not have

done so well in Norway and in the Mediterranean with big American submarines. He cites the poor performance of the US Subron 50 in European waters in 1942–3.

48. RN Submarine Museum, file A1945/45, papers of Lakin's. The letter is unsigned, but was clearly from Captain Ben Bryant, the celebrated CO of HMS *Safari* in 1941–3, and then a flotilla commander (in 1946 he was on board HMS *Adamant*). He mentions a compilation of lessons from the various technical missions on American boats, for FOSM. 'I think you have kept your head very well, and have not gone off the handle in praising the American boats, though there is much to praise in them, as well as the gallant men who drive them.'

49. Moore, *Building for Victory*, p 23. According to Moore, on the outbreak of war which submarines would be included in the 1940–1 Programme had not yet been decided. My text reflects Moore's descriptions of programmes as they were proposed and altered, but the numbers of ships in the programmes is taken from his tables at the back of the book. They generally *do not* match the text.

50. DNC official history, p 23.

51. ADM 1/15333 is RA(S)'s comments on planned 'S' and 'U'-class production, dated 19 June 1943. The current 1943 Programme called for thirty-six 'A' class, five 'S' class, and ten 'U' class, all of the latter to be built by the Vickers High Walker yard. The 'U' class were the quickest to build. On 14 June 1941 Churchill made the numbers and speed of construction the first factor in the submarine programme, as these vessels were wanted for the Mediterranean and for anti-invasion work. By the end of the 1942 Programme, fifty-five 'U' class would have been built. Now it was reasonable to look East. Experience with the 'U' class patrolling off Norway during the winter of 1942–3 had shown 'more than ever' that it was unsuited to distant and prolonged patrols 'and could not in any circumstances be used in the East'. Although the 'A' class was the best type for the Far East, High Walker could not build anything larger than the 'S' class. Their range was shorter than the 'T' class, and very much shorter than the 'A' class, 'yet they could play a part in the Eastern theatre'. RA(S) therefore proposed that the ten 'U' class in the 1943 Programme be replaced by as many 'S' class as possible.

52. Moore, *Building for Victory*, p 121, describes the three improved 'A' class as the residue of the 1944–5 Programme, changed from three of the 1944–5 units but taken as a new initiative. According to Moore, before the end of the war, twenty of the 1943–4 'A' class and seventeen of the 1944–5 'A' class were cancelled. Given the advances the Germans had made, at the end of the war the three improved 'A' class were cancelled and work began on a new 'B' class capable of 20 knots submerged. On 12 October 1945 the Board met to decide on further cancellations, which included ten rather than twelve 'A' class but also two 'T' class (*Thor* and *Tiara*) building at Portsmouth. Ultimately sixteen 'A' class were completed.

53. In a 15 November 1940 report the US Naval Attache (Captain E L Cochrane, who was soon to become chief of the US Bureau of Ships) reported a conversation with VA(S) and his staff in which the aft-firing amidships tubes in the 'T' class were mentioned. They were being installed in repeat 'T'-class submarines of the War Programme. These tubes were angled 7½° off the centreline, their gyros set to correct so that they emerged running right aft. This was an ONI Confidential report in a jacket marked 'British Submarines: General Notes Various 1939-40-41-42' coded 7489-A P-10-N Secret in RG 38, NARA II. Another report in this file, dated 15 September 1940, mentions all three aft-firing tubes in the 'T' class, including the external stern tube. The writer had been personally introduced to Admiral Horten by US Naval Attache Captain Alan Kirk. Horten mentioned his strong opposition to placing the submarine commanding officer anywhere but in the control room, as he should be in complete control of depth and should always be aware of what was going on. This was despite the fact that for the same length of periscope the submarine would have to be shallower than if it were being commanded from the conning tower. At this time the British had operational control of Dutch O-boats, which did use their conning towers for control (as did the US Navy), and some of Horten's staff liked the idea.

54. As described by Kemp, *T Class*, pp 19–21.

55. Cover 626, '1940 S Class'. Folio 1 is both the order for the modified S and the paper giving basic characteristics. The decisions were taken at a 22 January 1940 meeting presided over by VA(S); those present included L C Williamson, Assistant DNC, who was responsible for submarines. The five 'S'-class submarines had been ordered on 2 January 1940. Initially Deputy Controller wanted simply to repeat the last 'S' design to avoid delay. DNC had already prepared a sketch design, and it turned out that Vickers had sufficient drawing resources.

56. Cover 626, Folio 3 includes an account of the 30 January 1940 conference on required engine power. To complete a full charge in 8½ hours, a submarine had to supply 1000 amps per battery (2000 amps in all) for 3 hours. Cutting that to

800 per battery would extend the charging time, and at the minimum rate (200 amps per battery) 24 hours would be required. Pre-war practice had been to run one engine while using the other for charging, but under war conditions a submarine would try to run at maximum speed while charging, to make the best use of the dark hours. She might have to dive unexpectedly. Alternative engines considered at this time were seven and eight-cylinder versions of the *Sunfish* engine and four and five-cylinder Sulzers. This meeting considered the eight-cylinder version of the *Sunfish* engine (seven cylinders as installed), which would require 18in more engine room length. At 11 knots it would provide about 900 amps for charging. The conference decided that the design would proceed on the basis of 1500 BHP power, with a reserve sufficient to charge at 900 amps at 11 knots when 6 months out of dock. That meant the power available in *Sunfish*.

57. Vickers strongly advocated its own engine; EinC would have preferred to repeat the engine in *Sunfish*. Later he said that he would ask each builder to suggest the engine it preferred. Vickers claimed that its engine would save some space and weight.
58. As pointed out by Hezlet, *British and Allied Submarine Operations*, I, pp 264–5.
59. Miscellaneous Cover (483B), Folio 19, paper submitted by DNC dated 13 July 1941; Design A had been discussed with FOSM on 23 June. The small anti-invasion submarines were requested by Controller on 26 June. An enclosed Legend form dated 13 July 1941 described the three big designs, comparing them with the 'U' and 1940 'S' classes:

	'U' Class	1940 'S'	A	C	D
Length pp (ft)	180	185	–	185	191
Length oa (ft-in)	97	217	179-6	220	223
Beam Extreme (ft-in)	16-10	23-8¾	21-0	21-0	23-8½
Surface Draft (ft-in)					
Fwd	14-0½	12-10	13-0 mean	13-0 mean	13-9 mean
Aft	14-9	14-8			
Surface Dispt (tons)	632	830	540	795	885
Standard (tons)	552	715	–	685	755
Submerged (tons)	730	989	–	915	1060
BHP	800	1900	800	1900	2500
Speed surface (knots)	11.7	15	12	15.5	16.75
Oil Fuel (tons)	38.6	67	37.5	66	80
Of which external:	–	22	–	40	29
At 10 knots (nm)	4000	5800	4500	6000	6000
Cells 224	224	112	224		224
Motors	4	4	4	4	4
BHP of motors	825	1300	825	1300	1300
Submerged (knots)	8.7	9.7	9	9.8	9.3
For (hours)	1.8	1.1	1	1.1	1.1
Endurance (3 knots) (hours)	45	40	35 (2 knots)	40	35
TT					
Internal	4	6	4	4	4
External aft	–	–	–	1	2
External bow	–	–	–	2	2
Gun	12pdr	3in	–	3in	3in

Constructor's Notebook 492/6 (R D Cooper, 1941) gives details of A, B, and C designs which do not correspond with those above. In his book, A was 124ft 6in (pp) 160ft (oa) x 21ft 1in (13ft pressure hull diameter) with two 21in bow tubes, one above the other, and two (later four) reloads. Displacement would have been 462 tons surfaced and 540 tons submerged. She would have been driven by the diesels Vickers developed for the Estonian submarines, producing 500 BHP for 14 knots (submerged performance would have been 8.25 knots [later 8.75 knots] on 395 SHP). B was similar but smaller: 119ft 6in (pp) 152ft 5in (overall), with a surfaced displacement of 434 tons and a submerged displacement of 503 tons. Design C was enlarged to carry four bow tubes (two reloads): 124ft 6in (pp) 160ft (overall), 489 tons surfaced. At 8 knots surface endurance would be, respectively, 5360nm, 4450nm and 4800nm. These were probably the three anti-invasion designs.

60. Miscellaneous Cover (483B), Folio 19. This was when Vickers was told to stop laying down 'S'-class submarines. Material which had been partially fabricated at Barrow was moved to Cammell Laird and Scotts.
61. Unfortunately the Covers do not mention the change in gun armament.
62. This was the same conference at which changes to the 'T' class were ordered, and at which the decision to build the modified 'S' class was taken. Cover 626 (1940 S Class), Folio 1. It was decided that the 'U'-class submarines just ordered would be built, but that the next lot of 'U' and 'T' class would be replaced by the new

'S' class. An important factor in the decision to continue building the recently-ordered 'U' class was that they had Paxman engines not made by Vickers, that firm having only limited capacity due to gun-mounting work. It would therefore find production of new 'S'-class engines difficult (but Vickers saw no problem in producing more of the seven-cylinder Portuguese engines).
63. In the November 1940 interview with Captain Cochrane USN cited above.
64. DNC official history, p 25; these changes are not in the 'U' Class Cover.
65. I have not found Legends for these designs, which were designated X, Y, and Z. The DNC official history, p 34, states that all were about 160ft long, displacing 430 to 490 tons, with 1000 BHP engines (surface speed 13.5 knots, submerged speed 7.5 knots) and an endurance of 3000 to 3500nm at 9 knots. These seem to be the designs in the Cooper notebook.
66. Unfortunately the 'A' Class Cover (688) is missing. This account is therefore less complete than would be desirable. It is based largely on the DNC history.
67. A Legend is No 16 in the Brass Foundry's Legend Book; it is dated 5 March 1941 and is described as an 'improved *Cachalot*'. No notes are appended.
68. DNC official history, p 23. The next step up in power, adopted for the 'A' class, was supercharging, sometimes called pressure-charging in contemporary documents. The 600-ton figure is given in the official history as enough for three 'T'-class submarines, but their full fuel load was 134 tons.
69. 'T' Class Cover Vol 4 (542C), Folio 9, dated 8 January 1942. Proposals had been made by Admiral(S) in a 25 December 1941 memo.
70. DNC official history, p 24. This account is somewhat contradictory, and the account given here has been adapted from it, with changes suggested by the few surviving papers in the Covers.
71. DNC official history, p 33.
72. I have not found any statement of the Staff Requirements for the 'A' class. As an indication of what was happening at the time, a Miscellaneous Cover (483B) includes designs initially offered in July 1942 and then in modified form in September and October by Dutch naval constructor M F Gunning (Folio 32A), who had escaped the Netherlands and was working for DNC. He prefaced his own remarks by mentioning that 'as understood' two new types were under consideration, an operational type capable of long patrols in the tropics, and a cargo carrier which could also serve as a minelayer. Gunning was interested in using multiple hulls. Although nothing came of his proposal, afterwards the Royal Netherlands Navy built a class of triple-hull submarines he had designed. Presumably Gunning's ideas reflected the Staff Requirement of the time. His operational submarine had a diving depth of 500ft, his cargo/minelaying submarine 300ft.
73. A special air-conditioning compartment was introduced: air was drawn into it from the main body of the submarine and then expelled to be recirculated. Its temperature and humidity could be reduced, and, if necessary, CO_2 scrubbed out and oxygen added. Nearly all accommodation was forward, and a bunk was provided for every crewman. Other habitability features for the tropics were enlarged fresh-water stowage, electric distillers, cold cupboards and automatic refrigerators. During the discussion of the Sims paper, Engineer Rear Admiral S O Frew stated that in the early days of the war there was no air-conditioning, so under tropical conditions crews suffered from skin troubles and heat exhaustion. Crew conditions were so bad that two or three spare crews always had to be available. With the introduction of air-conditioning, humidity was vastly improved and temperature slightly reduced. This was absolutely essential for Pacific patrols lasting up to fifty days; when crews returned from patrol they were still fresh and could go out again. In response, Sims noted that the air-conditioning in use at the outbreak of war turned out to have 'certain disadvantages', and the British soon realised that they had to shift to Freon as a refrigerant. As a result, British submarine crews preferred to sleep on board rather than on board their non-air-conditioned depot ships, even though the latter were more spacious.
74. Sims, Institution of Naval Architects lecture 1947, p 151; he also states that existing submarines had become far too congested. The design was adapted to pre-fabrication in sections, assembled so as to employ downward welding as much as possible. The most difficult welds were the ones joining the pressure hull sections, each of which was either cylindrical or conical. Internal structures were welded into the sections on the slip. Sections of external tanks and superstructure were also prefabricated.
75. Data are based on Constructor's Notebook 492/9 (R D Cooper), which includes sketches of the pressure hulls associated with Designs II through VII. All seem to have been substantially smaller than the 'A' class as finally built. The earliest version shows a 213ft 3in pressure hull (but Design IV shows 208ft 9in, and a displacement of 1200 tons). Design VI showed a pressure hull 222ft long (216ft was crossed out) and a surface displacement of 1296 tons; in Design VII (26 November 1942) the pressure hull was lengthened 3ft to take a Q tank, and this version had saddle tanks derived from those of the 'S' class, but lengthened to

accommodate 60 tons of oil fuel, 20 tons of compensating water, and 6 tons of fresh water or ballast. Unlike earlier versions, this one showed four reloads for the two internal stern tubes. The design displacement of the 'A' class was 1360 tons surfaced; overall length was 227ft 6in. Length pp, which would somewhat exceed the length of the pressure hull, was 249ft 3in (pressure hull length is not given). Unfortunately the notebook does not give expected performance or, for that matter, machinery details.

76. Legend and covering note dated 24 February are in the Legend Book at the Brass Foundry. The covering note refers to Controller's instructions on TSD 861/42, which presumably gave initial Staff Requirements (no date is given). The Legend was sent for DNC's signature on 26 February 1942. Staff requirements were amended by TSD 2516/43 and 2519/43.

77. According to A J Sims, 'British Submarine Design During the War (1939-45)', in *Transactions* of the Institution of Naval Architects 1947, p 151, submerged battery charging had also been considered pre-war. I have not found any papers on this.

78. As reported by the US naval attaché, in a report dated 18 March 1945. The first of class HMS *Amphion* had made 18.4 knots with 4300 BHP. File marked P-10-h, 7489-C, in ONI (RG 38) Secret series, NARA II, in jacket marked 'British Submarines – General Notes 1945'. A second boat of the class was being completed at Chatham with a Chatham-built engine of the same type; its manifold trunking had been modified to reduce noise. At this time the British were working on a faster submarine, which would be driven by a higher-power (about 3000 BHP) faster-running diesel geared between motor and engine with the motor direct-coupled to the propeller shaft. The writer was Captain Albert G Mumma, a US submarine expert who would later be Chief of the Bureau of Ships.

79. Cover 483C, Folio 49. Brown, *Nelson to Vanguard*, p 116 ascribes the stability problem to the fact that the curve of righting arms (GZ) was not calculated due to a work overload; it seemed to be enough that GM was similar to that of the 'T' class. The rather lengthy calculation was done only after it was observed that the submarine sometimes hung at about 30° while rolling. Normally a submarine GZ curve has a maximum at about 40° and vanishes at an angle beyond 90°. However, the 'A'-class curve showed a maximum at 20°; it vanished at about 40°. The combined requirements of high surface speed, low silhouette, and sufficient GM when lightly loaded had caused the designers to choose a midship section similar to that of a deeply immersed surface ship with sharp tops to the ballast tanks. As the submarine heeled, the sharp top corner was soon immersed, reducing stability. Water trapped in the deep trough made by the tops of the ballast tanks worsened the situation. Corrections were to interchange the fuel and ballast tanks and to separate port and starboard tanks.

Chapter 16: A Glimpse of the Future

1. F H Hinsley, E E Thomas, C F G Ransom, and R C Knight, *British Intelligence in the Second World War* (London: HMSO, 1984), III Pt 1, p 244. The attaché messages are in an RG 457 file at NARA II (College Park).

2. Donald B Welbourn and Tim Crichton, 'The Schnorchel: A Short-Lived Engineering Solution to Scientific Developments', published in 2008 by the Newcomen Society (headquartered at the Science Museum). Welbourn spent the immediate post-war period in Germany as a Lieutenant Commander(E) RNVR. It was drafted in 1949 when he was developing auxiliaries for the Royal Navy at W H Allen Sons and Co Ltd, and later completed by Crichton. Data on German development is from this paper. Much of the paper shows that the snorkel idea was hardly new when the Germans exploited it; for example, during the First World War the commanding officers of *C 3* and *E 35* reportedly fitted their boats with 'breathing tubes'. When the Germans overran the Netherlands in 1940, their operational staff ordered the removal of the captured Dutch snorkels on safety grounds. The German submarine designers wanted to run trials. Welbourn and Crichton consider the lack of interest in anything new typical of the German Admiralty at that time; great U-boat successes in 1941–2 made them even more complacent. Presumably German policy was to avoid any change in design because it would slow U-boat production. Their attitude changed when the situation became desperate in the spring of 1943. During a 2 March 1943 visit to Dönitz, chief of the U-boat arm, Professor Walter mentioned the possibility of running diesels submerged. By May the Naval Technical Department had a design, which could automatically shut and reopen if the intake was temporarily drowned by a wave. Even at 17 knots the boat could keep running for 60 seconds with the valve shut off. Walter reiterated his ideas in a 19 May 1943 letter to Dönitz. Not only would U-boats generally be more effective if given snorkels, but the new device would be particularly valuable to the HTP U-boats he advocated, because they would be completely freed from the surface. Dönitz replied at once that he would try out the device. On 8 February 1944 he wrote to Walter that Hitler had decorated him for both

devising the Walter (HTP) submarine and for devising the schnorchel. Welbourn attributed German adoption of the snorkel to the great success the British were enjoying using Coastal Command aircraft against U-boats transiting the Bay of Biscay during the summer of 1943. It happened that a naval group sank the first snorkel U-boat there. Paper courtesy of George Malcomson, RN Submarine Museum. For an account of the Dutch invention and use of snorkels see Mark C Jones, 'Give Credit Where Credit is Due: The Dutch Role in the Development and Deployment of the Submarine Schnorkel', *Journal of Military History* 69 (October 2005), pp 987–1012. During the First World War, the Dutch fitted retractable ventilation tubes to their *0-2* through *0-7*, *K-II*, and *K-V* through *K-VII*. One ventilated the battery, and the other brought fresh air into the submarine. The Dutch did not consider the tubes sufficient to run diesels submerged, because when the top of the ventilating tube was awash it could admit water into the battery. However, they did use the tubes to run diesels when trimmed down, with only the conning tower awash, a procedure used in home waters in 1916 and in the Netherlands East Indies after 1922. Meanwhile an Italian naval engineer proposed a true snorkel in 1923, and it was tested on board the Italian *H-3* about November 1925. The main drawback seems to have been the visibility of the submarine due to exhaust. The Italians did not install a snorkel on board a new submarine until 1933–4, and in 1937 the new chief of their submarine service ordered all snorkels removed, without any surviving explanation (Crichton and Welbourn cite the rather visible smoke the snorkel produced). Meanwhile Lieutenant Commander J J Wichers RNLN submitted a formal proposal for a snorkel in 1933, but nothing was done until a mysterious object was observed on the surface, creating a wake and emitting smoke. The Dutch thought that it was the snorkel of a Japanese submarine (it was not), and included snorkels in the submarines *0-19* and *0-20*, which were being designed in 1936. Wichers later claimed compensation from the British for the snorkel they adopted, but the Admiralty argued that their valve, the key element, had been adapted from German designs which differed from the Dutch type. The two Dutch snorkel submarines entered service in July and September 1939. Their air intakes projected 1.5m above the surface, and their exhausts, which were at the after end of the superstructure, were well below the surface. Maximum snorkelling speed was 5 to 7 knots. As noted, there were serious problems, and the two submarines made only limited use of their snorkels operationally. Snorkels were, however, incorporated in the next class (*0-21* through *0-27*), of which the first four were either complete or nearly so when the Netherlands fell. They escaped to Great Britain; the Admiralty ordered their snorkels removed. At this time the commander of the Dutch submarines described snorkels as dangerous. However, the Dutch did like it as a ventilator, to be used when running on the surface in rough weather. The two boats equipped with snorkels in the Far East did not use them, the exception apparently being when *0-19* escaped from Java to Ceylon in March 1942 (her snorkel was removed during a 1943 refit). According to Jones, in 1943 the Germans modified the Dutch snorkel by using the entire volume of the submarine as a buffer to keep supplying air to the engine when the intake was briefly closed by a wave. They retained the Dutch ball float to close and open the intake. Like the Dutch, they could operate only at slow speed, their snorkel submarines suffered from vibration which made it difficult to use periscopes, and even with the buffer they suffered sudden drops in internal pressure when the intake valve closed. According to Jones, in July 1942 the British requested drawings of the Dutch snorkel, probably because they feared that the Axis, like the Allies, would develop effective radars which would limit surfaced submarine operation. Interest apparently began in June 1942; by October the British were concluding that there were serious problems. Depth-keeping near the surface became more vital, meaning that the snorkelling submarine had to run at higher speed. All components of the snorkel would have to be strengthened to withstand the rougher seas in which the Royal Navy operated (compared to those of the Netherlands East Indies). EinC listed disadvantages including increased noise (the Germans and Italians depended largely on hydrophones), increased visibility (e.g. from sparks in the exhaust), increased space and weight, greater complication, and increased onboard temperature and an increased risk of battery fire.

3. In ADM 223/320, a compilation of NID U-boat papers.

4. ADM 223/320. It was intended as a handbook for those continually handling U-boat material, and also as an overview for newcomers.

5. ADM 223/320. The next paper in the file is an urgent request dated 3 February 1944 for information about 'schnorchel' in connection with D-Day. Verification of German construction of midget submarines was also urgently needed. At about the same time NID and other intelligence agencies noted a sharp drop in the rate of U-boat construction, which they correctly associated with a shift in production to a new type or types. According to Hinsley et al, *British Intelligence in the Second World War*, III Pt 1, p 241, in January 1944 a prisoner of war from

U 841 said that a ventilation trunk was being developed. Other prisoners, however, talked of closed-cycle power plants for high underwater speed. NID therefore initially associated schnorchel with a closed-cycle diesel, an entirely separate project. On 24 January 1944 it reported that the Germans were going to fit existing U-boats with closed-cycle diesels. According to Hinsley, however, the naval section at Bletchley Park maintained that the schnorchel was simply a ventilation trunk enabling a U-boat to charge its batteries while submerged. It pointed to a report that a U-boat had conducted tests in December 1943 in the Strander Bucht near Kiel with a snorkel. There the water was only 8 to 9m deep, hardly enough for high-speed trials. The final evidence was a series of signals to *U 264* asking her to report her experience using the schnorchel, and thus revealing its character; the U-boat was sunk before she could do so. US ONI files include a report dated 20 March 1944 in which Coastal Command described the schnorchel in some detail. It is in ONI file 14731-A Register P-10-j, 'Submarines – German 1942-43-44' (Secret) in NARA II RG 38. This paper includes a description of the W-Boat, information on which was credited to prisoners of war. A few had been completed and were running trials in the Baltic.

6. By this time the British had the sensational Japanese account of U-boat policy intercepted on 30 May 1944. The 20 July 1944 summary mentioned both a long-range U-boat intended for the Atlantic and perhaps the Indian Ocean (Type XXI) and a short-range type for the Mediterranean and the coast around Britain. Type XXI was credited with exceptional speed surfaced and submerged – 20 knots surfaced and about 15 knots submerged, with a new-type Asdic to help fire torpedoes submerged. Type XXIII was credited with a speed of 12 knots surfaced and 13 knots submerged. Both would have schnorchels. The larger submarines had been seen on building ways since the autumn of 1943.

7. RN technical submarine history, p 23. I have not found any relevant documents either in PRO or in the 'U' Class Covers.

8. As suggested by a lengthy account of the Dutch installations, in the Foreign Submarines Cover (439A, Folio 19), a carbon copy of an enclosure to DNC's D.C. 12135/42 (i.e., a 1942 report, unfortunately without a precise date). The paper is headed 'submerged dieseling'. It states that the Dutch began fitting gear allowing them to run their diesels at periscope depth with *O-19–O-20*, and later fitted it to *O-21–O-27*. As initially intended it was considered unsuccessful. The air intake pipe created a wake visible from a considerable distance, and the exhaust head, 10ft below the surface, created an enormous disturbance. Thus the device made a submarine very vulnerable to air attack. Later the Dutch tried using it at night; they had just overcome problems with battery ventilation when war broke out in 1940. In its final form the system employed a streamlined induction pipe and an exhaust pipe with a spring-loaded valve. In the final version the induction was closed by a ball valve, which cut out when water came over it (the engine was stopped automatically). Air was led into a water separator under the floor of the control room, and then back through an outboard induction pipe back into the pressure hull and thence directly into the intake of the scavenging pump. Thus the entire system was cut off from the interior of the submarine. It was possible to run the engine but not to ventilate the battery. To solve that problem, a separate connection was made between the water separator and the battery ventilating duct. Suction in the boat was no great problem, but when it surfaced it took some time before the hatch could be opened. The water separator too often operated the wrong way around, soon bringing water into the diesel. The Dutch also found that the violent variations in air pressure in the induction system caused great condensation. The Dutch found that their two-stroke diesels required too much air. When war broke out, they were considering new designs using auxiliary diesels to charge the batteries, requiring only a sixth as much air as the main propulsion diesels. The single telescopic induction mast would connect directly to the interior of the submarine, without any water separator; air would be led into a large separate space such as the entrance over the engine room, where it would precipitate out unwanted moisture. According to Welbourn and Crichton, British trials showed that the snorkel boats were very wet internally. After arriving in England, Dutch submarine commanders asked that their snorkels be removed for safety. ADM 1/17549 is a US report summarising what was known about snorkels as of February 1945 (Op-16-Z Special Report 1-45: this is a Photostat of a US original). It was intended as background for research on snorkel detection. The report cited *U 1230*, which had recently brought two German agents to the United States after a 54-day submerged passage from Norway to Maine. Normal procedure was to run on snorkel twice every 24 hours, each time for 2½ to 3 hours.

9. Typed notes of the meeting are in Constructor's Notebook 492/12 (R D Cooper). Other attendees were DNE and DEE.

10. A paper on future submarines produced by A(S) early in January 1945 referred to separate proposals for fitting trial snort, which were being put into effect. *Truant* arrived at Barrow for installation on 5 March 1945; she was completed

on 5 May 1945, and arrived at Rothesay on 16 May for trials. She had gone out to the Far East and had been forced to return due to engine trouble. A US naval intelligence report dated 15 March 1945 reported official details of the snort then being manufactured for *Truant*. As an initial step, a fixed (not folding) jury-rigged snort was installed on board the old submarine *H 34*. She proceeded to the James Watt Dock at Greenock on 20 February 1945 for a special fitting which was surely the snort; she made her first post-fitting dive on 9 March. She tested her snort only either bottomed or suspended at fixed depth from floats. She ran tests on 10–13 March, the last day including a deep dive (presumably to test whether the piping would crush at depth). There is no indication of a second yard period to remove the proto-snort, and she was then used for ASW training with surface ships; it is not clear whether she used the snort or whether part of it was used to simulate a U-boat snort. *H 34* was decommissioned on 13 June 1945. A sketch of this installation is in M G Kitchener's constructor's notebook (no. 570/7). It shows an induction pipe replacing the after periscope, retracting into its well, and an exhaust pipe well abaft the conning tower, the exhaust substantially lower than the induction. In the sketch, the exhaust is at about the waterline, the induction considerably higher (it appears to be 12ft above the waterline, 8ft above the window of the remaining periscope). According to the US report, a snort installation was being prepared for a 'U'-class submarine. Plans were still subject to modification, and it was proposed to make the exhaust pipe fixed, terminating at the top of the periscope shears; the only folding pipe would be the intake extending above water. 'No attempt at ingenuity has been undertaken in this design, the directive being to install the nearest equivalent to the German schnorchel as possible in the shortest time.' As yet there were no immediate plans for an 'A'-class installation, as supercharged engines raised 'additional difficulties with the underwater exhaust'. The US report is in NARA II RG 38 ONI series 7489-B P-10-h (Secret series) in jacket 'British Submarines – General Notes 1943-44-45'. Unfortunately the file does not include any report of the outcome of the trials.

11. ADM 1/16396. The SIGINT side of schnorchel intelligence is laid out in the US SIGINT history of the Battle of the Atlantic, Chapter IV: Technical Intelligence from CI, in NARA II, RG 357 (5750/433-CN56). Terminology suggests this was a British report. The word 'schnorchel' was first encountered in German signal traffic in January 1944, but initially there was no indication of what it was, except that it was mechanical and that it was associated with diesel engines. Through early 1944 the German command was gaining experience with schnorchels, asking U-boats to report their experience. There was some fear that schnorchel U-boats felt too safe; in February and March they were warned that it was not immune to radar detection. A 31 May broadcast indicated that several U-boats had successfully schnorchelled for submerged cruises lasting several days. Schnorchels could be used for four or five hours per day to charge batteries, and radar detection range of a schnorchel was a fraction of that for a surfaced submarine. Given the noise of running diesels while schnorchelling, U-boat commanders were told to interrupt schnorchelling every twenty minutes to use their hydrophones. On 6 June the operational area for schnorchel U-boats was shifted to the southern coast of England and the Channel, for maximum interference with the Normandy invasion. Within a week U-boats in the Bay of Biscay *without* schnorchels were ordered into port because it was admitted that they could not survive if they had to surface to charge batteries. The schnorchel was considered so important that in August 1944 its installation was designated the chief task of U-boats in port. The first snorkel U-boat the Royal Navy obtained was *U 249*, which surrendered off the Lizard at the end of the war in Europe. *U 1105* had the 'Alberich' anti-sonar coating, and she was tested alongside the uncoated *U 1171*.

12. ADM1/16493, 'Appreciation of the Potential Menace of the "Walterboote"', 7 March 1944, from the Director of the ASW Division of the Naval Staff. This estimate of the threat presented to the Normandy Invasion ('Overlord') was produced by a panel consisting of DDOD(C), CAOR (Chief of Air Operations Research), DNI, and DEE, on which DAUD, DAWT, and Coastal Command were also represented. Hinsley et al, *British Intelligence in the Second World War*, III Pt 1, p 241 explains the background. At the end of November 1943 the Germans began broadcasting claims that they were about to revolutionise the U-boat war. Prisoners of war mentioned a 250-ton U-boat with a crew of fifteen to twenty. These two items were linked with three intelligence items. In September 1943 photo reconnaissance showed two 110ft U-boats in Kiel. Naval Attaché Stockholm reported that a 'Channel type' 250-ton U-boat was exercising in Kiel and that a 250-ton rubber-coated U-boat had been seen in Hamburg. Prisoners of war claimed that Germany was developing new methods of propulsion giving high underwater speed. All of these reports turned out to refer to prototype Walter (i.e., HTP) U-boats 130ft long, with a crew of nineteen. A month later NID stated that reports of U-boats with non-electric propulsion referred to craft of 500 tons or over; it suggested that the might refer to *U 792*

and *U 794*, which had been mentioned in German signals as undergoing trials. Decrypts indicated that they were of an unusual type. In fact they were the first full-sized Walter U-boats, Type XVII. I have used the German designation S-boat for coastal attack craft; the British called them E-boats, and that term was used in the paper.

13. Rössler, *The U Boat*, p 168. HTP did not figure at all in the work of the pre-war Admiralty submarine propulsion committee

14. This message also described Type XXI, and it referred to both (in the US version, anyway) as 'Walder' U-boats, after their inventor. Hinsley et al incorrectly refer to this message as an ambiguous description of Types XXI and XXIII. In the RG 457 version (Entry 9013), this message is SRNA Nos. 000738 – 000743. 'Since Germany has not yet released secret details concerning their new submarines, it is impossible to verify the same . . . request you Japanese naval headquarters. take special care to keep it secret.' Types 21 and 17B are described as larger and small versions of the same type of submarine, both with characteristic lobed hulls (circular-section main pressure hull, semi-circular lobe below it), the lower part containing batteries, WRT and other tanks, and fuel. The small boat was credited with an underwater speed of over 20 knots. Construction of the smaller boats was underway at three yards; the Japanese actually saw the small submarines under construction at two yards, though the information gathered was only superficial.

15. In a 13 February 1945 (translated on 20 February) message the attaché described Type 26, the first of which was to be completed at the end of August 1945, displacing 852 metric tons. It would have four bow tubes and six midships tubes, with no reloads. On Walter turbines it could cruise at 22 knots for 7 hours or at 19 knots for 10 hours. Maximum speed on electric motors was 10 knots. The Walter turbine was credited with 7500 HP (6500 SHP, 1000 HP for auxiliaries), and the submarine carried 97 tons of HTP (Ingolin) for it. The message included a detailed description of the internal arrangement of the submarine and a weight breakdown. A message translated on 21 February described the Walter engine in detail, and a 24 February message explained how the Walter system worked. These are US translations, but the British had the same information.

16. Malcolm Llewellyn-Jones, *The Royal Navy and Anti-Submarine Warfare 1917-49* (London: Routledge, 2006), p 81, citing March 1945 correspondence. Llewellyn-Jones was an experienced ASW officer who worked in the Royal Navy Historical Branch; this is a published version of his PhD thesis (King's College London).

17. Llewellyn-Jones, *The Royal Navy and Anti-Submarine Warfare*, p 84. His references include ADM 1/27774, a file on the project to develop an HTP engine and HTP production (which had no commercial value) in the UK. It includes an account by EinC of the project background, beginning with 1944 information that the Germans had submarines with high submerged speed. Clearly they were operating main engines while submerged. Two items, for a total of £1.1 million, were inserted into the list of research projects sent to the Admiralty's Director of Finance on 14 February 1945 (EinC did not describe them). He went on to credit HTP information to the Assault Team(s). A 17 July 1945 Controller meeting decided to bring *U 1407* to the UK. On 19 September Vickers representatives were given an outline of the work required. EinC estimated that the Germans had already spent over £8 million on building and research. EinC's project would replace that for which he had requested £1 million in February.

18. Hinsley et al, *British Intelligence in the Second World War*, III Pt 1, p 519 (their Appendix 11) is the message in full. This appendix also includes the text of an 11 October message from the attaché describing the Type XXI building programme (large-scale prefabrication) in some detail. It also gave technical details.

19. In accordance with the minutes of a 28 February 1944 conference chaired by ACNS(W), a panel was convened to consider implications of fast and/or deep diving U-boats under the chairmanship of DASW. ADM 1/16495 contains the paper the panel produced, dated 28 March 1944. One possibility was a homing torpedo. The panel set out three possibilities for future U-boats: deeper diving, higher submerged speed, and increased submerged endurance, all of which characterised Type XXI. It appeared that a compromise between diving depth and underwater speed would be necessary, current evidence emphasising the attempt to dive deeper. The target was said to be 400m (1300ft), which in turn would require a considerably thicker pressure hull. Evidence of increased underwater speed was 'not so conclusive', but it had to be expected before long. A combination of deeper diving and higher underwater speed would require a considerably larger submarine – as turned out to be the case. It appeared that a U-boat running at great depth would be unable to counter-attack, as it was most unlikely that torpedo tubes had been redesigned.

20. Llewellyn-Jones, *The Royal Navy and Anti-Submarine Warfare*, p 70, points out that work on *Seraph* began on 16 June 1944, one month after the first Type XXI (*U 2501*) was launched, and she ran trials seven months before the first Type

XXI (*U 2511*) made her first operational cruise. *Seraph* was chosen because she was limited to 200ft, possibly because she had damaged herself in the dive, requiring repairs. Drag was reduced by 55 per cent and propulsive power increased by 13 per cent. On trials, she maintained 12 knots for 40 minutes. Endurance at 10 knots was 2 hours. Llewellyn-Jones cites a November 1945 lecture by R N Newton RCNC of DNC Department on the trend of submarine design (RNSM A1991/058), and also an account of first in class trials; this trials data is also in the Cover. Post-war trials showed that HE did not decrease significantly with depth at 10 knots and above. Llewellyn-Jones points out that HE was sometimes loud enough to mask an echo, hence might be the only way to maintain contact. A fast submarine might quickly escape the Asdic beam, but Asdic could sweep about ten times more quickly for HE than waiting for an echo. To further complicate matters, the wake of a deep U-boat could mask the HE from its propeller if the ship listening was within 20° of dead astern.

21. ONI file (RG 38) at NARA II: 7480-C P-10-h (Secret series), 15 November 1944. The enclosed papers were provided by FOSM via VCNS, who stressed their highly secret nature. The official account of first-of-class trials was enclosed.

22. ONI file (RG 38) at NARA II (Confidential series) 25818 P-10-H. The 'S' Class Cover does not report any such performance.

23. ADM 1/16384. There was also interest in taking over large numbers of the new U-boats to operate in the Far East. A signal dated 3 May 1945 cut the number of Type XXI from 'maximum all available' to 'maximum 8'. The US Navy wanted examples of most types of U-boats plus 'two each of any further types which show promise for experiments and tests, excepting midgets'. The explicit list included Type XXVI. A 5 May amendment to the British list added 'all available parts, plans, and drawings' of Type XXVI, and this was also in the US list. FOSM also wanted examples of more conventional submarines.

24. Identifications from Hezlet, *British and Allied Submarine Operations*, I, p 349. On p 350, Hezlet writes that Type XXI was so impressive that a Joint Chiefs of Staff planning paper suggested scrapping all existing 'A' and 'T'-class submarines and taking over an equal number of Type XXIs from the Germans.

25. ADM 1/18949, a 4 October 1945 report of a hydrogen explosion on board *U 3017*, which had replaced *U 2502*.

26. ADM 1/18557.

27. Llewellyn-Jones cites British interest in coastal ASW, which seemed the most likely problem in the Far East. Otherwise, in his view, it is difficult to see why the Admiralty even cared about testing a Type XXIII. At least three had been able to operate in British coastal waters without being sunk.

28. Llewellyn-Jones, *The Royal Navy and Anti-Submarine Warfare*, p 85, in part citing a May 1947 lecture by A J Sims of DNC department on poor structural design (RNSM A1990/083).

29. Llewellyn-Jones, *The Royal Navy and Anti-Submarine Warfare*, pp 88–90. I have relied on Llewellyn-Jones to explain the collapse of the Type XXI trials programme.

30. ADM 1/18604. Attendees were DEE, DSR, and representatives of DNC, EinC, DNE, DNO, Director of Naval Operational Research, and DTM. Director of Tactical, Torpedo, and Staff Duties was also present, and Assistant Controller for R&D attended part of the meeting. The meeting generally agreed with the A(S) paper described here.

31. Cover 728 (1945 Experimental Submarine), Folio 3, January 1945. The pressure hull would have been 222ft long; length overall would have been 266ft 9in (262ft on the waterline), with an extreme beam of 23ft and an internal pressure hull diameter of 1ft. Submerged displacement would have been 1500 tons. Cover 727, Folio 3 (and Cover 728 Folio 4) is a summary of a 15 January 1945 meeting concerning this submarine. DNC estimated that to reach 20 knots submerged a submarine would need 8000 HP at about 300 RPM. Total battery weight would be about that of seven 'A'-class sections plus 60 tons; short-life batteries would be fitted (not over two years). DEE was to investigate a scheme for rapid switchover from group down to group up, as it was thought the ship might be difficult to control if switchover was prolonged. Cover 728, Folio 3 also includes the much shorter Design C, with a 177ft 9in pressure hull (231ft 9in overall), 231ft on the waterline), with a pressure hull internal diameter of 19ft (19ft 2in extreme beam) and submerged displacement of 1480 tons. It would have had the same power plant and the same performance submerged, but surface speed at full power would have been 14.5 knots. Design D, with six groups of cells, could produce 6900 BHP at the 20-minute rate, for a submerged speed of 19 knots. In its final form it would have had a 175ft 9in long pressure hull (229ft 9in overall) and would have displaced 1430 tons submerged. Cover 728 Folio 10 lists three alternative designs for an experimental submarine, unfortunately undated: Designs 1, 1A, and 2. All had two bow tubes, and could accommodate six torpedoes if their batteries were reduced. All had 8000 BHP motors for 18+ knots submerged (six sets, each of 131 'A' class cells). Endurance

BRITISH SUBMARINES IN TWO WORLD WARS

at 18 knots would be 1 hour. Designs 1 and 1A were 165ft overall with a 24ft diameter pressure hull; surface displacements were 1240 tons and 1200 tons (1320 tons and 1280 tons submerged; form displacements were 1400 tons and 1360 tons). They would have 1½in thick pressure hulls. Design 2 had a 1⅛in pressure hull and was 221ft long overall with a 19ft diameter pressure hull; displacement was 1285 tons surfaced and 1340 tons submerged (1420 tons form displacement). Diving depth was 600ft, rather than the 500ft of Designs 1 and 1A. In the table, they were compared to *Seraph* and to an improved *Seraph* with a welded rather than riveted hull, 0.625 in rather than 0.56in thick. The improved *Seraph* would have two rather than six bow torpedo tubes, with four rather than six reloads. Her 3200 BHP motors would drive her at 15.5 knots rather than 12.5 knots, and endurance at full speed would be an hour rather than 20 minutes. *Seraph* had two batteries (112 high-capacity 'S'-class cells each); the improved *Seraph* had 192 high-capacity 'S' class cells in each of her two batteries. Form displacements were 1110 tons for *Seraph* and 1030 tons for the improved *Seraph*; diving depths were 300ft and 350ft.

32. Cover 728, Folio 7. Notes dated 14 August 1945.
33. Papers on the Improved 'A' Class design are in Cover 727. A possible improvement soon dropped was accommodation for the CO and the attack team in the conning tower, as in most foreign submarines. It was dropped particularly because the AIO demanded so much space. The CO cabin did remain in the conning tower, as in the 'A' class. This double-hulled design could gain internal space by framing its pressure hull externally.
34. Cover 727, Folio 6 summarises a 15 May 1945 discussion on likely modifications to the 'A'-class design, including a telescopic (rather than folding) snort, which would require two extra frame spaces in the control room (which in turn would suffice for the additional radar and AIO requirements), and a modified gun armament: one 4in, one 6pdr and a twin Oerlikon, with the 6pdr at the after end of the bridge, the Oerlikon between the bridge and the 4in gun. The forward casing would be raised slightly. Shutters might have been fitted to the forward torpedo tubes to improve performance above and below the surface.
35. Cover 727, Folio 8.
36. Cover 728, Folio 9, notes of informal discussion dated 29 October 1945.
37. Cover 728, Folio 11.
38. The US Navy sought 25 knots and 15,000 SHP in its post-war closed-cycle submarines; hence its first nuclear power plant, in USS *Nautilus*, had that output.
39. Cover 728, Folio 9, discussion after that on the operational submarine.
40. ADM 1/19027.

Appendix A: Radio (W/T) and Submarines
1. The earliest wireless devices did use high-speed transformers directly, but they were gone by the time the Royal Navy was installing sets in submarines.
2. The first vacuum tube, the diode, was invented in 1904, followed by the triode, the key to amplification, in 1907. Early versions did not embody the hard vacuum which made later tubes effective. AT&T tested a high-vacuum triode in 1913 for its long-distance telephone network. During the First World War the United States and France led in tube technology, the Admiralty working hard to catch up. That was evident in, for example, the development of Asdic.
3. ADM 116/1361.
4. Type numbers applied to transmitters, not receivers. When war broke out, *Vernon* was working on a much more compact Type 11 similar to the Type 12 aircraft set then under development. After war broke out, Type 11 was relegated to patrol craft. During the First World War, submarines which could not accommodate Type 10 had the smaller Type S credited with 20nm by day and 35nm by night. According to a 1928 catalogue of existing sets (ADM 220/102), Type 10 used a 1 kW motor-alternator and operated at 375 to 1364 kHz. Typical current in its antenna was 2 amps, and nominal range was 20nm.
5. 1914 W/T Appendix to *Vernon* Annual Report, ADM 189/83.
6. ADM 1/8230 is the 18 June 1913 report on W/T lessons. It did *not* mention the danger that excessive transmission would give away the submarine's position, very much a wartime issue.
7. ADM 1/8471/241, on Long-Distance W/T in Submarines and Destroyers, dated 19 October 1916 but including a report on a 21 April 1915 conference. It is marked 'the First Sea Lord's view should be given effect to with the utmost urgency. The present situation is not satisfactory'. The paper dated 20 April 1915 asks for an immediate report on the W/T installations of the Harwich overseas submarines, the 'D' class, eleven 'E' class, and *S 1*. It asked which station in East Kent was fitted to send to them, at what distance they could receive and send (day and night) to shore stations and for inter-communication. What was being done to fit new boats with W/T? This sheet is marked 'RUSH'. All but *S 1* (which was too small) had Type 10.
8. The stations involved were Felixstowe, Grimsby, Tynemouth, Inchkeith and Cromarty. The maximum current wavelength for submarines was 2500ft (762m,

390 kHz). Ipswich was withdrawn from the fleet W/T organisation as a medium-power station on 26 April, to specialise in communication with submarines and destroyers in the North Sea. It would operate on R wave and keep watch on D wave.
9. The Admiralty's first Poulsen set was installed ashore, in 1913. According to the 1915 Vernon W/T *Appendix* (ADM 189/84), arrangements were being made to fit twenty submarines with such sets (Type 14, 3 kW) in addition to their Type 10 (1 kW) spark sets. Presumably the submarines involved were those which would conduct the observational blockade in the Heligoland Bight, the 'E' and 'J' classes. Some 'E'-class submarines had their beam torpedo tubes removed so that Poulsen sets could be fitted (it is not certain which). Type 14 was identical to the Type 15 destroyer set except for its motor-generator and deck insulator; it could use the variable voltage available on board a submarine charging her batteries. The first annual report of the Signal School (ADM 186/753, dated 1917 but published in 1919) described a new 100 watt submarine set using vacuum tubes (Type 32), one of a series of such sets. The 1928 list of W/T sets credits Type 14 with a nominal range of 300nm (6 amps in its antenna), powered by a 5 kW motor generator. Operating frequency was 125 to 187.5 kHz. The 1928 list of transmitters includes an obsolete Type 32, a valve set intended to replace Type 14; it was on board some submarines. Nominal range was 100nm (1.5 amps in antenna). In this list, Types 1–13 were spark sets, 14–19 were Arc sets, 20–29 were shore sets, 30–69 were tube sets, and 100–109 were reserved for S/T. The 1928 list includes Type 41X, for submarines with Type 14, an experimental ICW set to replace Type 10, operating at 375 to 1500 kHz, with a nominal range of 80nm (1 to 2 amps). ICW would indicate keying by interrupting the CW signal rather than by changing frequency. Type 40X was an exercise set associated with Type 14. The list did not include Types 42 – 45.
10. The trials would be conducted by an 'E'-class submarine (*E 16* was chosen) and a destroyer. The 'M' class destroyer would convoy the submarine to Devonport, exchanging signals with Ipswich en route and after arrival at prearranged times. Newhaven as well as Ipswich tried to receive signals.
11. The destroyers were *Lurcher*, *Firedrake*, the two 8th Flotilla destroyers and two 'M' class. These sets operated on a much longer wavelength than the usual destroyer (D) wave; standard destroyer aerials were not long enough, and had to be doubled up.
12. Ranges are for masts fore and aft with a large aerial strung between them. The alternative was a single mast amidships supporting an 'inverted V' aerial. In that case range in the best conditions would be reduced by 100nm and in moderate conditions by 50nm. That is why 10th and 11th Flotilla submarines needed two masts, even though they made quick diving difficult. Submarines generally had the single mast. By the end of the war several submarines had jumping wires usable as aerials; the 'J' class used 56ft of the after jumping stay for this purpose. ADM 137/1946, dated 4 March 1918, pp 208–9, remarks by Captain (S) 10th Flotilla for Admiral Beatty 'submitted in view of the importance of submarines on certain patrols reporting enemy movements'. The submarine wavelength was 2176m (7.25 kHz). As an alternative to the aerial strung between masts, a submarine could fly a kite trailing an aerial. If the submarine had to crash-dive, the kite could simply be released.
13. Admiralty Technical History and Index, TH 21 (submarines), October 1921, 17. The submarine would be submerged, with the top of the bridge bulwark 10 to 15ft under water. The report on the post-war experiments is from Submarine Newsletter No 1–22 (October 1922), Submarine Museum file A1922/5. Newsletter No. 2 (18 January 1923) describes further experiments to determine reliable range, a ship using Type 16 and Type 36 transmitters. At 30ft, *K 12* and *K 22* heard HMS *Conquest* at 15nm; *Queen Elizabeth* was heard at 90 to 95nm, in each case on 4000m wavelength. Adjustment of the receiver was critical. Every additional foot of submergence drastically affected reception. Submarine Museum A1922/5.
14. Submarine Newsletter No 8 (July 1924), Submarine Museum A1922/5
15. Submarine Newsletter No 2 (January 1923) described some early kite tests. Using a kite, on passage from the Dardanelles to Portsmouth, *L 52* managed to communicate with Gibraltar at a range of 1050nm, and after leaving Malta was constantly in communication with Gibraltar. She communicated with Ipswich at a range of 1150nm, and with Group Stations at Portsmouth and Devonport 1060nm away. Submarine Museum file A1922/5.
16. Submarine Newsletter No 13 (5 October 1925) describes initial trials on board *H 43*. Submarine Newsletter No 14 (January 1926) mentions that results varied because 'the short waves are very selective and at the receiving station the greatest care must be taken to adjust the receiving instrument carefully. This has not always been possible . . . ' Submarine Newsletter No 15 (April 1926) describes further experiments at 12m, 29m, 35m, 48m and 85m, the best results being obtained on 35m (the set on *H 43* had been designed for 27m). From Port Said, the cruiser *Yarmouth* transmitted successfully to Horsea, 2000nm away. Results in the Red Sea were very poor, but after Aden (3200nm),

396

results improved; signals could be read in the dark hours as far away as Hong Kong (6050nm). At 1900 daily Horsea could reliably hear the ship all the way between Aden and Hong Kong. These results were much better than those achieved by *H 43* during her cruise to Antwerp in October 1925. Newsletter 17 (October 1926) mentions that future submarines should be able to receive signals from Rugby or any other high-powered shore station using long waves at 2000nm. The best aerial was directional, so a submarine wishing to read (receive) Rugby when submerged would have to be heading in the direction parallel to the great circle bearing of England or its reciprocal; Rugby would broadcast at set times. The 1922–7 RA(S) newsletters are all in Submarine Museum file A1922/5.

17. Submarine Newsletter No 14 (January 1925), Submarine Museum file A1922/5.
18. Submarine Newsletter No 30 (January 1930), Submarine Museum A1927/17. She worked on 23,622 kHz (12.7m) and the aircraft operated at 26,067 kHz (11.5m).
19. Submarine Newsletter No 7 (April 1924), Submarine Museum A 1922/5.
20. According to the 1928 list, it operated on three bands: 100–750 kHz, 7500–16,667 kHz, and 18,750–30,000 kHz. Nominal range was 200nm on the low band, 1000nm on the second band, and 40nm on the very high band, which came close to VHF. This was Type 46X. Type 46Y was a follow-on for *L 12*, *L 16*, *L 21*, and *L 23*, covering the same bands, but with nominal ranges of, respectively, 300nm, 1500nm and 40nm. There was also a Type 46Z, but no application or data are given.
21. Submarine Newsletter No 18 (January 1927), Submarine Museum file A1922/5.
22. 'P' Class Cover (459), Folio 2, minutes of a 12 May 1927 conference at Fort Blockhouse, the main submarine base; also the communication section of Submarine Newsletter No 20 (July 1927) in Submarine Museum file A1922/5.
23. Submarine Newsletter No 21 (October 1927), Submarine Museum file A1927/17.
24. Submarine Newsletter No 27 (April 1929), Submarine Museum file A1927/17.
25. Submarine Newsletter No 36 (August 1931), Submarine Museum file A1927/17.
26. Submarine Newsletter No 38 (early 1932), Submarine Museum file A1927/17.
27. Submarine Newsletter No 39 (May 1932), Submarine Museum file A1927/17.
28. Submarine Newsletter No 40 (August 1932), Submarine Museum file A1927/17.
29. This seems to have been a widespread assumption. It explains why the Germans thought they could use HF radio so freely.
30. Submarine Newsletter No 41 (November 1932), Submarine Museum file A1939/39. Conclusions are summarised in a general submarine Cover (185C), Folio 11.
31. Submarine Newsletter No 42 (February 1933), Submarine Museum file A1939/39.
32. Submarine Newsletter No 43 (May 1933), Submarine Museum file A1939/39.
33. Submarine Newsletter No 46 (April 1934), Submarine Museum file A1939/39.
34. Submarine Newsletter No 47 (October 1934), Submarine Museum file A1939/39.
35. As mentioned in a 1931 newsletter reviewing foreign ASW measures. This was correct; the Italian Ginocchio sweep had been developed during the First World War, and was also used by the French.
36. Submarine Newsletter No 48 (April 1935), Submarine Museum file A1939/39.
37. Submarine Newsletter No 49 (November 1935), Submarine Museum file A1939/39.
38. From CAFO NS 04/38 of 20 January 1938, in ADM 182/95. The 1944 list is from ADM 220/1645, a nomenclature list. The 1928 list credits *Oberon*, *Oxley*, and *Otley* with Type 39I. It used a 20 kW motor alternator for 375 to 500 kHz, and a 1 kW motor alternator for 7500 to 16,667 kHz (HF). Nominal range was 1000nm (25 to 30 amps antenna current). *Odin* is credited with Type 47, operating at 107.1–666.7 kHz, 7500–16,667 kHz, and 18,750–30,000 kHz, with respective nominal ranges of 800nm, 3000nm and 40nm. A pencilled note states that this set is also in the 'O', 'P', and 'R' classes. The 'G' class is credited with Type 48, for which no details are given.
39. ADM 239/241, *Naval W/T Organisation*, a technical history published in 1948. A table of wartime sets in this book includes Type 47M/P as an obsolescent high-power set with a low-power LF attachment, operating at 100–500 kHz and 3–20 MHz. According to BR 3043, in 1935 *Odin*, *Parthian*, and *Rainbow* all had Type 47; *Swordfish* had 46Z; *Thames* and *Porpoise* had Type 47. The latter was credited with a range of 1000nm.

Appendix B: Midget Submarines

1. ADM 1/10176. Goodall's remarks were dated 8 December 1939. The assign-ment arose from a 20 November 1939 Admiralty conference. Goodall cautioned that sketch designs had not been prepared, so the many practical problems involved had not been solved. Goodall wrote that 25 tons was probably too large for a small self-destructive craft brought near its target by a mother ship; it could probably displace 15–20 tons, with an endurance of 50nm at 5 knots and a 1000lb explosive load. This and the larger low-end submarine would both be powered only by batteries and a motor; the larger ones would have diesels.
2. According to Chapter IX of the official Technical History of British submarines.
3. The designation *X 2* was used for the captured Italian submarine *Galilei*.
4. Details from a series of data sheets in a DNC folder marked 'Submarines & X Craft (Varley – Vickers, Wellman, etc) 1943' at the Brass Foundry. This file includes a Vickers midget of comparable size proposed in June 1940 but not built. It would have been armed with a single 24.5in torpedo, and its 88 SHP diesel would have sufficed to propel it at about 6 knots while charging its battery. Surface displacement would have been 43.6 tons (58ft 9in overall x 7ft ½in). The original Varley X-craft was somewhat smaller (30 tons surfaced with side cargo, 43ft 6in x 8ft including side cargo). The DNC folder also included November 1943 data sheets for Italian human torpedoes, an abortive proposal for a sub-mersible motor torpedo boat (April 1942), Chariot Mk II (Commander (E) Terry's design – November 1943), a Vickers design for an X-craft with conning tower, a Japanese midget submarine, an abortive Vickers high-speed small submarine (May 1940), the production version of the Welman (as of November 1943), Drigenko's High Speed Design (not dated), and Chariot Mk I.
5. ADM 1/12929.
6. ADM 1/18654 is a file on the employment of the XE-craft. Hezlet, *British and Allied Submarine Operations*, I, p 335, writes that the obvious targets were the surviving Japanese battleships and carriers in the Inland Sea; 'T'-class sub-marines could have towed the XE-craft from the Philippines. 'There is little doubt that the American high command regarded them almost as suicide machines and felt there was no need at this stage of the war for such sacrifices.' Elsewhere he points out that the Japanese would almost certainly have killed any crews they captured. To Hezlet, the real problem was that the X-craft had arrived too late; a year earlier an attack on Lingaa Roads would have been quite possible, and might well have been approved by the US command.
7. In June, it was agreed that the XE-craft would be used to cut the cables between Singapore and Saigon and Hong Kong, *Bonaventure* supporting them from Brunei Bay. There was some question as to whether that was practicable, the Admiralty having experimented unsuccessfully with submarine cable-cutting in 1941. The craft worked up using an old disused cable in the Brisbane area; *Bonaventure* and her craft arrived at Subic Bay on 20 July. They were towed by 'S'-class submarines adapted for the purpose.
8. This account of the British Chariots is based partly on the post-war submarine Staff History and partly on Robert W Hobson, *Chariots of War* (Church Stretton: Ulrich, 2004). On his father's death Hobson discovered that he had commanded the wartime Chariot organisation. His father's effects included wartime docu-mentation, and Hobson was able to meet ex-charioteers and their Italian equiva-lents. Some time in the early 1930s two Italian naval engineers proposed what they called a *Siluro lenta corsa* (SLC – low-speed torpedo). Their idea was endorsed in 1935 by the chief of the Italian naval staff. The SLC prototype was first tested in January 1936. The first volunteers were chosen a few months later. Security seems to have been excellent, as the British were unaware of the SLC until it was used in combat. According to Hobson, the British army, which was interested in commando operations against German-occupied Europe, was interested in early Italian operations against British shipping; a submersible with breathing apparatus was recovered in Gibraltar harbour. The British army copied the breathing device and began training with it. This was entirely separate from the naval Chariot. The first attempted operation was an abortive attack against Alexandria in August 1940, frustrated when the submarine carrying the devices was sunk. Two submarines were then converted into *Maiale* carriers: *Gondar* and *Scire*, with pressure-proof containers on deck. *Gondar* approached Alexandria on 29 September 1940, but discovered that the British fleet had left harbour. She was sunk. Meanwhile *Scire* approached Gibraltar, but again the British fleet had left. *Scire* finally conducted a *Maiale* attack on Gibraltar in October. A charge exploded in the harbour, without sinking anything. Gibraltar was attacked unsuccessfully again in May 1941, but an attack in September sank three merchant ships. *Scire* took the *Maiale* to Alexandria for the successful December 1941 attack on the two British battleships. References to equipment and sub-mersibles found at Gibraltar are presumably to the series of attacks there. *Maiale* were later based on the tanker *Olterra* across the bay from Gibraltar, and they attacked shipping in Algiers.
9. Hezlet, *British and Allied Submarine Operations*, I, p 130. According to Hobson, as VA(S) Admiral Horton demanded that the Royal Navy control the Chariot programme.

10. Hobson, *Chariots of War*, p 28, credits Commander G M Sladen RN with the suit, which was produced by the British company Siebe Gorman, which produced diver's suits. The Mk I Sladen suit was used on board Mk I Chariots (Mk II on board the Mk II version). Hobson notes that an Italian breathing device was recovered in Gibraltar, but considers the British Mk I suit much cruder. Like the Italian suit, the Sladen included two cylinders with enough oxygen for six hours. Initial trials revealed that breathing pure oxygen could be quite dangerous, the maximum safe depth being 10m (33ft).
11. ADM 1/12207, described as very rough figures.
12. Hobson's figures, presumably from the handbook, are 2.5 knots with a depth limit of 90ft; dimensions were 22ft 3in x 2ft9in, and weight with warhead was 350 lbs. Endurance was 5 hours.
13. My production figures are from Hobson's book. They are not sourced. A British official account of special craft (X, Welman, and Chariots) written in February 1947 (ADM 199/1890) gave a figure of fifty Mk I and sixteen Mk II (four for training, twelve operational). According to this source, Mk III was designed but not built. Production figures were described as approximate. This account was written to help produce requirements for post-war special craft. Hobson refers to minor modifications to Chariots *XXVII* to *LX*, and *LXII* to *LXXIV*, all Mk Is, suggesting that numbering was not at all consecutive. These are generally *not* the numbers Hezlet uses.
14. Hezlet, *British and Allied Submarine Operations*, I, p 137.
15. Hezlet, *British and Allied Submarine Operations*, I, p 179. Chariots were carried in big pressure-tight cylinders nearly 20ft long. *Trooper* had three (one forward, two aft) and *P 311* and *Thunderbolt* had two. Crews could board only on the surface, the submarine then trimming down to launch the Chariots. Hezlet points out that the cylinders themselves endangered submarines, by increasing their silhouettes, making them difficult to handle submerged, and considerably decreasing their seaworthiness on the surface. The two modified submarines could not be used for any other purpose.
16. Dimensions given by Hobson: 30ft 6in x 2ft 6in, 5200lbs with warhead. A data sheet (in a series of midget submarine sheets) in the Brass Foundry adds two other advantages: controls were better and, because the crew were in dead water they were under less strain. The submersible could therefore move faster without crushing their lungs. Diving depth was given as 300ft, although the maximum operational depth for the crew was 60ft. The battery could be moved fore and aft to adjust trim. According to the data sheet, dated November 1943, the prototype was undergoing trials, and a second model (9in shorter, total length 30ft 6in) was being built.
17. A US attaché report dated 13 September 1944 stated that a recent Admiralty dispatch ordered abandonment of all operational use of Chariots and training and procurement programs; commands could use stocks on hand if desired. US technical attaché TS series, NARA II. The writer added that all three Chariot operations in the Mediterranean had been successful, and that conditions there were ideal, the water being calm with little tide. All were carried out by Mk I Chariots. This report mentions the barbaric treatment by the Japanese of any prisoners they might capture as a reason that their employment was very doubtful. Unfortunately the first page of the enclosure to this report is missing. The Admiralty had declassified the Mk I Chariot on 18 April 1944, and an exhibition was held at Harrods, the department store, between 24 July and 29 August 1944. It featured both a Chariot and the breathing equipment.
18. ADM 1/13480.
19. Hobson, *Chariots of War*, p 59, reproduces an official drawing of the proposed device. He gives no information as to possible production. The drawing is labelled 'proposed new design of Chariot to carry lobster-pot charges'. Hobson claims that it was produced and used in the Far East late in the war, but he gives no details, and no other reference seems to mention this device. This was *not* the Welman one-man submarine, about 100 of which were made. The latter was an SOE project developed by that organisation's Inter-Services Research Bureau (ISRB); its name seems to have come from the fact that the prototype was built at Welwyn Garden City. Its single operator sat in an enclosed space surmounted by an armoured conning tower, and its 425lb warhead was to be attached magnetically to a target ship. Unlike a Chariot, whose operator could cut through an anti-submarine net, a Welman with its single on-board operator could not. A February 1943 order for 150 was cut to the 100 already built in October 1943 as analysis showed that the design was too flawed. Among other things, there was no periscope, and the operator had poor visibility. However, a Welman attack was mounted that autumn against a floating drydock in Bergen. It failed, and at least one of the Welman submersibles fell into German hands. After that the project was apparently dropped altogether.
20. ADM 1/12207. Hezlet, *British and Allied Submarine Operations*, I, p 130, writes that Horton and other submarine officers had been interested in midgets for years, but that their value was dramatised by Japanese use at Pearl Harbor.

21. According to Hobson, *Chariots of War*, p 137, one was flown to Fort Lauderdale in 1945 for trials. The US Navy tested two improved Italian *Maiale* (SSB) after the war; one survives in the submarine museum at Groton.
22. There is a Cover (768) in the Brass Foundry, although there is no Cover for the Chariots – which are not mentioned in the Cover. Most of the craft mentioned were means of inserting agents or Special Forces personnel into enemy territory. They included the one-man Sleeping Beauty submersible canoe.

Appendix C: The Export Market
1. This account is based largely on the Vickers' design and estimate (costing) books held by the Brass Foundry, supplemented by the submarine part of the Thurston design notebook (courtesy of Steve McLaughlin), by a sheet in the Brass Foundry which listed Vickers' export projects by design number, and by material in the Foreign Submarine Cover (439). There were at least three, unfortunately overlapping, series of numbers, presumably corresponding to three separate submarine design offices. Also, the sets of design book are quite incomplete. It appears that the Thurston series matches a later 'Barrow' series. A second series, with higher numbers, is labelled 'Walker' (presumably Walker High Yard) in one of the Vickers books. A third series, which does *not* correspond to anything in the surviving Vickers books, has lower numbers (high 700 series) dating to the 1920s such as Design 783 for Greece. Some of the submarine estimates are marked 'L.O.', meaning London Office, and probably intended mainly for use as what amounted to advertising. Material in the sole Estimate book stops at the end of 1930. Drawings of many of the designs are in the Brass Foundry collection.
2. Thurston notebook, courtesy of Steve McLaughlin. Another page states that 621 was like 619 but had two rather than four broadside tubes. Unfortunately these notes are undated. The notebook includes a series of submarine descriptions without any indication of expected buyers. Design 669 (probably spring 1913) was probably Vickers' proposal for the big steam ocean submarine; it seems to have been 300ft long. Design 668 may have been an alternative. The notebook shows a very fast steam submarine proposed to the Admiralty in November 1915, possibly No 743, developing 45,000 SHP (50,000 SHP boilers) using three-shaft geared turbines. No dimensions or supposed performance were given, but she would have had one 63ft 9in engine room, two 45ft boiler rooms and one 24ft boiler rooms, total machinery weight being 813 tons. A new series probably drawn up in 1923–4, with 200ft safe diving depth, would be powered either by conventional Vickers diesels or by Vickers vertical diesels, presumably double-acting or opposed-piston, with six or eight cylinders. The high-powered conventional or vertical diesel was rated at 6400 BHP. Another alternative was a horizontally-opposed (HO) piston engine: 1600 BHP on eight cylinders or 2400 BHP on twelve cylinders (the output of a six-cylinder version was not given). Design 841 was mentioned but not elaborated. The largest submarines in the series were 842 and 844 with, respectively, normal and vertical engines.
3. Cover 439 Folio 72 is a discussion of factors in their diving performance. It turned out that two-thirds of the total time to pass out of sight was taken up filling main ballast tanks and thus destroying buoyancy. The controlling factor seemed to be the size and form of the openings in the tank bottoms. The rate of diving after the water covered the forward superstructure was largely controlled by the down angle of the bow. Planes should be used slowly and *steadily* to put on and maintain this angle (emphasis in original), so they should be controlled by an officer, not left to the discretion of the petty officer working them. Vents were not overloaded except for the initial 2–3 seconds; it would help to trunk the vents to the top of the superstructure (casing), as otherwise the vents would be drowned at just the time the superstructure had to flood.
4. Unfortunately the Thurston notebook does not include these 700-series designs. Also unfortunately, the surviving Vickers compendia in the Brass Foundry do not include these numbers.
5. The dates indicate that these numbers were in the Thurston/Barrow series, but the designs apparently do not appear in the Thurston notebook.
6. Cover 439, Folio 50, which includes a lengthy discussion for DNC. Length was governed mainly by the armament requirement, but it did not help that the Poles wanted 12 weeks' provisions (8ft of length); three 350-ton salvage pumps, about three times the capacity the British would normally have; blowers sufficient to empty 400 tons of tankage in 6½ minutes (the British would allow at least 15 minutes). On the diameter of 15¼ft pressure hull plating (25 to 22lbs) seemed excessive for the 260ft diving depth; *Swordfish* had been down to 240ft with 17lb plating (diameter 14ft 11in). Vickers was bound by specification to offer a safety factor of 2 using particular formulas, which made its plating necessary. The frames were spaced 24in (the British used 21in) and the panels were 7in vs 6in for the British. On the whole the structure seemed heavy compared to British practice. The specified conning tower was considered very large: 12ft long and 9ft diameter placed longitudinally above the pressure hull. The bridge was about

10ft longer than that in the 1935 'T' class. A wide superstructure (casing) extended practically the full length of the ship. She had external tubes. All of that pushed up displacement to make it possible to carry these weights with reasonable stability. As for power, it seemed that Vickers was being optimistic in expecting 20 knots, even with bow shutters streamlining the torpedo tube muzzles. Based on *Thames* (10,000 BHP for 22.2 knots at 2165 tons, 345ft long), the proposed submarine needed 6000 BHP. With a prismatic coefficient approaching 0.8, the form was poorly adapted to speed. The situation could be improved by shortening her and increasing beam. Even then power (and machinery weight) would have to be increased, the increased weight offset by reduced hull weight. One of the DNC papers is dated 8/10/35.

7. A comparison is in Cover 439, Folio 34, MFO 267/35, referring to *Golfinho*. She was somewhat larger (880 tons vs 760 tons for *Shark* surfaced, 1091 tons vs 960 tons submerged, 227ft overall vs 208ft 8in) and faster on the surface (17 knots on 2300 BHP vs 14.5 knots on 1550 BHP) but slower submerged (9 knots vs 10 knots), with a considerably larger tactical diameter (355 yds vs 254 yds at 14 knots surfaced, 300 yds vs 281 yds submerged). She had a considerably wider superstructure, which was normally a disadvantage when diving due to the time it took to flood. In the Portuguese submarine the problem was solved by covering the top with wooden slats with spaces between them, but the British constructor reviewing the Portuguese submarine pointed out that under depth-charging they would tend to break away and give away the submarine. Venting by other means was being looked into for the 'T' class of the 1935 Programme. The underwater control of the Portuguese submarine was said to be exceptionally good. That could not be attributed to the shape of the submarine, but she did have much larger planes than the British: 60ft^2 vs 54ft^2 for the bow planes and 80ft^2 vs 45ft^2 for the stern planes. Vickers had saved considerable weight on main engines (50 tons vs 77 tons despite greater power) but it went not into fuel (30 tons vs 40 tons) but into a 'needlessly thick' pressure hull (465 tons vs 366 tons total hull weight) for the diving depth and the diameter of the pressure hull. A more centralised telemotor system saved weight but made the submarine more vulnerable if air got into any of it.

8. This was Electric Boat Design 307V. Vickers reviewed it (finding errors) and the estimate book includes it as Estimate 2926 of 1 December 1926.

9. Cover 439, Folio 78. This is a report of an 18 September 1938 Admiralty discussion, with a representative of the Vickers Engine Department present. The Turks wanted an Admiralty-type telescoping W/T mast like those in current British submarines; they could not be told that in British craft it was for MF only. Admiralty representatives informed the Turks verbally that they could have a light 4in gun instead of the 3in gun shown on drawings. Some changes to accommodation were discussed. The Turkish commission wanted the low pressure blowers to be adequate to empty main tanks in 5 minutes rather than the 10 to 15 usual in British submarines, so that the gun could be brought quickly into action; they did not consider it safe to use it (as the British did) in the low-buoyancy condition. The British explained to the Turkish commission that they provided a gun access truck specifically to enable the gun to be manned quickly and safely. The Turks stood by their 5-minute requirement. They also wanted a guaranteed time to flood main tanks, as that would indicate a diving performance independent of the efficiency of the crew. They stated a time of 30 seconds, and also stated that it was usual to get the top of the casing underwater was 45 seconds. Vickers would have to explain its 55-second figure. The Turks rejected the 1.9 factor safety as too low, wanted at least the 2.2 they had given as a requirement. They also considered 21 per cent reserve buoyancy too low, although Vickers pointed out that increasing that percentage would reduce submerged speed and increase surface GM; ultimately they accepted Vickers' figure. They accepted the 14-knot surface and 9-knot submerged speeds, as well as the firm's endurance (3900nm at 9 knots with normal fuel and 4500nm with reserve fuel; 80nm at 4 knots submerged). The four bow and one stern torpedo tubes (with four reloads forward) were also accepted, as well as the 3in gun (the Turkish commission would have preferred an anti-aircraft mounting). The commission preferred the Continental practice of controlling the submarine from within the conning tower, but after a vigorous defence of the British technique (underwater control from the Control Room) the matter was left undecided. It also developed that the Turkish commission was 'considerably impressed' by the speed with which British submarines dove and by their underwater manoeuvrability. The German-built Turkish submarines apparently lacked longitudinal stability. Dutch and German claims of diving in 40 seconds referred to a static dive to the point at which the upper deck was awash, the ship being stopped; the British argued this was meaningless.

10. Cover 439, Folio 18. On 26 July 1926 CinC Mediterranean wrote that the Yugoslavs would likely take both submarines, but wanted Armstrong to add stern tubes. He was told that would entail considerable modification, the submarine being lengthened by 16ft and aft surfaces completely rearranged, but it was done: they both emerged with two stern tubes. The displacement of the extended stern balanced the added weight.

11. Information from Dr Raymond Cheung.

12. These designs *do not* appear in the Thurston notebook, which has the only design numbers in this range.

13. This is the first submarine in the Vickers Estimate Book (it is Estimate 2773).

14. US Naval Intelligence report, 15 November 1919. This plan included two battleships and four battlecruisers. NARA RG 38 (ONI series) folder O-4-a Register 12455. About 1937 the Chileans wee in the market for more submarines, with a displacement of not less than 750 tons surfaced, a speed of at least 15 knots surfaced (endurance 4000nm at 10 knots) and 8 knots submerged, a minimum of six torpedo tubes and twelve torpedoes, one 4in gun and one or two anti-aircraft machine guns, and a diving depth of 120m (about 400ft). Submarines most nearly approaching what was wanted were the German *U 25*, the Italian *Glauco* the Dutch improved *K 14* and the Vickers-built Portuguese *Delfin*. This is from an undated paper (which must be late 1930s) in US ONI folder 'Chilean Naval Policy' 1930-32-37, O-4-a Register 14148-B. The submarines were part of a larger programme including a small cruiser, for which competition was fierce. A later file (O-4-a Register 14048-C, 'Chilean Naval Policy 1937-38-39') included a 31 May 1939 report that the programme then included two 900-ton submarines similar to the Dutch *K 18* or the German *U 37*. The Chileans then had a naval mission in London, which was authorised to get bids from as many countries as possible for these and other desired ships, including the two light cruisers. None of the US files covers the purchase from Vickers of the *Capitan O'Brien* class.

15. Cover 439, Folio 5.

BIBLIOGRAPHY

Primary Sources

Admiralty Technical History and Index (TH)

Compiled at the end of the First World War. All are in ADM 275 and in the Admiralty Library, Portsmouth.

TH 1: *Submarine v. Submarine* (March 1919).

TH 7: *The Anti-Submarine Division of the Naval Staff December 1916 – November 1918* (July 1919).

TH 21: *Submarine Administration, Training, and Construction* (October 1921).

TH 40: *Anti-Submarine Development and Experiments Prior to December 1916* (September 1920).

Admiralty Staff Histories

Naval Operations Connected with the Raid on the North-East Coast. December 16th, 1914 (Admiralty Staff Monograph in Vol II of Admiralty Staff Monographs [Fleet Issue], July 1921).

The Mediterranean 1914–15 (Vol VIII of Naval Staff Monographs [Fleet Issue], March 1923).

British Mining Operations 1939–45 Vol I (1973) (BR 1736(56)(1)).

H.M. Submarines 1939–45 (CB 3210, 1954: ADM 239/414).

Naval W/T Organization (1948: ADM 239/241).

Torpedoes (CB 03203, 1948); my copy was in the file of British documents from NHHC in NARA II.

Admiralty (PRO) Files

ADM 1/7515 Holland Submarines (papers about acquisition).

ADM 1/7522 Submarines (foreign and proposed British) 1901.

ADM 1/7618 Report on Italian submarine *Delfino*.

ADM 1/7717 Substitution of Submarines for Coast Defence Mines 1903–1904.

ADM 1/7719 Submarine Exercises 1 June to 31 December 1903.

ADM 1/7725 Report on Submarines 1903.

ADM 1/7795 Submarine Flotilla Annual Report 1904.

ADM 1/7988 Submarine Annual Report 1908.

ADM 1/8119 Submarine Exercise Rules 1910.

ADM 1/8128 Submarine Committee Report No. 4 (1910).

ADM 1/8230 W/T lessons of 1913 manoeuvres.

ADM 1/8331 War Duties of Submarines (by War Staff) 1913.

ADM 1/8374/93 Commodore (S) report on British submarine design 1914.

ADM 1/8424/171 New Construction 1915.

ADM 1/8428/209 Submarine New Construction Program July 1915.

ADM 1/8470/236 Conferences between CinC Grand Fleet and Third Sea Lord 1916.

ADM 1/8471/241 Long-range W/T in Submarines and Destroyers, 1916.

ADM 1/8547/340 Warship Construction 1914–18 (DNC history) including Submarines.

ADM 1/8549/18 Post-war Fleet.

ADM 1/8586/70 Report of Post-war Questions Committee 1920.

ADM 1/8672/230 New construction programme 1924.

ADM 1/8675/19 External Submarine Minelayer 1925.

ADM 1/8675/21 Fleet Submarine with Internal Combustion Engine (Vickers Proposal, 1925).

ADM 1/8678/69 Submarine Engine Development 1925–26.

ADM 1/8683/131 Naval disarmament 1924–25.

ADM 1/8715/188 Naval disarmament 1927.

ADM 1/8724/90 Submersible Aircraft Carrier 1928 (*M 2*).

ADM 1/9311 'G' Class Design 1930.

ADM 1/9312 Minelaying Submarine Sketch Design 1930.

ADM 1/9245 New Patrol Submarine 1923.

ADM 1/9328 *Porpoise* Class Design.

ADM 1/9343 Modifications to 1931 'S' Class.

ADM 1/9346 *Severn* Class.

ADM 1/9348 *Shark* and *Sealion* and 1932 'S' class.

ADM 1/9373 Sketch designs of 400 and 1000-ton submarines April 1934.

ADM 1/9389 'H' Class Replacement ('U' Class).

ADM 1/9728 Submarine Programme 1930–38.

ADM 1/10075 Asdic Operations 1937–39.

ADM 1/10171 Use of Large Submarines in Atlantic 1939.

ADM 1/10176 Potential of Midget Submarines 1941.

ADM 1/11969 Conversion of submarines to supply Malta 1941–42.

ADM 1/12207 Employment of Chariots and X Craft – Co-operation with USA, 1942.

ADM 1/12929 Simulated X-craft attack on HMS *Bonaventure* (depot ship).

ADM 1/13300 Use of foreign submarines for ASW training 1943.

ADM 1/13476 Radar in submarines 1943.

ADM 1/15114 Report of Submarine Propulsion Committee 1938.

ADM 1/15182 Submarine Propulsion Committee Papers 1936–39.

ADM 1/15333 Report on S and U Class Submarines 1943.

ADM 1/16396 Schnorkel 1944.

ADM 1/16384 Post-war experiments on U-boats.

ADM 1/16493 Potential of 'Walterboote' 1944.

ADM 1/16495 Deep fast U-boats (and countermeasures).

ADM 1/17003 Future of the Torpedo 1942–44.

ADM 1/17549 Snorkel (US report, Photostatted, 1945).

ADM 1/18032 Mine Detection Asdic on Submarines 1945.

ADM 1/18557 Types XXI and XXIII.

ADM 1/18604 Future Submarine Design and Development 1945.

ADM 1/18654 Pacific Plans for *XE*-Craft 1945.

ADM 1/18949 Explosion on board *U 3017*.

ADM 1/19027 Submarine programme 1945.

ADM 1/24219 Minelaying Submarine 1939 Programme Sketch Design (December 1938).

ADM 1/24278 STD I: nominally about an award for the invention, but it includes a preliminary handbook and an account of the request to Clausen for a design.

ADM 1/27774 Development of HTP engines in the UK, 1944–46.

ADM 116/1361 Fitting submarines with W/T through 1914.

ADM 116/1430 Ultrasonics vs submarines.

ADM 116/2060 Post-war Questions Committee source material 1920.

ADM 116/2522 Future Submarines and Submarine Depot Ships 1926–29.

ADM 116/3164 Submarine Policy 1924–25.

ADM 116/3441 Cabinet papers on naval building programme 1925.

ADM 116/3484 Submarines Carrying Aircraft 1930–33.

ADM 116/3493 CID discussion of defensive impact of submarines.

ADM 137/226 (*Eighth Submarine Flotilla Memoranda and Reports August–December 1914*).

ADM 137/289 Grand Fleet Battle Orders 1916–18.

ADM 137/500 Policy paper collection of VADM Sir Henry Oliver.

ADM 137/834 Operations Committee Minutes and Memoranda Sept 1917–Dec 1918.

ADM 137/1098 Admiralty policy Vol 2.

ADM 137/1247 Baltic Submarine Operations 1916, including transfer of submarines from Arctic.

ADM 137/1332 Admiralty policy Vol 7.

ADM 137/1926 Miscellaneous Submarine Operations; includes lessons of the 1913 manoeuvres.

ADM 137/1929 ASW Devices (hydrophone reports).

ADM 137/1946 includes proposed ASW measures by submarines.

ADM 137/1949 Grand Fleet Submarine Operations.

ADM 137/2067 Commodore (S) papers including 'Development of British submarines' 1914.

ADM 137/2077 Commodore (S) reports 1918.

ADM 167/50 Board Minutes 1916.

ADM 167/54 Board Minutes and Memos August–December 1917.

ADM 167/62 Board Minutes and Memos 1920.

ADM 167/66 Board Minutes 1923.

ADM 167/67 Board Memos 1923.

ADM 167/81 Board Minutes 1930.

ADM 182/95 CAFOs 1938.

ADM 186 *Quarterly Appropriation List of Gun Mountings for BL, QF, and Machine Guns* (November 1914, February 1915, May 1915, August 1915, November 1915, April 1916, July 1916, October 1916, July 1917, November 1917).

ADM 186/15 *War Vessels and Aircraft (British and Foreign)* (October 1915).

ADM 186/301 *Handbook of Torpedo Control* 1916 (CB 302).

ADM 186/440 *Handbook of Hydrophones in Submarines* 1924 (CB 1664).

ADM 186/450 *Handbook of Hydrophones in Submarines* 1926 (CB 1757).

ADM 186/456 Submarine Handbook 1927 Vol II.

ADM 186/462 Submarine Manual 1929.

ADM 186/497 Submarine Handbook 1933 Vol III.

ADM 186/499 Submarine Operations 1933.

ADM 186/512 Submarine Handbook 1933 Vol III Appendix I.

ADM 186/513 Submarine Handbook 1934 Vol III Appendix II.

ADM 186/514 Submarine Handbook 1934 Vol III Appendix III.

ADM 186/549 *Submarine Asdic Instructions* 1939 (CB 1991).

ADM 186/753 Report of Signal School 1917 (Fessenden signalling).

ADM 189/48 *Vernon* annual report 1928.

ADM 189/49 *Vernon* annual report 1929.

ADM 189/64 *Vernon* annual report 1944.

ADM 189/66 *Vernon* annual report 1946.

ADM 189/83 *Vernon* W/T appendix to annual report 1914.

ADM 189/84 *Vernon* W/T appendix to annual report 1915.

ADM 189/103 *Progress in Torpedo, Mining, Anti-Submarine and in Allied Subjects* 1926.

ADM 189/444 *Progress in Torpedo etc* 1924.

ADM 189/447 *Progress in Torpedo etc* 1925.

ADM 189/461 *Progress in Torpedo etc* 1927.

ADM 189/105 *Progress in Torpedo etc* 1928.

ADM 189/106 *Progress in Torpedo etc* 1929.

ADM 189/107 *Progress in Torpedo etc* 1930.

ADM 189/108 *Progress in Torpedo etc* 1931.

ADM 189/109 *Progress in Torpedo etc* 1932.

ADM 189/111 *Progress in Torpedo etc* 1934.

ADM 189/112 *Progress in Torpedo etc* 1935

ADM 189/113 *Progress in Torpedo etc* 1936.

ADM 189/114 *Progress in Torpedo etc* 1937.

ADM 189/115 *Progress in Torpedo etc* 1938.

ADM 189/116 *Progress in Torpedo etc* 1939.

ADM 189/1890 A(S) papers including STD II/TDC.

ADM 204/2239 Submarine Silencing 1941.

ADM 213/424 Submarine propulsion 1945, including comments on the earlier Propulsion Committee.

ADM 220/1645 List of W/T installations 1944.

ADM 223/320 Compilation of NID U-Boat papers.

ADM 226/116 Haslar (test tank) reports 1910–11.

ADM 234/434 Naval Staff Monograph: *The Naval Staff of the Admiralty: Its Work and Development* (September 1929).

ADM 239/45 *Handbook of Submarines* Vol 1 1943 (CB 1795A(1943)).

ADM 239/212 *Submarine Asdic Instructions* July 1945 (CB 3079) (and 1942 version from NARA II).

ADM 239/420 *Progress in Underwater Warfare* (December 1946).

ADM 239/421 *Progress in Underwater Warfare* (1947).

Covers Consulted (in numerical order).

Submarines, General including Holland type and foreign types through 1938 (185–185C).

'D' Class (212, 212A).

'V' Class (289); 'S' Class is 289A.

'E' class (291, 291A) (also 330 for repeat boats).

'R' Class (292).

Nautilus (306).

'W' Class (307).

'J' Class (326) (note that 345, possibly repeat 'J' class, is missing).

'E' Class 1914-15 (and 'G' Class) (330).

'K' Class (353, 353A).

'F' Class (Admiralty Coastals: 354).

'H' Class (368).

'M' Class (374, 374A).

'L' Class (393, 393A, 393B, 393C).

H 21 Class (401).

X 1 (419, 419A, 419B).

Oberon (424, 424A).

Submarine Minelayer (not built: 438).

Foreign Submarines (439, 439A: 1924–43, 1943–51).

Oxley and *Otway* (443).

Odin class (445, 445A).

'P' Class (459).

Thames class (458, 458A).

Regent and class (473)

Submarines general (483, 483A, 483B, 483C covering 1929–38, 1939–41, 1941–44, and not dated).

Severn and *Clyde* (503, 503A).

Snapper and *Seawolf* (514; 514A is *Sunfish*).

Minelaying submarines *Grampus* and *Narwhal* (523, 523A).

Minelaying submarine *Rorqual* (538).

'T' Class (542, 542A, 542B, 542C).

Minelaying submarines *Seal* and *Cachalot* (549).

'U' Class (548, 548A).

Minelaying and patrol submarine 1939 (603: modified 'S' Class).

Repeat 'U' Class (616, 616A).

War records (618, 618A).

'S' Class 1940 (626, 626A).

Note that the 'A' Class Cover (688) has not been found.

Improved 'A' Class (727).

Experimental Submarine (728).

Royal Navy Submarine Museum

Liaison with US Pacific Fleet (Lakin papers).

Repeat 'O' class (A1927/20).

Submarine Newsletters of RA(S) 1929–39 (A1922/5, A1927/17, A1939/39).

Submarine Situation October 1939 (A1938/16).

Miscellaneous Manuscripts.

Churchill Minutes II in Admiralty Library.

DEY/31 (D'Eyncourt submarine papers) in National Maritime Museum, Greenwich.

Draft Interwar Staff History in Admiralty Library.

Folder marked 'Submarines & X Craft (Varley – Vickers, Wellman, etc) 1943' in Brass Foundry.

Keyes papers in British Library.

Thurston notebook of Vickers designs, courtesy of Steve McLaughlin.

Vickers Design and Estimate Books in Brass Foundry.

US National Archives
NARA RG 38 (First World War files).
Folder C-26-118 to C-26-120: hydrophone reports.
Folder C-26-251 to -258: hydrophone reports.
Folder C-26-333: Inter-Allied Conference on Supersonic Detection (sonar) 1918.
Folder C-84-18 to 84–29: Sims report on 'R' Class.
Folder C-84-30 to 84-89, Confidential OpNav records 1917-19.
ONI series P-10-f Register No. 9644-C on a hydrophone visit to the UK.

Interwar ONI Series.
12455 O-4-a Chilean Navy 1919.
14148-B O-4-a Chilean Naval Policy 1930-32-37.
14148-B O-4-a Chilean Naval Policy 1937-38-39.

ONI Second World War Series.
Folder 7480-C P-10-H Confidential of 15 November 1944, including *Seraph* trials.
Folder 7489-A P-10-N Secret: British Submarines: General Notes Various 1939–40–41–42.
Folder 7489 P-10-H Confidential (British Submarines 1941–42).
Folder 7489-B P-10-H Secret 'British Submarines – General Notes 1943–44–45' including snorkel projects.
Folder 7489-C P-10-H Secret 'British Submarines – General Notes 1945'.
Folder 14731-A P-10-j Secret, 'Submarines – German 1942–43–44'.
Folder 25818 P-10-H Confidential giving post-war notes on *Seraph*.

NARA RG 38 NHHC File (ex-British material).
NARA RG 457 (NSA) SIGINT History of the Battle of the Atlantic, Chapter IV: Technical Intelligence from CI (5750/433-CN56).
NARA RG 457 Entry 9013, messages from Japanese naval attaché in Berlin, messages intercepted in 1943-45.
Report on "U 570" (HMS "Graph"), January 1943 (CB 4318R)
US Naval Technical Mission to Japan (NavTechJap) Report E-10 (December 1945): Japanese sonar.

Secondary Sources

Books

Ackermann, Paul, *Encyclopaedia of British Submarines 1901–1955* (privately published, 1989).
Bacon, Reginald, *From 1900 Onward* (London: Hutchinson, 1940).
Brown, D K, *The Grand Fleet: Warship Design and Development 1906–1922* (London: Chatham Publishing, 1999).
_____, *Nelson to Vanguard: Warship Design and Development 1923-1945* (London: Chatham Publishing, 2000).
Chesneau, Roger (ed), *Conway's All the World's Fighting Ships 1922-1946* (London: Conway, 1980).
Choong, Andrew, and Perkins, Richard (eds), *British Warship Recognition Vol VII: Submarines, Gunboats, Gun Vessels, and Sloops 1860-1939* (Barnsley: Seaforth, 2018).
Compton-Hall, Richard, *Submarine Boats: The beginnings of underwater warfare* (London: Conway, 1983).
Cummins, C Lyle, *Diesels for the First Stealth Weapon: Submarine Power 1902-1945* (Wilsonville OR: Carnot Press, 2007).
Dittmar, F J, and Colledge, J J, *British Warships 1914–1919* (London: Ian Allan, 1972).
Douglas, L H, *Submarine Disarmament 1919-1936*, Ph.D. thesis for Syracuse University, 1970.
Edmonds, Martin (ed), *100 Years of The Trade: Royal Navy Submarines Past, Present, and Future* (Lancaster: Centre for Defence and International Security Studies [of Lancaster University], 2001).
Field, Andrew, *Royal Navy Strategy in the Far East 1919–1939* (London: Frank Cass, 2004).
Franklin, George, *Britain's Anti-Submarine Capability 1919–1939* (London: Frank Cass, 2003).

Friedman, Norman, *U.S. Submarines Through 1945: An Illustrated Design History* (Annapolis: Naval Institute Press, 1995).
Gray, Randal (ed), *Conway's All the World's Fighting Ships 1906-1921* (London: Conway, 1985).
Groener, Erich, *German Warships 1815–1945, II (U-Boats and Mine Warfare Vessels)*, as revised and expanded by Dieter Jung and Martin Maas (London: Conway, 1991).
Hackmann, Willem, *Seek & Strike: Sonar, Anti-Submarine Warfare and the Royal Navy 1914-1954* (London: HMSO, 1984).
Harrison, A N, *The Development of H.M. Submarines from Holland No. 1 (1901) to Porpoise (1930)*, published by MoD as BR 3043, January 1979.
Hezlet, Arthur, *Electronics and Sea Power* (New York: Stein and Day, 1975) (British title: *The Electron and Sea Power*).
_____, *British and Allied Submarine Operations in World War II* 2 vols (Gosport: Royal Navy Submarine Museum, 2001).
Hinsley, F H, Thomas, E E, Ransom, C F G, and Knight, R C, *British Intelligence in the Second World War* (London: HMSO, 1984), III Pt 1.
Hobson, Robert W, *Chariots of War* (Church Stretton: Ulrich, 2004).
Kemp, Paul J, *The T Class Submarine: The Classic British Design* (Annapolis: Naval Institute Press, 1990).
_____, *Midget Submarines of the Second World War* (London: Chatham, 1999).
Lambert, John, and Hill, David, *Anatomy of the Ship: The Submarine Alliance* (London: Conway Maritime Press, 1986).
Lambert, Nicholas, *The Submarine Service 1900-1918* (Aldershot: Navy Records Society, 2001).
Lenton, H T, *British and Empire Warships of the Second World War* (London: Greenhill, 1998).
Lindell, Terry D, 'The Development of Torpedo Fire Control Computers in the Royal Navy', in Edmonds, Martin (ed), *100 Years of 'The Trade'* (Lancaster University: Centre for Defence and International Security Studies, 2001).
Llewellyn-Jones, Malcolm, *The Royal Navy and Anti-Submarine Warfare 1917–49* (London: Routledge, 2006).
Moore, George, *Building for Victory: The Warship-Building Programmes of the Royal Navy 1939-1945* (Gravesend: World Ship Society, n.d.).
Moss, Michael, and Russell, Iain, *Range and Vision: the First Hundred Years of Barr & Stroud* (Edinburgh: Mainstream Publishing, 1988).
Patterson, A Temple, *The Jellicoe Papers* (Naval Records Society, 1966).
Roskill, Stephen, *Naval Policy Between the Wars* (London: Collins), 2 vols (1968 and 1976).
Rössler, Eberhard, *The U-Boat: The Evolution and Technical History of German Submarines* (London: Arms and Armour, 1981).
Smith, Gaddis, *Britain's Clandestine Submarines 1914–1915* (Archon Books, 1975; reprint of 1964 book from Yale University Press in a series of Yale historical publications).

Articles

Brown, D K, 'Submarine Pressure Hull Design & Diving Depths Between the Wars', *Warship International* No 3 (1987), pp 279–86.
Llewellyn-Jones, Malcolm, 'Trials With H.M. Submarine *Seraph* and British Preparations to Defeat the Type XXI U-Boat, September–October 1944,' *Mariner's Mirror* 86 (2000), pp 434–51.
Jones, Mark C, 'Give Credit Where Credit is Due: The Dutch Role in the Development and Deployment of the Submarine Schnorkel,' *Journal of Military History* 69 (October 2005), pp 987–1012.
Welbourn, Donald B, and Crichton, Tim, 'The Schnorchel: A Short-Lived Engineering Solution to Scientific Developments', published in 2008 by the Newcomen Society (headquartered at the Science Museum). Royal Navy Submarine Museum copy.
Papers in *Transactions* of the Institution of Naval Architects (later the Royal Institution).
    Johns, A W, 'German Submarines' (1920).
    Sims, A J, 'British Submarine Design During the War (1939–45)' (1947).

SUBMARINE DATA

NOTE: Dimensions and displacements for 'Holland' through *Porpoise* are from BR 3043, which does *not* give weights. Weights for 'Holland' through *E 9* and for *Porpoise, Otway, Osiris, Perseus, Regent* and the wartime 'T' and 'U' classes are Vicker' data courtesy of Dr Ian Buxton, of which the first group (through *E 9*) were grouped very differently from the later ones (and the two wartime sets of data are grouped differently from the others). *H 41, K 11, M 3* and *R 9* data are from Vickers' notebooks of detailed warship data in the Brass Foundry. Data are also taken from Covers for 'F' class, 'L' class (588B, for a 1923 Legend of *L 50* class, based on surface displacement of 930 tons), 'M' class (design estimates), *Oberon* (Legend, 1924), Patrol and Minelaying Submarine 1939, 'S' class (various versions), 'T' class (as designed before the war), *Thames*, and 'W' class, plus General Submarine Cover 185B. 'A' class (1943) data are from John Lambert and David Hill, *Anatomy of the Ship: The Submarine Alliance*, somewhat modified; they seem more precise than the Legend data. Other data are from Covers. Data not given in great detail are from Legends, generally design figures. Hull weight generally includes fittings. Double-starred entries are much simplified, machinery being separated into engineers' and electricians' weights as noted. In some cases engines include auxiliaries but the data are not further simplified. Torpedo tube weight typically includes water in WRTs. In some cases ballast keel weight and lead weight are included in hull weight, but given separately in parentheses. Some equipment weight is included in hull weight. Triple stars indicate 'remainder of fittings'. This is presumably most of the usual equipment list, except for spares. It probably also includes auxiliary machinery. Crew and effects for these submarines includes provisions and stores. Fresh water generally includes a ton of distilled water to top up batteries. Detailed weights generally include hull plus a list of 'judgement items' which could be divided in various ways; I have decided how to do so. Complement is officers/ratings (or total). *K 26* weights are from a Legend dated 16 February 1923 (which received the Board Stamp) in the relevant Cover. Data for the 1941 'U' class (*P 55* [*Unsparing*] in particular) are from Constructor's Notebook 570/3 (W G Kitchener, opened 27 April 1943), a compilation for the DNC data sheet. The same book gives 'T'-class data for *P 339* (*Taurus*). 'H'-class data are US design data, and do not follow typical British weight conventions. Hull fittings are lumped with hull, as in British submarines. There was apparently no ballast keel. The Covers and other available materials (including extensive Vickers papers in the Brass Foundry) did not provide weights for *Nautilus* as built, for *Swordfish* (1913), for *S 1–S 3*, or for the 'J' class. Scotts' papers were destroyed in a 1941 air raid. I have approximated weights for *S 1* using the weights (in the Cover) of her Italian prototypes. *Nautilus* was clearly derived from the 1912 Vickers design described (which is from the Cover), but modified during construction.

Early Single-Hull Submarines

	'HOLLAND'	A 1	A 2
SURFACED	113	190	189
SUBMERGED	122	207	205.5
STANDARD	N/A	N/A	N/A
LOA	63-10	103-3	105-0½
LBP	61-9	102-6	102-6
BEAM (PRESSURE HULL)	11-9⅞	11-0	12-8¾
BEAM	SAME	SAME	SAME
DRAFT (MEAN)	9-11	10-1	10-8
ENGINE BHP	160	400	450
SPEED SURFACED	7.4	10.4	11
MOTOR SHP	70	150	150
CELLS	60	120	120
SPEED SUBMERGED	5.0	6	6
ENDURANCE SURFACED	236/7.4	489/10.4	325/11
ENDURANCE SUBMERGED	20/5	24/6	24/6
TORPEDO TUBES (TORPEDOES)	1(3)	1(3)	2(4)
GUNS	NONE	NONE	NONE
COMPLEMENT	2/6	2/9	2/9
WEIGHTS:			
HULL	49.02	68.05	72.52
BALLAST KEEL	–	–	–
EQUIPMENT			
STEERING, DIVING	0.43	0.64	0.65
WATER SERVICE	1.63	3.23	2.95
AIR SERVICE	2.95	4.03	3.60
KINGSTONS ETC	0.33	0.94	0.85
ELECTRICAL	2.52	4.27	4.28
CREW & EFFECTS	0.65	0.75	0.75
SPARES	0.31	4.80	0.72
ARMAMENT:			
TT ETC.	1.16	1.16	3.50

TORPEDOES	1.77	1.77	2.36
GUNS	–	–	–
AMMUNITION	–	–	–
MACHINERY:			
ENGINES	7.52	17.10	17.10
BATTERY	30.10	58.00	59.00
MOTORS	2.02	5.20	5.65
SHAFTS ETC	1.10	4.09	3.10
LIQUIDS:			
FUEL	1.95	7.0	7.1
LUBE OIL	0.23	0.74	0.74
FRESH WATER	0.05	0.15	0.17
AUX & TRIM WATER	0.20	1.40	1.90
LEAD	3.67	8.99	–

	B 1	C 1
SURFACED	287	287
SUBMERGED	316	316
STANDARD	N/A	N/A
LOA	142-2½	142-2½
LBP	139-4	139-4
BEAM (PRESSURE HULL)	13-7	13-7
BEAM	SAME	SAME
DRAFT (MEAN)	11-2	11-2
ENGINE BHP	600	600
SPEED SURFACED	12	12
MOTOR SHP	189	300
CELLS	159	166
SPEED SUBMERGED	6.5	7.5
ENDURANCE SURFACED	740/12	909/12
ENDURANCE SUBMERGED	24/6.5	18/7.5
TORPEDO TUBES (TORPEDOES)	2 (4)	2 (4)
GUNS	NONE	NONE
COMPLEMENT	15	16
WEIGHTS:		
HULL	117.95	117.95
BALLAST KEEL	–	–
EQUIPMENT:		
STEERING, DIVING	1.25	1.25
WATER SERVICE	3.10	3.10
AIR SERVICE	6.51	6.51
KINGSTONS ETC	1.75	1.75
ELECTRICAL FITTINGS	4.95	4.95
CREW & EFFECTS	0.95	0.95
SPARES	1.72	5.25
ARMAMENT:		
TT ETC	5.39	5.39
TORPEDOES	2.36	2.36
GUNS	–	–
AMMUNITION	–	–
MACHINERY:		
ENGINES	17.50	17.50
BATTERY	68.80	68.80
MOTORS	11.22	11.22
SHAFTS ETC	2.40	2.40
AUX MCHY	3.25	3.25
LIQUIDS:		
FUEL	14.6	14.6
LUBE OIL	1.20	1.20
FRESH WATER	0.20	0.20
AUX & TRIM WATER	4.50	4.50
LEAD	13.12	13.12

Overseas Submarines

	D 1
SURFACED	483
SUBMERGED	595
STANDARD	N/A
LOA	163-0
LBP	158-6
BEAM (PRESSURE HULL)	13-7
BEAM	20-6
DRAFT (MEAN)	10-5
ENGINE BHP	1200
SPEED SURFACED	14

MOTOR SHP	2 x 210		
CELLS	210		
SPEED SUBMERGED	9		
ENDURANCE SURFACED	1680/14		
ENDURANCE SUBMERGED	20/9		
TORPEDO TUBES (TORPEDOES)	3 (6)		
GUNS	NONE		
COMPLEMENT	25		
WEIGHTS:			
HULL	201.2		
BALLAST KEEL	–		
EQUIPMENT:			
STEERING, DIVING	3.1		
WATER SERVICE	11.2		
AIR SERVICE	19.6		
KINGSTONS ETC	3.9		
ELECTRICAL FITTINGS	13.1		
CREW & EFFECTS	1.7		
SPARES	1.0		
ARMAMENT:			
TT ETC	5.39		
TORPEDOES	2.36		
GUNS	–		
AMMUNITION	–		
MACHINERY:			
ENGINES	17.50		
BATTERY	68.80		
MOTORS	11.22		
SHAFTS ETC	2.40		
AUX MCHY	3.25		
LIQUIDS:			
FUEL	14.6		
LUBE OIL	1.20		
FRESH WATER	0.20		
AUX & TRIM WATER	4.50		
LEAD	13.12		

	D 2	D 3–D 8	E 1–E 8
SURFACED	489	495	655
SUBMERGED	603	620	796
STANDARD	N/A	N/A	N/A
LOA	162-1	164-7	178-1
LBP	158-2	160-0	173-0
BEAM (PRESSURE HULL)	13-8⅛	13-10⅞	15-1¾
BEAM	20-6½	20-5	22-8⅜
DRAFT (MEAN)	10-9½	11-5	12-6¼
ENGINE BHP	1200	1200	1600
SPEED SURFACED	14	14	15
MOTOR SHP	2 x 220	2 x 220	2 x 224
CELLS	220	220	224 (split)
SPEED SUBMERGED	9	9	10
ENDURANCE SURFACED	1460/14	1460/14	1680/15
ENDURANCE SUBMERGED	14/9	14/9	15/10
TORPEDO TUBES (TORPEDOES)	3 (6)	3 (6)	4 (8)
GUNS	NONE	NONE	NONE
COMPLEMENT	2/23	2/23	3/27
WEIGHTS:			
HULL	207.6	205.8	282.2
BALLAST KEEL	8.0	22.4	30.2
EQUIPMENT:			
STEERING, DIVING	4.6	2.8	4.9
WATER SERVICE	13.0	12.0	12.7
AIR SERVICE	19.2	19.7	19.3
KINGSTONS ETC	2.4	2.7	3.5
ELECTRICAL FITTINGS	7.0	7.4	13.0
CREW & EFFECTS	1.7	1.7	2.8
SPARES	6.1	8.0	7.1
ARMAMENT:			
TT ETC	10.0	9.4	16.0
TORPEDOES	3.5	3.5	4.8
GUNS	–	–	2.7
AMMUNITION	–	–	1.1
MACHINERY:			
ENGINES	40.6	40.7	54.5
BATTERY	81.0	85.3	95.0

MOTORS	19.0	19.0	23.0
SHAFTS ETC	8.5	8.4	14.0
AUX MCHY	8.1	8.9	10.0
LIQUIDS:			
FUEL	29	29.4	40
LUBE OIL	3.7	4.4	5.0
FRESH WATER	1.5	1.6	2.0
AUX & TRIM WATER	2.5	2.1	2.0
LEAD	–	–	–

	E 9–E 16, E 27–E 56	*E 17–E 26***	*G 8***
SURFACED	667	664	703
SUBMERGED	807	780	837
STANDARD	N/A	N/A	N/A
LOA	181-0	181-0	187-1
LBP	176-0	176-0	178-0
BEAM (PRESSURE HULL)	15-1¾	15-1¾	15-4
BEAM	22-8⅜	22-7⅞	22-8
DRAFT (MEAN)	12-6¼	12-9	13-4
ENGINE BHP	1600	1600	1600
SPEED SURFACED	15	15	14
MOTOR SHP	2 x 420	2 x 420	2 x 420
CELLS	224	224	200
SPEED SUBMERGED	10	10	10
ENDURANCE SURFACED	1680/15	2600/10	1900/14
ENDURANCE SUBMERGED	99/3	99/3	95/3
TORPEDO TUBES (TORPEDOES)	5 (10)	5 (10)	5
GUNS	1 x 12pdr	1 x 12pdr	1 x 3in HA
COMPLEMENT	3/27	3/27	3/27
WEIGHTS:			
HULL	297.2	320.7	371.7
BALLAST KEEL	30.2	(32.42)	(47.18)
EQUIPMENT:			
STEERING, DIVING	4.5	N/A	N/A
WATER SERVICE	12.5	N/A	N/A
AIR SERVICE	17.7	N/A	N/A
KINGSTONS ETC	3.5	N/A	N/A
ELECTRICAL	13.0	N/A	N/A
CREW & EFFECTS	3.0	1.50	2.50
(STORES)		0.50	2.00
SPARES	9.6	N/A	N/A
ARMAMENT:		8.70	13.50
TT ETC.	18.0	N/A	N/A
TORPEDOES	5.9	N/A	N/A
GUNS	2.7	N/A	N/A
AMMUNITION	1.1	N/A	N/A
MACHINERY:			
ENGINES	54.5	153.76**	155.67**
BATTERY	95.0	–	–
MOTORS	23.0	125.84**	118.58**
SHAFTS ETC	15.0	–	–
AUX MCHY	9.0	–	–
LIQUIDS			
FUEL	40	41.50	44.00
LUBE OIL	5.0	5.00	3.50
FRESH WATER	2.6	4.00	3.90
AUX & TRIM WATER	2.0	3.00	3.00
LEAD	–	(2.40)	(2.47)

	*L 1–L 8***	*L 9–L 33***	*L 50* CLASS
SURFACED	891	914	960
SUBMERGED	1074	1089	1150
STANDARD	N/A	760	845
LOA	231-1	238-7	235-0
LBP	225-6	233-0	230-6
BEAM (PRESSURE HULL)	15-8½	15-8½	15-8½
BEAM	23-5½	23-5½	29-10
DRAFT (MEAN)	13-3	13-6	13-2½
ENGINE BHP	2400	2400	2400
SPEED SURFACED	17.2	17.6	17.5
MOTOR SHP	2 x 800	2 x 800	2 x 800
CELLS	336	336	336
SPEED SUBMERGED	10.5	10.5	10.5
ENDURANCE SURFACED	3850/17.2	2950/17.6	3000/17.5
ENDURANCE SUBMERGED	200/2	200/2	80/3 200/2

TORPEDO TUBES (TORPEDOES)	6	6	6
GUNS	1 x 3in HA	1 x 4in	2 x 4in
COMPLEMENT	35	38	44
WEIGHTS:			
HULL	393.00	455.0	344.47
BALLAST KEEL	40.55	40.0	31.5
EQUIPMENT:	10.0	10.0	
STEERING, DIVING	N/A	N/A	13.2
WATER SERVICE	N/A	N/A	5.8
AIR SERVICE	17	N/A	17.5
KINGSTONS ETC	N/A	N/A	13.18
ELECTRICAL	N/A	N/A	N/A
CREW & EFFECTS	3.50	N/A	6.60
SPARES	15.00	N/A	N/A
ARMAMENT:			
TT ETC.	26	29.0	17.1
TORPEDOES			17.0
GUNS	5	6.0	6.0
AMMUNITION			3.0
MACHINERY:			
ENGINES	111	103.0	77.23
		(INCL ENGRG STORES)	
BATTERY	135	136.0	137.5
MOTORS	40	40.0	41.20
SHAFTS ETC	–	–	11.62
AUX MCHY	–	–	30.27
LIQUIDS:			
FUEL	51.40	76.0	78.4
LUBE OIL	6.00	7.0	6.4
FRESH WATER	8.80	8.0	11.1
AUX & TRIM WATER	8.70	20.0	20.3
LEAD	(3.50)	N/A	–

Coastal Submarines

Note: weights for *S 1–S 3* are those given in the Cover for the Laurenti submarine *Velella* and *Medusa*, which were similar, of about the same size, carrying about the same amount of fuel (possibly 8 tons rather than 8.5 tons).

	F 1	S 1–S 3	V 1
			(estimate 1912)
SURFACED	363	265	386 (364 as est)
SUBMERGED	441	324	453
STANDARD	N/A	N/A	N/A
LOA	151-0	148-1½	144-0
LBP	143-0	137-0	139-10
BEAM (PRESSURE HULL)	12-0	10-0	12-6
BEAM	16-1¼	14-5	16-6
DRAFT (MEAN)	10-7	10-4½	11-6
ENGINE BHP	900	2 x 365	800
SPEED SURFACED	14	13.25	14
MOTOR SHP	380	2 x 400	300
CELLS	128	240	132
SPEED SUBMERGED	9	8.5	8.5
ENDURANCE SURFACED	1200/14	1600/8.5	2000/12
ENDURANCE SUBMERGED	90/3	75/5	85/6
TORPEDO TUBES (TORPEDOES)	3 (5)	2 (4)	2 (4)
GUNS	1 x 3pdr	1 x 12pdr	–
COMPLEMENT	18	26	18
WEIGHTS:			
HULL	157.6	116.5	181.0
BALLAST KEEL	23.0	26.0	19.5
EQUIPMENT:			
STEERING, DIVING	6.2	N/A	3.0
WATER SERVICE	9.5	3.5	9.5
AIR SERVICE	3.2	6.0	9.7 (incl 0.5 ventilating)
KINGSTONS ETC	(in water service)	(in water service)	3.5
ELECTRICAL	3.5	(in motors)	6.0
CREW & EFFECTS	2.0	2.0	1.5
SPARES	1.0	NA	1.0
ARMAMENT:			
TT ETC.	6.7	3.0	4.9
TORPEDOES	3.5	3.0	3.0
GUNS	0.6	–	–
AMMUNITION		–	–
MACHINERY:			
ENGINES	39.3	14.5	26.0

BATTERY	47.2	47.0	54.0
MOTORS	15.0	10.8	10.4
SHAFTS ETC	(with engines)	4.7	8.0
AUX MCHY	7.5	N/A	4.0
LIQUIDS:			
FUEL	17.5	8.5	17.0
LUBE OIL	2.5	2.0	1.5
FRESH WATER	1.6	1.5	0.5
AUX & TRIM WATER	7.2	N/A	3.0
LEAD	2.0	N/A	–

	V 2–V 4 (as designed)	W 1–W 2	H 1 CLASS
SURFACED	391	331	364
SUBMERGED	457	499	434
STANDARD	N/A	N/A	N/A
LOA	144-0	171-11	150-6
LBP	139-10	N/A	N/A
BEAM (PRESSURE HULL)	12-9	11-0	15-9
BEAM	16-3	15-4¼	15-9
DRAFT (MEAN)	11-6	8-10½	12-3
ENGINE BHP	900	710	480
SPEED SURFACED	14	13	13
MOTOR SHP	380	340	320 (620 for 1hr)
CELLS	132	290	120
SPEED SUBMERGED	9	8.5	11
ENDURANCE SURFACED	1200/14	2500/9	2000/13
ENDURANCE SUBMERGED	74/5	68/5	30/5
TORPEDO TUBES (TORPEDOES)	2	2 (8)	4
GUNS	NONE	NONE	NONE
COMPLEMENT	2/16	2/16	2/23
WEIGHTS:			
HULL	N/A	138.4	197.1
BALLAST KEEL	N/A	4.7	N/A
EQUIPMENT:			7.79
(EQ & OUTFIT)			
STEERING, DIVING	N/A	6.7	N/A
WATER SERVICE	N/A	6.4	N/A
AIR SERVICE	N/A	8.0	N/A
KINGSTONS ETC	N/A	N/A	N/A
ELECTRICAL	N/A	1.6	N/A
CREW & EFFECTS	N/A	1.8	N/A
SPARES	N/A	2.1	N/A
ARMAMENT:			
TT ETC.	N/A	6.9	6.52
TORPEDOES	N/A	5.3	2.22
GUNS	N/A	–	–
AMMUNITION	N/A	–	–
MACHINERY:			
ENGINES	N/A	26.9	34.7
BATTERY	N/A	51.8	56.7
MOTORS	N/A	17.6	11.1
SHAFTS ETC	N/A	3.3 }	12.89
AUX MCHY	N/A	4.5	
LIQUIDS:			
FUEL	N/A	12.9	16.64
LUBE OIL	N/A	1.6	N/A
FRESH WATER	N/A	0.9	N/A
AUX & TRIM WATER	N/A	4.1	N/A
LEAD	N/A	30.1	–
		(incl 3.9 drop weight)	

	H 41	R 9
SURFACED	438	410
SUBMERGED	504	503
STANDARD	410	N/A
LOA	171-9	163-9
LBP	167-3	138-3
BEAM (PRESSURE HULL)	15-4	15-3
BEAM	15-9*	15-9*
DRAFT (MEAN)	13-2½	11-6
ENGINE BHP	480	420
SPEED SURFACED	13	9.5
MOTOR SHP	320 (620 for 1 hr)	500
SPEED SUBMERGED	10.5	15

ENDURANCE SURFACED	2000/13	2200/9.5
ENDURANCE SUBMERGED	70/3	15/15, 240/4
TORPEDO TUBES (TORPEDOES)	4 (6)	6 (7)
GUNS	1 x Lewis	1 x Lewis
COMPLEMENT	3/19	22
WEIGHTS:		
HULL	206.21	164.87
BALLAST KEEL	26.47	–
EQUIPMENT:		
STEERING, DIVING	12.08	8.65
WATER SERVICE	9.22	7.28
AIR SERVICE	15.38	15.34
KINGSTONS ETC	N/A	N/A
ELECTRICAL	4.55	5.34
CREW & EFFECTS	2.25	2.25
SPARES	–	–
ARMAMENT:		
TT ETC.	11.87	11.92
TORPEDOES	11.58	8.26
GUNS	0.57	0.41
AMMUNITION	0.36	1.50
MACHINERY:		
ENGINES	25.12	12.09
BATTERY	52.09	103.01
MOTORS	10.48	62.90
SHAFTS ETC	5.73	3.27
AUX MCHY	4.98	8.27
LIQUIDS:		
FUEL	14.75	11.80
LUBE OIL	1.67	2.50
FRESH WATER	3.80	3.42
AUX & TRIM WATER	21.83	5.76
LEAD	–	–

Ocean Submarines

	NAUTILUS	VICKERS DESIGN 619 (AS BID OCT 1912)
SURFACED	1441	1270
SUBMERGED	2026	1694
STANDARD	N/A	N/A
LOA	258-3¼	N/A
LBP	218-6	240
BEAM (PRESSURE HULL)	20-6	N/A
BEAM	26-0	26-0
DRAFT (MEAN)	17-9	13-4½
ENGINE BHP	3700	3700
SPEED SURFACED	17	17.5
MOTOR SHP	1000	1000
CELLS	352	
SPEED SUBMERGED	10	10
ENDURANCE SURFACED	5300/11	5300/11
ENDURANCE SUBMERGED	72	72
TORPEDO TUBES (TORPEDOES)	8 (16)	7 (14)
GUNS	1 x 3in HA	1
COMPLEMENT	4/37	N/A
WEIGHTS:		
HULL	N/A	568.5
BALLAST KEEL	N/A	100.0
EQUIPMENT:		
STEERING, DIVING	N/A	5.0
WATER SERVICE	N/A	14.0
AIR SERVICE	N/A	32.2
KINGSTONS ETC	N/A	7.5
ELECTRICAL	N/A	11.2
CREW & EFFECTS	N/A	7.0
SPARES, MISC	N/A	5.2
ARMAMENT:		
TT ETC.	N/A	26.0
TORPEDOES	N/A	12.5
GUNS	N/A	} 3.0
AMMUNITION	N/A	
MACHINERY:		
ENGINES	N/A	120.0
BATTERY	N/A	147.0
MOTORS	N/A	34.0

SHAFTS ETC	N/A	31.0	
AUX MCHY	N/A	15.1	
LIQUIDS:			
FUEL	N/A	100.0	
LUBE OIL	N/A	12.0	
FRESH WATER	N/A	5.0	
AUX & TRIM WATER	N/A	11.0	
LEAD	N/A	—	

*Indicates over rudders

	SWORDFISH (AS PROPOSED JUNE 1913)	'J' CLASS	K 11
SURFACED	932	1204	1980 (1764 design)
SUBMERGED	1105	1820	2566 (as built 932/1475 tons)
STANDARD	N/A	N/A	N/A
LOA	231-3½	275-6	330-0
LBP	218-6	262-0	328-6
BEAM (PRESSURE HULL)	16-0	18-0	21-7
BEAM	22-11	23-0	26-6¾
DRAFT (MEAN)	14-11	14-0	17-0
ENGINE BHP	4000	3600	10,000 steam 800 diesel
SPEED SURFACED	18	19.5	24
MOTOR SHP	400	1350	1400
CELLS	128		
SPEED SUBMERGED	10	9.5	9
ENDURANCE SURFACED	3000/8.5	2600/19.5	1950/full
ENDURANCE SUBMERGED	60/6	60/3	83/1.75
TORPEDO TUBES (TORPEDOES)	6 (12)	6	10 (incl twin UD tubes)
GUNS	1 x 12pdr	1 x 3in HA	1 x 3in HA, 2 x 4in
COMPLEMENT		5/39	5/54
WEIGHTS:			
HULL	N/A	N/A	992.64
BALLAST KEEL	N/A	N/A	165.04
(SAFETY WEIGHT)	–	–	19.54
EQUIPMENT:			
STEERING, DIVING	N/A	N/A	34.79
WATER SERVICE	N/A	N/A	14.72
AIR SERVICE	N/A	N/A	51.20
KINGSTONS ETC	N/A	N/A	9.06
ELECTRICAL	N/A	N/A	21.39
CREW & EFFECTS	N/A	N/A	7.90
SPARES	N/A	N/A	10
ARMAMENT:			
TT ETC.	N/A	N/A	30.72
TORPEDOES	N/A	N/A	14.92
GUNS	N/A	N/A	5.30
AMMUNITION	N/A	N/A	3.98
MACHINERY:			
ENGINES	N/A	N/A	171.11
STEAM			42.75
DIESEL			
BATTERY	N/A	N/A	137.84
MOTORS	N/A	N/A	24.9
SHAFTS ETC.	N/A	N/A	21.72
AUX MCHY	N/A	N/A	(IN STEAM PLANT)
LIQUIDS:			
FUEL	N/A	19.1	191.30 STEAM
DIESEL			
LUBE OIL	N/A	N/A	11.50
FRESH WATER	N/A	N/A	7.50
AUX & TRIM WATER	N/A	N/A	25.00
LEAD	N/A	N/A	30.94

	K 26	M 1	X 1
SURFACED	2140	1594	2759
SUBMERGED	2530	1946	3600
STANDARD	1786	N/A	2385
LOA	351-6	259-9	363-6

LBP	339-0	280-0	350-0
BEAM (PRESSURE HULL)	21-9	20-4	19-9½
BEAM	28-0	24-8	29-10
DRAFT (MEAN)	16-10	15-9	15-9
ENGINE BHP	10,000 (steam)	2400	6000
SPEED SURFACED	23.5	15.5–16	19.5–20
MOTOR SHP	1400	2000	2400
CELLS	333	552	330
SPEED SUBMERGED	9	9.5–10	9.5
ENDURANCE SURFACED	7500/12	4000/11	10,000/8
ENDURANCE SUBMERGED	80/1.75	10/10	18/4
TORPEDO TUBES (TORPEDOES)	10 (20)	4	6
GUNS	3 x 4in	1 x 12in, 1 x 3in HA	4 x 5.25in
COMPLEMENT	5/54	6/58	9/88
WEIGHTS:			
HULL	}1170	734.63	1490
BALLAST KEEL		179.32	170
EQUIPMENT:	40 (GEN EQ'T)		–
STEERING, DIVING	N/A	23.69	30
WATER SERVICE	N/A	23.02	N/A
AIR SERVICE	26	57.00	37
KINGSTONS ETC	N/A	N/A	34
ELECTRICAL	N/A	21.39	32
CREW & EFFECTS	N/A	8.00	35
SPARES	N/A	N/A	5
ARMAMENT:			
TT ETC.	}52	11.65	}35
TORPEDOES		14.98	
GUNS	}18	122.87	50
AMMUNITION		24.7	14
(WATER IN HYDRAULICS)	–	15.00	–
MACHINERY:			
ENGINES STEAM:	211	–	–
DIESEL/GENERATORS	60	64.37	286
BATTERY	156	152.10	210
MOTORS	22	42.49	62
(AUXILIARY DRIVE)	–	–	4
GENERATORS	–	–	36
SHAFTS ETC	(WITH ENGINES)	23.95	N/A
AUX MCHY	N/A	99.89	136
LIQUIDS:			
FUEL	285	72.50	219
LUBE OIL	15	11.50	44
FRESH WATER	}45	13.00	24
AUX & TRIM WATER		25.00	70
RESERVE FEED WATER	20	N/A	N/A
LEAD	20 (MARGIN)	0.65	–

Interwar Submarines

	OBERON	OTWAY	OSIRIS
SURFACED	1598	1636	1781
SUBMERGED	1831	1872	2038
STANDARD	1311	1349	1475
LOA	(design 1480/1805)	(design 1740)	
	269-8	275-0	283-6
LBP	260-0	264-6	273-0
BEAM (PRESSURE HULL)	16-1¾	16-1¾	16-10¾
BEAM	27-11½	27-7 5/8	29-10¾
DRAFT (MEAN)	15-6	15-8½	16-1¼
ENGINE BHP	2950	3000	4400
SPEED SURFACED	15	15.5	17–17.5
MOTOR SHP	1350	1350	1320
CELLS	330	330	336
SPEED SUBMERGED	9	9	9
ENDURANCE SURFACED	12,000/8	14,000/8	10,000/8
ENDURANCE SUBMERGED	60/4	60/4	60/4
TORPEDO TUBES (TORPEDOES)	8 (14)	8 (14)	8 (16)
GUNS	1 x 4in	1 x 4.7in	1 x 4.7in
COMPLEMENT	6/47	6/47	6/47
WEIGHTS:			
HULL	}830	538.8	819
BALLAST KEEL		151.9	104
EQUIPMENT:	73 (GEN EQ'T)	282.8***	292.5***
AIR SERVICE	26	N/A	27

CREW & EFFECTS	28	17.5	28.0
SPARES	5	9.6	5.0
W/T AND A/S	20		19.0
			(battery cooling plant 10)
ARMAMENT:			
TT ETC.	28.7	26.8	20.4
TORPEDOES	23.4	20.4	22.5
GUNS	5.1	5.0	9.4
AMMUNITION	3.4	3.3	6.6
MACHINERY:			
ENGINES	87.3	131.5	210
	(BATTERY COOLING 10)		
BATTERY	141.8	138.0	146
MOTORS	35	37.5	39.4
SHAFTS ETC	N/A	21.7	18.3
LIQUIDS:			
FUEL	111.0	133.0	145
LUBE OIL	13.0	29.7	24
FRESH WATER	20.0	39.0	N/A
AUX & TRIM WATER			49.7
LEAD	16 (MARGIN)	– 46.6	–

	PERSEUS	*REGENT*	*THAMES*
SURFACED	1760	1763	2165
SUBMERGED	2040	2030	2680
STANDARD	1475	1475	1805
LOA	289-2	287-2	345-0
LBP	273-0	271-0	325-0
BEAM (PRESSURE HULL)	16-10¾	16-10¾	18-6
BEAM	29-10¾	29-10¾	28-0
DRAFT (MEAN)	15-11	16-1	15-7½
ENGINE BHP	4640	4640	8750–10,000
SPEED SURFACED	17.5	17.5	20.5–21.75
MOTOR SHP	1320	1320	2500
CELLS	336	336	336
SPEED SUBMERGED	8.5	9	10
ENDURANCE SURFACED	10,000/8	10,000/8	10,000/8
ENDURANCE SUBMERGED	60/4	60/4	90/3
TORPEDO TUBES (TORPEDOES)	8 (14)	8 (14)	6 (12)
GUNS	1 x 4.7in	1 x 4.7in	1 x 4.7in
COMPLEMENT	53	53	61
WEIGHTS:			
HULL	595.0	646.0	922
BALLAST KEEL	185.6	121.4	85.7
EQUIPMENT:	258.4***	273.6***	48.0
AIR SERVICE	N/A	N/A	39.0
			(add to equipment)
			(also 5.5 CO_2 plant)
CREW & EFFECTS	15.1	18.0	28.0
SPARES	11.8	10.8	5.0
W/T AND A/S	N/A	N/A	12.5
ARMAMENT:			
TT ETC.	31.2	32.9	24.9
TORPEDOES	20.4	20.5	17.0
GUNS	9.6	11.6	11.7
AMMUNITION	6.0	4.6	5.4
MACHINERY:			
ENGINES	140.7	142.0	197.0
BATTERY	140.6	140.0	222.3
MOTORS	44.3	42.5	56.2
SHAFTS ETC	14.8	15.0	31.9
LIQUIDS:			
FUEL	158.5	156.5	215.0
LUBE OIL	32.0	30.0	36.0
FRESH WATER	41.4	41.4	41.3
AUX & TRIM WATER	44.3	43.0	45.5
LEAD	18.7	–	–

	PORPOISE	*SWORDFISH*	*SHARK*
SURFACED	1768	730	761
	(design 735/935 tons)		
SUBMERGED	2053	907	960
STANDARD	1500	640	670
LOA	289-0	202-6	208-6
LBP	267-0	187-0	193-0

BEAM (PRESSURE HULL)	16-9	14-11¾	14-11¾
BEAM	29-0¾	24-0⅜	24-0⅜
DRAFT (MEAN)	15-10	11-8	12-0
ENGINE BHP	3300	1550	1550
SPEED SURFACED	15	13.75	13.75
MOTOR SHP	1630	1300	1300
CELLS	336	224	224
SPEED SUBMERGED	8.75	10.0	10.0
ENDURANCE SURFACED	11,500/8	3800/9	3800/9
ENDURANCE SUBMERGED	64/4	72/2	72/2
TORPEDO TUBES (TORPEDOES)	6 (12)	6 (12)	6 (12)
GUNS	1 x 4in	1 x 3in HA	1 x 3in HA
COMPLEMENT	5/54	36	36
WEIGHTS:			
HULL	577.0	}372.2	}388.0
BALLAST KEEL	191.0		
EQUIPMENT:	293.9***	30 (GEN EQ'T)	30 (GEN EQ'T)
AIR SERVICE			
CREW & EFFECTS	17.6		
W/T AND A/S			
ARMAMENT:			
TT ETC.	23.4	}45.0	45.0
TORPEDOES	17.1		
GUNS	11.9	}6.7	7.0
AMMUNITION	4.4		
MACHINERY:			
ENGINES	107.3	74.5**	75**
BATTERY	137.7	100	98
MOTORS	42.4	23	29
SHAFTS ETC.	14.2	N/A	N/A
LIQUIDS:			
FUEL	151.0	44.5	45
LUBE OIL	20.6	6.2	6.5
FRESH WATER	34.5)	35.2	36.5
AUX & TRIM WATER	68.1)		
LEAD	3.9	–	–

Rearmament and War

	1939 PATROL/MINELAYER	1940 'S' CLASS
SURFACED	815	805
SUBMERGED	1025	995
STANDARD	727	715
LOA	218-0	217-0
LBP	N/A	N/A
BEAM (PRESSURE HULL)	N/A	N/A
BEAM	25-0	23-8 ¾
DRAFT (MEAN)	13-3	13-7
ENGINE BHP	1600	1500
	(1500 for propulsion; BHP is 1900)	
SPEED SURFACED	14	14
MOTOR SHP	1300	1300
CELLS	224	224
SPEED SUBMERGED	9	9 (1¼ hrs)
ENDURANCE SURFACED	4000/10	3800/10
ENDURANCE SUBMERGED	108/3	120/3
TORPEDO TUBES (TORPEDOES)	6 (12)	6 (12)
GUNS	1 x 3in	1 x 3in
COMPLEMENT	38	38
WEIGHTS:		
HULL	390	}439
BALLAST KEEL	61	
EQUIPMENT:	N/A	16 (Gen Eq't)
AIR SERVICE	15	12
CREW & EFFECTS	7.4	N/A
W/T AND A/S	5.3	N/A
ARMAMENT:		
TT ETC.	}43	}47
TORPEDOES		
(MINES	11)	NONE
GUNS	}4	}4
AMMUNITION		
MACHINERY:		
ENGINES	67**	74**
BATTERY	97	97
MOTORS	26	26

AUX MCHY		
LIQUIDS:		
FUEL	47	45
LUBE OIL	6	6
FRESH WATER	8	
AUX & TRIM WATER	26	39
LEAD	–	–

	TRITON (LEGEND 1935)	'T' CLASS 1943
SURFACED	1290	1304 (DRY MBTs: 17 TONS)
SUBMERGED	1560	1567
STANDARD	1090	1090
LOA	276-6	273-3
LBP	263-0	268-6 (LWL)
BEAM (PRESSURE HULL)	–	–
BEAM	25-6	26-6
DRAFT (MEAN)	14-0	14-6
ENGINE BHP	2500	2500
SPEED SURFACED	15.5	15.25
MOTOR SHP	1450	1450
CELLS	336	336
SPEED SUBMERGED	9	9
ENDURANCE SURFACED	4500/11	9300/8
ENDURANCE SUBMERGED	110/2	126/2.25
TORPEDO TUBES (TORPEDOES)	10 (16)	11 (17)
GUNS	1 x 4in	1 x 4in
COMPLEMENT	48	60
WEIGHTS:		
HULL/FITTINGS }	685	568
BALLAST KEEL }		139
EQUIPMENT:	23 (GEN EQ'T)	20 (GEN EQ'T)
AIR SERVICE	12	12
CREW & EFFECTS	N/A	18.9
W/T AND A/S	N/A	6.5
ARMAMENT:		
TT ETC. }	}64	70
TORPEDOES }		
GUNS }	}10	10
AMMUNITION }		
MACHINERY:		
ENGINES	110**	105**
BATTERY	146	146
MOTORS	36	39.5 (INCL 3.5 AUX DRIVE)
AUX MCHY	4 (CO_2 plant)	
LIQUIDS:		
FUEL	135	129.3
LUBE OIL	15	15.9
FRESH WATER }	50	33.6
AUX & TRIM WATER }		27.3
LEAD	–	–

	'A' CLASS (AS DESIGNED 1943)	1940 MINELAYER (IMPROVED CACHALOT)
SURFACED	1360	1737
SUBMERGED	1590	2085
STANDARD	1120	–
LOA	281-4¾	298-0
LBP	249-3	273-0
BEAM (PRESSURE HULL)	N/A	N/A
BEAM	22-3	27-9 (MLD)
DRAFT (MEAN)	17-0	16-4 (WITH MINES)
ENGINE BHP	4300	3300
SPEED SURFACED	19	15.75
MOTOR SHP	1250	1630
CELLS	224	336
SPEED SUBMERGED	8	8.75
ENDURANCE SURFACED	12,200/10	11,000/8
ENDURANCE SUBMERGED	80/4	100/2
TORPEDO TUBES (TORPEDOES)	10 (20)	6 (12) (50 MINES)
GUNS	1 x 4in	1 x 4in
COMPLEMENT	61	61
WEIGHTS:		
HULL	571.03	788

SUBMARINE DATA

BALLAST KEEL (INCLUDES Q TANK IN 'A' CLASS)	117.68	210
EQUIPMENT:		30 (GEN EQ'T)
AIR SERVICE	14.64 (INCL COOLING PLANT, 4)	N/A
CREW & EFFECTS	17.55	N/A
W/T AND A/S	11.10	N/A
ARMAMENT:		
TT ETC.	70.0 }	44
TORPEDOES		
GUNS	13.26 }	10
AMMUNITION		
MINES	N/A	54
MACHINERY:		
ENGINES	140.0**	135**
BATTERY	118.85	147
MOTORS (AND 1 TON FREON PLANT)	37.00	51 (INCL AUX DRIVE)
SHAFTS ETC	–	–
LIQUIDS:		
FUEL	61 (105 EXTERNAL)	140
LUBE OIL	18.66	23
FRESH WATER	27.78	72
AUX AND TRIM WATER	33.95	(IN FRESH WATER)
LEAD	–	–

	UNDINE	'U' CLASS 1940
SURFACED	631.46	6
SUBMERGED	732.54	732
STANDARD	540	540
LOA	191-0	196-10
LBP	180-0	180-0
BEAM (PRESSURE HULL)	16-0	16-1
BEAM	16-0	16-1
DRAFT (MEAN)	14-5	14-9
ENGINE BHP	720	615
SPEED SURFACED	11.25	11.25
MOTOR SHP	2 x 412	825
CELLS	224	224
SPEED SUBMERGED	9	9
ENDURANCE SURFACED	4450/8	5000/10
ENDURANCE SUBMERGED	120/2	120/2
TORPEDO TUBES (TORPEDOES)	6 (10)	4 (8)
GUNS	1 x Lewis	1 x 3in
COMPLEMENT	3/27	33
WEIGHTS:		
HULL	319.19	294 (INCL FITTINGS)
BALLAST KEEL	49.34	52.4
EQUIPMENT:	(IN HULL WEIGHT)	
AIR SERVICE	N/A	N/A
CREW & EFFECTS	6.94	9.67
W/T AND A/S	N/A	4.6
ARMAMENT:		35
TT ETC.	–	N/A
TORPEDOES	14.40	N/A
GUNS }	0.77	N/A
AMMUNITION }		N/A
MACHINERY:		
ENGINES	41.75**	41.8**
BATTERY	97.25	98.0
MOTORS	19.15	20.0
LIQUIDS:		
FUEL	38.19	55.17
LUBE OIL	4.28	5.03
FRESH WATER	8.42	8.50
AUX & TRIM WATER	29.16	22.9
LEAD	3.24	–

415

SUBMARINE LIST

For compactness, the builder's symbol appears under the name of the submarine. Launch date is under laying-down date.

Builders:

A	Armstrong Whitworth
B	Beardmore
BQ	Bethlehem Quincy (US yard)
CDY	Chatham Royal Dockyard
CL	Cammell Laird
CV	Canadian Vickers (Electric Boat components)
D	Denny
DDY	Devonport Royal Dockyard
F	Fairfield
FR	Fore River (US)
F/B	Launched by Fairfield, completed by Beardmore (similarly for similar entries)
JB	John Brown
P	Palmer
PDY	Portsmouth Royal Dockyard
PEDY	Pembroke Royal Dockyard
RDY	Rosyth Royal Dockyard
S	Scotts
SDY	Sheerness Royal Dockyard
SH	Swan Hunter
T	Thornycroft
UIW	Union Iron Works San Francisco
V	Vickers (later Vickers-Armstrong)
W	White
Y	Yarrow

Fates:

Boats listed as lost and then as target were raised and then used as targets, sunk on date indicated.

A	Accidental loss (not collision)
B	Bombed (lost to air attack)
BU	Broken Up
C	Collision (includes ramming)
CTL	Constructive Total Loss (write-off after surviving damage)
DC	Depth-charged
F	Foundered
G	Gunfire
I	Interned
M	Mine
PC	Converted to surface patrol craft (with name)
RAN	Royal Australian Navy (transfer)
RNLN	Royal Netherlands Navy (transfer)
RNN	Royal Norwegian Navy (transfer)
S	Sold
Sc	Scuttled
T	Torpedo
W	Wrecked

Construction Through 1921

NOTE: In some cases dates given by the Barrow Submariners' Association website, used here, give the day as the first of the month, where other sources do not give any day, only the month and the year.

'Hollands'

No 1	04/02/01	02/02/03	S 07/10/13
V	02/10/01		
No 2	04/02/01	01/08/03	07/10/13
V	21/02/02		
No 3	04/02/01	19/01/03	07/10/13
V	09/05/02		
No 4	04/02/01	02/08/03	F 03/09/12, target 1914
V	23/05/02		
No 5	04/02/01	19/01/03	S 1912
V	10/06/02		

'A' Class (*A 14* became *B 1*; *A 1* was originally *No 6*)

A 1	19/02/02	23/07/03	C 18/03/04, raised, target 08/11
V	09/07/02		
A 2	06/11/02	21/06/04	W 01/20
V	16/04/03		
A 3	06/11/02	13/07/04	F 02/02/12, target 17/05/12
V	09/05/03		
A 4	06/11/02	17/07/04	S 16/01/20
V	09/06/03		
A 5	01/09/03	11/02/05	BU 1920
V	03/03/04		
A 6	01/09/03	23/03/05	S 16/01/20
V	03/03/04		
A 7	01/09/03	13/04/05	F 16/01/14
V	23/01/05		
A 8	01/09/03	08/05/05	S 08/10/20
V	23/01/05		
A 9	1903	08/05/05	BU 1920
V	08/02/05		
A 10	1903	08/05/05	S 01/04/19
V	08/02/05		
A 11	1903	11/07/05	BU 5/20
V	08/03/05		
A 12	1903	23/09/05	S 16/01/20
V	03/03/05		
A 13	19/02/03	22/06/08	Diesel prototype. BU 1920
V	18/04/05		

'B' Class

B 1	N/A	16/04/05	S 25/08/21
V	25/10/04		
B 2	N/A	09/12/05	C 04/10/12
V	19/08/05		

Boat	Builder	Date 1	Date 2	Date 3	Fate
B 3	V	N/A	31/10/05	19/01/06	S 20/12/19
B 4	V	N/A	14/11/05	28/01/06	S 01/04/19
B 5	V	N/A	14/11/05	25/02/06	S 25/08/21
B 6	V	N/A	30/11/05	03/03/06	PC 08/17 *S.6*
B 7	V	N/A	30/11/05	27/03/06	PC 08/17 *S.7*
B 8	V	N/A	23/01/06	10/04/06	PC 08/17 *S.8*
B 9	V	N/A	26/01/06	28/04/06	PC 08/17 *S.9*
B 10	V	N/A	28/03/06	31/05/06	B 09/08/16
B 11	V	N/A	24/02/06	11/07/06	PC 08/17 *S.11*

'C' Class

Boat	Builder	Date 1	Date 2	Date 3	Fate
C 1	V	13/11/05	10/07/06	30/10/06	S 22/10/20
C 2	V	13/11/05	10/07/06	26/11/06	S 08/10/20
C 3	V	25/11/05	03/10/06	23/02/07	Expended Zeebrugge 23/04/18
C 4	V	25/11/05	18/10/06	13/03/07	S 28/02/22 (retained for experiments post-war)
C 5	V	24/11/05	20/08/06	15/12/06	S 31/10/19
C 6	V	24/11/05	20/08/06	21/01/07	S 20/11/19
C 7	V	09/12/05	15/02/07	23/05/07	S 20/12/19
C 8	V	09/12/05	15/02/07	23/05/07	S 22/10/20
C 9	V	30/01/06	03/04/07	18/06/07	S 22/10/20
C 10	V	30/01/06	15/04/07	13/07/07	S 07/22
C 11	V	06/04/06	27/05/07	03/09/07	C 14/07/09
C 12	V	27/11/06	09/09/07	19/01/08	S 02/02/20
C 13	V	29/11/06	09/11/07	19/02/08	S 02/02/20
C 14	V	04/12/06	07/12/07	13/03/08	S 05/12/21
C 15	V	07/12/06	21/01/08	01/04/08	S 28/02/22
C 16	V	14/12/06	19/03/08	05/06/08	S 12/08/22
C 17	CDY	11/03/07	13/08/08	13/05/09	S 20/11/19
C 18	CDY	11/03/07	10/10/08	23/07/09	S 26/05/21
C 19	CDY	01/06/08	20/03/09	09/11/09	S 02/02/20
C 20	CDY	01/06/08	27/11/09	31/01/10	S 26/05/21
C 21	V	04/02/08	26/09/08	18/05/09	S 05/12/21
C 22	V	04/02/08	10/10/08	05/05/09	S 02/02/21
C 23	V	07/02/08	26/11/08	05/05/09	S 05/12/21
C 24	V	12/02/08	26/11/08	05/05/09	S 26/05/21
C 25	V	27/02/08	10/03/09	28/05/09	S 05/12/21
C 26	V	14/02/08	20/03/09	28/05/09	Sc 04/04/18
C 27	V	04/06/08	22/04/09	14/08/09	Sc 05/04/18
C 28	V	06/03/08	22/04/09	14/08/09	S 25/08/21
C 29	V	04/06/08	19/06/09	17/09/09	M 29/08/15
C 30	V	10/06/08	19/07/09	11/10/09	S 25/08/21
C 31	V	07/01/09	02/09/09	19/11/09	M 04/01/15
C 32	V	12/01/09	29/09/09	19/11/09	Sc 22/10/17 (ran ashore)
C 33	CDY	29/03/09	10/05/10	13/08/10	M 04/08/15
C 34	CDY	29/03/09	08/06/10	17/09/10	T 17/07/17
C 35	V	03/03/09	02/11/09	01/02/10	Sc 05/04/18
C 36	V	03/03/09	30/11/09	01/02/10	S 25/06/19
C 37	V	07/04/09	01/01/10	31/03/10	S 25/06/19
C 38	V	05/04/09	10/02/10	31/03/10	S 25/06/19

'D' Class (*D 9* and *D 10* built as *E 1* and *E 2*)

Boat	Builder	Date 1	Date 2	Date 3	Fate
D 1	V	14/05/07	16/05/08	09.09	Target 23/10/18
D 2	V	10/07/09	25/05/10	29/03/11	German patrol craft 25/11/14
D 3	V	15/03/10	17/10/10	30/08/11	B (error) 12/03/18
D 4	V	24/02/10	27/05/11	29/11/11	S 19/12/21
D 5	V	23/02/10	28/08/11	19/01/12	M 03/11/14
D 6	V	24/02/10	23/10/11	19/04/12	T 28/06/18
D 7	CDY	14/02/10	14/01/11	14/12/11	S 19/12/21
D 8	CDY	14/02/10	23/09/11	23/03/12	S 19/12/21

'E' Class (*E 57* and *E 58* built as *L 1* and *L 2*) (Starred units are minelayers)

ID	Builder	Dates	Date	Fate
E 1	CDY	14/02/11 09/11/12	06/05/13	Sc 03/04/18
E 2	CDY	14/02/11 23/11/12	30/06/13	S 07/03/21
E 3	V	27/04/11 29/10/12	29/05/14	T 18/10/14
E 4	V	16/05/11 05/02/12	04/01/13	S 21/02/22
E 5	V	09/06/11 17/05/12	07/06/13	M 07/03/16
E 6	V	12/09/11 12/11/12	15/10/13	M 26/12/15
E 7	CDY	30/03/12 02/10/13	14/03/14	T 04/09/15
E 8	CDY	30/03/12 30/10/13	14/03/14	Sc 04/04/18
AE 1	V	03/11/11 22/05/13	20/01/14	RAN; accidental loss 19/09/14
AE 2	V	10/02/12 18/06/13	10/02/14	RAN; Sc 30/04/15 Dardanelles
E 9	V	01/06/12 29/11/13	16/06/14	Sc 04/04/18
E 10	V	10/07/12 29/11/13	10/08/14	Unknown cause 18/01/15
E 11	V	13/07/12 23/04/14	19/09/14	S 07/03/21
E 12	CDY	16/12/12 05/09/14	14/10/14	S 07/03/21
E 13	CDY	16/12/12 22/09/14	09/12/14	I after stranding 18/08/15
E 14	V	14/12/12 07/07/14	01/12/14	G 28/01/18
E 15	V	14/10/12 23/04/14	15/10/14	Stranded Dardanelles 17/04/15
E 16	V	14/10/12 23/09/14	26/02/15	M 22/08/16
E 17	V	29/07/14 16/01/15	07/04/15	W 06/01/16
E 18	V	01/04/14 04/03/15	06/06/15	G 24/05/16
E 19	V	27/11/14 13/05/15	12/07/15	Sc 03/04/18
E 20	V	25/11/14 12/06/15	30/08/15	T 06/11/16
E 21	V	29/11/14 24/07/15	01/10/15	S 06/09/22
E 22	V	25/11/14 27/08/15	08/11/15	T 25/04/16
E 23	V	01/12/14 28/09/15	06/12/15	S 06/09/22
E 24*	V	N/A 09/12/15	10/01/16	M 24/03/16
E 25	B	N/A 23/08/15	04/10/15	S 14/12/21
E 26	B	N/A 11/11/15	03/10/15	Unknown (prob M) 22/11/16
E 27	Y	N/A 09/06/17	01/08/17	S 06/09/22
E 28	Y	Cancelled (with *E 27*) 20/04/15, but *E 27* resumed 07/08/15		
E 29	A	04/12/14 01/06/15	13/10/15	S 21/02/22
E 30	A	08/12/14 26/09/15	08/12/15	Unknown (prob M) 22/11/16
E 31	S	01/12/14 23/08/15	27/12/15	S 06/09/22
E 32	W	24/12/14 16/08/16	01/10/16	S 06/09/22
E 33	T	01/01/15 18/04/16	01/11/16	S 06/09/22
E 34*	T	N/A 27/01/17	01/03/17	M 20/07/18
E 35	JB	07/12/14 20/05/16	14/07/16	S 06/09/22
E 36	JB	07/01/15 16/09/16	16/11/16	C 19/01/17
E 37	F	12/14 02/09/15	17/03/16	Unknown (prob M) 01/12/16
E 38	F	12/14 13/06/16	10/07/16	S 06/09/22
E 39	P	01/12/14 18/05/16	30/09/16	S 13/10/21
E 40	P	12/14 09/11/16	01/05/17	S 14/12/21
E 41*	CL	N/A 26/07/15	01/02/16	S 06/09/22
E 42	CL	12/14 23/10/15	01/06/16	S 06/09/22
E 43	SH	22/12/14 10/11/15	20/02/16	S 03/01/21
E 44	SH	08/01/15 21/02/16	18/07/17	S 13/10/21
E 45*	CL	N/A 25/01/16	01/08/16	S 06/09/22
E 46*	CL	N/A 04/04/16	01/10/16	S 06/09/22
E 47	F/B	01/01/15 29/05/16	01/10/16	Unknown, prob M 20/08/17
E 48	F/B	01.15 02/08/16	01/02/17	Target 1920, S/07/28
E 49	SH	15/02/15 18/09/16	14/12/16	M 12/03/17
E 50	JB	01/03/15 13/11/16	23/01/17	M 31/01/18
E 51*	S	01/03/15 30/11/16	27/01/17	S 13/10/21
E 52	D	01/03/15 25/01/17	13/03/17	S 03/01/21
E 53	B	01/02/15 30/01/16	30/01/16	S 06/09/22
E 54	B	01/02/15 30/03/16	01/05/16	S 14/12/21

E 55 D	01/12/14 05/02/16	25/03/16	S 06/09/22
E 56	01/12/14 19/06/16	08/08/16	S 09/06/23D

'F' Class (Admiralty Coastals)

F 1 CDY	01/12/13 31/03/15	14/08/15	BU 1920
F 2 W	30/11/14 07/07/17	22/08/17	S/07/22
F 3 T	12/10/14 19/02/16	07.16	BU 1920

Note: F 4–F 8 projected, not ordered.

'G' Class (G 15 ordered from W, cancelled 20/04/15)

G 1 CDY	01/10/14 14/08/15	07/12/15	S 14/02/20
G 2 CDY	01/10/14 23/12/15	18/03/16	S 16/01/20
G 3 CDY	01/10/14 22/01/16	13/04/16	S 04/11/21
G 4 CDY	12/10/14 23/10/16	03/02/16	S 27/06/28
G 5 CDY	12/10/14 23/11/16	17/01/16	S 25/10/22
G 6 A	08/12/14 17/12/15	07/05/16	S 04/11/21
G 7 A	08/12/14 14/03/16	19/08/16	Unknown 01/11/18
G 8 V	18/12/14 01/05/16	30/06/16	Unknown 14/01/18
G 9 V	08/12/14 15/06/16	22/08/16	C 16/09/17
G 10 V	12/03/15 22/02/16	13/05/16	S 20/01/23
G 11 V	28/03/15 24/03/16	13/05/16	W 22/11/18
G 12 V	07/04/15 24/03/16	15/06/16	S 14/02/20
G 13 V	09/04/15 18/07/16	23/09/16	S 20/01/23
G 14 S	01/12/14 31/08/16	17/05/17	S 11/03/21

Swordfish (renamed S 1 April 1916, then Swordfish as surface patrol vessel July 1917)

Swordfish S	28/02/14 18/03/16	27/07/16	S 07/22

'H' Class (US-built)
Note that H 1–H 10 were all credited with the same launch date.

H 1 CV	11/01/15 01/04/15	26/05/15	S 07/03/21
H 2 CV	11/01/15 01/04/15	04/06/15	S 07/03/21
H 3 CV	11/01/15 01/04/15	03/06/15	M 15/07/16
H 4 CV	11/01/15 01/04/15	05/06/15	S 30/11/21
H 5 CV	11/01/15 01/04/15	10/06/15	C 02/03/18
H 6 CV	14/01/15 01/04/15	09/06/15	Stranded, I, 19/01/16, RNLN 4/05/17

H 7 CV	1915 01/04/15	25/06/15	S 30/11/21
H 8 CV	1915 1915	25/06/15	S 29/11/21
H 9 CV	1915 01/04/15	29/06/15	S 3/11/21
H 10 CV	09/02/15 01/04/15	29/06/15	Unknown 19/01/18
H 11 FR		02/12/15	S 1921
H 12 FR		02/12/15	S/04/22
H 14 FR		15	RCN/02/19, S 1927
H 15 FR		15	RCN/02/19, S 1927

Note: H 13, H 16–H 20 ceded to Chile, never delivered to RN. Fore River boats were released to RN after the US entered the war in April 1917, but were held back as surplus to requirements; only H 11 and H 12 reached the UK before the Armistice. The other two were en route when the war ended, and were re-routed to Canada.

H 21 Class (British-built)

H 21 V	02/03/17 20/10/17	28/01/18	S 13/07/26
H 22 V	06/03/17 14/11/17	13/11/18	S 19/02/29
H 23 V	03/03/17 29/01/18	25/04/18	S 04/05/34
H 24 V	04/03/17 14/11/17	09/05/18	S 04/05/34
H 25 V	03/03/17 27/04/18	16/07/18	S 19/02/29
H 26 V	02/03/17 15/11/l7	20/03/18	S 21/04/28
H 27 V	20/03/17 25/09/18	02/01/18	S 30/08/35
H 28 V	18/03/17 12/03/18	29/06/18	S 18/08/44
H 29 V	19/04/17 08/06/18	21/02/19	F 09/08/26
H 30 V	20/04/17 09/05/18	27/05/19	S 30/08/35
H 31 V	20/11/17 16/11/18	17/05/19	Unknown 24/12/41
H 32 V	20/11/17 19/11/18	10/09/19	S 18/10/44
H 33 CL	20/11/17 24/08/18	17/05/19	S 10/44
H 34 CL	20/11/17 05/11/18	10/09/19	S/07/45 (snort test bed)
H 41 A	17/09/17 26/07/18	01/11/18	S incomplete 12/03/20
H 42 A	09/17 21/10/18	01/05/19	C 23/03/22
H 43 A	04/10/17 03/02/19	25/11/19	S 11/44
H 44 A	10/10/17 17/02/19	15/04/20	S 02/45

H 47 B	20/11/17 19/11/18	25/02/19	C 09/07/29
H 48 B	30/11/17 31/03/19	23/06/19	S 30/08/35
H 49 B	21/01/18 15/07/19	25/10/19	DC 18/10/40
H 50 B	23/01/18 25/10/19	03/02/20	S/07/45
H 51 PEDY	Oct 17 15/11/18	01/09/19	S 06/06/24
H 52 PEDY	01/18 31/03/19	16/12/19	S 09/11/27

Note: H 35–H 40 (Cammell Laird), H 45–H 46 (Armstrong), and H 53–H 54 (Devonport) were all cancelled before being laid down.

'J' Class

J 1 PDY	26/04/15 06/11/15	01/04/16	RAN 25/03/19, S 26/02/24
J 2 PDY	03/05/15 06/11/15	01/07/16	RAN 25/03/19, S 26/02/24
J 3 PEDY	02/03/15 04/12/15	02/03/17	RAN 25/03/19, S 01/26
J 4 PEDY	08/03/15 02/02/16	01/08/16	RAN 25/03/19, S 26/02/24
J 5 DDY	26/04/15 09/09/15	18/05/16	RAN 25/03/19, S 26/02/24
J 6 DDY	26/04/15 09/09/15	31/07/16	Sunk in error 15/10/18
J 7 DDY	05/08/16 21/02/17	01/11/17	RAN 25/03/19, S/11/29

Note: J 1–J 8 were ordered January 1915, but J 3 and J 4 were cancelled in April 1915. J 7 was reordered in May 1916 to a revised design. The reordered J 3 was originally to have been J 7; the reordered J 4 was originally to have been J 8.

'K' Class

K 1 PDY	01/11/15 14/11/16	01/04/17	C 18/11/17, sunk by gunfire
K 2 PDY	13/11/15 14/10/16	01/02/17	Sold 13/07/26
K 3 V	21/05/15 20/05/16	22/09/16	Sold 26/10/21
K 4 V	28/06/15 15/07/16	01/01/17	C 31/01/18
K 5 PDY	13/11/15 16/12/16	01/06/17	Accident 20/01/21
K 6 PDY	08/11/15 31/05/16	01/02/17	Sold 13/07/26
K 7 PDY	08/11/15 31/05/16	01/02/17	S 09/09/21
K 8 V	22/09/15 10/10/16	06/03/17	S 11/10/23
K 9 V	28/06/15 08/11/16	09/05/17	S 23/07/26
K 10 V	28/06/15 27/12/16	26/05/17	S 04/11/21
K 11 A	18/10/15 16/08/16	24/02/17	S 04/11/21
K 12 A	21/10/15 23/02/17	01/08/17	S 23/07/26
K 13 F	Oct 15 11/11/16	18/10/17	Lost on trials 29/01/17, raised as K 22
K 14 F	Nov 15 08/02/17	22/05/17	S 16/12/26
K 15 S	19/04/16 31/10/17	30/04/18	S 08/24
K 16 B	Jun 16 05/11/17	13/04/18	S 22/08/24
K 17 V	May 16 10/04/17	20/09/17	C 31/01/18

K 18–K 21 became M 1–M 4

K 22 K 23 – K 25	Renamed K 13 when raised Cancelled 26/11/18		S 16/12/26
K 26 K 27–K 28 V/CDY	01/06/18 Cancelled 26/11/18 26/08/19	28/06/23	S 03.31

'L' Class (Cancelled not laid down: Vickers L 24–L 31, Pembroke L 34–L 35, Fairfield L 36; L 13 and L 37–L 49 not ordered, L 50 class ordered instead) (Stars indicate minelayers)

L 1 V	18/05/16 10/05/17	18/11/17	S 03/30
L 2 V	18/05/16 06/07/17	18/12/17	S 03/30
L 3 V	21/06/16 01/09/17	31/01/18	S 02/31
L 4 V	21/06/16 17/11/17	26/02/18	S 02/34
L 5 SH	28/08/16 26/01/18	15/05/18	S 1931
L 6 B	19/10/16 14/01/18	10/07/18	S 1935
L 7 CL	28/05/16 24/04/17	22/12/17	S 1930
L 8 CL	28/05/16 07/07/17	12/03/18	S 07/10/30
L 9 D	10/16 29/01/18	27/05/18	S 30/06/27
L 10 D	26/02/17 24/01/18	01/06/18	G 03/10/18
L 11 V	17/01/17 26/02/18	27/08/18	S 16/02/32
L 12 V	22/01/17 16/03/18	30/06/18	S 16/02/32
L 14* V	19/01/17 10/06/18	18/10/18	S 05/34
L 15 F	16/11/16 16/01/18	27/03/18	S 02/32
L 16 F	21/11/16 09/04/18	31/05/18	S 02/32
L 17* V	24/01/17 13/05/18	30/09/18	S 02/34
L 18 V	22/06/17 04/02/19	15/05/19	S 10/36
L 19 V	18/07/17 04/02/19	02/08/19	S 1937
L 20 V	26/07/17 23/09/18	28/01/19	S 07/01/35

L 21 V	15/09/17 11/10/19	05/10/20	S 02/39
L 22 V	28/11/17 25/10/19	10/06/21	S 30/08/35
L 23 V/CDY	29/08/17 01/07/19	31/10/24	S 1946
L 24* V	25/02/18 19/02/19	24/02/20	C 10/01/24
L 25* V	23/02/18 13/02/19	29/07/20	S 1935
L 26* V/DDY	31/01/18 29/05/19	11/10/26	A/S target 24/09/46
L 27* V/SDY	31/01/18 14/06/19	24/03/26	S 1946
L 32 V	18 23/08/19	Hull sold 01/03/20	
L 33 SH	26/09/17 29/05/19	22/12/19	S 02/32

L 50 Class (L 59–L 66 and L 74 all cancelled by Admiralty Order 26/11/18, others 12/04/19)

L 50 CL	05.17	Cancelled 1919	
L 52 A	16/05/17 18/12/18	18/01/21	S 1935
L 53 A/CDY	19/06/17 12/08/19	06/01/25	S 1938
L 54 D/DDY	14/05/17 20/08/19	27/08/24	S 1938
L 55 F	01/05/17 21/09/18	19/12/18	M 04/06/19, salved by Soviets
L 56 F	16/10/17 25/05/19	03/09/19	S 25/03/38
L 57 F	01/18	Cancelled 1919	
L 58 F	22/04/18	Cancelled 1919	
L 65 SH	09/18	Cancelled 1918	
L 67 A	08/11/17 16/06/19	Canc/03/19, completed as Yugoslav *Hrabri* (bought by builder 10/1919)	
L 68 A	05/12/17 02/07/19	Canc/03/19, completed as Yugoslav *Nebojsa* (bought by builder 10/1919)	
L 69 B/RDY	07/07/17 06/12/18	18/04/23	S 02/39
L 70 B	01/07/17	Cancelled 04/19	
L 71 S	29/09/17 17/05/19	23/01/20	S 25/03/38
L 72 S	12/17	Cancelled 04/19	

'M' Class

M 1 V	01/07/16 09/07/17	17/04/18	C 12/11/25
M 2 V	13/07/16 15/04/19	14/02/20	F 26/01/32
M 3 A	08/12/16 19/10/18	14/07/20	S/02/32
M 4 A	08/12/16 20/07/19	Cancelled 26/11/18, launched to clear slip	

'N' Class (*Nautilus*, special; renamed N 1 in 1918)

Nautilus V	13/03/13 16/12/14	02/10/17	S 09/06/22

'R' Class

R 1 CDY	04/02/17 25/04/18	14/10/18	S 20/01/23
R 2 CDY	04/02/17 25/04/18	20/12/18	S 21/02/23
R 3 CDY	04/02/17 08/06/18	31/03/19	S 21/02/23
R 4 CDY	04/02/17 08/06/18	23/08/19	S 26/05/34
R 5 PEDY	03/18	Cancelled 28/08/19	
R 6 PEDY	03/18	Cancelled 28/08/19	
R 7 V	01/11/17 14/05/18	29/06/18	S 21/02/23
R 8 V	01/11/17 28/06/18	26/07/18	S 21/02/23
R 9 A	05/12/17 12/08/18	14/10/18	S 21/02/23
R 10 A	07/12/17 05/10/18	12/04/19	S 19/02/29
R 11 CL	01/12/17 06/03/18	08/08/18	S 21/02/23
R 12 CL	01/12/17 09/04/18	29/10/18	S 21/02/23

'S' Class (Scotts Coastals)

S 1 S	23/08/12 28/02/14	05/08/14	Italy 15/09/15
S 2 S	20/10/13 14/04/15	29/05/15	Italy 20/09/15
S 3 S	04/03/14 10/06/15	25/09/15	Italy 26/09/15

'V' Class (Vickers Coastals)

V 1 V	12/11/12 23/07/14	05/05/15	S 29/11/21
V 2 V	15/10/13 17/02/15	14/11/15	S 29/11/21
V 3 V	17/01/14 01/04/15	22/01/16	S 08/10/20
V 4 V	27/02/14 25/11/15	15/03/16	S 08/10/20

'W' Class (Armstrong Coastals)

W 1 A	19/10/13 19/11/14	06/01/15	Italy 23/08/16
W 2 A	04/12/13 15/02/15	18/05/15	Italy 23/08/16
W 3 A	07/03/14 28/07/15	04/02/16	Italy 23/08/16
W 4 A	20/03/14 11/09/15	27/06/16	Italy 23/08/16

X 1

X 1 CDY	02/11/21 16/06/23	23/09/25	BU 12/12/36

Interwar and Second World War Classes

Oberon (Originally *O 1*)

Oberon	22/03/24	24/08/27	BU 24/08/45
CDY	24/09/26		

Oxley Class (Originally *AO 1* and *AO 2*)

Otway	24/08/25	09/09/27	BU 24/08/45
V	07/09/26		
Oxley	24/08/25	22/07/27	T (friendly fire) 10/09/39
V	29/06/26		

Odin Class

Odin	23/06/27	21/12/29	DC 14/06/40
CDY	05/05/28		
Olympus	14/04/27	14/06/30	M 05/08/42
B	11/12/28		
Orpheus	14/04/27	23/09/30	M c. 19/06/40
B	26/02/29		
Osiris	12/05/27	27/02/29	BU/09/46
V	19/05/28		
Oswald	30/05/27	01/05/29	C 01/08/40
V	19/06/28		
Otus	31/05/27	05/07/29	Sc 09/46
V	31/08/28		

Parthian Class

Pandora	09/07/28	30/06/30	B 01/04/42
V	22/08/29		
Parthian	30/06/28	13/01/31	M (probable) c. 10/08/43
CDY	22/06/29		
Perseus	02/07/28	15/04/30	M 06/12/41
V	22/05/29		
Phoenix	23/07/28	03/02/31	DC 16/07/40
CL	03/10/29		
Poseidon	05/09/28	05/05/30	C 09/06/31
V	21/06/29		
Proteus	18/07/28	17/06/30	BU 26/02/46
V	23/07/29		

Rainbow Class

Rainbow	24/06/29	18/01/32	C 04/10/40
CDY	14/05/30		
Regent	19/06/29	11/11/30	M 18/04/43
V	11/06/30		
Regulus	17/07/29	17/12/30	Prob M c. 06/12/40
V	11/06/30		
Rover	24/07/29	29/01/31	BU 30/07/46
V	11/06/30		

Note: *Royalist* laid down 10/06/29, cancelled.

Grampus Class (minelayers)

Porpoise	22/09/31	11/03/33	B 19/01/45
V	30/08/32		
Cachalot	12/05/36	15/08/38	G, rammed 30/07/41
S	02/12/37		
Grampus	20/08/34	10/03/37	DC 16/06/40
CDY	25/02/36		
Narwhal	29/05/34	28/02/36	B 23/07/40
V	29/08/35		
Rorqual	01/05/35	10/02/37	BU 19/12/45
V	21/07/36		
Seal	09/12/36	24/05/39	Captured by Germans 05/05/40, became *UB*
CDY	27/09/38		

Note: *P 411*–*P 413* ordered from Scotts under 1940 Emergency War Programme, not built.

Thames Class (fleet submarines)

Clyde	15/03/33	12/04/35	BU 30/07/46
V	15/03/34		
Severn	27/03/33	12/01/35	BU 1946
V	16/01/34		
Thames	06/01/31	14/09/32	M 23/07/40
V	26/01/32		

'S' Class Pre-war Series

Seahorse	14/09/31	02/10/33	Prob M 29/12/39
CDY	15/11/32		
Starfish	26/09/31	27/10/33	DC 09/01/40
CDY	14/03/33		
Sturgeon	01/01/31	27/02/33	BU 01/47
CDY	08/01/32		
Swordfish	01/12/20	28/11/32	M 07/11/40
CDY	10/11/31		

Modified Boats:

Salmon	15/06/33	08/03/35	M 09/07/40
CL	30/04/34		
Sealion	16/05/33	21/12/34	ASW Target 03/03/45
CL	16/03/34		
Seawolf	25/05/34	12/03/36	BU 11/45
S	28/11/35		
Shark	12/06/33	31/12/34	Sc 06/07/40 after DC
CDY	31/05/34		
Snapper	18/09/33	14/06/35	DC 11/02/41
CDY	25/10/34		
Spearfish	23/05/35	11/12/36	T 01/08/40
CL	21/04/36		
Sterlet	14/07/36	06/04/38	DC 18/04/40
CDY	22/09/37		
Sunfish	22/07/35	02/07/37	To Soviet Navy/07/44
CDY	30/09/36		

'T' Class (stern tube added in starred boats 1942)

Taku*	18/11/37	03/01/40	S 11/46
CL	20/05/39		
Talisman	27/09/38	29/06/40	Probably M 17/09/42
CL	29/01/40		
Tarpon	05/10/37	08/03/40	DC 10/04/40
S	17/10/39		
Tetrarch	24/08/38	15/02/40	Unknown c. 27/10/41
V	14/11/39		
Thistle	07/12/37	04/07/39	T 10/04/40
V	25/10/38		
Thunderbolt*	21/12/36	01/11/40	Ex-*Thetis*, renamed/04/40 after she sank on trials 01/06/39, completed 11/40, DC 14/03/43
CL	29/06/38		
Tigris*	11/05/38	20/06/40	Probably DC 14/03/43
CDY	31/10/39		
Torbay*	21/11/38	14/01/41	S 19/12/45
CDY	09/04/40		
Triad	24/03/38	16/09/39	T 15/10/40
V	05/05/39		
Tribune*	03/03/37	17/10/39	S 07/47
S	08/12/38		

Trident* V	12/01/37 07/12/38	01/10/39	BU 17/02/46
Triton V	28/08/36 05/10/37	09/11/38	DC 18/12/40
Triumph V	19/03/37 16/02/38	02/05/39	Unknown C. 01/01/42
Truant* V	24/03/38 05/05/39	31/10/39	Snort prototype, S 19/12/45
Tuna* S	13/06/38 10/05/40	01/08/40	BU 24/06/46

(Group II: external bow tubes moved aft, bow fined, midships tubes turned aft, stern tube)

Tempest CL	06/01/40 10/06/41	06/12/41	DC 13/02/42
Thorn CL	20/01/40 18/03/41	26/08/41	DC 07/08/42
Thrasher CL	14/11/39 28/11/40	14/05/41	BU 09/03/47
Traveller S	17/01/40 27/08/41	10/04/43	Probably M c. 04/12/42
Trooper S	26/03/40 05/03/42	29/08/42	Probably DC c. 10/10/43
Trusty V	15/03/40 14/03/41	30/07/41	BU/07/47
Turbulent V	15/03/40 12/05/41	02/12/41	Probably DC 14/03/43

(Group III: partly or fully welded; stars indicate fully-welded)

Tabard ex-P 342* S	06/09/44 21/11/45	25/06/46	BU 14/03/74
Taciturn ex-P 334* V	09/03/43 07/06/44	08/10/44	BU 08/08/71
Tactician ex-P 314, ex-P 94 V	13/11/41 29/07/42	29/11/42	BU 06/12/63
Talent ex-P 322 V	13/10/42 17/07/43	04/12/43	RNLN 06/12/43
Talent ex-P 343* S	Cancelled		
Talent ex-Tasman, ex-P 337* V	21/03/44 13/02/45	27/07/45	BU 28/02/70
Tally-Ho ex-P 317, ex-P 97 V	25/03/42 23/12/42	12/04/43	BU 10/02/67
Tantalus ex-P 318, ex-P 98 V	06/06/42 24/02/43	02/06/43	BU/11/50
Tantivy ex-P 319, ex-P 99 V	04/07/42 06/04/43	25/07/43	ASW target 1951
Tapir ex-P 335 V	29/03/43 21/08/44	30/12/44	BU/02/66
Tarn ex-P 336* V	12/06/43 29/11/44	07/04/45	RNLN 06/04/45
Taurus ex-P 339, ex-P 313, ex-P 93 V	30/09/41 27/06/42	03/11/42	BU 04.60
Telemachus ex-P 321 V	25/08/42 19/06/43	25/10/43	BU 28/08/61

Templar ex-P 316, ex-P 96 V	28/12/41 26/10/42	15/02/43	Target 1950
Teredo ex-P 338* V	17/04/44 27/04/45	05/04/46	BU 05/06/65
Terrapin ex-P 323 V	19/10/42 31/08/43	22/01/44	Damaged 19/05/45, CTL
Theban ex-P 341* V	Cancelled		
Thermopylae ex-P 355* CDY	26/10/43 27/06/45	05/12/45	Sc 1970
Thor ex-P 349 PDY	05/04/43 18/04/44	Cancelled 1945, BU	
Thorough ex-P 324 V	26/10/42 30/10/43	01/03/44	BU 29/06/61
Threat ex-P 344* V	Cancelled 1945		
Thule ex-P 325 DDY	20/09/41 22/10/42	13/05/44	BU 14/09/62
Tiara ex-P 351 PDY	09/04/43 18/04/44	Cancelled	Cancelled 1945, BU
Tiptoe ex-P 332* V	10/11/42 25/02/44	12/06/44	BU 1975
Tireless ex-P 327 PDY	30/10/41 19/03/43	18/04/45	BU 11.68
Token ex-P 328 PDY	06/11/41 19/03/43	15/12/45	BU 03/70
Totem ex-P 352* DDY	22/10/42 28/09/43	09/01/45	Israel 10/11/67
Tradewind ex-P 329 CDY	11/02/42 11/12/42	18/10/43	BU 14/12/55
Trenchant ex-P 331 CDY	09/05/42 24/03/43	26/02/44	BU 23/07/63
Trespasser ex-P 312, ex-P 97 V	08/09/41 29/05/42	25/09/42	BU 26/09/61
Truculent ex-P 315, ex-P 95 V	04/12/41 12/09/42	31/12/42	C 12/01/50
Trump ex-P 333* V	31/12/42 25/03/44	08/07/44	BU 08/71
Truncheon ex-P 353* DDY	05/11/42 22/02/44	25/05/45	Israel 19/05/67
Tudor ex-P 326 DDY	20/09/41 23/09/42	16/01/44	BU 27/07/63
Turpin ex-P 354 CDY	24/05/43 05/08/44	18/12/44	Israel 19/05/67
P 311 ex-P 91 V	25/04/41 05/03/42	07/08/42	Probably M C. 02/01/43

'U'/'V' Class
(Initial Group; Ursula had 3in gun and eight rather than ten torpedoes)

Undine V	19/02/37 05/10/37	21/08/38	DC 07/01/40
Unity V	19/02/37 16/02/38	15/10/38	C 29/04/40
Ursula V	19/02/37 16/02/38	20/12/38	BU/05/50

(Group I: four torpedo tubes, 12pdr gun, 3in in *Unbeaten*, *Unique* as modified 1942. Flush bow in *Umpire* and *Una*; in *Unbeaten* and *Unique* 1942, also in all Group II)

Umpire CDY	01/01/40 30/12/40	10/07/41	C 19/07/41
Una CDY	07/05/40 10/06/41	27/09/41	BU 11/04/49
Unbeaten V	22/11/39 09/07/40	20/11/40	B (error) 11/11/42
Undaunted V	02/12/39 20/08/40	30/12/40	Unknown 13/05/41
Union V	09/12/39 01/10/40	22/02/41	DC 20/07/41
Unique V	30/10/39 06/06/40	27/09/40	Unknown 10/10/42
Upholder V	30/10/39 08/07/40	31/10/40	DC 14/04/42
Upright V	06/11/39 21/04/40	03/09/40	BU/03/46
Urchin V	09/12/39 30/09/40	28/01/41	Poland 19/01/41, to *P 97* on return 27/08/46, BU 1949
Urge V	30/10/39 19/08/40	12/12/40	B or M 29/04/42
Usk V	06/11/39 07/06/40	11/10/40	M 26/04/41
Utmost V	02/11/39 20/04/40	17/08/40	DC 25/11/42

(Group II, designed without external tubes, bows reshaped and lengthened)

Ultimatum ex-*P 34* V	19/06/40 11/02/41	29/07/41	BU 02/50
Ultor ex-*P 53* V	30/12/41 12/10/42	31/12/42	BU 22/01/46
Umbra ex-*P 35* V	19/07/40 15/03/41	02/09/41	S 09/07/46
Unbending ex-*P 37* V	30/08/40 12/05/41	05/11/41	BU 05/50
Unbroken ex-*P 42* V	30/12/40 04/11/41	29/01/42	BU 09/05/50
Unison ex-*P 43* V	30/12/40 04/11/41	19/02/42	BU 19/05/50
United ex-*P 44* V	25/02/41 18/12/41	02/04/42	BU 12/02/46
Universal ex-*P 54* V	05/09/41 10/11/42	08/03/43	BU/06/46
Unrivalled ex-*P 45* V	12/05/41 16/02/42	03/05/42	BU 22/01/46
Unruffled ex-*P 46* V	25/02/41 19/12/41	09/04/42	BU/01/46
Unruly ex-*P 49* V	19/11/41 28/07/42	03/11/42	BU/02/46
Unseen ex-*P 51* V	30/07/41 16/04/42	02/07/42	BU/09/49
Unshaken ex-*P 54* V	12/05/41 17/02/42	21/05/42	BU/03/46
Unsparing ex-*P 55* V	11/08/41 28/07/42	29/11/42	S 14/02/46

Unswerving ex-*P 63* V	17/02/42 02/06/43	03/10/43	BU 12/07/49
Untiring ex-*P 59* V	23/12/41 20/01/43	09/06/43	ASW Target 29/07/57
Uproar ex-*Ulleswater*, ex-*P 31* V	30/04/40 27/11/40	02/04/41	S 13/02/46
Upstart ex-*P 65* V	17/03/42 24/11/42	03/04/43	ASW Target 25/07/57
Usurper ex-*P 56* V	19/08/41 24/09/42	02/02/43	DC 03/10/43
Uther ex-*P 62* V	31/01/42 06/04/43	15/08/43	BU 04/50
Vandal ex-*P 64* V	17/03/42 23/11/42	20/02/43	Unknown (trials) 24/02/43
Varangian ex-*P 61* V	23/12/41 04/03/43	10/07/43	S 06/49
Varne ex-*P 66* V	29/04/42 22/01/43	03/04/43	RNN 28/03/43
Vitality ex-*Untamed*, ex-*P 58* V	09/10/41 S 08/12/42	14/04/43	As *Untamed*, F 30/05/43, salved as *Vitality*, 13/02/46
Vox ex-*P 67* V	29/04/42 23/01/43	02/05/43	BU 02/05/49
P 32 V	30/04/40 15/12/40	03/05/41	M 18/08/41
P 33 V	19/06/40 28/01/41	30/05/41	DC 18/08/41
P 36 V	26/07/40 28/04/41	24/09/41	B 01/04/42
P 38 V	02/09/40 09/07/41	17/10/41	DC 23/02/42
P 39 V	14/10/40 23/08/41	16/11/41	B 26/03/42
P 41 V	15/10/40 24/08/41	12/12/41	RNN 12/41
P 47 V	19/11/41 27/07/42	08/10/42	RNLN 11/42
P 48 V	30/12/41 15/04/42	16/12/42	DC 25/12/42
P 52 V	30/12/41 11/10/42	16/12/42	BU/04/58

(Group III: hull further fined, stern lengthened to improve angle of approach of water to screws; partly welded)
Ulex ex-*P 93*, *Unbridled* , *Upas* ex-*P 92* (laid down 10/08/43, not launched), *Upward*, *Utopia* ex-*P 94*, *Vehement*, *Venom*, *Verve*, *Veto* (laid down 28/1/43), *Virile* (laid down 02/11/43), *Visitant* ex-*P 91*, all by Vickers, cancelled. None was launched.

Upshot ex-*P 82* V	03/05/43 24/02/44	15/05/44	BU 22/11/49
Urtica ex-*P 83* V	27/04/43 23/03/44	20/06/44	BU 03/50
Vagabond V	23/04/43 19/09/44	27/02/45	BU 26/01/50
Vampire ex-*P 72* V	09/11/42 20/07/43	13/11/43	BU 05/03/50
Variance ex-*P 85* V	21/05/43 22/05/44	24/08/44	RNN 08/44

Name	Dates	Dates 2	Fate
Varne ex-P 81 V	18/11/42 24/02/44	30/07/44	BU 09/58
Veldt ex-P 71 V	02/11/42 19/07/43	01/11/43	BU 23/02/58
Vengeful ex-P 86 V	30/07/43 20/07/44	16/10/44	BU 22/03/58
Venturer ex-P 68 V	25/08/42 04/05/43	19/08/43	RNN 08/46
Vigorous ex-P 74 V	14/12/42 15/10/43	13/01/44	S 23/12/49
Viking ex-P 69 V	03/09/42 05/05/43	30/08/43	RNN 08/46
Vineyard ex-P 84 V	21/05/43 08/05/44	01/08/44	BU 06/50
Virtue ex-P 75 V	17/02/43 29/11/43	29/02/44	B 19/05/46
Virulent ex-P 95 V	30/03/43 23/05/44	01/10/44	BU 04/61
Visigoth ex-P 76 V	15/02/43 30/11/43	09/03/44	BU 04/50
Vivid ex-P 77 V	26/10/42 15/09/43	19/01/44	BU 10/50
Volatile ex-P 96 V	30/03/43 20/06/44	04/11/44	BU 23/12/58
Voracious ex-P 78 V	26/10/42 26/10/42	13/04/44	BU 19/05/46
Vortex ex-P 87 V	13/08/43 19/08/44	01/12/44	BU 08/58
Votary V	21/04/43 21/08/44	13/12/44	RNN 07/46
Vox ex-P 73 V	19/12/42 28/09/43	20/12/43	BU 19/05/46
Vulpine ex-P 79 V	18/11/42 28/12/43	02/06/44	S 06/59

'S' Class (1940 Type) Note original P numbers in some cases. P numbers changed to three-digit numbers July 1941, and to names January–April 1943.

Name	Dates	Dates 2	Fate
Safari (ex-P 211, ex-P 61) CL	05/06/40 18/11/41	14/03/42	S 07/01/46
Saga CL	05/04/44 14/03/45	14/06/45	Portugal 11/10/48
Sahib (ex-P 212, ex-P 62) CL	05/07/40 19/01/42	13/05/42	DC 24/04/43
Sanguine CL	10/01/44 15/02/45	13/05/45	Israel 10/58
Saracen (ex-P 247, ex-P 213, ex-P 63) CL	16/07/40 16/02/42	27/06/42	DC 14/08/43
Satyr (ex-P 214, ex-P 64) S	08/06/40 28/09/42	08/02/43	BU 04/04/62 fast target
Sceptre (ex-P 215, ex-P 65) S	08/06/40 28/09/42	08/02/43	BU 09/49 fast target
Scorcher CL	14/12/43 18/12/44	16/03/45	BU 14/09/62

Name	Dates	Dates 2	Fate
Scotsman (ex-P 243) S	15/04/43 18/08/44	09/12/44	BU 19/11/64 fast target
Scythian (ex-P 237) S	21/02/43 14/04/44	11/08/44	BU 08/08/60
Sea Devil (ex-P 244) S	05/05/43 30/01/45	12/05/45	BU 15/12/65
Sea Dog (ex-P 216, ex-P 66) CL	31/12/40 11/06/42	24/09/42	BU 08/48
Sea Nymph) (ex-P 233, ex-P 73) CL	06/05/41 29/07/42	03/11/42	BU 06/48
Sea Rover (ex-P 218, ex-P 68) S	14/01/41 25/02/43	07/07/43	BU 10/49
Sea Scout (ex-P 253) CL	01/04/43 24/03/44	19/06/44	BU 14/12/65
Selene (ex-P 254) CL	6/04/43 24/04/44	19/06/44	BU 06/06/61 Fast target
Seneschal (ex-P 255) S	01/09/43 23/04/45	06/09/45	BU 23/08/60
Sentinel (ex-P 256) S	15/11/43 27/07/45	28/12/45	S 28/02/62
Seraph (ex-P 219, ex-P 69) V	16/08/40 25/10/41	10/06/42	BU 20/12/65 fast target
Shakespeare (ex-P 221, ex-P 71) V	13/11/40 08/12/41	10/07/42	B/G 03/01/45, CTL
Shalimar (ex-P 242) CDY	17/04/42 22/04/43	22/04/44	BU 07/50
Sibyl (ex-P 217, ex-P 67) CL	31/12/40 29/04/42	16/08/42	BU 03/48
Sickle (ex-P 224, ex-P 74) CL	08/05/41 27/08/42	01/12/42	Probable M c. 16/06/44
Simoom (ex-P 225, ex-P 75) CL	14/07/41 12/10/42	30/12/42	M 15 or 20/11/43
Sirdar (ex-P 226, ex-P 76) S	24/04/41 20/09/43	20/09/43	BU 31/05/65 snort prototype
Sleuth CL	30/06/43 06/07/44	08/10/44	BU 15/09/58 fast target
Solent CL	07/05/43 08/06/44	07/09/44	BU 28/08/62 fast target
Spark (ex-P 236) S	10/10/42 28/12/43	28/04/44	S 28/10/49
Spearhead CL	18/08/43 02/10/44	21/12/44	Portugal 08/48
Spirit (ex-P 245) CL	27/10/42 20/07/43	25/10/43	BU 04/07/50
Spiteful (ex-P 227, ex-P 77) S	19/09/41 05/06/43	06/10/43	BU 15/07/63
Splendid (ex-P 228, ex-P 78) CDY	07/03/41 19/01/42	08/08/42	DC 21/04/43

Name			
Sportsman (ex-P 229, ex-P 79) CDY	01/07/41 17/04/42	21/12/42	To France
Springer CL	08/05/44 14/05/45	02/08/45	Israel 09/10/58
Spur CL	01/10/43 17/11/44	18/02/45	Portugal 11/48
Statesman (ex-P 246) CL	02/11/42 09/04/43	29/06/43	S 03/01/61 fast target
Stoic (ex-P 231) CL	18/06/42 23/03/43	15/06/43	S/07/50
Stonehenge (ex-P 232) CL	04/04/42 23/03/43	15/06/43	Unknown c. 16/03/44
Storm (ex-P 233) CL	23/06/42 18/05/43	23/08/43	BU 09/49
Stratagem (ex-P 234) CL	15/04/42 21/06/43	23/12/43	DC 22/11/44
Strongbow (ex-P 235) S	27/03/42 30/08/43	09/10/43	BU 04/46
Stubborn (ex-P 238, ex-P 88) CL	10/09/41 11/11/42	20/02/43	ASW Target 30/04/46
Sturdy (ex-P 248) CL	22/12/42 30/11/43	29/12/43	BU 09/05/58
Stygian (ex-P 249) CL	06/01/43 27/01/44	16/04/44	S 28/10/49
Subtle (ex-P 251) CL	01/02/43 27/01/44	16/04/44	BU 06/49
Supreme (ex-P 252) CL	15/02/43 24/02/44	20/05/44	BU 07/50
Surf (ex-P 239, ex-P 89) CL	02/10/41 10/12/42	18/03/43	S 28/10/49
Surface, Surge – CL, cancelled			
Syrtis (ex-P 241) CL	14/10/41 04/02/43	04/02/43	M 28/03/44
P 222 (ex-P 72) V	10/08/40 20/09/41	04/05/42	DC 12/12/42

Ex-Turkish Submarines (Comparable to 'S' Class)
Of four submarines ordered by Turkey, P 611 and P 612 were commissioned only for the delivery trip to Turkey. The other two served in the RN, one being lost and one returned to Turkey 17/01/46 as Murat Reis. There was no P 613.

P 614 V	24/05/39 19/10/40	10/03/42	Ex Burak Reis, returned 46
P 615 V	30/10/39 01/11/40	03/04/42	Ex Uluc Ali, T 18/04/43

'A' Class (1943)
All cancellations were on 29/10/45.
Cancelled without being laid down:
Portsmouth: Abelard, Acasta
Chatham: Adept
Cammell Laird: Agate, Aggressor, Agile, Aladdin, Alcestis
Scotts: Asgard, Assurance, Astarte
Vickers: Admirable, Adversary, Andromache, Answer, Antaeus, Antagonist, Anzac, Aphrodite, Approach, Arcadian, Ardent, Argosy, Atlantis, Austere, Awake, Aztec

Ace DDY	03/11/43 14/03/45	Cancelled	
Achates DDY	08/03/44 20/09/45	Cancelled	
Acheron CDY	26/08/44 25/03/47	17/04/48	BU 08/72

Aeneas CL	10/10/44 25/10/45	31/07/46	BU 13/12/74
Affray CL	16/01/44 12/04/45	02/05/46	F 16/04/51
Alaric CL	31/05/44 18/02/46	11/12/46	BU 05/07/71
Alcide V	02/01/45 12/04/45	18/10/46	S 1974
Alderney V	06/02/45 25/06/45	10/12/46	BU 08/72
Alliance V	13/03/45 28/07/45	14/05/47	Museum ship 1981
Ambush V	17/05/45 24/09/45	22/07/47	BU 05/07/71
Amphion (ex-Anchorite) V	14/11/43 31/08/44	27/03/45	BU 06/07/71
Anchorite (ex-Amphion) V	19/07/45 22/01/46	18/11/47	BU 24/08/70
Andrew V	13/08/45 06/04/46	16/03/48	BU 04/05/77
Artemis S	28/02/44 26/08/46	15/08/47	S 04/72
Artful S	08/06/44 22/05/47	23/02/48	BU 23/06/72
Astute V	04/04/44 30/01/45	30/06/45	BU 01/10/70
Auriga V	07/06/44 29/03/45	12/01/46	BU 11/02/75
Aurochs V	21/06/44 28/07/45	07/02/47	BU 07/02/67

Ex-US 'R' Class (First World War construction, transferred under Lend-Lease)

P 511 FR	11/12/17 18/01/19	17/04/19	Ex-R 3, to RN 04/11/41, returned 20/12/44
P 512 UIW	05/05/17 24/12/17	17/08/18	Ex-R 17, to RN 09/03/42, returned 06/09/44
P 514 UIW	23/06/17 28/01/18	17/08/18	Ex-R 19, C (error) 21/06/42

Ex-US 'S' Class (First World War construction, transferred under Lend-Lease)

P 551 BQ	26/10/18 29/05/22	09/07/23	Ex S 25, to RN 04/11/41, C 02/05/42
P 552 FR	11/12/17 26/10/18	05/06/20	Ex S 1, to RN 20/04/42, returned 16/10/44
P 553 BQ	19/12/18 18/08/20	24/08/21	Ex S 21, to RN 14/09/42, returned 11/07/44
P 554 BQ	06/01/19 15/07/20	23/06/24	Ex S 22, to RN 19/06/42, returned 11/07/44
P 555 BQ	01/11/18 27/06/22	24/08/23	Ex S 24, to RN 10/08/42, returned 20/12/44
P 556 BQ	17/04/19 09/11/22	22/05/24	Ex S 29, to RN 05/06/42, returned 26/01/45

Captured Submarines in British Service
The 710 series of designations was used for captured submarines temporarily in British service, mainly for test and evaluation: P 711 (formerly X 2, the Italian Galilei, captured 19/06/40), P 712 (ex-Italian Perla, taken 09/07/42, to Greece after trials), P 714 was the Italian Bronzo (to France after trials), and P 715 was the German U 570, afterwards named HMS Graph.

INDEX